CW01500162

Quality Control in Criminal Investigation

**Xabier Agirre, Morten Bergsmo,
Simon De Smet and Carsten Stahn
(editors)**

**2020
Torkel Opsahl Academic EPublisher
Brussels**

Front cover: *Master carpenter Lorenzo Corti fine-tuning a piece of European cherrywood in the CILRAP Bottega (office) in Florence. Recognized for the high quality of his work, he has restored churches and monasteries in Tuscany for many years. The books in CILRAP's Quality Control Project display contemporary Florentine artisans as symbols of the mindset of quality control which they seek to inspire. Photograph: © CILRAP 2020.*

Back cover: *Segment of the steps at the entrance of the San Miniato al Monte Basilica, a Romanesque church (from 1013 AD) on a hill-top in southern Florence. The surface of each stone is carefully carved by a mason's hand for water to run off and for better grip. Photograph: © CILRAP 2020.*

This and other publications in TOAEP's *Publication Series* may be openly accessed and downloaded through the web site http://www.toaep.org/, which uses Persistent URLs for all publications it makes available (such PURLs will not be changed). This publication was first published on 9 November 2020.

ISBNs: 978-82-8348-129-7 (print) and 978-82-8348-130-3 (e-book).

Dedicated to those in criminal justice for core international crimes
who never stop questioning the quality of their work

PREFACE BY THE CO-EDITORS

This volume contains a wealth of ideas, sources and information on how the investigation and preparation of fact-rich cases can be improved. Cases concerning core international crimes are often fact-rich. The book focuses on such crimes, but it is also relevant for those who work on certain forms of serious fraud, organized crime, and human trafficking. Fact-rich cases require time and teams of investigators, analysts and lawyers to prepare for trial. They consume resources, sometimes millions of euros. There is an immediate public interest in their efficiency and fairness. And they can always be improved – the challenge of professionalization is common to all criminal investigation and case-preparation. The theme of 'quality control' reflects this fact. It is a general theme; it does not point fingers at specific institutions or individuals. The theme invites mobilization around the question 'how can we do better in this investigation or case-preparation?'.

This simple question – how can we do better? – underpins the entire Quality Control Project which the Centre for International Law Research and Policy (CILRAP) and partners around the world have conducted in the period 2012-2020, with support from the Norwegian Ministry of Foreign Affairs. During the project, the term 'quality control' has started to take on prominence in the field of international criminal justice, most recently in the final report of the Independent Expert Review of the Assembly of States Parties of the International Criminal Court. The term should be further mainstreamed, to the extent that it becomes a common term of workplace discussions. This is one of the motives behind the project. To this end, the present book is dedicated to "those in criminal justice for core international crimes who never stop questioning the quality of their work". Empowering the working level and line managers in relevant criminal justice organizations has been at the forefront of the minds that have designed the Quality Control Project. Enabling existing staff in criminal justice agencies to work more critically – and by doing so triggering virtuous cycles of better performance – is not only a necessary supplement to recommendations on managerial or normative reform; it may in the longer term prove more important to sustainable change.

i

The Quality Control Project has had three legs, focusing on three distinct phases of fact-work prior to the criminal trial. The first leg concentrated on fact-finding and documentation outside (or prior to) criminal justice of violations that may amount to core international crimes, typically fact-finding by non-governmental organizations or United Nations human rights bodies. The anthology *Quality Control in Fact-Finding* was first published in November 2013, with a second, expanded edition in July 2020. The second leg focused on the stage of preliminary examination prior to the formal opening of a criminal investigation, leading to the publication of *Quality Control in Preliminary Examination: Volumes 1 and 2* in September 2018.

The present volume is the main outcome of the third leg of the project, focusing on the investigative and case-preparatory phase prior to the opening of trial. This first edition contains 24 chapters by some of the leading experts in the field, as well as forewords by Prosecutor Fatou Bensouda (International Criminal Court), Professor Manoj Kumar Sinha (Indian Law Institute), and Professor Gregory S. Gordon (Chinese University of Hong Kong). It is organized in five parts: Part I: The Context, Part II: Evidence and Analysis, Part III: Systemic Challenges in Case-Preparatory Work-Processes, Part IV: Investigation Plans as Instruments of Quality Control, and Part V: Judicial and Prosecutorial Participation in Investigation and Case Preparation.

We have sought to include a broad diversity of views in the book. We deliberately invited experts who hold very different views on, for example, the role of the judiciary in case-preparation or the extent to which information technology should be used in the presentation and analysis of potential evidence pre-trial. As co-editors we do not necessarily agree with all views in the chapters below – nor do the institutions we work for share all views. The clash of opinions – which was on display during the project conference held at the Indian Law Institute in New Delhi on 22-23 February 2019 – is important to avoid hegemonic or other imbalances in the discourse on these questions, whether by stealth or overt assertion. You can make use of the conference presentations through the films and podcasts that are available on the conference web page.[1] Each film has a persistent URL so it can be linked to in your own writing, as several authors in this book have done.

---

[1] See https://www.cilrap.org/events/190222-23-delhi/.

The concept paper for this third leg of the Quality Control Project[2] – as elaborated in the introductory chapter below – outlines seven 'bottlenecks' to effective and fair investigation and preparation of fact-rich cases. These 'bottlenecks' have informed the authors and co-editors of the present volume. Most of the subsequent chapters make reference to one or more of these 'bottlenecks'. It may therefore be useful to introduce this conceptual taxonomy already here, at the outset of the book:[3] (1) "The loss or fragmentation of overview of information and potential evidence in the possession of the team during investigation or case-preparation"; (2) "Inadequate analysis of factual propositions relevant to the prosecution's burden in the case and corresponding evidence"; (3) "Irregularity in the team's daily routine of assessing relevancy and possible weight of information or potential evidence"; (4) "Vague or non-substantial formulation of criminal responsibility within the team *after* it has in its possession enough potential evidence"; (5) "Broad use of cumulative charging of crimes and modes of liability – often pursuant to a precautionary fear of acquittals caused by failure to include a classification, not only a desire to ensure accountability for the full range of criminal conduct engaged in"; (6) "Excessively long exhibit- and witness-lists in the prosecution's part of the case"; and (7) "Prosecution disclosure to the defence of voluminous materials not clearly related to a central hypothesis of criminal responsibility".

These and other common challenges in the preparation of fact-rich cases are being discussed in considerable detail in this book. It is not for this foreword to highlight any particular contribution. But we see some trends of thought. Firstly, a number of contributors are concerned with investigation plans as a tool of continuous quality control from the start of a criminal justice agency's factual analysis of a situation or incident. Part IV of the book contains four chapters that discuss investigation plans. Secondly, several authors discuss the importance of proper evidence review, especially during the quality control of draft indictments. Chapter 3 provides a comprehensive overview of key methods. Thirdly, there is an emphasis on the importance of understanding the context in which the alleged crimes were committed, and on the necessity of using and developing proper methodologies for factual analysis. Fourthly, avoiding over-

---

[2] See Morten Bergsmo, "Towards a Culture of Quality Control in Criminal Investigations", FICHL Policy Brief Series No. 94 (2019), Torkel Opsahl Academic EPublisher, Brussels, 2019 (http://www.toaep.org/pbs-pdf/94-bergsmo/).

[3] Quoted from the above-mentioned concept paper (footnotes omitted).

collection of information and finding new, more rational ways of organizing disclosure are topics that are thoroughly analyzed, notably in Chapter 14. Fifthly, there are also detailed chapters on the interviewing of children and age determination of possible child soldiers. And sixthly, the quality of the legal guidance provided to fact-finders is a further recurring theme in the book. If prosecutors blame their investigators for why a case did not go well, there is usually cause to look more closely at the work of the prosecutors as well.

Recognizing that criminal justice is an ever-evolving field of practice, the book does not offer a casuistic or defined catalogue of proposals. Rather, the authors develop myriad suggestions and advice which, we are confident, will germinate among colleagues both in international and national criminal justice agencies over the coming years, a sprouting that will lead to further refinement and development of approaches. The book makes it clear that – although the International Criminal Court has much to offer other jurisdictions in this area, as detailed by several chapters – the exchange of thoughts and experience should be a two-way stream between international and national actors.

At the end of the day, the strongest assets of a criminal justice agency are the abilities, efforts and precision of its working-level analysts, investigators and prosecutors. More often than not, the leaders of the agency represent its greatest risk, as they select the staff, the cases and the charges. Perhaps the most important take-away from the book for leaders of investigations and case-preparation is their responsibility to build a *culture* of quality control within their agency, division, section or team. At a minimum, this means creating an office atmosphere where staff do not fear the consequences of raising concerns about quality. But managers should do more. They should devise incentive structures to actively encourage challenges by staff to the quality of work product. Individual analysts, investigators and prosecutors, on the other hand, should see it as their professional obligation to develop a *mindset* of quality control. This may require more courage to speak up, and a stronger preparedness to let institutional loyalties override inter-personal relations, even if this can be unpleasant.

The co-editors and the publisher are committed to releasing new, expanded editions of this anthology in the coming years, with a view to enhancing its usefulness and quality. We would like the volume to become a standard reference book in the field for many years to come. We see already now that topics that should be addressed through additional contributions in the second edition include digital evidence, more national perspectives on investigation planning, and possible IT-enabling of key work-processes in case-preparation.[4]

We would like to thank the Norwegian Ministry of Foreign Affairs for its financial support to the Quality Control Project, and the Indian Law Institute in New Delhi for co-organising and hosting the project conference on which the book is based. We are also grateful to CILRAP's many friends in New Delhi, in particular Professor Manoj Kumar Sinha (Director, Indian Law Institute), Justice Madan B. Lokur (former Judge, Supreme Court of India), Ambassador Narinder Singh (former Legal Adviser, Ministry of External Affairs of India), and Professor Usha Tandon (Delhi University) as well as the Indian co-operating partners for the New Delhi conference: the Campus Law Centre of University of Delhi, Maharishi Law School, Jindal Global University, and the Indian Society of International Law. Finally, we thank Mr. LEE Wai Chun, Mr. Subham Jain and Mr. Antonio Angotti of the Torkel Opsahl Academic EPublisher for meticulous and patient copy-editing.

Xabier Agirre Aranburu
Morten Bergsmo
Simon De Smet
Carsten Stahn
Co-Editors

---

4   See Morten Bergsmo, "Decomposition Works in Our Favour", Policy Brief Series No. 114 (2020), Torkel Opsahl Academic EPublisher, Brussels, 2020 (http://www.toaep.org/pbs-pdf/114-bergsmo/), who identifies some potential areas for such developments.

FOREWORD BY FATOU BENSOUDA

I was pleased to accept the co-editors' invitation to write a foreword for this volume – *Quality Control in Criminal Investigation* – as ensuring effective and efficient investigations have been a central focus of our efforts since I assumed my mandate as Prosecutor of the International Criminal Court ('ICC') in 2012. This volume is an impressive anthology of contributions by leading experts. I recognise in its pages the efforts to reach the highest quality and fairness in investigations. This is the same vision that has guided the Office of the Prosecutor ('OTP') at the ICC under my tenure.

To begin with, several chapters highlight the importance of having clear selection criteria, so that investigations follow from fair and consistent strategic choices. I am glad to see our OTP Policy Paper on Case Selection and Prioritisation (2016) repeatedly acknowledged throughout this volume, as I expected it to give clear direction in this area. It will hopefully also serve as a source of inspiration for practice in other jurisdictions.[1] My decisions on selection of situations and cases have always been guided by the legal criteria required by the ICC Statute, as is my duty. On occasion, I have been told that my decisions may not be well received by certain parties, particularly by those associated with the suspected conduct. I was never impressed with such suggestions. I have always acted on the basis of my legal duties – independently, objectively and consistently applied – and by the harm suffered by victims. This is what should influence the decisions of a responsible prosecutor.

The first OTP Strategic Plan that I issued in 2012 set the path for improvement in our investigations.[2] I directed the Office to move from a perspective of shorter-term impact, to the serious in-depth investigations that a court such as the ICC should undertake. Strengthening the investigations was necessary to meet the evidentiary standards under the ICC

---

[1]   ICC-OTP, Policy Paper on Preliminary Examinations, November 2013 (http://www.legal-tools.org/doc/acb906/) and ICC-OTP, Policy Paper on Case Selection and Prioritisation, 15 September 2016 (https://legal-tools.org/doc/182205).

[2]   ICC-OTP, Strategic Plan 2012-2015, 11 October 2013 (https://www.legal-tools.org/doc/954beb/).

Statute, to address the concerns expressed by judges and through our own self-assessment, and, more fundamentally, to make sure that we can deliver as effectively as possible in the discharge of our mandate and to bring a measure of justice to the victims of atrocity crimes and their communities.

This approach has led to important developments in our investigative model: I upgraded the areas of analysis and forensics with additional resources and responsibilities, and the newly established Investigative Analysis Section ('IAS') and Forensic Scientific Section ('FSS'); we implemented a planning cycle based on standard investigation plans and reviews (as explained by our Team Leader Markus Eikel in his Chapter 15 below); the investigation teams adopted the Fact Analysis Database, an all-source integrated database managed by our analysts; we invested in digital evidence and big data, including projects in relation to telephone data and Internet-based open sources, hiring experts, specific monitoring projects, advanced software, drafting technical guidelines, and developing co-operation with service providers; we adopted the 'PEACE model' for investigative interviewing (the same as explained in Chapter 5 below) and had our investigators trained by experts of the International Investigative Interviewing Research Group ('IIIRG'); we established Situation-Specific Investigations Assistants to help the teams bridging the distance with the situation countries; we implemented the Source Evaluation Guidelines, with corresponding templates and training (as explained in Chapter 3 by Xabier Agirre Aranburu, Head of IAS); and I obtained from the ICC Assembly of States Parties an important increase in the training budget for investigators and analysts, though pressures on resources are ever increasing and we are consistently obliged to reallocate and prioritise our limited resources. Mismatch between demands and resources is certainly part of the equation when one is genuinely concerned with the question of investigative and prosecutorial impact and performance.

I agree with the suggestions in this volume on the importance on internal review mechanisms. I have encouraged critical and open discussion in all important decisions under my responsibility. My staff know that they can express themselves with full freedom in any meeting or in direct communication with me. Analysts at the IAS are mandated to develop 'critical thinking' techniques by their Operational Guidelines. The investigation teams hold regular reviews in which all team members are invited to discuss and challenge the cases as much as necessary. The Director of the Investigations Division regularly convenes meetings with his managers to review the investigation plans proposed by every team, which facilitates peer-review among Team Leaders and identification of best practices.

The database of lessons-learned developed by the Legal Advisory Section, under the guidance of the Office's Executive Committee, captures our institutional memory based on critical review of our investigative and legal practices. The Prosecutions Division also calls mandatory evidence reviews with independent boards at key points of the process, as instructed since the OTP Strategic Plan 2012-2015. We have also instituted working groups to devise and map out how we are implementing specific Office policies, to assess our performance and to fill gaps where required. We initiated and engaged in *ad hoc* review processes with the assistance of independent external experts. Other examples include full engagement with evaluations carried out by the Court's Independent Oversight Mechanism on certain aspects of our work. In short, as an Office, we have espoused a culture of continuous self-assessment and improvement, and with this as our guide, we are looking actively to see what other mechanisms we can devise to assist us.

The emphasis in this volume on appropriate legal direction for investigations is not new to me. All our teams, including investigation and trial phases, are led by Senior Trial Lawyers who make the strategic decisions and supervise the progress of the investigations. The Investigations Division is not independently responsible for the conduct of investigations; they support them with the requisite expertise and resources, while legal direction and control is guaranteed by the Senior Trial Lawyers of the Prosecutions Division.

I announced my priority to investigate efficiently gender-based crimes in my very first intervention when I was appointed Prosecutor, as a form of thematic prosecution. My commitment shows in the OTP Policy Paper on Sexual and Gender-Based Crimes adopted in 2014, including specific instructions to my staff to engage with civil society and specialised training.[3] The Investigations Division followed up with training by leading experts, the development of focal points in the teams, and strengthening the Gender and Children Unit with a newly created legal officer position. In 2016, I issued our internal Gender Analysis Guidelines, expanding the focus from sexual crimes to all aspects of our work that require gender awareness. I engaged UN Women to benefit from specialised advice, and they generously seconded a number of highly qualified analysts and investigators – I am grateful for their support. The results of

---

[3] ICC-OTP, Policy Paper on Sexual and Gender-Based Crimes, June 2014 (https://www.legal-tools.org/doc/7ede6c/).

these efforts show, among others, in *Ntaganda*, after his conviction in 2019 on all charges of sexual crimes, as the Trial judges endorsed our arguments to close any legal loophole and protect intra-ranks victims of rape and sexual slavery.[4] I look forward to the judicial findings in other cases in which I have sought proactively the best possible protection for victims of gender crimes under the law, including forced pregnancy and gender persecution, such as *Ongwen* and *Al Hassan*. The situation in Afghanistan also requires serious investigation of gender-based crimes,[5] as we identified in our Preliminary Examination credible allegations of gender persecution, including attacks against schools for girls and murder of female leaders.

Several contributors to this volume have highlighted the uneven results in court, including some high-profile acquittals. These concerns are understandable and I am grateful for expert feedback, even when critical. Firstly, observers should strive to be objective, and bear in mind that even in difficult circumstances my Office has succeeded in a number of convictions of leading perpetrators. Limitations in the results are the consequence of several factors that may confront any prosecutor, such as an initial prosecutorial strategy that had to be transformed; co-operation challenges; security conditions; resource limitations; and lack of consistent judicial judgments, practice or clarity, in addition to the need for the Office to improve its own performance. As this volume rightly recognises, all criminal justice agencies can improve. The Court, notwithstanding the unique challenges it faces, is no exception.

Threats against witnesses are sadly common in our cases and have often obliged our Investigations Division to take specific protective measures for both witnesses and staff. I have also been obliged under Article 70 of the ICC Statute to develop additional investigative efforts and to file cases for "Offences under the administration of justice" for such conduct. This has been an important challenge in our investigations, much as national prosecutors find in cases of organised crime or terrorism.

Lately, threats and sanctions of a different kind have been publicly issued against me and one of my senior managers by the government of a non-State Party. I have taken strength from the strong support that I have

---

[4] The *Ntagantda* case is currently under appeal. See ICC, *Prosecutor v. Bosco Ntaganda*, Appeals Chamber, Defence Appeal Brief, 11 November 2019, ICC-01/04-02/06-2443 (Part I: https://www.legal-tools.org/doc/dstrmv/).

[5] At the time of writing, the investigation in Afghanistan situation is subject to a pending article 18 deferral request.

received from the ICC States Parties, from the world-wide civil society, as well as from my own staff.[6] By statutory definition, you can rest assured that such threats will have no impact on the conduct of our duties and the fulfilment of our mandate under the Rome Statute.

Most recently, I have also encouraged my staff to communicate without restrictions with the Independent Expert Review ('IER') mandated by the ICC Assembly of States Parties, including critical observations as much as they find necessary. As a result of this openness, many staff members of the OTP, as well as other ICC organs, spoke freely to the IER and gave them their best advice. The Investigations Division is developing the project 'Investigations 3.0' to guide the future of OTP investigations, and I am glad to see that the IER report has acknowledged and endorsed this project.[7] As I stated at a recent session of the Hague and New York Working Group convened on the 7 October 2020 to discuss the IER final report, we will be looking to the report of the Independent Experts for inspiration and fact-based actionable recommendations which we can then carry forward.

As with all things, there is always room for improvement, and that should come both from internal self-reflection and external feedback. I am grateful to the co-editors of this volume for the opportunity to reflect on the topic of *Quality Control in Criminal Investigation*, a much-needed process which I am confident will receive broad attention.

Fatou Bensouda
Prosecutor, International Criminal Court

---

[6]   See ICC, "ASP President, O-Gon Kwon, rejects US measures against ICC", Press Release, 2 September 2020 (available on the ICC's web site). See, for example, European External Action Service ('EEAS'), "International Criminal Court: Statement by the High Representative/Vice-President Josep Borrell on US sanctions", Press Release, Brussels, 3 September 2020 (available on the EEAS' web site); ICC, "ICC Prosecutor briefs annual ministerial meeting, at the UN General Assembly High-Level Week, expresses gratitude for strong show of support", Press Release, 24 September 2020, ICC-OTP- 20200924-PR1538 (available on the ICC's web site).

[7]   Independent Expert Review, "Review of the International Criminal Court and the Rome Statute System, Final Report", 30 September 2020, para. 744 (https://www.legal-tools.org/doc/cv19d5/).

FOREWORD BY MANOJ KUMAR SINHA

On 15 January 2019, Laurent Gbagbo was acquitted by the International Criminal Court ('ICC') of charges of crimes against humanity allegedly committed in the context of post-electoral violence in Côte d'Ivoire between 16 December 2010 and 12 April 2011 as the Prosecutor failed to submit sufficient evidence to demonstrate Gbagbo's responsibility. The acquittal raises important concerns of quality control in the international criminal justice system, as such cases are factually complex, fact-rich, and often span several years.

In the wake of this event, the Centre for International Law Research and Policy (CILRAP) and the Indian Law Institute organized a two-day conference on 'Quality Control in Criminal Investigation' ('QCCI') in New Delhi on 22 and 23 February 2019. This is the third leg of CILRAP's Quality Control Project, which was conceived in 2012. The present QCCI Project is led by Morten Bergsmo, together with Xabier Agirre, Simon De Smet, Carsten Stahn and myself.

The conference, from which this volume originates, registered an international gathering of Professors, ICC officials as well as international law practitioners, advocates and students from Indian and foreign universities. In his inaugural address, the Honourable Justice Madan B. Lokur, former judge of the Supreme Court of India, highlighted how topical the issue of quality control in criminal investigation is, and drew our attention towards the ineluctable fact that both national and international criminal justice systems are in need of quality control.

The contributors to the project offered practical solutions and a host of new ideas on how to address the bottlenecks of, and impart quality in, the process from the opening of a criminal investigation to the start of the trial. The presentations drew on anthropology, demography, history, psychology, linguistics and philosophy, making the conference a truly multi-disciplinary event, as this volume demonstrates.

Like the conference, this anthology is divided into five parts, addressing (i) the context of quality control in investigations and case preparation; (ii) evidence and analysis; (iii) systemic challenges in case-preparatory work-processes; (iv) investigation plans as instruments of quality control; and (v) prosecutorial and judicial participation in investigations and case preparation.

In his opening chapter, Carsten Stahn urges international law practitioners to adopt a critical look towards the very foundation on which the existing system is built, and emphasises how the QCCI Project attempts to do so. His contribution sets the theme for future debate on four broad points: (i) the structural difference between preliminary examinations and investigations; (ii) macro problems such as cognitive biases; (iii) different structures and steps of criminal investigations; and, lastly, (iv) the way forward. What follows from there is a critical engagement with the various aspects of criminal investigations, ranging from the efficacy of procedural norms and practical problems of collecting evidence, to more substantive issues like cognitive biases within criminal investigations.

Since most of the contributors are legal practitioners, they can draw on their personal experience as actors within the criminal justice system in demonstrating the hurdles an investigator encounters in the field: for example, how investigators must take into account and understand the culture that an informant belongs to during an interview, in order to put the information in the right perspective. In this context, Simon De Smet addresses the aspect of minimizing cognitive bias in investigations and judicial fact-finding. His chapter on "Controlling the Quality of Reasoning about the Link between Evidence and Factual Propositions" could be retitled "Quality Control of One's Own Thinking", as he candidly admitted at the conference. The basic premise of his chapter is that judicial fact-finding should be a rational process that is not based on what one believes, but rather on what is rationally acceptable. De Smet argues that the 'standard of proof' should be based on a rational approach to evidence: the judge who makes a certain finding after appreciating the evidence should be able to rationally explain his finding.

The contributors discuss the various 'bottlenecks' and offer suggestions as to the possible ways to overcome them. For example, issues of inadequate factual analysis and evidence-review by the prosecution lead to weaknesses in the formulation of charges and in the trial stage. In order to overcome them, contributors such as Olympia Bekou and Xabier Agirre suggest devising a structured approach to data and information collection from the very beginning of case preparation to avoid the fragmentation and the over-collection of evidence. Particularly, Bekou emphasises the importance of understanding the legal requirements from the earlier stages of case preparation. Agirre provides insights into various analytical tools like source evaluation and diagnostic techniques, which can help the prosecution during the investigation. Highlighting the importance of structured investigation and high-quality case development, Christian Axboe Nielsen points out that analysis not only enhances the quality of investigation, but can also help the prosecution in countering the narrative of the defence whenever it is argued that the preparation of a case has been chaotic, and hence full of loopholes.

Gregory S. Gordon, while synthesizing the chapters and the deliberations, offers an important insight: the problems that constitute the topics of the discussion are a product of the regime of the ICC's first Prosecutor. He expresses that broader participation in the QCCI Project and similar ones is the need of the day in order to facilitate course correction.

Indeed, the ICC has recently found itself mired in events such as States threatening to leave – with Burundi even formally withdrawing from the Rome Statute in October 2017 – and the Office of the Prosecutor under attack from the serious accusations against both the former and the current Prosecutors. Therefore, the importance of efforts such as the QCCI Project cannot be overemphasised. In fact, contributions like these are the epicentre where many brilliant minds of the field congregate to generate a ripple of ideas that will eventually help the institutions and the system to perform better.

Professor Manoj Kumar Sinha
Director, Indian Law Institute

PROLOGUE BY GREGORY S. GORDON

I have had the pleasure to participate in the second and third legs of the incredible Quality Control Project undertaken by the Centre for International Law Research and Policy ('CILRAP') and partners from around the world since its first conference in May 2013, held at the European University Institute in Florence, on 'Quality Control in International Fact-Finding Outside Criminal Justice for Core International Crimes'. The second was on 'Quality Control in Preliminary Examination: Reviewing Impact, Policies and Practices' (The Hague, June 2017), and the third focused on 'Quality Control in Criminal Investigation' (New Delhi, February 2019), on which this volume is based. I was honoured to deliver closing remarks at this last gathering. As I pointed out in delivering those remarks, alongside this three-prong Quality Control Project, CILRAP has undertaken other research projects of a distinct theoretical flavour, such as 'Philosophical Foundations of International Criminal Law: Its Intellectual Roots, Related Limits and Potential' (New Delhi, August 2017) and 'Power in International Criminal Justice: Towards a Sociology of International Justice' (Florence, October 2017).

In his policy paper[1] underpinning the 'Quality Control in Criminal Investigation' project, Morten Bergsmo made reference to 'seven bottlenecks' in investigation and case preparation of cases involving core international crimes. He invited us to think more deeply in respect of criminal investigation practices, and to get out of our comfort zones. I quote here various snippets of his policy paper, quite revealing in this regard, where he referred to the more abstract notions of "'*fact-rich*' cases" and "a *culture* of quality control" (both footnote 10), "the *freedom* [...] to challenge the quality of work" (footnote 11), "'micro-prioritization'" (footnote 16), "confirmation biases" (Section 3.2.), "'meta-evidence'" (Section 3.1.), "nuanced [...] narratives" (footnote 21), "subsumption-analysis capacity" (footnote 22), "[e]vidence-review should be multi-disciplinary" (footnote 33), and "social anthropology" (footnote 35). In that paper, he explicitly

---

[1] Morten Bergsmo, "Towards a Culture of Quality Control in Criminal Investigations", FICHL Policy Brief Series No. 94 (2019), Torkel Opsahl Academic EPublisher, Brussels, 2019, Section 3 (http://www.toaep.org/pbs-pdf/94-bergsmo/).

encouraged us "to develop new ideas for what can be done differently and how. Honest problem-descriptions", he reminded us, "are vital but not enough. To generate new ideas, minds from outside established criminal justice practice should also contribute: *In hora venit* [or 'the hour has come']" (Section 5) – his use of Latin there certainly enhanced the call for us to go on a more cerebral journey.

I think it is evident from this comprehensive volume that many of the project participants have answered the challenge and risen to the occasion. At the New Delhi conference, rather than merely focusing on the 'nuts and bolts' aspects of criminal investigation, we were treated to a whole host of new ideas and deeper thinking that one might well consider to be of the philosophical stripe of research in our field. I jotted down notes throughout the conference and, at various points, typed in references to reliance on different disciplines, such as anthropology, demography, history, psychology, linguistics, and, of course, philosophy itself. We have heard reference to persons such as Plato and Aristotle and terms such as 'epistemology', 'natural language theory', 'cognitive load', 'cognitive bias', 'confirmation bias', 'bounded rationality', 'virtual reality', 'taxonomies', 'group think', 'victim-perpetrator dichotomies', 'Zeno's paradox', 'quantum physics', the 'observer effect', and 'dialectical processes'.

Let me return to the project policy paper's 'seven bottlenecks' and, within that framework, ask, what is the outlook going forward? Clearly, the *Gbagbo* and *Blé Goudé* case casts a large shadow over discussions on the quality of international criminal investigations. Are ICC investigations doomed to follow the same pattern in the future? I remain optimistic in thinking about the longer trajectory of the field for several reasons.

First, many of the problems discussed in this volume are arguably the product of the regime of the ICC's first Prosecutor, Luis Moreno-Ocampo. There is currently a different prosecutor in place, Fatou Bensouda, and she will soon be replaced by another. Course corrections are taking place, as we see from some of the chapters in this book, and it is reasonable to assume that more are in the offing.

Second, the ideas presented in this volume, which, as noted above, are the fruit of deep thinking by some of the key experts and practitioners in our field, will help us course-correct. And this will be an integral part of building a foundation for future success. After all, this is merely the latest in a series of quality control projects that has already dealt with fact-finding and preliminary examinations. And this volume has only added to that growing body of knowledge. From this most recent project in the series, we can glean certain common themes and tensions:

- Tension 1: establishing truth that yields real justice versus promoting efficiency and results;
- Tension 2: the use of in-house vs. outside experts; and
- Tension 3: focusing on big-picture or holistic answers vs. keeping track of the important small pieces of evidence.

And I would propose two new areas of inquiry implicit in this volume's materials but not addressed explicitly: (1) What quality control is needed on the defence side? (2) How might we modify the investigative phase so as to better promote due process and victim's rights? For overall success in this endeavour, I believe it is paramount that we eschew too much of a prosecutor-centric approach.

At the same time, from the perspective of all participants in the process, I submit that other avenues of research should be considered. The materials herein consider effective evidence-gathering procedures and different legal traditions. But it is recommended that we also study human and inter-cultural dynamics in investigative and prosecution teams. In this regard, certain facets of organisational behaviour theory could be quite enriching: (a) considering *individuals* in organisations (micro-level analysis); (b) examining *work groups* (meso-level analysis); and (c) studying how *organisations* themselves behave (macro-level analysis). There could be much value as well in considering the anthropological side of organisational behaviour by dissecting organisational culture, organisational rituals, and symbolic acts within investigative and prosecutorial units.

Another potential important area of study in this field is its international dimension. International criminal investigation on behalf of international institutions will nearly always involve *international* work teams. Thus, it would behove us to examine and incorporate social psychologist Geert Hofstede's 'cultural dimensions theory', which describes national cultures along six dimensions: power distance, individualism, uncertainty avoidance, masculinity, long-term orientation, and indulgence vs. restraint. These inter-personal or cultural human dynamics may also factor into better understanding quality control in criminal investigations. Indeed, this is true for examining all phases of the international criminal law spectrum. And, of course, it is possible that CILRAP will undertake future quality control projects on the trial phase itself, as well as perhaps post-trial proceedings. So, the Quality Control Project itself should give us great grounds for optimism.

Finally, the other key reason for optimism derives from historical reflection. In his Chapter 13 on "Challenges in Charge Selection: Considerations Informing the Number of Charges and Cumulative Charging Practices", Cale Davis refers to the wise charging decisions taken in the *Karadžić* case. I have heard my good friend and colleague Serge Brammertz (former International Criminal Tribunal for the former Yugoslavia ('ICTY') chief Prosecutor and currently chief Prosecutor of the International Residual Mechanism for Criminal Tribunals ('MICT')) describe the thought-process that went into the charge prioritisation in that case. He has observed that, notwithstanding the public's focus on the siege of Sarajevo and the Srebrenica genocide, Karadžić had been tied to many other ethnic-cleansing offences. He has described the challenges of the prosecutor's charging strategy when there are so many different crime scenes over so many years and limited resources. It would be too unwieldy to charge them all and doing so creates a risk of the 'Slobodan Milošević scenario', that is, a trial with a tremendous number of counts that drags on for so long that the defendant dies before a verdict can be rendered. But, with such a wide range of horrific war crimes traceable to Karadžić, deciding exactly which charges to exclude was an agonising process.

In the end, Brammertz and his team chose to trim the potential universe of counts by about half. They then spoke with survivors whose loved ones were not victims of the offences featured in the indictment. The prosecutors were prepared for bitter complaints. Instead, much to their relief, the survivors were extremely supportive when learning that the charging strategy was motivated by assuring the most effective and winnable case could be brought against Karadžić. More than anything, they wanted justice for the representative crimes. And, in the end, they got justice. We can learn a lot from this. And it resonates with many of the recommendations made in this volume for enhancing quality control in international criminal investigations.

The other historical point that ought to make us feel sanguine about the prospects for international criminal law in this realm going forward is the work of the last living Nuremberg prosecutor, Benjamin Ferencz, who was a master of efficiency when prosecuting the *Einsatzgruppen* case. Judge David Re in his New Delhi presentation "Rethinking Disclosure in Core International Crimes Cases" talked about the document-intensive approach in Nuremberg (see Chapter 14 below). Dr. William H. Wiley spoke about the potential benefit of having a specific end-date in mind when one starts a case (see Chapter 8 below, co-authored by Dr. Wiley and Ewan Brown). The Associated Press ('AP') described the *Einsatzgruppen* case as the "biggest murder trial in history".

But after discovering secret files that documented the deliberate massacre of over a million innocent Jews, Gypsies, and other civilian 'enemies' of the Third Reich by these special *Schutzstaffel* ('SS') extermination squads, Ferencz concluded the investigation within a matter of months. He presented his case in chief against 22 *Einsatzgruppen* leaders in less than a week (22 defendants were indicted, but one committed suicide pre-trial and another was removed from the trial on medical grounds pre-verdict). In the words of Ferencz himself:

> I did not intend to call a single witness. I knew that every survivor of a concentration camp would be eager to testify that any one of the defendants was responsible for the murder of his or her family. But I also knew that witness testimony can be fallible, and I did not have to risk it. I would rely upon the captured official German documents to prove the guilt of each defendant. A typical EG Report, for example, said, "In the city of Minsk, about 10,000 Jews were liquidated on 28 and 29 July (1941), 6,500 of whom were Russian Jews – mainly old people, women, and children – the remainder consisted of Jews unfit for work [...]". We knew which unit made the report and who was in command. And we had hundreds of such statements, including totals for each unit that added up to more than a million executions. [...] [T]he Prosecution submitted its evidence and rested its case after two days.[2]

Not all cases are the same. It is unlikely in modern times that we would be able to successfully implement such an efficient strategy. But it provides a good rough model. Using the various reforms and techniques that have been suggested in this volume – such as in-depth evidence analysis tools, the equivalent of Rule 73 hearings, time limits, better use of local resources, evidence disclosure suites, and external peer review – we can aspire to achieve those kinds of results.

In concluding remarks at the December 2018 CILRAP conference on "Integrity in International Justice", I called on the participants to look back to our Nuremberg pioneers for best practices. As part of this project,

---

[2]   Benferencz.org, "Benny Stories", Story 33 (available on its web site).

Xabier Agirre has pointed out that, in later years, Telford Taylor observed that "nobody anticipated how complex the task would be to investigate international crimes". Perhaps that was true. But at Nuremberg, in spite of it all, they still managed to do it efficiently and effectively. Based on the wise insights in this volume, we can certainly achieve similar results on a consistent basis, as we work to develop model international criminal law investigative practices in the years to come.

Gregory S. Gordon
Professor, The Chinese University of Hong Kong, Faculty of Law
Research Fellow, CILRAP

TABLE OF CONTENTS

PART III:
SYSTEMIC CHALLENGES
IN CASE-PREPARATORY WORK-PROCESSES

PART IV:
INVESTIGATION PLANS
AS INSTRUMENTS OF QUALITY CONTROL

PART V:
JUDICIAL AND PROSECUTORIAL PARTICIPATION
IN INVESTIGATION AND CASE PREPARATION

Investigative Bottlenecks and the Mindset of Quality Control

Xabier Agirre Aranburu and Morten Bergsmo[*]

1. **Investigation and Preparation of Fact-Rich Cases: The Quality Control Framework**

1.1. **Some Words on the Context of the Discourse on Quality Control**

On 15 January 2019, the case against Laurent Gbagbo, former President of Côte d'Ivoire, collapsed before the International Criminal Court. This has caused a flurry of comments. In a tempered text, Richard J. Goldstone

---

[*] **Xabier Agirre Aranburu** is currently the Head of the Investigative Analysis Section at the Investigations Division ('ID'), Office of the Prosecutor ('OTP'), International Criminal Court ('ICC'), where he has served since 2004. Previously he was Analyst and Strategic Analyst at the OTP of the International Criminal Tribunal for the Former Yugoslavia ('ICTY') (1997–2003). He has contributed to multiple investigative and training projects with different international and national authorities, universities and NGOs. He is a member of the TOAEP Editorial Board and the Advisory Boards of the Master on International Crimes, Conflict and Criminology at the Vrije Universiteit Amsterdam, and the Berg Human Rights Institute (Madrid). He has co-authored Sections 2.-4. of this chapter in his personal capacity, and his views do not represent any of the above-mentioned institutions. **Morten Bergsmo** is Director of the Centre for International Law Research and Policy (CILRAP). He was formerly Legal Adviser, ICTY-OTP (1994-2002), Senior Legal Adviser, ICC-OTP (2002-2005), before serving as an academic. Relevant to the Quality Control in Criminal Investigation ('QCCI') Project, he worked on numerous ICTY cases by writing the applicable law section of pre-trial briefs and other motions. He also played a critical role in raising the importance given by the ICTY-OTP to documentary evidence (linked initially to the use of the archive of the UN Commission of Experts for the Former Yugoslavia (UNSC 780 (1992)), the Kotor Varoš municipal documents, municipal archives secured after the lifting of the siege of Bihać, and the archive of the International Conference for the Former Yugoslavia); in securing the co-operation of key insider-witnesses; and in conceptualising the non-military analysis function within the ICTY-OTP. Section 1. of this chapter is authored by Morten Bergsmo based on the concept paper of the conference held in New Delhi on 22-23 February 2019, whose papers are published in this anthology (see Morten Bergsmo, "Towards a Culture of Quality Control in Criminal Investigations", FICHL Policy Brief Series No. 94 (2019), Torkel Opsahl Academic EPublisher, Brussels, 2019 (http://www.toaep.org/pbs-pdf/94-bergsmo/)).

observed that it "cannot be doubted [that] mistakes have been made by organs of the ICC", and that the "challenge to the Office of the Prosecutor is to expend greater effort in ensuring that cases brought to trial are fully investigated and supported by sufficient evidence".[1] Referring to the acquittal of Gbagbo as "a stinging rebuke of OTP's *modus operandi*", Patryk Labuda opined that the response of the ICC Office of the Prosecutor ('OTP') to "the challenges of conducting effective investigations in the coming years will define the Court's future".[2] Highlighting the implications for the prosecution's "investigation methods and strategies", he called for a "thorough evaluation of the Prosecutor's performance".[3] The ICC Prosecutor has in turn indicated her disagreement with the decision.[4]

As an article in *Le Monde* pointed out,[5] the concern for quality control in international criminal justice more generally goes several years back to the 1990s. It is this long observation period – not any specific case or jurisdiction – that gave birth in 2012 to the 'Quality Control Project', a research project led by the Centre for International Law Research and Policy (CILRAP) with partners. As described in the foreword above by the four co-editors of this anthology, the project has already produced three volumes on quality control in documentation as well as preliminary examination.[6]

---

[1]   Richard J. Goldstone, "Acquittals by the International Criminal Court", *EJIL: Talk!*, 18 January 2019.

[2]   Patryk Labuda, "The ICC's 'Evidence Problem': The Future of International Criminal Investigations After the Gbagbo Acquittal", *Völkerrechtsblog*, 18 January 2019. Borrowing from a 2013-article by Christian M. De Vos, Labuda observed that the ICC "has an 'evidence problem'", see Christian M. De Vos, "Investigating from Afar: The ICC's Evidence Problem", in *Leiden Journal of International Law*, vol. 26, no. 4, pp. 1009–1024. Labuda traces the 'evidence problem' "directly to certain policies put in place by the first Prosecutor, Luis Moreno Ocampo".

[3]   *Ibid.*

[4]   ICC Press Release, "Statement of the ICC Prosecutor, Fatou Bensouda, following today's decision by Trial Chamber I in the case of Laurent Gbagbo and Charles Blé Goudé", 15 January 2019 (available on the Court's web site).

[5]   See Morten Bergsmo, "La CPI, l'affaire Gbagbo et le rôle de la France", *Le Monde*, 18 January 2019 (http://www.legal-tools.org/doc/d499f6/ (French) and http://www.legal-tools.org/doc/693bee/ (English)).

[6]   See Morten Bergsmo (ed.): *Quality Control in Fact-Finding*, Torkel Opsahl Academic EPublisher ('TOAEP'), Florence, 2013, 500 pp. (http://www.toaep.org/ps-pdf/19-bergsmo); a second, expanded edition was published in July 2020 (Morten Bergsmo and Carsten Stahn (eds.): *Quality Control in Fact-Finding*, TOAEP, Brussels, 2020, 650 pp. (http://

The third leg – the 'Quality Control in Criminal Investigation Project' ('QCCI') – was launched in the autumn of 2018, with a conference held in New Delhi on 22-23 February 2019. The conference presentations can be openly accessed as films or podcasts on the project web page.[7] It concerns the phase that encompasses criminal investigation and case preparation.[8] This is the period from the opening of criminal investigation until the start of the trial. As with the two previous legs of the Quality Control Project, the focus is on core international crimes,[9] but it also includes perspectives from other fact-rich criminal cases[10] such as serious fraud and organised crime (for example, human trafficking).

1.2.   The Need to Enhance Quality Control is Not Sensitive

The QCCI Project is premised on the assumption that there is room for improvement in the quality control of all investigation or preparation of fact-rich criminal cases. This is a common challenge both in international and national jurisdictions in cases that involve many alleged incidents,

---

www.toaep.org/ps-pdf/19-bergsmo-stahn-second); and Morten Bergsmo and Carsten Stahn (eds.): *Quality Control in Preliminary Examination: Volumes 1 and 2*, TOAEP, Brussels, 2018, 1,470 pp. (http://www.toaep.org/ps-pdf/32-bergsmo-stahn and http://www.toaep.org/ps-pdf/33-bergsmo-stahn). For films and podcasts on the latter, see https://www.cilrap.org/events/170613-14-the-hague/.

[7]   The QCCI Project has been led by the authors of this chapter in co-operation with Dr. Simon De Smet (Legal Officer, Chambers, ICC), Professor Carsten Stahn (Leiden University), and Professor Manoj Kumar Sinha (Director of the Indian Law Institute, New Delhi). The team is grateful for the financial support from the Norwegian Ministry of Foreign Affairs and for the kind co-operation on the project by the ICC Prosecutor. You find more information on the project web site (https://www.cilrap.org/events/190222-23-delhi/).

[8]   There is not a clear line between 'investigation' and 'case preparation'. Jurisdictions use different regulatory frameworks and terminology. The QCCI Project does not define the two terms, to avoid narrowing the discourse it convenes. Generally speaking, 'case preparation' includes 'investigation' in addition to the legal and other preparation of a case-file for trial. This chapter refers several times to both 'investigation' and 'case preparation', not to limit the analysis to 'investigation'. Moreover, the decision to open an investigation is prepared during the earlier phase which we often refer to as 'preliminary examination'. Ideally, the first investigation plan should be drawn up late in preliminary examination. Such preparatory steps that become investigatory tools or instruments do also fall within the scope of the QCCI Project.

[9]   For the purposes of this chapter, the term 'core international crimes' denotes war crimes, crimes against humanity, genocide and aggression.

[10]   Examples of 'fact-rich' cases include core international crimes, serious fraud and organised crime. Violent crime cases in peace-time national jurisdictions – such as isolated murders or sexual violations – normally lack the factual complexity to be considered 'fact-rich'.

---

acts, transactions, victims, perpetrators, witnesses and other potential evidence. "Prosecutorial professionalization – as other forms of professionalization in the public sector – requires awareness on the part of prosecutorial leaders of the importance of self-questioning and -improvement. This is a precondition for such professionalization to take proper hold in the practice of criminal justice teams."[11] Discussing quality control does therefore not imply criticism of specific jurisdictions or actors. Such discussions are important as the available literature for practitioners has up until now been limited.[12]

Inherent in criminal justice systems around the world are two fundamental mechanisms of quality control: the work of the defence and the assessment and decisions of the judges. Both should correct errors and expose weaknesses in the prosecution's investigation and case-preparation. Both are fundamental 'quality-control mechanisms' in criminal justice, for the outcome of the case as a whole. This is a part of the architecture of

---

[11] See Carsten Stahn, Morten Bergsmo and CHAN Icarus, "On the Magic, Mystery and Mayhem of Preliminary Examinations", in Morten Bergsmo and Carsten Stahn (eds.): *Quality Control in Preliminary Examination: Volume 1, supra* note 6, p. 3, which continues: "It is this awareness and culture of quality control, including the freedom and motivation to challenge the quality of work, that this project seeks to advance". This applies equally to the QCCI Project. See also: "This quality control approach recognises the importance of leadership in fact-finding mandates, the responsibility of individual fact-finders to continuously professionalise, and the need for fact-finders to be mandate-centred, as discussed above. It is an approach that invites consideration of how the quality of every functional aspect of fact-finding can be improved, including work processes to identify, locate, obtain, verify, analyse, corroborate, summarise, synthesise, structure, organise, present, and disseminate facts. It is a state of mind characterised by a will to professionalise, and not just by the *ad hoc* development and adoption of standard procedures or universal methodologies that come so easily to lawyers", Morten Bergsmo, "Foreword by the Editor", in Morten Bergsmo (ed.), *Quality Control in Fact-Finding, supra* note 6, p. viii.

[12] Further to the references in note 6 above, the following publications are among the relevant contributions: Martin Witteveen, "5. Dealing with Old Evidence in Core International Crimes Cases: The Dutch Experience as a Case Study", in Morten Bergsmo and CHEAH Wui Ling (eds.): *Old Evidence and Core International Crimes*, TOAEP, Beijing, 2012, pp. 65–108 (http://www.toaep.org/ps-pdf/16-bergsmo-cheah); Morten Bergsmo, "1. Institutional History, Behaviour and Development" (pp. 1–31) and Xabier Agirre, "2. The Role of Analysis Capacity", in Morten Bergsmo, Klaus Rackwitz and SONG Tianying (eds.): *Historical Origins of International Criminal Law: Volume 5*, TOAEP, Brussels, 2017 (http://www.toaep.org/ps-pdf/24-bergsmo-rackwitz-song); and Helge Brunborg, "12. The Introduction of Demographic Analysis to Prove Core International Crimes", in Morten Bergsmo, CHEAH Wui Ling, SONG Tianying and YI Ping (eds.): *Historical Origins of International Criminal Law: Volume 4*, TOAEP, Brussels, 2015, pp. 477–512 (http://www.toaep.org/ps-pdf/23-bergsmo-cheah-song-yi).

criminal justice. In order to focus more in-depth, the QCCI Project is primarily concerned with quality control in the prosecution's investigation and case-preparation, not in the work of the defence or during the trial, both of which deserve a separate, subsequent project. We have, however, included a Part V in this anthology that looks at what may be useful roles for prosecutors, investigating judges, judges and specialised military lawyers in investigation and preparation of cases.

The project zooms in on some systemic 'bottlenecks' or problems that give rise to the long duration and high cost of the majority of investigations of core international crimes – undermining the quality of work-processes in cases – and it asks whether we can improve the way we work, as stated in the co-editors' foreword at the outset of this volume. The main focus is not on the habitual reform of rules of procedure or evidence, but on the less visible work-processes that constitute the day-to-day reality of investigation and preparation of core international crimes.[13] They are negatively affected by several bottlenecks of varying degrees of seriousness. The expression of these challenges differs between jurisdictions, depending on factors such as whether lawyers lead the investigations or not.[14]

1.3. Seven Bottlenecks

Based on continuous observation and analysis of work-process problems in international and national war crimes jurisdictions since July 1994, the QCCI Project team has identified the following bottlenecks as particularly problematic in core international crimes cases. The list is obviously not exhaustive, and there might be significant variations between jurisdictions and teams. The nature of a team's challenges may also change over time

---

[13] This important distinction has escaped some of the colleagues who have considered the problem of length of proceedings in international criminal justice since the expert report prepared under the auspices of the preparatory team of the ICC Office of the Prosecutor in 2003, see Morten Bergsmo and Vladimir Tochilovsky, "Measures Available to the International Criminal Court to Reduce the Length of Proceedings", in Morten Bergsmo, Klaus Rackwitz and SONG Tianying (eds.): *Historical Origins of International Criminal Law: Volume 5, op. cit.*, pp. 651–693. Pages 660–661 discuss subsequent reports, with references. Most of the bottlenecks can be resolved by improving work-processes without changing rules of procedure or evidence.

[14] In international(ised) criminal jurisdictions, the investigators and prosecutors tend to be organised in one 'office of the prosecutor'. In many Civil Law jurisdictions, lawyers lead the investigations (despite a two-fold chain of authority), whereas in many Common Law jurisdictions there is more of a separation between investigators and lawyers.

as progress is made and staff rotate. The abilites of staff are at the centre of all seven bottlenecks.

The list of bottlenecks was compiled following consultation among a number of practitioners and experts in the field, with long accumulated experience from practice. We thank the colleagues who have contributed to this process. We mention here in particular Gilbert Bitti, Eleni Chaitidou, Cale Davis, Richard J. Goldstone, Teresa McHenry, Matthias Neuner, David Re, Bård Thorsen and William H. Wiley, as well as the co-editors of this volume, Simon De Smet and Carsten Stahn.

1.3.1.   Loss of the Overview of Information

The first bottleneck concerns the problem of loss or fragmentation of overview of information and potential evidence[15] in the possession of the team during investigation or case-preparation (a problem closely related to point 3.3. below). This problem can cause delays in the investigation or case-preparation, lack of awareness of gaps in the available potential evidence (including missing 'meta-evidence' demonstrating authenticity and reliability), and the problems described in 1.3.4.–1.3.7. below. It can also perpetuate weak evidence-overview at the stages of confirmation of charges and trial.[16]

It was detailed observations of problems related to loss of overview in teams at the ICTY Office of the Prosecutor between 1994 and 2002 that led to the development of the ICC Case Matrix application as an IT-enabled prototype of a more structured cognitive approach. Its methodol-

---

[15]   The distinction between 'information' and 'potential evidence' is not strict. But much of the materials that have come into the possession of the prosecution in several core international crimes jurisdictions have had limited potential to become evidence. Search and seizure operations or requests for information may have been too wide; state actors may have dumped large amounts of information of dubious relevancy on the prosecution; non-governmental organisations may not have been selective in what they have submitted; or the prosecution may have accessed a large amount of open source information, including audio-visual material, without a clear understanding of the limits of such material. The volume of materials directly impacts on translation and disclosure requirements.

[16]   Although war crimes cases do not exceed the largest serious fraud cases, the QCCI Project has considered how cases can be narrowed where it is doubtful that the investigation team has the capacity to proceed with proper overview (and in other situations), including the rationale for narrowing and how it can be implemented. Such narrowing entails a form of 'micro-prioritization' and needs careful reflection to avoid perceptions of confirmation-bias or target-driven investigation.

ogy has influenced experiments with in-depth analysis charts in different jurisdictions and more advanced software developments such as I-DOC.

1.3.2.   Inadequate Factual Analysis

The second bottleneck concerns inadequate analysis of factual propositions relevant to the prosecution's burden in the case[17] and corresponding evidence. This problem can lead to blind alleys, misleading confirmation biases, poor evaluation of source credibility and reliability,[18] factual errors,[19] wasteful over-collection of potential evidence, unawareness of possible counter-arguments,[20] unwitting reliance on unsustainable inferences or impeachable evidence, delayed exploration of alternative factual narratives, or lack of modesty in the assessment of the work done by the team and the quality of the evidence collected.[21]

1.3.3.   Uneven Evidence-Review

The third bottleneck included here concerns irregularity in the team's daily routine of assessing relevancy and possible weight of information or potential evidence. Such irregularity can undermine the quality of the evidence-review. The irregularity can have a variety of causes, such as unavailability of the skill-sets required for effective and reliable subsumption-analysis;[22] stationary evidence-review may be seen by team members

---

[17]   That is, the factual propositions that must be proven to the requisite level of proof in order to satisfy the applicable legal requirements under the legal classification or charges. These are the factual propositions that are material to, or necessary to sustain, the charges.

[18]   This can be a particular problem if reports by non-governmental organisations based in part on hearsay are relied upon.

[19]   In international(ised) criminal jurisdictions and in the exercise of universal jurisdiction by states, materials relevant to the prosecution may be in foreign language(s) and witnesses or crime scenes situated within locations and cultures with which team members are not familiar.

[20]   The manner in which the investigation team collects and analyses exculpatory evidence can significantly impact on this analytical work.

[21]   It is relevant whether the prosecution is investigating all sides to the conflict. Multi-front investigations may generate a more nuanced understanding and narrative. One-sided investigations may make it harder to get relevant information on the other side.

[22]   By 'subsumption-analysis' is meant analysis that subsumes (or sorts and assesses) potential evidence or related factual propositions under applicable legal standards in the jurisdiction in question, primarily subject-matter provisions. This form of analysis is vital to the success of fact-rich investigations. Teams should have adequate subsumption-analysis capacity at all times during case-preparation.

as a less attractive task delegated to inadequately qualified junior staff or even interns; relevant senior team members go on too many missions causing interruptions in the evidence-review; the team fails to avail itself of evidence-review mechanisms which may exist; or lack of senior oversight from levels above the investigation team and senior prosecutor assigned to the case.

This problem can weaken the efforts to build the case steadily, undermine a sense of dynamic progress in the team, and prevent that individual team members develop a proper overview of the case (1.3.1.), with subsequent delays and demotivation.[23]

1.3.4.   Formulation of Responsibility

A fourth bottleneck is vague or non-substantial formulation of criminal responsibility within the team *after*[24] it has in its possession enough potential evidence. The problem is the formulation is not properly informed by existing potential evidence. Several reasons can cause this problem, including a lack of overview of information (1.3.1.) or inadequate management of evidence-review (1.3.3.). This bottleneck can prevent proper prioritisation of team resources to focus on weak links; slow down work-processes for lack of clarity; prolong the fact-gathering period; and inundate the team's systems with information of limited value.[25]

1.3.5.   Charging Without Proper Focus in the Case

A fifth bottleneck is the broad use of cumulative or other forms of charging of crimes and modes of liability that have the effect of blunting the focus of the case.[26] Cumulative charging is often used pursuant to a pre-

---

[23]   Point 1.3.3. essentially concerns the role lawyers should play in the investigation, including in overall co-ordination.

[24]   This bottleneck scenario does not presuppose the problems of target-driven investigations or factual confirmation-bias: that is, the described bottleneck may be there even when these additional problems are absent.

[25]   There is obviously a difference (especially early in the investigation) between having specific investigative targets (which can facilitate a more efficient investigation, but may not be in keeping with the facts as they emerge during the investigation) or a more open-ended investigation (perhaps ultimately fairer, but possibly less efficient). But the challenge of vague formulation of criminal responsibility described in 1.3.4. needs to be addressed in both scenarios.

[26]   In some instances, there may even be an unwillingness to undertake an internal prosecution assessment of what the best-suited principal and subsidiary charges would be, as an exercise to better understand the core of the case under preparation. Jurisdictions that do

cautionary fear of acquittals caused by failure to include a classification,[27] not only a desire to ensure accountability for the full range of criminal conduct engaged in. Diffusing the focus of the case can swell both the prosecution and defence cases, and reduce the impact of the judgment.

1.3.6. Too Much Evidence

The sixth bottleneck included is made up of excessively long exhibit- and witness-lists in the prosecution's part of the case.[28] This can again be caused by a variety of reasons, including lack of focus in the framing of the case (1.3.4.); fear of not having enough evidence; misconstrued faith in the effect of voluminous evidence; and weak quality control in selecting the best-suited evidence. This practice can obviously delay proceedings significantly and make them costlier.

1.3.7. Voluminous Disclosure

The seventh and final bottleneck included here concerns prosecution[29] disclosure to the defence of voluminous materials not clearly related to a central hypothesis of criminal responsibility. The reasons may be those described in 1.3.1.–1.3.6. above; a perceived pressure to start the trial; fear of being accused of hiding materials; or the prosecution having received a large amount of materials collected by others. This problem can delay the case and raise questions of *de facto* fairness.

1.4. Further Challenges

Fact-rich war crimes investigations are of course confronted by other challenges than these seven, for example, a) context-specific difficulties in obtaining evidence in the first place because of factors such as ongoing

---

not have the principle of *iura novit curia* may sometimes be more constrained in their ability to avoid cumulative charging. There is, however, a difference between narrow and broad use of cumulative charges even then.

27 Frequently referred to as 'technical acquittals'.

28 Which is then often replicated by the defence.

29 It should be considered how appropriate it is that the prosecution – as opposed to the registry or judicial administration – is the central repository of materials that may only potentially be disclosable and is not its work-product (such as documents from archives in the country where the alleged crimes occurred). This does not refer to witness-related materials generated by the prosecution. The rapid increase in open source materials is also relevant in this connection. Chapter 14 below by Judge David Re discusses this bottleneck in detail.

conflict or time-consuming mutual legal assistance procedures; b) that the available personnel lack the experience or ability to effectively undertake these types of investigations, especially where lawyers are not involved at the earliest stages and do not oversee or supervise the investigation, or where the personnel is not so familiar with applicable core international crimes (which can contribute to, for example, vague formulation of criminal responsibility or evidence overload); c) co-ordination deficiencies between investigation teams that pursue different crimes in the same conflict; and d) personnel may be assigned to several inquiries at the same time (especially in domestic agencies), affecting their drive to bring the investigation forward.[30] These challenges should be kept in mind when analysing the core bottlenecks identified in Section 1.3., in order not to take a simplified or schematic view.

1.5.   Structuring an Open Inquiry

The QCCI Project has asked whether work-processes can be enhanced so as to reduce the negative impact of the seven bottlenecks described in Sections 1.3.1. to 1.3.7. above. Such inquiry requires open-minded analysis and new ideas on how we can work better, in manners that are not boxed in by the particulars of any one jurisdiction or by biases related to the familiar distinctions between Common and Civil Law procedure which too often become a distraction to innovative thinking.

The project has not been constrained by the traditional discourse-delimitation between procedural and evidentiary questions (for the lawyers) and police methods (for the police). Rather, it has sought to carve out and focus on a third discourse domain which we have called *key work-processes in investigation and case preparation*, with a pragmatic focus on high-quality results, cost-efficiency, and best project-management techniques, for critical and innovative input by lawyers, analysts, investigators and others. It is particularly important that lawyers participate in the discussion on the seven bottlenecks in Section 1.3., rather than retreating into comfortable shells of legalese.

The project has been structured into five main parts that are reflected in the New Delhi conference programme as well as this anthology: Part I: The Context of Quality Control in Investigations and Case Preparation,

---

[30]   A case law with judgments running into hundreds of pages, and a proliferation of separate and dissenting opinions, may increase the consequences of a less settled law.

Part II: Evidence and Analysis, Part III: Systemic Challenges in Case-Preparatory Work-Processes, Part IV: Investigation Plans as Instruments of Quality Control, and Part V: Judicial and Prosecutorial Participation in Investigation and Case Preparation.

The project has sought to promote attention to

- whether our use of existing quality-control instruments[31] such as a) investigation plans,[32] b) evidence-review panels,[33] c) draft indictments, d) indictments, and e) pre-trial briefs can be further developed;

- how newer tools such as f) analysis techniques[34] can be used more intuitively and consistently;

- whether a) to f) should be supplemented by additional instruments to avert the bottlenecks described in Section 1.3. or reduce their negative impact; and

- whether there are areas of expertise that could meaningfully be tapped into more actively during investigation.[35]

The Centre for International Law Research and Policy (CILRAP) and partner institutions have invited as broad participation as possible in the QCCI Project. Authors were asked to not only describe the best available practice as seen by him or her, but to develop new ideas for what could be done differently and how. Honest problem-descriptions are vital,

---

[31] These tools have the *capacity* to be used to enhance quality control. We are not suggesting that they are actually being used to that end, or that they have been designed to serve that purpose only.

[32] Due consideration should be given to the added importance of such plans when a team is composed of professionals from different national jurisdictions and cultures, and the common glue that binds them is not yet strong.

[33] By this is meant panels with senior officers, external to the team, to assess the strength of the case and its evidence. This entails 'stress-testing' of the evidence, including of crime-base incidents and linkage to persons higher in chains of authority. In some entrenched situations, experts from outside the organisation are used (persons who are not part of the chains of authority and who have no loyalty or other conflicts of interest). Proper evidence-review is multi-disciplinary when required, while led by competent lawyers.

[34] Such as statistics, mapping, analysis of organisational structures and telecommunications, and source evaluation.

[35] One example is social anthropology, which could be employed to shed light on what actually happened on a factual level, and develop case hypotheses and supplement evidence reviews.

but not enough. To generate new ideas, minds from outside established war crimes justice practice have been encouraged to contribute.

The QCCI Project never sought to produce a mere catalogue of proposals. Rather, its ambition has been to have a longer-term impact on our thinking about the appropriate mindset and culture of quality control in different jurisdictions. The project has already had some impact prior to the publication of this anthology. The Prosecutor of the International Criminal Court welcomed the debates in our conference in February 2019 and took into account some of the resulting advice when issuing her OTP Strategic Plan 2019-2021 in July 2019.

Further to her presentation and the lively discussions at the New Delhi conference, Moa Lidén was invited by the Investigative Analysis Section ('IAS') of the ICC Office of the Prosecutor to conduct two training sessions on confirmation bias (see Chapter 7 below), proposing specific methods to control such biases and build greater objectivity in investigations. The training was positively received, and subsequently the Investigations Division has decided to consolidate some of the relevant considerations into standard practice.

Inspired by the QCCI Project, two of the co-editors of this volume – Simon de Smet and Xabier Agirre Aranburu, with the assistance of researchers from Amsterdam Free University – organised on ICC premises a "Forum on witness assessments" in November 2019 with participation of staff from all ICC organs and the defence. Three experts on forensic psychology from the Universities of Maastricht and Amsterdam gave lectures, and the ensuing debate has assisted in raising awareness among organs and parties.[36] Given the positive feedback from participants, this 'forum' may well continue to explore issues of evidence and investigations related to the QCCI Project, seen in light of emerging ICC practice.

In September 2020, the Independent Expert Review ('IER') mandated by the ICC Assembly of States Parties made public its findings in a detailed report with 384 recommendations for improvement across the Court organs. The IER report included a number of references to 'quality control', including a section on "OTP Internal Quality Control Mechanisms", and references to relevant publications released by the Torkel Opsahl Academic Epublisher. Some of their recommendations are con-

---

[36] The event was possible thanks to the assistance of Barbora Hola and Gabrielle Chlevikaite from Vrije Univeristeit Amsterdam.

sistent with views expressed in this volume, as explained in the following pages. We are pleased to see that the emphasis on 'quality control' promoted by the QCCI Project – and CILRAP's wider Quality Control Project – is being increasingly endorsed by practitioners and experts in international justice.

2. Main Themes of the Anthology

Five main themes emerge from the subsequent 23 chapters of this volume, all of them relevant to quality control in investigation and case-preparation ('QCCI') in any criminal justice juridiction:

- rigorous internal review mechanisms;
- analysis techniques and professionals;
- contextual embedding;
- cognitive psychology and sound reasoning; and
- planning tools and processes.

Firstly, investigations need rigorous internal review mechanisms, within the investigation and prosecution agencies, to ensure their quality, and to adjust direction whenever necessary. We identified these reviews from the outset as one of the key bottlenecks (see Section 1.3.3. above), and several chapters have underlined their importance, whether in the form of 'evidence review boards' like those known since the late 1990s at the ICTY, or through adversarial tests like 'devil's advocates' or 'red teaming'. This emerges as a 'lesson learned' in chapters written by senior practitioners (including Chapter 3 below as well as the chapters by Christian A. Nielsen, William H. Wiley and Ewan Brown, and Markus Eikel), and it is also reinforced by the advice offered by legal and psychological experts (see Chapters 1 by Carsten Stahn and Chapter 7 by Moa Lidén). The above-mentioned Independent Expert Review on the ICC ('IER') has likewise emphasised this issue in its report of September 2020, inviting the OTP to strengthen its current practice.[37] Effective implementation of these mechanisms in any jurisdiction will require support and commit-

---

[37] See Independent Expert Review, "Review of the International Criminal Court and the Rome Status System, Final Report", 30 September 2020, section on "Evidence Reviews: Internal and Peer Review", and recommendations 305, 308, 309 and 310 ('IER Report') (https://www.legal-tools.org/doc/cv19d5/). See footnote 44 below.

ment from senior officers, including chief prosecutors themselves, and adequate analytical techniques.

Secondly, investigations need to use analysis strategically to find their way through masses of complex and often conflicting information, as identified in the bottlenecks defined as loss of overview of information (Section 1.3.1. above) and inadequate factual analysis (Section 1.3.2. above). Cognisant of the importance of analysis, the co-editors invited several former or current professional analysts and researchers as contributors to this volume (Bouwknegt, Nielsen, Wiley, Brown and Eikel, in addition to co-editor Xabier Agirre Araburu himself). The reader may appreciate the value of their methods, including elements of political analysis, organisational structures, critical evaluation of sources, and multiple structured techniques. The more talented lawyers have always valued the work of analysts, as we know from Telford Taylor's compliments for the analysts at Nuremberg, to Leila Bourghiba's similar praise in her Chapter 21, through the continuing support for analysis by CILRAP.[38]

The investigations of core international crimes need to embrace the 'intelligence-led model', which has been recommended as best practice among others by the Organisation for the Security and Cooperation in Europe ('OSCE'), based on "close co-operation between the analysts and the law enforcement decision-makers".[39] This is also consistent with the notion of "evidence-based decision making", which the International Organisation for Standardization ('ISO') identifies a one of the key 'quality management principles', since "[f]acts, evidence and data analysis lead to greater objectivity and confidence in decision making".[40] Furthermore, the IER in September 2020 issued several recommendations to strengthen analysis in the ICC-OTP investigations, including higher recognition for analysts, trusting analysts for collection planing and evidence reviews, engaging "analysts with specialised skills", and that the OTP "should

---

[38] See Telford Taylor, USA Brigadier General and Chief Counsel for War Crimes, "Final Report to the Secretary of the Army on the Nuernberg War Crimes Trials under Control Council Law No. 10", Washington, D.C., 15 August 1949, including acknowledgements of analysts on pp. 14, 18, 43, 44 and 345.

[39] See OSCE, "Guidebook on Intelligence-Led Policing", 3 July 2017 (available on its web site).

[40] See ISO, "Quality Management Principles", 2015, p. 12 (available on its web site).

make additional resources available for the IAS" [Investigative Analysis Section].[41]

The mass proliferation of digital data only emphasises the role of professional analysts. They are in the best position to lead the investigation, navigating in parallel the analogue and digital worlds, because of their comprehensive factual knowledge, critical thinking, and advance software skills. As has been observed by technology experts in reference to the ICC investigations: "Empowering analysts, in particular, by creating opportunities for learning, experimentation, and creativity, may be the best way to adapt to the new challenges".[42]

Thirdly, any crime emerges from a social context, and understanding that context is indispensable to investigate the crime effectively. If the investigators are foreign to the context, they will need to make a serious effort to educate themselves on the relevant cultural and societal issues prior to contact with potential witnesses. They will also need to engage local actors genuinely and respectfully, and hire area-experts on an ongoing basis. The importance of this knowledge and embedding cannot be over-emphasised. The investigation must breathe with the local society, and be guided by emotional intelligence towards its victims and perpetrators alike. It is necessary to understand the blend of factors that shape uniquely every situation (in a way similar to how inter-sectional feminism calls for a joint consideration of gender along with class, ethnicity, postcolonial legacy and other features).[43]

---

[41] IER Report, section on "Evidence Assessment and Analysis" and recommendations 299-304, see *supra* note 37.

[42] Jay D. Aronson and Enrique Piracés, contribution to the ICC Forum hosted by the University of California, Los Angeles ('UCLA'), School of Law, on the question "To what extent can cyber evidence repositories, and digital and open-source evidence, facilitate the work of the OTP, and the ICC more generally?", 2020 (available on the web site of the UCLA ICC Forum).

[43] For an early formulation of this concept, see Angela Davis, *Women, Race and Class*, Vintage Books, New York, 1983. For a more recent analysis, see Ana Martin Beringola "Intersectionality: A Tool for the Gender Analysis of Sexual Violence at the ICC", in *Amsterdam Law Forum*, 2017, vol. 9, No. 2. For a feminist critical discussion on the focus on sexual violence, see Karen Engle, *The Grip of Sexual Violence in Conflict*, Stanford University Press, 2020.

The IER Report has also highlighted this issue in the context of the ICC.[44] In the absence of proper contextual and inter-sectional knowledge, the serious consequences highlighted by several contributors to this volume (Bouwknegt, Wiley and Brown, Bourguiba, as well as Agirre Aranburu) may repeat again and again with every new international investigation.

Fourthly, investigations and prosecutions are highly conditioned by the psychology of the officers in charge. They are conducted by human beings, not by super-human robots; by people who think and feel essentially like any person in the street, including projections of their personal backgrounds, desire to be accepted by colleagues and superiors, and personal or institutional self-interest. International investigations need the scientific knowledge on cognitive psychology developed over decades in national systems, as Moa Lidén, Trond Myklebust, Gavin Oxburgh and William Webster, as well as Xabier Agirre Aranburu explain in their chapters, and Stahn and De Smet also endorse from a legal perspective. Practitioners need humble acknowledgment of their psychological frailties – modesty helps learning, and investigations are nothing else than learning processes.

Finally, it is clear that major investigations, like any major scientific or engineering project, need serious planning. This is firmly established in the chapters by Eikel, Angotti, Tandon and Lalit, and Butenschøn Skre on the basis of both national and international experience. There is not only a need to have clarity on the objectives, timelines and resources. Planning of a higher order will also be required to secure the appropriate budget and personnel, and to make the right decisions when selecting situations and cases, a point thoroughly addressed by Devasheesh Bais and Cale Davis in their chapters.

---

[44] The experts argue that there is "a substantial problem" with regard to sufficient expertise in the ICC-OTP on situation countries. See IER Report, para. 170 and recommendations 293-298, see *supra* note 37. At the time of writing, the ICC-OTP is carefully considering the IER report and its recommendations. For an earlier commentary on this subject, see Xabier Agirre Aranburu, "Measuring Distances – A Response to the Book 'Distant Justice' by Phil Clark", in *Opinio Juris*, 2 October 2019.

3. Overview of Subsequent Chapters of the Anthology

In Chapter 1 below, Carsten Stahn builds a bridge between the previous work on preliminary examination in the Quality Control Project[45] and this volume on investigations, based, *inter alia*, on his expert knowledge of ICC jurisprudence. His chapter outlines the commonalities and differences between these different stages, and proposes important points for further development, some of which are subsequently addressed in detail by other contributors to this volume, such as cognitive biases, the need of proper planning, and the crucial importance of peer-review systems.

Thijs B. Bouwknegt follows in Chapter 2 with a critique of the investigations by different international tribunals in Africa, including Rwanda (ICTR), Sierra Leone (SCSL), the Democratic Republic of Congo, Northern Uganda and Côte d'Ivoire (ICC). From his viewpoint as a historian and researcher, Bouwknegt finds that too often the arguments by the prosecution are simplistic and biased for the sake of incrimination. He suggests that investigations would be more reliable if trusted to some agency independent from the prosecution.

Part II: Evidence and Analysis contains six chapters. In Chapter 3, Xabier Agirre Aranburu explains the role of professional analysts and their QCCI tecniques. Most of this chapter is devoted to source evaluation, including a model with standard criteria to assess credibility and reliabiliy, and a critique of the reasoning adopted for this matter by some ICC chambers. He further recommends a number of diagnostic and adversarial techniques, such as Analysis of Competing Hypotheses, overview templates, 'devil's advocates' and Evidence Review Boards.

The reader may find some common ground between the second and the fourth chapter, both written by historians. In Chapter 4, Christian A. Nielsen, formerly an analyst at the ICTY and the ICC and currently a professor of history, deals with the key question of organisational structures. His insight is critical for leadership cases, beginning with his warning that organisations are never monolithical, no matter what legal theories may have been used to aggregate multiple suspects and incidents. Like Bouwknegt, Nielsen doubts the impartiality of investigations designed for

---

45. See Morten Bergsmo and Carsten Stahn (eds.), *Quality Control in Preliminary Examination: Volumes 1 and 2*, TOAEP, Brussels, 2018 (http://www.toaep.org/ps-pdf/32-bergsmo-stahn and http://www.toaep.org/ps-pdf/33-bergsmo-stahn).

prosecution. Both recommend greater organisational independence, particularly for analysts.

In Chapter 5, Trond Myklebust, Gavin Oxburgh and William Webster focus on investigative interviews, a fundamental issue as international criminal investigations continue to rely largely on witness testimony. They outline the best practices according to scientific research, the 'PEACE model' and the standards of the International Investigative Interviewing Research Group ('IIIRG'). These operational and training standards for witness interviewing have been adopted, among others, by the Investigations Division of the ICC-OTP and it is safe to recommend them to any investigative agency dealing with witnesses.

In Chapter 6, Moa Lidén brings a forensic perspective to the book with her assessment of the methods used to estimate age in cases of alleged child soldiers. Her review of eight cases from the SCSL and ICC identifies challenges and opportunities for every kind of evidence so far utilised, including forensics, testimony, images and documents. Those familiar with the difficulties in the first trial of the ICC, the *Lubanga* case, will appreciate the importance of the subject, and investigations on alleged child soldiers should consider Lidén's pioneering research for guidance and 'lessons learned'.

In a second comprehensive contribution to this anthology, Chapter 7, Moa Lidén takes the psychological research on confirmation bias, conducted in multiple national systems, to the international arena for the first time. Practitioners will recognise many of the cognitive problems described in this chapter, as the tendency to confirm incriminating allegations to the detriment of impartial assessments is a frequent problem in criminal investigations. The chapter identifies the main 'risk factors' and proposes 'debiasing techniques' for each of them, in ways that can be readily implemented by investigation and prosecution services.

William H. Wiley and Ewan Brown develop a sobering analysis of the current state of international investigations in Chapter 8. Both authors worked as analysts at the ICTY-OTP before joining the ICC-OTP in its early days, just like other contributors to this volume (Nielsen, Eikel and Agirre Aranburu), and they write with sound technical knowledge as well as a sense of disappointment with international tribunals. They make the case for privatisation of international investigations, which comes as no surprise after their work with the Commission for International Justice and Accountability, as well as different defence cases. Based on their intelligence background, they propose appointing 'collection managers'. They also advise internal review procedures, such as 'evidence reviews' and 'devil's advocates', in line with the recommendations in other chapters (Stahn, Agirre Aranburu, Lidén and others).

Part III: Systemic Challenges in Case-Preparatory Work-Processes also includes six chapters. Devasheesh Bais addresses in Chapter 9, case selection and prioritisation, which is the strategic issue *par excellence* in international investigations. The chapter builds on the experience of different jurisdictions, as well as pioneering work undertaken by CILRAP in this area since prior to 2008, leading, *inter alia*, to a 2009 TOAEP volume on this subject.[46] Bais shares an overview of some fourteen projects and reports on case selection and prioritisation in the period 1995-2019, from the ICTY, ICC, Bosnia and Herzegovina, Colombia, the Democratic Republic of the Congo, and the Central African Republic. As he concludes, the ICC-OTP Policy Paper on Case Selection and Prioritisation (2016) and its Strategic Plan 2019-2021 may be of some assistance to inform strategic decision-making on this matter, but more work needs to be done on prioritisation criteria.

With her Chapter 10, Olympia Bekou inaugurates a series of chapters dedicated to pre-trial techniques, exploring whether their earlier implementation could help investigation and case-preparation. Bekou chronicles the implementation of the 'in-depth analysis charts' at the ICC, a classification scheme designed to tabulate legal requirements with factual allegations and means of evidence. At the ICC this tool was adopted by some judges and dismissed by others, while the prosecution never favoured it in the specific manner that it was introduced by judges. Bekou highlights the potential benefits of the 'in-depth analysis chart' for disclosure and for investigations, and she suggests that the charts should be given due consideration, perhaps in an evolved form.

Simon De Smet is one of the three legal officers at ICC Chambers contributing to this volume, along with Gilbert Bitti and Eleni Chaitidou. In Chapter 11 he presents a prototype for an 'argumentation map' to plot the logical flows that could lead to judicial findings 'beyond reasonable doubt'. De Smet also discusses the trustworthiness of the sources of evidence, in terms that are comparable to the analytical methodology for

---

[46] Morten Bergsmo (ed.), *Criteria for Prioritizing and Selecting Core International Crimes Case*, TOAEP, Oslo, 2nd edition, 2010 (https://legal-tools.org/doc/f5abed).

source evaluation proposed in Chapter 3, only from the viewpoint of the judges. The chapter makes important contributions to the theory of legal reasoning, inviting the reader to join in further exploration.

Matthias Neuner reviews in Chapter 12 the practice of the ICC regarding modes of responsibility.[47] He suggests that the cases filed by the prosecution should be clearer about the alleged responsibilities, avoiding to charge multiple modes in ways that could swell the case unnecessarily or otherwise be unfair, and that have been discouraged by the judges. In view of the judicial record so far, Neuner advises caution for the prosecution, holding back the filing of draft charges until the modes of responsibility can be clearly identified. Following detailed analysis, he discourages the use of cumulative charges. Neuner concurs with Agirre Aranburu in recommending a policy of 'over-delivering' by operating with evidence standards higher than what is formally required in the early stages, which would be also consistent with the practice in Norway, as we will learn in the chapter by Butenschøn Skre.

Chapter 13 by Cale Davis discusses the selection of charges. He approaches this issue empirically, after interviewing a selection of senior prosecution lawyers in several international tribunals, and mastering statistically a large series of cases. He identifies ample variations across cases, as well as underlying factors that lead to more expansive or economic choices. Practitioners will recognise those factors from their experience, while this chapter may assist to acknowledge and manage them with greater fairness and efficiency.

The anthology would not be complete without the advice of a judge, and we were fortunate to have Judge David Re (of the Special Tribunal for Lebanon) address the issue of disclosure in Chapter 14. In his own words, "disclosure is a swamp, like a mire of quicksand that can rapidly swallow the unsuspecting". Judge Re offers a way out of this 'swamp', based on a detailed review of the experience of several international tribunals. He proposes specific methods and responsibilities for the parties and the judges as well as an important role for the court's neutral admin-

---

[47] While many authors and practitioners refer to 'modes of liability' in the context of the ICC, the term 'liability' is never mentioned in the ICC Statute, which refers instead consistently to 'responsibility', including in Article 25 on "Individual criminal responsibility", Article 28 on "Responsibility of commanders and other superiors", and Article 31 on "Grounds for excluding criminal responsibility", see Rome Statute of the ICC, 17 July 1998 (http://www.legal-tools.org/doc/7b9af9/).

istration, with appropriate electronic tools and protocols. Beyond investigations, this chapter will be of great technical interest for litigation lawyers and judges. It is an example of the kind of well-informed, critical and innovative thinking that the QCCI Project has invited.

Markus Eikel is one of the two contributors to this volume who work for the Investigations Division of the ICC-OTP, along with Agirre Aranburu. In Chapter 15 – the first of four chapters in *Part IV: Investigation Plans as Instruments of Quality Control* – he explains the importance of investigative planning based on the experience of the ICC-OTP, including his own as Investigations Team Leader. Having proper investigation plans, with standard templates and processes, is fundamental for the success of any complex investigation, as well as for cost-efficient management of resources. The bottlenecks of 'overview of information' (Section 1.3.1.), 'evidence review' (Section 1.3.3.) and 'too much evidence' (Section 1.3.6.) cannot be addressed without serious design and control of investigation plans. In this chapter the reader will find detailed guidance for this purpose, including specific reference to the ICC-OTP Regulations and practice.

Additional guidance for investigation planning follows in Chapter 16 by Antonio Angotti, who compares the original concept of investigation plans in the ICC-OTP Draft Regulations (2003) and some tools available in the Italian legal system. Interesting examples of prosecutorial planning, co-ordination and prioritisation have surfaced in Italy in recent years in areas such as environmental and gender-based crimes, with elements that partly resemble the tools designed for the ICC and may provide inspiration for any jurisdiction. He also highlights the detailed provisions on the Draft Regulations on investigation plans, including the required participation by the highest level of management in their discussion and adoption (which is echoed in the 2020 IER Report), and that an investigation should not be opened unless there is a draft investigation plan prepared. The Draft Regulations required that professional investigators and prosecutors should be responsible for its preparation.

More national references enrich the discussion on investigation plans in Chapter 17, as Usha Tandon and Shreeyash Uday Lalit share the experience in India with human trafficking crimes. A comparative consideration of the Indian Criminal Procedure Code and the ICC model shows both similarities and differences. While in India investigations are conducted independently by the police, in the ICC-OTP they are subordinated to trial attorneys. The Standard Operating Procedures ('SOPs') to investigate human trafficking crimes adopted by the Government of India in 2007 with the assistance of UNODC, and by the National Human Rights Commission of India in 2017, show tools and techniques that may be relevant for crimes in different jurisdictions. The authors argue that the ICC-OTP planning model could be "too onerous" for Indian practice, which needs more flexibility under broader SOPs. Perhaps every system needs to find the planning model that best suits its needs, combining appropriately efficiency, accountability and flexibility.

Alf Butenschøn Skre is the author of Chapter 18, the last one of Part IV dedicated to investigation plans. He explains in detail the planning process for criminal investigations in Norway, based on relevant documents and his experience as a Public Prosecutor. In the Norwegian system, the adoption of investigation plans is a standard practice based on clear instructions and requirements. The plans are used as 'living documents' handled through web-based electronic templates to facilitate sharing and updating as necessary. Instructions by the Director of Public Prosecutions outline the specific purposes of the investigation plans, including to implement national prosecutorial priorities, manage efficiently resources, guarantee legal compliance, keep investigative objectivity, and facilitate due diligence *vis-à-vis* victims. Factual hypotheses and legal considerations must also be captured in these plans. Butenschøn Skre explains methodically these processes and suggests rightly that this approach should assist in adressing bottlenecks identified by the QCCI Project.

Part V: Judicial and Prosecutorial Participation in Investigation and Case Preparation offers the last five chapters of the book. They consider the role judges, investigating judges, prosecutors and specialised military lawyers can and should play during investigation and preparation of core international crimes cases. This is an area where comparative perspectives can be particularly important.

In Chapter 19, Gilbert Bitti draws on his long experience at the ICC Pre-Trial Chambers that review the cases resulting from the OTP investigative and legal work. The author favours greater involvement of ICC judges in the investigations, a theory rooted in French national law, as Leila Bourguiba explains in her Chapter 21 about the French model. Bitti draws on his expert knowledge of the law of the ICC, having played a key role in the drafting of the ICC Statute, Rules of Procedure and Evidence, and Regulations. The chapter contains many propositions for the ICC-

OTP, some of them essential to its investigative duties, and others reflective of disagreements between Pre-Trial Chambers and the OTP.

Eleni Chaitidou adds, in Chapter 20, more advice for the ICC Prosecutor from the viewpoint of a lawyer who has several years of experience from the ICC Pre-Trial Chambers. She focuses on cases in which Pre-Trial Chambers decided to amend the charges proposed by the ICC Prosecutor. The comparison between the legal assessments of the OTP attorneys and the judges are helpful for the legal discourse, as well as for the OTP's general case-preparation. Based on the cases she discusses, the author emphasises the role of the Pre-Trial Chambers in case-preparation, especially as regards legal characterisations (where she offers some guidance also for the ICC-OTP).

Whereas Part IV offers some national perspectives on investigation planning (drawing on Italy, India and Norway), Chapter 21 by Leila Bourguiba analyses the role of investigating judges and judges in French investigations and case-preparation, supplementing the two preceding chapters which considered the role of the judiciary in case-preparation before the ICC. Bourguiba provides a thorough overview of the French experience, writing from her unique experience from both the ICC Pre-Trial Chambers and the French War Crimes and Crimes against Humanity Unit. Among the many valuable points in her chapter, we learn about the proactive efforts of the French judges to study the social context of the crimes, engaging experts *ex officio*, in ways that resemble the recommendations in earlier chapters by Bouwknegt and Nielsen to ensure contextual awareness and independent analysis. Bourguiba describes a solid system, as it operates in French law. There are obviously many aspects of the French and other well-functioning national systems from which criminal justice for core international crimes can learn. As stated in the co-editors' foreword to this book, there needs to be a two-way stream of ideas and approaches between national and international jurisdictions.

We are privileged to have Tor-Geir Myhrer (Norway Police University College) addressing, in Chapter 22, one of the most sensitive issues in the real world of criminal investigations: the role of prosecutors in investigation and case-preparation as well as the rapport between investigative and legal officers. Myhrer speaks with the wisdom of a senior prosecutor and doctor of law with some 40 years of professional experience, committed to building the best possible understanding between lawyers and investigators. In the Norwegian system, importantly, the initial prosecutorial work is done by lawyers embedded in the police force. The high level of education of Norwegian police officers allows them to interact most effectively with both the embedded lawyers as well as the more senior prosecutors. As Myhrer explains with multiple examples, legal direction and audit of the investigation are necessary for a number of activities that impact on due process, privacy rights, and overall legal relevance. Both investigative and legal staff can make good use of Myher's advice to build their co-operation on the basis of loyalty and respect.

Finally, in Chapter 23, Gilad Noam presents some reflections on the role of military lawyers in case-preparation based on the experience of Israel, which has a military justice system, as do countries like Nigeria, the United Kingdom and the United States. Noam reviews some of the recommendations by the 'Turkel Commission' established by the Government of Israel to examine the attack by Israeli forces on the humanitarian flotilla bound for Gaza.[48] The chapter highlights the question whether specialised criminal justice personnel should be used more in criminal justice for core international crimes, while respecting the integrity of the criminal justice process. For some elements of crime, it can obviously be an advantage to have detailed familiarity with and understanding of technical and operational military practice.

4. Some Thoughts on the Way Forward

We hope that this volume will help set the foundation for better quality control in the investigation of core international crimes, and foster dialogue among practitioners across jurisdictions and professional fields. There is certainly much more to say. Additional research and critical discussion are much needed. Different views among experts are not only understandable; they are prerequisites to progress through the contrast of

---

[48] In 2010, the Israeli Navy attacked a flotilla *en route* to Gaza, resulting in the death of ten flotilla members. In 2013, the Union of the Comoros referred to the ICC-OTP the situation concerning "the 31 May 2010 Israeli raid on the Humanitarian Aid Flotilla bound for [the] Gaza strip", and requested the OTP to initiate an investigation, see, ICC-OTP, "ICC Prosecutor receives referral by the authorities of the Union of the Comoros in relation to the events of May 2010 on the vessel 'MAVI MARMARA'", Statement, 14 May 2013 (https://www.legal-tools.org/doc/3434fe/). For the latest decision on this situation, see ICC, Decision on the 'Application for Judicial Review by the Government of the Comoros', Pre-Trial Chamber I, 16 September. 2020, ICC-01/13-111 (https://www.legal-tools.org/doc/mqu8bo/).

opinions. Even on highly specialised investigative issues, experts are frequently known to differ.[49]

Management issues have been addressed to some extent in our volume, but may deserve further attention in subsequent editions. A deliberate quality-control culture requires not only thoughtful planning, but also knowledge-management (as building knowledge is the core business of an investigation), recruitment, human resources, financial management, training, security (for information, premises, witnesses and staff), procurement, logistics, language skills, and co-operation with external partners. It is not an easy set of tasks. Good criminal justice practitioners do not necessarily make good managers, just like in any other business. It remains a key issue for discussion how to manage the workflow and interface between investigators and lawyers, a complex question that, as our volume shows, finds different answers in, for example, France, Norway, India, Italy or the ICC.

In some criminal justice agencies, it may be helpful to detail the 'quality control' notion with an articulation of pre-conditions for the desired high quality. Paramount among them will be the right choice of skills and personnel. This issue was the subject of much discussion in the initial stages of the ICC, leading to the conclusion that investigations require staff with higher levels of education and diverse backgrounds.[50] The large volumes of information, along with complex responsibilities, call for personnel that are not afraid to study hundreds of pages, and will be able to synthesise the main points while considering alternative hypotheses and

---

[49] See, for example, the diverging views between experts testifying about statistical crime-pattern analysis in the ICTY judgments of *Milutinović*, and about trauma and credibility in *Furundžija*, see ICTY, *Milutinović et al.*, Trial Chamber, 26 February 2009, IT-05-87-T (vol. 1: https://www.legal-tools.org/doc/9eb7c3/, vol. 2: https://www.legal-tools.org/doc/f0666a/, vol. 3: https://www.legal-tools.org/doc/d79e85/, vol. 4: https://www.legal-tools.org/doc/3b31aa/); ICTY, *Furundžija*, Trial Chamber, 10 December 1998, IT-95-17/1-T (https://www.legal-tools.org/doc/e6081b/). For an advanced discussion from a forensic viewpoint, see Moa Lidén and Itiel E. Dror, "Expert Reliability in Legal Proceedings: "Eeny, Meeny, Miny, Moe, With Which Expert Should We Go?"", in *Science and Justice*, 1 October 2020.

[50] See Morten Bergsmo, "Institutional History, Behaviour and Development", in Morten Bergsmo, Klaus Rackwitz and SONG Tianying (eds.), *Historical Origins of International Criminal Law: Volume 5*, TOAEP, Brussels, 2017, pp. 10-11 (https://www.toaep.org/ps-pdf/24-bergsmo-rackwitz-song); see also in the same volume, Morten Bergsmo and Klaus Rackwitz, "The First Budget of the Office of the Prosecutor", pp. 1009 ff.

perspectives. These are research skills typically acquired through university education.

To assume that investigations of this kind must rely exclusively on police officers, may well be perceived as regression to models that have been tried in the ICTY in 1990s, prior to management reforms made there. It may be correct that the first ICC Prosecutor, Luis Moreno-Ocampo, distrusted police and military, but this will come as no surprise if you come from a country in which historically the military and the police have been notorious perpetrators of human rights violations and corruption.[51] It is noteworthy that the first two investigators hired in 2003 by the first ICC Prosecutor – at the recommendation of a panel led by Morten Bergsmo – had law enforcement backgrounds. One of them, William H. Wiley, is a contributor to the present volume. Several police officers were subsequently hired by the first Prosecutor (including those who led the *Lubanga* investigation and most of the team leaders). A number of lawyers and other professionals with experience in criminal and human rights investigations were also hired as investigators, whenever they succeeded in competitive recruitment with candidates of different backgrounds.[52] Persons from NGOs were rarely recruited as investigators.

The staffing dilemma may be overcome in those systems where police investigations already include professionals with high levels of education, such as in Norway, or in specialised investigation agencies in different countries that also include analytical and scientific profiles. Another element of proactive 'quality assurance' is the strategic use of analysis following an 'intelligence-led model', which entails use of qualified methods and professionals with the support of higher management and decision-makers.

To determine whether an investigation meets the required quality standards can be seen as an auditing challenge. The assessment requires thorough knowledge of the context of the investigative decision-making,

---

[51] For an account of human rights violations in Argentina and the trial of the Juntas by the first ICC Prosecutor, see Luis Moreno-Ocampo, *Cuando el poder perdió el juicio*, Planeta, Buenos Aires, 1996, and Julio C. Strassera and Luis G. Moreno-Ocampo, *Será Justicia. Entrevistas*, Editorial Distal, Buenos Aires, 1986.

[52] For a volume edited by three former junior investigators with a legal background, see Adejoke Babington-Ashaye, Aimee Comrie and Akingbolahan Adeniran (eds.), *International Criminal Investigations: Law and Practice*, International Publishing, The Hague, 2018.

made possible through painstaking study of the relevant records and evidence, and through consultation with the officers involved. Absent such knowledge, caution is advisable, although this volume and the QCCI Project have welcomed highly critical approaches and questions. For example, ascertaining whether the investigation collected too much or too little evidence is not always straightforward, as the cases evolve and what today seems excessive evidence may offer the basis for additional cases beyond the original plan; or what appeared to be sufficient ended up not meeting unexpected requirements, defence challenges, or witness withdrawals due to personal or security issues. The German investigation of Reserve Police Battalion 101 interrogated 210 of its less than 500 members:[53] was that over-collecting? To answer this question would require analysis of the investigation in its original context. Modesty is advisable for any learning process, including both the actual investigation and any subsequent evaluation.

Assessing the cases made at trial is not enough to evaluate the quality of the underlying investigation. One thing is how the investigation was conducted. It is quite another what the prosecutors subsequently chose to present as the legal case. If the evidence ends up lacking, it is the responsibility of the prosecution lawyers to frame their charges accordingly – or not to file them at all, as several contributors to this volume have explained (mainly Bitti, Chaitidou, De Smet, Neuner and Agirre Aranburu). The advice offered by lawyers does not always penetrate the underlying investigative work. The true histories of investigations rest on larger and more intricate scopes of evidentiary and operational information, protected by layers of confidentiality. Progress may follow from deep case-studies more so than from sweeping assessments (much like 'thick descriptions' are increasingly appreciated in social sciences after a discrediting of 'big theories').[54]

A certain 'international exoticisation' may be another source of confusion. One sometimes gets the impression that observers consider that problems encountered in international investigations belong to a field that

---

[53] See Christopher R. Browning, *Ordinary Men. Reserve Police Battalion 101 and the Final Solution in Poland*, Harper Perennial, New York, 1993, p. xvii.

[54] For example, the independent expert review commissioned by the ICC Prosecutor on the Kenya investigation, see ICC-OTP, "Statement of the Prosecutor, Fatou Bensouda, on external expert review and lessons drawn from the Kenya situation", 26 November 2019 (available on the ICC's web site).

is vastly different and far-removed from the home turf. Fact-rich criminal investigations are complex, fragile and prone to human error in any known system, including in the countries that are reputed to have among the best criminal justice systems in the world.[55] For example, it took 34 years for the Swedish police to conclude the investigation of the murder of Prime Minister Olof Palme – which happened on a busy street right in the centre of the capital Stockholm – although the investigation was a top State priority involving hundreds of officers and millions of euros.[56] In Spain it is estimated that some 40% of the murders committed by the terrorist group ETA have not been solved, although again this issue was a top State priority with heavy resource investment over decades.[57] In England miscarriages of justice are known in cases of various kinds, from terrorism to mothers wrongly convicted for the accidental deaths of their infants, due to investigative or forensic malpractice.[58] Similar examples are known in many other countries.[59]

---

[55] For an early comment on the frailties of criminal justice, see André Gide, *Ne jugez pas*, Gallimard, Paris, 1930. Gide expresses candidly his doubts about the reliability of criminal procedure for fact-finding after his experience with several trials in France.

[56] See "Decision in the investigation into the murder of former Swedish Prime Minister Olof Palme", announced by the Swedish Prosecution Authority on 10 June 2020 (available on their web site). Palme was murdered on 28 February 1986. For an overview in English of the crime and multiple failed lines of enquiry, see Jan Bondeson, *Blood on the Snow: The Killing of Olof Palme*, Cornell University Press, Ithaca, 2005. For a detailed journalistic work on the person who was identified as the perpetrator by the Swedish police in 2020, see Thomas Pettersson, *Den osannolika mördaren: Skandiamannen och mordet på Olof Palme*, Offside Press, Stockholm, 2018.

[57] See Juanfer F. Calderín, *Agujeros del Sistema. Más de 300 asesinatos de ETA sin resolver*, Ikusager, 2014, Vitoria-Gasteiz (research based on investigative and judicial records). The author claims that the gap is due to "serious mistakes" by State authorities, including investigative malpractice and procedural neglect. For an account from the viewpoint of the Spanish *Guardia Civil*, see Manuel Sánchez (colonel of the *Guardia Civil*), Lorenzo Silva and Gonzalo Araluce, *Sangre, Sudor y Paz. La Guardia Civil Contra ETA*, Ediciones Península, Barcelona, 2017. In June 2018, the Prosecutor of the *Audiencia Nacional* established a special unit to address these unsolved crimes in response to the demands from victims' associations.

[58] See "The Case of Sally Clark: Motherhood Under Attack", Chapter 1 in Leila Schneps and Coralie Colmez, *Math on Trial. How Numbers Get Used and Abused in the Courtroom*, Basic Books, New York, 2013. For terrorism cases, see "Miscarriages of Justice and False Confessions", Chapter 7 in Gisli H. Gudjonsson, *The Psychology of Interrogations and Confessions: A Handbook*, Wiley, Chichester, 2003.

[59] For France, see Laurent Dibos *et al.*, *Grandes erreurs judiciaires*, Prat Éditions, Issy-les-Moulineaux, 2006. For the US see, among others, Brandon L. Garrett, *Convicting the In-*

As Tor-Geir Myhrer explains in Chapter 22, reflecting on national practice: "Most prosecutors have experienced that even indictments based on the most thorough investigation fall apart during court hearings. The reason is often that witnesses change their statements, do not any more remember, do not show up, or use their right".

The problems facing criminal investigations are, in other words, not confined to the international level. They can be found in any investigation because of inherent operational, cognitive and political challenges. Professionals know these difficulties, and understand that they can only increase exponentially in contexts of high threat and low resources. There is no excuse for incompetence, especially when public trust in, and the will to, justice is high. But setting the right standards requires a realistic understanding of how investigations actually work, starting from their foundation in the national domain.

Contextual embedding in close dialogue with local communities is one of the themes emerging from this volume. In view of the patent disparities and disproportionate influence of some States in the international society, we could paraphrase Anthea Roberts and ask the question: 'Are international investigations really international?'.[60] Closeness to the victimised communities should not just be a tool for the international investigation. It is essential for the legitimacy of the entire exercise, in order for the judicial outcome to be accepted and owned by victims and respected by the world at large. Feedback from victims and the victimised communities should also be considered a quality-control measure. Addressing their rights is what justifies the investigation in the first place. Organisations that call themselves 'international' should benefit from a truly international composition of the leadership, if they seek broad credibility in the eyes of the world. Genuine cross-cultural empathy, including post-

---

nocent. Where Criminal Prosecutions go Wrong, Harvard University Press, Cambridge, 2011, and Mark Godsey, *Blind Justice. A Former Prosecutor Exposes the Psychology and Politics of Wrongful Convictions*, University of California Press, Oakland, 2017.

[60] Anthea Roberts (with a foreword by Martti Koskenniemi), *Is International Law International?*, Oxford University Press, 2017. See also Wolgang Kaleck, *Double Standards: International Criminal Law and the West*, TOAEP, Brussels, 2015 (http://www.toaep.org/ps-pdf/26-kaleck).

colonial reckoning and specific research, will be required to facilitate this dialogue.[61]

Moreover, international investigations need to benefit from gender analysis to address the current disproportionate male share among investigators and witnesses and apply due diligence on all crimes regardless of their gender context. To the extent that prosecutorial excesses correlate with what may be perceived as male over-confidence, a measure of gender analysis may help for greater objectivity and efficiency. Inter-sectional analysis needs further development, as it responds to world-wide common sense, and the interplay of diverse factors among victims, perpetrators and investigating officers alike.[62]

Another area that may require further development concerns the investigation of the crime of aggression.[63] At the domestic level, violent crime is usually associated with poorer neighbourhoods and complex corruption with the richer ones. This imbalance led criminologists to develop the concept of 'white collar crime' in order to address corporate crimes, and to correct class biases in criminal justice.[64] Similar disparities show at the international level. The crime of aggression could be regarded as a kind of 'white collar crime' under international criminal law, committed by powerful State actors, at arm's length from actual physical violence. The widely perceived class and post-colonial imbalances in international

---

[61] For emerging research in this area, see Julie Fraser and Brianne McGonigle Leyh, *Intersections of Law and Culture at the International Criminal Court*, Edward Elgar Publishing Ltd, Cheltenham, 2020. See also Morten Bergsmo, Wolfgang Kaleck and Kyaw Yin Hlaing (eds.), *Colonial Wrongs and Access to International Law*, TOAEP, Brussels, 2020 (forthcoming).

[62] See ICC-OTP, "Policy Paper on Sexual and Gender-Based Crimes", 5 June 2014 (https://www.legal-tools.org/doc/7ede6c/) for a definition of gender analysis (p. 4) and inter-sectionality (p. 16 and footnote 25). In this Policy Paper the OTP made a commitment to "integrating a gender perspective and analysis into all of its work" (p. 10), and to "understand" the intersection of multiple factors in line with some recommendations from the Committee on the Elimination of Discrimination Against Women ('CEDAW') and some ICC jurisprudence (footnote 25).

[63] On the crime of aggression under the ICC Statute, see, among others, Deborah Ruiz Verduzco, "Fragmentation of the Rome Statute through and Incoherent Jurisdictional Regime for the Crime of Aggression: A Silent Operation", in Larissa van den Herik and Carsten Stahn (eds.), *The Diversification and Fragmentation of International Criminal Law*, Martinus Nijhoff Publishers, 2012, pp. 389-428.

[64] For the seminal work in this area, see Edwin Sutherland, *White Collar Crime. The Uncut Version*, Yale University Press, New Haven, 1983 (originally published in 1949).

criminal law are unlikely to be addressed appropriately by seeking to establish responsibility for mass violence in the rich countries, but rather by understanding and investigating correctly crimes that are characteristic of their power, including the crime of aggression and crimes related to military occupation. That may require investigative methods akin to those used in serious fraud investigations, with meticulous study of internal records and decision-making processes. 'How to investigate the crime of aggression' could be a useful subject to address in future editions of this anthology.

It is only natural that several authors in this volume and many observers in the field are concerned with the outcome of ICC cases, including the underlying investigations. This is understandable in view of the high expectations and the acquittals in several early cases before the Court. Critical interest mounted after the acquittal in *Gbagbo and Blé Goudé* in January 2019, shortly before the New Delhi conference on which this anthology draws, as discussed in Section 1. above.[65] Assessing the overall results of ICC cases falls outside the scope of this volume and the QCCI Project, which is not jurisdiction-specific and which considers both the international and national levels.[66]

Witness protection difficulties are a pervasive factor across cases and situations before the ICC. This topic was addressed at the New Delhi conference, but it is not covered by this first edition of the anthology. The leak of internal files and witness information at the Kosovo Specialist Chambers in September 2020 is a stark reminder of such difficulties in

---

[65] See, among others, Richard J. Goldstone, "Acquittals by the International Criminal Court", in *EJIL: Talk!*, 18 January 2019.

[66] Such assessments would have to look critically at the preparation and presentation of specific cases, as well as in some instances also analyse the reasoning of the judges, as the IER has indicated particularly in relation to the acquittal in *Bemba* by ICC appeal judges, see IER Report, see *supra* note 37, sections on "Standards of Review in Appeals" and "Departure from Established Practice and Jurisprudence", including para. 611:

Until the Bemba case, however, the Court had followed the jurisprudence of the ad hoc Tribunals, and had been applying 'a standard of reasonableness in reviewing' a Trial Chamber's factual findings, according to them a margin of deference. The decision to depart from that standard was unexpected. There is no clear explanation why that occurred. The decision has created a void of uncertainty about the applicable standard of review for error of fact. Uncertainty as to the applicable standard is undesirable.

different national and international jurisdictions.[67] Issues of prioritisation, selection and exercise of other forms of discretion during case-preparation merit further analysis, including presumptions about 'most responsible persons', 'representativity' in incident- and conduct-prioritisation,[68] and impartiality between parties to the conflict.[69] Government co-operation is a further area of research for a second edition of the volume, including the imposition of formal sanctions by States against individuals serving at war crimes courts, or similar informal measures.[70]

Part IV of the anthology invites further research on the use of investigation plans, in particular the arguments in favour of early preparation of such plans. It is suggested in the book that a decision to open a large investigation should not be made before a draft investigation plan has been prepared. This would seem rather obvious in some national jurisdictions, such as Norway. Further analysis should also be given to the involvement of the leadership in the preparation and adoption of such draft investigation plans, as well as the extent of continuity of operational staff involvement in their creation and maintenance. The Norwegian model of a *dynamic* investigation plan, implemented digitally, whereby the elements of the plan are continuously updated as the work advances – rather than a printed document frozen in time which is common in many agencies – is

---

[67] Hysni Gucati is accused of "intimidation" through public disclosure of witness identities, "violating the secrecy of proceedings", see KSC, Arrest Warrant for Hysni Gucati (public redacted version), 24 September 2020. For an early overview and commentary, see Dean B. Pineles, "Kosovo War Crimes File Leaks Deliver a Blow to Justice", *Balkan Insight*, 1 October 2020.

[68] See "Chapter 5: Case Selection and Prioritization Criteria", in Morten Bergsmo, Kjetil Helvig, Ilia Utmelidze and Gorana Žagovec, *The Backlog of Core International Crimes Case Files in Bosnia and Herzegovina*, TOAEP, Oslo, 2010, 2nd edition, pp. 79-127 (https://www.toaep.org/ps-pdf/3-bergsmo-helvig-utmelidze-zagovec-second).

[69] See, for example, the IER Report, section on "The Criteria for Case Selection and Prioritisation", see *supra* note 37.

[70] See United States, *Executive Order on Blocking Property Of Certain Persons Associated With the International Criminal Court*, 11 June 2020, No. 13928, signed by President Donald J. Trump (https://www.legal-tools.org/doc/dfkvpn/). On 2 September 2020, the US government in furtherance of this Executive Order designated sanctions against ICC Prosecutor Fatou Bensouda and her Head of the Jurisdiction Complementarity and Cooperation Division, Phakiso Mochochoko. For a legal analysis of this Executive Order under US law, note the law suit filed on 1 October 2020 by Open Society Justice Initiative ('OSJI') and four US law professors, see OSJI, "Open Society Justice Initiative Sues Trump Administration over International Criminal Court Executive Order", Statement, 1 October 2020 (available on its web site).

something that should be further elaborated in the second edition of this anthology.

Skills can at all times be improved in criminal justice agencies, and such institutions should always welcome constructive feedback and criticism, and use that as an opportunity to accelerate the work to enhance the internal culture of quality control. Contributing to the strengthening of such institutional cultures is a main objective of the QCCI Project. As the Foreword of the Co-Editors states:

> Perhaps the most important take-away from the book for leaders of investigations and case-preparation is their responsibility to build a *culture* of quality control within their agency, division, section or team. At a minimum, this means creating an office atmosphere where staff do not fear the consequences of raising concerns about quality. But managers should do more. They should devise incentive structures to actively encourage challenges by staff to the quality of work product. Individual analysts, investigators and prosecutors, on the other hand, should see it as their professional obligation to develop a *mindset* of quality control. This may require more courage to speak up, and a stronger preparedness to let institutional loyalties override inter-personal relations, even if this can be unpleasant.

This goes to the heart of this volume. We invite further submissions for the second edition specifically on these notions of *culture* and *mindset of quality control*, and how managers and staff members of relevant criminal justice agencies should act to give effect to this passage by the co-editors. This continuous query will benefit from contributions from different fields of expertise, including business management, psychology, anthropology and ethics.

This is not to diminish the importance of resource limitations, as the personnel available sometimes pales in comparison to the scale of fact-rich cases.[71] As the IER Report has found in the context of the ICC: "The ID [Investigations Division] is the most severely under-resourced Division, having 87 less full time staff than estimated to provide the basic

---

[71] For resource data and estimates, see ICC Assembly of the State Parties, "Report of the Court on the Basic Size of the Office of the Prosecutor", 17 September 2015, ICC-ASP/14/21, including section VII, "Resource comparison" with data from different national and international systems (https://www.legal-tools.org/doc/b27d2a/).

needs of the Division".[72] Conversely, some have contended that there may be an issue of over-reach, caused by the selection of an exceedingly large scope of work against finite resources.[73]

A second edition of this anthology could include more analysis of the technical forensic sciences, an area that merits detailed attention. The same applies to digital evidence, as a parallel reality of electronic data is growing in our lives.[74] The digital future has already arrived. Its investigation requires expertise on computer science, telecommunications, systematic monitoring and exploitation of Internet open sources, collection of satellite imagery and remote sensing data, and other evolving sources and techniques.[75] Continuing research on digital investigations is needed, along with efforts to educate practitioners and judges in this area.[76] This is an area where the ICC may be well-placed to engage confidently with IT-developers, building on the useful legal information services that the Court has made available to the public commons since many years.[77]

---

[72] IER Report, para. 178, see *supra* note 37.

[73] This is the view adopted by the IER Report which invites the OTP to apply a higher threshold of gravity for admissibility, and to focus on fewer situations; see *ibid.*, section "Narrower Standards for Admissibility" (paras. 646-650) and recommendation 227.

[74] See, for example, Council of Europe, "Electronic Evidence Guide. A Basic Guide for Police Officers, Prosecutors and Judges", version 2.1, March 2020, published with the support of the European Union, including the chapters on the collection, analysis and legal procedure for digital evidence (available on the cyber-crime page of the Coucil of Europe's web site).

[75] For some techniques of online investigations see, for example, Craig Silverman (ed.), "Verification Handbook", endorsed by different UN agencies and specialised organisations (available on the Verification Handbook's web site). For a meticulous discussion on evidence from call data records, see Special Tribunal for Lebanon, *Ayyash et al.*, Trial Chamber I, Judgment, 18 August 2020, STL-11-01/T/TC (https://www.legal-tools.org/doc/gcoqu8/). The Trial Chamber was presided over by Judge David Re, one of the contributors to the present volume.

[76] For ongoing research see, for example, Formobile Project, "From Mobile Phones to Court", an EU project funded under the Horizon 2020 programme (available on the Project's web site). For a strategic outline, including considerations of workforce, skills and governance, see United Kingdom, "Digital Forensic Science Strategy", July 2020, published by the National Police Chiefs' Council and other UK agencies.

[77] See Morten Bergsmo, "Decomposition Works in Our Favour", Policy Brief Series No. 114 (2020), TOAEP, Brussels, 2020 (https://www.toaep.org/pbs-pdf/114-bergsmo/).

PART I:
THE CONTEXT OF QUALITY CONTROL
IN INVESTIGATIONS AND CASE PREPARATION

1

From Preliminary Examination to Investigation: Rethinking the Connection

Carsten Stahn[*]

1.1. Introduction

International criminal justice has grown significantly as a field over the past decades. As Frédéric Mégret has noted, international criminal justice is not only "simply a set of laws or even an ideological project", but a social field constructed by agents and professional communities.[1] It is marked by investment in institutions and practices. The development of this field requires critical scrutiny.[2] Some methodologies of international criminal justice are in need of refinement.

The work on quality control is an attempt to provoke critical self-reflection and offer approaches to rethink existing practices.[3] This requires critical analysis of practices, questioning of existing hypotheses, openness for dialogue and formulation of recommendations that may unpack or remedy existing problems.

---

[*] **Carsten Stahn** is Professor of International Criminal Law and Global Justice, Leiden University, Programme Director, Grotius Centre for International Legal Studies and Professor of Public International Law and International Criminal Justice, Queen's University Belfast. This chapter is based on a presentation at the Indian Law Institute, see Carsten Stahn, "From Preliminary Examination to Criminal Investigation", CILRAP Film, New Delhi, 22 February 2019 (https://www.cilrap.org/cilrap-film/190222-stahn/).

[1] See Frédéric Mégret, "International Criminal Justice as a Juridical Field", in *Penal Field*, 2016, vol. 13, p. 9 ("One might say: it is international criminal lawyers who create international criminal justice, not the other way around").

[2] See Carsten Stahn, *A Critical Introduction to International Criminal Law*, Cambridge University Press, Cambridge, 2019.

[3] See Morten Bergsmo (ed.), *Quality Control in Fact-Finding*, Torkel Opsahl Academic EPublisher, Florence, 2013 (http://www.toaep.org/ps-pdf/19-bergsmo).

Our previous two volumes on preliminary examinations have left footprints in enhancing the work in the pre-investigative stage,[4] some of which are beginning to be reflected in OTP strategies.[5] The project on investigations is a natural continuation of this line of work. This contribution argues that the nexus between preliminary examinations and investigations deserves fresh attention in the practice of the International Criminal Court ('ICC').

In the existing policies, preliminary examinations and investigations have been treated as if they are separate normative universes. They are associated with distinct goals and methodologies, and have their own unique institutional infrastructure.[6] For instance, preliminary examinations are conducted by the Situation Analysis Section, which belongs to the Jurisdiction, Complementarity and Cooperation Division, while investigations are run largely independently by the Investigation Division. This separation may be explained by certain structural differences between preliminary examinations and investigations. However, there should not be a 'Great Wall' between them. The different phases of proceedings are inherently connected. Preliminary examinations and investigations share numerous synergies and forms of interaction, which merit attention from the perspective of quality control and improvement of investigative structures. For instance, a preliminary examination provides an important knowledge base for investigations and might gradually shape investigation plans.[7] Preliminary examinations rely heavily on external information

---

4   See Morten Bergsmo and Carsten Stahn (eds.), *Quality Control in Preliminary Examination: Volumes 1 and 2*, Torkel Opsahl Academic EPublisher, Brussels, 2018 (http://www.toaep.org/ps-pdf/32-bergsmo-stahn and http://www.toaep.org/ps-pdf/33-bergsmo-stahn).

5   The Draft Strategic Plan 2019–2021 expressly recognizes the importance of on-going quality control and recommends steps to 'optimize' preliminary examinations. See OTP, Strategic Plan 2019–21, 14 May 2019, para. 13. See also Alex Whiting "ICC Prosecutor Signals Important Strategy Shift in New Policy Document", in *Just Security*, 17 May 2019 (available on its web site).

6   See Carsten Stahn, "Damned If You Do, Damned If You Don't: Challenges and Critiques of Preliminary Examinations at the ICC", in *Journal of International Criminal Justice*, 2017, vol. 15, no. 3, pp. 413–34.

7   Morten Bergsmo, "Towards a Culture of Quality Control in Criminal Investigations", FICHL Policy Brief No. 94 (2019), Torkel Opsahl Academic EPublisher, Brussels, 2019, pp. 3–4 (http://www.toaep.org/pbs-pdf/94-bergsmo/). Morten Bergsmo, "Rethinking Instruments of Quality Control in the Investigation and Preparation of Core International Crimes Cases", CILRAP Film, New Delhi, 23 February 2019 (https://www.cilrap.org/cilrap-film/190222-bergsmo/).

providers. Investigations require a pre-investigative plan in order to set out operational details or secure the preservation of evidence even before the formal initiation of the investigations. Preliminary examinations may contribute important elements to the formulation of investigative plans.[8] Trial strategy benefits from the continued input of investigative teams. These lessons are gradually recognized in the Draft Strategic Plan 2019–2021, which expresses a commitment to: (1) "adapt the analytical products and information databases used during preliminary examinations to better reflect and anticipate investigative needs", (2) to "consider means and opportunities for preserving evidence at the earliest stage" (for example, through "interaction with first responders, preservation requests, statement-taking at the seat of the Court"), and to (3) increase the "integration between teams conducting preliminary examinations and investigations".[9]

This chapter analyses synergies and differences between preliminary examinations and investigations. It highlights two macro problems arising in practice ('cognitive bias' and 'bottlenecks'). It then discusses the structure of international criminal investigations and some ideas to improve the *status quo,* including means to address some of the ICC's evidentiary problems.

1.2. Structural Differences Between Preliminary Examinations and Investigations

Preliminary examinations differ from investigations in at least five ways: purpose, formalization, investigative power (coercive powers, co-operation duties), standard of proof and analytical methods.

To begin with, a preliminary examination is "a form of pre-investigation that precedes the actual formal investigation of a situation and subsequently a case".[10] It serves essentially as an analytical tool to determine whether there are sufficient grounds to commence an investigation. At the ICC, preliminary examinations have become a quasi-independent stage of the proceedings. It is governed by a four-stage ana-

---

[8] See Markus Eikel, "Nature and Use of Investigation Plans at the International Criminal Court", CILRAP Film, New Delhi, 23 February 2019 (https://www.cilrap.org/cilrap-film/190223-eikel/).

[9] OTP, Strategic Plan 2019–21, see above note 5, para. 24.

[10] See Kai Ambos, *Treatise on International Criminal Law: Volume III: International Criminal Procedure*, Oxford University Press, Oxford, 2016, pp. 335–36.

lytical process and a high degree of transparency. These four phases are: (1)"initial assessment of all information on alleged crimes received", which filters out information on crimes that are outside the jurisdiction of the Court; (2) analysis of jurisdiction, which leads to a report on crimes ('Article 5 report'); (3) analysis of the "admissibility of potential cases", including complementarity and gravity, which leads to a report on Article 17); and (4) examination of the interests of justice.[11] This implies that not all preliminary examinations may culminate in investigations.

In practice, the OTP has actively used preliminary examinations as a space to shape accountability policies, namely to foster deterrence and incentivize domestic investigations and prosecution.[12] A preliminary examination involves uncertainty as to whether or not a situation shall be dealt with internationally or domestically. From a policy perspective, the lack of predictability as to whether or not a preliminary examination will lead to an investigation may be an asset: it may increase the political leverage of the ICC to steer domestic justice approaches.[13]

The assessment is made on the basis of material submitted to the Prosecution or open-source material.[14] The OTP does not enjoy proper investigative power at this stage. It may invite other entities to co-operate; however, formal co-operation under Part 9 of the ICC Statute is not yet available. This makes the OTP comparable to a fact-finding body.[15] The

---

[11] OTP, Policy Paper on Preliminary Examinations, November 2013, paras. 77–83 (http://www.legal-tools.org/doc/acb906/).

[12] Carsten Stahn, Morten Bergsmo, and CHAN Icarus, "On the Magic, Mystery and Mayhem of Preliminary Examinations", in Morten Bergsmo and Carsten Stahn (eds.), *Quality Control in Preliminary Examination: Volume 1*, pp. 1–32, see above note 4; Elizabeth Evenson, "ICC Preliminary Examinations and National Justice: Opportunities and Challenges for Catalysing Domestic Prosecutions", in Morten Bergsmo and Carsten Stahn (eds.), *Quality Control in Preliminary Examination: Volume 2*, , pp. 713–29, see above note 4.

[13] See Mark Kersten, "Casting a Larger Shadow: Premeditated Madness, the International Criminal Court, and Preliminary Examinations", in Morten Bergsmo and Carsten Stahn (eds.), *Quality Control in Preliminary Examination: Volume 2*, pp. 655, 665, see above note 4.

[14] On open-source material, see Lindsay Freeman, "Digital Evidence and War Crimes Prosecutions: The Impact of Digital Technologies on International Criminal Investigations and Trials", in *Fordham International Law Journal*, 2018, vol. 41, no. 2, p. 283; Alexa Koenig, Felim McMahon, Nikita Mehandru, and Shikha Silliman Bhattacharjee, "Open Source Fact-Finding in Preliminary Examinations", in Morten Bergsmo and Carsten Stahn (eds.), *Quality Control in Preliminary Examination: Volume 2*, pp. 681–710, see above note 4.

[15] Ambos, 2016, p. 341, see above note 10.

initiation of preliminary examination requires an initial suspicion that crimes within the jurisdiction of the Court have been committed.[16] The aim is to determine whether there is a "reasonable basis to proceed".[17] Typically, no particular case hypothesis is developed. The focus is rather on the analysis of the situation and on the formulation of initial hypotheses that are developed based on "relatively untested information".[18]

Investigations are different. Transforming material into a criminal case is a more complex undertaking. It requires several steps: the collection and analysis of material, investigation and the formation of a case theory. It involves document collection and analysis, the collection of crime-base and linkage-witness statements, as well as the identification of individual suspects.[19] The purpose is to decide whether there is a sufficient basis for prosecution. The main difference from preliminary examinations is that the information and material is tested, for instance, through interrogatory processes, the taking of statements and witness interviews.[20]

Further, investigations are more formal. They may involve coercive action against suspects. While criminal investigators are tasked with establishing facts, they are also subject to formalized requirements. They are bound by professional duties, are required to disclose evidence, may be called to testify about investigative methods, and must balance their mandate against the rights of the Defence, as well as victims and witnesses. The legal framework serves as a basis to 'frame' investigations.[21]

---

[16] *Ibid.*, p. 336.

[17] Rome Statute of the International Criminal Court, 17 July 1998, Article 53(1) ('ICC Statute') (http://www.legal-tools.org/doc/7b9af9/).

[18] See Paul Seils, "Putting Complementarity in its Place", in Carsten Stahn (ed.), *The Law and Practice of the International Criminal Court*, Oxford University Press, Oxford, 2015, pp. 305, 319. According to Article 15(2) and Rule 47, the OTP may "receive written or oral testimony at the seat of the Court".

[19] Morten Bergsmo and William Wiley, "Human Rights Professionals and the Criminal Investigation and Prosecution of Core International Crimes", in Siri Skåre, Ingvild Burkey, and Hege Mørk (eds.), *Manual on Human Rights Monitoring: An Introduction for Human Rights Field Officers*, Norwegian Center for Human Rights, Oslo, 2010, pp. 1–27 (http://www.legal-tools.org/doc/8362d5/).

[20] See Seils, 2015, p. 319, see above note 18.

[21] On framing theories, see Fujiwara Hiroto and Stephan Parmentier, "Investigations", in Luc Reydams, Jan Wouters, and Cedric Ryngaert (eds.), *International Prosecutors*, Oxford University Press, Oxford, 2012, pp. 572, 585.

Moreover, investigations are primarily aimed at identifying evidence to hold individuals accountable before a court of law. This implies that they are subject to different safeguards and standards of proof.[22] The aim of the investigation is to reduce uncertainties. This requires more concrete case hypotheses and different plans: investigation plans, evidence collection plans and co-operation plans.

Lastly, analytical methods differ and might change in the course of the investigation. Investigations rely on a combination of inductive and deductive methods. For instance, crime-base evidence is often induced from facts and information. Linkage evidence is more commonly deduced from organizational structures and contexts. Investigators navigate between these two techniques.

Throughout the investigation, the collection of evidence is closely interrelated with analysis. Prosecutors must collect enough evidence to build a reliable case. However, the necessary scope, form and type of evidence depend on the formulation of a charging theory, and involve the identification of suspects, the formulation of specific charges and the identification of modes of liability. This theory is gradually refined throughout the investigation. Methodologies need to be adjusted in light of newly available evidence. As Alex Whiting has noted:

> with a limited budget and uncertain and changing investigative needs, the Prosecutor must constantly react to shifting priorities and opportunities.[23]

Ultimately, hastily investigated cases carry high chances of failure.

1.3. Two Macro Problems

Although preliminary examination and investigation differ in relation to aims and methods, they pose similar macro problems.

The first one relates to risks of cognitive bias.[24] Like all human beings, analysts and investigators are vulnerable to inherent biases that may shape their processing of information, consciously or unconsciously.

---

[22] *Ibid.*, pp. 572, 580–81.

[23] Alex Whiting, "Dynamic Investigative Practices", in *Law and Contemporary Problems*, 2016, vol. 76, no. 3, pp. 163, 179.

[24] See Moa Lidén, Minna Gräns, and Peter Juslin, "From devil's advocate to crime fighter: confirmation bias and debiasing techniques in prosecutorial decision-making", in *Psychol-*

1.3.1. Cognitive Bias

Due to their limited investigative resources, distance to crime sites, security constraints and lack of enforcement powers, international criminal institutions are highly dependent on third parties in relation to access to information and material. External entities have their own vested interests in sharing information and follow their own methodologies. The information and material that they supply is often heavily pre-selected or filtered. Time pressures, external expectations and the sheer stigma associated with atrocity crimes may provide a natural temptation to take certain context elements, causalities or crime patterns for granted. Investigations may focus too easily on individuals, rather than crimes. It is thus essential for analysts and investigators to

> remain aware of the interests and perspectives of the various agencies and to counter their influence by cultivating multiple information sources and always seek to corroborate all available information.[25]

Investigators require sufficient knowledge of the historical context of conflicts and the culture of societies in order to counter such potential biases and understand the broader causes of violence and dynamics between different agents in conflict. In situations such as Rwanda and Sierra Leone, cultural factors affected the evidence of witnesses. For instance, the *Akayesu* Trial Judgment noted that "cultural constraints" prompted different understandings as to "dates, times, distances and locations".[26]

A second potential bias relates to the relationship between the scale and seriousness of crimes and their probability of proof. International criminal justice relates to system criminality and collective crime. As Fujiwara Hiroto and Stephan Parmentier have argued, it is misguided that international crimes are 'easy to prove', because of their magnitude:

> While the crime base may be evident because of the large number of victims, perpetrators and resources involved, this is not necessarily the case when it comes to the issue of [...] responsibility, whose proof [...] requires more complex con-

---

ogy, *Crime & Law*, 2019, vol. 25, no. 5, pp. 494–526. See also Moa Lidén, "Prevention of Factual Confirmation-Bias During Offence-Driven Investigations", CILRAP Film, New Delhi, 22 February 2019 (https://www.cilrap.org/cilrap-film/190222-liden/).

25   See Fujiwara and Parmentier, 2012, pp. 572, 582, see above note 21.

26   International Criminal Tribunal for Rwanda, *Prosecutor v. Akayesu*, Trial Chamber, Judgment, 2 September 1998, ICTR-96-4-T, para. 156 (http://www.legal-tools.org/doc/b8d7bd/).

ceptual thinking and an elaborate strategy of evidence collection.[27]

1.3.2. Addressing Bottlenecks

Another macro problem is the risk of 'bottlenecks' referred to in the Policy Brief "Towards a Culture of Quality Control in Criminal Investigations".[28] In practice, both preliminary examinations and investigations have suffered from bottleneck problems.

A bottleneck is "a narrow place through which people must pass in order to reach many opportunities",[29] "a place where a road becomes narrow, or a place where there is often a lot of traffic, causing the traffic to slow down or stop".[30] In institutional terms, it is associated with the idea of delay, paralysis, or getting stuck in bureaucracy. This problem has become evident in relation to ICC preliminary examinations.

1.3.2.1. Bottlenecks in Preliminary Examinations

Preliminary examinations have suffered from different types of bottlenecks: indecision in relation to investigation, pitfalls of a phase-based approach, a mismatch between ends and means and the lack of a completion strategy.

The relationship between preliminary examinations and investigation has caused concern. There are more and more voices expressing fear that the OTP has made more of preliminary examinations than they are or ought to be. Situations like Colombia, Palestine, Afghanistan or Myanmar have shown that preliminary examinations can easily get stuck over years or decades in complicated analysis. The lack of a decision one way or the other is criticized by those who want see situations move to investigation as much as by States who want to see their situations 'delisted' from preliminary examination. Some voices argue that preliminary examinations have taken the space that investigations should occupy.[31] Long prelimi-

---

[27] Fujiwara and Parmentier, 2012, p. 582, see above note 21.

[28] Bergsmo, "Towards a Culture of Quality Control in Criminal Investigations", see above note 7.

[29] Joseph Fishkin, "The Anti-Bottleneck Principle in Employment Discrimination Law", in *Washington University Law Review*, 2014, vol. 91, no. 6, pp. 1429, 1472.

[30] See definition on Cambridge English Dictionary's web site.

[31] On the paradoxes, see Stahn, 2017, see above note 6. For a critique, see Ana Cristina Rodriguez Pineda, "Deterrence or Withdrawals? Consequences of Publicising Preliminary

---

nary examinations may also extend the periods during which potential witnesses are at risk.

In our volumes on preliminary examinations, we have identified several strategies to improve the *status quo*. One way to get out of such paralysis is to seek early guidance by the Pre-Trial Chamber in an inclusive process, in order to seek clarity on jurisdiction. This option has been used in the Myanmar context.[32] It requires further procedural clarification in the future. There are two different potential legal bases: Article 19(3) and inherent powers. Pre-Trial judges have remained divided on this point. Procedural aspects, such as potential prejudicial effect, right to appeal or impact on later challenges need to be addressed, if this avenue is used more systemically to unlock stalemate.

Another way out is to move ahead to investigation in relation to a particular segment of a situation, while keeping a broader focus under preliminary examination. For instance, if a preliminary examination is prolonged, such as in the situation in Afghanistan, it may be appropriate to consider strategies in relation to a partial opening of an investigation, in order to keep the 'golden hour' of evidence collection. Alternatively, individual situations may be defined more narrowly.

Another critique is that the OTP has created an overly restrictive framework for consideration of preliminary examinations, which deprives it of the flexibility needed to manage preliminary examinations more effectively. The phase-based approach introduces the same temporal sequence for all situations. It considers jurisdiction first, then admissibility and gravity and finally the interests of justice. This approach is grounded in the logic of Article 53, but it might be applied with more flexibility. These four criteria do not always have to be considered in a strictly sequenced fashion, but are often interrelated.[33] Overall, the OTP may have

---

Examination Activities", in Morten Bergsmo and Carsten Stahn (eds.), *Quality Control in Preliminary Examination: Volume 2*, pp. 321–91, see above note 4.

[32] See ICC, Decision on the "Prosecution's Request for a Ruling on Jurisdiction under Article 19(3) of the Statute", Pre-Trial Chamber, 6 September 2018, ICC-RoC46(3)-01/18-37 (http://www.legal-tools.org/doc/73aeb4/).

[33] On Gantt charts as alternative model, see Asaf Luban, "Politics, Power Dynamics, and the Limits of Existing Self-Regulation and Oversight in ICC Preliminary Examinations", in Morten Bergsmo and Carsten Stahn (eds.), *Quality Control in Preliminary Examination: Volume 2*, pp. 143–45, see above note 4.

created too much bureaucracy at this early stage, in an attempt to manage preliminary examinations.

In its highly controversial decision not to authorize the investigation in relation to Afghanistan, Pre-Trial Chamber II has proposed to use the "interest of justice" criterion to deal with bottleneck problems.[34] It has argued that

> an investigation would only be in the interests of justice if prospectively it appears suitable to result in the effective investigation and subsequent prosecution of cases within a reasonable time frame.[35]

Deviating from earlier jurisprudence, the Chamber has relied on three criteria to deny the request for authorization: (1) the time elapsed between the commission of crimes and the authorization, (2) the scope of co-operation obtained by the Prosecutor "even for the limited purposes of a preliminary examination", and (3) the "likelihood that both relevant evidence and potential relevant suspects might still be available and within reach of the Prosecution's investigative efforts and activities".[36]

This reading misconstrued the relationship between preliminary examinations and investigations and infringed on prosecutorial power. It turned the "interests of justice" into an 'interest of politics' test. The purpose of an investigation is to establish whether there is a sufficient basis to act in the first place. The level of co-operation cannot be reliably determined at the preliminary examination stage, since States lack a duty to co-operate under Part 9. Most fundamentally, making authorization dependent on alleged prospects of success, as determined by the Chamber, conflates the authorization to act with enforcement. It deprives the Prosecutor of the possibility to gather a case and seek co-operation from non-compliant States. The decision provides an incentive for States to obstruct preliminary examinations and refuse to co-operate, in order to successfully avoid *proprio motu* investigations. This result squarely contradicts the

---

[34] On the OTP understanding, see Maria Varaki, "Revisiting the 'Interests of Justice' Policy Paper", in *Journal of International Criminal Justice*, 2017, vol. 15, no. 3, pp. 455–70.

[35] ICC, Situation in the Islamic Republic of Afghanistan, Pre-Trial Chamber, Decision Pursuant to Article 15 of the Rome Statute on the Authorisation of an Investigation into the Situation in the Islamic Republic of Afghanistan, 12 April 2019, ICC-02/17-33, para. 89 (http://www.legal-tools.org/doc/2fb1f4/).

[36] *Ibid.*, para. 91.

purposes of the ICC and the interests of victims, which ought to be taken into account in the interpretation of the 'interests of justice' test.[37]

Getting rid of bottlenecks requires more investment in structures, including consultation, verification and monitoring of domestic action and, possibly, even more interaction with other human rights or accountability mechanisms. Currently, the OTP lacks the means to achieve the goals that it aspires to reach.[38] It is questionable whether the existing institutional structures allow OTP analysts and staff to gain sufficient context and expertise in relation to the uniqueness of each situation, in order to understand the factors and interests driving the conflict, or the potential ramifications of ICC action. As Paul Seils, former Head of Situation Analysis at the OTP, has argued:

> A longer presence on the ground should allow analysts to improve their understanding of the institutions that are of interest, both in terms of those providing information and those conducting national proceedings. Developing relationships in relation to both may help to create a sense of urgency at a national level that proceedings have to advance if ICC action is not to occur.[39]

Problems are likely to amplify in the future. The rise of new technologies and the availability of open-source material may create risks of overload of information.

Finally, the ICC requires a completion strategy for preliminary examinations. Many existing ICC situations are based on open-ended referrals and do not simply go away. It is key to develop strategies to end long-standing preliminary examinations successfully. Several preliminary examinations have been on the docket for years. Investigations have been 'open-ended'. Conceptual thinking in relation to completion strategies has

---

[37] For a critique, see Kevin Heller, "One Word for the PTC on the Interests of Justice: Taliban", in *Opinio Juris*, 13 April 2019 (available on its web site); Dapo Akande and Talita de Souza Dias, "The ICC Pre-Trial Chamber Decision on the Situation in Afghanistan: A Few Thoughts on the Interests of Justice", in *EJIL: Talk!*, 18 April 2019 (available on its web site).

[38] For a critique, see Human Rights Watch, *Pressure Point: The ICC's Impact on National Justice: Lessons from Colombia, Georgia, Guinea, and the United Kingdom*, 10 May 2018 (http://www.legal-tools.org/doc/442f1c/).

[39] Paul Seils, "Making Complementarity Work", in Carsten Stahn and Mohamed El Zeidy (eds.), *The International Criminal Court and Complementarity*, Cambridge University Press, Cambridge, 2011, pp. 989, 1000.

started more than a decade ago, in the context of work on 'positive complementarity'. The Statute provides indicators that can be used for 'closure'. The Draft Strategy Plan 2019–2021 entails a commitment to "seek a suitable 'closure ratio' by completing, over each three year period, as many as preliminary examinations as it opens".[40] However, completion is more than an arithmetic exercise. It requires a case-by-case strategy that is driven by situational context rather than a (budget-driven) equivalence of open and closed situations. In complex situations where the OTP has started to collect useful information and material, completion should not be a mere 'exit', but should be guided by the goals set by the Statute, including the prevention of crimes, complementarity strategies that facilitate knowledge-sharing, the strengthening of domestic accountability efforts and reverse co-operation under Article 93(10).[41]

1.3.2.2. Bottlenecks in Investigations

Investigations pose their own types of bottleneck problems. One of the main difficulties is to translate the large amount of material and evidence collected during investigations into successful cases. The record of the Court is mixed in this regard. Many cases have remained stuck in the 'bottle', rather than making it through the 'neck' at pre-trial or trial. Problems relate, among other things, to the timing of investigations, the organization of evidence, the amount of evidence and investigative strategy.

1.3.2.2.1. Timing of Investigations

The ICC has experimented with a number of approaches to enhance case preparation.[42] At the *ad hoc* tribunals, the Prosecution had the possibility to continue investigations beyond pre-trial. The ICC sets a stricter regime relating to the timing of investigations, due to the presence of the confirmation of charges procedure. It is deemed to make cases more focused and to protect the Defence against changing Prosecution narratives at trial. In *Mbarushimana*, the Appeals Chamber held that

---

[40] OTP, Strategic Plan 2019–2021, see above note 5, para. 24.

[41] See in relation to investigations, *Ibid.*, para. 26.

[42] On the ICTY experience, see Morten Bergsmo and Michael J. Keegan, "Case Preparation for the International Criminal Tribunal for the Former Yugoslavia", in Hege Araldsen and Øyvind W. Thiis (eds.), *Manual on Human Rights Monitoring: An Introduction for Human Rights Field Officers*, see above note 19.

the investigation should largely be completed at the stage of the confirmation of charges hearing. Most of the evidence should therefore be available, and it is up to the prosecutor to submit this evidence to the Pre-Trial Chamber.[43]

The key argument is that it is not in the interests of justice to allow the cases to go forward at pre-trial in the hope that sufficient evidence will materialize at trial. This ruling has been interpreted differently by different Chambers. Some Chambers have favoured a strict approach, requiring completion of the investigation at the confirmation hearing, whilst others have allowed greater flexibility.[44]

In the post-Ocampo era, the OTP expressed a commitment that, as a matter of policy, cases should be as trial-ready as possible by the confirmation of charges stage. The Draft Strategic Plan 2019–2021 rightly notes that "having cases trial-ready at the arrest warrant or confirmation stage" minimizes the "possibility of delays in order for the Office to complete its investigative activity, to secure witnesses and evidence, or otherwise to prepare for confirmation or trial proceedings".[45] This approach reflects recommendations found in the ICTY Manual on Developed Practices, which states:

> Ideally a case should be ready for trial before an indictment is issued and it should be the object of the Prosecutor's investigation to gather all necessary evidence before any charges are brought.[46]

However, in actual practice, this principle has caused problems. For instance, in *Kenyatta*, the Trial Chamber found that the OTP interviewed "at least 24 out of the Prosecution's 31 fact witnesses" for "the first time after the Confirmation Hearing".[47] The Prosecution has on several occa-

---

43 ICC, Situation in the Democratic Republic of the Congo, *Prosecutor v. Mbarushimana*, Appeals Chamber, Judgment on the Appeal of the Prosecutor Against the Decision of Pre-Trial Chamber I of 16 December 2011 entitled "Decision on the Confirmation of Charges", 30 May 2012, ICC-01/04-01/10-514, para. 44 (http://www.legal-tools.org/doc/6ead30/).

44 For a survey, see Whiting, 2016, pp. 168–73, see above note 23.

45 OTP, Strategic Plan 2019–2021, see above note 5, para. 28.

46 See ICTY and UNICRI, ICTY Manual on Developed Practices, UNICRI Publisher, Turin, 2009, p. 35 ('ICTY Manual on Developed Practices') (http://www.legal-tools.org/doc/0cc55d/).

47 See ICC, Situation in the Republic of Kenya, *Prosecutor v. Kenyatta*, Trial Chamber, Decision on Defence Application Pursuant to Article 64(4) and Related Requests', 26 April 2013, ICC-01/09-02/11-728, para. 122 (http://www.legal-tools.org/doc/da5089/).

sions failed to meet the threshold of Article 61. There is an assumption that the OTP "has simply moved too quickly in bringing some cases before the judges".[48] This raises questions as to the extent to which the "stated policy of completing as much of its investigation as possible prior to confirmation is being implemented as a practical matter".[49]

The main issue is whether a time-limit to complete the bulk of investigations before the confirmation hearing has a didactic effect on the Prosecution, namely to increase quality control of the case.

Such an approach places greater demands at the investigative stage, that is, to conduct more thorough investigations. It requires the Prosecution not to proceed until thorough investigations have been conducted. But it also has trade-offs. It might prolong the pre-trial phase, since the Prosecution might "wait until a case is trial ready or almost trial-ready before any charges are ever presented to a judge".[50] It also makes the confirmation hearing more central in the procedure as such since it may be

> understood as an implicit incentive for the Prosecutor to submit as much evidence as possible, including live witnesses, in order to secure confirmation, this in turn compelling the Defence to do the same.[51]

1.3.2.2.2. Organization of Evidence

Another issue relates to the better organization of evidence gathered during the investigation.[52] The ICC has taken new avenues in this regard.

In *Bemba*, the Pre-Trial Chamber introduced the idea of the "in-depth analysis chart" ('IDAC') in order to "streamline the disclosure of evidence, to ensure that the Defence be prepared under satisfactory condi-

---

[48] War Crimes Research Office, *Investigative management, Strategies, and Techniques of the International Criminal Court's Office of the Prosecutor*, 2012, p. 10.

[49] Susana Sácouto and Katherine Cleary Thompson, "Investigative Management, Strategies and Techniques of the ICC's OTP", in Carsten Stahn (ed.), *The Law and Practice of the International Criminal Court*, pp. 328, 347, see above note 18.

[50] War Crimes Research Office, 2012, p. 10, see above note 48.

[51] See ICC, Situation in the Republic of Côte d'Ivoire, *Prosecutor v. Gbagbo*, Pre-Trial Chamber, Dissenting opinion of Judge Silvia Fernández de Gurmendi, 3 June 2013, ICC-02/11-01/11-432-Anx-Corr, para. 27 (http://www.legal-tools.org/doc/9a3b94/).

[52] On evidence and reasoning, see Simon De Smet, "Enhancing the Quality of Reasoning about the Link Between Evidence and Factual Propositions", CILRAP Film, New Delhi, 22 February 2019 (https://www.cilrap.org/cilrap-film/190222-smet/).

tions, to expedite proceedings and to prepare properly for the confirmation hearing".[53] The chart is designed to increase the certainty and consistency of the disclosure process.[54] It is one of the innovations of ICC practice, which is considered for replication in other contexts (for example, the Kosovo Specialist Chambers). It requires the OTP to link each piece of evidence to each element of the charged crimes. It is designed to make proceedings more focused and transparent, and to highlight evidentiary weaknesses early on.

The introduction of the IDAC has caused an ideological divide. Much of the dispute is over the role of the pre-trial judge, rather than the IDAC's utility as a tool to facilitate proceedings. The OTP has remained opposed to the idea that such a chart should be required. It fears that such a chart may lock-in the evidence too firmly at pre-trial[55] and force the Chamber to look at the link between crimes and fact rather than the "relevance of the evidence in its totality".[56] In *Al-Hassan*, the OTP gave at least six substantial reasons why it rejects the IDAC:

1. it "is premature at this stage of the proceedings and would provide only a truncated, incomplete and inaccurate view of the charges as they will be presented during the confirmation of charges hearing, rendering the production of tables useless";

2. it "would necessarily and unduly delay the proceedings and, as a result, have a negative impact on the parties' right to the fair and expeditious conduct of proceedings";

---

[53] ICC, Situation in the Central African Republic, *Prosecutor v. Jean-Pierre Bemba Gombo*, Pre-Trial Chamber, Decision on the Evidence Disclosure System and Setting a Timetable for Disclosure between the Parties, 31 July 2008, ICC-01/05-01/08-55, para. 72 (http://www.legal-tools.org/doc/15c802/).

[54] Olympia Bekou, "Loss of Overview and In-Depth Analysis of Evidence During the Preparation of Fact-Rich Cases", CILRAP Film, New Delhi, 23 February 2019 (https://www.cilrap.org/cilrap-film/190222-bekou/).

[55] See also Alex Whiting, "Disclosure Challenges at the ICC", in Carsten Stahn (ed.), *The Law and Practice of the International Criminal Court*, p. 1027, see above note 18:
   Evidence in a criminal case does not come in neat, little packets that can be simply linked to individual elements. Rather the evidence supporting the elements of crimes charged is usually based on lots of pieces put together or inferences drawn from long transcripts or documents […].

[56] ICC, Situation in the Republic of Mali, *Prosecutor v. Al Hassan*, Pre-Trial Chamber, Decision on the In-Depth Analysis Chart of Disclosed Evidence, 29 June 2018, ICC-01/12-01/18-61-tENG, para. 14 (http://www.legal-tools.org/doc/d35cef/).

3. it "would unfairly burden and intrude into the Prosecution's ability to undertake its core work before the confirmation of charges hearing";

4. it "is not a substitute for the [D]efence's deontological obligation to assess each and every item of evidence";

5. it "does not facilitate the Defence's or the Chamber's understanding of the Prosecution's case, especially as the IDAC envisaged is law-driven rather than fact-driven, which inverts the logic of the three-stage process of evidence assessment, which – according to the Prosecution – is to be followed by the Pre-Trial Chamber"; and

6. it "departs from the practice of other international tribunals".[57]

The OTP insisted that the "most appropriate tool available to the Chamber to analyze the evidence is a document containing a detailed description of the charges and other documents provided in support of it".[58]

The Defence countered that many of these justifications lack merit. It stated that

> the disclosure of voluminous evidence with no indication of its relevance to the constituent elements of crime and modes of liability is, in fact, what could truly affect the expeditiousness of the proceedings.[59]

The ICC Chambers' Practice Manual rejected imposing the IDAC on the parties. It noted:

> there is no basis for the Chamber to impose on the parties a particular modality/format to argue their case and present their evidence. For example, no submission of any "in-depth analysis chart", or similia, of the evidence relied upon for the purposes of the confirmation hearing can be imposed on either of the parties.[60]

Currently, judges have preferred increasing the specificity of the document containing the charges, rather than insisting on the IDAC. Critics observe that the IDAC may fail to meet its purported objectives (namely to enhance transparency or provide necessary structural guid-

---

[57] *Ibid.*

[58] *Ibid.*, para. 15.

[59] *Ibid.*, para. 20.

[60] ICC, Chambers' Practice Manual, 12 May 2017, p. 14 ('ICC Chambers' Practice Manual') (http://www.legal-tools.org/doc/f0ee26/).

ance), in cases where the underlying OTP narratives and legal categorizations remain vague.[61] However, the jury is still out on the future of this approach.

The bigger point from the perspective of quality control is that a clear and well-structured case at pre-trial is ultimately in the interests of the Prosecution itself.[62] For instance, identifying the links between facts and elements on the one hand and the law (that is, crime labels and modes of liability) on the other early on allows the OTP to focus on the essence of the case and avoid identify evidentiary weaknesses and gaps.[63] This rationale can be realized without requiring the OTP to "present all of its evidence at the early stages of proceedings against a suspect".[64] As Morten Bergsmo and Olympia Bekou have argued:

> By requiring the Prosecution to structure the case according to a clear format, designed to enhance the understanding of the parties who have not been privy to the detailed investigations (for example, other teams within the OTP or other members of the same team), such charts will help them maintain an overview of the case, which will also assist, when presenting the case, in arguing it in a clear and logical fashion, thus improving its strength. When filled in, the charts highlight and help the Prosecution to identify the weak links in its case. They assist all members of a case preparation team to share a common understanding of the evidentiary state of the case. The charts also compel Prosecution team members to undertake fact-related work with the (draft) legal classification of the case in the forefront of their minds.[65]

---

[61] On alternative re-thinking of disclosure, see David Re, "Rethinking Disclosure in Core International Crimes Cases", CILRAP Film, New Delhi, 23 February 2019 (https://www.cilrap.org/cilrap-film/190222-re/).

[62] Gilbert Bitti, "Quality Control in Case Preparation and the Role of the Judiciary of the International Criminal Court", CILRAP Film, New Delhi, 23 February 2019 (https://www.cilrap.org/cilrap-film/190223-bitti/).

[63] See also Guénaël Mettraux et al., Expert Initiative on Promoting Effectiveness at the International Criminal Court, 2 December 2014, p. 13 (http://www.legal-tools.org/doc/3dae90/).

[64] See Sácouto and Thompson, 2015, pp. 345–46, see above note 49.

[65] See Morten Bergsmo and Olympia Bekou, "The In-depth Evidence Analysis Charts at the International Criminal Court", in Morten Bergsmo (ed.), *Active Complementarity: Legal Information Transfer*, Torkel Opsahl Academic EPublisher, Oslo, 2011, pp. 313, 324 (http://www.toaep.org/ps-pdf/8-bergsmo).

The form and modalities of the IDAC remain subject to debate and potential improvement. However, the idea behind it, that is, a better organizing of evidence at pre-trial, is essential in three respects: to filter charges, prepare trials and avoid bottlenecks.

1.3.2.2.3. Amount of Evidence

A further concern relates to the management of the amount of evidence gathered during investigations. Defence lawyers typically complain that they are drowning in material because of the amount of files and evidence disclosed. Overloaded charges may render cases unmanageable.

As the ICTY Manual stated,

> one the most important lessons to be learned from the ICTY experience is that, given the complex nature of war crime trials, there is a tendency for indictments to become overloaded with charges, thus making it difficult for the criminal process to cope with the extent of issues to be proved.[66]

It is thus essential to develop hypotheses, at the time of the investigation, on "how long it is likely to take to try the case".[67]

One strategy is to enhance evidence review within the OTP and to focus cases on the strongest charges since the outset. This possibility is foreseen in the Draft Strategic Plan 2019–2021, which openly recognizes that pursuing "narrower but stronger cases" may increase the "speed, efficiency and effectiveness of investigations and prosecution".[68] It marks a departure from previous practices, including the experiences in the Kenyan cases and *Gbagbo*, which showed the risks of evidentiary weaknesses at trial. It needs to be reconciled with the premise to reflect "key aspects of victimization" in the charges.[69]

Another strategy is to strengthen judicial oversight over prosecutorial action. One may contemplate the extent to which ICC judges should use their managerial powers to avoid that cases become unmanageable, as

---

[66] ICTY Manual on Developed Practices, p. 36, see above note 46.
[67] *Ibid.*
[68] OTP, Strategic Plan 2019–2021, see above note 5, para. 27.
[69] *Ibid.*

ICTY judges have done, after the experience of the *Milosević* trial, under Rule 73*bis*.[70]

In particular, the practice of alternative charging requires careful scrutiny. The ICC Chambers Practice Manual has allowed alternative charges at pre-trial, in an attempt to "limit the improper use of regulation 55 immediately after the issuance of the confirmation decision".[71] It states that

> the Prosecutor may plead alternative legal characterisations, both in terms of the crime(s) and the person's mode(s) of liability. In this case, the Pre-Trial Chamber will confirm alternative charges (including alternative modes of liability) when the evidence is sufficient to sustain each alternative. It would then be the Trial Chamber, on the basis of a full trial, to determine which one, if any, of the confirmed alternative is applicable to each case.[72]

However, the permission of alternative charges has caused confusion in relation to case theories at trial. Where alternative charging is allowed,

---

[70] See ICTY, Rules of Procedure and Evidence, 8 July 2015, Rule 73*bis* (http://www.legal-tools.org/doc/30df50/), which gives judges broad managerial powers:

   (B)   In the light of the file submitted to the Trial Chamber by the pre-trial Judge pursuant to Rule 65 *ter* (L)(i), the Trial Chamber may call upon the Prosecutor to shorten the estimated length of the examination-in-chief for some witnesses.

   (C)   In the light of the file submitted to the Trial Chamber by the pre-trial Judge pursuant to Rule 65 *ter* (L)(i), the Trial Chamber, after having heard the Prosecutor, shall determine

      (i)   the number of witnesses the Prosecutor may call; and

      (ii) the time available to the Prosecutor for presenting evidence.

   (D)   After having heard the Prosecutor, the Trial Chamber, in the interest of a fair and expeditious trial, may invite the Prosecutor to reduce the number of counts charged in the indictment and may fix a number of crime sites or incidents comprised in one or more of the charges in respect of which evidence may be presented by the Prosecutor which, having regard to all the relevant circumstances, including the crimes charged in the indictment, their classification and nature, the places where they are alleged to have been committed, their scale and the victims of the crimes, are reasonably.

[71] ICC, Chambers' Practice Manual, p. 19, see above note 60. For a discussion, see Eleni Chaitidou, "The Judiciary and Enhancement of the Classification of Alleged Conduct", CILRAP Film, New Delhi, 23 February 2019 (https://www.cilrap.org/cilrap-film/190223-chaitidou/).

[72] ICC, Chambers' Practice Manual, p. 19, see above note 60.

---

care should be taken to avoid listing multiple theories of responsibility in a way that obscures the main theory of the Prosecution.[73]

1.3.2.2.4. Investigative Strategy

It is clear from past experiences that some of the existing methodologies require a substantive makeover. OTP investigative practices have been under critique since *Lubanga*. Judges have taken issue with different aspects of investigations, including (1) the outsourcing of investigations, (2) reliance on intermediaries, and (3) heavy use of indirect evidence and witness testimony. Judge Van den Wyngaert has openly the criticized OTP for

> grave problems in the Prosecution's system of evidence review, as well as a serious lack of proper oversight by senior Prosecution staff.[74]

After the acquittals in *Bemba* and *Gbagbo*, one may openly speak of an "evidence problem",[75] which can be traced to investigative strategies.[76]

Initially, the OTP has followed a strategy of carrying out "short, focused investigations",[77] with reliance on a limited number of witnesses. This has resulted in "heavy reliance on indirect evidence gathered through secondary sources".[78] This approach was partially corrected in the Strategic Plan 2012–2015, which shifted its attention "from its previous 'fo-

---

[73] ICTY Manual on Developed Practices, p. 36, see above note 46. On charging practices, see Cale Davis, "Cumulative Charging and Challenges in Charge Selection", CILRAP Film, New Delhi, 22 February 2019 (https://www.cilrap.org/cilrap-film/190222-davis/).

[74] ICC, Situation in the Republic of Kenya, *Prosecutor v. Uhuru Muigai Kenyatta*, Trial Chamber, Concurring Opinion of Judge Christine Van den Wyngaert, 26 April 2013, ICC-01/09-02/11-728-Anx2, para. 4 (http://www.legal-tools.org/doc/917ec7/).

[75] See Patryk Labuda, "The ICC's 'Evidence Problem': The Future of International Criminal Investigations After the Gbagbo Acquittal", in *Völkerrechtsblog*, 18 January 2019 (available on its web site).

[76] See also Morten Bergsmo, "The Gbagbo case and the role of France", in *Le Monde*, 18 January 2019 ("The Gbagbo acquittal tells us there is a problem of quality control at the Court. This is not a new problem. As a matter of fact, the investigative capacity of the Court was downgraded from the start") (http://www.legal-tools.org/doc/693bee/).

[77] War Crimes Research Office, 2012, p. 12, see above note 48.

[78] *Ibid.*

cused' investigative approach to 'open-ended, in-depth investigations'".[79] The OTP acknowledged that it would, where appropriate, apply a "building upwards" strategy. [80] But this turn in strategy has not translated into reality.

The ICC has witnessed a significant increase in Article 70 cases. However, the main trial record has been disappointing.[81] In the *Kenyatta* case, the OTP had to withdraw charges due to witness interference. At trial, four of the seven cases have failed due to evidence deficits: *Ngudjolo*, *Bemba*, *Ruto and Sang* and *Gbagbo and Blé Goudé*. In two cases, the judges found that there was no 'case to answer' for the Defence. This motion is not even contemplated in ICC proceedings. It was permitted as to tool to enhance the expeditiousness and fairness of proceedings. The fact that there is not even a case to answer at trial after the filter of the confirmation hearing illustrates severe evidentiary shortcomings in the Prosecution's case, including insufficient linkage evidence and preparation for the fallout of witnesses at trial.

In reality, the ICC is thus mainly becoming a criminal court for members of non-State armed groups. The trials against *Lubanga*, *Katanga* and *Al Mahdi* have succeeded, because their prosecution matched State interests. However, all cases against acting State officials or former State leaders have failed. This raises serious legitimacy concerns. It exposes the ICC to critiques of one-sided justice. Victor Peskin has called this "new victor's justice",[82] namely the risk that the ICC becomes an instrument for States to get of their enemies or political opponents.

These findings have implications for investigative strategy. The lesson from *Bemba* and *Gbagbo* is that investigations and evidence collection require more in-depth engagement with individual situations and

---

[79] OTP, Strategic Plan 2016–2018, 16 November 2015, para. 13 (http://www.legal-tools.org/doc/2dbc2d/).

[80] *Ibid.*

[81] See also "The Gbagbo case and the role of France", 18 January 2019, see above note 76:
[T]he record of the International Criminal Court is unprecedented in international criminal justice: cases against 12 persons have collapsed, compared to three convictions of international crimes. Four suspects were acquitted, and charges were dismissed against four and withdrawn against four others.

[82] Victor Peskin, "Beyond Victor's Justice? The Challenge of Prosecuting the Winners at the International Criminal Tribunals for the Former Yugoslavia and Rwanda", in *Journal of Human Rights*, 2005, vol. 4, no. 2, pp. 213–31.

careful case-building. As scholars like Phil Clark[83] and Patryk Labuda have emphasized, the ICC has remained at the surface in these contexts. One of the critiques is that the Court has assumed too easily

> that evidence against high-ranking officials can or will eventually be found, rather than basing arrest warrants on actionable evidence developed over time against a larger group of suspects.[84]

The experience of the *ad hoc* tribunals has shown that it is difficult to immediately go after leaders, without gradually building a sequence of interrelated cases. The *Bemba* and *Gbagbo* cases have made it clear that it may be necessary to engage more fully and in depth with individual situations, before passing on to leadership responsibility. Such hypotheses should be factored in during the planning of investigations. This lesson is more prominently reflected in the Draft Strategic Plan 2019–2021. It expressly acknowledges the need to bring "cases against notorious or mid-level perpetrators who are directly involved in the commission of crimes', in order to "provide deeper and broader accountability" and also to "ultimately have a better prospect of conviction in potential subsequent cases against higher-level accused.[85]

Such an approach has drawbacks, since it may limit the overall number of situations where the ICC is investigating. But ultimately 'less may be more', as in the context of preliminary examinations.

1.4. The Structure of International Criminal Investigations

Planning investigation of international crimes requires different mindsets and multidisciplinary input. Success depends on the co-operation between legal experts and non-lawyers. Experiences from the ICTY suggest

> that in addition to investigators with a traditional police background, teams require the services of military, criminal and political analysts, historians, demographers, forensic specialists and linguists. All groups of investigators can learn from each other, and it is essential that all understand the le-

---

[83] See Phil Clark, *Distant Justice: The Impact of the International Criminal Court on African Politics*, Cambridge University Press, Cambridge, 2018.

[84] Labuda, 18 January 2019, see above note 75.

[85] OTP, Strategic Plan 2019–2021, see above note 5, para. 27.

gal structure of the cases and the legal requirements for gathering evidence.[86]

Emphases and needs shift at different stages of an investigation. Investigations cover context, structures and individuals. Dermot Groome has developed a model that divides investigations into roughly four phases: "casting the net", "discovering the case", "exploring the case" and "building the case".[87]

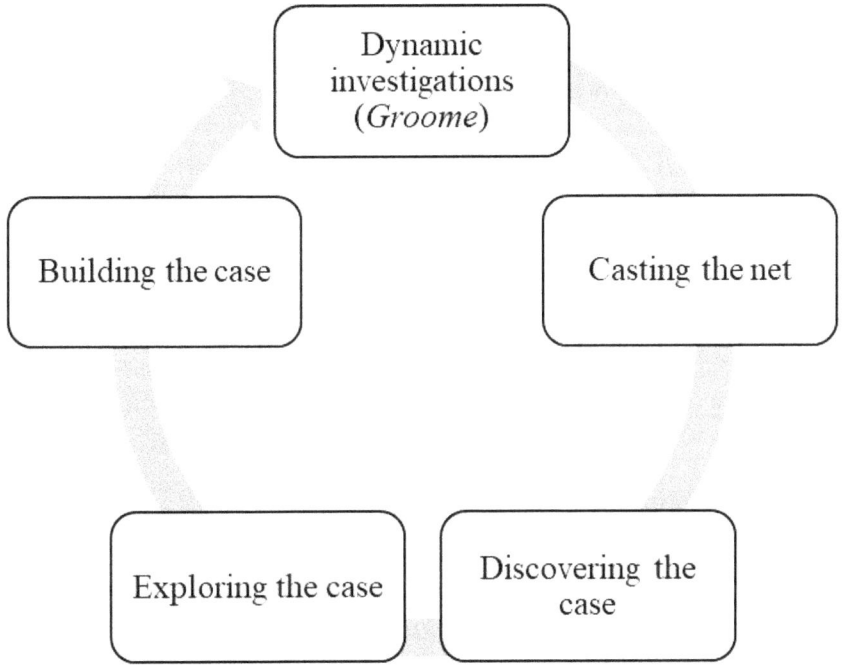

Figure 1: Four phases of investigation.

At the ICC, these four phases are connected to preliminary examination. At the very least, the first two phases may benefit from work done during preliminary examination.

The first step is to provide a 'fact-base', that is, to establish what actually happened. In this first phase, investigators often cast the net widely,

---

86   ICTY Manual on Developed Practices, p. 12, see above note 46.
87   Dermot Groome, "Evidence in cases of mass criminality", in Ilias Bantekas and Emmanouela Mylonaki (eds.), *Criminological Approaches to International Criminal Law*, 2014, Cambridge University Press, Cambridge, pp. 117, 121–22.

by trying to capture as much evidence as possible about events. This serves to limit cognitive biases, and requires a broad investigation plan.[88] At the ICC, this phase may be supported by the work done during preliminary examinations that involves fact-finding.

The second phase relates to 'discovering the case'. Investigators analyse the evidence in order to develop theories of events and to identify potential suspects.[89] This assessment may lead to early tentative conclusions or a theory of events. As Paul Seils has argued, this phase may also benefit from insights gathered during preliminary examination:

> If from the outset, the process of preliminary examination was seen as the development of potential cases through formulating initial hypotheses, once an investigation was opened the OTP would be potentially in a stronger position to allocate resources and identify areas of particular interest.[90]

The third phase is about 'exploring the case'. Investigators deepen the collection of evidence to pursue concrete lines of inquiry, eliminate doubt in relation to hypotheses and meet relevant standards of proof.[91] This requires close co-ordination between investigators and prosecutors, who need to rely on evidence at trial. It may require changes in the investigation plan.

The 'building of the case' is the last phase. It includes more detailed identification of the crime-base and modes of liability. It also serves to identify or remedy evidentiary gaps.

This sequence implies that investigative teams have to rely on 'legal direction' throughout the entire phase of the investigation, and not only during the 'case-building' stage.[92]

---

[88] *Ibid.*, p. 121.

[89] *Ibid.*, p. 122.

[90] Seils, 2015, p. 319, see above note 18.

[91] Groome, 2014, p. 122, see above note 87. See generally Simon de Smet, "The International Criminal Standard of Proof at the ICC – Beyond Reasonable Doubt or Beyond Reason?", in Carsten Stahn (ed.), *The Law and Practice of the International Criminal Court*, pp. 861–89, see above note 18.

[92] See also ICTY Manual on Developed Practices, p. 12, see above note 46 ("Experience has also shown that it is essential for investigative teams to have strong legal direction from the outset").

1.5. Some Thoughts on the Way Ahead

There are several ways in which existing practices can be improved. They relate to planning, the role and structure of investigative teams, investigative strategies and review.

1.5.1. Planning

Firstly, the ICTY Manual on Developed Practices has defended the use of investigation plans in order to "clarify the investigative objectives and evidence collection methods".[93] It has identified certain key elements that should be "developed, discussed and approved by senior management" prior to the start of any substantive investigative activity. They include

- fundamental questions, that is, questions that the "investigation will hopefully be able to answer through the collection of credible and reliable evidence";
- the legal framework, including theories of responsibility and "possible crimes that were committed and their legal elements";
- primary investigative avenues, including summaries of "what is presently known", "people whose activities will be examined", potential witnesses, physical evidence and potential documentary evidence;
- a summary of "investigative tasks to be undertaken"; and
- the "resources to be deployed to conduct" the investigative activities.[94]

These plans require periodic review in light of the different phases of the investigation, changing hypotheses and evolving "collective knowledge of a particular event".[95]

Careful planning is even more essential at the ICC, where situational analysis encompasses additional elements and where case selection and access to evidence have remained problematic. Successful investigations require not only different types of investigative plans, but also pre-

---

[93] *Ibid.*, p. 30.

[94] *Ibid.*

[95] *Ibid.*, p. 32:
  For example the class of people to be investigated should over time narrow as recent evidence inculpates some and exculpates others. Theories of how crimes were committed will similarly evolve and entire investigative avenues can be safely terminated and newer more precise avenues commenced.

investigative plans, which should be informed by preliminary examinations. In some situations, the formulation of investigative plans may be a desired outcome of preliminary examinations.[96] This requires close collaborative links between preliminary examination analysts and investigative experts not only after, but also during the preliminary examination.[97]

1.5.2. Role and Structure of Investigative Teams

Secondly, it has become evident that there should be limits and adequate control structures relating to the outsourcing of investigations.[98] At the ICC, the role of intermediaries went beyond establishing contact with potential witnesses. In the *Lubanga* case, the Trial Chamber reprimanded the Prosecution for its unchecked use of intermediaries and its "negligence in failing to verify and scrutinize" the work of intermediaries, which led to "inaccurate or dishonest" testimonies.[99] It found that "the prosecution should not have delegated its investigative responsibilities to the intermediaries in the way set out, despite the security difficulties it faced".[100] The Chamber suggested that some intermediaries exercised improper influence over witnesses, warranting contempt of court proceedings.[101]

One of the weaknesses of the 'contracting of intermediaries' is that it may introduce a filter between the locals and the 'internationals'. It may be more helpful to embed ICC investigators more deeply in local contexts or to consider mixed investigation teams, composed of domestic and international investigators. Such teams operate successfully in the context of regional systems, as seen in the ICTY's completion strategy.[102]

---

[96] See also Bergsmo, 2019, see above note 7.

[97] OTP, Strategic Plan 2019–21, see above note 5.

[98] Elena A. Baylis, "Outsourcing Investigations", in *UCLA Journal of International Law and Foreign Affairs*, 2009, vol. 14, no. 1, p. 121.

[99] ICC, Situation in the Democratic Republic of the Congo, *Prosecutor v. Lubanga*, Trial Chamber, Judgment pursuant to Article 74 of the Statute, 14 March 2012, ICC-01/04-01/06-2842, para. 482 (http://www.legal-tools.org/doc/677866/).

[100] *Ibid.*

[101] *Ibid.*, para. 483 ("there is a risk that P-0143 persuaded, encouraged, or assisted witnesses to give false evidence; there are strong reasons to believe that P-0316 persuaded witnesses to lie as to their involvement as child soldiers within the UPC").

[102] See War Crimes Research Office, 2012, p. 5, see above note 48:
Another option relating to the composition of investigation teams that may improve investigations is to hire nationals of the country being investigated and/or persons will-

Throughout the proceedings, it is essential to maintain a close link between investigative teams and trial teams. Investigators have unique insights into the situational context and may continue to provide useful input at pre-trial or trial. However, after the formal end of the investigation, investigators easily fall off the radar screen or may lack voice, since they operate under the leadership of trial team leaders. Institutionally, it might be helpful to re-introduce a Deputy Prosecutor for Investigations at the ICC (as in early OTP practice), in order to reinforce the importance of investigative work and to ensure that investigative knowledge and expertise is effectively and continuously present throughout the proceedings.

1.5.3. Place-based Approach

Thirdly, the 'evidence problem' of the ICC suggests that investigations require not only a "phase-based", but also a "place-based approach to evidence gathering".[103] The success of investigations depends on fostering meaningful relations with ground-level institutions and persons. The initial strategy to conduct investigations from abroad without a more developed field-based presence has had significant drawbacks. As Xabier Agirre has noted:

> Local expertise is indispensable to interpret the relevant information in its authentic social context, including aspects of culture, politics, economy and linguistics.[104]

Investigations require more investment in establishing long-term relationships with local agents and communities. They may benefit from greater field presence during preliminary examination.[105]

---

ing to be permanently located in the situation country for the duration of the investigation. Of course, this may not always be possible due to security concerns and will have to be evaluated on a case-by-case basis. In addition, the Office will need to be cautious about potential bias, be it real or perceived, when engaging local actors as part of its investigation team.

[103] Christian M. De Vos, "Investigating from Afar: The ICC's Evidence Problem", in *Leiden Journal of International Law*, 2013, vol. 26, no. 4, pp. 1009, 1011.

[104] Xabier Agirre, "Methodology for the Criminal Investigation of International Crimes", in Alette Smeulers (ed.), *Collective Violence and International Criminal Justice: An Interdisciplinary Approach*, Intersentia, 2010, pp. 353, 359.

[105] See War Crimes Research Office, 2012, p. 6, see above note 48:
[W]e recommend that, in most cases, the OTP send analysts to the country under examination for an extended period of time prior to the formal opening of an investigation, which may improve the OTP's understanding of the context in which the crimes

1.5.4. In-depth Investigation and Bottom-up Strategy

Fourthly, the strategy of targeted investigations needs to be complemented by more in-depth investigations in cases where investigative strategies aim at reaching the most responsible political leaders or State agents. In such contexts, it may be necessary to pursue a broad investigation strategy within a single situation that extends beyond a handful of cases. This means that the OTP must devote greater time and resources to investigations from the start. As now reflected in the Draft OTP Strategic Plan 2019–21, which is based on academic critique and work on quality control as well,[106] cases may need to be gradually and carefully built up, as was done in the context of the *ad hoc* tribunals.[107] The investigative fabric must be thick enough to succeed despite the risk of loss of witnesses or other evidence.

1.5.5. Peer Review System

Finally, it is key to ensure a rigorous 'peer review' process within the OTP to ensure quality control.[108] Internal reviews, involving other teams and lawyers, are required early on, in order to refresh minds and detect weaknesses.[109] They may guide analytical processes and the review of potential material and evidence.

During investigations, the OTP is mandated to investigate exculpatory evidence as well.[110] This is an important element of facilitating review. But peer review structures are needed much earlier. It is important to frame and question key assumptions already at the preliminary examination stage. For instance, the preparation of a pre-investigative plan re-

---

took place and its ability to gain the trust of those who may be in a position to provide useful information.

[106] See Bergsmo, 2013, see above note 3; Bergsmo and Stahn, 2018, see above note 4; Carsten Stahn, "The Times They Are A-Changin': Why the ICC Should Re-Visit Strategies on Preliminary Examination", in *Justice in Conflict* (available on its website).

[107] OTP, Strategic Plan 2019–21, see above note 5, para. 27.

[108] Such an approach was adopted at the ICTY. See Bergsmo and Keegan, 1997, p. 11, see above note 42.

[109] See War Crimes Research Office, 2012, p. 70, see above note 48:
Another measure that may help to expose potential weaknesses in the Prosecution's case and ensure that all necessary investigative steps have been undertaken before the OTP seeks an arrest warrant or summons to appear would be to implement a rigorous and formal "peer review" process within the OTP similar to that used at the ICTY.

[110] ICC Statute, Article 54, see above note 17.

quires effective anticipation of Defence challenges and development and consideration of alternative hypotheses. Structures, like 'devil's advocate' models or 'red team' approaches, may help to strengthen peer review during preliminary examinations and investigations.[111]

In addition, it is essential to nurture a 'culture of critical thinking' inside the OTP which allows dissident voices to be freely expressed and considered in working practices, without fear of marginalization or repression. It needs to be reflected not only in internal working structures and daily practice[112], but also applied in relation to critical voices from outside.[113] Such a culture requires careful and open-minded listening to outside voices, openness towards quality control, constructive engagement with critiques of OTP practices and policies, and their potential use as springboard for review and reform.

1.6. To be Continued

In criminal procedure, it is often said that time spent at pre-trial may be time gained at trial. In ICC practice, this promise has not yet come to fruition. There are numerous initiatives to promote the fairness and expeditiousness of judicial proceedings. However, the foundations must be laid much earlier, namely in prosecutorial practice. Saving time at pre-trial requires more investment into effective preliminary examinations and investigations by the OTP itself and ICC members and supporters. Quality control during preliminary examinations and investigation is essential for the Court as a whole. It has a double function. It serves as a filter at pre-trial and has preparatory function for trial. As the following chapters in this volume indicate, this aim requires critical engagement with existing practices and new pathways that go beyond classical procedural divides (that is, adversarial vs. inquisitorial), institutional standpoints or disciplinary silos.

---

[111] On OTP approaches, see Xabier Agirre, "On How Analysis Can Enhance the Quality of Investigation and Case Preparation", CILRAP Film, New Delhi, 22 February 2019 (https://www.cilrap.org/cilrap-film/190222-agirre/).

[112] OTP, Strategic Plan 2019–21, see above 5, para. 17.

[113] See for instance Morten Bergsmo, Wolfgang Kaleck, Sam Muller and William H. Wiley, "A Prosecutor Falls, Time for the Court to Rise", Policy Brief Series No. 86 (2017), Torkel Opsahl Academic EPublisher, Brussels, 2016 (http://www.toaep.org/pbs-pdf/86-four-directors/).

The Draft OTP Strategic Plan 2019–21 recognizes that it is important for the OTP to engage with quality control and adjust institutional structures, where necessary. Some of the proposed changes reflect recommendations voiced in the course of this project. The main test is to what extent they will be implemented in practice. This requires ongoing dialogue and an institutional culture which is open to listen and engage.

2

Investigating International Crimes: Pitfalls, Problems and Promises

Thijs B. Bouwknegt[*]

2.1. Introduction

International criminal justice for violent mass atrocity crimes has developed into a belief system, a political project, a scholarly field as well as a vibrant industry at an astonishing pace since 1993. In the last years, however, it is in relapse. Progressively, as Mark Drumbl reasons, there is a realisation that basically "law cannot solve the biggest problems we face".[1] Among myriad tribulations is the collection and ascertainment of facts about mass atrocity violence through preliminary examinations and criminal investigations. Investigative inhibitions and biases have explicitly come to light at the International Criminal Court ('ICC'). Its manifold investigations in a dozen African (post-)conflict situations have therefore led to only miniature truth(s), a few completed trials, and to hardly any convincing convictions.

Much criticism of the ICC has focused on the way it has conducted its investigations in Africa. This critique does not only come from human rights organisations, academics and Court observers. Judges too have raised serious concerns about the coalesced investigative and prosecutori-

---

[*] **Thijs B. Bouwknegt** is a Researcher at NIOD Institute for War, Holocaust and Genocide Studies (part of the Royal Netherlands Academy of Arts and Sciences, 'KNAW') and Assistant Professor at the University of Amsterdam ('UvA'). This chapter is an extended version of: Thijs B. Bouwknegt, "Gbagbo – An Acquittal Foretold", *JusticeInfo*, 31 January 2019 (available on its web site); Thijs B. Bouwknegt, "The International Criminal Trial Record as Historical Source", Nanci Adler (ed.), *Understanding the Age of Transitional Justice: Crimes, Courts, Commissions, and Chronicling*, Rutgers University Press, New Brunswick, 2018, pp. 118–46.

[1] Thierry Cruvellier (conducting a justiceinfo.net in-depth interview), "Mark Drumbl: 'Law Cannot Solve the Biggest Problems We Face'", *JusticeInfo*, 16 July 2019 (available on its web site).

al *status quo* of the ICC's Office of the Prosecutor ('OTP'). In 2011, for example, the Pre-Trial Chamber found that the prosecution did not make it through the basic evidentiary test of the confirmation of charges versus Callixte Mbarushimana. As the OTP's case was largely built on non-governmental organisation ('NGO') and United Nations ('UN') reports, the Chamber found that the case was riddled with "inconsistencies", "lack of any corroborating evidence" and "assumptions" from third parties.[2] In 2012, Judge Adrian Fulford, while reading a summary of the judgment in the trial of Thomas Lubanga Dyilo, lamented the prosecution's negligence in parts of its investigation:

> A series of witnesses have been called during this trial whose evidence, as a result of the essentially unsupervised actions of three of the principal intermediaries, cannot safely be relied on.[3]

As a result, the ICC's first judgment was also an indictment of the Prosecutor's investigation. Somewhat literally, the Chamber commanded better quality. A year later, however, the Pre-Trial Chamber adjourned the confirmation of charges hearing in the case against Laurent Gbagbo. Judges held that "the Prosecutor relied heavily on NGO reports and press articles with regard to key elements of the case, including the contextual elements of crimes against humanity", and that "[s]uch pieces of evidence cannot in any way be presented as the fruits of a full and proper investigation".[4] Seven years later, the collapse of the Prosecution's case was hardly surprising. Judge Cuno Tarfusser, in a ranting opinion, said:

> It is or should be obvious that the investigation constitutes the bedrock of any criminal case; as a consequence, flaws and shortcomings at the investigative stage are not suitable

---

[2] ICC, Situation in the Democratic Republic of the Congo, *The Prosecutor v. Callixte Mbarushimana*, Pre-Trial Chamber, Decision on the confirmation of charges, 16 December 2011, ICC-01/04-01/10-465-Red, paras. 120, 136 ('Decision on the confirmation of charges of Mbarushimana's case') (https://legal-tools.org/doc/63028f).

[3] ICC, Situation in the Democratic Republic of the Congo, *The Prosecutor v. Lubanga Dyilo*, Trial Chamber, Transcript, 14 March 2012, ICC-01/04-01/06-T-359-ENG, p. 5 (https://legal-tools.org/doc/4f82d2).

[4] ICC, Situation in the Democratic Republic of Côte d'Ivoire, *The Prosecutor v. Laurent Gbagbo*, Pre-Trial Chamber, Decision adjourning the hearing on the confirmation of charges pursuant to Article 61(7)(c)(i) of the Rome Statute, 3 June 2013, ICC-02/11-01/11-432, para. 35 ('Decision Adjourning the Hearing on the Confirmation of Charges of Gbagbo's Case') (https://legal-tools.org/doc/2682d8).

to be remedied in the courtroom and will inevitably com-
promise the chances of success of any resulting case.[5]

Judge Tarfusser's colleague, Judge Henderson, proposed institutional and strategic lessons to be learned:

> [T]he Prosecutor cannot be expected to bring cases of this
> level of complexity and scope within a reasonable time
> frame with the limited resources that are currently available
> to her. While it is important for the Prosecutor to be ambi-
> tious in the way that she approaches her mandate, she ought
> also to be realistic about what is feasible.[6]

Indeed, Prosecutors and ICC protagonists have generally lacked
modesty by promising more than what they could realistically achieve.
Carsten Stahn fairly writes that the field of international criminal justice
"requires critical scrutiny" and proposes that "[s]ome [of its] methodologies […] are in need of refinement".[7] Any such fine-tuning, however, can
only be achieved if one understands the intrinsic pitfalls and practical
obstacles of investigating international crimes, and if one determines the
ICC's investigative culture and *modus operandi*. In other words, only
through an investigation of investigations would it become possible to
conclude whether there is need for 'refinement', as Stahn suggests, or for
revolution, restructuring and reorganisation.

Morten Bergsmo points to an important precondition for international criminal justice to improve its investigation or preparation of fact-
rich criminal cases:

> Prosecutorial professionalization […] requires awareness on
> the part of prosecutorial leaders of the importance of self-
> questioning and -improvement.[8]

---

[5]   ICC, Situation in the Republic of Côte d'Ivoire, *The Prosecutor v. Laurent Gbagbo and Charles Blé Goudé*, Trial Chamber, Opinion of Judge Cuno Tarfusser, 16 July 2019, ICC-02/11-01/15-1263-AnxA, para. 95 ('Opinion of Judge Cuno Tarfusser') (https://legal-tools.org/doc/f6c6f3).

[6]   ICC, Situation in the Republic of Côte d'Ivoire, *The Prosecutor v. Laurent Gbagbo and Charles Blé Goudé*, Trial Chamber, Reasons of Judge Geoffrey Henderson, 16 July 2019, ICC-02/11-01/15-1263-AnxB-Red, para. 10 ('Reasons of Judge Geoffrey Henderson') (https://legal-tools.org/doc/j0v5qx).

[7]   Carsten Stahn, "From Preliminary Examination to Investigation: Rethinking the Connec-tion", Chap. 1 above.

[8]   See Morten Bergsmo, "Towards a Culture of Quality Control in Criminal Investigations", FICHL Policy Brief Series No. 94 (2019), Torkel Opsahl Academic EPublisher, Brussels,

As the OTP is not only tasked with prosecutions but also investigations, this practical repair approach to 'quality control on investigations' is fair. However, it omits questioning whether the OTP, as adversarial party to criminal proceedings, should be empowered, or burdened, with investigations in the first place. Arguably, a focus solely directed at improvement, or curing, existing practice may not necessarily lead to sustainable solutions, or more crucially to better investigations. Gauging a wider pallet of options for changing existing investigative practice is therefore warranted. Why not, amongst others, think about the creation of an investigative chamber, an autonomous investigative organ, or an independent permanent international investigative 'mechanism'? Considering an evidence-based rather than prosecution-based system of international criminal investigations may in itself be a form of quality control.

If one desires a "culture of quality control in criminal investigations"[9] one ought to start with an assessment of the existing culture of international criminal investigations, and understand its rationale, practice and outcomes. This requires a critical and empirical analysis. First, it makes sense to establish *what* international criminal investigations, *by whom*, seek to achieve, *when, why, how* and *for whom*? *Ergo*: what are the biases? Secondly, one should consider whether the existing approaches, methodologies and available (re)sources allow for standardised investigations. Thirdly, what have investigations resulted in? Truth, convictions, acquittals or something else?

This chapter analyses the pitfalls of the specific rationale and practice of international criminal justice on criminal investigations of international crimes. It does so by discussing a variety of investigative problems in Africa and analysing investigations in Rwanda, Sierra Leone, the Democratic Republic of the Congo, Uganda and Côte d'Ivoire. It concludes by discussing several promises for the way forward.

2019, p. 2 (http://www.toaep.org/pbs-pdf/94-bergsmo/). This publication has served as the concept paper for the research project that led to this anthology.

[9] See *ibid.*

2.2. Pitfalls and Problems

Historian Uğur Üngör finds that the study of mass violence must principally be shielded from moral, legal, political, and emotional constraints.[10] He classifies fundamental biases that may distort objective, neutral and meticulous investigation of mass atrocity violence. First, people find mass violence repulsive. They react with strong condemnatory emotions and pleas for righteousness. Involvement, attachment or empathy for victims are logical human traits, but they can also bias the forensic eye of a truth-seeker. A second logjam is moralisation (a sense of good versus evil), which can easily percolate into investigations and affect its core neutrality. 'Doing good' does not equal rigour, value-free inquisition and thus quality inquiry. A third pitfall is politics. Frequently, the lexicon of atrocity crimes is weaponised (by, *inter alia*, lobbyists, advocacy groups, critics, opposition groups and States) in service of political rhetoric, litigation, moral outcry, diplomatic interests and identity-politics. The wanton allegation of political atrocity violence does not always mean that there is unpolluted or unmanipulated evidence of crime.[11] A fourth pitfall in the study of mass violence is a strict legal approach. In international legal practice – a field that is the product of politics – the aim is to name and shame, accuse, condemn and punish individuals. Law's orientation is only determining individual criminal responsibility in the context of mass violence (within a clearly set legal, procedural and evidentiary straitjacket) which by itself is a heuristic bottleneck.

Reflecting soberly on the quality of criminal investigation of atrocities, we could consider that excellence is best secured if they are carried out in a dispassionate, amoral, apolitical and non-juridical way.[12] However, international criminal justice – in particular its epitome, the ICC – is performed by passionate agents, based on a particular moral worldview, stirred towards achieving liberal political goals, and curtailed by laws and regulations. Because of its inborn biases, international criminal justice seems to have become its own enemy.

---

[10] Uğur Ümit Üngör, "Studying Mass Violence: Pitfalls, Problems, and Promises", in *Genocide Studies and Prevention: An International Journal*, 2012, vol. 7, no. 1, pp. 68–80.

[11] Also see Alex de Waal, "Writing Human Rights and Getting it Wrong", in *Boston Review*, 6 June 2016 (available on its web site).

[12] Üngör, p. 73, see above note 10.

International criminal justice is a system of belief grounded in the human rights positivism of the 1990s. It was premised on liberal notions that it was finally possible to speak law to power, and that truth would prevail. On the macro-level, it is premised on a *liberal bias*, which favours democratic values and rule-of-law type political systems. However, its expressed goals of contributing to world peace, ending impunity, forging reconciliation, uncovering truth and repairing victims are not so much "assumptions of epistemology".[13] Rather, achieving universal 'justice' is an 'article of faith', rooted in the idea there is one justice, and that law would liberate humanity from repression and evil. This *ideological bias*, together with the idea that justice is globally applicable (*universalist bias*), trickles through generalised transitional justice ambitions into international criminal justice. Ultimately, these fields are rooted in a *human rights bias*. Not only do they address topical human rights issues, they are also informed by leads and information provided by human rights lobby groups (*NGO bias*).[14] Ultimately, international criminal justice is driven by a nearly religious zeal that the ICC would "heal the world".[15] Yet, if one recalls the realism of Hannah Arendt, one is reminded about the law's limited role:

> The purpose of a trial is to render justice and nothing else; even the noblest of ulterior purposes [...] can only detract from the law's main business: to weigh the charges brought against the accused, to render judgment, and to mete out due punishment.[16] [...] Justice demands that the accused be prosecuted, defended, and judged, and that all the other questions, though they may seem to be of greater import [...] be left in abeyance.[17]

When justice is overpromised, it risks ending up underdelivered. A fundamental bottleneck is the perception that law – and lawyers – could also fulfil non-judicial goals.

---

[13] Michael Ignatieff, "Articles of Faith", in *Index on Censorship*, 1996, vol. 25, no. 5, p. 111.

[14] Cf. Luc Reydams, "NGO Justice: African Rights as Pseudo-Prosecutor of the Rwandan Genocide", in *Human Rights Quarterly*, 2016, vol. 38, no. 3, pp. 547–88.

[15] Author's Observation, see below note 143, and accompanying text.

[16] Hannah Arendt, "A Reporter at Large: Eichmann in Jerusalem – V", *The New Yorker*, 16 March 1963, p. 101.

[17] *Ibid.*, p. 40.

As lawmakers appointed Prosecutors as drivers of international criminal justice, other bottlenecks came to light, including *accountability*, *punitive* and *responsibility biases*. OTP investigations are oriented towards prosecution, punishment and winning cases; they are not *per se* about establishing truth. Moreover, because their mandate may be limited to or focused on going after those 'most responsible', a particular category of public persons may become suspects by default. According to common knowledge and public opinion, they 'must be guilty'. This form of *cognitive bias* can lead to a presumption of guilt, until proven otherwise. In such a reversed situation, investigations may serve to corroborate assumptions of guilt, not to seek, find and ascertain facts. Because of this *prosecutorial bias* in the inquiry, the system chases targets by seeking evidence against them (top-down), rather than finding suspects by following the evidence (ground-up). Christian Nielsen has called this practice case perpetration.[18] This *confirmation bias* does not only pollute inquisitorial investigations, broadly understood. It also creates prosecutorial tunnel vision, and Manichean and unprovable case theories. Lastly, as a result of limited existence or availability of documentary evidence in certain situations (for example, in some countries in Africa), the chief evidentiary base for international criminal prosecutions is witness evidence. Apart from basic questions as to reliability and credibility, a bottleneck may be *witness bias*; the assumption that victims and survivors of the most horrible atrocities do not lie.

2.3. Investigating Atrocity

Besides prosecution, the ICC-OTP is also tasked with 'preliminary examination' and 'investigation'. However, the drafters of the Rome Statute and the Elements of Crimes document defined only sketchily what these words actually mean, and which actions and methodologies they require. The practice to date may differ fundamentally from other forms of inquisitorial, forensic fact-seeking, fact-finding and fact-ascertainment about mass violence.

According to the Cambridge Dictionary an 'examination' is the "act of looking at or considering something carefully in order to discover

---

[18] Christian Axboe Nielsen, "Analysis of Organisational Structures and Quality Control of Case Development", CILRAP Film, New Delhi, 22 February 2019 (www.cilrap.org/cilrap-film/190222-nielsen/).

something", while an 'investigation' means "the act or process of examining a crime, problem, statement, etc. carefully, especially to discover the truth".[19] At is its core, examinations (which in practice is a form of open source desk research) and investigations (in the field) are about discovery of facts and truth. Ideally, such an exercise would be done holistically, inquisitorially and without constraints. So far, however, the political authors of the Rome Statute judiciously straitjacketed the scope of the OTP's examinations and investigations. Although the Prosecutor shall "establish the truth", she is regulated to assess "whether there is criminal responsibility under this Statute, and, in doing so, investigate incriminating and exonerating circumstances equally".[20] The margins as to what the OTP is allowed to investigate are thus plenty.

First, as a judicial organisation, the ICC is not purposed – and arguably incapable – to establish forensic, historical '(Rankean) truth' (as it happened) about mass violence in each particular and unique situation. Rather, the ICC pursues judicial truth – a legal, argumentative, narration that is made compatible with its given mandate, procedures and evidentiary standards. Second, the ICC is after the judicial truth about a specific kind of micro agency (individual criminal responsibility) within a macro-reality (structure) of acts and events that fit complex definitions of genocide, crimes against humanity, war crimes, or aggression. Third, in doing so, the OTP is perhaps paradoxically constrained: besides looking for evidence to support its charges (which is its core business), it must also look for evidence that potentially undermines its charges. Prior to filing charges, it has the duty during the investigations to explore doubt about evidence that should prove charges beyond any reasonable doubt. Essentially, the OTP is tasked to undermine its own cases. Fourth, the OTP does not possess the investigative means and powers that are typically required for criminal investigations. Unlike professional police, the OTP cannot investigate and secure immediate crime scenes, hear witnesses on the spot, conduct search and seize operations, wiretap suspects or conduct under-cover operations. Its examinations and investigations may therefore resemble a form of secondary research, often depending largely on secondary sources, while its success depends on tertiary factors and agents (State

---

[19] Cambridge Dictionary, "Examination", "Investigation" (available on its web site).
[20] Rome Statute of the International Criminal Court, 17 July 1998, Article 54 ('ICC Statute') (https://legal-tools.org/doc/7b9af9).

co-operation, assistance from national police and military forces, peace-keepers, NGO lobby groups and local 'intermediaries').

Overall, one could consider that international criminal investigations present a particular, yet limited, way of fact-seeking, fact-finding and fact-ascertainment of atrocity crimes. Moreover, critique has been levelled against the manner in which, as well as by whom, such investigations are being carried out. Particularly in the early days of the ICC, investigative teams would hardly include of investigators with police background, skills or experience. Quite infamously, the first Prosecutor, Luis Moreno-Ocampo, distrusted police, almost as much as he distrusted staff who would express disagreement with him. This led to a situation in which investigators were recruited from a pool of NGO researchers, academics and human rights lawyers; people with remarkable skills in their own fields, but they were not necessarily professional crime investigators. Senior investigators lamented this reality in the beginning, saying it seriously impacted the quality of investigations. Moreover, some critiques have argued that the OTP's investigative units were too heavily controlled by prosecuting lawyers, who obviously had a specific interest in finding a particular kind of facts and evidence that would support their indictments and case scenarios against readily identified targets. Moreover, and quite crucially, OTP's investigations were often hampered by security concerns. By nature, police work in volatile contexts – and particularly in the context of war crimes and organised crime –is dangerous and risky. Investigating atrocity crimes requires risk taking, but so far, however, there has been a notable tilt towards safeguarding investigators over pursuing fact-finding opportunities. Other tribunals, like the International Criminal Tribunal for the former Yugoslavia ('ICTY'), also investigated during armed conflicts, but in comparison the ICC has been more risk averse to date. Overall, due to its limitations and rationale, the ICC's Investigation Division can hardly be compared to criminal investigative units in national police forces.[21]

Further to these rather basic observations about international atrocity crime investigations, there are certain challenges that are particular to

---

[21] See Thijs B. Bouwknegt, *Investigation, Prosecution and Adjudication of International Crimes in the Netherlands* (*Opsporing, Vervolging en Berechting van Internationale Misdrijven in Nederland*), NIOD Institute for War, Holocaust and Genocide Studies, Amsterdam, 2019.

the ICC. First, there is an issue with temporality. Legal responses, including investigations, often start a long time after crimes have occurred, sometimes even decades. Recently, in the ICC's decision not to allow the OTP to investigate atrocity crimes in Afghanistan (and in sub-text in Poland, Lithuania and Romania), judges expressed concerns about the timing of criminal investigations and especially the investigative risks related the expiration of evidence about old crimes.[22] In fact, international criminal investigations mostly deal with cold cases and old evidence. Such a cold-case situation poses epistemological, empirical and thus evidentiary challenges and requires a particular kind of expertise. It is hardly surprising that the investigative units at the *ad hoc* tribunals, but also in various national war crimes units, include(d) historians and social scientists with particular methodological and contextual expertise. At the International Criminal Tribunal for the former Yugoslavia, for instance, the Leadership Research Team, headed by an historian, was such an entity that assisted investigators and prosecutors in dealing with fact-finding, source-interpretation and contextualisation. At the ICC, no such specialised unit was set up, leaving key questions about the nature and context of crimes unanswered by professionals and left to lawyers. As seen in the prosecution of former history professor and President Gbagbo, ignoring the warnings of specialists and analysts (because, based on the evidence, they could advise against prosecution, charges or case narrative) contributed to a prosecution based on an unrealistic Manichean case scenario. Greater and genuine involvement of independent and unbiased experts, at both the examination and investigation stages, could arguably better inform the OTP on evidentiary and feasibility matters as well as the quality of evidence and the presentation of realistic case scenarios in charges and prosecutions.

2.4. Investigations in Africa

> Q: [Mr. Biju-Duval] [...] Can you tell us precisely on the basis of which document or what other source you can make such a claim?

---

22 ICC, Situation in the Islamic Republic of Afghanistan, Pre-Trial Chamber, *Decision Pursuant to Article 15 of the Rome Statute on the Authorisation of an Investigation into the Situation in the Islamic Republic of Afghanistan*, 12 April 2019, ICC-02/17-33 (https://legal-tools.org/doc/2fb1f4).

A: [Gérard Prunier] Well, sir, we're dealing with Africa. Pity, please, a little common sense. This isn't how things work there.[23]

2.4.1. International Criminal Tribunal for Rwanda

What lessons are learned from past investigations? Justice for international crimes tends to arrive belatedly, particularly if it is generated through international bureaucracies.[24] At the International Criminal Tribunal for Rwanda ('ICTR'), it took a year after the end of the civil war and genocide in Rwanda (1990-1994), before an investigative unit was set up in Kigali. Prosecutor Richard J. Goldstone reported in April 1995 that he was already processing about 400 cases.[25] His investigative team, however, faced tremendous administrative, leadership and operational problems.[26] One year after its establishment, the OTP had 52 staff members from 15 different countries, 28 of them on secondment.[27] Next to lawyers, intelligence analysts, advisers, a scientific director, experts in forensic medicine, statisticians, demographers, interpreters and support staff, the team comprised only a dozen investigators.[28] Experience and qualification was, however, lacking. Senior prosecutors came from academia or human

---

[23] ICC, Situation in the Democratic Republic of the Congo, *The Prosecutor v. Thomas Lubanga Dyilo*, Trial Chamber, Transcript, 26 March 2009, ICC-01/04-01/06-T-156-ENG, pp. 94–95 (https://legal-tools.org/doc/4bf97a).

[24] Megan M. Westberg, "Rwanda's Use of Transitional Justice After Genocide: The Gacaca Courts and the ICTR", in *Kansas Law Review*, 2011, vol. 59, no. 2, p. 343.

[25] Progress Report of the Secretary-General on the United Nations Assistance Mission for Rwanda, UN Doc. S/1995/297, 9 April 1995, para. 18 (https://legal-tools.org/doc/7tpba7).

[26] Financing of the ICTR: Report of the Secretary-General on the Activities of the Office of Internal Oversight Services, UN Doc. A/51/789, 6 February 1997, Annex, para. 19–25 (https://legal-tools.org/doc/59dqh2); Further Report of the Secretary-General Pursuant to Paragraph 5 of Security Council Resolution 955 (1994), UN Doc. S/1995/533, 30 June 1995, para. 4 (https://legal-tools.org/doc/573b94).

[27] Netherlands House of Representatives, "Rwanda; Brief van de Ministers van Buitenlandse Zaken en voor Ontwikkelingssamenwerking", 8 October 1996, kst-23727-25, p. 2; Frank Vermeulen, "Negen Miljoen voor Rwanda", *NRC Handelsblad*, 20 May 1995; "Nederlanders naar Rwanda", *Het Parool*, 26 September 1995; Hans Marijnissen, "Nederlandse politie brengt zaak voor Rwanda-tribunaal", *Trouw*, 24 October 1995; Hanneke de Wit, "Onderzoek in Rwanda traag", *Het Parool*, 2 November 1995.

[28] Report of the Office of Internal Oversight Services on the Review of the Office of the Prosecutor at the International Criminal Tribunals for Rwanda and for the former Yugoslavia, in Review of the Office of the Prosecutor at the International Criminal Tribunals for Rwanda and for the former Yugoslavia: Note by the Secretary-General, UN Doc. A/58/677, 7 January 2004, para. 6 (https://legal-tools.org/doc/nkowtt).

rights organisations and had neither criminal trial proficiency nor experience. Legal advisors had no experience in criminal investigations. And the investigators, drawn largely from police forces in the Netherlands, Canada, Norway and Sweden, hardly had experience in investigating genocide, crimes against humanity and war crimes. Many were in Africa for the first time[29] and were foreign to Rwandan society, culture and language.[30] Working conditions were hard and some staff left "in complete frustration" after being threatened or assaulted.[31] They also lacked vehicles – essential to visit crime scenes and witnesses – computers, phones, faxes and stationery, leaving some investigators to bring their own laptops to the field. Overall, the OTP was in disarray and had no strategy at all.[32]

As a result, self-organised teams set their own plans and strategies. But they made little effort to gather documentary and forensic evidence.[33] In the field, investigators were escorted by Rwandan officials, clergy, policemen or translators. They often worked on the basis of UN or human rights reports focussed on Rwandans who were captured already.[34] They further relied on witnesses identified and delivered to them by NGOs and survivor organisations.[35] The investigative strategy was suspect-based with a geographical focus on Butare, Kibuye, Cyangugu and Kigali.[36] Three investigators gathered the first survivor testimonies in May 1995.[37] They testified that it was not complicated to collect evidence. "In Rwanda, everyone knows everything, and everybody knows everybody", one of them explained in court.[38] However, sometimes, in the case no witnesses

---

[29] Also see Nick Louvel and Michele Mitchell, "The Uncondemned", *Film at Eleven*, 2015.

[30] Alison Des Forges, "Legal Responses to Genocide in Rwanda", in Eric Stover and Harvey M. Weinstein (eds.), *My Neighbor, My Enemy: Justice and Community in the Aftermath of Mass Atrocity*, Cambridge University Press, Cambridge, 2004, p. 53.

[31] Financing of the ICTR: Report of the Secretary-General on the Activities of the Office of Internal Oversight Services, 1997, para. 38, see above note 26.

[32] *Ibid.*, para. 56.

[33] *Ibid.*

[34] Nicholas A. Jones, *The Courts of Genocide, Politics and the Rule of Law in Genocide and Arusha*, Routledge, Abingdon, 2010, pp. 112–15.

[35] Des Forges, 2004, pp. 49–68, see above note 30.

[36] Larissa van den Herik, *The Contribution of the Rwanda Tribunal to the Development of International Law*, Martinus Nijhoff Publishers, Leiden, 2005, p. 65.

[37] Thierry Cruvellier, *Court of Remorse: Inside the International Criminal Tribunal for Rwanda*, Chari Voss trans., University of Wisconsin Press, Madison, 2010, p. 81.

[38] *Ibid.*, p. 96.

could be found, professional witnesses would offer their fairly priced "testimonial services".[39] From early on there were rumours of denunciation syndicates, groups of opportunistic people, who allegedly organised testimony against rich persons.[40] This investigatory *modus operandi* would sow the seeds, in part, for the troublesome process of truth-ascertainment at the ICTR. It was only late in the ICTR's history that these investigative impediments came to light and were addressed by judges.[41]

2.4.2. Special Court for Sierra Leone

Some of the lessons learned at the ICTR were taken aboard at the Special Court for Sierra Leone ('SCSL'), which was to:

> [I]nitiate the research on the history of the conflict ("map the conflict"), take into possession existing evidence from the Sierra Leone Police, UNAMSIL [United Nations Mission in Sierra Leone] and NGOs, and establish an evidentiary basis from which investigations could be launched [...].[42]

Soon, however, the missions' interim prosecutor and investigators found that the available evidentiary material was of "limited utility".[43] They found that the only reliable material available was held by the Sierra Leonean police but was collected only after 1999. With few exceptions, there was "virtually no evidentiary material for the bulk of the crimes committed against the people of Sierra Leone in the decade-long conflict".[44] Thus, the paucity of detailed, reliable evidentiary material would place a significant burden on the investigative functions of the Prosecutor.[45] When Prosecutor David Crane arrived in Freetown[46] he recruited

---

[39] André Sirois, "Les mauvais débuts du Tribunal international pour le Rwanda", *Mondialisation.ca*, 13 November 2014 (available on its web site).

[40] See "The trial of Jean-Paul Akayesu, former mayor of Taba commune", *Hirondelle News Agency*, 1 September 1998.

[41] Doris Buss, "Expert Witnesses and International War Crimes Trials: Making Sense of Large-Scale Violence in Rwanda", in Dubravka Zarkov and Marlies Glasius (eds.), *Narratives of Justice in and Out of the Courtroom: Former Yugoslavia and Beyond*, Springer, Cham, 2014, pp. 23–44.

[42] Letter dated 6 March 2002 from the Secretary-General addressed to the President of the Security Council, UN Doc. S/2002/246, 8 March 2002, Annex, para. 60(b)(ii) (https://legal-tools.org/doc/usgtwc).

[43] *Ibid.*, para. 26.

[44] *Ibid.*

[45] *Ibid.*, para. 27.

among his personal connections, former ICTR and ICTY staff members, Sierra Leonean expatriates[47] and Human Rights Watch ('HRW') activists.[48] Four Sierra Leonean police officers joined the investigations team within the first two weeks of operations to provide local insights and follow-up leads throughout the process.[49] Like at the ICTR, chief investigator Alan White assumed that "[p]eople are the best source of information and your best source of evidence", and in "this case, our best evidence is going to be good, credible witness testimony".[50] His methodology was "getting out and talking to people, letting them know what our mission is and soliciting their support".[51]

In the following months, the investigation team increased to some 20 investigators, including interns, alongside almost 50 analysts and lawyers. The team carried out one forensic examination[52] and focused mainly on finding witnesses.[53] In chasing its predetermined suspects, soon the old prosecutorial trick of flipping potential suspects to testify against their superiors became the standard.[54] On that testimonial basis, the first round of investigations that lasted about six months, the first indictments were drawn up, approved and (partially) executed during two targeted mis-

---

[46] David M. Crane, "Dancing with the Devil – Prosecuting West Africa's Warlords: Building Initial Prosecutorial Strategy for an International Tribunal after Third World Armed Conflicts", in *Case Western Reserve Journal of International Law*, 2005, vol. 37, no. 1, p. 3.

[47] Thierry Cruvellier and Marieke Wierda, *The Special Court for Sierra Leone: The First Eighteen Months*, International Center for Transitional Justice, March 2004, p. 4.

[48] For instance, West Africa Researcher Corrine Dufka of Human Rights Watch. See her testimony: SCSL, *The Prosecutor v. Charles Ghankay Taylor*, Trial Chamber, Transcript, 21 January 2008, pp. 1749–50 (https://legal-tools.org/doc/541e5b).

[49] Tom Perriello and Marieke Wierda, *The Special Court for Sierra Leone Under Scrutiny*, International Centre for Transitional Justice, 5 March 2006, p. 21.

[50] Charles Cobb Jr., "Sierra Leone's Special Court: Will it Hinder or Help?", *AllAfrica*, 21 November 2002 (available on its web site).

[51] *Ibid.*

[52] SCSL, *First Annual Report of the President of the Special Court for Sierra Leone for the Period 2 December 2002 - 1 December 2003*, pp. 14–15 (https://legal-tools.org/doc/5c5175).

[53] Author's interview with Corrine Dufka, 15 March 2015.

[54] Eric Stover, Victor Peskin and Alexa Koenig, *Hiding in Plain Sight: The Pursuit of War Criminals from Nuremberg to the War on Terror*, University of California Press, Oakland, 2017, p. 261.

---

sions.[55] Like pursuing the mafia, the investigators went on undercover operations, posing as diamond dealers, in refugee camps to track informants whom they would offer a deal: "[t]estify and you'll be safe. In return, we'll take care of you and your family".[56] This mode of investigations resembled practice at other hybrid constructions, such as the Special Panels in East Timor, but has not resurfaced after the SCSL experience. Particularly the ICC departed from police-style investigations.

2.4.3. Democratic Republic of the Congo: Pandora's Box

> On the fact that humanitarian groups are lousy investigators,
> I will not go that far. However, one must concede that the
> procedure of investigation of humanitarian groups, in my
> opinion, is more a sort of a general journalism rather than le-
> gal-type activities of investigators.
>
> Bernard Lavigne, Investigator[57]

In all respects, the Democratic Republic of the Congo ('DRC') seemed to be the perfect case file for the ICC. But it turned out to become the ICC's Pandora's Box. In the year before the set-up of the OTP, 6 out of 499 'communications' related to Ituri.[58] In March 2004, Joseph Kabila outsourced the well-reported atrocities to Prosecutor Luis Moreno-Ocampo who then announced the start of a criminal inquiry.[59] The troubled Congolese province had been on his radar from the very beginning.[60]

---

[55] David M. Crane, "The Take Down: Case Studies Regarding 'Lawfare' in International Criminal Justice: The West African Experience", in *Case Western Reserve Journal of International Law*, 2010, vol. 43, no. 1, pp. 201–14.

[56] Stover, Peskin and Koenig, 2017, p. 261, see above note 54.

[57] ICC, Situation in the Democratic Republic of the Congo, *The Prosecutor v. Thomas Lubanga Dyilo*, Trial Chamber, Transcript, 17 November 2010, ICC-01/04-01/06-Rule68Deposition-T-2-Red2-ENG, p. 47 (https://legal-tools.org/doc/318f82).

[58] ICC Assembly of States Parties ('ASP'), *Second Assembly of States Parties to the Rome Statute of the International Criminal Court: Report of the Prosecutor of the ICC, Mr Luis Moreno-Ocampo*, 8 September 2003 ('Report of the Prosecutor of the ICC 2003') (https://legal-tools.org/doc/8873bd). OTP, "Communications Received by the Office of the Prosecutor of the ICC", 16 July 2003, pids.009.2003-EN, sect. III.a. (https://legal-tools.org/doc/df602e).

[59] OTP, "The Office of the Prosecutor of the International Criminal Court Opens Its First Investigation", 23 June 2004, ICC-OTP-20040623-59 (https://legal-tools.org/doc/b68535).

[60] Report of the Prosecutor of the ICC 2003, see above note 58; OTP, Statement of the Prosecutor Luis Moreno Ocampo to Diplomatic Corps, 12 February 2004 (https://legal-tools.org/doc/6dvm3d).

Congo appeared to be a politically convenient and feasible pick.[61] But it was also challenging. Former Deputy Prosecutor Serge Brammertz told the United States embassy in Kinshasa that his probe ought not to "derail" Congo's delicate peace process.[62] It would hence only "focus on abuses committed by actors outside the transition, such as the Ituri armed groups".[63] Brammertz also raised concerns about the working terrain: the DRC was "difficult and complex [...] for logistical and political reasons".[64] And indeed, throughout their first field mission to Bunia in September 2004, investigators heard gunshots in the regional capital. Bunians greeted them with suspicion, unsure what and who these foreigners were after. Roadblocks prevented them from leaving the city to visit crime scenes and potential witnesses.[65] Amidst these security concerns and start-up issues,[66] the first witness in the investigation was not heard before 2005 or mid-2005.[67] Around this time, the Congolese army arrested eight Iturian warlords, including Thomas Lubanga Dyilo and Germain Katanga, who were charged with serious charges including genocide and crimes against humanity.[68]

Meanwhile, Bosco Ntaganda – who since April 2005 also faced a Congolese arrest warrant[69] – fled to his home country Rwanda.[70] Ntagan-

---

[61] ICC, Situation in the Democratic Republic of the Congo, Presidency, Decision assigning the Situation in the Democratic Republic of the Congo to Pre-Trial Chamber I, 5 July 2004, ICC-01/04-1 (https://legal-tools.org/doc/218294).

[62] USA Embassy in Kinshasa, "ICC Gearing up to Start Ituri Investigation", *WikiLeaks*, 4 August 2004, para. 6.

[63] *Ibid.*, para. 3.

[64] *Ibid.*

[65] See ICC, Situation in the Democratic Republic of the Congo, *The Prosecutor v. Thomas Lubanga Dyilo*, Trial Chamber, Transcript, 16 November 2010, ICC-01/04-01/06-Rule68Deposition-T-1-Red2-ENG, p. 35 ('Lubanga Rule 68 Deposition Transcript – Session 1') (https://legal-tools.org/doc/2f1389).

[66] ICC, Situation in the Democratic Republic of the Congo, *The Prosecutor v. Thomas Lubanga Dyilo*, Trial Chamber, Judgment pursuant to Article 74 of the Statute, 14 March 2012, ICC-01/04-01/06-2842, para. 151–68 ('Lubanga Trial Judgment') (https://legal-tools.org/doc/677866).

[67] Lubanga Rule 68 Deposition Transcript – Session 1, p. 43, see above note 65.

[68] Human Rights Watch, *Democratic Republic of Congo and the International Criminal Court Hearing to Confirm the Charges against Thomas Lubanga Dyilo: Questions and Answers*, November 2006 (https://legal-tools.org/doc/vfs22n).

[69] Since 12 April 2005, Bosco Ntaganda was under a DRC arrest warrant, issued by the Prosecutor of the Tribunal de Grande Instance of Bunia. The arrest warrant details charges

da was featured as the 'terminator' in many HRW reports and ICC investigators spent most of their time tracking down 'Bosco' and lobbying for his arrest with the United Nations Organization Mission in the Democratic Republic of the Congo ('MONUC'). But without results, Moreno-Ocampo's mood swung and:

> [S]uddenly, because of a political decision by Louis or his political committee, we were obliged to change our planning and our investigative work and concentrate on a new target. It was completely crazy. [...] We put in danger a lot of people.[71]

As a result, the cases "barely scratched the surface of the conflict".[72] But it was exactly that very conflict that also brought along substantial hurdles for the investigators; continuing violence, no permanent office. Besides, the United States restricted MONUC's assistance to a minimum. While security concerns dragged down investigations, the lack of police experience arguably affected its quality. Only two out of the twelve investigators had a police background. The Congo team included former NGO researchers, who were instructed to refrain from local contact with chiefs, priests or school teachers. It was to protect the identities of witnesses and informants, but it barred them from gaining useful 'field knowledge'.[73]

The team's immobility obstructed their core business: collecting information and impartially verifying prospective evidence. Instead, the Ituri investigation was outsourced. Intelligence was borrowed from the notes of MONUC police officers and NGO researchers. The very first

---

of joint criminal enterprise, arbitrary arrest, torture and complicity in assassination pursuant to Articles 156 to 158, 67, 44 and 45 of the DRC Criminal Code. ICC, Situation in the Democratic Republic of the Congo, Pre-Trial Chamber, Annex 2 to "Decision on the Prosecutor's Application for Warrants of Arrest, Article 58", 10 February 2006, ICC-01/04-02/06-20-Anx2, para. 34 ('Decision on the Prosecutor's Application for Warrants of Arrest') (https://legal-tools.org/doc/d68b07).

[70] Jason Stearns, *Strongman of the Eastern DRC: A Profile of General Bosco Ntaganda*, Rift Valley Institute, 12 March 2013.

[71] James Verini, "The Prosecutor and the President", *The New York Times*, 22 June 2016 (available on its web site).

[72] *Ibid.*

[73] Caroline Buisman, "Delegating Investigations: Lessons to be Learned from the Lubanga Judgment", in *Northwestern Journal of International Human Rights*, 2013, vol. 11, no. 3, pp. 30–82.

witness was heard in The Hague "through an NGO, which acted as an intermediary",[74] a *modus operandi* that was soon exported to Bunia. On the advice of the human rights researchers, the OTP commissioned locals to liaise between investigators and potential witnesses. These 'intermediaries' carried out the ICC's essential fact-finding mandate: selecting witnesses, recording their statements and corroborating the information. A Congolese lawyer summarised that "investigating cases of child soldiers in Ituri is like picking a ripe mango that fell at your feet. It could not be any easier".[75] This methodology was soon criticised by observers as being "amateurish" and "mediocre".[76]

Based on its delegated enquiry, Moreno-Ocampo requested the ICC Pre-Trial Chamber to issue arrest warrants for Lubanga and Ntaganda for child soldering.[77] But pre-trial judges were hardly impressed by the evidence and found that Ntaganda was not a key actor or most responsible in the DRC situation and only approved the indictment against Lubanga,[78] who was already in prison.[79] His case, however, was riddled by evidentiary hurdles. Just before the Lubanga trial was to start, in July 2008, the Chamber ordered his release. Moreno-Ocampo refused to – and argued he could not – disclose to them and the defence more than 200 documents he had obtained under confidentiality agreements, including from the UN. As some of the material was believed to contain exculpatory evidence, the Chamber believed in these circumstances a fair trial was impossible without the judges seeing it. By use of first-aid solutions and legal gymnastics by the Appeals Chamber, the trial went forward.

---

[74] Lubanga Rule 68 Deposition Transcript – Session 1, p. 53, see above note 65.

[75] Franck Petit, "Minimalist investigation in Lubanga's case", *International Justice Tribune*, 23 September 2006, no. 53, p. 1 (on its web site).

[76] *Ibid.*, p. 1; Thierry Cruvellier, "Lessons from the Lubanga Trial", *International Justice Tribune*, 15 March 2012, no. 147, pp. 2–3; author's interview with Anneke van Woudenberg, 27 February 2014.

[77] ICC, Situation in the Democratic Republic of the Congo, Pre-Trial Chamber, Prosecutor's Application for a Warrant of Arrest, Article 58, 13 January 2006, ICC-01/04-98-US-Exp.

[78] Decision on the Prosecutor's Application for Warrants of Arrest, paras. 87–89, see above note 69.

[79] *Ibid.*, para. 33; ICC, "ICC - First arrest for the International Criminal Court", 2 March 2006, ICC-CPI-20060302-125 (https://legal-tools.org/doc/eef265).

"Lubanga's armed group recruited, trained and used hundreds of young children to kill, pillage, and rape",[80] said Moreno-Ocampo. "They cannot forget what they suffered".[81] But the OTP narrative was soon shattered, when he called a former child soldier as his first witness. The timid boy, who could not remember his date of birth, testified that:

> I would like to say what actually happened myself, not say what some other person intended me to say. [...] At the time there was an NGO which was helping children. My friends went there. I also went there, and they took our addresses and told us that they could help us. [...] They told me things which did not help me to remember what happened, but now that I'm here I will tell you exactly what happened.[82]

With such a shaky evidentiary start, the trial forged on and only in the ninth week did the Prosecution turn to historian Gérard Prunier. He was to go through the details of the origins of the ethnic conflicts in Ituri. But he constantly reminded the court of the difficulties of investigations in Africa:

> I cannot be more reliable than the UN for the simple reason that there are a lot of things in the history of that region that you cannot elucidate [...] sometimes you have to resign yourself to the fact that it's difficult to elucidate these things and you may not know everything.[83]

The same precision was lacking in the testimony in the evidence by forensic expert witnesses. Discussing x-ray images taken from 9 former child soldiers, who were witnesses in the trial, radiologist Catherine Adamsbaum said that age determination "is not a totally exact science".[84]

---

[80] ICC, Situation in the Democratic Republic of the Congo, *The Prosecutor v. Thomas Lubanga Dyilo*, Trial Chamber, Transcript, 26 January 2009, ICC-01/04-01/06-T-107-ENG, p. 4 (https://legal-tools.org/doc/bc5f5e).

[81] *Ibid.*

[82] ICC, Situation in the Democratic Republic of the Congo, *The Prosecutor v. Thomas Lubanga Dyilo*, Trial Chamber, Transcript, 28 January 2009, ICC-01/04-01/06-T-110-ENG, pp. 40–41 (https://legal-tools.org/doc/7e62d3).

[83] ICC, Situation in the Democratic Republic of the Congo, *The Prosecutor v. Thomas Lubanga Dyilo*, Trial Chamber, Transcript, 27 March 2009, ICC-01/04-01/06-T-157-ENG, pp. 13–14 (https://legal-tools.org/doc/d35011).

[84] ICC, Situation in the Democratic Republic of the Congo, *The Prosecutor v. Thomas Lubanga Dyilo*, Trial Chamber, Transcript, 12 May 2009, ICC-01/04-01/06-T-172-Red3-ENG, p. 80 (https://legal-tools.org/doc/73e93c).

Her colleague, Caroline Rey-Salmon, a paediatrician and forensic doctor, testified that the x-ray images she had to analyse were of relatively bad quality, only showed hard-to-interpret jawbones and that their methodology could not always produce the exact age of a person.[85]

In July 2010 judges again stayed the proceedings.[86] This time it was because Moreno-Ocampo refused to reveal the name of an intermediary. The Appeals Chamber reversed the release order, but rebuked Moreno-Ocampo for flouting court orders.[87] On that notice the trial resumed with the testimony of Barnard Lavigne, two investigators and several intermediaries, who shed light on the investigations. The trial continued and finally, at its closure in August 2011, Fatou Bensouda insisted that Lubanga's guilt was "beyond any possible doubt".[88] But Defence lawyer Catherine Mabille alleged that the Chamber must have seen a product of organised manipulation of witnesses. "[T]he intermediaries knew exactly what story needed to be told",[89] she said, accusing them of going to Congolese towns "recruiting children, and they would tell the children what they had to say".[90]

Lubanga heard his judgment in March 2012. But to some extent, it was also levelled against the OTP. Judge Fulford lamented the prosecution's negligence in parts of its investigation, which ultimately led the Chamber to find the nine 'child soldiers' who had testified for the prose-

---

[85] ICC, Situation in the Democratic Republic of the Congo, *The Prosecutor v. Thomas Lubanga Dyilo*, Trial Chamber, Transcript, 13 May 2009, ICC-01/04-01/06-T-173-ENG, pp. 26–28 (https://legal-tools.org/doc/7fbfc0).

[86] ICC, Situation in the Democratic Republic of the Congo, *The Prosecutor v. Thomas Lubanga Dyilo*, Trial Chamber, Redacted Decision on the Prosecution's Urgent Request for Variation of the Time-Limit to Disclose the Identity of Intermediary 143 or Alternatively to Stay Proceedings Pending Further Consultations with the VWU, 8 July 2010, ICC-01/04-01/06-2517-Red, para. 31 (https://legal-tools.org/doc/cd4f10).

[87] ICC, Situation in the Democratic Republic of the Congo, *The Prosecutor v. Thomas Lubanga Dyilo*, Appeals Chamber, Judgment on the appeal of Prosecutor against the oral decision of Trial Chamber I of 15 July 2010 to release Thomas Lubanga Dyilo, 8 October 2010, ICC-01/04-01/06-2583 (https://legal-tools.org/doc/230492).

[88] ICC, Situation in the Democratic Republic of the Congo, *The Prosecutor v. Thomas Lubanga Dyilo*, Trial Chamber, Transcript, 25 August 2011, ICC-01/04-01/06-T-356-ENG, p. 4 (https://legal-tools.org/doc/01302c).

[89] ICC, Situation in the Democratic Republic of the Congo, *The Prosecutor v. Thomas Lubanga Dyilo*, Trial Chamber, Transcript, 26 August 2011, ICC-01/04-01/06-T-357-ENG, p. 15 (https://legal-tools.org/doc/16241d).

[90] *Ibid.*, p. 10.

cution "unreliable".[91] Lubanga's conviction and sentence were upheld by the Appals Chamber. However, Judge Anita Ušacka, found that Lubanga should not have been convicted at all. In her view, the evidence relied upon by the Trial Chamber to convict Lubanga was not sufficient to reach the threshold of beyond any reasonable doubt. In practice they have applied a lower standard.[92]

Ušacka expressed her hope that "future prosecutions [...] will adduce direct and more convincing evidence".[93] Her dissent was a sharp indictment against the court's fact-ascertainment dilemmas. She found the OTP levelled insufficiently detailed charges – which did not contain reference to identified victims, while "dates and locations were framed in unacceptably broad terms",[94] and had relied too much on the testimony of nine former child soldiers. Even "the factual conclusions of the Trial Chamber suffered from the same level of imprecision",[95] she said. Moreover, Ušacka, considered "that the evidence in this case was, in particular, not sufficient to establish that at least some of the children in the UPC [Union of Congolese Patriots]/FPLC [Patriotic Forces for the Liberation of Congo] were under the age of fifteen".[96] Ušacka reminded the court of the testimony of two alleged child soldier, who featured in a video excerpt heavily relied on by the Trial Chamber, who testified they were aged between 17 and 20 years at time that the video was filmed.[97]

---

[91] Lubanga Trial Judgment, para. 502, see above note 66.

[92] ICC, Situation in the Democratic Republic of the Congo, *The Prosecutor v. Thomas Lubanga Dyilo*, Appeals Chamber, Dissenting opinion of Judge Anita Ušacka, 1 December 2014, ICC-01/04-01/06-3121-Anx2, pp. 15–16 (https://legal-tools.org/doc/df4480).

[93] *Ibid.*, p. 38.

[94] ICC, Situation in the Democratic Republic of the Congo, *The Prosecutor v. Thomas Lubanga Dyilo*, Appeals Chamber, Transcript, 1 December 2014, ICC-01/04-01/06-T-364-ENG, p. 15 (https://legal-tools.org/doc/abead3).

[95] *Ibid.*

[96] *Ibid.*, p. 16.

[97] *Ibid.*, p. 17.

2.4.3.1.   Bogoro

> [D]eclaring that an accused person is not guilty does not necessarily mean that the Chamber has been convinced of the person's innocence.[98]

Judge Bruno Cotte elucidated that "[s]uch a decision merely shows that the evidence adduced is insufficient to convince the Chamber beyond all reasonable doubt".[99] His carefully chosen words were the pretext of the acquittal of Ngudjolo. The prosecution had alleged he had intended and planned to "wipe out Bogoro" during an attack that killed around 200 civilians.[100] Out of a total of 54, the OTP relied heavily on three "key" witnesses who had themselves been taking part in the attack. The prosecutor ensured they had "testified as best they could and in light of their own personal situations".[101] But for the Chamber "their remarks were too contradictory or too hazy, too imprecise […] to base itself on".[102]

With the uncertain start of Lubanga's trial in mind, the judges in this case selected the first witness, the head of the team that had investigated the Bogoro case since May 2006, themselves. The Chamber questioned her about their methodologies: "Could you tell us how you assess the objectivity and credibility of these intermediaries?".[103] It was a query that poured salt in an open wound. Ngudjolo, since his acquittal was upheld,[104] was sent back to Kinshasa.[105]

---

[98]   ICC, Situation in the Democratic Republic of the Congo, *The Prosecutor v. Mathieu Ngudjolo Chui*, Trial Chamber, Transcript, 18 December 2012, ICC-01/04-02/12-T-1-ENG, p. 6 ('Ngudjolo Chui Trial Transcript – Session 1') (https://legal-tools.org/doc/713344).

[99]   *Ibid.*

[100]   ICC, Situation in the Democratic Republic of the Congo, *The Prosecutor v. Germain Katanga and Mathieu Ngudjolo Chui*, Decision on the Confirmation of Charges, 30 September 2008, ICC-01/04-01/07-717 (https://legal-tools.org/doc/67a9ec); ICC, Situation in the Democratic Republic of the Congo, *The Prosecutor v. Germain Katanga and Mathieu Ngudjolo Chui*, Trial Chamber, Transcript, 24 November 2009, ICC-01/04-01/07-T-80-ENG, p. 23 (https://legal-tools.org/doc/0f399df).

[101]   Ngudjolo Chui Trial Transcript – Session 1, p. 7, see above note 98.

[102]   *Ibid.*

[103]   ICC, Situation in the Democratic Republic of the Congo, *The Prosecutor v. Germain Katanga*, Trial Chamber, Transcript, 25 November 2009, ICC-01/04-01/07-T-81-Red-ENG, p. 37 (https://legal-tools.org/doc/fd1869).

[104]   ICC, Situation in the Democratic Republic of the Congo, *The Prosecutor v. Mathieu Ngudjolo Chui*, Appeals Chamber, Judgment on the Prosecutor's appeal against the decision of Trial Chamber II entitled "Judgment pursuant to article 74 of the Statute", 7 April 2015, ICC-01/04-02/12-271-Corr (https://legal-tools.org/doc/efb111).

Meanwhile, his former co-accused Germain Katanga was found guilty based on the same evidence.[106] But the outcome in his case was controversial. In his case, the judges – with Christine van den Wyngaert dissenting "in the strongest possible terms"[107] – experimented with Regulation 55.[108] In its final considerations, the bench changed the contours of the jigsaw puzzle, in order to fit in the pieces at hand.[109] In effect Katanga was only officially informed about the exact nature of the charges on the day he was found guilty. Had the balance of power shifted from the Prosecution to the Judges and did the judges take over the role of the prosecutor?[110] On the surface, it appears so. At least to the point where some judges have favoured a more inquisitorial approach.[111] This was the case for Trial Chamber II. Like in Lubanga, the Ngudjolo and Katanga case was based on "witness statements and reports by MONUC investigators or representatives of various NGOs",[112] while OTP investigators had never travelled to the home-villages of the accused or places where preparations for the very attack allegedly took place. A forensic investigation in Bogoro was only concluded in late March 2009, six years after the massa-

---

[105] Netherlands Council of State, Administrative Jurisdiction Division, *de vreemdeling v. de staatssecretaris van Veiligheid en Justitie*, Uitspraak 201310217/1/V1, 27 June 2014, ECLI:NL:RVS:2014:2427.

[106] ICC, Situation in the Democratic Republic of the Congo, *The Prosecutor v. Germain Katanga*, Trial Chamber, Judgment pursuant to article 74 of the Statute, 7 March 2014, ICC-01/04-01/7-3436-tENG ('Katanga Trial Judgment') (https://legal-tools.org/doc/f74b4f).

[107] See ICC, Situation in the Democratic Republic of the Congo, *The Prosecutor v. Germain Katanga*, Trial Chamber, Dissenting Opinion of Judge Christine van den Wyngaert, in Decision on the implementation of regulation 55 of the Regulations of the Court and severing the charges against the accused persons, 21 November 2012, ICC-01/04-01/07-3319, paras. 1, 19, 20 (https://legal-tools.org/doc/b0367a).

[108] ICC, Situation in the Democratic Republic of the Congo, *The Prosecutor v. Germain Katanga*, Trial Chamber, Decision on the implementation of regulation 55 of the Regulations of the Court and severing the charges against the accused persons, 21 November 2012, ICC-01/04-01/07-3319-tENG/FRA (https://legal-tools.org/doc/85f380).

[109] See Katanga Trial Judgment, p. 658, see above note 106.

[110] Dov Jacobs, "A Shifting Scale of Power: Who is in Charge of the Charges at the International Court and the Uses of Regulation 55", in *Grotius Centre Working Paper Series*, 13 December 2011.

[111] *Ibid.*

[112] ICC, Situation in the Democratic Republic of the Congo, *Prosecutor v. Matthieu Ngudjolo Chui*, Trial Chamber, Judgment Pursuant to Article 74 of the Statute, 18 December 2012, ICC-01/04-02/12-3-tENG, para. 117 ('Ngudjolo Chui Trial Judgment') (https://legal-tools.org/doc/2c2cde).

cre.[113] But its findings were filed too late and lacked "probative value".[114] The Chamber acknowledged that the OTP:

> would have encountered difficulties in locating witnesses with sufficiently accurate recollections of the facts and able to testify without fear, as well as in the collection of reliable documentary evidence necessary for determining the truth in the absence of infrastructure, archives and publicly available information.[115]
>
> [...]
>
> In all probability, the Prosecution's [case] would have benefitted from a more thorough investigation of these issues, which would have resulted in a more nuanced interpretation of certain facts, a more accurate interpretation of some of the testimonies taken and, again, an amelioration of the criteria used by the Chamber to assess the credibility of various witnesses.[116]

It was against this background that the Trial Chamber travelled to the Iturian towns of Bogoro, Aveba, Zumbe and Kambutso.[117] The Chamber found it essential to "make its own findings and verify various witness accounts".[118] They did not want to judge the case file from an armchair in The Hague.[119] To see is to believe seemed to be their adage.[120] Katanga

---

[113] ICC, Situation in the Democratic Republic of the Congo, *The Prosecutor v. Germain Katanga*, Trial Chamber, Decision on the Disclosure of Evidentiary Material Relating to the Prosecutor's site visit to Bogoro on 28, 29 and 31 March 2009 (ICC-01/04-01/07-1305, 1345, 1360, 1401, 1412 and 1456), 9 October 2009, ICC-01/04-01/07-1515-Corr ('Decision on the Disclosure of Evidentiary Material Relating to the Prosecutor's site visit to Bogoro') (https://legal-tools.org/doc/514321).

[114] Ngudjolo Chui Trial Judgment, fn. 266, see above note 112, citing Decision on the Disclosure of Evidentiary Material Relating to the Prosecutor's site visit to Bogoro, paras. 27–36, see above note 113.

[115] Ngudjolo Chui Trial Judgment, para. 115, see above note 112.

[116] *Ibid.*, para. 123.

[117] See ICC, Situation in Democratic Republic of the Congo, *The Prosecutor v. Germain Katanga and Mathieu Ngudjolo Chui*, Registrar, Enregistrement au dossier du procès-verbal du transport judiciaire en République démocratique du Congo, 3 February 2012, ICC-01/04-01/07-3234 (https://legal-tools.org/doc/c40ed0).

[118] ICC, "ICC judges in case against Katanga and Ngudjolo Chui visit Ituri", 27 January 2012, ICC-CPI-20120127-PR765 (https://legal-tools.org/doc/7408a0).

[119] "It was important to us to go to these places, in order to see where the events took place, and to see, with our own eyes, places from the testimonies of some of the witnesses", said Trial Chamber II Presiding Judge Bruno Cotte. ICC, "Site visit in the DRC - ICC Trial

did not appeal his conviction – and was brought before the Congolese judiciary for a range of other crimes against humanity[121] – and therefore the 'Bogoro dossier' came to a close.[122] But it did not put a lid on the Pandora's Box in Ituri altogether.

2.4.3.2.   Ntaganda

> Bosco was someone who would kill people easily; he was a nasty man. [...] He would kill people very easily. For example, if a soldier killed another soldier, he would be killed.
>
> 'Dieumerci', Witness[123]

The first witness in the Lubanga trial already talked about one of the ICC's key suspects: Bosco Ntaganda. Many other witnesses followed, and in the videos shown during the Lubanga trial he was seen several times. After chasing Ntaganda since 2004, his case file had effectively been dormant for many years.[124] But amidst the pandemonium of the Congo proceedings, Ntaganda's unexpected surrender was more an inconvenience than a present. Investigators had to go back to Ituri to track down the old case-witnesses and find new ones to support additional charges.[125] While the OTP has had time to rethink its investigative methodologies and

---

Chamber II, January 2012", *YouTube*, 27 February 2012, 02:16–02:32 mins. (available on its web site).

[120] See Katanga Trial Judgment, paras. 106–08, see above note 106:

> Aside from the opportunity thus afforded to the Chamber to gain a better understanding of the context of the events before it for determination, the main purpose of the site visit was to enable the Chamber to conduct the requisite verifications in situ of specific points and to evaluate the environment and geography of locations mentioned by witnesses and the Accused persons.

[121] Bienvenu-Marie Bakumanya, "DR Congo to prosecute militia leader Katanga, convicted by ICC", *AFP*, 18 January 2016.

[122] ICC, "Defence and Prosecution discontinue respective appeals against judgment in Katanga case", 25 June 2014, ICC-CPI-20140625-PR1021 (https://legal-tools.org/doc/5f85b5).

[123] ICC, Situation in the Democratic Republic of the Congo, *The Prosecutor v. Thomas Lubanga Dyilo*, Trial Chamber, Transcript, 10 February 2009, ICC-01/04-01/06-T-123-Red3-ENG, p. 20 (https://legal-tools.org/doc/8bead3).

[124] ICC, Situation in the Democratic Republic of the Congo, *The Prosecutor v. Bosco Ntaganda*, OTP, Prosecution's Urgent Request to Postpone the Date of the Confirmation Hearing, 23 May 2013, ICC-01/04-02/06-65, paras. 2, 21 (https://legal-tools.org/doc/3fc08c).

[125] ICC, Situation in the Democratic Republic of the Congo, *The Prosecutor v. Bosco Ntaganda*, Pre-Trial Chamber, Decision on the Prosecutor's Application under Article 58, 13 July 2012, ICC-01/04-02/06-36-Red (https://legal-tools.org/doc/18c310).

"unfinished business",[126] 'intermediaries' were again looking for witnesses in the field.[127]

After these renewed investigations, which delayed most of the proceedings, Ntaganda went on trial in 2015. His case was riddled with controversies and allegations against him of witness tampering.[128] From its advent, it was likely to be poisoned by the investigations and strategies in the other Congo trials.[129] The evidentiary foundations in Ntaganda are again embedded mostly in witness testimony.[130] In seeking to add meat to the case, the prosecution also tendered tangible evidence, including Ntaganda's radio communications logbook; internal reports, requests, orders, letters, decrees and statutes; photographs; and video. Introducing this documentary evidence seemed promising. However, from the beginning of the trial the OTP mainly called witnesses in closed session. Like in another cases, the Trial Chamber also raised concerns about the use of NGO sources, including the testimony of HRW researcher Anneke van Woudenberg. Judge Robert Fremr had reservations about admitting her report into evidence. The Chamber would

> exercise really high caution in relation to this document because in fact it's mainly based on anonymous sources. And as we already expressed in I would say similar case concerning the previous similar witness, we really see very low relevance on this kind of information coming from that kind of sources.[131]

Fremr's reasoning was informed by the ICC's Kivu-probe. In 2011 the Court released Callixte Mbarushimana[132] as the OTP did not make it through the test of the confirmation of charges hearings. Their case was

---

[126] Elizabeth Evenson, *Unfinished Business: Closing Gaps in the Selection of ICC Cases*, Human Rights Watch, September 2011 (https://legal-tools.org/doc/738f10).

[127] Author's interview with ICC investigator, 12 February 2014.

[128] Stéphane Bourgon, "'Bosco Ntaganda: 12 days without eating at the ICC prison'", *Press Release*, 19 September 2016.

[129] Wairagala Wakabi, "Overview of the Ntaganda Trial", *International Justice Monitor*, 15 December 2015 (available on its web site).

[130] Author's observations of the trial.

[131] ICC, Situation in the Democratic Republic of the Congo, *The Prosecutor v. Bosco Ntaganda*, Trial Chamber, Transcript, 22 June 2016, ICC-01/04-02/06-T-107-Red-ENG, p. 58 (https://legal-tools.org/doc/2850f8).

[132] ICC, "Callixte Mbarushimana is released from the ICC custody", 23 December 2011, ICC-CPI-20111223-PR760.

built largely on NGO and UN reports, barely on its own investigations on the ground. In his case, the Chamber issued a damning decision citing "inconsistency", "lack of any corroborating evidence" and "assumptions" from third parties.[133] Ntaganda was convicted on 18 counts of crimes against humanity and war crimes.

2.4.4. Uganda

While the Ituri investigations were problematic, the situation in Uganda was slightly different. Although the investigation was announced at a very early stage of the ICC's life, considerable time passed by as Moreno-Ocampo was still hiring lawyers, analysts and investigators. A so-called 'Uganda joint team' – including a dozen investigators, analysts and trial lawyers – was recruited in early 2004.[134] There was no scarcity of sources. Uganda was a key investigating partner and shipped piles of reports and evidence of Lord's Resistance Army ('LRA') activities to The Hague, including intercepted radio and satellite phone communications. With a strong appetite to start trials, OTP lawyers went into overdrive. Tight deadlines left no time for thorough collection and broad analysis of existing information. Moreno-Ocampo's hand-picked case-leader, Christine Chung, opined: "many think for too long – [and] at some point you need to go to the field".[135]

In the event that the LRA militants suddenly came out of the bush, Moreno-Ocampo wanted indictments 'ready-to-go'. Rushing to produce arrest warrants, the OTP lawyers selected six crimes scenes, handpicked six specific crime types, and identified several targets. Under that blue-printed directive, a small team was sent into the field. However, none of the seven on-ground investigators had police background. As the six crime scenes were already deemed too old, forensic evidence was not trailed. Instead, during over 50 missions in little more than half a year, the investigators identified, heard and collected testimonies from victims in refugee camps, LRA defectors within the Ugandan Army, and former child soldiers. Amongst other things, the investigation recorded at least 2,200 and 3,200 abductions in over 850 attacks between July 2002 and

---

[133] Decision on the confirmation of charges of Mbarushimana's case, see above note 2.

[134] OTP, "Statement by Chief Prosecutor Luis Moreno-Ocampo", 14 October 2005, p. 3 (https://legal-tools.org/doc/d9b3cb).

[135] Katie Glassborow, *ICC Investigative Strategy Under Fire*, Institute for War and Peace Reporting, 27 October 2008.

June 2004.[136] In contrast to the Ituri-probe, witnesses were directly accessible, and recourse to 'intermediaries' was unnecessary. In Uganda, the biggest challenge was to keep the number of witnesses small but of 'smoking gun' quality, something that, according to former investigators, worked out rather well.[137]

Ten months after the start of the investigation, the Court's first-ever arrest warrants were issued on 8 July 2005, against five senior commanders of the LRA.[138] However, only Dominic Ongwen made it to trial. Both a victim and (alleged) perpetrator of LRA atrocities,[139] and facing no fewer than 70 counts of war crimes and crimes against humanity,[140] Ongwen's trial, which is ongoing at the time of writing, has seen substantial introduction of documentary evidence.[141]

2.4.5. Côte d'Ivoire

> First, let me be clear: I have not yet opened an investigation. But, if serious crimes under my jurisdiction are committed, I will do so. For instance, if as a consequence of Mr. Charles

---

[136] OTP, "The Investigation in Northern Uganda", 14 October 2005 (https://legal-tools.org/doc/zlp4tr).

[137] Author's interview with ICC investigator, 14 January 2015.

[138] ICC, Situation in Uganda, *The Prosecutor v. Dominic Ongwen*, Pre-Trial Chamber, Decision on the Prosecutor's Application for Warrants of Arrest under Article 58, 8 July 2005, ICC-02/04-01/15-5 (https://legal-tools.org/doc/9870dd); ICC, Situation in Uganda, *The Prosecutor v. Joseph Kony and Vincent Otti*, Pre-Trial Chamber, Warrant of Arrest for Joseph Kony issued on 8 July 2005 as amended on 27 September 2005, 27 September 2005, ICC-02/04-01/05-53 (https://legal-tools.org/doc/b1010a); ICC, Situation in Uganda, *The Prosecutor v. Joseph Kony and Vincent Otti*, Pre-Trial Chamber, Warrant of Arrest for Vincent Otti, 8 July 2005, ICC-02/04-01/05-54 (https://legal-tools.org/doc/f7c78c); ICC, Situation in Uganda, *The Prosecutor v. Joseph Kony and Vincent Otti*, Pre-Trial Chamber, Warrant of Arrest for Raska Lukwiya, 8 July 2005, ICC-02/04-01/05-55 (https://legal-tools.org/doc/97466a); ICC, Situation in Uganda, *The Prosecutor v. Joseph Kony and Vincent Otti*, Pre-Trial Chamber, Warrant of Arrest for Okot Odhiambo, 8 July 2005, ICC-02/04-01/05-56 (https://legal-tools.org/doc/313f9b); ICC, Situation in Uganda, *The Prosecutor v. Joseph Kony and Vincent Otti*, Pre-Trial Chamber, Warrant of Arrest for Dominic Ongwen, 8 July 2005, ICC-02/04-01/05-57 (https://legal-tools.org/doc/7a2f0f).

[139] Thijs B. Bouwknegt, "Dominic Ongwen: born at the time of the white ant, tried by the ICC", *African Arguments*, 20 January 2015 (available on its web site).

[140] ICC, Situation in Uganda, *The Prosecutor v. Dominic Ongwen*, Pre-Trial Chamber, Decision on the confirmation of charges against Dominic Ongwen, 23 March 2016, ICC-02/04-01/15-422-Red (https://legal-tools.org/doc/74fc6e).

[141] Thijs B. Bouwknegt and Barbora Holá, "Dominic Ongwen: The ICC's Poster and Problem Child", *JusticeInfo*, 16 March 2020 (available on its web site).

Blé Goudé's speeches, there is massive violence, he could be prosecuted. [...] [V]iolence is not an option. Those leaders who are planning violence will end up in the Hague.

Luis Moreno-Ocampo, Prosecutor[142]

When the ICC's new building was officially inaugurated by Dutch King Willem-Alexander in April 2016, the celebratory ceremony ended with a performance of children singing Michael Jackson's *Heal the World* in one of the courtrooms.[143] Three months earlier, there was a totally different atmosphere. In front of the building a crowd was chanting "Libérez Gbagbo!" ("Free Gbagbo!").[144] Outside the guarded entrance, Ivorians from the diaspora community had assembled to demand the release of Laurent Gbagbo. Inside, while the Court clerk read out the charges at the opening of the trial, some spectators on the Public Gallery uttered praises when Gbagbo and his companion in the dock, former youth leader Charles Blé Goudé, did "not recognize [the] charges" and pleaded not-guilty to crimes against humanity charges.[145] Absent from the hearings were victims of the post-electoral crisis that shocked the West African nation between late 2010 and early 2011.[146] Inside the courtroom, the atmosphere was tense. One could hear a pin drop.

Conscious of the highly politicised public discourse, controversies and conspiracy theories concerning, the trial Judge Tarfusser explained: "This is a criminal trial. [...] This is not a game in which one side wants to win and the other side shall be defeated. Côte d'Ivoire is not on trial either here. The people of Côte d'Ivoire are not on trial".[147] Instead, he articulated, "[t]he task of this bench is to determine on the basis of the

---

[142] OTP, "Statement by ICC Prosecutor Luis Moreno-Ocampo on the situation in Côte d'Ivoire", 21 December 2010, ICC-OTP-20101221-PR617 (https://legal-tools.org/doc/3ffcf8).

[143] ICC, "Official Opening of the ICC Permanent Premises - 19 April 2016", *YouTube*, 22 April 2016, 52:00–56:20 (available on its web site).

[144] Author's Observations, 28 January 2016.

[145] ICC, Situation in the Republic of Côte d'Ivoire, *The Prosecutor v. Laurent Gbagbo and Charles Blé Goudé*, Trial Chamber, Transcript, 28 January 2016, ICC-02/11-01/15-T-9-ENG, p. 19 ("Gbagbo and Blé Goudé Trial Transcript – Session 9") (https://legal-tools.org/doc/73746b).

[146] Report of the International Commission of Inquiry on Côte d'Ivoire, UN Doc. A/HRC/17/48, 1 July 2011 (https://legal-tools.org/doc/9d910a).

[147] Gbagbo and Blé Goudé Trial Transcript – Session 9, p. 3, see above note 145.

evidence adduced by the parties and participants for our assessment whether the charges are, indeed, well-established or not".[148]

Like Ituri, the ICC had its eyes on Côte d'Ivoire from 2003. Although not yet a Rome Statute subscriber,[149] the country had been under preliminary examination since 2003. It was sparked because of an invitation from Gbagbo's government to identify, investigate and try "the perpetrators and accomplices of acts committed on Ivorian territory since the events of 19 September 2002".[150] It took until 2010 for the ICC to move into action. It was a response to the violent aftermath of the contested presidential elections on 28 November 2010. Soon after the final round of elections, perceived supporters of Alassane Ouattara, who had claimed victory, were attacked.[151] By February 2011, the country had descended into an intra-State conflict between forces loyal to Gbagbo and Ouattara. An estimated 3,000 civilians were killed and more than 150 women were raped in a conflict waged along political, ethnic, and religious lines. With French and United Nations military assistance, Gbagbo was defeated and arrested on 11 April 2011.[152] Amidst the turmoil, the OTP responded to Ouattara's 2010 invitation to initiate a *proprio motu* investigation.[153]

The ICC's move into Côte d'Ivoire was supported by human rights lobbyists and international political figureheads. Experts, however, raised serious concerns about the way the OTP operated. The late historian and West-Africa expert Stephen Ellis said they "sometimes run ahead of their ambitions". He and other experts on mass violence in Côte d'Ivoire warned that a criminal case against Gbagbo for the political violence be-

---

[148] *Ibid.*

[149] ASP, "Côte d'Ivoire ratifies the Rome Statute", 18 February 2013, ICC-ASP-20130218-PR873 (https://legal-tools.org/doc/d79e54).

[150] Côte d'Ivoire, *Déclaration de reconnaissance de la Compétence de la Cour Pénale*, 18 April 2003 (https://legal-tools.org/doc/036bd2).

[151] UN Office for the Coordination of Humanitarian Affairs ('OCHA'), "Côte d'Ivoire: Electoral Violence and Displacement", 25 March 2011 (https://legal-tools.org/doc/h5yrj6).

[152] See Report of the International Commission of Inquiry on Côte d'Ivoire, 2011, see above note 146; ICC, Situation in Côte d'Ivoire, OTP, Request for authorisation of an investigation pursuant to article 15, 23 June 2011, ICC-02/11-3, para. 14 (https://legal-tools.org/doc/1b1939); Mike McGovern, *Making War in Côte d'Ivoire*, Hurst, London, 2011.

[153] In particular with respect to crimes and abuses committed since March 2004, See, Côte d'Ivoire, *Confirmation de la Déclaration de Reconnaissance*, 14 December 2010 (https://legal-tools.org/doc/8b188c); Côte d'Ivoire, *Letter confirming acceptance of jurisdiction*, 3 May 2011 (https://legal-tools.org/doc/le9iw0).

---

tween December 2010 and April 2011 would not fly.[154] But the OTP followed suit nonetheless. In May 2011, Fatou Bensouda, the Deputy Prosecutor at that time, said the ICC was "poised to receive" the file from Abidjan.[155] For then Prosecutor Moreno-Ocampo, Gbagbo was the obvious target: he was in prison, he featured as a bad guy in the press, and the new regime provided access to presidential records and insider witnesses.

In Paris on 24 November 2011, President Ouattara and Prosecutor Moreno-Ocampo orchestrated Gbagbo's prompt transfer to The Hague, based on a sealed indictment.[156] Crucially, the field investigations would follow only *after* Gbagbo's arrest and transfer to The Hague. For a case against a president, the inquiry was marginal.[157] By February 2012, the OTP had only eight investigators on the ground. Working with Côte d'Ivoire's main human rights groups to record witness testimonies, they were focusing on preparing for Gbagbo's confirmation of charges hearing.[158] Fatou Bensouda wanted to "send out a strong message to those who intend to attempt to get to power, or to remain in power, by use of force and brutality, to tell them that they shall henceforth be answerable for their actions".[159] Like in Kenya, the OTP sought to only deal with contemporary messy political violence in the chaotic, blurry wake of contested elections. And indeed, at first sight, the charges against Gbagbo seemed clear-cut: four violent attacks against unarmed civilians in Abidjan. It could have worked if the underlying case theory was not the OTP's

---

[154] Richard Walker, "Gbagbo: where to next?", *International Justice Tribune*, 13 April 2011, no. 126, p. 6.

[155] Thijs B. Bouwknegt and Richard Walker, "Fatou Bensouda: ICC crimes monitor", *International Justice Tribune*, 25 May 2011, no. 129, p. 6.

[156] ICC, Situation in the Republic of Côte d'Ivoire, Pre-Trial Chamber, Warrant Of Arrest For Laurent Koudou Gbagbo, 23 November 2011, ICC-02/11-26 (https://legal-tools.org/doc/12e4cc); Pierre Hazan, "Scandal Rocks International Criminal Court", *JusticeInfo*, 8 October 2017 (available on its web site).

[157] Thijs B. Bouwknegt, "Gbagbo ICC File: Fit for a President?", *International Justice Tribune*, 7 December 2011, no. 141, p. 1.

[158] Author's interview with OTP Investigator, 10 March 2012.

[159] ICC, Situation in the Republic of Côte d'Ivoire, *The Prosecutor v. Laurent Gbagbo*, Pre-Trial Chamber, Transcript, 19 February 2013, ICC-02/11-01/11-T-14-ENG, p. 44 (https://legal-tools.org/doc/8bcccd).

Manichean narrative on Gbagbo's decade-long presidency and his virtually despotic determination to cling on to power by criminal means.[160]

> Madam President, my entire life, and this is a known fact not only back in Côte d'Ivoire but throughout Africa, and throughout France, throughout political France notably, I have been fighting for democracy. I asked my counsel only last week, and I said that I wanted to bring you all the books that I've written, and they said that it was too late to introduce these books, but once we have finished, whatever the result may be, whatever you decide, I will send a batch of books written by Gbagbo to the Office of the Prosecution, and I will send you also a batch of my books, because, well, that is the man that I am.[161]

On 28 February 2013, at the end of the ICC's confirmation of charges hearings, Gbagbo told the Pre-Trial Chamber he would share a batch of his history books with the Prosecutor's office. He reinforced his position as the all-knowing leader and central agent in recent Ivoirian history as well as his supreme expertise as a history professor.[162] In his opinion, Bensouda had distorted the facts and "constructed a mere caricature of the history of Côte d'Ivoire, which made it impossible for them to fully grasp the issues at stake or to understand the reality of the crisis in this country".[163] Nearly six years later, after finishing writing two additional books in The Hague's Scheveningen prison,[164] he may want to keep his promise to send the OTP his books.

On 15 January 2019, Gbagbo and his former Youth Minister Blé Goudé were acquitted by the Trial Chamber. They did not even have to

---

[160] See Thijs B. Bouwknegt, "Gbagbo: Lost in History", *International Justice Tribune*, 5 July 2016.

[161] ICC, Situation in the Republic of Côte d'Ivoire, *The Prosecutor v. Laurent Gbagbo*, Pre-Trial Chamber, Transcript, 28 February 2013, ICC-02/11-01/11-T-21-ENG, p. 47 ('Gbagbo Pre-Trial Transcript – Session 21') (https://legal-tools.org/doc/6bb8b1).

[162] Gbagbo was a professor of history and geography at the University of Abidjan and director at the Institute of History, Art, and Archaeology of Africa ('IHAAA'). Cyril K. Daddich, *Historical Dictionary of Côte d'Ivoire (The Ivory Coast)*, 3rd edition, Rowman & Littlefield, London, 2016, p. 261.

[163] Gbagbo Pre-Trial Transcript – Session 21, pp. 44–45, see above note 161.

[164] See Mark Kersten, "A Portrait from The Hague: All You Need to Know About What Laurent Gbagbo Wants You to Know", *Justice in Conflict*, 20 January 2016 (available on its web site).

present their case. It was a bitter start of the year for the ICC. It was its first hearing in 2019 and the only people revelling in The Hague were Ivorians. On the Court's crisp doorsteps, they were drinking champagne and singing, rejoicing the acquittal.[165] For the international justice community, and for victims back in Côte d'Ivoire too, it was a moment of tremor, defeat, disillusion, and despair. Once again – following an acquittal of Jean Pierre Bemba Gombo – the world's court of last resort that is to speak justice to power had ordered the release of government officials suspected of mass atrocity crimes. Since its beginning, the trial was politicised, theatrical, emotional, controversial and uneasy. However, its abrupt ending midway – after two years of prosecution evidence and one year for the judges to make an evaluation of it – was barely surprising. Overall, the trial suffered from an implausible case theory, lack of evidence, and paradoxical testimonies.

Should it have gone to trial at all? If it was for Christine van den Wyngaert to answer, it would have been a decisive 'no'. The former ICC judge echoed how profoundly feeble she found the evidence in the case, which she called "a fiasco".[166] She said she had seen the acquittal looming in the air, like a dark cloud, for more than five years. From the beginning, the Prosecution had built its crimes against humanity case on anonymous hearsay evidence from NGO reports and press articles. Such pieces of evidence may serve as first drafts of history, sketch context and provide leads, but they cannot, wrote the Pre-Trial Chamber in June 2013, "in any way be presented as the fruits of a full and proper investigation".[167] In a somewhat unexpected move of judicial lenience, the same Pre-Trial Chamber – of which van den Wyngaert was a member – gave the OTP five extra months to collect evidence that would withstand the lowest threshold of legal scrutiny required to confirm the charges. But the writing on the wall was clear of what was going to happen if the Prosecutor could not deliver. The rest is history.

---

[165] Author's Observations at ICC, 15 January 2019.

[166] Ine Roox and Bart Beirlant, "Het Strafhof moet dringend in de spiegel kijken", *De Standaard*, 26 January 2019.

[167] Decision Adjourning the Hearing on the Confirmation of Charges of Gbagbo's Case, para. 35, see above note 4.

While the charges against Gbagbo were confirmed, by majority,[168] Abidjan chose to transfer Charles Blé Goudé to The Hague on 22 March 2014. The former sports and youth minister was charged with the same – and one additional count – crimes as the Gbagbo.[169] Laurent Gbagbo's wife, Simone, who was charged as well,[170] was never transferred to The Hague as she has faced national investigations and proceedings.[171] She, alongside with 82 other defendants including her son, was convicted to 20 years imprisonment in early 2015 for undermining State security.[172] A year later, in January 2016, Gbagbo and Blé Goudé were tried in a joint trial.[173] Getting presidents and ministers convicted of mass atrocities might have felt easy to the OTP.[174] But practice, so far, has demonstrated the opposite. Proving that political responsibility also amounts to criminal responsibility may require sound expertise on the political history of a 'situation', systematic inquisitorial investigations, and bringing realistic

---

[168] The Pre-Trial Chamber I confirmed four charges of crimes against humanity (murder, rape, other inhumane acts or – in the alternative – attempted murder, and persecution) against Gbagbo ICC, Situation in the Republic of Côte d'Ivoire, *The Prosecutor v. Laurent Gbagbo*, Pre-Trial Chamber, Decision on the Confirmation of Charges against Laurent Gbagbo, 12 June 2014, ICC-02/11-01/11-656-Red (https://legal-tools.org/doc/5b41bc).

[169] ICC, Situation in the Republic of Côte d'Ivoire, *The Prosecutor v. Charles Blé Goudé*, Pre-Trial Chamber, Decision on the confirmation of charges against Charles Blé Goudé, 12 December 2014, ICC-02/11-02/11-186 (https://legal-tools.org/doc/0536d5).

[170] ICC, Situation in the Republic of Côte d'Ivoire, *The Prosecutor v. Simone Gbagbo*, Pre-Trial Chamber, Warrant of Arrest for Simone Gbagbo, 29 February 2012, ICC-02/11-01/12-1 (https://legal-tools.org/doc/1ac0b4).

[171] ICC, Situation in the Republic of Côte d'Ivoire, *The Prosecutor v. Laurent Gbagbo*, Côte d'Ivoire, Requête de la République de Côte d'Ivoire sur la recevabilité de l'affaire le Procureur c. Simone Gbagbo, et demande de sursis à exécution en vertu des articles 17, 19 et 95 du Statut de Rome, 30 September 2013, ICC-02/11-01/12-11-Red (https://legal-tools.org/doc/89790b).

[172] Maureen Grisot, "Côte d'Ivoire: Simone Gbagbo écope de vingt ans de prison", *Le Monde*, 10 March 2015 (available on its web site).

[173] ICC, Situation in the Republic of Côte d'Ivoire, *The Prosecutor v. Laurent Gbagbo*, Trial Chamber, Decision on Prosecution requests to join the cases of The Prosecutor v. Laurent Gbagbo and The Prosecutor v. Charles Blé Goudé and related matters, 11 March 2015, ICC-02/11-01/11-810 (https://legal-tools.org/doc/d30097); ICC, Situation in the Republic of Côte d'Ivoire, *The Prosecutor v. Charles Blé Goude*, Trial Chamber, Decision on Prosecution requests to join the cases of The Prosecutor v. Laurent Gbagbo and The Prosecutor v. Charles Blé Goudé and related matters, 11 March 2015, ICC-02/11-02/11-222 (https://legal-tools.org/doc/ea0e7d).

[174] OTP, "ICC Prosecutor's statement at press conference, ahead of the trial-start of the Prosecution's case against Messrs. Laurent Gbagbo and Charles Blé Goudé", 27 January 2016.

charges. This is not what we saw in the Gbagbo-Blé Goudé case – as well as in previous ICC cases from Africa.

In reality, the prosecution's case theory relied on such a simplistic understanding of Côte d'Ivoire's political history that it was bound to fail. No reasonable judge, or first year history student, could be convinced of the following propositions about Gbagbo, his wife Simone and his protégé Blé Goudé:

> Upon assuming the Presidency of Côte d'Ivoire in October 2000, G[bagbo] harboured the objective of retaining power by, *inter alia*, repressing or violently attacking those who challenged his authority.
>
> In the following years, knowing that a freely-contested presidential election was inevitable, G[bagbo] and the Inner Circle jointly conceived and implemented a common plan to keep him in power by all means, including by committing the crimes charged ("Common Plan"). By 27 November 2010, the implementation of the Common Plan had developed to include a State or organisational policy aimed at a widespread and systematic attack against perceived Ouattara supporters.[175]

Particularly informed by a pile of reports from activist group HRW – which summarise anonymised witness testimony, media reports and selected interviews[176] – and "a rather unsophisticated general hypothesis on the workings of the African state",[177] which even commences two years before the start of the ICC's temporal jurisdiction from 1 July 2002, the allegations culminate in the core charge that from November 2010:

> G[bagbo] and members of the Inner Circle jointly planned, organised, coordinated, ordered, induced, authorised and allowed various measures to implement the Common Plan and the crimes charged. In pursuance of the Common Plan, pro-

---

[175] ICC, Situation in the Republic of Côte d'Ivoire, *The Prosecutor v. Laurent Gbagbo and Charles Blé Goudé*, OTP, Corrected version of Prosecution's pre-trial brief, 16 July 2015, ICC-02/11-01/15-148-Anx1, 28 July 2015, ICC-02/11-01/15-148-Anx1-Corr, paras. 5–6 ('Gbagbo and Blé Goudé – Prosecution's Pre-Trial Brief Annex 1') (https://legal-tools.org/doc/d840ab).

[176] Decision Adjourning the Hearing on the Confirmation of Charges of Gbagbo's Case, see above note 4.

[177] Author's interview with Scott Straus, 26 February 2016.

G[bagbo] forces attacked, killed, injured, raped and persecuted hundreds of civilians.[178]

The criminal incidents alleged[179] were committed in the past, but
not in historical isolation.[180] They took place in the immediate aftermath
of the first presidential elections in a decade of rising nationalism ('Ivoirité' or 'Ivorianness') ,[181] a preceding civil war, prior political and ethnic
animosity, and anti-Western – particularly French – sentiments.[182] This
broader historical context – arrested by these real social, political and
historical dimensions in which Gbagbo had acted – actually appear to
matter more than Prosecutor Bensouda would have liked. In linking
Gbagbo to widespread and systematic crimes against humanity, she elected to show the Trial Chamber that Gbagbo (and his wife Simone, also a
trained historian[183]) had always been driven by an insatiable appetite for
power. Once they were served the main dish (the Presidency), the couple
was not about breaking bread, up to the point that they became criminal
minded. Moreover, Gbagbo's intent to commit crimes, writes Bensouda, is
partly demonstrated by "his historical repression of his political opposition".[184] That is the red thread in the case against him: from the day
Gbagbo was elected President in October 2000, he "intended to stay in
power at any cost".[185] First he used the defence forces to quell demonstra-

---

[178] Gbagbo and Blé Goudé – Prosecution's Pre-Trial Brief Annex 1, para. 7, see above note 175.

[179] These crimes were allegedly committed between 16 and 19 December 2010 during and after a pro-Ouattara march on the RTI headquarters, on 3 March 2011 at a women's demonstration in Abobo, on 17 March 2011 by shelling a densely populated area in Abobo, and on or around 12 April 2011 in Yopougon.

[180] The Prosecution relied on acts committed against civilians during the course of 38 incidents, but charged only 4 thereof. See Gbagbo and Blé Goudé – Prosecution's Pre-Trial Brief Annex 1, para. 288–358, see above note 175.

[181] Francis Akindès, "Côte d'Ivoire: Socio-political Crises, 'Ivoirité' and the Course of History", in *African Sociological Review*, 2003, vol. 7, no. 2, pp. 11–28.

[182] Scott Straus, *Making and Unmaking Nations. War, Leadership, and Genocide in Modern Africa*, Cornell University Press, Ithaca, 2015, pp. 123–68; McGovern, 2011, see above note 152.

[183] Daddich, 2016, p. 264, see above note 162; Robey Corey-Boulet, "Gbagbo's Trial Is the Latest Sign of Victor's Justice in Côte d'Ivoire", *World Politics Review*, 4 May 2016 (available on its web site).

[184] Gbagbo and Blé Goudé – Prosecution's Pre-Trial Brief Annex 1, para. 439.i., see above note 175.

[185] *Ibid.*, para. 19–23.

tions. But after a failed coup attempt in 2002, he employed militias, foreign mercenaries and "pro-Gbagbo youth".[186] Indeed, the civil war that plagued and divided Ivory Coast in the early 2000s was extremely violent, included massacres and some observers said even bordered on genocide,[187] but that episode was not a part of the ICC charges.

One day before the Gbagbo trial started in January 2016, Bensouda told journalists "that the purpose of the trial [...] is to uncover the truth through purely a legal process [...], for the sake of doing justice for the victims; and to prevent mass atrocities recurring in the future".[188] However, during the entire trial, the judges signalled that they found the Prosecution narrative – which went beyond the scope of the charges – implausible, unclear, and unsubstantiated. Halfway through trial, the Chamber even asked the Prosecution to file a trial brief

> containing a detailed narrative of her case in light of the testimonies heard and the documentary evidence submitted at trial. More specifically, she should indicate to the Chamber in which way she thinks the evidence supports each of the elements of the different crimes and forms of responsibility charged.[189]

During trial, the OTP presented 2,679 documents, including the presidential palace logbooks, police records, UN reports, medical reports and Simone Gbagbo's diary. None of these documents contained a single Nazi-style meticulously kept record of crimes against humanity, let alone presidential orders to commit such acts. In the absence of a documentary trail of primary sources, the OTP resorted to secondary sources: human rights reports, a documentary, press footage, and erratic testimonies.

At trial, hardly anyone corroborated the case theory or linked the charges to Gbagbo. From day one, in January 2016, witness testimonies

---

[186] *Ibid.*, para. 36.

[187] Straus, 2015, pp. 123–68, see above note 182; Stephen Smith, "En Côte d'Ivoire, le spectre du Rwanda", *Le Monde*, 24 October 2002.

[188] OTP, "ICC Prosecutor's statement at press conference, ahead of the trial-start of the Prosecution's case against Messrs. Laurent Gbagbo and Charles Blé Goudé", 27 January 2016 (https://legal-tools.org/doc/zuqhi2).

[189] ICC, Situation in the Republic of Côte d'Ivoire, Trial Chamber, *The Prosecutor v. Laurent Gbagbo and Charles Blé Goudé*, Trial Chamber, Order on the further conduct of the proceedings, 9 March 2018, ICC-02/11-01/15-1124, para. 10 (https://legal-tools.org/doc/66a934).

were laborious, non-sensical, and at times even absurd. The trial faced hurdles and promised to take a long breath. Already when the Chamber heard the first prosecution witness on 8 February 2016, Tarfusser could not hide his annoyance with lawyers asking the same questions "three, four, five, ten times",[190] or the witness being unable to estimate a distance, only to jokingly observe that "at this pace we finish this trial in 2050".[191] While hearing only the sixth prosecution witness three months later, almost half an hour was spent on questioning whether he was washing a kettle or if he was washing himself with water at 09:00 on a Friday morning in February 2011, more than five years previously.[192] Then Tarfusser became increasingly impatient.[193] After the trial he concluded:

> For almost two years, I assisted [sic] to the Prosecutor's case unravelling before my eyes in the courtroom, where witness after witness, from the humblest of victims up to the highest echelons of the Ivorian Army, systematically weakened, when not outright undermined, the case they were 'expected', and had been called, by the Prosecutor to support.[194]

The Chamber had heard testimony from a variety of witnesses. Among the crime base witnesses, there were victims, a fishmonger, the owner of two pubs, an electrician, a truck driver, a seamstress and an educator. Among the insider witnesses were several members of the Rassemblement des Républicains ('RDR') and senior officers from the military, special units and the gendarmerie. Their testimony was contextualised by a HRW researcher, two documentary producers, a forensic expert, and a former UN volunteer. However, the OTP did not produce experts to testify about Côte d'Ivoire's political history, culture and language – evidence that could potentially support the OTP case narrative. If getting as close to truth as possible on even the most basic facts about peripheral events in 2011 was not attempted, and already seemed impossible, how then to ass-

---

[190] ICC, Situation in the Republic of Côte d'Ivoire, *The Prosecutor v. Laurent Gbagbo and Charles Blé Goudé*, Trial Chamber, Transcript, 8 February 2016, ICC-02/11-01/15-T-18-Red2-ENG, p. 39 (https://legal-tools.org/doc/mok5ud).

[191] *Ibid.*, p. 51.

[192] ICC, Situation in the Republic of Côte d'Ivoire, *The Prosecutor v. Laurent Gbagbo and Charles Blé* Goudé, Trial Chamber, Transcript, 10 May 2016, ICC-02/11-01/15-T-36-Red-ENG, pp. 43 ff. (https://legal-tools.org/doc/8b92af).

[193] Author's Observations.

[194] Opinion of Judge Cuno Tarfusser, para. 4, see above note 5.

es witness testimony that turns the trial into somewhat of a carnival-like operetta? After hearing harrowing detailed testimony from four Ivoirian victims, the OTP called to the stand their fifth witness, Mohammed Sam Jichi, better known in Côte d'Ivoire as 'Sam the African'. As a former 'insider' he was to testify against Gbagbo and corroborate the prosecution's case theory. On the stand, however, the witness turned 'hostile', changed the incriminating story he had told ICC investigators a year before, and started to apologetically exonerate Gbagbo:

> He is a professor. He knows the history of Africa. […] [H]e was a great head of state […]. That's my personal analysis. And in the investigations and in many documents, you will read that this is the truth what I say to you.[195]

Nodding in agreement, for Gbagbo, the historian, it was a narrative he would subscribe to. But moments later, the witness drifted on to say:

> When I see the history of President Gbagbo it reminds me a little of that of Jesus and Barnabas […]. It's history repeating itself […]. This is my analysis. This is what's happening to Gbagbo, Jesus and Barnabas.[196]

Playing along the game, Gbagbo's lawyer then staunchly asked, "and who is Jesus?". Only to wait for the presiding judge to interrupt, "I think we're going a little bit too far with this questioning on the Holy Bible. We should come back a bit to the facts. Please".[197] In trying to do so, the OTP called their prime witness, former HRW researcher Matt Wells, an American who was to testify on the investigations he had carried out immediately after the crisis and published in a report relied upon by the Prosecution.[198] Yet, the precise contents of his reports, which formed the core of the OTP's case, were hardly discussed at the hearings, which were dominated by belligerent cross-examination by the defence on the investi-

---

[195] ICC, Situation in the Republic of Côte d'Ivoire, *The Prosecutor v. Laurent Gbagbo and Charles Blé Goudé*, Trial Chamber, Transcript, 15 March 2016, ICC-02/11-01/15-T-30-ENG, pp. 73–74 (https://legal-tools.org/doc/ff8970).

[196] *Ibid.*, p. 74.

[197] *Ibid.*, pp. 74–75.

[198] Matt Wells and Corinne Dufka, *"They Killed Them Like It Was Nothing": The Need for Justice for Côte d'Ivoire's Post-Election Crisis*, HRW, New York, 5 October 2011 (https://legal-tools.org/doc/2dvuab).

gative methodology and alleged bias of his organisation.[199] This line of questioning continued when the Trial Chamber heard from Nigel Walker (and later his translator), a British-American documentary producer who made a film, *Shadow Work*, about the rise of Goudé's youth movement in 2006,[200] events from four years before the alleged crimes occurred.[201]

Increasingly irritated by the trial's endless dwelling on the past, Judge Tarfusser, while hearing the twelfth witness, former Cabinet Minister for Human Rights Joël Kouadio N'Guessan,[202] could no longer hide his impatience. On 28 June 2016, after 05:43 hours of questioning, he urged the prosecution to finally move forward with its examination to the post-electoral violence, exclaiming:

> And I really, and it's not the first time that I said that I would urge you to move towards what are – towards the period of the charges, otherwise, I mean, we're really making history. And I understand the context, we have to know the context, but we have enough context I think. Please go ahead.[203]

Thus, five months into the trial, the proceedings had been riddled with historical questions outside of the scope of the indictment, but had

---

[199] ICC, Situation in the Republic of Côte d'Ivoire, *The Prosecutor v. Laurent Gbagbo and Charles Blé Goudé*, Trial Chamber, Transcript, 17 May 2016, ICC-02/11-01/15-T-40-Red-ENG (https://legal-tools.org/doc/9e4d05); ICC, Situation in the Republic of Côte d'Ivoire, *The Prosecutor v. Laurent Gbagbo and Charles Blé Goudé*, Trial Chamber, Transcript, 18 May 2016, ICC-02/11-01/15-T-41-Red2-ENG (https://legal-tools.org/doc/f55d69); ICC, Situation in the Republic of Côte d'Ivoire, *The Prosecutor v. Laurent Gbagbo and Charles Blé Goudé*, Trial Chamber, Transcript, 19 May 2016, ICC-02/11-01/15-T-42-ENG (https://legal-tools.org/doc/c36cf4).

[200] Nigel Walker, "Shadow Work", *Walkerfilm*, 2008.

[201] ICC, Situation in the Republic of Côte d'Ivoire, *The Prosecutor v. Laurent Gbagbo and Charles Blé Goudé*, Trial Chamber, Transcript, 24 May 2016, ICC-02/11-01/15-T-43-Red2-ENG (https://legal-tools.org/doc/b3r3ds); ICC, Situation in the Republic of Côte d'Ivoire, *The Prosecutor v. Laurent Gbagbo and Charles Blé Goudé*, Trial Chamber, Transcript, 25 May 2016, ICC-02/11-01/15-T-44-Red2-ENG (https://legal-tools.org/doc/o88nvt).

[202] At the time he was testifying, he was "a management consultant", the assistant secretary general of RDR and "responsible for communications and public relations"; ICC, Situation in the Republic of Côte d'Ivoire, *The Prosecutor v. Laurent Gbagbo and Charles Blé Goudé*, Trial Chamber, Transcript, 27 June 2016, ICC-02/11-01/15-T-53-ENG, p. 2 (https://legal-tools.org/doc/0ef0c7).

[203] ICC, Situation in the Republic of Côte d'Ivoire, *The Prosecutor v. Laurent Gbagbo and Charles Blé Goudé*, Trial Chamber, Transcript, 28 June 2016, ICC-02/11-01/15-T-54-ENG, p. 41 (https://legal-tools.org/doc/c8e44a).

---

not touched upon the heart of the matter: the individual criminal responsibility of Gbagbo and Blé Goudé for the specific incidents charged. All this window-dressing on broader questions of history may have been interesting for the judges, but the process failed to address whether or not Gbagbo committed the crimes as charged. Besides the HRW researcher, the documentary producer, and a UN investigator, no real independent expert was called to outline what exactly had happened in Côte d'Ivoire, who had actually been involved in violence, and how.[204] Thus, after hearing 82 witnesses, it remained forensically unclear who did what to whom.

Who killed 150 people, raped 17 women, and injured 111 others, as listed in the indictment, during the attacks on the national Radio and Television headquarters, Abobo's women march, and the shelling of Abobo's market? Nobody questioned that this violence had taken place, including the trial judges. But insider witnesses, including a score of police officials, generals and politicians, could not provide a beyond-reasonable doubt picture of who was ultimately responsible. Their testimonies were generally unspecific, ambiguous, evasive or even exonerative, particularly concerning Gbagbo's role – and of course their own – in the events. Other witnesses, including 'Sam the African', took the stand for opportunistic reasons.

After 231 hearing days, many of which behind closed doors (thus disallowing public scrutiny of the trial evidence), the OTP closed its case in January 2018. The prosecutors involved must have felt confident, as they cancelled 44 witnesses initially announced to testify in The Hague. The Trial Chamber, however, was not. It soon requested the OTP to file a trial brief in which it was to summarise, organise and clarify how the evidence presented related to the charges and the theory of criminal responsibility. This was an uncommon request. And it was obviously telling of the Trial Chamber's confusion over the relevance of what they had heard during the course of two years. But the OTP's mid-trial brief offered the Chamber no remedy.[205]

---

[204] Bouwknegt, 2016, see above note 160.

[205] ICC, Situation in the Republic of Côte d'Ivoire, *The Prosecutor v. Laurent Gbagbo and Charles Blé Goudé*, OTP, Public Redacted Version of "Corrected version to Annex 1 of Prosecution's Mid-Trial Brief", 19 March 2018, ICC-02/11-01/15-1136-Conf-Anx1-Corr, 29 March 2018, ICC-02/11-01/15-1136-Anx1-Corr-Red (https://legal-tools.org/doc/b25eea).

It took the Chamber a mere 15 minutes to render an oral decision to acquit, and order the release of Gbagbo and Blé Goudé, saying that there was no need for the Defence to submit further evidence "as the Prosecutor has not satisfied the burden of proof in relation to several core constitutive elements of the crimes as charged".[206]

It took six months from the oral acquittal decision until each of the judges published their reasons.[207] Particularly Tarfusser's opinion was uncompromising, even personal. It reads like an indictment of international criminal justice, the ICC, ICC judges, the OTP and the Defence. The Italian Judge generally found the case scenario "Manichean and simplistic"[208] and the evidence in the case to support it of "exceptional weakness".[209] He aims his arrows at the OTP's investigation, which he found "far from being completed",[210] lamenting that "much of the evidence was essentially provided by the current [Ivorian] government, which is headed by political opponents of the accused".[211] Moreover, he critiqued the OTP for only photocopying – at times illegible – original items, continuing: "Even more troubling, it seems that staff with limited mastery of French was selected as responsible for carrying out interviews of critical importance for the case".[212]

While agreeing in substance with Tarfusser, Judge Henderson's opinion is more structured, elaborate and substantive, carefully combing through the evidence. At the core, however, he also found that the OTP's case failed because the way "the Prosecutor depicted their [Gbagbo and Blé Goudé's] actions and omissions from a legal point of view could not be sustained by the evidence".[213] Crucially, judge Henderson observed:

---

[206] ICC, Situation in the Republic of Côte d'Ivoire, *The Prosecutor v. Laurent Gbagbo and Charles Blé Goudé*, Trial Chamber, Transcript, 15 January 2019, ICC-02/11-01/15-T-232-ENG, p. 3 (https://legal-tools.org/doc/4fe93a).

[207] See also, Maxence Peniguet, "Gbagbo/Blé Goudé: Why Judge Herrera-Carbuccia Refused to Acquit Them", *JusticeInfo*, 19 September 2019 (available on its web site); Maxence Peniguet, "Why the ICC Acquitted Laurent Gbagbo and Charles Blé Goudé", *JusticeInfo*, 17 September 2019 (available on its web site).

[208] Opinion of Judge Cuno Tarfusser, para. 12, see above note 5.

[209] *Ibid.*, para. 3.

[210] *Ibid.*, para. 17.

[211] *Ibid.*, para. 92.

[212] *Ibid.*, para. 93.

[213] Reasons of Judge Geoffrey Henderson, para. 2, see above note 6.

The main concern is that the Prosecutor seems to have presented a rather one-sided version of the situation in Côte d'Ivoire. There is a reason why we ask witnesses to undertake to tell the 'whole truth'. This is because withholding part of the relevant information may be highly misleading. Although it would be unfair to suggest that the Prosecutor deliberately withheld important information, her narrative – wittingly or unwittingly – systematically omits or downplays significant elements of the political and military situation. This has resulted in a somewhat skewed version of events that may be inspired by reality but does not fully reflect it.[214]

Henderson's opinion, which is not directed against the OTP *per se*, uncovers the consequences of simultaneously tasking prosecutors with investigations and with prosecutions, while they are also being part of the proceedings. In this case, this issue became readily apparent, as the prosecutor "seems to have started from the premise that her case theory is correct and that this theory provides the necessary coherence to link the disparate evidentiary elements she relies upon".[215] In the Gbagbo case, the OTP put "the cart in front of the horse",[216] and has "on occasion, been selective in the evidence she collected".[217] In fact, the Prosecutor was led by proving a theory, not by following evidence:

While it is recognised that the Prosecutor does not have limitless resources, it is important to stress that the Prosecutor should not cherry-pick those (parts of) exhibits that support her narrative and ignore the rest.[218]

Moreover, while the OTP retains the burden of proof, Henderson found that "the Prosecutor sometimes seems to want to shift the burden of proof onto the Defence for missing evidence".[219] Henderson concludes, that "because of the Prosecutor's 'everything-proves-everything' approach, it has proved impossible to conduct a linear analysis of the evidence".[220]

---

[214] *Ibid.*, para. 66.
[215] *Ibid.*, para. 79.
[216] *Ibid.*
[217] *Ibid.*, para. 81.
[218] *Ibid.*
[219] *Ibid.*, para. 83.
[220] *Ibid.*, para. 91.

The OTP appealed the majority's decision to acquit on one procedural matter and on the Chamber's application of its standard of proof and approach to assessing the sufficiency of the evidence.[221] But it does not raise any substantive matter. They may want to rely on the dissenting opinion of Judge Olga Herrera-Carbuccia. Contrary to her colleagues, she found: "In the case at bar I find that there is sufficient evidence, if accepted, on which a reasonable Trial Chamber could convict the accused".[222] Her human rights approach to the facts, evidence and purpose of international criminal justice differs from the majority's approach. She underscores the rights of participating victims who's "interest in the proper and transparent administration of justice and the establishment of the truth" should not be ignored.[223] She opined:

> Establishing the truth behind events and preventing all forms of revisionism have always been the underlying objectives of all international criminal justice systems. If we allow a president in a democratic society who refuses to step down in the aftermath of a contested election to target citizens of that society and commit crimes against humanity with impunity, we fail to comply with the values and purposes enshrined in the Rome Statute ("Statute") and espoused by the international community.[224]

For Herrera-Carbuccia, the purpose of the trial goes beyond Hannah Arendt's adage that is must focus solely on the criminal responsibility of the accused. Instead, she focused on the State's responsibility by default. "The State has a duty to protect its citizens, and the principle of proportionality applies in every case where civilians are harmed", she writes, adding that "[w]hen the State apparatus targets citizens of the State without fear of sanction, it acts against the fundamental values of a democratic society, and the individuals at the head of the State apparatus must be held

---

[221] ICC, Situation in the Republic of Côte d'Ivoire, *The Prosecutor v. Laurent Gbagbo and Charles Blé Goudé*, OTP, Corrected version of "Prosecution Notice of Appeal", 16 September 2019, ICC-02/11-01/15-1270, 17 September 2019, ICC-02/11-01/15-1270-Corr, paras. 4–7 (https://legal-tools.org/doc/2d15e0).

[222] ICC, Situation in the Republic of Côte d'Ivoire, *The Prosecutor v. Laurent Gbagbo and Charles Blé Goudé*, Trial Chamber, Public Redacted Version of Dissenting Opinion Judge Herrera-Carbuccia, 16 July 2019, ICC-02/11-01/15-1263-AnxC-Red, para. 5 (https://legal-tools.org/doc/6ak9rf).

[223] *Ibid.*, para. 7.

[224] *Ibid.*, para. 6.

accountable".[225] In Côte d'Ivoire, according to her, there was evidence that unjustifiable violence was committed and that State institutions – led by Gbagbo – failed to protect civilians and took no action to punish those responsible for perpetrating the crimes. Herrera-Carbuccia implies that Gbagbo and Blé Goudé bear some criminal responsibility, and finds that "[o]n the basis of the evidence submitted into the record, the seriousness of the charges and the interests of the victims participating in these proceedings, the trial should have continued with the presentation of the Defence case".[226]

At the time of writing, it is impossible to gauge what the Appeals Chamber may do. However, it is safe to conclude that during the combative trial proceedings, virulent cross-examinations in front of a public gallery filled with Gbagbo supporters, the OTP fought the case as if it were the underdog. In so doing, it held on to its bone for too long, blindly believing in its case theory.

More fundamentally, the Gbagbo case is eventually emblematic of the OTP's inability to forensically investigate atrocity crimes in Africa. The problem is widespread and systematic as evidenced by the ICC's feeble conviction record. Should we fault the OTP for it? Yes, to some extent. The OTP needs to consider whether it should continue to act as the executive, prosecutorial, arm of major international human rights NGOs, or work in a more inquisitorial, independent manner. That includes deciding not to push cases if there is insufficient evidence. On the other hand, and in fairness, the OTP is hamstrung by its mandate to simultaneously act as truth-finder, prosecutor and litigator. Enhanced quality control in international criminal investigations may therefore require a balanced division of labour, which unburdens, in the first place, the OTP from carrying out the investigations.

At the same time, as Judge Henderson remarks, we must be aware of financial constraints. States supporting the Court have maintained it on a shoestring budget. By 2018, the ICC only had 61 investigators, 23 analysts, and 9 staff in its forensic science section.[227] That is modest for a

---

[225] *Ibid.*, para. 13.

[226] *Ibid.*, para. 648.

[227] ASP, *Assembly of States Parties to the Rome Statute of the International Criminal Court: Seventeenth Session: The Hague, 5–12 December 2018: Official Records, Volume II*, Part A, paras. 299–301 (https://legal-tools.org/doc/1d6o4f).

court that deals with no less than 21 situations across the globe. By comparison, the ICC says that the ICTY deployed between 20 and 30 investigators per case – excluding lawyers and other support functions.[228] One could argue that the financial and political backers of the Court have been very successful at maintaining a court that is imperfect when it comes to holding to account government officials. The Gbagbo trial reassured them that they have little to worry from the ICC. As to Gbagbo, while he may have to wait for the appellate proceedings, he now stands among an illustrious group of powerful figures who have benefitted from the shoestring investigations at the ICC.

2.5. Conclusion: Promises

Much criticism from the quarters of observers, activists, lawyers, academics and ICC judges of the ICC has focused on the way in has conducted its investigations in Africa. As regards investigations, it is clear that the system of international criminal justice has created an enemy from within. It suffers from ingrained pitfalls, inherent problems and inborn biases, each of which are impediments to its objectives, in particular in truth-finding abilities.

Essentially, international criminal justice is heavily restrained by its limited investigatory mandate, power and resources – more so than, for example, truth commissions. In thinking about quality control, the question is thus whether the field requires *refinement* or *revolution* in order to come to sustainable solutions, or more crucially to better investigations. If we analyse the quality of judicial investigations of atrocity crimes in light of how historical sciences approach mass violence, we may consider that its excellence is best secured if carried out in a dispassionate, amoral, apolitical and non-juridical manner.

Arguably, while looking at the past *modus operandi* of international criminal investigations, one could make a case that investigations ought to be done independently and not by an adversarial party to the proceedings with a specific orientation, the OTP. Considering an evidence-based rather than prosecution-based system of international criminal investigations

---

[228] ASP, *Assembly of States Parties to the Rome Statute of the International Criminal Court: Twelfth Session: The Hague, 20–28 November 2013: Official Records, Volume II*, p. 39, fn. 45 (https://legal-tools.org/doc/236cad).

may in itself represent a form of quality control. This requires a separation of powers in international criminal justice.

In this sense it may be worthwhile to think about the creation of an investigative chamber – like in the Extraordinary Chambers in the Courts of Cambodia and Extraordinary African Chambers – that carries out the investigation, including site visits. In national jurisdictions too, like in the Netherlands, there is a clear division between war crimes prosecutors, war crimes police, specialised war crimes investigative magistrates, the defence, and trial judges. In the entire process, each party plays a role in the truth-finding exercise. This may not always lead to prosecutions and convictions, but that too is a realistic outcome of an inquiry. Checks and balances safeguard the quality of the investigation at different stages, and ultimately the prosecutions.

Alternatively, States Parties could consider establishing an independent inquisitorial investigative organ within the ICC. This could not only solve external perceptions that investigations are biased, but also allow the OTP to carefully consider charges in the case if it finds that there is enough evidence to commence prosecutions. In both scenarios (neither of which would obviate the need for the parties to conduct their own additional investigations), the ICC would have the benefit of an independent expert unit, along lines similar to the ICTY, which could advise on historical, sociological, linguistic, cultural, and political contexts. The past has shown that these areas are insufficiently and unprofessionally covered by trial lawyers, who are not professionally trained in these fields.

If international criminal justice is to improve its investigation or preparation of fact-rich criminal cases, perhaps the solution is not "prosecutorial professionalization",[229] but rather *investigative* professionalisation: a move towards an inquisitorial investigative process, independent from the OTP.

---

[229] Bergsmo, 2019, p. 2, see above note 8.

PART II:
EVIDENCE AND ANALYSIS

3

The Contribution of Analysis to the
Quality Control in Criminal Investigation

Xabier Agirre Aranburu[*]

3.1. Introduction: The Role of Analysts

This chapter will explain different analysis techniques that are instrumental for quality control in criminal investigations ('QCCI') and the contributions that analysts should make for that matter as part of their professional duties within the investigations. The proposed methods are based on the experience of different national and international tribunals over the last 25 years as well as research in the fields of criminology and other social sciences, intelligence studies, and cognitive psychology.

Jerome Frank, judge and law professor, observed by 1949 based in his own extensive legal experience that "fact-finding is the toughest part of the judicial function. It is there that court-house government is least satisfactory. [...] but the legal profession has done next to nothing about the problem of fact-finding".[1] He suggested that "law-suits are misnamed:

---

[*] **Xabier Agirre Aranburu** is currently the Head of the Investigative Analysis Section at the Investigations Division ('ID'), Office of the Prosecutor ('OTP'), International Criminal Court ('ICC'), where he has served since 2004. Previously he was Analyst and Strategic Analyst at the OTP of the International Criminal Tribunal for the Former Yugoslavia ('ICTY') (1997–2003). He has contributed to multiple investigative and training projects with different international and national authorities, universities and NGOs. He is a member of the Editorial Board of Torkel Opsahl Academic EPublisher (TOAEP) and a member of the Advisory Boards of the Master on International Crimes, Conflict and Criminology at the Vrije Universiteit Amsterdam, and the Berg Human Rights Institute (Madrid). The author wrote this chapter in his personal capacity, his views do not represent any of the abovementioned institutions. The author is grateful to Moa Lidén, Adina Nistor, Simon De Smet, Alejandro Kiss, Matteo Butera, Helena Martinsone, Helen Brady, Frank Leibovici and Julien Seroussi for their bibliographical suggestions, comments and corrections.

[1] Jerome Frank, *Courts on Trial: Myth and Reality in American Justice*, Princeton University Press, Princeton, 1949, p. 4. For a critique of the mystification of the law by lawyers, see *ibid.*, chap. IV "Modern Legal Magic", pp. 37–61, and *ibid.*, chap. V, "Wizards and Lawyers", pp. 62–79. Frank bases his findings anthropological research by Malinowski and others, as well as the works by Hans Gross and Wigmore.

They should rather be called 'fact suits'".[2] In more recent times, Sarah M.H. Nouwen followed in Frank's footsteps and highlighted the "empirical weakness" of research on academic literature about international criminal law and "transitional justice", a remarkable gap since "after all, the job of international criminal tribunals itself is, or should be, largely empirical".[3] Most analysts working in investigations will share the concerns expressed by Frank and Nouwen, they also struggle to call everybody's attention to the facts in a world dominated by legal rhetoric, as they do their best to bring empirical rigour to the procedures.

The primary role of analysts in investigations is to make sense of the factual information, processing large volumes of data, most often incomplete and conflicting, to give strategic direction to the investigation, and to present valid factual findings relevant to the legal case. Contributions to the Quality Control ('QC') of the investigative findings are inherent to the duties of the analysts, to avoid situations in which "criminal investigations lack a quality control supervisor on the job. There is no process for collecting and analysing information about errors" and "[t]he farther a case moves down the assembly line [...] the harder it is to undo an error".[4]

Already in Nuremberg, professional analysts made significant contributions to the investigations and prosecutions under the direction of Franz Neumann, Chief of Analysis with the United States ('US') prosecution.[5] In the 1980s, the Office of Special Investigations ('OSI') of the US

---

[2] *Ibid.*, p. 32.

[3] Sarah M.H. Nouwen, "'*As You Set out for Ithaka*': Practical, Epistemological, Ethical, and Existential Questions about Socio-Legal Empirical Research in Conflict", in *Leiden Journal of International Law*, 2014, vol. 27, no. 1, p. 228.

[4] Brandon L. Garrett, *Convicting the Innocent: Where Criminal Prosecutions Go Wrong*, Harvard University Press, Cambridge, 2011, p. 270.

[5] See Franz Neumann, Herbert Marcuse and Otto Kirchheimer, in Raffaele Laudani (ed.), *Secret Reports on Nazi Germany: The Frankfurt School Contribution to the War Effort*, Princeton University Press, Princeton, 2013. Compilation of reports produced by Franz Neumann, Herbert Marcuse and Otto Kirchheimer while working of the Office of Strategic Services (OSS) and supporting the US prosecution in Nuremberg. For an overview of their experience, including their conflict with the US Chief Prosecutor Jackson, see *ibid.*, "Introduction", pp. 1–23. See also David Kettler and Thomas Wheatland, *Learning from Franz L. Neumann: Law, Theory and the Brute Facts of Political Life*, Anthem Press, London, 2019, and Petra Marquardt-Bigman, "Behemoth revisited: The research and analysis branch of the office of strategic services in the debate of us policies towards Germany, 1943–46", in *Intelligence and National Security*, 1997, vol. 12, no. 2, pp. 91–100.

Department of Justice ('DOJ') hired historians to work as analysts in their investigations on World War II crimes.[6] Soon afterwards the role of professional analysts was included in the work of the ICTY-OTP (1993–2017), thanks to the support from Morten Bergsmo and other experts in international criminal law.

The Investigations Division at the ICTY-OTP included analysts with different profiles and functions. From the outset in 1994, it had an Special Advisory Section with experts on "military matters including chains of command and order of battle; and the cultural, historical and political background relating to the Balkans" whose function was described as "providing the Prosecution and Investigations Sections with the necessary background knowledge and information".[7] The Special Advisory Section operated independently, along with the Investigations Section and the Prosecutions Section. In 1995 the OTP reported that this section, now referred to as Strategy Team, grew from 3 to 15 staff because of "the tremendous amount of extant and potentially critical information relating to the conflict in the former Yugoslavia and the importance of providing strategic guidance to the investigative teams".[8] The Strategy Team included the Intelligence Analysis Unit, "responsible for disseminating information to other units within the Office of the Prosecutor and analysing information, intelligence and other material received by the Office", and the Special Projects Unit "analysing the power and legal structures within the former Yugoslavia and providing a chronology of events pertaining to the former Yugoslavia".[9]

---

[6] See Lawrence Douglas, *The Right Wrong Man: John Demjanjuk and the Last Great Nazi War Crimes Trial*, Princeton University Press, 2016, p. 50. For an account by a former OSI researcher, who later became the head of the LRT at ICTY-OTP (1997–2009), see Patrick J. Treanor, "Old Documents and Archives in Core International Crimes Cases", in Morten Bergsmo and CHEAH Wui Ling (eds.), *Old Evidence and Core International Crimes*, Torkel Opsahl Academic EPublisher, Beijing, 2012, pp. 141–53 (http://www.toaep.org/ps-pdf/16-bergsmo-cheah). Treanor served in the DOJ OSI as Historian (1980–89) and Senior Historian (1989–94), he joined ICTY-OTP from the outset in 1994, and became the head of its Leadership Research Team ('LRT') throughout its existence from 1997 to 2009.

[7] ICTY, *First Annual Report of the ICTY*, 29 August 1994, p. 40 (https://www.legal-tools.org/doc/cacdb7/).

[8] ICTY, *Second Annual Report of the ICTY*, 23 August 1995, p. 14 ('Second Annual Report of the ICTY') (https://www.legal-tools.org/doc/9a66a1/).

[9] *Ibid.*, p. 15.

As the OTP grew, more analysts were recruited and two specialized analysis units were established in 1997, the Leadership Research Team ('LRT') and the Military Analysis Team ('MAT'). The LRT was:

> responsible for the identification of persons from the civilian and military leadership structures of the relevant Yugoslav entities believed to be responsible for crimes committed during the conflict. [...] Within its area of expertise, the Section makes recommendations to the Chief of investigations on the selection of appropriate cases for investigation.[10]

The LRT was led by a former Senior Historian at the US DOJ OSI and it comprised mainly historians and social scientists with advanced knowledge of the former Yugoslavia, and fluent in the local languages.[11] The investigation teams had Crime Analysts and Strategic Analysts operating under the supervision of a Team Leader, usually a senior police officer, or a Senior Trial Attorney when the teams moved to the prosecution phase. The MAT comprised analysts with a background of military intelligence mainly, "to provide specialized analysis of military aspects".[12] The Demographics Unit employed researchers focused on demographic and crime pattern analysis.

A few analysts were assigned to support the tracking of fugitives at the Fugitive Intelligence and Sensitive Sources Team (FISST, focused on operational intelligence, initially created in 1996 as FIST or Fugitive Intelligence Support Team). Continuing this precedent, as recently as May 2020 the work of professional analysts was decisive for the arrest of the ICTR fugitive Félicien Kabuga, on the basis on phone, financial and surveillance data.[13] Some analysis resource was also assigned to support the

---

[10] ICTY, *Statement of Functions and Organization*, undated, *circa* 1997, p. 5 ('ICTY Statement of Functions and Organization').

[11] On the experience of the LRT and related analysis issues, see Christian Axboe Nielsen, "Leadership Analysis in International Criminal Justice", in Adejoke Babington-Ashaye, Aimee Comrie and Akingbolahan Adeniran (eds.), *International Criminal Investigations: Law and Practice*, Eleven International Publishing, The Hague, 2018, pp. 207–30.

[12] ICTY Statement of Functions and Organization, p. 5, see above note 10. See also the chapter by Peter Nicholson, who led the MAT from 1997 to 2004, "The Function of Analysis and Analysts", in Morten Bergsmo, Klaus Rackwitz and SONG Tianying (eds.), *Historical Origins of International Criminal Law: Volume 5*, Torkel Opsahl Academic EPublisher, Brussels, 2017, pp. 121–35 (http://www.toaep.org/ps-pdf/24-bergsmo-rackwitz-song).

[13] See Adam Ciralsky, "How a High-Tech Dragnet Nabbed the Alleged Financier of the Rwandan Genocide – After He'd Spent 26 Years on the Lam", *Vanity Fair*, 22 May 2020, including an interview with Serge Brammertz, where he explains the role of analysis in

Appeals Section, since some factual issues became unavoidable event at the appeals stage.[14]

By 1995, the ICTY-OTP had 20 "researchers and analysts" along with 35 investigators and 29 lawyers, which is a significant share for analysis in the overall composition of the office.[15] As the ICTY annual reports indicate, OTP senior management chose an investigative model with a fairly large analytical component because of the need to process large volumes of complex information, as well as regional and military expertise. The number of analysts grew in the period 1997–2000 upon request from the investigation and prosecution teams. At the highest point of staffing around the year 2000 the Investigations Division ('ID') at the ICTY-OTP employed some 50 professional analysts across the above-mentioned categories. In the final completion stage the workload of the ICTY-OTP shifted from investigations to trials, the ID was disbanded, and its staff transferred to the Prosecutions Division including all analysts and the LRT and MAT in full.

Many of the ICTY-OTP analysts joined other international tribunals and investigation bodies and carried with them the ICTY experience in the analysis of sources, crime patterns and organisational structures. Among them are five contributors to this volume: Christian Nielsen (formerly with the LRT, and then ICC analyst), William H. Wiley and Ewan Brown (formerly MAT, and later ICC investigators), Markus Eikel (formerly Crime Analyst with ICTY, and later investigations Team Leader in the ICC), and myself.

Most of the contributions by analysts at the ICTY are not public, they are part of confidential investigations, but some of it has become public through a number of trial exhibits and testimonies. Among others, the Head of LRT Patrick Treanor contributed to the *Perišić* trial and LRT researchers Christian Nielsen (co-author of this volume), William Tomlja-

---

this operation (available on its web site). Brammertz is the Chief Prosecutor of the International Residual Mechanism for Criminal Tribunals since 2016 and previously, among others, ICTY Prosecutor (2008–17) and ICC Deputy Prosecutor for Investigations (2003–06).

[14] For public research conducted by a former analyst assigned to the ICTY-OTP Appeals Section, see Uwe Ewald, "Large-Scale Victimisation and the Jurisprudence of the ICTY. Victimological Research Issues", in Uwe Ewald and Ksenija Turković (eds.), *Large-Scale Victimisation as a Potential Source of Terrorist Activities: Importance of Regaining Security in Post-Conflict Societies*, IOS Press, Amsterdam, 2006, pp. 171–96.

[15] Second Annual Report of the ICTY, p. 13, see above note 8.

novich and Dorothea Hanson to *Krajišnik, Karadžić, Stanišić and Župljanin, Prlić et al.* and *Mladić.*[16] Examples of testimony by MAT analysts include the co-author of this volume Ewan Brown in *Brđanin,* and *Stanišić and Župljanin,* Richard Philipps in *Galić,* and Reynaud Theunens in *Gotovina* and *Šešelj.*[17] Contributions on analysis of demographics and crime patterns became public mainly through the reports and testimonies by Helge Brunborg and Ewa Tabeau in *Blagojević and Jokić, Krstić, Mladić,* in *Milutinović, Galić* and *Prlić et al.*[18] By 2003 one of the most experienced ICTY Senior Trial Attorneys assessed based in his experience

---

[16] ICTY, *Prosecutor v. Perišić,* Trial Chamber, Decision on Admissibility of Expert Report of Patrick Treanor, 27 November 2008, IT-04-81-T (https://www.legal-tools.org/doc/d317dd/); ICTY, *Prosecutor v. Krajišnik,* Trial Chamber, Decision on Two Expert Witnesses (Nielsen and Riedelmayer), 31 March 2004, IT-00-39-T (https://www.legal-tools.org/doc/2d5562/); ICTY, *Prosecutor v. Karadžić,* Prosecution, Prosecution's Notice of Disclosure of Expert Reports by Christian Nielsen and His Curriculum Vitae, 12 March 2009, IT-95-5/18-PT (https://www.legal-tools.org/doc/11h9vl/); ICTY, *Prosecutor v. Prlić et al.,* Trial Chamber, Judgement, 29 May 2013, IT-04-74-T, para. 528 ('Prlić et al. Trial Judgment') (https://www.legal-tools.org/doc/2daa33/); ICTY, *Prosecutor v. Mladić,* Trial Chamber, Transcript, 29 October 2012, IT-09-92-T, p. 4137 (https://www.legal-tools.org/doc/cw1f5l/).

[17] ICTY, *Prosecutor v. Brđanin,* Trial Chamber, Decision on Prosecution's Submission of Statement of Expert Witness Ewan Brown, 3 June 2003, IT-99-36-T (https://www.legal-tools.org/doc/8e3882/); ICTY, *Prosecutor v. Stanišić and Župljanin,* Trial Chamber, Decision pursuant to Rule 94*bis* accepting Ewan Brown and Affirming Ewa Tabeau as Prosecution Expert Witnesses, and Written Reasons for the Oral Ruling accepting Andras Riedlmayer as an Expert Witness, 29 September 2010, IT-08-91-T, para. 18 (https://www.legal-tools.org/doc/ab4f2c/); ICTY, *Prosecutor v. Galić,* Trial Chamber, Decision concerning the Expert Witnesses Ewa Tabeau and Richard Philipps, 3 July 2002, IT-98-29-T ('Galić Trial Decision concerning the Expert Witnesses Ewa Tabeau and Richard Philipps') (https://www.legal-tools.org/doc/3937e8/); ICTY, *Prosecutor v. Gotovina et al.,* Trial Chamber, Decision and Guidance with regard to the Expert Report, Addendum, and Testimony of Reynaud Theunens, 17 November 2008, IT-06-90-T, para. 25 (https://www.legal-tools.org/doc/5d595a/); ICTY, *Prosecutor v. Šešelj,* Trial Chamber, Decision on Expert Status of Reynaud Theunens, 12 February 2008, IT-03-67-T, para. 36 (https://www.legal-tools.org/doc/42881c/).

[18] ICTY, *Prosecutor v. Blagojević and Jokić,* Trial Chamber, Judgement, 17 January 2005, IT-02-60-T, para. 291 ('Blagojević and Jokić Trial Judgment') (https://www.legal-tools.org/doc/7483f2/); ICTY, *Prosecutor v. Krstić,* Trial Chamber, Judgement, 2 August 2001, IT-98-33-T, para. 82 (https://www.legal-tools.org/doc/440d3a/); ICTY, *Prosecutor v. Mladić,* Trial Chamber, Decision pursuant to Rule 94*bis* in relation to proposed expert Helge Brunborg, 19 July 2013, IT-09-92-T (https://www.legal-tools.org/doc/d83f80/); ICTY, *Prosecutor v. Milutinović et al.,* Trial Chamber, Judgement: Volume 2 of 4, 26 February 2009, IT-05-87-T, para. 565 (https://www.legal-tools.org/doc/f0666a/); Galić Trial Decision concerning the Expert Witnesses Ewa Tabeau and Richard Philipps, see above note 17; Prlić et al. Trial Judgment, paras. 296–355, see above note 16.

that "it is the analyst, in my view, who has the most important job of assisting the prosecutor in building a case against high-ranking superiors".[19]

At the ICC analysts so far have testified twice, also on the basis of their reports, first in relation to telephone data analysis in *Bemba et al.*, and for issues of military telecommunications in Ongwen.

The Special Tribunal for Lebanon ('STL') also hired a number of professional analysts for its investigations, including several from ICTY-OTP, particularly for the analysis of large volumes of telephone data. Other agencies investigating international crimes that have employed former ICTY analysts, include multiple UN commissions of inquiry, the ECCC, the IIIM for Syria, Organisation for the Prohibition of Chemical Weapons (OPCW), The Court of Bosnia and Hercegovina, Commission for International Justice and Accountability (CIJA), and the International Crisis Group (ICG).

By 2012, the International Best Practices Project acknowledged the role of analysts based on the experience of five international or hybrid tribunals (ICTY, ICTR, SCSL, ECCC and STL): "Analysts who have specialized knowledge and expertise may be vitally important to a successful investigation and prosecution and their analytical output must be accessible and usable throughout the process".[20] A recommended best practice, essential for their role in QCCI, was that "[a]nalysts must adopt an objective approach, highlighting both information that supports and undermines the prosecution case", since "an analyst should always be objective and should formulate his or her views and opinions on the basis of all the available source materials".[21] To further strengthen the role of analysts the International Best Practices Project mentioned the options to have a dedicated analysis section to manage analysts deployed across teams, and specialized analysis units (military, political or other specialized domains), and having in each team along with a lead prosecutor and a lead investiga-

---

[19] Peter McCloskey, "Leadership and Control of Investigations", in Morten Bergsmo, Klaus Rackwitz and SONG Tianying (eds.), *Historical Origins of International Criminal Law: Volume 5*, Torkel Opsahl Academic EPublisher, Brussels, 2017, p. 209 (http://www.toaep.org/ps-pdf/24-bergsmo-rackwitz-song).

[20] Robert Petit, David Akerson and Maria Warren (eds.), *Prosecuting Mass Atrocities: Lessons from the International Tribunals: A Compendium of Lessons Learned and Suggested Practices from the Offices of the Prosecutors*, 2012, sect. "Evidence Analysis", p. 144. See also *ibid.*, sect. "Ongoing Analysis of Collected Material", p. 62.

[21] *Ibid.*, p. 146.

tor, and at the same level, "a lead analyst in charge of the analysis of the material and the identification of what the prosecution does not have and should collect".[22] The stronger the mandate and institutional safeguards for the analysts, the better they will be able to contribute to QCCI.

Among the national investigations on international crimes, the Fiscalía General de la Nación in Colombia has been probably most advanced in the use of analysts, since the late 1990s, as well as with the Unidad de Análisis y Contextos established in 2012.[23] Multiple national units for the investigation of international crimes in third countries have also employed analysts, including those in Canada and the Netherlands.[24]

The ICC-OTP was given since its first budget in 2003 an Analysis Section in the Investigations Division. This section today, the Investigative Analysis Section ('IAS'), comprises 21 professional analysts and 11 junior Analysis Assistants, deployed to support multiple investigation and prosecution teams across 13 situations. Analysts design and sustain all-source collation databases and they contribute regularly to the identification of investigative leads, strategic decision-making, Source Evaluation,[25] analysis of crime patterns and organisational structures (including elements of statistics, Geographic Information Systems, military and network analysis), and systematic monitoring and exploitation of internet open sources and social media. The Investigations Division benefits from the experience of other international and national investigations and conducts highly competitive recruitment processes which, along with continuing training and standardisation programs, has led to a high level of technical skill among analysts, as assessed by feedback from the investigation teams as well as external peer-review. IAS also has engaged the co-

---

[22] *Ibid.*, p. 14.

[23] See their official web site "Unidad de Análisis y Contextos", *Fiscalía General de la Nación*.

[24] For publications by Canadian analysts in this area (historians), see Norman G. Finkelstein and Ruth Bettina Birn, *A Nation on Trial: The Goldhagen Thesis and Historical Truth*, Owl Books, New York, 1998 (Birn was the Chief Historian in the War Crimes and Crimes Against Humanity Section of the Department of Justice); and Ralf Ogorreck, *Les Einsatzgruppen: Les groupes d'intervention et la "genèse de la solution finale"*, Olivier Mannoni trans., Calman-Lévy, Paris, 2007 (translation of the original in German of 1996, Ogorreck was a historian in the same Section).

[25] See below Section 3.2.

---

operation of UN Women, and thanks to their generous support has received in secondment several analysts specialised on gender issues.

3.1.1. The Cycle

Analysts look at their work as part of an iterative cycle, anticipating the need to review multiple times the findings as a process of development, verification and QC. A merely linear model, which is how usually criminal procedure is conceived, would be too simplistic and positivistic, because investigations are creative processes in which cases morph constantly until they reach a stage of evidential maturity. This cyclical approach is common among scientist, engineers or software designers, combining inductive and deductive techniques, and planning ahead for multiple tests and iterations.[26] Sherman Kent, considered 'the founding father of intelligence analysis', proposed similarly in 1949 the adoption for intelligence research of a cyclical framework borrowed from social sciences, for "the development of new concepts from observations and that the new concepts in turn indicate and lead to new observations".[27] In the words of Catrien Bijleveld, an expert in criminology, "[t]he empirical cycle is therefore not a cycle, but a spiral, with each answer generating new research ideas".[28]

The essence of the investigation needs to be the implementation of the well-known principles of scientific methodology to the matter of the crimes and the relevant evidence.[29] As the Italian prosecutor Gherardo Colombo explained based on his experience with large-scale corruption cases: "Investigation must be carried out in a scientific manner. [...] Fact-finding in an investigation must be carried out using the same methods as

---

[26] For software engineering, see the classic work by Frederick P. Brooks Jr., *The Mythical Man-Month: Essays on Software Engineering*, anniversary edition, Addison-Wesley, Boston, 1995 (originally published in 1975).

[27] Sherman Kent, *Strategic Intelligence for American World Policy*, Princeton University Press, Princeton, 1949, pp. 156–57.

[28] Catrien Bijleveld, *Conflicts and International Crimes: An Introduction to Research Methods*, Eleven International Publishing, Amsterdam, 2017, sect. 2.2. "Empirical Cycle", p. 15. Bijleveld is professor of Research Methods in Criminology at the Vrije Universiteit Amsterdam and director of the Netherlands Institute for the Study of Crime and Law Enforcement.

[29] For general reference on scientific methodology, see Karl Popper, *The Logic of Scientific Discovery*, Routledge, London, 2005 (originally in German, 1935).

in an experiment carried out in any sector of science".[30] In the context of criminal procedure, unlike other domains, the 'spiral' of the scientific cycle will not roll endlessly, it has discrete purpose and it shall stop when the investigation is completed. The subsequent litigation can be also understood as a new round or iteration in the cycle, only then integrating evidence delivered by the opposing party.

Such cycles have gained currency in police and intelligence agencies around the world.[31] Agencies have adopted different versions, more or less elaborate depending on their needs and their organisational culture. The following cycle may be appropriate for the needs of investigating complex or international crimes:

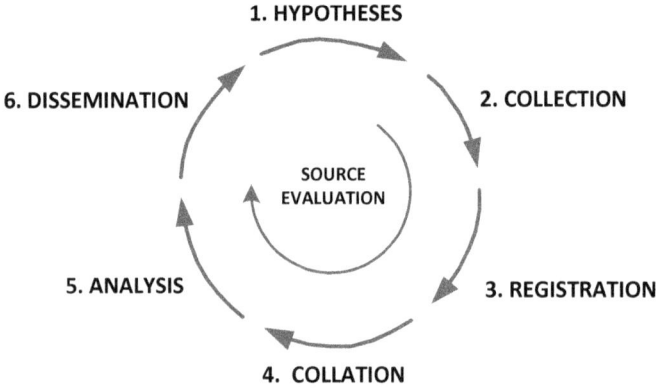

Figure 1. Cycle of investigating complex or international crimes.

The first step is identifying the relevant hypotheses to guide the investigation, to be critically tested and verified, much like any scientific process. Pretending instead to start from some blank slate or *tabula rasa* would be a fallacy, because any action is always based on some knowledge, which is best stated and treated properly rather than letting it govern the investigation implicitly and free of audit. In the words of Karl

---

[30] Gherardo Colombo, "Investigating and Prosecuting Large-scale Corruption: The Italian Experience", in *Journal of International Criminal Justice*, 2006, vol. 4, no. 3, p. 516.

[31] See Don McDowell, *Strategic Intelligence: A Handbook for Practitioners, Managers and Users*, Istana Enterprises, Pambula, 1998, p. 18; Europol, *Analytical Guidelines*, The Hague, 1999, insert 2; Howard Atkin, "Criminal Intelligence Analysis: A Scientific Perspective", in *Journal of Intelligence and Analysis*, 2000, vol. 13, no. 1, pp. 1–15; and Mark Pythian (ed.), *Understanding the Intelligence Cycle*, Routledge, London, 2013.

Popper: "it is not only impossible to avoid a selective point of view, but also wholly undesirable to do so; for if we could do so, we should get not a more 'objective' description, but only a mere heap of entirely unconnected statements".[32] Hypotheses need to be formulated impartially and objectively, assuming these criteria as fundamental requirements of the investigation from the outset.[33]

The second step refers to the collection of relevant evidence, which shall follow in accordance to proper investigation plans.[34] This is primarily the duty of professional investigators, trained in the relevant techniques for interviewing witnesses among other means, as well as the required standards for operational and information security.

Thirdly, 'registration' shows as a specific step because of the needs of 'chain of custody' for the evidence, as a reminder for this fundamental investigative duty, as also because good registration meta-data are very useful for investigative analysis.

Fourthly, 'collation' is the step of summarising and integrating data from multiple sources, a necessary foundation for the actual analysis. The use of all-source databases is considered best practice, to integrate information from any kind of source (statements, reports, videos, phone data, and so on) around factual entities (mainly persons, events, organisations and locations), with and Entity-Attribute-Value data model, and links between related entities. The implementation of such databases may grow into a major project, with specific protocols and dedicated inputters and database managers.

The fifth step is the analysis as such, assigned to professional analysts for key factual issues of the investigation. The most common areas of analysis include the following: crime pattern analysis about the common features among large series of incidents and victims; analysis of organisational structures and networks with the systems of command and communications; and Source Evaluation (see Section 3.2. below). The relevant techniques include both quantitative and qualitative methods, as

---

[32] Karl R. Popper, *The Open Society and Its Enemies, Volume II: The High Tide of Prophecy: Hegel, Marx and the Aftermath*, Princeton University Press, 1966, p. 261.

[33] For a more detailed discussion on investigative hypotheses, see below Section 3.3.2. "Analysis of Competing Hypotheses ('ACH')".

[34] See Markus Eikel, "Investigation Plans in International Criminal Investigations: The Example of the ICC Office of the Prosecutor", Chap. 14 below.

well as Geographic Information Systems (GIS), applied both for tactical support in operations, and for strategic advice when selecting situations, cases, suspects and charges.

The sixth and last step is 'dissemination', fundamental to make sure that the analytical findings are properly communicated and understood by the end-users, typically investigators, prosecutors and management for operational, legal and strategic decisions. Proper standards for archival storage, report drafting, visual aids and briefings are required for effective dissemination.

The model above shows a 'cycle within the cycle' for Source Evaluation because of the importance of this aspect across investigative steps, as Section 3.2. below explains. References to multiple judgments are included in relation to Source Evaluation to illustrate the expectation of the judges, not necessarily to endorse those findings.

Concerning specifically the role of analysis for QCCI, Sections 3.3. and 3.4. below propose two sets of techniques known as 'diagnostic', focused on the descriptive evaluation of a given case or hypothesis, and 'adversarial', designed to test critically hypotheses and findings. Diagnostic techniques are reminiscent of scientific methodology, while adversarial techniques anticipate the dialectics of litigation.[35]

Finally, Section 3.5. will propose Evidence Review Boards as a fundamental tool for QC, with the input of the analysts and their techniques, in close co-operation with legal officers, investigators and investigation managers.

3.2. Source Evaluation

> One quarter of [the guilt of] an unjust [decision] falls on him who committed [the crime], one quarter on the [false] witness, one quarter on all the judges, one quarter on the king.
>
> *Manusmriti*, verses 8.18.

> We learn what happened by ruling out unreliable testimony; and we know what testimony to rule out as unreliable by learning what happened.
>
> M.C. Otto, "Testimony and human nature" (1918)

---

[35] For a catalogue of analytical techniques and their classification, see Richards J. Heuer Jr. and Randolph H. Pherson, *Structured Analytic Techniques for Intelligence Analysis*, SAGE, Los Angeles, 2015.

> La pratique judiciaire devra désormais choisir entre deux at-
> titudes possibles vis-à-vis des témoignages: ou bien conti-
> nuer à les apprécier routinièrement, *intuitu personnæ,* sans
> méthode, au risque d'erreurs grossières; ou bien mettre à
> profit les nouvelles données de la science du témoignage
> s'édifiant par le labeur accumulé de tant de savants (psycho-
> logues, médecins, psychiatres, juristes, etc.), pour tenter de
> soumettre les témoignages à une critique psycho-judiciaire
> méthodique et d'en tirer le maximum de vérité avec le mini-
> mum d'erreur.
>
> François Gorphe, *La critique du Témoignage* (1924)

3.2.1. The Concept

Source Evaluation ('SE') is the domain of investigative analysis dedicated to assess the quality of the evidence, with standard criteria related to its providers and its content. The equivalent terms of 'source assessment', 'source criticism' (*Qellenkritike* in German historiography), 'verifica-tion'[36], 'evidence about the evidence', 'probative efficiency' or 'infor-mation quality' are known in various technical and legal domains.[37] Con-cerning witnesses the key question is "how do you know if the witness is speaking the truth?". Concerning other means of evidence (documents, objects, forensics, and so on) SE will address questions of documentary or physical authenticity and integrity. The SE criteria and methods com-prised in this section refer mainly to witnesses, but they may be relevant also for any type of evidence, and their authors.

Mistakes in the evaluation of witnesses and other sources may oc-cur due to multiple conflict-related biases, the dramatic nature of the crimes and various operational limitations. Anybody growing up in a

---

[36] For 'verification' in historiography, see Jacques Barzun and Henry F. Graff, "Verification", in *The Modern Researcher*, 5th edition, Harcourt Brace Jovanovich, New York, 1992, p. 99. For 'verification' of internet sources, see Craig Silverman (ed.), *Verification Handbook: A Definitive Guide to Verifying Digital Content for Emergency Coverage*, European Journal-ism Centre, Maastricht, 2014 (available on Verification Handbook's web site), including reference to multiple examples, techniques and tools.

[37] For 'evidence about the evidence', see Fernando Gascón Inchausti, *El control de fiabilidad probatoria: "Prueba sobre la prueba" en el proceso penal*, Ediciones Revista General del Derecho, Valencia, 1999. On 'information quality', see Craig Fisher, Eitel Lauria, Shobha Chengalur-Smith and WANG Richard, *Introduction to Information Quality*, AuthorHouse, London, 2006; and Global Privacy and Information Quality Working Group (GPIQWG), *Information Quality: The Foundation for Justice Decision Making*, US DOJ, 2010.

country affected by violent conflict, as I did, is used to hear regularly different versions of the same event from different media, friends or relatives: the so-called 'Rashomon effect' is part of your daily life.[38] I further dealt with SE issues through my research and field work in the former Yugoslavia (1992–95), and I became acutely aware of such problems in criminal investigations through my work as an analyst at the ICTY-OTP (1997–2003). Section 3.2.2. below summarising the "most frequent biases and limitations" is inspired largely, but not exclusively, by my experience with ICTY investigations. It appeared to me that those investigations did not have a proper system to evaluate the quality of witness evidence, which is also noticeable in the lack of any reference to the subject in the *ICTY Manual on Developed Practices*.[39]

I decided to develop a methodology for Source Evaluation upon joining the ICC-OTP investigations in 2004. This was in line with the vision of Morten Bergsmo and other ICTY veterans who joined the ICC determined to carry 'lessons learned' and improve previous practice. In any event, problems with the evaluation of the evidence are well-known in domestic practice, where "[t]he objectivity of the evaluation is key to the integrity of any investigation. Yet the most ubiquitous form of biased reasoning occurs through a distorted evaluation of evidence".[40]

Difficulties in SE may arise under the pressure of operational or litigation deadlines. Hans Gross already observed in relation to the evaluation of witnesses the 'rapidity' affecting the quality of the interviews, and advised "for the Officer to carefully prepare his interrogatory, not to be afraid to remind the witness at length that he must speak the truth, and to

---

[38] *Rashōmon* is the story of four conflicting witness accounts of the same alleged crimes of killing and rape, as told by different witnesses to the same judge, as shown in Kurosawa's famous film *Rashōmon* (1950), based on the story by AKUTAGAWA Ryūnosuke, *In a grove* (1922). See Wendy D. Roth and Jal D. Mehta, "The Rashomon Effect Combining Positivist and Interpretivist Approaches in the Analysis of Contested Events", in *Sociological Methods and Research*, 2002, vol. 31, no. 2, pp. 131–73; and Robert Anderson, "The Rashomon Effect and Communication", in *Canadian Journal of Communication*, 2016, vol. 41, no. 2, pp. 249–69. For context, see Peter Wild, *Akira Kurosawa*, Reaktion Books, London, 2014, particularly pp. 64–73.

[39] ICTY and United Nations Interregional Crime and Justice Research Institute ('UNICRI'), *ICTY Manual on Developed Practices*, UNICRI Publisher, Turin, 2009 ('ICTY Manual on Developed Practices') (https://www.legal-tools.org/doc/0cc55d/).

[40] Dan Simon, *In Doubt: The Psychology of the Criminal Justice Process*, Harvard University Press, Cambridge, 2012, p. 38.

---

probe him to the bottom, especially if he has the slightest suspicion that his statement is false".[41] Rushed evaluations are unlikely to save time, they may instead lead to waste and mistakes in the longer run. Insufficient professional experience may also lead to errors in SE, which should be trusted as much as possible to experienced officers, and those who have the most advanced knowledge of the case and the context. Definition of standard criteria, specific training and mentoring should help to shorten the learning curve.

Criteria for SE are known historically in every major culture around the world, including the Indian civilisation. The classic canon *Manusmriti* dictated detailed rules for the qualifications of witnesses.[42] The *Nyāya Sūtra*, the treaty on logics and epistemology, included rules for 'verbal testimony', defined as the "instructive assertion of a reliable person".[43] By the second century CE, the *Arthashastra* also referred to criteria for the admissibility and evaluation of witnesses, including issues of 'honesty', independence and corroboration.[44] More recently in December 2018, the High Court of Delhi in *Sajjan Kumar et al.*, a case related to mass violence against Sikhs in the 1980s, issued a conviction only after evaluating thoroughly the key witnesses and their testimonies.[45]

---

[41] Hans Gross, *Criminal Investigation: A Practical Handbook for Magistrates, Police Officers, and Lawyers: Translated and Adapted to Indian and Colonial Practice from the SYSTEM DER KRIMINALISTIK*, John Adam and J. Collyer Adam eds. and trans., A. Krishnamachari, Chennai (Madras), 1906 (original in German from 1893), p. 97.

[42] See *Manusmriti in Sanskrit with English Translation*, verses 8.61.–8.78., 8.95. and 8.254. (available on Internet Archive's web site).

[43] *The Sacred Books of the Hindus: Translated by Various Sanskrit Scholars: Vol. VIII: The Nyaya Sutras of Gotama*, B.D. Basu ed., Mahamahopadhyaya Satla Chandra Vidyabhusana trans., The Panini Office, Allahabad, 1913, sutra 7, p. 4. In other versions translated as "testimony is instruction by a trustworthy authority". The *Nyāya Sūtra* is the foundational canon of the *Nyāya* school of philosophy, focused on methodology, logics and epistemology, written at some point between sixth century BCE and second century CE. For an annotated version, see Matthew Dasti and S. Phillips, *The Nyāya-sūtra: Selections with Early Commentaries*, Hackett Publishing Company, Indianapolis, 2017.

[44] See Kautilya, *The Arthashastra*, Penguin Books India, New Delhi, 1992, sect. "Law of Evidence", pp. 356–58 and sect. "Guidelines to Judges", pp. 358–59. It is estimated that Kautilya, also known as Chanakya or Vishnugupta, authored the Arthashastra treatise at some point between the second century BCE and third century CE.

[45] Delhi High Court, *State Through CBI v. Sajjan Kumar and Others*, Judgment, 17 December 2018, Criminal Appeal No. 1099/2013 ('Delhi High Court Sajjan Kumar and Others Judgment') (https://www.legal-tools.org/doc/b08482/). See in particular sect. "Analysis of the Evidence of PW-1", paras. 178–220.

Methods for SE have been developed in a range of fields, from psychology to intelligence, as explained in Section 3.2.3. below, and their multi-disciplinary consideration offers the best foundation to define appropriate standards for international criminal law. This is the approach that I took when I drafted the SE guidelines for the ID of the ICC-OTP, proposing the method presented and discussed in Section 3.2.4. below. The Director of the ID issued these guidelines to assist the work of analysts and investigators, and this chapter benefits from the experience of this implementation since 2006.

Abundant national and international jurisprudence underscores the importance of critical Source Evaluation. For example, in the very first case before the ICTY, it became apparent that a witness for the prosecution had given false testimony.[46] The issue was reported in the ICTY annual report of 1997 as follows:

> The Defence, having researched the witness's family situation, found discrepancies in his testimony and confronted him with relatives who he had claimed in Court were dead. After a conversation with his family, witness L, who had testified for the Prosecution on 14 and 15 August 1996, stated that he had lied when testifying before the Trial Chamber and that he had not witnessed Duško Tadić committing any of the acts with which the latter was charged. The Trial Chamber instructed the Prosecutor to conduct an investigation into the circumstances surrounding this testimony. On 8 May 1997, the Prosecutor informed the Judges that it did not consider the case of witness L – whose name was now disclosed as Dragan Opacić – to be an appropriate one for prosecution for false testimony under rule 91.[47]

This incident in *Tadić*, the first ICTY trial, is remarkably similar with the problems in *Lubanga*, the first ICC trial, about 15 years later, with some intermediaries engaged by the prosecutor: the judges also decided to dismiss the evidence facilitated by these intermediaries and asked the prosecutor to investigate them for their falsehood, and the prosecutor

---

[46] See ICTY, *Prosecutor v. Tadić*, Trial Chamber, Opinion and Judgement, 7 May 1997, IT-94-1-T, paras. 33, 553 and 554 ('Tadić Trial Opinion and Judgement') (https://www.legal-tools.org/doc/0a90ae/).

[47] ICTY, *Fourth Annual Report of the ICTY*, 18 September 1997, p. 13 (https://www.legal-tools.org/doc/6bc14e/).

equally declined to prosecute them because of insufficient evidence, in spite of the judicial record of their wrongdoing.[48]

Also in *Tadić*, the defence questioned "the reliability as witnesses" of victims on grounds of eventual subjectivity and resentment; the Judges dismissed this claim, indicating that "the reliability of witnesses, including any motive they may have to give false testimony, is an estimation that must be made in the case of each individual witness".[49]

For the ICC Source Evaluation is required within the following legal framework:

- Article 54(1)(a) ICC Statute – the Prosecutor has the duty to investigate with impartiality "in order to establish the truth", "considering equally incriminating and exonerating circumstances", which requires necessarily objective evaluation of the merits and limitations of the different means of evidence.

- Article 74(2) ICC Statute – "[t]he Trial Chamber's decision shall be based on its evaluation of the evidence and the entire proceedings". In the context of a trial judgment issued at the end of the trial, the ICC judges have indicated that this provision implies the need for evaluating the credibility and reliability of the evidence.

- Rule 140(2)(b) of the ICC Rules of Procedure and Evidence ('RPE') – "[t]he prosecution and the defence have the right to question that witness about relevant matters related to the witness's testimony and its reliability, the credibility of the witness and other relevant matters".

- OTP Regulation 24:

    In the analysis of information and evidence regarding alleged crimes, the Office shall develop and apply a consistent and objective method for the evaluation of sources, information and evidence. In this context, the Office shall take into account *inter alia* the credibility and reliability of sources, information and evidence, and shall examine information and evidence from multiple sources as a means of bias control.

---

[48] ICC, Situation in the Democratic Republic of the Congo, *Prosecutor v. Lubanga*, Trial Chamber, Judgment Pursuant to Article 74 of the Statute, 14 March 2012, ICC-01/04-01/06-2842, para. 291 ('Lubanga Trial Judgment') (https://www.legal-tools.org/doc/677866/).

[49] Tadić Trial Opinion and Judgement, para. 541, see above note 46.

3.2.1.1. Note on Terminology: 'Credibility' and 'Reliability'

As explained below, to follow a dual approach distinguishing between provider and content is a commonly accepted approach in jurisprudence and investigations, but the terminology for those two parameters has not always been used consistently. In ICTY and ICTR jurisprudence the meaning attributed to the terms 'reliability' and 'credibility' varied across cases. For example, the Trial Chamber in *Kunarac* held that "credibility depends upon whether the witness should be believed. Reliability assumes that the witness is speaking the truth, but depends upon whether the evidence, if accepted, proves the fact to which it is directed".[50] The Appeals Chamber (AC) in *Aleksovski* adopted the opposite view. It held that it is for the Trial Chamber "to consider whether a witness is reliable and whether evidence presented is credible".[51] The same definition was utilized by the Appeals Chamber in *Delalić et al.*[52] In other cases, including *Tadić*, the ICTY judges used 'reliability' and 'credibility' interchangeably or referring both to the witnesses and to their evidence.[53]

The ICTR Chambers used 'credibility' for witness and 'reliability' for testimony in some but not all cases. For example, the Trial Chamber in *Rwamakuba* stated that "[w]hen a witness is found to be credible, a Chamber must also determine whether his or her evidence is reliable".[54] The Appeals Chamber in *Ntagerura*, and the Trial Chambers in *Kayishema et al.* and *Ndindabahizi* used the same terminology.[55] However, in

---

[50] ICTY, *Prosecutor v. Kunarac et al.*, Trial Chamber, Decision on Motion for Acquittal, 3 July 2000, IT-96-23-T and IT-96-23/1-T, para. 7 ('Kunarac et al. Trial Decision on Motion for Acquittal') (https://www.legal-tools.org/doc/70edc1/).

[51] ICTY, *Prosecutor v. Aleksovski*, Appeals Chamber, Judgment, 24 March 2000, IT-95-14/1-A, para. 63 (https://www.legal-tools.org/doc/176f05/).

[52] ICTY, *Prosecutor v. Delalić et al.*, Appeals Chamber, Judgment, 20 February 2001, IT-96-21-A, para. 491 (https://www.legal-tools.org/doc/051554/).

[53] Tadić Trial Opinion and Judgement, paras. 232, 253, 255, 259, 268, 275, 536, and so on, see above note 46.

[54] ICTR, *Prosecutor v. André Rwamakuba*, Trial Chamber, Judgement, 20 September 2006, ICTR-98-44C-T, para. 35 ('Rwamakuba Trial Judgment') (https://www.legal-tools.org/doc/b6ffa6/).

[55] ICTR, *Prosecutor v. André Ntagerura, Emmanuel Bagambiki, and Samuel Imanishimwe*, Appeals Chamber, Judgement, 7 July 2006, ICTR-99-46-A, para. 174 (https://www.legal-tools.org/doc/816b44/); ICTR, *Prosecutor v. Kayishema et al.*, Trial Chamber, Judgement, 21 May 1999, ICTR-95-1-T, para. 397 ('Kayishema et al. Trial Judgment') (https://www.legal-tools.org/doc/0811c9/); ICTR, *Prosecutor v. Ndindabahizi*, Trial Chamber, Judge-

---

Bagilishema the Appeals Chamber changed the meaning of the terms, to determine whether "the witness was reliable and his evidence credible"[56]. In *Akayesu* the Trial Chamber used the term 'credibility' both for witness and for testimony.[57] The Appeals Chamber in the same case referred to "the credibility and reliability of the relevant witness, the same usage as the Trial Chamber did in *Semanza*".[58]

ICC RPE Rule 140(2)(b) establishes the use of 'credibility' for witness and 'reliability' for testimonies, while the drafting history of this rule does not provide any precise definition or factor for these two parameters. The ICC judges have followed subsequently this terminology to a large extent. In *Lubanga* trial judgment and in *Ngudjolo* trial judgment, the judges used both terms interchangeably, or jointly for witnesses. By 2014 the Appeals Chamber operated in line with Rule 140(2)(b):

> Thus, although a witness may be honest, and therefore credible, the evidence he or she gives may nonetheless be unreliable because, *inter alia*, it relates to facts that occurred a long time ago or due to the "vagaries of human perception".[59]

Most recently, *Ntaganda* follows this guidance and confirms:

> Credibility relates to whether a witness is testifying truthfully, while the reliability of the facts testified to by the witness may be confirmed or put in doubt by other evidence or the surrounding circumstances. Therefore, although a witness

---

ment and Sentence, 15 July 2004, ICTR-01-71-T, para. 23 (https://www.legal-tools.org/doc/272b55/).

[56] ICTR, *Prosecutor v. Bagilishema*, Appeals Chamber, Judgement (Reasons), 3 July 2002, ICTR-95-1A-A, para. 78 (https://www.legal-tools.org/doc/e4786a/).

[57] ICTR, *Prosecutor v. Jean-Paul Akayesu*, Trial Chamber, Judgement, 2 September 1998, ICTR-96-4-T, para. 47 ('Akayesu Trial Judgment') (https://www.legal-tools.org/doc/b8d7bd/).

[58] ICTR, *Prosecutor v. Jean-Paul Akayesu*, Appeals Chamber, Judgment, 1 June 2001, ICTR-96-4-A, para. 292 (https://www.legal-tools.org/doc/c62d06/); and ICTR, *Prosecutor v. Laurent Semanza*, Trial Chamber, Judgement and Sentence, 15 May 2003, ICTR-97-20-T, paras. 119, and so on (https://www.legal-tools.org/doc/7e668a/).

[59] ICC, Situation in the Democratic Republic of the Congo, *Prosecutor v. Lubanga*, Appeals Chamber, Judgment on the Appeal of Mr Thomas Lubanga Dyilo Against His Conviction, 1 December 2014, ICC-01/04-01/06-3121-Red, para. 239 ('Lubanga Appeals Judgment') (https://www.legal-tools.org/doc/585c75/).

> may be credible, the evidence he or she gives may nonetheless be unreliable.[60]

This convention seems contrary to the practice of most national models for SE, when 'reliability' is used most often for the source, and 'credibility' for the evidence.[61] It may be also contrary to common semantics, since 'reliability' (*fiabilité, fiabilidad, Glaubwürdigkeit*) is usually understood in relation to 'trustworthiness' for a method, a tool or a person and the expected or actual behavior over time, while 'credibility' (*credibilité, credibilidad, Glaubhaftigkeit*) is most commonly used to refer to a single item of information or allegation at a given point of time.[62] In any event, the usage of these two terms might be of lesser importance as long as the specific underlying indicators are properly addressed.[63]

3.2.2. Most Frequent Biases and Limitations

For the purpose of Source Evaluation 'bias' is commonly understood as a systematic conditioning of the information, because of the sources' background, purpose, or methodology. Biases can be deliberate and conscious or not.[64] For example, deliberate biases are common in propaganda, while unconscious biases may show in rumours resulting from fear, anxiety or

---

[60] ICC, Situation in the Democratic Republic of the Congo, *Prosecutor v. Bosco Ntaganda*, Trial Chamber, Judgment, 8 July 2019, ICC-01/04-02/06-2359, para. 53 ('Ntaganda Trial Judgment') (https://www.legal-tools.org/doc/80578a/).

[61] See, for example, judgment on the terrorist attacks in Madrid on 11 March 2003, when referring to the "fiabilidad de la fuente" and "contraste de la informacion" as the two main parameters for source evaluation used by the Spanish Guardia Civil. Spain National High Court (Audiencia Nacional), Criminal Chamber (Sala de lo Penal), Sección Segunda, *The Prosecutor v. Jamal Zougam et al.*, Sentencia no. 65/2007, 31 October 2007, ECLI:ES:AN:2007:4398, p. 332 ('Spain National High Court Zougam Sentencia') (https://www.legal-tools.org/doc/b6mvfl/).

[62] For common usage, see definition in the dictionaries by Oxford, Cambridge, Merriam-Webster, Larousse (French), Real Academia Española (Spanish), and so on. All of them refer to 'reliability' and the equivalent terms as related to the ability of the source, rather than a description of the outcome. For example, the *Trésor de la Langue Française informatisé* defines 'fiabilité' as "qualité d'un appareil, d'un équipement fiable" and 'crédibilité' as "caractère, qualité rendant quelque chose susceptible d'être cru ou digne de confiance".

[63] See below Sections 3.2.4. and 3.2.5.

[64] For a viewpoint from cognitive psychology, see among others Rüdiger F. Pohl (ed.), *Cognitive Illusions: A Handbook on Fallacies and Biases in Thinking, Judgement and Memory*, Psychology Press, New York, 2004. For an authoritative reference from social science research, see Stathis N. Kalyvas, "Appendix A: Data Sources", in *The Logic of Violence in Civil War*, Cambridge University Press, 2006, pp. 393–411; and sect. "Bias", pp. 405–07.

different assumptions. A biased source is not necessarily lying, in a conscious deliberate sense, the source may be just conveying what seems truthful from its viewpoint.[65]

The investigation should operate on the assumption that there are no 'bias-free sources', they all carry biases of one type or another. Instead the purpose of Source Evaluation is to identify the relevant biases, and to control them through systematic analysis and triangulation with other sources.[66]

The following pages outline the most frequent biases and difficulties related to SE in order to raise awareness and readiness among professionals. The issues highlighted below are not theoretical, they follow from real investigative experience, while some historical or domestic examples are used as proxies for more current realities in international investigations. Different biases[67] may affect both the sources and the evaluating officers, hence the corresponding paragraphs on 'advice' propose measures at different substantive and operational levels. For example, cultural biases are likely to show both in witnesses, as well as among investigators, analysts and judges evaluating their statements. Evaluating officers should be wary of their own personal and institutional biases, as well as those of those from the source.

Sections 3.2.2.4. and 3.2.2.5. refer to some operational difficulties related to the perception by the investigating officers, which would require from them specific awareness, training and careful implementation of the proposed Source Evaluation model.

3.2.2.1. Partisan Biases

Biases related to the parties in the conflict are frequent, because of partisan links, kinship or shared ideology. They may take different degrees, from the most obvious forms of propaganda, to more subtle forms of under-rep orting or emphasizing different crimes. The information may contain exaggerations or inflammatory language and images constituting

---

[65] For some recent research on actual lies, as well as data biases, in the context of internet, see Seth Stephens-Davidowitz, *Everybody Lies: What the Internet Can Tell Us About Who We Really Are*, Bloomsbury, London, 2017. The author is a former data scientist at Google and an expert on 'big data'.

[66] Paulette M. Rothbauer, "Triangulation", in Lisa M. Given (ed.), *The SAGE Encyclopedia of Qualitative Research Methods*, SAGE Publications, Los Angeles, 2008, pp. 892–94.

[67] Below Sections 3.2.2.1. to 3.2.2.3.

'atrocity propaganda'.[68] Information conveyed by a partisan or sensation-alist source may still be truthful to some extent, once the exaggerated or dramatic elements are identified and neutralized. Consider the following examples:

- *Nazi reports on war crimes*: Nazi sources were keen on reporting thoroughly about German victims, while ignoring the victims of their own crimes. For example, in 1940 the German Foreign Office published an elaborate volume in English on "the Polish atrocities against the German minority in Poland", "based on documentary evidence" from the Military Commission "for the investigation of breaches of International Law", and including detailed information and pictures of a number of alleged civilian victims.[69] It may be that some of that evidence was truthful, but the notorious suppression from the record of the Nazi invasion of Poland and their subsequent crimes would call for some additional verification. The Nazi regime had already started using such selective reporting of war crimes by 1937 in relation to the Spanish Civil War, emphasizing crimes committed by government forces while ignoring those committed by the fascist uprising and the Luftwaffe.[70]

- *Rigoberta Menchú Tum*: In 1983 the authors of a widely distributed documentary about the genocide committed by the Guatemalan Army featured the Maya K'iche' indigenous activist Rigoberta Menchú Tum stating: "I am going to tell you my story, which is the

---

[68] For a classic study on the subject, see Arthur Ponsoby, *Falsehood in Wart-Time: Containing an Assortment of Lies Circulated Throughout the Nations During the Great War*, George Allen and Unwin, London, 1928. See also Paul Morrow, "A Theory of Atrocity Propaganda", in *Humanity: An International Journal of Human Rights, Humanitarianism, and Development*, 2018, vol. 9, no. 1, pp. 45–62, and the article by Jo Fox, "Atrocity propaganda", *British Library*, 29 January 2014 (available on its web site).

[69] Hans Schadewaldt (ed.), *The Polish Atrocities Against the German Minority in Poland: Edited and Published by Order of the German Foreign Office and Based upon Documentary Evidence: Second Revised Edition*, Volk und Reich Verlag, Berlin, 1940. For methodology, see *ibid.*, chap. II "Sources of information and explanations".

[70] See Xabier Agirre Aranburu, "Goebbels en el pais de San Ignacio: Reflexiones sobre Espana, fascismo y propaganda", Joseph Paul Goebbels, in Xabier Agirre Aranburu (ed.), *La verdad sobre España* [The Truth About Spain], Iralka, Irun, 1998. "The Truth About Spain" is a speech delivered by Joseph Paul Goebbels in the annual congress of the Nazi Party in Nuremberg on 9 September 1937, originally published by M. Muller & Sohn in Berlin, 1937.

---

story of all the Guatemalan people".[71] In 1984 Menchú Tum became widely known after the publication of her biography, which included an array of episodes of marginalization and violence.[72] In 1992, the Norwegian Nobel Committee awarded her the Peace Nobel Prize. Subsequent research revealed by 1994 that in her biography Menchú Tum had fabricated or appropriated a number of facts to craft a narrative supportive of the guerrillas, of which she had been an associate.[73] She responded explaining that she acted as a collective spokeswoman, and whether her individual account was accurate is not important as long as it is valid to tell the experience of her community. Anthropologists and others have debated extensively about the ethics, the politics and the credibility of her account. The prevailing view is that her narrative makes useful advocacy, but poor evidence.[74]

---

[71] Peter Kinoy (Prod.), Pamela Yates and Thomas Newton Sigel (Dirs.), "When the Mountains Tremble" [motion picture], 1983, United States, Skylight Pictures. The documentary was designed to expose the crimes committed by the Guatemalan Army, while in one instance it attributed mistakenly to it a massacre committed by the guerrillas, as the Commission for Historical Clarification (Comisión para el Esclarecimiento Histórico) established in 1999, and the authors were compelled to acknowledge in 2014; see their statement: Pamela Yates, "Preliminary investigation results by Pamela Yates and Skylight Pictures", *Skylight Pictures*, 6 July 2014 (available on its web site). For context, see the report of the Commission for Historical Clarification, *Guatemala: Memoria del Silencio: Conclusiones y Recomendaciones*, United Nations Office for Project Services, 1999 (https://www.legal-tools.org/doc/c0c4af/); and the judgement and conviction of José Efraín Ríos Montt and José Mauricio Rodríguez Sánchez by the Guatemalan Tribunal Primero de Sentencia Penal, 10 May 2013, C-1076-2011-00015, finding the accused guilty of genocide and crimes against humanity ('Ríos Montt and Rodríguez Sánchez Tribunal Primero de Sentencia Penal Judgment') (https://www.legal-tools.org/doc/riztst/).

[72] Elisabeth Burgos, *Me llamo Rigoberta Menchu y asi me nacio la conciencia*, Casa de las Americas, Havana, 1984. For context, see Commission for Historical Clarification, 1999, see above note 71; and Ríos Montt and Rodríguez Sánchez Tribunal Primero de Sentencia Penal Judgment, see above note 71.

[73] See David Stoll, *Rigoberta Menchú and the Story of All Poor Guatemalans: Expanded Edition*, Routledge, New York, 2008. Including a foreword by Elisabeth Burgos in which she explains how she and other activists linked to the guerrillas chose Menchú Tum as she "would make and ideal witness" for their advocacy campaign.

[74] For an overview of the controversy, see Mario Roberto Morales (ed.), *Stoll-Menchú: la invención de la memoria*, Consucultura, Guatemala, 2001, including chapters by David Stoll, Elisabeth Burgos, Jennifer Schirmer and others. For a view supportive of Menchú, see Leigh Gilmore, "Jurisdictions and Testimonial Networks: Rigoberta Menchú", in *Tainted Witness: Why We Doubt What Women Say About Their Lives*, Columbia University Press, New York, 2017, pp. 59–84.

- *UN Security Council ('UNSC')*: On 11 March 2004 a bomb attack killed 191 people in Madrid. The Spanish government immediately attributed the attack to the Basque terrorist group ETA, led apparently by two considerations. Firstly, because indeed ETA and no other group had carried out a number of murderous bomb attacks in Madrid in previous years.[75] Secondly, because of partisan bias, since this hypothesis was more convenient for the government than the alternative of blaming the attack on Jihadi militants, in the given political context and three days before the general elections.[76] The position of the Spanish government led the UNSC to adopt unanimously Resolution 1530 (2004) stating erroneously that it *"[c]ondemns* in the strongest terms the bomb attacks in Madrid, Spain, perpetrated by the terrorist group ETA".[77] Police investigations indicated soon that the authors were associated to Al Qaeda, which was confirmed by the judgment and conviction issued by the Audiencia Nacional in Madrid in 2007.[78] The UNSC resolution and public statement containing this factual mistake is still today available in their official site (as of October 2020).

A source should not be discarded just because of an alleged or real association to a party in the conflict, as different judges have indicated. In 1997, the ICTY judges indicated in their very first judgment:

---

[75] Among several other bomb attacks in Madrid, on 29 July 1979, ETA exploded a bomb in the Atocha train station, the same station attacked by the Jihadi group on 11 March 2004, killing three persons. For an account based on police and judicial investigative records, see Juanfer F. Calderín, *Agujeros del Sistema: Más de 300 asesinatos de ETA sin resolver*, Ikusager Ediciones, Vitoria, 2014, pp. 79–91.

[76] For context, see the conclusions of the Commission of Investigation of the Spanish Cortes Generales (Comisión de Investigación sobre el 11 de marzo de 2004), 22 June 2005, session no. 50 (available on Cortes Generales' web site). Also, Fernando Reinares, *Al Qaeda's Revenge: The 2004 Madrid Train Bombings*, Woodrow Wilson Center Press, Washington, D.C., 2016. See Bruce Riedel, "Foreword", in *ibid.*, p. xiii for UNSC Resolution 1530 (2004).

[77] UNSC, "Security Council Condemns Madrid Terrorist Bombings, Urges All States to Join Search for Perpetrators", 11 March 2004, SC/8022 (available on UN Meetings Coverage and Press Releases' web site).

[78] Spain National High Court Zougam Sentencia, see above note 61. The alternative hypothesis of commission by ETA was raised by the defence, and dismissed by the judges after considering multiple means of evidence, including testimony of senior police officers (see *ibid.*, p. 346, and so on). For an explanation by the presiding judge, see Javier Gómez Bermúdez, *No destruirán nuestra libertad*, Planeta, Madrid, 2010.

> It is neither appropriate, nor correct, to conclude that a witness is deemed to be inherently unreliable solely because he was the victim of a crime committed by a person of the same creed, ethnic group, armed force or any other characteristic of the accused. That is not to say that ethnic hatred, even without the exacerbating influences of violent conflict between ethnic groups, can never be a ground for doubting the reliability of any particular witness. Such a conclusion can only be made, however, in the light of the circumstances of each individual witness, his individual testimony, and such concerns as the Defence may substantiate either in cross-examination or through its own evidence-in-chief.[79]

In 2019, an ICC judge found in similar terms:

> [...] the fact that victims and witnesses were ethnically or politically related to Mr Ouattara is not per se sufficient to raise doubts concerning their credibility. It would thus be unreasonable to exclude their testimony solely on that basis.[80]

3.2.2.2.   Cultural Biases

Culture is likely to affect both the production of information by the witness, and its interpretation by the investigating and judicial officers. Difficulties of cross-cultural understanding are common in international investigations, when investigating officers are foreign to the relevant communities.[81] Research in the fields of anthropology, linguistics, 'cross-cultural communication', and international management should help for the evidence not going 'lost in translation', as the pages below shall illustrate.[82]

---

[79]   Tadić Trial Opinion and Judgement, p. 186, para. 541, see above note 46.

[80]   ICC, Situation in the Republic of Côte d'Ivoire, *Prosecutor v. Laurent Gbagbo and Charles Blé Goudé*, Trial Chamber, Public Redacted Version of Dissenting Opinion by Judge Herrera Carbuccia, 16 July 2019, ICC-02/11-01/15-1263-AnxC-Red, para. 33 (https://www.legal-tools.org/doc/6ak9rf/).

[81]   For a compilation of relevant cases studies, see Richard A. Wilson (ed.), *Human Rights, Culture and Context: Anthropological Perspectives*, Pluto Press, London, 1997.

[82]   For the view from management studies, see among others David C. Thomas, *Cross-Cultural Management: Essential Concepts*, 2nd edition, SAGE Publications, Los Angeles, 2008; and Erin Meyer, *The Culture Map: Decoding How People Think, Lead, and Get Things Done Across Cultures*, Public Affairs, New York, 2014. For a view from law and linguistics, see "The Discourses of Law in Cross-Cultural Perspective", in John M. Conley, William M. O'Barr and Robin Conley Riner, *Just Words: Law, Language and Power*, 3rd edition, Chicago University Press, 2019, pp. 101–20. Among the many references in anthropological studies that are highly relevant for international investigations, note Nigel

---

Insufficient contextual knowledge is very likely to lead to investigative mistakes. For example, Justice Jackson, the Chief US Prosecutor in Nuremberg, when interrogating Joachim Ribbentrop, the former Nazi Minister of Foreign Affairs, accused him of denying passports to Jews who wanted to flee Germany, and refused angrily to believe Ribbentrop's denial on this point: Jackson's interpreter, a native German, had to tell him discreetly that Ribbentrop was being truthful since in Germany, unlike in the US, passports are issued by the police and not by the Ministry of Foreign Affairs, and Ribbentrop may have committed many crimes but not that particular one.[83]

Officers dealing with asylum applications face similar problems, as explained in the United Nations High Commissioner for Refugees ('UNHCR') and EU guidelines for their 'credibility assessments':

> Multi-lingual and cross-cultural communication in the asylum procedure increases scope for misunderstandings and errors. Though interpreters may help to overcome the linguistic barriers, decision makers' lack of familiarity with the cultural backgrounds of applicants as well as the social mores and gender norms of their societies of origin, and the linguistic barriers may remain a challenge.[84]

Among many other cultural dimensions, cross-cultural communication may be affected by the different perceptions of individuality and hierarchy. World-wide variations about these two dimensions are known at

---

Barley, *The Innocent Anthropologist: Notes from a Mud Hut*, London, Penguin, 1983. For some pioneering anthropological work by African researchers, see Jomo Kenyatta, *Facing Mount Kenya*, Heinemann Educational Books, Nairobi, 1982 (first published in 1938). Kenyatta's book describes the culture of his own community, the Kenyan Kikuyu, and has an introduction by Branislaw Malinowski, who had mentored him in the London School of Economics. Jomo Kenyatta was the first President of independent Kenya, and the ICC Prosecutor indicted his son Uhuru in 2011 and withdrew the charges in 2014, see "Kenyatta Case", *ICC* (available on its web site). See also Susan Thomson, An Ansoms and Jude Murison (eds.), *Emotional and Ethical Challenges for Field Research in Africa: The Story Behind the Findings*, Palgrave Macmillan, New York, 2013.

[83] See the memoirs by Richard W. Sonnefeldt, *Witness to Nuremberg: The Chief American Interpreter at the War Crimes Trials*, Arcade Publishing, New York, 2002, p. 24.

[84] UNHCR, *Beyond Proof: Credibility Assessment in EU Asylum Systems*, Brussels, May 2013, p. 30 (https://www.legal-tools.org/doc/i4racg/). This report is based on extensive research, including practice in different national systems, relevant asylum jurisprudence, academic research, as well as ICTY and ICTR jurisprudence on the assessment of witness testimony.

least since Geert Hofstede published his influential book *Cultures and Organisations*.[85] Hofstede's data show a certain correlation between these two dimensions, that is, the more hierarchical cultures tend to be also more collectivistic, as the scatter plot below from his book illustrates, with his data for hierarchy (defined as 'power distance') and 'individualism'(Figure 2 below).[86]

Furthermore, according to these data the countries that have suffered mass violence in recent decades appear to belong in the cluster with high values for both hierarchy and collectivism (upper right quarter in the scatter plot below).[87] People from such victimized countries are likely to offer relatively hierarchical and collectivistic narratives. Conversely, persons from the minority of countries at the other end of the spectrum (lower left quarter), some of which are often over-represented in international institutions, are likely to be biased towards high individualism and low-hierarchy, which could impair their understanding of the rest of the world. 'WEIRD people' is how some researchers call the people from "Western Educated Industrialized Rich and Democratic" societies, who are "a truly

---

[85] Geert Hofstede and Gert Jan Hofstede, *Cultures and Organizations: Software of the Mind: Intercultural Cooperation and Its Importance for Survival*, 2nd edition, McGraw Hill, New York, 2005 (1st edition published in 1991). For a discussion on Hofstede's research and comparison with other global surveys, see: Thomas, 2008, chap. 3 "Comparing Cultures: Systematically Describing Cultural Differences", pp. 47–69, see above note 82; Peter B. Smith, Ronald Fischer, Vivian L. Vignoles and Michael H. Bond, *Understanding Social Psychology Across Cultures: Engaging with Others in a Changing World*, SAGE, Los Angeles, 2013, chap. 2, sect. "The Hofstede Project", pp. 26–31; and Daphna Oyserman, Heather M. Coon and Markus Kemmelmeier, "Rethinking Individualism and Collectivism: Evaluation of Theoretical Assumptions and Meta-Analyses", in *Psychological Bulletin*, 2002, vol. 128, no. 1, pp. 3–72. Hofstede's model is part of the induction program for ICC staff delivered by the Registry as they join the institution, to raise their multi-cultural awareness. For Hofstede on gender, see Geert Hofsted et al., *Masculinity and Femininity: The Taboo Dimension of National Cultures*, SAGE, London, 1998. For the latest research in the field, see the *Journal of Cross-Cultural Psychology*. For a review of research trends and limitations in this field, see Jüri Allik, Koorosh Massoudi, Anu Realo and Jérôme Rossier, "Personality and Culture: Cross-Cultural Psychology at the Next Crossroads", in *Swiss Journal of Psychology*, 2012, vol. 71, no. 1, p. 5–12.

[86] Hofstede and Hofstede, 2005, p. 83, see above note 85. The level of aggregation is one of the main limitations of this research: variations between persons and regions within the same State are under-represented, while data from Africa and Arab countries are aggregated at an even larger level ("Arab ctrs", "W Africa" and "E Africa").

[87] On the implications of different perceptions of hierarchy around the world, see Meyer, 2014, chap. 4 "How Much Respect Do You Want? Leadership, Hierarchy, and Power", pp. 115–42, partly based on Hofstede's research, see above note 82.

unusual group" within the overall world population, hence their perspective may not be suitable to understand many societies around the world.[88]

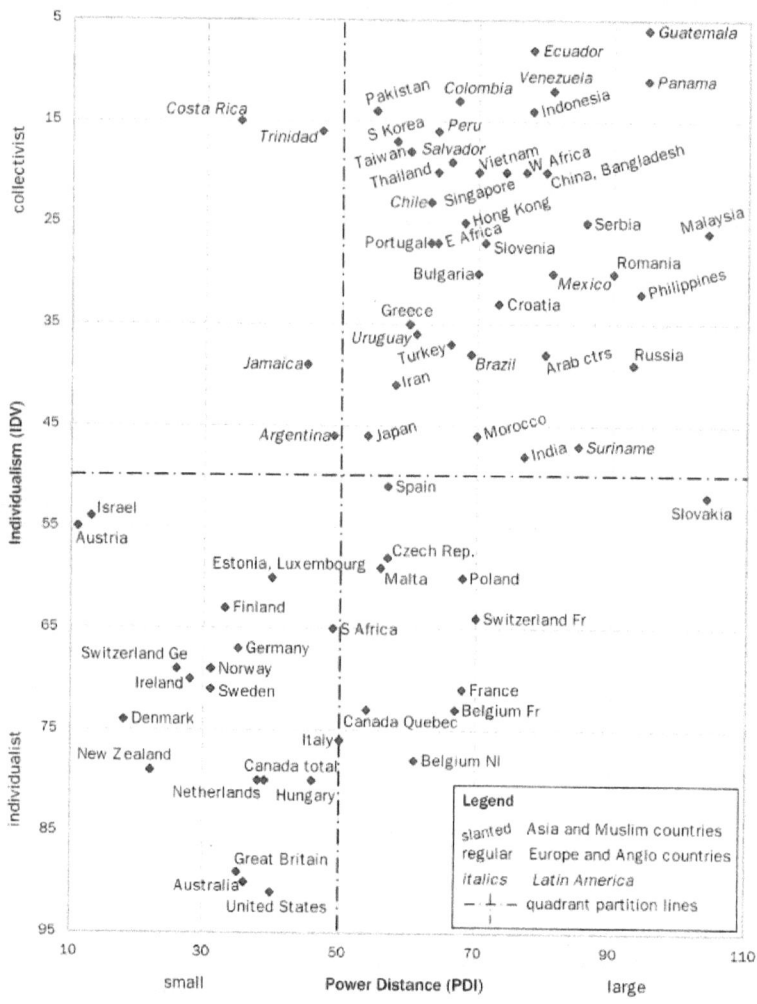

Figure 2. Correlation between power distance and individualism.

[88] Joseph Henrich, Steven J. Heine and Ara Norenzayan, "The Weirdest People in the World?", in *Behavioral and Brain Sciences*, 2010, vol. 33, nos. 2–3, p. 61. In the view of these authors, "[t]he findings suggest that members of WEIRD societies, including young children, are among the least representative populations one could find for generalizing about humans".

Remembering is a form of thinking, and people that think collectively are likely to remember the same way.[89] This is a very common cultural choice around the world, but it may conflict with the production of individualized knowledge expected by criminal procedure, particularly in Western criminal law. As mentioned above, this issue surfaced with the biography of Rigoberta Menchú Tum and the ensuing controversy, while she justified certain inaccuracies in her account because she intended to speak collectively. The ICTR addressed similar issues in its first judgment, *Akayesu*, under a brief section on "cultural factors affecting the evidence of witnesses". The judges observed, based on expert testimony, "that most Rwandans live in an oral tradition in which facts are reported as they are perceived by the witness, often irrespective of whether the facts were personally witnessed or recounted by someone else". Still the chamber found that Rwandan witnesses were capable of differentiating direct from indirect knowledge in the courtroom context, and they made a "consistent effort to ensure that this distinction was drawn throughout the trial proceedings".[90] In ICTR *Musema*, the judges echoed and cited *Akayesu* and noted:

> While there appears, as the Defence argued, to be in Rwandan culture a "tradition that the perceived knowledge of one becomes the knowledge of all", the Chamber notes that, as in other cultures, Rwandan individuals are clearly able to distinguish between what they have heard and what they have seen.[91]

The concerns with cross-cultural understanding in international procedures are legitimate, but some authors appear to emphasize differences in ways that are not loyal to the judicial record, nor consistent with the ability to truly communicate across cultures. Nancy A. Combs in particular misquotes the above lines from *Musema* in her book when discussing 'cultural divergences'. She attributes to the Trial Chamber the sentence "tradition that the perceived knowledge of one becomes the knowledge of

---

[89] See Joël Candau, *Anthropologie de la mémoire*, Presses Universitaires de France, Paris, 1996, particularly chap. V "Mémoires et amnésie(s) collectives"; and David Middleton and Derek Edwards (eds.), *Collective Remembering*, SAGE Publications, London, 1990.

[90] Akayesu Trial Judgment, para. 155, see above note 57.

[91] ICTR, *Prosecutor v. Alfred Musema*, Trial Chamber, Judgement and Sentence, 27 January 2000, ICTR-96-13-T, para. 103 ('Musema Trial Judgment and Sentence') (https://www.legal-tools.org/doc/1fc6ed/).

all", while that was not the finding of the judges, it was only the allegation of the defence that the judges actually dismissed, as quoted above from the judgment.[92] This author also fails to mention the solution that the judges adopted on this issue, which shows in the last sentence of the paragraph above; that Rwandans "are clearly able" to overcome that tradition and to distinguish between direct and indirect knowledge in the context of the proceedings.

The Special Panels for Serious Crimes in East Timor ('SPSC') encountered similar difficulties, with some witnesses failing to differentiate individual from collective knowledge in their testimonies. It appears that most SPSC judgments "largely ignore or only deal cursorily with matters impacting credibility", while a more detail evaluation can be found in *Florencio Tacaqui*, including indications of "the court's frustration at trying to sort out what witnesses actually saw and what they later decided had occurred".[93] In that case a key point was eyewitness identification of the alleged perpetrator, reported by a number of witnesses only after the suspect was arrested, which in the given context the judges attributed to "the power of collective suggestion".[94] David Cohen has explained this phenomenon as follows:

> this is a problem of traditional societies, especially in overwhelmingly oral cultures like that of East Timor, where literacy was low and Tetun, the most widely spoken indigenous language, was at the time for the most part not a written language.[95]

This observation could be seen as consistent with Hofstede's data, while Indonesia features among the highest values for authority and collectivism in his scheme.[96] Nevertheless situations of 'collective sugges-

---

[92] Nancy A. Combs, *Fact-Finding Without Facts: The Uncertain Evidentiary Foundations of International Criminal Convictions*, Cambridge University Press, 2010, p. 94.

[93] See David Cohen, "The Passage of Time, the Vagaries of Memory, and Reaching Judgment in Mass Atrocity Cases", in Morten Bergsmo and CHEAH Wui Ling (eds.), *Old Evidence and Core International Crimes*, Torkel Opsahl Academic EPublisher, Beijing, 2012, p. 18 (http://www.toaep.org/ps-pdf/16-bergsmo-cheah). Note within Cohen's chapter, Section 2.2. "Collective Memory and 'Cultural Factors'", pp. 13–22.

[94] Timor-Leste District Court of Dili, *Prosecutor v. Florencio Tacaqui*, Special Panel for the Trial of Serious Crimes, Judgement, 9 December 2004, Case No. 20/2000, p. 43 (https://www.legal-tools.org/doc/864bbe/).

[95] Cohen, 2012, p. 17, see above note 93.

[96] See Figure 2 above.

tion' or contamination are known in any society, not only in 'traditional' ones, as for example, the research by Wagenaar and others shows in The Netherlands.[97] Researchers should resist the temptation to exoticize behaviour that they find problematic.

Another relevant cultural dimension is how explicitly people communicate or not. In the so-called 'low-context cultures' explicit and direct communication is the norm, which requires limited knowledge of the context. In the 'high-context cultures', to the contrary, people avoid explicit communication and tend to use indirect or metaphorical expressions that are only understandable with proper contextual knowledge.[98] Western cultures are typically regarded as 'low-context cultures', while high-context is common in the rest of the world. High-context communication style tends to correlate with collectivistic and hierarchical values, which in turn coincides with countries suffering mass violence. Furthermore, particularly sensitive issues may lead to high-context or euphemistic expressions in any culture, out of a sense of embarrassment, fear, or respect for other persons or superiors.

ICTR judges dealt with this issue, among others, in *Musema*, when they decided not to draw "any adverse conclusions regarding the credibility of witnesses when cultural constraints appeared to induce them to answer indirectly certain questions regarded as delicate".[99] This is a valid position, in order to avoid cultural biases in the procedure, but contextual communication tends to understate the information, and it requires reconstructing the original context to be able to retrieve the message, which may be a sensitive and laborious exercise. 'High-context' communication is an *opera aperta*, as Umberto Eco would say for semiotics, a creative piece open to many interpretations.[100]

Some recent research may help for greater understanding of the rapport between local culture and international evidence. Tim Kelsall has discussed extensively cultural issues affecting litigation at the SCSL, in-

---

[97] See Willem Albert Wagenaar and Hans Crombag, *The Popular Policeman and Other Cases: Psychological Perspectives on Legal Evidence*, Amsterdam University Press, 2005, chap. 10, sect. "Collaborative storytelling", pp. 166–68.

[98] See Meyer, 2014, chap. 1 "Listening to the Air: Communicating Across Cultures", pp. 29–60, see above note 82.

[99] Musema Trial Judgment and Sentence, para. 103, see above note 91.

[100] See Umberto Eco, *Opera aperta: Forma e indeterminazione nelle poetiche contemporanee*, Bompiani, Milano, 1962.

cluding command structures, magic beliefs and credibility challenges.[101] Mark Osiel has discussed some cultural factors in relation to what he calls "Non-western military organisation".[102] Julien Seroussi, based on his unique 'participant observation' while working for the ICC Trial Chamber in *Katanga and Ngudjolo*, believes that 'international lawyers' suffer from 'structural ignorance' when dealing with evidence from cultures foreign to them.[103] Leigh Swigart has identified a number of sensitive cultural-linguistic issues after interviewing multiple ICC staff members and defence teams.[104] Perhaps languages with limited phonetic and verbal systems are ill-suited to convey the meaning of expressions in languages with richer repertoires. For example, English has an 'ergativity problem' in its inability to translate languages with ergative forms marking nouns and pronouns for transitive verbs, such as Georgian, Hindi and Basque.[105]

On the other hand, while the above-mentioned authors and others seem interested on finding differences between cultures, common elements maybe equally real and relevant. For example, to assume that conventional military hierarchies are characteristic of the global West would be misleading, actually a sign of lacking world-wide knowledge, since such systems are known in every major civilisation, at least since the times of the *Arthashastra* some twenty centuries ago.[106] Joseph Campbell has identified universal values and archetypes in his research since the 1950s.[107] Attitudes towards truth also show both universal features and

---

[101] Tim Kelsall, *Culture under Cross-Examination: International Justice and the Special Court for Sierra Leone*, Cambridge University Presss, 2009.

[102] Mark Osiel, "Ascribing Individual Liability Within a Bureaucracy of Murder", in Alette Smeulers (ed.), *Collective Violence and International Criminal Justice: An Interdisciplinary Approach*, Intersentia, Antwerp, 2010, pp. 105–30.

[103] Julien Seroussi, "How Do International Lawyers Handle Facts? The Role of Folk Sociological Theories at the International Criminal Court", in *British Journal of Sociology*, 2018, vol. 69, no. 4, pp. 962–83. See also Franck Leibovici and Julien Seroussi, *Bogoro*, Questions théoriques, Paris, 2016.

[104] Leigh Swigart, "Now You See It, Now You Don't: Culture at the International Criminal Court", in *Intersections of Law and Culture at the International Criminal Court*, forthcoming (available on ResearchGate's web site).

[105] Conley, O'Barr and Conley Riner, 2019, chap. 6, sect. "Ergativity", pp. 115–16, see above note 82.

[106] See Kautilya, 1992, sect. "Military Organisation", pp. 640–62, including regulations for "Organisational Structure", duties of commanders, and so on, see above note 44.

[107] See his classic work, Joseph Campbell, *The Hero with a Thousand Faces*, 3rd edition, New World Library, Novato, 2008.

cross-cultural variations.[108] A large body of research in psychology and anthropology has identified both commonalities and differences across cultures in relation to multiple individual and social aspects.[109]

A certain emphasis on cultural differences leads some commentators to raise doubts referring typically to Western officers and non-Western witnesses. Nancy A. Combs elaborated on issues of 'cultural divergences' in relation to witnesses from Rwanda, Sierra Leone and Timor-Leste, assuming that they would have "very different worldviews than the Western court personnel who hear their testimony. Those differences create numerous barriers to understanding and assessing witness testimony".[110] The fact is that ICTR, SCSL and the Special Panels for Timor-Leste had judges and personnel from all regions of the world, not just 'Western personnel'. Combs insists based in the precedent of *Akayesu* that Trial Chambers hear experts on the local cultures "so that they do not inappropriately assess the credibility of non-Western witnesses by Western cultural norms".[111] It is not clear how this would be consistent with *Akayesu*, since the Trial Chamber was presided by a judge from Senegal,

---

[108] For commonalities, see Charles F. Bond, Jr. and Sandhya R. Rao, "Lies Travel: Mendacity in a Mobile World", in Pär Anders Granhag and Leif A. Strömwall (eds.), *The Detection of Deception in Forensic Contexts*, Cambridge University Press, 2004, sect. "Universality", pp. 128–30. For differences, see Edward Westermarck, "The Regard for Truth and Good Faith", in *The Origin and Development of the Moral Ideas*, 2nd edition, vol. 2, McMillan, London, 1917, pp. 72–108; and Edward Westermarck, "The Regard for Truth and Good Faith (Concluded)", in *ibid.*, pp. 109–36, including multiple examples from different cultures showing apparently varying degrees of truthfulness in their social and historical context.

[109] See, for example, regarding cross-cultural commonalities and differences about causality Sieghard Beller, Andrea Bender and Michael R. Waldmann (eds.), *Diversity and Universality in Causal Cognition*, Frontiers Media, Lausanne, 2017; on emotions, see SHAO Bo, Lorna Doucet and David R. Caruso, "Universality Versus Cultural Specificity of Three Emotion Domains: Some Evidence Based on the Cascading Model of Emotional Intelligence", in *Journal of Cross-Cultural Psychology*, 2015, vol. 46, no. 2, pp. 229–51; and Hugo Mercier, "On the Universality of Argumentative Reasoning", in *Journal of Cognition and Culture*, 2011, vol. 11, nos. 1–2, pp. 85–113. I am grateful to Moa Lidén for bibliographic advice on this point.

[110] Combs, 2010, p. 81, among multiple references to Western standards in section 3.C. "Cultural Divergences", pp. 79–100, see above note 92.

[111] *Ibid.*, p. 99.

with another one from South Africa, and only the third one from a Western country (Sweden).[112]

The cultural landscape of international tribunals is more complex indeed, with different combinations of officers and witnesses across regions, multi-cultural teams within the institutions, and also often staff from anywhere in the world trained in Western universities. Besides, issues that are regarded as 'cultural differences' may have quite universal roots, such as personality traits, security concerns, socio-economic class, peer-pressure, sexual taboos and economic incentives, hence proper intersectional analysis should be more truthful, and a safeguard against stereotypes. Additional research seems necessary to explore the potential impact of cross-cultural issues, controlling for the background of the different judges and officers, and considering other concurring factors.

A related issue is suggestibility and acquiescence, because the imbalance of power or expectations between international officers and witnesses.[113] Acquiescence is understood as "the tendency of an individual to answer questions in the affirmative irrespective of the content".[114] It is known that, depending of different personality and operational factors, some witnesses may be very sensible to suggestion or tending to say what they think the investigators want to hear. For example, one empirical study showed that regarding suggestibility "Afro-Caribbean police detainees scored significantly higher than their Caucasian counterparts" after controlling for other factors.[115]

Nancy A. Combs has raised the issue of acquiescence in relation to ICTR and SCSL witnesses, under the heading of "a cultural component to perjury?", as follows: "Some interviewees contended only that Rwandan and Sierra Leonean witnesses were inclined to tailor their testimony to

---

[112] Akayesu Trial Judgment, see above note 57. Trial Chamber presided by judge Laïty Kama (Senegal), with judges Navanethem Pillay (South Africa, ICTR judge 1995–2003 and its President 1999–2003, ICC judge 2003–08 and UN High Commissioner for Human Rights 2008–14) and Lennart Aspegren (Sweden).

[113] For a pioneering study, see Alfred Binet, *La suggestibilité*, Schleisher Frères, Paris, 1900; and for an influential, more recent handbook, see Gisli H. Gudjonsson, "Suggestibility: Historical and Theoretical Aspects", in *The Psychology of Interrogations and Confessions: A Handbook*, Wiley, London, 2003, pp. 332–59; and Gisli H. Gudjonsson, "Interrogative Suggestibility: Empirical Findings", in *ibid.*, pp. 360–414.

[114] *Ibid.*, p. 376.

[115] *Ibid.*

convey what they believed the Western investigator, lawyer or judge questioning them wished to hear".[116] This approach shows three main limitations: the author ignores prior experience and research from national systems and presents the issue erroneously as characteristic of international tribunals and related to 'cultural differences', while allegedly "lying is more accepted in Rwandan and Sierra Leonean cultures";[117] the author refers to Western officers when those tribunals comprised officers from all regions of the world, including many Africans; and she relies mainly on the information from the defence teams, who have an interest on highlight any actual or hypothetical evidentiary weakness. Combs also quotes a senior ICTR-OTP officer stating that in Rwandan culture "lying is not only tolerated but sometimes encouraged":[118] this quotation is not correct, in the media article used by Combs these were not the words used by the OTP officer, they were only the words of the journalist who interviewed him.[119]

It may be the case that evaluating officers carry ethno-centric biases, tending to give greater credibility to persons that are culturally closer to them. Some research on asylum procedures in the Netherlands indicates that "there seems to be a relation between ethnicity and credibility", based on a comparison between the evaluation of asylum seekers from different countries, particularly Bosnia and DRC:

> Bosnians were often not asked about their flight motives apparently because they were considered self-evident. When Bosnian applicants were interviewed, credibility was not raised. In Zairian cases, incredibility is routinely invoked against applicants; in 23 or the 37 Zairian cases in the sample, credibility was a central argument given for rejecting the claim.[120]

---

[116] Combs, 2010, p. 131, see above note 92.

[117] *Ibid.*, p. 131, quoting five interviewees (see fn. 576), four of them from the defence and one from the prosecution, including Howard Morrison (UK, formerly defence counsel in ICTR and ICTY, then judge at the ICC), Peter Robinson (USA, defence counsel at ICTR, ICTY, SCSL and ICC), and Michiel Pestman (The Netherlands, defence counsel at SCSL and ECCC).

[118] *Ibid.*, p. 131, fn. 577; citing Karen Palmer, "It's a Lying Shame", *South China Morning Post*, 22 March 2006 (available on its web site).

[119] See *ibid.*

[120] Thomas Spijkerboer, "Stereotyping and Acceleration: Gender, Procedural Acceleration and Marginalised Judicial Review in the Dutch Asylum System", in Gregor Noll (ed.), *Proof,*

The researchers found some indications of "generally negative attitude towards Zairian applicants" and some "incredulous attitude" among interviewing officers, who considered Bosnians as most credible, Congolese as the least credible, and others in between (from Turkey, Iran, China and Sri Lanka in the given sample).[121] The same research found that the Dutch immigration officers tended to perceive the violence in the Bosnian accounts as systematic and the violence in the accounts from the DRC and other countries as random, a difference not necessarily granted by the available information.[122] This comparatively more restrictive standards for DRC people may have been related to multiple issues, from the availability of contextual information (the average Dutch person would have been much more exposed to information about Bosnia than about the DRC) to cultural distance, language issues or merely 'sloppiness'.[123] It appears however that credibility and the perception on alleged violence "are constructed in part by gendered and ethnic notions" in a way that may call for intersectional analysis:

> They [notions of gender and ethnicity in place] do not work per se against women. They work to the benefit of women who succeeded in fitting the mould, and to the detriment of women who don't. It seems that for Zairian women it was particularly difficult (but not impossible) to do so, and for Bosnian women it was relatively easy. However, the use of (sometimes blatant) stereotypes turns out to be crucial in fact finding, credibility assessments and deciding what has been proven.[124]

The above-mentioned research, including the comparison between the evaluation of accounts from Bosnia and the DRC, suggests a hypothesis of 'ethno-centric bias' that may be worth exploring in relation to the

---

Evidentiary Assessment and Credibility in Asylum Procedures, Martinus Nijhoff Publishers, Leiden, 2005, p. 82. Researcher based on the analysis of the relevant interview records and reports.

[121] *Ibid.*

[122] *Ibid.*, p. 88.

[123] *Ibid.*, p. 82. The author mentions particularly language and translation issues, and procedural "sloppiness", as main causal factors.

[124] *Ibid.*, p. 88.

---

evaluation of DRC witnesses and alleged patterns by some ICC judges,[125] and in comparison with the ICTY.

Issues like eventual suggestibility, acquiescence or perjury need to be assessed on an *ad hoc* basis, taking into account multiple concurring factors, and considering equally elements of resilience and incentives for veracity, otherwise the analysis may easily lead to stereotypes and unreasonable discredit of any and all witnesses, from all parties.[126]

3.2.2.2.1. Advice

a) Training on implicit biases and cross-cultural communication, and use of tools to raise awareness about cultural biases;[127]

b) serious background analysis and preparation on the given situation prior to the contact and collection of any source;

c) hiring or consultation with area experts, local staff and translators; and

d) multi-cultural team composition to combine different perspectives.

3.2.2.3. Other Personal Biases

The officer(s) in charge of the evaluation may carry personal biases due to various other issues, including gender, social extraction, professional background or ideology, as well as confirmation bias.

Gender assumptions may condition the perception of the source and the information in relation to all relevant issues, from the substantive gravity of the crime, to various elements of credibility. For example, it

---

[125] See below Section 3.2.5.

[126] For a more rigorous approach to the issue, see Bond Jr. and Rao, 2004, sects. "Cross-Cultural Variation", "Worldwide Beliefs About Deception", and "Cross-Cultural Deceptions", see above note 108.

[127] See, for example, the Implicit Association Test ('IAT'), on the web site of Project Implicit, with different tests available in relation various race, religion and gender issues. Economic issues are not considered in the IAT, which is conceived from a US perspective. There are different views about the scientific validity of the IAT, but at least it may help to raise awareness on unconscious biases, which is why I have recommended it over the years to my staff and members of recruitment panels. For a discussion on the limited predictive validity of the IAT, significantly conditioned by social expectations just like any self-reporting exercise, see Anthony G. Greenwald, T. Andrew Poehlman, Eric Luis Uhlmann and Mahzarin R. Banaji, "Understanding and Using the Implicit Association Test: III. Meta-Analysis of Predictive Validity", in *Journal of Personality and Social Psychology*, 2009, vol. 97, no. 1, pp. 17–41.

may happen that male sources dismiss crimes involving male perpetrators of sexual assault, because of some conscious or unconscious association with the perpetrator or a sense of embarrassment. Other combinations and factors may also be conducive to different kinds of gender biases.

Prejudice against women's testimony is known from a number of classic works. John Henry Wigmore, probably the single most influential authority on the law of evidence in the US, noted in his *Principles of Judicial Proof* that "woman does not reason and infer" and "objectivity is another property that women lack".[128] He also states, without any reference to scientific sources or reasoning, that "[d]ishonesty is, however, a especially feminine characteristic; in men it occurs only when they are effeminate".[129] F. Gorphe warned against female witnesses in *La critique du Témoignage* because women would lie more often and more effectively than men:

> Les femmes, par des considérations de pudeur, ont davantage l'habitude de cacher, et, pour des raisons de faiblesse physique et de subordination sociale, elles ont davantage recours à la tromperie. Aussi est-il généralement plus difficile de découvrir leurs mensonges habilement et audacieusement présentés, sans souci de la vérité ni de la justice.[130]

This prejudice against women is likely to persist in patriarchal societies, to the extent that credibility correlates with social status. From a viewpoint of socio-linguistics this problem has been fully exposed by Robin Lakoff in her influential study *Language and Woman's Place*.[131] Other authors have brought this linguistic analysis to the legal field and found that for cultural reasons "women project deference and uncertainty" and their "language style did indeed influence the credibility of their testimony".[132] The testing of Lakoff's observations in experimental settings

---

[128] John Henry Wigmore, *The Principles of Judicial Proof: As Given by Logic, Psychology, and General Experience, and Illustrated in Judicial Trials*, Little, Brown, and Company, Boston, 1913, p. 341.

[129] *Ibid.*, p. 343.

[130] François Gorphe, *La critique du Témoignage*, Librairie Dalloz, Paris, 1924, p. 165.

[131] Robin Tolmach Lakoff, in Mary Bucholtz (ed.), *Language and Woman's Place: Text and Commentaries*, revised and expanded edition, Oxford University Press, 2004 (original from 1975). See also Leigh Gilmore, *Tainted Witness: Why We Doubt What Women Say About Their Lives*, Columbia University Press, New York, 2017.

[132] Conley, O'Barr and Conley Riner, 2019, chap. 4 "Speaking of Patriarchy", p. 67, see above note 82.

has led to the conclusion that a kind of 'powerless language' is "associated primarily with the speaker's status in society", and in certain societies "most women, most of the time, were speaking in a style that the legal system devaluated; men, by and large, did not suffer this disadvantage".[133] Such gender bias may have deeper implications in those societies in which the law carries "a preference for a characteristically male epistemology" favoring typically male assertiveness and 'rule-oriented accounts', in detriment of more realistic 'relational accounts' usually expressed by women.[134] Hence some experts have concluded that "the law displays a deep gender bias in the way it performs such basic tasks as judging credibility and defining narrative coherence".[135]

The record of the trial testimonies in different international tribunals shows a large majority of male witnesses, approximately some 80 per cent. This is likely to result from both underlying social factors (higher visibility, availability and trust on men in patriarchal societies) and operational factors related to the investigations and prosecutions (including reliance on insider and expert witnesses, most often male), all of which requires additional research.[136] Among many efforts in this area around the world, for example, the Supreme Court of Mexico issued in 2013 comprehensive guidelines to include gender perspective in the evaluation of evidence and other procedural requirements.[137]

Concerning political, religious or ethnic ideology, experience indicates that the background of the investigating officers may easily influence the evaluation of sources. A number of examples could be mentioned

---

[133] *Ibid.*

[134] *Ibid.*, p. 77.

[135] *Ibid.*, p. 4. See also Deborah Epstein and Lisa A. Goodman, "Discounting Women: Doubting Domestic Violence Survivors' Credibility and Dismissing Their Experiences", in *University of Pennsylvania Law Review*, 2019, vol. 167, no. 2, p. 399–461; and Deborah Tuerkheimer, "Incredible Women: Sexual Violence and the Credibility Discount", in *University of Pennsylvania Law Review*, 2017, vol. 166, no. 1, p. 1–58.

[136] Data and analysis produced by Investigative Analysis Section (IAS) as part of a Gender Analysis project supported by UN Women. Similarly, Nancy Amoury Combs found 74.5 per cent of male witnesses in a sample of 342 witnesses from 19 ICTR cases, see See Nancy A. Combs, "Grave Crimes and Weak Evidence: A Fact-Finding Evolution in International Criminal Law", in *Harvard International Law Journal*, 2017, vol. 58, no. 1, p. 65.

[137] Mexico Suprema Corte de Justicia de la Nación, *Protocolo para Juzgar con Perspectiva de Género: Haciendo Realidad el Derecho a la Igualdad*, Mexico City, 2013, further to the work of the Unidad de Igualdad de Género established in 2008.

in relation to left-right political conflict in Latin America, as well as religious and ethnic cleavages in any region of the world.

Concerning professional background (police, humanitarian, military, NGOs, legal, and so on), the evaluating officer may perceive more positively persons with similar backgrounds, which may contribute to overestimate their credibility. The opposite negative effect can equally take place, with under-estimation across different backgrounds.

Confirmation bias arises if the officer(s) in charge of evaluating the source are driven, consciously or not, by an interest to corroborate allegations, hypotheses or charges, which may lead to look for and accept corroborating information and to exclude systematically conflicting information. This is a rather frequent problem for all parties in the procedure, including particularly in suspect-driven investigations, and under the pressure of adversarial litigation. I identified this problem from the outset of my work at the ICC-OTP, and I included specific references to it in different analytical protocols. I remain concerned with this cognitive problem, which is why we invited Dr. Lidén to join the New Delhi conference on which this book is initially based, and I defer to her expertise for this matter.[138]

3.2.2.3.1. Advice

Officers involved in investigations and Source Evaluation must conduct some 'self-evaluation', on their own or preferably with the advice of others, to anticipate which aspects of their background may carry relevant biases and affect the evaluation of the source. As it has been observed by experienced officers, in the same way that psychoanalysts need to be psychoanalyzed themselves as a requirement to start practicing, in criminal investigations officers need to subject themselves to analysis in relation to their potential biases.[139]

---

[138] Moa Lidén, "Confirmation Bias in Investigations of Core International Crimes: Risk Factors and Quality Control Techniques", Chap. 7 below.

[139] See Richards J. Heuer, Jr., *The Psychology of Intelligence Analysis*, Center for the Study of Intelligence, 1999. For advice regarding confirmation bias, see Moa Lidén, "Confirmation Bias in Investigations of Core International Crimes: Risk Factors and Quality Control Techniques", Chap. 7 below.

3.2.2.4. Insider Witness Issues

Witnesses with internal knowledge of the criminal groups are usually referred to in investigative practice as 'insider witnesses', including most often active members of the group and perpetrators, but also possibly persons that happened to gain such knowledge by virtue of their work or persistent victimisation. Insiders have always been important in the investigation of crimes involving multiple perpetrators, examples abound from cases of organized crime, terrorism and surely core international crimes. The ICTY-OTP identified from an early stage the need to foster cooperation with insiders, which shows in its Regulation no. 1 on the "Prosecutor's Policy on *Nolle Prosequi* of Accomplices". By 2006, ICTY Prosecutor Carla del Ponte advised: "Insiders can and must be used in complex criminal cases because proof of a complex criminal enterprise and its leadership can otherwise be extremely difficult and time/resource consuming".[140]

Insiders and suspects may cause a certain fascination because of the high value of their evidence. Hans Gross already warned about the difficulties with insiders and suspects in his handbook, referring to persons who perhaps "are afraid of being suspected of being themselves the perpetrators, or that they are conscious of negligence which may have facilitated the perpetration, or that they may be considered as abettors or accessories of the accused, & c.".[141] His advice for this kind of witness remains relevant today:

> the witnesses will, despite their best intention to speak the truth, fashion it the way apparently most useful to themselves. They will rely on certain details, they will slur over others, they will arrange the various incidents in a new manner, and if the Investigating Officer examines attentively all the depositions he will recognize the existence of a group of persons deposing inaccurately; the group of frightened people, always imagining themselves suspected and constantly shuffling.[142]

---

[140] Carla Del Ponte, "Investigation and Prosecution of Large-scale Crimes at the International Level: The Experience of the ICTY", in *Journal of International Criminal Justice*, 2006, vol. 4, no. 3, p. 546.

[141] Gross, 1906, p. 89, see above note 41.

[142] *Ibid.*

The officer(s) in charge of collecting the evidence may involve themselves personally in the process in ways that affect their objectivity. Some research indicates that when comparing evaluations conducted by interviewers and observers, "the observers were more accurate in their assessment of the target than were those who engaged in the conversation".[143] Operational experience also suggests that trusting the evaluation only to the same officer that carried out the interview or collection may cause over-rating. This can be explained as cognitive dissonance, that is, an interpretation of the reality biased towards justifying our prior actions and decisions.[144]

3.2.2.4.1.   Example: Rudolf Höss, SS Auschwitz Commander

The officers that conducted the first interrogation of Rudolf Höss, a psychologist and a lawyer, praised his 'frank answers' and evaluated that "his statements were generally true".[145] They spent very long time with him and took upon themselves to learn about his whole life, including happy childhood memories, and to record not only his statement about the alleged crimes, but also his whole biography. Subsequent research proved that Höss had been fairly truthful about the crime as such, but he had lied about his own role. Among other issues, Höss never mentioned Eleonore Hodys, the prisoner with whom he had sex, and once she got pregnant was put in an isolation cell to die of starvation.[146] It appears that the interviewers failed to distance themselves sufficiently from the interviewee,

---

[143]   Saul Kassin, "True or False: 'I'd Know a False Confession If I Saw One'", in Pär Anders Granhag and Leif A. Strömwall (eds.), *The Detection of Deception in Forensic Contexts*, Cambridge University Press, 2004, p. 176.

[144]   On cognitive dissonance associated to confirmation bias, see Moa Lidén, *Confirmation Bias in Criminal Cases*, Uppsala University, Uppsala, 2018, pp. 189 and 191; and Carol Travis and Elliot Aronson, *Mistakes Were Made (But Not by Me): Why We Justify Foolish Beliefs, Bad Decisions, and Hurtful Acts*, Harvest, Orlando, 2007, particularly chap. 1 "Cognitive Dissonance: The Engine of Self-Justification" and chap. 5 "Law and Disorder".

[145]   Jerzy Rawicz, "Foreword", in Rudolf Höss, Pery Broad and Johann Paul Kremer, *KL Auschwitz Seen by the SS*, Publications of Państwowe Muzeum Oświęcimiu, Auschwitz, 1978, p. 16.

[146]   On Eleonore Hodys, see the book by Herlinde Pauer-Studer and J. David Velleman, "Rudolf Höss and Eleonore Hodys", in *Konrad Morgen: The Conscience of a Nazi Judge*, Palgrave Macmillan, London, 2015.

and that they "did not manage to avoid a certain overestimation of the allegedly absolute credibility of his reminiscences".[147]

3.2.2.4.2. Example: Mafia Insiders

Italian investigators and judges have interviewed hundreds of insiders, commonly known as *pentiti*, over the last forty years, after the legal and investigative measures adopted in the 1980s for cases of terrorism and organized crime.[148] In any given year around 1,000 *pentiti* from different groups may be under the national witness protection programme.[149]

Tommaso Buscetta is perhaps the single most influential one among them. The late judge Giovanni Falcone, who interviewed him extensively, explained how Buscetta provided with multiple details on the Sicilian mafia, "[b]ut above everything he gave a global vision, ample, far-reaching of the phenomenon [the mafia]. He gave an essential key for reading, a language, a code", so that Buscetta allowed Falcone to see "il carattere unitario de la Cosa Nostra", as a unified hierarchy.[150] This 'uni-

---

[147] Jerzy Rawicz, 1978, p. 17, see above note 145.

[148] See Italy, Misure per la difesa dell'ordinamento costituzionale, 29 May 1982, Law no. 304, conceived originally for terrorism cases, then used extensively also for organised crime, including Article 3 granting attenuation for accused "in case of co-operation" (https://www.legal-tools.org/doc/xzzva7/). For an analysis of the history and investigative practice with the *pentiti*, see Gruppo Abele, *Dalla mafia allo Stato: I pentiti: analisi e storie*, EGA Editore, Torino, 2005. For a compilation of Italian authors (mainly Sicilian, University of Palermo professors), see Alessandra Dino (ed.), *Pentiti: I collaboratori di giustizia, le istituzioni, l'opinione pubblica*, Donzelli Editore, Rome, 2006. For analysis techniques in Italy, see Tiziana Montefusco, *L'analisi di contesto per la lotta al crimine*, Laurus Robuffo, Rome, 2007; and Ultimo (pseudonym), *La lotta anticrimine: Intelligence e azione*, Laurus Robuffo, Rome, 2006. For the legal framework, see Salvatore Aleo, *Sistema penale e criminalità organizzata: Le figure delittuose associative*, Giuffrè Editore, Milan, 2005.

[149] See figures for the period 1994-2002 in Abele, 2005, p. 134, Graph "Grafico 1. Numero totale de pentiti (1994-2002)", in a range from 899 (1994) to 1214 (1996), see above note 148. In 2016, the Italian Ministry of Interior (Ministero dell'Interno) reported to the parliament having 1277 "justice collaborators" under the protection programme: see Michele Ciervo, "Protezione testimoni e collaboratori di giustizia, Minniti: "I minori sono la priorità da tutelare"", *Ministero dell'Interno*, 11 December 2018 (available on its web site).

[150] Giovanni Falcone, *Cose di Cosa Nostra*, RCS Libri, Milano, 1998, p. 41. First published in 1991, based on interviews with the journalist Marcelle Padovani conducted in 1987. The mafia killed Falcone on 23 May 1992. For Buscetta's account, see Saverio Lodato, *La Mafia ha vinto: Intervista con Tommaso Buscetta*, Mondadori, Milano, 2017. For the memoirs of one of the judges that ruled over related cases, see Pietro Grasso, *Storie di sangue, amici e fantasmi: Ricordo di mafia*, Feltrinelli, Milano, 2017, including his hom-

tarian theory', referred by some observers critically as 'il teorema Buscetta', was confirmed in the judgment of the Maxi Trial in 1987 and further by the Italian Supreme Court in 1992.[151] As one of the judges of the Maxi Trial would say, thanks to Falcone "[f]rom that point on, for the other judges everything became easier because it was enough to prove the belonging in the mafia association", and it was accepted that "the full use of the justice collaborators, equated with trial witnesses, unlike in the past, when they were simple police informants inefficient for the purpose of evidence, and the myth of the impunity for Mafiosi is definitely broken".[152]

Nevertheless, there are different views among researchers and judges about this unified vision of the mafia, as well as the credibility of the insiders who supported it. By the late nineteenth century, a senior police officer assessed based on his investigative experience that considering the Sicilian mafia as a unified group would be a "gravissimo errore".[153] A

---

age to Falcone (chap. 1 "Caro Giovanni", pp. 8–14) and chap. 7 on the *pentiti* (pp. 68–84). For an anthropological assessment, see Deborah Puccio-Den, "L'ethnologue et le juge: L'enquête de Giovanni Falcone sur la mafia en Sicile", in *Ethnologie française*, 2001, vol. 37, no. 1, pp. 15–27. For his methodological approach, with an emphasis on financial investigations, see Giovanni Falcone and Giuliano Turone, "Tecniche di indagine in materia di mafia", in *Rivista di Studi e Ricerche Sulla Criminalità Organizzata*, 2015, vol. 1, no. 1, pp. 116–53 (paper delivered in June 1982). The co-author Giuliano Turone, investigating judge from Milano known for his role in high-profile corruption cases, and colleague of Gherado Colombo, would become later Senior Trial Lawyer in the ICTY-OTP, acting particularly in *Delalic et al.* For Turone on the ICC, see Giuliano Turone, "Powers and Duties of the Prosecutor", in Antonio Cassese, Paola Gaeta and John R.W.D. Jones (eds.), *The Rome Statute of the International Criminal Court: A Commentary*, Oxford University Press, 2002. For a highly qualified and comprehensive study of contemporary legal history, see Giuliano Turone, *Italia occulta: Dal delitto Moro alla strage di Bologna: Il triennio maledetto che sconvolse la Repubblica (1978-1980)*, Chiarelettere, Milano, 2019, including chaps. 5 and 6 about the alleged links of Giulio Andreotti with the mafia and chap. 11 on Falcone's investigations.

[151] The so-called Maxi Trial (*maxiprocesso*) included 475 accused, with Buscetta as the main witness for the prosecution, starting in 1986 and concluding after appeals in last instance with the judgment of the Supreme Court of 30 January 1992. See Salvatore Lupo, *1986: Il maxiprocesso*, Editori Laterza, Rome, 2008, and Sarah Mazzenzana, "Il maxiprocesso di Palermo", in *Rivista di Studi e Ricerche Sulla Criminalità Organizzata*, 2016, vol. 2, no. 1, pp.117–69.

[152] Grasso, 2017, p. 35, see above note 150.

[153] Antonino Cutrera, *La mafia e i mafiosi: Origini e manifestazioni*, Alberto Reber, Palermo, 1900, p. 127:

---

number of researchers have reached similar conclusions, considering the mafia merely a series of autonomous local gangs with a common culture and methods.[154] Charles Tilly noted in 1974: "Sicily has never had any single organization one could properly call The Mafia. The Mafia supergang is a simplifying fiction".[155] Henner Hess warns that "Mafia is neither an organisation nor a secret society, but a method" and "[t]here are organisations, but not 'the organisation'".[156] Maurizio Catino proposes a more complex interpretation, with different degrees of centralization depending on periods, activities and regions.[157] In 1984 the expert on organized crime Pino Arlacchi discussed the issue with Falcone, advised him that "the scientific literature on the issue, in Italy and the US, is virtually unanimous in excluding the existence of the 'mafia' intense in these terms", and warned him "to be alert with his 'sources', who were perhaps more cunning than what he thought".[158] By 1991 Arlacchi changed his views after the revelations by Buscetta and other insiders and acknowledged

---

Trattandose adunque di associazione di malfatori autonome, indipendenti, non legate da vincoli di commune responsabilità o complicità, esse non possono costiture un'unica e grande associazione. Se questa fosse vera, con conseguenza ne sarebbe che la mafia di tutta l'isola altro non sarebbe che un'inmmensa associazione a delinquere; allora avrebbero pienamente ragione coloro che nella mafia hanno vista una vasta associazione segreta: e il ritener questo sarebbe un gravissimo errore.

[154] Among others, see Judith Chubb, *The Mafia and Politics: The Italian State Under Siege*, Cornell University Press, Ithaca, 1989; Henner Hess, *Mafia and Mafiosi: Origin, Power and Myth*, C. Hurst & Co., London, 1998; Letizia Paoli, *Mafia Brotherhoods: Organized Crime, Italian Style*, Oxford University Press, 2008; and Maurizio Catino, *Mafia Organizations: The Visible Hand of Criminal Enterprise*, Cambridge University Press, 2019.

[155] Charles Tilly, "Foreword", in Anton Blok, *The Mafia of a Sicilian Village, 1860-1960: A Study of Violent Peasant Entrepreneurs*, Waveland Press, Prospect Heights, 1974, p. xiv.

[156] Hess, 1998, pp. 132 and 191, see above note 154. Pietro Grasso, one of the judges of the Maxi Trial, refers to Hess and his theories and claims that Falcone proved him wrong through the Maxi Trial:

[I]t should not be overlooked that, until then, the most widespread book on the mafia theme had been that of the sociologist Henner Hess, according to which the mafia was a subculture inherent in the soul of the Sicilians, while for others it was a set of criminal gangs not connected to each other, or the result of a romantic reality borrowed from the film The Godfather.

See Grasso, 2017, p. 35, original in Italian, see above note 150.

[157] Catino, 2019, sect. 3.1.1 "The Sicilian Cosa Nostra", pp. 153–60, see above note 154.

[158] Pino Arlacchi, *Addio Cosa Nostra: I segreti della mafia nella confessione di Tommaso Buscetta*, Biblioteca Universale Rizzoli, Milan, 1994, p. vii. Arlacchi advised Falcone and the Italian government on related issues, and in 1997 was appointed Executive Director of the UN Office on Drugs and Crime ('UNODC').

Falcone's findings.[159] The issue has been indeed extensively discussed in Italy at all levels of social research, litigation and legal doctrine.

Some observers refer to 'il innamoramento del pentito' to question the reliance on such insider witnesses by prosecutors, a critique favoured often by the accused and their counsel.[160] The prosecutors would respond that there is no alternative to the insider evidence, or as an Italian prosecutor would explain:

> You have to understand that the so-called pentiti represent a strategy for us that is irreplaceable. [...] Hearing them is like a little load of explosives in a wall of stone, or marble. It creates an opening for us to excavate inside. This is why the judges are enamored of them.[161]

In any event, Falcone did emphasize that their testimony was "only one of many means", to be subject to "critical examination", "rigorously" with "wisdom and caution".[162] Even Buscetta himself advised that he needed to be corroborated: "The word of a *pentito* is never cast gold. Investigators must verify whether the facts told are the truth. This is the correct way to use *pentiti* and not to destroy their statements".[163]

A different aspect of the debate concerns the links to higher political levels. The testimony of Buscetta and other *pentiti* led to numerous con-

---

[159] *Ibid.*, p. ix.

[160] See Fernando Díaz Cantón, "Breves notas críticas sobre la figura del 'arrepentido'", in *Pensar en Derecho*, 2018, no. 13, sect. V "El peligro de la sobrevaloración probatoria de las manifestaciones del arrepentido", p. 26 (available on Facultad de Derecho, Universidad de Buenos Aires' web site).

[161] Jance C. Schneider and Peter T. Schneider, *Reversible Destiny: Mafia, Antimafia and the Struggle for Palermo*, University of California Press, Oakland, 2003, sect. "The Justice Collaborators as Flash Points", p. 135.

[162] Falcone as quoted in Abele, 2005, p. 75, see above note 148:

> Falcone sosteneva l'importanza del 'vaglio critico' delle dichiarazione dei pentiti che doveva essere particolarmente 'rigoroso', condotto con 'saggeza e oculatezza', senza mai trascurare la ricerca di riscontri obiettivi [...] La dichiarazione del pentito 'è solo uno dei tanti mezzi' di cui dispone il magistrato inquirente.

[163] Interview with Tommaso Buscetta by Liana Milella, "Di Andreotti non parlerei più", *La Repubblica*, 24 October 1999 (available on its web site). Buscetta was interviewed in the US, where he was in a witness protection program, shortly after Andreotti's first acquittal for alleged complicity in the murder of journalist Mino (Carmine) Pecorelli.

victions of gangsters, but when they implicated former prime minister Giulio Andreotti the cases resulted in acquittal.[164]

The Italian authorities faced similar difficulties with the investigations and trials about the Neapolitan *camorra*. It appears that in the initial stages of proceeding and trials in 1983–86 the judges "relied excessively on the *pentiti*'s testimony and allowed them great latitude, frequently uncritically accepting their claims", while by 1986:

> The appellate judges' careful and more antagonistic scrutiny revealed many distortions and lies in the *pentiti*'s previous testimonies, with the result that the verdicts of the first set of trials were almost completely overturned.[165]

The appellate judges, "followed three fundamental factors in deciding the credibility of the *pentiti*: consistency, good knowledge of details, and ability to provide contextual embedding for their testimony", while "hard evidence [*riscontri oggettivi*] became to be seen as the only possible way to determine the pentito's credibility".[166] Some cases of terrorism from the 1970s had also showed difficulties with the *pentiti* evidence, such as the case against some leaders of *Lotta Continua*, convicted and acquitted in different instances based on the testimony of a single *pentito*.[167]

The perception of the *pentiti* evolved over time. In the 1980s they were increasingly valued, as there was a sense of urgency to confront the escalation in mafia violence and Falcone and other judges showed im-

---

[164] Buscetta and other *pentiti* alleged that Andreotti was knowingly associated with local Sicilian politicians of his party who were part of the mafia. These allegations led to two trials, one with charges of mafia association and the second one about the murder of the journalist Mino Pecorelli. In both cases Andreotti was acquitted in 1999, as the defence counsel succeeded to discredit the *pentiti* evidence. For the murder of Pecorelli, Andreotti was first acquitted (1999), then convicted (2002) and finally acquitted in last instance (2003). See the records of judgements and hearings for both cases at the web site of Archivio Antimafia. For an analysis of the Andreotti cases, see Salvatore Lupo, *Storia della maffia: dalle originia ai giorni nostri*, Donzelli, Rome, 1993, pp. 302–11.

[165] See Marco Jacquemet, *Credibility in Court: Communicative Practices in the Camorra Trials*, Cambridge University Press, 1996, p. 6. See also Felia Allum, "Pentiti di camorra", in Alessandra Dino (ed.), *Pentiti: I collaboratori di giustizia, le istituzioni, l'opinione pubblica*, Donzelli Editore, Rome, 2006, pp. 185–205.

[166] Jacquemet, 1996, p. 184, see above note 165.

[167] For a detailed critical review of the case against the leaders of *Lotta Continua*, see Carlo Ginzburg, *The Judge and the Historian: Marginal Notes on a Late-Twentieth-Century Miscarriage of Justice*, Verso, London, 1999 (original in Italian 1991).

portant results. This trend led to the approval in 1991 of a law establishing a new system for witness protection, which facilitated crucially insider co-operation.[168] Towards the late 1990s the climate grew more sceptical, when the level of violence decreased and the problems with insider evidence showed in different procedures, including the two acquittals of Andreotti in 1999. The Italian parliament reacted modifying the Law 82/1991 and approving, after four years of intense debate, a new law in 2001 to impose more restrictive regulations in the acceptance and protection of *pentiti*.[169] The new restrictions included a time limit of 180 days after the expression of the intention to co-operate, for the *pentito* to state the relevant evidence, in order to avoid the so-called 'instalment declarations' used in some cases by the witnesses to bargain or to manipulate the investigation.[170] Many judges and prosecutors were disappointed with these restrictions or, as the former Maxi Trial judge Pietro Grasso stated,

---

[168] Italy, Conversione in legge, con modificazioni, del decreto-legge 15 gennaio 1991, n. 8, recante nuove misure in materia di sequestri di persona a scopo di estorsione e per la protezione di coloro che collaborano con la giustizia (based on the law decree no. 8 of 15 January 1991, new rules on kidnappings for the purpose of extortion and for the protection of witnesses of justice, as well as for the protection and sanctioning of those who collaborate with justice), 15 March 1991, Law no. 82 (https://www.legal-tools.org/doc/vj77ee/).

[169] Italy, Modifica della disciplina della protezione e del trattamento sanzionatorio di coloro che collaborano con la giustizia nonche' disposizioni a favore delle persone che prestano testimonianza [Modification of the discipline of protection and sanctioning of those who collaborate with justice as well as provisions in favor of people who testify], 13 February 2001, Law no. 45 ('Law no. 45 of 2001') (https://www.legal-tools.org/doc/631z2v/). On this evolution from 1991 to 2001, see the interview with the Director of the Division of Justice Collaborators in the Central Protection Office, Colonel R. Scuzzarello conducted in 2002, "Aspetti evolutivi del servizio centrale de protezione: dalla lege del 1991 a quella riforma del 2001", in Abele, 2005, pp. 535–37, see above note 148.

[170] Law no. 45 of 2001, Article 14-1, see above note 169:

[L]a persona che ha manifestato la volonta' di collaborare rende al procuratore della Repubblica, entro il termine di centottanta giorni dalla suddetta manifestazione di volonta', tutte le notizie in suo possesso utili alla ricostruzione dei fatti e delle circostanze sui quali e' interrogato nonche' degli altri fatti di maggiore gravita' ed allarme sociale di cui e' a conoscenza oltre che alla individuazione e alla cattura dei loro autori ed altresi' le informazioni necessarie perche' possa procedersi alla individuazione, al sequestro e alla confisca del denaro, dei beni e di ogni altra utilita' dei quali essa stessa o, con riferimento ai dati a sua conoscenza, altri appartenenti a gruppi criminali dispongono direttamente o indirettamente.

the new law was not conducive to generate insider witnesses, and "[i]f I were a Mafioso, I would not co-operate".[171]

Much like in the abovementioned Italian cases, insider evidence was a major difficulty in the ICC investigations in Kenya. The cases relied on a limited number of insiders that had inspired the investigations through their 'theorems', and once those insiders were not available anymore as the result of serious threats and attacks, the cases were not sustainable.[172] Insiders are often high-maintenance witnesses, like some *pentiti* regarded as 'collaborante in evoluzione' or 'pentito in osservazione' as their commitment and truthfulness may evolve over time depending on various factors, including security.[173] In *Ruto and Sang*, for example, after serious threats upon them and their relatives, key insider witnesses for the prosecution recanted the evidence given during the investigation and "testified that they had deliberately implicated the Accused falsely, partly motivated by material gains, including relocation abroad".[174]

The scenario in the Kenyan cases resembles the experience in mafia cases, since "[t]he typical end of any trial of a *mafioso*, acquittal for lack of evidence" follows among other factor from the fact that "incriminating testimony is sometimes given in the preliminary investigation, but this as a rule is later retracted".[175] The same problems are common in cases of terrorism, also due to pressure and threats on insider and co-accused wit-

---

[171] Felice Cavallaro, interview with Pietro Grasso, "Allarme del magistrato sulla lotta a Cosa Nostra: con le nuove regole, a parità di condizioni, è meglio fare l'imputato: "Se fossi un mafioso non mi pentirei": Il procuratore di Palermo Grasso: legge cambiata, ora non conviene più collaborare con lo Stato", *Corriere della Sera*, 18 March 2001.

[172] See ICC-OTP, "Annex 1: ICC OTP Kenya Cases: Review and Recommendations: Executive Summary of the Report of the External Independent Experts", in "Full Statement of the Prosecutor, Fatou Bensouda, on external expert review and lessons drawn from the Kenya situation", 26 November 2019, paras. E.19 and E.20 ('Kenya Cases: Review and Recommendations: Executive Summary of the Report of the External Independent Experts') (https://www.legal-tools.org/doc/32p2hy/).

[173] Abele, 2005, p. 90, see above note 148.

[174] ICC, Situation in the Republic of Kenya, *The Prosecutor v. William Samoei Ruto and Joshua Arap Sang*, Trial Chamber, Lesser Public Redacted Version of Decision on Joint Defence Application for Further Prosecution Investigation Concerning the Asylum Application Records of Certain Prosecution Witnesses, 11 December 2017, ICC-01/09-01/11-1655-Red2, para. 2 (https://www.legal-tools.org/doc/7b843a/).

[175] Hess, 1998, p. 142, see above note 154.

nesses.[176] In the Kenyan cases the prosecution found those 'insider theorems' credible and consistent with other evidence, whether they were true should have been determined through the trials and due process. The extent of the witness tampering and threats against Kenyan insider witnesses shows in the investigations conducted by the OTP under Article 70 and the corresponding warrants of arrest issued by the ICC judges in 2013 and 2015.[177]

3.2.2.4.3. Advice

Thorough handling and evaluation of insider witnesses is fundamental for international investigations, including:

a) extensive preparation and background analysis prior to the interviews;

b) emphasis on verification with other sources, including communications and financial records whenever possible;

c) including an analyst with advanced knowledge of the case in the interviewing team;

d) equipping the interviewing team with analytical tools, such as chronologies, maps, indexes of key individuals, and so on; or support them during the interview with relevant databases;

e) building some distance in the time, space and personnel, between interviewing and evaluation;

f) sharing the evaluation with officers that have not had personally involvement with the witness;

g) keeping in mind the actual crime while carrying out the interview, and confronting the witness with details of the crime and the suffering of the victims, as a means to control the 'fascination effect';

h) planning ahead the need to have multiple interviews; and

---

[176] See, for example, Gómez Bermúdez, 2010, pp. 138–46, see above note 78. *Ibid.*, pp. 139–40: "[…] este problema de la valoración de la prueba de los coimputados […] es muy frecuente en terrorismo, incluido el yihadista"; and *ibid.*, p. 145: "[…] hubo imputados que se retractaron de sus anteriores declaraciones".

[177] See ICC, "Barasa Case" and ICC, "Gicheru and Bett Case" (available on ICC's web site), with arrest warrants issued in 2013 and 2015, the relevant individuals remain at large.

i)   other specific de-biasing techniques.[178]

3.2.2.5.   Victim Witness Issues

The officer(s) in charge of collecting the evidence may experience a feeling of compassion because of the human suffering caused by the crimes, which may affect the objectivity of the evaluation.

This issue is most common when interviewing victims. Investigators will often interview persons with appalling experiences of suffering, including grave physical pain, sexual violence, mutilations, extreme cruelty, miserable conditions of life, death of close relatives, destruction of the entire family or social environment with long-standing consequences, and so on. A reaction of empathy and compassion by the interviewer is understandable, but it is also necessary to keep a certain distance for the sake of objectivity and greater investigative quality. On a related legal note, Cesare Beccaria warned against lowering the standards of evidence for atrocious crimes, and he considered "a cruel imbecility" the classic dictum *in atrocissimis leviores conjecturae sufficient, et licet iudice iura trasgredi*.[179]

It may happen that victims are truthful and accurate regarding the personal experience of victimization (what they suffered directly), but not necessarily so accurate when reporting on the perpetrators regarding their identification, methods and organization.[180] Regarding the perpetrators, a victim may tend to express greater certitude than granted by his or her knowledge and experience, because such rationalization is psychologically comforting, or possibly out of resentment. It may happen that a victim

---

[178]   See Moa Lidén, "Confirmation Bias in Investigations of Core International Crimes: Risk Factors and Quality Control Techniques", Chap. 7 below.

[179]   Cesare Beccaria, *Dei delitti e delle pene: Edizione Rivista, corretta e disposta secondo l'ordine della Traduzione francese*, Presso la Società dei Filosofi, Londra, 1774 (corrected and rearranged version of the original book of 1764), p. 20: "In the very atrocious crimes the lightest conjectures suffice, and it is legitimate for the judge to breach the law".

[180]   On the difficulties of eyewitness identification in domestic investigation, see Simon, 2012, chap. 3 ""Officer, That's Him!": Eyewitness Identification of Perpetrators", pp. 50–89, and chap. 6 ""We Find the Defendant Guilty": Fact-Finding at Trial", section on "Eyewitness Identification Testimony", pp. 150–57, see above note 40. For the international context, see Andrew Smith, Roderick Lindsay and Brian Cutler, "Eyewitness Psychology in the Context of International Criminal Law", in Ilias Bantekas and Emmanouela Mylonaki (eds.), *Criminological Approaches to International Criminal Law*, Cambridge University Press, 2014, pp. 159–91, including sections on "Distance and Lighting", "Emotions and Stress" and "Post-event Information".

does not have knowledge of the internal functioning of the structure of the perpetrators, and in his or her account tends to exaggerate the coherence of such structure and the role of a given suspect.

3.2.2.5.1. Example

In an ICTY case the Trial Chamber based the conviction of an accused largely on the testimony of a witness who was deemed reliable by the Prosecutor and the judges, but the Appeals Chamber made a different evaluation of the same witness, considered her not reliable and acquitted the accused. The witness was a victim that apparently had made a strong impression on the investigators because of her personal experience of suffering and her very assertive expression. In spite of defence objections and objective difficulties at the time of the events (low visibility, limited length of observation), the investigators as well as the Trial Chamber evaluated positively the witness impressed by her "confident and force-ful" demeanour. The Appeals Chamber found that, "very often, a confi-dent demeanour is a personality trait and not necessarily a reliable indica-tor of truthfulness or accuracy", and actually the witness had not been in a position to know the facts that she reported, concerning in particular eye-witness identification.[181] The Appeals Chamber concluded that

> the Trial Chamber erred in relying so heavily upon Witness H's confident demeanour. There are several strong indica-tions on the trial record that her absolute conviction in her identification evidence was very much a reflection of her personality and not necessarily an indicator of her reliabil-ity.[182]

The expert testimony of a cognitive psychologist, as well as contra-dictions with earlier statements by the same witness, was considered to this effect.

Conversely, it may also happen that the interviewer or any other op-erator evaluating a victim may develop a tendency of disbelief as a coping mechanism, to protect him or herself from the psychological impact of the narrative. As the UNHCR research has observed in relation to asylum procedures:

---

[181] ICTY, *Prosecutor v. Kupreškić et al.*, Appeals Chamber, Appeal Judgement, 23 October 2001, IT-95-16-A, para. 138 ('Kupreškić et al. Appeals Judgment') (https://www.legal-tools.org/doc/c6a5d1/).

[182] *Ibid.*, para. 154.

> If interviewers and decision-makers suffer psychological distress from their exposure to such evidence – so-called vicarious trauma – they risk employing natural coping strategies that involuntarily compromise their fact-finding and impartiality. [...] Examiners may find the content of the evidence so horrific that they are tempted to reject it as unimaginable, fabricated and therefore not credible. [...] Disbelief is a very human coping strategy that undermines objectivity and impartiality.[183]

Continuing exposure to victims may cause a "compassion fade effect", if officers grow dismissive over time due to their fatigue, regardless of the quality of the information.[184]

3.2.2.5.2.   Advice

To differentiate aspects of the victimization as such (the suffering caused by the victims), and aspects of related to the perpetrators (identification, *modus operanda*, organizational structures), and be particularly rigorous in the evaluation of the latter.

3.2.3.   Multi-Disciplinary Overview of Methods

Different domains of investigation and research have developed diverse approaches to Source Evaluation. Structured methods focused on alphanumeric codes are common in some police and intelligence agencies. The models known as '4 x 4', '5 x 5', '6 x 6', or Admiral, consist on a matrix to rank the sources by two scales related to the source and the information. See below an example of a '4 x 4' matrix.[185]

---

[183]   UNHCR, 2013, p. 40, see above note 84.

[184]   See Philip Pärnamets, Alexander Tagesson and Annika Wallim, "Inconsistencies in Repeated Refugee Status Decisions", in *Journal of Behavioral Decision Making*, 2020 (forthcoming), pp. 1–10.

[185]   Image from Pierre Aepli, Olivier Ribaux and Everett Summerfied, *Decision Making in Policing: Operations and Management*, EPFL Press, Lausanne, 2011, p. 31.

Evaluation of information

		1 Accuracy is not in doubt	2 Personal experience by the source	3 Indirect source but corroborated by other information	4 Indirect and not corroborated
Evaluation of the source	A No doubt.	A1	A2	A3	A4
	B Source proved to be reliable in most instances.	B1	B2	B3	B4
	C Source proved to be unreliable in most instances.	C1	C2	C3	C4
	X Reliability cannot be assessed.	X1	X2	X3	X4

Figure 3. An example of a '4 x 4' matrix for Source Evaluation.

The Criminal Intelligence Manual for Analysts published by the UN Office on Drugs and Crime ('UNODC') in 2011 includes the '4 x 4' model, and a '6 x 6' variant, based on the following fundamental principles for the "evaluation of sources and information":

1. It must not be influenced by personal feelings but be based on professional judgment.

2. Evaluation of the source must be made separately to the information.

3. It must be carried out as close to the source as possible.[186]

This UNODC manual illustrates the second principle and "the evaluation process" with the graphic below.[187]

---

[186] UNODC, *Criminal Intelligence Manual for Analysts*, Vienna, 2011, p. 25.
[187] *Ibid.*

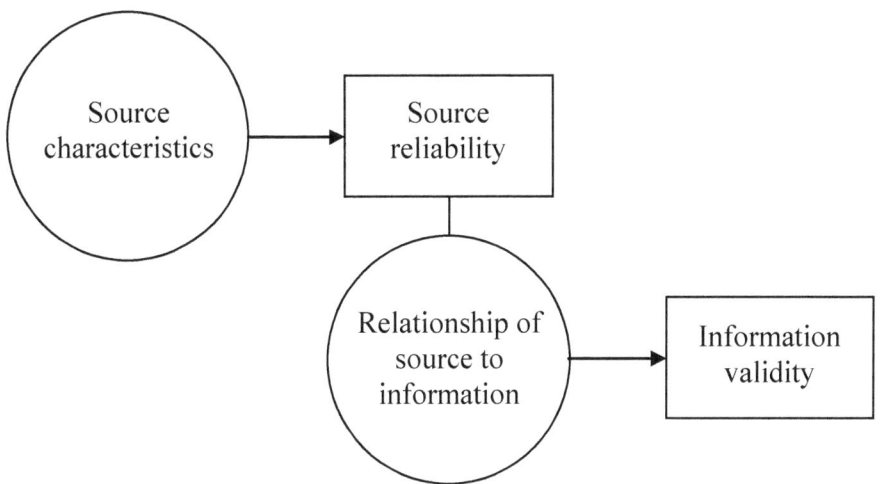

Figure 4. The evaluation process.

The '4 x 4' model is also part of the methodology for the EUROPOL Serious and Organised Crime Threat Assessment ('SOCTA') adopted in 2012, described as follows:

> In general, information will be evaluated using the "four by four (4x4)" system, in which both the source and the information are independently assessed, and every combination of a source and its information is assigned a value ranging from A1 to X4.[188]

The same document defines as an assumption that all source from EUROPOL, the contributing agencies from EU member States and EU institutions (Eurojust, Frontex, and so on) shall be rated A1 and that "[t]he information that can be used for the SOCTA should have an evaluation of B3 or higher (A1, A2, A3, B1, B2)".[189] In the version of the '4 x 4' model adopted by INTERPOL the sources codes are: A – Always reliable; B – Sometimes reliable; C – Unreliable; X – Untested. The information codes

---

[188] Council of the European Union, "Serious and Organised Crime Threat Assessment (SOCTA) – Methodology", 4 July 2012, ST 12159 2012 INIT, p. 19 (available on the Open Data web site of the European Council).

[189] *Ibid.*

define the top value 1 as 'known to be true', and lower values are similar to Figure 3 above.[190]

A main merit of this model is evaluating separately source and information, which contemplates the possibility that a 'bad source' can provide 'good information' and vice versa. As indicated from historiography, "[t]he most honest witness may misstate; the worst may tell the truth".[191] This distinction departs from classic jurisprudence that conditioned entirely the validity of the evidence on the honesty of the witness. The principle *testibus se, no testimoniis creditor* (believe the witness, not the testimony), known in Roman and other ancient traditions, was characteristic of systems with limited means of evidence that relied exclusively on witness testimony.[192] A certain emphasis on witness traits could also lead to an *argumentum ad hominem*, that is, disqualifying an argument by attacking its proponent, which is considered as a classic fallacy.

The analytical distinction between the two parameters source–information was already acknowledged by Jeremy Bentham in his *An Introductory View of the Rationale of Evidence* when he referred to two aspects relevant to the "increase or diminution of probative force" for the evidence:

1. The *source from* which the evidence – the information – sprints, and is delivered; and

2. The *shape* in which it is delivered.[193]

Hans Gross would also indicate that, for different reasons, "[w]e must not imagine that an honest witness will at all hazard stick to the

---

[190] See INTERPOL, *Practical Guidelines: Sharing Information with Law Enforcement*, sect. 3 "Providing High Quality Information" and template in sect. 6 (available on INTERPOL's web site). See also Agreement between Interpol and Europol, 5 November 2001, Article 9, adopting the 4 x 4 model.

[191] Thomas Spencer Jerome, "The Case of the Eyewitnesses: 'A Lie Is a Lie Even in Latin'", in Robin W. Winks (ed.), *The Historian as Detective: Essays on Evidence*, Harper Colophon Books, New York, 1968, p. 187.

[192] See János Jany, *Judging in the Islamic, Jewish and Zoroastrian Legal Traditions: A Comparison of Theory and Practice*, Routledge, New York, 2012, pp. 96–97.

[193] Jeremy Bentham, in John Bowring (ed.), *An Introductory View of the Rationale of Evidence; for the Use of Non-lawyers as well as Lawyers*, vol. VI, William Tait, Edinburgh, 1843, p. 14. For a commentary on Bentham, see William Twining, *Theories of Evidence: Bentham and Wigmore*, Weidenfeld and Nicolson, London, 1985 and William Twining and Terence Anderson, *Analysis of Evidence*, Butterworths, London, 1991.

---

truth".[194] ICTY jurisprudence concurs, particularly for eyewitness identification of perpetrators, when referring to "the possibility that even completely honest witnesses may have been mistaken in their identification".[195] As it has been observed from national practice: "[h]ence testimony should not be understood as a mere *dictum*, but rather as an act made of two elements: the *testis* and the *dictum*".[196] This broad acceptance in contemporary investigative and judicial practice led to incorporate the dual approach in the method adopted by OTP ID in 2006.[197]

The method of the structured matrix also helps developing awareness and standard practice for agencies comprising large numbers of officers and sources. The officer is forced to adopt a scale in the quality of the sources and to carry out the evaluation accordingly. This model has two main limitations for the needs of a criminal investigation. Firstly, the source codes are based on the experience with the source, assuming a series of previous or ongoing engagements. This is consistent with the practice of handling informants by police and intelligence officers, for continuing monitoring of criminal or hostile activities, but it may not apply the same way for a criminal investigation when the witness is assessed in relation to a single event.

Secondly, merely assigning a code is insufficient to address the complexity of the relevant issues, usually requiring more detailed assessment. For example, in the judgment on the terrorist attack in Madrid on 11 March 2003, the judges considered as a relevant indicator the classification of some information as A1, according to the handling of an informant by the police, but they further discussed extensively credibility and reliability issues in the context of the alleged crime.[198]

Furthermore, assumptions of highest validity merely because of the formal status of the provider, like in the above-mentioned EUROPOL

---

[194] Gross, 1906, p. 90, see above note 41.

[195] Kunarac et al. Trial Decision on Motion for Acquittal, para. 8, see above note 50.

[196] Alejandro Solís Espinoza, "Psicología del testigo y del testimonio", in *Derecho PUCP: Revista de la Facultad de Derecho*, 2000, vol. 53, p. 1015. The author elaborates on the procedure of Perú, with references from Spanish-speaking countries.

[197] See below Section 3.2.4.

[198] Spain National High Court Zougam Sentencia, pp. 331–32, based on the testimony of the *guardia civiles* who had handled the informant and produced relevant reports rated A1, see above note 61.

model, are certainly not appropriate for a criminal investigation, let alone one that may have to confront State actors.

At the other end of the methodological spectrum is the unstructured approach, consisting on some free commentary and assessment according to broadly defined criteria, or trusted to the experience of a seasoned professional. This is typical of researchers and lawyers acting individually, as opposed to teams that need common standards, and claiming a degree of authority or expertise on the relevant subjects and procedures.

Historians have a solid tradition of Source Evaluation, including exegesis and hermeneutics in Biblical studies, and the school of *Quellenkritik* (source criticism) in German historiography. Their approach is often sophisticated, but not necessarily with a uniform methodology. For example, Raul Hilberg, leading authority in the history of the holocaust, explained his very elaborate practice for Source Evaluation in his book *Sources of Holocaust Research* based on a multitude of *ad hoc* examples, rather than an overall standard system.[199] The historian Carlo Ginzburg has discussed thoroughly issues of Source Evaluation when reviewing the investigation and trial of some leaders of *Lotta Continua* in his book *The Judge and the Historian*.[200] Stathis N. Kalyvas, another leading researcher, explains thoroughly his experience handling multiple sources and their biases in his major work *The Logic of Violence in Civil Wars*, in a way that similarly is very sophisticated, but not easy to replicate in standard team work.[201] In the words of a classic study in this area, "[v]erification is required of the researcher in a multitude of points [...] verification is accordingly conducted on many planes, and its technique is not fixed".[202] Taken to the field of philosophy, this would be similar to

---

[199] Raul Hilberg, *Sources of Holocaust Research: An Analysis*, Ivan R. Dee, Chicago, 2001. More on his experience, including exchanges with Franz Neumann and Hannah Arendt, in his memoirs, Raul Hilberg, *The Politics of Memory: The Journey of a Holocaust Historian*, Ivan R. Dee, Chicago, 1996.

[200] Ginzburg, 1999, see above note 167.

[201] See Kalyvas, 2006, pp. 393–411, including detailed methodological observations about archives, judicial records and witnesses and their biases, see above note 64.

[202] Barzun and Graff, 1992, p. 99, see above note 36. For historiographic methodology, see Robin W. Winks (ed.), *The Historian as Detective: Essays on Evidence*, Harper Colophon Books, New York, 1968; Louis R. Gottschalk, *Understanding History: A Primer of Historical Method*, 2nd edition, Alfred A. Knopf, New York, 1969; and Jerzy Topolsky, *Metodologia de la Historia*, Cátedra, Madrid, 1992 (translation of the original in Polish, 1973),

Paul Feyerabend's 'epistemological anarchism', a radical critique of universal scientific methodologies.[203] Only that Feyerabend means to challenge rationalism, and criminal justice rests axiomatically on rationalist positivism, that is, the assumption that there is a positive factual reality that can be determined through universal rational methods.

Legal practitioners are often reluctant to adopt clear methodologies for Source Evaluation. For example, John Henry Wigmore dedicated more than 400 pages to "testimonial evidence" in his massive work (1179 pages) *The Principles of Judicial Proof*, identifying multiple factors relevant from jurisprudence and scientific research, but he never produced a methodology to assess them systematically.[204] Another legal expert of this period, Charles C. Moore quoted in his *A Treatise on Facts or the Weight and Value of Evidence* several judges and authors dismissing the idea of having any set methodology for the evaluation of witnesses.[205] One judge found that when deciding to believe or not a witness, for each juror "this belief is personal, individual, and depends upon an infinite variety of circumstances; any attempt to regulate or control it by a fixed rule is impracticable, worse than useless, inconsistent and repugnant to the nature of a trial by jury [...]".[206] Another judge noted: "[i]t is one of the difficulties attending all tribunals passing upon facts, that the reasons for believing particular witnesses or particular testimony in preference to others cannot be defined".[207] Jerome Frank, another influential judge and legal theorist would summarise: "the methods used by trial judges in determining whether or not to believe particular witnesses cannot be formulated in rules and rendered systematic".[208]

---

particularly chap. XVIII "La autenticidad de las fuentes y la fiabilidad de los informants", pp. 333–49.

[203] Paul Feyerabend, *Against Method*, Verso, London, 1975.

[204] Wigmore, 1913, part II "Testimonial Evidence", pp. 312–744, including title I "Generic Human Traits Affecting the Trustworthiness of Testimony", title II "The Elements of the Testimonial Process Itself as Affecting the Trustworthiness of Testimony", and so on, see above note 128.

[205] Charles C. Moore, "Introductory", in *A Treatise on Facts or the Weight and Value of Evidence: Volume I*, Edward Thompson Company, New York, 1908, sect. 3 "Judicial Statements Concerning Standards of Belief", pp. 4–7.

[206] *Ibid.*, p. 5.

[207] *Ibid.*

[208] Jerome Frank, ""Short of Sickness and Death": A Study of Moral Responsibility in Legal Criticism", in *New York University Law Journal*, 1951, vol. 26, no. 4, p. 559.

This kind of holistic and intuitive free evaluation has the advantage of flexibility to address multiple factors and scenarios, but its validity seems to be subject to at least four premises. Firstly, the person conducting the evaluation should be a true expert on evidence, with advanced skills derived from serious training and investigative or judicial experience. Secondly, the evaluator would need to be free of confirmation bias and be able to evaluate source and information impartially, regardless of their consistency with the litigation arguments: this is very hard to achieve for the parties, whether defence or prosecution, in a polarized litigation context. Thirdly, the evaluator should be very knowledgeable about the personal and social context of the witness, which is not always the case with foreign investigating and judicial officers. Fourthly, for auditing purposes, the evaluator would have to be ready to communicate and explain the assessment conducted every time, by the *ad hoc* reasoning developed for each source.

Some semi-structured methods have emerged in forensic psychology, asylum procedures and Internet research. By the late nineteenth and early twentieth century a number of psychologists and lawyers developed in Europe what they called 'the science of testimony', beginning with the Austrian criminologist Hans Gross, as he explained in his handbook *Criminal Investigations*, the French lawyer and psychologist Alfred Binet and his seminal book *La suggestibilité*, and followed among others by Francois Gorphe with his influential handbook *La critique du Témoignage*.[209]

Gross addressed in detail "the examination of witnesses and accused" based on investigative practice, jurisprudence and research on psychology. His original handbook in German was translated into English and published in Chennai in 1906 with some adaptation to the context of

---

[209] Binet, 1900, see above note 113; and Alfred Binet, "La science du témoignage", in *L'Année psychologique*, 1904, vol. 11, pp. 128–36. For a commentary on Binet's historical importance, see Serge Nicolas, Yannick Gounden and Rasyid Bo Sanitioso, "Alfred Binet, Founder of the Science of Testimony and Psycho-legal Science", in *L'Année psychologique*, 2014, vol. 114, no. 2, pp. 209–29. For that period, see also Hugo Münsterberg, *On the witness stand: Essays on Psychology and Crime*, Doubleday, Page & Co., New York, 1909. Münsterberg refers to Binet's experiments, and further highlights problems with witness memory and suggestibility. Also very critical of witness testimony, M.C. Otto, "Testimony and Human Nature", in *Journal of Criminal Law and Criminology*, 1918, vol. 9, no. 1, pp. 98–104.

India.[210] He identified many relevant factors and scenarios, but gave no clear guidance for operational implementation. His outline for Source Evaluation shows in the table of contents of his handbook as follows:

Examination of Witnesses and Accused.

Table 1. Outline for Source Evaluation.

Gorphe went one step beyond and proposed a *tableau synoptique* to assess testimonies from four points of view: moral, intellectual, emotional, and psychological, see below:[211]

---

[210] Gross, 1906, see above note 41. The editors adapted this edition to "combine and include therewith a mass of information of peculiar interest in India" ("Preface", in *ibid.*, p. v). See *ibid.*, chap. II "Examination of Witnesses and Accused", pp. 52–122.

[211] Gorphe, 1924, p. 386, see above note 130.

— 386 —

II. — Quelle est la propriété de *l'objet* à déclancher un bon témoignage ?

1. Objet perçu par les sens inférieurs.
2. Objet *auditif* : nécessitant plus ou moins d'interprétation (sons, paroles).
3. Objet *visuel* : selon sa catégorie. Particularités pour le signalement et ses divers éléments.
4. *Reconnaissance* : dans quelles conditions a-t-elle eu lieu ? Difficultés pour les cadavres et pour les photographies.
5. *Évaluations* : leur subjectivité. Epreuves des capacités.

III. — Dans quelles *conditions* s'est formé le témoignage ?

1. Au moment de la *perception* :

Au point de vue objectif
1. temps d'obs. ?
2. perspective ?
3. éclairage ?

subjectif (fix. des souvenirs)
1. attention ?
2. émotion ?
3. intégrité cérébrale (bles., ivresse, etc.) ?

2. Dans la *mémoire* (conservation des souvenirs) :
a) Temps ou ancienneté des souvenirs ?
b) Suggestions reçues
d'autres témoins ? du milieu ou de la presse ?
c) Dépositions antérieures ?

3. Lors de la *déposition* :
a) Etat d'esprit du témoin (ébriété, approche de la mort, etc.) ?
b) Caractère plus ou moins sérieux du serment ?
c) Assurance des déclarations ?
d) Ont-elles été faites spontanément, ou sur questions et quelles sortes de questions ?

Il est évident que toutes ces questions n'ont pas à être résolues dans chaque cas ; chaque espèce a ses particularités. Mais il y a un ordre logique à suivre pour essayer de ne rien omettre.

Au terme de ce long travail, basé autant que possible sur les faits et sur des expériences de toutes sortes, nous avons à nous demander quel est le chemin parcouru. La nécessité de

Table 2. *Tableau synoptique.*

As forensic psychology evolved, more elaborate methods emerged, such as the Statement Validity Assessment ('SVA'). This method is based on the so-called 'Undeutsch hypothesis', as formulated by the German psychologist Udo Undeutsch, according to which "a statement derived from memory of an actual experience differs in content and quality from a statement based on invention or fantasy".[212]

The German Supreme Court ruled first in 1954 that expert witnesses, such as psychiatrists or psychologists, could be called to assess the credibility of statements by alleged child victims of sexual abuse, particularly in the absence of any other evidence. Then in 1999 it declared SVA as the standard expert procedure for such cases.[213]

The SVA was designed to assess statements given by children about alleged sexual abuse, which were considered particularly sensitive and prone to suggestion or false allegations, and in many cases the only available evidence.[214] This origin is comparable to the context of international investigations, with various reliability issues and often allegations sustained by a single witness, hence the need of some methodology of that kind is understandable in the international context. Some proponents of the SVA claim that it can be used also with adults and any crime.[215]

The SVA considers multiple hypotheses about the factual validity of a statement, including 'deliberate lie' and 'non-intentional mistakes', and it includes the Criteria-Based Content Analysis ('CBCA') as a standard check-list for evaluating statements under the hypothesis of 'deliberate

---

[212] Aldert Vrij, *Detecting Lies and Deceit: Pitfalls and Opportunities*, 2nd edition, Wiley, Chichester, 2008, p. 209.

[213] Valerie Hauch, Siegfried L. Sporer, Jaume Masip and Iris Blandon-Gitlin, "Can Credibility Criteria Be Assessed Reliably? A Meta-Analysis of Criteria-Based Content Analysis", in *Psychological Assessment*, 2017, vol. 29, no. 6, p. 820.

[214] See Günter Köhnken, "Statement Validity Analysis and the 'Detecion of Truth'", in Pär Anders Granhag and Leif A. Strömwall (eds.), *The Detection of Deception in Forensic Contexts*, Cambridge University Press, 2004, pp. 41–63; Josep Baqués Cardona, "Otras técnicas en psicología forense: detección de mentiras en la declaración de testigos", in Miguel Angel Soria Verde (coord.), *Manual de psicología penal forense*, Atelier, Barcelona, 2002, pp. 335–60; and Eugenio Carlos Fernández-Ballesteros González, "Evaluación de la credibilidad y de la validez del testimonio de menores", in Miguel Angel Soria Verde (coord.), *Manual de psicología penal forense*, Atelier, Barcelona, 2002, pp. 581–622.

[215] See Köhnken, 2004, p. 60, see above note 214.

lie'. See below outline of the main hypotheses, as presented by proponents of this method.[216]

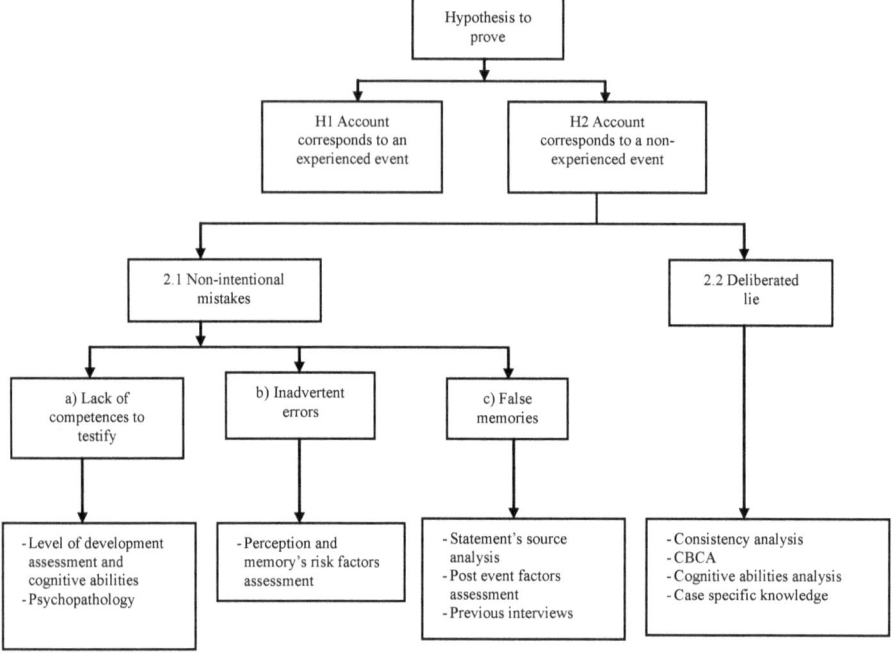

Figure 5. Outline of the main hypotheses.

See overview of the 19 CBCA criteria in Table 3 below.[217]

General characteristics:
1. Logical structure
2. Unstructured production
3. Quantity of details

Specific contents:
4. Contextual embedding
5. Descriptions of interactions
6. Reproduction of conversation
7. Unexpected complications during the incident
8. Unusual details
9. Superfluous details

---

[216] Günter Köhnken, Antonio L. Manzanero, and M. Teresa Scott, "Statement Validity Assessment: Myths and Limitations", in *Anuario de Psicología Jurídica*, 2015, vol. 25, p. 17.

[217] From Pär Anders Granhag, Aldert Vrij and Bruno Verschuere, *Detecting Deception: Current Challenges and Cognitive Approaches*, Wiley, Chichester, 2015, p. 8.

10. Accurately reported details misunderstood
11. Related external associations
12. Accounts of subjective mental state
13. Attribution of perpetrator's mental state

Motivation-related contents:
14. Spontaneous corrections
15. Admitting lack of memory
16. Raising doubts about one's own testimony
17. Self-deprecation
18. Pardoning the perpetrator

Offence-specific elements:
19. Details characteristic of the offence

Table 3. Overview of the 19 CBCA criteria.

SVA and CBCA are meant to be applied by certified psychologists who have been trained specifically in the method. They are expected to rate each CBCA criterion in three-level or five-level scales (practice varies), and to produce an overall score aggregating the ratings of all indicators.[218] In some countries, particularly Germany, the SVA and its CBCA have been admitted as evidence in court while, beyond formal admissibility, their actual probative value may vary across cases, practitioners, and jurisdictions.[219]

This method appears to show several limitations: the underlying 'Undeutsch hypothesis' is taken as an axiomatic premise rather than as a hypothesis; each indicator is fairly open to interpretation; some of the indicators have dubious scientific foundation, such as 'quantity of details' (see discussion in Section 3.2.4.8.2. below). Some research and laboratory tests suggest that the CBCA may be able to determine the truthfulness of a statement with about 70 per cent of success: this is slightly above the 50 per cent of a random guess, which could be helpful but far from conclu-

---

[218] Vrij, 2008, p. 208, see above note 212.

[219] According to Köhnken, "SVA has now [2004] been widely accepted by many courts in continental Europe (Germany, Switzerland, Austria, the Netherlands, Sweden) as well as in the United Kingdom", including a ruling to that effect by the German Supreme Court. See Köhnken, 2004, p. 60, see above note 214. Still, as Moa Lidén rightly observed in her review of my draft, one thing is to be procedurally 'accepted' as evidence, another thing is the actual probative value, and yet a different thing is acceptance by the scientific community. For an example and critical assessment of CBCA applied in a case in the Netherlands, see Wagenaar and Crombag, 2005, pp. 113–14, see above note 97.

sive.[220] Hence the method may be useful tentatively at the investigation stage, but not as categorical evidence on its own right. The proponents of SVA-CBCA argue that it is preferable to the alternatives of merely impressionistic assessments, reliance on non-verbal cues, or the polygraph, which is probably a fair point but it doesn't say much about the validity of the method as such.[221]

Following the SVA method, psychologists are expected to run the results of the CBCA with a Validity Checklist comprising another 11 indicators related to the witness' motives and psychological profile, the conduct of the interview, and consistency with other statement and evidence.[222] This Validity Checklist then would take the assessment to a whole different area, including verification against other sources.

Reality Monitoring is another model developed by experts in cognitive psychology. It resembles SVA-CBCA in some respects, and some authors recommend to use both jointly.[223]

Similar models have been proposed for evaluating asylum applications, including with the support of UNHCR and the European Union.[224] For example, the European Asylum Support Office proposed in 2018 a check-list with four 'credibility indicators': 'internal consistency', 'external consistency', 'sufficiency of detail' and 'plausibility'.[225]

3.2.4. Recommended Method

Based on a review of the abovementioned methods, the relevant jurisprudence, and consultation with colleagues, I concluded in the early years of the ICC-OTP that a semi-structured approach would be most suitable for

---

[220] Vrij, 2008, p. 256, see above note 212.

[221] See Köhnken, 2004, p. 61, see above note 214. For a critical assessment of CBCA, see Wagenaar and Crombag, 2005, pp. 189–92, see above note 97.

[222] Vrij, 2008, chap. 8 "Statement Validity Assessment", sect. "Stage 4: Evaluation of the CBCA Outcome: The Validity Checklist", pp. 213–18, see above note 212; *ibid.*, sect. "Validity Checklist: Reflections", pp. 241–51.

[223] See Siegfried L. Sporer, "Reality Monitoring and Detection of Deception", in Pär Anders Granhag and Leif A. Strömwall (eds.), *The Detection of Deception in Forensic Contexts*, Cambridge University Press, 2004, pp. 64–102.

[224] UNHCR, 2013, p. 30, see above note 84.

[225] European Asylum Support Office (EASO), *Evidence and Credibility Assessment in the Context of the Common European Asylum System*, 2018, p. 188; *ibid.*, sect. 4.5 "Credibility Indicators".

our investigations. I drafted accordingly the Source Evaluation Guidelines, based on a check-list of standard indicators to be addressed with a brief description of the relevant facts, and a rating for each indicator. This method was designed to assist the investigations both prospectively, to select the best sources for collection, and also for subsequent analysis and quality control. This section reflects largely the content of these guidelines, while departing on some issues for the purpose of academic discussion, and further critical review and improvement.

The 15 proposed indicators (see Table 4 below) were meant to assess jointly different dimensions. Some indicators relate to the likelihood of 'the truth' in a fundamental sense, trying to assess whether 'the source is telling the truth'.[226] Other indicators have the more modest purpose to contribute to 'the judicial truth', assessing whether the sources are suitable for the communicative procedure of the investigations and trials. Certainly 'the judicial truth' is meant to correspond with 'the truth', but the judicial process is based on the principles of evidential 'orality', 'immediacy' and reasonability in ways that call for specific communicative skills.[227] First the witness is expected to be fundamentally able and willing to convey the truth; additionally, a good witness is also expected to be convincing, which usually requires good oral communication and reasoning skills, in order to pass the test of cross-examination and the 'immedi-

---

[226] For epistemological reference, see Jacobo Munoz and Julián Velarde (eds.), *Compendio de Epistemología*, Editorial Trotta, Madrid, 2000; Juan Antonio Nicolás and María José Frápolli (eds.), *Teorías de la verdad en el siglo XX*, Tecnos, Madrid, 1997; and Feyerabend, 1975, see above note 203.

[227] For a discussion about 'judicial truth' and empirical truth, see Michele Taruffo, "Prueba y verdad en el proceso civil", in *La prueba de los hechos*, Trotta, Madrid, 2002 (Spanish translation of the original in Italian of 1992), pp. 21–88; and HO Hock Lai, "Truth, Justice and Justification", in *A Philosophy of Evidence Law: Justice in the Search of Truth*, Oxford University Press, 2008, pp. 51–84. For the Dutch system, see Marc S. Groenhuijsen and Hatice Selçuk, sect. III "The Concept of Truth in the Dutch Criminal Procedure", in "The Principle of Immediacy in Dutch Criminal Procedure in the Perspective of European Human Rights Law", in *Zeitschrift für die gesamte Strafrechtswissenschaft*, 2014, vol. 126, no. 1, pp. 251–52. For communication requirements in common-law procedure, see Emily Henderson, Christopher Heffer and Mark Kebbell, "Courtroom Questioning and Discourse", in Gavin Oxburgh, Trond Myklebust, Tim Grant and Rebecca Milne (eds.), *Communication in Investigative and Legal Contexts: Integrated Approaches from Forensic Psychology, Linguistics and Law Enforcement*, Wiley Blackwell, Chichester, 2016, pp. 181–208.

ate' perception by the judges.[228] These different dimensions can be explained as follows:[229]

A. *Truthfulness*: Whether the information is fundamentally true, it corresponds with tangible positive facts. To be addressed mainly through 'internal consistency', 'external verification', and 'detail', which are three of the four indicators relevant to the information.

B. *Competence*: As a pre-condition for truthfulness, whether the source is capable to acquire truthful knowledge. This is equivalent to what historians may call 'competence', in relation to "degree of expertness, state of mental and physical health, age, education, memory, narrative skill, etc.".[230] Also related to what Wigmore referred to as 'perception', including sight, hearing and other sensory considerations.[231] To be evaluated through 'language', 'knowledge' and 'medical condition'.

C. *Authenticity*: Whether the knowledge is authentic, not determined by undue self-serving design or external influence. To be evaluated through 'motivation', 'independence', 'contamination' and 'immediacy'. These indicators are related to the perspective of the source *vis-à-vis* the reported facts, comparable partly to the concept of 'positionality' in gender studies or 'personal equation' in astronomy.[232]

D. *Pragmatic performance*: As a practical consideration and subordinate to the above substantive issues, whether the witness is able to communicate effectively, during the investigation, and also potentially to the judges after adversarial cross-examination. Once the truthful and authentic sources are identified, the parties may want to prioritize for trial among them those who communicate best, particularly in common-law systems that rely heavily on oral perfor-

---

[228] On legal procedure as communication, see Frank, 1949, chap. XIII "A Trial as Communicative Process", pp. 186–89, see above note 1.

[229] For the specifics on each indicator, see below Sections 3.2.4.7. and 3.2.4.8.

[230] See Gottschalk, 1969, p. 151, see above note 202.

[231] See John Henry Wigmore, *The Principles of Judicial Proof, or the Process of Proof: As Given by Logic, Psychology and General Experience and Illustrated in Judicial Trials*, 2nd edition, Little, Brown, and Company, Boston, 1931, sect. "Perception", pp. 335–93.

[232] See Gottschalk, 1969, p. 148, see above note 202. On positionality, see, for example, Frances A. Maher and Mary Kay Tetreault, "Frames of Positionality: Constructing Meaningful Dialogues About Gender and Race", in *Anthropological Quarterly*, 1993, vol. 66, no. 3, pp. 118–26.

mance. This is similar to what Wigmore referred to as "narration or communication", defined as "accurately reproducing and expressing the actual and sincere recollection" and "intelligibility to the tribunal of the witness's utterance".[233] To be evaluated possibly on the basis of 'prior experience', 'communication', 'behaviour', and 'criminal record', as explained below.

The model below aggregated requirements related to both the investigation and trial performance, which is consistent with the 'integrated' model adopted by the ICC-OTP, with early anticipation of trial requirements at the investigation stage. To an extent this reflects the US model since, in the words of a former US prosecutor, in the US "the line between investigation and trial is non-existent", and "this adversarial mentality sees the investigation and trial as one undifferentiated process".[234] Since at least the times of Bentham and Wigmore "the central tradition of Anglo-American evidence scholarship is closely connected to the discourse of lawyers and of the courts", hence evidence tends to be evaluated in a utilitarian perspective, for prospect litigation effectiveness, rather than from an autonomous viewpoint of empirical validity and accuracy.[235] The US influence on international prosecutorial practice is noticeable, dating back to the precedents of Nuremberg, Tokyo, ICTY, ICTR and SCSL, through the influence of a large number of senior officers and advisors. For example, by 2003 an experienced ICTY Senior Trial Attorney ('STA') from the US, previously a prosecutor in his country, advised ICC that an "experienced attorney should be in charge of the overall investigation and responsible for carrying it out" because:

> The experienced senior trial attorney is the person in the best position to understand what evidence he or she will need to charge and successfully prosecute an accused person. This is especially true in a new, developing system like the ICC.[236]

---

[233] See Wigmore, 1931, sect. "Narration", p. 455, see above note 231.

[234] William T. Pizzi, *Trials Without Truth: Why Our System of Criminal Trials Has Become and Expensive Failure and What We Need to Do to Rebuild It*, New York University Press, 1999, p. 60.

[235] Twining, 1985, p. 178, see above note 193. The author, an English law professor, comments approvingly on Wigmore, and considers his method "solidly grounded in one intellectually respectable tradition" and unmatched "in sophistication and clarity".

[236] McCloskey, 2017, p. 207, see above note 19.

Another ICTY STA from the US also advised the ICC in the same direction, arguing that "[i]t is vital, therefore, that the prosecutors be actively involved in the investigation and oversee the manner in which evidence is developed and collected".[237] A word of caution may be needed here because anticipating the argument for incrimination as the guiding principle for investigations may undermine their impartiality. As observed by a former US prosecutor, the US system tends to "permit and encourage extreme behaviour from lawyers" and such aggressive adversarial competition "ends up undervaluing truth".[238] A safer alternative could be to address separately the investigative and trial needs when evaluating sources, in order to focus more accurately on empirical fact-finding, and discuss separately suitability for trial performance.

Following the dual approach adopted in the practice by jurisprudence, police and intelligence, I arranged the indicators under two categories, as they are relevant to the provider of the evidence (under 'source' in Table 4 below) or to the substantive content (under 'information' in Table 4 below). The check-list includes 11 indicators for 'source' and 4 for 'information'. This does not mean that 'information' is less important. 'External verification' in particular is often a crucial issue, requiring extensive work for cross-checking against multiple sources. See below the 15 indicators with their summary descriptions:

		Summary Description
1.	**Source**	
1.1	Motivation	Motives that lead the source to offer the information.
1.2	Prior experience	Prior experience of interaction, or earlier records.
1.3	Independence	Association with any actor relevant to the matter under investigation.

---

[237] Clint Williamson, "On Charging Criteria and Other Policy Concerns", in Morten Bergsmo, Klaus Rackwitz and SONG Tianying (eds.), *Historical Origins of International Criminal Law: Volume 5*, Torkel Opsahl Academic EPublisher, Brussels, 2017, p. 413 (http://www.toaep.org/ps-pdf/24-bergsmo-rackwitz-song).

[238] Pizzi, 1999, p. 3, see above note 234. More on the US prosecutorial system in Garrett, 2011, see above note 4.

1.4	Contamination	Influence by other sources or actors.
1.5	Self-restraint	Ability to restrain to areas of actual valid knowledge.
1.6	Language	Knowledge of languages material to the investigation.
1.7	Communication	Ability to communicate clearly.
1.8	Knowledge	Prior knowledge of the relevant context or areas of expertise.
1.9	Behaviour	Interaction and co-operation with the interviewers or the investigation.
1.10	Criminal record	Legitimate record of criminal behaviour, for crimes of any kind.
1.11	Medical condition	Physical or psychological issues relevant to cognition.
2.	**Information**	
2.1	Immediacy	Distance to the reported facts, primary or secondary knowledge.
2.2	Detail	Specificity regarding names, dates, locations, figures, actions, and so on.
2.3	Internal consistency	Logical consistency of the information.
2.4	External verification	Verification with other sources relevant to the same facts.

Table 4. The 15 indicators of the Source Evaluation Guidelines with their summary descriptions.

3.2.4.1. Standard Template

The evaluation should be completed through a 'Source Evaluation Report' ('SER') based on a standard template. That template would include a table comprising the indicators in the check-list above, along with two more columns: one for a concise description of the relevant facts, and another one for the rating of each indicator. The evaluator is expected to rate the indicators following a simple code as follows: 'positive' for a positive evaluation of the source or the information under that indicator; 'negative' for the opposite; 'intermediate' in case of ambivalent data; 'undetermined' if the indicator cannot be assessed due to insufficient or conflicting data.

In addition to the table described above, the standard template would have a section for free commentary, if the evaluator wishes to share some additional observation that does not fit under the check-list or explain some specifics, and for recommendations in order to address issues revealed by the evaluation through additional evidence collection or analysis.

The resulting Source Evaluation Report shall contain an elaborate qualitative description, in which the ratings are meant to assist the description, rather than producing a quantitative measurement. The overall evaluation would not be quantified because the indicators are not homogeneous enough for mathematical aggregation.

The evaluation should assist making the following decisions:

- To believe or not the information;
- to take additional actions to verify the information, such as a new interview of the witness, collection of other additional evidence, or specific analytical checks;
- selection of witnesses for appearance before the trial chamber; and
- protection measures, along with specific risk assessment procedures.

These decisions would be made considering the specifics of the case and the source, and the available alternatives, after considering all indicators 'in the round' or holistically.[239]

Beyond the standard Source Evaluation Report some sources may require a more elaborate and detailed report because they are particularly complex and important for the investigation. For example, a standard report may require two pages, and it can be filled relatively quickly, while a more extensive report on a key insider may take several days of work and many more pages.

The quality of a source may evolve over time, as new information emerges about the source or the subject-matter, or the behaviour of the source evolves. Hence the evaluation of a source may need to be run dy-

---

[239] On the concept of determination 'in the round', see Allan Mackey and John Barnes, *Assessment of Credibility in Refugee and Subsidiary Protection Claims Under the EU Qualification Directive: Judicial Criteria and Standards*, International Association of Refugee Law Judges ('IARLJ'), Haarlem, 2013, p. 41 (available on IARLJ's web site).

namically, for example, if a witness is interviewed several times, after every new interview.

3.2.4.2. Implementation

The Director of the ID issued the Source Evaluation guidelines in 2006 for mandatory reference of our Division, including analysts and investigators, and he asked me to reinforce the implementation in 2012 in response to the acquittal in *Ngudjolo*. The OTP Legal Advisory Section also conducted research on the relevant jurisprudence by 2008 and the Situation Analysis Section followed-up with a version of the guidelines adapted to their duties at the Preliminary Examination stage.

The ID SE Guidelines were marked as an internal confidential OTP document, only to assist at the investigation stage, not intended to bear probative value at the litigation stage. The evaluation, ratings and SERs are considered internal operational information, not subject to mandatory disclosure at the litigation stage. Some 'facts' (under the column 'facts' in the SER) identified through the evaluation and their underlying evidence may require disclosure at the litigation stage under certain circumstances. For example: under 'medical condition' the SER identifies some sight impairment that is relevant for an eyewitness selected for trial by the prosecution; this fact may need to be disclosed to the judges and the defence, along with relevant medical diagnostic records, to the extent that it affects the evidence of that eyewitness, but not the SER as such, which is merely a document for internal investigative reference. The above would apply to ICC procedure, while rules of disclosure vary across legal systems and the practice would need to be adjusted to the legal system in question.

3.2.4.3. Training

I have conducted the mandatory training on SE over the years for analysts and investigators at the ID. This training lasts some four hours, starting with a briefing based on the ID guidelines and real examples from different investigations and trials. Then participants are asked to evaluate a fictional statement inspired on real experience with a key insider (11 pages, a summarised and simplified version of an original statement of 60 pages). The insider was not a perpetrator, he had been both a member and a victim of the perpetrating group. Participants are given a copy of this fictional statement, along with a one-page summary of 'available evidence' to check 'external verification', and information about the circumstances of the interview to assist evaluating 'self-restraint', 'communication' and 'behaviour'. Then participants are divided in small groups to fill the SE table and evaluate the witness following the guidelines. The training concludes with a review of the evaluations, and further instructions for implementation. The training is most often evaluated positively by the participants, and a common feedback observation is that it should be longer to go into greater detail on the different examples, indicators and instructions.

3.2.4.4. Inter-Rater Reliability

I have recorded the ratings resulting from the practical exercises through multiple trainings to assess consistency among the raters, as a tentative inter-rater reliability test. The results of this test, as conducted by staff of the ID immediately after the training and based on the given scenario, showed consistency for most but not all indicators (see below specifics about the results of this testing for each indicator). Inter-rater reliability tests conducted for CBCA indicate similar variations across criteria, with higher consistency for "criteria that have more straightforward or intuitive operationalizations" and lower for "criteria with more complicated or less clearly defined operationalizations".[240] Low inter-rater consistency in any event may be due to a number of factors, related to the validity of the method, the available information or the skills of the evaluators. A proper inter-rater reliability test with valid statistical results could well be developed with additional research support.

3.2.4.5. Additional Criteria

There are more criteria that could be added to the check-list for further thoroughness. For example, in 2016 Chlevickaite and Hola identified 20 criteria, including 9 for the 'credibility of a witness' and 11 for 'the reliability of information provided', see Table 5 below.[241]

---

[240] See Hauch, Sporer, Masip and Blandon-Gitlin, 2017, p. 820, see above note 213.

[241] Gabriele Chlevickaite and Barbora Hola, "Empirical Study of Insider Witnesses' Assessments at the International Criminal Court", in *International Criminal Law Review*, 2016, vol. 16, no. 4, pp. 687–88; *ibid.*, Table "Testimony Assessment Factors in International Criminal Tribunals", p. 688.

Credibility		Reliability	
1	Motivation	1	Ability to understand the language of the events
2	Potential bias (independence)	2	Knowledge of the facts
3	Contamination	3	Detail
4	Demeanour	4	Consistency (internal and to prior statements)
5	Criminal record	5	External corroboration
6	Medical condition	6	Time-lapse between the events and the testimony
7	Character	7	Impact of translation and interpretation
8	Existence of plea agreement	8	Social and cultural factors
9	Status of witness's case (awaiting trial, already sentenced)	9	Age and vulnerability
		10	Impact of traumatic events
		11	Proximity to or involvement in the events in question

Table 5. The 20 criteria identified by Chlevickaite and Hola.

Twelve of these 20 criteria had been already included in the pre-existing ID Source Evaluation model.[242] The procedural status of the witness could be a very relevant factor (suspect, accused, plea agreement, convict, and so on), which could be assessed specifically, as Chlevickaite and Barbora suggest, or be captured under 'motivation'. Translation issues are certainly important, and they could be considered specifically or as a matter of 'immediacy' (a translation is strictly speaking a secondary source). The 'time-lapse between the events and the testimony' (SCSL jurisprudence, and Chlevickaite and Hola) could be considered, under the assumption that recency helps reliability.

---

[242] While the article does not include definitions of the criteria, it appears that the following 12 would be consistent with the ID Source Evaluation model: 'Motivation', 'Potential Bias (Independence)', 'Contamination', 'Demeanour', 'Criminal Record', 'Medical Condition', 'Ability to Understand the Language of the Events', 'Knowledge of the Facts', 'Detail', 'Consistency (Internal and to Prior Statements', 'External Corroboration' and 'Proximity to or Involvement in the Events in Question'.

'Impact of traumatic events' (no. 10 under 'reliability' in Table 5 above) is common in situations of violence, and the issue has been litigated in a number of cases (ICTY *Kunarac*, *Furundžija*, ICTR *Akayesu*, *Kayishema*, SCSL *Fofana and Kandewa*, and so on). Nevertheless, there is no scientific consensus on the impact of trauma on memory. A review of scientific literature would show that "there is no clear consensus as to whether stress improves or worsens memory" while the issue is conditioned by "many individual psychosocial and biological factors".[243] The existing jurisprudence does not show any consensus either on the matter, as judges have tended to dismiss it as a relevant factor for specific findings.

Different authors (Gross 1893 and others) have proposed psychological criteria, including on individual memory and intellectual skills, some jurisprudence refers to the 'personality' of the witness, similar possibly to 'character' (no. 7 under 'credibility' in Table 5 above, proposed by Chlevickaite and Hola).[244] The relevance of such psychological traits cannot be excluded, but its scientific foundation and practical implementation would need to be critically discussed.

3.2.4.6.   Fewer Criteria

Alternatively, one could consider a more simple and robust model, with less criteria. An option could be to decide that "what matters is the information and its corroboration" and reduce or eliminate the source indicators. The problem is that in the context of international investigations corroboration opportunities are often limited, because of the complexity of the facts and operational limitations, and with facts alleged by a single source the source-specific indicators become indispensable. This is precisely in the origins of the SVA-CBCA, which was invented to evaluate child testimony in cases when that was the only source of evidence, and the methods developed for asylum procedures, also often reliant only on the account of the applicant.[245]

---

[243] Anya Topiwala and Seena Fazel, "Memory and Trauma", in Morten Bergsmo and CHEAH Wui Ling (eds.), *Old Evidence and Core International Crimes*, Torkel Opsahl Academic EPublisher, Beijing, 2012, p. 164 (http://www.toaep.org/ps-pdf/16-bergsmo-cheah).

[244] See for example, Rwamakuba Trial Judgment, paras. 102 and 135, dismissing a witness among other reasons because of "her particular personality", see above note 54.

[245] See Gregor Noll (ed.), *Proof, Evidentiary Assessment and Credibility in Asylum Procedures*, Martinus Nijhoff Publishers, Leiden, 2005.

Still, for the sake of operational expediency, the source indicators could be limited to those that appear to be most relevant and reliable. As explained bellow, this could be 'independence', 'contamination', 'language', 'communication', 'knowledge' and 'medical condition', which are related mainly to competence. This would reduce the source indicators from 11 to 6, and the total from 15 to 10.

3.2.4.7.   Source Indicators

3.2.4.7.1.   Motivation

Often prosecutors, judges, or any observer for that matter, wonder about why a given witness decides to co-operate. Already in the times of the Maurya Empire the *Arthashastra* referred to "persons known for their honesty" as 'trustworthy witnesses'.[246] Cesare Beccaria proposed in his classic work *Dei delitti e delle pene* that for any witness "the true measure of his credibility is none other than the interest that he may have in telling the truth or not".[247] For Hans Gross, as he explained in his handbook *Criminal Investigations*, the first consideration in evaluating a witness was to assess his or her intentions, defining a method based on two main scenarios, A. "when the witness desires to speak the truth", and B. when they do not.[248] In some legal systems the trial testimony of a co-accused can be dismissed if the motives are related to revenge, 'personal hatred', blackmail or similar.[249] For example, in the trial for the terrorist attack in Madrid on 11 March 2004, the judges evaluated positively the testimony of a key insider because "[i]t has been also confirmed the absence of spurious motives, such as revenge, hatred, animosity or price".[250] In ICC-OTP investigations, among many others, witnesses are regularly asked about their motives to speak in the beginning of interviews, and their answer may show in their statements. This indicator would be similar to the point of "questionable motives to report" in the SVA Validity Checklist.[251]

---

[246] See Kautilya, 1992, p. 356, see above note 44.

[247] Beccaria, 1774, sect. VIII "Dei testimoni", p. 18, see above note 179.

[248] Gross, 1906, chap. II "Examination of Witnesses and Accused", pp. 52–122, see above note 41.

[249] See Gascón Inchausti, 1999, pp. 125–26, referring to jurisprudence of the Spanish Tribunal Supremo (Supreme Court), see above note 37.

[250] Spain National High Court Zougam Sentencia, p. 334, see above note 61.

[251] Vrij, 2008, p. 217, see above note 212.

This emphasis on motivation is arguable for several reasons: motives are culturally conditioned, particularly by the weight given to the individual or the collective in each culture (see Section 3.2.2.2. above regarding *cultural biases*), and open to culturally-biased interpretation;[252] different motives, no matter how benign or pernicious, are not mutually exclusive, they may well coexist and evolve; establishing the motive requires a degree of psychological speculation; sometimes the focus on motives brings inappropriately moral judgment into the technical assessment; and the record from jurisprudence is far from conclusive on the weight given to different motives. While I had my doubts about the validity of 'motivation' as a reliable empirical parameter, I agreed to include it in the model because of the precedents in jurisprudence and suggestion by some legal officers.

Table 6 below summarises motives to give a statement that are often self-reported by witnesses, or otherwise identified through investigation, in the context of international crimes.

1.	Contribution to justice and truth.
2.	Wish to put an end to impunity.
3.	Wish to prevent future crimes.
4.	Pre-existent personal conflict with the suspect or associates.
5.	Revenge, intention to damage the alleged suspect or associates.
6.	Political or war propaganda, discrediting opposing party or suspects.
7.	Personal profit or self-promotion, including penal benefits.
8.	Group loyalty or pressure.
9.	Asylum application for reasons related to the case.
10.	Advocacy agenda for victims or particular issues.
11.	Reparations because of relevant crimes.

---

[252] See Thomas, 2008, chap. 4, section on "Motivation Across Cultures", pp. 87–89, see above note 82.

12.	Protection because of relevant procedures or other.
13.	Financial support because of relevant procedures or other.

**Table 6. Motives of witnesses to give a statement
in the context of international crimes.**

The top three motives above are often self-reported by victims and other witnesses and they are consistent with the purpose of the procedure. They may express their genuine commitment to justice, which is often the case, or their wish to please the interviewer, or some combination of both. In a survey of ICTY witnesses conducted in 2001, 90 per cent of the respondents indicated that their motivation to testify was a sense of 'moral obligation', including "to speak for those who were missing or dead" and to make sure that they "would never be forgotten".[253] A word of caution may be still be granted since, as indicated for interviewing methodology in anthropology, "[i]nterviews are social encounters [...] [e]xpect people to over-report socially desirable behavior and to under-report socially undesirable behavior".[254]

Motives related to personal agendas, revenge or propaganda (4 to 8 in Table 6 above) are rarely self-reported by witnesses, but they are not uncommon in view of the human suffering and polarization in situations of mass violence. For example, in ICTY *Vasiljević* the Trial Chamber dismissed the evidence from a witness because she appeared to have "considerable animus against the accused".[255]

Penal benefits as a motive is common in scenarios of plea bargain, or for convicts seeking reduction of terms or improvement of penitentiary conditions. Defence attorneys are likely to object to such witnesses, but often judges have dismissed such objections and accepted their evidence. In ICTY *Simić* the Trial Chamber did not consider a co-accused who pleaded guilty and who appeared as a witness for the Prosecution unrelia-

---

[253] Eric Stover and Harvey M. Weinstein (eds.), *My Neighbor, My Enemy: Justice and Community in the Aftermath of Mass Atrocity*, Cambridge University Press, 2004, p. 105.

[254] See H. Russel Bernard, "Interviewing: Unstructured and Semistructured", in *Research Methods in Anthropology: Qualitative and Quantitative Approaches*, Altamira Press, Walnut Creek, 2002, p. 237.

[255] ICTY, *Prosecutor v. Vasiljević*, Trial Chamber, Judgment, 29 November 2002, IT-98-32-T, fn. 190 (https://www.legal-tools.org/doc/8035f9/). The judgment does not explain the basis of this finding, nor its relevance in the given context.

ble, since the witness was sentenced prior to giving his oral testimony.[256] In *Blagojević* the Trial Chamber accepted evidence from a prosecution witness that had given his plea agreement, and the Appeals Chamber confirmed the validity of this decision in spite of objections from the defence.[257] In *Kordić and Čerkez* the defence challenged the credibility of a key insider and co-perpetrator, who had been convicted before for the same crimes by ICTY judges, because of his interest to get his sentence reduced, as well as established falsehood in his own previous trial: the Trial Chamber deemed his testimony reliable because of circumstantial corroboration and "his demeanour".[258] Similarly in ICTR *Ntakirutimnana et al*, the Appeals Chamber observed: "the mere fact that an incarcerated suspect had a possible incentive to perjure himself on the stand in order to gain leniency from the prosecutorial authorities is not sufficient, by itself, to establish that the suspect did in fact lie".[259] In *Niytegeka*, the Appeals Chamber also took into consideration that accomplice witnesses may have motives or incentives to implicate the accused person, but found that "accomplice testimony is not *per se* unreliable, especially where an accomplice may be thoroughly cross-examined".[260]

In some cases, the judges have presumed that insiders involved in the crimes have an interest in avoiding self-incrimination, which may disqualify their testimony. For example, in ICTR *Bagambiki et al.* the Chamber found certain Defence witnesses not to be "credible or reliable" because they were "biased and self-interested" after they had served under the command of the accused, and because acknowledging the crimes could incriminate them.[261] The Trial Chamber in *Muvunyi* found the tes-

---

[256] ICTY, *Prosecutor v. Simić et al.*, Trial Chamber, Judgement, 17 October 2003, IT-95-9-T, para. 21 (https://www.legal-tools.org/doc/aa9b81/).

[257] Blagojević and Jokić Trial Judgment, para. 117, see above note 18.

[258] ICTY, *Prosecutor v. Kordić and Čerkez*, Trial Chamber, Judgement, 26 February 2001, IT-95-14/2-T, para. 630 ('Kordić and Čerkez Trial Judgment') (https://www.legal-tools.org/doc/d4fedd/).

[259] ICTR, *Prosecutor v. Elizaphan Ntakirutimana and Gérard Ntakirutimana*, Appeals Chamber, Judgement, 13 December 2004, ICTR-96-10-A and ICTR-96-17-A, para. 181 (https://www.legal-tools.org/doc/af07be/).

[260] ICTR, *Prosecutor v. Niyitegeka*, Appeals Chamber, Judgement, 9 July 2004, ICTR-96-14-A, para. 98 (https://www.legal-tools.org/doc/35cd4f/).

[261] ICTR, *Prosecutor v. Ntagerura, Bagambiki and Imanishimwe*, Trial Chamber, Judgement and Sentence, 25 February 2004, ICTR-99-46-T, para. 399 (https://www.legal-tools.org/doc/60036f/).

---

timony of one witness to be "unreliable" because he was a militiaman who "had reason to enhance the accused's role in order to diminish his own role", and "his evidence on the issue was not corroborated".[262]

There are other motives that are also frequent and they do not necessarily have a positive or negative impact (9 to 13 in Table 6 above). They may be legitimate, but they need to be reported in order to determine whether they have influenced the resulting information.

The prospect of reparations is legitimate for genuine victims under any regime, including the ICC Statute, but it may also prompt false victims or exaggerated allegations. For example, ICC Trial Chamber I found in the *Lubanga* judgment that "there is a real possibility" that some pretended victims "stole the identities" of other actual victims "in order to obtain the benefits they expected to receive as victims participating in these proceedings".[263]

Financial allowances for witnesses related to the procedures are common, for example, to facilitate transportation, to compensate for the disruption of economic activities, or because of relocation out of the normal social and work environment. What seems a reasonable amount of money from the viewpoint of the administration of the procedures, may constitute a reward in the eyes of witnesses with limited means. In a number of cases defence counsel has raised this issue to challenge the credibility of witnesses and to allege that somehow the prosecution is 'buying witnesses'. In SCSL *Taylor*, the judges addressed this issue as follows: they agreed with the defence that theoretically such allowances may impact on the credibility of witnesses;[264] they referred to the standard policy approved by the Court Registrar for such allowance;[265] they assessed on a case by case basis, taking into account the records disclosed by the Witness and Victims Section ('WVS') and the prosecution for each witness, whether the allowances were justified in view of the specific needs of

---

[262] ICTR, *Prosecutor v. Muvunyi*, Trial Chamber, Judgement and Sentence, 12 September 2006, ICTR-2000-55A-T, para. 156 (https://www.legal-tools.org/doc/fa02aa/).

[263] Lubanga Trial Judgment, para. 502, see above note 48.

[264] SCSL, *Prosecutor v. Taylor*, Trial Chamber, Judgement, 18 May 2012, SCSL-03-01-T, paras. 184–95 ('Taylor Trial Judgment') (https://www.legal-tools.org/doc/8075e7/).

[265] *Ibid.*, paras. 190–91, in reference to the *Practice Direction on Allowances for Witnesses and Expert Witnesses*, issued by the SCSL Registrar on 16 July 2004, valid for all parties (https://www.legal-tools.org/doc/078448/).

each witness;[266] ultimately they dismissed the defence objections for every witness that they evaluated individually.[267]

3.2.4.7.1.1. ICC Jurisprudence

In their assessment published in 2016, focused on insider witnesses from both prosecution and defence, Chlevickaite and Hola found that the ICC judges had given low weight to "potential bias and motivations" when compared to previous practice "in both national proceedings and other ICTs".[268]

3.2.4.7.1.2. Training Test

'Motivation' was the indicator that showed the lowest consistency among raters. Against the given information, the evaluators often disagreed in the identification of the motives, as well as their evaluation. This may be related to both limited information and differing understanding about the motives as such. In spite of the expectations about 'motive', it appears that assessing it may require a degree of speculation, in ways that may question its validity as an indicator.

---

[266] Taylor Trial Judgment, para. 195, see above note 264.

[267] *Ibid.*, for example, para. 240 for insider witness Foday Lansana, who received some USD 300 from the prosecution "for expenses including medication, meals, communication, his children's education and uniforms", and some USD 6,000 from WVS "to cover rent, utility bills, subsistence, medical care, child care, transportation and other miscellaneous expenses", and the judges found "that the promise of early release from prison for protective reasons and the support he received for his and his family's expenses did not influence his testimony"; para. 250 similar for insider witness TF1-362, who had received some USD 8,500 from the prosecution and WVS "for various items such as lost wages, accommodation and transportation. For a period of a few months it appears that the witness lived on Prosecution funds at a "Safe House" along with her three children and her sister. During that period, she received a mobile phone, expenses for child care and school fees for her children."; para. 287 for Alimamy Bobson Sesay, an insider witness and perpetrator who also worked as an intermediary for the prosecution: "WVS provided him a weekly allowance for meals and accommodation in addition to payments made by the OTP. The Trial Chamber does not find these payments to be unreasonable, nor did they appear to influence his testimony"; and para. 346 for insider witness Dauda Aruna Fornie, who received some USD 3,470 over two years from OTP and WVS for "transportation, medical expenses, rent payments and witness attendance allowances […] The Trial Chamber finds that these payments do not appear to be unreasonable, and did not influence his testimony".

[268] Chlevickaite and Hola, 2016, p. 694, see above note 241.

3.2.4.7.2. Prior Experience

In cases when there is prior experience with the witness, the question is whether that experience was positive regarding the needs of the investigation, and whether the information provided at the time is consistent with the information currently under evaluation. The *Arthashastra* already mentioned "contradiction between earlier or later statements" as one of the circumstances that "shall go against a party".[269]

That prior experience may refer to the same agency, or to other agencies that worked on the same or related allegations. For example, before testifying ICTR witnesses in some cases had been interviewed by the Rwandan authorities, the Gacaca proceedings, foreign agencies, the ICTR investigations, as well as previous ICTR trials.[270] In the ICC Kenya investigations key witnesses had been interviewed, among others, by the national Commission on Inquiry on Post-Election Violence (CIPEV), the Kenya National Commission on Human Rights (KNCHR), and the national police. A word of caution is necessary in relation to prior experience with other actors, since there may be significant differences in the timing, evidentiary standards or methods. Often prior experiences and statements are less demanding than the full engagement in an international investigation and testimony, hence the predictive or validating value may be limited.

At the investigation stage the interviewers need to identify and study prior statements as much as possible prior to interviewing a witness. The witnesses shall be given the opportunity to tell their accounts afresh, without being conditioned by earlier statements. Once the witness completes the account, the interviewer may want to review earlier statements with him or her, to authenticate them, and to ask about eventual contradictions. At the trial stage the parties are expected to disclose all available statements from a given witness, whether they have been collected by the party or by others, and they may well raise questions about contradictions in adversarial cross-examination. This is common practice in many systems, international or national, for example, as provided by the Spanish Law of Criminal Procedure.[271]

---

[269] See Kautilya, 1992, p. 358, see above note 44.
[270] See Combs, 2017, p. 80, see above note 136.
[271] Spain, Ley de Enjuiciamiento Criminal, 14 September 1882, Article 714 (https://www.legal-tools.org/doc/227b70/):

The jurisprudence of international tribunals indicates that some factual discrepancies between multiple statements may be acceptable if they do not affect the central elements of the case. Peripheral details might well drop out and new ones appear when a person truthfully retells an event. Arguably a lack of any discrepancy could be rather regarded with suspicion, possibly indicative of a fabricated story, because a degree of variation or evolution is perfectly normal in human cognition and memory. Still, what is 'central' and what 'peripheral' in a given account will require *ad hoc* consideration.

3.2.4.7.2.1.   Example: ICC *Kenyatta*

A key insider gave a statement for asylum seeking purposes that was not consistent with his ICC statement is some key points: the issue affected seriously his reliability and had litigation consequences. Statements given by the witness for asylum applications or other purposes need to be thoroughly analysed and cross-checked as part of the source evaluation process.

3.2.4.7.2.2.   Training Test

The evaluators were highly consistent regarding this indicator, while the information given to them conveyed prior positive experience of the witness with a commission of enquiry. On the basis of the underlying real experience, a word of caution was advisable here for two reasons: firstly, that prior experience was relatively superficial compared to the deeper engagement required for proper criminal investigations; and secondly, the situation deteriorated over time with increased pressure and threats on the witness, in ways that made difficult to predict behaviour on the basis of a less stressful prior situation.

3.2.4.7.3.   Independence

The question is whether the provider of the evidence is acting independently or influenced by some specific association, formal or informal, to relevant parties in the conflict or the proceedings, through organizational, business, family or other links. The *Arthashastra* mentioned "his

---

Cuando la declaración del testigo en el juicio oral no sea conforme en lo sustancial con la prestada en el sumario, podrá pedirse la lectura de ésta por cualquiera de las partes. Después de leída, el presidente invitará al testigo a que explique la diferencia o contradicción que entre sus declaraciones se observe.

[business] partner, a dependent, a creditor, a debtor" and "an enemy of his" among "those who shall not be cited as witnesses".[272] Cesare Beccaria indicated that "the credibility of a witness must diminish in proportion to the hatred, or friendship, or close relationships existing between him and the accused".[273] The relevance of eventual links shows in those legal systems that provide for *las preguntas generales de la ley* (the general questions of the law), to be asked to the witness at the outset of an interview or testimony, about any personal links, friendship or animosity, or interest on the subject-matter.[274]

If a witness is associated with a suspect or party to the conflict it is advisable to follow-up with specific questions on the circumstances (extent, period and duration of group membership or relevant link). For example, the fact that a witness is a member of an armed group involved in the group may certainly be very relevant to the evaluation, and worth clarifying in detail regarding the role or rank within the group, reasons for joining, chronology and other circumstances.

The ideology of the source may be relevant to evaluate independence, including political and religious beliefs, feelings of group belonging (ethnic, national, tribal, and so on), gender, cultural or other.

3.2.4.7.3.1. Training Test

The results were somehow consistent, with most participants giving a negative rating. This was a valid assessment, since the scenario indicated that the witness was a member of a key group and had some specific links to relevant institutions. There was not a single positive rating, but some were 'undetermined' or 'intermediate'. That hesitation among some respondents seems surprising, because the information showed clearly the lack of independence, for more than one reason. It appears that some evaluators, a minority within this sample, may hesitate to give a negative rating when the reported links are related to the victimized group or legit-

---

[272] See Kautilya, 1992, p. 356, see above note 44.

[273] Beccaria, 1774, p. 20, see above note 179.

[274] See Gascón Inchausti, 1999, pp. 78–86, referring to the criminal procedure in Spain, Italy and Germany, see above note 37. For a discussion in the procedure of Paraguay, including also references for several Latin-American countries, see Juan Marcelino González Garcete and Guzmán Esteban Orué Prieto, *La Prueba Testimonial*, Lexijuris, Asunción, 2017, particularly chap. VI "Tipos de testigos", pp. 63–138, and fn. 68.

imate institutions, as if they would 'feel sorry for the witness', and they would not want to 'punish the witness' because of legitimate relationships. Experience shows that indeed sometimes evaluators over-estimate independence out of respect for the witness or the interview, not to be dismissive about apparently legitimate witnesses and procedures. Evaluators need to be instructed clearly to avoid moral or instrumental considerations, and to focus on the narrow question on to what extent the source was independent or not as a matter of fact.

3.2.4.7.4. Contamination

Whether the source has been contaminated by other actors that influenced his or her information, to the point that is not possible to determine whether the information belongs genuinely with the source or it has been conveyed indirectly by others. Such contamination may be spontaneous or deliberate, and it may result from communication between witnesses, tampering designed to harm the case, or media influence.

Communication between witnesses could contaminate the evidence only if they influence each other in a way that makes impossible to distinguish between direct and hearsay knowledge, or causes some significant distortion. Research in psychology has referred to this phenomenon variously as 'collaborative narration', 'co-narration', 'joint remembering' or 'conversational remembering', while "through dialogue people actually pool their recollections".[275] An intensified form of contamination can become 'collaborative storytelling', when witnesses reinforce gradually each other accounts towards a common goal, possibly aiming at a given claim or suspect.[276]

For example, in *Fedorenko*, a key issue was the identification of the suspect by several eyewitnesses, which was dismissed by the judges because of contamination:

> The court was convinced the witnesses were discussing the trial among themselves, at least; and at worst someone was coaching them. [...] because of the obvious discussion of the

---

[275] Wagenaar and Crombag, 2005, p. 175, and experimental findings in chap. 8, sect. "Misleading Post-event Information", pp. 135–38, see above note 97.

[276] *Ibid.*, chap. 10, sect. "Collaborative Storytelling", pp. 166–68.

case by the witnesses in violation of the rule, the court rejects the in-court identification *in toto*.[277]

Conversely, in *Bemba* the ICC Trial Chamber dismissed allegations of 'collusion' between two witnesses, although they had been in contact in circumstances related to the proceedings, because "the contact between P42 and P23 prior to and after their testimonies is, in itself, insufficient to cast doubt on their credibility or the reliability of the entirety of their evidence".[278]

The review conducted by independent experts about the ICC Kenya investigations found that key insider witnesses "had been relocated to the same locations for extended periods of time, raising the possibility that they had talked among themselves and tainted each other's evidence".[279] This issue was indeed specifically investigated and analysed by the OTP at the time. Unfortunately, the cases did not proceed to completion, which otherwise could have shed some light on this and other related issues.

Deliberate tampering is a different and more serious issue. It may require specific investigation and prosecution in many national systems, and also under Article 70(1)(c) of the ICC Statute (offences against the administration of justice) for "corruptly influencing a witness". It also shows in the SVA Validity Checklist under "pressures to report falsely", defined as: "whether there are indications that others suggested, coached, pressured, or coerced the witness to make a false report or to exaggerate certain elements in an otherwise truthful report".[280] Such undue influence originating from the accused or their associates is frequent in ICC cases, as found by the prosecutor and reported to the judges among other cases in *Bemba*, *Ruto and Sang*, *Ntaganda* and *Gbagbo and Ble-Goude*.

---

[277] US District Court for the Southern District of Florida, *United States v. Fedorenko*, Judgment, 25 July 1978, 455 F. Supp. 893. Case on the denaturalisation of Feodor Fedorenko, a US citizen of Ukrainian origin suspected of having been involved in Nazi crimes, dismissed first in 1978, and granted on appeal by the US Supreme Court in 1981. Fedorenko was then extradited to USSR, sentenced to death, and executed in 1987.

[278] ICC, Situation in the Central African Republic, *The Prosecutor v. Jean-Pierre Bemba Gombo*, Trial Chamber, Judgment Pursuant to Article 74 of the Statute, 21 March 2016, ICC-01/05-01/08-3343, para. 335 ('Bemba Trial Judgment') (https://www.legal-tools.org/doc/edb0cf/).

[279] See Kenya Cases: Review and Recommendations: Executive Summary of the Report of the External Independent Experts, paras. E.19 and E.20, see above note 172.

[280] Vrij, 2008, p. 217, see above note 212.

In *Lubanga* similar problems surfaced with an intermediary working for the prosecution, which led Trial Chamber I to dismiss the evidence from four alleged child soldiers. The judges found that the intermediary introduced a "pattern of unreliability" and "it is likely that as the common point of contact he [the intermediary] persuaded, encouraged or assisted some or all of them to give false testimony" particularly regarding their age.[281] Subsequently the OTP reviewed this experience and introduced more strict standards for hiring, managing and auditing intermediaries.

Witnesses may be also be influenced by media reports on the relevant events. This is plausible with widely-reported reported incidents, but the mere exposure to media reports should not be tantamount to contamination, while it may be difficult to determine to what extent the knowledge by the witness is authentic or suggested by media.

In the very first case before the ICTY the defence argued that the identification of the accused by the prosecution witnesses was contaminated by the pictures of him published extensively in media. The defence also presented Professor Willem A. Wagenaar (Leiden University), a leading expert on cognitive psychology that had already testified for the defence in *Israel v. Demjanjuk*,[282] to challenge the methods utilized for the visual identification of the accused. The judges acknowledged that this was a relevant issue, they took it into account when raised by the defence in cross-examination, they granted that some of Wagenaar's critique was legitimate, and yet they dismissed the defence allegations because in the given context the individual witnesses did not appear to have been influenced by the images of the suspect published by different media.[283]

3.2.4.7.4.1. Training Test

The results were not consistent for this indicator. About half of the participants rated 'contamination' as 'undetermined' because, in the given scenario, it was clear that the witness interacted with other witnesses and relevant actors, but it was not established whether such interactions 'contaminated' his knowledge. The other half assessed that there was no con-

---

[281] Lubanga Trial Judgment, para. 291, see above note 48.

[282] Israel, *State of Israel v. Ivan (John) Demjanjuk*, Criminal Case no. 373/86, Criminal Appeal no. 347/88.

[283] Tadić Trial Opinion and Judgement, section on "Pre-trial Media Coverage and the Infection of Testimonial Evidence", paras. 542–44, and para. 552, see above note 46.

tamination, since that was not specifically reported in the scenario. Not a single participant identified the existence of 'contamination', although this could have been inferred from the circumstances, and in the true underlying case this was very plausible. These results seem indeed a reflection of the real difficulties with this indicator: contamination is a real risk, often witnesses will be exposed to communication with multiple actors about the relevant facts, but whether such interaction 'contaminated' or not their account may be difficult to determine. Notwithstanding the difficulties with this indicator, it may still be worth keeping it because of the likelihood of such situations, and its potentially serious impact, as indicated among others by the ICC precedent in *Lubanga*.

3.2.4.7.5.   Self-Restraint

Whether the source acknowledges the limitations of his or her own knowledge. The purpose of this indicator is to identify sources are most realistic and tempered with their information, as opposed to those that may be overly assertive, beyond their actual knowledge, for reasons of personality, acquiescence, fabrication or other. Having categorical answers for all questions is usually not considered a good sign, on the assumption that no witness 'knows everything'. To control possibly for issues of acquiescence the witness should be told before, and reassured throughout the interview that "it is ok to the say 'I don't know'", or "we don't expect you to have answers for all our questions", or "it is ok to acknowledge ignorance or limitations".

When genuine, acknowledging the following limitations is generally considered as positive signs:

- *Ignorance*: Whether the sources acknowledge it when they do not know the answer, perhaps simply stating 'I don't know'.

- *Doubts*: Whether the sources use 'maybe', 'I am not sure' and similar expressions when appropriate to qualify their account.

- *Spontaneous corrections*: Whether the source corrects him or herself spontaneously. Defined in the CBCA model as "corrections are made or information is added to material previously provided in the statement without having been prompted by the interviewer".[284]

---

[284] Vrij, 2008, p. 212, see above note 212.

- *Memory limitations*: Whether the source acknowledges memory gaps or limitations when appropriate. Similar to "admitting lack of memory" in the CBCA model.[285]

- *Self-critique*: Including details that are self-critical or self-incriminating is usually considered as a positive sign because it suggests that the source is not driven merely by self-interest, and it is more likely to be objective. In some systems this is referred to as "declarations (or statements or utterances) contrary to self-interest". Similar to "self-deprecation" in the CBCA model, defined as "the witness mentions personally unfavourable, self-incriminating details".[286] Historians may concur that "when a statement is prejudicial to a witness, his dear ones, or his causes, it is likely to be truthful".[287]

3.2.4.7.5.1. Training Test

The results were consistent, most evaluators agreed on a negative rating, since the information given to them suggested that the witnesses spoke in an overly confident manner. This is probably consistent with real investigative experience, where usually interviewers are able to evaluate fairly the degree of 'self-restrain' of the witness. After several hours of methodical conversation, it is often possible to spot a bragger.

3.2.4.7.6. Language Skill

The question is whether the source had the ability to gather the information in its original language or not. The level of knowledge of a language may be a relevant issue, as well as whether the source acquired the information through translation. A person that is fluent in the relevant language would be more reliable to convey information originated in that language, rather than someone who has only limited knowledge of the language or has obtained the information through translation.

This may apply to victim accounts about statements made by perpetrators in a given language. For example, in ICC *Ruto and Sang* the alleged perpetrators communicated among themselves and made public statements in Kalenjin, while the level of knowledge of this language

---

285   *Ibid.*
286   *Ibid.*, p. 209.
287   Gottschalk, 1969, p. 161, see above note 202.

among victims was uneven, and sometimes an important issue to be evaluated. Similar linguistic issues arose in ICC *Bemba* in view of the different languages spoken by victims and perpetrators. The linguistic gap can be even bigger with foreign witnesses or international observers.

3.2.4.7.6.1. Training Test

The results were fully consistent, while this was a very relevant issue, and clearly exposed in the given scenario.

3.2.4.7.7. Communication

The question is the ability of the witnesses to convey effectively their knowledge, and to respond clearly to the questions raised in the investigative interview. In linguistic studies, this would be a point of 'pragmatics', that is, about the impact of the language and its reception by the audience, which is different from 'semantics' as substantive meaning.[288] The investigations need 'pragmatic' results from 'good communicators' that convey readily understandable information. Whether that information is true or not is a different question, closer to linguistic 'semantics', but it can only be addressed if the witness makes the information available properly in the first place.

Giving clear answers, focused on the actual questions, is desirable, as opposed to confusing, evasive or ambiguous answers. On a related note, some judges consider spontaneity as a good sign. For example, in *Bemba* the ICC judges referred to 'lack of spontaneity' negatively when evaluating three witnesses: "the Chamber found D19's demeanour and testimony to demonstrate evasion, and a lack of spontaneity and impartiality"; "[t]he Chamber finds that the nature of these notes casts significant doubt on the credibility of D45, in particular his spontaneity and impartiality"; "D21's testimony – which was generally evasive, lacking spontaneity [...]".[289] This may merit some discussion, since spontaneity may be conditioned by various factors, including the courtroom adversarial setting, not necessarily related to truthfulness.

---

[288] See Gennaro Chierchia, "Linguistics and Language", in Robert A. Wilson and Frank C. Keil (eds.), *The MIT Encyclopedia of the Cognitive Sciences*, The MIT Press, Cambridge, 1999, pp. xci–cix; *ibid.*, entry "Pragmatics", pp. 661–64.

[289] *Bemba* Trial Judgment, paras. 359, 363 and 435, see above note 277.

3.2.4.7.7.1. Training Test

The evaluators were divided between 'negative', 'undetermined' and 'intermediate', while none of them gave a positive evaluation. This may be a valid set of observations, since the information provided to the evaluators did convey some negative elements, but it was not entirely conclusive, and assessing this point usually requires direct knowledge of the interaction with the witness, hence it could well remain 'undetermined' for those who did not participate in the interview. Indicators of this kind, including 'communication skill' and 'behaviour', would be better tested with a simulation of an interview, giving the evaluator the opportunity to observe the interaction.

3.2.4.7.8. Knowledge

On the source's prior knowledge qualifications, how much did the source know beforehand about the relevant area, people, institutions, or issues. Consider, for example:

- whether the source knew well the area and population under attack, including topology and society;
- whether the source had a qualified knowledge of the group by virtue of his or her internal position or interaction; and
- whether the source has any military expertise when reporting about military operations or weapons.

3.2.4.7.8.1. Expert Witnesses

Expert witnesses, whether scientific or area experts, require detailed evaluation of their knowledge credentials, experience, and so on; and they are subject to specific procedures before the judges.

3.2.4.7.8.2. Training Test

The results were largely consistent, with positive ratings. The available information indicated that the witness was a long-term local resident, socially very active, and very knowledgeable about the relevant area and actors.

3.2.4.7.9. Behaviour

The question would be whether the witness behaved in a co-operative and reassuring way during the interview or other contacts. The views of psychologists and litigators tend to differ on this point: most psychologists will warn against considering behaviour as an indicator of credibility; most litigators will look at behaviour to predict witness performance before the judges.

If accepted as a relevant consideration, the behaviour of a witness during the interview should be evaluated with caution. Methods that rely on behaviour or body language to determine truthfulness, such as the 'Behavioral Analysis Interview', lack scientific foundation and have been discredited.[290] Witnesses may give a negative impression through their behaviour perhaps because of discomfort or insecurity when not telling the truth, or for many other reasons, including the following: personal circumstances unknown to the interviewer; cross-cultural issues; mistrust or rapport with the interviewer, the interpreter or the organisation; time pressure.

However, at trial judges are expected to listen and observe directly the expressions and conduct of witnesses, and this direct appreciation is considered as an epistemic guarantee and part of the 'principle of immediacy', particularly in common-law procedure.[291] By 1949 Jerome N. Frank warned that inevitably the witness' demeanour and manners are always in evidence, the judge will never be able to ignore their human conduct when evaluating the testimony, consciously or unconsciously, and this is actually part of 'the principle of immediacy' in the procedure. For that matter judges "are themselves witnesses of what goes on in courtrooms. They must determine the facts from what they see and hear, from the gestures and other conduct of the testifying witnesses as well as from their words", and "as silent witnesses of the witnesses, the trial judges and juries suffer from the same human weaknesses as other witnesses".[292] Frank insisted that that for witnesses "their demeanor, while testifying,

---

[290] See Simon, 2012, chap. 5 ""Just Admit It, You're Guilty": Interrogating Suspects", section on "The Behavioral Analysis Interview", pp. 127–32, see above note 40. This method is focused on the interrogation of suspects.

[291] See Richard Volger, "The Principle of Immediacy in English Criminal Procedural Law", in *Zeitschrift für die gesamte Strafrechtswissenschaft*, 2014, vol. 126, no. 1, pp. 239–47. In Volger's view, "[t]hese aspects of the English trial methodology have over many years offended continental Positivist sensibilities as illogical, excessively theatrical and showing little respect for the serious pursuit of truth". For the Dutch system, see Groenhuijsen and Selçuk, 2014, see above note 227.

[292] Frank, 1949, p. 22, see above note 1.

counts heavily in appraising their credibility – their observable demeanor, as 'wordless language', being an important part of the evidence".[293]

Among other international examples, in ICTY *Strugar* the Trial Chamber was critical about a witness because they "gained the clear impression that he was very uneasy and uncomfortable about his testimony".[294] In ICTR *Akayesu* the Trial Chamber acknowledged among other factors "the witness's demeanour".[295] In ICTR *Kayishema et al.* the Trial Chamber noted that:

> having observed the demeanour of the witnesses and listened closely to their oral testimony the Trial Chamber is satisfied that the eyewitnesses were credible and did not attempt to invent facts. This credibility was helpful in determining the reliability of the identification of the accused at the massacre site.[296]

In ICC *Ngudjolo* Trial Chamber II assessed negatively that P-0250 (key insider) "behaved oddly during his testimony", including that "he threatened to interrupt his testimony and even, on one day, refused to appear in court", while "none of the other witnesses considered to be vulnerable behaved in such a peculiar manner".[297] In the case of P-0250 the issue would not be just some subtle signs, his odd behaviour was very noticeable and impacting on the interaction with the court.

Similar dilemmas surface in asylum procedures. The International Association of Refugee Law Judges (IARLJ) advices caution:

> using demeanour as a basis for credibility assessment should be avoided in virtually all situations. If demeanour is used as a negative factor the judge must give sustainable reasons as to why and how the demeanour and presentation of the claimant contributed to the credibility assessment, taking in-

---

[293] Frank, 1951, p. 559, see above note 208.

[294] ICTY, *Prosecutor v. Strugar*, Trial Chamber, Judgement, 31 January 2005, IT-01-42-T, para. 148 (https://www.legal-tools.org/doc/927ba5/).

[295] Akayesu Trial Judgment, para. 47, see above note 57.

[296] Kayishema *et al.* Trial Judgment, para. 397, see above note 55.

[297] See ICC, Situation in the Democratic Republic of the Congo, *The Prosecutor v. Mathieu Ngudjolo Chui*, Trial Chamber, Judgment Pursuant to Article 74 of the Statute, 18 December 2012, ICC-01/04-02/12-3-tENG, sect. VII "Analysis of the Credibility of Specific Witnesses", para. 141 ('Ngudjolo Chui Trial Judgment') (https://www.legal-tools.org/doc/2c2cde/).

to account relevant capacity, ethnicity, gender and age factors.[298]

For example, "[i]n many cultures, it is a sign of respect not to make eye contact. In Western culture avoiding eye contact is a sign of shame". And yet they acknowledge: "However, it must be recognised that in reality, demeanour can always have some impact in an oral hearing", because of the principle of orality that informs hearings with the applicant.[299]

3.2.4.7.9.1. Emotions

Emotional reactions by the witness may be indicative of truthfulness, particularly if they appear to be a consequence of the alleged crimes. For example, a victim of the genocide in Guatemala started crying when telling how her eight-year-old daughter was killed, and the judges assessed as one of the reasons "to give probative value" the fact that "the witness' crying was apparent when recalling what happened to his daughter".[300] For several others witnesses the same judges considered positive for 'probative value' that they "could observe the witness' pain when recalling what happened".[301]

This should not lead to a negative reading of the lack of emotional expression, because such behaviour may be conditioned by multiple factors unrelated to truthfulness. Concerning female victims of rape in particular, it seems that "distressed rape complainants are perceived to be more credible than complainants who present with controlled affect",

---

[298] Mackey and Barnes, 2013, p. 41, see above note 239.

[299] *Ibid.*, p. 42.

[300] Ríos Montt and Rodríguez Sánchez Tribunal Primero de Sentencia Penal Judgment, part IV "Razonamientos que inducen al tribunal a condenar o absolver", sect. B "Prueba testimonial", para. 46, see above note 71: "Fue manifiesto el llanto del testigo al recordar lo ocurrido a su hija de ocho años".

[301] *Ibid.*, part IV, sect. B, para. 55: "El tribunal, pudo observar el dolor de la testigo al recordar lo ocurrido"; *ibid.*, part IV, sect. B, para. 47: "Para los juzgadores ha sido visible el dolor experimentado por el testigo al recordar lo que le ocurrió"; *ibid.*, part IV, sect. B, para. 57: "Es evidente el dolor de la testigo, al recordar los hechos"; *ibid.*, part IV, sect. B, para. 63: "Los jueces observamos el grado de afectación del testigo, al recordar todo lo ocurrido"; *ibid.*, part IV, sect. B, para. 65: "Bañada en llanto, indicó como mataron a su hermano e hijos"; *ibid.*, part IV, sect. B, para. 68: "Los juzgadores observamos y escuchamos el llanto desgarrador de la testigo, al recordar las violaciones sexuales de las cuales fue objeto"; *ibid.*, part IV, sect. B, para. 95: "Evidencia dolor y tristeza al relatar lo ocurrido"; and so on.

which could lead to discredit unfairly the less emotionally expressive victims.[302]

3.2.4.7.9.2. Assertiveness

Assertiveness is not necessarily indicative of accuracy. For example, in one ICTY case the Trial Chamber issued a conviction largely on the strength of a victim witness who showed a "confident and forceful" demeanour before investigators, prosecutors and judges. The Appeals Chamber reversed this evaluation and indicated that:

> very often, a confident demeanour is a personality trait and not necessarily a reliable indicator of truthfulness or accuracy [...] an enormous amount of research has determined that the relationship between the certainty expressed by a witness and the correctness of the identification is very weak. [...] Even witnesses who are very sincere, honest and convinced about their identification are very often wrong.[303]

The finding referred particularly to eyewitness identification. Research on national cases shows confident witnesses being particularly influential although "the observed confidence-accuracy relationship is close to zero".[304] And yet for litigation purposes "confident witnesses are likely to be overrepresented at trial because prosecutors are more likely to try cases when they have confident eyewitnesses".[305]

Chlevickaite and Hola found that "[e]ven though identified as one of the most fundamental factors in the judicial assessments of witness credibility in the literature, demeanour did not play a leading role at the ICC".[306] As these authors indicate, this "can be seen as a positive devel-

---

[302] See Faye T. Nitschke, Blake M. McKimmie and Eric J. Vanman, "A Meta-Analysis of the Emotional Victim Effect for Female Adult Rape Complainants: Does Complainant Distress Influence Credibility?", in *Psychological Bulletin*, 2019, vol. 145, no. 10, pp. 953–79. On the credibility assessments of female victims of rape in India, see Ravinder Barn and Ved Kumari, "Understanding Complainant Credibility in Rape Appeals: A Case Study of High Court Judgments and Judges' Perspectives in India", in *British Journal of Criminology*, 2015, vol. 55, no. 3, pp. 435–53.

[303] Kupreškić *et al.* Appeals Judgment, para. 138, see above note 181. The expert testimony of a cognitive psychologist, as well as contradictions with earlier statements by the same witness, was considered to this effect.

[304] Simon, 2012, p. 167, see above note 40.

[305] *Ibid.*, p. 154.

[306] Chlevickaite and Hola, 2016, p. 694, see above note 241.

opment, since behaviour-related factors are particularly difficult to assess appropriately in judicial proceedings, and may be easily misinterpreted".[307] It appears that the ICC judges focus instead on "on more tangible aspects of the testimonies, though not dismissing demeanour altogether".[308] This is similar to the approach taken by the ID SE guidelines, considering behaviour only as one among many factors, to be assessed with caution.

This caution could consist on limiting any consideration of behaviour only to the most apparent and disruptive actions by the witness, while avoiding speculation on minor signs or 'body language'. An alternative could be to train judges to ignore the behaviour of the witnesses when perceiving and assessing their testimony. Some authors do recommend in relation to rape "that effective methods of reducing reliance on emotional demeanor to make credibility judgments about rape complainants should be investigated to make credibility assessments fairer and more accurate".[309] One author has recommended for asylum procedures "prohibiting entirely the use of nonverbal cues or demeanor in credibility assessments".[310]

3.2.4.7.9.3. Training Test

The results were not consistent, possibly reflecting the different behavioural aspects reported in the scenario, which were not necessarily amenable to a single overall conclusion. This result is probably a valid proxy of the true difficulties to assess behaviour in real life, as per the above-mentioned caveats and differing judicial record. The reliance on behavioural indicators by judges would merit some additional research.

3.2.4.7.10. Criminal Record

The question is whether the witness has been involved in the commission of crimes, whether related to the matter under investigation, or others. It is a common assumption that a criminal record is detrimental for the credi-

---

[307] *Ibid.*

[308] *Ibid.*, p. 695.

[309] See Nitschke, McKimmie and Vanman, 2019, see above note 302.

[310] Michael Kagan, "Is Truth in the Eye of the Beholder? Objective Credibility Assessment in Refugee Status Determination", in *Georgetown Immigration Law Journal*, 2003, vol. 17, no. 3, p. 380.

bility of a witness, but in reality, criminals may be as knowledgeable of many facts as anybody else, and there are many kinds of criminal conduct that may be more or less relevant to the quality of a witness for a particular case. The judicial record across international tribunals is not consistent when evaluating this factor.

For example, in one ICTY case the judges considered that prior criminal record, criminal conduct and history of personal drug use, weighs "very negatively in an assessment of the trustworthiness" of a witness. Such a record, together with the witness' association with the armed group of the accused, left the judges with an "extremely negative view of the credibility of this witness".[311] The judges required corroboration for any fact reported by this witness. In another ICTY case the defense challenged the credibility of an insider witness because of his criminal record, since the witness had confessed to robbing and then murdering two fellow soldiers, but the Trial Chamber considered the witness credible, with the subsequent endorsement by the Appeals Chamber.[312] ICTY judges dismissed similar objections by the defence in another case, while the witness had contributed to the crimes, and the defence argued that blaming the accused was in the exculpatory self-interest of the witness.[313]

Similar differences show across cases in ICTR. In *Kajelijeli*, the Trial Chamber found credible a witness who was a convicted co-perpetrator, and furthermore accused by his brother acting as witness for the defence of being "a liar and a thief who had previously stolen things from his own family".[314] In *Rwamakuba*, after careful discussion the Trial Chamber relied on the testimony of two witnesses with a criminal record, while dismissing another witness who also had a criminal record but was considered dishonest and not trustworthy in relation to "her particular personality".[315] Some research on ICTR shows that the judges have found

---

[311] ICTY, *Prosecutor v. Limaj et al.*, Trial Chamber, Judgement, 30 November 2005, IT-03-66-T, para. 28 (https://www.legal-tools.org/doc/4e469a/).

[312] ICTY, *Prosecutor v. Naletilić and Martinović*, Appeals Chamber, Judgement, 3 May 2006, IT-98-34-A, para. 174 (https://www.legal-tools.org/doc/94b2f8/).

[313] ICTY, *Prosecutor v. Delalić et al.*, Trial Chamber, Judgement, 16 November 1998, IT-96-21-T, paras. 759 and 762 (https://www.legal-tools.org/doc/6b4a33/).

[314] ICTR, *Prosecutor v. Kajelijel*, Trial Chamber, Judgment and Sentence, 1 December 2003, ICTR-98-44A-T, para. 467 (https://www.legal-tools.org/doc/afa827/).

[315] Rwamakuba Trial Judgment, paras. 102 and 135, see above note 54.

much more often that witnesses are credible when they were not involved in the genocide, or they were not co-accused, that when they were.[316]

3.2.4.7.10.1. Insiders

Persons with direct internal knowledge of the perpetrating group are commonly referred to as 'insider witnesses'. Most often they are members of the group, eventually involved in the crimes or related operations, but victims or other persons may have also gained internal knowledge as the result of their confinement or work with the group.

Some ICC judges have tended to see the criminal record of insiders as detrimental to their credibility, while others to the contrary appreciate their qualified knowledge of the criminal actions. For example in the confirmation procedure for *Ruto and Sang* the prosecution presented four insider witnesses and argued that "'insiders' commonly provide highly relevant information accessible only to individuals involved in the crime or close to the accused", the defence responder that "they should not be considered by the Chamber as reliable or credible because they are self-confessed criminals".[317] The judges found these insiders reliable and based their decision to confirm the charges to a large extent on their evidence.[318]

3.2.4.7.10.2. Subsequent Criminal Conduct

Crimes or lesser offences committed after the person became a witness may be relevant to the evaluation, they may need to be specifically recorded, and in some cases communicated to the judges and the defence. For example, in one case a witness that was under a protection scheme attacked violently a protection officer, which constituted a criminal offence, and the witness was arrested, prosecuted and convicted for this matter: this situation required specific evaluation and disclosure.

---

[316] See Combs, 2017, p. 95, see above note 136.

[317] ICC, Situation in the Republic of Kenya, *Prosecutor v. Ruto and Sang*, Pre-Trial Chamber, Decision on the Confirmation of Charges Pursuant to Article 61(7)(a) and (b) of the Rome Statute, 23 January 2012, ICC-01/09-01/11-373, para. 91 ('Ruto and Sang Pre-Trial Decision on the Confirmation of Charges') (https://www.legal-tools.org/doc/96c3c2/).

[318] *Ibid.*, paras. 168 and 218.

3.2.4.7.10.3. Training Test

The participants rated this indicator consistently as 'undetermined', which is fair since the scenario did not contain any relevant information. If judges consider this a relevant indicator, as in the examples above, it is advisable for the investigation to address such issues specifically.

3.2.4.7.11. Medical Condition

Did the witness have, at the time of the events or at the time of the interview, any medical condition that may affect his or her cognitive ability or memory (sight, hearing, psychological, psychiatric, or other)?

For example, in one ICTY case the psychological diagnosis and treatment of a victim was seen by the judges as a relevant fact that should have been disclosed to the defence, as a matter of fairness for the accused, even if ultimately there is no scientific consensus on whether that condition affects the credibility of the witness or not.[319] Such diagnosis or treatment should show in the evaluation as a relevant fact, but it does not lead necessarily to a positive or negative assessment.

If needed the investigation may seek medical (sight, hearing, physical), psychological or psychiatric assessments of witnesses on issues relevant to their cognitive ability.

3.2.4.7.11.1. Training Test

The participants rated this indicator consistently as 'undetermined', since the scenario did not contain any relevant information. Whenever visual ability is essential for the evidence, or there are reasons for doubt, it is probably advisable to verify it specifically, so that the information would show in the statement and the evaluators would be able to make a valid assessment.

3.2.4.8. Information Indicators

3.2.4.8.1. Immediacy

On the cognitive distance between the source and the reported facts. In principle direct knowledge is considered more credible than indirect or

---

[319] ICTY, Prosecutor v. Furundžija, Judgement, 10 December 1998, IT-95-17/1-T, para. 92 (https://www.legal-tools.org/doc/e6081b/).

hearsay knowledge. It is crucial to determine whether a source is direct or indirect, and who is the original source of the given information.

'Primary source' is a term for direct witness, original records, or any other kind of source that conveys direct, immediate knowledge of the facts. Conversely 'secondary sources' are those that convey indirect knowledge, whether as hearsay witnesses, or copies of documents, or documents that are based on other primary sources. There is abundant case-law from ICC and other jurisdictions indicating that direct sources have higher probative value than indirect ones.

3.2.4.8.1.1. Degrees and Modes of Hearsay

There are different degrees and modes of hearsay or secondary information. For example, some hearsay may be very credible, if the direct witness is reliable, he or she conveyed the information immediately after fact, in a very detailed way, and to several persons that corroborate each other in their hearsay accounts. On the other hand, 'double hearsay' refers to two or more degrees of separation from the direct source, which will require identifying the specifics of every step of separation, and it will be less credible.

3.2.4.8.1.2. Secondary Reports

Some ICC judges have considered NGO and human rights fact-finding reports as indirect evidence about the crimes of only limited probative value. Detailed Source Evaluation is advisable for sources of this kind to determine their methods, degree of closeness to the primary sources, qualifications of the authors, and so on. If such reports were conveyed to the suspects they might constitute direct evidence about their knowledge of the crime.

3.2.4.8.1.3. Translations

Translating the information may be seen as detrimental in terms of immediacy: an original document is preferable than a translated version, when possible.

3.2.4.8.1.4. Training Test

The ratings were not consistent, possibly because the witness reported many different facts, based variously on direct and indirect knowledge. A better evaluation would require to test 'immediacy' on specific facts, rather that the account as a whole.

3.2.4.8.2. Detail

Detailed information is usually perceived as more credible than generic information, including specific locations, time, persons and descriptions. This is commonly accepted in many systems, including, for example, in the Italian jurisprudence about the testimony of the *pentiti*, and also emphasized in the SVA-CBCA and Reality Monitoring models.[320]

The focus on details is based on two assumptions: first, substantially, that a more detailed account is more likely to be true; second, methodologically, that more details offer more factual points for verification. The first assumption is arguable; a very detailed account may well be false, for different reasons of cognitive mistake or deliberate deception. A common strategy among deliberate liars, known as 'embedded lies', is to take a true and detailed story, and to add or change only some detail, such as a name or a date, to achieve the desired deception. A different type of 'embedded lie' could occur when a source appropriates a story known only to another source, hence presenting as direct knowledge what is only hearsay. Such 'embedded lies' are well-known from scientific research as well as investigative practice.[321]

By 1900, Alfred Binet had observed that a recollection, even in good faith, can be "detailed and entirely false [...] an unprepared observer could consider these details so clear, so specific, as evidence of the accuracy of the memory; we see now that the detail of the recall is not incompatible with its falsehood".[322] Still, some seventy years later CBCA in-

---

[320] See Giacomo Cavalli, *La chiamata in correità*, Giuffrè Editore, Milan, 2006, sect. 3.2.2.5. "Precisione o articolazione", p. 106: "La chiamata in correità è tanto più credibile quanto più ricca di particolari, anche marginali, poiché il guidice ha maggiori possibilità di verificare la dichiarazione accusatorial".

[321] I am grateful to Moa Lidén for calling my attention to 'embedded lies' in scientific literature, the phenomenon indeed is also known in international investigations.

[322] Binet, 1900, pp. 284–85, see above note 113:

Les erreurs commises par les élèves ont ce caractère singulier: ils ont la précision de détails des souvenirs exact. Toutes nos observations montrent qu'un souvenir peut être précis quoique entièrement faux; [...] Un esprit not prévenu pourrait considérer ces détails si nets, si circonstanciés comme un prévue de l'exactitude du souvenir. Nous voyons maintenant que la précision des souvenirs n'est pas incompatible avec leur fausseté.

---

cluded the criterion of "quantity of details", defined as "the statement is rich in detail and includes specific descriptions of place, time, persons, objects and events".[323] Those experts that are critical with CBCA have observed that this criterion, which is one of the most decisive ones within CBCA, has no scientific validity because "[i]t has never been shown that a detailed testimony is more often true than one with fewer details".[324] It is a well-known technique in literary fiction to add detail to impress realism, as Julio Cortazar observed about Edgar Allan Poe's horror stories.[325] Conversely, a relatively vague account may be truthful, while the vagueness is related to the source's methods or skills, or the circumstances of the communication.

The second assumption seems valid as a matter of methodology, since more details means more information, and more opportunities for testing external verification and internal consistency. In other words, more detailed sources are preferable because they contain more information and they are more verifiable, not necessarily because they are more truthful.

Evaluating this criterion should take into account the background of the source, which may be more or less inclined to give details because of their personality, rapport, and so on; and the circumstances when collecting the information, including the available time and methods.

3.2.4.8.2.1. Training Test

The results were not consistent, apparently because the witnesses referred to many different issues, with varying degrees of detail, hence the information was not necessarily suitable for a single overall conclusion. A better evaluation would require to test 'detail' on specific issues of fact, rather that the account as a whole. Alternatively, in view of the abovementioned critical considerations, perhaps 'details' could be dropped entirely as an indicator, and the available details simply be utilized as relevant for the rest of the indicators about the information.

---

[323] Vrij, 2008, p. 209, see above note 212.

[324] Wagenaar and Crombag, 2005, p. 190, see above note 97.

[325] Edgar Allan Poe, *Cuentos/1: Prólogo, traducción y notas de Julio Cortazar*, Alianza, Madrid, 1994.

3.2.4.8.3. Internal Consistency

The question is whether the information is consistent, factually and logically, in its own terms. This would be equivalent to "logical structure" in the CBCA, defined as "the statement is coherent and does not contain logical inconsistencies or contradictions".[326] Similarly multiple Italian cases related to *pentiti* refer to the "*logicità o coerenza del racconto*" as an element of credibility.[327]

Consider the following examples:

- A witness reported seeing the perpetrator at the crime scene, but this was not plausible giving the insufficient light, obstacles in the line sight, or distance;

- An insider reported that he had participated in multiple attacks quite far away from each other within a short period of time. The account was not plausible because it would have been impossible to travel to those locations in the given conditions and timeframe.

- ICC Trial Chamber II in *Ngudjolo* assessed negatively some 'contradictions' within the testimony of P-0250 (key insider) in relation to the command status of the accused:

> Within a short time span in the course of his testimony, Witness P-250 stated that soldiers were not authorised to meet Mathieu Ngudjolo on an individual basis, only to claim in apparent contradiction or at the very least extemporaneously, that even an ordinary soldier could report to the Accused or provide him with information directly.[328]

Internal consistency also needs to be evaluated with caution, only to exclude propositions that are factually implausible within a well-known or safely predictable material context, for example, for a specific chronolog-

---

[326] Vrij, 2008, p. 209, see above note 212.

[327] See Cavalli, 2006, sect. 3.2.2.4. "Logicità o coerenza del racconto", p. 106, quoting multiple judgments from the Italian Corte Suprema di Cassazione (Supreme Court of Cassation) from 1971 to 1999, see above note 320: "La chiamata en correità deve essere strutturata in modo tale da rispondere alle regole della commune esperienza, della logica e della fisica".

[328] See Ngudjolo Chui Trial Judgment, sect. VII "Analysis of the Credibility of Specific Witnesses", para. 138, see above note 297. Note fns. 305 and 306 for the corresponding transcripts quoted by the Chamber in support of this finding.

---

ical sequence, or some discrete physical action, or predictable functioning of different artefacts (vehicles, weaponry, and so on). Internal consistency will be more open to interpretation in relation to higher-level logical arguments or complex factual scenarios. Plausibility is context and culture-specific, as John Locke indicated already in his classic work *An essay concerning human understanding* with the story of the king of Siam and the Dutch Ambassador:

> As it happened to a Dutch ambassador, who entertaining the king of Siam with the particularities of Holland, which he was inquisitive after, amongst other things told him that the water in his country would sometimes, in cold weather, be so hard that men walked upon it, and that it would bear an elephant, if he were there. To which the king replied, Hitherto I have believed the strange things you have told me, because I look upon you as a sober fair man, but now I am sure you lie.[329]

A number of judgments and experts on asylum procedures have made this point, since "[a]sylum seekers' claims may be rejected because the accounts of their experiences fail to satisfy decision-makers' expectations as to how persecuted people 'ought' to behave or react".[330] In the words of one expert "[t]oo often officials assume that the way they think is also the way the asylum-seeker thinks".[331]

A different kind of consistency issues may appear with contradictions, or additional allegations, among multiple statements by the same witness. Regarding rape in particular the international judges, including ICTR, SCSL and ICC, have stated in several cases that the fact that the allegation was not included in the first statement should not be a reason to doubt its veracity. A situation of this kind surfaced in ICC *Ntaganda*, with the statements of three victims who reported being raped only in their second statement given in 2013, not in their first one from 2005.[332] The

---

[329] John Locke, *An Essay Concerning Human Understanding and a Treatise on the Conduct of the Understanding*, Heys & Zell, Philadelphia, 1860 (original edition of 1690), p. 429.

[330] Douglas McDonald, "Credibility Assessment in Refugee Status Determination", in *National Law School of India Review*, 2014, vol. 26, no. 2, p. 123.

[331] *Ibid.*, citing Walter Kälin, "Troubled Communication: Cross-Cultural Misunderstandings in the Asylum Hearing", in *International Migration Review*, 1986, vol. 20, no. 2, p. 234.

[332] Ntaganda Trial Judgment, para. 88 "Delayed reporting of rape", including fns. 192 and 195 referring to the testimony and reports by prosecution's expert witness Ms. Maeve Lewis, see above note 60.

OTP team identified this issue and took the additional steps of conducting two expert assessments, one medical in order to assess some injuries reported in the statement, and another one psychological to assess the credibility of the witness. The psychologist who interviewed the witnesses and conducted the assessments concluded that "delayed reporting of their rapes is consistent with the 'experience of raped women worldwide'", and that the allegations were credible.[333] This psychologist testified in court, the prosecution submitted her reports and three other witnesses corroborated her assessment on the difficulties to report rape by victims.[334] The judges accepted this assessment, and further considered the rapes proved on the strength of the testimonies of these victims.[335]

Nancy A. Combs takes a critical stand towards the acceptance of delayed rape reporting for two reasons. Firstly, she claims that "[a] Western victim's credibility would be in shreds if she failed to mention that she had been raped until a late stage of the investigation".[336] There are several problems with this statement. Combs does not present any source of academia nor jurisprudence to support this notion, this shows only as her opinion. Research indicates a more complex and evolving picture in Western national systems, including instances in which national judges are equally understanding towards delayed rape allegations.[337] Furthermore, even if the comment were true, it does not mean that it is fair, it could be related to prejudice prevailing in national systems, and the practice advanced by international judges could be more truthful and fair than many a national precedent.[338]

---

[333] *Ibid.*, fn. 195.

[334] *Ibid.*, fn. 192.

[335] *Ibid.*, para. 88 "Delayed reporting of rape" for the general conclusion, and paras. 599–601 for the specific crimes.

[336] Combs, 2010, p. 87, see above note 92. Note that the author refers to victims of rape exclusively as "she".

[337] See among others Louise Ellison, "Closing the Credibility Gap: The Prosecutorial Use of Expert Witness Testimony in Sexual Assault Cases", in *The International Journal of Evidence and Proof*, 2005, vol. 9, no. 4, pp. 239–68, including on "Delayed Reporting" pp. 248–50, focused on England and Wales; and Melissa S. Morabito, Linda M. Williams and April Pattavina, *Decision Making in Sexual Assault Cases: Replication Research on Sexual Violence Case Attrition in the U.S.*, US National Criminal Justice Reference Service, February 2019.

[338] For the state of the issue in India, including on delayed reporting, see Barn and Kumari, 2015, see above note 302.

Secondly Combs claims that although the acceptance of delayed rape allegations may be justified because of "widespread taboo", in her view "it likewise could have the effect of encouraging witnesses to embellish or to lie outright about their experiences".[339] Combs does not offer any justification, nor basis of research to support this statement. Hypothetically witnesses may have incentives to "embellish or to lie" for any crime, just as they may have important incentives to speak the truth. Combs proposes a teleological interpretation of the argument anticipating some hypothetical negative consequences, but she does not consider the implications of the alternative argument, while the consequence of rejecting delayed reporting would be the impunity for many instances of true rape that are subject to reporting delays and difficulties for understandable reasons.

The judgment by the High Court of Delhi in *Sajjan Kumar et al.* offers another example of accepting the veracity of delayed allegations. The key witness referred to police officers as "killers and murderers" only during the trial testimony, and never in the previous investigative interviews. She acknowledged this contradiction under cross-examination and explained that it was due to lack of trust on the police officers.[340] The judges accepted her testimony as truthful in the following terms:

> the investigation was completely botched-up. [...] The atmosphere of distrust created as a result of these developments would have dissuaded the victims from coming forward to speak about what they knew. In the context of these cases, the factum of delay cannot be used to the advantage of the accused [...] Nothing in the deposition of PW-1 points to either untruthfulness or unreliability. Her evidence deserves acceptance.[341]

3.2.4.8.3.1. Training Test

The participants were divided between positive and 'undetermined' ratings, with not a single negative rating. This seems understandable because in the given scenario some general features were consistent, particularly a good chronological flow, and plausible cause-effect accounts, while the information included some internal contradictions in relation to specific

---

[339] Combs, 2010, p. 87, see above note 92.
[340] Delhi High Court Sajjan Kumar and Others Judgment, paras. 210–12, see above note 45.
[341] *Ibid.*, paras. 219–20.

issues. That may well happen with complex narratives involving multiple facts.

3.2.4.8.4. External Verification

Verification is a test of consistency with the rest of the evidence that has been positively evaluated and originate from separate independent sources. This is a particularly important aspect, checking against multiple sources is a fundamental requirement for proper investigations. 'Verification' is a neutral term, literally aiming at a determination about the truth, hence preferable to define an impartial parameter, rather than 'corroboration' which means positive confirmation: the evaluation must aim at verifying impartially the validity of the evidence, with no prejudice towards confirming or dismissing it. The approach should not be driven by 'confirmation bias' or 'asymmetrical scepticism', it needs to look impartially for points of either confirmation or contradiction.[342]

Corroboration is not a legal requirement in most systems, and a single good source may produce conclusive evidence. Even the classic rule *testis unus testis nullus* (one witness, no witness) accepted exceptions in its original context. As Mirjan Damaška has explained: "contrary to the widespread opinion on the mechanical nature of Roman-canon evidence [...] even under mainstream Roman-canon doctrine, two eyewitnesses were not always required for the imposition of sanguinary punishments".[343] At the international level the SCSL trial judgment in *Taylor* stated, while quoting several ICTY precedents: "[a]s a matter of law, the testimony of a single witness on a material fact does not require corroboration".[344]

Corroboration is not a guarantee either, because several sources may be equally wrong about a point of fact. As explained in ICTY jurisprudence:

> corroboration of testimonies, even by many witnesses, does not establish automatically the credibility, reliability or weight of those testimonies. Corroboration is neither a con-

---

[342] See Moa Lidén, "Confirmation Bias in Investigations of Core International Crimes: Risk Factors and Quality Control Techniques", Chap. 7 below.

[343] Mirjan Damaška, *Evaluation of Evidence: Pre-Modern and Modern Approaches*, Cambridge University Press, 2019, p. 85.

[344] Taylor Trial Judgment, para. 166, with reference in fn. 414 to ICTY *Tadić*, *Aleksovski*, and *Kupreškić et al.*, see above note 264.

> dition nor a guarantee of reliability of a single piece of evidence. It is an element that a reasonable trier of fact may consider in assessing the evidence.[345]

The ICC judges have explained in similar terms:

> Depending on the circumstances, a single piece of evidence, such as a video image of a person, may suffice to establish a specific fact. However, as recognised by the Trial Chamber, this does not mean that any piece of evidence provides a sufficient evidentiary basis for a factual finding.[346]

Evidence needs to be impartially checked against other sources by the principle of 'follow the best source', that is, take as a starting point the information that has been evaluated as most credible. The assessment of which one is the 'best source' may evolve along with the investigation.

It is highly advisable, as recommended by the ICC judges, to check witness allegations against documentary or forensic records (personal records, pictures, communication data, and so on), which might be 'the best source' to be followed. Allegations of injuries or death should be checked as much as possible with existing medical or death records, or with medical examinations or exhumations conducted specifically for the purpose of the investigation.

3.2.4.8.4.1. Corroboration of Co-Perpetrators

Some national systems consider that the evidence by a co-perpetrator alone is insufficient to justify a conviction, which would be an exception to the general rule of validity of single-witness allegations.[347] The Italian Code of Criminal Procedure suggests a requirement of corroboration for co-perpetrators as follows: "3. The statements made by the accused of the same crime or by a person accused in a connected procedure pursuant to

---

[345] ICTY, *Prosecutor v. Limaj et al.*, Appeals Chamber, Judgement, 27 September 2007, IT-03-66-A, para. 203 (https://www.legal-tools.org/doc/6d43bf/).

[346] Lubanga Appeals Judgment, para. 218, see above note 59.

[347] See Cavalli, 2006, sect. 3.3. "La credibilità estrinseca della chiamata in correità", p. 108, see above note 320: "Qualora si stato superato il controllo sulla attendibilità intrinseca della chiamata in correità, il giudice, data l'insufficiente forza probatoria della stessa, deve individuare 'altri elementi di prova', ossia i c.d. riscontri estrinseci, che siano idonei a confermare l'attendibilità della dichiarazione accusatoria"; Gascón Inchausti, 1999, p. 126, referring to jurisprudence of the Spanish Constitutional Court (Tribunal Constitucional), ECLI:ES:TC:1997:153, ECLI:ES:TC:1998:49, and ECLI:ES:TC:1998:115, see above note 37.

Article 12 are valued together with the other elements of proof that confirm their reliability".[348] Similarly, in the trial for the terrorist attack in Madrid on 11 March 2004, the judges evaluated the testimony of a key insider "as if it were the testimony of a co-accused, so that they are given the value of incriminating evidence after being corroborated by sources of evidence or objective external data, as required by jurisprudence".[349]

ICTY judges considered this issue in *Kordić and Čerkez*, and taking into account, among others, the Italian procedure and jurisprudence in relation to *pentiti*, they decided that the testimony of co-perpetrators does not require corroboration.[350] Nevertheless, in the case in question the judges did verify the testimony by a key co-perpetrator with some circumstantial indicia and found it reliable.[351] The SCSL judges took the same position in *Taylor*, echoing several SCSL and ICTR precedents, and stating that the Trial Chamber "may convict on the basis of the evidence of a single witness, even an accomplice, provided such evidence has been viewed with caution".[352]

3.2.4.8.4.2. Circumstantial Corroboration

The ICTY jurisprudence has admitted two types of corroboration, which can be defined as substantive and circumstantial. Substantive corroboration is the most common and compelling understanding of corroboration, when two independent sources report consistently the same fact. Circumstantial corroboration takes place when one source reports the substantive fact, and other sources report some accessory facts in a way that makes the primary account plausible. As mentioned above, *Kordić and Čerkez* is a remarkable example of circumstantial corroboration, as follows: a co-perpetrator testifying for the prosecution reports, on the basis of hearsay, the crucial fact that a certain meeting took place to plan the massacre with

---

[348] Italy, Codice di Procedura Penale (Code of Criminal Procedure), Article 192 "Valutazione della prova" (Evaluation of the Evidence), para. 3. Article 12 "Casi di connessione" (Connected Cases) defines the criteria to connect cases with the same actions or perpetrators (https://www.legal-tools.org/doc/513152/, https://www.legal-tools.org/doc/aee4e8/).

[349] Spain National High Court Zougam Sentencia, p. 334, see above note 61.

[350] Kordić and Čerkez Trial Judgment, para. 628, see above note 258.

[351] *Ibid.*, para. 630.

[352] Taylor Trial Judgment, para. 183, with reference in fn. 445 to SCSL *AFRC* and *RUF*, and ICTR *Nchamihigo* and *Muvunyi*, see above note 264.

the participation of the accused;[353] "the Trial Chamber must determine to what extent his evidence is confirmed by other evidence";[354] "there is no direct evidence supporting his account of the meeting";[355] "[h]owever, there is circumstantial evidence which does so", including three elements; that the events "followed the plan which he described"; that "no such plan could have been put into operation without prior meetings and without political approval"; and that given the power of the accused in the area no such meeting would have taken place without him.[356] Hence the judges found that those circumstantial elements corroborated the core fact alleged by the witness. The defence challenged this evidence in appeal, arguing that the Trial Chamber erroneously relied on "the uncorroborated hearsay testimony of a convicted murderer and admitted liar" and that "alternative inferences favourable to the Accused ought to have been drawn".[357] The Appeals Chamber discussed this issue thoroughly and endorsed the findings by the Trial Chamber because "[i]t is incorrect to suggest that circumstantial evidence cannot be regarded as corroborative" and otherwise the Trial Chamber did not err in its evaluation of the evidence.[358]

3.2.4.8.4.3.   Circular Reporting

Only sources that are different and independent among themselves can provide corroboration. For example, when a media or intelligence report and an insider witness are giving the same information, this may constitute corroboration only if the insider was not the source of the media or intelligence report in the first place. If the source is anonymous it may not be possible to assess whether it provides with corroboration or it is merely a case of duplication, or circular reporting.

---

[353] Kordić and Čerkez Trial Judgment, para. 610, see above note 258: "The witness was not present himself but was some of those who did attend […] He was told about it by Paško Ljubičić (the Commander of the IV Battalion Military Police) while it was going on".

[354] *Ibid.*

[355] *Ibid.*

[356] *Ibid.*

[357] ICTY, *Prosecutor v. Kordić and Čerkez*, Appeals Chamber, Judgement, 17 December 2004, IT-95-14/2-A, para. 247 (https://www.legal-tools.org/doc/738211/).

[358] *Ibid.*, paras. 276–84.

3.2.4.8.4.4. Fabricated Corroboration

Mechanically echoing known allegations may be a negative indicator; it may be that the providers of the information aims at corroborating the allegation and giving us 'what they think we want to hear' rather than his or her true knowledge. Including details that are counter-intuitive, and contrary to the expected or most popular version of the events, might be in some cases a positive indicator.

3.2.4.8.4.5. Internal Tools

Checking external corroboration requires specific and laborious checks with analytical products, evidence databases, and possibly open sources.

3.2.4.8.4.6. Training Test

The participants gave consistently negative ratings for external corroboration, which was a valid assessment in view of the information contained in the scenario.

3.2.4.8.5. Evolution

The evaluation often evolves over time, because of the behaviour of the source, or new information. Hence the evaluation needs to be dated and time-specific, and it may need to be updated. It is advisable to review periodically the evaluation and correct or adjust to the new information when appropriate.[359]

3.2.5. The Practice of the ICC Chambers

The sections above focus on the methodology to conduct Source Evaluation at the investigation stage. At the litigation stage SE issues will surface in similar terms, with the benefit of the adversarial test, and judges will need to address them with criteria and methods of their choice.

The ICC judges have paid attention extensively to SE in multiple decisions and judgments, which is a sign of high professional standards. They have discussed at length the relevant issues even at the pre-trial stage and Confirmation Hearings. In *Ruto and Sang*, for example, the judges of the Pre-Trial Chamber (PTC) discussed in detail the evaluation of insider witnesses and dismissed the prosecution's argument that "for

---

[359] See below Section 3.4. on the process.

purposes of confirmation, the Pre-Trial Chamber should accept as reliable the Prosecution's evidence, so long as it is relevant", and defer to the trial judges for "a careful weighing and evaluation of the credibility of the witnesses".[360]

Table 7 below illustrates the extensive consideration of SE issues in the five main judgments by different Trial Chambers (TC) from 2012 to 2019:

Year	TC	Case	Source Evaluation Considerations
2012	I	Lubanga	130 pages on the issue of the intermediaries, which was relevant to the alleged "contamination" of some victims who testified for the prosecution; 35 pages to discuss specifically issues of "witness credibility" and age determination for 15 different witnesses.
2012	II	Ngudjolo	2 pages to outline their criteria for the "assessment of oral testimony" and 62 pages for the "analysis of credibility of specific witnesses", including 32 pages for the prosecution's main 2 insider witnesses.
2014	II	Katanga	13 pages on "the Chamber's criteria for the evaluation of witnesses", 99 pages on "analysis of credibility of specific witnesses", including 22 pages for the prosecution's main 2 insider witnesses.
2016	III	Bemba	12 pages on "the criteria for the weight to be accorded to the evidence"; 32 pages on "issues of witness credibility".
2019	VI	Ntaganda	12 pages on "evaluation of evidence"; 89 pages on "specific issues of witness credibility", including individual evaluation of 16 witnesses and 9 pages on alleged collusion.

**Table 7. Consideration of SE issues in the five main judgments
by different TC from 2012 to 2019.**

In four of the above judgments the TCs outlined their evaluation criteria, with similar language, but some differences in the choice of criteria. See below the list of the criteria identified by these TCs (with the judgments of *Ngudjolo* and *Katanga* by TC II sharing the same criteria),

---

[360] Ruto and Sang Pre-Trial Decision on the Confirmation of Charges, paras. 55–58, see above note 317.

and their correspondence with the criteria of the OTP ID Source Evaluation Guidelines:[361]

		TC II	TC III	TC VI	OTP ID
1	"indicia suggesting that witnesses may have been pressurised or influenced".	X			1.4
2	"or whether there was a risk that they were colluding with other witnesses".	X			1.4
3	"the consistency and precision of the accounts".	X	X	X	
4	"whether the information provided was plausible".	X	X	X	2.3
5	"whether the evidence conflicted with a witness's prior statement".	X	X	X	1.2
6	"any possible contradictions with the evidence of other witnesses".	X			2.4
7	"conduct during their testimony, including their readiness, willingness, and manner of responding to questions".	X	X	X	1.9
8	"the fact that the charges relate to events that occurred in 2002 and 2003".	X	X	X	
9	"and that witnesses who suffered trauma may have had particular difficulty in providing a coherent, complete, and logical account".	X	X	X	
10	"relationship to the Accused".	X			1.3

---

[361] Ngudjolo Chui Trial Judgment, paras. 49, 51 and 53, see above note 297; ICC, Situation in the Democratic Republic of the Congo, *Prosecutor v. Katanga*, Trial Chamber, Judgment Pursuant to Article 74 of the Statute, 7 March 2014, ICC-01/04-01/07-3436-tENG, paras. 83, 85 and 87 (https://www.legal-tools.org/doc/f74b4f/); Bemba Trial Judgment, para. 230, see above note 278; Ntaganda Trial Judgment, paras. 78 and 79, see above note 60. In *Prosecutor v. Bemba et al.*, TC VII indicated some of the same criteria, in the context of Article 70 offences, and citing the precedents of the abovementioned judgements and paragraphs, see ICC, Situation in the Central African Republic, *The Prosecutor v. Bemba et al.*, Trial Chamber, Public Redacted Version of Judgment Pursuant to Article 74 of the Statute, 19 October 2016, ICC-01/05-01/13-1989-Red, paras. 202 and 203 (https://www.legal-tools. org/doc/fe0ce4/).

11	"sincerity".	X			
12	"possible bias towards or against the Accused".	X			1.1
13	"motives for telling the truth or giving false testimony".	X			1.1
14	"other potential reasons why a witness's evidence may have been flawed".	X	X		

Table 8. List of the criteria identified by TCs and their correspondence with the criteria of the OTP ID Source Evaluation Guidelines.

The criteria above are partly consistent with those adopted by the OTP ID independently in 2006.[362] As Table 8 above shows, the judges identified explicitly 7 of the 15 criteria adopted previously by OTP ID. On the other hand, the judges adopted criteria that were not in the OTP ID model, such as trauma and passage of time (criteria 8 and 9 in Table 8 above). I had decided not include them in the OTP ID model because they did not appear to be settled in scientific research nor in jurisprudence, hence they would not make reliable parameters. Another difference could be using "sincerity" as a criterion by TC II (criteria 11 in Table 8 above), which may be repetitive with "motives" (criteria 13 in Table 8 above) or otherwise rather speculative.

Concerning consistency across chambers, TC II adopted a longer list of criteria (14 as opposed to 6 or 7), and defined them in more demanding terms. TC II defined several of their additional criteria by reference to potential rather than actual issues, as follows: "indicia suggesting" (criterion no. 1 in Table 8 above), "may have been" (criterion no. 1 in Table 8 above), "risk" (criterion no. 2 in Table 8 above), "possible contradictions" (criterion no. 6 in Table 8 above), "possible bias" (criterion no. 12 in Table 8 above), and "other potential reasons" (criterion no. 14 in Table 8 above). That hypothetical and suggestive language is not present in the criteria defined by TC III and TC VI, who use descriptive impartial language, as Table 8 above shows.

The approach proposed by TC II presents two problems. Firstly, it does not seem in accordance to the required legal standard and practice for the prosecution's evidence, since under the ICC Statute judges are bound to decide "beyond reasonable doubt" (Article 66(3)) based on the

---

[362] See above Section 3.2.4.

actual evidence, as opposed to any potential doubt or mere "risk".[363] This issue was already addressed by the ICTY Appeals Chamber in *Tadić*, the very first ICTY case, in 1999. The Trial Chamber had acquitted the accused of certain killings because they "may have been" committed by other perpetrators, as a "bare possibility" and other elements "could suggest" different conclusions.[364] The prosecutor appealed considering that "the proof must be such as to exclude not every hypothesis or possibility of innocence, but every fair or rational hypothesis which may be derived from the evidence, except that of guilt".[365] The Appeals Chamber agreed with the prosecutor, since the participation of the accused in the killings was the only reasonable inference from the available evidence and no witness had suggested an alternative hypothesis.[366] Several ICTY chambers endorsed this doctrine.[367]

Secondly, the focus on "suggestion/risk/potential" may lead to an area of theoretical speculation that is not verifiable or, in terms of scientific epistemology, the method is not valid because it is not falsifiable. As Karl Popper would say: "We cannot search the whole world in order to establish that something does not exist, has never existed, and will never exist".[368] In classic jurisprudence this kind of impossible proof is known as *probatio diabolica* and considered fallacious.[369]

---

[363] For a discussion on the standard "beyond reasonable doubt" and scientific methodology, see Elena Maria Catalano, "Logica della prova, *statistical evidence* e applicazione della teoria delle probabilità nel processo penale", in *Diritto Penale Contemporaneo*, 2013, vol. 4, pp. 132–51.

[364] ICTY, *Prosecutor v. Tadić*, Appeals Chamber, Judgement, 15 July 1999, IT-94-1-A, p. 77 (https://www.legal-tools.org/doc/8efc3a/).

[365] *Ibid.*, p. 76.

[366] *Ibid.*, p. 79.

[367] See Mark Klamberg, "Fact-finding in International Criminal Procedure: How Collection of Evidence may Contribute to Testing of Alternative Hypotheses", paper presented during lecture at the Amsterdam Center for International Law, 30 May 2011, pp. 10–11.

[368] Popper, 2005, p. 49, see above note 29. See also *ibid.*, chap. 4 "Falsifiability", pp. 57–73.

[369] See for example in ICJ, *Legality of Use of Force (Serbia and Montenegro v. France)*, Preliminary Objections of the French Republic, 5 July 2000, para. 25, about the Yugoslav claim for France to prove in the negative that the alleged facts would not fall under the Genocide Convention, and para. 33, denying the validity of such *probatio diabolica* (https://www.legal-tools.org/doc/waseth/). See also Antônio Augusto Cançado Trindade, *The Construction of a Humanized International Law: A Collection of Individual Opinions (1991-2013): Volume 1*, Brill, Leiden, 2014, chap. 18, sect. IV "The Inadmissibility of the Probatio Diabolica", pp. 771–72.

One of the speakers in our conference, a Legal Officer with the ICC Chambers, suggested an approach similar to the one adopted by TC II.[370] According to him the duty of the judges is "identifying all potential sources of doubt".[371] Then the speaker, outlined the different "potential sources of doubt" related to logical consistency, plausibility and evidence validity.[372] Unfortunately the speaker did not quote any relevant source of law or jurisprudence, which would help to assess the legal validity of this argument.

An earlier version of this theory addressed witness credibility emphasising all potential problems, rather than defining impartial parameters and tools. The author starts by elaborating on the different reasons why "witnesses may lack credibility", warning the reader that "[w]itnesses may be mistaken about the facts they testify to for a wide variety of reasons" and "many things can go wrong".[373] Then the author describes various types of potential biases. We are warned, for example, that "[a]nother very powerful type of bias is the witness's self-interest", assuming that this may distort the evidence:[374] the author ignores the equally plausible scenario in which speaking the truth may be in the 'self-interest' of the witness, particularly victims. The author carries on warning about all kinds of possible "deception" since apparently "research suggests that it may be equally difficult for international investigators to detect when witnesses are trying to deceive them".[375] Again, this is a very theoretical observation, biased towards doubting the investigative skills, when an impartial empirical research most likely would show different results, including many instances of successful identification of deception. More warnings follow about "mendacious witnesses" and all thinkable difficul-

---

[370] See presentation by Simon De Smet, Legal Officer at the ICC Chambers, "Enhancing the Quality of Reasoning about the Link Between Evidence and Factual Propositions", CILRAP Film, New Delhi, 22 February 2019 (https://www.cilrap.org/cilrap-film/190222-smet/).

[371] *Ibid.*, 05:51 and corresponding slide.

[372] *Ibid.*, 05:58 and corresponding slide.

[373] Simon De Smet, "Justified Belief in the Unbelievable", in Morten Bergsmo (ed.), *Quality Control in Fact-Finding*, Torkel Opsahl Academic EPublisher, Florence, 2013, p. 121 (http://www.toaep.org/ps-pdf/19-bergsmo). For the 2020 second, expanded edition, co-edited by Morten Bergsmo and Carsten Stahn, see http://www.toaep.org/ps-pdf/19-bergsmo-stahn-second.

[374] *Ibid.*, p. 122.

[375] *Ibid.*, p. 123.

ties, to conclude with the rather obvious statement that "[e]ven after thorough testing, testimony therefore remains essentially defeasible evidence".[376] All evidence is defeasible by definition, this is why we have adversarial processes, with the parties dedicated to defeat each other's evidence and argument, and the judicial officers hopefully presiding impartially.

The same speaker from the ICC Chamber continued with his sceptical discourse explaining that some "holistic assessment of the evidence" is not possible because of the sheer volume of the evidence or "cognitive load", so that when dealing, for example, with "25000 data points" if someone is claiming to have assessed holistically the evidence this person would be "lying to me".[377] This statement would run contrary to the longstanding experience in social sciences managing large volumes of information and producing holistic assessments based on multiple qualitative and quantitative methods. Such complex cognitive tasks should be feasible, as long as they are trusted to properly trained professionals using the appropriate empirical methods.[378]

Different authors refer to the distinction between 'holistic' and 'atomistic' approaches to the evaluation of evidence.[379] From the viewpoint of scientific research this is a false dilemma: complex large phenomena always require a multi-level approach addressing both the whole at the macro level, the atoms at the micro level, and various intermediate levels. This is similar to the distinction between the macro, meso and micro levels that is common in social sciences. International cases comprise most often both 'big questions' that require macro holistic methods and reasoning, as well as 'smaller questions' for specific victims or items of evidence. That should be regarded as an ontological issue, inherent to the underlying reality, rather than a methodological choice. For large-scale

---

[376] *Ibid.*, p. 126.

[377] De Smet, 2019, 12:47, see above note 370.

[378] For an overview of empirical methods applied to international crimes, see Bijleveld, 2017, p. 15, see above note 28.

[379] See among others Taruffo, 2002, chap. IV, sect. 5. "Concepción holista y método analítico", pp. 307–19, see above note 227; Twining, 1985, pp. 183–84, see above note 193; Mark Schweizer, "Comparing Holistic and Atomistic Evaluation of Evidence", in *Law, Probability and Risk*, 2014, vol. 13, no. 1, pp. 65–89; and Yvonne McDermott, "Strengthening the Evaluation of Evidence in International Criminal Trials", in *International Criminal Law Review*, 2017, vol. 17, no. 4, pp. 682–702.

cases the equivalent of the *macro* level could be the pattern of crime as a whole, the *meso* level would correspond with the multiple incidents that constitute the alleged pattern, and the *micro* level would speak to the individual victim or source. All the three levels would need to be specifically proved and tested through litigation with sources and methods appropriate to their scope.

Besides the tools available from scientific methodology, other logical solutions for 'complex facts' are also known from jurisprudence and legal expertise, including certain forms of 'evidence by sampling', 'evidence by absence of evidence to the contrary', and 'reducing complexity' by focusing selectively on key defining elements.[380]

What some jurisprudence has accepted as 'evidence by absence of evidence to the contrary' is the equivalent of the classic *reductio ad absurdum*, whereby the alternative explanations are identified and discarded if they are not logical, a well-known scientific principle since the times of Euclid and Archimedes.[381] This is also similar to 'differential diagnosis' in medicine, a process of finding the right diagnosis by eliminating the alternatives, as well as the concept of 'inference to the best explanation' promoted by some authors in logics and law, and the technique of Analysis of Competing Hypotheses.[382] With this approach the holistic conclusion does not need to be perfect in every element to be valid 'beyond reasonable doubt', it only needs to be the single reasonable answer left when other reasonable alternatives have been duly identified, fairly considered, and discarded if they are not plausible.

The same speaker presented "bounded rationality" along with the notion that "human mind is prone to make reasoning errors (fallacies, heuristics)".[383] This proposition is misleading because, unlike fallacies, heuristics and 'bounded rationality' are not essentially erroneous, they are reasoning strategies that may be valid or not, depending among other fac-

---

[380] See among others Taruffo, 2002, chap. II, sect. 5.1. "El hecho complejo", pp. 143–49, including references from Italy and other countries on *prova per campione* ('evidence by sampling') and *prova per mancanza del contrario* ('evidence by absence to the contrary'), see above note 227.

[381] See John Losee, "The Ideal of Deductive Systematization", in *A Historical Introduction to the Philosophy of Science*, 3rd edition, Oxford University Press, Oxford, 1993, pp. 23–26.

[382] See below Section 3.3.2.

[383] De Smet, 2019, 13:14, see above note 370.

tors on the expertise of the observer.[384] Even Daniel Kahneman, most vocal among experts in the critique of heuristics, does not consider them essentially wrong. In his view rather "[t]here is a heuristic alternative to careful reasoning, which sometimes works fairly well and sometimes leads to serious errors".[385] Other experts, and particularly Gerd Gigerenzer, question the premise that there must be a "careful reasoning" preferable to heuristics, since any reasoning, including legal reasoning, is context-specific and it cannot be assessed by merely formal abstract standards.[386]

As explained above a differential approach ('evidence by absence of evidence to the contrary', *reductio ad absurdum*, 'differential diagnosis', 'inference to the best explanation' or Analysis of Competing Hypothesis) could be valid heuristics at the holistic level, which coupled with proper Source Evaluation at the atomistic level, would suffice to reach certainty 'beyond reasonable doubt'. An approach of abstract formal logic is not necessarily any more reasonable, it is only more grandiloquent, or perhaps a heuristic path to dismiss the cases, which would be a legitimate strategy for the defence counsel, but not for impartial judges.

Dismissing certain forms of reasoning and suggesting the theoretical risk of logical mistakes contributes to raise 'reasonable doubts', which is the task of the defence counsel, rather than determining impartially whether such doubts are present or not, which is the task of the judge. During our conference a judge responded to the presentation by the abovementioned speaker indicating indeed that it seemed to reflect the

---

[384] For a discussion on bounded rationality and heuristics in relation to prosecutions, see Barbara O'Brien, "Recipe for Bias: An Empirical Look at the Interplay Between Institutional Incentives and Bounded Rationality in Prosecutorial Decision Making", in *Missouri Law Review*, 2009, vol. 74, no. 4, pp. 999–1050. For an overview on heuristics, history of the concept and related controversies, see Ulrich Hoffrage, Sebastian Hafenbrädl and Julian N. Marewski, "The Fast-and-Frugal Heuristics Program", in Linden J. Ball and Valerie A. Thompson (eds.), *The Routledge International Handbook of Thinking and Reasoning*, Routledge, London, 2018, pp. 325–45. For broader reference, see also Patrick Nerhot (ed.), *Law, Interpretation and Reality: Essays in Epistemology, Hermeneutics and Jurisprudence*, Kluwer Academic Publishers, Dordrecht, 1990.

[385] Daniel Kahneman, *Thinking, Fast and Slow*, Penguin, London, 2011, p. 98.

[386] On legal reasoning, see Gerd Gigerenzer and Christoph Engel (eds.), *Heuristics and the Law*, The MIT Press, Cambridge, 2006. For broader reference applicable to different fields, see Gerd Gigerenzer, Peter M. Todd and the ABC Research Group, *Simple Heuristics that Make Us Smart*, Oxford University Press, 1999.

---

way of thinking of the defence, committed to dismantle the case for the prosecution, rather than that of judges with a duty to assess it impartially.

Cultural preferences amount to another aspect that would need to be taken into account when discussing 'holistic v. atomistic'. 'Analytical thinking', in the sense of dissecting the elements of an argument or an image is typical of Western culture, while the alternative of 'holistic thinking' is common in the rest of the world, along with more collective and contextual thinking.[387]

Beyond the formal definition of criteria, the most difficult question is assessing their actual implementation in specific cases. This would require extensive analysis of the judicial decisions and their underlying evidence, which is beyond the scope of this chapter. A comprehensive study would reveal variations among judges and chambers, which is otherwise noticeable in multiple dissenting options that refer to issues of evidence, as well as contradictions between Trial Chambers and the Appeals Chambers. Just like in any fair national or international judicial system, clearly there is a broad scope of standards and practice among ICC judges, some being more conservative than others with the evidence.

Let us consider the example of TC II with the *Katanga* and *Ngudjolo* judgments, which appears to be an outlier when compared with the criteria adopted by other chambers. Table 9 below summarises the information contained in these judgments comparing the OTP evidence and allegations, and the findings of the Source Evaluation conducted by the chamber in relation to the five key insider witnesses presented by the prosecution (the evaluation is the same in both judgments for all of them, except for P-28):

---

[387] Henrich, Heine and Norenzayan, 2010, sect. 4.3 "Analytic Versus Holistic Thinking", pp. 71–73, see above note 88.

	OTP Evidence/Allegation	TC II Source Evaluation
P-28	Abducted, Katanga's personal escort, witnessed preparations and participated in the Bogoro attack.	*Ngudjolo* – Not credible on issues specific to the accused, dismissed. *Katanga* – Credible on some details of the Aveba militia and commanders. On key responsibility issues his testimony alone will not suffice and must be corroborated.
P-219	Lived with a member of Katanga's family, access to the camp and commanders.	Not credible, contradictions with 5 defence witnesses.
P-250	Member of a delegation that Ngudjolo dispatched to Katanga, when they decided to attack Bogoro.	Not credible on his membership of the militia, lacking internal consistency.
P-279	Abducted, witness of Katanga discussing Bogoro with Ngudjolo, order to attack Bogoro.	Not credible, "trop imprécis et contradictoires", denial of his precise age and his relationship, and contradictions with another witness.
P-280	Abducted, Katanga one of the FRPI leaders.	Not credible, "trop imprécis et contradictoires", he may have transposed what he knew of Aveba to add value to his description of Zumbe, contradictions with other witnesses.

Table 9. Comparison between the OTP evidence and allegations, and the findings of the Source Evaluation conducted by the chamber in relation to the five key insider witnesses presented by the prosecution.

The discrepancy is remarkable, with the chamber quashing all five of the prosecution's key insider witnesses. The assessment by the chamber would suggests that the OTP had a very poor understanding of their witnesses, while the view of the OTP was rather that the chamber was exceedingly dismissive with these witnesses.

Some comparative pattern analysis may shed additional light. In 2016 Chlevickaite and Hola published some initial findings about the evaluation of insider witnesses by ICC judges based on the three judgments issued at the time (*Lubanga, Katanga* and *Ngudjolo*) and the relevant 21 insider witnesses (12 for the prosecution and 9 for the defence).

They assessed the value given to these witnesses regarding their 'witness credibility' and 'information reliability', as well as the 'probative value' for 'linkage evidence' and 'crime base evidence', see below their overview table:[388]

	Witness Code	Credibility	Reliability	Probative Value: Linkage Evidence	Probative Value: Crime base Evidence
TC I – Lubanga	D-0007	High	High	High	High with exceptions
	D-0011	Low	Low	Low	Low
	D-0019	Low	High	Low	High
	D-0037	High	High	High	High
	P-0002	High	High	High	High
	P-0012	High	High	High	High
	P-0016	High with exceptions	High with exceptions	High with exceptions	High with exceptions
	P-0017	High	High	High	High
	P-0038	High with exceptions	High with exceptions	High with exceptions	High
	P-0041	High	High	High	High
	P-0055	High	High with exceptions	High	High with exceptions
TC II – Katanga and Ngudjoo	P-250	Low	Low	None	None
	P-279	Low	Low	None	None
	P-280	Low	Low	None	None
	P-28	Low	Medium	Medium	Low
	P-219	Low	Low	None	None
	D03-88	Low	High	Low	High
	D02-176	High	High	High	High

[388] Chlevickaite and Hola, 2016, Table 2 "Link Between Credibility/Reliability Assessments and Weight Given to Linkage/Crime-Base Evidence", p. 696, see above note 241. The first column is added to facilitate identifying visually the witnesses of the two trials. Witnesses D02-176, D02-228, D02-236 and D02-350 were assessed only for *Katanga*.

D02-228	Medium	High	High	High
D02-236	Medium	High	Medium	High
D02-350	High	High	High	High

Table 10. Overview table of the value of insider witnesses based on the *Lubanga*, *Katanga* and *Ngudjolo* judgments issued.

Concerning the association of the witnesses with the prosecution or the defence, this dataset shows a quite different distribution of values for the witnesses evaluated by TC I (witnesses D-0007 to P-0055), and those evaluated by TC II (witnesses P-250 to D02-350). TC I gave positive and negative values for both prosecution and defence witnesses, with a distribution that does not correlate clearly with any of the two parties. TC II evaluated negatively every one of the prosecution witnesses (see above P-250, P-279, P-280, P-28 and P-219), with remarkably more positive evaluations for defence witnesses (see above D03-88, D02-176, D02-228, D02-236 and D02-350). These results coincide with the different formulation of the evaluation criteria by TC II, which are more demanding and leaning to side with the defence in their proactive exploration of potential doubts, as explained above. Furthermore, one of the judges in TC II was even more dismissive than the majority with the prosecution's witnesses, as she indicated in her dissenting opinion and vote for acquittal.[389]

Taking into account the unusually expansive criteria adopted by TC II, and the results in the judgments as explained above, the fact that the chamber was so dismissive selectively with the prosecution's witnesses appears to be the result of applying some high standard akin to 'beyond reasonable doubt' at the atomistic level for each witness, instead that at the holistic level for the case as a whole. These two judgments give the impression that TC II projected the overall standards for the defence and prosecution cases on their individual witnesses: defence witnesses were evaluated more positively as if the standard for them was merely to raise doubts about the prosecution's case, while prosecution witnesses were dismissed because they were evaluated individually with a higher stand-

---

[389] See ICC, Situation in the Democratic Republic of the Congo, *The Prosecutor v. Germain Katanga*, Trial Chamber, Minority Opinion of Judge Christine van den Wyngaert, 7 March 2014, ICC-01/04-01/07-3436-AnxI, sect. III.A.3. "Unconvincing Credibility Analysis", pp. 87–98 ('Katanga Trial Minority Opinion of Judge Christine van den Wyngaert') (https://www.legal-tools.org/doc/9b0c61/).

ard equivalent to 'beyond reasonable doubt'. This would be a legal and logical mistake, because judges must be convinced 'beyond reasonable doubt' about the ultimate question of individual responsibility, after having evaluated all the evidence holistically, they are not expected to apply the ultimate standard to the primary items of evidence individually. This approach of deconstruction and fragmentation would make impossible to understand complex phenomena, and it would set an impossible standard of a 'perfect case' for the prosecution, highly conducive to quash any and all possible cases.

Concerning the validity and implementation of the two main parameters, for the witness and for the information, Table 10 above by Chlevickaite and Hola shows a remarkable correlation for most witnesses across the four columns, for both chambers, very often receiving the same value. Not a single witness given 'high credibility' is assessed with 'low reliability', and only two witnesses show the reverse combination. This pattern begs the question of to what extent there is a 'halo effect' in place, that is, once they get a good impression about the witness, the judges might be inclined to assess positively their evidence and give it good probative value for all purposes. Some 'witness halo effect' might have operated for the judges when trying to find their way through the mass of evidence. This could be regarded as a hypothesis for further research, with a larger dataset from more cases.

Chlevickaite and Hola found that the ICC judges had focused primarily on the content of the testimony ("reliability of the information"), while issues related to the background of the witness ("credibility of the witness") appeared to be secondary, only relevant in case of doubt about the evidence as such.[390] These authors find that the judges may have underestimated the importance of "witness credibility" issues since insiders often are conditioned by subjective or self-serving motives and biases.

Chlevickaite and Hola found that judges had focused particularly on 4 of the 11 criteria relevant to the "reliability of the information": consistency, corroboration, detail and knowledge.[391] This focus is in my view appropriate, since these appear to be indeed the most relevant criteria for this matter. These four criteria coincide largely with the four criteria in the

---

[390] Chlevickaite and Hola, 2016, p. 691, see above note 241.
[391] *Ibid.*, p. 689.

ID model for 'information', which appears to validate the design adopted by ID in 2006.

A more complete assessment of the judicial practice will require additional research of the kind that Chlevickaite and Hola have initiated, including both pattern analysis and statistics across cases, as well as qualitative case studies fully embedded in the factual and cultural context of the cases and the chambers. In addition to the context of justification, on how judges or prosecutors justify their decisions, research on the context of discovery may be equally important to explore how such decisions are truly developed in the first place.

Another issue that would merit additional research is the impact of tampering and pressure on witnesses from the accused and their associates. Problems of this kind have surfaced in every ICC case brought to trial, including threats against witnesses, public defamation, coaching and bribery. When the OTP has raised these issues before the judges, some of them have declined to consider their impact on the validity of evidence, and directed instead the prosecution to a different procedure. This policy adopted by some ICC judges may run contrary to the need to conduct proper Source Evaluation at the trial stage, because it may exclude from the scrutiny information relevant to, among others, 'motivation', 'independence' and 'contamination' (as explained in Section 3.2.4. above under criteria 1.1, 1.3 and 1.4 in the ID model).

3.2.6. Conclusion

The investigation of international crimes requires a proper methodology for Source Evaluation, with a set of standard criteria to be systematically tested against individual sources of evidence. The model adopted by the Investigations Division at the ICC-OTP may assist investigations by national and international agencies, with appropriate adjustments to the operational and legal context as necessary. No model is perfect and the above-recommended model may also benefit from additional review and feedback from researchers and practitioners, as explained in reference to different indicators.[392] Once a model is adopted, proper training, implementation and compliance control will be required.

---

[392] See above Section 3.2.4.

3.3. Diagnostic Techniques

Diagnostic techniques aim at dissecting the content of the tentative case or proposition, breaking it down into tangible elements that can be subject to individual examination. These techniques are most relevant to address the bottlenecks no. 1 "information overview", no. 3 "evidence review" and no. 4 "formulation of responsibility" identified in the QCCI project, see the introductory chapter above by Bergsmo and the present author. The term 'analysis' is known in Western culture since Aristotle and his works *Prior Analytics* and *Posterior Analytics*, which are considered as foundations of Western epistemology. The original meaning and etymology of 'analysis' in this tradition is actually to dissect and break in smaller pieces a phenomenon to better understand it.[393] The four techniques in this section are known from analytical practice and they are largely consistent with principles of scientific methodology, as well as the requirements of legal procedure.

3.3.1. Key Assumptions Check

This method requires: a) To identify the underlying factual assumptions of a given investigative hypothesis; b) To check specifically their factual and logical validity.[394]

There are a number of factual assumptions that the investigation may have accepted axiomatically, because they were implicit in the sources, because of insufficient contextual knowledge, or for various operational reasons. Because these assumptions operate as building blocks for the investigation, it is advisable to check them in the best interest of the whole construct, particularly for the first cases in a new situation. Questioning such assumption may be difficult if they follow from cultural consensus, precedent in other cases, policy orientation, or 'groupthink'. Consider the following examples:

- *Group identity*: In the context of an 'ethnic conflict' various reports refer to different 'ethnic groups' as well-defined entities. The investigation in based on the assumption of the existence and belonging in these 'ethnic groups'. There may be a need to check this assump-

---

[393] See Losee, 1993, chap. 1 "Aristotle's Philosophy of Science", pp. 5–15, see above note 381.

[394] See Heuer Jr. and Pherson, 2015, sect. 8.1 "Key Assumptions Check", pp. 209–14, see above note 35.

tion in view of fuzzy belonging boundaries, mixed types, sub-groups, and stereotypical reporting for propaganda of journalistic purposes. Perhaps the 'ethnic' image is an epiphenomenon and the true drives are other economic or political factor, which could explain some contradictions with the profiles of victims or other investigative issues.

- *Military organisation*: The investigation may have assumed that a military group follows conventional schemes because of their appearance, denomination, ranks or uniforms. It is advisable to check this assumption against the real functioning of the group, key personalities, internal processes, and actual operations. It could be that a self-proclaimed military group is actually a cover for pre-existing structures, or a proxy for other actors.

- *Authority*: Assumptions about the mandate of different government branches from the national background of the investigation team may conflict with the realities of other countries.[395]

- *Ideology*: Major political and religious belief-systems are defined in binary terms, with negative assumptions about opposing creeds. Assumptions of 'fundamentalism' or 'authoritarianism' may follow implicitly, when the reality is that major political or religious creeds comprise many different trends and experiences.

Best practice is to identify and check the key assumptions from the outset of the investigation, when defining investigative hypotheses, through specific brainstorming, consultation and analysis tasks. This check may lead to confirm, dismiss or adjust the assumptions, or it may trigger specific efforts of collection or analysis if the issue is particularly important. For example, checking assumptions about group identity typically requires context-specific research and group-specific victim data, while organisational assumptions most often require documentary or witness internal sources.

Alternatively, if the team is not able to check certain assumptions, or they do not consider them critical for the case, at least those assumptions should be stated clearly for the record, so that it is understood that

---

[395] Like in the example of the interrogation of a former Nazi Foreign Affairs Minister by a US prosecutor, see above Section 3.2.2.2.

the investigative findinsg are subject to the validity of those underlying premises.

3.3.2. Analysis of Competing Hypotheses ('ACH')

Causality, as Hannah Arendt indicated, is one of the most difficult and elusive questions in science.[396] It is also the ultimate question in criminal investigations, focused on causal attribution and individual responsibility.[397] It is useful to identify causal hypotheses from the early stages of the investigation,[398] to the extent supported by the available information. Hypotheses, in investigations as much as in science, are meant to be tested critically and compared with alternative or concurring factors.[399] They should be phrased in factual plain terms, as the most plausible factual explanation of the alleged crimes, and as a syllogism or chain of discrete propositions that lead logically to a conclusion of responsibility. By 2003 Patrick J. Treanor, Head of the ICTY Leadership Research Team, advised the nascent ICC-OTP as follows:

> It is extremely important that investigations, especially of leadership figures on a higher level, begin and continue to

---

[396] See her essay: Hannah Arendt, "Understanding and Politics (the Difficulties of Understanding)", in *Essays in Understanding, 1930-1954: Formation, Exile, and Totalitarianism*, Harcourt, Brace & Co., New York, 1994, p. 319: "Causality, however, is an altogether alien and falsifying category in the historical sciences". On her scepticism about causal thinking, see Annette Vowinckel, "Hannah Arendt and Martin Heidegger: History and Metahistory", in Steven E. Aschheim (ed.), *Hannah Arendt in Jerusalem*, University of California Press, Berkeley, 2001, pp. 338–46. See also entry "Causation", in Robert. A. Wilson and Frank. C. Keil (eds.), *The MIT Encyclopedia of the Cognitive Sciences*, The MIT Press, Cambridge, 1999, pp. 108–10.

[397] See among others Carlo Brusco, *Il rapporto di causalità: prassi e orientamenti*, Giuffré Editore, Milan, 2006. For a case study of alternative hypotheses and argumentation theory, see E.T. Feteris, "An Argumentative Analysis and Evaluation of Complex Cases in Dutch Criminal Law", in C.M. Breur, M.M. Kommer, J.F. Nijboer and J.M. Reijntjes (eds.), *New Trends in Criminal Investigation and Evidence: Volume 2*, Intersentia, Antwerpen, 2000, pp. 225–38; the author focuses on the "ballpoint case", in which a conviction was reversed by the appeals judges because they found that the judges in the first instance had not considered the alternative hypothesis presented by the defence. For more on this high-profile Dutch case, see Roland Bal, "How to Kill with a Ballpoint: Credibility in Dutch Forensic Science", in *Science, Technology, and Human Values*, 2005, vol. 30, no. 1, pp. 52–75.

[398] As indicated in the general cycle, see above Section 3.1.

[399] See Brooke Noel Moore and Richard Parker, "Causal Explanation", in *Critical Thinking*, 9th edition, McGraw-Hill, Boston, 2009, pp. 385–413. For related issues of statistical evidence, see Leila Schneps and Coralie Colmez, *Math on Trial: How Numbers Get Used and Abused in the Courtroom*, Basic Books, New York, 2013.

proceed on the basis of a substantive hypothesis (for example, the party leader was in control) developed through the analysis of all information and evidence available on the given leadership structure. That is, all relevant knowledge must be integrated through analysis into a consistent hypothesis or, if inconsistent with it, put aside but not forgotten for later re-evaluation and possible use. The hypothesis may, indeed most likely will, change over time, but the changes must reflect a deepening of knowledge and constant analysis. Analysis will in fact serve to point up gaps and other weaknesses in the hypothesis and the available knowledge and serve as a guide to the investigative process, that is, the turning of mere information into evidence and the gathering of fresh information and evidence.[400]

The Regulations of the ICC-OTP direct the teams to identify an overall "case hypothesis (or hypotheses)" at an initial stage, as a tool to guide the investigation, and to "be reviewed and adjusted on a continuous basis taking into consideration the evidence collected".[401] Similarly in Colombia, where the Fiscalía General de la Nación has decades of experience with complex investigations (numerous cases of organized crime, corruption, war crimes, and so on since its establishment in 1992), the "prosecutor in charge of co-ordinating the investigation" is required at the outset of the investigation to "determine the objectives of the investigation" on the basis of a "crime hypothesis" as part of a "methodological program".[402]

---

[400] Patrick J. Treanor, "Research and Analysis in the Investigation, Prosecution and Adjudication of Crimes", in Morten Bergsmo, Klaus Rackwitz and SONG Tianying (eds.), *Historical Origins of International Criminal Law: Volume 5*, Torkel Opsahl Academic EPublisher, Brussels, 2017, p. 138 (http://www.toaep.org/ps-pdf/24-bergsmo-rackwitz-song).

[401] ICC, Regulations of the Office of the Prosecutor, 23 April 2009, ICC-BD/05-01-09, Regulations 24 and 35 (https://www.legal-tools.org/doc/a97226/).

[402] Colombia, Código de Procedimiento Penal Colombiano (Law 906 of 2004), 31 August 2004, Article 207 "Programa metodológico" (https://www.legal-tools.org/doc/96af08/):

el fiscal, con el apoyo de los integrantes de la policía judicial, se trazará un programa metodológico de la investigación, el cual deberá contener la determinación de los objetivos en relación con la naturaleza de la hipótesis delictiva; los criterios para evaluar la información; la delimitación functional de las tareas que se deban adelantar en procura de los objetivos trazados; los procedimientos de control en el desarrollo de las labores los recursos de mejoramiento de los resultados obtenidos.

Hypotheses are necessary to guide investigations, but they are also dangerous if poorly designed or handled. What Chimamanda Ngozi Adichie calls "the danger of a single story", harmful simplifications based on limited information and stereotypes, resembles the stories that sometimes the parties tell in adversarial litigation.[403] This issue surfaced, for example, in ICTY *Milutinović et al.*, when an expert for the prosecution presented statistical analysis about the mass displacement of Albanian population in Kosovo.[404] He argued that the displacement was "consistent" with the hypothesis of an attack against civilians by the Serbian forces, but the defence challenged this finding because the expert never considered other alternative hypotheses that could have also been "consistent" with the data. The judges agreed with the defence in that the prosecution's analysis "still leaves a number of potentially plausible options unexplored", besides other methodological flaws, and they dismissed this expert evidence.[405] Additionally the accused in a related case had questioned the same analysis because it had excluded the exodus of Serbian civilians from the population to be analysed, which could suggest some fundamental bias, or otherwise it should have been checked as a "key assumption". The need to consider alternative factual hypotheses has also been indicated by ICC judges in different cases.[406]

A way to counter 'the danger of a single story' is to consider simultaneously several investigative hypotheses. But this is not easy, psychologically and operationally, or as F. Scott Fitzgerald would say, "[t]he test of a first-rate intelligence is the ability to hold two opposing ideas in mind at the same time and still retain the ability to function".[407] That challenge

---

[403] Chimamanda Ngozi Adichie, "The Danger of a Single Story", *TED*, July 2009 (available on TED's web site).

[404] For the analytical report, see Patrick Ball, Wendy Betts, Fritz Scheuren, Jana Dudukovich and Jana Asher, *Killings and Refugee Flow in Kosovo, March - June 1999: A Report to the International Criminal Tribunal for the Former Yugoslavia*, American Association for the Advancement of Science (AAAS) and American Bar Association Central and East European Law Initiative (ABA/CEELI), Washington, D.C., 2002.

[405] See ICTY, *Prosecutor v. Milutinović et al.*, Trial Chamber, Judgement: Volume 3 of 4, 26 February 2009, IT-05-87-T, pp. 13–17 (https://www.legal-tools.org/doc/d79e85/).

[406] See, for example, in Katanga Trial Minority Opinion of Judge Christine van den Wyngaert, sect. C. "Another Reasonable Reading of the Evidence Is Possible", pp. 100–42, see above note 389.

[407] F Scott Fitzgerald, in Edmund Wilson (ed.), *The Crack-UP*, New Directions Books, New York, 1945, p. 69.

can be addressed with Analysis of Competing Hypotheses, a method developed for intelligence analysis that can be equally helpful in criminal investigations, applied for the case as a whole (case hypothesis) or for specific elements.

ACH is essentially a table to check comparatively different hypotheses against the relevant items of evidence.[408] The logic is similar to the methods of differential diagnosis in medicine: a process of elimination, first identifying different potential diagnoses, and then checking them against the available medical evidence. The original public formulation by Richards J. Heuer indicated the following 8 steps:[409]

	Step-By-Step Outline of Analysis of Competing Hypotheses
1	Identify the possible hypotheses to be considered. Use a group of analysts with different perspectives to brainstorm the possibilities.
2	Make a list of significant evidence and arguments for and against each hypothesis.
3	Prepare a matrix with hypotheses across the top and evidence down the side. Analyse the 'diagnosticity' of the evidence and arguments – that is, identify which items are most helpful in judging the relative likelihood of the hypotheses.
4	Refine the matrix. Reconsider the hypotheses and delete evidence and arguments that have no diagnostic value.
5	Draw tentative conclusions about the relative likelihood of each hypothesis. Proceed by trying to disprove the hypotheses rather than prove them.
6	Analyse how sensitive your conclusion is to a few critical items of evidence. Consider the consequences for your analysis if that evidence were wrong, misleading, or subject to a different interpretation.
7	Report conclusions. Discuss the relative likelihood of all the hypotheses, not just the most likely one.
8	Identify milestones for future observation that may indicate events are taking a different course than expected.

Table 11. The original public formulation of ACH.

---

[408] See Heuer Jr. and Pherson, 2015, sect. 7.3 "Analysis of Competing Hypotheses", pp. 181–92, see above note 35; and Morgan D. Jones, "Hypothesis Testing", in *The Thinker's Toolkit: 14 Powerful Techniques for Problem Solving*, Three Rivers Press, New York, 1999, pp. 178–216.

[409] Heuer, Jr., 1999, p. 97, see above note 139.

The first step requires defining through analysis several plausible hypotheses, beyond merely echoing the allegations from victims and other actors. In the second step the key items of evidence, those most relevant and credible, need to be also identified systematically. These two initial steps need to be conducted impartially, regardless of eventual incriminating or exonerating implications. The exercise needs to integrate as much as possible the hypotheses and evidence proposed by or expected from the viewpoint of the alleged perpetrators. The team might consider at least three different hypotheses, two of them mutually exclusive representing the most likely scenarios for incrimination and exoneration (hypotheses A and B), and a third hypothesis C to anticipate variations partially compatible with A and B. The hypotheses might be suspect-specific, if justified by the available information, in the understanding that this process should help to control for suspect-driven biases. ACH can also be used to test comparatively several suspect-specific hypotheses about different suspects, if relevant.

The third and fourth steps require to identify those items of evidence and propositions that appear to carry the highest diagnosticity, that is, those who make a difference for the diagnosis, and to remove those of lesser value, in order to consolidate a robust model. Otherwise the model could become too cumbersome and not workable.

The fifth step can be covered by coding the cells in the matrix with a positive or negative assessment on whether each item of evidence supports each hypothesis or not. A simple coding scheme can be applied as follows (colour coding for the ease of visual synopsis, or with figures for tentative scores) in the tables, and similarly for 'links' in relational charts:[410]

Finding	Explanation	Link
(green)	Conclusively positive, the item of evidence supports clearly the hypothesis.	**Solid** = Confirmed
(amber)	Undetermined. Ambivalent, the item of evidence is compatible with the hypothesis, but also open to other interpretations or compatible with other hypotheses.	**Broken** = Unconfirmed: compatible with the evidence but not conclusive, because the evidence is incomplete or conflicting.
		Dotted = Tentative: mere hypothesis proposed by the analyst, or unverified allegation.
(red)	Conclusively negative, the item of evidence contradicts clearly the hypothesis.	No link.
	Irrelevant. Evidence not relevant to the hypothesis.	No link.

Table 12. Coding scheme for tables and relational charts.

For a more elaborate version, this step can also be covered with different formulas in spread-sheets, adding possibly a scale for the Source Evaluation of each evidence item (that is, attributing them different weights), and aggregated scores for each hypothesis.

Steps number 6 and 7 will allow to identify the most plausible hypothesis. If more than one hypothesis is equally valid, this can mean that they are too vague, or that the evidence is not specific enough, which may help to refine the hypothesis or to search for additional and more specific evidence. The last step should contribute to the collection plan, by identifying key points and facts and sources for further verification.

---

[410] As for Case Evaluation Charts, see below Section 3.3.4.

The initial design of ACH has led to different versions and implementations, as well as software tools and video tutorials, all of which readily available online. Clearly identifying multiple hypotheses and comparing them systematically is a good idea for any complex investigation, and the ACH model may help for this purpose, while other models and combinations of methods should also be explored. For large cases it could be that an overall 'case hypothesis' is too complex to be subsumed under a table with a few rows, but still the method can be used for general orientation, or otherwise applied on discrete propositions within the case. Ultimately having a hypothesis or an explanation as 'the best' does not mean that it is factually correct, it only means that it is better than the alternatives under consideration, hence hypotheses are tools and not findings, always in need of further inductive and deductive verification.[411] The preferred hypothesis still will be subject to the critical test of the investigation, and the resulting findings subject to Evidence Review.[412]

Beyond and after the investigation, this comparative approach could help in the stage of litigation, towards a finding 'beyond reasonable doubt', as a method to identify the 'inference to the best explanation'. The judges could use the ACH method in their deliberations, but with a higher standard of certainty, so that a conviction would require not just that the alternative hypotheses are less compelling, but rather that they are not reasonable in view of the available evidence.

3.3.3. Case Evaluation Table

Once one or more hypotheses have been selected for investigation after the ACH or similar process, a subsequent step would be to apply a similar test to each element of the hypothesis. The Case Evaluation Table ('CET') is meant to test the premises of the case hypothesis against specific items of evidence and to produce a synopsis that should help to identify investigative priorities, and ultimately to decide on the sufficiency of the evidence for eventual charges. As the example below shows, the case hypothesis is specified with one row for each of its premises, stated in pre-

---

[411] See Larry Laudan, "Strange Bedfellows: Inference to the Best Explanation and the Criminal Standard of Proof", in *International Journal of Evidence and Proof*, 2007, vol. 11, no. 4, pp. 292–306. The author questions similarly the validity of 'inference to the best explanation' based on history of the sciences, and considers it insufficient to warrant certainty 'beyond reasonable doubt'.

[412] See below Section 3.5.

cise factual terms, while the columns show the different sources of evidence that have been assessed positively as a matter of Source Evaluation.

	Case Hypothesis	Insiders					Victims	Intl. Witness	Documents	Videos	Forenscis	Total	Comment
		1	2	3	4	5							
1	X was the Head of the Police in [period].											5	
2	Y was the Head of the Prison system in [period].											5	
3	Z was the top leader above X and Y.											4	
4	X directed and controlled effectively the police.											2	
5	Y directed and controlled effectively the prison system.											3	
6	Z issued orders to arrest opposition civilians.											4	
7	Police arrested some 5000 opposition civilians.											7	
8	Police and prison guards tortured some 300 prisoners.											7	
9	Police and guards tortured to death some 20 prisoners.											7	
10	Police and prison guards raped some 25 prisoners.											4	
11	X, Y and Z knew about the arrests, torture and rapes.											2	
12	X, Y and Z did not prevent nor punish their subordinates.											3	
	Total	8	1	4	4	8	8	6	9	2	2	5	

Table 12. Example of Case Evaluation Table.

The CET can be read horizontally, to see which elements of the hypothesis are confirmed with the available evidence or not. It can also be read vertically, to show the number of positive hits per item of evidence.

The 'total' figures per source (count in the lowest row) and per element of the hypothesis should help understanding the degree of confirmation of the hypothesis, and the relative weight of each source, but operational decisions cannot be based on quantitative thresholds because of the multiple qualitative issues at stake. The colour-code for the 'total' column is based on a holistic assessment of all relevant evidence, not necessarily dictated by the count of positive hits because of variations in the value of different sources. The 'comment' column is open for analytical commentary on the sources or other issues not captured by the coding.

The example above, inspired in Cold-War situations of political conflict from the 1970s, illustrates some common scenarios in international investigations, which the CET should help identifying and managing:

- Wide discrepancies among insider witnesses, some highly incriminating (like insiders 1 and 5) and others highly exonerating (like insider 2);

- highest value of international witnesses (confirming 9 of the 12 points of the hypothesis), which is not uncommon assuming different types of international witnesses with significant access to the relevant area, actors and victims;

- highest corroboration, including forensics, for the criminal acts (rows 7 to 10, except for rape), often the least contested part of the case;

- lowest corroboration for individual responsibilities (rows 11 and 12), including mixed evidence from insiders;

- more corroboration for formal authority (rows 1 to 3) than for effective control (rows 4 to 6).

The example above pays particular attention to insider witnesses, with specific columns for each one of them, on the assumption that their evidence is critical to assess individual responsibilities. The evidence from all victim-witnesses is aggregated under a single column, assuming broadly that the victimisation as such is a less contested issue, and it is corroborated with forensic evidence.

Table 12 above could suggest, among others, the following investigative decisions: to interview more insiders, since they have only five and there are important contradictions among them; to conduct advanced

Source Evaluation on the items of evidence that may be most decisive (such insiders 1, 2 and 5, documents and international witnesses); to try to obtain more videos, if possible in the given context, since they are so far relevant to only two points; to investigate specifically issue of knowledge and means of reporting, since this point (row 11) is only corroborated by two sources.

The CET will need to be kept and updated regularly by a designated analyst. It should be used as a reporting tool to be shared with the team, management, as well as in Evidence Reviews (see Section 3.5. below). Multiple versions over time should be kept to monitor progress. Best practice is to accompany the CET with a report justifying the assessment in detail. Similar tables can be developed for specific incidents, accused or offences, applying the method to smaller scopes of information and greater detail.

3.3.4. Case Evaluation Chart

The Case Evaluation Chart ('CEC') is a relational chart designed as a synopsis of the case linking suspects, alleged criminal actions, and all persons related to them as alleged perpetrators, victims or witnesses. The chart should help to diagnose the strength of the case hypothesis by using the existing diagramming conventions for actors, groups and links, including the following:

- Title indicating the subject, version no., and date of the evaluation, since the case will require multiple versions of the chart, and it will evolve over time;

- sober style, avoiding visual manipulation, no pictures of persons, no red colour associated to persons, sober colour palette, no sensational language or icons;

- only one icon per entity (mainly persons and incidents), no repetition;

- attributes or shapes to show the profile of the persons, as relevant to the investigation, including possibly gender, ethnicity, and so on;

- boxes to show organisational units, while persons within boxes indicate organisational membership;

- links witness-incident to visualize the number of relevant witness and to identify them easily; links between perpetrators and suspects to visualize their network or hierarchy;

- different strengths of links to show the strength of the information, typically a solid line for 'confirmed', broken for 'unconfirmed', and dotted 'tentative' (see explanations in Table 12 above).

Relational charts of this kind are very valuable to produce a graphic synopsis that integrates aspects of hierarchy (the links between a senior suspect, multiple direct perpetrators, and intermediate levels), crime pattern (visualising multiple incidents as entities, as well as relevant attributes of victims and perpetrators) and Source Evaluation (by the strength of the links). Their dissemination needs to be accompanied by a briefing with the analyst that produced the chart, at least for those officers who are not familiar with this kind of graphic language. Databases designed around entities and links (the Entity-Attribute-Value models or graph databases) may facilitate processing datasets about large numbers of persons, and they may be the foundation to plot relational charts of this kind. Consolidated versions could well be used as visual aids in trial, since the judges and the accused may equally benefit from a synoptic view of the alleged case.

3.4. Adversarial Techniques

Adversarial techniques are designed as a 'stress test', to challenge the investigative findings in order to control for 'tunnel vision' and 'confirmation bias', and to anticipate the counter-arguments of adversarial litigation. They are similar to the 'resistance test' that the Italian investigating judge Gherardo Colombo proposes, based in his experience in large corruption cases:

> When no alternatives to the current outcome of the investigation emerge, and evidence seems therefore conclusive, the outcome should nonetheless be checked again against a 're-sistance test', so as to ascertain whether it can resist imaginable contrary evidence that might contradict it.[413]

The purpose of these techniques is not to challenge or weaken managers and decision-makers, rather to the contrary the purpose is to empower them "to make better decisions by providing them with a more objective analysis" and "alternative options to consider".[414]

---

[413] Colombo, 2006, p. 517, see above note 30.
[414] Bryce G. Hoffman, *Red Teaming: How Your Business Can Conquer the Competition by Challenging Everything*, Crown Business, New York, 2017, p. 59.

The following conditions are necessary for the success of any adversarial technique in QCCI:

- *Independence*: The designated officers must operate with full independence, and with the institutional guarantee that no adverse consequences will follow, no matter how controversial the exchange. In other words, "you can't red team in the *Führerbunker*",[415] and such groups must be "licensed to be troublesome".[416] If the officers are members of the investigation team, or otherwise closely related to its members, a sense of peer-pressure may prevent them from developing a full critique. Higher management must intervene communicating clear support for this kind of critical intervention, sheltering the designated officers, and acknowledging such contributions in their performance reviews as appropriate.

- *Choice of staff*: Not all good officers are suitable for that contrarian task, the exercise requires those who are not afraid to contradict colleagues and popular assumptions, and can handle the stress involved in the exercise. Professional analysts are often well prepared for this kind of work, but surely one can find good candidates also among lawyers and investigators. The following attributes should be taken into account when choosing the staff for an adversarial exercise:[417]

  a. ability to see things from alternative perspectives, imagination;

  b. familiarity with different cultural perspectives, cultural capability and empathy;

  c. confidence and assertiveness to challenge conventional or established thinking;

  d. ability to communicate effectively.

- *Preparation*: The designated officers need to have sufficient time, tools and access to the evidence to prepare properly for the exercise.

---

[415] *Ibid.*, p. 95.

[416] The Commission on the Intelligence Capabilities of the United States Regarding Weapons of Mass Destruction, *Report to the President of the United States*, 31 March 2005, p. 170.

[417] Adapted and summarised from Development, Concepts and Doctrine Centre of the UK Ministry of Defence, *A Guide to Red Teaming: DCDC Guidance Note*, February 2010, pp. 2-16 and 2-17.

The exercise should be anticipated and planed from an early stage; it should not be a mere afterthought.

- *Equality of arms*: The designate officers should be offered the same opportunities to present the critique as others have to present the proposed case, taking into account allocated time and access to decision-makers. Only officers with the required qualifications and seniority should be asked to act as Devil's Advocate.

- *Focus*: Adversarial techniques need to focus on the key elements of the case, a selective high-quality focus is likely to be more useful than a broad review of any and every element.

- *Receptiveness*: The investigation team and management must be committed to actually listen to the Devil's Advocate and take into account the resulting feedback.

Absent the above-mentioned conditions, adversarial techniques may fail, or worse, they may reinforce 'groupthink' among those who may feel victorious without having been really challenged, and to comfort management after a merely cursory test. As indicated from military doctrine: "Poorly conducted red teaming is pointless, may be misleading and engender false confidence".[418]

There are two main techniques of this kind, known from the practice of investigations and intelligence, among other fields: Devil's Advocate and Red Teams.[419]

3.4.1. Devil's Advocate

Advocatus diaboli is a technique known in the Catholic procedures for beatification since centuries ago, with an officer tasked to challenge systematically the heavenly merits of the candidate. The Devil's Advocate should play a role equivalent and anticipating that of a defence counsel, arguing *ex parte* anything that could help challenging the accusation.[420] Rather than an extraordinary procedure for problematic cases, this should

---

[418] *Ibid.*, p. 1-8.

[419] See Heuer Jr. and Pherson, 2015, chap. 9 "Challenge Analysis", pp. 233–70, see above note 35.

[420] See *ibid.*, sect. 9.5 "Devil's Advocacy", pp. 260–62; and Jones, 1999, chap. 12 "Devil's Advocacy", pp. 217–23, see above note 408.

be considered a standard QC test for every major investigation because of the serious budgetary and procedural consequences of eventual mistakes.

The advantage of this technique is that the designated officer will deliberately depart from the accepted position and aim at questioning any point in the proposed facts or case. This should be a safeguard against 'groupthink' and 'confirmation bias', with the help of an officer specifically tasked to 'think against the group' and carry a 'contrarian bias'. Any officer in the investigation team may be asked to play this role, on an *ad hoc* basis, or within Evidence Reviews (see Section 3.5. below), while analysts may be particularly well equipped because of their overall knowledge of the case (if they are part of the team), and their training in 'critical thinking' (including fallacies, Source Evaluation, and so on) which usually is part of their standard professional training.

3.4.2. Red Teaming

A Red Team is similar to a Devil's Advocate but more demanding: beyond challenging the proposed argument, a Red Team is expected to build an alternative argument or scenario with the same information.[421] Red Teams have grown from the field of military, intelligence, security as well as some private sector companies interested on testing their systems and achieving greater certainty and efficiency. They can be defined as follows:

> Red Teaming is the art of applying independent structured critical thinking and culturally sensitised alternative thinking from a variety of perspectives, to challenge assumptions and fully explore alternative outcomes, in order to reduce risks and increase opportunities.[422]

Techniques used by Red Teams in different fields vary, from strengthened versions of Devil's Advocate, to hiring external consultants or 'tiger teams', to full simulations designed to test security systems. In a broad sense Red Teams comprise techniques of simulation, vulnerability

---

[421] See Hoffman, 2017, see above note 414; and Micah Zenko, *Red Team: How to Succeed by Thinking like the Enemy*, Basic Books, New York, 2015. For a list of references, see Micah Zenko, "Red Team Reading List", *Council on Foreign Relations*, 26 October 2015 (available on its web site). For historical background and precedents in 'war game' simulations, see Manuel De Landa, *War in the Age of Intelligent Machines*, Swerve Editions, New York, 1991.

[422] Development, Concepts and Doctrine Centre of the UK Ministry of Defence, 2010, p. 1-1, see above note 417.

tests and alternative analyses.[423] While the Devil's Advocate is usually associated with a single senior officer, by definition the Red Team refers to several officers, which in the context of criminal investigations could well comprise analysts, investigators and lawyers working for the same strategy.

3.5. Evidence Review Boards

An Evidence Review Board ('ERB') is a board of senior officers that shall review critically the case resulting from the investigation to advise on whether the available evidence is sufficient to file charges or not. This is similar to the concept of 'testing team' in software design and other industries, where it is accepted that "[t]he project manager's best friend is his daily adversary, the independent product-testing organization", and "[e]very development organization needs such an independent technical auditing group to keep it honest".[424] Their task is to "check machines and programs against specifications and serves as a devil's advocate, pinpointing every conceivable defect and discrepancy", and they act as "the surrogate customer, specialized for finding flaws".[425] In criminal procedure the ultimate 'customer' of the investigation would be the judge, and its 'surrogate' the ERB. Methods of this kind are sometimes referred to as 'murder boards', because of the merciless approach expected from the reviewers, which have been defined as "a group charged with the responsibility to slam a candidate or proposer of an idea up against the wall with tough questioning".[426]

The ERB is a fundamental mechanism of QC for the investigation and the proposed legal case. Senior management would convene ERBs at key moments of the process, typically when the investigation is considered as completed and a legal case or indictment is proposed for submission before the judges. It is not uncommon that officers that have been involved in the investigation over-estimate the strength of the case, as they often work under internal and external pressure to 'show results' for

---

[423] Zenko, 2015, p. xxi, see above note 421.

[424] Brooks Jr., 1995, p. 69, see above note 26.

[425] *Ibid.*

[426] See William Safire, "On Language; Murder Board at the Skunk Works", *The New York Times*, 11 October 1987. For example, for the 'murder boards' adopted by NASA researchers in the 1970s, see Glenn E. Bugos, *Atmosphere of Freedom: 75 Years at the NASA Ames Research Center*, NASA History Office, Washington, D.C., 2014, p. 10-11.

incrimination. Prosecutions and investigations tend to attract assertive personalities, which may be necessary to lead complex projects and confront criminals, but it comes with a risk of insufficient self-reflection. As indicated by an experienced prosecutor "a tragic lack of humility" on the part of investigating and prosecuting officers is a key factor in cases of judicial miscarriage, the remedy for which may be simply to show "humility and the ability to accept our human limitations".[427] This internal self-reflection is crucial because of the consequences of prosecutorial decisions on the lives of indicted persons, as well as witnesses and victims, and their impact on the resources and the credibility of the institution.

In national systems researchers and practitioners that have focused on prosecutorial decision-making have advised greater accountability and review procedures of different kinds.[428] In Canada in 2005, the Working Group on the Prevention of Miscarriages of Justice included among its recommendations that "[s]econd opinions and case review should be available in all areas".[429] In 2008 the American Bar Association recommended that "[g]enerally, the prosecutor engaged in an investigation should not be the sole decision-maker regarding the decision to prosecute matters arising out of that investigation".[430]

At the international level the ICTY-OTP adopted from its early years mandatory 'Indictment Reviews', defined by the ICTY-OTP Charging and Indictment Guidelines as "the formal, authorised OTP procedure for testing all proposed indictments".[431] These guidelines presented the reviews as mandatory and essential for the Office, and regulated them in detail:

---

[427] Mark Godsey, "Seeing and Accepting Human Limitations", in *Blind Justice: A Former Prosecutor Exposes the Psychology and Politics of Wrongful Convictions*, University of California Press, Oakland, 2017, p. 213.

[428] O'Brien, 2009, p. 1047, see above note 384.

[429] See FPT Heads of Prosecutions Committee, "Tunnel Vision", in *The Path to Justice: Preventing Wrongful Convictions: Report of the Federal/Provincial/Territorial Heads of Prosecutions Subcommittee on the Prevention of Wrongful Convictions*, 2011, sect. II "2005 Recommendations", and sect. VI "Discussion of Recommendations". This recommendation was included both in the 2005 report and the 2011 review.

[430] ABA, *ABA Standards for Criminal Justice: Prosecutorial Investigations*, 3rd edition, 2014, p. 8.

[431] ICTY-OTP, *Charging and Indictment Guidelines*, internal document, undated, *circa* 1995, section 4 "Indictment Reviews", p. 13. Copy on file with author. Every staff member received a copy of these guidelines, I have kept mine.

Every proposed indictment must go through a review. If there are security concerns or exigencies, then the Deputy Prosecutor can convene a confidential or expedited review, but it is essential that the proposed indictment be reviewed by a group of attorneys who have not participated in the investigation. The OTP is committed to subjecting all of its charging proposals to an objective and critical internal review in order to ensure fairness, accuracy and consistency with OTP policies and strategies.[432]

See below an excerpt from the ICTY-OTP Charging and Indictment Guidelines:[433]

4.0   INDICTMENT REVIEWS

The indictment review is the formal, authorised OTP procedure for testing all proposed indictments. If a proposed amendment to an existing indictment expands the charges or adds a new accused, then the trial team should consult with the legal commander in order to arrange a review.

The legal commander sets the time for the review, recruits participants for the review and ensures that the investigation/trial team has provided the reviewers with sufficient material to evaluate the case. The legal commander chairs the review and, upon its conclusion, is responsible for preparing detailed, written minutes and recommendations to the Prosecutor and Deputy Prosecutor.

In reviewing the proposed targets and charges, the reviewers can make the following recommendations, among others:

i   Accept the proposed targets and charges;
ii   Omit certain targets and/or charges;
iii   Include additional targets and/or charges;
iv   Modify the charging theories to better reflect the underlying crimes and culpability of the targets or OTP policy concerning legal issues;
v   Conduct additional investigations into designated matters and submit the indictment to a second review; and
vi   Conduct additional follow-up work and simply report back to the legal commander before presenting the case to the Prosecutor and the Deputy;

Figure 6. Excerpt of ICTY-OTP Charging and Indictment Guidelines.

The guidelines mandated the OTP 'legal commander' to call and chair the reviews, designate the reviewers, and to prepare "detailed, writ-

---

[432]   *Ibid.*
[433]   *Ibid.*

ten minutes and recommendations to the Prosecutor and Deputy Prosecutor".[434] The Legal Advisory Section would advise on legal issues, with its head or a representative participating as a reviewer. The Special Project Unit, with a focus on analysis, was requested to participate, to "provide special expertise concerning, among other things, historical, contextual, constitutional, political and hierarchical information", and to "review the draft indictment to ensure that the allegations are accurate and are placed in proper context".[435]

Under the section on "team preparation for reviews" these guidelines indicated that "[t]he team leader and legal advisor are responsible for presenting the case to the indictment review committee".[436] The teams had to present a draft indictment and a memorandum including the following eight sections: "summary of the case"; "review of proposed accused" including issues of command and knowledge; "general proof of incidents and analysis of the charges" to "outline the evidence supporting each alleged incident and charge"; "factual difficulties", the guidelines advising wisely to "[k]eep in mind, it is always preferable to get an objective and critical evaluation of the weaker aspects of your case in an OTP review, as opposed to a cross-examination at trial"; "legal problems and affirmative defences"; "additional investigation"; "special policy issues"; and "recommendations".[437]

The mandate for the reviewers was to accept, omit or add "targets and charges", advise on the legal characterisation of the alleged crimes and responsibilities, and recommend additional investigative or legal work if necessary.[438] The only issue for which the reviewers were given a specific threshold was suspect identification: "If the team has not compiled sufficient and reliable identification information on a proposed accused, the reviewers will not recommend proceeding with the indictment".[439]

---

[434] *Ibid.*

[435] *Ibid.* This unit hosted analysts prior to the establishment of the Leadership Research Team and the Military Analysis Team in 1997.

[436] *Ibid.*, sect. 5 "Team Preparation for Reviews", p. 15.

[437] *Ibid.*, pp. 15–16.

[438] *Ibid.*

[439] *Ibid.*, p. 15.

The standard of evidence for the 'indictment reviews' was defined as "trial ready", as a matter of office-wide policy:

> When an investigation team proposes an indictment, the evidence should be sufficient to proceed to trial immediately. The OTP has adopted a policy of requiring investigation teams to develop the case to a "trial ready" status before seeking the confirmation of an indictment.[440]

Under the section on "post-review procedures" the guidelines instructed the team and the 'legal commander' to brief the Prosecutor and Deputy Prosecutor and plan subsequent investigative or procedural steps, including possibly operational issues and arrest opportunities. In case of disagreement the 'legal commander' was asked "to present all views to the Prosecutor and Deputy". The 'legal commander' also had to communicate relevant policy decisions "to all legal advisors for application to future indictments and reviews".[441]

The ICTY-OTP implemented these 'indictment reviews' indeed. As Morten Bergsmo and Michael Keegan wrote in 1997:

> The OTP has developed an internal review procedure for draft indictments which aims at eliminating factually or legally deficient charges. [...] When the drafting and internal team review is concluded, the draft indictment with supporting material is evaluated by a general OTP review to which all lawyers working for the Office are invited to participate. As many as 20–25 lawyers, who have been provided with and reviewed the relevant material, can participate in such reviews, which tend to be very thorough and can sometimes last several days. In most cases a number of changes are made in the draft indictment following the review.[442]

I attended myself several of these reviews as observer or participant. The reviewers used to be a number of senior lawyers, including often the Head of the Legal Advisory Section, Commander William J. Fenrick and Dr. Vladimir Tochilovsky, known for his expertise on procedure and evi-

---

[440] *Ibid.*, "Introduction", p. 4.

[441] *Ibid.*, sect. 6 "Post-review Procedures", p. 18.

[442] Morten Bergsmo and Michael J. Keegan, "Case Preparation for the International Criminal Tribunal for the former Yugoslavia", in Hege Araldsen and Øyvind W. Thiis (eds.), *Manual on Human Rights Monitoring: An Introduction for Human Rights Field Officers*, Norwegian Institute of Human Rights, 1997, p. 10 (https://www.legal-tools.org/doc/bfbba0/).

dence.[443] I drafted an indictment and presented it for review in 1998, and I still remember the very cold and incisive comments by some senior reviewers. I had been very involved in that investigation for some two years, including multiple missions and interactions with victims and insiders, which gave me both the best knowledge of the facts, and the highest risk of overstating them because of my personal biases and self-interest. Sometimes when discussing internally the strength of cases you hear that 'the team knows best', which is true for the team that conducted the investigation and proposed the legal characterisation because of their extensive work with the evidence, but it is equally true that sometimes 'the team knows worst' because their personal involvement and the all-too-human confirmation biases and defensive reactions. The feedback from the reviewers was for me first irritating, and ultimately helpful. I believe it did help to improve the draft, and to develop higher professional standards. That indictment led to a successful arrest, prosecution and conviction of the accused.

The evidence reviews in the ICTY-OTP had four main limitations, which are likely to surface similarly in any other institution: cognitive load, forecast uncertainty, suspect-driven biases, and weak implementation. Firstly, the cognitive load for the reviewers is very high, possibly beyond the ability of many of them, because it is very difficult for an external observer to command the evidence of a complex case in short notice.

Secondly, as explained when defining the standard of review, in addition to being certain about the facts, the reviewers need to conduct a prospective assessment on the likelihood of success of the case in the court. This is similar to the notion of 'realistic prospect of conviction' required for prosecutions in England and Wales, which calls for a forecast

---

[443] Fenrick is a former military lawyer in the Canadian armed forces (1974–94), member of the UN Commission of Experts investigating war crimes allegations in the former Yugoslavia, and then Head of the Legal Advisory Section at the ICTY-OTP. Tochilovsky is a former Deputy Regional Attorney for judicial matters, and as District Attorney in the Ukraine (1976–94) and then investigation team leader and trial attorney in the ICTY-OTP (1994–2010), as well as official representative of the ICTY to the UN negotiations for the establishment of the ICC (1997–2001). Among Tochilovsky's publications, note his books *Indictment, Disclosure, Admissibility of Evidence: Jurisprudence of the ICTY and ICTR*, Wolf Legal Publishers, Nijmegen, 2004; and *The Law and Jurisprudence of the International Criminal Tribunals and Courts: Procedure and Human Rights Aspects*, 2nd edition, Intersentia, Amsterdam, 2014.

on the cogency of the evidence by both prosecution and defence.[444] This is not an easy task, even with the best intentions and skills. As judge Jerome Frank explained, and practitioners know well:

> Trials are often full of surprises. The adversary introduces unanticipated testimony. Witnesses, on whom the lawyer relied, change their stories when they take the witness-stand. The facts as they appeared to the lawyer when, before a trial, he conferred with this client and his witnesses, frequently are not at all like the facts as they later show up in the courtroom.[445]

The "surprises" that Frank found in national practice will only increase in international cases because of multiple investigative and communicative difficulties. There is a real risk of erring on the side of overconfidence with this kind of procedural forecast exercise, if the institution is under pressure to file charges, the teams carry their confirmation biases, and the reviewers do not want to be too harsh with their colleagues. Hence the forecast on the viability of the case will require some careful methods, including design of different scenarios, and using adversarial techniques within the review sessions.[446] Methods developed in management studies to facilitate decision-making could be of assistance, including different kinds of diagrams and 'decision-trees'.[447]

Thirdly, the ICTY-OTP had a policy focused on 'targets' – for "reviewing the proposed targets and charges" – further to the official criteria for "selection of targets", and such target-driven mind-set usually breeds confirmation bias.[448] Target- or suspect-driven cases are common when arrests are difficult, hence the cases may focus on whoever is arrestable or already arrested instead of those who are truly the key perpetrators, in

---

[444] Director of Public Prosecutions of the Crown Prosecution Service, "The Evidential Stage", in *The Code for Crown Prosecutors*, 2018, sect. 4.6.

[445] Frank, 1949, p. 17, see above note 1.

[446] See above Section 3.4.

[447] See for example Peter Mcnamee and John Celona, *Decision Analysis for the Professional*, 4th edition, SmartOrg, San Jose, 2008, particularly section on "Litigation Decision Analysis", pp. 190–92; and Philip Meissner, Olivier Sibony and Torsten Wulf, "Are You Ready to Decide?", *McKinsey Quarterly*, 1 April 2015, including a decision-making checklist to consider "different points of view" and "downside risk", and integrating the resulting scores in a screening matrix.

[448] See ICTY-OTP, *circa* 1995, sect. 3 "Selection of Targets", and several references to 'targets' in sect. 4 "Indictment Reviews", see above note 431.

order to make the trials possible (unless trial *in absentia* is accepted, which is usually not the case in international tribunals). The focus on 'most responsible' senior suspects (which was the policy in the ICTY and ICTR and a statutory duty for the IMT, IMTFE, ECCC and SCSL) would also contribute to this suspect-driven pressure.

Fourthly, the design of the review model was very thorough, but its implementation was uneven. Some ICTY Prosecutors supported these reviews, while others found them an unnecessary infringement on their discretion or burden on limited resources. In some instances, the teams disregarded the findings of the reviewers and succeeded to brief the Prosecutor directly and get their proposals approved. The gap between the stated policy and the real practice was at times noticeable.

Many former officers, including contributors to this volume,[449] are critical about the efficiency of these reviews at the ICTY-OTP. They would not agree with the above-mentioned assessment that they "tend to be very thorough". Overall, the quality of the ICTY indictments was not very impressive, in view of the multiple amendments that were often required, and frequent critical observations by ICTY judges on their quality.[450] I believe these 'indictment reviews' proved to be useful as a QC mechanism to a certain extent, but the Office would have benefited from a more robust review system. This was also the assessment and advice of Mark B. Harmon, one of the most experienced ICTY-OTP Senior Trial Attorneys, when he recommend in 2003 the adoption of 'indictment reviews' by the ICC-OTP.[451] The reviews were popular among the junior staff, who were allowed to attend as observers, and they could learn from the discussions with senior officers about multiple issues of evidence and procedure.

---

[449] See Ewan Brown and William H. Wiley, "International Criminal Investigative Collection Planning, Collection Management and Evidence Review", Chap. 8 below.

[450] See some examples of judicial decisions criticising the quality of the prosecutor's indictments and cases in Xabier Agirre, "The Role of Analysis Capacity", in Morten Bergsmo, Klaus Rackwitz and SONG Tianying (eds.), *Historical Origins of International Criminal Law: Volume 5*, Torkel Opsahl Academic EPublisher, Brussels, 2017, p. 96 (http://www.toaep.org/ps-pdf/24-bergsmo-rackwitz-song).

[451] Mark B. Harmon, "Preparation of Draft Indictments and Effective Indictment Review", in Morten Bergsmo, Klaus Rackwitz and SONG Tianying (eds.), *Historical Origins of International Criminal Law: Volume 5*, Torkel Opsahl Academic EPublisher, Brussels, 2017, pp. 385–90 (http://www.toaep.org/ps-pdf/24-bergsmo-rackwitz-song).

Subsequent accounts have presented the ICTY-OTP evidence reviews in a somehow idealized way, perhaps echoing the 'official history' of the institution, without a proper appraisal of the above-mentioned limitations. The ICTY Manual on Developed Practices, published in 2009 by the ICTY and UNICRI, acknowledged the OTP 'indictment reviews' as follows:

> The Office of the Prosecutor eventually adopted its own internal procedures for reviewing indictments before they are finalised and presented to a Judge for confirmation. Using a peer-review process, the prosecution team presented a draft indictment to colleagues from other teams, and defended their product against the colleague's questions. These internal indictment reviews helped produce a consistent approach, and often exposed problems with an indictment. The reviews also served to highlight the need for better evidence or further investigation, and produced suggestions for improvement.[452]

By 2012, the International Best Practices Project, based on the experience of five international or hybrid tribunals (ICTY, ICTR, SCSL, ECCC and STL) recommended categorically: "Every indictment should only be approved after review and recommendation to the chief prosecutor by a review panel".[453] The aim should be to achieve "the highest quality" and:

> The panel will ensure that the indictment under review is trial ready (although that standard may differ from one tribunal to another), supported by strong sufficient evidence, is consistent with other indictments and is in line with the indictment policy and charging directives.[454]

The practice of the ICC-OTP has evolved over time. The Regulations of the ICC-OTP issued by the first ICC Prosecutor in 2009 (six years after the beginning of his mandate) do not include any reference to evidence review boards. During the mandate of the first Prosecutor such reviews took place occasionally, without standard methodology and subject to the participation and evaluation by the Prosecutor himself. Strengthen-

---

[452] ICTY Manual on Developed Practices, p. 39, see above note 39.
[453] Petit, Akerson and Warren (eds.), 2012, p. 169, sect. "Indictment Review Panel", see above note 20.
[454] *Ibid.*

ing the review system was one of the priorities of the second Prosecutor, well aware of the need to improve the results after the feedback received from the judges, as well as OTP staff, in different cases. Hence, the ICC-OTP Strategic Plan 2012-2015 announced her decision "to organize an internal review committee that is independent of the joint team which will advise Excom on the strength of the presented case and on the desirability to proceed with it".[455] The ICC-OTP, particularly its Prosecution Division, started indeed to convey regularly ERBs, with a model similar to the practice of the ICTY-OTP, including senior lawyers and analysts as reviewers, prior to filing any Application for a Warrant of Arrest, or Document Containing the Charges. The next ICC-OTP Strategic Plan (2016-2018) reiterated the commitment to "[s]tandardising and enhancing the system of internal evidence review prior to a case being presented for prosecution".[456]

Taking into account the above-mentioned experiences and others, the best practice for ERBs in the investigation of international crimes, whether in national or international jurisdictions, can be summarised in the following points.

3.5.1. Status

The ERB must be considered as a mandatory procedure and a safeguard of quality control, particularly for the decisions whether or not to file an indictment. There should be no exceptions to this mandatory rule. No chief prosecutorial authority should issue or request an indictment or similar filing without having received the qualified opinion of an independent evidence review board. The advice of the ERB is not necessarily binding for the decision-maker (chief prosecutor or other), but a departure from this advice should be regarded as exceptional, requiring specific justification.

3.5.2. Scope

The purpose of the review would be primarily to assess the strength of the proposed case and answer the basic question "do we have the evidence or not?". Broader considerations of policy or opportunity should not distract

---

[455] ICC-OTP, *Strategic Plan 2012-2015*, 2013, p. 26 (https://www.legal-tools.org/doc/954beb/).

[456] ICC-OTP, *Strategic Plan 2016-2018*, 2015, p. 22 (https://www.legal-tools.org/doc/2dbc2d/).

the team and the reviewers from this technical assessment. They should be discussed separately. This is similar to the double test required by the Code for Crown Prosecutors in England and Wales to decide whether or not to file charges, including two stages to be discussed separately: 'the evidential stage', on whether the evidence suffices for a conviction; and 'the public interest stage', on whether the prosecution is worth the effort in an utilitarian perspective, taking into account the limited resources, the priorities of the community, and the circumstances of the suspect.[457] The question about the evidence needs to be discussed specifically for every proposed charge, incident and accused, a broad aggregated assessment would not be sufficient nor reliable.

3.5.3. Standard of Evidence

Given the seriousness of the decision at hand, the reviewers should aim at a high standard of certainty, based only on the actually available and admissible evidence. The question for the reviewers is not only about their personal certainty ("are you certain about the alleged facts and responsibilities?"). In addition to that, reviewers need to assess whether the prosecution is able to communicate that certainty to the chamber and prove successfully the case after adversarial challenge based on the actual evidence, which is a complex prospective assessment. Hence the question for the reviewers becomes: "are you certain about the alleged facts and responsibilities, *and* is the office able to prove this case beyond reasonable doubt with the actually available and admissible evidence"?

Effectively this calls for a standard of 'beyond reasonable doubt' in the eyes of the prosecution, assuming that only prosecutors who are fully convinced of their case will be able to lead the judges to the same conclusion. This standard is not procedurally required, but it is operationally highly advisable, and it should apply to every person and charge included in the proposed indictment. It requires an approach of 'inference to the best explanation', so that the prosecution, after having considered impartially multiple alternative hypotheses, will aim at the most cogent, logical and truthful causal explanation of the alleged crimes, not merely at the one that may seem most convenient for incrimination.

---

[457] Director of Public Prosecutions of the Crown Prosecution Service, 2018, sect. 4 "The Full Code Test", see above note 444.

This standard, in a sense 'beyond the reasonable doubt of the prosecutor', is similar to the 'trial ready' standard required by the ICTY-OTP Charging and Indictment Guidelines, as well as the International Best Practices Project, since the prosecution's goal in trial is actually to achieve certainty 'beyond reasonable doubt'.[458] This is also similar to the standard recommended by the American Bar Association ('ABA') for this purpose: "A prosecutor should not seek an indictment unless the prosecutor reasonably believes the charges are supported by probable cause and that there will be admissible evidence sufficient to support the charges beyond reasonable doubt at trial".[459]

The excerpt below from the ICTY-OTP guidelines, from its very first page, contains the explanation of their 'trial ready' standard and its specific requirements:[460]

The selection of charges and accused should provide a secure foundation for our trials. If we mistakenly pursue charges that are not founded in fact and law, or if we proceed on technically permissible, but ill-advised, charges or inappropriate accused, we will undermine the credibility of the ICTY. If we proceed on incomplete evidence, we place the trial attorneys in the untenable position of investigating the case while they are preparing for trial. When an investigation team proposes an indictment, the evidence should be sufficient to proceed to trial immediately. The OTP has adopted a policy of requiring investigation teams to develop the case to a "trial ready" status before seeking the confirmation of an indictment.

For a case to be trial ready, it must have all of the necessary evidence in an admissible and authenticated format. The team should know which witnesses are to be called at trial and the basic outline of how the case is to be presented to the court. All fundamental charging issues should be resolved. While there will always be some follow-up work necessary to prepare the case for trial once the accused is arrested, the investigation team should make every effort to have the case as complete as possible before seeking confirmation of an indictment.

Figure 7. Excerpt of the first page of the ICTY-OTP guidelines.

---

[458] For the International Best Practices Project, see their report Petit, Akerson and Warren (eds.), 2012, p. 169, see above note 20.

[459] ABA, *Criminal Justice Standards for the Prosecution Function*, 4th edition, 2017, Standard 3-4.6 "Quality and Scope of Evidence Before a Grand Jury".

[460] ICTY-OTP, *circa* 1995, p. 1, see above note 431.

3.5.4. Team Preparation

The team proposing the indictment must submit before the ERB a fully finalized and sourced draft indictment, ready to be submitted without further elaboration, and meeting in their view the required standard of certainty. The draft indictment must be sourced in detail, for every significant factual proposition, against discrete items of evidence referenced after their registration in an evidence management system with guarantees of 'chain of custody'. The team must also submit analytical reports and other products (relational charts, maps, and so on) that justify the factual findings in the draft indictment. Relevant key witnesses, such as insiders, must be subject to individual Source Evaluation, so that the reviewers can endorse a case only if these witnesses are considered sufficiently credible and reliable. The team must report candidly the limitations in the evidence, as well as the known or most predictable lines of defence, and the corresponding responses. The analysts in the team must assist in the preparation and lead the production of reports and presentation on key analytical issues, such as crime patterns, organisational structures, the role of the accused, documentary evidence, and Source Evaluation. The analysts should also use diagnostic tools and tables to assist the review.[461] The team must submit the relevant materials with sufficient time for the reviewers to study them properly, for example, no less than one week prior to the review.

3.5.5. Reviewer Preparation

The reviewers must allocate an adequate amount of time to study the proposed case and the underlying evidence. A superficial review or merely legal commentary is of little assistance. This may oblige senior officers to block their agendas and postpone other duties, which may be well-justified in view of the importance of the task.

3.5.6. Composition

The reviewers should be a few senior officers with extensive experience in investigations and litigation, including attorneys, analysts and investigators. They should have not participated in the investigation, for the sake of objectivity and independence. Top managers responsible for the ultimate decision, such as the chief prosecutor or the next senior management

---

[461] See above Section 3.3.

level, may abstain from participating, or participate only as observers, since they will have their chance to review the case subsequently on their own, and they might influence the technical assessment with policy considerations (suggesting the accused and charges that are more desirable, rather than those who are more truthful and viable in court).

3.5.7. Independence

The ERB must act with full independence from the team and from higher levels. Top managers should not influence the ERB directly or indirectly with suggestions about the desired outcome. Reviewers need to be reassured that they will not suffer any adverse consequence from their fair assessment. Reviewers need to act with utter objectivity and technical focus on the evidence, free of any influence or pressure.

3.5.8. Method

The review as such could take a few hours or a whole day, including a presentation by the team, questions by reviewers and ensuing discussion. A designated officer should act as a facilitator, to help ensure focus on the core questions and manage time and participation. After the presentation and discussions, the reviewers should meet separately to reach their conclusions, much in the way a jury would do, and to prepare their evaluation report. The reviewers must state clearly in this report their opinion on whether the proposed case and its different elements meet the required standard, as well as possible legal and operational recommendations. The report may well include different opinions and votes if there is no unanimity.

4

Analysis of Organisational Structures and Quality Control of Case Development

Christian Axboe Nielsen[*]

Serious international crimes of the type investigated and prosecuted by international criminal courts and tribunals are by definition complex phenomena that typically involve a multitude of actors, a broad geographical area and a wide chronology. Crimes against humanity, to take one major category of serious international crimes, are by statutory definition 'widespread and systematic' and genocides typically involve thousands of actors and detailed planning and execution. War crimes can, unlike the other two categories of major international crimes against humanitarian law, be discrete, but they are by definition committed within the context of complicated armed conflicts, many of which feature not just two opposing standing armies but a variety of regular and irregular forces. And while one of the major tenets of modern international criminal justice is individual criminal responsibility, it is to date unheard of that those individuals prosecuted are lone wolves. Rather, all accused perpetrators of international crimes prosecuted by international courts and tribunals since the end of the Second World War have belonged to some type of regime or organisation through which criminal acts have been committed. The challenges posed to investigators, analysts and prosecutors by the scope of these crimes has been evident since the Nuremberg and Tokyo trials which gave birth to modern international criminal justice. But as we slowly approach the centenary of these trials, questions of how best to investigate these crimes and their perpetrators remain important.

Based on my own experience since 2002 – both as a full-time analyst and as an external consultant and expert witness – with investigations and prosecutions at the International Criminal Tribunal for the former

---

[*] **Christian Axboe Nielsen** is Associate Professor, Aarhus University. He worked as Research Officer, ICTY-OTP, and Associate Analyst, ICC-OTP. He holds a doctorate from Columbia University.

Yugoslavia ('ICTY'), International Criminal Court ('ICC'), Special Tribunal for Lebanon ('STL'), as well as with domestic proceedings (in Canada and Germany) focused on serious crimes and more general knowledge of other recent international judicial proceedings, I will in this paper address key features and typical pitfalls occurring in the analysis of organisational structures. Through this analysis, I hope to raise some relevant and practically useful points regarding quality control in international case development, though I believe that a number of the comments I will make here would also be relevant for complex domestic criminal investigations in cases involving terrorism or organised crime. I write this chapter inspired by – and, I hope, in the spirit of – Morten Bergsmo's policy brief on quality control in criminal investigations.[1] Needless to say, all thoughts and opinions expressed herein are attributable to me and not to any of the aforementioned instances or jurisdictions.

As anyone who has ever worked with international criminal investigations and prosecutions will know, any meaningful analysis of organisational structures presupposes an initial identification and categorisation of those organisations which are germane to the particular situation being investigated. Those familiar with more well-organised States tend to assume that the civilian, military and police structures that are relevant for such investigations will be more or less universally recognisable. That is to say, there will be a state with a government, ministries, a standing army and security organisations with clear structures operating on the basis of relevant laws and regulations. Such a situation would be ideal from the point of view of analysis and investigation, but even when such clear structures exist, they are almost always adversely affected, modified and obfuscated by the processes that generate the malicious behaviour that also leads to criminal conduct.[2] Moreover, to the degree that actors are cognisant of the risk of investigations and prosecutions because of their own criminal actions, these actors have a vested interest in obscuring their structures, whether through manufacturing 'plausible deniability' or other avenues.

---

[1] Morten Bergsmo, "Towards Culture of Quality Control in Criminal Investigations", FICHL Policy Brief Series No. 94 (2019), Torkel Opsahl Academic EPublisher, Brussels, 2019 (https://legal-tools.org/doc/65157b).

[2] On the wide array of military organisations and structures, see John Keegan, *A History of Warfare*, Vintage, New York, 1994.

The case of the former Yugoslavia illustrates that even when a very well-organised modern army – the Yugoslav People's Army ('JNA') – is one of the principal actors in the violent dissolution of a state, organisational analysis can be extremely difficult and time-consuming. For on the same side of the conflict a multitude of other actors quickly emerged whose roles and relationship to the JNA were far from clear. For example, a large number of volunteer forces appeared on the scene in Croatia and Bosnia and Herzegovina in 1991 and 1992. Although legislation existed regarding the incorporation of these forces into the JNA and their subsequent deployment in combat, investigation and analysis revealed that this process was to a considerable extent highly improvised and localised and was very contingent on the personalities of key officers in the JNA and the self-appointed leaders of these volunteer units.[3]

Many conflicts feature a large number of paramilitary groups, most of which are self-proclaimed and very loosely organised and which may exist for relatively short periods of time. As seen in cases against both Bosnian Serb and Bosnian Croat perpetrators at the ICTY, these amorphous, ephemeral and highly contingent groups may or may not be coherent. Their relationships with various official (even if self-proclaimed) government, military and police actors can vary greatly over time and may veer from complete co-operation to antagonism and even open conflict. Indeed, the very names of paramilitary groups and their colloquial usage in the affected area may or may not be indicative of their actual existence. In both Croatia and Bosnia and Herzegovina, a particularly good example of this phenomenon was the 'Red Berets'. Many witnesses reported that this group has perpetrated criminal acts in a considerable number of municipalities. The name obviously emerged as a result of their distinct headgear, but it remained for a long time fundamentally unclear whether all those actors wearing red berets actually belonged to the same unit. Additionally, many victims' accounts exaggerated the consistency and uniformity of these groups. In the end, investigators and analysts were able to prove that a unit wearing red berets did actually exist – though it formally bore another name. However, it also became apparent that a number of the actors wearing red berets had no real affiliation with this

---

[3] Reynaud Theunens, "Military Aspects of the Role of Jovica Stanišić and Franko Simatović in the Conflict in Croatia and Bosnia-Herzegovina (BiH) (91-95)", in Prosecution's Submission of the Expert Report of Reynaud Theunens Pursuant to Rule 94*bis* With Annexes A and B, 2 July 2007, IT-03-69.

unit. Indeed, it seemed instead likely that some had adopted this headgear as a way of becoming 'copycats' and sponging off the notoriety of the actual unit. It is easy to see how mistakes could have been made in the investigation of the 'Red Berets' without careful analysis.

The point here is that preconceived notions or assumptions regarding the organisations involved can impact negatively upon the analysis that is essential to investigations of major international crimes.[4] There is of course nothing at all wrong with assembling available information regarding orders of battle, established institutions, leadership structures, etc. However, doing so is the beginning and not the end of the analytical investigative process. The analysis of organisations is affected by whether they have existed prior to the alleged commission of crimes or whether they emerged only subsequent to the emergence of armed conflict or autocratic rule. In other words, are these regimes or organisations inherently criminal or have they been transformed or perverted in such a way that previously 'ordinary' and legitimate organisations and institutions have now become vehicles for the perpetration of criminal acts? Again, in the case of the former Yugoslavia, a relatively stable and highly-bureaucratic federal State – though one also characterised by chronic human rights abuses typical of party-States – disintegrated into mutually warring States in which the army and the police were among the chief perpetrators of criminal acts. However, during that same process elements of these organisations voluntarily outsourced policing and combat activities to newly-established paramilitary organisations whose entire purpose was based on illicit economic gain and by extension violent criminal conduct. Analysing these two types of organisational structures requires different modalities, not least because the interrelationship between them was to a large extent deliberately obfuscated in order that the former type could achieve and maintain plausible deniability with respect to the activities of the latter type.

Having established an approximate and initial understanding of the quantity and types of significant structures operating in the particular situation, the next obvious challenge is to begin the analysis of the interrelationship of these organisations. This challenge is in turn interlinked with the analysis of the *de jure* and *de facto* operation of previously existing

---

[4]   See Gareth Morgan, *Images of Organization, Updated Edition*, Sage Publications, London, 2006.

organisations. Essentially this entails comparing the way in which these organisations are supposed to function according to existing laws and regulations and comparing this with how they actually functioned. Here it should be noted that anyone who has ever worked in any kind of organisation or who has interacted with the authorities even in a stable and peaceful environment will recognise that the actual functioning of such organisations and authorities differs from the official way in which they are supposed to function. Inevitably, the events leading to the commission of crimes lead to much more considerable deviations from the *de jure* structures and manner of functioning, and it may well be that deputies, temporarily appointed or even completely official actors are more significant than the ones officially in charge. Struggles for power and resources also exacerbate the functioning, as does bureaucratic turf warfare. In some cases, the most powerful actors may be difficult to detect because they deliberately try to shield their power and activity from public view.

For analyses of organisations to have a chance of succeeding and become useful in investigations and subsequent trials, the analysts performing them must demonstrate that they are primarily interested in understanding the genesis, operations and internal structures and logics of these organisations. Here a delicate and difficult balance needs to be struck: if the analysts performing this work are exclusively focused on examining questions which pertain to the case theory being developed by investigators and prosecutors, then the analysis risks being tainted by prosecutorial agendas. Conversely, analysts must realise and accept that the main reason they are being asked to perform analysis is to assist not just the prosecutors and investigators but also the lawyers representing the accused and – not least – the trial chamber. Both the relevant document collection process and the subsequent analysis can therefore not be allowed to exist in an intellectual vacuum. Document collection plans must of course exist, but these document collection plans must be focused primarily on the relevant organisational structures rather than on specific investigative or prosecutorial theories. This requires a bit of a tightrope walk. Put differently, the goal should be able to provide the most objective analysis of the designated organisations and their structures while recognising that the primary focus must be on the role and legal responsibility of these structures with respect to potential commission of serious international crimes. That having been said, from the perspective of leadership analysis and organisational structures, overly narrow document collection and evidence review based primarily on elements of crime can also create serious problems, particularly if the use of expert reports produced by analysts at trial is being contemplated.

One of the mistakes routinely made in the investigation of major international crimes is to assume that the organisations responsible for the commission of these crimes are monolithic, possessing at all times the same (criminal) intent and purpose. (Given the amount of personal and professional rivalries and bureaucratic infighting that characterise large organisations – and in this sense international criminal courts and tribunals are certainly no exception – it is rather ironic that some employees of these courts and tribunals commit the fallacy of believing in monolithic criminal enterprises.) At the ICTY, the decision to espouse the doctrine of joint criminal enterprise ('JCE') probably to a significant extent exacerbated this fallacy and has led critics to claim that the doctrine possessed an inherent pro-conviction bias.[5] Somewhat paradoxically, separate trials of various members of the alleged JCE also at times resulted in contradictory prosecution theories in the sense that in each separate case prosecutors had a vested interest in portraying the accused in the given case as primarily responsible for criminal acts. Hence, a regional governor might be prosecuted in one case and be portrayed as nearly omnipotent in his area of responsibility. Later, at the same judicial institution, the president or prime minister of the country in which the regional governor served might in turn be prosecuted, yet in this case the regional governor's role is downplayed in order to increase the perception of culpability on the part of the president or prime minister. Such contradictory case theories and prosecutions should be thwarted by proper quality control in analysis. Absent this the prosecutions, even if successful, will be suboptimal and will moreover also lead to the emergence of problematic historical narratives. Of course, similar mistakes can also be identified on the part of defence teams representing the accused in international criminal cases, who also labour under the constant risk of succumbing to myopic understandings of the overall context.

---

[5] For a constructive criticism of JCE, see Kai Ambos, "Joint Criminal Enterprise and Command Responsibility", in *Journal of International Criminal Justice*, 2007, vol. 5, no. 1, pp. 159–83. On organisational liability and alleged pro-conviction bias, see Nancy A. Combs, *Fact-Finding without Facts: The Uncertain Evidentiary Foundations of International Criminal Convictions*, Cambridge University Press, Cambridge, 2010, chap. 8.

It may be argued that the presentation of seamless joint criminal enterprises may be a conscious choice made by prosecutors to streamline their cases and hence convince trial chambers of their overarching case theory. Yet international trial chambers are not juries composed of lay persons in a domestic court of law. Although it is true that a number of judges at international criminal courts and tribunals have lacked previous trial and criminal law experience, it is equally true that the prosecutors have in several cases at both the *ad hoc* tribunals and the ICC seen their cases collapse because they oversimplified analysis and tried in a sense to engage in incriminating heuristics.

4.1. Strategic vs. Case-Based Analysis

By strategic analysis I refer to the type of analysis that focuses on an entire set of crimes in a geographical area over a certain span of time, or 'situation analysis', as it is also called at the ICC. Conducting such analysis also leads us to a better overview of the possible drawbacks of focusing on certain crimes, organisations or perpetrators. This is important because all international criminal courts and tribunals must operate within the constraints of finite resources: personnel, time, and money. Even in the best-case scenario, only a small fraction of the crimes committed in any given situation will be investigated, and therefore only a small minority of the actual perpetrators will face prosecution. Strategic analysis can help ensure that those investigations and prosecutions that are carried out deliver 'the best bang for the buck'.

A particular risk when choosing to focus on certain organisations is whether those organisations are primarily responsible for the conflict or whether they are rather symptomatic of the conflict. With respect to paramilitary, proxy and other irregular forces, special care is necessary in analysis and investigation. If too much emphasis is placed on these forces, a substantial risk exists that subsequent prosecutions will treat the symptoms rather than addressing the root cause of criminal conduct. We can see this danger both in domestic prosecutions that focus on low or mid-level criminal conduct and at the ICC where certain State sponsors of rebel militias have for various reasons largely avoided prosecution. For example, in the Democratic Republic of the Congo ('DRC') and more generally the Great Lakes Region of Africa, some of the groups committing crimes against humanity and war crimes were essentially established as proxy groups for States in the region, though some of them later broke with their erstwhile sponsors and subsequently acted more independently or sought out other sponsors. While there is no doubt that the level of criminality perpetrated to proxy groups reached the threshold triggering investigation and possible prosecution, it is at least worth questioning the overall strategic value of such cases, regardless of their success or failure in court. These cases can of course have significant inherent value, not least from the perspective of the victims of these crimes. Yet in a world of finite resources, if such cases are pursued, then they should preferably yield increasing returns to scale for subsequent investigations of those States or regimes which have established the proxy groups. Otherwise, the entire international criminal justice process risks treating the symptoms while ignoring the underlying disease.

The example of some of the early cases at the ICTY illustrate this point. The Tribunal's very first case, against a lowly perpetrator named Duško Tadić, was in some senses a fluke. Compared to later cases against other accused, neither Tadić's crimes nor his importance rose to anywhere near the level that the UN Security Council had in mind when talking about the Tribunal's obligations to pursue the most serious cases. Indeed, had Tadić been found just a few years later, he almost certainly would not have been prosecuted at the ICTY. Yet at the particular time of his discovery and arrest in Germany, he was a 'godsend' to a tribunal casting about for its first case. The same to some extent holds true for Jean Paul Akayesu at the International Criminal Tribunal for Rwanda ('ICTR').

Nonetheless, the Tadić case was put to great effect by the Office of the Prosecutor ('OTP') at the ICTY. The documentation gathered and the analysis and investigations carried out for the Tadić case were used to build the base of knowledge from which other cases could subsequently be constructed. Evidence – documentary, as well as witness statements, forensic and other material – could in effect be recycled and reused in cases that worked their way up the chain of responsibility. From the Tadić case, in which the focus was on a rather randomly selected guard at a Bosnian concentration camp, the evidence and the prosecutions wound their way up to the mayor and governor of the area in which this and similar camps were located, and from there up to the 'national' level of *Republika Srpska* and ultimately to the leadership in Serbia (at the time a part of the Federal Republic of Yugoslavia) which had instigated and supported the criminal activities perpetrated by the Bosnian Serbs.

The first case which went to court at the ICC, the case of Thomas Lubanga, suffered from the same flaws as the Tadić case. Lubanga, who at the time of the investigation conducted against him was already languishing in prison in Kinshasa, was the head of a paramilitary force called the Union of Congolese Patriots (*Union des Patriotes Congolais*, 'UPC'), one of many proxy forces present in the eastern provinces of the DRC. (Admittedly, the UPC had elements of both a proxy group and an independent group, having been founded by Uganda then subsequently switching to Rwandan patronage.) The mere fact that Lubanga had been neutralised did not necessarily invalidate his prosecution for some of the grave crimes the UPC had committed in the DRC's Ituri province.

However, unlike in the case of Tadić, there are few indications that significant returns to scale were obtained from the Lubanga case. In particular, even though the UPC and several other similar groups were at least during some periods acting as proxies for Uganda or Rwanda, the ICC did not prove capable or willing to pursue the leads provided by the investigations of proxy groups. Whether the failure to do so was rooted in politically influenced decisions or political pressure, or whether it was a strategic error or a decision informed by a narrow-minded cost-benefit calculation is immaterial here. The end result to date has been that the ICC has failed to achieve the types of increased returns to scale seen at the ICTY. Of course, to be fair to the ICC, that court has faced tremendous pressure to deal with situations in several countries, whereas the ICTY as a geographically defined *ad hoc* court enjoyed the relative luxury of being able to focus on crimes committed in one (former) country. And the ICTY has also been criticised for not succeeding sufficiently in prosecuting and convicting those leaders in Serbia and Croatia who were most responsible for funding, supplying and to some extent commanding Bosnian Serb, Croatian Serb and Bosnian Croat forces. Yet with a bit of poetic license, one can compare the above problem to applying lotion to cosmetic treatment of skin moles while ignoring the underlying skin cancer.

Successful investigations and prosecutions of paramilitary groups are not by definition bad, but if the ICC does not move beyond these, the results of its work will be very limited. The ICC has in the Darfur situation shown that it can pursue investigations and prosecutions which build on local or regional atrocities and then reach all the way to the top of a state, as evidenced by the indictment of Sudanese President Omar Hassan Ahmad Al Bashir. Yet as a truly international criminal court, the ICC also labours under the structural problem of having to address numerous situations that may be completely detached from one another. Although there are certainly investigative, analytical and prosecutorial lessons learned which can be transferred from one situation to another, it can be argued that even in the best of circumstances, the ICC will not be able to generate the kinds of investigative and prosecutorial returns to scale which the two most productive *ad hoc* tribunals could achieve in the former Yugoslavia and Rwanda.

At the opposite end of the spectrum, another risk exists if we devote too much attention to the ultimate sponsors of proxy forces. By doing so, we risk not seeing the disagreements regarding means and goals, contradictions and power struggles that may inform the relationship between them. There is a certain seductiveness that attaches to the simplicity of hegemonic control and monolithic actors. After all, if one actor is in near total control, both investigations and prosecutions should all things equal be easier. Yet here we skirt the danger of assuming the existence of a well-formulated and implemented master plan and – by extension – the existence of a hegemonic mastermind.[6] By contrast, historical research informs us that even those regimes most notoriously identified with one individual – Hitler in the case of Nazi Germany, Stalin in the case of the Soviet Union – were much more complicated and nuanced than they seem at first glance.[7]

In this respect it may also be useful to entertain the competing explanations that have informed much of Holocaust scholarship, intentionalism and functionalism.[8] Briefly put, adherents of intentionalism believed

---

[6] Patrick J. Treanor, "Old Documents and Archives in Core International Crimes Cases", in Morten Bergsmo and CHEAH Wui Ling (eds.), *Old Evidence and Core International Crimes*, Torkel Opsahl Academic EPublisher, Beijing, 2012 (https://legal-tools.org/doc/f130e1).

[7] Ian Kershaw's biography of Hitler summarises much of the research on the Nazi regime, and the same is true of Stephen Kotkin's biography of Stalin. Ian Kershaw, *Hitler: 1889–1936: Hubris*, W.W. Norton, New York, 1999 and Ina Kershaw, *Hitler: 1936–1945: Nemesis*, W.W. Norton, New York, 2000; Stephen Kotkin, *Stalin: Paradoxes of Power, 1878–1928*, Penguin Random House, 2014; and Stephen Kotkin, *Stalin: Waiting for Hitler, 1929–1941*, Penguin Random House, 2017.

[8] For an overview of the debate see Christopher R. Browning, "Beyond 'Intentionalism' and 'Functionalism': The Decision for the Final Solution Reconsidered", in Christopher R. Browning (ed.), *The Path to Genocide: Essays on Launching the Final Solution*, Cambridge University Press, Cambridge, 1992, pp. 88–101.

that Hitler as the leader of Nazi Germany possessed a clear intent to destroy European Jewry. All subsequent criminal actions committed followed from his dictatorial role and this criminal intent. By contrast, while not denying the existence of Hitler's intent, functionalists argued that a significant portion of subsequent actions could better be explained by the bureaucratic apparatus. Competition among bureaucrats and other Nazi officials inexorably contributed to a ratcheting up effect in which criminal actions resulted not so much out of intent as out of careerist and egotistical motivations. Of course, for victims of the regime, whether they were being persecuted and ultimately killed based on intentionalist or functionalist reasons mattered little. But in terms of better understanding how such regimes work – and how they can be prevented and their crimes subsequently investigated and prosecuted – is of great import.

This in turn leads us to the question of whether serious international crimes are committed in an environment of chaos or well-planned conspiracy. If one indulges a bit of generalisation based on cases tried at international courts and tribunals since the mid-1990s, it could be said that whereas the defence in complex (international) cases argues that the situation – particularly where armed conflict was involved – was chaotic, the prosecution tends to argue that everything was entirely (too) well-organised. As with so many things, quality control in analysis requires recognising that all situations reviewed by international courts include elements of both chaos and conspiracy. The entire point of analysis is not to succumb to either end of the chaos-conspiracy spectrum, but instead to break down the dichotomy and analyse what actually transpired.[9] At a much more fundamental level, this also leads to questions regarding our understanding of the relationship between human nature and violence.[10]

4.2. Remembering the Flip Side

In the vast majority of situations which give rise to the commission of serious international crimes, the complexity and multitude of factors underlying these crimes is augmented by the existence of misdeeds on 'the other side'. It is exceedingly rare that conflicts are completely one-sided.

---

[9] Xabier Agirre, "Methodology for the Criminal Investigation of International Crimes", in Alette Smeulers (ed.), *Collective Violence and International Criminal Justice: An Interdisciplinary Approach*, Intersentia, Antwerp, p. 363.

[10] Siniša Malešević, *The Sociology of War and Violence*, Cambridge University Press, Cambridge, 2010.

Even if one side's forces commit the lion's share of crimes during the actual conflict, it is entirely possible that the other side has previously committed crimes or does so later, particularly if the conflict is marked by a reversal of fortunes. From an analytical point of view, the challenge that must be grasped and confronted is to ensure that alleged criminal activity is investigated *per se*, and not because a particular side or set of actors have allegedly committed crimes.

Analysis of organisational structures therefore also need to take into account the existence and performance of opposing organisations: flip-side cases. At the same time, we must recognise that analysts will almost inevitably end up developing a particularly deep knowledge of one or several – but not all – parties to a conflict. The mere fact that a particular analyst has been assigned to work on a particular side of the conflict cannot and must not serve to disqualify that analyst in the eyes of the court. Rather, such compartmentalised tasking is simply a recognition that no one analyst can reasonably be expected to cover all sides of the conflict *equally*. Those analysts must however be able to cover all sides of the conflict *objectively*, that is, they should apply precisely the same standards to their analysis and scrutiny of one side as they would to all others.

By way of example, both the leadership research team ('LRT') and the military analysis team ('MAT') at the ICTY featured research subunits working on a particular side of the conflict. Within the LRT, the Bosnian Serb unit, composed of several analysts, worked on analysing the leadership of the Bosnian Serbs. Importantly, these analysts co-operated not just within their subunit, where the analyst focusing on the Bosnian Serb Assembly exchanged knowledge and sources with the analysts concentrating on the Bosnian Serb's primary political party or their self-proclaimed 'crisis staffs'. Upon encountering information that was *prima facie* relevant for an investigation of the Bosnian Croats' leadership, the analysts would pass this on to their colleagues. And, of course, the analysts would work on producing products that conformed to the same standards and were quality-checked by the chief analyst. In principle, analysts could be reassigned to another subunit if there was no longer sufficient work for them on their present assignment.

It is not unusual that one side commits more crimes than the other in a conflict, and the plea not to neglect flip side cases should not be construed as a misguided call for equivocation or what-about-ism. Rather, analysis of both (or all sides) of a conflict should contribute to better quality of investigations and prosecutions. Moreover, to the extent that international courts and tribunals are to have any chance at contributing to long-term reconciliation, it is essential that they treat allegations of criminal conduct on all sides of any given conflict. To not do so is to succumb to the reification of the victor-perpetrator dichotomy.[11] And analysis that ignores flip side cases has real costs for the reputation of international judicial institutions in the long run, as the relative neglect at the ICTY of crimes perpetrated by Kosovo Albanians, at the ICTR of crimes perpetrated by Tutsis and at the ICC of crimes perpetrated by Ugandan government security forces show. We must be extremely wary of reifying and appropriating the analytical categories employed by parties to a conflict.

4.3. Evidence-Based, Not Target-Based

As pointed out in the concept note by Morten Bergsmo underpinning this volume, avoiding target-based investigations requires strategizing in order "to avoid perceptions of confirmation-bias or target-driven investigation".[12] Quality control in analysis in international criminal investigations is of cardinal importance. However, the best analysis in the world can end up being an exercise in futility if the wrong strategical decisions are taken. A notorious example of this in newer history is the analytical work carried out by American and British intelligence agencies regarding possible weapons of mass destruction possessed by Saddam Hussein in Iraq. Although most reports indicate that the intelligence analysts carried out thorough and effective analysis, the political leadership in both the US and the UK had arrived at their own preordained conclusions, thereby in effect neutralising the analysis performed.[13]

Similar observations can be made at international criminal courts and tribunals. All of those judicial institutions established since the mid-1990s have to some degree struggled with the problems created by investigations that were at least initially driven by a focus on particular indi-

---

[11] Margarida Hourmat, "Victim-Perpetrator Dichotomy in Transitional Justice: The Case of Post-Genocide Rwanda", in *Narrative and Conflict: Explorations of Theory and Practice*, 2016, vol. 4, no. 1, pp. 43–67.

[12] Bergsmo, 2019, see above note 1.

[13] James P. Pfiffner and Mark Phythian (eds.), *Intelligence and National Security Policymaking on Iraq*, Manchester University Press, Manchester, 2018. For a contrarian view, see Robert Jervis, "Reports, Politics, and Intelligence Failures: The Case of Iraq", in *Journal of Strategic Studies*, 2006, vol. 29, no. 1, pp. 3–52.

viduals rather than on the evidence collected. Indeed, it is common knowledge that the Lubanga and Ntaganda cases at the ICC were a result of a target-driven investigation ordained by the Court's first prosecutor and persist to some extent in later cases such as in the Mali situation.

Target-driven investigations are notorious for creating situations of severe cognitive bias.[14] Information and evidence collection are distorted because investigators, analysts and lawyers from a very early stage collect data that pertains to a particular target. Moreover, in practice the collection is further skewed so that it focuses predominantly on the culpability of the target in question. This makes it, often unconsciously and implicitly, much more difficult to comply with the (statutory) obligations to investigate potentially exonerating leads equally.

It is of course theoretically possible that target-driven investigations can point at individuals who are genuinely guilty of committing serious international crimes. Taking this possibility into consideration, analysis of these targets can still be useful and lead to better investigations and prosecutions. However, the risk of prosecutorial bias and blindness not only to the potential innocence of the targets but also the potentially greater culpability of others not targeted should be enough to dissuade any international judicial institution from pursuing target-driven investigations.

Quality analysis, properly done, instead constitutes an essential part of evidence-based investigations. As Patrick J. Treanor, the head of the LRT has argued, investigations must:

> [B]egin and continue to proceed on the basis of a substantive hypothesis [...] developed through the analysis of all information and evidence available on the given leadership structure. That is, all relevant knowledge must be integrated through analysis into a consistent hypothesis or, if inconsistent with it, be put aside but not forgotten for later re-evaluation and possible use.[15]

---

[14] Moa Lidén, "Prevention of Factual Confirmation-Bias during Offence-Driven Investigations", CILRAP Film, New Delhi, 22 February 2019 (https://www.cilrap.org/cilrap-film/190222-liden/).

[15] Patrick J. Treanor, "Research and Analysis in the Investigation, Prosecution and Adjudication of Crimes", in Morten Bergsmo, Klaus Rackwitz and SONG Tianying (eds.), *Historical Origins of International Criminal Law: Volume 5*, Torkel Opsahl Academic EPublisher, Brussels, 2017, p. 138 (https://legal-tools.org/doc/ea5269).

Needless to say, the hypothesis can involve mention of the roles of various individuals, units, organisations, etc. However, the hypothesis should not be target-driven *per se*, rather targets should emerge organically based on the objective collection and rigorous analysis of information and evidence. Simply put, those who commit the error of conducting target-driven investigations ended up perpetrating cases instead of preparing cases.

4.4. Breadth vs. Depth

Quality in major criminal investigations requires energy, resources, objectivity and time. Reprioritising scarce resources is a key aspect of sound investigative management, but all too often we see that resources are reprioritised in a manner that resources are spread too thin or that reprioritisation is done in a reactive rather than proactive and strategic manner, putting out fires instead of planning to prevent future fires. Quality control in analysis requires robust and decisive managers who are willing to shield analysts from menial tasks that are sloughed off on them because they are viewed by others as undesirable, as well as from tasks that threaten to derail or severely delay the production of in-depth analytical work product. This is not to say that analysts should somehow be isolated or be permitted to exist in a cocoon from which they emerge only when they finish their major analytical tasks. It is legitimate to expect analysts to be accessible to pressing relevant questions from investigators and lawyers, as long as those posing these questions do so in a manner that does not fundamentally distract analysts from fulfilling their primary tasks.

Another challenge that undoubtedly exists at the ICC is that of analytical depth. Unlike the *ad hoc* tribunals who had a fixed mandate concerning a particular region and timeframe, the ICC must cover a wide variety of countries and regions, none of which it will conceivably focus on permanently. There are undoubtedly analysts who have started their careers by becoming experts on a particular region, and who have subsequently become agile and competent analysts in situations that have little or nothing to do with their own original areas of expertise. The ICC at present employs quite a number of analysts who began their careers as experts on the former Yugoslavia, worked for the LRT at the ICTY and subsequently moved on to work on the DRC, Uganda, Côte d'Ivoire, etc. However, most if not all of these analysts and their colleagues in similar situations are acutely aware of the empirical and linguistic gap that they must overcome when compared to their previous assignments. To give but one highly relevant example: in all international criminal investigations, the total quantity of available material in the relevant languages of the country or region being investigated is larger than the amount of this material that has been translated into the working languages of the judicial institution. Moreover, notwithstanding the often very high quality of translation work done at these institutions, it is an absolute certainty that mistakes will be made, and that the best and most reliable analysis is performed on the basis of the documentation in its original language.[16] It is therefore absolutely essential that the institution employ analysts who do not have to rely on translations in order to perform their analytical work.

Building up a roster of expert analytical knowledge is crucial but often difficult to justify if a court or tribunal must deal with a wide array of situations, as opposed to ICTR or ICTY, which had the opportunity to delve much deeper into a particular time and geographical area. If it is not possible to establish in-house analytical expert knowledge, then it will be necessary to retain relevant outside experts, which comes with its own disadvantages. Country or area experts who work in academia or other professions have their own hectic schedules, and experience with external experts at the ICTY shows that not all such experts are able to prioritise adequately the work they are retained to perform for international courts and tribunals. (Let it be noted that whereas publication deadlines are often highly relative and routinely ignored by many scholars, prosecutors and judges are much less likely to indulge external experts' requests for extended deadlines.) Moreover, just as it is a truism in academia that not all excellent scholars make excellent teachers – and vice versa – so it is absolutely the case that not all excellent scholars make excellent analysts. For this reason, there is often a considerable cost and risk attached to retaining outside experts on an *ad hoc* basis instead of relying on more permanently appointed analysts to produce analytical products and expert reports for judicial institutions.

In terms of securing the best quality of analysis in investigations while simultaneously operating within the multiregional environment of the ICC, it might well therefore be necessary to craft a hybrid analytical unit, juxtaposing career analysts with country experts. Such a unit could

---

[16] Ellen Elias-Bursać, *Translating Evidence and Interpreting Testimony at a War Crimes Tribunal: Working in a Tug-of-War*, Palgrave Macmillan, 2015.

employ a combination of permanent analysts who have seasoned experience performing analysis for international courts and tribunals. In addition, a less permanent category of analysts could be hired to ensure that the necessary linguistic and area expertise was available. Finally, if no other alternative existed, and if there was a higher likelihood of a particular case being a 'one off' in a given region, outside experts with relevant competencies could be retained for this case.

4.5. Navigating Tensions During Verification Analysis

A substantial portion of analysis involves checking the veracity of witness and suspect statements against relevant documentation. Doing so is part and parcel of the investigation or intelligence cycle, variations of which are widely used by law enforcement and intelligence agencies.[17] As I have explained elsewhere, there is very good reason to rely on documentation as a mechanism for checking whether witnesses are being honest or not. Simply put, although it is entirely plausible that documents contain false or mendacious assertions, the content of any given document should not change over time. By contrast, a witness may constantly alter his or her account. Moreover, to the degree that the documents in question are produced in what I call the halcyon days of a particular regime, such documents are likely to include evidence of criminal conduct. Simply put, many regimes are at their apex proud of their accomplishments, even when the acknowledgement of such accomplishments constitutes admission of criminal acts. Such documentation can later be used to considerable effect when questioning members of these regimes who are suspected of having participated in the commission of these crimes.

It is worth noting briefly that this can lead to certain tensions between those who gather information and those who verify it. This topic is tangentially related to the main subject at hand here, but it is enough of a problem that it deserves mention. There is, all things equal, at international judicial institutions a tendency to overvalue field missions, with laborious analysis in headquarters being commonly perceived by many as a less prestigious or desirable activity. As Xabier Agirre has observed, these preferences can lead to what he calls 'the paratrooper syndrome', where

---

[17] On the investigation cycle, see Xabier Agirre, "The Role of Analysis Capacity", in Morten Bergsmo, Klaus Rackwitz and SONG Tianying (eds.), *Historical Origins of International Criminal Law: Volume 5*, Torkel Opsahl Academic EPublisher, Brussels, 2017, pp. 41–42 (https://legal-tools.org/doc/59ec97).

investigative staff deploy frequently to the field to engage in unfocused and often redundant collection of information.[18] Going on mission becomes a goal in and of itself and the material collected is not properly plugged into the intelligence cycle and analysed.

It is also imperative that those persons engaged in collecting evidence from witnesses must accept that the verification and cross-checking of this information, regardless how enamoured they become of a certain collection or source. This is particularly worth emphasising with respect to insider witnesses. Experience at the *ad hoc* tribunals teaches that there is a very real risk that those persons dealing with high-ranking and powerful insider witnesses romanticise these sources in a way that exaggerates their importance and underestimates the amount of criticism that the information they provide should be subjected to subsequently. Those handling insider witnesses must be constantly reminded that no lower standards of analytical scrutiny and quality control apply to the information provided by these witnesses.

4.6. For Whom is Analysis Produced?

In writing a chapter such as this one, it is all too easy to summarise and repeat the wise words on the matter which knowledgeable colleagues have shared with the public in the past. In order to stir the pot and be a bit more provocative, I would like to submit that some problems linked to quality control of analysis in international criminal investigations are structural. By 'structural', I am not as above referring to questions related to the structure of the organisations or institutions under investigation but rather to the structure of analysis or rather analytical structures at international criminal courts and tribunals.

In a memo written at the request of the Director of Common Services at the nascent ICC, Xabier Agirre, who subsequently became a Senior Analyst at the Court, provided a detailed examination of the role of analysis in international criminal investigations and prosecutions.[19] According to Agirre, experience from the International Military Tribunal and the *ad hoc* tribunals of the 1990s has shown that:

---

[18] *Ibid.*, p. 45.

[19] *Ibid.*, p. 37. Morten Bergsmo led this expert-consultation process in the preparatory team establishing the ICC Office of the Prosecutor.

[A] better use of the analyst would be secured by grouping them in an analytical unit, and having them under the guidance of legal officers rather than investigators, which seems to be the first choice of the ICC structure, as indicated by the first budgetary period.[20]

Agirre went on to propose that the ICC's OTP include an analysis section which should:

[F]ulfil an advisory role on factual issues (as opposed to legal issues), at the strategic level of planning and decision-making, for the benefit of the prosecutor, deputy prosecutor and the chief of investigations.[21]

[...]

The analysis section should fulfil a support role to evidence-gathering operations, trials and appeals, on an *ad hoc* basis, at a level of tactical analysis focused on the specific operation or procedure.[22]

The analysis section would be led by a senior (chief) analyst who would be able to implement quality control of analytical products and to ensure that analysts were tasked in a rational manner commensurate with their skill sets and with the needs of the relevant cases. The analysis section had to possess a clear mandate.

Analysis needs to be central to ICC investigations in order to avoid dysfunctionality and waste in operations-led practice. The analysis section should cover three main functions: advisory-strategic, support-tactical and source exploitation.[23]

[...]

In order to preserve its integrity, operate as a safeguard for objectivity and best perform its advisory-strategic function, the analysis section needs to maintain its organisational autonomy under the chief of investigations, but without being subordinated to any particular line of investigation or proceeding.[24]

---

[20] *Ibid.*, p. 95.
[21] *Ibid.*, p. 103.
[22] *Ibid.*, p. 106.
[23] *Ibid.*, p. 117.
[24] *Ibid.*, p. 118.

In February 2019, the investigative analysis section ('IAS') at the ICC produced as set of guidelines on structural analysis which summarise many state-of-the-art reflections and lessons learned.[25]

Agirre was not alone in highlighting the need for analytical autonomy. Writing in the same volume as Agirre, Peter Nicholson, who served as the head of the MAT at the ICTY, agreed that the role of the analyst had often been misunderstood in the early days of the *ad hoc* tribunals, and that:

> [H]istorically the effective use of analysis had been from outside the investigative team environment, where the analyst nevertheless supported the team, but the tasks were identified, allocated and supervised by the analytical management structure.[26]

Nicholson therefore proposed that:

> [T]he analyst should have a separate management chain in terms of the execution of his or her professional obligations to the Office of the Prosecutor, namely objectivity, ethical analytical process, qualitative contribution and proper utilisation of the resource.[27]

Similar thoughts about the use of analysis were shared by Patrick J. Treanor, who had headed the LRT, also at the OTP of the ICTY.

Taking the thoughts of Agirre, Nicholson and Treanor a bit further, it is worth considering whether it would be desirable and beneficial to not only have a strong and dedicated analytical unit at international criminal courts and tribunals, but to actually have this unit exist independently of the OTP. This would conceivably involve placing the analytical unit so that it would be directly subordinate to the Chambers.

Why place the analytical unit in Chambers? To begin with, doing so would to a significant extent counter the perception that analysts working for the OTP produce analytical products that are designed to prove prose-

---

[25] ICC OTP, "IAS Guidelines for the Analysis of Structures v1", 1 February 2019 (on file with the author).

[26] Peter Nicholson, "The Function of Analysis and Analysts", in Morten Bergsmo, Klaus Rackwitz and SONG Tianying (eds.), *Historical Origins of International Criminal Law: Volume 5*, Torkel Opsahl Academic EPublisher, Brussels, 2017, p. 131 (https://legal-tools. org/doc/fe6c90).

[27] *Ibid.*

cution case theories. Many defence lawyers believe that analysts employed by the OTP are at the very least over time contaminated by a prosecutorial mindset, and that the analysts therefore suffer from collection and confirmation bias leading to inferior and subjective analysis. Of course, lawyers working for the OTP often have a similar opinion of the analysts who have been retained by the defence.

If analysts instead worked directly for judges, the analysts would have an increased chance of producing analysis for the court as opposed to producing analysis that would – explicitly or implicitly – speak to the interests of one party to a given case.

In terms of recruitment, it could be made possible for the parties to a case to nominate experts in the field to fixed-term employment in the analytical unit for the duration of a particular case or situation. A panel of judges could then decide whether the academic and professional qualifications of the proposed expert warranted retaining him or her as a member of the analytical unit.

Once retained, the analysts would interact with other, more experienced analysts working for the analytical unit. Tasking of the analyst would occur through the relevant pre-trial or trial chambers. These chambers would be responsible for collating all pertinent analytical questions posed by all parties to the case. At the ICC, this would mean that the judges, the prosecution, the defence and victims' representatives would all have the ability to pose questions or propose analytical tasks that could be handled by the analysts. For example, in the case of expert reports, analysts could be tasked with answering the questions not just of the prosecutor but of all parties to the case. Both the judges and the analytical unit's chief would be able to vet the questions being posed, but the burden would be on the analysts in question to explain why they could not answer some of the questions posed.

In German criminal courts a similar model exists. Both defence and prosecution can identify and propose expert witnesses to the trial chamber in a case. The appointment of experts takes place at the discretion of the trial chamber. Once appointed, the expert works on behalf of the trial chamber for all parties to the case. As just explained, the expert would then prepare his or her report based on questions posed by all parties, and would through the trial chamber have access to all information that the trial chamber deems relevant. In addition, the expert has the opportunity for *ex parte* communication with the trial chamber if the need for this should arise.

In my specific case I was initially retained by the German federal prosecutor who gave me an initial list of questions to which I was asked to respond. The questions were to some degree case-specific but quite a number of them were more general and structural in nature. Once the case proceeded to trial, I was presented by the prosecution to the court, where the judges in the trial chamber decided to retain me as an expert witness for the trial. At that point in time, I became the expert witness of the court rather than the prosecution. Effectively, I was transformed from being the instrument of one party of the court to being a resource for all parties to the court. Reflecting this situation, I now received questionnaires from all parties to the case: the judges, the prosecution, the defence and the representatives of the victims. Compare this to the ICTY, where every appearance of a prosecution expert witness in cases led to a ritualistic dance on cross-examination regarding whether the experts had merely sought to prove the prosecution's case.

Obviously, making the analysts into court witnesses requires a different statutory setting than the one which obtains in some jurisdictions. In terms of assuring proper quality control in international courts, however, it is worth considering the extent to which such a status could at the very least be emulated. A chief analyst could set the overall research agenda and ensure that the analysts produced analysis that was sufficiently open-minded and broad to ensure proper quality and objectivity but conversely specific enough that it addressed the needs of the parties to the court.

Expert analytical reports should be produced for the court – or in other words for all parties to the court case and should therefore be salient and useful for all. The point of a report on a given army and ministry of defence should therefore not be proving the prosecution's or defence's case theory but instead on providing as complete and objective as possible of the subject matter. If a prosecution analyst has succeeded in this endeavour, this will become visible when both the judges and defence counsel use the opportunity of courtroom examination to elicit information that is pertinent to their case. Thinking back to the internal electronic file of analytical memos produced by the LRT at the ICTY, it seems to me that a very significant portion of these memos could have been disclosed to the defence and thereby assisted them as well as the prosecution.

In terms of document and source collection, analysts working in such an analytical unit would be able to draft document collection plans based on the analytical tasks that they were given by all parties to the court. This would in principle give them extra assurance that they were casting an objective net and collecting as much relevant information as possible. If relocating analysts or an analytical unit outside of the OTP is too radical, then at the very least analysts should be shown to be primarily interested in explaining the topic of analytical focus – which should be organisations, structures, etc. and not the (potential) criminal charges. It should also be examined to which degree analytical products can at as early a stage as possible be informed by and be exposed to outside input in order to encompass/envelope the questions of the chambers and – very importantly – also the defence.

Placing an analytical unit in the jurisdiction of the judges at international institutions is no panacea. Just as not all lawyers and investigators in the OTP have a proper understanding of the role of analysis, so it must be said that not all judges taking up appointments at international courts and tribunals understand this role, either.[28] Indeed, those who have attended workshops and conferences on international criminal justice will be familiar with the *sotto voce* sentiment that these fora address a wide arrange of challenges in international criminal justice but tend to shy away from addressing the shortcomings of chambers, particularly as regards judges appointed to the international bench without little or no practical relevant experience.

4.7. Conclusion

I am quite well aware that a considerable number of the problems highlighted herein and related to quality control in analysis of serious international crimes have been identified and discussed elsewhere by very knowledgeable authors. The fact that these challenges nonetheless persist in international criminal investigations indicates that we must continue to flag their existence and to discuss how to surmount them. By doing so we will help to increase the likelihood that the vast and ambitious experiment

---

[28] For a criticism of lacking contextual knowledge by lawyers and judges at the ICC, see Julien Seroussi, "How Do International Lawyers Handle Facts? The Role of Folk Sociological Theories at the International Criminal Court", in *The British Journal of Sociology*, 2018, vol. 69, no. 4, pp. 962–83.

of international criminal justice will not just survive but also prove successful.

When speaking of quality control in international criminal investigations, it is important that we ask what kind of quality is actually being controlled? From the perspective of analysts, it becomes problematic if quality control is linked too closely to issues of culpability, as these will impact upon the objectivity of the analysis. It might therefore also be considered whether quality control of analysis in international investigations should also involve some kind of internal peer review mechanism, where a panel of analysts, investigators and lawyers not working on particular case would have the ability to independently review the quality of the analysis produced.

At the ICC, it was frequently said that the prosecution should be investigating cases as if it were simultaneously also pursuing exculpatory information and hence complying with its statutory obligations to investigate potentially exculpatory avenues equally. The track record of the ICC raises questions as to whether that has been happening in practice or not.

It will surprise no one who knows me and my professional record that I believe that strong analytical teams interacting closely with prosecutors and investigators but also insulated from both prosecutorial and investigative pressures are a prerequisite for high-quality complex investigations. An analytical team can, among other things, provide expert knowledge on several fronts and ensure standardisation of analytical output, thereby militating against the loss or fragmentation of overview of information and potential evidence. From an analytical perspective, this also helps against having to reinvent the wheel.

5

Interviewing Victims and Witnesses of Crime

Trond Myklebust, Gavin Oxburgh and William Webster[*]

Communication in investigative settings with vulnerable victims and witnesses (and suspected offenders) is a vitally important area of practice and research. This chapter outlines a significant paradigm-shift in interviewing practices relating to victims and witnesses, highlighting that such interviewing requires enhanced sensitivity and advanced training. There is strong, international consensus on which interviewing skills are currently deemed to be the most effective and appear to yield the most accurate accounts, some of which are presented and discussed in this chapter. Although these skills can be learned, it has been continually found across scientific research that, for (as yet) unknown reasons, many interviewers do not appear to use these skills reliably during interviews.

We discuss elements of current interview methods currently available internationally and provide an overall consensus that the use of structured interview protocols appears to be the most effective. Several aspects of our approach to investigative interviewing that are now considered conventional wisdom, were once contested, challenged and debated. In this chapter we have examined and presented some of the debate surrounding the complex nature of investigative interviewing of victims and

---

[*] **Trond Myklebust** is Assistant Chief of Police, Research Department, The Norwegian Police University College. He holds a Ph.D. from the Department of Psychology, University of Oslo. He is an Executive Board member of the IMPACT Section, The International Association of Chiefs of Police (IACP). He was the co-founder of the International Investigative Interviewing Research Group (iIIRG) and its deputy chair and co-director from its inception in 2007 until August 2019. **Gavin Oxburgh** (Ph.D.) is Professor of Applied Forensic Psychology, Newcastle University, a registered Forensic Psychologist and an Expert Witness. He is a 22-year veteran detective of the Royal Air Force Police specialising in child protection and sexual offences. He was the co-founder, chair and co-director of iIIRG from its inception in 2007 until August 2019. **William Webster** (Ph.D.) is a Lecturer in Psychology at the University of Sunderland, with a particular research interest in vulnerable victims and witnesses of crime.

witnesses, specifically those who are deemed vulnerable, and the key aspects with which all interviewers should be familiar.

5.1. Background to Investigative Interviewing

In its 'Quality Control in Criminal Investigation' project ('QCCI'), the Centre for International Law Research and Policy (CILRAP) has identified seven bottlenecks as particularly problematic in the investigation of core international crimes or war crimes (dating back to 1994).[1] In the voluminous case materials collected, analysed and presented in all crime cases, the investigative interview has a central role. This chapter outlines a significant paradigm-shift in interviewing practices relating to victims and witnesses.

Knowledge about communication in investigative settings is of major importance in the prevention of the first four of the seven bottlenecks presented by Bergsmo.[2] In the areas of research and practice, there is a strong international consensus about interviewing skills that are currently deemed to be the most effective, some of which are presented and discussed in this chapter.

Investigative interviewing requires great sensitivity. Investigative interviewing of victims and witnesses (and suspects in criminal cases) is cognitively demanding.[3] Consequently, information elicited must be accurate and reliable with the main objective of obtaining the best *quality* and *quantity* of information possible that will assist in determining what has happened, when, and by whom.[4] In addition, interviewers are required to

---

[1] See Morten Bergsmo, "Towards Culture of Quality Control in Criminal Investigations", FICHL Policy Brief Series No. 94 (2019), Torkel Opsahl Academic EPublisher, Brussels, 2019 (https://legal-tools.org/doc/65157b). Based on continuous observation and analysis of work-process problems in international and national war crimes jurisdictions since July 1994, the QCCI project team has identified the following seven bottlenecks as particularly problematic: (i) overview of information, (ii) factual analysis, (iii) evidence-review, (iv) formulation of responsibility, (v) cumulative charging, (vi) too much evidence, and (vii) disclosure.

[2] *Ibid.*: (i) overview of information, (ii) factual analysis, (iii) evidence-review, and (iv) formulation of responsibility.

[3] Gavin Oxburgh and Ian Hynes, "Investigative Practice", in Pamela Radcliffe, Gisli Gudjonsson, Anthony Heaton-Armstrong and David Wolchover (eds.), *Witness Testimony in Sexual Cases: Evidential, Investigative and Scientific Perspectives*, Oxford University Press, Oxford, 2016, p. 221.

[4] Rebecca Milne and Ray Bull, "Interviewing Victims of Crime, Including Children and People with Intellectual Difficulties", in Mark Kebbell and Graham Davies (eds.), *Practi-*

possess professional integrity, be appropriately trained in the use of effective models, and follow relevant policy and procedures.[5]

5.2. Interview Models

Interview models around the world differ in many ways, however, the principles are very similar.[6] For example, in the United Kingdom there are two different models: in Scotland, the 'PRICE' model is utilised (**P**lanning and preparation; **R**apport building; **I**nformation gathering; **C**onfirming the content; **E**valuate and action); it has very similar principles to that of the 'PEACE' model used in England and Wales.[7] PEACE is the mnemonic acronym used for the five phases:

- Planning and preparation: This should take place prior to the interview itself and is a vital part of all investigative interviews. Interviewers must first consider how the interview might contribute to the overall investigation and they should have a clear understanding of the purpose of the interview. They should also consider when and where it will take place. If there is more than one interviewer, they should be clear what each other's roles are and have a clear knowledge of relevant legislation. Before commencing the interview, he or she should make any necessary arrangements for the attendance of other persons.[8]

---

cal Psychology for Forensic Investigations, Wiley, Chichester, 2006, pp. 7–24; Ole Thomas Bjerknes and Ivar A. Fahsing, Etterforskning: Prinsipper, metoder og praksis (Investigation: Principles, Methods and Practice), Vigmostad og Bjørke, Bergen, 2018; Gavin Oxburgh, James Ost and Julie Cherryman, "Police Interviews with Suspected Child Sex Offenders: Does Use of Empathy and Question Type Influence the Amount of Investigation Relevant Information Obtained?", in *Psychology, Crime and Law*, 2012, vol. 18, no. 3, p. 259.

[5]   Oxburgh and Hynes, 2016, see above note 3.

[6]   Dave Walsh, Gavin E. Oxburgh, Allison D. Redlich and Trond Myklebust, *International Developments and Practices in Investigative Interviewing and Interrogation, Volume 1: Victims and Witnesses*, Routledge, London, 2016; Dave Walsh, Gavin E. Oxburgh, Allison D. Redlich and Trond Myklebust, *International Developments and Practices in Investigative Interviewing and Interrogation, Volume 2: Suspects*, Routledge, London, 2016.

[7]   Central Police Training and Development Authority, *Practical Guide to Investigative Interviewing*, 2004; Central Planning and Training Unit, *The Interviewer's Rulebook*, Harrogate, 1992; National Crime Faculty, *A Practical Guide to Investigative Interviewing*, National Police Training College, Bramshill, 1996, 1998 and 2000.

[8]   For example, an interpreter or intermediary, see below Section 5.5.5.

- Engage and explain: The first main phase of the actual interview is all about the opening stage of the interview and is crucial to its overall success. Interviewers should use appropriate language, be flexible in their approach, and try to create a relaxed atmosphere. The reason for the interview should be explained, together with the procedures that will be followed during the interview, including how long it will last, a basic outline of the interview, who will ask the most questions, and who will be taking notes etc. Rapport-building and adopting an empathic approach in this stage are key to the overall success of the interview.[9]

- Account, clarify and challenge: This is where the interviewer(s) obtain the person's version of events (or account) using one of two ways: (i) the cognitive approach,[10] or (ii) the conversation management approach. If the latter approach is used, he or she should obtain an initial account from the interviewee and then sub-divide his or her account into a number of sub-sections in order to probe for further detail or clarify any details provided.

- Closure: This phase involves the interviewers summarising what occurred during the interview to ensure there is a mutual understanding about what has taken place. This is an ideal opportunity to verify that all aspects have been sufficiently covered (with the witness and the second interviewer if appropriate). The interviewers should also explain what will happen after the interview is completed.

- Evaluation: This is not just about an evaluation of the interview that has just taken place, or about how much information was obtained, rather, it includes an evaluation of the interviewer(s) own performance during the interview.

The PEACE model is depicted in Figure 1 as a linear model that includes the processes before the interview commences (for example, the planning and preparation phase) all the way through until after the interview is completed (the evaluation phase). The actual interview itself includes: (i) engage and explain; (ii) account, and (iii) closure. Figure 1 shows the links between the three main phases of the interview, indicated

---

[9] See below Section 5.4. for an outline of these concepts.
[10] See below Section 5.5.1.

with solid lines, showing there is a natural forward movement from one phase to the next, whereas the dotted lines indicate that the interviewer can move backwards and forwards between any of the three main phases as required in order to remain as flexible as possible during the course of the interview. For example, if the interviewer reaches the closure stage and is provided with new information, he or she can move back to the engage and explain, and/or the account phase(s) as required.

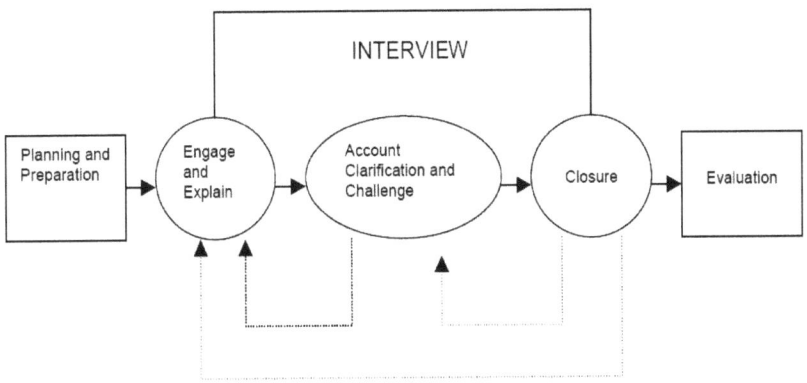

Figure 1. The PEACE model[11] of interviewing.

The PEACE model, which was introduced in 1992, was based on collaborative work with academic researchers, psychologists, police practitioners, and lawyers, and was intended to take into account the vulnerabilities of some interviewees.[12] The model also integrated two other interview methods based on reputable psychological principles: (i) the cognitive interview ('CI'),[13] and (ii) the conversation management ('CM') approach.[14] The focus of the PEACE model is based on fairness, openness, workability, accountability, and fact (truth) finding rather than the obtain-

[11] Central Planning and Training Unit, 1992, see above note 7; National Crime Faculty, 2000, p. 27, see above note 7.

[12] Andrea Shawyer, Rebecca Milne and Ray Bull, "Investigative Interviewing in the UK", in Tom Williamson, Rebecca Milne and Stephen Savage (eds.), *International Developments in Investigative Interviewing*, Willan, Devon, 2009, p. 24.

[13] Ronald Fisher and Edward Geiselman, *Memory-Enhancing Techniques for Investigative Interviewing: The Cognitive Interview*, Charles Thomas, Springfield, 1992.

[14] Gisli Gudjonsson and John Pearse, "Suspect Interviews and False Confessions", in *Current Directions in Psychological Science*, 2011, vol. 20, no. 1, p. 33.

ing of a confession (involving suspects).[15] The PEACE model is now a widely-resourced method of interviewing and is used throughout England and Wales in addition to many other countries including Australia, New Zealand, Norway (known as KREATIVE) and some parts of Canada.

5.3. Interview Training

Effective training in the various interview models is required and there is no doubt it has been enhanced considerably during the past two decades.[16] The investigative interviewing of vulnerable (and intimidated) witnesses requires additional, advanced training (over and above foundation level training) together with enhanced sensitivity to ensure the information obtained is accurate, reliable and untainted in any way. This is equally important when it comes to interviewing reluctant and/or 'insider' witnesses.

There are many methods of training used throughout the world. In England and Wales, the Initial Police Learning and Development Programme ('IPLDP') was introduced in 2005, designed to ensure quality and to support student officers throughout their two-year probationary period, thereby meeting their individual development. In 2007, investigative interview training was enhanced and incorporated into the Professionalising the Investigation Programme ('PIP'; see Table 1). This development was intended to increase professionalism amongst all police investigators and to establish a structured, professional approach to investigations and interviewing. The IPLDP provides all uniformed police officers and supervisors with the necessary accreditation at PIP level 1, with PIP level 2 designed for dedicated investigators (for example, detectives) who investigate serious and complex investigations, including victims, witnesses and suspected offenders. PIP level 3 was designed for Senior Investigating Officers ('SIOs') in cases of murder, stranger rape, kidnap, or crimes of similar complexity, with PIP level 4 designed for SIOs and Officers in Overall Command ('OIOC') who manage critical, complex or protracted and/or linked serious crime.

---

[15] *Ibid.*

[16] Gavin Oxburgh and Coral Dando, "Psychology and interviewing: What Direction Now in Our Quest for Reliable Information?", in *The British Journal of Forensic Practice*, 2011, vol. 13, no. 2, pp. 135–44.

Table 1. PIP levels.

PIP level	Example of role	Investigative responsibility
1	Uniformed constable or police staff or supervisors	1. Conduct priority and volume crime investigations. 2. Interview suspects, witnesses and victims for priority and volume crime investigations.
2	Dedicated investigator (that is, Detective)	1. Plan and conduct serious and complex investigations. 2. Plan, conduct and evaluate interviews with witnesses and victims for serious and complex investigations. 3. Plan, conduct and evaluate interviews with suspects for serious and complex investigations.
3[17]	SIO	1. Lead investigator in cases of murder, stranger rape, kidnap or crimes of similar complexity. 2. Manage major investigations.
4	SIO or OIOC	1. Manage critical, complex, protracted and/or linked serious crime. 2. Responsible for the review of investigations in other force areas (as appropriate).

It is important to note, that although such enhancements in training will doubtlessly continue, Powell, Fisher and Wright[18] outlined the elements of training that have been found to be the most successful which include the use of:

- structured interview protocols;[19]
- multiple opportunities to practice over an extended period;

---

[17] This PIP level is split into various core and specialist roles including the interviewing of vulnerable witnesses and the specialist interviewing of suspects, some of which would have been categorised at the old tier level 3.

[18] Martine B. Powell, M.B. Ronald, P. Fisher and Rebecca Wright, "Investigative Interviewing", in Neil Brewer, and Kipling D. Williams (eds.), *Psychology and Law. An Empirical Perspective*, The Guilford Press, London, 2005, pp. 11–42.

[19] See below Section 5.5.2.

- expert feedback and ongoing supervision; and
- internal motivation by the interviewer to enhance his or her individual performance.

5.4. Recurring Themes Across Interview Research

A plethora of research has been conducted by many academic researchers and practitioners in numerous countries across the world incorporating many different jurisdictions. The research to date has been overwhelmingly consistent with regards to best practice across all types of interviews (for example, victims, witnesses and suspected offenders) which include: (i) the use of a humane and non-coercive interview approach incorporating legal safeguards, procedural justice and international human rights; (ii) the use of rapport-building; (iii) the use of empathy; and (iv) the use of appropriate questions.

5.4.1. Humane and Non-Coercive Interviewing Approach

Previous research[20] has highlighted how a humanitarian style of interviewing, characterised by the use of supportive or humane interview techniques (for example, rapport-building and the use of empathy), can facilitate communication and improve the quality of the interaction between interviewer and interviewee. Indeed, all interviewees, regardless of country or legal jurisdiction, must never be subjected to any form of physical or psychological abuse. Every individual regardless of the type of crime they are being interviewed about, have the fundamental right[21] to be treated in accordance with international human rights, which by virtue, pro-

---

[20] Alison J. Laurence, Emily Alison, Geraldine Noone, Stamatis Elntib and Paul Christiansen, "Why Tough Tactics Fail and Rapport Gets Results: Observing Rapport-Based Interpersonal Techniques (ORBIT) to Generate Useful Information From Terrorists", in *Psychology, Public Policy, and Law*, 2013, vol. 19, no. 4, pp. 411–31; Ulf Holmberg and Sven-Åke Christianson, "Murderers' and Sexual Offenders Experiences of Police Interviews and Their Inclination to Admit or Deny Crimes", in *Behavioral Sciences and the Law*, 2002, vol. 20, nos. 1–2, pp. 31–45; Miet Vanderhallen, Geert Vervaeke and Ulf Holmberg, "Witness and Suspect Perceptions of Working Alliance and Interviewing Style", in *Journal of Investigative Psychology and Offender Profiling*, 2011, vol. 8, no. 2, pp. 110–30.

[21] See Interim report of the Special Rapporteur on torture and other cruel, inhuman or degrading treatment or punishment, in Torture and other cruel, inhuman or degrading treatment or punishment: Note by the Secretary-General, UN Doc. A/71/298, 5 August 2016 (https://legal-tools.org/doc/luww5z).

vides[22] procedural justice. To this end, in 2016, the former United Nations ('UN') Special Rapporteur on Torture, Juan E. Mendez, presented a report to the UN General Assembly on the need for the development of a universal protocol ('UP') to provide practical guidance to police, law-enforcement officials and other state authorities on the conduct of effective, ethical, and non-coercive interviews/interrogations, grounded in the absolute legal prohibition of torture and ill-treatment.

The Association for the Prevention of Torture (APT), together with Anti-Torture Initiative (ATI) and the Norwegian Centre for Human Rights (NCHR) are (at time of writing this chapter) co-ordinating the development of this UP which will embed the implementation of associated legal safeguards. The expert-driven, multi-disciplinary process for developing the protocol consists of a Steering Committee, Drafting Group and Advisory Council, and involves the participation of legal, medical, psychological, law enforcement and criminological professionals from dozens of countries around the world.

5.4.1.1. Procedural Justice Theory ('PJT')

PJT derives from social psychology and relates to the notion of fairness, dignity, respect, and due process in legal proceedings. With interviewees, it relates to their personal experiences of interacting with the police or law enforcement agency and how the behaviour of an officer could potentially influence their level of co-operation throughout the investigation – in other words, the fairness with which an interviewee is treated and whether this influences whether they co-operate or resist authority. The earliest studies regarding the psychology of procedural justice recognised that the opportunity to present information relevant to a decision enhances judgements relating to the fairness of the decision-making procedures.[23] Early theories regarding PJT attempted to explain procedural justice by referring to the assumptions made by the perceiver about the potential out-

---

[22] Allan E. Lind and Tom R. Tyler, "Procedural Justice in Organizations", in Allan E. Lind and Tom R. Tyler (eds.), *The Social Psychology of Procedural Justice*, Plenum, New York, 1992, pp. 173–202.

[23] John Thibaut and Laurens Walker, *Procedural Justice: A Psychological Analysis*, Erlbaum, New York, 1975; Laurens Walker, Stephen Latour, Allan E. Lind and John Thibaut, "Reactions of Participants and Observers to Modes of Adjudication", in *Journal of Applied Social Psychology*, 1974, vol. 4, no. 4, pp. 295–310.

comes that could be the result of different procedures.[24] Key components of PJT include:[25]

- Participation (being allowed to speak) – which involves having the opportunity to present one's own side of the dispute and be heard by the decision maker.
- Dignity – which includes being treated with respect and politeness, having one's rights acknowledged by the decision maker.
- Trust – that the authority is concerned with one's welfare.

Lind and Tyler[26] also suggest that people want to be treated fairly by authorities, independent of the outcome of the interaction. Fair treatment by an authority, defined in terms of voice (by coming forward and disclosing the crime to the authorities), dignity and trust, directly shapes procedural justice judgements and signifies that the individual in question is a valued member of the group. Tyler and Blader[27] argued that this, in turn, would then facilitate co-operation by strengthening a person's tie to the social order. The strengthening of the tie promotes the value of membership within the group, which then increases the level of confidence in the authorities (that is, the interviewer), which subsequently provides encouragement to others. In other words, as a result of perceived fair treatment, interviewees may be more willing to report crimes.

Conversely, if officers show disrespectful behaviour, this will reduce the likelihood of citizen co-operation.[28] These findings could also be

---

[24] Gerald S. Leventhal, "What Should be Done with Equity Theory? New Approaches to the Study of Fairness in Social Relationships", in Kenneth Gergen, Martin S. Greenberg and Richard H. Willis (eds.), *Social Exchange: Advances in Theory and Research*, Plenum Press, New York, 1980, pp. 27–55; Thibaut and Walker, 1975, see above note 23; Walker, Latour, Lind and Thibaut, 1974, see above note 23.

[25] For a full review see Lind and Tyler, 1992, pp. 173–202, see above note 22.

[26] *Ibid.*

[27] Tom R. Tyler and Steven L. Blader, "The Group Engagement Model: Procedural Justice, Social Identity and Cooperative Behaviour", in *Personality and Social Psychology Review*, 2003, vol. 7, no. 4, pp. 349–61.

[28] Stephen D. Mastrofski, Jeffrey B. Snipes and Anne E. Supina, "Compliance on Demand: The Public's Response to Specific Police Requests", in *Journal of Research in Crime and Delinquency*, 1996, vol. 33, no. 3, pp. 269–305; John D. McCluskey, Stephen D. Mastrofski and Roger B. Parks, "To Acquiesce or Rebel: Predicting Citizen Compliance with Police Requests", in *Police Quarterly*, 1999, vol. 2, no. 4, pp. 389–416.

associated with those of Bull and Cherryman[29] who found that specific qualities, similar to those antecedents that make up the PJT (for example, voice, dignity and trust), were also present within 'skilful' police interviews. Similarly, in terms of interviews with suspects of crime, many authors have highlighted the importance of being empathic, respectful and humane when interviewing suspects, again, comparable to the procedural justice framework antecedents.[30]

5.4.2. The Use of Rapport

Rapport building is an established part of the interaction during investigative interviews, regardless of whether it is with a victim, witness or suspect.[31] Scientific findings indicate that interviewers who utilise rapport-building techniques elicit significantly more detailed and accurate memory reports from child and adult victims, witnesses and suspects.[32]

---

[29] Ray Bull and Julie Cherryman, *Identifying Skills Gaps in Specialist Investigative Interviewing*, Home Office, London, 1995; Julie Cherryman and Ray Bull, "Police Officers' Perceptions of Specialist Investigative Interviewing Skills", in *International Journal of Police Science and Management*, 2001, vol. 3, no. 3, pp. 199–212.

[30] Holmberg and Christianson, 2002, pp. 31–45, see above note 20; Mark Kebbell, Laurence Alison, Emily Hurren and Paul Mazerolle, "How Do Sex Offenders Think the Police Should Interview to Elicit Confessions from Sex Offenders?", in *Psychology, Crime and Law*, 2010, vol. 16, no. 7, pp. 567–84; Oxburgh, Ost, Cherryman, 2012, see above note 4; Eric Shepherd, "Ethical Interviewing", in *Policing*, 1991, vol. 7, no. 1, pp. 42–60.

[31] Ministry of Justice, *Achieving Best Evidence in Criminal Proceedings: Guidance on Interviewing Victims and Witnesses and Using Special Measures*, Her Majesty's Stationery Office ('HMSO'), London, 2011.

[32] Alison, Alison, Noone, Elntib and Christiansen, 2013, pp. 411–31, see above note 20; Jehanne Almerigogna, James Ost, Lucy Akehurst and Mike Fluck, "How Interviewers' Nonverbal Behaviors Can Affect Children's Perceptions and Suggestibility", in *Journal of Experimental Child Psychology*, 2008, vol. 100, no. 1, pp. 17–39; Ray Bull and Stavroula Soukara, "Four Studies of What Really Happens in Police Interviews", in G. Daniel Lassiter and Christian A. Meissner (eds.), *Police Interrogations and False Confessions: Current Research, Practice, and Policy Recommendations*, American Psychological Association, Washington, 2010, pp. 81–95; Kimberly Collins and Nikki Carthy, "No Rapport, No Comment: The Relationship Between Rapport and Communication During Investigative Interviews with Suspects", in *Journal of Investigative Psychology and Offender Profiling*, 2019, vol. 16, no. 1, pp. 18–31; Roger Collins, Robyn Lincoln and Mark G. Frank, "The Effect of Rapport in Forensic Interviewing", in *Psychiatry, Psychology and Law*, 2002, vol. 9, no. 1, pp. 69–78; Ulf Holmberg, *Police Interviews with Victims and Suspects of Violent and Sexual Crimes: Interviewee's Experiences and Interview Outcomes*, Doctoral Dissertation, Department of Psychology, Stockholm University, 2004; Jenna Mitchell Kieckhaefer, Johnathan Patrick Vallano and Nadja Schreiber Compo, "Examining the Positive Effects of Rapport Building: When and Why Does Rapport Building Benefit Adult Eyewitness

However, there appears to be no shared definition on the exact meaning of 'rapport', with the concept being traditionally referenced by therapists in a clinical setting, citing the importance of establishing a 'therapeutic alliance'.[33] It is, however, generally accepted that rapport does not exist solely with one individual, rather it is a relationship between two or more individuals.[34] In addition, some definitions of 'rapport' appear to conflict, as in practitioner guidelines offered in England and Wales and the United States respectively: "a positive mood between interviewer and interviewee",[35] and "the establishment of a relationship, which does not have to be friendly in nature".[36] Some academic researchers believe that 'rapport' involves a "harmonious, sympathetic connection to another",[37] whereas other, more theoretically-driven conceptualisations identified and described attentiveness, positivity and co-ordination as the non-verbal components associated with the relationship between interacting individuals.[38] Although definitions of rapport are sometimes conflicting, most indicate interconnecting components of openness and an 'interest' in the other party (sometimes referred to as 'mutual attentiveness').[39]

During the early stages of an interaction with two or more individuals, mutual attention is important for the purpose of building a relationship as it is essential to show an interest in the other party (parties). It is argued that attentiveness facilitates the creation of focused and interacting

---

Memory?", in *Memory*, 2014, vol. 22, no. 8, pp. 1010–23; Lina Leander, Pär Anders Granhaga and Sven-Åke Christianson, "Children's Reports of Verbal Sexual Abuse: Effects of Police Officers' Interviewing Style", in *Psychiatry, Psychology and Law*, 2009, vol. 16, no. 3, pp. 340–54.

[33] Robinder P. Bedi, Michael D. Davis and Meris Williams, "Critical Incidents in the Formation of the Therapeutic Alliance from the Client's Perspective", in *Psychotherapy: Theory, Research, Practice, Training*, 2005, vol. 42, no. 3, pp. 311–23.

[34] Fiona Gabbert, Gordon Wright, Lorraine Hope, Gavin E. Oxburgh, NG Magdalene and Kirk Luther, "Exploring the Use of Rapport in Professional Information-Gathering Contexts via Systematically Mapping the Evidence-Base", in *Psychology, Public Policy and Law*, forthcoming.

[35] Ministry of Justice, 2011, p. 70, see above note 31.

[36] US Department of the Army, *Human Intelligence Collector Operations*, Washington, D.C., 2006, sect. 8.3.

[37] James J. Newberry and Carol A. Stubbs, *Advanced Interviewing Techniques*, Bureau of Alcohol Tobacco and Firearms National Academy, Glynco Georgia, 1990, p. 14.

[38] Linda Tickle-Degnen and Robert Rosenthal, "The Nature of Rapport and Its Nonverbal Correlates", in *Psychological Inquiry*, 1990, vol. 1, no. 4, pp. 285–93.

[39] *Ibid.*; Newberry and Stubbs, 1990, see above note 37.

---

engagement.[40] Paying attention is synonymous with active listening, whereby the listener, without interrupting, interprets what the other party is expressing, and through demonstrating active listening behaviour encourages the other party to talk and interact.[41] In addition to active listening, another type of behaviour that helps facilitate the mutual attentiveness during an interaction and has been used as a measure to define 'rapport' is reflective listening.[42] This is characterised by the listener being able to accurately reflect something that the other party has expressed to encourage further discussion or clarification.[43]

Given that there is no agreed definition on the exact meaning of 'rapport', and whether it is used mutually between parties, it comes as no surprise that difficulties are evident when attempting to define the concept within an operational setting (that is, an investigative interview). To this end, Gabbert et al.[44] proposed that when describing rapport which is often present in a professional interaction, such as an investigative interview, the term 'professional rapport' could be used. This term can be understood as an intentional use of rapport behaviours to facilitate positive interactions and build a relationship that is not necessarily mutual. It differs distinctly from the idea of 'genuine mutual rapport'.[45] As such, Gabbert et al. propose that the cultivation of rapport is a key skill within investigative interviews.

5.4.3. The Use of Empathy

Similar to rapport, there are various definitions that attempt to describe the multi-dimensional construct of empathy throughout counselling and

---

[40] Ulf Holmberg and Kent Madsen, "Rapport Operationalized as a Humanitarian Interview in Investigative Interview Settings", in *Psychiatry, Psychology and Law*, 2014, vol. 21, no. 4, pp. 591–610; Michel St-Yves, "The Psychology of Rapport: Five Basic Rules", in Tom Williamson (ed.), *Investigative Interviewing: Rights, Research, Regulation*, Willan, Cullompton, 2006, pp. 87–106.

[41] Michel St-Yves, 2006, pp. 87–106, see above note 40.

[42] Laurence Alison, Susan Giles and Grace McGuire, "Blood from a Stone: Why Rapport Works and Torture Doesn't in 'Enhanced' Interrogations", in *Investigative Interviewing: Research and Practice*, 2015, vol. 7, no. 2, pp. 5–23.

[43] Alison, Alison, Noone, Elntib and Christiansen, 2013, pp. 411–31, see above note 20.

[44] Gabbert, Wright, Hope, Oxburgh, NG and Luther, forthcoming, see above note 34.

[45] Bella M. DePaulo and Kathy L. Bell, "Rapport Is Not So Soft Anymore", in *Psychological Inquiry*, 1990, vol. 1, no. 4, pp. 305–08.

clinical psychology, in addition to medical writings.[46] However, there is an absence of a clear operational explanation that professional interviewers can understand. Davis termed empathy as "a reaction of one individual to the observed experiences of another".[47] It is important to consider the various types of reactions that can range from simply understanding the other's perspective, to a more intuitive or emotional reaction.[48] Therefore, when used in an investigative interview, it is not just about the interviewer 'showing' empathy to the interviewee, it is also about having the ability to understand their perspective appreciating their emotions and then communicating that directly, or indirectly.[49]

To explain the multi-dimensional nature of empathy, Barrett-Lennard[50] developed an empathy cycle in 1981 that Oxburgh and Ost[51] amended in 2011 for use in relation to an investigative interview (see Figure 2).

---

[46] See Simon Baron-Cohen, *Zero Degrees of Empathy: A New Theory of Human Cruelty*, Penguin Books, Milton Keynes, 2011, pp. 1–181; Godfrey T. Barrett-Lennard, "The Empathy Cycle: Refinement of a Nuclear Concept", in *Journal of Counselling Psychology*, 1981, vol. 28, no. 2, pp. 91–100; Mark H. Davis, "Measuring Individual Differences in Empathy: Evidence for a Multidimensional Approach", in *Journal of Personality and Social Psychology*, 1983, vol. 44, no. 1, pp. 113–26; Gerald A. Gladstein, "Understanding Empathy: Integrating Counselling, Developmental and Social Psychology Perspectives", in *Journal of Counselling Psychology*, vol. 30, no. 4, pp. 467–82; Stephanie D. Preston and Frans B.M. de Waal, "Empathy: Its Ultimate and Proximate Bases", in *The Behavioral and Brain Sciences*, 2002, vol. 25, no. 1, pp. 1–72.

[47] Davis, 1983, p. 114, see above note 46; See also Gavin E. Oxburgh and James Ost, "The Use and Efficacy of Empathy in Police Interviews with Suspects of Sexual Offences", in *Journal of Investigative Psychology and Offender Profiling*, 2011, vol. 8, no. 2, pp. 178–88.

[48] Davis, 1983, p. 114, see above note 46.

[49] *Ibid.*; Oxburgh and Ost, 2011, see above note 47.

[50] Barrett-Lennard, 1981, see above note 46.

[51] Oxburgh and Ost, 2011, p. 182, see above note 47.

Step 1	Step 2	Step 3	Step 4	Step 5
Empathic set	**Empathic resonation**	**Expressed empathy**	**Received empathy**	**Feedback, fresh expression**
A actively listens (conditions for empathic process)	*Phase 1 Empathy* (vicarious resonation)	*Phase 2 Empathy* (*A* shows awareness)	*Phase 3 Empathy* (*B* aware of response)	Return to Phase 1 (in repeat form)

Figure 2. Diagrammatical illustration of the empathy cycle.

The 'empathy' demonstrated by an interviewer during an investigative interview differs considerably to that demonstrated by other individuals in less complex and cognitively demanding exchanges (that is, in clinical settings). Oxburgh *et al.*[52] developed a model for measuring empathic responses within such interviews that was based on the theoretical principles of the empathy cycle outlined by Barrett-Lennard[53] in 1981. Their model focused on four key variables (empathic opportunities, empathic continuers, empathic terminators and spontaneous empathy) that were central to the interaction between interviewer and interviewee (see Figure 3). During an investigative interview, the interviewee might provide information (consciously or otherwise) that could be deemed empathic (the 'opportunity'). The interviewer then has one of two options in how to deal with this information, either he or she can resonate some, or all aspects, of the information received (for example, "I understand, please don't worry") and 'continue' the opportunity presented. Alternatively, the interviewer could ignore the comments made or information received completely, or ask an unrelated question in response, thus 'terminating' the opportunity.[54] Finally, an interviewer may use empathy without any prompting (or 'opportunities') from the interviewee, something which Oxburgh *et al.* termed spontaneous empathy.

---

[52] Gavin E. Oxburgh, James Ost, Paul Morris and Julie Cherryman, "The Impact of Question Type and Empathy on Police Interviews with Suspects of Homicide, Filicide and Child Sexual Abuse", in *Psychiatry, Psychology and Law*, 2013, vol. 21, no. 6, pp. 903–17.

[53] Barrett-Lennard, 1981, see above note 50.

[54] Oxburgh, Ost, Morris and Cherryman, 2013, see above note 52.

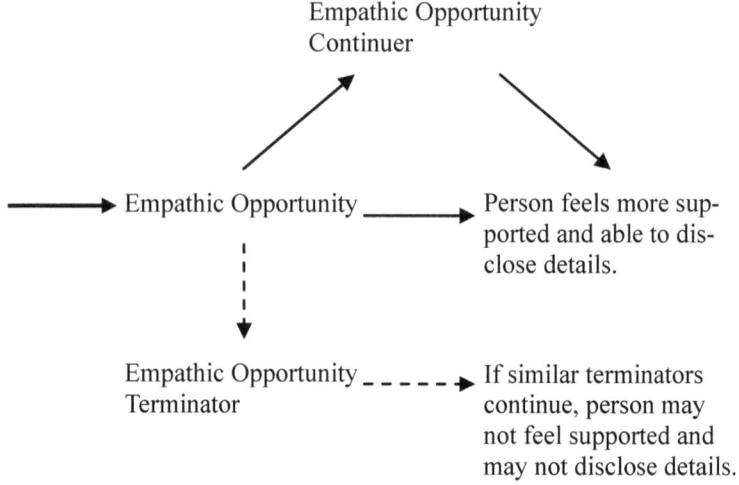

Figure 3. Model for measuring empathic responses in police interviews.[55]

5.4.4. Question Typologies

There has been a large amount of research that has concentrated on assessing the efficacy of different questioning techniques used during investigative interviews with suspects, victims and witnesses.[56] It is now widely accepted that using *open-ended* questions (for example, those starting with 'tell me', 'explain', 'describe') and more *probing* forms of questions (for example, five 'WH questions' – 'what', 'where', 'when', 'why', 'who' and 'how') are the most productive and encourage interviewees to

---

[55] Adapted from Anthony Suchman, Kathryn Markakis, Howard B. Beckman and Richard Frankel, "A model of empathic communication in the medical review", in *The Journal of the American Medical Association*, 1997, vol. 277, no. 8, pp. 678–82.

[56] Colin Clarke, Becky Milne and Ray Bull, "Interviewing Suspects of Crime: The Impact of PEACE Training, Supervision and the Presence of a Legal Advisor", in *Journal of Investigative Psychology and Offender Profiling*, 2011, vol. 8, no. 2, pp. 149–62; Trond Myklebust and Roald A. Bjørklund, "The Effect of Long-Term Training on Police Officers' Use of Open and Closed Questions in Field Investigative Interviews of Children (FIIC)", in *International Journal of Investigative Psychology and Offender Profiling*, 2006, vol. 3, no. 3, pp. 165–81; Trond Myklebust and Roald A. Bjørklund, "The Child Verbal Competence Effect in Court: A Comparative Study of Field Investigative Interviews of Children in Child Sexual Abuse Cases", in *Journal of Investigative Psychology and Offender Profiling*, 2009, vol. 6, no. 2, pp. 117–28; Oxburgh, Ost and Cherryman, 2012, see above note 4; Oxburgh, Ost, Morris and Cherryman, 2013, pp. 903–917, see above note 52. See below note 57 for a full review of the use of question typologies.

---

freely recall events, that in turn, are also associated with more fulsome and accurate accounts.[57] However, interviewers do not appear to be using *appropriate* questions.[58] A notable concern is the more regular use of *inappropriate* questions (that is, *closed, leading, multiple, forced choice, opinion or statement*) by interviewers that encourage interviewees to respond on the basis of recognition memory, rather than on the basis of free recall which can dramatically increase the probability of error in the provided answers.[59] The classification of question types does not adhere to a universally accepted protocol and consequently this can result in confusion when trying to compare different research findings.[60]

---

[57] Jan Aldridge and Sandra Cameron, "Interviewing Child Witnesses: Questioning Techniques and the Role of Training", in *Applied Developmental Science*, 1999, vol. 3, no. 2, pp. 136–47; Ann-Christin Cederborg, Yael Orbach, Kathleen J. Sternberg and Michael E. Lamb, "Investigative Interviews of Child Witnesses in Sweden", in *Child Abuse and Neglect*, 2000, vol. 24, no. 10, pp. 1355–61; Graham M. Davies, Helen L. Westcott and Noreen Horan, "The Impact of Questioning Style on the Content of Investigative Interviews with Suspected Child Sexual Abuse Victims", in *Psychology, Crime and Law*, 2000, vol. 6, no. 2, pp. 81–97; Elizabeth F. Loftus, "Interrogating Eyewitnesses – Good Questions and Bad", in R. Hogarth (ed.), *Question Framing and Response Consistency*, Josey-Bass, San Francisco, 1982, pp. 51–63; Milne and Bull, 2006, pp. 7–24, see above note 4; Myklebust and Bjørklund, 2006, pp. 165–81, see above note 56.

[58] John Baldwin, "Police Interview Techniques: Establishing Truth or Proof?", in *British Journal of Criminology*, 1993, vol. 33, no. 3, pp. 325–52; Davies, Westcott and Horan, 2000, pp. 81–97, see above note 57; Michael E. Lamb, Irit Hershkowitz, Kathleen J. Sternberg, Barbara Boat and Mark D. Everson, "Investigative Interviews of Alleged Sexual Abuse Victims with and Without Anatomical Dolls", in *Child Abuse and Neglect*, 1996, vol. 20, no. 12, pp. 1251–59; Myklebust and Bjørklund, 2006, pp. 165–81, see above note 56.

[59] Helen R. Dent, "The Effects of Interviewing Strategies on the Results of Interviews with Child Witnesses", in Arne Trankell (ed.), *Reconstructing the Past*, Kluwer, Deventer, 1982, pp. 279–98; Helen R. Dent, "An Experimental Study of the Effectiveness of Different Techniques of Questioning Mentally Handicapped Child Witnesses", in *British Journal of Clinical Psychology*, 1986, vol. 25, no. 1, pp. 13–17; Helen R. Dent and Geoffrey M. Stephenson, "An Experimental Study of the Effectiveness of Different Techniques of Questioning Child Witnesses", in *British Journal of Social and Clinical Psychology*, 1979, vol. 18, no. 1, pp. 41–51; Yael Orbach and Michael E. Lamb, "The Relationship Between Within-in-Interview Contradictions and Eliciting Interviewer Utterances", in *Child Abuse and Neglect*, 2001, vol. 25, no. 3, pp. 323–33.

[60] Debra A. Poole and Michael E. Lamb, *Investigative Interviews of Children: A Guide for Helping Professionals*, American Psychological Association, 1998.

5.5. Interviewing Vulnerable Witnesses

During the last three decades, an impressive body of research has been published about the capacity of vulnerable witnesses to provide reliable information about their experiences.[61] Within the extant literature-base, a witness can be broadly defined as 'vulnerable' by:

- reason of their age;
- their psychological state;
- having a mental disorder;
- being significantly impaired in relation to intelligence and social functioning;
- intellectual functioning; or
- having a physical disability.

In general terms, being vulnerable refers to a witness' ability in giving evidence and to give answers which address the questions put to them and can be understood both individually and collectively.[62] As outlined by Gudjonsson, a vulnerable witness has "psychological characteristics or mental state which render a witness prone, in certain circumstances, to providing information which is inaccurate, unreliable or misleading".[63]

The capacity of the interviewee to cope with an interview also depends on many other circumstances, including culture, interactions (or sense-making), personality, and health.[64] Today we are leaning from a

---

[61] For an overview see for example, Stephen J. Ceci and Maggie Bruck, *Jeopardy in the Courtroom: A Scientific Analysis of Children's Testimony*, American Psychological Association, Washington, D.C., 1995; Kevin R.H. Smith and Steve Tilney, *Vulnerable Adult and Child Witnesses*, Oxford University Press, 2007; Joyce Plotnikoff and Richard Woolfson, *Intermediaries in the Criminal Justice System: Improving Communication for Vulnerable Witnesses and Defendants*, Policy Press, Bristol, 2013, pp. 1–352; Gavin E. Oxburgh, Trond Myklebust, Tim D. Grant and Rebecca Milne (eds.), *Communication in Investigative and Legal Contexts: Integrated Approaches from Psychology, Linguistics and Law Enforcement*, Wiley, Chichester, 2016; Michael E. Lamb, Deirdre A. Brown, Irit Hershkowitz, Yael Orbach and Phillip W. Esplin, *Tell Me What Happened: Questioning Children About Abuse*, John Wiley & Sons, Chichester, 2018.

[62] Ministry of Justice, 2011, see above note 31.

[63] Gisli H. Gudjonsson, "The Psychological Vulnerabilities of Witnesses and the Risk of False Accusations and False Confessions", in Anthony Heaton-Armstrong, Eric Shepherd, Gisli Gudjonsson and David Wolchover (eds.), *Witness Testimony: Psychological, Investigative and Evidential Perspectives*, Oxford University Press, Oxford, 2006, p. 68.

[64] Gisli H. Gudjonsson and James MacKeith, *Disputed Confessions and the Criminal Justice System*, Meudsley Discussion Paper, Institute of Psychiatry, London, 1997; see also, Lind-

---

large body[65] of scientific research that has investigated various elements of the investigative interview, including:

- the interviewer;
- the interviewee;
- the context of the interview (and where it takes place); and
- the interplay between these factors.

One of the first scientists to study various elements of an interview was the German-born William Stern.[66] In his early studies of children in 1903, he demonstrated the importance of the distinction between different question typologies in achieving the most valid information from the interviewee. His research was the starting point for the focus on the way to phrase questions during legal proceedings, especially among vulnerable witnesses. Now, there are three main models that have been thoroughly researched, developed and scientifically-proven to elicit information through questioning without generating inaccurate accounts or confabulations: (i) the CI; (ii) the National Institute of Child Health and Human Development ('NICHD') protocol; and (iii) Achieving Best Evidence ('ABE'). Each will now be discussed.

5.5.1. Cognitive Interview

The CI technique was developed by Fisher and his colleagues[67] in the early 1980s and is based on four memory retrieval rules:

1. Mental reinstatement of environmental and personal contexts.

   The interviewee is asked to mentally revisit the 'to-be-remembered' ('TBR') event. The interviewer may ask them to form a mental picture of the environment in which they witnessed the event. The participant is also asked to revisit their personal mental state during the event and then describe it in detail. The purpose of this process is to

---

say D.G. Thompson, "Disputed Confessions and the Criminal Justice System, Maudsley Discussion Paper No. 2.", in *Psychiatric Bulletin*, 1998, vol. 22, no. 4, p. 270.

[65] See, for example, Ceci and Bruck, 1995, see above note 61; Neil Brewer and Kipling D. Williams (eds.), *Psychology and Law: An Empirical Perspective*, Guilford Press, New York, 2005; Oxburgh, Myklebust, Grant and Milne, 2016, see above note 61.

[66] William Stern, *Beiträge zür Psychologie der Aussage*, Verlag von Johann Ambrosius Barth, Leipzig, 1903–04.

[67] Ronald P. Fisher and Edward R. Geiselman, *Memory-Enhancing Techniques for Investigative Interviewing: The Cognitive Interview*, Charles Thomas, Springfield, 1992.

---

increase the feature overlap between initial witnessing and subsequent retrieval contexts.

2. In-depth reporting – report everything.

    The interviewer encourages the reporting of every detail, regardless of how peripheral it may seem to the main incident.

3. Describing the to-be-remembered event in several orders.

    This process may provide a new perspective of the event which subsequently provides an opportunity for new information to be recalled.

4. Change perspective technique – reporting the TBR event from different perspectives.

    The participant is asked to report the event from several different perspectives; like that of another witness or even a participant. If the participant witnessed a robbery, for example, the interviewer may ask, "what do you think the cashier saw?", and then ask for the participant's perspective.

5.5.2. NICHD Protocol

Elaborating on the CI's four elements, the NICHD protocol was one of the first to translate the recommendations from the CI into practice, focusing on how to interview children effectively. This tool was developed through the intensive efforts of US Government Scientists at the National Institutes of Health in the 1990s and has been the subject of intensive evaluation and research ever since.[68]

The advantage of using the NICHD protocol is to have the same standardised step-wise approach with all children, regardless of whether they are a victim or witness. It 'levels the playing field', giving every child who is interviewed an equal opportunity to disclose or not disclose the TBR event. Personal biases such as underestimating children's capabilities, or those resulting from certain case characteristics, are also minimised. Forensic interviewers sometimes also lack self-awareness or self-

---

[68] For a review, see, for example, David La Rooy, Sonja P. Brubacher, Anu Aromäki-Stratos, Mireille Cyr, Irit Hershkowitz, Julia Korkman, Trond Myklebust, Makiko Naka, Carlos E. Peixoto, Kim P. Roberts, Heather Stewart and Michael E. Lamb, "The NICHD Protocol: A Review of an Internationally-Used Evidence-Based Tool for Training Child Forensic Interviewers", in *Journal of Criminological Research, Policy and Practice*, 2015, vol. 1, no. 2, pp. 76–89.

monitoring regarding their own interviewing practices and, thus, a stand-ardised format aids in efforts to maintain desirable interview standards. The NICHD protocol is validated in over 40,000 interviews worldwide.[69] Based on the same psychological principles, other step-wise approaches and guidelines have been designed to interview a wider segment of vul-nerable or intimidated victims and witnesses (for example, adults with different disabilities such as a mental disorder, are impaired in relation to intelligence and social functioning, or have a physical disability).

5.5.3. ABE in Criminal Proceedings Guidelines

One of the most referred-to guidelines in use is the ABE guidelines that were first published in England and Wales in 2002[70] and a large number of the special measure provisions in their 1999 Youth Justice and Criminal Evidence Act[71] were implemented and replaced the previous guidance set out in the 1992 Memorandum of Good Practice for video-interviewing children.[72] The ABE guidance was later updated in 2007, with the most recent revision, to date, being released in 2011 (although a further update is due imminently).[73] This guidance document is predominantly aimed at officers conducting visually-recorded interviews with vulnerable, intimi-dated and significant witnesses or victims. It is also utilised by those of-ficers that are tasked with preparing and supporting witnesses or victims during the criminal justice process and those involved at the trial, both in supporting and questioning the witness or victim in Court. While the guidance is not compulsory, it is advised. Compliance (in conjunction with effective training) with the guidance is likely to enhance the quality of the interview, which is likely to benefit the interviewer, the interviewee, practitioners and the Court.

---

[69] See *ibid.*; Lamb, Brown, Hershkowitz, Orbach and Esplin, 2018, see above note 61.

[70] Home Office, *Achieving Best Evidence in Criminal Proceedings: Guidance for Vulnerable or Intimidated Witnesses, Including Children, Implementing the Speaking Up for Justice Report*, Home Office Communication Directorate, January 2002.

[71] UK, Youth Justice and Criminal Evidence Act 1999, 27 July 1999 (https://legal-tools.org/doc/3eb20e).

[72] Home Office in conjunction with Department of Health, *Memorandum of Good Practice on Video Recorded Interviews with Child Witnesses for Criminal Proceedings*, HMSO, London, 1992.

[73] Ministry of Justice, 2011, see above note 31.

The revised edition of the ABE includes amendments that account for legislative changes to the 1999 Youth Justice and Criminal Evidence Act, that were introduced to eradicate some of the difficulties associated with giving oral evidence by granting 'vulnerable' and 'intimidated' witnesses or victims the use of alternative trial arrangements (with limitations and conditions attached). There are a wide variety of modifying measures that can be used to protect witnesses or victims from recognised court related stressors, including the erection of temporary screens to shield them from the view of the defendant, or the use of live-links to allow them to give evidence from a room remote from the main courtroom in a comparatively informal, relaxed environment (all the while remaining visible and audible to those in Court). Previous research has identified the positive impact that special measures can have on cases involving vulnerable victims with almost half of the sampled victims stating that special measures had enabled them to give evidence and that they would not otherwise have been willing or able to give.[74]

Finally, given the importance of visually-recorded statements, it is imperative that they are of good quality so as to ensure that where a prosecution takes place this can be conducted as effectively as possible. Therefore, it is advised that officers read the guidance *Advice on the Structure of Visually Recorded Witness Interviews*[75] in conjunction with the ABE as this will further reinforce good practice. This guidance was developed based on feedback from a range of sources about recurrent problems with the way visually recorded interviews had been conducted and how they then were used as evidence in Court. The next section will detail what guidance the ABE provides officers with on how they should conduct an interview.

The ABE guidance document given to officers has four recommended phases that fall under the section related to 'conducting the interview' and these include:

1. Establishing rapport;

---

[74] Mandy Burton, Roger Evans and Andrew Sanders, *Are Special Measures for Vulnerable and Intimidated Witnesses Working? Evidence from the Criminal Justice Agencies*, 2006, Home Office, London; Becky Hamlyn, Andrew Phelps, Andrew Phelps, Jenny Turtle and Ghazala Sattar, *Are Special Measures Working? Evidence from Surveys of Vulnerable and Intimidated Witnesses*, 2004, Home Office, London.

[75] The National Police Chiefs' Council (NPCC) and the College of Policing, *Advice on the Structure of Visually Recorded Witness Interviews*, 3rd edition, 1 October 2016.

2. free narrative account;
3. questioning; and
4. closing the interview.

Phase one is a process whereby the interviewer should establish rapport with the witness or victim to personalise the interview and put them at ease. The initial interaction is recognised as determining the success of the interview, as well as assisting in the *quantity* and *quality* of information gained in the interview, by establishing a sense of trust that can help in laying the foundations for future, successful, communication.[76] Through this process, the interviewer is reducing any possible tension and insecurity felt by the witness or victim, treating them with a unique set of needs, as opposed to being 'just another witness or victim'. The significance of building rapport within the investigative interview is highlighted straight away in this first phase of the ABE and was previously discussed in this chapter.

Phase two of the interview recommends that the interviewer should initiate an uninterrupted free narrative account from the witness or victim through the use of an *open-ended* invitation. This would be through an *open* question framed in such a way that the witness or victim is able to give an unrestricted answer, which in turn enables them to control the flow of information in the interview (that is, "tell me", "explain" or "describe"). The free narrative account allows the interviewer to gain a better understanding of the way in which the witness or victim holds the information about the event in their memory. Thus, note taking is recommended at this stage. However, the detail of note taking is down to the interviewer, too many notes may distract the witness or victim, which subsequently could hinder the flow of recall. On the other hand, if the interviewer slows the witness or victim down in order to record detailed notes, this could potentially hinder maximum retrieval.

Phase three focuses on the questioning of the witness or victim, as most will not be able to recall everything relevant to the event that is in their memory. Therefore, their accounts could greatly benefit from the interviewer asking *appropriate* questions related to the event that could assist in further recall. Those officers conducting the interviews need to fully appreciate that there are various types of questions that vary in how direct they are (as previously discussed). The questioning phase should,

---

[76] Ministry of Justice, 2011, see above note 31.

whenever possible, commence with *open-ended* questions and then proceed, if necessary, to specific *closed* questions. These are the second-best type of question (to *open-ended* questions) and should be used to obtain information not provided by the witness or victim in the free narrative account and not elicited through the use of *open-ended* questions. A specific *closed* question is one that allows only a relatively narrow range of responses.

Finally, phase four centres around closing the interview by briefly summarising what the witness or victim has said, using words and phrases used by them as much as possible. By adopting such practices allows the witness or victim to check the interviewer's recall for accuracy. The interviewer must explicitly tell the witness or victim to correct them if they have missed anything out or have got something wrong.

These four phases are basic for most communication models in investigative interviewing, however, from our perspective, the ABE is the one, at present, presenting the most theoretical approach from various disciplines including psychology, linguistics and law. However, there is another model which takes account of the entire 'whole' process of being interviewed and providing testimony at Court: the Nordic Model.

5.5.4. The Nordic Model

There is a model that has been implemented in the Nordic countries for more than a decade which attempts to meet children's needs by offering multiple services in child-friendly premises and 'under one roof': the Nordic Barnahus model.[77] This model was first introduced in Iceland and drew on experiences from Children's Advocacy Centres (CAC) in the United States. The implementation of the Barnahus model is linked to a long-lasting concern for the protection of children at risk and for the way children's needs are met during a criminal investigation, increasing the likelihood of obtaining complete and precise information as well as a lack of co-ordinated follow-up services for children and families that need treatment or support related to the child's experiences.

The primary aim is to reduce the stress of being part of a much larger legal process for victimised children and their families, but also for

---

[77] Susanna Johansson, Kari Stefansen, Elisiv Bakketeig and Anna Kaldal (eds.), *Collaborating Against Child Abuse, Exploring the Nordic Barnahus Model*, Palgrave Macmillan, 2017.

adult victims that suffer with mental health problems. The Barnahus is generally staffed with a manager, four to six employees, and a part time medical examiner. The main functions are:

- to facilitate the forensic interview and the medical examination;
- to evaluate the child and family's need for social assistance; and
- to provide short-term treatment and support.

At the Barnahus, the vulnerable victim is met by a specially trained police officer (the interviewer) and representatives from the Barnahus, together with representatives from the prosecution, defence lawyers, State-funded counsel to the complainant, and, in some cases, the Social services monitoring the interview from an adjoining room. In this way, the interview is planned and conducted based on a team approach from specialists within different areas of communication with vulnerable victims and witnesses.

5.5.5. Registered Intermediaries

Another approach for improving communication for vulnerable persons is by using Registered Intermediaries ('RI') – currently used within England, Wales and Northern Ireland.[78] The central part of the RI's role is to assist in communication in its widest sense. In other words, to assist the legal process, both prior to (at police interviews) and during the giving of evidence by the witness in Court, by facilitating two-way communication in order to achieve best evidence.[79] The role can be specifically defined as to communicate to the witness, any questions put to the witness, and to any persons asking such questions, the answers given by the witness in reply to them; and to explain such questions or answers so far as necessary to enable them to be understood by the witness or the questioner.[80]

5.6. Conclusion

There is no doubt that a good quality interview with victims, witnesses or suspects is conducted in a fair, compassionate manner using appropriate

---

[78] Plotnikoff and Woolfson, 2013, see above note 61.

[79] Ministry of Justice, *Registered Intermediary Procedural Guidance 2019*, Crown Publishing Service, London, 2019. For more detailed information, see Johansson, Stefansen, Bakketeig and Kaldal, 2017, see above note 77, and The Advocated Gateway, "Intermediaries" (available on its web site).

[80] Youth Justice and Criminal Evidence Act, Section 29, see above note 71.

questions, empathy and rapport throughout. Researchers have argued that there are clear indications that the use of non-humane tactics in investigative interviews is wholly ineffective and that more empathic, rapport-based strategies have more of an effect in generating relevant information from the interviewee.[81] These findings are reflected in the discovery of specific qualities that have been found in 'skilful' police interviews, amongst which positive communication skills, empathy and open-mindedness were all present.[82]

However, to date, empirical research examining empathic interviewing styles in relation to its impact and efficacy during the interviewing process is in its relative infancy. The research that has been conducted has tended to focus more on the interviewing of suspected offenders and their perceptions of their specific police interview.[83] However, the absence of having a precise operational explanation that professional interviewers can understand, arguably leaves the term 'empathy' and 'rapport' open to interpretation, with potential negative consequences relating to how it is researched, understood, trained, and practiced. More research is needed in this fundamental area of psychology and communication.

---

[81] Alison, Alison, Noone, Elntib and Christiansen. 2013, pp. 411–31, see above note 20.

[82] Bull and Cherryman, 1995, see above note 29.

[83] Holmberg and Christianson, 2002, pp. 31–45, see above note 20; Mark Kebbell, Emily J. Hurren and Paul Mazerolle, "Sex Offenders' Perceptions of How They Were Interviewed", in *Canadian Journal of Police and Security Services*, 2006, vol. 4, pp. 67–75; Kebbell, Alison, Hurren and Mazerolle, pp. 567–84, see above note 30; Oxburgh and Ost, 2011, pp. 178–88, see above note 47; Oxburgh, Ost, Morris and Cherryman, 2013, pp. 903–17, see above note 52; Gavin E. Oxburgh, James Ost, Paul Morris and Julie Cherryman, "Police Officers' Perceptions of Interviews in Cases of Sexual Offences and Murder Involving Children and Adult Victims", in *Police Practice and Research: An International Journal*, 2015, vol. 16, no. 1, pp. 36–50.

6

Child Soldier or Soldier?
Estimating Age in Cases of Core International
Crimes: Challenges and Opportunities

Moa Lidén[*]

6.1. Introduction

> [...] the children were smaller than the Kalashnikovs they
> were carrying[1]

In 2006, Witness P-0046 testified before Pre-trial Chamber I at the International Criminal Court ('ICC') regarding her observations while working in MONUC's child protection program in Ituri, the Democratic Republic of the Congo ('DRC').[2] As part of an ongoing investigation into war crimes allegedly committed by Mr. Lubanga, P-0046 had conducted interviews with young individuals believed to be child soldiers and she described some of them as smaller than the Kalashnikovs they were carrying. When P-0046's testimony was presented in Court, the defence claimed

---

[*]   **Moa Lidén** is Postdoctoral Research Fellow, funded by Ragnar Söderberg Foundation and The Swedish Research Council, at the Department of Security and Crime Science, Centre for the Forensic Sciences, University College London, London. She holds a Ph.D. in Jurisprudence from the Law Faculty of Uppsala University and her doctoral thesis was on the topic "Confirmation Bias in Criminal Cases". For more on this topic in relation to investigations of core international crimes, see Moa Lidén, "Confirmation Bias in Investigations of Core International Crimes: Risk Factors and Quality Control Techniques", Chapter 7 below; Moa Lidén, "Prevention of Factual Confirmation Bias During Offence-Driven Investigations", CILRAP Film, New Delhi, 22 February 2019 (https://www.cilrap.org/cilrap-film/190222-liden/). The author is grateful to Xabier Agirre Aranburu, Marie Allen and Fredrik Tamsen for their valuable inputs on this chapter.

[1]   International Criminal Court ('ICC'), Situation in the Democratic Republic of the Congo, *The Prosecutor v. Thomas Lubanga Dyilo*, Testimony of P-0046 before Pre-Trial Chamber I, video excerpt EVD-OTP-00479; and the respective Transcript of Testimony, T-37-FR, p. 23, lines 8–12.

[2]   *Ibid.*

---

she "showed obvious bias in favor of the prosecution".[3] However, according to the Trial Chamber, P-0046 had not exaggerated any material facts or otherwise provided biased or unreliable evidence,[4] an assessment which the Appeal's Chamber agreed with.[5]

Mr. Lubanga was convicted for the war crimes of enlisting and conscripting children under the age of 15 years and using them to participate actively in hostilities, to a total of 14 years of imprisonment.[6] Both the judgment and the sentence were upheld on appeal.[7] A crucial and heavily disputed question in this case was whether the prosecution had proven beyond reasonable doubt that the individuals enlisted or conscripted by Lubanga were younger than 15 years within the time frame of the charges. The Court considered the age element proven, primarily on the basis of video evidence, but also oral evidence from witnesses such as P-0046 and forensic as well as documentary evidence was available.

Age estimations are necessary in all jurisdictions, whether international or national, and they also have consequences for a range of legal questions in distinct legal areas including for instance criminal law,[8] asy-

---

[3]   *Ibid.* On appeal, the defence also claimed that her testimony was hearsay evidence, a claim which the Appeals Chamber did not consider substantiated, see ICC, *The Prosecutor v. Thomas Lubanga Dyilo*, Appeals Chamber, Judgment, 1 December 2014, ICC-01/04-01/06-3121-Red, paras. 244–46 ('Lubanga Appeals Chamber Judgment') (https://www.legal-tools.org/doc/585c75/).

[4]   ICC, *The Prosecutor v. Thomas Lubanga Dyilo*, Trial Chamber, Judgment, 14 March 2012, ICC-01/04-01/06-2842, para. 648 ('Lubanga Trial Chamber Judgment') (https://www.legal-tools.org/doc/677866/). However, the Trial Chamber rejected the admission into evidence of a document entitled "*Histoires individuelles*" which were witness P-0046's notes of interviews with 34 individuals who were allegedly under 15 years since the Prosecutor intended to introduce the document for the limited purpose of establishing the working methods of P-0046 and, given that this could be explained during her testimony, the Chamber considered "the merits of the suggested purpose for introducing this document are so slight that the arguments as regards prejudice are persuasive". See ICC, *The Prosecutor v. Thomas Lubanga Dyilo*, Trial Chamber, Transcript, 7 July 2009, ICC-01/04-01/06-T-205-ENG, p. 3 (https://www.legal-tools.org/doc/083fc3/). During the course of her testimony, P-0046 relied on a database of 687 individuals with whom she met rather than on the "*Histoires individuelles*". Lubanga Appeals Chamber Judgment, p. 92, see above note 3.

[5]   *Ibid.*, paras. 92–94.

[6]   Lubanga Trial Chamber Judgment, see above note 4.

[7]   Lubanga Appeals Chamber Judgment, see above note 3.

[8]   Since many crimes require that an individual is classified as a child such as child trafficking or sexual exploitation or rape of a child. There is lots of variation in what more specific age limits are applicable across different jurisdictions. For instance, the range at which an

lum law[9] and some parts of civil law.[10] Although all legal age elements have potentially far-reaching consequences, this Chapter uses as a case study the 15-year threshold entailed in the war crime of conscripting, enlisting and/or using child soldiers in armed forces or groups, see, for example, The Rome Statute of the ICC Article 8(e)(vii) and Elements of Crimes Element 8(2)(b)(xxvi) and the Special Court of Sierra Leone ('SCSL') Statute Article 4(c). Given the gravity of the crime in question and the associated controversiality, this legal age element has received relatively little scientific attention. There are many legal as well as official debates about whether alleged child soldiers are to be considered victims or perpetrators.[11] This is likely to be a false dilemma, as individuals can

---

individual can provide legally acceptable sexual consent varies from 14 to 18 years and for criminal responsibility some US states do not legislate a minimum age at all, whereas others apply, for example, 8, 10, 12, 14,15,16 or 18-year limits. For more on this see, for example, ZHU Guangxing and Suzan van der Aa, "Trends of Age of Consent Legislation in Europe: A Comparative Study of 59 Jurisdictions on the European Continent", in *New Journal of European Criminal Law*, 2017, vol. 8, no. 1, p. 21; Helmut Graupner, "Sexual Consent: The Criminal Law in Europe and Outside of Europe", in *Journal of Psychology and Human Sexuality*, 2004, vol. 16, no. 2, pp. 117–18.

[9] For instance, an individual's chances of being granted asylum are influenced by the individual's age, and age can also be decisive for whether and in what way he or she may be detained. For more on this see Daja Wenke, *Age Assessments: Council of Europe member States' Policies, Procedures and Practices Respectful of Children's Rights in the Context of Migration*, Council of Europe, 2017, p. 18; Karin Schittenhelm, "Implementing and Rethinking the European Union's Asylum Legislation: The Asylum Procedures Directive", in *International Migration*, 2018, vol. 57, no. 1, pp. 229–44; Tara Magner, "Refugee, Asylum, and Related Legislation in the US Congress: 2013-2016", in *Journal on Migration and Human Security*, 2018, vol. 4, no. 4, pp. 166–89. Overall, age is also relevant to determine an individual's access to fundamental rights and safeguards that children under 18 years are entitled to in line with the UN Convention on the Rights of the Child and other relevant international and European standards, see Maria Antonia Di Maio, *Position Paper of Age Assessment in the Context of Separated Children in Europe*, Separated Children in Europe Programme, 2012, p. 12; Devyani Prabhat, Ann Singleton and Robbie Eyles, "Age is Just a Number? Supporting Migrant Young People with Precarious Legal Status in the UK", in *The International Journal of Children's Rights*, 2019, vol. 5, no. 2, pp. 228–50.

[10] For instance, age estimations may be necessary in relation to questions of legal capacity and legal guardianship. For more on this see Sevastian Cercel and Stefan Scurtu, "Full Legal Capacity Acquired Before the Age of Majority", in *Revista de Stiinte Politice*, 2015, vol. 4, no. 46, pp. 279–304; Amy Weatherburn and Yvonne Eloise Mellon, "Child Trafficking Victims and Legal Guardians: Exploring the Fulfilment of the EU Trafficking Directive in the Context of the UK Modern Slavery Act 2015: Best Practice of Not Fit for Purpose? 2019", in *New Journal of European Criminal Law*, vol. 10, no. 2, pp. 102–27.

[11] For instance, some argue that child soldiers are viewed either as helpless passive victims or irreparably damaged good, which is a false dilemma, as we can't rely on stark divisions

be both victims and perpetrators simultaneously,[12] but the debates have been refuelled by the ongoing ICC proceedings against the former child soldier Dominic Ongwen for having committed child soldiering crimes himself.[13] Also, the 15-year threshold deviates from the so-called "straight 18" position which is gaining ground[14] and which raises questions as to

between passivity and agency if we wish to judge these cases well and fairly, see Mark Drumbl, *Reimagining Child Soldiers in International Law and Policy*, Oxford University Press, Oxford, 2012, pp. 143–44. Much of this debate has also centred on the reasons why young individuals may choose to join the army, and whether there can be any real voluntariness. For instance, some argue that children perceive armed groups as a way to escape from domestic violence or ensure their protection from attacks by other groups, see Rachel Brett and Irma Specht, *Young Soldiers: Why They Choose to Fight*, Lynne Reinner Publishers, Geneva, 2004.

[12] For instance, in the Holocaust, Jewish inmates had become so-called 'Kapos' or Ghetto Police in the extermination camps under the Nazis, and some of them were brought to trial in Israel. These trials have been described by Dan Porat, *Israel Tries Holocaust Survivors as Nazi Collaborators*, Harvard University Press, 2019.

[13] ICC, Situation in Uganda, *The Prosecutor v. Dominic Ongwen*, ICC-02/04-01/15. Closing statements took place from 10 to 12 March 2020 and the Trial Chamber will now deliberate. For a discussion relating to Ongwen's case see, for example, Jill Stauffer, "Law, Politics, the Age of Responsibility, and the Problem of Child Soldiers", in *Law, Culture and the Humanities*, 2020, vol. 16, no. 1, pp. 42–52. Stauffer poses the question: "[a]t what point did he pass the line between too young to be responsible and old enough to have known better?" Furthermore, Stauffer argues that from one angle Ongwen's case is about international criminal law: that is, whether Ongwen is legally guilty of any of the crimes with which he is charged. From another angle it is about politics, will he be found guilty of crimes of which he is also a victim, crimes committed as part of a struggle where all sides used child soldiers and resorted to criminal means, but only some sides find their leaders indicted by the ICC. And from yet another angle it is about the limits of these two field to get at the heart of the questions: have either of these ways of understanding what is at stake in Ongwen's case helped us clarify what it means to find someone with Ongwen's background guilty, or to understand what the conditions are that allow a case as complicated as Ongwen's to end up at the ICC.

[14] For instance, UN agencies aim to replace 15 with 18-year thresholds, advancing the "Straight 18" position. The first UN Special Representative for Children in Armed Conflict had this goal in the context of recruitment of children in hostilities and the conviction has since been consolidated and expanded within the Office of the Special Representative. The Integrated Disarmament, Demobilization and Reintegration Standards identify as the "UN's advocacy position" that "no person under 18 shall be recruited into or used in armed forces or groups". Rosen remarks that "most human rights groups […] declare that there is now a universal ban on the recruitment of children under age eighteen". David M. Rosen, "Who is a Child? The Legal Conundrum of Child Soldiers", in *Connecticut Journal of International Law*, 2009, vol. 25, no. 1, p. 100. The Coalition to Stop the Use of Child Soldiers has spearheaded and international campaign to establish 18 years as the minimum age of recruitment, see David M. Rosen, "Review of Child Soldiers: From Violence to Protection", in *Studies in Social Justice*, 2010, vol. 4, no. 1, pp. 93–95. According to the *Child*

when children have reached a sufficient cognitive and developmental maturity to be held criminally responsible for their acts.[15] Although many jurisdictions have acknowledged the 15-year age limit as a reasonable threshold and are still using it today,[16] a few debaters express dissatisfaction with legal rules that enable the prosecution of soldiers younger than 18 years.[17] Yet, it should be noted that the ICC does not have any such jurisdiction.[18]

Soldiers International Annual Report 2017-18, 109 countries have a Straight 18 policy for military recruitment in practice, meaning a minimum age of 18 for enlistment as well as deployment while 46 States (23 per cent) still recruit under 18's into their armed forces in practice, see pp. 18–23. Drumbl notes that as an international community we seem to be headed towards a Straight 18 position and poses the question: "Might it be counterproductive, however, to chronologically expand the membership of the protected class while statically relying on uniform, atrophied, and infantilized assumptions of the capacities of class members?". Drumbl, 2012, p. 143, see above note 11. Thus, as a first step, it seems reasonable to attempt to better understand the factors which make individuals capable or incapable of bearing responsibility for their actions, and only after that discuss and evaluate whether applicable age thresholds are fit for their purposes.

[15] Clearly this question has been answered differently across differently jurisdictions, see above note 8, and the debate in the literature is still ongoing. For instance, Rosen argues that viewing childhood as something uniform ignores variations across culture, gender, history and location and therefore clashes with many local standards not only about age but about responsibility and justice, and thereby it ignores the real-world experience of child soldiers as well as their victims, see Rosen, 2009, pp. 81–118, see above note 14; David M. Rosen, *Armies of the Young: Child Soldiers in War and Terrorism*, Rutgers University Press, New Jersey, 2005. Along similar lines, some argue that individual variation among children make it virtually impossible to determine a fixed age at which a child develops sufficiently rational and reasonable senses, and this questions has been discussed with respect to executive functions specifically, see, for example, Tyler Fagan, William Hirstein and Katrina Sifferd, "Child Soldiers, Executive Functions, and Culpability", in *International Criminal Law Review*, 2016, vol. 16, no. 2. pp. 258–86.

[16] For more on this as well as variation across different jurisdiction, see ZHU and van der Aa, 2017, see above note 8.

[17] For instance, Drumbl argues that in ICL there is an unwillingness to prosecute child soldiers (younger than 18) and that the reluctance to exercise jurisdiction over minors is more than just a procedural technicality or admissibility criterion. It is also more than just a gravity limitation or leadership requirement. In fact, Drumbl argues, it instrumentalizes, reflects and contributes to the substantive notion within international legal imagination that it is unimportant, embarrassing, and unhelpful for child soldiers to answer for their involvement in acts of atrocity in a courtroom, see Drumbl, 2012, p. 127, see above note 11. Also, David Crane, commenting on the Khadr prosecution states that: "No child has the *mens rea*, the criminal mind, to commit war crimes" (referring to children under the age of 18), cited in *ibid.*

[18] The ICC does not have any jurisdiction over any person who was under the age of 18 at the time of the alleged commission of a crime, see The Rome Statute of the International

While age is a legal question, to be answered ultimately by legal actors, their assessments often rely on scientific, medical or other expertise as well as witnesses, and so on. Across different jurisdictions, there is also large variation in how age estimations are usually made, involving several different experts such as radiologists, odontologists, paediatricians, pathologists, psychologists and social workers who use different methods[19] to answer the same question.[20] Thus, there is no internationally accepted framework specifying best practices, save for recommendations to use multidisciplinary and holistic approaches.[21] This also means that legal actors like prosecutors and judges are faced with the challenge of understanding, accurately integrating and evaluating multidisciplinary evidence which is not only outside of their typical expertise but is also sometimes uncertain, vague or even contradictory. Hence, the age element, being only one element of the crime, can in itself result in several investigative and evaluative difficulties. These difficulties can easily be underestimated, especially if there is not much precedent, which was the case for instance at the outset of the Lubanga investigation.[22] Thus, in line with the more

---

Criminal Court, 17 July 1998, Article 26 ('ICC Statute') (https://www.legal-tools.org/doc/7b9af9/).

[19] This includes *non-medical methods* such as documents (passports, ID documents, residence cards, travel documents, certificates, and so on), age assessment interviews and psychological assessment, *radiation free medical methods* including, for example, dental observation, MRI/MR and observations of physical development, and as a measure of last resort, *other medical methods with radiation*, including, for example, wrist (carpal) X-ray, collar bone X-ray and dental X-ray, see European Asylum Support Office ('EASO'), *EASO Practical Guide on Age Assessment*, 2018, p. 33. The methods used also vary depending on what age limit (15, 18 or 21, and so on) is being assessed.

[20] For more on this see, for instance, *ibid.*, pp. 1–116.

[21] The Study Group on Forensic Age Diagnostics ('AGFAD'), an international assembly of experts, with approximately 18 years' experience, have issued recommendations to use dental X-rays, wrist X-rays and collar bone X-rays for forensic age estimations, see, for example, Andreas Schmeling *et al.*, "Criteria for Age Estimation in Living Individuals", in *International Journal of Legal Medicine*, 2008, vol. 122, no. 6, pp. 457–60 and Andreas Schmeling *et al.*, "Forensic Age Estimation: Methods, Certainty, and the Law", in *Deutsches Ärzteblatt International*, 2016, vol. 113, no. 4, pp. 44–50.

[22] The case against Lubanga, see Lubanga Trial Chamber Judgment, above note 4 and Lubanga Appeals Chamber Judgment, above note 3, was focused on child soldiers because it was assumed that this was easier to prove than other crimes. In other words, it was only plan B, while plan A was to investigate and charge a series of attacks resulting in massacres and mass-destruction, charges that were later brought against Ntaganda. However, it is likely that the investigative difficulties associated with child soldiering, including the age element, were underestimated, and that this contributed to the "significant pressure" which

general observation of investigations into war crimes which Taylor made already in 1949, properly investigating and evaluating the age element is "far bigger and far more difficult [...] than anyone had anticipated".[23] Taking this challenge on, as is mandated by their roles, legal actors are also dealing with a politically and emotionally sensitive part of law. One major reason for this is that their decisions may influence the lives of a typically very well protected group, that is, children. Today, there is no framework supporting legal actors in their collection and evaluation of age evidence. Ideally, such a framework should help legal actors answer the following essential questions: 1) Where do doubts regarding age evidence stem from (challenges) and what can be done to reduce it (opportunities)? and 2) How to deal with the remaining doubt (diagnostic accuracy)?

Hence, the purpose of this research is two-folded:

1. It provides a potential framework for collection and evaluation of age evidence in the legal setting. This framework is designed to help answer the essential questions described above: Firstly, what are the causes of doubt regarding age evidence and what can be done to reduce it? This is addressed in Section 6.2. "Challenges and Opportunities with Age Estimations". Secondly, how should legal actors deal with the remaining doubt? This is discussed in Section 6.3. "Diagnostic Accuracy of Age Estimations".

2. It applies this framework in relation to age estimations in child soldiering cases (Section 6.4.) by addressing challenges and opportunities with estimations in this specific context. This requires an empirical review of cases dealing with child soldiering charges to identify what types of evidence were used for age estimation purposes (Section 6.4.2.). This is followed by an examination of the challenges and opportunities relating to each type of evidence, including forensic, video, oral and documentary evidence (Section 6.5.). Thereafter, the diagnostic accuracy of age estimations in child soldiering cases will be discussed (Section 6.6.).

---

the investigation team was under, see Lubanga Trial Chamber Judgment, paras. 134 and 142, see above note 4.

23 Telford Taylor, *Final Report to the Secretary of the Army on The Nuernberg War Crimes Trials under Control Council Law No. 10*, U.S. Government Printing Office, Washington, 1948, p. 124.

6.2. Challenges and Opportunities with Age Estimations

This section addresses the questions; where do doubts regarding age evidence stem from (challenges) and what can be done to reduce it (opportunities)? Although it is clear that challenges can take many shapes this research will focus primarily on challenges of three specific kinds namely; validity, reliability and biasability. The working definitions are provided below.

Validity: the extent to which inferences can be made from 'operationalizations' of chronological age.[24] Legal age elements, including that entailed in child soldiering crimes, are exclusively interested in one type of age; chronological age, that is, the number of years since a person was born.[25] However, since chronological age is often unknown, there is a need for operationalizations, or 'proxies' of it. As will be outlined in the following, this usually entails *biological*, *apparent* and/or *social age*. In this research, *biological age* connotes results from forensic age estimations (FAEs) of, for example, bone and teeth,[26] *apparent age* refers to how old an individual appears to be based on his or her physical appearance or demeanour and *social age* refers the age of an individual as determined by social or cultural factors rather than the number of days since birth. Hence, validity is the extent to which biological, apparent and social age fit the construct of interest here, the chronological age. In other words,

---

[24] Hence, this definition is borrowed from so-called construct validity which in psychological research is taken to mean the degree to which a test measures what it claims, or purports, to be measuring, see, for example, William R. Shadish, Thomas D. Cook and Donald T. Campbell, *Experimental and Quasi-Experimental Designs for Generalized Causal Inferences*, Houghton Mifflin, Boston, 2002, pp. 64–82.

[25] See, for instance, Ording Muller *et al.*, "Bone Age of Chronological Age Determination: Statement of the European Society of Pediatric Radiology Musculoskeletal Task Force Group", in *Pediatric Radiology*, 2019, vol. 49, no. 7, pp. 979–82; Lloyd Rhodri *et al.*, "Chronological Age vs. Biological Maturation: Implications for Exercise Programming in Youth", in *Journal of Strength and Conditioning Research*, 2014, vol. 28, no. 5, pp. 1454–64.

[26] Bone age is often defined as the general degree of maturation of bone that subjects of a population reach at a certain average age, often based on the hand or wrist and dental age is defined as the general degree of development of teeth that subjects of a population reach at a certain average age. Also, skeletal age is used when referring to the entire skeleton, and is this the defined as the general degree of maturation of the skeleton that subjects of a population reach at a certain average age. Thus, unlike in this research, different kinds of biological age will be distinguished from one another, see Edel Doyle *et al.*, "Guidelines for Best Practice: Imaging for Age Estimation in the Living", in *Journal of Forensic Radiology and Imaging*, 2019, vol. 16, pp. 38–49.

---

what is the more specific relationship between chronological age on the one side and biological, apparent and social age on the other side.[27]

Reliability: although there are many types of reliability the term is here used primarily to refer to *Between Expert Reliability*. This connotes the extent to which different experts examining the exact same evidence make the same observations and draw the same conclusions in relation to that evidence.[28] Some examples are whether two radiologists examining the same individual's wrist or hand to estimate age make the same observations and draw the same conclusions regarding biological age, or whether two observers of the same individual's physical appearance will make the same assessments as regards the individual's apparent age. There may be corresponding reliability issues for one and the same expert who examines the same evidence at different points in time (*Within Expert Reliability*).[29] However, this research will focus on Between Expert Reliability since this type of reliability has direct implications for questions such as the necessity of a second opinion and/or how to properly integrate and understand dissent between different experts in legal proceedings.

Biasability: similar to reliability this can be understood both as *Between* and *Within Expert Biasability*, whereof this Chapter will focus on the former category. Between Expert Biasability is the extent to which experts make the same observations and reach the same conclusions, depending on what knowledge they have of potentially biasing contextual information such as a case hypothesis[30] or the type of crime in question.[31] Importantly, bias often operates on a subconscious level and it may there-

---

[27] Clearly, it may also be important to think of the relationship between biological, apparent and social age respectively, especially in cases of contradictions.

[28] This definition comes from Itiel E. Dror, "A Hierarchy of Expert Performance (HEP)", in *Journal of Applied Research in Memory and Cognition*, 2016, vol. 5, no. 2, pp. 121–27.

[29] Also this definition comes from *ibid*.

[30] See, for example, Saul Kassin, Itiel E. Dror and Jeff Kukucka, "The Forensic Confirmation Bias: Problems, Perspectives, and Proposed Solutions", in *Journal of Applied Research in Memory and Cognition*, 2013, vol. 2, no. 1, pp. 42–52; Moa Lidén, *Confirmation Bias in Criminal Cases*, Uppsala University Press, Uppsala, 2018.

[31] See Dror, 2016, pp. 121–27, see above note 28.

fore be present despite individuals' best efforts to remain objective.[32] Also, the risk of bias is greater in relation to ambiguous material.[33]

The term *opportunities* refers to current and ongoing research which is relevant in the sense that it may help to overcome some challenges with age estimations. Thereby it may also help to reduce, although not completely remove, doubts regarding someone's chronological age. For instance, this research offers new technologies or scientific methods for age estimations or suggest procedures on how to improve Between Expert Reliability or prevent bias. As such, the research is relevant for the experts or individuals involved in conducting the actual age estimations but also for legal actors who collect, integrate and evaluate age evidence within the context of a criminal case. Furthermore, the Chapter also identifies opportunities for researchers to contribute with more field specific empirical investigations.

6.3. Diagnostic Accuracy of Age Estimations

After having considered what doubts are present in relation to age evidence (challenges) and what could have or should have been done to reduce such doubts (opportunities), it is likely that some doubts about an individual's chronological age will still remain. This section introduces the question of how to deal with such remaining doubts. Although there are no general answers to this question and the considerations will vary between different legal areas (criminal, asylum, etc.), this section will consider the question primarily in relation to criminal law and more specifically the war crime of conscripting, enlisting or using child soldiers in armed forces or groups.[34]

Since the age element of interest is an element of a (war) crime, most lawyers are likely to intuitively say that any remaining doubts about

---

[32] For more on this see Raymond Nickerson, "Confirmation Bias: A Ubiquitous Phenomenon in Many Guises", in *Review of General Psychology*, 1998, vol. 2, no. 2, pp. 175–220; and Lidén, 2018, see above note 30.

[33] See, for instance, Kassin, Dror and Kukucka, 2013, pp. 42–52, see above note 30; Nikola K.P. Osborne and Rachel Zajac, "An Imperfect Match? Crime-related Context Influences Fingerprint Decisions", in *Applied Cognitive Psychology*, 2016, vol. 30, no. 1, pp. 126–34.

[34] As defined by ICC Statute, Article 8(e)(vii), see above note 18; ICC, Elements of Crimes, 11 June 2010, Article 8(2)(b)(xxvi) (https://www.legal-tools.org/doc/3c0e2d/); and the Special Court of Sierra Leone ('SCSL') Statute, 16 January 2002, Article 4(c) (https://www.legal-tools.org/doc/aa0e20/).

an alleged child soldier's age should be to the advantage of the accused. Legally speaking, this intuition is uncontroversial as it is clearly in line with fundamental principles of the criminal procedure such as *in dubio pro reo* ('when in doubt for the accused') and *in dubio mitius* ('more lenient in cases of doubt'). However, in line with the beyond reasonable doubt standard, following the Rome Statute of the International Criminal Court (ICC), Article 66(3),[35] it is equally clear that the accused shall not have the advantage of virtually *any* doubt, but only the *reasonable* doubt, neither more nor less.[36] Certainly, the assessment of what constitutes reasonable doubt in a single case falls within the discretion of the judges[37] and given the inherently open character of this standard it is impossible to say exactly what should be considered reasonable or unreasonable doubt.[38] Simultaneously, it is essential to promote a uniform application of the law, so that like cases are treated alike in practice and that predictability and legal security are promoted in a more general sense.[39] While there are no

---

[35] While the ICC Statute describes this standard as "beyond reasonable doubt" in English, the French translation is "audelà de tout doute raisonnable.'and in Spanish 'más allá de toda duda razonable'. Also, in other contexts different English versions are used, including "beyond all reasonable doubt" and "beyond a reasonable doubt". For historical perspectives on this topic see, for example, Barbara J. Shapiro, *Beyond Reasonable Doubt and Probable Cause, Historical Perspectives on the Anglo-American Law of Evidence*, University of California Press, Berkeley, 1991.

[36] This was addressed specifically by the International Criminal Tribunal for the former Yugoslavia ('ICTY'), *The Prosecutor v. Duško Tadić*, Appeals Chamber, Judgement, 15 July 1999, IT-94-1-A, p. 77 (https://www.legal-tools.org/doc/8efc3a/). The Trial Chamber had acquitted the accused of certain killings because they "may have been" committed by other perpetrators as a "bare possibility" and other elements "could suggest" different conclusions. On appeal, the Appeals Chamber agreed with the prosecutor that the participation of the accused in the killings was the only reasonable inference from the available evidence and no witness had suggested an alternative hypothesis. *Ibid.*, p. 79. For more on this, see Xabier Agirre Aranburu, "The Contribution of Analysis to the Quality Control in Criminal Investigation", Chapter 3 of this volume.

[37] See, for instance, Jon Newman, "Quantifying the Standard of Proof Beyond Reasonable Doubt: A Comment on Three Comments", in *Law, Probability and Risk*, 2006, vol. 5, pp. 267–69. Quite a few scholars have attempted to quantify this evidentiary standard or in other ways understand it numerically, see, for example, Svein Magnussen *et al.*, "The Probability of Guilt in Criminal Cases: Are People Aware of Being "Beyond Reasonable Doubt"?", in *Applied Cognitive Psychology*, 2013, vol. 28, no. 2, pp. 196–203.

[38] For more on this topic see, for example, Larry Laudan, "Is Reasonable Doubt Reasonable?", in *Legal Theory*, 2003, vol. 9, no. 4, pp. 295–331.

[39] There are quite a few critical reviews challenging the notion that like cases are treated alike in practice, see, for instance, Gerald Seniuk, "Systemic Incoherence in Criminal Justice: Failing to Treat Like Cases Alike", in *Canadian Bar Review*, 2006, vol. 93, no. 3, pp.

general answers as to the meaning of the BARD standard neither in criminal law generally, nor in relation to the age element specifically, it may be helpful to think of the BARD standard in terms of *diagnostic accuracy*.

The term diagnostic accuracy is commonly used in for instance the medical field as an expression of the extent to which a result of a medical test can be trusted. More specifically, diagnostic accuracy refers to whether a test accurately and fully identifies those carrying a disease as carrying the disease, while simultaneously excluding accurately and fully those who are tested for the disease but do not carry the disease.[40] Hence, diagnostic accuracy is divided into two components: *sensitivity* and *specificity*. The sensitivity of a measurement instrument is the probability that a diagnostic test or instrument will be positive in persons who have a disease or condition.[41] Sensitivity is also referred to as true positive rate. Tests or instruments that have high sensitivity *are more likely to rule in, or accurately confirm, the disease or condition* when the disease or condition exists.[42] By contrast, specificity is the ability of a measurement instrument to correctly identify persons without a disease or condition. In statistical terms, this is the probability that diagnostic tests or instruments will give negative results in individuals who do not have the disease or condition.[43] Tests or instruments that have high specificity are able to *more accurately rule out a disease or condition.* Specificity is often referred to as the true negative rate, meaning that a test is negative in persons without the disease or condition.[44]

In the medical field, the importance of reasoning in terms of diagnostic accuracy is fairly straightforward since diagnostic errors (false positives and false negatives) can lead to inaccurate treatment, patient harm, and suffering both on a human level and in terms of financial costs due to

---

747–92 as well as questions being asked about what cases really are to be considered alike, see, for instance, Kenneth I. Winston, "On Treating Like Cases Alike", in *California Law Review*, 1974, vol. 62, no. 1, pp. 1–39.

[40] Stephen B. Hulley, *Designing Clinical Research*, Wolters Kluwer, Philadelphia, 2007.

[41] See, for instance, *ibid.*

[42] Stacey Plichta *et al.*, *Munro's Statistical Methods for Health Care Research*, Wolters Kluwer, Philadelphia, 2005; MA Xiaoye *et al.*, "Statistical methods for multivariate meta-analysis of diagnostic tests: an overview and tutorial", in *Statistical Methods in Medical Research*, 2016, vol. 25, no. 4, pp. 1596–619.

[43] Plichta *et al.*, 2005, see above note 42; MA *et al.*, 2016, see above note 42.

[44] Hulley, 2007, see above note 40.

law suits, and so on. Empirical research indicates that physicians' over-confidence in the own ability to reach accurate diagnosis is a contributing factor to diagnostic errors.[45] Thus, there is a potential issue with *diagnostic calibration*, that is, the relationship between the diagnostic accuracy and confidence in that accuracy.[46] Diagnostic errors may occur when the relationship between accuracy and confidence is miscalibrated or misaligned so that confidence is higher than it should be.[47] It is unknown exactly how physicians' confidence relate to the accuracy of their diagnosis, and how common this problem is,[48] but there are indications that physicians, fairly regularly, are overconfident, that is, they are more confident than they are accurate.[49]

Although age evidence may come from actors in a range of disciplines or fields, it is the legal actors, and ultimately the judges, who integrate and draw conclusions from the evidence. In child soldiering cases, these legal actors use the evidence they collected and/or had presented for

---

[45] Eta Berner and Mark L. Graber, "Overconfidence as a Cause of Diagnostic Error in Medicine", in *The American Journal of Medicine*, 2008, vol. 121, no. 5, pp. 22–23.

[46] *Ibid.*

[47] *Ibid.*

[48] The more specific relationship between diagnostic accuracy and confidence is discussed by, for instance, Donald A.B. Lindberg, "Introduction", in *The American Journal of Medicine*, 2008, vol. 121, no. 5, S1. If confidence and accuracy were perfectly aligned, then lower levels of confidence could cue physicians to deliberately seek diagnostic help and/or conduct additional tests.

[49] Daniel P. Davis *et al.*, "The Association between Operator Confidence and Accuracy of Ultrasonography Performed by Novice Emergency Physicians", in *Journal of Emergency Medicine*, 2005, vol. 29, no. 3, pp. 259–64; Charles Friedman *et al.*, "Are Clinicians Correct When They Believe they are Correct? Implications for Medical Decision Support", in *Studies in Health Technology and Informatics*, 2001, vol. 84, no. 1, pp. 454–58; Charles P. Friedman *et al.*, "Do Physicians Know When Their Diagnoses are Correct? Implications for Decision Support and Error Reduction?", in *Journal of General Internal Medicine*, 2005, vol. 20, no. 4, pp. 334–39; Matej Podbregar *et al.*, "Should we Confirm Our Clinical Diagnosis Certainty by Autopsies?", in *Intensive Care Medicine*, 2001, vol. 27, pp. 1750–55; J. Yazbek *et al.*, "Confidence of Expert Ultrasound Operators in Making a Diagnosis of Adnexal Tumor: Effect on Diagnostic Accuracy and Interobserver Agreement", in *Ultrasound in Obstetrics and Gynaecology*, 2010, vol. 35, no. 1, pp. 89–93. See also Saul J. Weiner and Alan Schwartz, "Contextual Errors in Medical Decision Making: Overlooked and Understudied", in *Academic Medicine*, 2016, vol. 91, no. 5, pp. 657–62. These authors present empirical data suggesting that whereas physicians provided error-free care in 73 per cent of uncomplicated encounters, their care was appropriate in only 38 per cent of biomedically complex encounters, 22 per cent of contextually complex encounters and just 9 per cent of the combined biomedically and contextually complicated encounters.

---

them to categorize an alleged child soldier as either having reached a chronological age of 15 years or not. This process has similarities with how a physician categorizes a patient as either having a disease or condition or not. As such, just like physicians, legal actors may benefit from reasoning in terms of diagnostic accuracy. More specifically, the diagnostic accuracy in relation to the age element in child soldiering cases would be the extent to which the 'test', that is, the process of determining age, *accurately and fully identifies all those younger than 15 years as being under 15 years*, as well as the extent to which the process is capable of *accurately and fully excluding those aged 15 years or older*. A perfect diagnostic accuracy would require that the process is fully *sensitive*; all those under 15 years are identified and legally classified as under 15 years, while the process is also fully *specific*: all those 15 years or older are legally classified as 15 years or older.[50] Thus, there are four possible outcomes of an age estimation and this entails two correct and two incorrect outcomes, see Table 1.

The two correct outcomes are:

- A true negative: an individual 15 years or older is estimated to be 15 years or older; and

- A true positive: an individual younger than 15 years is estimated to be younger than 15 years.

The two incorrect outcomes are:

- A false positive: an individual 15 years or older is estimated to be younger than 15 years; and

- A false negative: an individual younger than 15 years is estimated to be 15 years or older.

---

[50] The diagnostic accuracy or predictive value of age estimations can also be understood and illustrated using the so-called *signal detection theory*, see David Green and John Swets, *Signal Detection Theory and Psychophysics*, John Wiley, 1996. Most of the early research relating to signal detection theory aimed to determine how humans distinguish a 'signal' (more specifically a radar signal) from 'noise'. Identifying a signal among noise would then be similar to identifying someone younger than 15 years among others who are 15 years and above. In the process of identifying a 'signal', it seems humans have different subjective thresholds, as some want to feel more confident than others before calling something a signal.

Table 1. Four possible outcomes of age estimations in child soldering cases.

	Real Chronological Age	
Estimated Chronological Age	*15 or older*	*Younger than 15*
15 or older	True negative	False negative
Younger than 15	False positive	True positive

Since tests can usually not guarantee both sensitivity and specificity simultaneously there are often trade-offs between the two in practice. In this trade-off, whether sensitivity or specificity is prioritized is strongly context dependent. Since reasonable doubts should be to the advantage of the accused, this seems to imply that in the criminal context, specificity, the ability to accurately rule out those who are over 15 years, is somewhat prioritized over sensitivity. If evidentiary thresholds are set or applied in a way that requires a lot from the evidence, false positives are unlikely but there is also a substantial risk of false negatives. Hence, constantly resorting to the burden of proof in criminal cases may make criminal justice inefficient as it is likely that there will always be some doubt (reasonable or not) in relation to the question of chronological age.

It can be discussed whether and to what extent evidentiary difficulties stemming from, for example, the inherent uncertainties in forensic age estimations are relevant in this context. There is no general answer as to how scientific uncertainty relates to the BARD standard.[51] It can also be noted that the European Court of Human Rights ('ECHR') have approved of presumptions that are in fact to the disadvantage of the accused, since the crime in question otherwise would result in unreasonable evidentiary difficulties. For instance, in *Salabiaku v France*[52] and the related case *Pham Hoang v France*,[53] the ECHR considered a French rule according to which a person who has passed the customs with illegal goods is presumed to have had intent to smuggle the goods. The ECHR did not con-

---

[51] For more on this topic see, for example, Charles Weiss, "Expressing Scientific Uncertainty", in *Law, Probability and Risk*, 2003, vol. 2, pp. 25–46.

[52] European Court of Human Rights ('ECHR'), *Salabiaku v. France*, Judgment, 7 October 1988, ECLI:CE:ECHR:1988:1007JUD001051983 (https://www.legal-tools.org/doc/af3734/) ('ECHR Salabiaku Judgment').

[53] ECHR, *Pham Hoang v. France*, Judgment, 25 September 1992, ECLI:CE:ECHR:1992:0925JUD001319187 (https://www.legal-tools.org/doc/hxjbrh/) ('ECHR Pham Hoang Judgment').

sider this rule contradictory to the presumption of innocence while it added that Article 6(2) requires states to confine legal presumptions "within reasonable limits which take into account the importance of what is at stake and maintain the rights of the defense".[54] In asylum law, the scientific uncertainty of age assessments have resulted in a *presumption of minor age* which benefits the individual whose age is being estimated[55] and, in civil cases, evidentiary thresholds for establishing age elements are lower.[56] While age estimations for the purpose of deciding someone's criminal guilt are clearly different, it seems reasonable to include considerations like these into the interpretation of what constitutes reasonable doubt regarding someone's chronological age.

---

[54] ECHR Salabiaku Judgment, para. 28, see above note 52. These reasonable limits had not been trespassed since the French Courts had taken into consideration circumstances indicating that the defendants had in fact acted unintentionally. Thus, the presumption was rebuttable. Similarly, a presumption that the owner of a car is guilty of traffic offences committed using the car, was not considered a breach in, for example, ECHR, *Falk v. Netherlands*, Decision, 19 October 2004, ECLI:CE:ECHR:2004:1019DEC006627301 (https://www.legal-tools.org/doc/jsmie5/) and ECHR, *Krumpholz v. Austria*, Judgment, 18 March 2010, ECLI:CE:ECHR:2010:0318JUD001320105 (https://www.legal-tools.org/doc/vn3bnz/), since the defence had been able to offer evidence in disproof. Neither the French rule according to which defamatory statements were presumed to be in bad faith was considered a breach, in ECHR, *Radio France and others v. France*, Judgment, 30 March 2004, ECLI:CE:ECHR:2004:0330JUD005398400 (https://www.legal-tools.org/doc/ea66ee/).

[55] The ECHR has stated, for instance, in *Yazgül Yilmaz v. Turkey*, Judgment, 1 February 2011, ECLI:CE:ECHR:2011:0201JUD003636906 (https://www.legal-tools.org/doc/7bl57z/), that due to the scientific inaccuracy and unreliability of age assessments methods, age assessment results have to be presented with a margin of error. Furthermore, the Court has emphasized that due the presumption of minor age and the best interest of the child, the margin of error should always be applied in favour of the person who has undergone age assessment. In addition, this individual shall be treated as a child until any further evidence is provided to substantiate the age of the person. It can of course be discussed whether a presumption of minor age is always to the advantage of the examined individual. For instance, children may claim to be adults to be allowed to work, to marry or because they consider themselves to be adults responsible for the well-being of siblings, and so on. See EASO, 2018, p. 17, see above note 19.

[56] For more on this topic see, for instance, Cercel and Scurtu, 2015, pp. 297–304, see above note 10 and LOO Wee Ling, "Full Contractual Capacity: Use of Age for Conferment of Capacity", in *Singapore Journal of Legal Studies*, 2010, pp. 328–51. This delimitation does not mean that age estimations are only relevant in relation to such charges of war crimes. It can be noted that also other charges refer to 'children' such as forcibly transferring children of the group to another group, as part of a genocide, ICC Statute, Article 6(e), see above note 18.

6.4. Age Estimations in Child Soldiering Cases

6.4.1. Method

The purpose of this as well as the following sections is to apply the suggested framework to age estimations in child soldiering cases. To this end, an empirical review of Court cases was conducted to identify the cases dealing with child soldiering charges, as defined by Article 8(b)(xxvi) and (e)(vii) of the ICC Statute and Article 4 of the SCSL Statute. This resulted in the identification of 11 cases, 4 from the SCSL and 7 from the ICC, all of which are outlined in Table 2. For the more specific question of what age evidence was used, only cases which had resulted in at least a first judgment, whether this judgment was appealed or not, were included. This was in total 8 cases, 4 from the SCSL and 4 from the ICC, see Table 3. In appealed cases which had already been handled by two instances, both of the judgments were examined. Among the cases outlined in Table 3, the ICC Lubanga case entailed the widest range of age evidence including forensic, video, oral and documentary evidence. The Lubanga case was also the only case which dealt exclusively with child soldiering charges,[57] enabling a more in-depth evaluation of the age evidence specifically. Therefore, in Table 4, the age evidence available for each of the 19 alleged child soldiers in the Lubanga case is outlined. This includes different kinds of contradictions as regards age, namely between different evidence types (external), between different items of the same evidence type (internal) and other types of contradictions, as well as the Court's conclusions.

The discussion of challenges (validity, reliability and biasability) and opportunities attributable to the different types of age evidence (Section 6.5.) was based on a literature review. This entailed database searches for relevant literature on age estimations based on forensic evidence, doc-

---

[57] For the specifics of the charges, as well as the confirmation of the charges, ICC, *The Prosecutor v. Thomas Lubanga Dyilo*, Pre-Trial Chamber, Decision on the Confirmation of Charges, 29 January 2007, ICC-01/04-01/06-803-tEN, pp. 6–7 (https://www.legal-tools. org/doc/b7ac4f/) ('Lubanga Decision on the Confirmation of Charges'). Mr. Lubanga was charged as a co-perpetrator jointly with other FPLC officers and UPC members and supporters for conscripting and enlisting children under the age of 15 years into the FPLC military wing of the UPC since September 2002, and using them to participate actively in hostilities. The Prosecution submitted that the crimes occurred in the context of an armed conflict not of an international character, and this was also the conclusion reached by the Trial as well as Appeals Chambers.

umentary evidence, oral evidence and video evidence or physical appearance.

6.4.2. Results

This section outlines the results of the review of cases which involved allegations of conscripting, enlisting or using child solders. As noted below Table 2 there are also other more or less well documented both historical and contemporary examples of child soldiering crimes worldwide which have not been considered suitable for this analysis (see more below).

Table 2. Cases involving charges of conscripting, enlisting and/or using child soldiers by court in chronological order (by date of last verdict with ongoing cases last).[58]

Court	Case	Time	Place	Charges	Status
SCSL	BRIMA, KAMARA and KANU 'The AFRC case'	1996– 2000	Sierra Leone	C, E &/ U	All three convicted for C &/ U[59] in 2006. Upheld on appeal 22 February 2008.[60]
SCSL	NORMAN, FOFANA and KONDEWA 'The CDF case'	1996– 1999	Sierra Leone	E/U	Norman deceased before end of trial, proceedings terminated against him in May 2007.[61]

---

[58] Under "Charges" and "Status", "C" = Conscripting, "E" = Enlisting, "U" = Using, "&" = and, "/" = or, "&/" = and/or. The "Status" column refers to the outcome and present status in relation to child soldiering charges exclusively while this was often different in relation to other charges, that is, the defendant was acquitted for child soldiering charges but convicted for other charges that fall outside the scope of this research.

[59] SCSL, *The Prosecutor v. Alex Tamba Brima, Brima Bazzy Kamara and Santigie Borbor Kanu*, Trial Chamber, Judgment, 20 June 2007, SCSL-2004-16-T, pp. 569–72 ('SCSL Brima *et al*. Trial Chamber Judgment') (https://www.legal-tools.org/doc/87ef08/).

[60] It can be noted that neither of the defendants appealed specifically in relation to the ages of the alleged child soldiers but rather on points of location of child recruitment, see SCSL, *The Prosecutor v. Alex Tamba Brima, Brima Bazzy Kamara and Santigie Borbor Kanu*, Appeals Chamber, Judgment, 22 February 2008, SCSL-2004-16-A, pp. 13–19, paras. 27–49 ('SCSL Brima *et al*. Appeals Chamber Judgment') (https://www.legal-tools.org/doc/4420ef/).

[61] SCSL, *The Prosecutor v. Sam Hinga Norman, Moinina Fofana and Allieu Kondewa*, Trial Chamber, Judgment, 2 August 2007, SCSL-04-14-T, pp. 1–2 ('SCSL Norman *et al*. Trial Chamber Judgment') (https://www.legal-tools.org/doc/025645/). The Trial against Norman began in June 2004. Norman died in hospital on 22 February 2007, after the completion of

					Fofana acquitted and Kondewa convicted for E/U in 2007.[62]
					Kondewa's conviction overturned on Appeal, 28 May 2008.[63]
SCSL	SESAY, KALLON, GBAO 'The RUF case'	1996–2000	Sierra Leone	C/E/U	Sesay and Kallon convicted for planning U,[64] Gbao acquitted in 2009.[65]
					Upheld on appeal 26 October 2009.[66]

trial but before pronouncement of Judgment. According to the indictment as well as the SCSL, Norman was the "National Coordinator" of the CDF while Fofana was "Director of War" and Kondewa was the CDF's "High Priest" (*Ibid.*, p. 1). Norman was first indicted in March 2003 and Fofana and Kondewa were indicted in June 2003. In February 2004, the Trial Chamber ordered a joint trial of the three accused. For more on the timeline see Residual Special Court for Sierra Leone ('RSCSL'), "The CDF Trial" (available on its web site).

62 SCSL Norman *et al.* Trial Chamber Judgment, see above note 61.

63 SCSL, *The Prosecutor v. Sam Hinga Norman, Moinina Fofana and Allieu Kondewa*, Appeals Chamber, Judgment, 28 May 2008, SCSL-04-14-A ('SCSL Norman *et al.* Appeals Chamber Judgment') (https://www.legal-tools.org/doc/b31512/).

64 Both Sesay and Kallon were found guilty for planning the use of persons under the age of 15 to participants actively in hostilities in Kailahun, Kono and Bombali District between 1997 and September 2000, under the Statute of the Special Court for Sierra Leone, Article 6(1), but not for personal commission, see SCSL, *The Prosecutor v. Issa Hassan Sesay, Morrie Kallon, Augustine Gbao*, Trial Chamber, Judgment, 2 March 2009, SCSL-04-15-T, paras. 2230–37 ('SCSL Sesay *et al.* Trial Chamber Judgment') (https://www.legal-tools.org/doc/7f05b7/).

65 *Ibid.*

66 SCSL, *The Prosecutor v. Issa Hassan Sesay, Morris Kallon and Augustine Gbao*, Appeals Chamber, Judgment, 26 October 2009, SCSL-04-15-A (https://www.legal-tools.org/doc/133b48/). In their appeals, both Sesay and Kallon claimed that the Trial Chamber erred in finding them liable for planning the use of child soldiers since their acts did not amount to planning (substantial contribution to the crime). The acts in question were, for Sesay, for instance, ordering the training of child soldiers, receiving reports on such training, personally visiting the Camp Lion training camp, addressing and threatening the child soldier conscripts there, see *ibid.*, pp. 272–74. For Kallon's reasoning in these parts see *ibid.*, pp. 324–28. The Appeals Chambers dismissed these grounds for appeal both in relation to Sesay and Kallon. The Trial Chamber had acquitted Gbao since, while it had found that Gbao loaded former child soldiers onto a truck and removed them from the Interim Care Centre in Makeni in May 2000, this was insufficient to constitute a substantial contribution to the widespread system of child conscription or the consistent pattern of using children to

SCSL	TAYLOR	1996–2000	Sierra Leone	C, E & U	Convicted for C/E/U in 2012.[67] Upheld on appeal 26 September 2013.[68]
ICC	KATANGA	2003	DRC	U	Acquitted 7 March 2014.[69] Parties discontinued their appeals.
ICC	LUBANGA	2002–2003	DRC	C, E & U	Convicted for C, E & U in 2012.[70] Upheld on appeal 1 December 2014.[71]
ICC	NGUDJOLO	2003	DRC	U	Acquitted in 2012.[72] Upheld on appeal 7 April 2015.[73]
ICC	NTAGANDA	2002–2003	DRC	C, E & U	Convicted for C, E & U in 2019.[74] Now in the appellate phase.[75]

actively participate in hostilities. While the acquittal was appealed by the Prosecution, its grounds for appeal were dismissed in this regard (*ibid.*, pp. 414–23).

[67] SCSL, *The Prosecutor v. Charles Ghankay Taylor*, Trial Chamber, Judgment, 18 May 2012, SCSL-03-01-T ('SCSL Taylor Trial Chamber Judgment') (https://www.legal-tools.org/doc/8075e7/).

[68] SCSL, *The Prosecutor v. Charles Ghankay Taylor*, Appeals Chamber, Judgment, 26 September 2013, SCSL-03-01-A (https://www.legal-tools.org/doc/3e7be5/).

[69] ICC, Situation in the Democratic Republic of the Congo, *The Prosecutor v. Germain Katanga*, Trial Chamber, Judgment, 7 March 2014, ICC-01/04-01/07-3436-tENG ('Katanga Trial Chamber Judgment') (https://www.legal-tools.org/doc/f74b4f/).

[70] Lubanga Trial Chamber Judgment, see above note 4.

[71] Lubanga Appeals Chamber Judgment, see above note 3.

[72] ICC, Situation in the Democratic Republic of the Congo, *The Prosecutor v. Mathieu Ngudjolo Chui*, Trial Chamber, Judgment, 18 December 2012, ICC-01/04-02/12-3-tENG ('Ngudjolo Chui Trial Chamber Judgment') (https://www.legal-tools.org/doc/2c2cde/).

[73] ICC, *The Prosecutor v. Mathieu Ngudjolo Chui*, Appeals Chamber, Judgment, 7 April 2015, ICC-01/04-02/12-271-Corr (https://www.legal-tools.org/doc/efb111/).

[74] ICC, Situation in the Democratic Republic of the Congo, *The Prosecutor v. Bosco Ntaganda*, Trial Chamber, Judgment, 8 July 2019, ICC-01/04-02/06-2359 ('Ntaganda Trial Chamber Judgment') (https://www.legal-tools.org/doc/80578a/).

[75] The next session is scheduled for 12 October 2020, see ICC, "Ntaganda Case" (available on its web site).

ICC	ONGWEN	2002–2005	Uganda	C & U	Trial phase, Trial Chamber now deliberating.[76]
ICC	YEKATOM and NGAÏSSONA	2013–2014	CAR	C, E & U	Charges confirmed in relation to YEKATOM 11 December 2019.[77]
ICC	KONY and OTTI	2002–2004	Uganda	E	Execution of arrest warrants pending.[78]

As suggested above, Table 2 does not entail a complete list of all the historical and contemporary examples of child soldiering crimes or suspicions worldwide. This is because many of those situations never resulted in Court cases and for those that did, the focus was not on child soldiering, let alone age estimations of alleged child soldiers. However, for the purpose of a more complete record, some of these examples will be outlined briefly below.

While the Extraordinary Chamber in the Courts of Cambodia ('ECCC') was tasked with bringing the surviving members of the Khmer Rouge to justice and child recruitment was widespread during the late 1970's regime,[79] no charges relating to child recruitment were brought

---

[76] Closing statements took place from 10 to 12 March 2020, see ICC, "Ongwen Case" (available on its web site).

[77] ICC, Situation in the Central African Republic II, *The Prosecutor v. Alfred Yekatom and Patrice-Edouard Ngaïssona*, Pre-Trial Chamber, Decision on the Confirmation of Charges against Alfred Yekatom and Patrice-Edouard Ngaïssona, 11 December 2019, ICC-01/14-01/18-403-Red-Corr (https://www.legal-tools.org/doc/314uw9/). However, the initial charges included individual criminal responsibility for the child soldiering crimes both for Yekatom and Ngaïssona, see ICC, The Prosecutor v. Alfred Yekatom and Patrice-Edouard Ngaïssona, Pre-Trial Chamber, Public Redacted Version of "Document Containing the Charges", 18 September 2019, ICC-01-14-01/18-282-AnxB1-Red, pp. 11–12 (https://www.legal-tools.org/doc/fdgouu/).

[78] Hence, Kony and Otti remain at large, 10 years after the issuance of the warrants of arrest, see ICC, Situation in Uganda, *The Prosecutor v. Joseph Kony and Vincent Otti*, ICC-02/04-01/05. Because of this, on 6 February 2015, Pre-Trial Chamber II severed the proceedings against Dominic Ongwen from the case against Kony and Otty: Decision Severing the Case Against Dominic Ongwen, ICC-02/04-01/05-424 (https://www.legal-tools.org/doc/16fb19/). Dominic Ongwen was surrendered to the ICC's custody on 16 January 2015. For more on this see, for example, ICC, "Kony et al. Case", Case Information Sheet (available on its web site).

[79] Cambodian League for the Promotion and Defense of Human Rights ('LICADHO'), *Child Soldiers in Cambodia*, Briefing Paper, June 1998.

before this Court.[80] There were reports of children as young as five years being trained while the majority of soldiers were up to 17 years.[81] It is likely that omission of such charges was to avoid claims of retrospective law-making,[82] since child soldiering was not specifically criminalized in Cambodian national legislation at the time of interest.[83] Similarly, in Vietnam, during the Vietnam war, children under 15 years referred to as 'tiny guerrilla' were learning guerrilla warfare tactics and were also involved in armed struggle.[84] Also, some evidence has emerged of the use of child soldiers in Laos, by Hmong armed opposition groups.[85] Similarly,

---

[80] Like the SCSL, the Extraordinary Chambers in the Courts of Cambodia ('ECCC') is a hybrid institution, which was established in 2006. The interested reader can have a look at the following cases which do not entail any child soldiering charges or mentioning of child soldiers: ECCC, *The Prosecutor v. Kaing Guek Eav*, Supreme Court Chamber, Appeal Judgment, 3 February 2012, 001/18-07-2007-ECCC/SC (https://www.legal-tools.org/doc/681bad/); ECCC, *The Prosecutor v. Khieu Samphan and Nuon Chea*, Judgment, 7 August 2014, 002/19-09-2007/ECCC/TC (https://www.legal-tools.org/doc/4888de/).

[81] LICADHO, 1998, see above note 79.

[82] For more on this see Julie McBride, *The War Crime of Child Soldier Recruitment*, Springer, p. 106. The recruitment and use of children as soldiers were not specifically criminalized in national legislation. Only in July 2004 did Cambodia ratify the Optional Protocol to the Convention on the Rights of the Child on the involvement of children in armed conflict, referring in its declaration to Article 42 of the Law on General Statutes for the Military Personnel of the Royal Cambodian Armed Forces, which set 18 as the minimum age for contractual-service military personnel, see "Optional Protocol to the Convention on the Rights of the Child on the involvement of children in armed conflict", sect. "Declarations and Reservations" (available on United Nations Treaty Collection's web site). However, it has been acknowledged that recruitment of children as soldiers and cadres was very common in the Khmer Rouge period (1975–79), see, for example, LICADHO, 1998, see above note 79.

[83] Only in July 2004 did Cambodia ratify the Optional Protocol, referring in its declaration to Article 42 of the Law on General Statutes for the Military Personnel of the Royal Cambodian Armed Forces, which set 18 as the minimum age for contractual-service military personnel, see "Optional Protocol to the Convention on the Rights of the Child on the involvement of children in armed conflict", sect. "Declarations and Reservations" (available on United Nations Treaty Collection's web site).

[84] For instance, children were in the Nguyễn Văn Trỗi Youth Group in the Quảng Nam province, see *Việt Nam*, 1969, no. 141, 6, p. 29 (British Library, SU216). Many of these children were decorated with awards and "glorious titles" such "Iron Font Children" or "Valiant Destroyer of the Yanks", see *ibid*. See also Brenda M. Boyle and Jeehyun Lim (eds.), *Looking Back on the Vietnam War: Twenty-first-Century Perspectives*, Rutgers University Press, 2016.

[85] This included evidence from journalists who visited Laos clandestinely and photographed children with guns in jungle areas, see, for example, Andrew Perrin, "Welcome to the Jungle", *TIME Asia Magazine*, 5 May 2003 (available on its web site). In 2003, Amnesty In-

a Sri Lankan rebel group, the Liberation Tigers of Tamil Eelam ('LTTE') made extensive use of children in its war against the Sinhalese government, recruiting more than seven hundred child soldiers during 2003 alone.[86] Children have also played active roles in armed conflicts in Kashmir, the Philippines and Burma/Myanmar.[87] In Afghanistan, child fighters were involved in the successive insurgencies against the Soviets, the Taliban, and the American and European Coalition forces.[88]

In Rwanda, child soldiering cases were fairly well documented but never dealt with by the International Criminal Tribunal for Rwanda ('ICTR') since this tribunal was more concerned with adjudicating high-level conspiracies to commit genocide.[89] Instead, adolescent children were prosecuted and convicted by the domestic Courts of Rwanda, including the Gacaca Courts,[90] even though there seem to have been doubts regard-

---

ternational urged opposition groups not to permit children to participate in combat, see Coalition to Stop the Use of Child Soldiers, "Laos", in *Child Soldiers: Global Report 2004*, 2004, p. 183 (https://www.legal-tools.org/doc/f96pr8/).

[86] United Nations Children's Fund ('UNICEF'), *The State of the World's Children*, 1996. See also Chris Hobbs *et al.*, "Conscription of Children in Armed Conflict: A Form of Child Abuse. A Study of 19 Former Child Soldiers", in *Child Abuse Review*, 2001, vol. 10, no. 5; Alejandro Sanchez Nieto, "A War of Attrition: Sri Lanka and the Tamil Tigers", in *Small Wars and Insurgencies*, 2009, vol. 19, no. 4, pp. 573–87, Harendra de Silva, "The Use of Child Soldiers in War with Special Reference to Sri Lanka", in *Paediatrics and International Child Health*, 2013, vol. 33, no. 4, pp. 273–80; Alcinda Manuel Honwana, *Child Soldiers in Africa*, University of Pennsylvania Press, Philadelphia, 2006.

[87] For more on this see, for example, *ibid.*

[88] *Ibid.*

[89] Sara Rakita, *Rwanda, Lasting Wounds: Consequences of Genocide and War for Rwanda's Children*, Human Rights Watch, New York, 2003, p. 18.

[90] Rwanda was the first country to hold individuals accountable for genocide committed as minors, see *ibid.* According to the Rwandan Penal Code a minor is defined as an individual aged 14 to 18 years when the crime was committed, see The Rwandan Penal Code, 18 August 1977, Article 77 (https://www.legal-tools.org/doc/71507b/). This means that children under the age of 14 cannot be held criminally responsible but can instead be placed in rehabilitation centres. In December 1996, the first trails of genocide suspects began in the national Courts. To deal with the large number of individuals charged with genocide, the Government established the Gacaca Courts, which, unlike the national courts, rely on traditional processes of addressing disputes within the community as well as national law. For more on this see Constance Morrill, "Reconciliation and the Gacaca: The Perceptions and Peace-Building Potential of Rwandan Youth Detainees", in *Online Journal of Peace and Conflict Resolution*, 2004, vol. 1, no. 1, pp. 1–66, citing, *inter alia*, statistics originally from the Rwandan Ministry of Justice, see "Q & A: Rwanda's Long Search for Justice", 18 December 2008, *BBC News* (available on its web site). Of the 121,500 people in detention at the end of 1999, 4,454 were children, according to the Report on the Situation of Human

ing their ages.[91] Traditionally, such doubts should have been to their advantage as criminal defendants.[92] Also, the use of child soldiers has been well documented in countries like Mozambique and Angola[93] as well as Algeria, Ethiopia, Eritrea and Sudan.[94]

There are examples also from other parts of the world. In Indonesia, the Special Panels for Serious Crimes ('SPSC') in Dili, East Timor, allowed for the prosecution of individuals younger than 15 years following mass political violence in 1999 that involved children in armed groups.[95] There are also a few examples of children being convicted for, for exam-

---

Rights in Rwanda, UN Doc. E/CN.4/2000/41, 25 February 2000 (https://www.legal-tools.org/doc/tsm2j8/). The majority of the genocide suspects were dealt with by these more informal jurisdictions.

[91] For more on this see Jastine Barret's field research in Rwanda, Jastine C. Barett, "What a Difference a Day Makes: Young Perpetrators of Genocide in Rwanda", in *University of Cambridge Faculty of Law*, 2014, Research Paper No. 24, pp. 1–31, noting that this research defines someone younger than 18 years as a child. Barret points out that the Rwandan birth certificates usually only contained the year of birth but not the exact date and also that many documents were destroyed during the genocide. As such, the Courts were sometimes unable to verify a defendant's age.

[92] Through field research in the Rwandan Courts, Barett finds that the accused were not always given the benefit of doubt, see *ibid.*, p. 6. For example, a defendant's file stated 1980 as year of birth but the prosecutor argued that his sources had confirmed the year of birth as 1975. Despite doubt over his age, the Court continued to hear witnesses without investigating further. In another case, an accused had two conflicting pieces of evidence; a census form stating 1974 as the year of birth and an identity card showing 1976. The Court relied on the census form as this pre-dated the identity card and the accused was sentenced as an adult.

[93] In Mozambique and Angola large numbers of children were used as soldiers by rebels and government forces. RENAMO exploited at least 1,000 child soldiers some as young as six years old. In Angola, a 1995 survey found that 36 per cent of children had accompanied or supported soldiers and 7 per cent of Angolan children had fired at somebody, see UNICEF, *The State of World's Children 1996: Children in War*, 1996 and Honwana, 2006, see above note 86.

[94] *Ibid.*

[95] See United Nations Transitional Administration in East Timor ('UNTAET'), Regulation 2001/25 on The Amendment of UNTAET, 14 September 2001, UNTAET/REG/2001/25 (https://www.legal-tools.org/doc/b35f1b/), UNTAET, Regulation No. 2000/11 on the Organization of Courts in East Timor, 6 March 2000, UNTAET/REG/2000/11 (https://www.legal-tools.org/doc/2bedb8/) and UNTAET, Regulation No. 2000/30 on the Transitional Rules of Criminal Procedure, 25 September 2000, UNTAET/REG/2000/30 (https://www.legal-tools.org/doc/f3e141/). However, the Special Panels for Serious Crimes ('SPSC') stipulated a specific legal regime for offenders under 16 years.

ple, war crimes by military tribunals,[96] while the mixed State Court in Bosnia and Herzegovina ('BiH') allowed prosecution of individuals over 15 years at the time of the offence.[97] In Latin America, children have been directly involved in civil wars since the 1980s, for instance in Peru,[98] Guatemala, El Salvador, Nicaragua[99] and more recently Colombia.[100] In fact, already the youth factions of the Nazi Party in Germany, the *Hitler-jugend*[101] and the *Deutsches Jungvolk in der Hitler Jugend*[102] consisted of boys aged 10 to 18 years.[103]

For more on any of these cases, the reader is referred to the cited literature. In the following, these cases will not be further considered. Table 3 only includes those cases from Table 2 which have resulted in a

---

[96] A prominent as well as controversial example is the case of Omar Khadr, who was the first child to be prosecuted and tried before a military tribunal for alleged war crimes, after his transfer to Guantanamo Bay, Cuba, in September 2002, see, for example, Chris Lewis, "Abu Ykhiel to Guantanamo Bay and Beyond: The Paper Trials of Omar Khadr 2002-2017", in *Social Identities: War and Visual Technologies*, 2019, vol. 25, no. 4, pp. 476–95. There are also examples from the DRC. For instance, Amnesty International reports about a 14-year old child soldier who was tried by a military court for murder and executed 30 min later, see Amnesty International, "Democratic Republic of Congo: Massive Violations Kill Human Decency", 31 May 2001, AFR 62/011/2000, p. 1.

[97] See the Criminal Code of Bosnia and Herzegovina, Article 1(11), 1(12), Article 10 (https://www.legal-tools.org/doc/46b8dc/), albeit with special rules regarding treatment and punishment of juvenile offenders. ICTY focused on deterring the adult leadership in the Balkans, see, for example, Jaimey Fisher, *Disciplining Germany: Youth, Reeducation, and Reconstruction after the Second World War*, Kritik, 2007, pp. 1–59.

[98] In Peru, children and youth fought in the Shining path rebellion, see, for example, Pino H. Ponciano, "Family, Culture and Revolution: Everyday Life with Sendero Luminoso", in Steve J. Stern (ed.), *Shining and Other Paths: War and Society in Peru, 1980-1995*, Duke University Press, 1998, pp. 158–92.

[99] In civil wars in Guatemala, El Salvador, Nicaragua armed groups and paramilitaries, including irregular forces that support existing governments and those that oppose the, continue to recruit and use children under the age of fifteen, see Honwana, 2006, p. 30, see above note 86.

[100] Human Rights Watch, *You Will Learn Not to Cry: Child Combatants in Colombia*, 2003 (https://www.legal-tools.org/doc/f44978/). According to the report more than 11,000 children were fighting in irregular armies, including paramilitaries and urban militias, in regions such as Alto Naya and Tierradentro.

[101] The Hitler Youth.

[102] German Youngsters in the Hitler Youth.

[103] See, for example, Philip Baker, *Youth led by Youth: Some Aspects of the Hitlerjudgend*, Vilmor, London, 1989; Brenda Lewis and Staffan Olsson, *Hitlerjugend: I Krig och Fred*, Svenskt Militärhistoriskt Bibliotek, Hallstavik, 2007.

first judgment, whether this judgment was appealed or not. Table 3 outlines the different types of age evidence that were present in these cases. Descriptions and examples of these different evidence types are provided below Table 3.

Table 3. Evidence used for estimating age of alleged child soldiers by court and case.[104]

Court	Case	Verdict	Evidence			
			Forensic	Video or Photo	Oral	Documentary
SCSL	BRIMA, KAMARA and KANU 'The AFRC case'	Convicted (Final)			X	X
SCSL	NORMAN, FOFANA and KONDEWA 'The CDF case'	Acquitted (Final)			X	
SCSL	SESAY, KALLON, GBAO 'The RUF case'	SESAY and KALLON convicted, GBAO acquitted (Final)			X	X
SCSL	TAYLOR	Convicted (Final)			X	X
ICC	LUBANGA	Convicted (Final)	X	X	X	X
ICC	NGUDJOLO	Acquitted (Final)			X	X

---

[104] Evidence categories marked as "X" indicate the presence of this type of evidence in the case. For an "X" mark, it suffices that this evidence was available for one of the alleged child soldiers. The "Verdict" column refers to the verdict in relation to child soldiering charges exclusively while the verdict might have been different in relation to other charges.

ICC	KATANGA	Acquitted (Final)		X	X	X
ICC	NTAGANDA	Convicted (Appealed)		X	X	X

Forensic evidence. This evidence type entails experts' estimations of ages based on visual assessments of X-rays of hands or wrists and teeth and was only present in the Lubanga case before the ICC. In this case, two experts; one professor in paediatric radiology and one paediatrician and forensic doctor, provided estimations in relation to nine UPC child soldiers.[105] While the first expert had the main responsibility for the hand or wrist assessments and the second expert had the main responsibility for the teeth assessments, they presented joint conclusions in a report jointly signed.[106] The experts regularly worked together on age assessment matters.[107] When assessing the hands or wrists the experts used the so-called Greulich and Pyle index.[108]

While forensic evidence was not referred to in any of the SCSL cases, there are odd examples of witnesses themselves describing that they've undergone less invasive age assessment forensic methods. For instance, in the RUF case one alleged child soldier described that a nurse had examined his teeth and only then did he find out that he was 14 years.[109] Since this examination was not made part of the case material, the Court could not consider it directly and it has therefore not been in-

---

[105] ICC, *The Prosecutor v. Thomas Lubanga Dyilo*, Trial Chamber, Transcript, 12 May 2009, ICC-01/04-01/06-T-172-ENG, p. 80 ('Lubanga Transcript of 12 May 2009') (https://www.legal-tools.org/doc/e522af/).

[106] ICC, *The Prosecutor v. Thomas Lubanga Dyilo*, Trial Chamber, Transcript, 13 May 2009, ICC-01/04-01/06-T-173-ENG, pp. 46–47 ('Lubanga Transcript of 13 May 2009') (https://www.legal-tools.org/doc/3acffb/). After a question from the defence on this matter, the second expert indicated that she did look at the hand or wrist X-rays as well, although her conclusions in the report bore only on the dental age assessments.

[107] *Ibid.*, p. 22.

[108] *Ibid.*, pp. 44–45.

[109] SCSL Sesay *et al.* Trial Chamber Judgment, para. 1628, see above note 64. The SCSL notes that: "[…] during the DDR process it was established through the use of verification of age methods such as the physical inspection of teeth that many of the children who had fought with the RUF and AFRC forces were under 15 years at that time, which was towards the end of the Indictment period" (*ibid.*, p. 487, para. 1628). Thus, it is not clear from the verdict what other age verification methods were used but presumably, the Court is here referring to other types of forensic evidence.

cluded in Table 3, while it is commented on in Section 6.5.3. on oral evidence.

Video or Photo evidence. In the Lubanga case, the prosecutor relied "on a number of video excerpts to establish that some of the UPF/FPLC recruits were 'visibly' under the age of 15".[110] The Trial Chamber agreed with the prosecution that children who are undoubtedly less than 15 years can be distinguished from those undoubtedly over 15,[111] while it also noted the defence's contention that "it is impossible to distinguish reliably between a 12 or 13 year-old and a 15 or 16 year-old on the basis of a photograph or video extract alone".[112] In its own assessment of the video excerpts the Trial Chamber identified specific individuals who, in its opinion, were "evidently",[113] "clearly"[114] or "significantly"[115] under the age of 15 years. This approach was also approved by the Appeals Chamber which stated that: "[…] given the margin of error applied by the Trial Chamber, its approach was not unreasonable".[116]

Also in the Ntaganda case, video evidence was referred to and used for age estimation purposes. For instance, on the basis of three video extracts, the Trial Chamber identified two individuals whom it considered "manifestly under the age of 15"[117] at the time the extracts were recorded, around February 2003.[118] In relation to another video extract the Chamber considered "in particular, the facial features of the relevant individual"[119] and while it allows for "a wide margin of error, the Chamber is satisfied beyond reasonable doubt that this individual was manifestly under 15 years of age around May 2003, the time when the video extract was recorded".[120] In its appeal of Ntaganda's conviction, the defence suggested

---

[110] Lubanga Trial Chamber Judgment, para. 644, see above note 4.
[111] *Ibid.*, para. 643.
[112] *Ibid.*, para. 644.
[113] *Ibid.*, para. 861.
[114] *Ibid.*, paras. 713, 792, 854, 858, 862, 869, 912, 915, 1348.
[115] *Ibid.*, paras. 1249, 1251–52.
[116] Lubanga Appeals Chamber Judgment, para. 222, see above note 3.
[117] Ntaganda Trial Chamber Judgment, paras. 386–87, see above note 74.
[118] *Ibid.* Before this, the Chamber points out that witness testimonies were insufficient for establish the age element.
[119] *Ibid.*, paras. 388.
[120] *Ibid.*, paras. 388–99. However, the Chamber also adds that there was other evidence provided by witnesses who were in regular contact with, or had sufficient opportunities to ob-

that the Trial Chamber only relied on video images,[121] which was contested by the Prosecution suggesting that the Chamber also relied on other corroborating evidence.[122] The defence also claimed that the Trial Chamber did not explain its approach to age assessments based on visual images and also disputed the Chamber's age assessments of three individuals depicted in the "Rwampara" video.[123] Also this was contested by the prosecution, which argued that the Chamber's findings were reasoned and based on the size and physical appearance (including the facial features of one individual) of the alleged child soldiers.[124] Also, the prosecution pointed out that the Chamber allowed for a wide margin of error.[125] Only time can tell what the Appeal's Chamber will think of these claims.[126]

In the Katanga case there was no systematic references to video or photo evidence but in relation to one alleged child soldier, Katanga's youngest bodyguard[127] there was one photograph. Katanga himself had described his bodyguard as a young man whom he put at around 22 years old in 2004, while witness P-28 described the bodyguard as young and

---

serve, individuals serving within Mr. Ntaganda's escort, which also demonstrates that Mr. Ntaganda's escort comprised Kadogos, including individuals under 15 years of age.

[121] But, as pointed out by the Prosecution in its response, the Defence later conceded that the Chamber had also relied on testimonial evidence, referring to ICC, *The Prosecutor v. Bosco Ntaganda*, Defence, Corrigendum of the "Public Redacted Version of 'Defence Appeal Brief – Part II', 31 January 2020, ICC-01/04-02/06-2465", 27 March 2020, ICC-01/04-02/06-2465-Red, 30 June 2020, ICC-01/04-02/06-2465-Red-Corr, paras. 232–33, 243, 246 ('Ntaganda Defence Appeal Brief – Part II') (https://www.legal-tools.org/doc/krrzxw/).

[122] More specifically the Prosecution here refers to oral evidence and "the Chamber's own assessment of four video extracts in which P-0010 and P-0898 identified three individuals in Ntaganda's escort as under the age of 15", see ICC, *The Prosecutor v. Bosco Ntaganda*, OTP, Public Redacted Version of "Prosecution Response to 'Defence Appeal Brief – Part II'", 3 April 2020, ICC-01/04-02/06-2500-Conf, 14 April 2020, ICC-01/04-02/06-2500-Red, para. 176 ('Prosecution Response to 'Defence Appeal Brief – Part II') (https://www.legal-tools.org/doc/p24gqr/)

[123] Ntaganda Defence Appeal Brief – Part II, paras. 238–40, citing video excerpt DRC-OTP-0120-0293, see above note 121.

[124] Prosecution Response to 'Defence Appeal Brief – Part II', p. 77–78, paras. 178–79, see above note 122.

[125] *Ibid.*, p. 78, para. 179.

[126] For updates see ICC, "Ntaganda Case" (available on its web site).

[127] As acknowledged by Katanga himself, see Katanga Trial Chamber Judgment, para. 1079, see above note 69.

that he did not yet have a beard. From the photograph, the Chamber itself stated that "he resembled an adult".[128] It then added:

> In the light of these two contradictory testimonies from, on the one hand, the Accused and, on the other, P-28, whose evidence requires corroboration on this vital point since it has a direct bearing on Germain Katanga's criminal responsibility, the Chamber is not in a position to ascertain whether, at the material time, one of the Accused's bodyguards was under the age of 15 years.[129]

No other cases before the ICC or SCSL involved video or photo evidence, but clearly, prosecutors and judges can, consciously or subconsciously, make assessments based on the physical appearance and/or demeanour of anyone present physically, present via video link or similar arrangements. In the Taylor case, the SCSL Trial Chamber explicitly took physical appearance into account when it stated that "he looked young at the time he gave evidence in 2008 ten years after the incidents he testified about".[130] It is possible that physical appearance has had an impact on age assessments also in other cases, although more subtly and implicitly. Importantly, such an impact is not necessarily conscious to legal actors but rather based on more or less subconscious processing of physical appearance, which is a relatively dominant aspect of our perceptions of others.[131]

Oral evidence. As outlined in Table 3, oral evidence was referred to in all of the cases. This entails both the testimony of the alleged child soldiers themselves as regards their own ages and/or the ages of other alleged

---

[128] *Ibid.*, para. 1080.

[129] *Ibid.*

[130] SCSL Taylor Trial Chamber Judgment, para. 1431, see above note 67.

[131] For more on this see, for example, the conceptual framework on social perception, Leslie Zebrowitz and Joann Montepare, "Social Psychological Face Perception: Why Appearance Matters", in *Social and Personality Psychology Compass*, 2008, vol. 2, no. 3, pp. 1–16; Leslie Zebrowitz, *New Directions in Social Psychology, Reading Faces: Window to the Soul?*, Westview Press, 1997. Also, there are several studies suggesting that facial appearance predicts criminal justice decisions, see, for example, Jennifer L. Eberhardt *et al.*, "Looking Deathworthy: Perceived Stereotypicality of Black Defendants Predicts Capital-Sentencing Outcomes", in *Psychological Science*, 2006, vol. 17, no. 5, pp. 383–86; John Wilson and Nicholas O Rule, "Facial Trustworthiness Predicts Extreme Criminal-Sentencing Outcomes", in *Psychological Science*, vol. 26, no. 8, pp. 1325–31; Leslie Zebrowitz and Susan M. McDonald, "The Impact of Litigant's Baby-Facedness and Attractiveness on Adjudications in Small Claims Courts", in *Law and Human Behavior*, 1991, vol. 15, no. 6, pp. 603–23.

child soldiers, as well as the testimony of for instance parents, social workers or insider witnesses. In the following all of these testimonies are referred to as *age statements*.

To illustrate, in the RUF case, the alleged child soldier TF1-314 testified that she was 10 years when she was captured and raped by the RUF in Masingbi, Tonkolili District.[132] Both the Sesay and the Gbao defence asserted that TFI-314 was not to be relied upon, for example, because there were significant inconsistencies in her evidence.[133] However, the Chamber opined that her evidence was "largely credible" and that "slight variations" between prior statements and those made at trial were immaterial.[134]

When it comes to the age statements provided by others than the alleged child soldiers themselves, these varied in their degree of specificity. For instance, in the AFRC case some of the age statements were not specific at all but describing, for example, a "young boy"[135] or indicating relatively wide age spans like "between the ages of 10 and 14 years old"[136] or "some no older than 12 years".[137] In the CDF case, both the prosecution witnesses and the defence witnesses indicated the presence of children younger than 15.[138] Witness TFI-334 stated that among those captured were "many"[139] small boys, including some as young as 9 or 10 years old.[140] They were later trained as SBUs (Small Boys Unit) and the witness himself had two SBUs. In the RUF case, a witness estimated that "45 per cent" of those taken to train at Bunumbu were under the age of 15.[141] Occasionally, there were defence witnesses who disputed the pres-

---

[132] SCSL Sesay *et al.* Trial Chamber Judgment, paras. 592–94, see above note 64.

[133] *Ibid.*

[134] *Ibid.*

[135] This was the statement of Witness TF1-023 who testified that she was captured by a "young boy" holding a gun on 22 January 1999, see the SCSL Brima *et al.* Trial Chamber Judgment, para. 1262, see above note 59.

[136] This was Witness TF1-227, see *ibid.*, para. 1263.

[137] Witness TF1-122 about the use of children in Kenema District. This witness testified that during the Junta period he saw child soldiers, "some no older than 12 years old [...]", *ibid.*, para. 1265.

[138] Although these witnesses said that the abductees ranged in "age from 14 to 18 years old", see *ibid.*, para. 1269.

[139] *Ibid.*, para. 1272.

[140] *Ibid.*

[141] SCSL Sesay *et al.* Trial Chamber Judgment, para. 1438, see above note 64.

ence of soldiers younger than 15 years in the armed groups, for example, the Zumbe group and the Bedu-Ezekere group in the Ngudjolo case before the ICC.[142] However, in the Ngudjolo case, the Chamber considered that the presence of child soldiers had been established, on the basis of other witnesses and documentary evidence, while it acquitted Ngudjolo for other reasons.[143]

Also, there are connections between the video or photo evidence and the age statements in the sense that some witnesses based their age statements on the physical appearance of the alleged child soldiers. For instance, in the Katanga case, the Trial Chamber relied on the observations of various eyewitnesses as proof of the age element in relation to children involved in the attack on Bogoro in February 2003.[144] The Chamber noted that:

> P-132 stated without hesitation, on the basis of their physical appearance – specifically, their size and facial features – that the attackers, whom she had seen and estimated to be 'small children', were in her view, from 10 to 13 years old, and she explained in this regard that 'you can see a child's face, and from that you can easily tell that he or she is still a child.[145]

Similarly, in Ntaganda, witness P-0017 testified that alleged child soldiers acting as bodyguards appeared to be between 12 and 13 years old.[146] P-0017 based this on the "physiognomy" (own addition: facial features or expression), their sizes and the fact that they played, and that "they looked more like young boys because they didn't have any breasts".[147]

When comparing the evaluations made by the SCSL and the ICC, it appears the SCSL has trusted the provided age statements – particularly those of the alleged child soldiers themselves – to a greater extent than the

---

[142] Ngudjolo Chui Trial Chamber Judgment, paras. 515–16, see above note 72. The Chamber was unable to establish beyond reasonable doubt a link between the accused and the children who were in Bogoro on 24 February 2003.

[143] *Ibid.*

[144] Katanga Trial Chamber Judgment, para. 1060, see above note 69.

[145] *Ibid.*, para. 1062.

[146] Ntaganda Trial Chamber Judgment, p. 235, fn. 1508, see above note 74.

[147] *Ibid.* The Trial Chamber, whose conviction of Ntaganda is now appealed, used this, as well as other witness testimony as its basis for concluding that soldiers younger than 15 years participated in the assaults forming part of the First Operation, see *ibid.*, p. 235, para. 511.

ICC. The likely main explanation of this is that while the age statements presented before the SCSL were largely uncontested,[148] many of the age statements presented before the ICC were strongly contested.[149] For instance, in the AFRC case the Trial Chamber[150] simply noted that TF1-157 and TFI-158 were 20 and 18 years old when they testified before the Court.[151] None of these witnesses could remember the precise year of the alleged crimes but the Court inferred their ages at the relevant time on the basis of information provided by the witnesses, for example, "given the precision with which the witness described his journey [...]",[152] in relation to TFI-157.[153] While the AFRC case, the Taylor case and the RUF case all resulted in convictions (save for Gbao), the final verdict in the CDF case was an acquittal. As outlined in Table 2, the only age evidence in the CDF case was oral evidence. The Trial Chamber had accepted and considered oral evidence of several witnesses including three former child soldiers in determining Kondewa's responsibility for child enlistment. However, it relied solely on the evidence of Witness TF2-021 in arriving at its conclusion. The Trial Chamber found that the evidence of witness TF2-021 was pivotal in making its factual findings and noted that the events in questions occurred when he was very young and that his testimony came many years after the events in question. Nevertheless, the Trial Chamber found the testimony of Witness TF2-021 "highly credible

---

[148] Although in the AFRC case, the defence questioned the legal 15-year threshold in a wider sense, since it considered it arbitrary as "the ending of childhood (in the traditional African setting) has little to do with achieving a particular age more to do with physical capacity to perform acts reserved for adults". See SCSL Brima *et al.* Trial Chamber Judgment, para. 730, see above note 59; SCSL, *The Prosecutor v. Alex Tamba Brima, Ibrahim Bazzy Kamara and Santigie Borbor Kanu*, Defence, Kanu – Defence Trial Brief, 8 December 2006, SCSL-2004-16-T, para. 75 ('Brima *et al.* Kanu Defence Trial Brief'), referring to exhibit D-37, Defence Expert Research Report on the Use of Child Soldiers in the Sierra Leone Conflict by Mr. Osman Gbla, paras. 9–11. This contention is discussed in more detail in Section 6.5.3.1.1.1. "Social Age".

[149] Not the least in case of Lubanga, in which many of the alleged child soldiers were believed to have been influenced in their age statements by an intermediate.

[150] SCSL Brima *et al.* Trial Chamber Judgment, para. 1253, 1256, see above note 59. The Trial Chambers' convictions in relation to all three defendants were upheld on appeal, see SCSL Brima *et al.* Appeals Chamber Judgment, see above note 60.

[151] SCSL Brima *et al.* Trial Chamber Judgment, para. 1254, see above note 59.

[152] *Ibid.*

[153] However, it should also be noted that three other former child soldiers testified before the Trial Chamber, TF1-199 TF1-180 and TF1-085 but the Trial Chamber concluded that their testimonies were problematic, see *ibid.*

and reliable"[154] and on this basis alone, it concluded that he was 11 years old at the time of the first enlistment and 13 years old at the time of the second enlistment.[155] Subsequently, it convicted Kondewa for having enlisted this one child soldier.[156] However, the Appeals Chamber acquitted Kondewa of enlisting TF2-021 since it considered that TF2-021 had already been enlisted when Kondewa initiated him into the Kamajors (and the initiation could therefore not be considered enlistment).[157] There were also other alleged child soldiers and TF2-021 had testified that they were of the same age as him but the Appeal's Chamber referred to "the lack of evidence of the ages of the boys who were initiated along with witness TF2-021"[158] and upheld the Trial Chamber's acquittal in these parts.[159] Hence, an overall observation on the basis of the SCSL practice is that while age statements, together with documentary evidence, have been sufficient for proving the age element at the SCSL, the single testimony of one alleged child soldier was considered insufficient as regards the ages of others.[160] When it comes to the ICC cases, regardless of whether they have resulted in convictions or acquittals, the Court has not considered the age element proven on the basis of age statements. In its assessments, the Court has placed emphasis on whether the age statements were consistent

---

[154] SCSL Norman *et al.* Trial Chamber Judgment, para. 282, see above note 61.

[155] *Ibid.*, para. 970.

[156] *Ibid.*

[157] SCSL Norman *et al.* Appeals Chamber Judgment, paras. 145–46, see above note 63. Justice Winter was dissenting.

[158] *Ibid.*, para. 132.

[159] In relation to Fofana, neither the Trial Chamber nor the Appeals Chamber discusses the age element in any detail as they both find that the Prosecution did not establish beyond reasonable doubt that Fofana was individually responsible for any child soldiering crime, see SCSL Norman *et al.* Trial Chamber Judgment, paras. 959 and 963, see above note 61 and SCSL Norman *et al.* Appeals Chamber Judgment, paras. 153–54, see above note 63. Fofana had acknowledged that the CDF as an organization enlisted child soldiers, but submitted that this was insufficient proof that he was personally involved in the crime of enlistment. His mere presence at events and his position of authority in the CDF do not amount to encouragement or assistance for the purpose of aiding and abetting, see SCSL, *The Prosecutor v. Sam Hinga Norman, Moinina Fofana and Allieu Kondewa*, Defence, Fofana Response to Prosecution Appeal Brief, 21 January 2007, SCSL-04-14-A, paras. 60 and 76.

[160] Although it should be reinforced that the Appeals Chamber did not acquit Kondewa because they didn't consider the age element to have been proven on the basis of TF2-021's age statement, but rather that he had already been enlisted when Kondewa initiated him into the Kamajors.

---

over time as well as consistent with other age evidence. This is most clearly spelled out in the Lubanga case,[161] but also the Katanga[162] and Ntaganda[163] cases illustrate this point.

Documentary evidence. The documentary evidence entailed a range of different document types that provided information about the age of specific alleged child soldiers or more generally about groups of alleged child soldiers.

In the former category were for instance *ad hoc* birth certificates,[164] electoral cards,[165] school registers[166] and lists of recruits[167] which were common in many of the ICC cases (for example, Katanga and Lubanga) but also in some of the SCSL cases (for example, Taylor and RUF). There were often discrepancies between the ages indicated by these different documents,[168] and/or in relation to the statement of the alleged child sol-

---

[161] Lubanga Trial Chamber Judgment, para. 406, see above note 4 where the Trial Chamber states that "the extent of the inconsistencies and the other problems with this witness's evidence supports the suggestion that he provided an account that was false, at least in part", and para. 479: "Nonetheless, for the reasons identified in the relevant analysis for each witness, the inconsistencies or other problems with their evidence has led to a finding that they are unreliable as regards the matters that are relevant to the charges in this case".

[162] In this case, several alleged child soldiers appeared in Court but their testimonies were considered problematic, see Katanga Trial Chamber Judgment, pp. 1086–87, see above note 69. The Chamber considered there was an absence of evidence regarding Katanga's direct involvement in the use of child soldiers and therefore acquitted him.

[163] For instance, P-0809 testified that he joined the UPC when he was "between 13 and a half and 14 years of age", see Ntaganda Trial Chamber Judgment, para. 202 and fn. 482, see above note 74 which was consistent with his statement concerning his date of birth, which, in turn, corresponded to the information provided in several documents: an electoral card, a citizenship certificate and a birth certificate. In the light of this, and absent any specific challenges concerning the witness's date of birth, the Chamber found that he was under 15 years old at the relevant time. Thus, when the witness was consistent with himself and age was not disputed, the age element was considered proven.

[164] For instance, Lubanga Trial Chamber Judgment, paras. 231 and 248, see above note 4.

[165] *Ibid.*, para. 248, citing evidence EVD-D01-00762 (electoral card).

[166] *Ibid.*, for instance, paras. 266 and 397.

[167] See, for example, SCSL Sesay *et al.* Trial Chamber Judgment, para. 1639, see above note 64. The lists of recruits had been drawn up by adjutants at the base including their names, ages and other personal data.

[168] For details on this see Table 3 but, for example, there were inconsistencies in the documentary evidence used to establish P-0007's age. While the voter card indicated 1987, the birth certificate indicated 1990 as his year of birth, see Lubanga Trial Chamber Judgment, para. 236, see above note 4.

dier him or herself.[169] Occasionally, there were also questions relating to the veracity of the documents.[170] In the Lubanga case the discrepancies were believed to have resulted from interference by an intermediary and this resulted in that the age element was not considered proven for many of the alleged child soldiers. In the SCSL cases, discrepancies were accepted to a somewhat greater extent, and a contributing cause of this difference is probably that these discrepancies were not believed to originate from interference by an intermediary or similar. For instance, in the Taylor case, the Trial Chamber accepted, in relation to "Sumana", that he "may not himself have known his exact age at the time of his abduction, he was "very small" at the time and did not yet have facial hair. His father 'used to tell him' that he was 14, whereas according to his recently acquired birth certificate he was actually only 13".[171] The age stated in the birth certificate was also inconsistent with the exact age in Sumanas voter ID card, but since both documents suggested he was 13 at the time of his abduction, the Chamber considered it proven beyond reasonable doubt that he was under 15 years at the time of interest.[172]

The latter more general category of documents include for instance different kinds of reports, like a UN ('United Nations') Report in the AFRC case.[173] This report was released in the wake of the January 1999 invasion of Freetown and stated that "a significant number of rebel combatant were children. Reports were received of death and injuries being inflicted by boys as young as 8 to 11 years old".[174] Together with the evidence provided by the alleged child soldiers themselves, as well as that of other witnesses, the Trial Chamber considered this sufficient to establish

---

[169] This is outlined in detail in Table 3, but, for example, P-007, at different points in time stated that he was born in 1986, 1987 and that he did not know his age, while his voter card indicated 1987 and his birth certificate indicated 1990 as his year of birth, see *ibid.*

[170] For example, in *ibid.*, para. 397, a school register indicated that P-0213 was born in 1989 but it was established by expert evidence that the entry for the year 1989 overwrote a previous entry which was partially visible underneath and the underlying reference could not be made out. The Trial Chamber considered this entry potentially unreliable and placed little reliance on it.

[171] SCSL Taylor Trial Chamber Judgment, para. 1391, see above note 67.

[172] *Ibid.*, paras. 1392–93.

[173] SCSL Brima *et al.* Trial Chamber Judgment, para. 1274, see above note 59, Exhibit P-46, "Fifth Report of the Secretary-General on the United Nations Observer Mission in Sierra Leone", UN Doc. S/1999/237, 4 March 1999.

[174] *Ibid.*

---

that children younger than 15 years had been conscripted and/or used during the period covered by the indictment.[175] However, in the Taylor case, the Trial Chamber evaluated similar documentary evidence somewhat differently. The Chamber discussed the significance of several reports, for example, one from the Coalition to Stop the Use of Child Soldiers according to which 10 per cent of the armed forces which attacked Freetown in January 1999 were children.[176] There was also a UN Secretary-General report stating that a significant number of rebel fighters in the Freetown attack were children and that boys as young as 8 to 11 years were killing and inflicting injuries.[177] The Trial Chamber found that the information contained in these, as well as a few other exhibits,[178] was based on hearsay and did not provide sufficient information about the age element.[179] Reports of a similar nature were also present in the ICC case Katanga. More specifically, there was a MONUC report on events in Ituri in 2002–03 according to which 40 per cent of each militia consisted of children under the age of 18 years, with a significant minority below the age of 15.[180] In the same case, also an internal register of children admitted to a demobilization centre ("the Log Book") was tendered into evidence.[181] It contained 952 names of children aged from 9 to 17 years, about 40 of whom were under the age of 15 years.[182] Although there were doubts as to the number of these who were to be considered demobilized child soldiers, the Trial Chamber considered itself to be:

> in a position to find that children under the age of 18 years, some of whom were under 15 years of age, joined the armed

---

[175] *Ibid.*, para. 1275.

[176] SCSL Taylor Trial Chamber Judgment, paras. 1566–68, see above note 67.

[177] *Ibid.*

[178] More specifically, the Chamber discusses a confidential report (Exhibit P-0077) according to which during the rebels' attack on Freetown, 8 to 11 year old boys raped, killed and amputated the hands of civilians, as well as a Human Rights Watch report (Exhibit P-328, *Getting Away with Murder, Mutilation, and Rape: New Testimony from Sierra Leone*, July 1999) suggesting that RUF child combatants, armed with pistols, rifles and machetes, were seen actively participating in killings and amputations during the Freetown attack, see *ibid.*, paras. 1566–68.

[179] *Ibid.*, para. 1573.

[180] Katanga Trial Chamber Judgment, para. 1052, see above note 69.

[181] *Ibid.*, para. 1054 and fn. 2532, citing evidence EVD-OTP-00120: Admissions log book of the Aveba transit site.

[182] *Ibid.*, para. 1054.

> groups within the Ngiti community of Walendu-Bindi collec-
> tivité from 2002 and that some of these, also under the age of
> 15 years, were 'combatants' within Walendu-Bindi collec-
> tivité at the material time.[183]

It reached this conclusion based on both the documentary evidence and witness evidence,[184] but still acquitted Katanga from the child soldiering charges for other reasons than the age element not being proven.[185] Also in the Ngudjolo case, a MONUC Report, together with oral evidence, was relied upon for the finding of children younger than 15 years in the armed groups. According to this report, there could be "no doubt that all of the armed groups [...] systematically recruited [...] children – ranging from 7 to 17 years old – through the district of Ituri".[186] It further stated that "at least 40 per cent of each militia force are children below the age of 18, with a significant minority below the age of 15".[187]

In two cases from the SCSL; the AFRC case and the Taylor case there were also what the Court referred to as "expert witness reports".[188] While it was never made clear in what way the individuals writing these reports had expertise in age estimations specifically, the Court did refer to their reports when determining the age element. This is manifested in the AFRC case when the Trial Chamber "stresses that both experts agree that persons under the age of 15 were used for military purposes by all fac-

---

[183] *Ibid.*, para. 1059.

[184] *Ibid.*, pp. 399–400.

[185] As such, the Trial Chamber found that there was evidence beyond reasonable doubt that there were children within the Ngiti militia and among the combatants who were in Bogoro on the day of the attack. However, the Chamber concluded that the evidence presented in support of the accused's guilt did not satisfy it beyond reasonable doubt of the accused's responsibility for these crimes, see ICC, "Katanga Case", Case Information Sheet (available on its web site). Yet, in relation to some alleged child soldiers present in, for example, the Ngiti militia's camps on or around 24 February 2003, the Chamber did not find the age element substantiated since there was only one eye-witness testimony which it considered insufficiently detailed. Katanga Trial Chamber Judgment, paras. 1070–73, see above note 69.

[186] Ngudjolo Chui Trial Chamber Judgment, para. 511, fn. 1182, citing evidence EVD-OTP-00285: MONUC Report on the Events in Ituri, para. 138, as well as paras. 6, 39, 141, 143, 147, see above note 72.

[187] *Ibid.*

[188] SCSL Brima *et al.* Trial Chamber Judgment, fn. 2243, citing testimony of expert witness TF1-296, Transcripts of 4 October 2005 and 5 October 2005, see above note 59.

tions, including the AFRC".[189] A closer examination of these reports shows that the prosecution's expert based the report on "sources",[190] some of which has referred to child soldiers as individuals under the age of 18 rather than 15.[191] While this limitation is acknowledged by the Court,[192] there is no questioning of whether the sources have any type of proficiency in estimating age. The defence expert report has similar issues as regards its probative value in relation to the age element, since it is based on interviews with individuals in the security forces,[193] documents[194] and on secondary sources.[195]

Among the cases outlined in Table 3, the ICC Lubanga case entailed the widest range of age evidence, including forensic, video, oral and documentary evidence. Since the Lubanga case was also the only case which dealt exclusively with child soldiering charges,[196] the evaluation of the age evidence was more in-depth. Therefore, in Table 4, the Court's evaluation of each piece of evidence available for each respective child soldier

---

[189] *Ibid.*, para. 1251.

[190] *Ibid.*, para. 1248.

[191] *Ibid.*

[192] *Ibid.*

[193] Especially the Republic of Sierra Leone Armed Forces ('RSLAF') and the Sierra Leone ('SLP') as well as the personnel at the Special Court of Sierra Leone and representative of child protection agencies, see SCSL, *The Prosecutor v. Alex Tamba Brima, Ibrahim Bazzy Kamara and Santigie Borbor Kanu*, Defence, Research Report: The Use of Child Soldiers in the Sierra Leone Conflict, 11 October 2006, SCSL-2004-16-T, p. 10 ('Brima *et al*. Defence Research Report on the Use of Child Soldiers in the Sierra Leone Conflict').

[194] The author cites international documents like the UN Convention on the Rights of the Child ('UNCRC'), the Graca Machel Reports (1996 and 2001) and the Sierra Leone Military Forces Act of 1961, see Brima *et al*. Defence Research Report on the Use of Child Soldiers in the Sierra Leone Conflict, p. 11, see above note 193.

[195] Such as desk research and review of relevant documents including books, journal articles, reports and newspapers bearing relevance to the issue of child soldiers in the Sierra Leone conflict, see *ibid.*

[196] For the specifics of the charges, as well as the confirmation of the charges, see Lubanga Decision on the Confirmation of Charges, see above note 57. Lubanga was charged as a co-perpetrator jointly with other FPLC officers and UPC members and supporters for conscripting and enlisting children under the age of 15 years into the FPLC military wing of the UPC since September 2002, and using them to participate actively in hostilities. The Prosecution submitted that the crimes occurred in the context of an armed conflict not of an international character, and this was also the conclusion reached by the Trial as well as Appeals Chambers.

in the Lubanga case is outlined. In Appendix 1 more details about the evidence items, contradictions and the Court's evaluations are provided.

Table 4. Implications of age evidence, contradictions and conclusions in relation to alleged child soldiers in the Lubanga case.[197]

Alleged Child Soldier	Evidence Type				Contradictions	Court's Conclusion
	Forensic	Video	Oral	Documentary		
P-0007	Under[198]	NA	Under[199]	Under or over[200]	Yes *Internal*: D *External*: F and O v. D *Other*: O (own testimony)	Not proven
P-0008	Under	NA	Under[201]	Under or over[202]	Yes *Internal*: D *External*: F and O v. D *Other*: F v. O	Not proven

---

[197] In the table: "Under" = Any age below 15 years within the time frame of the charges, "Over" = 15 years or any age above 15 within the time frame of the charges, "Under/Over" = For this evidence type, different evidence items contradicted each other so that some indicated that the individual was under 15 years and some indicated that the individual was 15 years or over. Furthermore, "NA" = This evidence type was not available, "X" = No conclusion was offered. In the column "Contradictions", "F" = Forensic evidence, "V" = Video evidence, "O" = Oral evidence and "D" = Documentary evidence. "External" = External contradiction, that is, contradictions between different evidence types some suggesting under and other 15 years or older, "Internal" = Internal contradiction, that is, contradictions between different evidence items within the same evidence type some suggesting under and other 15 years or older. "Other" = Other types of contradictions about the specific birth year or day while both still suggested either under or 15 years or older or an initially retracted testimony. In the column "Court's conclusion", "Not proven" = It was not established beyond reasonable doubt that the individual was under 15 years within the time frame of the charges and "Proven" = It was established beyond reasonable doubt that the individual was under 15 years within the time frame of the charges.

[198] For all alleged child soldiers in relation to whom forensic evidence was available, this forensic evidence was hand or wrist as well as dental X-rays. When evaluating the hand or wrist X-rays, the experts used the Greulich and Pyle Atlas.

[199] Contradictions but all accounts suggested under 15 years.

[200] Contradictions, some documents suggested under and other over 15 years.

[201] Contradictions but all accounts suggested under 15 years.

P-0010	Un-der[203]	X	Under or Over[204]	Under or over[205]	Yes *Internal*: O and D *External*: F and O v. D *Other*: O (own testimony or defence witness)	Not proven
P-0011	Under	NA	Under[206]	Under	No *Other*: O (own testimony or defence witness)	Not proven
P-0157	Over	NA	Under[207]	Over	Yes *External*: F and D v. O	Not proven
P-0213	Under	NA	Under[208]	Under[209]	No	Not proven
P-0294	Under	NA	Under	Over[210]	Yes *External*: F and O v. D	Not proven
P-0297	Un-der[211]	NA	Under[212]	Over	Yes *External*: F and O v. D	Not proven

[202] Contradictions, some documents suggested under and other over 15 years.

[203] The forensic experts stated it was "scientifically possible" that P-0010 was under 15 years at the time of her recruitment.

[204] Contradictions but all own accounts suggested under 15 years. Accounts from defence witnesses contradicted this and suggested P-0010 was 15 or older.

[205] Contradictions, some documents suggested under and other over 15 years.

[206] Contradictions but all accounts suggested under 15 years.

[207] According to P-0157's own testimony he was under 15 years. Defence witnesses were unspecific about the age of P-0157.

[208] According to P-0213's own testimony he was under 15 years. Defence witnesses were unspecific about the age of P-0213.

[209] P-0213 had a school register suggesting he was under 15 years but according to expert evidence this was unreliable and the Trial Chamber placed little reliance on it.

[210] Contradictions but all documents suggested over 15 years.

[211] Hand, wrist, dental examination suggested P-0297 was under 15 years within the time frame of the charges but between 16 and 17 years in January 2008.

P-0298	Under	NA	Under[213]	Under	No *Other*: O (initially retracted testimony)	Not proven
D-0040	NA	Under[214]	Over[215]	Over	Yes *External*: V v. O and D	Proven
D-0041	NA	Under[216]	Over[217]	Over	Yes *External*: V v. O and D	Proven
'Bodyguard 1'	NA	Under[218]	Over[219]	NA	Yes *External*: V v. O	Proven
'Bodyguard 2'	NA	Under[220]	Over[221]	NA	Yes *External*: V v. O	Proven
Individual 1	NA	Under[222]	Under[223]	NA	No	Proven

---

[212] According to P-0297's own testimony he was under 15 years. Defence witnesses unspecific about his age.

[213] Although there were some contradictions in P-0298's own testimony, first stated he was born in 1989 and then couldn't remember, and also compared to his father's testimony, according to which he was born in 1991. P-0298 initially retracted his testimony in Court but maintained his original testimony when appearing in Court two weeks later.

[214] Video excerpt EVD-OTP-00574, filmed at Lubanga's office, 24 February 2003, 01:49:02.

[215] According to D-0040's own testimony, introduced by the defence, he was born on 8 April 1983 and therefore 20 years at the time the footage was shot.

[216] "Manifestly under the age of 15 years", according to the Trial Chamber. Video excerpt EVD-OTP-00571, taken during a presidential rally at the Bunia city stadium, 11 January 2003, 02:47:15 to 02:47:19.

[217] According to D-0041's own testimony, introduced by the defence, he was born on 2 December 1984 and therefore 19 years at the time the footage was shot.

[218] "Clearly under the age of 15" according to the Trial Chamber. Video excerpt EVD-OTP-00572, showing a group from the UPC meeting with Lendu representatives near the city of Lipri, 14 January 2003, 00:00:50, 00:02:47 and 00:28:42.

[219] A witness estimated the age of 'Bodyguard 1' to 16 years.

[220] "Clearly under the age of 15", according to the Trial Chamber. Video excerpt EVD-OTP-00572, showing a group from the UPC meeting with Lendu representatives near the city of Lipri, 14 January 2003, 00:00:50, 00:02:47 and 00:28:42.

[221] A witness estimated the age of 'Bodyguard 2' to be 16.

Individual 2	NA	Under[224]	NA	NA	No	Proven
Individual 3	NA	Under[225]	NA	NA	No	Proven
Individual 4	NA	Under[226]	NA	NA	No	Proven
Individual 5	NA	Under[227]	NA	NA	No	Proven
Individual 6	NA	Under[228]	NA	NA	No	Proven
Total: **19 individuals**	**9 of 19** 8 under 15	**10 of 19** 10 under 15	**14 of 19** 9 under 15	**11 of 19** 3 under 15	**12 of 19**	**Proven: 10 of 19**

As outlined in Table 4, contradictions were relatively common, especially external contradictions between different evidence types (10 out 19), followed by other types of contradictions (5 out of 19) and lastly internal contradictions (3 out of 19). Seemingly, these contradictions impacted differently on the Court's conclusions in relation to the 15-year threshold, probably because some contradictions were believed to arise from interference by an intermediary. For 8 out of 19 alleged child soldiers, there was forensic evidence suggesting they were younger than 15 years but for all of these individuals, save for one (P-0213), this was contradicted by oral and/or documentary evidence or there were internal con-

---

222 "Significantly below 15 years of age" according to the Trial Chamber, Video excerpt EVD-OTP-00571, taken during a presidential rally at the Bunia city stadium, 11 January 2003, 02:22:52 to 02:22:54.

223 According to P-0010 Individual 1 was below 12 years.

224 Video excerpt EVD-OTP-00570, shot at Rwampapra training camp, 12 February 2003, 00:06:57 . The Trial Chamber specified that, in its view, the person was a "young male who is well below the age of 15".

225 "Evidently under the age of 15" according to the Trial Chamber. Video excerpt EVD-OTP-00571, taken during a presidential rally at the Bunia city stadium, 11 January 2003, 02:02:44.

226 "Plainly under the age of 15" according to the Trial Chamber. Testimony of P-0002, evidence EVD-OTP-00410; and video excerpt EVD-OTP-00676, showing a UPC/FPLC rally at the stadium in the centre of Bunia, opposite the Ituri Hotel, 26 February 2003, 00:52:14.

227 "Clearly under the age of 15 years" according to the Trial Chamber. Video excerpt EVD-OTP-00574, filmed at Lubanga's office, 24 February 2003, 00:36:21.

228 "Clearly under the age of 15 years" according to the Trial Chamber. *Ibid.*

tradictions between the oral or documentary items. For none of these individuals, the age element was considered proven beyond reasonable doubt. For the remaining 1 alleged child soldier with forensic, oral and documentary evidence all suggesting he was younger than 15 years (P-0213), the result was the same, that is, the Court decided it had not been established beyond reasonable doubt that this individual was under 15 years within the time frame of the charges.

The Court seems to have accepted contradictions only for 4 of the alleged child soldiers. For these 4 individuals, the video evidence suggested they were younger than 15 years, while the oral and documentary evidence introduced by the defence suggested they were over 15 years (D-0040, D-0041, Bodyguard 1, Bodyguard 2). This contradictory evidence did not seem to impact significantly on the Court's conclusions since the Court found it proven beyond reasonable doubt that these individuals were younger than 15 years. The same conclusion was reached in relation to the 6 remaining alleged child soldiers (Individuals 1–6). For these individuals only video evidence was available, save for 1 witness in relation to Individual 1, and there were no contradictions.

Hence, from Table 4 it is evident that the Court placed trust in its own age assessments based on the physical appearance of alleged child soldiers, as they appeared in the video evidence. These assessments were considered more reliable than contradictory evidence introduced by the defence (D-0040, D-0041, Bodyguard 1, Bodyguard 2) and were also considered sufficient even lacking any other age evidence (Individuals 1–6). Conversely, forensic evidence was not trusted, neither when the other evidence offered no contradictions (P-0213), nor when it was wholly or partially contradicted by oral and/or documentary evidence introduced by the prosecution. Since this analysis only pertains to 19 alleged child soldiers in Lubanga, the generalizability of these findings is unknown. One important development in this regard will be the Appeal Chamber's assessments of similar issues in the Ntaganda case.[229] As such, the data presented here, as well as the prospect of future similar assessments motivate a thorough examination of challenges and opportunities pertaining to each of the relevant evidence types. Such examination is offered in the next Section.

---

[229] For more on this see Ntaganda Trial Chamber Judgment, see above note 74.

6.5.   Challenges and Opportunities with Age Estimations

This Section examines challenges and opportunities for each of the evidence types that were present in the cases outlined in Table 3, as well as in the LUBANGA case specified in Table 4, that is, forensic evidence (Section 6.5.1.), video or photo evidence (Section 6.5.2.), oral evidence (Section 6.5.3.) and documentary evidence (Section 6.5.4.).

6.5.1.   Forensic Evidence

6.5.1.1.   Challenges

6.5.1.1.1.   Validity

> [...] this approach will only provide an approximate answer, particularly given it is not an exact science.[230]

Forensic age estimation (FAE) has an inherent challenge to validity, namely that forensic methods enable assessments of physiological or biological age, rather than chronological age.[231] Hence, there is a mismatch between the construct of interest here; the chronological age and the forensic 'proxies' or operationalizations of it. Although the more specific forensic age indicators and methods used vary extensively across different jurisdictions, the three most common ones among EU states are assessments including the hand or wrist, that is, bone age,[232] teeth, that is, dental age[233] and clavicle or collarbone (also bone age).[234] As outlined in Table 4, the Lubanga case entailed hand or wrist and dental X-rays in relation to 9 alleged UPC child soldiers and when assessing the hands or wrists the experts used the so-called Greulich and Pyle (GP) index.[235]

One major reason for the lacking validity is that for instance bone age and dental age are general in the sense that they indicate trends in a

---

[230] Lubanga Trial Chamber Judgment, para. 176, see above note 4.

[231] See, for example, Doyle *et al.*, 2019, pp. 38–49, see above note 26.

[232] Bone age is defined as the general degree of maturation of bone that subjects of a population reach at a certain average age. This term may be used when referring to the bone age of a specific anatomical region such as the bone age in the hand and wrist, see *ibid.*

[233] Dental age is defined as the general degree of development of teeth that subjects of a population reach at a certain average age, see *ibid.*

[234] Dental X-rays, wrist X-rays and collar bone X-rays are all age indicators included in the recommendations by The Study Group on Forensic Age Diagnostics, see Schmeling *et al.*, 2008, see above note 21; Schmeling *et al.*, 2016, see above note 21.

[235] Lubanga Transcript of 12 May 2009, pp. 44–45, see above note 105.

population and it is uncertain whether and to what extent such trends are informative for individual assessments such as legal age estimations. This means that FAEs are properly understood as estimations of the most probable chronological age of an individual considering their skeletal and dental age, as well as their specific demographic characteristics such as sex, health, nutrition, and so on. As such, it is unknown exactly how bone age and dental age correlate with chronological age.[236] Consequently, it has been widely acknowledged that estimating chronological age is complex, some say "at best an educated guess"[237] and when possible, multiple techniques from different forensic disciplines should be used.[238]

Hence, the research available today does not allow safe conclusions about how much or little the results of FAEs deviate from the chronological ages of individuals or whether over- or under-estimations are more likely. While research has enabled the identification of error intervals and/or the proportion of false positives/negatives, these studies use different methodologies, for example when it comes to imaging techniques and/or the applied assessment scales as well as different samples,[239] and they also define and express error somewhat differently.[240] Hence, the more specific error which is most relevant for an individual assessment will vary. Appendix 2 provides an overview of meta-analyses and other studies outlining error intervals and/or the risk of false positives/negatives

---

[236] In other words, chronological age, dental age and bone age are not necessarily the same in a given individual, see, for example, Francesco Introna and Carlo P. Campobasso, "Biological vs Legal Age of Living Individuals", in Aurore Schmitt, Eugénia Cunha and João Pinheiro (eds.), *Forensic Anthropology and Medicine*, Humana Press, 2006, pp. 57–82.

[237] Wenke, 2017, p. 29, see above note 9.

[238] See, for example, EASO, 2018, p. 17, see above note 19.

[239] As implied above, the errors identified in research stem from studies using different kinds of methodologies, as a result of the disparities and lack of incorporated best practices for FAEs. This also means that it is unknown to what extent the error rates will be representative for the specific assessment in question, for example, in a real criminal case. Even though more specific information of the respective studies is provided in Appendix 2, this research is not necessarily sufficient to establish sound error intervals for each specific methodology. For that purpose, more studies with the exact same methodology would have to be conducted. For more on how error rates are often a problematic construct, see Itiel E. Dror, "The Error in 'Error Rate': Why Error Rates Are So Needed, Yet so Elusive", in *Journal of Forensic Sciences*, 2020, vol. 65, no. 4, pp. 1–27.

[240] For instance, some of the studies define and express error as a deviation from the exact known chronological age while other studies use percentages to express how many false positives or false negatives were obtained in relation to a specific age threshold (15, 18, 21) using a certain methodology to study a certain skeletal area in a certain sample.

---

in this regard. Research is still being conducted as regards the most appropriate methodological choices[241] as well as which skeletal areas to assess.[242]

Due to the large variation in how research studies have been conducted, it is uninformative to present average errors in estimations of chronological age based on hand/wrist, dental, clavicle as well as combined assessments. However, it is possible to outline factors that are likely to influence the error interval/risk of a false positive or negative. Legal actors should aim to gain an understanding of these factors for example by asking the hired and/or other experts. These factors include, but are not limited to, the following three.

To begin with, it varies whether and to what extent the applied methods/scales etc. have been validated in relation to the population of interest. In this regard, it can be noted that while the GP Index, which was used by the experts in Lubanga, is the most commonly used index today,[243] there are indications that it results in over-estimations of age for

---

[241] For instance, when it comes to which imaging modalities to use. Some modalities that are discussed are *ultrasound, CT, DXA/DEXA* and *MRI*. See Sara Larsen, Arge Tangmose and Niels Lynnerup, "The Danish Approach to Forensic Age Estimation in the Living: How, How Many and What's New? A Review of Cases Performed in 2012", in *Annals of Human Biology: Age Estimation*, 2015, vol. 42, no. 4, pp. 342–47; Fukran Ufuk, Kadir Agladiogl and Nevzat Karabulut, "CT Evaluation of Medial Clavicular Epiphysis as a Method of Bone Age Determination in Adolescents and Young Adults", in *Diagnostic and Interventional Radiology*, 2016, vol. 22, no. 3, pp. 241–46; Denise Heppe, "Bone Age Assessment by Dual-energy X-ray Absorptiometry in Children: An Alternative for X-ray", in *British Journal of Radiology*, 2012, vol. 85, no. 1010, pp. 114–20; Dedouit *et al.*, "Age Assessment by Magnetic Resonance Imaging of the Knee: A Preliminary Study", in *Forensic Science International*, 2012, vol. 217, pp. 232.e1-232.e7; Krämer *et al.*, "Forensic Age Estimation in Living Individuals using 3.0 T MRI of the Distal Femur", in *International Journal of Legal Medicine*, 2014, vol. 128, pp. 509–14.

[242] Apart from the already mentioned skeletal areas, reference data sets and atlases exists also for knees, foot/ankle, elbow and iliac crest. For more on this, see Sarah Pyle and Normand Louise Hoerr, *Radiographic Atlas of Skeletal Development of the Foot and Ankle: A Standard of Reference*, Blackwell Scientific Publications, 1957; Herman Grossman, "Radiology of the Pediatric Elbow", in *Pediatric Annals*, 1982, vol. 11, no. 6, pp. 560–62; Sven Schmidt *et al.*, "Sonographic Evaluation of Apophyseal Ossification of the Iliac Crest in Forensic Age Diagnostics in Living Individuals", in *International Journal of Legal Medicine*, 2011, vol. 125, no. 2, pp. 271–76.

[243] The Greulich and Pyle (GP) Atlas is based on Dr. William Walter Greulich and Dr. Sara Ideel Pyle's *The Radiographic Atlas of Skeletal Development of the Hand and Wrist* which was first published in 1959, but remains today the most commonly used atlas for skeletal age measurement by radiologists. The GP Atlas contains reference images of the left

some populations.[244] Therefore, it is often recommended that the GP is combined with other methods to promote a more accurate result. Although the GP approach is considered applicable and reliable for children in the UK,[245] Australia[246] and the Middle East,[247] disparities have been noted with for example Asian children,[248] and Afro-American and Hispanic samples.[249] For this reason, the GP approach has been adapted to a few populations, for example, from the Basque Country (used as a national reference in Spain)[250] and Germany,[251] but not for populations in any of

---

hand/wrist for male and female standard from birth till 18 years of age for females and 19 years of age for males. There are also written explanations of gradual age-related changes observed in the bone structure that accompany each standard image. To calculate bone age, a non-dominant wrist radiograph of the subject is compared with the nearest matching reference radiographs in the atlas. For more on this, see Cree M. Gaskin *et al.*, *Skeletal Development of the Hand and Wrist: A Radiographic Atlas and Digital Bone Age Companion*, Oxford University Press, 2011; William W. Greulich and S. Idell Pyle, *Radiographic Atlas of Skeletal Development of hand and Wrist*, Stanford University Press, 1959; Abdul M. Zafar, "An Appraisal of Greulich-Pyle Atlas for Skeletal Age Assessment in Pakistan", in *Journal of Pakistan Medical Association*, 2010, vol. 60, no. 7, pp. 552–55.

[244] Vilma Pinchi *et al.*, "Skeletal Age Estimation for Forensic Purposes: A Comparison of GP, TW2 and TW 3 Methods on an Italian Sample", in *Forensic Science International*, 2014, vol. 238, pp. 83–90.

[245] Lucina Hackman and Sue Black, "Age Estimation from Radiographic Images of the Knee", in *Journal of Forensic Sciences*, 2013, vol. 58, no. 3, pp. 732–37.

[246] LIN Ni-Hung, "New Growth References for Assessment of Stature and Skeletal Maturation in Australians", in *Australasian Orthodontic Journal*, 2015, vol. 22, no. 1, pp. 1–10.

[247] Michalle Soudack *et al.*, "Bone Age in the 21st Century: is Greulich and Pyle's Atlas Accurate for Israeli Children", in *Pediatric Radiology*, 2012, vol. 42, no. 3, pp. 343–48.

[248] Bora Buken *et al.*, "Is the Assessment of Bone Age by the Greulich-Pyle Method Reliable at Forensic Age Estimation for Turkish Children", in *Forensic Science International*, 2007, vol. 173, no. 2, pp. 146–53; Zafar, 2010, pp. 552–55, see above note 243.

[249] Pedro Manuel Garamendi *et al.*, "Reliability of the Methods Applied to Assess Age Minority in Living Subjects Around 18 years Old – A Survey on a Moroccan Origin Population", in *Forensic Science International*, 2005, vol. 154, no. 1, pp. 3–12; Randall T. Loder *et al.*, "Applicability of the Greulich and Pyle Skeletal Age Standards to Black and White Children of Today", in *American Journal of Diseases of Children*, 1993, vol. 147, no. 12, pp. 1329–33; Stefano Mora *et al.*, "Skeletal Age Determinations in Children of European and African Descent: Applicability of the Greulich and Pyle Standards", in *Pediatric Research*, 2001, vol. 50, no. 5, pp. 624–28; Francesca K. Ontell, "Bone Age in Children of Diverse Ethnicity", in *American Journal of Roentgenology*, 1996, vol. 167, no. 6, pp. 1395–98.

[250] Manuel Hernández, *Skeletal Maturation and Height Prediction: Atlas and Scoring Methods*, Ediciones Diaz de Santos, 1991.

[251] Hans-Heinrich Thiemann, Inna Nitz and Andreas Schmeling, "Röntgenatlas Der Normalen Hand im Kindesalter" (Radiographic Atlas of the Normal Hand At an early Age), in *International Journal of Legal Medicine*, 2007, vol. 12, p. 149.

the countries in which the child soldiering crimes allegedly have taken place (see Table 2).

Secondly, it is essential to find out whether and how demographic factors (sex, health, nutrition etc.) pertaining to the examined individual have been taken into account by the expert. There is no universally accepted standard for how to quantify demographic factors, although evidence-based guidelines[252] encourage forensic practitioners to find out as much assessment-relevant information as they possibly can.[253] This does not eliminate the issue since compliance rates are unknown[254] and it is far from self-evident how experts should integrate and express such factors.

Thirdly, so-called *age mimicry*, means that the specific age distribution in the studied population influences the results obtained for different

---

[252] A number of guidelines exist in age estimation in living individuals, see, for example Sue Black, Anil Aggrawal and Jason Payne-James, *Age Estimation in the Living: The Practitioner's Guide*, Wiley-Blackwell, 2010; EASO, 2018, p. 17, see above note 19; Daniel Franklin *et al.*, "Forensic Age Estimation in Living Individuals: Methodological Considerations in the Context of Medico-Legal Practice", in *Research and Reports in Forensic Medical Science*, 2015, vol. 5, no. 5, pp. 53–66; Michael J. Thali, Mark D. Viner and Gil Brogdon, *Brogdon's Forensic Radiology*, CRC Press, 2012. There are also guidelines on how to formulate the expert witness statement, see, for example American College of Radiologists, *ACR Practice Parameter on the Physician Expert Witness in Radiology and Radiation Oncology*, 2014; Royal College of Radiologists, *Providing Expert Advice to the Court: Guidance for Members and Fellows*, 2012.

[253] Forensic practitioners are encouraged to ensure that they have knowledge of all of the information that is available about the individual in questions, including but not limited to: sex, ancestry, geographical background, socio-economic status, health status, medication, diet, and lifestyle habits. Furthermore, these factors are to be taken into account when undertaking the skeletal age assessment. For more on this, see, for example, Robert Cameriere *et al.*, "Effects of Nutrition on Timing of Mineralization in Teeth in a Peruvian Sample by the Cameriere and Demirjian Methods", in *Annals of Human Biology*, 2007, vol. 34, no. 5, pp. 547–66; Lynn Meijerman *et al.*, "Variables Affecting the Probabiliy of Complete Fusion of the Medial Clavicular Epiphysis", in *International Journal of Legal Medicine*, 2007, vol. 121, no. 6, pp. 463–68; Andreas Olze *et al.*, "Forensic Age Estimations in Living Subjects: The Ethic Factor in Wisdom Tooth Mineralization", in *International Journal of Legal Medicine*, 2004, vol. 118, no. 3, pp. 170–73; Andreas Schmeling *et al.*, "Effects of Ethnicity on Skeletal Maturation: Consequences for Forensic Age Estimation", in *International Journal of Legal Medicine*, 2000, vol. 113, no. 5, pp. 252–58; Andreas Schmeling, "The Impact of Economic Progress and Modernization in Medicine on the Ossification of Hand and Wrist", in *International Journal of Legal Medicine*, 2006, vol. 120, no. 2, pp. 121–26.

[254] Overall, there is a need for better co-ordination in the field of forensic age estimations.

ossification/mineralization stages.[255] To illustrate, the ossification of a skeletal area may be graded on a scale from 1 to 5 and researchers try to understand at what age stage 4 is reached. In a study, the ages of the studied population are evenly distributed between 15 and 20 years, and the result is that stage 4 is reached at 17 years with a 2-year dispersion. Later, the study is extended to also include 12 to 14-year olds so that the ages in the studied population are evenly distributed between 12 and 20 years. Now, the average age at which stage 4 is reached is 16 years with a diversion of 2.5 years. This is because the extended study also included individuals whose skeleton ossified unusually early, and thereby they reach stage 4 before they turn 15 years. These individuals will then decrease the average age at which stage 4 is reached and also increase the diversion.

Since legal age elements such as the 15-year threshold of interest here entail dichotomous decisions; either someone is considered younger than 15 years or instead 15 years or older, it is not necessarily a requirement to know someone's exact age. In other words, it does not matter whether an alleged child soldier is 13 or 14 years as long as he or she is younger than 15 years and vice versa; it does not matter if he or she is 17 or 18 years as long as he or she has turned 15 years or more. Consequently, the error intervals are only a problem if they comprehend the 15-year threshold (for example, 13–16 years) or if the crime in question is a continuous crime and it is relevant to establish whether someone turned 15 years in the duration of the crime. The war crime(s) of conscripting, enlisting and/or using child soldiers is indeed a continuous crime[256] and it is possible that such questions will arise. However, the dichotomous nature of the age element means that not all types of uncertainty are necessarily legally relevant, even if they come from a science that is inexact.[257] Argu-

---

[255] For more on age mimicry and possible methods for researchers to prevent it, see, for example, Øyvind Bleka et al., "BioAlder: A Tool for Assessing Chronological Age Based on Two Radiological Methods", in International Journal of Legal Medicine, 2019, vol. 133, pp. 1177–89. See also The Norwegian Institute of Public Health (NIPH), "Demirjian's Development Stages on Wisdom Teeth for Estimation of Chronological Age: A Systematic Review", March 2017 (available on its web site).

[256] As such, it only ends when the child reaches the 15-year threshold or leaves the force or group, see Lubanga Trial Chamber Judgment, para. 618, see above note 4.

[257] It can be noted that the statement from the Trial Chamber that forensic age estimations can only provide approximate answers since they do not come from an exact science, is likely to originate from the testifying expert herself, since she, fully accurately and in line with provided guidelines draws the Court's attention to sources of variation in the estimations,

ably, *there is no such thing* as an exact science, but rather scientific fields or scientists that are more or less effective in communicating uncertainty and what uncertainty means.[258] In this specific context, a prerequisite for communicating uncertainty effectively is for experts to state their conclusions as age intervals with minimum and maximum ages rather than one single age.[259] While such conduct is in line with guidelines developed to promote international best practice among forensic practitioners, it is unknown to what extent the guidelines are abided by in practice.[260] In the Lubanga case the experts did not offer any specific age intervals but did express uncertainty in their estimations, for instance that it was "scientifically possible"[261] that an alleged child soldier was under 15 years. In relation to other alleged child soldiers, the experts provided more general statements like someone being "born before December 1988".[262] Presumably, this is an indication that the experts knew that December 1988 was

---

see Lubanga Transcript of 12 May 2009, see above note 105, p. 34, lines 15–20: "[…] But you must understand that this is not a precise science […] There are a number of variation factors, and they are well known". Whether the expert and the Court understands preciseness or exactness in the same way is a different topic.

[258] The topic of communicating scientific uncertainty between scientific experts and legal experts has received more attention in recent years as this has proven to be relatively challenging, see, for example, Agnes S. Bali *et al.*, "Communicating Forensic Science Opinion: An Examination of Expert Reporting Practices", in *Science and Justice*, 2020, vol. 60, no. 3, pp. 1–9; Rafael Urbaniak *et al.*, "Decision-theoretic and Risk-based Approaches to Naked Statistical Evidence: Some Consequences and Challenges", in *Law, Probability and Risk*, 2020, vol. 19, no. 1, pp. 1–17. A topic that seems particularly relevant is how uncertainty reported from different scientific fields relate to 'reasonable doubt'. Although age estimations will always be associated with doubts, some doubts may be unreasonable given that there may not be more certain scientific methods available and in an epistemological sense it might not make sense to doubt this knowledge. Similarly, if scientific uncertainty is regularly understood as reasonable doubt, this may make criminal justice inefficient.

[259] For more on this see Doyle *et al.*, 2019, pp. 38–49, see above note 26.

[260] See *ibid*. Some argue that the so-called minimum age concept is a useful approach in the forensic setting, see Schmeling *et al.*, 2016, pp. 44–50, see above note 21.

[261] Experts P-0358 and P-0359: "it is scientifically possible for P-0010 to have been under the age of 15 at the time of her recruitment in late 2002". ICC, *The Prosecutor v. Thomas Lubanga Dyilo*, OTP, Prosecution's Closing Brief, 1 June 2011, ICC-01/04-01/06-2748-Red, para. 400, fn. 1156, citing expert report EVD-OTP-00430 ('Lubanga Prosecution's Closing Brief') (https://www.legal-tools.org/doc/92ecf9/); and Lubanga Trial Chamber Judgment, para. 264, see above note 4.

[262] See *ibid.*, para. 177, fn. 452, citing expert report EVD-OTP-00428, T-172-Red-ENG, p. 47, lines 7 ff. The expert concluded that the witness was aged at least 19 on 5 December 2007 and was therefore born before December 1988.

---

an important date in relation to the 15-year threshold, and it can be questioned whether their assessments would have been different without such knowledge (for more on this see Section 6.5.1.1.3. "Biasability").

Yet another potential challenge with using FAE's is the frequently long time-span from the point in time when the alleged war crime(s) involving child soldiers took place to the point in time when the ages of the alleged child soldiers are to be estimated. In the Lubanga case, the official documents do not indicate when the dental and hand or wrist X-rays were taken, but as outlined in Table 2, approximately 10 years had passed since the beginning of the alleged crime (2002) up until the first conviction (2012). Even though such a time span is common in child soldiering cases[263] and unsurprising given the complexities associated with such investigations[264] it poses a risk that FAEs are no longer informative. More specifically, alleged child soldiers who were younger than 15 years at the time of the alleged crimes will have matured physically to the extent that examining their wrists, teeth or collarbones is pointless. Their hands or wrists and collarbones may already have fully fused and their teeth may have fully emerged as well as mineralized. Although there is clearly individual variation as to when this happens, research suggests that hand or wrist ossification as well as third molar ("wisdom teeth") mineralization are commonly completed at some point between 18 and 20 years.[265] Also,

---

[263] See, for instance, the Taylor case in which approximately 16 years passed between the commencement of the crime and the first conviction (1996–2012) and the Ntaganda case in which approximately 17 years had passed (2002–19), although neither of these cases entailed forensic evidence about the alleged child soldiers' ages.

[264] See, for example, Elinor Fry, "The Nature of International Crimes and Evidentiary Challenges", in Elies van Sliedregt and Sergey Vasiliev (eds.), *Pluralism in International Criminal Law*, Oxford University Press, Oxford, 2014, pp. 251–72; Mark Klamberg, *Evidence in International Criminal Procedure: Confronting Legal Gaps and the Reconstruction of Disputed Events*, Stockholm University, Stockholm, 2012.

[265] Different studies show different results, and age mimicry is one possible explanation of this. For more on the topic, see Mattias Haglund and Håkan Mörnstad, "A Systematic Review and Meta-analysis of the Fully Formed Wisdom Tooth as a Radiological Marker of Adulthood", in *International Journal of Legal Medicine*, 2019, vol. 133, no. 1, pp. 231–39, according to which 50 per cent of the studied individuals had fully matured wisdom teeth when 20 years old; Petter Mostad and Fredrik Tamsen, "Error Rates for Unvalidated Medical Age Assessment Procedures", in *International Journal of Legal Medicine*, 2019, vol. 133, pp. 613–23, suggesting that this occurs at 19.5 years for 50 per cent of the studied individuals; Manzor Mughal, Arsalan Hassan and Anwar Ahmed, "Bone Age Assessment Methods: A Critical Review", in *Pakistan Journal of Medical Sciences*, 2014, vol. 30, no. 1, pp. 211–15, implying that some individuals have fully matured bones at 18 years.

---

the medial epiphysis of the clavicle or collarbone fuses around the age of 22 years.[266] Therefore, a CT of the medial end of the clavicle is the most commonly used and extensively developed modality for assessing individuals aged 18–22 years.[267] It is therefore possible that further evaluation based on the clavicle could have provided more relevant information in the Lubanga case for some of the alleged child soldiers. For instance, based on the hand or wrist assessment of one alleged child soldier, the expert noted that:

> It is a simple case here. There is no growth cartilage any longer, and there is no clear or light line around the radius of the ulna. Therefore, we can conclude that this young individual has finished growing, has reached the last stage of the Greulich and Pyle index. That is, he is at least 19 years of age. From that point onward, we cannot determine whether he's 19, 25, or 90 years old, because once the bones have fused, it's forever.[268]

Other possibilities to estimate age in situations like these, including for example DNA methylation are discussed in Section 6.5.1.2. Opportunities.

6.5.1.1.2. Reliability

Since X-rays are depictions of human skeleton made using more or less accurate and precise technologies, X-rays can often be quite ambiguous. The task difficulty stemming from the X-ray itself is likely to result in a more or less serious lack of *Between Expert Reliability*.[269] In other words,

---

[266] Although this is dependent on the biological sex of the individual, see Louise Scheuer and Sue M. Black, *Developmental Juvenile Osteology*, Academic Press, London, 2000; Andreas Schmeling *et al.*, "Studies on the Time Frame for Ossification of the Medial Clavicular Epiphyseal Cartilage in Conventional Radiography", in *International Journal of Legal Medicine*, 2004, vol. 118, no. 1, pp. 5–8.

[267] See Doyle *et al.*, 2019, pp. 38–49, see above note 26; Mughal, Hassan and Ahmed, 2014, pp. 211–15, see above note 265.

[268] Lubanga Transcript of 12 May 2009, pp. 44–45, see above note 105.

[269] For more on the topic of why experts disagree with one another see, for example, Moa Lidén and Itiel E. Dror, "Expert Reliability in Legal Proceedings: "Eeny, Meeny, Miny, Moe, With Which Expert Should We Go?"", in *Science and Justice*, 2020, pp. 1–21; Itiel E. Dror and Daniel C. Murrie, "A Hierarchy of Expert Performance (HEP) Applied to Forensic Psychological Assessments", in *Psychology, Public Policy, and Law*, 2018, vol. 24, no. 1, pp. 11–23; Lucy A. Guarnera, Daniel C. Murrie and Marcus T. Boccaccini, "Why Do Forensic Experts Disagree? Sources of Unreliability and Bias in Forensic Psychology

experts examining the exact same X-ray to estimate the age of the exact same individual, are likely to make different observations and also draw different conclusions. There is no worldwide study on the prevalence and extent of this problem. However, field data from asylum cases dealt with by the Swedish Board of Forensic Medicine shows that two independent odontologists examining the exact same dental X-rays to make determinations in relation to the 18 year threshold reached different conclusions as to whether the third molars ("the wisdom teeth") were fully matured or not in 9.29 per cent of the cases.[270] Similarly, radiologists examining the exact same knee X-rays disagreed about whether the knees were fully fused in 8.05–55.00 per cent of the cases.[271] Notably, also *across* these different categories of experts there was disagreement in 11.98–42.66 per cent of the cases.[272] In other words, age estimation in relation to the same individual may vary depending on whether an odontologist or radiologist is asked to conduct the assessment,[273] as well as which more specific odontologist or radiologist makes the assessment. Similar results have been found under controlled experimental conditions for age estimations based on knee X-rays[274] and wrist X-rays,[275] other types of radiological interpre-

---

Evaluations", in *Translational Issues in Psychological Science*, 2017, vol. 3, no. 2, pp. 143–52; Daniel C. Murrie and Janet Warren, "Clinician Variation in Rates of Legal Sanity Opinions: Implications for Self-Monitoring", in *Professional Psychology: Research and Practice*, 2005, vol. 36, no. 5, pp. 519–24; Marcus T. Boccaccini, Darrel B. Turner and Daniel C. Murrie, "Do Some Evaluators Report Consistently Higher or Lower PCL-R Scores than Others? Findings from a Statewide Sample of Sexually Violent Predator Evaluations", in *Psychology, Public Policy, and Law*, 2008, vol. 15, no. 4, pp. 262–83.

[270] For more on the Swedish data and the problem of lacking between expert reliability see Lidén and Dror, 2020, pp. 1–21, see above note 269.

[271] *Ibid.*

[272] *Ibid.*

[273] As regards the national context, it can be noted that most European countries use two or more age indicators but which these two indicators are vary somewhat, see EASO, 2018, p. 58, see above note 19.

[274] More specifically, this related to estimations based on the proximal tibial epiphyses, in relation to which interobserver agreement of $\kappa = 0.941$–0.951, see Christian Ottow *et al.*, "Forensic Age Estimation by Magnetic Resonance Imaging of the Knee: the Definite Relevance in Bony Fusion of the Distal Femoral- and the Proximal Tibial Epiphyses using Closest to Bone TI TSE Sequence", in *European Radiology*, 2017, vol. 27, no. 12, pp. 5041–48.

[275] Hans Henrik Thodberg and Lars Sävendahl, "Validation and Reference Values of Automated Bone Age Determination for Four Ethnicities", in *Academic Radiology*, 2010, vol. 17, no. 11, p. 1428.

---

tations relating to wrist X-rays[276] as well as in specialist neuroradiology.[277]

Unlike in the studies cited above, it seems like the experts involved in the Lubanga case were not strictly speaking independent of one another as they regularly worked together on age assessment matters[278] and while they had different main responsibilities, they presented joint conclusions in a report jointly signed.[279] Although the more specific circumstances of their assessments are unknown, it is possible that they were aware of each other's conclusions and were influenced by them, and such influence is not necessarily conscious at all. Reasonably, the evidence from two or more independent examiners who reach the same conclusions has a stronger probative value. Yet, it should also be noted that one of the experts testifying in the Lubanga case herself pointed out the potential problem of lacking Between Expert Reliability (as well as Within Expert Reliability). More specifically, she stated that the likely variability in relation to the interpretation of hand X-rays between experts is one year, while the variation between one and the same experts at different points in time is less.[280] Clearly, neither the Trial nor the Appeals Chamber trusted the forensic evidence as a bases for age estimations of the alleged child soldiers, see Table 4, since this evidence was believed to come from an inexact science. While this is obviously true, an alternative approach would have

---

[276] More specifically, this was for the detection of bone erosion in rheumatoid arthritis and disagreement varied depending on what radiological technique was used, see Richard Waver *et al.*, "Carpal Pseudoerosions: A Plain X-ray Interpretation Pitfall", in *Skeletal Radiology*, 2014, vol. 43, no. 10, pp. 1377–85.

[277] Gaving Briggs *et al.*, "The Role of Specialist Neuroradiology Second Opinion Reporting: Is there Added Value?", in *Clinical Radiology*, 2008, vol. 63, no. 7, pp. 791–95.

[278] Lubanga Transcript of 13 May 2009, p. 22, see above note 106.

[279] *Ibid.*, pp. 46–47. After a question from the defence on this matter, the second expert indicated that she did look at the hand or wrist X-rays as well, although her conclusions in the report bore only on the dental age assessments.

[280] See *ibid.* The expert is asked what the limits of the conclusions are and answers *inter alia* that: "[…] you must understand that this is not a precise science […]" (*ibid.*, p. 34). Then she specifies: "First of all, there is what we call intra-or inter-individual variability […]" (*ibid.*) and later on explains that "We deemed that the inter-variability is about one year […] and we know that this intra-variability, individual variability, is lower, shorter than one year". (*ibid.*, p. 35). As other factors that limit the conclusions, she states, for example, socio-economic conditions and geographical origin and the fact that the Atlas used assess age was based on other populations than those of interest in the Lubanga case.

been to include more experts, and independent experts, for example, from different countries. This is elaborated on in Section 6.5.1.2.

6.5.1.1.3. Biasability

Today, there is ample research into the so-called *forensic confirmation bias*.[281] This research highlights how the assessments of forensic examiners can be biased by knowledge of different types of contextual information, for instance that the suspect confessed,[282] what the investigators' hypothesis is[283] or other evidence available in the case,[284] especially if such evidence has strong emotional content (for example, pictures of wounded children). [285] Effects of contextual information have been demonstrated in relation to fingerprint analysis,[286] comparisons of shoe prints,[287] bite marks,[288] bullets[289] and handwriting samples.[290] It has also

---

[281] For an overview of this field see Kassin, Dror and Kukucka, 2013, pp. 42–52, see above note 30. For a response by a forensic examiner see Leonard Butt, "The Forensic Confirmation Bias: Problems, Perspective, and Proposed Solutions: Commentary by a Forensic Examiner", in *Journal of Applied Research in Memory and Cognition*, 2013, vol. 2, no. 1, pp. 59–60. For other parts of this debate see Jeff Kukucka, "People Who Live in Ivory Towers Shouldn't Throw Stones: A Refutation of Curley et al.", in *Forensic Science International*, 2020, vol. 2, pp. 1–11.

[282] See, for example, Jeff Kukucka and Saul Kassin, "Do Confessions Taint perceptions of Handwriting Evidence? An Empirical Test of the Forensic Confirmation Bias", in *Law and Human Behavior*, 2013, vol. 38. no. 3, pp. 1–15.

[283] See, for example, Kassin, Dror and Kukucka, 2013, pp. 42–52, see above note 30.

[284] See, for example, Itiel E. Dror and David Charlton, "Why Experts Make Errors", in *Journal of Forensic Identification*, 2006, vol. 56, no. 4, pp. 600–16; and Itiel E. Dror, David Charlton and Ailsa E. Péron, "Contextual Information Renders Experts Vulnerable to Making Erroneous Identifications", in *Forensic Science International*, 2006, vol. 156, no. 1, pp. 74–78.

[285] See, for example, Itiel E. Dror *et al.*, "When Emotions Get the Better of Us: The Effect of Contextual Top-down processing on Matching Fingerprints", in *Applied Cognitive Psychology*, 2005, vol. 19, no. 6, pp. 799–809.

[286] Osborne and Zajac, 2016, pp. 126–34, see above note 33.

[287] José H. Kerstholt, Roos Passhuis and Marjan Sjerps, "Shoe Print Examinations: Effects of Expectation, Complexity and Experience", in *Forensic Science International*, 2007, vol. 165, no. 1, pp. 30–34.

[288] Nikola K.P. Osborne *et al.*, "Does Contextual Information Bias Bitemark Comparisons?", in *Science and Justice*, 2014, vol. 54, no. 4, pp. 267–73.

[289] José H. Kerstholt *et al.*, "Does Suggestive Information Cause a Confirmation Bias in Bullet Comparisons?", in *Forensic Science International*, 2010, vol. 198, no. 1, pp. 138–42.

[290] Kukucka and Kassin, 2013, pp. 1–15, see above note 282.

---

been noted in bloodstain pattern analysis ('BPA'),[291] dog detection evidence,[292] evaluations of skeletal remains,[293] arson investigations,[294] forensic pathology[295] and a range of forensic reconstructions.[296] Also, a bias may be introduced because of base rate expectations, that is, the bias does not originate from anything related to the specific case at hand but instead on past experience of other cases in the past, which results in expectations about the nature of this specific case.[297] Such expectations may impact on examiners' perceptions of a specific piece of evidence, even if logically speaking, the expectations cannot change the nature of the evidence.

While the question of bias in relation to interpretations of X-rays or MRI-images specifically has not been empirically evaluated yet, the cited

---

[291] Nikola K.P. Osborne, Michael C. Taylor and Rachel Zajac, "Exploring the Role of Contextual Information in Bloodstain Pattern Analysis: A Qualitative Approach", in *Forensic Science International*, 2016, vol. 260, pp. 1–8.

[292] Lisa Lit, Julie B. Schweitzer and Anita M. Oberbauer, "Handler Beliefs Affect Scent Detection Dog Outcomes", in *Animal Cognition*, 2011, vol. 14, no. 3, pp. 387–94. Also, since the ultimate determination that an alert has been signalled by the dog rests solely with the human handler, the process is highly dependent on human judgments and therefore also potentially fallible in this regard, see Sherri Minhinnick *et al.*, "Training Fundamental and the Selection of Dogs and Personnel for Detection Work", in Tadeusz Jezierski, John Ensminger, L.E. Papet (eds.), *Canine Olfaction Science and Law: Advances in Forensic Science, Medicine, Conservation, and Environmental Remediation*, CRC Press, 2016, pp. 155–71.

[293] Sherry Nakhaeizadeh, Ian Hanson and Nathalie Dozzi, "The Power of Contextual Effects in Forensic Anthropology: A Study of Biasability in the Visual Interpretations of Trauma Analysis on Skeletal Remains", in *Journal of Forensic Sciences*, 2014, vol. 59, no. 5, pp. 1177–83; Sherry Nakhaeizadeh *et al.*, "Cascading Bias of Initial Exposure to Information at the Crime Scene to the Subsequent Evaluation of Skeletal Remains", in *Journal of Forensic Sciences*, 2018, vol. 63, no. 2, pp. 403–11.

[294] Paul Bieber, "Fire Investigation and Cognitive Bias", in Allan Jamieson and Andre Moenssens (eds.), *Wiley Encyclopedia of Forensic Science*, Wiley, 2014, pp. 1–13.

[295] William R. Oliver, "Effect of History and Context on Forensic Pathologist Interpretation of Photographs of Patterned Injury of the Skin", in *Journal of Forensic Sciences*, 2017, vol. 62, no. 6, pp. 1500–05.

[296] See, for instance, Emma A. Levin *et al.*, "A Comparison of Thresholding Methods for Forensic Reconstruction Studies Using Fluorescent Powder Proxies for Trace Materials", in *Journal of Forensic Sciences*, 2019, vol. 64, no. 2, pp. 1–10; Rachael Carew, Ruth M. Morgan and Carolyn Rando, "A Preliminary Investigation into the Accuracy of 3D Modelling and 3D Printing in Forensic Anthropology Evidence Reconstruction", in *Journal of Forensic Sciences*, 2008, vol. 64, no. 2, pp. 342–52.

[297] See, for example, Itiel E. Dror, "Human Expert Performance in Forensic Decision Making: Seven Different Sources of Bias", in *Australian Journal of Forensic Sciences*, 2017, vol. 49, no. 5, p. 544.

research about similar complex and visual assessments do indeed highlight a risk of bias. For this reason, it is important not only to conduct research into X-ray interpretation specifically but also, in the meantime, to be aware of what type of information is available to odontologists, radiologists or other forensic experts that are consulted. It is likely that cases concerning child soldiering charges contain many potential sources of bias. In fact, the crime type itself is likely to generate emotional reactions, for instance because it, potentially, involves children and very vulnerable children. Experts may, more or less subconsciously, be motivated to reach certain conclusions, for example, that an individual is a child soldier rather than a soldier, and this motivation may lead them to subconsciously attend to and emphasize more the aspects of the X-rays supporting the conclusion that the individual was younger than 15 years within the time frame of the charges.[298]

Another possible source of bias in relation to child soldiering charges is base rate expectations. For instance, the experts may be aware that the examined individual lived in a village from which many child soldiers were recruited or kidnapped or that the individual belonged to a group in which the prevalence of children is known. In the cases dealt with by the SCSL, it was accepted as an established fact that the Revolutionary United Front ('RUF') or Armed Forces Revolutionary Council ('AFRC') had Small Boys Units ('SBUs') and Small Girls Units ('SGUs'). According to testimony known at the time, these units consisted of young or even very young children. In the Taylor case some witnesses testified to seeing children as young as five years in these units.[299] Similarly, in the Lubanga case it was accepted that there were "Kadogos", that is young fighters, although compared to the SCSL cases, there was more uncertainty due to the multiple age ranges suggested by witnesses. The Trial Chamber stated that the military wing of the UPC, under Lubanga's leadership, was known to recruit young people, regardless of age, in schools and in villages. Some of these recruitment efforts were coercive, including abductions. This meant that children under 15 years old were recruited – in violation of international law – whether or not this was specifically

---

[298] For more on the topic of motivated reasoning as well as the so-called compassion fade effect see Moa Lidén, "Emotions in International Criminal Justice: A Threat and a Promise?", in *Forensic Science International: Mind and Law*, 2020, pp. 1–17 (forthcoming).

[299] SCSL Taylor Trial Chamber Judgment, para. 1597, see above note 67.

intended. The children were sent to training camps where "they were beaten, whipped, imprisoned and inadequately fed". Young female recruits were raped. The children were encouraged to smoke cannabis and "drink alcohol" and were frequently intoxicated.[300]

It is unknown whether and to what extent experts in, for example, the Lubanga case were aware of such information. To a certain extent, it has been acknowledged that base rates are in fact relevant for forensic decision making.[301] This is in line with Bayes theorem which is used and incorporated into many types of forensic assessments. However, it is important to remember the distinction between observations and conclusions. Statistically speaking, it may be reasonable to incorporate base rates into, for example, the stated certainty of a certain conclusion. Yet, a known base rate cannot, regardless of how accurate it is, change the nature of the evidence. The X-ray is exactly the same regardless of whether there were "Kadogos", SBUs or SGUs or not. Hence, if base rate expectations bias examiners in the sense that they perceive of the X-rays differently than someone without such base rate expectations, this is neither rational nor desired applying Bayes theorem. In practice, this could mean that the base rate is triple counted, first in the observations, then in the stated certainty of the conclusion, and then also by the judges who are to integrate all the information, including the age estimation and knowledge that the individual was considered a "Kadogo" or belonged to a SBU or SGU.

6.5.1.2. Opportunities

To the extent that traditional FAEs based on, for example, wrists and teeth are still informative at the time when alleged child soldiers are examined, recently developed and tested deep learning approaches can be useful since they seem to entail smaller risks of error. Such results have been obtained using hand X-rays in the age range of 3 to 17 years,[302] pelvic X-

---

[300] Lubanga Trial Chamber Judgment, para. 32, see above note 4.

[301] See the vast literature on the base rate fallacy, see, for example, Gunnar Goude, "Base-rate Fallacy: Who is Wrong About What in What Way?", in *Uppsala Psychological Reports*, Uppsala, 1981.

[302] KIM Jeong Rye *et al.*, "Computerized Bone Age Estimation Using Deep Learning: Based Program: Evaluation of the Accuracy and Efficiency", in *American Journal of Roentgenology*, 2017, vol. 209, no. 6, pp. 1374–80. See also LEE Jang Hyung *et al.*, "Bone Age Estimation Using Deep Learning and Hand X-ray Images", in *Biomedical Engineering Letters*, 2020, vol. 10, no. 3, pp. 1–10.

rays in the age range of 10 to 25 years[303] as well as MRI-images of knees in the age range of 14 to 21 years.[304] To illustrate, with the automated approach used in the last study (MRI knee), 98.10 per cent of male subjects and 95.00 per cent of female subjects were correctly classified in relation to the 18 year threshold.[305] One automated approach which address specifically the problem of lacking Between Expert Reliability as well as issues stemming from ethnical variations is the BoneXpert software[306] which replaces the Greulich and Pyle (GP) assessment.[307] This software was developed and validated with data from European Caucasian children[308] but more recently it has also been validated with a large dataset from Los Angeles including images of children's wrists recorded on

---

[303] LI Yuan *et al.*, "Forensic Age Estimation for Pelvic X-ray Images using Deep Learning", in *European Radiology*, 2018, vol. 29, no. 5, pp. 2322–29.

[304] Ana Dallora *et al.*, "Age Assessment of Youth and Young Adults Using Magnetic Resonance Imaging of the Knee: A Deep Learning Approach", in *JMIR Medical Informatics*, 2019, vol. 7, no. 4, pp. 1–17. MRI examinations were conducted for 402 volunteer subjects, 221 males and 181 females. The method comprised two convolutional neural network ('CNN') models: the first one selected the most informative images of MRI sequence for age assessment purposes. These were then used in the second module, which was responsible for the age estimation. Different CNN architectures were tested, both training from scratch and employing transfer learning. The CNN architecture that provided the best results was that referred to as 'GoogLeNet', pretrained on the ImageNet database.

[305] For the male subjects in the range of 14-20.5 years, the mean absolute error ('MAE') was 0.793 years, and for the female subjects in the range of 14-19.5 years, the MAE was 0.988 years.

[306] See BoneXpert's web site. This software is a commercially available medical device in Europe and an investigation device in the US has been certified for use in the clinical setting in Europe. For more see Hans Henrik Thodberg, "Clinical Review: An Automated Method for Determination of Bone Age", in *The Journal of Clinical Endocrinology and Metabolism*, 2009, vol. 94, no. 7, pp. 2239–44; Rick R. van Rijn, Maarten H. Lequin and Hans Henrik Thodberg, "Automatic Determination of Greulich and Pyle Bone Age in Healthy Dutch Children", in *Pediatric Radiology*, 2009, vol. 39, no. 6, pp. 591–97; Hans Henrik Thodberg *et al.*, "The BoneXpert Method for Automated Determination of Skeletal Maturity", in *IEEE Transactions on Medical Imaging*, 2009, vol. 28, no. 1, pp. 52–66; Thodberg and Sävendahl, 2010, pp. 1425–32, see above note 275.

[307] *Ibid.*; Hans Henrik Thodberg *et al.*, "Automated Determination of Bone Age from Hand X-rays at the End of Puberty and Its Applicability for Age Estimation", in *International Journal of Legal Medicine*, 2017, vol. 131, no. 3, pp. 771–80.

[308] Thodberg *et al.*, 2009, pp. 2239–44, see above note 306; David D. Martin *et al.*, "Clinical Application of Automated Greulich-Pyle Bone Age in Children with Short Stature", in *Pediatric Radiology*, 2009, vol. 39, no. 6, pp. 598–607; van Rijn, Lequin and Thodberg, 2009, pp. 591–97, see above note 306.

multiple occasions between 1993 and 2006 with children from four ethnicities; Caucasian, African American, Hispanic and Asian.[309]

The automated approaches described above are likely to help also
with issues such as lacking Between Expert Reliability as well as Biasability. When it comes to Between Expert Reliability it is also, from the
perspective of the legal actors, desirable to include more experts, and independent experts, for example, from different countries. Should these
experts disagree it may constitute reasonable doubt regarding the alleged
child soldiers' ages. However, should these experts agree, it is likely that
at least some of the uncertainty has been removed and it may no longer be
reasonable to doubt the experts' opinions, particularly not if they are expressed as age intervals. As discussed in Section 6.3. on diagnostic accuracy, there are no general answers as to how scientific uncertainty relates
to the BARD-standard,[310] but, it should be viewed in the light of how
much uncertainty other types of age assessments such as those based on,
for example, physical appearance or oral evidence entail. Furthermore,
from the perspective of the forensic practitioners, it is essential to engage
in continuous training, including attempts to calibrate assessments of different practitioners within the same discipline. There are many reasons as
to why experts may disagree including differences in training, experience,
personality, task difficulty, and so on. This also means that some types of
disagreement are more desirable than others. If the disagreement stems
from task difficulty, it is essential that legal actors are made aware of the
disagreement as it is directly relevant for their legal assessments. Clearly,
disagreement between experts does not have to be an indication that the
experts lack proper experience or assessment tools. Interpreting X-rays is
a difficult task and radiology is a medical specialty in relation to which
the need for continuous training, including calibration attempts, has been
noted for several different types of interpretations.[311] Forensic practition-

---

[309] Thodberg and Sävendahl, 2010, pp. 1425–32, see above note 275.

[310] See, for example, David B. Allison, Pavela Gregory and Ivan Oransky, "Reasonable Versus
Unreasonable Doubt", in *American Scientist*, 2018, vol. 106, no. 2, p. 84; Weiss, 2003, pp.
25–46, see above note 51.

[311] See, for example, S. Wentzel *et al.*, "E-learning for Chest X-ray Interpretation Improves
Medical Student Skills and Confidence Levels", in *BMC Medical Education*, 2018, vol. 18,
pp. 1–8. In this study, the findings demonstrated a modest improvement in basic chest X-
ray interpretation skills and confidence among first year graduate entry medical school
students following the introduction of an e-learning module. For similar studies see Chris-
tiane M. Nyhsen *et al.*, "Undergraduate Radiology Teaching from Student's Perspective",

ers are also encouraged to engage in continued education and training.[312] Also, of international recognition is the German Study Group on Forensic Age Diagnostics ('AGFAD') of the German Society of Legal Medicine which offers proficiency tests on annual basis to promote quality.[313]

When it comes to the question of Biasability specifically, it is important that forensic practitioners, as far as possible conduct contextual information management ('CIM'), whereby a context manager makes assessment of whether information is relevant or irrelevant for the forensic assessment as well as potentially biasing or not.[314] On this basis, the context manager will then chose what information to disclose to forensic examiners, and when. While implementing CIM is the primary responsibility of forensic laboratories, contextual information may be provided in communication with legal actors, who should therefore also be aware of the potential issues stemming from this.

In situations where traditional FAEs are unlikely to be informative, or as an alternative or complement to them in other situations, one possibility which is currently being researched is based on genetics and called DNA methylation. In the past five years a number of reports have shown that distinct epigenetic changes, that is, altered methylation levels, occur during the process of aging, and these changes show a high degree of correlation (both increased and decreased methylation levels) with chrono-

---

in *Insights into Imaging*, 2013, vol. 4, no. 1, pp. 103–09; Martin Maleck *et al.*, "Do Computers Teach Better? A Media Comparison Study for Case-Based Teaching in Radiology", in *Radiography*, 2013, vol. 21, no. 4, pp. 1025–32.

[312] For instance, in the case of radiographers, such professional training is outlined by the International Association of Forensic Radiographers ('IAFR'), in conjunction with professional bodies like the Irish Institute of Radiography and Radiation Therapy ('IIRRT') and The Society and College of Radiographers ('SOR'). For more on this see, for example, The Society and College of Radiographers and the International Association of Forensic Radiographers, *Guidance for Radiographers Providing Forensic Radiography Services*, 2014 and the Irish Institute of Radiography and Radiation Therapy, *Forensic Imaging: Best Practice Guidelines*, 2013.

[313] This certification ensures at a global level, although especially European level, that the forensic practitioners have the skills to assess age and regularly review these skills to ensure they are up to date, valid and admissible. For more on this see, for example, Schmeling *et al.*, 2008, see above note 21.

[314] See, for example, Michael C. Taylor and Nikola K.P. Osborne, "Letter to the Editor: A Contribution to Contextual Information Management in Bloodstain Pattern Analysis: Preliminary Ideas for a Two-Step Method of Analysis", in *Journal of Forensic Sciences*, 2018, vol. 63, no. 1, p. 341.

logical age.[315] Human and mouse studies indicate that using a small set of biomarkers measuring DNA methylation can provide a way to measure chronological age across the entire age spectrum and in all tissues, despite the fact that patterns of DNA methylation vary considerably across tissues.[316] For instance, the data obtained by Horvath and colleagues suggests that their so-called *epigenetic clock*[317] predicts ages fairly accurately with 1 year error intervals for individuals younger than 30 years and with a 3 year error interval for individuals older than 30 years.[318] Apart from

---

[315] Steve Horvath and Kenneth Raj, "DNA Methylation-based Biomarkers and the Epigenetic Clock Theory of Ageing", in *Nature Reviews Genetics*, 2018, vol. 19, no. 6, pp. 371–84; Ana Freire-Aradas *et al.*, "Tracking Age-correlated DNA Methylation Markers in the Young", in *Forensic Science International: Genetics*, 2018 vol. 36, pp. 50–59; Ana Freire-Aradas *et al.*, "Development of a Methylation Marker set for Forensic Age Estimation using Analysis of Public Methylation data and the Agena Bioscience EpiTYPER system", in *Forensic Science International: Genetics*, 2016, vol. 24, pp. 65–74.

[316] Vallentina Bollati, "Decline in Genomic DNA Methylation through Aging a Cohort of Elderly Subjects, Mechanisms of Ageing and Development", in *Mechanisms of Ageing and Development*, 2009, vol. 130, no. 4, pp. 234–39; LIM Unhee and SONG Min-Ae, "DNA Methylation as a Biomarker of Aging in Epidemological Studies", in Ramona G. Dumitrescu and Mukesh Verma (eds.), *Cancer Epigenetics for Precision Medicine: Methods and Protocols*, Humana Press, New York, 2018, pp. 219–31; Steve Horvath, "DNA Methylation Age of Human Tissues and Cell Types", in *Genome Biology*, 2013, vol. 14, no. 1, pp. 1–19; Horvath and Raj, 2018, pp. 371–84, see above note 315.

[317] For more on the term "epigenetics" see Aaron D. Goldberg, C. David Allis and Emily Bernstein, "Epigenetics: A Landscape Takes Shape", in *Cell*, 2007, vol. 128, no. 4, pp. 1–4. These authors describe epigenetics as a bridge between genotype and phenotype, a phenomenon that changes the final outcome of locus or chromosome without changing the underlying DNA sequence. Historically, the word "epigenetics" was used to describe events that could not be explained by genetic principles. Conrad Waddington (1905–75), who is given credit for coining the term, defined epigenetics as "the branch of biology which studies the causal interactions between genes and their products, which bring the phenotype into being", see Conrad Hal Waddington, "The Epigenotype", in *Endeavour*, 1942, vol. 1, pp. 18–20; Conrad Hal Waddington, *The Strategy of the Genes: a Discussion of Some Aspect of Theoretical Biology*, Allen and Unwin, 1957. Over the years, numerous biological phenomena, some considered bizarre and inexplicable, have been lumped into the category of epigenetics. Today, a simplified definition of epigenetics for the uninitiated is that epigenetics is the study of biological mechanisms that will switch genes on and off, see, for example, Shelley L. Berger *et al.*, "An Operational Definition of Epigenetics", in *Genes and Development*, 2009, vol. 23, no. 7, pp. 781–83.

[318] The Horvath clock is based on the weighted average of 353 CpGs correlated with age, whereby methylation of 193 CpGs is positively correlated (hypermetylated) with age, while methylation of the other 160 CpGs is negatively correlated (hypomethylated) with age, see Horvath, 2013, pp. 1–19, see above note 316; Steve Horvath *et al.*, "Epigenetic Clock for Skin and Blood Cells Applied to Hutchinson Gilford Progeria Syndrome and *Ex Vivo* Studies", in *Aging*, 2018, vol. 10, no. 7, pp. 1758–75. An interesting feature of the ep-

this being a potential solution to the time issue, DNA methylation may also be associated with fewer practical difficulties, since obtaining buccal swabs or blood from alleged child soldiers may be easier than to have them taken to facilities with X-rays or MRI machines. However, to better understand the usefulness of DNA methylation for age estimations of alleged child soldiers specifically, careful evaluation is needed in relation to, for example, environmental factors such as poor nutrition, trauma, and so on.[319] Clearly, this technique, like other forensic methods, also requires that the alleged child soldiers have been identified and agree to being swabbed in the mouth or to have a blood sample taken. Such examinations should not jeopardize the security of alleged child soldiers and their families or others. As exemplified by the evidence available in the Lubanga case, see Table 4, forensic evidence was not obtained for all alleged child soldiers. For some of them, the age assessments were instead based on documentary, oral and video evidence, whereof the last category was given most weight by the judges. Hence, the next Section discusses the challenges and opportunities with age estimations based on video or photo evidence.

6.5.2. Video or Photo Evidence

6.5.2.1. Challenges

6.5.2.1.1. Validity

> Video images are routinely admitted as evidence in international tribunals because 'the video footage contained therein will usually speak for itself.'. – Office of the Prosecutor, *The Prosecutor v. Thomas Lubanga Dyilo*, 2013

In line with the prosecutor's statement in Lubanga, video evidence is regularly admissible, meaning that, as a matter of law, the age element can be

---

igenetic clock is that it does not seems to be restricted to specific tissue, but that it is instead a tissue independent correlation with similar are estimates regardless of tissue type including brain, skin, kidney, colon, lung etc, see Horvath, 2013, see above note 316. There is also data today suggesting that epigenetic clock is maintained in the retina, as a strong correlation, $r = 0.80$, between the epigenetic age and chronological age in the fetal retina.

[319] For instance, it is clear that some factors may lead to accelerated DNA methylation, as exemplified by Steve Horvath *et al.*, "Accelerated Epigenetic Aging in Down Syndrome", in *Aging Cell*, 2015, vol. 14, no. 3, pp. 491–95. Analyses of samples with Down syndrome show the pronounced acceleration of the DNA methylation age even in fetal stages, similar to what has been observed in adult tissues.

established beyond reasonable doubt on the basis of such evidence. This is consistent with national as well international jurisprudence and specifically Rule 63(4) of the Rules of Procedure and Evidence, according to which a Chamber shall not impose a legal requirement that corroboration is required in order to prove any crime within the jurisdiction of the Court.[320]

Yet, as regards the second half of the prosecutor's statement, that the "video footage contained therein will usually speak for itself", there seems to be more room for discussion. Certainly, how old an individual appears to be based on his or her physical appearance, demeanour, and so on, here referred to as *apparent age*, is not necessarily a valid operationalization of the individual's chronological age. While this may seem self-evident, it deserves to be emphasized that conclusions about chronological age are drawn on the basis of apparent age, and it is unknown whether, how and to what extent these two correlate, neither in a general population nor in the population of alleged child soldiers involved in these cases. Compared to the correlation between biological age and chronological age (see Section 6.5.1.), the relationship between apparent age and chronological age has received relatively little scientific attention so far. Hence, it should be carefully considered in which situations and for which more specific purposes video or photo evidence is used, even if the evidence is admissible as such.

In the national cases referred to by the Appeals Chamber in the Lubanga case, video footage was used in somewhat different contexts and for somewhat different purposes. For instance, the national cases concerned child pornography, the relevant age thresholds were 16 or 18 years, and none of the alleged child victims had been identified, meaning that they were not present before the Court and no other methods for estimating their ages could be used. Furthermore, and importantly, in the national cases, the video evidence was not used to establish objective crime elements of chronological age, but rather subjective crime elements of ap-

---

[320] It can also be noted that when it comes to the identification of a child as an unaccompanied and separated child, the UN Committee on the Rights of the Child ('CRC')'s General Comment No. 6: Treatment of Unaccompanied and Separated Children Outside Their Country of Origin, 2005, states that the age assessment should take into account the individual's physical appearance as well as psychological maturity. It is also pointed out that the assessment must be conducted in a scientific, safe, child and gender sensitive and fair manner, avoiding any risk of violation of the physical integrity of the child, giving due respect to human dignity. *Ibid.*, para. 31.A. (https://www.legal-tools.org/doc/6fb257/).

parent age, that is, the intent of the accused in relation to the depicted individuals' apparent ages. This is clearly spelled out in, for example, *Police v. Kennedy*[321] in which it is noted that:

> The prosecution did not attempt to prove that any of the persons depicted in the material were in fact under the age of 16 years. The source of the material and the identity of the persons in the photographs were quite unknown. Therefore it would have been impossible to have proved the actual age of the persons by any acceptable evidence. The prosecution relied on the photographs themselves together with some parts of the written text as depicting or describing a person or persons apparently under the age of 16 years.[322]

Also, some of the cited cases, such as *R. v. Loring*[323] and *R. v. Garbett*,[324] refer to whether the depicted individuals would be perceived by a "reasonable observer" as being under the age of 18 years.[325] If so, the

---

[321] Supreme Court of South Australia, *Police v. Peter Melbourne Kennedy*, Decision, 28 April 1998, [1998] SASC 7122 (https://www.legal-tools.org/doc/1ba636/).

[322] *Ibid.*, p. 12.

[323] Supreme Court of British Columbia, *R. v. Loring*, Decision, 5 February 2001, [2001] BCSC 200 (https://www.legal-tools.org/doc/d277c2/).

[324] Ontario Court of Justice, *R. v. Garbett*, Judgment, 4 March 2008, [2008] ONCJ 97 (https://www.legal-tools.org/doc/765fd2/).

[325] In *R. v. Loring*, Justice Wilson observed:

> In the absence of any evidence of the ages of the other persons depicted in these video recordings, Mr. Lauder submits that it is open to me to make a finding of "apparent age" by looking at the video recording.
>
> I have no expertise in assessing the age of young persons. I have no confidence that I would be able to give a reliable opinion on "apparent age" or otherwise, which would permit a distinction between one aged seventeen years and nine months, and one aged eighteen years one month. My confidence is in no way enhanced if I am asked to distinguish between an eighteen year old and a fifteen, sixteen or seventeen year old. These matters ought not to be determined on a guess. I decline Mr. Lauder's invitation to speculate on the apparent age of the unidentified persons depicted in the video recording.

Supreme Court of British Columbia Loring Decision, paras. 14–15, see above note 323. In *R. v. Garbett*, the Justice states, *inter alia*, that the test:

> requires a consideration of whether I am satisfied beyond a reasonable doubt that a reasonable observer, looking at this photograph, would perceive either of these females as being under 18. In this respect, the nature of the bedding, which appears to be of a kind favoured by an adolescent or a child, and the child-like ring on the second female's finger together with the matching bracelet are relevant circumstances. They are part of the context to consider in relation to the perception that a reasonable observer

intent of the accused was to be assumed. While the connection between subjective crime elements, the "reasonable observer" and apparent age is relatively straightforward, the connection between objective crime elements (aimed at chronological age) and apparent age is more complex and probably weaker. If the applicable law asks to determine apparent age, as in the national cases, apparent age is a valid operationalization, even if there may still be reliability and biasability issues. However, if the applicable law asks to determine chronological age as in child soldiering cases, apparent age is less of a valid operationalization. Hence, save for the differences in crime types, the contexts are fairly similar, since also in the child soldiering cases some individuals had not been identified and other types of age estimations were not possible. Yet, the purposes of the age estimations are quite distinct. In the national cases, the purpose was to establish apparent age and in the child soldiering cases, the purpose was to establish chronological age. The relevance of apparent age for objective rather than subjective crime elements needs further discussion, not the least when it comes to the probative value.[326]

---

would form of the age of the females. So too, however, is the logo in the bottom corner, which suggests that the image comes from the web site of someone who is 18, and the inset photograph. As I have said, I do not believe that a reasonable observer would perceive the person in the inset photograph, who resembles the first female in picture #41, as being under 18 years of age.

Taking all of these circumstances into account, and applying the test set forth by Chief Justice McLachlin in Sharpe, I am not satisfied that "a reasonable observer [would] perceive [either] person in the representation as being under 18". It seems to me to be just as likely that a reasonable observer would be unable to form an opinion one way or the other.

I am left with a reasonable doubt with respect to whether either person in picture #41 "is or is depicted as being under the age of eighteen years". Accordingly, the Crown has not proved that picture #41 constitutes child pornography.

For these reasons Mr. Garbett was found not guilty of both charges before the Court. Ontario Court of Justice Garbett Judgment, paras. 91–93, see above note 324.

[326] The Court expresses related, although not the same, limitations with such age estimations. For instance, in Lubanga Trial Chamber Judgment, para. 711, see above note 4, the Trial Chamber stated that it has "independently assessed the ages of the children identified in the video footage and about whom this witness expressed a view, to the extent it is possible to draw a safe conclusion based on their appearance". Also, the Lubanga Appeals Chamber Judgment, para. 222, see above note 3, expresses a similar view, that it "considers that the Trial Chamber was indeed aware of the limitations of determining age on the basis of physical appearance, including video images, and expressed caution with regard to age assessment on that basis. [...] The Appeals Chamber notes that the Trial Chamber indicated that it applied a large margin of error and made findings as to the age of the children only

As implied above, both the SCSL and the ICC have used apparent age to establish objective crime elements, as defined by Article 4(c) of the Statute of the SCSL and Article 8 of the Rome Statute of the ICC. Seemingly, these Courts have had different strategies in dealing with the potential mismatch between apparent age and chronological age. In the Taylor case, the SCSL Trial Chamber noted that: "he [the alleged child soldier] looked young at the time he gave evidence in 2008 ten years after the incidents he testified about".[327] This does not make any explicit reference as to the required subjective certainty regarding the alleged child soldier's age, but presumably the Court applied the BARD-standard. However, in the Lubanga case before the ICC, the prosecutor relied on "a number of video excerpts to establish that some of the UPF/FPLC recruits were "visibly" under the age of 15".[328] In other words, the prosecution here claimed that, for some of the recruits, the chronological ages were visible, that is, there was a strong positive correlation between apparent and chronological age. The Trial Chamber agreed with the prosecution that children who are undoubtedly less than 15 years can be distinguished from those undoubtedly over 15 years,[329] while it also noted the defence's contention that "it is impossible to distinguish reliably between a 12 or 13 year-old and a 15 or 16 year old on the basis of a photograph or video extract alone".[330] In its own assessment of the video excerpts the Trial Chamber identified specific individuals who, in its opinion, were "evidently",[331] "clearly"[332] or "significantly"[333] under the age of 15 years. This approach was also approved by the Appeals Chamber which stated that: "[…] given the margin of error applied by the Trial Chamber, its approach was not unreasonable".[334] While the Appeals Chamber does not spell out precisely its view on how these requirements relate to the BARD-standard, re-

---

where the children were, in its assessment, "clearly" under age of fifteen years. The Appeals Chamber considers that such an approach is not unreasonable, even though the reasoning of the Trial Chamber in that regard could have been more extensive [...]".

[327] SCSL Taylor Trial Chamber Judgment, para. 1431, see above note 67.

[328] Lubanga Trial Chamber Judgment, para. 644, see above note 4.

[329] *Ibid.*, para. 643.

[330] *Ibid.*, para. 644.

[331] *Ibid.*, para. 861, 1254.

[332] *Ibid.*, paras. 713, 792, 854, 858, 862, 869, 912, 915, 1348.

[333] *Ibid.*, paras. 1251–52.

[334] Lubanga Appeals Chamber Judgment, para. 236, see above note 3.

quirements such as "evidently", in a literal sense, seem to require more of the evidence. It can be questioned what this means in terms of the risk of false negatives, that is, that someone younger than 15 years, but not "evidently" so, is classified as 15 years or older, see Table 1 in Section 6.3. and Section 6.6. on diagnostic accuracy. In the Katanga case, only one photo of Katanga's youngest bodyguard was used for age assessment purposes and the Trial Chamber believed it was "not in a position to ascertain [...]"[335] whether this individual was under 15 years, especially in the light of other contradictory testimony.

From a scientific point of view, the available research suggests that when individuals try to estimate chronological age based on someone's physical appearance, the error intervals are fairly large and chronological age can be both underestimated and overestimated. The earliest research in this field focused on age estimations based on faces and used relatively small samples.[336] These studies suggest errors in the range of three to four years.[337] In more recent research, with larger samples and wider age ranges, the errors were larger, with a mean error around six years.[338] The today most extensive research study, using a database of standardized passport images of individuals of heterogenous ages (n = 3948) found that the average age estimation error was approximately 8 years.[339] Looking only at the estimations of individuals in the age range 12 to 19 years, the average estimation error was 5.39 years.[340] The cited research concerns age guess-

---

[335] Katanga Trial Chamber Judgment, para. 1080, see above note 69.

[336] Small samples both in terms of the faces used and the participants who were asked to estimate age on the basis of those faces.

[337] Michael Burt and David I. Perrett, "Perception of Age in Adult Caucasian Male Faces: Computer Graphic Manipulation of Shape and Colour Information", in *Proceedings of the Royal Society*, 1995, vol. 259, no. 1355, pp. 137–43; Patricia A. George and Graham J. Hole, "The Role of Spatial and Surface Cues in the Age-processing of Unfamiliar Faces", in *Visual Cognition*, 2000, vol. 7, no. 4, pp. 485–509; Patrik Sörqvist and Mårten Eriksson, "Effects of Training on Age Estimation", in *Applied Cognitive Psychology*, 2007, vol. 21, no. 1, pp. 131–35.

[338] Manuel C. Voelkle *et al.*, "Let Me Guess How Old You Are: Effects of Age, Gender, and Facial Expression on Perceptions of Age", in *Psychology and Aging*, 2012, vol. 27, no. 2, pp. 265–77; Evelyn Moyse and Serge Brédart, "An Own-age Bias in Age Estimation of Faces", in *European Review of Applied Psychology*, 2012, vol. 62, no. 1, pp. 3–7.

[339] Colin Clifford, Tamara Watson and David White, "Two Sources of Bias Explain Errors in Facial Age Estimation", in *Royal Society Open Science*, 2018, vol. 5, no. 10, pp. 1–10.

[340] This data was obtained through personal contact with Colin Clifford, Tamara Watson and David White who kindly shared the data they collected and towards whom the author of

---

es in relation to faces of individuals living in Australia, the US and the UK and while these countries are multicultural or ethnical, the generalizability of the findings to a more general world population or a population of alleged child soldiers is uncertain. Similarly, the assessments of crowd sourced responses deviated from the chronological age by 4.57 years on average, suggesting there is not really any "wisdom of the crowd" in this context.[341] Unsurprisingly, this research also suggests that for some individuals the age is even more difficult to estimate. For instance, for a 14-year-old girl, the mean estimated age was 20.10 years and the age guesses varied widely from 14 to 29 years.[342] Also outside of the laboratory similar findings have been made. For instance, shopkeepers asked to estimate whether 16-year-old boys and girls had reached legal drinking age (18), misjudged 38 per cent of the boys and 56 per cent of the girls to be at least 18 years.[343]

As noted, it is unknown whether the errors identified in the cited research are representative for the population of alleged child soldiers. However, the research still seems relevant in relation to the margin of error applied in Lubanga. The Trial Chamber did not outline any specific age range to be used, but simply described a "wide" margin of error.[344]

---

this chapter is grateful. For more on the research in relation to which the data was collected see *ibid*. The average 5.39 was obtained when each individual experiment included in this research was given equal weight. If instead, one gives equal weight to each rater, the average estimation error would be 5.32.

[341] Jared Rondeau and Marco Alvarez, "Deep Modeling of Human Age Guesses for Apparent Age Estimation", in *2018 International Joint Conference on Neural Networks (IJCNN)*, IEEE, 2018, pp. 1–8.

[342] These results were obtained using the so-called Appa-Real database in which each face image is labelled with a number of human guesses, on average 38 per image, see *ibid*. The APPA-real database is considered a state-of-the art dataset, for more see Eirikur Agustsson *et al*., "Apparent and Real Age Estimation in Still Images with Deep Residual Regressors on Appa-Real Database", in *2017 12th IEEE International Conference on Automatic Face & Gesture Recognition (FG 2017)*, IEEE, 2017, pp. 87–94. This dataset provides a large number of face images labelled with real and apparent age annotations. APPA-real contains 7.6k face images with an associated number of nearly 300k human guesses.

[343] Paul Wilner and Gavin Rowe, "Alcohol Servers' Estimates of Young People's Ages", in *Drugs: Education, Prevention and Policy*, 2001, vol. 8, no. 1, pp. 375–83.

[344] Lubanga Trial Chamber Judgment, paras. 643–44, see above note 4 and Lubanga Appeals Chamber Judgment, para. 222, see above note 3. The Appeals Chamber notes that the Trial Chamber indicated that it applied a *large* margin of error and made findings as to the age of the children only where the children were, in its assessment, "clearly" under the age of fifteen years. Furthermore, the Appeals Chamber noted that the reasoning of the Trial

---

Among the error intervals found in the cited research, the most relevant one seems to be that found for individuals in the age range 12 to 19 years, where the mean estimation error was 5.39 years.[345] Hence, from a scientific perspective, a "wide enough" margin should probably be around at least 5.39 years.

This bring us back to the defence's claim in the Lubanga case, namely that it is impossible to distinguish reliably between 12 or 13 year olds and 15 or 16 year olds on the basis of their physical appearance alone.[346] There are today no systematic empirical studies evaluating whether and how the discriminatory ability changes as one moves closer to and away from the 15-year age threshold. A reasonable prediction is that error would be at its peak in the interval of 13 to 17 years, thus leaving error fairly normally distributed around the 15-year threshold, as illustrated in Figure 1 below. The reader should note that this prediction is made solemnly on the notion expressed by the Trial Chamber in Lubanga that, generally, children with chronological ages clearly under or clearly over 15 years are likely to look a lot more like children or adults (apparent ages) than those closer to the 15-year threshold.[347] Certainly, individual variation means that, in practice, several factors may influence what the estimation error curves look like, including, for example, biological sex and what more specific aspects of an individual's appearance are used to estimate age. In both the SCSL and the ICC cases, witnesses were sometimes asked to explain the more specific bases for their age estimations. The responses include a range of physical or developmental cues such as size,[348] the change in a boy's voice when he reaches puberty[349] and

---

Chamber in that regard "could have been more extensive" (*ibid.*, para. 222) as this would have facilitated appellate review.

[345] Clifford, Watson and White, 2018, see above note 339.

[346] Lubanga Trial Chamber Judgment, para. 644, see above note 4.

[347] The Trial Chamber states that:

> Given the undoubted differences in personal perception as regards estimates of age, and most particularly in the context of this case, the difficulties in distinguishing between young people who are relatively close to the age of 15 (whether above or below), the Chamber has exercised caution when considering this evidence.

See *ibid.*, para. 643.

[348] P-0046 recalled holding the hand of a younger child when crossing the street. Her evidence was that "he was so small". *Ibid.*, para. 654.

[349] P-0014 observed there was "no age limit" in regard to the children recruited into the UPC/FPLC and he saw 8–15-year olds who had been forcibly recruited. He stated that

whether a girl has developed breasts.[350] One witness, who used to be a teacher, described that his estimation that a specific child was five years old was based on that a six year old should be able to reach over his head and touch his opposite ear, and the child in question was unable to do so.[351] Also, the witnesses sometimes referred to behavioural cues like: "[s]ome would cry for their mother when they were hungry"[352] or their manner of playing, for instance young girls at Mandro Camp had "braided a particular type of grass in the way that young girls who have not reached the age of maturity tend to do, as if they are braiding the hair of a doll".[353] When it comes to the Court's own reasoning about age it is not specified in the verdicts why an individual is considered to be "evidently", "clearly", or "significantly" under 15 years. However, the Appeals Chamber in Lubanga noted that the estimations in the lower instances had been based on the size and general appearance of the individuals, rather than their specific facial features.[354] It is unknown whether and to what extent the cues described here (physical or developmental or behavioural) are good age indicators and also whether age estimations based on the different cues may result in different types of errors or error rates.

In this regard it deserves to be emphasized that legal age elements are dichotomous. Hence, they only require determinations of whether the 15-year threshold has been reached or not. As such, through pure guessing without even looking at the evidence (the alleged child soldier), one has a 50 per cent chance of getting it right. Overall, it seems reasonable to claim that legal determinations should be, or at least seriously aim to be, far more accurate than chance. Otherwise it seems difficult to make any serious legitimacy claims. Consequently, an accuracy level significantly

---

when estimating the ages of children, he took into account, *inter alia*, the children's psychical characteristics, including such things as the change in a boy's voice when he reaches puberty. See *ibid.*, para. 708.

[350] *Ibid.*, para. 680.

[351] This was the testimony of P-0014. See *ibid.*, para. 708.

[352] P-0017 indicated "you could see it from their behaviour. Some would cry for their mother when they were hungry. They would whine at night, and during the day they were playing games, children's games, even if they had their weapon next to them [...]". See *ibid.*, para. 681.

[353] *Ibid.*, para. 807. This was the statement of P-0016 who indicated there were young girls at Mandro camp and although he did not give an exact indication of their ages he said "they must have been very young" as they behaved "like girls who were still at home".

[354] Lubanga Appeals Chamber Judgment, para. 229, see above note 3.

above 50 per cent and as close to 100 per cent as possible, would be desirable. Just how close to the 15-year threshold one can get before the discriminatory ability is getting unacceptably close to 50 per cent (or even lower) is a question that requires empirical research.

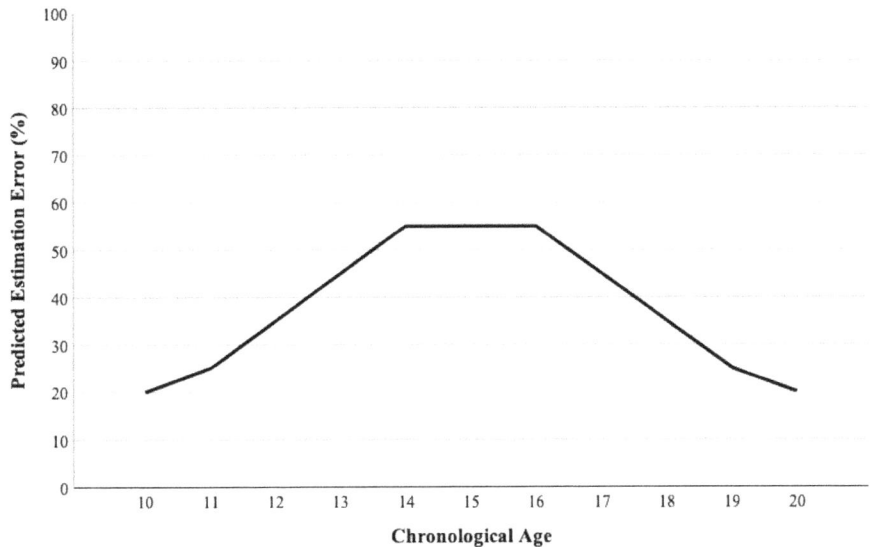

Figure 1. Predicted normally distributed error around the 15-year threshold in estimations of chronological age based on apparent age.

If the above general prediction is correct, age estimations on the basis of apparent age are likely to provide a better protection for individuals who are clearly younger than 15 (for example, 9–10 years), compared to those closer to 15 (for example, 12–14 years), even if both groups are considered equally worthy of protection, from a legal normative point of view.

Hence, if forensic age estimations are an inexact science,[355] then it seems fair to conclude that so are estimations of chronological age based on apparent age. Generally, legal proceedings are not under the same scientific scrutiny as sciences are. However, if legal actors choose to not place trust in forensic evidence because it stems from an inexact science, it appears to put some burden of explanation on them as to why visual age

---

[355] Lubanga Trial Chamber Judgment, para. 176, see above note 4.

assessments are more valid.[356] It is possible that some individuals can be safely identified as under 15 years but, using scientific terminology, what *method* is used to establish this? The method used to reach the conclusion is decisive for the validity of the conclusion. In the Lubanga case, the Appeals Chamber touches upon this, whether intended or not, when it states that the Trial Chamber's reasoning in relation to the video evidence was "not unreasonable" but "could have been more extensive" as this "would have facilitated appellate review".[357] Possible ways to extend this reasoning would be to include age intervals, rather than a single age, as is recommended to forensic practitioners. Other appropriate questions to address would be what more specific aspects of the physical appearance were used and why. Of course, transparency in the reasoning of a legal verdict opens up for criticism, particularly if the reasoning is very specific and extensive as regards how the Court reached its conclusions. But that is the point.

6.5.2.1.2. Reliability

Already the Court cases themselves illustrate the possibility of lacking 'Between Observer Reliability', that is, that different observers make different observations and/or draw different conclusions as regards the age of the same individual based on his or her physical appearance.[358] In the Lubanga case the Trial Chamber explicitly states that a margin of error is indeed called for due to: "the undoubted differences in personal perception as regards estimates of age"[359] on the basis of video excerpts. This raises follow-up questions such as what more specific factors may cause such differences, whether some individuals are better observers than others and if so, what this tells us about whose estimations to trust.

---

[356] As illustrated in Table 4, in the case of Lubanga, the forensic and the video evidence pertained to different alleged child soldiers and the Court has therefore not directly chosen to prioritize one type of evidence over the other in relation to the same individual. However, the estimated ages implied by the forensic evidence was often not trusted because the science was not trusted and because of inconsistencies with other evidence types as well as inconsistencies in oral as well as documentary evidence. Logically speaking, the validity of the forensic evidence should remain the same regardless of such inconsistencies.

[357] Lubanga Appeals Chamber Judgment, para. 222, see above note 3.

[358] Note that 'Between Observer Reliability' is an adjustment of 'Between Expert Reliability', as defined by the HEP framework, in relation to human observers, rather than experts. For more on the HEP framework see Dror, 2016, pp. 121–27, see above note 28.

[359] Lubanga Trial Chamber Judgment, para. 643, see above note 4.

Both the SCSL and the ICC express some notions as to which individuals would be better observers than others. For instance, in several of the SCSL cases, the Chambers rely on the notion that witnesses who have children themselves or in other ways obtained experience of children (such as school teachers) should be trusted in their age estimations. This is apparent for instance in Taylor, where the Court trusts the witness Conteh as "he was the father of three children and had been a secondary school teacher for several years prior to his capture"[360] as well as the testimony of Gbonda who was the "father of several children"[361] and yet another witness who was "the mother of four children".[362] Also in the ICC practice, the experience of having worked as a teacher[363] has been considered beneficial, as well as having worked close to the children and/or on a daily basis.[364] Although the Courts do not specify what this notion is based on, it will be presumed that the Courts believe that the experience of being a parent exposes you to children, not only your own but other children as well. Potentially, this would provide some relevant empirical data, that is, knowledge of the range of possible physical appearances of children with, presumably, known chronological ages. However, the lack of birth records in Sierra Leone, as well as the countries investigated by the ICC was the very justification for conducting age estimations to begin with. It can still be the case that parents and teachers have better access to such age relevant data than individuals who do not regularly interact with children. Yet, if the Courts hold this notion to be true for the stated reasons,[365] then

---

[360] SCSL Taylor Trial Chamber Judgment, para. 1419, see above note 67.

[361] *Ibid.*, para. 1486.

[362] *Ibid.*, para. 1489.

[363] See, for example, the evaluation of P-0014's testimony who used to be a teacher and had been in daily contact with individuals within this age group, and his evidence on the subject of age was considered credible and reliable, see Lubanga Trial Chamber Judgment, para. 709, see above note 4.

[364] For instance, the Trial Chamber in the case of Lubanga stated in relation to P-0024 that he gave honest, consistent and reliable evidence as regards his work with demobilized children. Although he did not train as a social worker, he spent over a year working with children and "although he did not give evidence as to how he assesses the children's ages, his interaction with them during those months provided a solid and credible basis for his assessments". See *ibid.*, para. 662.

[365] Certainly, it is unknown whether the notions expressed by the Courts are correct. The idea that some individuals have capacitates to conduct more accurate age estimations resemble the notion that there are so-called 'Super Recognizers'. These are individuals believed to be exceptionally good at recognizing faces and therefore particularly suitable for investiga-

should not the 'gold standard' for an age estimation be a paediatrician who is likely to be in possession of more such empirical data than most other people?[366] Also, a paediatrician would be less likely to have strong emotional or societal ties to the alleged child soldiers (see next Section 6.5.2.1.3. on Biasability).

The available psychological research does not address the effect of living with or working with children, or whether some individuals are inherently better at visual age assessments than others,[367] but the research has some other implications. More specifically, it suggests that *in-group age estimations* are usually superior to *out-group estimations*. Thus, age estimations are more accurate when observers make estimates of individuals belonging to their own age groups.[368] There is also some data indicat-

tive tasks such as recognizing individuals from CCTV. Although it is relatively uncontroversial to claim that there *are* differences in what individuals observe and conclude on the basis of the exact same stimuli, given experience, it is more controversial given the lack of data, to claim which individuals have superior abilities than others. For more on this see University of Greenwich, described briefly online, "Super Recognisers Greenwich" (available on its web site). See also Andrew W. Young and Eilidh Noyes, "We Need to Talk About Super-recognizers: Invited Commentary on: Ramon, M., Bobak, A.K., and White, D. Super-recognizers: From the Lab to the World and Back Again.", in *British Journal of Psychology*, 2019, vol. 110, no. 3, pp. 492–94.

[366] Children's' chronological ages are likely to be apparent in medical journals, and so on, and this, together with observing the children's' physical appearance is likely to give paediatricians overall quite good references/bases for estimating ages also of other, non-clinical, children. Also, a more specific context in which children's' ages are used is to predict their weight in emergency departments, where it is not always feasible to measure weight but the children require weight-based resuscitative measures. For more on this see, for example, Daming Pan *et al.*, "How Well Does the Best Guess Method Predict Children's Weight in an Emergency Department in 2018-2019?", in *Emergency Medicine Australasia*, 2020, vol. 32, no. 1, pp. 135–40; Katie Tinning and Jason Acworth, "Make your Best Guess: An Updated Method for Paediatric Weight Estimation in Emergencies", in *Emergency Medicine Australasia*, 2007, vol. 19, no. 6, pp. 528–34.

[367] An interesting finding in this regard is that individuals who do not possess the ability to identify faces, so-called Developmental Prosopagnosia, nevertheless seem to have normal ability to estimate the age of faces, see Garga Chatterjee and NAKAYAMA Ken, "Normal Facial Age and Gender Perception in Developmental Prosopagnosia", in *Cognitive Neuropsychology*, 2012, vol. 29, no. 5, pp. 482–502.

[368] George and Hole, 2000, pp. 485–509, see above note 337; Voelkle *et al.*, 2012, pp. 265–77, see above note 338; Moyse and Brédart, 2012, pp. 3–7, see above note 338. See also Jeffrey S. Anastasi and Matthew G. Rhodes, "Evidence for an Own-age Bias in Face Recognition", in *North American Journal of Psychology*, 2006, vol. 8, no. 2, pp. 237–53; Burt and Perrett, 1995, pp. 137–43, see above note 337. This effect may be present in children as well. For example, George and Hole showed children pairs of faces from nine age catego-

ing that age estimates are more accurate when observers assess individuals of the same race or ethnicity as their own, but this evidence is inconsistent.[369] There are some occasional acknowledgments of these in-group and out group effects in the Courts' practice. For instance, in the Ntaganda case, the Trial Chamber mentions in passing that the assessments a witness provided "related to individuals who were in the same age range as the witness" and this was a reason for considering the witness' age estimation reliable.[370]

6.5.2.1.3.   Biasability

The existing research suggests that age estimations based on physical appearance (facial images) show a serial dependency whereby estimates are systematically biased towards the age of the preceding face, that is, a *serial positioning bias*.[371] More specifically, this entails a tendency to underestimate age when the previous face was younger than the present one and to overestimate age when the previous face was older. This research also found a *bias towards middle-aged faces*, resulting in that younger faces appeared older than they were and older faces appeared younger.[372] Further, the strength of these biases was modulated by the degree of visual noise present in the stimulus so that their combined effect was strongest when perceptions were most uncertain. These findings, par-

---

ries ranging in age from 1 to 80 and asked participants to identify the oldest face in each pair. In general, discrimination was better when both faces in a pair were children than when both were adults. George and Hole, 2000, see above note 337. See also Arthur Weinberger, "Stereotyping the Elderly: Elementary School Children's Responses", in *Research on Aging*, 1979, vol. 1, no. 1, pp. 113–36.

[369] See Hedwidge Dehon and Serge Brédart, "An 'Other-race' Effect in Age Estimation of Faces", in *Perception*, 2001, vol. 30, no. 9, pp. 1107–13. In this study, white and black participants made age estimates for white and black faces ranging from 20 to 45 years of age. Results showed that white participants' age estimates were reliably more accurate for white faces compared to black faces. By contrast, black participants' estimation accuracy did not differ based on the race of the face, a finding that Dehon and Brédart attributed to the fact that all of the black participants tested had lived in a predominantly white country (Belgium) for at least five years. See also Christian A. Meissner and John C. Brigham, "Thirty Years of Investigating the Own-race Bias in Memory for Faces: A Meta-analytic Review", in *Psychology, Public Policy, and Law*, 2001, vol. 7, no. 1, pp. 3–35.

[370] Ntaganda Trial Chamber Judgment, para. 203, see above note 74. However, there is more uncertainty as relates to the bases for this witnesses' assessments, namely the "size and other physical features of the relevant individuals".

[371] Clifford, Watson and White, 2018, pp. 1–10, see above note 339.

[372] *Ibid.*

ticularly the serial positioning bias, are in line with research into the so-called *anchoring effect*.[373] This is a bias in relation to an anchor; an initial piece of information upon which decision makers seem to rely heavily as they only make small adjustments or deviations from it.[374] Importantly, this happens even when the anchor is explicitly random and irrelevant for the judgment task at hand. Taken together, this research underlines that estimations of ages based on physical appearance are likely to be strongly context dependent.[375] For instance, if judges look at the exact same individual with the exact same characteristics in a picture but the context of the picture changes, for example, who is standing next to the individual, there is a risk that also the judges' observations of this individual's characteristics will vary, just like their conclusions regarding his or her age.[376]

In child soldiering cases, for instance Lubanga, many individuals were depicted together and some of them stood out, for example, because they were shorter than the rest of the individuals. Possibly, these individuals would have come across as older or younger if presented together with other individuals or alone. In fact, it is explicit in the reasoning of the Trial Chamber that the context was taken into account, for instance in relation to the second video excerpt showing Mr. Lubanga returning to his residence after an event at the Hellenique Hotel on 23 January 2003.[377] Mr. Lubanga was travelling in a vehicle accompanied by members of the presidential guard who were armed and wearing military clothing and on the

---

[373] Daniel Kahneman, Paul Slovic and Amos Tversky, *Judgment under Uncertainty: Heuristics and Biases*, Cambridge University Press, 1982, pp. 1124–30.

[374] *Ibid*. In their pioneering studies, Tversky and Kahneman asked participants about the percentage of African nations in the UN. In a first comparative question, participants indicated whether the percentage was higher or lower than an arbitrary number (the anchor) that had been determined by spinning a wheel of fortune, showing 65 per cent or 10 per cent. In a subsequent absolute anchoring question, participants gave their best estimate of this percentage. Results showed that the absolute judgments were assimilated to the explicitly random anchor values. For more on this in the legal context see, for example, Birte Englich, "Blind or Biased? Justitia's Susceptibility to Anchoring Effects in the Courtroom Based on Given Numerical Representations", in *Law and Policy*, 2006, vol. 28, no. 4, pp. 497–514.

[375] The context dependency is also emphasized by Clifford, Watson and White, 2018, pp. 1–10, see above note 339.

[376] Apart from the research cited in the main text, this is also related to so-called carry-over bias, see, for example, Steven J. Ferris *et al.*, "Carryover Bias in Visual Assessment", in *Perception*, 2001, vol. 30, no. 11, pp. 1363–73.

[377] Lubanga Trial Chamber Judgment, para. 862, see above note 4.

---

back of a truck there were two individuals, alleged child soldiers, in camouflage clothing. The Trial Chamber compared these two individuals with the other individuals present in the video excerpt and found that the latter individuals were "taller".[378] This was taken into account when reaching the conclusion that the two individuals were significantly under the age of 15 years.[379] The fact that the Chamber explicitly took this information into account does not necessarily mean that their assessments were not biased. Knowledge of contextual information is always conscious in one way or another, but decisions makers are not necessarily in control over how such information influences their perceptions.[380]

Furthermore, the context of the video excerpt may introduce base rate expectations. For instance, knowing that a video was recorded in a training camp where children were present can be a biasing factor since it suggests that the likelihood of children appearing in the video is relatively high.[381] There are also many other possible sources of bias in the interpretation of visual evidence including, for example, selective attention[382] or a hypothesis at hand[383] causing the examiners to "see what they expect to see", as exemplified by research into perceptions of body-worn camera ('BWC') recordings.[384]

Clearly, biases like those discussed here constitute risk factors in relation to the accuracy of age estimation based on video evidence. Any such risks can be empirically evaluated and such research should also take into account how any biases play out and interact with other factors pre-

---

[378] *Ibid.*

[379] *Ibid.*

[380] For more on the topic of whether conscious and subconscious parts of decision making processes can be distinguished see, for example, Kahneman and Fredrick's dual process theory of probability judgment, describing how the so-called System 1 and System 2 interact in the decision making process, Daniel Kahneman and Shane Fredrick, "A Model of Heuristic Judgment", in Keith J. Holyoak and Robert G. Morrison (eds.), *The Cambridge Handbook of Thinking and Reasoning*, Cambridge University Press, 2005, pp. 267–94.

[381] See, for example, Dror, 2017, p. 544, see above note 297.

[382] See, for example, Sherry Nakhaeizadeh, Itiel E. Dror and Ruth M. Morgan, "Cognitive Bias in Forensic Anthropology: Visual Assessment of Skeletal Remains is Susceptible to Confirmation Bias", in *Science and Justice*, 2014, vol. 54, no. 3, pp. 208–14.

[383] See, for example, Lidén, 2018, see above note 30.

[384] See, for instance, Kristyn A. Jones, William E. Crozier and Deryn Strange, "Believing is Seeing: Biased Viewing of Body-worn Camera Footage", in *Journal of Applied Research in Memory and Cognition*, 2017, vol. 6, no. 4, pp. 460–74.

sent in these assessments, such as gender and ethnical differences between the observer and the observed individual.

6.5.2.2. Opportunities

Today, there is a growing number of research studies examining possibilities of estimating age on the basis of facial images by using handcrafted algorithms or deep learning technology.[385] In this research chronological age is considered a significant personal feature that can be derived from the emerging of patterns of the facial appearance.[386] Thus, the purpose of this research is to "label a face image automatically with the exact age (year) or the age group (year range) of the individual face".[387] So far, this approach has been evaluated in relation to areas such as aged-based access control for websites or mobile applications, and so on,[388] that is, fields that are distinct from legal age determinations. Hence, its value in the legal context still needs to be evaluated, empirically and systematically.

Although only time can tell what the more specific challenges of this approach may be,[389] the viability of this research depends on its ability to identify relevant large-scale data sets in which the ground truth in

---

[385] For an overview of this research see Arwa S. Al-Shannaq and Lamiaa A. Elrefaei, "Comprehensive Analysis of the Literature for Age Estimation from Facial Images", in *IEEE Access*, 2019, vol. 7, pp. 1–21. The main difference between handcrafted algorithms and deep learning technology is the process of features extraction and selection which is accomplished manually for handcrafted models.

[386] FU Yun, GUO Guodong and HUANG Thomas S., "Age Synthesis and Estimation via Faces: A Survey", in *IEEE Transactions on Pattern Analysis and Machine Intelligence*, 2010, vol. 32, no. 11, pp. 1955–76.

[387] *Ibid.*; GENG Xin, YIN Chao and ZHOU Zhi-Hua, "Facial Age Estimation by Learning from Label Distributions", in *IEEE Transactions on Pattern Analysis and Machine Intelligence*, 2013, vol. 35, no. 10, pp. 2401–12.

[388] See, for example, Ali Elmahmudi and Hassan Ugail, "Deep Face Recognition Using Imperfect Facial Data", in *Future Generation Computer Systems*, 2019, vol. 99, pp. 213–25; HUANG Jin *et al.*, "Age Classification with Deep Learning Face Representation", in *Multimedia Tools and Applications*, 2017, vol. 76, pp. 20231–47; and Narayanan Ramanathan, Rama Chellappa and Soma Biswas, "Computational Methods for Modelling Facial Aging: A Survey", in *Journal of Visual Languages and Computing*, 2009, vol. 20, no. 3, pp. 131–44.

[389] For an overview of challenges relating to the more general field of facial analysis that have already been identified see, for example, FU, GUO and HUANG, 2010, pp. 1955–76, see above note 386; Ramanathan, Chellappa and Biswas, 2009, pp. 131–44, see above note 388.

---

relation to chronological age is known.[390] As manifested by the lack of birth certificates to establish ground truth for many alleged child soldiers, this may prove to be difficult, although not necessarily impossible. Furthermore, there may be some general similarities in the aging process of all people, but it remains to be seen whether and to what extent this research can integrate individual differences due to internal factors (health status, gender, genetics, ethnicity) and external factors (life style, environment).[391]

Since the aging process is unique to every individual, and individuals also generally look quite different, two individuals with the exact same chronological age can have quite different facial appearances.[392] Clearly, this may complicate extraction of information from group level data to the individualized assessments. When it comes to the early stages of life, from birth to adulthood, the available research suggests that the main change in a human face is so-called craniofacial growth, that is, changes in the face shape and geometry. Craniofacial studies indicate that with age there is a modification from a circular to an oval face shape.[393]

The research focusing on specific facial characteristics as indicators of age is particularly interesting given that it seems to vary to what degree such characteristics have been incorporated into the visual age assess-

---

[390] Currently there are several databases, some of them available online, that can be used for this purpose. For more on such databases see, for example, Al-Shannaq and Elrefaei, 2019, pp. 1–21, see above note 385; Sergio Escalera *et al.*, "ChaLearn Looking at People 2015: Apparent Age and Cultural Event Recognition Datasets and Results", in *IEEE International al Conference on Computer Vision Workshop (ICCVW)*, IEEE, 2015.

[391] For more on this topic see, for example, Zebrowitz, 1997, see above note 131; Midori Albert, Karl Ricanek and Eric Patterson, "A Review of the Literature on the Aging Adult Skull and Face: Implications for Forensic Science Research and Applications", in *Forensic Science International*, 2007, vol. 172, pp. 1–9; LI Ya *et al.*, "Facial Age Estimation by Using Stacked Feature Composition and Selection", in *The Visual Computer*, 2016, vol. 32, no. 12, pp. 1525–36; DUAN Mingxing, LI Kenli and LI Kegin, "An Ensemble CNN2ELM for Age Estimation", in *IEEE Transactions on Information Forensics and Security*, 2018, vol. 13, no. 3, pp. 758–72.

[392] HAN Hu, Charles Otto and Anil K. Jain, "Age Estimation from Face Images: Human vs. Machine Performance", in *International Conference on Biometrics*, 2013, vol. 6, pp. 1–8.

[393] Narayanan Ramanathan and Rama Chellappa, "Face Verification Across Age Progression", in *IEEE Transactions on Image Processing*, 2006, vol. 15, no. 11, pp. 3349–61; Mohammad Dehshibi and Azam Bastanfard, "A New Algorithm for Age Recognition from Facial Images", in *Signal Processing*, 2010, vol. 90, no. 8, pp. 2431–44. For the stage from adulthood to old age, primarily texture change in the skin are relevant, but also slight changes in face shape may occur.

ments made by the Courts. For instance, in the Lubanga case, the Appeals Chamber explicitly recognizes "size and general appearance" as valid age estimation indicators while simultaneously noting that the Trial Chamber did not make any reference to the facial features of the individuals concerned.[394] In the Ntaganda case, the Trial Chamber mentions in relation to one video extract that it considers: "in particular, the facial features of the relevant individual".[395] It is unknown why the Chambers have decided to focus more or less on size, general appearance and facial features. From a research perspective, it is essential to better understand how and why different observers may vary in their observations as well as what types of contextual information may be biasing. Paediatricians' ability to estimate age should also be evaluated.

Clearly, the extent to which facial features can even be accurately perceived is dependent on image quality and focus, which was problematic in Lubanga. Preliminary empirical data suggests that even with relatively poor image quality, machine learning approaches can make sound classifications.[396] If an alleged child soldier is participating, photos can also be taken at a later stage under controlled conditions and then be used for age estimation. Such an approach requires that the time frame for the alleged crime can be established reasonably well.[397] This is to allow subtraction of the years that have passed by since then and use this to calculate the chronological age of the individual in question at the time period during which the crime(s) was (were) allegedly committed.

Although there seems to be some potential in age estimations based on faces, it is uncertain whether and to what extent it can help with the specific problem of distinguishing, for example, a 14-year-old from a 16-year old alleged child soldier. In this small age interval, there are probably

---

[394] Lubanga Appeals Chamber Judgment, para. 228, see above note 3.

[395] Ntaganda Trial Chamber Judgment, para. 388, see above note 74.

[396] So far, this has been tested primarily in the medical field, see, for example, LEE Hyunk-wang et al., "Pixel-Level Deep Segmentation: Artificial Intelligence Quantifies Muscle on Computed Tomography for Body Morphometric Analysis", in Journal of Digital Imaging, 2017, vol. 30, no. 4, pp. 487–98; Martina Sollini et al., "Towards Clinical Application of Image Mining: A Systematic Review on Artificial Intelligence and Radiomics", in European Journal of Nuclear Medicine and Molecular Imaging, 2019, vol. 46, no. 13, pp. 2656–72; Ahmed Hosny et al., "Artificial Intelligence in Radiology", in Nature Reviews Cancer, 2018, vol. 18, no. 8, pp. 500–10.

[397] Certainly, the prosecutor would have to establish the time frame anyways, in order to prove the crime(s) beyond reasonable doubt.

very gradual changes that are not necessarily visible at all, not the least considering all individual variation. Hence, it remains to be seen whether sufficiently nuanced and detailed estimations can be made to tackle this problem. Also, the relative accuracy of human age perceptions based on faces vs. the estimations obtained by using machine learning approaches has not been systematically and empirically evaluated.[398] Psychological research suggests that also humans who assess age on the basis of facial features rely on similar features as those identified to be the most reliable indicators through deep learning research.[399] In this regard, it is interesting

---

[398] Although early research suggests that deep learning approaches outperform humans, see HAN, Otto and Jain, 2013, see above note 392.

[399] For an overview of this research see Matthew G. Rhodes, "Age Estimation of Faces: A Review", in *Applied Cognitive Psychology*, 2009, vol. 23, no. 1, pp. 1–12. This research examines that facial cues individuals use for age estimations, consciously or subconsciously. For assessments of young individuals, up until approximately 20 years, age estimates seem to be sensitive to the level of *cardioidal strain*, that is, regularities in craniofacial growth which are sometimes described as a geometric transformation of the face. As cardioidal strain (and perceived age) increases, the skull casing is less pronounced and slopes further backward, the chin becomes more prominent and 'juts out' to a greater degree and the nose is placed higher in the face, see John B. Pittenger and Robert E. Shaw, "Aging Faces as Viscal-Elastic Events: Implications for a Theory of Non-rigid Shape Perception", in *Journal of Experimental Psychology: Human Perception and Performance*, 1975, vol. 1, no. 4, pp. 374–82. For more on cardioidal strain see, for example, Leonard S. Mark *et al.*, "Wrinkling and Head Shape as Coordinated Sources of Age Level Information", in *Perception and Psychophysics*, 1980, vol. 27, pp. 117–24; Leonard S. Mark *et al.*, "Perceptions of Growth: A Geometric Analysis of How Different Styles of Change are Distinguished", in *Journal of Experimental Psychology: Human Perception and Performance*, 1981, vol. 7, no. 4, pp. 855–68; John B Pittenger and Robert E. Shaw, "Perception of Relative and Absolut Age in Facial Photographs", in *Perception and Psychophysics*, 1975, vol. 18, pp. 137–43; Vicki Bruce *et al.*, "Further Experiment on the Perception of Growth in Three Dimensions", in *Perception and Psychophysics*, 1989, vol. 46, pp. 528–36. Interestingly, cardioidal strain also predicted the majority of variability in facial development evident in longitudinal studies of growth. For example, using X-rays of the skull of the same individual taken at several ages, a cardioidal strain transformation applied to growth at 4 years of age could predict the majority of the variability in facial growth at age 19, see James T. Todd and Leonard S. Mark, "Issues Related to the Prediction of Craniofacial Growth", in *American Journal of Orthodontics*, 1981, vol. 79, no. 1, pp. 63–80. A rounded skull, with a small chin and nose situated at a lower position are characteristics of early development (low levels of strain). Not surprisingly, also the skin texture among children is different than that of adults. The effect of contextual factors such as impoverished viewing conditions and clothing as well as training have on age estimations still need to be further examined. For more on these findings see Rhodes, 2009, pp. 1–12, see above note 399; Diane S. Berry and Leslie Z. McArthur, "Perceiving Character in Faces: The Impact of Age-related Craniofacial Changes on Social Perception", in *Psychological Bulletin*, 1986, vol. 100, pp. 3–18. See also Sörqvist and Eriksson, 2007, pp. 131–35, see above note 337.

to note that deep learning approaches to age estimations have already been tested on a preliminary basis in child pornography cases.[400] Here, the algorithms are used to identify a minor in a given image or video.[401] While this research still needs to be replicated it indicates that "the machines" outperform humans.[402] To properly evaluate such opportunities also in relation to age estimations of alleged child soldiers seem all the more important provided that it may be impossible to obtain other age evidence than video or photo evidence in relation to some alleged child soldiers, while the applicable law still requires objective elements of the crime to be determined. Also, even if there is other evidence such as oral evidence it is often fraught with serious challenges as well, as discussed in the next Section.

6.5.3. Oral Evidence

6.5.3.1. Challenges

6.5.3.1.1. Validity

This section focuses on *age statements*, that is, claims or estimations of age put forward either by the alleged child soldiers themselves or by other individuals like parents, social workers, NGO personnel, insiders or other witnesses. As such, this section has a different and more specific interest than the oral evidence presented by alleged child soldiers in a wider sense.[403] When the mentioned individuals provide their age statements, it

---

In this study, participants made age estimates for groups of young (15–24 years of age), middle-aged (34–46 years of age) and older (56–65 years of age) adults. Participants in a training group made age estimates and were given feedback in the form of the actual age of the individual. A control group practised making age estimates but was not provided feedback. Results showed that the provision of feedback improved performance relative to participants who were not given feedback. Yet, the improvements were restricted to estimates of the ages of older adults, limiting the utility of this training programme for age estimation of children and young adults.

[400] Jared Rondeau, *Deep Learning of Human Apparent Age for the Detection of Sexually Exploitative Imagery of Children*, University of Rhode Islands, 2019.

[401] *Ibid.*

[402] See, for example, HAN, Otto and Jain, 2013, see above note 392. These results were obtained using a database of 2200 face images in relation to which human age estimation (M-Turkers), 10 for each image, were obtained and compared to the accuracy obtained using machine learning approach.

[403] That more general question has already been empirically evaluated by See Barbora Holá and Thijs Bouwknegt, "Child Soldiers in International Courtrooms: Unqualified Perpetra-

---

is often unknown what the bases for their statements are. As outlined and discussed in the following, age statements *can be* based on chronological age but they can also or alternatively be based on biological age (Section 6.5.1.), apparent age (Section 6.5.2.) and/or social age, that is, a socially constructed age which is more strongly related to life events and to other people[404] or functional and physiological attributes[405] than the time that has passed since birth. It is today fairly widely acknowledged that age[406] is constructed, understood and used differently across different cultures and that this can result in communicational issues cross-culturally.[407] The child soldiering cases provide a perfect example of this. Importantly, this is not because the SCSL and the ICC hold a Western understanding of the age concept while the interviewed individuals do not. Both at the SCSL and the ICC the staff was or is multicultural as mandated and exemplified by, for example, the election rules for the ICC judges (Article 36 of the Rome Statute of the ICC).[408] Rather, the *legal culture* or context in which

---

tors, Erratic Witnesses and Irreparable Victims?", in Mark A. Drumbl and Jastine C. Barrett (eds.), *Research Handbook on Child Soldiers*, Edward Elgar, 2019, pp. 1–21.

[404] Ashish Vaska *et al.*, "Age Determination in Refugee Children: A Narrative History Tool for Use in Holistic Age Assessment", in *Journal of Paediatrics and Child Health*, 2016, vol. 5, p. 527.

[405] Terry Smith and Laura Brownless, *Age Assessment Practices: A Literature Review and Annotated Bibliography*, UNICEF, 2011; Deborah Durham, "Youth and the Social Imagination in Africa: Introduction to Parts 1 and 2", in *Anthropological Quarterly*, 2000, vol. 73, no. 3, pp. 113–20 and Derrick B. Jelliffe, "Age Assessment in Field Surveys of Children of the Tropics", in *The Journal Pediatrics*, 1966, vol. 69, no. 5, pp. 826–28.

[406] As well as time in a more general sense.

[407] This has been explored in relation to refugee children and this research demonstrates, *inter alia*, that age can be a significant factor but understood and remembered differently with knowledge of an exact date not required for functioning in participant's home societies. The researchers found that information regarding age was embedded in narrative accounts related to events and other people. Since birth was not always registered, birth and age-containing documentation was only obtained later in life. These documents often reflected cultural ideas regarding age, rather than recording true chronological age. See Vaska *et al.*, 2016, p. 527, see above note 404. See also Carla Willig, "Beyond Appearances: A Critical Realist Approach to Social Constructionist Work", in David J. Nightingale and John Cromby (eds.), *Social Constructionist Psychology: A Critical Analysis of Theory and Practice*, Open University Press, Philadelphia, 1999, pp. 37–51.

[408] For instance, according to Article 36(8) the State Parties shall, in the selection of judges, take into account the need, within the membership of the Court for: the representation of the principal legal systems of the world, equitable geographical representation and a fair representation of female and male judges. Also, in accordance with Article 36(7) no two judges may be nationals of the same country. For more on the topic of multiculturalism at

this staff operates has one very specific understanding of what kind of age is relevant, that is, chronological age, and for its legal determinations it is ultimately interested in in chronological age exclusively. Social age as an operationalization of chronological age will be discussed in more detail in this Section (Section 6.5.3.1.1.1. "Social Age"). Furthermore, age statements can also be false or honestly mistaken. Given this complexity, a few steps have to be taken in order to understand and evaluate the validity of an age statement as a measure of chronological age, namely:

1. The basis (or bases) for the age statement needs to be established. For age statements based on biological and/or apparent age, the reader is referred to these respective Sections (Section 6.5.1. and 6.5.2.). For age statements based on chronological age, the reader is referred to question 2 below. For age statements based on social age the reader is referred to the issues discussed in the subsequent text (Section 6.5.3.). Regardless of what the claimed basis (or bases) for the estimation is, it will always be relevant to answer question 3 below.

2. If an interviewee claims that the basis for the age statement is the chronological age an essential question is of course to establish whether the interviewee can be and is knowledgeable about his or her own chronological age or the chronological age of the alleged child soldier. If an unknowledgeable interviewee happens to guess the right age, this is a matter of luck rather than validity. The possibility that the interviewee confuses chronological age with social age should be evaluated (Section 6.5.3.1.1.1.).

3. How can legal actors know whether the interviewee providing the age statement is telling the truth, lying or is simply mistaken? Note that honest mistakes as regards chronological age are not defined as lies here.[409] To fully distinguish these three possibilities, legal actors would need a fool proof method distinguishing between individuals who are telling the truth, lying and making honest mistakes in their age statements, see Section 6.5.3.1.1.2.

---

the ICC, see, for example, YEE Sienho and Jacques-Yvan Morin, *Multiculturalism and International Law: Essays in Honour of Edward McWhinney*, Martinus Nijhoff Publishers, 2009.

[409] Neither are they defined as such in lie detection research, see Aldert Vrij, *Detecting Lies and Deceit: Pitfalls and Opportunities*, Wiley, 2008.

The legal cases themselves as well as relevant empirical research strongly suggests that the three questions posed above are usually very difficult to answer in practice. It might not even be possible to pass through question 1. These challenges are not any news to international criminal justice today, as manifested by that the ICC judges tend to not rely upon age statements, see, for example, the Lubanga case and Table 4.[410] However, it can be noted that the SCSL judges did in fact trust the child soldier's own age statements to a relatively large extent. The most likely reason for this difference between the Courts is that age was rarely contested in the SCSL cases.[411] Despite these challenges, oral evidence are still extensive in these cases and individuals, especially those under the age of 15 years, should be interviewed in ways that promote their rights.[412]

6.5.3.1.1.1. Social Age

Since age is constructed, understood and used differently across different cultures, and the legal culture's understanding of age as something entirely chronological can deviate from the understandings of age held by interviewees, there may be communicational issues when conducting and evaluating interviews with for instance victims and witnesses. Instead of focusing on a particular date of birth as legal age elements do, age may be considered to exist within a time span or bracket, which is more strongly related to significant life events and to other people[413] or functional and physiological attributes.[414] Also, apart from cultural differences, break-

---

[410] This was largely because of contradictions and the possible interference of an intermediate, see the discussion in Section 6.4.1.

[411] As will be discussed later, the age was often not heavily contested by the defence in these cases, there was no other evidence available and the SCSL also seem to have inferred ages of alleged child soldiers on the basis of them having been part of Small Boys Units ('SBU') or Small Girls Units ('SGU').

[412] See, for example, the Convention on the Rights of the Child and two of its Optional Protocols: CRC-OPAC and CRC-OPSC. There are also commitments to follow a child-sensitive approach, see, for example, ICC-OTP, *Policy on Children*, 2016, pp. 30–33 (https://www.legal-tools.org/doc/c2652b/). The latter document describes, for example, the OTP's "commitment to follow a child-sensitive approach" (p. 30) and that "[a]ll interviews with children will be conducted by staff members with expertise in interviewing and interacting with children, seeking the support of external experts if and when required" (pp. 31–32).

[413] Vaska *et al.*, 2016, p. 527, see above note 404.

[414] Smith and Brownless, 2011, see above note 405; Durham, 2000, pp. 113–20, see above note 405; and Jeliffe, 1966, see above note 405.

downs of structures such as education, healthcare and employment or of families and communities, memories and records may leave individuals with neither a socio-relational nor a record-based means of recalling age.[415] This means that age statements are often a measure of socially constructed age or inferred age, here referred to as social age, and it is unknown how this correlates with chronological age. In other words, this is a question of how valid social age is as a measure of chronological age.

At the SCSL, and more specifically the AFRC case, the potential mismatch between social age and chronological age was expressed and discussed by the Kanu defence expert. According to this expert opinion, the 15-year threshold is arbitrary because the "traditional African setting"[416] offers a different conception of childhood in which:

> the ending of childhood has little to do with achieving a particular age and more to do with physical capacity to perform acts reserved for adults. Marriage and the establishment of a new homestead are traditionally two prime indications of an adult male. As such, childhood refers more to a position in a societal hierarch than to biological age[417] and in order to become an adult it is necessary to ascend this hierarchy.[418]

Hence, this expert opinion challenges the conception of childhood, as expressed by SCSL (as well as ICC) Statutes. While the Trial Chamber in the AFRC rejected any defence based on cultural distinctions regarding the definition of childhood,[419] it is obvious in the statements of some of

---

[415] Vaska *et al.*, 2016, p. 527, see above note 404. Also, children may have false documents or may not know their age, or they may have no documentation to prove their identity or literally may not know their date of birth, see Laura Brownlee and Terry Smith, *Lives in the Balance: The Quality of Immigration Legal Advice Given to Separated Children Seeking Asylum*, Refugee Council, 2011.

[416] Brima *et al.* Defence Research Report on the Use of Child Soldiers in the Sierra Leone Conflict, p. 6, see above note 193.

[417] Own addition: Presumably, what the expert is referring to here is chronological age, not biological age as it is used in this research.

[418] Brima *et al.* Defence Research Report on the Use of Child Soldiers in the Sierra Leone Conflict, p. 6, see above note 193.

[419] The more specific arguments of the defence in the AFRC case was that the practice of recruiting and involving child soldiers was extensive and used by all the warring factions in the Sierra Leone conflict, that is, RUF-SL, the AFRC/SLA, West Side Boys and the pro-government forces including the Civil Defence Forces ('CDF's'), see Brima *et al.* Defence Research Report on the Use of Child Soldiers in the Sierra Leone Conflict, p. 18, see above note 193. According to the KANU defence this practice impacted on KANU's

the alleged child soldiers, that they simply did not know their chronological age at the time of interest. Rather, from their statements it is clear that they had *inferred* their chronological ages wholly or partially from what others had told them or other external events. For instance, in the Taylor case, Sumana told the SCSL that his father "used to tell him"[420] that he was 14 years at the relevant time. Furthermore, Sumana stated that he was abducted during the "mango season"[421] and that this was "at the time we were finally driven out of Koidu Town".[422] Similarly, Tholley testified that she had not yet had her menses when she was raped.[423] When age is inferred from external events, the validity will depend on whether 1) the individual is telling the truth or not making any subconscious mistakes in relation to the external events and when they took place and 2) that the dates of the external events can be corroborated. In some situations this can be made somewhat easier, for example, if cultural traditional events regularly take place within a certain time frame from birth, for example, celebrations seven days after child birth in Burundi[424] or traditional head shaving referred to as *chawar* in Bhutan.[425] If such events take place, which is often at the instigation of the parents of the child,[426] it may be easier to remember or infer chronological age. Other examples highlight that social age can sometimes also have strong ties to other types of ages, for example, biological age. For instance, in the RUF case, TFI-141 informed the Court that he only learned of his age "during his demobilization in 2000, when a nurse counted his teeth and determined he was 14

---

awareness as to the unlawfulness of conscripting, enlisting or using child soldiers below the age of 15. The defence submitted that such conduct was not on its face manifestly illegal and therefore no conviction should be entered on the ground of mistake of law. The Trial Chamber dismissed this submission stating that it was not persuaded that the defence of mistake of law could be invoked, since the rules of customary international law are not contingent on domestic practice in the given country, see SCSL Brima *et al.* Trial Chamber Judgment, pp. 226–27, see above note 59.

[420] SCSL Taylor Trial Chamber Judgment, para. 1378, see above note 67.

[421] *Ibid.*

[422] *Ibid.*

[423] *Ibid.*, para. 1454.

[424] Martha Nemes Fried and Morton H. Fried, *Transitions: Four Rituals in Eight Cultures*, Norton, New York, 1980; Henry Harald Hansen, *The Kurdish Woman's Life: Field Research in a Muslim Society*, Nationalmuseets Skrifter, 1961.

[425] *Ibid.*

[426] *Ibid.*

years old".[427] Hence, all of the issues associated with the different types of ages may be intertangled in an age statement.

6.5.3.1.1.2. Truths, Lies and Honest Mistakes

Apart from the potential mismatch between chronological age and social age, or social age intertangled with biological and apparent age, the SCSL and ICC cases also highlight another potentially problematic aspect of relying on age statements. This is when there is a real possibility that age statements are false or honestly mistaken. As indicated above, age statements can be false for many reasons. It could be that the person providing the statement is consciously lying, is honestly mistaken and/or has been led to provide a certain statement, whether he or she realizes that the statement is false or not. The possibility of *interviewer generated statements* has been widely acknowledged in the psychological literature and also in individual cases in national jurisdictions. Interestingly, this possibility was noted by the Trial Chamber in the Lubanga case in relation to Intermediary 143 and the alleged child soldiers he introduced to the Office of the Prosecutor ('OTP').[428] More specifically, the Chamber stated that:

> [...] there is a real risk that he [own addition: the Intermediary] played a role in the markedly flawed evidence that these witnesses provided to the OTP and to the Court [...] it is likely that as the common point of contact he persuaded, encouraged or assisted some or all of them to give false testimony. The Chamber accepts that the accounts of P-0007, P-0008, P-0010 and P-0011 were or may have been truthful and accurate in part, but it has real doubts as to critical aspects of their evidence, in particular their age at the relevant time. Although other potential explanations exist, the real possibility that Intermediary 143 corrupted the evidence of the four witnesses cannot be safely discounted.[429]

While this provides an example of a seemingly conscious influence on behalf of the interviewer, there are also more subtle forms of influences to take into account here, not the least provided the different understandings of age that might be at play during an interview. Presume that

---

[427] SCSL Sesay *et al.* Trial Chamber Judgment, p. 78, see above note 64.
[428] Lubanga Trial Chamber Judgment, para. 291, see above note 4.
[429] *Ibid.*

an interviewee has never or only very rarely had to speak about his or her chronological age, since this type of age has never been a big deal, or even a deal at all, in the individual's community. Is it even reasonable to expect that the interviewee could him or herself provide a specific age? As outlined in Table 3 many of the alleged child soldiers, also those who were not introduced by Intermediary 143, did provide own oral testimony as to their year of birth and/or specific age when they were abducted.

This raises questions in relation to *investigative interviewing*,[430] which is today a well-established and respected interview framework, as well as an accepted part of the ICC's investigative practice.[431] The overall aim of this framework is to conduct sound interviews that generate accurate and reliable information. This presupposes that the interview is conducted without impacting on the interviewee's memory retrieval or statement.[432] To this end, it is often recommended to establish so-called *ground rules* of the interview to ensure that the interviewee understands for instance what the difference between a truth and a lie is.[433] When it comes to interviews seeking to establish someone's chronological age, it seems

---

[430] Investigative interviewing is based on systematic and replicated empirical research, see, for example, Tom Williamson (ed.), *Investigative Interviewing: Rights, Research, Regulation*, Routledge, 2006; Ray Bull (ed.), *Investigative Interviewing*, Springer, New York, 2014. It includes interview models such as the PEACE model. For a summary see, for example, Becky Milne and Martine Powell, "Investigative Interviewing", in Jennifer M. Brown and Elizabeth A. Campbell (eds.), *The Cambridge Handbook of Forensic Psychology*, Cambridge University Press, 2010, pp. 208–14.

[431] For more on this see, for example, International Investigative Interviewing Research Group's web site.

[432] See, for example, Genevieve Waterhouse, Anne Ridley, Rachel Wilcock and Ray Bull, "Investigative interviewing in England and Wales: Adults, Children and the Provision of Support for Child Witnesses", in David Walsh, Gavin E. Oxburgh, Allison D. Redlich and Trond Myklebust (eds.), *International Developments and Practices in Investigative Interviewing and Interrogation, Volume 1: Victims and Witnesses*, Routledge, 2016, pp. 112–29; Bull (ed.), 2014, see above note 430.

[433] Several others describe ground rules but see, for instance, NAKA Makiko, "A Training Program for Investigative Interviewing of Children", in Ray Bull (ed.), *Investigative Interviewing*, Springer, New York, 2014, pp. 103–22. Other ground rules are, for instance, to encourage that the child says "I don't know" if the child does not know the answer and that the child should correct the interviewer if he or she makes a mistake. It has also been acknowledged by Naka, as well as several other authors that with repetitive interviews, children may say untrue things, consciously or subconsciously. For more on this see TAKAOKA Masako *et al.*, "False Memories in Children Created Through a Series of Interviews: Who Took a Boy Away?", in *International Journal of Police Sciences and Management*, 2002, vol. 4, no. 1, pp. 62–72.

relevant to also establish ground rules in relation to temporal aspects, for instance by asking questions such as: "What is a month?", "What is a year?", "What year is it now?" and "If I say that I am 7 years old, what am I doing then?".[434] The interviewees' answers to such questions would be indicative of whether the interviewee is at all capable of providing accurate information about chronological age. If ground rules have not been established, this is one possible explanation of differences between statements of the same or different individuals. Although it is unknown exactly why deviations occur, the Lubanga case has multiple examples of internal contradictions between the same alleged child soldier's statement at different points in time,[435] see Table 4.

If an interviewer tries to establish ground rules relating to temporal aspects and it becomes clear that the interviewee does not understand the relevant terms, guiding the interviewee in providing his or her own age statement will probably entail a very delicate balancing act. On the one hand, the interviewee needs support but on the other hand, the risk of leading the interviewee is probably quite large. Given the complexity of eliciting reliable age statements from individuals with age concepts fundamentally different from the legal age concept, the understanding of what constitutes a leading question in this specific context has to be more carefully examined.[436] An important aspect of this is of course that while

---

[434] This last question is intended to test the understanding of a lie in relation to age specifically. Note that none of these questions have been empirically evaluated but are rather suggestions based on similar suggestions primarily for interviews with children, for example, to determine whether the child understands the difference between lying and telling the truth, an interviewer could ask: "If I tell you that I am wearing a red shirt, what am I doing then?", presuming that the interviewer is wearing a shirt of some other colour. The usage of such questions to establish ground rules has been accepted as an important part of investigative interviewing, see, for example, Rebecca Milne and Ray Bull, *Investigative Interviewing: Psychology and Practice*, John Wiley and Sons, Chichester, 1999.

[435] Also, there were differences between the accounts of P-0298 who said he spent about four months at the camp and his father P-0299 who gave evidence that P-0298 left school and went to training camp for two months, see Lubanga Trial Chamber Judgment, para. 434, see above note 4.

[436] Especially considering that other suggestive elements may also be at play, for instance that the interviewee perceives of the interviewer as an authority figure. Suggestibility in children has been discussed at length, not the least in relation to events that occurred a long time ago and with interviewers who the children perceive as authority figures, when there is a tangible risk that the child feels that he or she has to answer in accordance with the interviewer's suggestion, see, for example, Milne and Bull, 1999, see above note 434; Barry

---

the ICC staff has training in conducting investigative interviewing, this is not necessarily the case for intermediaries, social workers and other individuals who conduct age interviews.[437] Importantly, the interviewer will not necessarily be aware that he or she is impacting on the individual's statement. But, since the interviewer is aware of what type of age statement is required for the statement to be used and relied upon by the prosecution or in Court, it is possible that the interviewer will subtly steer the interviewee towards providing an age statement he or she otherwise would not have provided.[438]

While there is emerging research into statement analysis in the context of international criminal law, see Chapter 3 by Agirre Aranburu in this volume,[439] most of the existing research has focused on national ju-

---

Feld, "Cops and Kids in the Interrogation Room", in Ray Bull (ed.), *Investigative Interviewing*, Springer, New York, 2014.

[437] For more on the research that has already been conducted focusing on the cultural aspects on investigative interviewing see, for example, Melanie O'Brien and Mark Kebbel, "Interview Techniques in International Criminal Court and Tribunals", in Ray Bull (ed.), *Investigative Interviewing*, Springer, New York, 2014, pp. 91–103. As pointed out by these authors much of the evidence in trials concerning international criminal law is elicited from witnesses, victims and suspects, and therefore, the way in which they are interviewed is critical to successful prosecutions of the guilty. The participants in this research report challenges of cultural differences in interviews because the method of storytelling and concept of time differ in some parts of Africa from those in Western cultures, seeking successfully to develop a rich and detailed narrative by the suspect or witness. However, a story as told by an African storyteller may not be told chronologically. Time is not measured by a clock or calendar but in reference to events. For example, a person in the UK might recount an event as occurring on 7 April 2009, whereas an event in the DRC might be mentioned relative to the rains. Also, a meaningful body of work on interviewing vulnerable witnesses of international crimes has been produced by scholars and NGO's on topics such as victims of sexual and gender-based violence and children, see Morten Bergsmo and William H. Wiley, "Human Rights Professional and the Criminal Investigation and Prosecution of Core International Crimes", in Siri Skåre, Ingvild Burkey and Hege Mørk (eds.), *Manual on Human Rights Monitoring: An Introduction for Human Rights Field Officers*, Norwegian Centre for Human Rights, Oslo, 2008, pp. 18–21 (https://www.legal-tools.org/doc/8362d5/).

[438] This should be seen against the background that cases have previously 'collapsed' before the Court because witness testimonies are considered unreliable. Also, the Court's reluctance to trust specifically the statements of alleged child soldiers has been documented in recent empirical research, see Holá and Bouwknegt, 2019, pp. 1–21, see above note 403.

[439] Xabier Agirre Aranburu, "The Contribution of Analysis to the Quality Control in Criminal Investigation", Chapter 3 above; Xabier Agirre Aranburu, "On How Analysis Can Enhance the Quality of Investigation and Case Preparation", CILRAP Film, New Delhi, 22 February 2019 (https://www.cilrap.org/cilrap-film/190222-agirre/); Gabriele Chlevickaite and

risdictions and statements in a more general sense, rather than age statements.[440] Since evidence corroborating or disproving witness statements is sometimes scarce or even non-existent, many national as well as international tribunals have established criteria upon which evaluations of reliability and credibility should be made.[441] The extent to which such criteria (like detail, consistency criteria, and so on) are indicative of a truthful, deceptive (or mistaken) testimony has also been the topic of much research into so-called statement analysis techniques such as Statement Validity Assessment ('SVA')[442] and Reality Monitoring ('RM').[443] These techniques all have a notion in common, namely that there are qualitative and quantitative differences between truthful and deceptive testimony. Research into these techniques suggest that statement analysis techniques have overall error rates of 25–30 per cent,[444] that is, when the criteria are used to decide whether someone is lying or telling the truth, these decisions are wrong in 25–30 per cent of the cases. Among the specific criteria

---

Barbora Holá, "Empirical Study of Insider Witnesses' Assessments at the International Criminal Court", in *International Criminal Law Review*, 2016, vol. 16, no. 4, pp. 673–702.

[440] See, for example, Richard A. Wise, Giuseppe Sartori, Svein Magnussen and Martin A. Safer, "An Examination of the Causes and Solutions to Eyewitness Error", in *Frontiers in Psychiatry*, 2014, vol. 5, pp. 1–8; Richard A. Wise, Kirsten A. Dauphinais and Martin A. Safer, "A Tripartite Solution to Eyewitness Error", in *The Journal of Criminal Law and Criminology*, 2007, vol. 97, no. 3, pp. 807–71.

[441] For more information about what criteria are used for Source Evaluation by the ICC-OTP see Agirre Aranburu, 2020, see above note 439.

[442] See, for example, Gunther Köhnken, "Statement Validity Analysis and the "Detection of Truth", in Pär Anders Granhag and Leif A. Strömwall (eds.), *The Detection of Deception in Forensic Contexts*, Cambridge University Press, 2004, pp. 41–63.

[443] See, for example, Marcia K. Johnson and Carol L. Raye, "Reality Monitoring", in *Psychological Review*, 1981, vol. 88, no. 1, pp. 67–85 and Sigfried L. Sporer, "Reality Monitoring and Detection of Deception", in Pär Anders Granhag and Leif A. Strömwall (eds.), *The Detection of Deception in Forensic Contexts*, Cambridge University Press, 2004, pp. 64–102. See also the so-called Multivariable Adults' Statements Assessment Model ('MASAM'), which has been tested in one study with suspect statement but still needs more evaluation, Bartosz Wojciechowski, Minna Gräns and Moa Lidén, "A True Denial or a False Confession? Assessing Veracity of Suspects' Statements using MASAM and SVA", in *PloS One*, 2018, vol. 13, no. 6.

[444] The overall error rate for SVA is estimated to 30 per cent, for a summary see Bartosz Wojciech Wojciechowski, "Content Analysis Algorithms: An Innovative and Accurate Approach to Statement Veracity Assessment", in *European Polygraph*, 2014, vol. 8, no. 3, p. 121. The overall error rate for RM is 25 per cent, see Jaume Masip *et al.*, "The Detection of Deception with the Reality Monitoring Approach: A Review of the Empirical Evidence", in *Psychology, Crime and Law*, 2005, vol. 11, no. 1, pp. 99–122.

entailed in statement analysis techniques, the detail criterion (the number of details) has gained the strongest scientific support, in both field and experimental studies.[445] Furthermore, a recent expert evaluation of the criteria previously used by the Swedish Supreme Court suggests that a truthful statement is significantly longer than a false statement.[446] Moreover, according to the expert evaluation, the fact that a statement is clear and detailed can suggest that the statement is truthful, whereas there is no real support for the notion that lacking consistency indicates deception.[447]

---

[445] While this is accurate of the research available, it does not necessarily mean that the detail criterion is useful in applied settings, for example due to embedded lies or that it is difficult to determine when a statement is detailed enough to satisfy this criterion. For a critical analysis of the detail criterion, see Xabier Agirre Aranburu, "The Contribution of Analysis to the Quality Control in Criminal Investigation", Chapter 3 in this volume. For research pertaining to the detail criterion in controlled experimental setting and some field studies, see Galit Nahari *et al.*, "Language of Lies: Urgent Issues and Prospects in Verbal Lie Detection Research", in *Legal and Criminological Psychology*, 2019, vol. 24, pp. 1–23. As pointed out by these authors: "There seems to be an emerging consensus among scholars about the validity of a limited number of cues. For example, ample research has shown that truthful statements are more detailed than deceptive statements". *Ibid.*, p. 10. However, they also emphasize difficulties in measuring the level of detail in practice as well as academic research, for instance, because coding schemes may produce arbitrary choices. See also Wendy L. Morris and Bella M. DePaulo, "Discerning Lies from Truths: Behavioral Cues to Deception and the Indirect Pathway of Intuition", in Pär Anders Granhag and Leif A. Strömwall (eds.), *The Detection of Deception in Forensic Contexts*, Cambridge University Press, 2004, pp. 15–40; Aldert Vrij *et al.*, "Detecting Deceit via Analysis of Verbal and Nonverbal Behavior", in *Journal of Nonverbal Behavior*, 2000, vol. 24, pp. 239–63. For more on the detail criteria in the context of investigations into core international crimes, the reader is referred to Agirre Aranburu, 2020, see above note 439.

[446] See Lena Schelin, *Bevisvärdering av utsagor i brottmål*, Norstedts Juridik, Stockholm, 2007, p. 86. This is based on research by, for example, Maria Alonso-Quecuty, "Deception Detection and Reality Monitoring: A New Answer to an Old Question?", in Friedrich Lösel, Doris Bender and Thomas Bliesener (eds.), *Psychology and Law: International Perspectives*, Walter De Gruyter, 1992, pp. 328–32; Vrij, 2008, see above note 409; Morris and DePaulo, 2004, see above note 445.

[447] The expert evaluation was made in relation to The Swedish Supreme Court case NJA 2010 p. 671, the Swedish Supreme Court, NJA 2010 p. 671, *Bevisvärdering i mål om sexualbrott*, 28 December 2010. For the full expert evaluation see the Swedish Government Official Reports, SOU 2017:7 appendix 7. In this case, the Court had stated that a reliable statement is characterized by that it is clear, long, vivid logical, rich in detail, proven to be true in relation to important details, free from errors, contradictions, exaggerations, details that are difficult to explain, lack of consistency/context or hesitation in important parts. The purpose of the review was to evaluate whether and to what extent these criteria were consistent with findings in lie detection research. The result of the expert evaluation made the Supreme Court revise its criteria, as acknowledged by the Court in NJA 2017 s. 316.

Even if some of the statement criteria have empirical support, their usefulness and accuracy in an applied setting can be discussed. The research findings often come from controlled experimental studies that may be relatively different to real-world contexts, and, the studies usually compare statements that are fully true to those that are fully false. This means that they largely disregard the possibility of so-called embedded lies, that is, when a liar takes an otherwise truthful statement and changes one detail that completely alters the significance of the account, for instance changing the date of when something happened or the identity of an individual.[448] While this strategy is believed to be fairly common in practice, little is known about whether and how it changes the characteristics of the statement.[449] Furthermore, it is difficult to decide when the criteria are fulfilled, as it is unclear what is long or detailed enough. In relation to the length criteria, research studies enable words and syllables to be counted and compared in written statements. This is clearly different from for example Court deliberations when the assessments usually have to be made only on the bases of a specific or several oral statements, without any possibility of comparing it to any objective length measure, or the witness's individual baseline. On top of this, verbal cues to deception are culturally specific[450] as well as age specific.[451]

---

[448] See, for example, Drew A. Leins, Ronald P. Fisher and Stephan J. Ross, "Exploring Liars' Strategies for Creating Deceptive Reports", in *Legal and Criminological Psychology*, 2013, vol. 18, pp. 141–51; Galit Nahari and Aldert Vrij, "Systematic Errors (Biases) in Applying Verbal Lie Detection Tools: Richness in Detail as a Test Case", in *Crime Psychology Review*, 2015, vol. 1, no. 1, pp. 98–107; Aldert Vrij, Pär Anders Granhag and Stephen Porter, "Pitfalls and Opportunities in Nonverbal and Verbal Lie Detection", in *Psychological Science in the Public Interest*, 2010, vol. 11, no. 3, pp. 89–121.

[449] *Ibid.*

[450] Cross cultural variations in the language of liars have been found that are consistent with known cultural difference in self-construction and episodic memory, see Paul J. Taylor *et al.*, "Culture Moderates Changes in Linguistic Self-Presentation and Detail provision When Deceiving Others", in *Royal Society Open Science*, 2017, vol. 4, no. 8, pp. 1–11. For example, participants considered to come from an individualistic culture (White and British), reduced their first-person pronoun use when lying compared to telling the truth. By contrast, collectivist North African participants increased their use of the first-person pronoun when lying, in part to compensate for their reduction in use of third-person pronouns and references to family.

[451] For instance, Reality Monitoring ('RM') cannot be used with younger children because they have more difficulties distinguishing facts from fantasy, see, for example, Stephan Lindsay, "Children's Source Monitoring", in Helen L. Westcott, Graham M. Davies and Ray H.C. Bull (eds.), *Children's Testimony: A Handbook of Psychological Research and*

When it comes to age statements specifically, they come with a special set of concerns. Given the social and cultural dimensions, any differences that may exist between truthful and deceptive statements may not be the same as for statements in a more general sense. Against this background, it seems reasonable to ask what *internal consistencies or inconsistencies* in age statements really mean.[452] According to the SCSL in the RUF case, inconsistency (in a general sense) is certainly a factor to take into consideration but alone it does not mean that the whole of the testimony is unreliable,[453] and here it refers to the ICTY Čelebići Appeal Judgment.[454] This view is clearly different from the fairly heavy reliance on inconsistencies (external, internal and other) as a cue to unreliability in the Lubanga case, see Table 4. However, this difference is likely to be due to the interference of an intermediary in the latter but not the former case. As suggested by the expert evaluation of the Swedish Supreme Court criteria, there is no real support that inconsistency is a good cue to deception in general.[455] Also, for age statements, inconsistencies may have a different and relatively unique meaning.

Forensic Practice, Wiley-Blackwell, 2002, pp. 83–98; Stephan Lindsay and Marcia K. Johnson, "Reality Monitoring and Suggestibility: Children's Ability to Discriminate Among Memories from Different Sources", in Stephan J. Ceci, Michael P. Toglia and David F. Ross (eds.), *Children's Eyewitness Memory*, Springer, New York, 1987, pp. 91–121.

[452] Clearly, failure to provide a fully consistent age statement could also have to do with, for example, memory issues, as highlighted by the Separate and Dissenting Opinion of Judge Odio Benito, para. 32 in the Lubanga Trial Chamber Judgment, see above note 4:

These witnesses (and anyone under those circumstances) could explicably and logically have difficulties in recollecting events since the time elapsed between the events (2002-2003), the first interviews with OTP investigators (2005) and the actual trial (2009-2010). In fact, with such elapses of time it would be suspicious if the accounts would remain perfectly alike and unchanged. Memory is faulty. This is more the case for children and adults have suffered any traumatic events.

[453] SCSL Sesay *et al.* Trial Chamber Judgment, para. 490, see above note 64.

[454] ICTY, *The Prosecutor v. Mucić et al.*, Appeals Chamber, Judgement, 20 February 2001, IT-96-21-A (https://www.legal-tools.org/doc/051554/). The trial related to events that took place in 1992 in a prison camp near the town of Čelebići, in central Bosnia and Herzegovina. The accused were charged with numerous counts of grave breaches of the Geneva Conventions of 1949 under Article 2 of the Tribunal's Statute. For more on the case see ICTY, "Appeal Judgement in the Čelebići case", 20 February 2001, JL/P.I.S./564-e (available on its web site).

[455] This is even more so if ground rules relating to temporal aspects have not been established.

6.5.3.1.2. Reliability

Between Expert Reliability can be discussed in relation to age statements primarily in two regards: 1) *Between Interviewer Reliability*, that is, that interviewers may have different approaches that results in different age statements and 2) *Between Evaluator Reliability*, that is, analysts or judges who evaluate age statements using statement validity criteria may make different observations and draw different conclusions.

It is well-established that the quality of communication between interviewer and interviewee can vary depending on a number of factors, for instance the personal attributes of the interviewer[456] and the amount of social support shown by the interviewer.[457] Similarly, given the inherently open character of statement criteria, different evaluators are likely to emphasize different criteria and also interpret these criteria differently. As implied above, even if criteria such as the detail criterion have some predictive value of a truthful statement this does not help the assessment of *what is* a detailed (or consistent, clear, etc.) statement, considering, for example, how an individual usually speaks and the context of the statement. Accordingly, research suggests that the level of agreement between different raters who rate the same statement for the detail criteria, is low.[458]

---

[456] See, for example, Gail S. Goodman *et al.*, "Mother Knows Best: Effects of Relationship Status and Interviewer Bias on Children's Memory", in *Journal of Experimental Child Psychology*, 1995, vol. 60, no. 1, pp. 195–228; David F. Björklund *et al.*, "Social Demand Characteristics in Children's and Adults' Eyewitness Memory and Suggestibility: The Effect of Different Interviewers of Free Recall and Recognition", in *Applied Cognitive Psychology*, 2000, vol. 14, no. 5, pp. 421–33.

[457] See, for example, Molly Carter Imhoff and Lynne Baker-Ward, "Preschoolers' Suggestibility: Effects of Developmentally Appropriate Language and Interviewer Supportiveness", in *Journal of Applied Developmental Psychology*, 1999, vol. 20, no. 3, pp. 407–29; Bette L. Bottoms, Jodi A. Quas and Suzanne L. Davis, "The Influence of Interviewer-provided Social Support on Children's Suggestibility, Memory, and Disclosures", in Margaret-Ellen Pipe, Michael E. Lamb, Yael Orbach and Ann-Christin Cederborg (eds.), *Child Sexual Abuse: Disclosure, Delay, and Denial*, Lawrence Erlbaum Associates Publishers, 2007, pp. 135–58; TEOH Yee San and Michael Lamb, "Interviewer Demeanor in Forensic Interviews of Children", in *Psychology, Crime and Law*, 2013, vol. 19, no. 2, pp. 145–59.

[458] Leif Strömwall and Pär Anders Granhag, "How to Detect Deception? Arresting the Beliefs of Police Officers, Prosecutors and Judges", in *Psychology, Crime and Law*, 2003, vol. 9, no. 1, pp. 30–34; Pär Anders Granhag and Leif Strömwall, "Deception Detection: Examining the Consistency Heuristic", in C.M. Breur, M.M. Kommer, J.F. Nijboer and J.M. Reijntjes (eds.), *New Trends in Criminal Investigation and Evidence*, Intersentia, 2000, p. 215.

Certainly, it can be discussed whether and to what extent lacking Between Expert Reliability in this context is a problem, or in fact an asset. In situations where there is only one interviewer or one evaluator, disparities can be problematic since the result of the interview or evaluation may become more dependent on the involved individual than anything else. However, when it comes to, for example, investigative teams and Court deliberations, it is possible that many evaluators can examine the same statement and, if dissent is successfully integrated into the decision-making process, it can in fact be an asset. This presupposes that the group climate allows such open discussions where group members dare to state their opinions freely. This is not always the case since groups and group climate can be quite complex.[459]

6.5.3.1.3. Biasability

There are many potential sources of bias in interviews and evaluations of age statements. For instance, an interviewer who has a clear hypothesis about the age of a certain individual might conduct the interview in a way that, as far as possible, confirms this hypothesis, for instance through the usage of leading questions.[460] Similar tendencies have been noted not the least in relation to child interviews.[461] Also, as implied by research on so-called *asymmetrical scepticism*, reliability and credibility assessments may be biased by, for example, case hypotheses.[462] More specifically,

---

[459] This is clear from research into group think and group polarization. For a summary of this research relating to the legal setting and more specifically Court deliberations see Lidén, 2018, pp. 129–43, see above note 30.

[460] See the related discussion on suggestibility in the validity Section 6.5.3.1.1.

[461] See, for instance, Stephan Ceci and Maggie Bruck, "The Role of Interviewer Bias", in Stephen J. Ceci and Maggie Bruck (eds.), *Jeopardy in the Courtroom: A Scientific Analysis of Children's Testimony*, American Psychological Association, 1995 pp. 87–108; Jessica Sparling *et al.*, "Effects of Interviewer Behavior on Accuracy of Children's Responses", in *Journal of Applied Behavior Analysis*, 2011, vol. 44, no. 3, pp. 587–92; William C. Thompson, Alison Clarke-Stewart and Stephan J. Lepore, "What Did the Janitor Do? Suggestive Interviewing and the Accuracy of Children's Accounts", in *Law and Human Behavior*, 1997, vol. 21, no. 4, pp. 405–26.

[462] The framework on asymmetrical scepticism essentially holds that decision makers perceive of evidence consistent with their hypothesis as more reliable and credible than evidence which is inconsistent with their hypothesis, even if there are no other differences between these statements. For more on this see Tamara Marksteiner *et al.*, "Asymmetrical Scepticism Towards Criminal Evidence: The Role of Goal- and Belief Consistency", in *Applied Cognitive Psychology*, 2011, vol. 25, no. 4, pp. 541–47. For a review of this research see, for example, Karl Ask and Laurence J. Alison, "Investigators' Decision Mak-

interviewers or evaluators tend to uncritically approve of information supporting their hypothesis, while critically scrutinizing hypothesis inconsistent information. Similarly, research on *coherence-based reasoning* suggests that premises and conclusions are sometimes blurred so that the premises are interpreted in the light of a preferred conclusion and, only in this way, the conclusion is 'supported' by the premises.[463]

Furthermore, alleged child soldiers may have experienced severe trauma and hardship, and interacting with them is likely to have an emotional impact. In the reports from, for example, social workers and NGO-workers who have conducted such interviews there are some examples of this. One such example was cited in the introduction of this chapter, namely P-0046 who worked in MONUC's child protection program and who had conducted interviews with alleged child soldiers in Ituri in 2003–04, within the context of the Lubanga case.[464] Apart from her disputed testimony that some children were smaller than the Kalashnikovs they were carrying,[465] she also reported that two boys, 11 and 13 years old, had been frightened by the military and when she began asking questions one of them broke down in tears. P-0046 recalled holding the hand of the younger child when crossing the street. Her evidence was that "he was so small".[466] It is possible that such emotional impact makes individuals motivated to reach certain conclusions,[467] suggesting a possible emotional bias in this context.

---

ing", in P.A. Granhag (ed.), *Forensic Psychology in Context: Nordic and International Perspectives*, Routledge, 2010, pp. 35–55.

[463] Andreas Glöckner and Christoph Engel, "Can We Trust Intuitive Jurors? Standards of Proof and the Probative Value of Evidence in Coherence-Based Reasoning", in *Journal of Empirical Legal Studies*, 2013, vol. 10, no. 2, pp. 230–52.

[464] Lubanga Trial Chamber Judgment, paras. 644–45, see above note 4.

[465] *Ibid.*, para. 648, fn. 1839, citing ICC, *The Prosecutor v. Thomas Lubanga Dyilo*, Defence, Closing Submissions of the Defence, 15 July 2011, ICC-01/04-01/06-2773-Red-tENG, para. 645 (https://www.legal-tools.org/doc/ca1fcd/), referring to Testimony of P-0046 before Pre-Trial Chamber I, video excerpt EVD-OTP-00479; and the respective Transcript of Testimony, T-37-FR, p. 23, lines 8–12.

[466] Lubanga Trial Chamber Judgment, fn. 1840, see above note 4, citing Testimony of P-0046 before Pre-Trial Chamber I, video excerpt EVD-OTP-00490; and the respective Transcript of Testimony, T-38-ENG, p. 83, lines 18–25.

[467] However, see also research on the compassion fade effect. For an overview of both motivated reasoning and compassion fade effect in the context of international criminal law, see Lidén, 2020, pp. 1–17, see above note 298.

6.5.3.2. Opportunities

From a research perspective, one appropriate first step is to evaluate whether and how the investigative interviewing framework can be used to promote accurate age statements, for example, through establishment of ground rules. Today, there are also interviewing frameworks introduced and/or used in asylum cases as well as by health professionals, in order to conduct appropriate interviews in relation to the question of age specifically. An example is the Age Assessment Tool Questionnaire.[468] It is possible that aspects of such interviewing tools can be useful to incorporate into the investigative interviewing framework used with alleged child soldiers, since such questionnaires have previously enabled age estimations within ranges that approximate chronological age.[469] As regards the evaluation of age statements, an appropriate first step would be to conduct experimental studies addressing the question of whether, in a controlled environment, there are any systematic, quantitative or qualitative differences between truthful, deceptive and mistaken age statements. Furthermore, and similar to forensic and video evidence, issues of lacking Between Expert Reliability and Biasability can be mitigated through training and calibration as well as CIM procedures.

6.5.4. Documentary evidence

6.5.4.1. Challenges

6.5.4.1.1. Validity

Similar to oral evidence, the more specific validity challenges relating to documentary evidence depends on what constitutes the basis for the age stated in the document. As outlined in the Results Section (6.4.2.) the category documentary evidence includes a range of different types of documents, for instance *ad hoc* birth certificates, electoral cards, school records, lists of recruits as well as more general reports regarding the prevalence of individuals under 15 years who actively participated in armed conflict. It is relatively uncommon for the courts to spell out explicitly what the basis for the provided ages are but this seems to entail all of the ages that have been discussed above, that is, biological, apparent and social age as well as combinations of these. Also, it is of course possible that

---

[468] Vaska *et al.*, 2016, p. 527, see above note 404.
[469] *Ibid.*

documents contain plainly false age information, a problem which over-laps with that described in relation to oral evidence (Section 6.5.3.1.1.). For instance, in the Lubanga case, P-0213 had a school register suggesting he was under 15 years but this document was considered unreliable as an expert had established that the age information overwrote a previous entry which was partially visible underneath (see Table 4 in Section 6.4.2.). Similarly, as was noted by the SCSL Trial Chamber in the Taylor case, more general reports regarding the prevalence of child soldiers may be based on hearsay.[470] The range of possible bases for ages stated in docu-ments is one possible explanation for the many contradictions found be-tween different documents in the Lubanga case (see Table 4 in Section 6.4.2.). Additionally, this can be because administrative procedures are flawed and that it is possible for anyone to obtain identity documentation "containing information which may or may not have been accurate, at his or her convenience",[471] as suggested in the Lubanga case. As such, there may not be any authenticity issues with the document itself, but the age information contained therein is still inaccurate. Since the document is simply the carrier of the age information, validity issues with documen-tary evidence largely coincide with the validity issues described in the previous sections. Taken together this seems to suggest that evaluating validity in relation to documentary evidence is about answering two ques-tions:

1) *Is the document authentic?* Depending on how the document is believed to have been produced there are many possible methods for evaluating its authenticity, including for instance different types of analy-

---

[470] The Chamber discussed the significance of several reports, one from the Coalition to Stop the Use of Child Soldiers according to which 10 per cent of the armed forces which at-tacked Freetown in January 1999 were children. There was also a UN Secretary-General report stating that a significant number of rebel fighters in the Freetown attack were chil-dren and that boys as young as 8 to 11 were killing and inflicting injuries. SCSL Taylor Trial Chamber Judgment, p. 566, paras. 1566–68, see above note 67.

[471] Counsel submitted that the voting cards and the personal information contained in the database of the DRC Independent Electoral Commission lacked probative value because, at the time in Ituri, the administrative procedure for issuing identity documents were seri-ously flawed and it was possible for anyone to obtain identity document "containing in-formation which may or may not have been accurate, at his or her convenience", see ICC, *The Prosecutor v. Thomas Lubanga Dyilo*, Office of Public Counsel for Victims, Closing Submissions of the Legal Representative of Victims a/0047/06, a/0048/06, a/0050/06 and a/0052/06, 31 May 2011, ICC-01/04-10/06-2744-Red-tENG, para. 33 (https://www.legal-tools.org/doc/5859d9/).

sis of the chemical composition of ink[472] and forensic handwriting examination ('FHE').[473]

2. *What is the basis for the age stated in the document?* As suggested above, apart from chronological age, the basis could be biological, apparent, social age or combinations of these. It could also be plainly false information in an authentic document, or information based on hearsay, and so on. This research provides a basis for analysis for the three first possibilities, see Sections 6.5.1.–6.5.3.

6.5.4.1.2. Reliability

Many forensic pattern examinations, including, for example, Forensic Handwriting Examination (FHE), use human perceptual and cognitive processes almost exclusively to form opinions regarding evidence.[474]

---

[472] Such as Easy Ambient Sonic-spray Ionization Mass Spectrometry ('EASI-MS'), infrared spectroscopy and laser desorption ionization mass spectrometry ('LDI-MS'). See, for example, Romao Wanderson *et al.*, "Analyzing Brazilian Vehicle Documents for Authenticity by Easy Ambient Sonic-Spray Ionization Mass Spectrometry", in *Journal of Forensic Sciences*, 2012, vol. 57, no. 2, pp. 539–43.

[473] FHEs are common and include the examination of cursive writing, hand printing, signatures, and numbers, and is part of a broader field of forensic document examination. An examiner may be called upon to assist fact finders to answer questions such as: are these writing samples written by the same or different people, or whether the writings in question were all written by one individual.

[474] Nikola Osborne, Carolyne Bird and Reinoud Stoel, "Forensic Handwriting Examination and Cognitive Bias: Recommendations from the NIST Expert Working Group on Human Factors", in *Australian Journal of Forensic Sciences*, 2019, vol. 51, no. 1, pp. 141–44; Bryan Found and John Ganas, "The Management of Domain Irrelevant Context Information in Forensic Handwriting Examination Casework", in *Science and Justice*, 2013, vol. 53, no. 2, pp. 155–58. In fact, in US District Court for the Southern District of New York, *US v. Starzecpyzel*, Memorandum and Order, 3 April 1995, 880 F. Supp. 1027, Judge McKenna ruled that forensic document examination ('FDE') was technical rather than scientific. Judge McKenna argued this is because forensic document examiners (FDEs) have no feedback as to whether their opinions are correct or not. The FDE's opinion may have been wrong even if the side for which they testify win the case. As pointed out by Mohammed, this way of reasoning seems to be related to Popper's criteria for determining whether a method is scientific, namely whether it is falsifiable, see Linton A. Mohammed, *Forensic Examination of Signatures*, Academic Press, 2019, pp. 129–30. In other words, there should be a way to test that the method is wrong. However, it is also clear that a method can be falsifiable even if the expert cannot reasonably know whether he or she is right in an individual case, where the basis for their examination is that the ground truth is not known. Also, research suggests that Forensic Handwriting Examiners develop specialist skills as they outperform lay persons on blind comparison tasks, see, for example, Moshe Kam, Joseph Wetstein and Robert Conn, "Proficiency of Professional Document

Therefore, there is room for experts making different observations and reaching different conclusions also in relation to this type of evidence. Indeed, research suggests that this is the case, as for instance the interpretation of handwriting varies between different handwriting examiners who have different years of experience.[475] There are also variations between handwriting examiners in their selections of different features of the handwriting.[476]

6.5.4.1.3. Biasability

The inherently open nature of forensic document examination,[477] also means that these examinations are prone to bias. This can be manifested in, for example, evaluations involving comparisons of the number and quality of similarities and differences between a questioned sample and the reference, in relation to which explicit and transparent criteria are sometimes lacking.[478] For instance, participants who were aware of a suspect's confession rated non-matching handwriting samples from the suspect and perpetrator as more similar to each other and were also more likely to misjudge them as having been authored by the same individual.[479] Also, since handwriting examination usually requires a comparison between the questioned and known handwriting, the features contained in one could influence the selection and interpretation of the features contained in the other.[480]

Examiners in Writer Identification", in *Journal of Forensic Sciences*, 1994, vol. 39, no. 1, pp. 5–14; Bryan Found, Jodi C. Sita and Doug Rogers, "The Development of a Program for Characterising Forensic Handwriting Examiner's Expertise: Signature Examination Pilot Study", in *Journal of Forensic Document Examination*, 1999, vol. 12, p. 69–80 and Jodi Sita, Bryan Found and Douglas K. Rogers, "Forensic Handwriting Examiner's Expertise for Signature Comparison", in *Journal of Forensic Sciences*, 2002, vol. 47, no. 5, pp. 1117–24.

[475] LI Bing and MA Tiantian, "Research on Subjective Bias Cognition Effect in Handwriting Identification", in *Journal of Forensic Sciences and Medicine*, 2018, vol. 4, no. 4, p. 212.

[476] *Ibid.*, p. 210.

[477] Found and Ganas, 2013, pp. 155–58, see above note 474.

[478] LI and MA, 2018, pp. 203–12, see above note 475.

[479] Jeff Kukucka, *An Investigation of Factors that Create and Mitigate Confirmation Bias in Judgments of Handwriting Evidence*, City University of New York, 2014.

[480] Dan E. Krane *et al.*, "Sequential Unmasking: A Means of Minimizing Observer Effects in Forensic DNA Interpretation", in *Journal of Forensic Sciences*, 2008, vol. 53, no. 4, pp. 1006–07; Itiel E. Dror *et al.*, "Letter to the Editor: Context Management Toolbox: A Linear

6.5.4.2. Opportunities

For the questions of whether a document is authentic, there are some relevant developments in recent research. The convolutional neural network ('CNN') is a state-of-the art deep learning tool that extracts spatial features from images.[481] It has improved image classification systems in a wide range of settings,[482] and has also evolved as an effective tool for classification of so-called hyperspectral images ('HSIs'), which provides broad spectral information that allows for identification of the underlying material in images using signal-processing techniques.[483] HSI analysis has gained enormous interest in forensic science as it adds to the potential of forensic experts for viewing and interpreting various forensic traces such as fingerprints, inks, bloodstains, hair and drugs.[484] Being a non-destructive tool, HSI analysis has also been widely used in document imaging for improving readability and determination of ink age, backdating and forgery in documents,[485] recovery of erased and overwritten scripts[486] and identification of inks and pigments for dating of manuscripts.[487] As

---

Sequential Unmasking (LSU) Approach for Minimizing Cognitive Bias in Forensic Decision Making", in *Journal of Forensic Sciences*, 2015, vol. 60, no. 4, pp. 1111–12.

[481] Yann LeCun *et al.*, "Gradient-based Learning Applied to Document Recognition", in *Proceedings of the IEEE*, 1998, vol. 86, no. 11, pp. 2278–324.

[482] Such as military target detection, speech recognition, character recognition, natural language processing, gaming, large-scale video classification and breast cancer detection, see, for example, Gyrgalcon Technology Inc., *Natural Language Processing using CNN Based Integrated Circuit*, 2018; Mahesh Gour, Sweta Jain and T. Kumar Sunil, "Residual Learning Based CNN for Breast Cancer Histopathological Image Classification", in *International Journal of Imaging Systems and Technology*, 2020, vol. 30, no. 3, pp. 621–35.

[483] Muhammad Jaleed Khan *et al.*, "Modern Trends in Hyperspectral Image Analysis: A Review", in *IEEE Access*, 2018, vol. 6, pp. 14118–29.

[484] The portability and speed of hyperspectral sensing systems has increased tremendously over the last few decades, thus making it the appropriate choice for investigation of forensic traces at crime scenes. See Muhammed Jaleed Khan *et al.*, "Deep Learning for Automated Forgery Detection in Hyperspectral Document Images", in *Journal of Electronic Imaging*, 2018, vol. 27, no. 5, pp. 1–9.

[485] KIM Seon Joo, DENG Fanbo and Michael S. Brown, "Visual Enhancement of Old Documents with Hyperspectral Imaging", in *Pattern Recognition*, 2011, vol. 44, no. 7, pp. 1461–69.

[486] Costas Balas *et al.*, "A Novel Hyper-spectral Imaging Apparatus for the Non-destructive Analysis of Objects of Artistic and Historic Value", in *Journal of Cultural Heritage*, 2003, vol. 4, pp. 330–37.

[487] Anastasia Giakoumaki, Kristalia Melessanaki and Demetrios Anglos, "Laser Induced Breakdown Spectroscopy and Hyper-spectral Imaging Analysis of Pigments on an Illumi-

such, HIS analysis has significantly improved the efficiency of forgery detection systems over the recent years. Various HIS-based techniques for automated forgery detection are proposed in the literature.[488] HIS bears a tremendous potential for accurate differentiation of materials based on their unique spectral signatures.[489] For instance, ink mismatch detection is a key step in document forgery detection, and using a deep-learning method effectively identifies different ink types in a hyperspectral document image for forgery detection and achieves an overall accuracy of 98.20 per cent for blue and 88.00 per cent for black inks.[490]

Automated approaches may help with the problem of lacking Between Expert Reliability and Biasability but in this regard, it is also desirable to undertake other measures such as training, calibration as well as hiring of more than one expert. It is also recommended that examiners should analyse the questioned material before the reference material, using so-called linear sequential unmasking.[491] Task-irrelevant case information, for example, background circumstances of investigator's theories[492] can be managed by a context manager who passes on to the examiner only the information that is task-relevant.[493] Interestingly, one study suggests that most handwriting examiners (75 per cent) believe that their examinations involve subjective influences. However, they still believe that it is necessary to understand the context when conducting an examination and that, in fact, it is something that can promote professional ex-

---

nated Manuscript", in *Spectrochimica Acta Part B: Atomic Spectroscopy*, 2001, vol. 56, no. 12, pp. 2237–346.

[488] Eric Brauns and Brian R. Dyer, "Fourier Transform Hyperspectral Visible Imaging and the Nondestructive Analysis of Potentially Fraudulent Documents", in *Applied Spectroscopy*, 2006, vol. 60, no. 8, pp. 833–40; Roberto Padoan *et al.*, "Quantitative Hyperspectral Imaging of Historical Documents: Techniques and Applications", in *9th International Conference on NDT of Art*, Jerusalem, 2008.

[489] David Landgrebe, "Information Extraction Principles and Methods for Multispectral and Hyperspectral Image Data", in CHEN C.H. (ed.), *Information Processing for Remote Sensing*, World Scientific Publishing, River Edge, 1999, pp. 3–37.

[490] Khan *et al.*, 2018, pp. 1–9, see above note 484.

[491] Krane *et al.*, 2008, pp. 1006–07, see above note 480; Dror *et al.*, 2015, pp. 1111–12, see above note 480.

[492] For instance, Miller proposed that Forensic Document Examiners may be influenced by their interactions with police, see Larry S. Miller, "Bias Among Forensic Document Examiners: A Need for Procedural Change", in *Journal of Police Science and Administration*, 1984, vol. 12, no. 4, pp. 407–11.

[493] Found and Ganas, 2013, pp. 154–58, see above note 474.

---

aminers to formulate correct expert opinions.[494] Such views do not necessarily contradict CIM procedures since these suggest to blind examiners not to virtually all information but only the potentially biasing and irrelevant information. The context manager can also choose to postpone the disclosure of potentially biasing but relevant information.

6.6. Diagnostic Accuracy of Age Estimations in Child Soldiering Cases

Building on the previous Sections, this Section will summarize and round off with a discussion about the diagnostic accuracy of age estimation in child soldiering cases. As a reminder from Section 6.3., diagnostic accuracy in relation to the age element in child soldiering cases is here defined as the extent to which the process of determining age *accurately and fully identifies all those younger than 15 years as being under 15 years*, as well as the extent to which the process is capable of *accurately and fully excluding those aged 15 years or older*. A perfect diagnostic accuracy would require that the process is fully *sensitive*; all those under 15 years are identified and legally classified as under 15 years, while the process is also fully *specific*: all those 15 years or older are legally classified as 15 years or older.[495] Deviations from perfect diagnostic accuracy are the result of two types of errors:

- False positives: Individuals 15 years or older is estimated to be younger than 15 years; and

- False negatives: Individuals younger than 15 years is estimated to be 15 years or older.

As outlined in Table 3 (Section 6.4.) age estimations in the child soldiering cases were based on forensic, video or photo, documentary and oral evidence. The two most common evidence types used for age estimation purposes were oral evidence (eight out of eight of cases) and docu-

---

[494] LI and MA, 2018, pp. 210–12, see above note 475.

[495] The diagnostic accuracy/predictive value of age estimations can also be understood and illustrated using the so-called signal detection theory, see Green and Swets, 1966, see above note 50. Most of the early research relating to signal detection theory aimed to determine how humans distinguish "signal" (more specifically radar signals) from "noise". Identifying a signal among noise would then be similar to identifying someone younger than 15 among others who are 15 and above. In the process of identifying a "signal", it seems humans have different subjective thresholds, as some want to feel more confident than others before calling something a signal.

mentary evidence (seven out of eight cases). Two of the ICC cases also had video evidence. Only one case involved forensic evidence, namely the Lubanga case. Also, following from Table 4 (Section 6.4.), in the Lubanga case, there were often external contradictions between these different evidence types, but also internal contradictions between different evidence items within the same evidence type as well as other types of contradictions, like an individual stating different years of birth even if they all indicate that the individual was younger than 15 years at the time of interest. The Court seems to have accepted contradictions only for four of the alleged child soldiers. For all of these four individuals, the video evidence suggested they were younger than 15 years, while the oral and documentary evidence introduced by the defence suggested they were over 15 years (D-0040, D-0041, Bodyguard 1, Bodyguard 2). The Court considered it proven beyond reasonable doubt that these individuals were younger than 15 years. This conclusion was also reached in relation to the six remaining individuals (1–6). For these individuals only video evidence was available, save for 1 witness in relation to Individual 1, and there were no contradictions. Hence, the Court placed trust in its own age assessments based on the physical appearance of alleged child soldiers, as they appeared in the video evidence. These assessments were considered more reliable than contradictory evidence introduced by the defence (D-0040, D-0041, Bodyguard 1, Bodyguard 2) and were also considered sufficient even lacking any other age evidence (Individuals 1–6). Conversely, forensic evidence was not trusted, neither when the other evidence offered no contradictions (P-0213), nor when it was wholly or partially contradicted by oral and/or documentary evidence introduced by the prosecution.

As summarized in Table 5, there are many challenges with age estimations based on each of the evidence types. These challenges will increase the risks of false positives as well as false negatives, and thereby they are detrimental to the diagnostic accuracy. Today, or within a reasonable future, it may be possible to use some of the currently developing methods for age estimations outlined under opportunities and thereby decrease the risk of false positives and false negatives. As mentioned throughout the text, it is likely that automated approaches can help overcome human factors including Between Expert Reliability and Biasability.[496] However, it is essential that such methods are tested and evaluated in the child soldiering context specifically.

Table 5. Summary of challenges and opportunities with age estimations based on forensic, video, oral and documentary evidence.

Type of Evidence	Challenges	Opportunities
Forensic	**Validity**	1) Deep Learning approaches (hand/wrist, teeth, knees etc.).
	Biological v. Chronological age.	2) DNA methylation.
	Reliability	3) Calibration training.
	Disagreement between, for example, radiologists and odontologists.	4) Contextual Information Management (CIM). 5) Independent second opinions.
	Biasability	
	Forensic confirmation bias.	
Video or Photo	**Validity**	1) Deep Learning approaches based on facial features.
	Apparent age v. Chronological age.	2) Empirical research into observer differences, including paediatricians.
	Reliability	3) Empirical research into more specific sources of bias.
	Disagreement between observers.	
	Biasability	
	Serial positioning bias, anchoring effects, base rate bias, etc.	
Oral	**Validity**	1) Elaborate interview framework with ground rules investigative relating to temporal aspects and, for example, Age Assessment Tool Questionnaires.
	Social, Biological and Apparent age v. Chronological age.	2) Experimental research into criteria for statement analysis specifically addressing age
	Reliability	

---

[496] Although this depends on the quality of the data that is used to train the artificial intelligence to make accurate predictions. Some data may have inherited biases from human decision making.

	Differences between interviewers and disagreements between evaluators.	statements. 3) Calibration training. 4) Contextual information management (CIM).
	Biasability	
	Emotional bias, base rate bias.	
Documentary	**Validity**	1) Deep Learning approaches to, for example, ink-mismatch detection. 2) Calibration training. 3) Contextual Information Management (CIM).
	Biological, Apparent and Social age v. Chronological age.	
	Reliability	
	Disagreement between examiners of, for example, handwriting.	
	Biasability	
	Forensic confirmation bias.	

Before new methodologies have been sufficiently evaluated, and even after this has happened, it is likely that some doubts regarding alleged child soldiers' ages will still remain. As implied by the discussion on forensic evidence in Section 6.5.1.1.1., forensic age estimations entail risks both of false negatives and false positives. With the developing deep learning approaches, the estimations become gradually more accurate and DNA methylation in those under 30 years has an error rate of ±1 year (±3 years for those over 30 years). Such developing methods may be able to provide answers which make it unreasonable to doubt the ages of alleged child soldiers. For instance, if the result of DNA methylation suggests that an individual was 12–13 years or 17–18 years at the time of interest, it seems sensible for the Court to trust these results. It seems unlikely that scientists or anyone else will be able to provide more exact answers within in a reasonable time period. Accepting such evidence, even if it comes with an error interval, is not to be considered a presumption to the disadvantage of the accused[497] but rather it expresses a balanced interpretation

---

[497] Although such presumptions have been accepted by the ECHR in relation to smuggle offences, in for example, ECHR Salabiaku Judgment, see above note 52 and the related case ECHR Pham Hoang Judgment, see above note 53.

of what reasonable as well as unreasonable doubt means in relation to forensic age evidence. However, if such a result suggests that someone was 14–15 years at the time of interest, a possible approach would be to also require more age evidence, whether forensic or of a different type.

Just like forensic evidence, video or photo evidence entails risks of false negatives as well as false positives. While this topic has received less attention, and it is unknown whether and how results will change with time, the most relevant error interval available today seems to be that of $\pm$ 5.39 years obtained in relation to 12–19-year olds. However, it deserves to be emphasized that the relative risk of such errors is not solemnly dependent on error intervals identified in research but also how the Courts deal with the uncertainty they are faced with. As outlined and discussed in detail in Section 6.5.2.1. the approach adopted by the Trial Chamber in Lubanga, which was approved by the Appeals Chamber, and which is also disputed with the appeal of Ntaganda's conviction, is a cautionary approach. More specifically, this means that the Court applies criteria by which only those alleged child soldiers who are "clearly" or "manifestly" under the age of 15 years are recognized as being under 15 years.[498] It is likely that the Chambers considered these criteria appropriate because of the rights of the accused that uncertainty should be to his or her advantage. However, this raises several questions. The criteria seem to require a very high degree of subjective certainty, probably higher than *beyond reasonable doubt*. Clearly, the BARD-standard is already an outlet for the accused's benefit of doubt as well as an expression of how extensive this benefit should be from a legal normative perspective. The Trial Chamber's judgment also explicitly excludes individuals who do not make the judges sufficiently certain, as it states for instance that a two-second video excerpt depicts "children who could be under the age of 15 but they appear too briefly to enable a definite finding".[499] This cautionary approach seems to entail a larger risk for false negatives than false positives. Since the threshold for agreeing to call someone "under 15" is set high, it is unlikely that individuals older than 15 years will be categorized as under

---

[498] See Lubanga Appeals Chamber Judgment, para. 222, see above note 3.

[499] See Lubanga Trial Chamber Judgment, fn. 2432, see above note 4, referring to video excerpt EVD-OTP-00571, taken during a presidential rally at the Bunia city stadium, 11 January 2003, 02:47:15 to 02:47:19, and stating that "In addition the Chamber observes that at 02:22:52–02:22:54 there are children who could be under the age of 15 but they appear too briefly to enable a definite finding".

15 years (false positives) but this comes at the cost that some individuals who are under 15 years may be categorized as 15 years or older (false negatives). Hence, the procedure's sensitivity may become an issue, since this decreases the probability that the procedure will identify someone under 15 years as being under 15 years. This is particularly the case if the Court relies heavily on video or photo evidence for age estimation purposes, which was the case in Lubanga, and, according to the defence, this is also the situation in Ntaganda.[500] Hence, it is possible that such a cautionary approach is problematic considering what Article 8 of the Rome Statute of the ICC sets out to protect, namely all individuals under 15 years, not just those "clearly" or "evidently" so.

Furthermore, the cautionary approach presupposes that judges' confidence in their assessments and the accuracy of their assessments are well calibrated. In other words, when judges determine that a certain individual is "clearly" or "manifestly" under 15, they are very unlikely to be wrong and all, or nearly all, of the individuals classified as younger than 15, will also have actual chronological ages below 15 (true positives). There is no data on this issue specifically but some predictions can be made, taking into consideration the already existing research suggesting that, in other contexts, such as the medical field, experts' confidence and accuracy levels are not necessarily well calibrated.[501] For instance, overall, it is likely that confidence and accuracy is better calibrated in relation to individuals whose chronological ages are further away from the 15 year threshold, for example, 6, 8 or 10, 20, 23, 25 year olds, compared to individuals whose chronological ages are closer to the threshold, for example, 13, 14, 16 or

---

[500] This is contested by the Prosecution which suggests that the Trial Chamber also relied on other corroborating evidence for age estimation purposes. More specifically the Prosecution here refers to oral evidence and the Chamber's own assessment of four video extracts in which P-0010 and P-0898 identified three individuals in Ntaganda's escort as under the age of 15, see Lubanga Trial Chamber Judgment, see above note 4 and Prosecution Response to 'Defence Appeal Brief – Part II', para. 176, see above note 122. Also, as pointed out by the Prosecution in its response, the Defence later conceded that the Chamber had also relied on testimonial evidence, referring to Ntaganda Defence Appeal Brief – Part II, paras. 232–33, 243, 246, see above note 121.

[501] Davis et al., 2005, pp. 259–64, see above note 49; Friedman et al., 2001, pp. 454–58, see above note 49; Friedman et al., 2005, pp. 334–39, see above note 49; HUANG Haiyan and DENG Min, "Ultrasound Operators' Confidence Influences Diagnosis of Ovarian Tumors: a Study in China?", in Asian Pacific Journal of Cancer Prevention, 2011 vol. 12, no. 5, pp. 1275–77; Podbregar et al., 2001, pp. 1750–55, see above note 49; Yazbek et al., 2010, pp. 89–93, see above note 49.

17 year olds. Just how close or far away from the threshold individuals have to be, for the calibration between confidence and accuracy to be on an acceptable level is unknown. However, it can be noted that, if anything, the applied criteria is likely to result in false negatives in the age group of 13 to 14 years or similar, that is, individuals very close to the threshold, but still younger. This is related to what Judge Ušacka expresses in her dissenting opinion in the Lubanga case, namely that there are inherent difficulties in establishing age based on physical appearance exclusively and that it is unclear whether the Trial Chamber has, in effect, applied the said "cautious approach" as well as how this approach relates to the beyond reasonable doubt standard.[502]

Compared to forensic and video or photo evidence, less is known about errors in relation to oral evidence (age statements). More specifically, there is no empirical data on individuals' tendencies to under – or overestimate the chronological age of an individual based on the statement of this individual. Yet, it is unknown what is the relative importance of what the interviewee says during the interview compared to the interviewee's physical appearance or demeanour. Since physical appearance is a relatively dominant aspect of our perceptions of others, both on conscious and subconscious levels,[503] it is possible that physical appearance, in fact, is more decisive than what is being said.[504] Hence, it is possible that the error interval of 5.39 years indicated above for video or photo evidence is relevant also for this category of age evidence. If this is fairly representative it would mean that also oral evidence entails risks of both false positives and false negatives. Nevertheless, these respective risks are also dependent on the Court's way of dealing with the uncertainty. As noted in Section 6.4.2. the SCSL trusted the age statements, particularly those provided by alleged child soldiers themselves, to a larger degree

---

[502] ICC, *The Prosecutor v. Thomas Lubanga Dyilo*, Appeals Chamber, Dissenting opinion of Judge Anita Ušacka, 1 December 2014, ICC-01/04-01/06-3121-Anx2, paras. 35-51 (https://legal-tools.org/doc/df4480).

[503] For more on this see, for example, Zebrowitz and Montepare, 2008, pp. 1–16, see above note 131; Zebrowitz, 1997, see above note 131. Also, there are several studies suggesting that facial appearance predicts criminal justice decisions, see, for example, Eberhardt, 2006, pp. 383–86, see above note 131; Zebrowitz and McDonald, 1991, pp. 603–23, see above note 131.

[504] When it comes to oral evidence provided by others than the alleged child soldiers themselves, these have often been based, explicitly, on the physical appearance of the alleged child soldier.

than what the ICC has done so far.[505] This is explained by that the ages of the alleged child soldiers were contested to a much larger degree at the ICC, and many of the testimonies also entailed contradictions (internal, external or other types, see Table 4 in Section 6.4.2.). Yet, in line with the above, an overly cautionary approach will result in an increased risk of false negatives (while the risk of false positives is greatly reduced). While such an approach is obviously in line with the idea that doubts should be to the advantage of the accused, it seems reasonable to seriously evaluate what can be expected from statements that alleged child soldiers or others provide. Inconsistencies may have other explanations than deceit or manipulation, for instance that the interviewer and the interviewee do not have the same understanding of temporal aspects since ground rules have not been established (see Section 6.5.3.1.1. on investigative interviewing). If an interviewee is interviewed on repeated occasions but it is uncertain whether he or she is able to provide (own) free accounts of his or her chronological age, inconsistencies between different interviews are unsurprising.[506]

Also, the oral evidence raises questions regarding the relevance or irrelevance of social age for legal age determinations. In a strict sense, it is clear that legislators have had chronological not social age in mind when creating legal age elements. However, the purposes behind legal age thresholds are usually to protect individuals who have not yet reached a sufficient level of psychological maturity to properly protect their own best interests.[507] Psychological maturity is likely to often coincide with what roles and responsibilities an individual has in a society. Just like chronological age, social age is directly related to the expectations a society has on the individuals living in it when it comes to schooling, home duties, and so on. As such, it is possible that relying on social age can also help promote the purposes behind the law. Hence, it can be argued that social age is in fact legally relevant, not just as an estimation of chrono-

---

[505] However, the SCSL clearly did not accept any testimony. As illustrated by *The Prosecutor v. Sam Hinga Norman, Moinina Fofana and Allieu Kondewa*, a single testimony of one alleged child soldier was considered insufficient as regards the ages of other alleged child soldiers, see SCSL Norman *et al.* Appeals Chamber Judgment, para. 132, see above note 63.

[506] Also, in such situations, interviewers will have to provide guidance, and even if this is done with the best intentions, it can still influence the interviewee's response.

[507] Or more specifically what the law considers to be their best interests.

logical age, but on its own merits.[508] This question has not been addressed specifically by the Courts, although it was raised to a certain extent by the Kanu defence in the AFRC case at the SCSL.[509]

Given that documentary evidence is simply the carrier of age information, which can be based on biological, apparent and social age or combinations of these (as well as false information or hearsay), many of the doubts relating to documentary evidence coincide with doubts described in relation to forensic, video or photo and oral evidence. In addition, there may be doubts relating to whether the document is authentic or not and recently developed deep learning approaches may be helpful in this regard.

In sum, it is likely that there will always be uncertainties pertaining to legal age elements and these uncertainties are clearly unsettling, particularly when they are an element of a crime with potentially far-reaching consequences both for the defendant and the alleged victims, including, for example, whether someone is entitled to victim reparations. Since this is indeed the case when it comes to child soldiering charges, it is essential that investigation agencies establish procedures that as safely and accurately as possible determine individuals' ages. While many different actors, including radiologists, odontologists, paediatricians, social workers and witnesses may be involved in this process and measures certainly should be undertaken among some of these actors as well, the legal actors are those ultimately responsible for collecting, integrating and evaluating the age evidence. This research has suggested a framework for doing so. While one important part of this framework is about ensuring that there is as little doubt as possible regarding the age evidence (see challenges and opportunities) another equally important part discussed in this section is what to do with any remaining doubts (diagnostic accuracy). This framework can aid both the formulation of best practices for collecting age evidence during the investigation and the evaluation of such evidence pre-

---

[508] Clearly, this possibility makes the question of the validity of social age as an operationalization of chronological age come into somewhat different light.

[509] The defence questioned the legal 15-year threshold in a wider sense, since it considered it arbitrary as "the ending of childhood (in the traditional African setting) has little to do with achieving a particular age more to do with physical capacity to perform acts reserved for adults". See Brima *et al.* Kanu Defence Trial Brief, para. 75, see above note 148, referring to exhibit D-37, Defence Expert Research Report on the Use of Child Soldiers in the Sierra Leone Conflict by Mr. Osman Gbla, paras. 9–11, 39.

sented in Court. Although it is likely that at least some of the scientific aspects on this issue fall outside of legal actors' typical expertise, understanding, integrating and applying such aspects indeed fall within their professional roles and responsibilities. This goes for age estimations of alleged child soldiers which this chapter has focused on, but also for age estimations in other legal contexts, whether national or international, and to which the suggested framework can be adjusted and applied.

Appendix 1: Detailed descriptions of age evidence for child soldiers in the Lubanga case

This appendix provides more detailed information about the age evidence outlined in Table 4 above pertaining to child soldiers in the Lubanga case.

P-0007

Oral Evidence

P-0007 provided somewhat different accounts of his age as he first stated he was born in 1986, then 1987 and then that he didn't know. P-0007 testified during meetings with the ICC Office of the Prosecutor ('OTP') that all of his answers were accurate but later, he said that he did not know his true date of birth. In August 2004, he told the IEC that his year of birth was 1986 and gave them a name that differed from the one he had provided to the OTP. See ICC, *The Prosecutor v. Thomas Lubanga Dyilo*, Trial Chamber, Transcript, 13 March 2009, ICC-01/04-01/06-T-148-Red2-ENG, p. 18, lines 14–17 (https://www.legal-tools.org/doc/5a6e16/); and Lubanga Trial Chamber Judgment, para. 223, see above note 4.

According to a defence witness P-0007 was never in the military.

Documentary Evidence

P-0007's voter card indicated that his year of birth was 1987 while his birth certificate indicated 1990. Intermediary 143 had provided the birth certificate. See Lubanga Trial Chamber Judgment, para. 593, see above note 4.

P-0008

Oral Evidence

Contrary to the forensic expert testimony, P-0008's account was that he was born in 1989 (although both indicated that P-0008 was under 15 years). See ICC, *The Prosecutor v. Thomas Lubanga Dyilo*, Trial Chamber, Transcript, 25 February 2009, ICC-01/04-01/06-T-135-Red3-ENG, p. 64, lines 12–14 (https://www.legal-tools.org/doc/1a6a08/). The prosecution relied on the evidence of the witness (P-0008) as to his age. See Lubanga Prosecution's Closing Brief, para. 245, see above note 261. Overall, the Trial Chamber considered his statement to be "contradictory and implausible". See Lubanga Trial Chamber Judgment, para. 232, see above note 4.

According to a defence witness P-0008 was never in the military.

Documentary Evidence

P-0008's electoral card indicated he was born in 1987 and his birth certificated indicated he was born in 1991. See Lubanga Trial Chamber Judgment, para. 231, see above note 4; and *ibid.*, fn. 613, citing extract of the IEC database, EVD-D01-01028, and the declaration of the electoral card, EVD-OTP-00658. There was also a record from P-0031 suggesting that P-0008 was 11 years old when he arrived at the center. See Lubanga Trial Chamber Judgment, para. 236, see above note 4.

P-0010

Forensic Evidence

Experts P-0358 and P-0359 stated that: "it is scientifically possible for P-0010 to have been under the age of 15 at the time of her recruitment in late 2002". See Lubanga Prosecution's Closing Brief, para. 400, see above note 261; and *ibid.*, fn. 1156, referring to expert report EVD-OTP-00430; and Lubanga Trial Chamber Judgment, para. 264, see above note 4.

Video Evidence

The witness recognised herself in a portion of a video recording as the figure standing in the centre of the screen with her hands together in front of her body. See video excerpt EVD-OTP-00570, shot at Rwampara training camp, 12 February 2003; and Lubanga Trial Chamber Judgment, para. 254, see above note 4. The witness also recognized one of her friends whom she said was an escort. In another video section (EVD-OTP-00570), the witness said the people moving toward a vehicle in the video were leaving and also identified a bodyguard in the video: a uniformed soldier who was shorter than the others. She did not know his name or age but said he was young and a 'Kadogo', probably around 10 years old. According to the Trial Chamber: "a body of evidence undermines the reliability of the witness account but the video material speaks for itself and falls into a separate category". See Lubanga Trial Chamber Judgment, para. 257, see above note 4.

Oral Evidence

According to P-0010's own testimony she was born in 1989. Defence witnesses suggested that P-0010 was born in 1985 or 1986 or that they didn't know. At one point, P-0010 said she was born in 1989, and also stated a particular month but later said she did not know the day or month.

If she was born in 1989, she would have been 13 years when she was abducted. See Lubanga Trial Chamber Judgment, para. 250, see above note 4.

D-0005 stated that P-0010 was born in 1985 and D-0006 said P-0010 was either his age or he was a year older than her and he was born on 18 April 1985, although he later stated he did not know her age. See Lubanga Trial Chamber Judgment, paras. 259–61, see above note 4; and ICC, *The Prosecutor v. Thomas Lubanga Dyilo*, Trial Chamber, Transcript, 8 March 2010, ICC-01/04-01/06-T-255-Red3-ENG, p. 12, lines 22–24 (https://www.legal-tools.org/doc/7d812b/).

Documentary Evidence

P-0010's birth certificate indicated she was born in 1988, the electoral card indicated 1986 and the individual case story indicated 1987. See Lubanga Trial Chamber Judgment, paras. 248–50, see above note 4; and evidence EVD-D01-01102 (birth certificate), EVD-D01-00762 (electoral card), EVD-D01-00082 (individual case story).

Not Proven

While the Trial Chamber accepted that P-0010 at some stage may have served as a soldier within the UPC, it did not consider it proven beyond reasonable doubt that this occurred when she was under 15 years of age. See Lubanga Trial Chamber Judgment, para. 480, see above note 4. Due to the internal contradictions in her accounts, including the unexplained differences as to her date of birth in both her testimony and the documentary evidence, together with the strength of the conflicting external evidence, the Chamber was unable to rely on her testimony. However, the Chamber points out that the: "video material and her comments on it remain essentially unaffected by these criticisms". See Lubanga Trial Chamber Judgment, para. 268, see above note 4.

P-0011

Oral Evidence

According to P-0011's own testimony he was born in 1992 but he also provided other dates to the investigators. Although he stated 1992, this date differed from the date in his original statement, provided to the investigators in July 2005. P-0011 stated that this date had been indicated to him by members of his family, and in particular his grandmother had suggested it prior to his first meeting with one of the representatives of the OTP and that this latter date was a mistake that he had made. See Lubanga Trial Chamber Judgment, para. 270, see above note 4. The Trial Chamber noted inconsistencies in the stated name of this witness as well as in information about where he attended school. The witness also said he joined the UPC in July 2003, although with inconsistencies across his statements. Lubanga Trial Chamber Judgment, paras. 269–72, see above note 4.

According to defence witnesses P-0011 was born in 1990–91.

Documentary Evidence

According to a birth certificate, P-0011 was born in 1992.

Not Proven

Given the internal contradictions and the confusion within the evidence of P-0011 and taking into account the evidence of D-0024, the Chamber had real doubts as to the suggestions that P-0011 served as child solider with the UPC in the circumstances he described, namely when he was under 15 years of age and during the period covered by the charges. See Lubanga Trial Chamber Judgment, para. 480, see above note 4. Due to the internal contradictions in his account and conflicting external evidence, the Chamber did not rely on his account. See Lubanga Trial Chamber Judgment, para. 288, see above note 4.

P-0157

Forensic Evidence

This evidence suggested that P-0157 was born before December 1988. See expert report EVD-OTP-00435; and Lubanga Transcript of 12 May 2009, p. 53, lines 13–22, see above note 105. The Trial Chamber noted: "Although of limited value, the X-ray evidence tends to support the suggestion that P-0157 was over the age of 15 at the time of his alleged conscription". See Lubanga Trial Chamber Judgment, para. 512, see above note 4.

Oral Evidence

Contrary to the forensic expert testimony, P-0157's account was that he was born in 1991 and therefore younger than 15 years old. See ICC, *The Prosecutor v. Thomas Lubanga Dyilo*, Trial Chamber, Transcript, 3 June 2009, ICC-01/04-01/06-T-185-Red2-ENG, p. 63, line 7 (https://www.

legal-tools.org/doc/52f1e0/). Also, P-0157 stated that he did not know his date of birth. See ICC, *The Prosecutor v. Thomas Lubanga Dyilo*, Trial Chamber, Transcript, 9 June 2009, ICC-01/04-01/06-T-188-Red2-ENG, p. 66, lines 1–6 ('Lubanga Trial Transcript of 9 June 2009') (https://www. legal-tools.org/doc/612a86/). When shown a document from the general inspectorate for secondary and professional education stating that he was born in 1986 and asked whether it was possible that in 1998 he was in 6th grade at a certain primary school, he answered: "It could be true. It's a certified document, a document that states that". See Lubanga Trial Transcript of 9 June 2009, p. 67, lines 7–11. The prosecution argued that school records were unreliable and appeared to have been altered. See Lubanga Trial Chamber Judgment, para. 463, see above note 4. The Prosecution relied on the evidence of the witness as to his age. See Lubanga Prosecution's Closing Brief, para. 511, see above note 261.

D-0025 said him and P-0157 went to school together and that he was younger than P-0157 but that he did not know P-0157's age. Lubanga Trial Chamber Judgment, para. 468, see above note 4.

P-0031 simply described P-0157 as a child who had been a member of the FNI. Lubanga Trial Chamber Judgment, para. 472, see above note 4.

Documentary Evidence

The documentary evidence in relation to the age of P-0157 (voter's card, school register, certificate award) suggested that in 2002 and 2003, P-0157 was over 15 years of age. THE IEC database demonstrated that P-0157 had a voter's card bearing his photograph and a date of birth in 1986. See evidence EVD-D01-01031 (voter's card). Moreover, his name appeared on the enrolment register for a particular school and, at what was seemingly his entry, it was recorded that P-0157 was born on an identified date in 1986. See Lubanga Trial Transcript of 9 June 2009, p. 63, line 24 to p. 65, line 14; evidence EVD-D01-00170 (enrolment register for a particular school); and evidence EVD-D01-00257 (extract of the complete enrolment registry for a particular school, EVD-D01-00170). Also, a 1991–2002 certificate award register for this school indicates that a certificate was awarded to P-0157, born on the same date in 1986. See Lubanga Trial Transcript of 9 June 2009, p. 66, lines 1–6. There was also a document from the general inspectorate for secondary and professional education which comprised a list of students in the 6th grade in the same primary school for the year 1998, in which it was also recorded that P-0157 was born in 1986. See Lubanga Trial Transcript of 9 June 2009, p. 66, lines 15–22; and evidence EVD-D01-00258.

P-0213

Oral Evidence

According to P-0213's own testimony he was born in 1991. See ICC, *The Prosecutor v. Thomas Lubanga Dyilo*, Trial Chamber, Transcript, 20 February 2009, ICC-01/04-01/06-T-132-ENG, p. 6, lines 12–13 (https://www.legal-tools.org/doc/0058ac/).

Defence witnesses were unspecific about P-0213's age.

A school teacher, D-0029, testified for the defence, stating that there was no primary school with the name referred to by P-0213 where he claimed he attended his first years of schooling. D-0029 also stated that P-0213 was not a child soldier. See Lubanga Trial Chamber Judgment, para. 399, see above note 4.

Documentary Evidence

P-0213 had a school register suggesting he was born in 1989 but expert evidence established this was unreliable. According to the expert evidence, the entry for the year 1989 in the school register overwrote a previous entry which was partially visible underneath. The Trial Chamber placed little reliance on the school register.

Not Proven

According to the Trial Chamber the extent of the inconsistencies and the other problems with this witness evidence supported the suggestion that he provided a false account, at least in part. See Lubanga Trial Chamber Judgment, para. 480, see above note 4. Moreover, the fact that he was introduced to the prosecution's investigators by P-0321 raised additional concerns that the latter may have influence his testimony. In light of all these circumstances, the Chamber concluded that P-0213 was not a witness who could safely be relied upon. See Lubanga Trial Chamber Judgment, para. 406, see above note 4.

P-0294

Forensic Evidence

This evidence suggested P-0294 was born before December 1989. See expert report EVD-OTP-00440; and Lubanga Transcript of 12 May 2009, p. 69, line 23 to p. 70, line 11, see above note 105.

Oral Evidence

Contrary to the forensic expert testimony, P-0294's own testimony was that he was born in December 1991 (although both suggest under 15 years). See ICC, *The Prosecutor v. Thomas Lubanga Dyilo*, Trial Chamber, Transcript, 18 March 2009, ICC-01/04-01/06-T-150-Red3-ENG, p. 44, lines 13–14 (https://www.legal-tools.org/doc/0f8cd1/) and ICC, *The Prosecutor v. Thomas Lubanga Dyilo*, Trial Chamber, Transcript, 19 March 2009, ICC-01/04-01/06-T-151-Red2-ENG, p. 53, lines 15–17 (https://www.legal-tools.org/doc/64a0fa/).

Documentary Evidence

According to a voter registration card, P-0294 was born in 1987. See evidence EVD-D01-00764 (extract of the register of the independent electoral commission) and EVD-D01-01006 (voter registration card). According to a certificate of family reunification, P-0294 was born in 1988. See evidence EVD-D01-00069 (certificate of family reunification) at page DRC-OTP-0160-0188. When asked about this document P-0294 said he did not give his correct age and he did not really know how old he is or was. According to a school register, P-0294 was born in 1988.

Not Proven

The Trial Chamber stated that this evidence, considered cumulatively, raised serious questions as to the reliability of P-0294. The documentary and oral evidence established that he did not tell the truth about his age and there were also real concerns he had lied about his military service. Moreover, the fact that P-0294 was introduced to the prosecution's investigators by P-0321 raised additional concerns because of the real possibility the he may have influenced this witness testimony. Given P-0294's credibility and that the reliability of his evidence was seriously at issue, the Chamber was unable to rely on his account. See Lubanga Trial Chamber Judgment, para. 415, see above note 4.

P-0297

Forensic Evidence

Examination of hand and wrist bones along with the dental records suggest that P-0297 was under 15 years within the time frame of the charges. See Lubanga Prosecution's Closing Brief, paras. 442 and 444, see above note 261. The experts concluded he was between 16 and 17 years old in January 2008. See expert report EVD-OTP-00618, p. 435. The Trial Chamber stated: "However, these forensic assessments of age lack precision and they provide an inadequate basis, taken alone, for determining an individual's age". See Lubanga Trial Chamber Judgment, para. 423, see above note 4.

Oral Evidence

According to P-0297's own testimony, he was born in 1990.

Other witnesses were unspecific about P-0297's age.

According to defence witnesses, a school teacher and D-0036, P-0297 was never a child soldier. In response to this, P-0297 suggested that two defence witnesses were sent to the Court by Cordo in order to state falsely that one of them and P-0297 had not served as child soldiers in the UPC. See Lubanga Trial Chamber Judgment, paras. 399–421, see above note 4.

Documentary Evidence

The school documents suggested that P-0297 was significantly over 15 years of age in 2002. Furthermore, these records suggested that someone with P-0297's identity attended one of the schools in October 1997 when he was allegedly living elsewhere. However, The Trial Chamber did not see any credible evidence to support the contention that it was a forgery. See Lubanga Trial Chamber Judgment, paras. 419–23, see above note 4.

Not Proven

The Chamber recognised that this witness may have been confronted with difficult circumstances but considered his account to be unreliable. Notwithstanding the allegation made by P-0297 against some of the other witnesses, the Chamber considered it likely that P-0321 persuaded or encouraged him to give false evidence and was therefore unable to rely on his account. See Lubanga Trial Chamber Judgment, para. 429, see above note 4.

P-0298

Oral Evidence

P-0298 provided different accounts about his age; that he did not remember and that he was born in 1989. Initially he retracted his testimony in Court but then maintained his original testimony when reappearing in Court two weeks later. When retracting his testimony, P-0298 stated that he, together with his friends, had been promised clothes and many other things. He had never been to training camp, but instead been taught the details of his account, and although he said he would do what they had asked, when he came to Court he decided to speak the truth. The Trial Chamber noted that, presumably, he was influenced by the presence of the accused in the Courtroom. Upon return two weeks later, P-0298 again stated that he had been enlisted by UPC soldiers, in line with his original statement. See Lubanga Trial Chamber Judgment, paras. 430–31, see above note 4.

P-0299, the father of P-0298 said that P-0298 was born in 1991 and that he was in a possession of a birth certificate which showed this year of birth. See Lubanga Trial Chamber Judgment, para. 438, see above note 4.

Documentary Evidence

Various school documents suggested P-0298 was born in 1989, although the implications of these documents were contested by the defence. Lubanga Trial Chamber Judgment, para. 438, see above note 4.

Not Proven

The Trial Chamber noted that, notwithstanding the prosecution's suggestion that P-0298's initial testimony in Court (where he retracted his previous statement) was merely the result of his anger, the evidence created a real doubt as to his honesty and reliability. Additionally, the Chamber considered there was a real possibility that he was encouraged and assisted by P-0321 to give false evidence. P-0298 was therefore not a witness on whom the Chamber was able to rely. See Lubanga Trial Chamber Judgment, para. 441, see above note 4.

D-0040

Video Evidence

Video filmed at Lubanga's office, 24 February 2003. See video excerpt EVD-OTP-00574, 01:49:02.

Oral Evidence

According to D-0040's own testimony, introduced by the defence, he was born on 8 April 1983 and therefore 20 years at the time the footage was shot.

Documentary Evidence

The voting card and a state diploma, introduced by the defence, confirmed D-0040's own testimony, that he was born on 8 April 1983. See evidence EVD-D01-01111 (voter registration card); and ICC, *The Prosecutor v. Thomas Lubanga Dyilo*, Trial Chamber, Transcript, 13 June 2012, ICC-01/04-01/06-T-360-Red2-ENG, p. 22, lines 5–23 (https://www.legal-tools. org/doc/02a5ae/).

Proven

In the assessment of D-0040's age, based on the video evidence, the Chamber determined that he was much younger than 15 years when the footage was shot, even when a wide margin of error was applied. See Lubanga Trial Chamber Judgment, para. 643, see above note 4.

D-0041

Video Evidence

According to the Trial Chamber, the individual in the foreground of the excerpt clad in camouflage clothing, wearing a beret and bearing a rifle on the right shoulder was "manifestly under the age of 15 years". Video excerpt EVD-OTP-00571, taken during a presidential rally at the Bunia city stadium, 11 January 2003, 02:47:15 to 02:47:19.

Oral Evidence

According to D-0041's own testimony, introduced by the defence, he was born on 2 December 1984 and therefore 19 years at the time the footage was shot.

Documentary Evidence

According to a voting card, D-0041 was over 15. Evidence DRC-D01-0003-5983 (voting card).

Proven

The Chamber considered that the individual in the foreground of the video excerpt (D-0041) wearing camouflage clothing, a beret and bearing a rifle on the right should was "manifestly under the age of 15 years". See Lubanga Trial Chamber Judgment, paras. 713, 860, 915, 1251, see above note 4.

Bodyguard 1

According to the defence, Bodyguards 1 and 2 were in fact the same individual. See ICC, *The Prosecutor v. Thomas Lubanga Dyilo*, Defence, Mr. Thomas Lubanga's Appellate Brief Against the 14 March 2012 Judgment Pursuant to Article 74 of the Statute, 3 December 2012, ICC-01/04-01/06-2948-Red-tENG, p. 49, para. 172 (https://www.legal-tools.org/doc/23428f/).

Video Evidence

This is footage shot during a meeting between a UPC delegation and representative from the Lendu community in the Lipri region on 14 January 2003. See video excerpt EVD-OTP-00572, 00:00:50, 00:02:47 and 00:28:42. According to the Trial Chamber, these individuals were "clearly under the age of 15".

Oral Evidence

A witness had indicated to the investigators of the OTP that he estimated the age to 16 years. See ICC, *The Prosecutor v. Thomas Lubanga Dyilo*, Trial Chamber, Transcript, 26 May 2009, ICC-01/04-01/06-T-178-Red3-ENG, p. 46, line 7 to p. 47, line 4 (https://www.legal-tools.org/doc/fe35bc/).

Proven

The Trial Chamber found that the excerpts show soldiers "clearly under the age of 15 years". See Lubanga Trial Chamber Judgment, para. 915, see above note 4.

Bodyguard 2

According to the defence, Bodyguards 1 and 2 were in fact the same individual. See ICC, *The Prosecutor v. Thomas Lubanga Dyilo*, Defence, Mr. Thomas Lubanga's Appellate Brief Against the 14 March 2012 Judgment

Pursuant to Article 74 of the Statute, 3 December 2012, ICC-01/04-01/06-2948-Red-tENG, p. 49, para. 172 (https://www.legal-tools.org/doc/23428f/).

Video Evidence

This is footage shot during a meeting between a UPC delegation and representative from the Lendu community in the Lipri region on 14 January 2003. See video excerpt EVD-OTP-00572, 00:00:50, 00:02:47 and 00:28:42. According to the Trial Chamber, these individuals were "clearly under the age of 15".

Oral Evidence

A witness had indicated to the investigators of the OTP that he estimated the age of Bodyguard 2 to be 16 years. See ICC, *The Prosecutor v. Thomas Lubanga Dyilo*, Trial Chamber, Transcript, 26 May 2009, ICC-01/04-01/06-T-178-Red3-ENG, p. 46, line 7 to p. 47, line 4 (https://www.legal-tools.org/doc/fe35bc/).

Proven

The Trial Chamber found that the excerpts show soldiers "clearly under the age of 15 years". See Lubanga Trial Chamber Judgment, para. 915, see above note 4.

Individual 1

Video Evidence

Video excerpt EVD-OTP-00571, taken during a presidential rally at the Bunia city stadium, 11 January 2003, 02:22:52 to 02:22:54. The Trial Chamber found one of the soldiers appearing in the excerpt to be "significantly below 15 years of age".

Proven

The Chamber found one of the soldiers appearing in the excerpt to be "significantly below 15 years of age". See Lubanga Trial Chamber Judgment, para. 1249, see above note 4.

Individual 2

The Trial Chamber concluded that this person was a "young male who is well below the age of 15". The defence pointed out that this finding was at odds with the statements of one of the Prosecution witnesses who testified that the soldier was female and argued that this erroneous finding on behalf of the Chamber made clear that it is impossible even to determine the sex of the individual concerned from the footage. The Appeals Chamber found that, an error as to biological sex does not affect the reasonableness of the Trial Chamber's finding that the individual was clearly under the age of 15 years.

Video Evidence

Video excerpt EVD-OTP-00570, shot at Rwampara training camp, 12 February 2003, 00:06:57. The Trial Chamber specified that, in its view, the person was a "young male who is well below the age of 15".

Proven

The Chamber stated that this individual was a "young male who is well below the age of 15". See Lubanga Trial Chamber Judgment, para. 1242, see above note 4.

Individual 3

Video Evidence

Video excerpt EVD-OTP-00571, taken during a presidential rally at the Bunia city stadium, 11 January 2003, 02:02:44. According to the Trial Chamber, this individual was "evidently under the age of 15".

Proven

The Chamber found that the young man in camouflage clothing and bearing a weapon was "evidently under the age of 15". See Lubanga Trial Chamber Judgment, para. 861, see above note 4.

Individual 4

Video Evidence

Testimony of P-0002, evidence EVD-OTP-00410; and video excerpt EVD-OTP-00676, showing a UPC/FPLC rally at the stadium in the centre of Bunia, opposite the Ituri Hotel, 26 February 2003, 00:52:14.

Proven

The Chamber found that the young man in camouflage clothing and in the middle of the frame was "plainly under the age of 15". See Lubanga Trial Chamber Judgment, para. 779, see above note 4.

Individual 5

The defence argued that this individual and Individual 6 below could be the same individual.

Video Evidence

The Chamber found that the excerpt showed two soldiers "clearly under the age of 15 years". See Lubanga Trial Chamber Judgment, paras. 712, 862, 915 and 1252, see above note 4.

Individual 6

The defence argued that this individual and Individual 5 above could be the same individual.

Video Evidence

Video excerpt EVD-OTP-00574, filmed at Lubanga's office, 24 February 2003, 00:36:21. The Chamber found that the excerpt showed two soldiers "clearly under the age of 15 years". See Lubanga Trial Chamber Judgment, paras. 712, 862, 915 and 1252, see above note 4.

Appendix 2: Meta-analyses and other studies on forensic age estimations including error intervals and/or the proportion of false positives/negatives.

Table A1 below summarizes meta-analysis as well as a few other studies considered relevant for the context of child soldiering cases. The table should not be considered an exhaustive list of all available research in the area and the reader is recommended to do additional literature searches, depending on the more specific case at hand. Table A1 includes research in which chronological age (CA) has been estimated on the basis of hand or wrist, dental, collarbone as well as combined assessments. Sometimes also other assessments of, for example, knees or pelvic bones are made for these purposes.

Table A1. Meta-analyses and other studies on forensic age estimations including error intervals and/or the proportion of false positives/negatives.

Type of Assess-ment	Study: Authors *Study Type*	Exact (E) or Threshold Assess-ment (T)	Sample	Method, Scale, etc.	Error
Hand or Wrist	Brush Founda-tion Study[510]	E	American, 3 months to 17 years, N = 999	Greulich and Pyle ('GP')	Boys 10–17 yrs: 9.79–13.05 months Girls 10–17 yrs: 7.31–11.73 months deviation from CA.
	Stuart Data[511]	E	Ameri-can,[512] 1–17 years, N ≈ 300	GP	Boys 10–17 yrs: 10.4–15.4 months

---

[510] Elisabeth Ebert and Katherine Simmons, *The Brush Foundation Study of Child Growth and Development: II. Physical Growth and Development*, Wiley, 1943. See also Greulich and Pyle, 1959, see above note 243; Gaskin *et al.*, 2011, see above note 243.

[511] Ebert and Simmons, see above note 510, Greulich and Pyle, 1959, see above note 243 and Gaskin *et al.*, see above note 243.

[512] However, this sample consisted of a more diverse body of children (compared to the Brush Foundation Study), many of whom were from less privileged socioeconomic groups, see Gaskin *et al.*, p. 1, see above note 243.

				Girls: 10.8–14.6 months deviation from CA.
Alshamrani, Messina and Offiah (2019)[513] *Meta-analysis*	E	Multiple,[514] 35 studies, 0–19 years, N = 21 081	GP	0.37 yrs[515] to 0.50–1.35 yrs[516] deviation from CA.
Benjavongkul-chai and Pitta-yapat (2018)[517] *Other*	T (10, 13, 15, 18)	Thai, 8–20 years, N = 365	GP, TW3-RUS, Fishman	Average error for all thresh-olds:[518] 19.54–38.07 per cent (lowest for Fishman, highest for GP).

---

[513] Khalaf Alshamrani, Fabrizio Messina and Amaka C. Offiah, "Is the Greulich and Pyle Atlas Applicable to All Ethnicities? A Systematic Review and Meta-analysis", in *European Radiology*, 2019, vol. 29, pp. 2910–23.

[514] Caucasian, Asian, African, Hispanic.

[515] In African females. Hence, in African females, bone was significantly advanced when compared to the Greulich and Pyle standard.

[516] In Asian males. Hence, in Asian males, bone age was significantly delayed between six and nine years old and significantly advanced at 17 years old when compared to the Greulich and Pyle standard. Thus, the ethnicity or origin of the child seemed to influence the applicability of the Greulich and Pyle standard.

[517] Sunpatch Benjavongkulchai and Pisha Pittayapat, "Age Estimation Methods Using Hand and Wrist Radiographs in a Group of Contemporary Thais", in *Forensic Science International*, 2018, vol. 287, pp. 218.e1–218.e8.

[518] Hence, in this study, the average error, including both under and overestimations, for all age thresholds ranged between 19.54–38.07 per cent of all individuals, depending in which more specific method was used.

	Pinchi *et al.* (2014)[519] *Other*	T (18)	Italian, 6–20 years, N = 307	GP, TW2, TW3	Average error: 14.26–21.72 per cent (lowest GP, highest TW2).[520]
Dental	Melo and Ata-Ali (2016)[521] *Other*	E	Spanish, 7–21 years, N = 2 641	X-rays or Demirjian and Nolla (all stages)	-0.213 yrs (Nolla) to +0.853 yrs (Demirjian) deviation from CA.[522]
	Meinl *et al.* (2007)[523] *Other*	T (18)	Austrian, 12–24 years, N = 610	Third molar X-ray/ Demirjian stage H	0.50–0.70 per cent.[524]
	Jayaraman *et al.* (2013)[525] *Meta-analysis*	E	Multiple,[526] 274 studies, 2–21 years, N = 19 599	X-rays/ Demirjian (all stages)	+0.60 yrs (males) to +0.65 (females) deviation from CA.

---

[519] Pinchi *et al.*, 2014, pp. 83–90, see above note 244.

[520] Thus, 14.26–21.72 per cent were classified inaccurately depending on which more specific method was used.

[521] Maria Melo and Javier Ata-Ali, "Accuracy of the Estimation of Dental Age in Comparison with Chronological Age in a Spanish Sample of 2641 Living Subjects using the Demirjian and Nolla Methods", in *Forensic Science International*, 2017, vol. 270, pp. 276.e1–276.e7.

[522] However, when combining Nolla and Demirjian the percentage of true positives was 99.20 per cent.

[523] Alexandra Meinl *et al.*, "The Chronology of Third Molar Mineralization in the Austrian Population: A Contribution to Forensic Age Estimation", in *Forensic Science International*, 2007, vol. 169, no. 2, pp. 161–67.

[524] Hence, when using stage H, 99.3–99.5 per cent of all the individuals were accurately classified.

[525] Jayakumar Jayaraman *et al.*, "The French-Canadian Data Set of Demirjian for Dental Age Estimation: A Systematic Review and Meta-analysis", in *Journal of Forensic and Legal Medicine*, 2013, vol. 20, no. 5, pp. 373–81.

[526] For instance, Australia, Brazil, Finland, France, Netherlands, New Zealand, Norway, Senegal, Spain, Sweden, Turkey, UK, Venezuela.

Esan, Yengopal and Schepartz (2017)[527] *Meta-analysis*	E	Multiple,[528] 28 studies, 3–18 years, N = 24 941	X-rays or Demirjian/ Willem	+0.62–0.72 yrs males/femal es (Demirjian) +0.26–0.29 yrs males/femal es (Willem) deviation from CA.
Yusof (2017)[529] *Meta-analysis*	E	Multiple,[530] 23 studies, 3–16.9 years, N = 13 915	X-rays/ Willem	+0.09–0.10 years (fe-males/ males) deviation from CA.
Franco et al. (2020)[531] *Meta-analysis*	E	Brazilian, 10 studies, <16 years, N = 7 538	Haavikko, Demirijian,	-0.87 to +0.74 yrs SD (Haa-viko, Demi-rijian) deviation from CA.
Sehrawat et al. (2016)[532] *Meta-analysis*	E	Multiple,[533] 12 studies, 3–18 years, N = 5 813	Nolla	-0.35 yrs (males) to -0.20 yrs (females) deviation

[527] Temitope Ayodejj Esan, "The Demirjian versus the Willems Method for Dental Age Esti-mation in Different Populations: A Meta-analysis of Published Studies", in *PloS one*, 2017, vol. 12, no. 11, pp. 1–23.

[528] For instance, Macedonia, Portugal, Serbia, Spain, India, Nigeria, Iran, Turkey, Malaysia, France, South Africa.

[529] Mohd Yusof et al., "Performance of Willem's Dental Age Estimation Method in Children: A Systematic Review and Meta-analysis", in *Forensic Science International*, 2017, vol. 280, pp. 245.e1–245.e10.

[530] For instance, China, Serbia, South Korea, Malaysia, India, Japan, Bosnia-Herzegovina.

[531] Ademir Franco et al., "Assessment of Dental Age Estimation Methods applied to Brazilian Children: A Systematic Review and Meta-analysis", in *Dento-Maxillo-Facial Radiology*, 2020, vol. 6, pp. 1–9.

[532] Jagmahender Singh Sehrawat et al., "Forensic Dental Age Estimation of Sub-adult Indi-viduals Using Nolla's Radiographic Method: A Systematic Review and Meta-analysis", in *Brazilian Journal of Forensic Sciences*, 2016, vol. 6, no. 1, pp. 32–46.

[533] For instance, Turkey, India, UK, Malaysia, Brazil and Pakistan.

				from CA
Sehrawat and Singh (2017)[534] *Meta-analysis*	E	Multiple,[535] 31 studies, 2.2–18 years, N = 17 741	Willem	+0.07 (females) to +0.16 (males) yrs deviation from CA.
Haglund and Mörnstad (2019)[536] *Meta-analysis*	T (18)	Multiple,[537] 82 studies, 15–25.9 yrs, N = 19 690	Third molar in the fully mature stage, Demirjian (H), Köhler (Ac), Moorrees (Ac), Nolla (10)	29 per cent.[538]
Esan and Schepartz (2018)[539] *Other*	E	South African, 5–20 years, N = 642	Demirjian	+1.25 years (male) to + 1.36 yrs (female) deviation from CA.

---

[534] Jagmahender Singh Sehrawat and Monika Singh, "Willems Method of Dental Age Estimation in Children: A Systematic Review and Meta-analysis", in *Journal of Forensic and Legal Medicine*, 2017, vol. 52, pp. 122–29.

[535] For instance, Belgium, Egypt, India, Malaysia, Serbia, Thailand, UK and Venezuela.

[536] Haglund and Mörnstad, 2019, see above note 265.

[537] Asian, Middle East, African, African-American, European and Caucasian, Latin American and Hispanic.

[538] Diagnostic accuracy was 71 per cent and the false positive rate was 3.1 per cent.

[539] Temitope Esan and Lynne A. Schepartz, "The Timing of Permanent Tooth Development in a Black Southern African Population using the Demirjian Method", in *International Journal of Legal Medicine*, 2018, vol. 133, no. 1, pp. 1–13.

Clavicle	Hermetet et al. (2018)[540] *Meta-analysis*[541]	T (18, 21)	Multiple,[542] 13 studies, 10–35 yrs, N = 5 605	Thin-slice computed tomography (TSCTs) of the medial clavicular epiphysis (MCE), Schmeling classification	0 per cent All individuals classified as stages 4 and 5[543] were aged 18 yrs or older.[544]
	Kellinghaus et al. (2009)[545] *Other*	E	Patients examined in German hospital, 10–35 yrs, N = 592	Thin-slice multidetector CT images, Schmeling classification	Stage 4 found in both sexes at 21 yrs. Earliest observation of stage 5 at age 26.
	Gurses et al. (2017)[546] *Other*	E	Patients examined in Turkish university, 13–28 years, N = 254	Thin-section CT images, Kellinghaus substage method	Earliest appearance for stage 3c was 19 yrs for both sexes.
	Garamendi et al. (2011)[547]	E	Spanish, 5–75 years,	Schmeling classifica-	Minimum CA of com-

---

[540] Coralie Hermetet *et al.*, "Forensic Age Estimation using Computed Tomography of the Medial Clavicular Epiphysis: A Systematic Review", in *International Journal of Legal Medicine*, 2018, vol. 132, pp. 1415–25.

[541] Referred to by the authors as "systematic review".

[542] Turkey, Germany, China, Australia, Thailand and France.

[543] The minimum age of stage four individuals was 18.1 years in the male population and 19.5 years in the female population.

[544] Same result was obtained concerning stage 3c, except in one article (Thailand).

[545] Manuel Kellinghaus *et al.*, "Forensic Age Estimation in Living Subjects Based on the Ossification Status of the Medial Clavicular Epiphysis as Revealed by Thin-slice Multidetector Computed Tomography", in *International Journal of Legal Medicine*, 2010, vol. 124, pp. 149–54.

[546] Murat Serdar Gurses *et al.*, "Evaluation of the Ossification of the Medial Clavicle according to the Kellinghaus Substage System in Identifying the 18-year-old Age Limit in the Estimation of Forensic Age. Is it Necessary?", in *International Journal of Legal Medicine*, 2017, vol. 131, pp. 585–92.

	Other (also examining the first rib)		N = 123	tion	plete fusion of medial clavicle <20 years (19.7).[548]
	Ufuk *et al.* (2016)[549] *Other*	E	Turkish, 10–30 years, N = 354	CT	Minimum CA of complete fusion of medial clavicular epiphysis 18 (male) and 19 (female).[550]
	Vieth *et al.* (2014)[551] *Other*	E	German (only males), 18–22 years, N = 152	Schmelling classification	Full ossification of medial clavicular epiphyseal plate was found only in individual of 21.2 years.[552]
Combined	Gelbrich *et al.* (2015)[553] Hand or Wrist and teeth *Other*	E	Patients examined in German university, 7.8–19.1 years, N = 383	Hand/ wrist and dental panoramic images	Combined = 0.79 yrs deviation from CA (hand = 0.97 yrs, teeth = 1.35 yrs)

---

[547] Pedro Garamendi *et al.*, "Forensic Age Estimation on Digital X-ray Images: Medial Epiphyses of the Clavicle and First Rib Ossification in Relation to Chronological Age", in *Journal of Forensic Sciences*, 2011, vol. 56, no. s1, pp. S3–S12.

[548] This was analysed because complete fusion of the medial clavicle is a parameter recommended by AGFAD for a FAE around 21 years.

[549] Ufuk, Agladiogl and Karabulut, 2016, pp. 241–46, see above note 241.

[550] Also, the probability of an individual being 18 years or older was 70.80 per cent in Stage III A and 100 per cent in Stages III B, IV and V in females and males.

[551] Volker Vieth *et al.*, "Age Estimation in U-20 Football Players using 3.0 Tesla MRI of the Clavicle", in *Forensic Science International*, 2014, vol. 241, pp. 118–22.

[552] Thus, the presence of a fully ossified clavicular epiphyseal plate appeared to provide evidence of completion of the 20th year of life.

[553] Biance Gelbrich *et al.*, "Combining Wrist Age and Third Molars in Forensic Age Estimation: How to Calculate the Joint Age Estimate and its Error Rate in Age Diagnostics", in *Journal of the Society for the Study of Human Biology*, 2015, vol. 42, no. 4, pp. 389–96.

Santoro *et al.* (2009)[554] Hand and wrist and teeth *Other*		E		Multiple,[555] immigrants, Bari, Italy, N = 52	Radiologic examination of hand or wrist and inspection of oral cavity	Greatest discrepancy: 5 years 10 months[556] from self-reported age (not known CA).
Mostad and Tamsen (2019)[557] *Teeth/Knees*		T (18)		Multiple, asylum seekers, Sweden N = 9954	X-ray third molar, MRI distal femoral epiphysis	CA <18 yrs approx. 33 per cent risk classified as >18 yrs, CA>18 yrs approx. 7 per cent risk classified as <18 yrs.

---

[554] Valeria Santoro *et al.*, "Forensic Age Estimation in Living Individuals: A Retrospective Analysis", in *Forensic Science International*, 2009, vol. 193, pp. 129.e1–129.e4.

[555] Slovenia, Serbia, Croatia, Albania, Palestine, Lebanon, Iran, Iraq, Egypt, Algeria, Morocco and Nigeria.

[556] Note that this is the difference between the estimated age and the age reported by the subject, thus not a known chronological age.

[557] Mostad and Tamsen, 2019, pp. 613–23, see above note 265.

7

Confirmation Bias in Investigations of Core International Crimes: Risk Factors and Quality Control Techniques

Moa Lidén[*]

> If one were to attempt to identify a single problematic aspect of human reasoning that deserves attention above all others, the *confirmation bias* would have to be among the candidates for consideration.[1]

7.1. Introduction

Although the historical roots, contemporary challenges, material as well as procedural law vary across different jurisdictions, all jurisdictions have one common and continuous denominator; they are all fundamentally dependent on the decision-making processes of humans operating inside of them. As such, the topic of bias in human decision making is directly related to issues of legitimacy, not the least when it comes to decision making in criminal case procedures.

This chapter examines the more specific context of investigations into core international crimes. Although the literature describes a range of

---

[*]   **Moa Lidén** is Postdoctoral Research Fellow, funded by Ragnar Söderberg Foundation and The Swedish Research Council, at the Department of Security and Crime Science, Centre for the Forensic Sciences, UCL, London. She holds a Ph.D. in Jurisprudence from the Law Faculty of Uppsala University and her doctoral thesis was on the topic "Confirmation Bias in Criminal Cases". This chapter is based on a presentation at a conference organised by the Centre of International Law Research and Policy (CILRAP) at the Indian Law Institute in New Delhi, see Moa Lidén, "Prevention of Factual Confirmation Bias During Offence-Driven Investigations", CILRAP Film, New Delhi, 22 February 2019 (https://www.cilrap.org/cilrap-film/190222-liden/). The author is grateful to Xabier Agirre Aranburu for his review of this chapter.

[1]   Raymond Nickerson, "Confirmation Bias: A Ubiquitous Phenomenon in Many Guises", in *Review of General Psychology*, 1998, vol. 2, no. 2, p. 175.

---

biases,[2] research since the 1960's into the so-called *confirmation bias* illustrates its pervasive and multifaceted nature as well as its potentially devastating consequences,[3] rendering it a top candidate for consideration.

The definition of confirmation bias, which was first presented by Raymond Nickerson in 1998 and is today well-established, describes it as a human "tendency to search for and interpret information in ways that are partial to existing hypotheses".[4] At the same time, opposing information is ignored or interpreted in ways that do not threaten the predetermined conclusion.[5] Thus confirmation bias entails one-sidedness both in how decision makers search for information and in how they evaluate the information. Importantly, this one-sidedness in reasoning happens more or less subconsciously. Today, 21 years later, the research on confirmation bias

---

[2] See, for example, Amos Tversky and Daniel Kahneman, "Judgment under Uncertainty: Heuristics and Biases", in *Science*, 1974, vol. 185, no. 4157, pp. 1124–31; Martin Hilbert, "Toward a Synthesis of Cognitive Biases: How Noisy Information Processing can Bias Human Decision Making", in *Psychological Bulletin*, 2012, vol. 138, no. 2, pp. 211–37; Jonathan Baron, *Thinking and Deciding*, Cambridge University Press, New York, 2008; Eugeniusz Pronin, "Perception and Misperception of Bias in Human Judgment", in *Trends in Cognitive Science*, 2006, vol. 11, no. 1, pp. 37–43; Steven Schwartz and Martin F. Kaplan, *Human Judgment and Decision Processes*, Academic Press, London, 1975. For a summary of a range of cognitive tendencies and biases overlapping confirmation bias, see Moa Lidén, *Confirmation Bias in Criminal Cases*, Uppsala University Press, Uppsala, 2018, pp. 106–08.

[3] This research has primarily been conducted by cognitive psychologists using experimental methods. The research began with Peter Cathcart Wason's today famous 2-4-6 task with which he illustrated that people tend to use evaluation strategies that can potentially confirm their hypothesis, but not strategies that can potentially disconfirm their hypothesis, see Peter Cathcart Wason, "On the Failure to Eliminate Hypotheses in a Conceptual Task", in *Quarterly Journal of Experimental Psychology*, 1960, vol. 12, no. 3, pp. 129–40. Although this task has been criticised, for example, for creating artificial results, the findings have since then been replicated in a range of settings and with more realistic tasks. The two most important meta-analyses which summarise these studies are William Hart, Dolores Albarracín, Alice H. Eagly, Inge Brechan, Matthew J. Lindberg and Lisa Merrill, "Feeling Validated Versus Being Correct: A Meta-Analysis of Selective Exposure to Information", in *Psychological Bulletin*, 2009, vol. 135, no. 4, pp. 555–88; Alice H. Eagly, Serena Chen, Shelly Chaiken and Kelly Shaw-Barnes, "The Impact of Attitudes on Memory: An Affair to Remember", in *Psychological Bulletin*, 1999, vol. 125, no. 1, pp. 64–89.

[4] Nickerson, 1998, pp. 175–76, see above note 1.

[5] *Ibid.*

has not only been widely replicated but the bias has also been found in a range of distinct contexts[6] including criminal investigations.[7]

On a general level, it can be noted that confirmation bias strongly contradicts legal demands on decision making, such as the presumption of innocence[8] and, in the context of the International Criminal Court ('ICC'), the prosecutor's duty to investigate both incriminating and exonerating circumstances equally.[9] Given the largely subconscious nature of confirmation bias, even legal actors who make every effort to remain objective and who might even perceive of themselves as objective, can in fact display this one-sidedness. As such, confirmation bias can result in wrongful suspicions, or even convictions, as well as the loyal companions of these problems, namely that the real perpetrator(s) remain at large or that investigation into their guilt is initiated too late, when it is unlikely that evidence sufficient for a conviction will be found. Alternatively, even if a hypothesis is correct in the sense that a certain suspect has committed a crime, the hypothesis might be wrong, for example, in relation to the course of event or the hierarchical structure that was used for a criminal

---

[6] One example is found within medicine, namely that physicians who are aware of a patient's medical diagnosis tend to make more diagnosis-consistent interpretations of information regarding the patient, as compared to physicians who are unaware of the diagnosis, see Tanya Lyn Eadie, "Does Knowledge of Medical Diagnosis Bias Auditory-perceptual Judgments of Dysphonia?", in *Journal of Voice: Official Journal of the Voice Foundation*, 2015, vol. 25, no. 4, pp. 420–29. However, there are also examples of non-experimental research studies, such as historical studies of the witch hunt between the 16th and 19th centuries in Western Europe, which is sometimes described as a consequence of confirmation bias on a societal level, that is, an example of how a dominating general belief that some women were witches, had devastating consequences, in this case the execution of tens of thousands of women, see Craig Cabell, *Witchfinder General: The Biography of Matthew Hopkins*, Sutton Publishing Ltd., Stroud, 2006; Bror Gadelius, *Häxor och Häxprocesser*, Prisma, Stockholm, 1986; Bror Gadelius, *Tro och Öfvertro i Gångna Tider*, Geber, Stockholm, 1912.

[7] This research will be discussed in detail in the chapter but some examples of such research studies are Willem A. Wagenaar, Peter J. van Koppen and Hans F.M. Crombag, *Anchored Narratives: The Psychology of Criminal Evidence*, St Martin's Press, New York, 1994; Saul M. Kassin, Itiel E. Dror and Jeff Kukucka, "The Forensic Confirmation Bias: Problems, Perspectives, and Proposed Solutions", in *Journal of Applied Research in Memory and Cognition*, 2013, vol. 2. no. 1, pp. 42–52; Lidén, 2018, see above note 2.

[8] Rome Statute of the International Criminal Court, 17 July 1998, Article 66 ('ICC Statute') (https://legal-tools.org/doc/7b9af9)

[9] *Ibid.*, Article 54(1)(a).

conduct,[10] as well as the associated legal labels. The potential consequences of confirmation bias in criminal investigations highlight an important part of quality control, namely to find effective debiasing techniques that prevent or at least mitigate the bias. Such debiasing techniques promote proper factual analysis and evidence-review, including careful and balanced evaluations of strengths and weaknesses in existing hypotheses as well as thorough exploration of alternative hypotheses. The techniques are therefore relevant in relation to the second and third bottlenecks ('factual analysis' and 'evidence-review') identified in Morten Bergsmo's policy brief "Towards a Culture of Quality Control in Criminal Investigations" that serves as the concept paper of the research project of which this anthology is part.[11] Due to the multifaceted nature of confirmation bias, finding effective debiasing techniques requires knowledge of, not only how the bias might manifest itself, but also why the bias occurs. Such knowledge can then be used to tailor-make debiasing techniques for the context in which they are intended to be used.

To address these questions, this chapter consists of two main parts:

1) *Manifestations of confirmation bias*: What is known about how confirmation bias manifests itself in criminal investigations and how can this knowledge be used to identify risk factors in investigations

---

[10] The importance of establishing hierarchical structures in investigations into core international crimes is discussed by, for example, Xabier Agirre Aranburu, "Gravity of Crimes and Responsibility of the Suspect", in Morten Bergsmo (ed.), *Criteria for Prioritizing and Selecting Core International Crimes*, Torkel Opsahl Academic EPublisher ('TOAEP'), Oslo, 2010, p. 234; Elinor Fry, "The Nature of International Crimes and Evidentiary Challenges – Preserving Quality While Managing Quantity", in Elies van Sliedregt and Sergey Vasiliev (eds.), *Pluralism in International Criminal Law*, Oxford University Press, Oxford, 2014, pp. 264–65. See also Ohlin who describes international criminal law as a "constant balancing of collective elements and individual responsibility", see Jens David Ohlin, "Meta-Theory of International Criminal Procedure: Vindicating the Rule of Law", in *UCLA Journal of International Law and Foreign Affairs*, 2009, vol. 14, no. 1, p. 92.

[11] Morten Bergsmo, "Towards a Culture of Quality Control in Criminal Investigations", FICHL Policy Brief No. 94 (2019), TOAEP, Brussels, 2019, pp. 2–3 (http://www.toaep. org/pbs-pdf/94-bergsmo/). See also Morten Bergsmo, "Rethinking Instruments of Quality Control in the Investigation and Preparations of Core International Crimes Cases", CILRAP Film, New Delhi, 23 February 2019 (https://www.cilrap.org/cilrap-film/190222-bergsmo/). Furthermore, Carsten Stahn describes two macro problems that are similar in preliminary examinations and investigations: 1) cognitive bias, including confirmation bias, and 2) addressing bottlenecks, see Carsten Stahn, "From Preliminary Examination to Investigation: Rethinking the Connection", chap. 1 above.

---

into core international crimes (war crimes, crimes against humanity, genocide)?

2) *Explanations of confirmation bias and debiasing techniques*: What are the explanations of confirmation bias and how can these be used to identify potential debiasing techniques? How can debiasing techniques be tested as to allow sound and accurate evaluations of their potential?

7.2. Manifestations of Confirmation Bias in Criminal Investigations

7.2.1. Suspect-Driven Investigations

> On February 14, 2005, at 12:50 p.m., former Lebanese Prime Minister Hariri and 22 other individuals were killed in an explosion in downtown Beirut. A United-Nations fact-finding mission arrived in Beirut to investigate the assassination on February 25, 2005. [...] By December 17, 2005, the chief UN investigator, Detlev Mehlis, had told an Arab newspaper he believed that Syria was directly responsible for Hariri's assassination. By the end of 2005, 19 suspects had been identified, including 5 high-level Syrian security officials and 4 Lebanese generals.[12]

The assassination of former Lebanese Prime Minister Rafik Hariri[13] and the events following it, not the least the so-called 'Mehlis Report' which implicated Syrian and Lebanese officials,[14] illustrate how powerful sus-

---

[12] Robert M. Bosco, "The Assassination of Rafik Hariri: Foreign Policy Perspectives", in *International Political Science Review*, 2009, vol. 30, no. 4, p. 354.

[13] Rafik Hariri took over as Lebanon's Prime Minister in 1992 with the support of Saudi Arabia and the United States. For more about Hariri's rise to power, Lebanon's civil war (1975–90) and the two distinct power alliances that, by 2004, the year before Hariri's assassination, had emerged between on the one hand Syrian President Bashar al-Assad, Lebanese President Émile Lahoud, and the cross-border security forces, and, on the other, Lebanese Prime Minister Rafik Hariri and his domestic and international supporters, Bosco, 2009, pp. 351–53, see above note 12.

[14] For more on this, see, for example, William Harris, "Investigating Lebanon's Political Murders: International Idealism in the Realist Middle East", in *The Middle East Journal*, 2013, vol. 67, no. 1, pp. 9–27. In October and December 2005, the inquiry produced two reports under the signature of United National International Independent Investigation Commission ('UNIIIC') chief Detlev Mehlis. According to Harris, Mehlis had the unanimous support of all seven international prosecutors in his team for the findings. After receiving death threats, he was advised by the United Nations ('UN') that he could no longer lead the inquiry and declined renewal of his contract. After this, he was replaced by Belgian prosecutor Serge Brammertz in January 2006.

pect identification can be.[15] Shortly after the assassination, the UNIIIC was established, initially led by senior German prosecutor Detlev Mehlis, to assist the Lebanese authorities in their investigation, including "identifying perpetrators, sponsors, organizers and accomplices".[16] However, the decision to create a commission of inquiry focusing on one specific bombing was soon heavily criticised for being politically selective, much due to the early identification of certain suspects in the Mehlis Report.[17] The report resulted in that four allegedly pro-Syrian Lebanese generals were arrested and detained in September 2005.[18] In November 2005, a key witness of the report publicly recanted his testimony saying he had been coerced,[19] only days after another witness allegedly was paid to testify.[20] However, the four generals were held in Lebanese prison for almost four years.[21] It was not until 2009, after the Hariri file had been transferred to the Special Tribunal of Lebanon ('STL'),[22] that the STL Prosecu-

---

[15] Although the official Mehlis report only pointed to 'Lebanese and Syrian involvement', an unedited version which found its way into the hands of journalists carried the names of several senior Lebanese and Syrian officials, see Nicholas Blanford, *Killing Mr Lebanon: The Assassination of Rafik Hariri and Its Impact on the Middle East*, Bloomsbury Publishing, New York, 2006, pp. 178–79.

[16] See Security Council Resolution 1595, UN Doc. S/RES/1595 (2005), 7 April 2005, para. 1 (https://legal-tools.org/doc/4a0623); Amal Alamuddin and Anna Bonini, "The UN Investigation of the Hariri Assassination", in Amal Alamuddin, Nidal Nabil Jurdi and David Tolbert (eds.), *The Special Tribunal for Lebanon: Law and Practice*, Oxford University Press, Oxford, 2014, p. 52.

[17] Alamuddin and Bonini, 2014, p. 52, see above note 16. Another part of the criticism was that other assassinations and crimes in Lebanon had gone un-investigated and unpunished before, during and after the Commission's life. The expansion of the Commission's mandate to cover other terrorist bombings that took place in Lebanon after 1 October 2004 only partially addressed this concern. See also Amnesty International, *The Special Tribunal for Lebanon: Selective Justice?*, London, 27 February 2009 (https://legal-tools.org/doc/rj32ah).

[18] Alamuddin and Bonini, 2014, pp. 60–61, see above note 16.

[19] This key witness was Hussam Hussam who said he was coerced by Saad Hariri and other March 14 coalition leaders, see Blanford, 2006, p. 184, see above note 15.

[20] This witness was Zuahir Ibn Mohammed Said Saddik who allegedly was paid to testify by Rifaat al-Assad, Bashar's uncle, who still had an eye on the presidency, see Blanford, 2006, p. 184, see above note 15.

[21] Alamuddin and Bonini, 2014, pp. 60–61, see above note 16.

[22] STL, which is sometimes referred to as the 'Hariri Tribunal' was established following a request by the government of Lebanon to the UN and its primary mandate is to hold trials for the people accused of carrying out the attack of 14 February 2005 which killed Hariri as well as 22 other people, see STL, "About the STL" (available on its web site).

---

tor requested that the generals be released based on, *inter alia*, the "inconsistencies in the statements of key witnesses and of a lack of corroborative evidence to support these statements".[23] As a result, the pre-trial judge ordered the generals' immediate release.[24]

Although it is difficult to assess conclusively the workings of any criminal investigations, always complex and confidential, according to the judicial record and the prevailing view among experts, it appears that the initial fact-finding on the Hariri assassination was strongly influenced by the expectations of key stakeholders and the early identification of suspects, offering a compelling example of this kind of bias in international investigations. Later, based on, for example, forensic expert statements of how the bombings happened[25] as well as analysis of telephone communications believed to be instrumental for the planning of the assassination,[26] four other suspects were identified and their guilt tried *in absentia* by the STL.[27] Still today the STL is deliberating whether the Prosecution has proved its case beyond reasonable doubt.[28]

Even though identifying suspects are both desired and necessary parts of criminal investigations, early suspect identification can be prob-

---

[23]   STL, Pre-Trial Judge, Order Regarding the Detention of Persons Detained in Lebanon in Connection with the Case of the Attack Against Prime Minister Rafiq Hariri and Others, 29 April 2009, CH/PTJ/2009/06, para. 34(vi) ('Order Regarding the Detention of Persons Detained in Lebanon in Connection with the Case of the Attack Against Prime Minister Rafiq Hariri and Others') (https://legal-tools.org/doc/60381f); Alamuddin and Bonini, 2014, p. 61, see above note 16.

[24]   Order Regarding Detention of Persons Detained in Lebanon in Connection with the Case of the Attack Against Prime Minister Rafiq Hariri and Others, see above note 23.

[25]   These statements came from experts from Germany, the Netherlands and Japan, see Marwan Iskandar, *Rafiq Hariri and the Fate of Lebanon*, Saqi, London, 2006, pp. 207–08. Previously there had been discussions about whether the bomb blast was above-ground or subterranean. According to Blanford, the Lebanese authorities were pressing the idea of an above-ground blast caused by a suicide bomber, citing the mysterious Abu Adas video confession, but those who firmly believed Syria was responsible for the assassination pinned their hopes on a subterranean blast, as digging a hole in the main road outside the St Georges Hotel would require the collusion of the authorities. For more on this, see Blanford, 2006, pp. 150–51, see above note 15.

[26]   According to the prosecution, the cell site-records demonstrate that the cellular phones using the identified six calling cards were placed to cover any route that Hariri would have taken that day. Iskandar, 2006, p. 207, see above note 25.

[27]   STL, *The Prosecutor v. Ayyash et al.*, STL-11-01.

[28]   See the current status of the *Ayyash et al.* case: STL, "Ayyash et al. (STL-11-01)" (available on its web site).

lematic as it may steer the investigation towards searching for, only or primarily, evidence supporting the hypothesis that the suspect is guilty.[29] Thus, in such investigations, the mindset of investigators is not to carefully evaluate the hypothesis by searching for both incriminating and exonerating information, but instead to "find the evidence"[30] that supports the hypothesis. Logically speaking, it is of course possible to find hypothesis-consistent evidence, even if the hypothesis is wrongful. However, given the one-sidedness of the investigation, it cannot properly evaluate whether this is the case or not. These so-called *suspect-driven investigations*, which were first described by Wagenaar, van Koppen and Crombag in 1993, are, today, widely acknowledged manifestations of confirmation bias.[31]

Wagenaar and colleagues based their framework regarding suspect-driven investigations on an analysis of Dutch criminal cases that were dubious in the sense that they contained legal or logical problems and were later reversed by the Court of Appeals (due to a different evaluation of the evidence, or that the defence attorney remained strongly convinced of a client's innocence).[32] Some of the cases were acknowledged wrongful convictions. Wagenaar and colleagues found that all these cases had something in common; a suspect had been identified at an early stage of the investigation and, from there on, this guilt hypothesis dictated the investigation as its only aim was to find hypothesis confirming information. They also distinguished suspect-driven investigations from *offence-driven investigation*s, the latter in which it is the available information, rather than a predetermined conclusion, which guides the search for further information and, eventually, the formation of the case's hypothesis.[33] Hence,

---

[29] Wagenaar, van Koppen and Crombag, 1993, p. 11, see above note 7.

[30] This determinative mindset has been described, using the same words, by, for example, Eric Rassin, Anita Eerland and Ilse Kuijpers, "Let's Find the Evidence: An Analogue Study of Confirmation Bias in Criminal Investigations", in *Journal of Investigative Psychology and Offender Profiling*, 2010, vol. 7, no. 3, pp. 231–46. Interestingly, this is similar to how a former International Criminal Court ('ICC') attorney describes the first Prosecutor of the ICC, Mr. Luis Moreno-Ocampo, to a New York Times magazine journalist, that is: "He would see the leader of a state and say: 'There must be evidence out there. Go get it for me'". See James Verini, "The Prosecutor and the President", *The New York Times*, 22 June 2016 (available on its web site).

[31] Wagenaar, van Koppen and Crombag, 1993, p. 11, see above note 7.

[32] *Ibid.*

[33] *Ibid.*

in offence-driven investigations, case hypotheses are formulated at later stages and on the basis of more information than in suspect-driven investigations.

Although postponing the formulation of a case hypothesis makes the accuracy of the hypothesis less dependent on chance and more dependent on sound investigation, a criminal investigation can of course not proceed without any hypothesis for too long. This would not only be draining in terms of resources, but also defeat the purpose of finding out whether any crime has been committed and by whom. In many investigations, and particularly those into core international crimes, there is a potentially endless amount of information of different degrees of relevance. Such investigations sometimes face allegations implying the killing of tens of thousands of civilians, the forcible displacement of several hundred thousand persons, and the unlawful destruction of more than one hundred thousand homes. In practice, it is rarely or never possible to take all of this information into account.

There are no specific answers as to exactly how this balancing should be made. Yet, the investigation should, as far as possible, help evaluate and potentially eliminate alternative hypotheses in relation to the beyond reasonable doubt standard.[34] If a confirmation bias is at play, this ability is greatly undermined as investigators, subconsciously, fail to see that there are other reasonable hypotheses and therefore do not initiate investigation into them. Alternatively, investigators do search for and find evidence in favour of another hypothesis, but systematically downgrade this evidence so that it does not threaten their predetermined conclusion. As such, the working hypothesis may appear essentially impeccable to investigators whereas others can more easily see that this is not the case.

Thus, the aim of preventing confirmation bias is not to ensure that literally all information is taken into account, but instead to promote careful and balanced evaluations of strengths and weaknesses of existing hy-

---

[34] See, for example, Mark Klamberg, "Fact-Finding in International Criminal Procedure – How Collection of Evidence May Contribute to Testing of Alternative Hypotheses", in *SSRN Electronic Journal*, 2011, pp. 1–20; Mark Klamberg, "The Alternative Hypothesis Approach, Robustness and International Criminal Justice: A Plea for a 'Combined Approach' to Evaluation of Evidence", in *Journal of International Criminal Justice*, 2015, vol. 13, no. 3, pp. 535–53.

potheses as well as genuine and through exploration of alternative hypotheses.[35]

Against this background, the usage of investigation plans[36] and the tradition of focusing on the most responsible perpetrators[37] in investigations of core international crimes, are of interest. On the one hand, there is no doubt that this helps the management, planning and allocation of investigative and prosecutorial efforts and resources.[38] On the other hand, it seems reasonable to ask whether and to what extent this triggers a confirmation bias, manifested in, for example, a suspect-driven investigation.

When it comes to investigation plans specifically, these may, of course, vary in how open or closed they are. For instance, there are variations in when and on what bases individuals are identified as suspects. In the first Darfur case,[39] the initial plan adopted in 2005 did not identify any suspect, as this only happened after about one year and then on the basis of ICC evidence.[40] However, in the Kenya investigation,[41] suspects were

---

[35] This is a crucial part of quality control, particularly in relation to the second and third bottlenecks 'factual analysis' and 'evidence-review', see Bergsmo, 2019, pp. 2–3, see above note 11.

[36] See, for example, Markus Eikel, "Nature and Use of Investigation Plans at the International Criminal Court", CILRAP Film, New Delhi, 23 February 2019 (https://www.cilrap.org/cilrap-film/190223-eikel/).

[37] Agirre Aranburu, 2010, p. 218, see above note 10.

[38] See ICC, *Paper on some policy issues before the Office of the Prosecutor*, 5 September 2003, p. 7 (https://legal-tools.org/doc/f53870), in which it is stated that the Office of the Prosecutor ('OTP') should focus "investigative and prosecutorial efforts and resources on those who bear the greatest responsibility, such as the leaders of the State or organization allegedly responsible for those crimes", cited by Agirre Aranburu, 2010, p. 222, see above note 10.

[39] ICC, Situation in Darfur, Sudan, Presidency, Decision Assigning the Situation in Darfur, Sudan to Pre-Trial Chamber I, 21 April 2005, ICC-02/05-1 (https://legal-tools.org/doc/8e8a93). On 1 June 2005, the Prosecutor determined that there was a reasonable basis to initiate an investigation and notified the Chambers and Presidency accordingly, see William A. Schabas, *An Introduction to the International Criminal Court*, Cambridge University Press, London, 2017, p. 48.

[40] See, for example, Xabier Agirre Aranburu and Roberta Belli, "The ICC and the Darfur Investigation – Progress and Challenges", in Mangai Natarajan (ed.), *International and Transnational Crime and Justice*, Cambridge University Press, Cambridge, 2019, and OTP, *First Report of the Prosecutor of the ICC to the Security Council Pursuant to UNSCR 1593 (2005)*, 29 June 2005.

[41] On 26 November 2009, the Prosecutor requested the Pre-Trial Chamber for authorisation to conduct investigations in Kenya. See ICC, Situation in the Republic of Kenya, OTP, Request for Authorisation of an Investigation Pursuant to Article 15, 26 November 2009,

---

identified early on in 2009, on the basis of prior investigations of two different fact-finding commissions.[42] Thus, adopting an investigation plan is not necessarily a trigger of confirmation bias in itself. Yet, recent research highlights the risk that investigators' minds "seize and freeze"[43] already with decisions about who should be investigated and through what tactics,[44] or with the identification[45] and/or apprehension or arrest of a suspect.[46] This means that the extent to which an investigation plan constitutes a risk factor is dependent on its more specific content, and also on its nature. If, for example – as Morten Bergsmo suggested at the New Delhi conference on which this anthology is based – the investigation plan is a dynamic, online knowledge-base for the investigation team, it may evolve on a daily basis and not be a one-off document early in an investigation.

ICC-01/09-3 (https://legal-tools.org/doc/c63dcc). This was after the Kenyan government, in breach of the so-called 'complementarity contract', failed to establish a special tribunal. For more on the different phases of these investigations see, for example, Lionel Nichols, *The International Criminal Court and the End of Impunity in Kenya*, Springer, London, 2015, pp. 69–86.

[42] *Ibid.*, pp. 69–70, see above note 41, and information obtained through personal communication with current and former ICC officers at the CILRAP conference "Quality Control in Criminal Investigation", 22–23 February 2019, New Delhi, India. After the Parliament voted against establishing the proposed special tribunal in February 2009 and subsequent revised proposals were rejected, the Prosecutor responded by using the *proprio motu* powers, and findings and materials from the Waki commission were delivered to the OTP. This led to the identification of the so-called 'Ocampo Six' (which then became the 'Ocampo Four' and the 'Ocampo Three', one of which had been elected President, Uhuru Kenyatta, and one Vice President, William Ruto). The second commission, the National Commission on Human Rights, named Kenyatta, saying, for example, that he repeatedly "attended meetings to plan for retaliatory violence by the Kikuyus", and also "contributed funds for the attacks", see Peter Leftie, "Poll violence was well planned: report", *Daily Nation*, 4 March 2010 (available on its web site).

[43] Arie W. Kruglanski and Donna M. Webster, "Motivated Closing of the Mind: "Seizing" and "Freezing"", in *Psychological Review*, 1996, vol. 103, no. 2, pp. 263–83.

[44] Leslie C. Griffin, "The Prudent Prosecutor", in *Georgetown Journal of Legal Ethics*, 2001, vol. 14, no. 249, pp. 259–307.

[45] Ivar Fahsing and Karl Ask, "Decision Making and Decisional Tipping Points in Homicide Investigations: An Interview Study of British and Norwegian Detectives", in *Journal of Investigative Psychology and Offender Profiling*, 2013, vol. 10, no. 2, pp. 155–65.

[46] Moa Lidén, Minna Gräns and Peter Juslin, "The Presumption of Guilt in Suspect Interrogations: Apprehension as a Trigger of Confirmation Bias and Debiasing Techniques", in *Law and Human Behavior*, 2018, vol. 42, no. 4, pp. 336–54; Fahsing and Ask, 2013, pp. 155–65, see above note 45.

The soundness of the hypothesis that someone is guilty will of course depend on the quality of the prior investigation leading up to the identification of the suspect(s).[47] It can be argued that developing a confirmation bias in relation to a guilt hypothesis that is correct is less of a problem. Although this seems reasonable in respect to a conviction, it can be noted that the duty to investigate incriminating and exonerating circumstances in the context of the ICC applies equally in all situations, and that the soundness of a guilt hypothesis can usually only be properly evaluated after finalising an investigation.

In comparison to investigation plans, the focus on the most responsible perpetrators,[48] is more unambiguously linked to suspect identification and, as such, a more potent risk factor.[49] Such a focus on one or a few responsible individuals may make prosecutors downgrade exculpatory evidence, for instance by categorising it as irrelevant.[50] This, in turn, can

---

[47] In this regard, it is relevant to evaluate how initial case hypotheses are developed during preliminary examinations and then tested during the subsequent investigations. For more on this topic see Carsten Stahn, "From Preliminary Examination to Criminal Investigation", CILRAP Film, 22 February 2019 (https://www.cilrap.org/cilrap-film/190222-stahn/).

[48] For more about the origins and definition of this concept as well as a review of the practice of different international tribunals on this matter, see Xabier Agirre Aranburu, "Prosecuting the Most Responsible for International Crimes: Dilemmas of Definition and Prosecutorial Discretion", in Joaquín González (ed.), *Protección Internacional de Derechos Humanos y Estado de Derecho*, Grupo Editorial Ibañez, Bogotá, 2009, pp. 381–404. Even if elements to identify the most responsible perpetrator (formal position, actual role, and so on) have been proposed (for example, by Pre-Trial Chamber I in their review of the Prosecutor's application to issue arrest warrants against Lubanga and Ntaganda, see ICC, Situation in the Democratic Republic of Congo, *The Prosecutor v. Thomas Lubanga Dyilo*, Public Redacted Version of Decision on the Prosecutor's Application for a warrant of arrest, Article 58, 10 February 2006, ICC-01/04-01/06-1-Corr-Red (https://legal-tools.org/doc/af6679)), one cannot state in general terms when precisely someone is to be considered as 'most responsible'.

[49] It can be noted that this focus is mandated at the ICC by, *inter alia*, the reference to 'degree of participation' as a sentencing factor, see ICC Rules of Procedure and Evidence, 9 September 2002, Rule 145(1)(c) (https://legal-tools.org/doc/8bcf6f) ('ICC RPE'); Agirre Aranburu, 2010, pp. 222–23, see above note 10.

[50] Alafair S. Burke, "Improving Prosecutorial Decision Making: Some Lessons of Cognitive Science", in *William and Mary Law Review*, 2006, vol. 47, no. 5, pp. 1588–631; Randolph N. Jonakait, "The Ethical Prosecutor's Misconduct", in *Criminal Law Bulletin*, 1987, vol. 23, no. 6, pp. 550–67; James McCloskey, "Convicting the Innocent", in *Criminal Justice Ethics*, 1989, vol. 8, no. 1, pp. 140–41; Colin Wastell, Nicole Weeks, Alexander Wearing and Piers Duncan, "Identifying Hypothesis Confirmation Behaviors in a Simulated Murder Investigation: Implications for Practice", in *Journal of Investigative Psychology and Offender Profiling*, 2012, vol. 9, no. 2, pp. 184–98; Ellen Yaroshefsky, "Cooperation with

influence their judgments of whether to press charges, what charges, what sentence to seek upon conviction, and so on.[51] Other research implies that this psychological shift only happens when the guilt hypothesis has become more consolidated, for example, with a charging decision.[52] This is manifested in that the charging decision in itself (*ceteris paribus*), seems to make prosecutors less likely to conduct additional investigation and if such investigation is undertaken, it is more often aimed at confirming the suspect's guilt.[53] Possibly, this is because they then anticipate the prospects of a conviction[54] and become more focused on proving the suspect's guilt at Court.[55]

Although it is impossible to say exactly at what point the hypothesis becomes consolidated enough to produce a confirmation bias, there are some specifics of investigations into core international crimes that may indicate an early onset. To begin with, often, the suspects are not any individuals but heads of State that enjoy diplomatic immunities in their national jurisdictions and towards whom popular opinions may be that of

Federal Prosecutors: Experiences of Truth Telling and Embellishment", in *Fordham Law Review*, 1999, vol. 68, no. 3, pp. 917–64.

[51] Angela J. Davis, "The American Prosecutor: Independence, Power, and the Threat of Tyranny", in *Iowa Law Review*, 2001, vol. 86, no. 2, pp. 393–465; Bruce A. Green, "Prosecutorial Ethics as Usual", in *University of Illinois Law Review*, 2003, vol. 2003, no. 5, pp. 1573–604.

[52] Moa Lidén, Minna Gräns and Peter Juslin, "From Devil's Advocate to Crime Fighter: Confirmation Bias and Debiasing Techniques in Prosecutorial Decision Making", in *Psychology, Crime and Law*, 2019, vol. 25, no. 5, pp. 1–33. See also Burke, 2006, pp. 1588–631, see above note 50.

[53] Lidén, Gräns and Juslin, 2018, pp. 1–33, see above note 52.

[54] Emelie Ernberg, Inga Tidefors and Sara Landström, "Prosecutors' Reflections on Sexually Abused Preschoolers and Their Ability to Stand Trial", in *Child Abuse and Neglect*, 2016, vol. 57, pp. 21–29; Denise Lievore, "Prosecutorial Decisions in Adult Sexual Assault Cases", in *Trends and Issues in Crime and Criminal Justice*, 2005, no. 291, pp. 1–6; Åsa Wettergren and Stina Bergman Blix, "Empathy and Objectivity in the Legal Procedure: The Case of Swedish Prosecutors", in *Journal of Scandinavian Studies in Criminology and Crime Prevention*, 2016, vol. 17, no. 1, pp. 19–35.

[55] Eric M. Freedman, "Innocence, Federalism, and the Capital Jury: Two Legislative Proposals for Evaluating Post-Trial Evidence of Innocence in Death Penalty Cases", in *New York University Review of Law and Social Change*, 1990, vol. 18, no. 2, pp. 315–23; Bennett L. Gershman, "The Prosecutor's Duty to Truth", in *Georgetown Journal of Legal Ethics*, 2001, vol. 14, no. 2, pp. 309–54.

strong support or dissent. Also, there is the more general historical[56] and contemporary[57] context and the associated controversy in relation to the *proprio motu* powers[58] as well as the critique that certain countries are being targeted, or even that twenty-first century neo-colonialism is at play.[59] The claim of neo-colonialism was put forward, for example, after the arrest warrant against President Al-Bashir had been issued over alleged criminal conduct in the Darfur conflict.[60] This context is important

---

[56]   See, for example, Michael Crowder, *West Africa under Colonial Rule*, Northwestern University Press, Evanston, 1968; Jürgen Osterhammel, *Colonialism: A Theoretical Overview*, Shelley L. Frisch trans., Markus Wiener Publishers, Princeton, 2005.

[57]   See, for example, Res Schuerch, *The International Criminal Court at the Mercy of Powerful States: An Assessment of the Neo-Colonialism Claim Made by African Stakeholders*, T.M.C. Asser Press, The Hague, 2017.

[58]   Schabas, 2017, pp. 16–22, see above note 39.

[59]   This term first became popular in the post-colonial period to describe continuing political and economic dependency of African States to their former colonial masters. For more on this and neo-colonialism allegations in relation to the ICC, see, for example, Schuerch, 2017, pp. 2–6, see above note 57; Jean-Baptiste Jeangène Vilmer, "The African Union and the International Criminal Court: Counteracting the Crisis", in *International Affairs*, 2016, vol. 92, no. 6, pp. 1319–42.

[60]   ICC, Situation in Darfur, Sudan, *The Prosecutor v. Omar Hassan Ahmad Al Bashir*, Pre-Trial Chamber, Warrant of Arrest for Omar Hassan Ahmad Al Bashir, 4 March 2009, ICC-02/05-01/09-1 (https://legal-tools.org/doc/814cca). The critique is addressed in detail by Schuerch, 2017, see above note 57. For instance, Schuerch cites the Rwandan President Paul Kagame, who commented that:

>   With ICC all the injustices of the past including colonialism, imperialism, keep coming back in different forms. They control you. As long as you are poor, weak there is always some rope to hang you. The ICC is made for Africans and poor countries.

A statement found in David Kezio-Musoke, "Kagame tells why he is against ICC charging Bashir", *Daily Nation*, 3 August 2008 (available on its web site). Similarly, Mahmood Mamdani, a respected Ugandan scholar of anthropology and political science has described the ICC as "a Western Court to try African crimes against humanity" whose 'responsibility to protect' is being turned into an assertion of neocolonial domination, see Mahmood Mamdani, "Darfur, ICC and the new humanitarian order", *Pambazuka News*, 17 September 2008 (available on its web site). These statements were made after the Court had opened investigations into four situations, all of which were African countries, more specifically concerning the situations in the Democratic Republic of Congo (ICC, The Office of the Prosecutor of the International Criminal Court Opens its First Investigation", 23 June 2004, ICC-OTP-20040623-59 (https://legal-tools.org/doc/b68535)); Northern Uganda (ICC, "Prosecutor of the International Criminal Court Opens an Investigation into Northern Uganda", 29 July 2004, ICC-OTP-20040729-65 (https://legal-tools.org/doc/cfe941)); Central African Republic (ICC, "Prosecutor Opens Investigation in the Central African Republic", 22 May 2007, ICC-OTP-20070522-220 (https://legal-tools.org/doc/7c1d44));

provided the Court's dependency on State co-operation to investigate and prosecute suspects.[61] Despite the general obligations of State parties to co-operate fully with the Court,[62] there is a risk of non-co-operation[63] resulting in difficulties with executing arrest warrants,[64] seizing evidentiary material,[65] and so on, sometimes even to the extent that the prospects of conducting a proper investigation seem very low.[66] The described context,

---

and Darfur, Sudan (ICC, "The Prosecutor of the ICC Opens Investigation in Darfur", 6 June 2005, ICC-OTP-0606-104 (https://legal-tools.org/doc/99180f)).

[61] As pointed out by La Haye, the lack of own enforcement agencies has the overall effect that the Court is dependent on national authorities to, for example, execute arrest warrants, to seize evidentiary material or to compel witnesses to give testimony, Eve La Haye, *War Crimes in Internal Armed Conflicts*, Cambridge University Press, Cambridge, 2008, p. 349.

[62] ICC Statute, Articles 86, 87, 89, 93, see above note 8.

[63] As well as documented situations of non-co-operation, for example, in Sudan, see OTP, "Statement of the Prosecutor of the International Criminal Court, Fatou Bensouda, to the United Nations Security Council on the situation in Darfur, the Sudan, pursuant to UNSCR 1593 (2005)", 13 December 2012, para. 7 (https://legal-tools.org/doc/rzcsx6). In 2012, a report from the Court showed overall compliance rates of 72 per cent, see Report of the International Criminal Court: Note by the Secretary-General, UN Doc. A/67/308, 14 August 2012, para. 9 (https://legal-tools.org/doc/f0ahnn).

[64] See, for example, Robert Cryer, Håkan Friman, Darryl Robinson and Elizabeth Wilmshurst, *An Introduction to International Criminal Law and Procedure*, Cambridge University Press, Cambridge, 2014, pp. 450–51. These authors perceive of the absence of any coercive means (although referral to the Assembly of States Parties or the Security Council is possible) as particularly worrying since this will leave the Court toothless if the State party where the internal conflict took place does not co-operate (through, for example, military or police forces) and the Security Council chooses to not take any coercive measures. They also point out that evidence obtained in contravention of the Statute or internationally recognised human rights may be declared inadmissible, which applies also to items seized by national authorities or international peacekeepers.

[65] See, for example, La Haye, 2008, p. 349, see above note 61.

[66] This is explicit in ICC, Situation in the Islamic Republic of Afghanistan, Pre-Trial Chamber, Decision Pursuant to Article 15 of the Rome Statute on the Authorisation of an Investigation into the Situation in the Islamic Republic of Afghanistan, 12 April 2019, ICC-02/17-33 (https://legal-tools.org/doc/2fb1f4). In its determination on the interests of justice of such investigation, the Chamber states that it is "extremely difficult to gauge the prospects of securing meaningful cooperation from relevant authorities" (*ibid.*, para. 94), that "[…] suffice it to say that nothing in the present conjuncture gives any reason to believe such cooperation can be taken for granted" (*ibid.*) and that the investigation "[…] far from honouring the victims' wishes and aspiration that justice be done, would result in creating frustration and possibly hostility [*vis-à-vis*] the Court and therefore negatively impact its very ability to pursue credibly the objective it was created to serve" (*ibid.*, para. 96). In popular media this decision has been linked to a US refusal to give the Court's staff the necessary visas, see, for example, Marlise Simons, Rick Gladstone and Carol Rosenberg,

combined with the explicit investment of investigative and prosecutorial efforts and resources into a certain line of inquiry, are relevant for the risk of confirmation bias primarily for two reasons.

Firstly, having to justify a view publicly, or even anticipating having to justify that view, increases commitment to that view.[67] This, in turn increases *defence motivation*, that is, the desire to defend one's existing beliefs, behaviours, and so on, rather than *accuracy motivation*, the desire to form accurate appraisals of stimuli.[68] This distinction between how people strive to *feel validated*, rather than to *be correct*, is crucial, especially since the distinction is not necessarily represented in the consciousness of individual decision makers.[69] More specifically, defence motivation is a strategy to relieve or avoid discomfort stemming from the presence of hypothesis inconsistent information (cognitive dissonance).[70] This discomfort can arise from the mere presence of cognitive conflict[71] like a perceived self-threat stemming from a fear that one is poorly informed.[72]

"Hague Court Abandons Afghanistan War Crimes Inquiry", *The New York Times*, 2019 (available on its web site).

[67] Hart, Albarracín, Eagly, Brechan, Lindberg and Merrill, 2009, pp. 555–88, see above note 3.

[68] *Ibid.*, p. 557.

[69] The distinction was made in a meta-analysis comprising 67 reports, which contained 91 studies incorporating 300 statistically independent groups with a total of just under 8,000 participants, see *ibid.*, p. 559.

[70] The theory of cognitive dissonance was first presented by Leon Festinger in 1957, see Leon Festinger, *A Theory of Cognitive Dissonance*, Stanford University Press, Stanford, 1957. Since then, the theory has gained substantial support and become one of the most influential and extensively studied theories in, for example, social psychology. For more on this, see, for example, Roope Oskari Kaaronen, "A Theory of Predictive Dissonance: Predictive Processing Presents a New Take on Cognitive Dissonance", in *Frontiers in Psychology*, 2018, vol. 9, pp. 1–15.

[71] Jean-Léon Beauvois and Robert-Vincent Joule, *A Radical Dissonance Theory*, Taylor and Francis Group, Bristol, 1996; Eddie Harmon-Jones, "Cognitive Dissonance and Experienced Negative Affect: Evidence that Dissonance Increases Experienced Negative Affect Even in the Absence of Aversive Consequences", in *Personality and Social Psychology Bulletin*, 2000, vol. 26, no. 12, pp. 1490–501; Eddie Harmon-Jones, Jack W. Brehm, Jeff Greenberg, Linda Simon and David E. Nelson, "Evidence that the Production of Aversive Consequences is not Necessary to Create Cognitive Dissonance", in *Journal of Personality and Social Psychology*, 1996, vol. 70, no. 1, pp. 5–16.

[72] Elliott Aronson, "Dissonance Theory: Progress and Problems", in Robert P. Abelson, Elliott Aronson, William J. McGuire, Theodore M. Newcomb, Milton J. Rosenberg and Percy H. Tannenbaum (eds.), *Theory of Cognitive Consistency: A Sourcebook*, Rand McNally, Chicago, 1968, pp. 5–27; Anthony, G. Greenwald and David L. Ronis, "Twenty

Thus, experiencing or anticipating cognitive dissonance motivates people to defend themselves by seeking more hypothesis-consistent than hypothesis-inconsistent information.

In investigations into core international crimes, this is likely to be manifested in the search for linkage evidence, as linking the crime to the alleged perpetrator is often more determinative for the outcome of the case than crime-based evidence which may be less disputed at trial.[73] The crimes in question are usually quite blatant due to their massive scale.[74] Hence, linkage issues and theories of liability such as superior and command responsibility, and aiding and abetting as a form of complicity in crime,[75] may be important outlets for confirmation bias. Thus, it is crucial that hierarchical structures are dealt with as the hypotheses they are.[76] Hierarchical structures are rarely well-defined and meticulously documented, but instead vague and complex, for example, because there are differences between formal and informal leaderships, responsibilities may be shared horizontally and vary from time to time.[77] As such, hierarchical

---

Years of Cognitive Dissonance: Case Study of the Evolution of a Theory", in *Psychological Review*, 1978, vol. 85, no. 1, pp. 53–57; Barry R. Schlenker, "Self-Presentation", in Mark R. Leary and June Price Tangney (eds.), *Handbook of Self and Identity*, The Guilford Press, New York, 2003, pp. 492–518; Claude M. Steele, "The Psychology of Self-affirmation: Sustaining the Integrity of the Self", in Berkowitz (ed.), *Advances in Experimental Social Psychology*, Academic Press, San Diego, 1988, pp. 261–302.

[73] Elinor Fry, "The Nature of International Crimes and Evidentiary Challenges", in *Pluralism in International Criminal Law*, Oxford University Press, Oxford, 2014, p. 264; Mark Klamberg, *Evidence in International Criminal Procedure: Confronting Legal Gaps and the Reconstruction of Disputed Events*, Stockholm University Press, Stockholm, 2012, p. 97. This can also be related to the acknowledgement that some investigations had been insufficiently thorough, as expressed by that the objective of conducting 'focused investigations' in the OTP's Strategic Plan was replaced by a principle of 'in-depth, open-ended investigations while maintaining focus' when a new strategic plan for 2012–15 was adopted, see the report Guénaël Mettraux, Shireen Avis Fisher, Dermot Groome, Alex Whiting, Gabrielle McIntyre, Jérôme de Hemptinne and Göran Sluiter, *Expert Initiative on Promoting Effectiveness at the International Criminal Court*, December 2014, p. 51 (https://legal-tools.org/doc/3dae90).

[74] Xabier Agirre Aranburu, "Methodology for the Criminal Investigation of International Crimes", in Alette Smeulers (ed.), *Collective Violence and International Criminal Justice*, Intersentia, Antwerp, 2010, p. 353.

[75] Fry, 2014, pp. 264–65, see above note 73.

[76] Agirre Aranburu, 2010, p. 234, see above note 10.

[77] *Ibid.*

structures do not necessarily fit theoretical notions.[78] A prediction from dissonance theory is that, when faced with such complex information, decision makers tend to interpret it in a hypothesis-consistent way as to avoid cognitive dissonance. It deserves to be said again, this 'goal-oriented' interpretation happens more or less subconsciously. As such, the warning from an ICC officer in 2010 to "beware of the risk of confirmation bias in suspect-driven investigations and take measures to control it",[79] should be emphasised.

Secondly, the manifest investment of time, efforts and resources into a specific line of investigation (or suspect), comes with the associated risk of so-called *escalation of commitment* and the *sunk cost effect*, tendencies that overlap and fuel confirmation bias.[80] Escalation of commitment is a tendency to adhere to a prior course of action, even when there are indications that the previous action was wrong.[81] This means that people prefer retroactive information that speaks to the decision already made, rather than prospective information about the decision to be made and that they interpret incoming information in a distorted manner that serves to justify previous decisions.[82] Similarly, the sunk cost effect refers to a tendency to continue an investment or take an action after a previous investment in money, effort or time has been made, even though the in-

---

[78]   *Ibid.*, pp. 228–34.

[79]   *Ibid.*, p. 234.

[80]   This relationship is discussed more closely in Hart, Albarracín, Eagly, Brechan, Lindberg and Merrill, 2009, p. 558, see above note 3; Lidén, 2018, pp. 106–08, see above note 2.

[81]   This was first described by Staw in 1976, see Barry M. Staw, "Knee-Deep in the Big Muddy: A Study of Escalating Commitment to a Chosen Course of Action", in *Organizational Behavior and Human Performance*, 1976, vol. 16, no. 1, pp. 27–44. The tendency has been noted, for example, in managers rating of employees they originally hired in which they tended to inflate the ratings of the employees effectiveness, likelihood of improvement and potential for promotion, see David F. Schoorman, "Escalation Bias in Performance Appraisals: An Unintended Consequence of Supervisor Participation in Hiring Decisions", in *Journal of Applied Psychology*, 1988, vol. 73, no. 1, pp. 58–62. Another example is that bank managers tend to be committed to bad loans that they themselves had approved, see Barry M. Staw, Sigal G. Barsade and Kenneth W. Koput, "Escalation at the Credit Window: A Longitudinal Study of Bank Executives' Recognition and Write-Off Problem Loans", in *Journal of Applied Psychology*, 1997, vol. 82, no. 1, pp. 130–42.

[82]   Jesse D. Beeler and James E. Hunton, "The Influence of Compensation Method and Disclosure Level on Information Search Strategy and Escalation of Commitment", in *Journal of Behavioral Decision Making*, 1997, vol. 10, no. 2, pp. 77–91.

---

vestment has higher future costs than benefits.[83] It has also been described as "throwing good money after bad".[84] The risk of such tendencies should be seen in the light of the usually very high costs of investigations into core international crimes, which have not only been widely acknowledged but also often criticised.[85] Hence, investing in a certain line of inquiry is likely to generate a will for the investment to become successful, perhaps primarily defined by whether it results in a conviction or not, because if not, then the investment may be even more criticised.[86]

Taken together, these factors may result in a suspect-driven investigation and more specifically, that the investigation only or primarily focuses on finding hypothesis-consistent evidence. It should also be noted that the discussion so far has examined the potential consequences of identifying a 'suspect', whereas the term 'target' is sometimes used in investigations of core international crimes.[87] One could argue that this is a purely terminological difference. However, this is unlikely to be the case as the term 'target' is not only more assertive in relation to an individual's guilt, but also, to a greater extent than the term 'suspect', it implies that the individual in question is dangerous and/or blameworthy. Therefore, it seems reasonable to expect that the identification of a 'target', can, potentially, triggers an even more hypothesis-confirming mindset.

---

[83] This term was first used by Arkes and Blumer in 1985. See, for example, Hal R. Arkes and Catherine Blumer, "The Psychology of Sunk Cost", in *Organizational Behavior and Human Decision Processes*, 1985, vol. 35, no. 1, pp. 125–40; Elmer Anita Thames, "The Sunk Cost Effect: The Importance of Context", in *Journal of Social Behavior and Personality*, 1996, vol. 11, no. 4, pp. 817–26.

[84] Hal R. Arkes, "The Psychology of Waste", in *Journal of Behavioral Decision Making*, 1996, vol. 9, no. 3, p. 124.

[85] For more on this topic see for example, Osvaldo Zavala, "The Budgetary Efficiency of the International Criminal Court", in *International Criminal Law Review*, 2018, vol. 18, no. 3, pp. 461–88; Jonathan O'Donohue, "Financing the International Criminal Court", in *International Criminal Law Review*, 2013, vol. 13, no. 1, pp. 269–96.

[86] This can be related to criticism according to which the costs of the ICC are disproportionate in relation to its conviction rates, see for example, Tom Mbakwe, "ICC gets first conviction after 10 years in existence", *New African*, 1 April 2012 (available on its web site); David Davenport, "International Criminal Court: 12 years, $ 1 Billion, 2 Convictions", *Forbes*, 12 March 2014 (available on its web site).

[87] See International Criminal Tribunal for the Former Yugoslavia ('ICTY'), OTP Charging and Indictment Guidelines, sect. 3, which deals with 'selection of targets', including, for example, 'personal characteristics of the target', sect. 3.1.

Apart from that 'target' identification is likely to generate a stronger guilt hypothesis and therefore a greater risk of confirmation bias, an added effect can also be predicted from research into the so-called *framing effect*[88] as well as the *anchoring effect*.[89] The framing effect is an effect of how a decision problem is framed, that is, presented, labelled or described.[90] For instance, frames presented by the media seem to effect individuals' attitudes about crime as well as their support for the criminal justice system.[91] Furthermore, the anchoring effect is an effect of an initial piece of information, an anchor, upon which decision makers seem to rely heavily as they only make small adjustments in relation to the introduced anchor.[92] To exemplify, judges' sentencing decisions seem to be influ-

---

[88] Amos Tversky and Daniel Kahneman, "The Framing of Decisions and the Psychology of Choice", in *Science*, 1981, vol. 211, no. 4,481, pp. 453–58

[89] Amos Tversky and Daniel Kahneman, "Judgment under Uncertainty: Heuristics and Biases", in *Science*, 1974, vol. 185, no. 4157, pp. 1124–30.

[90] Tversky and Kahneman, 1981, pp. 453–58, see above note 88. Most of this research has compared decision problems in which alternatives are framed either as potential gains or losses. However, there is also research looking into the effect of frames in, for example, negotiations. See YAO Shuguang, WANG Yanhua, PENG Jiaxi and SONG Lei, "The Framing Effect of Negation Frames", in *Journal of Risk Research*, 2018, vol. 21, no. 6, pp. 800–08, and frames introduced by the media, see Wayne R. Dunham, "Framing the Right Suspects: Measuring Media Bias", in *Journal of Media Economics*, 2013, vol. 26, no. 3, pp. 122–47. Also, gradually more research is looking into situational and individual factors influencing the susceptibility to framing effects, see, for example, Paul M. Miller and Nancy S. Fagley, "The Effects of Framing, Problem Variations, and Providing Rationale on Choice", in *Personality and Social Psychology Bulletin*, 1991, vol. 17, no. 5, pp. 517–22; Takemura Kazuhisa, "The Effect of Decision Frame and Decision Justification on Risky Choice", in *Japanese Psychological Research*, 1993, vol. 35, no. 1, pp. 36–40; Shoshana Shiloh, Efrat Salton and Dana Sharabi, "Individual Differences in Rational and Intuitive Thinking Styles as Predictors of Heuristic Reponses and Framing Effects", in *Personality and Individual Differences*, 2002, vol. 32, no. 3, pp. 415–29.

[91] Lisa A. Kort-Butler and Patrick Habecker, "Framing and Cultivating the Story of Crime: The Effects of Media Use, Victimization, and Social Networks on Attitudes About Crime", in *Criminal Justice Review*, 2018, vol. 43, no. 2, pp. 127–46.

[92] Tversky and Kahneman, 1974, pp. 1124–30, see above note 89. Tversky and Kahneman asked participants about the percentage of African nations in the UN. In a first comparative question, participants indicated whether the percentage was higher or lower than an arbitrary number (the anchor) that had been determined by spinning a wheel of fortune (showing 10 per cent or 65 per cent). In a subsequent absolute anchoring question, participants gave their best estimate of this percentage. Results showed that the absolute judgments were assimilated to the explicitly random anchor values. For more on this, see, for example, Birte Englich, "Blind or Biased? Justitia's Susceptibility to Anchoring Effects in the Courtroom Based on Given Numerical Representations", in *Law and Policy*, 2006, vol. 28, no. 4, pp. 497–514.

---

enced by demands (anchors) that are not only non-binding[93] but also completely irrelevant and determined at random, like the toss of a dice.[94] Similar anchors have been found in relation to, for example, damage awards.[95] Thus, this research implies that the more specific presentation of an individual as a 'suspect' or a 'target' can set different frames for the investigation and also, to different degrees, anchor the investigators' mindsets to the guilty hypothesis. Presumably, such stronger tendencies can be further fuelled if also other assertive language apart from 'target' is used. For instance, when describing crimes and responsibilities, these may be presented as established facts ('the crimes committed', 'target Y was responsible for') rather than allegations under investigation ('the alleged crimes', 'according to source X, target Y was responsible for'). Yet, it should be noted that neither the potential differences between using the terms 'target' and 'suspect' nor the effect of using assertive language in relation to crimes and responsibilities have been systematically and empirically evaluated.[96] This appears to be an important task for future re-

---

[93] See, for example, Birte Englich and Thomas Mussweiler, "Sentencing Under Uncertainty: Anchoring Effects in the Courtroom", in *Journal of Applied Social Psychology*, 2001, vol. 31, vol. 7, pp. 1535–51; Birte Englich, Thomas Mussweiler and Fritz Strack, "The Last Word in Court – A Hidden Disadvantage for the Defense", in *Law and Human Behavior*, 2005, vol. 29, no. 6, pp. 705–22. These studies used real judges, prosecutors or junior lawyers as participants. Also, analyses of actual court files show similar data patterns, see for example, Eugenio Garrido Martin and Carmen Herrero Alonso, "Influence of the Prosecutor's Plea on the Judge's Sentencing in Sexual Crimes: Hypothesis of the Theory of Anchoring by Tversky and Kahneman", in Santiago Redondo, Vicente Garrido and Jorge Perez (eds.), in *Advances in Psychology and Law: International Contributions*, Walter de Gruyter, Berlin, 1997.

[94] Birte Englich, Thomas Mussweiler and Fritz Strack, "Playing Dice with Criminal Sentences: The Influence of Irrelevant Anchors on Experts' Judicial Decision Making", in *Personality and Social Psychology Bulletin*, 2006, vol. 32, no. 2, pp. 188–200.

[95] See, for example. Reid Hastie, David A. Schkade and John W. Payne, "Juror Judgments in Civil Cases: Effects of Plaintiff's Requests and Plaintiff's Identity on Punitive Damage Awards", in *Law and Human Behavior*, 1999, vol. 23, no. 5, pp. 445–70; John Malouff and Nicola S. Schutte, "Shaping Juror Attitudes: Effects of Requesting Different Damage Amounts in Personal Injury Trials", in *Journal of Social Psychology*, 1989, vol. 129, no. 4, pp. 491–97.

[96] However, several scholars have noted that language is an important part, for example, in constructing blame. See James Murphy, *The Discursive Construction of Blame: the Language of Public Inquiries*, Palgrave Macmillan, London, 2019; Lawrence M. Solan and Peter M. Tiersma, *Speaking of Crime: The Language of Criminal Justice*, University of Chicago Press, Chicago, 2005; Mason Marianne, "The 'Preparatory' and 'Argumentation' Stages of Police Interrogation: A Linguistic Analysis of a Criminal Investigation", in *Language and Communication*, 2016, vol. 48, pp. 79–87. There is also research into the effect

search, as it would help answering whether it is motivated to speak not only of suspect-driven investigations but also of *target-driven investigations*, and the potentially more specific and/or larger problems associated with the latter type of investigation.

Whereas the research on suspect-driven investigations taps in well with the search component of confirmation bias, it is largely silent about another equally, or sometimes even more important component, namely the evaluative component. Thus, the next section deals with how hypotheses can make also the evaluation of evidence one-sided.

7.2.2. Asymmetrical Scepticism

> Day after day, document by document, witness after witness, the 'Prosecutor's case' has been revealed and exposed as a fragile, implausible theorem relying on shaky and doubtful bases, inspired by a Manichean and simplistic narrative of an Ivory Coast depicted as a 'polarised' society [...] a caricatured 'one-sided' narrative [...].[97]

An effective mechanism that enables criminal investigators to maintain their hypothesis, even in the face of hypothesis inconsistent information, is so-called *asymmetrical scepticism*.[98] As implied by the terminology, this refers to how decision makers tend to uncritically approve of hypoth-

---

of so-called 'distorted terminology' on closure of investigations into alleged torture and inhuman treatment, see Elizabeth Stubbins Bates, "Distorted Terminology: The UK's Closure of Investigations into Alleged Torture and Inhuman Treatment in Iraq", in *International and Comparative Law Quarterly*, 2019, vol. 68, no. 3, pp. 719–39.

[97] Judge Cuno Tarfusser describing his observations in the Courtroom. See ICC, Situation in Côte d'Ivoire, *The Prosecutor v. Laurent Gbagbo and Charles Blé Goudé*, Trial Chamber, Opinion of Judge Cuno Tarfusser, 16 July 2019, ICC-02/11-01/15-1263-AnxA, para. 12 ('Opinion of Judge Cuno Tarfusser') (https://legal-tools.org/doc/f6c6f3).

[98] Asymmetrical scepticism has been documented in a range of settings but in the legal context the Swedish researchers Ask and Granhag were the first to use it in 2005. See, for example, Karl Ask and Pär-Anders Granhag, "Motivational Bias in Criminal Investigators Judgments of Witness Reliability", in *Journal of Applied Social Psychology*, 2007, vol. 37, no. 3, pp. 561–91. Marksteiner and colleagues summarise research examining investigators' cognitive processing of criminal evidence, see Tamara Marksteiner, Karl Ask, Marc-André Reinhard and Pär-Anders Granhag, "Asymmetrical Scepticism Towards Criminal Evidence: The Role of Goal- and Belief-Consistency", in *Applied Cognitive Psychology*, 2011, vol. 25, no. 4, pp. 541–47. For a review of this research see for example, Karl Ask and Laurence Alison, "Investigators' Decision Making", in Pär-Anders Granhag (ed.), *Forensic Psychology in Context: Nordic and International Perspectives*, Cullompton, Willan, 2010, pp. 35–55.

---

esis-consistent information, whereas they critically scrutinise hypothesis inconsistent information.[99] This happens even though the only difference between the pieces of information is their content (implications) rather than differences when it comes to, for example, source reliability or other factors that may, objectively, influence whether and to what extent the information should be trusted. In investigations where asymmetrical scepticism is at play, the result can be one-sided narratives formed on the basis of insufficient evidence, similar to how Judge Tarfusser, in his concurring opinion, described the narrative presented by the prosecution in the ICC case of *The Prosecutor v. Laurent Gbagbo and Charles Blé Goudé*.[100] In its acquittal, the majority also presented criticism in relation to this narrative,[101] although to a lesser extent, while Judge Herrera Carbuccia considered the evidence sufficient for a conviction.[102] As manifested by the Prosecutor's notice of appeal, the OTP disagrees with the majority on issues of substance and procedure and the case is currently in the appeal phase.[103]

To illustrate the characteristics of asymmetrical scepticism as well as the research methodology used to study it, an example study is described in the following.[104] Criminal investigators were presented with a case vignette regarding a murder. The vignette indicated a certain female perpetrator but also opened up for the possibility of a male perpetrator (as implied by the statement of the suspected female perpetrator). The inves-

---

[99] Ask and Granhag, 2005, pp. 561–591, see above note 98.

[100] Opinion of Judge Cuno Tarfusser, para. 12, see above note 97.

[101] See ICC, Situation in the Republic of Côte d'Ivoire, *The Prosecutor v. Laurent Gbagbo and Charles Blé Goudé*, Trial Chamber, Reasons for oral decision of 15 January 2019 on the Requête de la Défense de Laurent Gbagbo afin qu'un jugement d'acquittement portant sur toutes les charges soit prononcé en faveur de Laurent Gbagbo et que sa mise en liberté immédiate soit ordonnée, and on the Blé Goudé Defence no case to answer motion, 16 July 2019, ICC-02/11-01/15-1263 (https://legal-tools.org/doc/440017).

[102] ICC, Situation in the Republic of Côte d'Ivoire, *The Prosecutor v. Laurent Gbagbo and Charles Blé Goudé*, Trial Chamber, Dissenting Opinion of Judge Herrera Carbuccia, 10 December 2018, ICC-02/11-01/15-1229-Anx (https://legal-tools.org/doc/39a71d).

[103] See ICC, Situation in the Republic of Côte d'Ivoire, *The Prosecutor v. Laurent Gbagbo and Charles Blé Goudé*, Appeals Chamber, Corrected version of "Prosecution Notice of Appeal", 16 September 2019, ICC-02/11-01/15-1270 (https://legal-tools.org/doc/2d15e0). See also Appeals Chamber, Decision on the Prosecutor's Request for Time Extension for the Notice of Appeal and the Appeal Brief, 19 July 2019, ICC-02/11-01/15-1268 (https://legal-tools.org/doc/949945).

[104] Ask and Granhag, 2005, pp. 561–91, see above note 98.

tigators were then informed about a witness who, at the time of the incident, had heard two loud voices from the apartment in which the female murder victim had been found. Without the investigators' knowledge, they had been divided into two groups, one which received the *incriminating* version of the witness testimony, stating that the loud voices came from two females, and the other which received the *exonerating* version, stating that the loud voices came from one female and one male. Then, investigators were asked to rate how reliable and credible the witness was, as well as how favourable the background and witnessing conditions were. Even though all these factors were exactly the same for both groups, the investigators who received the incriminating version perceived of the witness as significantly more reliable and credible and also thought that the background and witnessing conditions were more favourable.

There is no doubt that accurate assessments of witness reliability and credibility, both for insider witnesses and other witnesses, are often crucial in investigations of core international crimes,[105] and the most recent example of this is the ICC case of *The Prosecutor v. Bosco Ntaganda*.[106] Thus, the risk of asymmetrical scepticism in these assessments

---

[105] For an empirical study on the assessments of insider witnesses specifically, see Gabriele Chlevickaite and Barbora Hola, "Empirical Study of Insider Witnesses' Assessments at the International Criminal Court", in *International Criminal Law Review*, 2016, vol. 16, no. 4, pp. 673–702.

[106] ICC, Situation in The Democratic Republic of Congo, *The Prosecutor v. Bosco Ntaganda*, Trial Chamber, Judgment, 8 July 2019, ICC-01/04-02/06-2359 (https://legal-tools.org/doc/ 80578a). In this case 102 witnesses were called by the prosecution, the defence and on behalf of the victims (as well as the victims who testified as witnesses), regarding the situation in the Democratic Republic of the Congo. However, also earlier cases highlight the need for accurate assessment of witness credibility. See, for example, Situation in the Central African Republic, *The Prosecutor v. Jean-Pierre Bemba Gombo, Aimé Kilolo Musamba, Jean-Jacques Mangenda Kabongo, Fidèle Babala Wandu and Narcisse Arido*, ICC-01/05-01/13. On 19 October 2016, Trial Chamber VII found the five accused guilty of various offences against the administration of justice related to the false testimonies of defence witnesses in another case before the ICC: ICC, Situation in the Central African Republic, *The Prosecutor v. Jean-Pierre Bemba Gombo, Aimé Kilolo Musamba, Jean-Jacques Mangenda Kabongo, Fidèle Babala Wandu and Narcisse Arido*, Trial Chamber, Judgment pursuant to Article 74 of the Statute, 19 October 2016, ICC-01/05-01/13-1989-Red (https://legal-tools.org/doc/fe0ce4). On 8 March 2018, the Appeals Chamber rejected the appeals submitted by the five accused against their conviction. It confirmed the convictions in respect of most of the charges. However, it acquitted Mr. Bemba, Mr. Kilolo and Mr. Mangenda of the charge of presenting evidence that a party knows is false or forged (ICC Statute, Article 70(1)(b), finding that this provision only applies to the presentation of documentary evidence, not to the calling of witnesses, as in the case at hand, see above

---

should be noted. More specifically, this constitutes a risk that criteria used for reliability and credibility assessments are differently applied depending on whether the witness statement is consistent or inconsistent with a case hypothesis. For a hypothesis-consistent witness statement, factors such as the time that has passed since the incident, whether the witness has suffered trauma, the relationship to the accused, possible bias against the accused and motives for telling the truth or lying[107] would be perceived as less problematic, compared to a hypothesis inconsistent witness statement.[108] Just like in the example study outlined above, this could happen even if the hypothesis-consistent and inconsistent statements were identical save for, for example, whom the witness identified as the perpetrator.

The example study, together with replications in other legal settings[109] and for other types of assessments,[110] suggest that asymmetrical scepticism is more pronounced in relation to so-called *elastic* evidence, that is, evidence in relation to which there is a wide range of possible subjective interpretations that can be justified.[111] For instance, witness evi-

---

note 8). The convictions and acquittals in relation to the accused are now final, see ICC, Situation in the Central African Republic, *The Prosecutor v. Jean-Pierre Bemba Gombo, Aimé Kilolo Musamba, Jean-Jacques Mangenda Kabongo, Fidèle Babala Wandu and Narcisse Arido*, Case Information Sheet, September 2018, ICC-PIDS-CIS-CAR-02-014/18_Eng (https://legal-tools.org/doc/33n2us).

[107] These factors were applied in for example, ICC, Situation in the Democratic Republic of Congo, *The Prosecutor v. Thomas Lubanga Dyilo*, Trial Chamber, Judgment pursuant to Article 74 of the Statute, 14 March 2012, ICC-01/04-01/06-2842, para. 106 (https://legal-tools.org/doc/677866); ICC, Situation in the Central African Republic, *The Prosecutor v. Jean Pierre Bemba Gombo*, Trial Chamber, Judgement pursuant to Article 74 of the Statute, 21 March 2016, ICC-01/05-01/08-3343, paras. 202, 229 (https://legal-tools.org/doc/edb0cf); ICC, Situation in the Democratic Republic of Congo, *The Prosecutor v. Germain Katanga*, Trial Chamber, Judgment pursuant to Article 74 of the Statute, ICC-01/04-01/07-3436-tENG, 7 March 2014, para. 85 (https://legal-tools.org/doc/f74b4f); ICC, Situation in the Democratic Republic of Congo, *The Prosecutor v. Mathieu Ngudjolo Chui*, Trial Chamber, Judgment pursuant to Article 74 of the Court, 18 December 2012, ICC-01/04-02/12-3-tENG, para. 51 (https://legal-tools.org/doc/2c2cde).

[108] What more specific criteria are being used to assess reliability and credibility can of course vary between investigation and trial phases.

[109] Rassin, Eerland and Kuijpers, 2010, pp. 231–46, see above note 30.

[110] Lauren Alison, Matthew Smith and Keith Morgan, "Interpreting the Accuracy of Offender Profiles", in *Psychology, Crime and Law*, 2003, vol. 9, no. 2, pp. 185–95.

[111] Karl Ask, Anna Rebelius and Pär-Anders Granhag, "The 'Elasticity' of Criminal Evidence: A Moderator of Investigator Bias", in *Applied Cognitive Psychology*, 2008, vol. 22, no. 9, pp. 1245–59. See also Karl Ask, Marc-Andre Reinhard, Tamara Marksteiner and Pär-

dence is on average more elastic than DNA evidence. However, it can be noted that also DNA evidence and other types of forensic evidence, regardless of their scientific foundation, do have relatively strong elastic elements when it comes to the formulation of criminal responsibility (for example, because DNA on a crime scene can have many other explanations than a criminal act).

Thus, apart from witness evidence, the research regarding asymmetrical scepticism may also have implications for other types of evidence, which are assessed after the formulation of a case hypothesis. Clearly, re-evaluating the case hypothesis in the light of new evidence is an important part of the investigation cycle.[112] However, if decision makers are asymmetrically sceptical in relation to evidence that contradicts the case hypothesis, this would make them unwilling to make the necessary updates. Certainly, not any single piece of hypothesis inconsistent evidence will justify that a case hypothesis is changed. This is in line with reactions to anomalous data in scientific research, where the usual strategy is to first challenge the data (for example, by explaining it with methodological flaws) because it contradicts lots of other data. This approach may be rational at the outset, but can soon become irrational if theories are maintained even in the face of accumulated anomalous data.

Thus, in line with Kuhn's suggestion, when a scientist faces anomalies, that is, evidence that are inconsistent with a paradigm (basic beliefs about entities in the world), the initial reaction is not to abandon the paradigm but rather to view the anomalies as problems to be solved or somehow accommodate within the paradigm.[113] It is only when anomalies accumulate over time that they may come to be seen as counter-instances, which in the long run may lead to a paradigm shift. In scientific research, finding more anomalous data, which may eventually lead to a 'paradigm shift', is not necessarily dependent on the workings of one single individual or group of individuals, as virtually any researcher or group of re-

---

Anders Granhag, "Elasticity in Evaluations of Criminal Evidence: Exploring the Role of Cognitive Dissonance", in *Legal and Criminological Psychology*, 2011, vol. 16, no. 2, pp. 289–306; Marksteiner, Ask, Reinhard and Granhag, 2011, pp. 541–47, see above note 98.

[112] Markus Eikel, "Nature and Use of Investigation Plans at the International Criminal Court", CILRAP Film, New Delhi, 23 February 2019 (https://www.cilrap.org/cilrap-film/190223-eikel/).

[113] Thomas S. Kuhn, *The Structure of Scientific Revolutions*, University of Chicago Press, Chicago, 1962.

---

searchers may decide to conduct studies with the potential of obtaining such data.[114] Yet, if an inquiry leader or a group of criminal investigators decide that the anomalous data does not render any further inquiry necessary, it is unlikely that someone else will. The exception from this is if the defence has both a procedural right to insight into the investigation and sufficient resources to undertake its own investigation. In this regard it can be noted that many defence counsels have commented that:

> [W]hatever their legal background and professional experience, they are often insufficiently equipped to meet the challenges posed by Defence investigations, in both practical and ethical terms.[115]

This, in turn, may mean that not enough anomalous data will be presented to justify an update of the case hypothesis, even if such anomalous data exists. In line with this, and the prosecutor's duty to investigate incriminating and exonerating circumstances equally, it seems appropriate to set the threshold for changing case hypotheses in criminal investigations lower than a 'paradigm shift'. Even if it is unreasonable to change case hypothesis on the basis of any hypothesis inconsistent evidence, it is vital that such evidence is evaluated in a balanced manner as this may result in the allocation of investigative resources into another or supplementary line of inquiry. This can, in due time, give reason to update (or maintain) the original case hypothesis. Apart from promoting accuracy, this is also in the interest of procedural fairness. Any evidence discovered

---

[114] However, since scientific journals are sometimes unwilling to publish null results, it is not certain that such anomalous data will be communicated to other researchers, which highlights another potential type of bias. For more on this topic see, for example, Robert Rosenthal, "The 'File Drawer Problem' and Tolerance for Null Results", in *Psychological Bulletin*, 1979, vol. 86, no. 3, pp. 638–41; Hannah Rothstein, Alexander J. Sutton and Michael Borenstein, *Publication Bias in Meta-Analysis*, Wiley, 2005, pp. 1–7; Lidén, 2018, p. 63, see above note 2.

[115] Defence Office of STL (ed.), *Practitioner's Handbook on Defence Investigations in International Criminal Trials*, Leidschendam, 2017, p. 9. A related problem, that suspects of rape have insufficient assistance from legal counsel has been addressed in the documentary "Justice for Sale", by Ilse van Velzen and Femke van Velzen, which deals with struggles for fair trials and due process of law in the Democratic Republic of the Congo. In the documentary, this problem is explained by that 'the struggle against sexual violence' has largely favoured the plaintiffs who, unlike the suspects, do receive adequate legal representation. This is believed to result in rape convictions without concrete evidence, like in the case of the soldier Masamba. For more on this documentary see IFproductions, "Justice for Sale", 2011 (available on its web site).

at a late point in time (which could have been discovered earlier) and which, due to its nature, requires a change of a case theory, can make the defence perceive of the allegations as 'radically altered'[116]. This was the situation in the *Kenyatta* case, where the defence reacted in relation to the large number of witnesses identified only after the confirmation hearing.[117] Thus, there is a reciprocal action between a suspect-driven investigation and asymmetrical scepticism. If investigators primarily search for and find hypothesis-consistent information, this will make any hypothesis inconsistent evidence appear less important and therefore met with more scepticism. If such evidence is met with more scepticism, it is unlikely that alternative lines of inquiries will be carefully examined, with the result that the original case hypothesis is maintained.

Since logical consistency between a hypothesis and evidence does not necessarily exclude the possibility that the evidence can also be consistent, or even more consistent, with other hypotheses, it is difficult or even logically impossible to evaluate a theory in isolation. In any context where there is a limit to the number of hypotheses that are being tested, there will always be some uncertainty.[118] This issue is sometimes referred to as *underdetermination*.[119] In essence, this means that perhaps it is

---

[116] ICC, Situation in the Republic of Kenya, *The Prosecutor v. Francis Kirimi Muthaura and Uhuru Muigai Kenyatta*, Defence, Observations on the Conduct, Extent and Impact of the Prosecution's Investigation and Disclosure on the Defence's Ability to Prepare for Trial, 20 February 2013, ICC-01/09-02/11-655-Corr, para. 11 (https://legal-tools.org/doc/c8c5e9).

[117] Although the Chamber in large part rejected this assertion since the prosecution is not required to rely on the same evidence at trial that it had already during the confirmation process, it nevertheless expressed concern regarding the "substantial volume of new evidence that was gathered by the Prosecution" after confirmation. See ICC, Situation in the Republic of Kenya, *The Prosecutor v. Uhuru Muigai Kenyatta*, Trial Chamber, Decision on Defence Application Pursuant to Article 64(4) and Related Requests, 26 April 2013, ICC-01/09-02/11-728, para. 112 (https://legal-tools.org/doc/da5089). The Chamber also introduced the requirement that all investigations that reasonably could have been completed before confirmation must be and that the Defence will have remedies available in respect to failures to do so. See, *ibid.*, para. 121.

[118] This was pointed out already by Karl Popper who suggested that, logically speaking, confirmation of deductive inferences merely establishes that the hypothesis is not rejected, not that it is confirmed, see Karl Popper, *The Logic of Scientific Discovery*, Hutchinson & Co, Vienna, 1959. In other words, consistency with a hypothesis does not establish the truth of the hypothesis.

[119] Whereas some refer to this as underdetermination, others refer to it as *the fallacy of affirming the consequent*. For more on this see for example, Robert W. Proctor and John E. Ca-

---

equally likely that some other hypothesis or several hypotheses in combination better explain the result. A given body of data (or evidence) can in fact be compatible with an infinite number of theories and therefore be explained in many ways. The acknowledgment of this issue and the fact that it is usually impossible to evaluate all alternative hypotheses, have, in scientific research, resulted in attempts to ensure that a chosen hypothesis explains the evidence better than other propositions, a way of reasoning referred to as *inference to the best explanation* ('IBE').[120] The IBE has clear similarities with the standard of proof beyond reasonable doubt, and the criminal investigation should, preferably, contribute to the testing of alternative hypotheses required for the application of this standard.[121] Importantly, and as implied by the usage of *reasonable* in the standard of proof, this does not entail pure speculation but fair or rational hypotheses. As explained by The ICC Appeals Chamber in the al-Bashir decision (concerning the arrest warrant), the "requiring that the existence of genocidal intent must be the *only* reasonable conclusion amounts to requiring the Prosecutor to disprove any other reasonable conclusions and to eliminate any reasonable doubt".[122] Thus, even though there is no inherent contradiction between working on the basis of a case hypothesis and remaining open to alternative hypotheses, it is crucial to be attentive to the risk that the case hypothesis spell-bounds the investigators without them being aware of it, and thereby also dictates the investigation.

So far, the potential influence of a hypothesis has been discussed in relation to how information is sought and evaluated, on a general level, during criminal investigations. In practice, these general trends will interact with the results of more specific investigative measures, such as foren-

---

paldi, *Why Science Matters: Understanding the Methods of Psychological Research*, Blackwell Publishing, Malden, 2005, pp. 65–66, 122–25.

[120] The IBE is a basic point of scientific reasoning, stemming from Popper, 1959, see above note 118. Since then it has been developed by several authors within theory of science such as Gilbert G. Harman, "The Inference to the Best Explanation", in *The Philosophical Review*, 1965, vol. 74, no. 1, pp. 88–95.

[121] The connection between the IBE and the beyond all reasonable doubt standard has been pointed out by several legal scholars for example, Klamberg, 2011, pp. 2–3, see above note 34; Lidén, 2018, p. 38, see above note 2.

[122] ICC, Situation in Darfur, Sudan, *The Prosecutor v. Omar Hassan Ahmad Al Bashir*, Appeals Chamber, Judgment on the Appeal of the Prosecutor against the "Decision on the Prosecution's Application for a Warrant of Arrest against Omar Hassan Ahmad Al Bashir", 3 February 2010, ICC-02/05-01/09-73, para. 33 (https://legal-tools.org/doc/9ada8e).

sic investigation and analyses, and this interaction is particularly interesting provided that such investigations can also be tainted by case hypotheses.

7.2.3. Specific Investigative Settings

7.2.3.1. Forensic Investigation and Analyses

> Justice will only reach the highest level of effectiveness if it relies on the best scientific evidence.[123]

Although forensic evidence is usually considered the 'gold standard' in criminal cases,[124] a growing body of research illustrates the risk of confirmation bias in the information processing of both crime scene investigators ('CSIs') and forensic analysts. For instance, some studies suggest that a case hypothesis can dictate how a crime scene investigation is conducted and therefore also its results.[125] CSIs who, before entering a mock crime scene where a deceased woman was found, received different kinds of prior information (history of domestic violence or documented suicide risk or no information at all) secured different types and numbers of traces and also made different assessments regarding the most likely scenario.[126] More specifically, CSIs in the respective groups secured evidence and made assessments that were consistent with the prior information they received. For instance, CSIs who received information about a documented suicide risk were more likely to miss that the deceased victim had a hair from another person on her body. Thus, the CSIs ways of working were influenced by their expectations of what they would find. This influence can, in turn, result in that only or primarily evidence which confirms a hypothesis is secured and sent off for forensic analyses, whereas evi-

---

[123] Professor Duarte Nuno Vieira, cited in ICC OTP, "The Scientific Advisory Board of the Office of the Prosecutor holds its 5th Annual Meeting", 8 August 2018, ICC-OTP-20180808-PR1401 (https://legal-tools.org/doc/c6d45e).

[124] See, for example, Michael Lynch, "God's Signature: DNA Profiling, the New Gold Standard in Forensic Science", in *Endeavour*, 2003, vol. 27, no. 2, pp. 93–97.

[125] Claire A.J. van den Eeden, Christianne J. de Poot and Peter J. van Koppen, "Forensic Expectations: Investigating a Crime Scene with Prior Information", in *Science and Justice*, 2016, vol. 56, no. 6, pp. 475–81. See also Claire A.J. van den Eeden, Christianne J. de Poot and Peter J. van Koppen, "From Emergency Call to Crime Scene: Information Transference in the Criminal Investigation", in *Forensic Science Policy and Management: An International Journal*, 2017, vol. 8, nos. 3–4, pp. 79–89.

[126] van den Eeden, de Poot and van Koppen, 2016, pp. 475–81, see above note 125.

dence likely to disconfirm or challenge the hypothesis remains undetected or un-prioritised.

When forensic analysts conduct their examinations, they may have more or less knowledge of what the case hypothesis is and the associated contextual information, for example, what other evidence is available. Research into the so-called *forensic confirmation bias*[127] has highlighted the need to carefully evaluate what information is made available to the analysts. This is because contextual information, for example, that a suspect confessed or was identified by a witness, seems to bias the analysts' judgments so that they are more likely to confirm the conclusion implicated by the contextual information. The forensic confirmation bias has been documented in relation to fingerprint analysis,[128] comparisons of shoe prints,[129] bite marks,[130] bullets[131] and handwriting samples.[132] It has also been noted in bloodstain pattern analysis (BPA),[133] dog detection evidence,[134] evaluations of skeletal remains,[135] arson investigations,[136] foren-

---

[127] Saul Kassin, Itiel E. Dror and Jeff Kukucka, "The Forensic Confirmation Bias: Problems, Perspectives, and Proposed Solutions", in *Journal of Applied Research in Memory and Cognition*, 2013, vol. 2, no. 1, pp. 42–52.

[128] Nikola K. Osborne and Rachel Zajac, "An Imperfect Match? Crime-related Context Influences Fingerprint Decisions", in *Applied Cognitive Psychology*, 2016, vol. 30, no. 1, pp. 126–34.

[129] José H. Kerstholt, Roos Paashuis and Marjan Sjerps, "Shoe Print Examinations: Effects of Expectation, Complexity and Experience", in *Forensic Science International*, 2007, vol. 165, no. 1, pp. 30–34.

[130] Nikola K. Osborne, Sally Woods, Jules Kieser and Rachel Zajac, "Does Contextual Information Bias Bitemark Comparisons?", in *Science and Justice*, 2014, vol. 54, no. 4, pp. 267–73.

[131] José H. Kerstholt, Aletta Eikelboom, Tjisse Dijkman, Reinoud Stoel, Rob Hermsen and Bert van Leuven, "Does Suggestive Information Cause a Confirmation Bias in Bullet Comparisons?", in *Forensic Science International*, vol. 198, nos. 1–3, pp. 138–42.

[132] Jeff Kukucka and Saul Kassin, "Do Confessions Taint Perceptions of Handwriting Evidence? An Empirical Test of the Forensic Confirmation Bias", in *Law and Human Behavior*, 2014, vol. 38, no. 3, pp. 1–15.

[133] Nikola K. Osborne, Rachel Zajac and Michael C. Taylor, "Bloodstain Pattern Analysis and Contextual Bias", in Allan Jamieson and Andre Moenssens (eds.), *Wiley Encyclopedia of Forensic Science*, John Wiley & Sons, 2015, pp. 1–8.

[134] Lisa Lit, Julie B. Schweitzer and Anita M. Oberbauer, "Handler Beliefs Affect Scent Detection Dog Outcomes", in *Animal Cognition*, 2011, vol. 14, no. 3, pp. 387–94. Also, since the ultimate determination that an alert has been signalled by the dog rests solely with the human handler, the process is highly dependent on human judgments and therefore also potentially fallible in this regard, see Sherri Minhinnick, "Statistical Reliability Confounders and Improvement in Advanced Dog Training: Patterns, Routines, Targets, Alerts, Dis-

sic pathology[137] and a range of forensic reconstructions.[138] Furthermore, early research outlines risks of bias in digital forensics,[139] that is, how contextual information such as inferences made by others[140] or information found on a digital device (for example, Internet search logs),[141] influence the digital forensics practitioners' (DFP) perceptions of images, documents or chat conversations found on the same digital device. This, as well as other research,[142] also points to the importance of so-called

---

tractors, Reinforcement, and Other Issues", in Tadeusz Jezierski, John Ensminger, L.E. Papet (eds.), *Canine Olfaction Science and Law: Advances in Forensic Science, Medicine, Conservation, and Environmental Remediation*, CRC Press, Boca Raton, 2016, pp. 197–212.

[135] Sherry Nakhaeizadeh, Ian Hanson and Nathalie Dozzi, "The Power of Contextual Effects in Forensic Anthropology: A Study of Biasability in the Visual Interpretations of Trauma Analysis on Skeletal Remains", in *Journal of Forensic Sciences*, 2014, vol. 59, no. 5, pp. 1177–83; Sherry Nakhaeizadeh, Ruth M. Morgan, Carolyn Rando and Itiel E. Dror, "Cascading Bias of Initial Exposure to Information at the Crime Scene to the Subsequent Evaluation of Skeletal Remains", in *Journal of Forensic Sciences*, 2017, vol. 63, no. 2, pp. 403–11.

[136] Paul Bieber, *Measuring the Impact of Cognitive Bias in Fire Investigation*, 2012, pp. 1–13.

[137] William R. Oliver, "Effect of History and Context on Forensic Pathologist Interpretation of Photographs of Patterned Injury of the Skin", in *Journal of Forensic Sciences*, 2017, vol. 62, no. 6, pp. 1500–05.

[138] See, for example, Emma A. Levin, Ruth M. Morgan, Lewis D. Griffin and Vivienne J. Jones, "A Comparison of Thresholding Methods for Forensic Reconstruction Studies Using Fluorescent Powder Proxies for Trace Materials", in *Journal of Forensic Sciences*, 2019, vol. 64, no. 2, pp. 431–42; Rachael M. Carew, Ruth M. Morgan and Carolyn Rando, "A Preliminary Investigation into the Accuracy of 3D Modelling and 3D Printing in Forensic Anthropology Evidence Reconstruction", in *Journal of Forensic Sciences*, 2019, vol. 64, no. 2, pp. 342–52.

[139] Nina Sunde and Itiel E. Dror, "Cognitive and Human Factors in Digital Forensics: Problems, Challenges, and the Way Forward", in *Digital Investigation*, 2019, vol. 29, pp. 101–08. See also Nina Sunde, *Non-Technical Sources of Errors When Handling Digital Evidence within a Criminal Investigation*, 2017.

[140] Patricia A. Zapf and Itiel E. Dror, "Understanding and Mitigating Bias in Forensic Evaluation: Lessons from Forensic Science", in *International Journal of Forensic Mental Health*, 2017, vol. 16, no. 3, pp. 227–38.

[141] Sunde and Dror, 2019, see above note 139.

[142] Adversarial allegiance has been evaluated and confirmed both in field studies and experimental studies, see, for example, Daniel C. Murrie, Marcus T. Boccaccini, Darrel B. Turner, Meredith Meeks, Carol Woods and Chriscelyn Tussey, "Rater (Dis)agreement on Risk Assessment Measures in Sexually Violent Predator Proceedings: Evidence of Adversarial Allegiance in Forensic Evaluation?", in *Psychology, Public Policy and Law*, 2009, vol. 15, no. 1, pp. 19–53; Daniel C. Murrie and Marcus T. Boccaccini, "Adversarial Allegiance among

adversarial allegiance, that is, that forensics' observations and conclusions may be influenced by whether they work for (or believe they work for) the prosecution or the defence.[143]

Interestingly, contextual information seems to result in both *within expert biasability*, that is, the same experts make different assessments in relation to the same evidence when provided with different contextual information at different points in time, and *between expert biasability*, that is, different experts assessing the same evidence make different assessments when they have different contextual information.[144] When it comes to within expert biasability specifically, experts that in the past had concluded that fingerprints matched, were presented with the same fingerprints again, now within the context that "someone else confessed to the crime" or that "the suspect has a solid alibi".[145] These experts changed their conclusions between 17 per cent and 80 per cent of the time. Similarly, in another study, experts were shown fingerprints and told that the prints were from a highly publicised erroneous identification, suggesting that the fingerprints in front of them were an exclusion.[146] However, the fingerprints were, in fact, not only matches but also matches made by the same experts that were now being tested. Although the experts were instructed to ignore all the contextual information and to focus solely on the actual prints, most of the experts (80 per cent) seem to have been affected

---

Expert Witnesses", in *Annual Review of Law and Social Science*, 2015, vol. 11, no. 1, pp. 37–55.

[143] Murrie, Boccaccini, Turner, Meeks, Woods and Tussey, 2009, pp. 19–53, see above note 142. It also occurred when experts' beliefs about for whom they were working (defence or prosecution) were manipulated, see Daniel C. Murrie, Marcus T. Boccaccini, Lucy A. Guarnera and Katrina A. Rufino, "Are Forensic Experts Biased by the Side that Retained Them?", in *Psychological Science*, 2013, vol. 24, no. 10, pp. 1889–97.

[144] These terms stem from Itiel Dror's so-called 'hierarchy of expert performance', a framework for systematically evaluating the biasability as well as reliability of experts, primarily forensic experts, see Itiel E. Dror, "A Hierarchy of Expert Performance", in *Journal of Applied Research in Memory and Cognition*, vol. 5, no. 2, pp. 121–27. This framework has also been used, for example, for forensic psychological assessments, see Itiel E. Dror and Daniel C. Murrie, "A Hierarchy of Expert Performance Applied to Forensic Psychological Assessments", in *Psychology, Public Policy and Law*, 2018, vol. 24, no. 1, pp. 11–23.

[145] Itiel E. Dror and David Charlton, "Why Experts Make Errors", in *Journal of Forensic Identification*, 2007, vol. 56, no. 4, pp. 600–16; Itiel E. Dror, David Charlton and Alisa E. Péron, "Contextual Information Renders Experts Vulnerable to Making Erroneous Identifications", in *Forensic Science International*, 2006, vol. 156, no. 1, pp. 74–78. All of the experts included in the study were considered effective and competent by their employer.

[146] *Ibid.*, pp. 74–78.

by the contextual information, as they made decisions that were inconsistent with their own previous decisions regarding the same prints. Furthermore, between expert biasability has been noted for instance when two DNA experts assessed a DNA-mixture in an actual adjudicated gang rape case, knowing that one of the assailants testified against another suspect as part of a plea bargain and that, without corroborating evidence, the plea bargain would be deemed inadmissible in Court.[147] These two experts concluded that the suspect in question could not be excluded from being a contributor to the DNA mixture. Their conclusion was later on contradicted by 16 out of 17 experts who examined the same DNA mixture, but without the biasing information.[148] Later research suggests that the noted differences are due to that the *observations* leading up to the conclusions varied in relation to the previous examination.[149] Similarly, fingerprint analysts examining the same fingerprints mark different minutia (characteristics such as enclosures, ridge endings and bifurcations) as relevant and also come to different conclusions regarding their clarity.[150] This highlights how the bias drives the experts to selectively attend to hypothesis confirming features of the evidence. These findings are consistent with decades of psychological research on *selective visual attention*[151] and the drive for *cognitive coherence*,[152] that is, to make sense of information, which is sometimes both complex and ambiguous, by making it coherent. The results also draw attention to the more specific perceptual processes involved in making visual comparisons, where studies suggest that variables such as low image quality (for example, low intensity or contrast

[147] Itiel E. Dror and Greg Hampikian, "Subjectivity and Bias in Forensic DNA Mixture Interpretation", in *Science and Justice*, 2011, vol. 51, no. 4. pp. 204–08.

[148] *Ibid.*

[149] Bradford T. Ulery, Austin R. Hicklin, JoAnn Buscaglia and Maria Antonia Roberts, "Repeatability and Reproducibility of Decisions by Latent Fingerprint Examiners", in *PLoS ONE*, 2012, vol. 7, no. 3; Bradford T. Ulery, Austin R. Hicklin, George I. Kiebuzinski, Maria Antonia Roberts and JoAnn Buscaglia, "Understanding the Sufficiency of Information for Latent Fingerprint Value Determinations", in *Forensic Science International*, 2014, vol. 230, nos. 1–3, pp. 99–106.

[150] Ulery, Hicklin, Buscaglia and Roberts, 2012, see above note 149; Ulery, Austin, Hicklin, Kiebuzinski and Roberts and Buscaglia, 2014, see above note 149.

[151] Marisa Carrasco, "Visual Attention: The Past 25 Years", in *Vision Research*, 2011, vol. 51, no. 13, pp. 1484–525; Jason Rajsic, Daryl E. Wilson and Jay Pratt, "Confirmation Bias in Visual Search", in *Journal of Experimental Psychology*, 2015, vol. 41, no. 5, pp. 1353–64.

[152] Dan Simon, "A Third View of the Black Box: Cognitive Coherence in Legal Decision Making", in *The University of Chicago Law Review*, 2004, vol. 71, no. 2, pp. 511–86.

information and low information quantity, for example, the total finger-print area), are important predictors of error.[153]

The above-described findings highlight the necessity to take human factors into account also in forensic sciences that are often portrayed as objective and immune to bias.[154] Although information that someone confessed or has a solid alibi clearly is relevant in relation to an overall case hypothesis, it obviously does not change the characteristics of the finger-prints to be compared or the DNA-mixture to analyse. Although such information is logically separated from the forensic evidence, it is clear that this separation is difficult to maintain in practice. This highlights the risks of so-called *bias cascade effects*[155] and *bias snowball effects*.[156] *The bias cascade effect* is when bias arises as a result of irrelevant information cascading from one stage to another, for example, from the initial evidence collection to the evaluation and interpretation of the evidence. For instance, in some jurisdictions, the CSIs are the same people who also do the forensic work back in the laboratory. In such cases, the analysis, evaluations, interpretations, and conclusions at the forensic laboratory may be influenced by irrelevant contextual information that analysts or CSIs may have been exposed to at the crime scene (and which may have biased them already during the crime scene investigation). With the *bias snowball effect*, bias is not only cascading from one stage to another, but bias increases as irrelevant information from a variety of sources is integrated and influences each other.[157] The issue is not only that forensic work can be biased by other sources (for example, that a suspect has confessed) but also that it can bias other lines of evidence. For instance, a DNA match

---

[153] Phillip J. Kellman, Jennifer L. Mnookin, Gennady Erlikhman, Patrick Garrigan, Tandra Ghose, Everett Mettler, David Charlton and Itiel E. Dror, "Forensic Comparison and Matching of Fingerprints: Using Quantitative Image Measures for Estimating Error Rates through Understanding and Predicting Difficulty", in *PLoS ONE*, 2014, vol. 9, no. 5, pp. 1–14.

[154] For more on developments in this regard over the past decade, see Itiel E. Dror, "Human Expert Performance in Forensic Decision Making: Seven Different Sources of Bias", in *Australian Journal of Forensic Sciences*, 2017, vol. 49, no. 5, pp. 541–47.

[155] See Itiel E. Dror, Ruth M. Morgan, Carolyn Rando and Sherry Nakhaeizadeh, "Letter to the Editor – The Bias Snowball and the Bias Cascade Effects: Two Distinct Biases that May Impact Forensic Decision Making", in *Journal of Forensic Sciences*, 2017, vol. 62, no. 3, pp. 832–33.

[156] *Ibid.*

[157] *Ibid.*

---

can bias a forensic analyst who is examining a bite mark. Also, an eyewitness may be influenced by knowing about forensic evidence implicating the suspect, and in turn, then the eyewitness can influence the interpretation of other evidence.[158]

The research discussed above has not taken into account the specifics of forensic evidence in investigations of core international crimes. It is unknown whether such forensic assessments or analyses are associated with other types of cognitive errors, but this possibility deserves more attention, not the least considering that such evidence has to be interpreted in the light of the very complex legal elements (material as well as mental) required for criminal responsibility.[159] The existing research points to some possible risk factors, for example, when it comes to analyses which fundamentally depend on visual judgments and which are conducted by analysts with contextual knowledge. In these situations, the contextual information is likely to steer analysts' attention to some aspects of an item or document, and so on, rather than others. This, in turn, makes them perceive of it differently than what would have been the case if they had no information at all, or information indicating something else. Possible outlets for this could be *crime pattern analysis* used most commonly in investigations of large-scale killings, mass destruction and displacement.[160] Such pattern analysis is essential since international crimes often comprise a large number of incidents that can only be characterised as a pattern if they share certain common features (relating to the perpetrators, victims, geographical and chronological distribution, and so on).[161] This stems from the material constructions of the crimes, for example, for genocide by killing, that the "conduct took place in the context of a manifest pattern of similar conduct".[162] In this aggregation of multiple incidents into a (potential) pattern, there is, just like with other complex cognitive

---

[158] *Ibid.*

[159] See, for instance, Werle Gerhard and Florian Jeßberger, *Principles of International Criminal Law*, T.M.C. Asser Press, The Hague, 2005, pp. 165–286.

[160] Xabier Agirre Aranburu, "Sexual Violence beyond Reasonable Doubt: Using Pattern Evidence and Analysis for International Cases", in *Law and Social Inquiry*, 2010, vol. 35, no. 4, pp. 609–27.

[161] *Ibid.*, p. 610.

[162] ICC, Elements of Crimes, 11 June 2010, Article 6(a), Element 4 (https://legal-tools.org/doc/3c0e2d).

tasks, ample room for bias.[163] This is because human cognition is driven by expectations in so-called *top down processes*[164] and also strives towards *cognitive coherence*.[165] Some related tendencies are the *clustering illusion*, that is, how people tend to perceive of random clusters in small samples as non-random,[166] and *pareidolia*, a tendency to project something not actually present onto a vague object.[167] Such tendencies influence the perception of whether there is a pattern at all, and also what that pattern is, with a good head start for what the analyst expects to see. Reasonably, this risk should be considered both in relation to data collection, that is, crime mapping used to identify 'hot spots' or areas with highest concentrations of crime[168] and in relation to the actual analysis of the data,[169] including, for example, analysis of satellite imagery.[170]

Furthermore, other types of assessments in investigations of core international crimes, which resemble those already studied, are, for example, the testing of the authenticity of documents using chemical tests,[171] and

---

[163] For more on this research see the previous section in this chapter and Lidén, 2018, pp. 118–21, see above note 2.

[164] Top down processes integrate sensory information (visual, auditory, and so on) with expectations, experience, and so on, and makes it possible for humans to 'see' more than what a stimulus, in a strict sense, conveys. This is different from bottom up processes which build on analysis of stimulus without adding other information and therefore is more clearly data driven. For more on this, see, for example, Emiliano Macaluso, Uta Noppeney, Durk Talsma, Tiziana Vercillo, Jess Hartcher-O'Brien and Ruth Adam, "The Curious Incident of Attention in Multisensory Integration: Bottom-Up vs. Top-Down", in *Multisensory Research*, 2016, vol. 29, nos. 6–7, pp. 557–83; Jess Hartcher-O'Brien, Salvador Soto-Faraco and Ruth Adam, "Editorial: A Matter of Bottom-Up or Top-Down Processes: The Role of Attention in Multisensory Integration", in *Frontiers in Integrative Neuroscience*, 2017, vol. 11, pp. 1–2.

[165] Simon, 2004, pp. 511–86, see above note 152.

[166] See, for example, Thomas Gilovich, *How We Know What Isn't So: The Fallibility of Human Reason in Everyday Life*, Free, New York, 1991.

[167] Joel L. Voss, Kara D. Federmeier and Ken A. Paller, "The Potato Chip Really Does Look Like Elvis! Neural Hallmarks of Conceptual Processing Associated with Finding Novel Shapes Subjectively Meaningful", in *Cerebral Cortex*, 2012, vol. 22, no. 10, pp. 2354–64. This can be any vague object, but some examples are clouds and shadows. It is also captured by the interpretation of inkblots using the Rorschach test, see Hermann Rorschach, *Psychodiagnostik*, Verlage Hans Huber, Bern, 1921.

[168] Agirre Aranburu, 2010, p. 215, see above note 10.

[169] For more on data collection and analysis in this regard see Agirre Aranburu, 2010, pp. 618–23, see above note 160.

[170] Agirre Aranburu, 2010, p. 360, see above note 74.

[171] *Ibid.*, pp. 367–72.

---

physical evidence from exhumations of mass graves.[172] Based on previous research, the most reasonable prediction is that also these assessments are sensitive to contextual information. Hence, it is motivated to do a critical analysis of the flow of information, focusing on what analysts *need* to know to conduct their analyses as well as what information may potentially bias their assessments. In this regard, it can be noted that international investigations are often preceded by inquiries made by fact-finding commissions or bodies,[173] which are potential sources of biasing contextual information.[174] Although the prevalence of confirmation bias in forensic analyses is, by far, the most well-researched area, there are also studies regarding confirmation bias in other specific investigative settings, namely identifications and interviews, which are summarised below.

7.2.3.2. Identifications and Interviews

The most common purpose of conducting a line-up identification is to test whether a witness can identify a suspect as the perpetrator. In other words, the line-up aims to test the guilt hypothesis and the validity of this test is strongly related to how it is carried out. One of the most notorious cases of mistaken identity in legal history is that of 'Ivan the Terrible' of Treblinka.[175] There are also more recent examples of line-up identifications that national courts have considered more or less void of evidentiary value due to how they were conducted, including the identification of a suspect-

---

[172] Exhumations of mass graves were conducted for instance for the Srebrenica and Kosovo ICTY investigations, see *ibid.*, p. 360.

[173] For instance, this was the case with ICTY and the previous fact-finding UN Commission of Experts, see MICT, "The Tribunal – Establishment" (available on its web site) and the ICC investigation in Darfur (The UN Commission of Inquiry), see for example, Samuel Totten, "The UN International Commission of Inquiry on Darfur: New and Disturbing Findings", in *Genocide Studies and Prevention*, 2009, vol. 4, no. 3, pp. 354–78.

[174] See also Jason M. Chin, Gianni Ribeiro and Alicia Rairden, "Open Forensic Science", in *Journal of Law and the Biosciences*, 2019, vol. 6, no. 1, pp. 1–34. Chin and colleagues emphasise the need for transparency in how forensic analyses are conducted. Furthermore, they point to communication problems between scientific experts and legal experts for example, because legal experts lack the scientific training that they would need in order to appropriately question forensic practices.

[175] Lawrence Douglas, *The Right Wrong Man: John Demjanjuk and the Last Great Nazi War Crimes Trial*, Princeton University Press, Princeton, 2016, pp. 36–38.

ed murderer of the Swedish Prime Minister Olof Palme.[176] Although there are lots of possible psychological explanations of this,[177] confirmation bias seems to have an important role. For instance, studies suggest that when an administrator of a line-up is aware of the suspect's identity this information seems to be subtly transferred to the witness who is more likely to identify the suspect as the perpetrator, compared to when the administrator is unaware of the suspect's identity.[178] This so-called *hypothesis leakage*[179] happens without the administrator's awareness of communicating any information to the witness. Its impact varies with the witness' susceptibility to leading information,[180] and whether the administrator also uses *verbal cues* like leading questions that direct attention to a certain person in the line-up[181] and/or *non-verbal cues* like facial gestures (rolling the eyes, smiling) or body movements (moving toward or away from the witness, nodding the head).[182]

Furthermore, research implies that confirmation bias may be at play in suspect interviews, as a result of expectations that the suspect is

---

[176] For more on this, see the Swedish Government Official Reports, *Brottsutredningen efter Mordet på Statsminister Olof Palme: Granskningskommissionens Betänkande*, Stockholm, 1999, SOU 1999:88, pp. 727–37.

[177] There is a range of factors that potentially can bias the outcome of a line-up identification including for example, improperly chosen foils and simultaneous rather than sequential presentation formats. For more on this see, for example, Roderick Cameron L. Lindsay, Harold Wallbridge and Daphne Drennan, "Do Clothes Make the Man? An Exploration of the Effect of Lineup Attire on Eyewitness Identification Accuracy", in *Canadian Journal of Behavioural Science*, 1987, vol. 19, no. 4, pp. 463–78; Nancy Steblay, Jennifer Dysart, Solomon Fulero and Roderick Cameron L. Lindsay, "Eyewitness Accuracy Rates in Sequential and Simultaneous Lineup Presentations: A Meta-Analytic Comparison", in *Law and Human Behavior*, 2001, vol. 25, no. 5, pp. 459–73.

[178] See, for example, Mark R. Philips, Bradley D. McAuliff, Margaret Bull Kovera and Brian L. Cutler, "Double-Blind Photoarray Administration as a Safeguard against Investigator Bias", in *Journal of Applied Psychology*, 1999, vol. 84, no. 6, pp. 940–51; Ryann M. Haw and Ronald P. Fisher, "Effects of Administrator-Witness Contact on Eyewitness Identification Accuracy", in *Journal of Applied Psychology*, 2004, vol. 89, no. 6, pp. 1106–12.

[179] Sarah M. Greathouse and Margaret Bull Kovera, "Instruction Bias and Lineup Presentation Moderate the Effects of Administration Knowledge on Eyewitness Identification", in *Law and Human Behavior*, 2009, vol. 33, no. 1, p. 71.

[180] See, for example, Gillian Murphy and Clara M. Greene, "Perceptual Load Affects Eyewitness Accuracy and Susceptibility to Leading Questions", in *Frontiers in Psychology*, 2016, vol. 7, 2016, pp. 1–10.

[181] See, for example, Philips, McAuliff, Kovera and Cutler, 1999, pp. 940–51, see above note 178.

[182] *Ibid.*

guilty,[183] for example, due to a previous apprehension.[184] The bias is here manifested in that the interviewer asks more guilt-presumptive questions and perceives of the suspect's statement as less credible. Guilt expectations seem to set in motion a process of behavioural confirmation influencing not only the interviewers' behaviours but also those of the suspects.[185] For outside observers, suspects who were interviewed by interviewers with guilt expectations appeared to be more nervous, more defensive, less plausible and therefore more likely to be guilty. Furthermore, guilt expectations potentiate the risk of confrontational or manipulative interrogations[186] and nonstrategic use of evidence.[187] In this regard, it can be noted that the Pre-Trial Chamber, when declining to confirm the charges against Callixte Mbarushimana in the *Democratic Republic of the Congo* situation, expressed concern regarding interview techniques that "seem[ed] utterly inappropriate when viewed in the light of the objective set out in Article 54 (1)(a) ICC Statute, to establish the truth by "investigating incriminating and exoneration circumstances equally"".[188] Similarly, in witness interviews, when the interviewer believes that the suspect is guilty, this belief is more or less subtly transferred to witnesses, for example, through disclosure of suggestive information (such as a suspect's con-

---

[183]   Guilt expectations were manipulated by providing different base rates of guilt and innocence, see Saul M. Kassin, Christine C. Goldstein and Kenneth Savitsky, "Behavioral Confirmation in the Interrogation Room: On the Dangers of Presuming Guilt", in *Law and Human Behavior*, 2003, vol. 27, no. 2, pp. 187–203; Carol Hill, Amina Memon and Peter McGeorge, "The Role of Confirmation Bias in Suspect Interviews: A Systematic Evaluation", in *Legal and Criminological Psychology*, 2008, vol. 13, no. 2, pp. 357–71.

[184]   Lidén, Gräns and Juslin, 2018, pp. 336–54, see above note 46.

[185]   Hill, Memon and McGeorge, 2008, pp. 357–71, see above note 183.

[186]   Deborah Davis and Richard A. Leo, "Strategies for Preventing False Confessions and their Consequences", in Mark R. Kebbell and Graham M. Davies (eds.), *Practical Psychology for Forensic Investigations and Prosecutions*, Wiley & Sons, San Francisco, 2006, pp. 121–49; Richard A. Leo and Steven A. Drizin, "The Three Errors: Pathways to False Confession and Wrongful Conviction", in Daniel Lassiter and Christian A. Meissner (eds.), *Police Interrogations and False Confessions: Current Research, Practice, and Policy Recommendations*, American Psychological Association, Washington, D.C., 2010, pp. 9–30.

[187]   Maria Hartwig, Pär-Anders Granhag, Leif A. Strömwall and Aldert Vrij, "Detecting Deception via Strategic Disclosure of Evidence", in *Law and Human Behavior*, 2005, vol. 29, no. 4, pp. 469–84; Saul M. Kassin, "On the Psychology of Confessions: Does Innocence Put Innocents at Risk?", in *American Psychologist*, 2005, vol. 60, no. 3, pp. 215–28.

[188]   ICC, Situation in the Democratic Republic of Congo, *The Prosecutor v. Callixte Mbarushimana*, Pre-Trial Chamber, Decision on the Confirmation of Charges, 16 December 2011, ICC-01/04-01/10-465-Red, para. 51 (https://legal-tools.org/doc/63028f).

---

fession) or leading questions that may make the witness (including alibi witnesses) adjust his or her account making it consistent with the police's belief.[189] Suggestibility may be more pronounced in vulnerable victims.[190]

7.3. Explanations of Confirmation Bias and Possible Debiasing Techniques

The term confirmation bias is *descriptive*, that is, a name of a behaviour, not an *explanation* of that behaviour.[191] This is a crucial distinction since only studying the behaviour will not provide information about why it occurs. Yet, understanding why confirmation bias occurs is an essential step in understanding how it, potentially, can be prevented. In the following, the explanations of confirmation bias identified through empirical research have been categorised into three main groups: 1) cognitive explanations, 2) emotional and motivational explanations, and 3) social and organisational explanations. Since humans do not only have cognitive limitations but are also emotional creatures that work within social groups as well as organisational settings, these explanations are to be considered mutually supportive rather than mutually exclusive.

7.3.1. Cognitive Explanations

> Over the course of 248 days of hearing, the Chamber heard 102 witnesses called by the Prosecution, the Defence and on behalf of the victims. 1791 items were admitted into evi-

---

[189] See, for example, Lisa E. Hasel and Saul M. Kassin, "On the Presumption of Evidentiary Independence: Can Confessions Corrupt Eyewitness Identifications?", in *Psychological Science*, 2009, vol. 20, no. 1, pp. 122–26; Saul M. Kassin, Daniel Bogart and Jacqueline Kerner, "Confessions that Corrupt: Evidence from the DNA Exoneration Case Files", in *Psychological Science*, 2012, vol. 23, no. 1, pp. 41–45; Martine Powell, Maryanne Garry and Neil Brewer, "Eyewitness Testimony", in Ian Freckelton and Hugh Selby (eds.), *Expert Evidence: Law, Practice, Procedure and Advocacy*, Law Book Co., North Ryde, 2009, pp. 1–42; Amanda H. Waterman, Mark Blades and Christopher Spencer, "Indicating When You Do Not Know the Answer: The Effect of Question Format and Interviewer Knowledge on Children's 'Don't Know' Responses", in *British Journal of Developmental Psychology*, 2004, vol. 22, no. 3, pp. 335–48; Jessica Sparling, David A. Wilder, Jennifer Kondash, Megan Boyle and Megan Compton, "Effects of Interviewer Behavior on Accuracy of Children's Responses", in *Journal of Applied Behavior Analysis*, 2011, vol. 44, no. 3, pp. 587–92.

[190] Although individual differences should not be disregarded, see for example, Kim Drake and Ray Bull, "Individual Differences in Interrogative Suggestibility: Life Adversity and Field Dependence", in *Psychology, Crime and Law*, 2011, vol. 17, no. 8, pp. 677–87.

[191] For more on this see Lidén, 2018, pp. 106–08, see above note 2.

dence and 2129 victims have been authorised to participate in this trial, and in addition to several victims testifying as witnesses before the Chamber, five further victims presented their views and concerns in person.[192]

Cognition refers to human information processing, including perception, memory, thought and language.[193] Decision making primarily falls within the subcategory of thought, but is also closely related to other subcategories since humans, for instance, have to use information stored in memory to make decisions.[194] All humans have limitations in cognitive capacities (for example, in working memory capacity and attention), and these limitations can separately or together influence the susceptibility to confirmation bias.[195] This is because the limitations simply make it too cognitively demanding to seriously consider more than one hypothesis at the time.[196] Thus, studies suggest that confirmation bias is stronger in relation to cognitively more demanding tasks.[197]

As exemplified by the citation from the Ntaganda case at the beginning of this section, investigations into core international crimes regularly

---

[192] Judge Robert Fremr giving a procedural overview in the Judgment of Trial Chamber VI in the *Ntaganda* case, see ICC, Situation in the Democratic Republic of the Congo, *The Prosecutor v. Bosco Ntaganda*, Trial Chamber, Transcript, 8 July 2019, ICC-01/04-02/06-T-265-ENG, p. 4 (https://legal-tools.org/doc/fa8f8f).

[193] Lars-Gunnar Lundh, Henry Montgomery and Yvonne Wærn, *Kognitiv Psykologi*, Studentlitteratur, Lund, 1992; Michael W. Passer and Ronald Edward Smith, *Psychology: The Science of Mind and Behavior*, McGraw-Hill Higher Education, Boston, 2009, p. 16.

[194] Lundh, Montgomery and Wærn, 1992, see above note 193.

[195] Michael E. Doherty and Clifford R. Mynatt, "Inattention to P(H) and to P(D|~H): A Converging Operation", in *Acta Psychologica*, 1990, vol. 75, no. 1, pp. 1–11.

[196] *Ibid.*, pp. 1–11.

[197] Moa Lidén, Minna Gräns and Peter Juslin, "'Guilty, No Doubt': Detention Provoking Confirmation Bias in Judges' Guilt Assessment and Debiasing Techniques", in *Psychology, Crime and Law*, 2019, vol. 25, no. 3, pp. 219–47; Moa Lidén, Minna Gräns and Peter Juslin, "The Presumption of Guilt in Suspect Interrogations: Apprehension as a Trigger of Confirmation Bias and Debiasing Techniques", in *Law and Human Behavior*, 2018, vol. 42, no. 4, pp. 336–54; Jonathan St. B.T. Evans, "The Heuristic-Analytic Theory of Reasoning: Extension and Evaluation", in *Psychonomic Bulletin and Review*, 2006, vol. 13, no. 3, pp. 378–95; Wim De Neys, "Dual Processing in Reasoning: Two Systems but One Reasoner", in *Psychological Science*, 2006, vol. 17, no. 5, pp. 428–33. See also Clifford R. Mynatt, Michael E. Doherty and William Dragan, "Information Relevance, Working Memory, and the Consideration of Alternatives", in *Quarterly Journal of Experimental Psychology*, 1993, vol. 46, no. 4, pp. 759–78; Clifford R. Mynatt, Michael E. Doherty and James A. Sullivan, "Data Selection in a Minimal Hypothesis Testing Task", *Acta Psychologica*, 1991, vol. 76, no. 3, pp. 293–305.

---

encompass enormous amounts of information.[198] It is therefore not an exaggeration to claim that cognitive load, that is, the efforts used by working memory to actively process the case relevant information,[199] is *sky-high*. In fact, even the connotation *sky-high* seems quite modest considering that the average digit span that humans can actively process and remember is 7.[200] This is fewer digits than what most phone numbers have. The large quantity of information is of course related to the complex construction of crimes under the ICC Statute, for example, because a single specific charge is often assessed as one part of a much wider criminal charge, like that of genocide. It is also related to the pronounced need for corroboration to prevent a case from collapsing due to, for example, unreliable witness testimony.[201] This generally high cognitive load will probably always be present in investigations into core international crimes. Evidentiary rules – such as rules on agreed facts[202] and facts of common knowledge[203] – are likely to only have a marginal limiting effect.

Since the risk of confirmation bias is stronger in relation to cognitively more demanding tasks, a reasonable conclusion, which has been confirmed by empirical research, is that reducing cognitive load can be effective as a debiasing technique. The effectiveness of reducing cognitive load has been tested in relation to, for example, suspect interviews, which can be made less cognitively demanding by employing a standardised interview model.[204] Using such a model means that the interviewer does not constantly have to come up with new open-ended questions but can instead use standardised phrases to direct the interrogation, such as

---

[198] Simon de Smet also deals with the topic of information overload or cognitive load in relation to holistic assessments of evidence, see Simon de Smet, "Enhancing the Quality of Reasoning about the Link Between Evidence and Factual Propositions", CILRAP Film, New Delhi, 22 February 2019 (https://www.cilrap.org/cilrap-film/190222-smet/).

[199] John Sweller, Paul Ayres and Slava Kalyuga, *Cognitive Load Theory*, Springer, 2011.

[200] For adults without cognitive impairments, the average digit span that can be hold in working memory is 7 (± 2), see George A. Miller, "The Magical Number Seven, Plus or Minus Two: Some Limits on Our Capacity for Processing Information", in *Psychological Review*, 1955, vol. 101, no. 2, pp. 81–97.

[201] Fry, 2014, p. 266, see above note 10. The difficulty of finding and holding on to reliable witnesses is illustrated by, for example, the ICC acquittal of Mathieu Ngudjolo Chui in the Situation in the Democratic Republic of Congo.

[202] ICC RPE, Rule 69, see above note 49.

[203] ICC Statute, Article 69(6), see above note 8.

[204] Lidén, Gräns and Juslin, 2018, pp. 336–54, see above note 46.

"Please tell me everything you remember about".[205] Such phrases are not only inherently less guilt presumptive but also make the interrogation less cognitively demanding for the interrogator.[206] An associated benefit is that the interrogation becomes *more* cognitively demanding for the suspect, who therefore has less cognitive resources available for, for example, making untrue statements appear credible. Furthermore, continuous education and training in asking open-ended questions reduces cognitive load in the applied setting.[207]

When it comes to reducing cognitive load in the evaluation or assessment of evidence, conducting structured evaluations rather than unstructured evaluations seems to function as a debiasing technique.[208] More specifically, with a structured evaluation, decision makers rate or assess each piece of evidence separately before assessing the total evidence (rather than just conducting one total assessment).[209] This appears to make them more resistant to confirmation bias, a finding in line with the so-called *Divide and Conquer principle*, that is, that complex decision problems should be decomposed into smaller, more manageable parts, to improve decision quality.[210] Reducing cognitive load in this way makes differences in the implications of the different pieces of evidence more sali-

---

[205] John Yarbrough, Hugues F. Hervé and Robert Harms, "The Sins of Interviewing: Errors Made by Investigative Interviewers and Suggestions for Redress", in Barry S. Cooper, Dorothee Griesel and Marguerite Ternes (eds.), *Applied Issues in Investigative Interviewing, Eyewitness Memory, and Credibility Assessment*, Springer Science, New York, 2013, p. 87

[206] See Gisli H. Gudjonsson and John Pearse, "Suspect Interviews and False Confessions", in *Current Direction in Psychological Science*, 2011, vol. 20, no. 1, pp. 33–37; Christian A. Meissner, Maria Hartwig and Melissa B. Russano, "The Need for a Positive Psychological Approach and Collaborative Effort for Improving Practice in the Interrogation Room", in *Law and Human Behavior*, 2010, vol. 34, no. 1, pp. 43–45; Lidén, Gräns and Juslin, 2018, pp. 336–54, see above note 46.

[207] See Martine B. Powell, Carolyn H. Hughes-Scholes and Stefanie J. Sharman, "Skill in Interviewing Reduces Confirmation Bias", in *Journal of Investigative Psychology and Offender Profiling*, 2012, vol. 9, no. 2, pp. 126–34.

[208] Lidén, Gräns and Juslin, 2018, see above note 197.

[209] *Ibid.*

[210] Nils Kolling and Laurence Hunt, "Divide and Conquer: Strategic Decision Areas", in *Nature Neuroscience*, 2015, vol. 18, no. 5, pp. 616–18; Osvaldo F. Morera and David V. Budescu, "A Psychometric Analysis of the 'Divide and Conquer' Principle in Multicriteria Decision Making", in *Organizational Behavior and Human Decision Processes*, 1998, vol. 75, no. 3, pp. 187–206.

---

ent to decision makers.[211] It is therefore more likely that their assessments become more nuanced compared to when they only conduct one overall assessment.

A context in which it is particularly important that diversity and nuances in the evidence are not overlooked, is when analysts try to 'make sense' of the evidence that an investigation has resulted in so far. The outcome of such analyses will be the basis for strategic directions to investigators in charge of collecting the evidence.[212] As this entails the processing of large volumes of data, a best recommendation is to first divide the data into smaller pieces and only thereafter attempt to conquer it. This can be done, for example, through the usage of so-called *case evaluation tables*, which help to produce a synopsis matching the elements of the hypothesis with the different sources of the evidence and *case evaluation charts*, that link suspects, criminal actions, victims, witnesses, and so on.[213] This is likely to reduce cognitive load in similar ways as other types of structured evaluations and thereby make the implications of different types of evidence more salient to analysts. However, the tables and charts only ask the analysts to evaluate and link in relation to *one* hypothesis, whereas the soundness of a hypothesis is better determined in the light of also other hypotheses.[214] Thus, whereas the tables and charts do a good job in improving the evaluation of a single hypothesis, they do not logically exclude that the data is also compatible, perhaps even better compatible, with other hypotheses. This highlights the need to combine different debiasing techniques. For instance, the use of tables and charts can effectively be combined with comparative tests such as the *analysis of competing hypotheses* ('ACH'), a method developed from intelligence studies, with the aim to help systematic comparison of multiple causal hypothe-

---

[211] For more on the relationship between cognitive salience and cognitive load, see, for example, Rimvydas Rukšėnas, Jonathan Back, Paul Curzon and Ann Blandford, "Verification-guided Modelling of Salience and Cognitive Load", in *Formal Aspects of Computing*, 2009, vol. 21, no. 6, pp. 541–69.

[212] For more on the role of analysts see Xabier Agirre Aranburu, "On How Analysis Can Enhance the Quality of Investigation and Case Preparation", CILRAP Film, New Delhi, 22 February 2019 (https://www.cilrap.org/cilrap-film/190222-agirre/).

[213] *Ibid.*

[214] For more on this, see above Section 7.2.2. about underdetermination and inference to the best explanation, as well as the Baconian Approach to Probability in Klamberg, 2011, pp. 4–5, see above note 34.

ses.[215] ACH requires an analyst to explicitly identify all the reasonable alternatives and have them compete against each other, rather than evaluating their plausibility one at a time.[216]

The cognitive explanations can also be used to understand the effects of exposure to contextual information, for example, when it comes to the forensic confirmation bias.[217] As illustrated by the cited research, the subconscious influence of contextual information is well established. Given that this influence is subconscious, it is insufficient to try and prevent it using instructions to disregard the contextual information and only focus on the evidence. Although such disregard instructions are often trusted in other legal contexts, research systematically shows that they are not only inefficient but possibly also counterproductive.[218] Disregard instructions are a bit like saying: "Whatever you do, do not think about a large pink elephant", which is likely to lead the instructed person to do just that, that is, think about the elephant, and quite stubbornly so. This is because in order for the individual to check his or her status, that is, to monitor whether he or she is thinking about the elephant, he or she in fact has to think about the elephant. Thus, somewhat paradoxically, such instructions can make individuals pay even greater attention to the information they are supposed to disregard. Another strategy with better odds of success is to never tell the individual about the elephant, or if that information is considered relevant, then delay the disclosure of the information. This is also referred to as *contextual information management*

---

215 Richard J. Heuer, *Psychology of Intelligence Analysis*, Center for the Study of Intelligence, 1999, pp. 95–110.

216 *Ibid.*

217 However, there are also explanations of this found in social psychology and motivational psychology and their relevance are likely to depend on what the nature of the contextual information is. For more on this, see Joel D. Lieberman and Jamie Arndt, "Understanding the Limits of Limiting Instructions: Social Psychological Explanations for the Failures of Instructions to Disregard Pretrial Publicity and Other Inadmissible Evidence", in *Psychology, Public Policy and Law*, 2000, vol. 6, no. 3, pp. 677–711; Nancy K. Steblay, Harmon M. Hosch, Scott E. Culhane and Adam McWethy, "The Impact on Juror Verdicts of Judicial Instructions to Disregard Inadmissible Evidence: A Meta-Analysis", in *Law and Human Behavior*, 2006, vol. 30, no. 4, pp. 469–92.

218 The possibility of such instructions becoming counterproductive is also referred to as *the backfire effect*, Lieberman and Arndt, 2000, see above note 217; Steblay, Harmon, Hosch, Culhane and McWethy, 2006, pp. 469–92, see above note 217.

('CIM').[219] The main objective of CIM is to shield individuals from potentially biasing irrelevant information, while still allowing access to task-relevant (but potentially biasing) information. In the literature, three main CIM procedures have been reported which can be effectively combined. These are: 1) the context-manager model,[220] 2) (linear) sequential unmasking, and 3) blind peer review.

A context-manager, previously used in, for example, forensic document and firearm examinations, has access to all of the contextual information, but only passes on to the analyst the information that is relevant for the analysis.[221] This enables the analyst to conduct the analysis in the absence of potentially biasing information. Simultaneously, the context-manager can determine the type of examination that might be necessary and also choose to disclose potentially biasing (but relevant) information at a later stage, after the analysis has been conducted. This is directly connected to (linear) sequential unmasking, which specify the optimal order in which to examine forensic material.[222] For instance, fingerprint analysts

---

[219] See, for instance, Kassin, Dror and Kukucka, 2013, pp. 42–52, see above note 7; Gary Edmond, Alice Towler, Bethany Growns, Gianni Ribeiro, Bryan Found, David White, Kaye Ballantyne, Rachel A. Searston, Matthew B. Thompson, Jason M. Tangen, Richard I. Kemp and Kristy Martire, "Thinking Forensics: Cognitive Science for Forensic Practitioners", in *Science and Justice*, 2017, vol. 57, no. 2, pp. 1–27; Simon A. Cole, "Implementing Counter-Measures Against Confirmation Bias in Forensic Science", in *Journal of Applied Research in Memory and Cognition*, 2013, vol. 2, no. 1, pp. 386–401; William C. Thompson, "What Role Should Investigative Facts Play in the Evaluation of Scientific Evidence?", in *Australian Journal of Forensic Sciences*, 2011, vol. 43, nos. 2–3, pp. 123–34; Nikola K.P. Osborne and Michael C. Taylor, "Contextual Information Management: An Example of Independent-Checking in the Review of Laboratory-Based Bloodstain Pattern Analysis", in *Science and Justice*, 2018, vol. 58, no. 3, pp. 226–31; Sunde and Dror, 2019, see above note 127.

[220] For example, see Erwin Mattijssen, Wim Kerkhoff, Charles E. Berger, Itiel E. Dror and Reinoud Stoel, "Implementing Context Information Management in Forensic Casework: Minimizing Contextual Bias in Firearms Examination", in *Science and Justice*, 2016, vol. 56, no. 2, pp. 113–22; Bryan Found and John Ganas, "The Management of Domain Irrelevant Context Information in Forensic Handwriting Examination Casework", in *Science and Justice*, 2012, vol. 53, no. 2, pp. 154–58.

[221] Nikola K. Osborne and Michael Taylor, "Contextual Information Management: An Example of Independent-Checking in the Review of Laboratory-Based Bloodstain Pattern Analysis", in *Science and Justice*, 2018, vol. 58, no. 3, pp. 226–31.

[222] Dan E. Krane, Simon Ford, Jason R. Gilder, Keith Inman, Allan Jamieson, Roger Koppl, Irving L. Kornfield, D. Michael Risinger, Norah Rudin, Marc Scott Taylor and William C. Thompson, "Sequential Unmasking: a Means of Minimizing Observer Effects in Forensic DNA Interpretation", in *Journal of Forensic Sciences*, 2008, vol. 53, no. 4, pp. 1006–07;

would first examine the fingerprint from the crime scene and only thereafter be exposed to the suspect's fingerprint. This can promote that they work from the evidence to the suspect, rather than the other way around. Linear sequential unmasking also requires analysts to state levels of confidence in their opinion regarding the material under examination and to be transparent about how contextual information has been incorporated into the analysis.[223] To further check the validity of the analyst's findings, the process can be complemented with a blind peer review, where the peer-reviewer,[224] preferably assigned by the context-manager rather than the analyst, functions as a control in relation to the original assessment. If there, despite the previous control mechanisms, are reasons to believe that the prior analysis has been biased, then the peer-reviewer should conduct his or her analysis without the biasing information, in order to allow conclusions about its effects.[225] To effectively safeguard the co-ordination of these control mechanisms, it is advisable to create protocols that can be implemented with a minimal impact on the current workflow, while still effectively preventing bias. Clearly, such protocols have to be tailor-made for the context in which they are supposed to be used.

7.3.2. Emotional and Motivational Explanations

> For these crimes no punishment is severe enough. It may well be essential to hang Göring, but it is totally inadequate. That is, this guilt, in contrast to all criminal guilt, oversteps and shatters all legal systems [...]. We are simply not

---

Itiel E. Dror, William C. Thompson, Christian Meissner, Irv Kornfield, Dan Krane, Michael Saks and Michael Risinger, "Letter to the Editor: Context Management Toolbox: A Linear Sequential Unmasking (LSU) Approach for Minimizing Cognitive Bias in Forensic Decision Making", in *Journal of Forensic Sciences*, 2015, vol. 60, no. 4, pp. 1111–12.

[223] Dror, Thompson, Meissner, Kornfield, Krane, Saks and Risinger, 2015, pp. 1111–12, see above note 222.

[224] For an example, see Bradford T. Ulery, Austin Hicklin, JoAnn Buscaglia and Maria Antonia Roberts, "Accuracy and Reliability of Forensic Latent Fingerprint Decisions", in *Proceedings of the National Academy of Sciences of the United States of America*, 2011, vol. 108, no. 19, pp. 7733–38.

[225] Thus, this debiasing technique can benefit from more specific knowledge about between expert biasability for specific types of assessments. For more on this topic, see above Section 7.2.3.1.

equipped to deal, on a human level, with a guilt that is beyond crime.[226]

Although the words 'emotions' and 'motivation' are better known than
'cognition', the everyday uses of these words differ in important ways
from how they are used in the field of Emotion and Motivation Psychology. The subjective feeling such as anger, fear or joy, is only one of four
parts of an emotion,[227] and emotions are held to be strongly associated
with motivation.[228] According to these explanations of confirmation bias,
humans reason in one-sided ways in order to maintain control and self-
esteem.[229] The specific emotions that have been linked to increased levels
of confirmation bias are anger,[230] fear,[231] anxiety and worry.[232] Although
there are methodological challenges with studying the impact of emotions
on information processing[233] and some of these findings concern contexts

---

[226] Hannah Arendt writing about the Nuremberg trials, cited in Douglas, 2016, p. 7, see above
note 175. Originally published in Hannah Arendt, *Eichmann in Jerusalem: A Report on the
Banality of Evil*, The Viking Press, New York, 1963.

[227] See, for instance, Carroll E. Izard, "Four Systems for Emotion Activation: Cognitive and
Noncognitive Development", in *Psychological Review*, 1993, vol. 100, no. 1, pp. 68–90;
John Marshall Reeve, *Understanding Motivation and Emotion*, John Wiley & Sons, Hobo-
ken, 2018, p. 299. Emotions also encompass biological reactions, agents of purpose and a
social phenomenon.

[228] Izard, 1993, pp. 68–90, see above note 227 and Reeve, 2018, p. 299, see above note 227.

[229] Tom Pyszczynski and Jeff Greenberg, "Toward an Integration of Cognitive and Motivational Perspectives on Social Inference: A Biased Hypothesis-Testing Model", in *Advances
in Experimental Social Psychology*, 1987, vol. 20, pp. 297–340.

[230] Karl Ask and Pär-Anders Granhag, "Hot Cognition in Investigative Judgments: The Differential Influence of Anger and Sadness", in *Law and Human Behavior*, 2008, vol. 31, no.
6, p. 547.

[231] See, for instance, Peter J. de Jong, Marie-Anne Haenen, Anton Schmidt and Birgit Mayer,
"Hypochondriasis; The Role of Fear-Confirming Reasoning", in *Behaviour Research and
Therapy*, 1998, vol. 36, no. 1, pp. 65–74; Peter J. de Jong, Birgit Mayer and Marcel van
den Hout, "Conditional Reasoning and Phobic Fear: Evidence for a Fear-Confirming Reasoning Pattern", in *Behaviour Research and Therapy*, 1997, vol. 45, no. 6, pp. 507–16.

[232] See, for instance, Peter Muris, Suradj Debipersad and Birgit Mayer, "Searching for Danger:
on the Link between Worry and Threat-related Confirmation Bias in Children", in *Journal
of Child and Family Studies*, 2014, vol. 23, no. 3, pp. 604–09; Lourdes Suarez and Debora
Bell-Dolan, "The relationship of Child Worry to Cognitive Biases: Threat Interpretation
and Likelihood of Event Occurrence", in *Behavior Therapy*, 2001, vol. 32, no. 3, pp. 425–
42.

[233] For instance, there is likely to be a discrepancy between experimentally induced emotions
and emotions as experienced in real life criminal cases. However, if effects are found with
experimentally induced emotions, it is unlikely that these effects will be weaker in real life.

relatively distinct from the legal context, the studies do highlight the risk of such an impact.

The described risk appears to be relevant for investigations into core international crimes since these investigations, by necessity, concern crimes of extreme gravity, such as genocide. This is evident already in the requirement of 'sufficient gravity' for case selection and admissibility[234] as well as the qualifiers of gravity in the legal definitions of the core crimes, for example, 'grave breaches' that are differentiated from "other, presumably less grave violations" in relation to war crimes[235] or the "intent to destroy one of the protected groups" for genocide.[236] The gravity of the crimes can be expressed both in quantitative terms, for example, the number of victims or deaths,[237] and in qualitative terms, for example, abuse of power, victim vulnerability and particular cruelty.[238] Also, the general context of the alleged crimes is often that of public unrest and polarisation (post-electoral violence, armed conflict or other political conflict). Furthermore, media reports often focus on the suffering of the victims[239] or portray the suspect(s) in ways that are likely to elicit emotions like anger. An associated specific issue is that the extreme gravity of these crimes may – due to, *inter alia*, the emotional components – completely turn the priorities of the criminal investigations around.[240] This notion of changed priorities due to crime severity has not been systematically and

---

[234] ICC Statute, Article 17(1)(d), see above note 8.

[235] *Ibid.*, Article 7.

[236] *Ibid.*, Articles 2; Agirre Aranburu, 2010, pp. 208–09, see above note 10.

[237] ICC RPE, Rule 145(2)(b)(ii)–(iv), see above note 49.

[238] *Ibid.*; Agirre Aranburu, 2010, pp. 216–17, see above note 10.

[239] Agirre Aranburu, 2010, p. 358, see above note 74.

[240] See, for instance, Agirre Aranburu, 2010, p. 356, see above note 74; Peter A. Joy, "The Relationship Between Prosecutorial Misconduct and Wrongful Convictions: Shaping Remedies for a Broken System", in *Wisconsin Law Review*, 2006, vol. 3, no. 2, pp. 399–405; Herbert L. Packer, *The Limits of Criminal Sanction*, Stanford University Press, Stanford, 1968, p. 237; Stuart MacDonald, "Constructing a Framework for Criminal Justice Research", in *New Criminal Law Review: An International and Interdisciplinary Journal*, 2005, vol. 11, no. 2, p. 257. In a similar vein, J. Vincent Aprile II argues that American citizens tend to view investigative and charging decisions by the police and prosecution as the equivalent of a verdict of guilt. As a result, the function of the jury trial is simply to rubber stamp the conclusions of law enforcement and the prosecution. This results in a presumption of guilt, rather than that of innocence, among the public. For more on this, see J. Vincent Aprile II, "Presumption of Innocence Now an Assumption of Guilt", in *Criminal Justice*, 1995, vol. 10, no. 4, p. 32.

---

empirically evaluated, but is in line with the so-called *signal detection theory*.[241] According to this theory, the *cost* of making a mistake (a false positive or a false negative) will influence a decision maker's way of reasoning, as to avoid the mistake that costs the most.[242] More specifically, this may lead the decision maker to perceive that there is a 'hit' (a signal) when there, in fact, is none.[243] Although the legal doctrine prescribes that the costs of false positives (wrongful convictions) outweigh the cost of false negatives (wrongful acquittals), there are no guarantees that this maxim is reflected in legal actors' reasoning and decision making. If, on the contrary, it is true that the costs of allowing "the real Ivan to go free"[244] by far outweighs the cost of convicting an innocent person, then criminal investigators may in practice abide by a presumption of guilt.[245]

---

[241] Thomas D. Wickens, *Elementary Signal Detection Theory*, Oxford University Press, New York, 2002.

[242] *Ibid.*

[243] *Ibid.*, pp. 36–37.

[244] Agirre Aranburu, 2010, p. 356, see above note 74, citing Willem A. Wagenaar, *Identifying Ivan: A Case Study in Legal Psychology*, Harvester, Wheatsheaf, 1988, p. 170.

[245] See also Thijs Bouwknegt, *Cross-Examining the Past – Transitional Justice, Mass Atrocity Trials and History in Africa*, Faculty of Humanities, Amsterdam School for Heritage and Memory Studies, 2017, p. 210. However, this possibility should, be seen in the light of so-called 'vicarious trauma' which has been noted in asylum cases and means that decision makers who suffer psychological distress from exposure to evidence they sometimes use coping strategies involving rejecting the evidence as unimaginable, see the UNHCR, *Beyond Proof – Credibility Assessment in EU Asylum Systems*, pp. 79–82. If also applicable in criminal cases, it could mean that the gravity of the crime does not contribute to confirmation bias but rather a type of sceptical bias. A more specific manifestation of vicarious trauma in asylum cases is that examiners may seek to avoid exposure to evidence causing further distress and this may distort their questioning of the applicant during interview and/or their pursuit of further relevant supporting evidence, see Diana Bogner, Jane Herlihy and Chris R. Brewin, "Impact of Sexual Violence on Disclosure during Home Office Interviews", in *The British Journal of Psychiatry*, 2007, vol. 191, no. 1, pp. 75–81. This is also related to research into so-called 'compassion fatigue', suggesting that encounters with multiple victims or persons in need, compared to single individuals, changes valuation processes during decision making, see Marcus M. Butts, David C. Lunt, Traci L. Freling and Allison S. Gabriel, "Helping One or Helping Many? A Theoretical Integration and Meta-Analytic Review of the Compassion Fade Literature", in *Organizational Behavior and Human Decision Processes*, 2019, vol. 151, pp. 16–33. Furthermore, prolonged exposure to persons in need may lead to permanent deficits in emphatic capacities, known as 'compassion fade'. It may become increasingly difficult to "approach each case afresh and avoid creating hierarchies of persecution which demand ever higher levels of suffering to incite sympathy", see Helen Baillot, Sharon Cowan and Vanessa E. Munro, "Second-

Importantly, such a presumption does not necessarily mean that a person will in fact be wrongfully convicted, but can also mean that the investigators, due to their strong belief that the person in question is guilty, tend to evaluate the evidence against the defendant as stronger than someone without the belief would, and/or that they even downgrade or overlook exonerating information.[246] As a result, the suspected person may go free, rightly or wrongly, and in the former case it may be too late to try and find and prosecute the real perpetrator. This is particularly important considering the high expectations raised on getting a person convicted for a hideous crime and the disappointment or critique that can result when this is not fulfilled.

This raises the question whether emotional content of criminal investigations or proceedings can be reduced in ecologically valid ways? In other words, even if removing emotional content has a debiasing potential in controlled experiments, what meaning do such results have for a reality in which emotional content, often of a strong kind, is ever-present? Regularly, information that carries emotional content is also information that legal actors will have to be exposed to because it is relevant to their work. Although it can be debated whether relevant and irrelevant emotional content can be separated (and if so, this would be the job for a context manager), it is probably better to consider the emotional content an inherent characteristic of these investigations, that is, a baseline from which all debiasing attempts have to be made. However, this does not render research findings on this topic superfluous, rather the contrary, as it may draw decision makers' attention to situations in which these risks are at play. A finding that may be of particular interest provided the rather complex legal constructions in question, is that emotions seem to play a role not only in the fact-finding process but also in how legal actors chose to legally classify acts. For instance, American judges' assessments of whether an act – pasting a false US entry visa into a genuine foreign passport – constituted "forging an identification card" under Ohio Statutes varied significantly depending on the level of sympathy elicited by the

---

hand Emotion? Exploring the Contagion and Impact of Trauma and Distress in the Asylum-Law Context", in *Journal of Law and Society*, 2013, vol. 40, no. 4, p. 532.

[246] This clearly relates to asymmetrical scepticism, see above Section 7.2.2.

description of the defendant.[247] The defendant was either described as a hired killer who had sneaked into the US to track down and kill someone who had stolen drug proceeds from a cartel (killer condition) or a father trying to earn money for a liver transplant for his critically ill nine-year-old daughter (father condition). Of the judges in the killer condition, 60 per cent ruled that the act constituted forgery as compared to 44 per cent in the father condition, and the average sentence was also higher for the killer than the father. Thus, this study suggests that emotions can influence also the interpretation and application of the law (apart from fact-finding). It is likely, although not systematically and empirically evaluated, that this influence is often difficult to detect as legal actors are likely to argue in conventionally relevant terms such as the language of the statute, the legislative history, and so on. The reasons why they choose one interpretation of the law rather than another, are not necessarily clear, neither to the legal actors themselves nor for outside observers. Often both, or several, interpretations can be justified using the same sources but emphasising different aspects of the sources. This notion is in line with research on so-called *motivated reasoning* or *motivated cognition*, where affective preferences trigger the operation of cognitive processes that shifts reasoning to reach the desired conclusion.[248] There is no doubt that the legal classification, and the potential emotional influence on it, are relevant at many stages of investigations into core international crimes. For instance, the question of whether an act constitutes a certain crime is not only decisive for the question of jurisdiction,[249] but is also a requirement, *inter alia*, for the Pre-Trial Chamber to, for example, issue an arrest warrant or a summons to appear[250] as well as for the confirmation of charges and the trial on the charges as confirmed.[251]

---

[247] Andrew J. Wistrich, Jeffrey J. Rachlinski and Chris Guthrie, "Heart versus Head: Do Judges Follow the Law or Follow their Feelings?", in *Texas Law Review*, 2015, vol. 93, no. 4, 1993, pp. 856–911.

[248] Ziva Kunda, "The Case for Motivated Reasoning", in *Psychological Bulletin*, 1990, vol. 108, no. 3, pp. 480–98.

[249] ICC Statute, Articles 5–8, see above note 8.

[250] *Ibid.*, Article 58.

[251] *Ibid.*, Article 61.

7.3.3. Social and Organisational Explanations

> When men wish to construct or support a theory, how they
> torture facts into their service![252]

Social psychologists aim to understand and explain how the thought, feeling and behaviour of individuals are influenced by the actual, imagined or implied presence of others.[253] The social explanations of confirmation bias essentially hold that humans do not reason to find the truth but instead to convince others that they are right.[254] Consequently, research in this area implies that confirmation bias is stronger in relation to self-generated hypotheses than hypotheses generated by others.[255] This has resulted in a notion of confirmation bias as a self-enhancement or ego enhancement bias.[256] In the context of criminal investigations and proceedings this means that police officers who *themselves* have previously apprehended a suspect ask more guilt presumptive questions and perceive of the suspect as less credible during a subsequent interrogation, as compared to police officers who only conduct the interrogation.[257] Similarly, judges who *themselves* have detained a suspect prior to the main hearing, perceive of the suspect's credibility as lower, the evidence against the suspect as stronger and are 2.79 times more likely to convict, as compared

---

[252] Charles Mackay, *Extraordinary Popular Delusions and the Madness of Crowds*, Bentley, 1852, p. 552.

[253] This influential definition was provided by Allport in 1954, see Gordon Willard, *The Nature of Prejudice*, Anchor Books, Abridged, 1958, p. 3. The term 'implied presence' refers to the many activities the individual carries out because of his or her position (role) in complex social structures and because of his or her membership in a cultural group.

[254] Hugo Mercier, "The Argumentative Theory: Predictions and Empirical Evidence", in *Trends in Cognitive Science*, 2016, vol. 20, no. 9, pp. 689–700; Hugo Mercier and Dan Sperber, "Why Do Humans Reason? Arguments for an Argumentative Theory", in *Behavioral and Brain Sciences*, 2011, vol. 34, no, 2, pp. 57–111.

[255] Kevin Dunbar and David Klahr, "Developmental Differences in Scientific Discovery Processes", in David Klahr and Kenneth Kotovsky (eds.), *Complex Information Processing: The Impact of Herbert A. Simon*, Lawrence Erlbaum Associates, Hillsdale, 1989, pp. 109–43; David Klahr, "Designing Good Experiments to Test 'Bad' Hypotheses", in *The Artificial Intelligence and Psychology Project*, 1989, pp. 355–402; Christian D. Schunn and David Klahr, "Self vs. Other-Generated Hypotheses in Scientific Discovery", in Songer W. Kintsch (ed.), *Proceedings of the 15th Annual Conference of the Cognitive Science Society*, 2013; Beth E. Haverkamp, "Confirmatory Bias in Hypothesis Testing for Client-Identified and Counselor Self-Generated Hypotheses", in *Journal of Counseling Psychology*, 1993, vol. 40, no. 3, pp. 303–15.

[256] For more on this, see Lidén, Gräns and Juslin, 2018, pp. 336–54, see above note 46.

[257] *Ibid.*

---

to judges who are only in charge of the main hearing (*ceteris paribus*).[258] This is, and has been, connected to rules on disqualification of judges as well as the defendants right to an impartial tribunal, for example, in the case *Hauschildt v. Denmark*[259] (concerning pre-trial detentions as a basis for non-competence). However, in practice, the same legal actor often makes several decisions in relation to the same suspect for efficiency reasons, for example, that this specific legal actor already knows the case as opposed to a colleague who would have to take time and resources to learn about the case specific circumstances.[260]

Apart from the notion of confirmation bias as a self-enhancement bias, social psychological research also provides other perspectives that are important for understanding why confirmation bias occurs. These perspectives come from research examining group decision making. Intuitively, it seems reasonable to believe that the group setting[261] would prevent confirmation bias, for example, because the bias is more or less subconscious and therefore easier to detect in others than in oneself.[262] How-

---

[258] Lidén, Gräns and Juslin, 2018, pp. 1–29, see above note 197.

[259] European Court of Human Rights (ECHR), *Hauschildt v. Denmark*, Judgment, 24 May 1989 (https://legal-tools.org/doc/ee1c41).

[260] Lidén, Gräns and Juslin, 2018, pp. 1–29, see above note 197.

[261] A commonly accepted definition of a group is people who are interdependent and have at least potential for mutual interaction, see Shelley E. Taylor, Letitia Anne Peplau and David O. Sears, *Social Psychology*, Prentice Hall, Upper Saddle River, 2006, p. 345. Also, in most groups, people have regular face-to-face contact. However, the studied groups have varied in many respects, such as the group size. Most group research has focused on groups ranging from 3 to 20 people, although 2 people (a couple) is also included in the definition. As such, the definition of a group is narrower and more technical than in everyday language where the term is used to refer to all kinds of social units. Yet, in accordance with research using an experimental methodology called the minimal group paradigm (the minimal conditions required for group behaviour to occur), merely being arbitrarily categorised into groups using random criteria such as 'blue team' and 'red team' is sufficient for group members to display group behaviours, see Henri Tajfel, "Experiments in Intergroup Discrimination", in *Scientific American*, 1970, vol. 223, no. 5, pp. 96–102; Henri Tajfel, "Cognitive Aspects of Prejudice", in *Journal of Social Issues*, 1969, vol. XXV, no. 4, pp. 79–97; Marilynn B. Brewer and Rupert J. Brown, "Intergroup Relations", in Daniel Todd Gilbert, Susan T. Fiske and Gardner Lindzey (eds.), *The Handbook of Social Psychology*, McGraw-Hill, New York, 1998, pp. 554–94. For instance, such categorisation makes group members show more favourable attitudes and behaviours towards members of the own group than toward members of another group.

[262] See, for example, Emily Pronin, Thomas Gilovich and Lee Ross, "Objectivity in the Eye of the Beholder: Divergent Perceptions of Bias in Self Versus Others", in *Psychological Review*, 2004, vol. 111, no. 3, pp. 781–99.

ever, contrary to these expectations, research suggests that biases may even be produced or exacerbated in groups,[263] as groups often fail to successfully pool the information held by different members[264] and can have very restricted information-processing patterns.[265] The more specific mechanisms that can produce or exacerbate confirmation bias in groups are, for instance, the emergence of group norms, conformity and role-induced bias, mechanisms that were identified already in early social psychology studies.[266] Although their relationship to confirmation bias as well as the applicability to the legal setting needs to be further evaluated, these findings, together with more recent replications, highlight potential risk factors. These are, for example, *group polarisation*, that is, when a group of like-minded people discusses an issue and the average opinion of

---

[263] Susan M. Houghton, Mark Simon, Karl Aquino and Caren B. Goldberg, "No Safety in Numbers: Persistence of Biases and their Effects of Team Risk Perception and Team Decision Making", in *Group and Organization Management*, 2000, vol. 25, no. 4, pp. 325–53; Norbert L. Kerr and Scott Tindale, "Group Performance and Decision Making", in *Annual Review of Psychology*, 2004, vol. 55, pp. 623–55; R.S. Tindale, *Decision Errors Made by Individuals and Groups*, pp. 109–24.

[264] Garold Stasser and Dennis Stewart, "Discovery of Hidden Profiles by Decision-making Groups: Solving a Problem versus Making a Judgment", in *Journal of Personality and Social Psychology*, 1992, vol. 63, no. 3, pp. 426–34.

[265] Irving L. Janis, *Groupthink; Psychological Studies of Policy Decisions and Fiascoes*, Houghton Miffin, Boston, 1982.

[266] See, for instance, Muzafer Sherif's (1936) pioneering studies demonstrating that in uncertain and ambiguous situations, people tend to conform to group norms, Muzafer Sherif, *The Psychology of Social Norms*, Harper, Oxford, 1936. See also Solomon Asch's (1952) subsequent studies which illustrated conformity in stimulus situations where the correct answers were as plain as day, Solomon Asch, "Opinions and Social Pressure", in *Scientific American*, 1952, vol. 193, no. 5, pp. 31–35, as well as Stanley Milgram (1963) who criticized Asch's studies of conformity because he believed that Asch used trivial tasks in which there were no significant consequences for the participants or for others, Stanley Milgram, "Behavioral Study of Obedience", in *The Journal of Abnormal and Social Psychology*, 1963, vol. 67, no. 4, pp. 371–78. Influenced by a wider social issue, namely Nazi officials' obedience to Hitler's orders, he used a famous task were participants ('teachers') were told to apply electric shocks of increasing strength (75–450 V) to another person (a 'learner') when this person erred in a word association assignment. Overall, 100 per cent of the participants exceeded 180V and 65 per cent continued obeying all the way to 450V. Both Milgram and other have replicated these findings in a range of settings, groups of participants and also using other types of tasks, see, for example, Michael A. Hogg and Graham M. Vaughan, *Essentials of Social Psychology*, Pearson, New York, 2010, pp. 141–50.

group members tend to become more extreme.[267] Possibly, this is because group interaction enables each individual to feel less personally responsible for the consequences of the decisions and they therefore become more daring.[268] It can also be because group members provide each other with persuasive arguments supporting a certain preferred alternative, and contradicting a non-preferred alternative, resulting in a bargaining-like process where group members continuously bid above each other with hypothesis-consistent arguments.[269] Thus, the advantages of the preferred alternative are emphasised and disadvantages downplayed, increasing the individual members' previous beliefs and simultaneously decreasing the likelihood of anyone presenting opposing ideas, because of the fear of making a fool of oneself in front of the group majority.[270] This means that the group comes to function as one large individual with a very strong confirmation bias. Similarly, groups sometimes display a way of thinking where the will to reach consensus overshadows the motivation to use rational decision making procedures, which is referred to as *group-think*.[271]

---

[267] See Serge Moscovici and Marisa Zavalloni, "The Group as a Polarizer of Attitudes", in *Journal of Personality and Social Psychology*, 1969, vol. 12, no. 2, pp. 124–35; Daniel J. Isenberg, "Group Polarization: A Critical Review and Meta-Analysis", in *Journal of Personality and Social Psychology*, 1986, vol. 50, no. 6, pp. 1141–51.

[268] Moscovici and Zavalloni, 1969, p. 126, see above note 267. This is also aligned with the theory of diffusion of responsibility, see Michael A. Wallach and Nathan Kogan, "The Roles of Information, Discussion, and Consensus in Group Risk Taking", in *Journal of Experimental Social Psychology*, 1965, vol. 1, no. 1, pp. 1–19.

[269] See, for instance, Choong-Ling Sia, Bernard Tan and Kwok-Kee Wei, "Group Polarization and Computed Mediated Communication: Effects of Communication Cues, Social Presence, and Anonymity", in *Information Systems Research*, 2002, vol. 13, no. 1, pp. 70–90; Craig McGarthy, John C. Turner, Michael A. Hogg, Barbara David and Margaret S. Wetherell, "Group Polarization as Conformity to the Most Prototypical Group Member", in *British Journal of Social Psychology*, 1992, vol. 31, no. 1, pp. 1–20. Yet another explanation is that individuals who are attracted to a group may be motivated to adopt a more extreme position to gain the group's approval.

[270] Sia, Tan and Wei, 2002, pp. 70–90, see above note 269; McGarthy, Turner, Hogg, David and Wetherell, 1992, pp. 1–20, see above note 269.

[271] The term 'group-think' was first used by Irving Janis in 1982 to describe a series of political decisions that had been made by groups and which according to Janis were fiascos, since the groups failed to realise the moral and practical consequences of their decisions, see Janis, 1982, see above note 265. An example is Kennedy and his advisors' decision to invade the Bay of Pigs in Cuba in 1961. Since 1982, group-think has been studied experimentally in a variety of settings and meta-analysed in 1994, see Brian Mullen, Tara Anthony, Eduardo Salas and James E. Driskell, "Group Cohesiveness and Quality of Decision

This mindset results in, for example, that decision alternatives are not adequately considered and that the group fails to consult outside expertise.[272] According to a meta-analysis from 1994, the two strongest contributing factors to group-think are strong group cohesiveness and directive leadership.[273] As such, research on group-think challenge the notion that group members point out errors in one another's reasoning and instead suggest that such errors might be consolidated in groups. Although the risks of group polarisation and group-think are dependent on group specific factors (such as group cohesion), this research implies that a disregard of alternative hypothesis on an individual level may be reinforced by the will to reach consensus on a group level.

As a response to findings of group polarisation and groupthink, researchers have examined so-called 'devil's advocate' ('DA') procedures as potential debiasing techniques. However, these findings have been mixed as the success of the procedures seem to be dependent on how devilish the DA really is,[274] for example, whether the dissent is genuine or contrived.[275] Thus, for a DA to have the intended effect, rather than become a pointless ritual, the DA should actively research and advocate a contrary position, not just pose rhetorical questions and make insincere or unsubstantiated comments before slipping back into the mainstream of conventional thought. Some suggestions on how to do this, which have not yet been empirically evaluated, are, for example, to rotate the DA role among the members of the group and/or assigning the role to more than one group member.[276] Another way to avoid that the DA is at a numerical dis-

---

Making: An Integration of Tests of the Groupthink Hypothesis", in *Small Group Research*, 1994, vol. 25, no. 2, pp. 189–204.

[272] *Ibid.*

[273] *Ibid.*

[274] This was hypothesized already by Irving L. Janis, *Crucial Decisions, Leadership in Policymaking and Crisis Management*, The Free Press, 1989, p. 248 but has also been acknowledged more recently by for example, Morgan D. Jones, *The Thinker's Toolkit, 14 Powerful Techniques for Problem Solving*, Crown Business, 1995, p. 218.

[275] Stefan Schulz-Hardt, Marc Jochims and Dieter Frey, "Productive Conflict in Group Decision Making: Genuine and Contrived Dissent as Strategies to Counteract Biased Information Seeking", in *Organizational Behavior and Human Decision Processes*, 2002, vol. 88, no. 2, pp. 563–86.

[276] Irving L. Janis, *Victims of Groupthink: A Psychological Study of Foreign-Policy Decisions and Fiascoes*, Houghton Mifflin, Oxford, 1972, p. 216; Randall Kiser, *Beyond Right and Wrong, The Power of Effective Decision Making for Attorneys and Clients*, Springer, Berlin, 2010, p. 389.

---

advantage is to instead have a red team or similar unit, although this is more demanding in terms of resources.[277]

The cited research seems relevant, for example, for the choice between a 'horizontal' or 'vertical' model of investigation and prosecution. With the horizontal model, a crime moves through different sections of a prosecution office depending on the stage of proceedings, resulting in, for example, that different prosecutors make the charging decision and act as the defendant's counter party in court.[278] This is different from the vertical prosecution model, in which a prosecutor is assigned at the start of the process and remains with the case until the trial is completed.[279]

In 2013, the ICC-OTP announced the implementation of a vertical model giving the direction of its teams at all stages of investigation and prosecution to the prosecutions division, hence appointing a senior trial lawyer as the most senior officer in charge of each team starting from the investigation and the same person would also lead the case in court.[280] In 2014, a group of experts further recommended to the ICC-OTP to adopt the vertical model, considering jointly investigations and prosecutions under the concept of 'processing cases',[281] so that "once an incoming complaint has been preliminary screened it is assigned to a core team of qualified prosecutors, investigators and analysts who remain constant and make recommendations to the chief prosecutor at each stage of the case".[282] Furthermore, the core team would remain in charge of the case all through the proceedings.[283] In 2015, the ICC-OTP confirmed that "sen-

---

[277] For more on this see, for example, Gary Adkins, "Red Teaming the Red Team: Utilizing Cyber Espionage to Combat Terrorism", in *Journal of Strategic Security*, 2013, vol. 6, no. 3, pp. 1–9.

[278] Mettraux, Fisher, Groome, Whiting, McIntyre, de Hemptinne and Sluiter, 2014, p. 63, see above note 73.

[279] *Ibid.*, p. 64.

[280] See ICC-OTP, *Strategic Plan June 2012-2015*, 11 October 2013, para. 54 (https://legal-tools.org/doc/954beb).

[281] Mettraux, Fisher, Groome, Whiting, McIntyre, de Hemptinne and Sluiter, 2014, see above note 73.

[282] *Ibid.*

[283] *Ibid.*, pp. 64–65.

ior trial lawyers were placed in charge of the integrated teams"[284] concerning both investigations and prosecutions.[285]

Although the vertical model is considered advantageous, for example, because it promotes continuity and limits the number of different people that victims encounter through the court process,[286] it entails a substantial risk that prosecutors and investigators, who have been working with the hypothesis already from the outset of a case, fail to reason independently of it. This is implied by the notion of confirmation bias as a self-enhancement bias, research of group polarisation and group-think, as well as emotional explanations of confirmation bias. As suggested by the research cited in Section 7.2.1., a guilt hypothesis is likely to become consolidated, in a subjective sense, at the latest with the charging decision, and possibly before that.[287] The consolidation of the hypotheses can be manifested in that the prosecutor is less likely to initiate additional investigation, and if such investigation is undertaken, it is more often aimed at confirming the defendant's guilt.[288] Also, since confirmation bias is exacerbated by an individual's will to convince others that he or she is right, this is likely to be fuelled by a confirmation of the charges on which the prosecutor intends to seek trial by the Pre-Trial Chamber.[289]

---

[284] See ICC OTP, *Strategic Plan 2016-2018*, 16 November 2015, p. 9 (https://legal-tools.org/doc/2dbc2d).

[285] *Ibid.*, pp. 40–41.

[286] *Ibid.*

[287] Lidén, Gräns and Juslin, 2019, pp. 494–526, see above note 24.

[288] *Ibid.*

[289] ICC Statute, Article 61, see above note 8. In this regard it is interesting to note that prosecutors, pursuant to Article 42(7) of the ICC Statute, are disqualified from participating in cases if they have previously been involved, in any capacity, in proceedings against the suspected person, for example, criminal cases against the same person at the national level or in other international jurisdictions, see Yvonne McDermott, in Mark Klamberg, *Commentary on the Law of the International Criminal Court*, TOAEP, Brussels, 2017 p. 361 (https://www.legal-tools.org/doc/aa0e2b/). However, this does not refer to any previous action which the OTP has taken pursuant to the Statute. It seems reasonable to ask why prior involvement on a national level would make prosecutors less capable of remaining impartial than when it comes to involvement based on the Statute. Rule 34 of the ICC RPE sets out four additional grounds that may give rise to disqualification: the existence of a personal or professional relationship that might call their impartiality into question; the involvement with legal proceedings involving the suspect or the accused; the existence of a prior employment that may have led him or her to form opinions about the case, the accused, or counsel; or the expression of opinions that suggest a lack of impartiality, see above note 49.

Furthermore, the findings that self-generated hypotheses are 'stickier' than hypotheses generated by others, may have implications for appropriate ways to work with, for example, investigation plans or techniques such as the ACH. When reassessing whether an investigation plan needs to be updated in the light of new evidence, it is probable that an individual who has not been part of formulating the initial case hypothesis is better capable of reasoning independently of it. Therefore, such a person, or groups of persons (for example, evidence review panels), are less likely to be asymmetrically sceptical in relation to the new evidence and consequently, also more likely to update the investigation plan when this is mandated by the evidence. Similarly, the ACH distinguishes between generation of hypotheses and evaluation of the hypotheses. If the same individual both formulates and evaluates the hypotheses, the risk of confirmation bias is larger than if two different individuals are assigned these tasks.[290]

The organisational explanations of confirmation bias stem from organisational psychology, where an essential finding is that organisational values reinforce certain behaviours that promote goal fulfilment.[291] Thus, a primary defining characteristic of an organisation is *patterned* human behaviour,[292] which means that a structure, typically derived from formal job descriptions and organisational policies, is imposed. In the context of criminal investigation, organisational efficiency demands as well as external expectations to be 'tough on crime', can result in a guilt presumptive

---

[290] For instance, it can be noted that the ACH did not seem to constitute an effective remedy against serial position effects or confirmation bias in a study by Martha Whitesmith, "The Efficacy of ACH in Mitigating Serial Position Effects and Confirmation Bias in an Intelligence Analysis Scenario", in *Intelligence and National Security*, 2019, vol. 34, no. 2, pp. 225–42. Of the participants that exhibited confirmation bias, half were in the non-ACH condition (did not use the ACH) and half were in the ACH condition (did use the ACH). There are many possible explanations of this. One possible explanation is that the participants, when using the ACH both generated and evaluated their own hypotheses. Another explanation is that the ACH simply is not as effective as it is believed to be, a topic which needs further empirical evaluation. It should also be noted that the participants in this study were staff and students from King's College London (n=32) as well as staff from multiple departments within the British Government (n=7), who were asked to role-play the part of an intelligence analyst.

[291] Daniel Katz and Robert Kahn, *The Social Psychology of Organizations*, Wiley, New York, 1966.

[292] *Ibid.*.

---

mindset.[293] The presence of external expectations in relation to investigations of core international crimes is evident from, for example, the ICTY case of Vojislav Šešelj[294] and the ICC case of Laurent Gbagbo.[295] For instance, media reports that Gbagbo is "now widely regarded as a leader who was willing to destroy his country by refusing to accept defeat at the ballot box".[296] The potentially biasing effects as well as source memory errors stemming from pre-trial publicity ('PTP') are well researched.[297] Also, demands and/or expectations to respond effectively and promptly are likely to create time pressure, which, in turn, increases selectivity in information processing, illustrated in a range of decision making situations,[298] including criminal investigations.[299] Furthermore, being per-

---

[293] See, for example, Karl Ask, Pär-Anders Granhag and Anna Rebelius, "Investigators under Influence: How Social Norms Activate Goal-Directed Processing of Criminal Evidence", in *Applied Cognitive Psychology*, 2011, vol. 25, no. 4, pp. 548–53.

[294] ICTY, *The Prosecutor v. Vojislav Šešelj*, IT-03-67. Media reported on, for example, the behaviour of Mr. Šešelj including, for example, hunger strikes, dismissive language in pre-trial hearings, that he remained the figurehead of the Serbian Radical Party (SRS) while awaiting trial; for a summary, see "Serb Accused at War Crimes Trial", *BBC*, 7 November 2007 (available on its web site). Mr. Šešelj also filed a motion for contempt against members of the Office of the Prosecutor claiming that they had resorted to threats, intimidation and bribes in order to ensure the testimony of certain witnesses, see ICTY, *Prosecutor v. Vojislav Šešelj*, Trial Chamber, Decision on Vojislav Šešelj's Motion for Contempt Against Carla Del Ponte, Hildegard Uertz-Retzlaff and Daniel Saxon and on the Subsequent Requests of the Prosecution, 22 December 2011, IT-03-67-T, p. 2 (https://legal-tools.org/doc/686cc1). The Chamber concluded that sufficient grounds did not exist to instigate proceedings for contempt against any members of the Prosecution.

[295] ICC, *The Prosecutor v. Laurent Gbagbo and Charles Blé Goudé*, ICC-02/11-01/15.

[296] See "Laurent Gbagbo Profile: Ivory Coast's Defiant 'Cicero'", *BBC News*, 15 January 2019 (available on the web site).

[297] Although primarily in relation to jurors. For a summary see Christine Ruva, Cathy McEvoy and Judith Becker Bryant, "Effects of Pre-Trial Publicity and Jury Deliberation on Juror Bias and Source Memory Errors", in *Applied Cognitive Psychology*, 2007, vol. 21, pp. 45–67. According to the authors, measures to prevent biasing effects of PTP, such as judicial instruction, *voir dire* and deliberation are largely ineffective but measures such as change of venue (which reduces the PTP) and bench trial (which eliminates the jury) may be effective, although they have not yet been studied by experimenters.

[298] The effects of time pressure on human decision making are well-researched. Apart from selectivity in information processing (so-called 'filtering'), time pressure seems to decrease flexibility, which deteriorates the ability to generate alternative hypotheses and strategies and also make people rely more heavily on their previous views and stereotypes and less likely to assimilate new information. For literature on selectivity in information processing see, for example, Anne Edland and Ola Svensson, "Judgment and Decision Making under Time Pressure", in Ola Svensson and John Maule (ed.), *Time Pressure and Stress in Human Judgment and Decision Making*, Plenum Press, 1993, pp. 27–40; Rik Pie-

ceived as an effective criminal investigator or similar can help fulfil career goals, which is desirable for individuals with high needs to realise their potential and maximise capability, so-called *self-actualisation*.[300] Although efficiency demands as well as career goals will probably always be present, better time management can prevent time pressure and, as such, function as a debiasing technique.

7.4. Concluding Remarks

In investigations of core international crimes there are some inherent structural issues that exacerbate the risk of confirmation bias. These are, for example, the historical as well as contemporary context and the explicit and often large investments into specific lines of inquiry, as well as suspects, which increase, for example, commitment and defence motivation. The risk of confirmation bias is also enhanced by that, in these investigations, cognitive load is regularly sky-high, the emotional components are strong, ways of working such as the vertical prosecution model may trigger self-enhancement aspects and the organisational as well as external efficiency demands are pronounced. Depending on to what extent an investigation plan is closed or open, it entails different levels of risk of confirmation bias, while the focus on the most responsible perpetrators is a

---

ters, Luk Warlop and Michel Hartog, "The Effect of Time Pressure and Task Motivation on Visual Attention to Brands", *in Advances in Consumer Research*, 1997, vol. 24, pp. 281–87; Takeo Tsuji and Shigeru Watanabe, "Neural Correlates of Belief-Bias Reasoning Under Time Pressure: A Near-Infrared Spectroscopy Study", in *NeuroImage*, 2010, vol. 50, no. 3, pp. 1320–26. For literature on the decreased ability to generate alternative hypotheses, see, for example, Jerome Seymour Bruner and George Allen Austin, *A Study of Thinking*, Transaction Publishers, 1986, pp. 1091–97; and literature on stereotypes, see Galen V. Bodenhausen, "Stereotypes as Judgmental Heuristics: Evidence of Circadian Variations in Discrimination", in *Psychological Science*, 1990, vol. 1, no. 5, pp. 319–22; John S. Hulland and Don M. Kleinmunts, "Factors Influencing the Use of Internal Summary Evaluations versus External Information in Choice", in *Behavioral Decision Making*, 1994, vol. 7, no. 2, pp. 79–102; Martin F. Kaplan, Tatian Wanshula and Mark P. Zanna, "Time Pressure and Information Integration in Social Judgment: The Effect of Need for Structure", in Ola Svensson and John Maule (eds.), *Time Pressure and Information Integration in Social Judgment*, Springer, 1993, pp. 255–67; Abraham Tesser and Mary C. Conlee, *Some Effects of Time and Thought on Attitude Polarization*, in *Journal of Personality and Social Psychology*, 1975, vol. 31, no. 2, pp. 262–70.

299 See, for example, Ask and Granhag, 2007, pp. 561–91, see above note 98; Fahsing and Ask, 2013, pp. 155–65, see above note 45.

300 See, for example, Steve M. Jex and Thomas W. Britt, *Organizational Psychology: A Scientist-Practitioner Approach*, John Wiley & Sons, 2015, p. 294.

---

more unambiguous risk factor. Such case hypotheses can trigger suspect-driven investigations as well as asymmetrical scepticism in relation to hypothesis-inconsistent evidence, which, in turn, can result in case hypotheses not being challenged enough. This is further emphasised by the risk of hypothesis-consistent searching and securing of evidence on crime scenes, forensic analyses biased by hypotheses, or contextual information as well as line-ups and interviews that are largely driven by case hypotheses.

Yet, formulating and working on the basis of a case hypothesis is usually inevitable. Possibly, even if a case hypothesis was not made explicit, the drive for cognitive coherence would probably make investigators formulate such a hypothesis in their minds anyways. Clearly, an explicit formulation of a case hypothesis will make the hypothesis more open to scrutiny. This in itself does not mean that the hypothesis will also be *scrutinised*, as this requires that investigators are capable of reasoning independently of the hypothesis. Like the research cited in this chapter illustrates, this is indeed challenging. An aspect of confirmation bias that strongly contributes to this, is its largely subconscious nature. Since it is unlikely that decision makers will detect confirmation bias *when it occurs*, especially not in their own reasoning, preventing it by using proactive debiasing techniques is necessary and an important part of quality control.

The above-described inherent structural issues in investigations of core international crimes are to be considered risk factors of confirmation bias. However, many of these issues are difficult to address in other ways than making structural changes, which may be impossible or undesirable for other reasons. It is therefore better to focus on those risk factors that can be addressed more effectively. These risk factors are summarised in Table 1 together with corresponding debiasing techniques identified through cognitive, social or organisational as well as emotional or motivational psychology.

Table 1. Risk Factors and Corresponding Debiasing Techniques.

Risk Factor	Debiasing Technique
Information overload (*cognitive explanations*)	3. Structured analytical techniques 4. Models for suspect interviews
Access to contextual biasing information (*cognitive, emotional or motivational explanations*)	5. Contextual information management (CIM)
Vertical models of investigation and prosecution (*social and emotional or motivational explanations*)	6. Changing decision makers 7. Evidence review panels
Group polarisation and group-think (*social explanations*)	8. Genuine, substantiated dissent through, for example, Devil's advocate procedures or red teams
Time-pressure (*organisational explanations*)	9. Better time management, longer timelines
Multiple (*cognitive, emotional or motivational, social or organisational explanations*)	10. Specific training on confirmation bias and cognitive, emotional or motivational, social or organisational explanations 11. Combining debiasing techniques, for example, structured analytical techniques, contextual information management and changing decision maker

As illustrated by Table 1, when it comes to identifying debiasing techniques, the explanations of confirmation bias can be helpful to different extents and in different ways. The cognitive explanations provide rather specific guidelines. Since confirmation bias is enhanced in relation to cognitively more demanding tasks, reducing cognitive load can prevent the bias. More specifically, this can be done by using structured analytical techniques, such as case evaluation tables and charts. Such techniques break down a large and difficult decision or assessment task into smaller components, which, in line with the divide and conquer principle, reduces cognitive load. In the specific context of suspect interviews, cognitive load is reduced by using an accepted model for how to conduct these interviews, together with continuous training and education in asking open-ended questions.

Cognitive psychological research also suggests that it is very difficult or even impossible to disregard known contextual information. For instance, the research into forensic confirmation bias systematically shows biasing effects of analysts' knowledge of case hypothesis, other evidence, and so on. As such, confirmation bias can also be prevented by implementing protocols for management of contextual information. In teams of investigators that have been working on the same case continuously throughout the proceedings, the access to or knowledge of contextual information is likely to be large. A context-manager or similar is assigned the role to decide what information is necessary and relevant for decision makers to know, and also when they have to know of it (sequential linear unmasking). To avoid that such techniques interrupt the workflow more than necessary, it is advisable to use protocols that establish, step by step, how such context management should be conducted. Ideally, this protocol should be tailor-made for the context in question.

The explanations stemming from Emotion and Motivation Psychology highlight the potentially biasing influence of emotions not only in the fact-finding process, but also in legal interpretation. As this may greatly impact investigations into core international crimes, knowledge of the risk factor is in itself important. Although mere knowledge of this risk factor is insufficient for preventing confirmation bias, such knowledge can be helpful in identifying situations where the bias might be at play, which in turn can be informative of appropriate decision structures. For instance, a context manager can help in the process of avoiding exposure to irrelevant emotional information (or ensuring that relevant but potentially biasing emotional information is only disclosed at a later point in time). Also, knowledge of emotional risk factors, can help identify situations in which a change of decision maker is appropriate, even if these situations as such do not fall within the frames of the non-competence provisions.

Apart from that decision makers who have already been involved in an investigation might have formed emotional ties to a hypothesis, also the social explanations of confirmation bias imply that changing decision maker is a plausible debiasing technique. This is because confirmation bias seems to be stronger in relation to self-generated hypotheses than hypotheses generated by others. This research highlights that vertical models for investigation and prosecution are risk factors of confirmation bias, as these models require that the same individuals remain on the case through all stages. Being involved at several stages of an investigation increases the risk of self-enhancement issues (of which the subconscious types are of interest here). More specifically, this means that decision makers become less interested in the truth and more interested in proving to others that their hypothesis is right. As such, they may fail to see the relevance of hypothesis inconsistent information. This risk should not be underestimated, especially not in investigations of core international crimes, in which the large amounts of complex crime relevant information can result in a strong (subconscious) temptation to take cognitive shortcuts. Changing decision maker between different situations or stages triggers more of a critical stance and is therefore a possible debiasing technique. This debiasing technique can also be considered in relation to more specific tasks such as working with an investigation plan or using methods such as the ACH. It is preferable that the generation of hypotheses and the subsequent evaluation of the hypotheses are conducted by different individuals or teams of individuals. Similarly, evidence review panels consisting of individuals who have not previously been involved in the investigation are likely to be more critical and therefore better capable at providing alternative perspectives. Yet, the overall effect of having such panels is also dependent on how the presented alternative perspectives are received by those working with the investigation. Furthermore, social psychological research looking into group decision making highlights how group processes such as group polarisation and group-think can become risk factors of confirmation bias. Although more research is still needed, genuine and substantiated dissent, for example, through devil's advocate procedures or red teams can function as potential debiasing techniques.

When it comes to the organisational explanations of confirmation bias, these are relatively complex to convert into plausible debiasing techniques, primarily because organisational values such as efficiency demands are unlikely to change in practice. Yet, since there is a close relationship between time pressure and narrow searches for information, better time management and longer timelines can function as a debiasing technique.

Since humans do not only have cognitive limitations, but are also emotional creatures that work within social groups as well as organisational settings, the outlined explanations are, as pointed out in Section 7.3., to be considered mutually supportive rather than mutually exclusive. Understanding this complex interplay between different factors in producing the bias can be better understood through training on the nature of the bias. Furthermore, the identified debiasing techniques should be combined to provide effective quality control from a wider perspective. For instance, case evaluation tables and charts only ask decision makers to evaluate the evidence in relation to one hypothesis (under-determination), and it is therefore necessary to combine such methods with, for example, comparative methods such as the ACH. Additionally, methods such as contextual information management and changing decision maker should also be used simultaneously to address risk factors in other parts of the investigation.

Although previous research provides a good foundation for assessing what types of debiasing techniques will function, it is crucial that any implementation of debiasing techniques in a specific context is preceded by tailor-making the debiasing techniques for that context. To begin with, this entails practical considerations – that is, what techniques or methods would be practically feasible to implement, considering, for example, current workflows and mandatory decision structures. It also entails careful empirical evaluation, usually using experimental methods, of the techniques directly in the context where they are intended to be used. Such evidence-based prevention, that is both practically informed and oriented, is the best remedy available against confirmation bias.

The time that has passed since Nickerson introduced the currently most influential work on confirmation bias, has resulted in the realisation among researchers that there is no single fool-proof method to prevent confirmation bias. Yet, since the understanding of its context-specificity as well as its explanations have improved and become more nuanced, it is fair to say that we today know more about how to prevent it. To continue this work into specific contexts is important, not the least when it comes to the context of investigation of core international crimes. This is because, inspired by the quotation from Nickerson at the beginning of the chapter, if one were to attempt to identify a single problematic context in which all the risk factors of confirmation bias are pronounced, criminal investigation of core international crimes must be a leading candidate.

8

International Criminal Investigative Collection
Planning, Collection Management
and Evidence Review

Ewan Brown and William H. Wiley[*]

8.1. Introduction

The January 2019 collapse of the prosecution cases against Mr. Laurent
Gbagbo, the erstwhile President of Côte d'Ivoire, and his co-accused, Mr.
Charles Blé Goudé, constituted the latest in a series of debacles befalling
the Office of the Prosecutor ('OTP') of the International Criminal Court
('ICC'). In looking at the rather thin docket compiled since the establishment of the Court in 2003, even the casual observer will note the substantial number of ignominious OTP breakdowns. In four instances to date,
ICC pre-trial chambers have refused to confirm *any* of the prosecution
charges.[1] In two further instances, pre-trial chambers confirmed some of

---

[*] **Ewan Brown** is Senior Analyst at the Commission for International Justice and Accountability ('CIJA'); his prior service includes appointments as head of the Military Analysis
Team at the ICTY-OTP, as Darfur Team Leader at the ICC-OTP and as an officer in the
British Army. **William H. Wiley** is the Executive Director of the CIJA; he has also served
variously as an intelligence analyst, investigator and legal advisor with the Canadian war-
crimes programme, the ICTY-OTP, the ICTR-OTP and the Iraqi High Tribunal, additional
to his service as a Canadian Army officer.

[1] ICC, Situation in Darfur, Sudan, *The Prosecutor v. Bahr Idriss Abu Garda*, Pre-Trial
Chamber, Decision on the Confirmation of Charges, 8 February 2010, ICC-02/05-02/09-
243-Red (https://legal-tools.org/doc/cb3614); ICC, Situation in the Democratic Republic of
the Congo, *The Prosecutor v. Callixte Mbarushimana*, Pre-Trial Chamber, Decision on the
confirmation of charges, 16 December 2011, ICC-01/04-01/10-465-Red (https://legal-tools.
org/doc/63028f); ICC, Situation in the Republic of Kenya, *The Prosecutor v. Mohammed
Hussein Ali*, Pre-Trial Chamber, Decision on the Confirmation of Charges Pursuant to Article 61(7)(a) and (b) of the Rome Statute, 23 January 2012, ICC-01/09-02/11-382-Red
(https://legal-tools.org/doc/4972c0); ICC, Situation in the Republic of Kenya, *The Prosecutor v. Henry Kiprono Kosgey*, Pre-Trial Chamber, Decision on the Confirmation of
Charges Pursuant to Article 61(7)(a) and (b) of the Rome Statute, 23 January 2012, ICC-
01/09-01/11-373 (https://legal-tools.org/doc/96c3c2).

the OTP charges, only to see the Prosecutor formally withdraw the cases – including that brought against the President of Kenya – on the grounds that the OTP lacked sufficient evidence to secure a conviction.[2] In another case, Mr. Mathieu Ngudjolo was acquitted of all charges by Trial Chamber II at the conclusion of his trial,[3] after he had spent nearly five years in custody; and, it will be recalled, in mid-2018 the ICC Appeals Chamber vacated the conviction of Mr. Jean-Pierre Bemba on all charges arising from his alleged perpetration of core international crimes, after Mr. Bemba had spent ten years in custody.[4] Against this record, the OTP has successfully prosecuted only four individuals for war crimes and crimes against humanity, one of whom pleaded guilty.[5] Similarly, the Extraordinary Chambers in the Courts of Cambodia ('ECCC') have registered just three convictions since the first judges were sworn in during July 2006.[6] For its part, the Special Tribunal for Lebanon ('STL') has not (at January 2020) issued a single judgement on a criminal charge; the investigative body which gave rise to the Tribunal commenced its work in 2005.[7] In a similar vein, the Kosovo Specialist Chambers and Specialist Prosecutor's Office ('KSC') have not brought any charges, the investigations informing that body having commenced in 2011.[8]

---

[2] ICC, Situation in the Republic of Kenya, *The Prosecutor v. Francis Kirimi Muthaura*, OTP, Prosecution notification of withdrawal of the charges against Francis Kirimi Muthaura, 11 March 2013, ICC-01/09-02/11-687 (https://legal-tools.org/doc/4786c1); ICC, Situation in the Republic of Kenya, *The Prosecutor v. Uhuru Muigai Kenyatta*, OTP, Notice of withdrawal of the charges against Uhuru Muigai Kenyatta, 5 December 2014, ICC-01/09-02/11-983 (https://legal-tools.org/doc/b57a97).

[3] ICC, Situation in the Democratic Republic of the Congo, *The Prosecutor v. Mathieu Ngudjolo Chui*, Trial Chamber, Judgement pursuant to Article 74 of the Statute, 18 December 2012, ICC-01/04-02/12-3-tENG (https://legal-tools.org/doc/2c2cde).

[4] ICC, Situation in the Central African Republic, *The Prosecutor v. Jean-Pierre Bemba Gombo*, Appeals Chamber, Judgment on the appeal of Mr Jean-Pierre Bemba Gombo against Trial Chamber III's "Judgment pursuant to Article 74 of the Statute", 8 June 2018, ICC-01/05-01/08-3636-Red (https://legal-tools.org/doc/40d35b).

[5] Thomas Lubanga Dyilo, Germain Katanga, Ahmad Al Faqi Al Mahdi and Bosco Ntaganda.

[6] See ECCC's web site.

[7] The United Nations International Independent Investigation Commission ('UNIIIC') was established in April 2005 pursuant to United Nations Security Council Resolution 1595 (2005), UN Doc. S/RES/1595 (2005), 7 April 2005 (https://legal-tools.org/doc/4a0623).

[8] The Special Investigative Task Force ('SITF'), established in 2011, evolved into the Special Prosecutor's Office in 2016; see KSC's web site.

Factors unique to any given casefile will explain why (i) an investigation does not give rise to a prosecution and, where allegations are brought before a panel of judges, (ii) the prosecution fails to secure a conviction. This chapter is concerned primarily with the second phenomenon; and it will be noted that a consistent set of shortcomings invariably informs unsuccessful prosecutions. The principal problems identified by pre-trial (at the ICC) and trial chambers more generally are summarised here as being an insufficiency of evidence as well as the failure of prosecutors to assess properly such *prima facie* evidence which an OTP chooses to adduce. By way of example, the reasons given by ICC Trial Chamber I for the dismissal of the charges against Messrs. Blé Goudé and Gbagbo are representative. In the relevant decision, the trial panel noted the lack of evidence supporting the contextual narrative advanced by the prosecution as well as the paucity of evidentiary support for many of the key assertions made by the OTP. In particular, the trial chamber pointed to insufficiently-supported OTP allegations concerning, *inter alia*, the development of a common plan, the existence of an inner circle and the shared intent underlying the alleged common plan formulated by the ostensible members of the said inner circle.[9] Taken as a whole, the written reasons offered by the majority of the trial panel for the dismissal of the charges against both accused were withering – and justifiably so, given the palpable weakness of the prosecution case as well as the fact that Mr. Blé Goudé and Mr. Gbagbo had spent, respectively, roughly five and seven years in custody. As things stand, it is difficult to rebut the arguments of those who hold that ICC-OTP expenditures since 2003, along with the paucity of convictions relative to collapsed cases, together point to a record of prosecutorial failure.

It is undoubtedly the case that the underlying reasons for the undesirable state of affairs set out in the prior paragraph do not all lie with the ICC-OTP. For instance, any international chief prosecutor charged with the investigation of complex crimes in politically unstable environments which present significant physical-security challenges will encounter difficulties in securing sufficient evidence to warrant formal allegations of individual criminal responsibility for the perpetration of core international

---

[9] ICC, Situation in the Republic of Côte d'Ivoire, *The Prosecutor v. Laurent Gbagbo and Charles Blé Goudé*, Trial Chamber, Reasons of Judge Geoffrey Henderson, 16 July 2019, ICC-02/11-01/15-1263-AnxB-Red, paras. 66–77 (https://legal-tools.org/doc/j0v5qx).

crimes. Transcending the obstacles posed by political instability and physical risk will always prove to be especially difficult where an international court or tribunal lacks a United Nations Security Council Chapter VII mandate. These mitigating factors having been noted, it is nonetheless to be recalled that it is the ethical obligation of prosecutors – domestic and international – to refrain from bringing to trial any suspect where there is not a reasonable prospect of conviction. The limited collective caseload of the ECCC, STL and KSC would suggest that the chief prosecutors who have served in those institutions understand this ethical requirement. Ms. Fatou Bensouda, the ICC chief Prosecutor, presumably does as well, insofar as most of the cases which have collapsed on her watch were initiated by her predecessor, Mr. Luis Moreno Ocampo.

Given the wide-ranging responsibilities of any chief prosecutor charged with overseeing operations of significant scope, it follows that he or she will only be effective where subordinate investigators, analysts and counsel conform collectively to the highest standards of evidence collection, analysis and case management. Indisputably, it is the first duty of a chief prosecutor to ensure that such standards are upheld by his or her subordinates. This truism aside, the fact that the ICC-OTP has lost (or otherwise seen collapse) more cases than it has won would suggest to some that there is disconnect between the threshold for a conviction set by the ICC judges and the standard prevailing within the OTP. What is more likely is that the OTP grasps in theory the burden of proof established by the judicial chambers of the Court whereas in practice the OTP is, as a body, unable to determine consistently whether it holds sufficient evidence to meet the requisite evidentiary standards for a conviction on a particular charge.

If the latter assertion is correct – and the litany of OTP failures at the pre-trial, trial and appellate levels would suggest that it is – this deleterious situation points to three overlapping sets of problems. First, the OTP has experienced difficulties on a consistent basis in collecting information of *prima facie* evidentiary value which, in turn, might be transformed into relevant evidence through analytical processes. The suspicion of the authors of this chapter is that, more often than not, the obstacles encountered by the OTP where it has sought to collect high-quality *prima facie* evidence have led, in a misguided attempt to demonstrate internal progress, to the over-collection of more easily accessible forms of information, in particular, crime base testimony. Secondly, there is apparently an inability on the part of a plurality of OTP investigators, analysts and lawyers to grasp fully the depth, quality and quantities of evidence required to ensure a reasonable prospect of conviction where a decision is taken to send a case to trial. Thirdly, the evidence-review processes of the ICC-OTP are often not functioning properly. Were this not the case, convictions rather than prosecutorial failure would be the norm. Absent these three considerations, there is no logical explanation for the fact that the OTP chief and senior prosecutors have so often found themselves buried in the rubble of cases which have collapsed atop them.

Notwithstanding these introductory remarks, this chapter should not be seen as an indictment of the ICC-OTP, the evidence collection efforts of which have been undermined not infrequently by political chicanery and seemingly insurmountable physical risk. Rather, it takes certain of the shortcomings of that institution only as its starting point, offering, as the ICC-OTP performance does, an object lesson in the fate which awaits any prosecutor, appearing before an independent judiciary, where he or she proceeds to trial in a complex case armed with insufficient evidence. The policy brief of Mr. Morten Bergsmo, which informs this entire volume, serves as an important guide, not least through its reference to the indispensability of effective evidence collection and review as well as the pitfalls of collecting too much evidence – or, rather, the wrong sorts of evidence.[10] To these ends, what follows places particular emphasis upon planning for the collection of crime base as well as linkage evidence whilst making a case for innovation in the gathering of contextual evidence. The substantive discussion closes with a call for more robust evidence review processes.

8.2. Evidentiary Challenges

The building of prosecution cases against senior leadership personnel within the framework of international criminal and humanitarian law ('ICHL'), or domestic variants thereof, is time consuming, resource intensive and requires considerable attention to detail on the part of the investigators, analysts and counsel assigned to a given file. It is worth recalling that the focus of ICHL investigations and prosecutions frequently falls

---

[10] Morten Bergsmo, "Towards a Culture of Quality Control in Criminal Investigations", FICHL Policy Brief Series No. 94 (2019), Torkel Opsahl Academic EPublisher, Brussels, 2019 (https://www.toaep.org/pbs-pdf/94-bergsmo/).

upon individuals well removed from the underlying physical acts of a criminal nature; and, whether the suspects are of low or high rank, they will invariably be operating (or have operated) in the midst of military conflicts which often give rise to extreme levels of societal breakdown. The presence of an array of belligerent parties, including those foreign to the territory on which a conflict takes place, further complicates the challenges facing those tasked with the building of prosecution cases.

As a rule, investigative and prosecutorial bodies – particularly those operating internationally – find themselves grappling with an array of perpetrating structures of a political, military, police, security-intelligence, paramilitary and, occasionally, commercial nature. In the post-*ad hoc* Tribunal era, domestic and international investigations are in the main undertaken in and around ongoing armed conflicts; this reality complicates significantly the challenges inherent in the collection of high-quality, *prima facie* evidence, most especially by public authorities with their necessarily limited capacity to adapt to the physical risks presented by theatres of war. What is more, international criminal investigative teams are invariably compelled to take into account broad temporal parameters and wide geographical areas, within which multiple offences have taken place. Notwithstanding these challenges, there is (and can be) no lessoning of the requirement that, where a case is brought to trial, the prosecutor must demonstrate beyond a reasonable doubt that all of the elements of the crimes alleged as well as the legal requirements of the modes of liability alleged in the prosecution complaint.

It was the early practice of the OTPs of the International Criminal Tribunals for Rwanda ('ICTR') and the former Yugoslavia ('ICTY') to collect key evidence during trial; that is, after the accused had habitually spent significant periods of time in pre-trial custody and hard-pressed senior trial attorneys came to realise, time and again, that they were arguing cases which, absent significant additional evidence collection, would collapse. For the most part, both OTPs got away with this risky approach to case building insofar as the number of acquittals witnessed at the ICTY and the ICTR was remarkably few. At these institutions, prosecutorial disaster was consistently averted only because they both operated with Chapter VII mandates in secure, post-conflict environments characterised by levels of domestic-political interference which, in the main, did not present competent investigative efforts with insurmountable difficulties. These relative advantages have rarely made themselves available in such abundance to the OTPs established since 2000 – and, most especially, not to the ICC-OTP. Given the ethical requirement to investigate incriminating and exonerating evidence related to all the elements of every offence and mode of liability alleged *prior* to trial, investigators, analysts and counsel are today routinely confronted with potentially overwhelming evidentiary challenges.

During the investigative phase of ICHL cases, it has become commonplace for investigative and prosecutorial authorities to distinguish between crime base and linkage evidence. While there is at times a degree of important overlap between these categories, the distinction, which has gained traction in the practice of ICHL over the last 15 years, serves to focus the minds of investigators, analysts and counsel upon the relevance and value of every specific piece of evidence as well as its place within the overall case. The authors of this chapter suggest that the time has come to add a third category of evidence to those of crime base and linkage – that of contextual evidence. These three classifications of evidence shall now be considered in turn.

8.2.1. Crime Base Evidence

Defined in purely legal terms, crime base evidence is used to satisfy the physical elements of the offences alleged; as such, it does not concern itself with the mental elements of crimes nor the mental and material legal requirements of the modes of liability set out in ICHL. The collection of crime base information is designed to establish that acts of a criminal nature have been perpetrated and the context in which they were committed; to this end, crime base collection generally involves the identification of victims, eyewitnesses to physical acts and the institutional affiliation of the physical perpetrators of those acts. Additionally, crime base inquiries will frequently address the broader actions of perpetrating structures, not least prior to and following key incidents.

The focus of crime base inquiries upon the details pertaining to underlying physical acts of a potentially criminal nature, gleaned principally from witnesses to such events (that is, crime base witnesses), has come to be well understood by the investigators, analysts and counsel employed by national as well as international investigative bodies. However, individual investigative teams demonstrate at times an insufficient grasp of the multiple sub-themes of crime base collection – that is, the finding of material pertaining to selected incidents, including that which pre- and post-dates the key events – all of which require highly detailed, unique and demanding collection activities. For instance, it is invariably advisable that investigative teams secure location and geospatial data; identify all targets attacked during the key incident(s); obtain details regarding the weapons (or weapon systems) employed during the perpetration of offences; prepare a detailed account – including the full biographical details – of casualties and bystanders; establish the wider patterns of combat activity at the time of the relevant incident(s); secure information regarding the presence in the vicinity, if any, of armed groups hostile to the suspected perpetrating structures; determine whether ranking personnel were present at the incident location(s) prior to, during or after the key event(s); establish whether any threats or warnings were issued by the suspected perpetrating structure(s) prior to the incident(s); and identify any post-incident inquiries undertaken by officials associated with the said perpetrating structure(s).

These and other questions need to be explored systematically and exhaustively in order to arrive at a comprehensive and objective account of any suspected criminality. At times, it is relatively easy to establish, at least to a *prima facie* standard of evidence, that criminal acts were perpetrated, for example, in instances where military forces appeared in a village and, in the absence of armed opposition, proceeded to execute some or all of the civilians found in the settlement. However, in other instances the loss of civilian life, in and of itself, cannot reasonably give rise to a working hypothesis that one or another party to the fighting perpetrated criminal acts. This is most especially the case where sizeable opposing forces engaged one another in built-up areas in which large numbers of civilians were present. To conclude solely upon the basis of the loss of civilian life in the midst of battle that a criminal offence was perpetrated is to forget that international humanitarian law makes considerable allowance for such losses where civilians have not been targeted directly.

8.2.1.1. Crime Base Collection Planning

It is essential that crime base information-*cum*-evidence should be sought in accordance with a properly prepared and detailed collection plan. The undertaking of crime base collection activities in the absence of such a plan – which was almost uniformly the practice at the *ad hoc* Tribunals and remains a distressingly common practice – will invariably lead to the diversion of finite investigative resources from more pressing evidentiary requirements whilst serving to bury an investigative team in superfluous information. Material collected in the field is not, strictly speaking, evidence or even *prima facie* evidence; rather, what is collected is information which becomes evidence only after it has been analysed in the context of the applicable substantive law. What is more, analytical resources are invariably limited within investigative teams, which is to note that they should not be redirected from significant evidentiary questions towards the assessment of mountains of information which may, upon analysis, turn out to have the evidentiary value of mattress stuffing.

There is no fixed format for a crime base collection plan; such documents are organic in nature in that they are subject to ongoing amendment in accordance with the findings of the investigation as the latter evolves. In producing the first iteration of a collection plan, the investigative team will invariably turn to reports coming from the human rights world, for instance, those issued by non-governmental organisations and United Nations fact-finding missions. Although human rights reports are habitually produced for advocacy purposes – and conform to standards of evidence falling well below those demanded by criminal courts – they nonetheless tend to identify with reasonable accuracy the simple fact of critical incidents. As such, human rights reports offer something in the way of initial guidance to a criminal investigation at its outset. That noted, criminal investigative teams should look to open sources of this nature as guides rather than as gospel. For this reason, the leads taken from human rights reports will, in the first draft of a collection plan, be supplemented by lengthy lists of questions appropriate to the likely challenges identified at the outset by properly led investigative teams.

It is critical that such questions are posed *from the outset* of an investigation where, amended as necessary, they must remain at the heart of the collection plan, not least in order to focus the minds of investigators, analysts and counsel on to the key evidentiary requirements. Each theme and sub-theme in a crime base collection plan should generate detailed questions which, as they are answered, will facilitate the building of an objective as well as complete picture of what might be termed the what, where, when and how of an incident or incidences. For instance, an investigation concerned with one or more security-intelligence structures suspected of perpetrating ICHL offences in static locations (for instance, detention facilities) will pose to an extent different questions than an inquiry focused upon ground forces suspected of having violated the principles of distinction and the law of proportionality in the context of otherwise lawful military operations. Nonetheless, every crime base collection plan will set out clearly a number of key themes, not least: the identification of the chronology of the key incident(s); the establishment of the pertinent actions, along with the details of the physical perpetrators of the incident(s) as well as the units, formations and organisations with which the suspected physical authors of the *prima facie* criminal acts served; the material elements of the suspected *prima facie* offences; and the identification of a comprehensive contextual narrative taking into account key events which occurred prior to, during and following the relevant incident(s).

It is worth reiterating that collection plans take the form of a large number of specific questions to be answered with critical detachment; concomitantly, these questions are matched with potential sources – human and material – which are to be exploited to this end. This practice might be illustrated with reference to a single example, in particular, torture as a crime against humanity as this is set out in the Rome Statute at Article 7(1)(f) and, more specifically, the physical element of the offence which requires proof that the person was in the custody of the perpetrator. The questions arising during any effort to satisfy what is only one of the numerous elements of this offence necessarily revolve around when, where and how the person was taken into custody; an extremely detailed physical description of the relevant holding, detention and interrogation facilities used for the duration of the detention; the feeding, sanitary and medical arrangements; the allowance (if any) for prison visits, not least by international monitors such as representatives of the International Committee of the Red Cross; the nature of the prisoner routine, if a routine of sorts was imposed upon the detainees by the administration of the facility; the precise process of interrogation, questioning and detainee processing; the questions put to person(s) during interrogation sessions and the nature of any physical as well as mental suasion brought to bear during these sessions or at any other time; and the more general conduct and routines of the facility staff, whether guards, interrogators or persons in positions of higher authority. Each one of these themes and sub-themes demands a set of detailed (and different) questions to be asked if the whole story is to be ascertained. The potential sources of answers to these and other pertinent questions should be identified alongside each query and might include other persons incarcerated in the relevant facilities; persons who served in any capacity in the facilities; imagery (in all its forms); electronic and primary documentation, particularly that generated contemporaneously to the key incident(s) by the institution(s) and organisation(s) ultimately responsible for the detention of the person(s) subjected to *prima facie* acts of torture.

The aforementioned – though by no means complete – selection of questions to be answered in order to satisfy only one of the elements of a commonly perpetrated offence points to the complexity and indeed the typical length of crime base collection plans. Under the circumstances, the drafting and maintenance of collection plans is very time consuming given the demand for forensic attention to detail in a situation where investigators, analysts and counsel must collaborate closely. As such, an investigation manager who fails to ensure the utmost rigour in collection planning is remiss in the execution of one of his or her core duties and correspondingly runs the risk of failing to meet detailed collection requirements.

8.2.1.2. Excessive Crime Base Collection

It is the experience of the authors of this chapter that ICHL investigations have, on various grounds, oftentimes been blighted by the serious over-collection of crime base evidence. The reasons for this tendency reflect the relative (to linkage evidence collection) ease of securing crime base evidence; the generally emotive nature of crime base materials; a belief that any form of evidence collection constitutes a demonstration of progress; the widespread understanding of basic crime base collection requirements combined with a lack of awareness of the varied nature and critical importance of linkage evidence; and the mistaken belief that cases must necessarily be built from the ground up, that is, from crime scene to perpetrator. As a rule of thumb, properly conducted international-criminal investigations ultimately giving rise to the prosecution of high-level accused need to invest only a small amount (for instance, 10 per cent) of their resources to the establishment of the crime base. The investigation of lower-ranking suspects is principally the domain of national war-crimes units which invariably find themselves dealing with suspects who are alleged to have been the physical perpetrators of criminal acts. It logically follows that during the investigation of low-ranking perpetrators within domestic jurisdictions a great deal more emphasis is placed upon the establishment of the crime base, given the general absence of a requirement to collect linkage evidence.

The establishment of crime bases is very much the forte of police officers who have developed their skills in a non-international setting; this observation reflects the fact that the investigation of serious domestic criminality – most especially, murders and physical assaults where the perpetrator and victim had a relationship of some sort – place a great deal of emphasis upon the satisfaction of the physical elements of the offences. As such, when domestic police officers migrate to the international, criminal-investigative domain, their existing skills are, in the main, well suited to crime base work, where these investigators are managed properly in accordance with a detailed collection plan. More specifically, domestic practitioners are skilled at identifying, and interviewing with considerable attention to detail, the victims, eyewitnesses and the perpetrators of physical acts of a criminal nature. Police officers likewise tend to be adept at exploiting photographic and other forms of imagery as well as handling forensic, medical and other technical sources. Whereas these same people are generally unfamiliar with documentary analysis, unless they have worked domestically within specialised teams addressing allegations of complex fraud and transnational crime, this shortcoming can (or ought to) be addressed by investigative team analysts.

The system of international-criminal justice has learned through trial and a great deal of error that it is likely that difficulties will arise where police officers with insufficient international experience seek to execute complex international-criminal investigations without substantial input or management from analysts and trial counsel. Such is the lesson drawn by a great many informed observers who have engaged in the dissection of the formative investigations undertaken by the OTPs of the ICTY and ICTR. The majority of these early investigations were characterised by the massive over-collection of crime base information-*cum*-evidence – and little, if any, corresponding collection of the sort of linkage evidence required to secure the conviction of persons alleged to share criminal responsibility for offences perpetrated at oftentimes considerable physical and temporal distances from the headquarters and offices from which they directed their subordinates.

On the face of it, such over collection of crime base materials might be characterised as largely harmless – if, and only if, investigative team resources were not finite and the challenges posed by linkage evidence collection not a great deal more complicated than those presented when seeking to establish a crime base. In the event, the over-collection of crime base witness testimony will frequently serve to create witness-protection issues to a degree incommensurate with institutional capacity. Furthermore, the excessive collection of crime base witness evidence tends to raise the expectations of the victims of war that the sort of justice they seek will be realised, with concomitant reputational damage to the judicial institution concerned where such expectations are not met – which is generally the case. More immediately, excessive crime base collection will tend to overwhelm team analysts and counsel with large volumes of information which, even where it has evidentiary value, is superfluous to requirements. If the failings of the ICC-OTP are indicative, what is still more certain is that international judges are sufficiently savvy that they cannot be tricked into registering a conviction where an OTP adduces, in the hope of securing a conviction, a tsunami of crime base material as an alternative to linkage evidence specific to the accused. Given the foregoing, it must be reiterated that careful collection planning throughout the course of an investigation is the key to avoiding any tendency towards crime base over-collection.

8.2.2. Linkage Evidence

Linkage evidence can be defined in legal terms as that which is required to meet the mental and material elements of the alleged modes of liability as well as the mental elements of the offences. Put in layman's terms, linkage evidence collection seeks to connect acts of a criminal nature to individuals operating as part of institutions and like structures; this objective is realised through the analysis of the actions as well as inactions of the suspects and their subordinates in the context of their formal (that is, institutional) responsibilities. Given that international criminal investigations are not (or ought not to be) individual-target driven, the bulk of the collection and analytical effort within a given investigative team must necessarily be assigned to ensuring a comprehensive understanding of key linkage themes, including: the relevant military, security, political and paramilitary structures and their activities; the commanders, staff officers and other key personalities operating within these structures; the command, control and communications ('C3') apparatus linking command and staff headquarters to deployed units; and the disciplinary procedures at the disposal of the command, both *de jure* and *de facto*. As might be imagined, the building of linkage cases against high-ranking suspects requires considerable collection and analytical capacity. However, once the functioning of the relevant structures has been understood in significant detail – an effort which should absorb the overwhelming majority of the resources assigned to a complex criminal investigation – it is a relatively straightforward matter to identify the top leaders of the said structures and, in turn, link them through the C3 arrangements to the underlying criminal acts.

Whereas the crime base of any given case is invariably established to the requisite standard, notwithstanding the previously discussed tendency towards over-collection of crime base information, the same cannot often be said of the linkage component of international investigations. The problems which OTPs have experienced (and continue to experience) in establishing effective linkage cases would appear to stem from an insufficient understanding by many within the profession of ICHL investigations of: (i) the legal requirements of the modes of liability; (ii) how political, military, security-intelligence and paramilitary bodies function during operations; and, in particular, (iii) the detailed and oftentimes technical nature of the evidence needed to satisfy the legal requirements of a winning case. It is very difficult to understand – at least for the authors of this chapter – why international-criminal investigators, analysts and counsel, taken together, remain so deficient in these crucial respects. Redressing this shortcoming once and for all is a matter of the utmost urgency if the international practice of ICHL is not to be called into further and ultimately irreparable disrepute.

8.2.2.1. Linkage Case Collection Planning

As the above legal definition of linkage evidence would suggest, the starting point for all linkage collection efforts must be a consideration of the legal requirements of the modes of liability which are most likely to be alleged at the juncture that one or more suspects is identified. The collection planning process should be built around the relevant legal requirements, ideally with reference to the commentary built into easily accessible platforms such as the Case Matrix, where the legal requirements as well as a great many sub-themes of the legal requirements are hyperlinked in a user-friendly manner to relevant international jurisprudence. Armed with an understanding of how evidence and law have come together in prior litigation, investigators, analysts, counsel and investigations managers should be able at once to formulate and amend detailed collection plans whilst seeing to their proper execution. Why such practice has not emerged as a profession-wide standard operating procedure constitutes yet another mystery of the study of the practice of ICHL – albeit one in which the ramifications of failure could not be clearer.

Just as with crime base collection, the core linkage themes (for instance, structures, chains of command, commanders, communications systems and disciplinary processes) will each generate detailed lists of questions which need to be answered if a complete picture of the institutional context, and ultimately the actions of key actors, is to be built. By way of an example designed to illustrate the complexity of linkage collection planning, one might consider a single legal requirement relevant to Article 28(a) of the Rome Statute, which is concerned with command and superior responsibility, that is, the requirement that the prosecution demonstrate that an alleged perpetrator had effective command and control, or effective authority and control, over the forces which committed the crime. A review of the wealth of jurisprudence addressing the evidence which supports allegations of effective command and control makes it clear that this element might be demonstrated in numerous ways; and, if the requisite evidence is to be collected, it is essential that an investigative team grasp fully the approaches which have worked in the past. It follows that where such an understanding is absent, so too will be the ability of the team to generate the necessary questions during the collection-planning process; in turn, critical linkage evidence pertaining to the legal requirement shall not be gathered, leading to prosecutorial claims with respect to effective command and control remaining unproven.

Efforts to establish the existence of effective command and control should at the outset seek evidence concerning, amongst other matters: the identity of all relevant commanders and staff; the superior as well as subordinate structures; the types and functioning of the communications systems used by these structures; the operational as well as administrative relationships between the superior and subordinate structures; and the operational, administrative, disciplinary and logistical activity of the relevant structures. Each of the foregoing themes should be explored through the identification of several sub-themes, each of which require detailed questioning. For instance, the issue of discipline can be broken down into questions regarding contemporaneous notice of alleged criminal activity within one or more subordinate units, the investigation of the latter and the punishment (if any) of miscreants. In looking at the matter of communications, the investigative team should consider the communication systems and processes of every subordinate formation and unit within a given chain of command as well as that of the higher headquarters. These collection questions should encompass, not least: an examination of the communications procedures and their form (for instance, radio, e-mail, hard-copy documentation, meetings and briefings); a consideration of which key personnel utilised which systems; the capability and limitations of the communications systems; the frequency of communications and their formal regulation; a consideration of any redundancies built into the systems; and the security features of the latter, including callsigns and codewords. As with crime base collection planning, the various themes and sub-themes should be linked to potential sources of information and evidence which, in the assessment of the investigative team, might be exploited by OTP analysts.

Collection and analysis during the investigative phase should target as much primary source documentation as exists, specifically documentation generated by the structures suspected of having engaged in the perpetration of the core international crimes which constitute the crime base. Such materials can take the form of hard-copy documents or, as is increasingly common, materials in electronic form, such as email and databases. In this context, it will be recalled that the sources of crime base evidence are rarely of any use to efforts to establish individual criminal responsibility. The sort of witness testimony which is sought to establish a linkage case is that of insiders (one category of linkage witness), these being individuals who themselves served in some capacity within the perpetrating structures, ideally at the same time as the targets of the investigation. As individual investigative targets of higher rank are identified only relatively late in the investigative cycle – at least where an investigative team knows what it is doing and is consequently keen not to overlook exculpatory information and evidence – linkage witnesses of any sort should be interviewed only following the careful study of the primary documentation and well into the life of an investigation, in particular, once suspects have been identified, however tentatively, with an eye to their prosecution.

8.2.2.2. Linkage Collection Staffing in the Context of Evidentiary Requirements

The collapse of the ICC-OTP cases against Messrs. Gbagbo and Kenyatta, amongst others, suggests that (i) the accused were not criminally culpable, in which case these investigations should not have given rise to prosecutions or (ii) the OTP did (and does) not possess sufficient numbers of skilled personnel to build solid prosecution files against high-ranking suspects. The investigation of top-level suspects is best approached with humility as well as a realisation that the volume and variety of linkage factors to be considered in building cases rooted in ICHL shall invariably render daunting any given collection effort even before it has commenced. As *Gbagbo* and *Kenyatta* have shown, this is most especially the case where it is envisioned that an investigation shall ultimately lead to charges being brought against senior leaders operating at considerable physical and temporal distance from the underlying criminal acts, that is, suspects controlling numerous subordinate entities which, for senior most leaders, will frequently encompass military, security-intelligence, police and political structures.

Securing enough inculpatory evidence to warrant the prosecution of high-level suspects is highly challenging, even where an institution is adequately skilled to commence an investigation on the basis of a properly-structured collection plan – particularly where the investigative body is confronted with a need to operate in and around an ongoing armed conflict whilst dealing additionally (or alternatively) with substantial political-diplomatic resistance. Challenges of this nature constitute a chronic problem for public-sector authorities, not least the ICC-OTP. Recent non-public sector initiatives, especially the CIJA, are designed to execute successful criminal investigations rooted in ICHL and domestic variants thereof by overcoming the obstacles presented by physical risk as well as political difficulties. However, the private criminal-investigative sector remains very much in its infancy. As such, it is necessary to ask what the public sector might do on its own to strengthen its ability to build effective linkage cases in a timely as well as cost-effective manner. Answering this question is an exceptionally pressing matter for international criminal-investigative bodies such as the ICC-OTP, given the demands being placed upon them by Western donors who are anxious to see more cost-effective investigations and successful prosecutorial output.

The position taken here is that public-sector, international criminal-investigative bodies would do well to look at their current approach to recruitment. First, it will be observed that, as a rule, the relevant international institutions employ too many investigators and too few analysts. While the distinction between these two disciplines has, over the last 15 years, improved to the extent that investigators are often trained to engage in analytical work and vice-versa, a great many investigators and analysts continue to enter the international system (or otherwise move between international bodies) with a mind-set which holds that investigators ought to do little more than collect *prima facie* evidence in the field whilst analysts should remain chained to their computers collating material at headquarters. Analysts have the critical function of giving meaning to the material collected, although this primary purpose is frequently inappropriately subordinated to information-management tasks assigned by more senior personnel. When it comes to linkage evidence collection, it is essential that investigators and analysts have a detailed understanding of the entire case file, with analysts needing to be prepared to deploy alongside investigators to participate in, amongst other activities, the interviewing of insider witnesses and the exploitation at the point of acquisition of physical materials. In order to break down further the distinction between the investigator-collector and analysis roles, it is recommended in the strongest possible terms that investigator recruitment should in every case target the ranks of police officers with backgrounds in the fields of serious fraud and transnational crime. Bearing in mind the thematic core of most ICHL investigations, it remains surprising to the authors of this chapter just how few ICHL practitioners are possessed of prior military experience. Stated simply, more investigators as well as analysts with military- and security-intelligence backgrounds need to be taken into the international OTPs.

Secondly, it is the assessment of the authors of this chapter that the ranks of international trial counsel have come to be filled to an unhealthy degree with lawyers who have a brilliant understanding of ICHL which is not accompanied by a corresponding degree of excellence when it comes to matters of evidence. Whereas the ranks of international investigators and analysts do include the occasional professional with a legal education, it is rare that any of the people with such qualifications have practiced law, either domestically or internationally. As such, it falls to trial counsel – for reasons of crucial quality control – to take ultimate responsibility for the marrying of fact to law, that is, to ensure that the elements of the offences as well as the legal requirements of the modes of liability alleged are always properly supported by sufficient evidence. The lead trial attorneys employed at the remaining international bodies are, with very few exceptions, highly skilled in this respect. However, the complexity of any investigation and prosecution which encompasses a substantial linkage component is such that lead trial counsel are necessarily dependent upon subordinate attorneys in determining whether the marriage of fact to law is sufficient in every respect. The international OTPs have come to employ substantial numbers of counsel who have never practiced law outside of the international domain and, as a result, are unfamiliar with the culture of domestic criminal practice, where immense attention must be paid to questions of evidence, with legal niceties constituting a relevant, albeit secondary, matter. Finally, it will be noted that whilst there is absolutely no requirement for the hiring of more lawyers to international OTPs, the preponderance of international investigations involving military and paramilitary actors generates an immense need within these institutions for more counsel with military experience, secured as legal officers or through other military occupations.

8.2.3. Contextual Evidence

Crime base and, most especially, linkage evidence together rest at the heart of all international criminal cases brought against suspects of any substantive rank. However, the view taken here is that the field of international-criminal investigations and prosecutions – and, more to the point, the demands which trial judges now place upon prosecutors – has evolved to the point that it is necessary to consider a third category of evidence, that being of a contextual nature. Whereas contextual evidence has long been collected in the course of international-criminal inquiries, it has tended to be afforded insufficient priority by investigative teams and prosecutors. This absence of prioritisation reflects their general failure to grasp its relevance or, more simply, the tendency to fold the collection of contextual evidence into the building of the crime base and linkage cases.

8.2.3.1. The Dual Importance of Detailed Case Narratives

Contextual evidence collection can be used to formulate and inform detailed case narratives, in particular, prosecutorial narratives setting out the wider background, development and description of events within which the criminality and more general conduct of the alleged perpetrator(s) is assessed as having taken place. In formal allegations (for instance, indictments) as well as trial briefs, it is the practice of prosecutors to offer trial panels, by way of introduction to core prosecutorial arguments, what are purported to be comprehensive contextual narratives touching upon, as prosecutors deem relevant, questions of ethnicity, religion, political-geography and military matters. Such narratives will invariably (or ought to) address matters relating to the general context within which a conflict or crisis unfolded, and the relevant organisational structures involved, for instance, political parties as well as military, security-intelligence, para-military and police organs.

Notwithstanding the importance of this contextual argumentation, it is the practice of investigative-*cum*-prosecutorial teams to prepare only at the last minute those aspects of the case narrative which stand metaphorically furthest from the alleged misconduct of the accused. Often, the drafting of these components of formal allegations and trial briefs comes to rely upon secondary-source information collected haphazardly from the public domain, with a correspondingly slipshod critical engagement by the trial team with much of the source material. Equally problematic is the oft-seen folly which involves the building of contextual narratives from what is termed (by those engaging in such practices) the victim perspective. In international cases replete with highly charged political, ethnic, religious and historical elements, this flawed approach can (and frequently does) give rise to highly subjective contextual narratives. To cite a single example, it was the practice of the ICTR-OTP to allege in the preamble to its indictments that a pre-planned genocide was triggered when Hutu extremists shot down the aircraft carrying the then-President of Rwanda, killing all aboard. Incredibly, this feature of the standard OTP case narrative persisted well after elements of the OTP had collected substantial evidence which pointed to the killing of the said President by Tutsi-led, armed-opposition forces. Likewise, to be noted in this context is the fact that at no time did the OTP possess convincing evidence that the genocide had been pre-planned. The latter canard featured prominently in the then-available secondary literature concerning the Rwandan genocide, one piece of which was regarded widely as being sacrosanct and correspondingly not engaged with critically by the OTP as a whole.[11]

International trial panels – or at any rate, the ICC trial chamber which heard *Gbagbo and Blé Goudé* – are a good deal less tolerant than those of the ICTR when presented with shoddy or otherwise misleading contextual narratives. In *Gbagbo and Blé Goudé*, one of the majority on the trial panel was withering in his critique of the flawed OTP contextual narrative in his written reasons for ordering the acquittals of the accused.[12]

---

[11] Alison Des Forges, *Leave None to Tell the Story: Genocide in Rwanda*, Human Rights Watch, New York, 1999.

[12] ICC, Situation in the Republic of Côte d'Ivoire, *The Prosecutor v. Laurent Gbagbo and Charles Blé Goudé*, Trial Chamber, Opinion of Judge Cuno Tarfusser, 16 July 2019, ICC-02/11-01/15-1263-AnxA, noted how the "level of 'overall disconnect' [...] between the

This critique begs the question of whether the OTP viewed and packaged its core information-*cum*-evidence in the context of a flawed narrative developed at the commencement of the investigation. More likely, the narrative was cobbled together at the eleventh hour, on the basis of long-held, team-wide assumptions, in a manner designed to lend weight to assertions more immediately germane to the alleged criminal culpability of the accused. In either event, there is a high probability that the flawed narrative had been dictated, at least in part, to OTP personnel by partial witnesses without sufficient (or any) objective scrutiny on the part of those taking the said testimony. The more important assertion, which transcends the *Gbagbo and Blé Goudé* debacle, is this: there is metaphorical profit to be made where, at the outset of an inquiry, the investigative team commences the process of crafting a contextual narrative supported by properly analysed evidence.

8.2.3.2. Contextual Evidence Collection Planning

For the reasons above, contextual evidence which supports the prosecution narrative matters a great deal; it needs to be collected, rigorously analysed and presented in a thoroughly objective manner, that is, in the same way as *prima facie* crime base and linkage evidence. Contextual evidence should be collected from the outset of an investigation, not least for reasons of quality control within the investigative team. In particular, it is imperative that a team committed to a criminal investigation for a prolonged temporal period avoid backing itself into a conceptual corner. It is the experience of the authors of this chapter that investigative teams, working from the outset of an investigation on the basis of flawed assumptions (that is, those unsupported by evidence) with respect to the

---

Prosecutor's narrative and the facts as progressively emerging from the evidence, kept increasing", para. 5. Judge Tarfusser added that:

> Day after day, document by document, witness after witness, the 'Prosecutor's case' has been revealed and exposed as a fragile, implausible theorem relying on shaky and doubtful bases, inspired by a Manichean and simplistic narrative of an Ivory Coast depicted as a 'polarised' society where one could draw a clear-cut line between the 'pro-Gbagbo', on the one hand, and the 'pro-Ouattara', on the other hand, the former from the South and of Christian faith, the latter from the North and of Muslim faith; a caricatured, 'one-sided' narrative, 'built around a unidimensional conception of the role of nationality, ethnicity, and religion (in the broadest sense) in Côte d'Ivoire in general and during the post-electoral crisis in particular', progressively destroyed by the innumerable elements to the contrary emerging from the testimonies.

Ibid., para. 12 (https://legal-tools.org/doc/f6c6f3).

overall context will, after a prolonged period, find themselves trapped by these same assumptions because *prima facie* crime base and linkage evidence has been gathered in accordance with insufficient (or no) regard to exculpatory materials – to the point that an accused has been indicted or, worse, the trial has commenced. To cite a single example, such a situation was witnessed within the investigative-*cum*-prosecutorial team assembled to handle the Croatia phase of *Milošević* at the ICTY. In this instance, the team in question built its case upon the unsupported conclusion that military operations launched by federal forces from Serbia and Montenegro into Dalmatia during 1992 did so in the context of a grand strategic plan, formulated in Belgrade, to annex large chunks of the Croatian coast to what remained at that time of the Federal Socialist Republic of Yugoslavia. Concomitantly, the investigative-*cum*-prosecutorial team dealing with *Jokić, et al.*, which was concerned with the siege of Dubrovnik by these same federal forces, rejected this contextual narrative. As might be imagined, the ICTY-OTP leadership concluded that it was inadvisable for the OTP to present conflicting contextual narratives in distinct cases which nonetheless were concerned in large part with the same underlying event (that is, Yugoslavian military operations in Dalmatia during 1992). The situation was ultimately resolved at the OTP leadership level through the negotiation of a plea deal with *Jokić* and the timely (from an OTP perspective) death of Milošević during the trial of the latter.

As far as the authors of this chapter are aware, no international institution has yet formulated a contextual evidence collection plan at the outset (or near to the outset) of an investigation. Precisely how this might be done effectively must, therefore, be a matter of some speculation. That noted, it can be stated with confidence that the elements of offences and the legal requirements of modes of liability which lend backbone to crime base and linkage collection planning are not going to be as immediately relevant to contextual evidence collection plans. Indeed, the collection of contextual evidence will, at least at the outset, be approached from the perspectives of a criminal investigation as well as scholarly inquiry. By way of a start, investigative teams building a contextual evidence collection plan would do well to study previous prosecutions – be they successful or, most especially, where they were not – to get a sense of how trial panels have responded to *prima facie* contextual evidence adduced by both prosecution and defence advocates. This has been the approach taken by students of ICHL in order to understand how crime base and, most especially, linkage cases should best be constructed.

Whereas analysts working in the field of ICHL usually possess graduate degrees in the humanities which at one time exposed these personnel to academic research on matters of politics, military affairs, anthropology, sociology or comparative religion, academic backgrounds of this nature are less often seen within the ranks of investigators and trial counsel. What is more, analysts employed by international institutions are often possessed of a great deal of specialised knowledge regarding the States upon whose territory an investigation is concentrated. It logically follows that the crafting of contextual narratives should, at least in the first instance, be left to analysts rather than investigators and counsel. What is more, there is no reason that the *modus operandi* of criminal investigations and scholarly inquiry should not be reconciled. For instance, where at the outset of an investigation the *prima facie* crime base is suggestive of the mass killing of members of one ethnic group by another, the contextual evidence collection plan would logically seek (i) to document to a high standard previous outbreaks of inter-ethnic violence of a like nature and (ii) to identify lingering societal tensions following earlier pogroms which may have persisted until the point of the perpetration of the *prima facie* offences more immediately relevant to the investigative team. In a similar vein, if an investigation is centred at the start upon the conduct of security-intelligence structures during, for instance, the period since 2011, the investigative team would do well to examine the professional culture of those same structures during the decade or more preceding 2011. In taking contextual questions of this nature as a starting point, a skilled and well-led investigative team will, not least through reference to whatever secondary sources are found, identify with relative ease a wide range of sub-questions, the answers to which must ultimately be secured from primary sources.

8.3. Collection Management

The size of international criminal-investigative teams dealing with cases involving complex linkage components can be considerable. In the experience of the authors of this chapter, such teams will range in size from eight to ten persons, not all of whom might be assigned full-time to the team (for instance, in the case of early ICC-OTP investigation of Mr. Thomas Lubanga and his associates), to several dozen personnel (for example, during the prosecution of Mr. Slobodan Milošević, when a great deal of investigative work was undertaken in the midst of trial). Within even small investigative teams, there tends to be a great deal of division of labour, for instance, between those assigned to crime base work and the personnel dealing with building the linkage case. From the point at which suspects are identified during an investigation, counsel will frequently find their attention diverted from evidentiary to procedural matters, even where there remain significant evidentiary gaps in the casefile. For various reasons, the explanation of which lies beyond the scope of this chapter, effective command and control over complex international-criminal investigations was frequently lacking at the *ad hoc* Tribunals and, in the main, uneven levels of investigative management remain a problem within the international OTPs operating at the present time. Investigative management practices are altogether better within domestic war-crimes units, principally owing to the relative simplicity of building prosecutable cases against low-level perpetrators insofar as such cases are invariably characterised by the absence of a linkage component.

The sheer volume of crime base, contextual and, most especially linkage evidence required to mount a successful prosecution against a high-level suspect constitutes an immense challenge which the majority of those employed within international OTPs as investigators, analysts and counsel – assigned as most are only to specific parts of a casefile – would appear to fail to recognise. For this reason, investigative team managers, be they formally employed as counsel or in another capacity, would do well to remind themselves as well as their charges of the high stakes involved for an OTP where insufficient evidence is collected in support of a given prosecution – or, indeed, the negative ramifications for an OTP where there is a paucity of prosecutions notwithstanding tens of millions of dollars in annual investigative expenditures. It is here held that the addition of collection managers, seated metaphorically at the right hand of investigative team leads, would go a considerable way towards keeping investigative teams abreast of their shared progress whilst at the same time rectifying the twin problems of unfocussed as well as superfluous information-*cum*-evidence collection.

8.3.1. Defining Collection Management

Collection management is not to be confused with investigative management. Investigative management has a far wider scope than collection management. The former is concerned with, amongst other matters, the establishment of the overall direction of a case; the tasking of investigators; the work of team analysts, language and support staff; the general monitoring and direction of the collection effort; mission planning and execution; security and witness-protection issues; the production of reports and updates for higher OTP management and leadership cadres; and personnel-management issues. Collection management has a far narrower focus. More specifically, collection management deals with the production and maintenance of detailed collection plans, including the generation of key themes and questions, and the matching of these collection requirements to potential sources of information and evidence. Most critically, collection management involves responsibility for monitoring the overall collection effort through an ongoing review of whether the themes, issues, elements of offences and the legal requirements of the modes of liability set out in the collection plan are being addressed adequately in evidentiary terms. In this regard, effective collection management will identify (i) what precisely needs to be collected; (ii) how these needs might best be met in a timely manner; (iii) the remaining evidentiary gaps as they appear during the course of an investigation; and (iv) the filling of these gaps. In realising these objectives, effective collection management will concomitantly ensure the avoidance of over-collection.

Notwithstanding the foregoing, the establishment of collection management as an explicit, stand-alone function within investigative teams in not currently a feature of complex international-criminal investigations. This is not to say that collection management within investigative teams does not exist. Manifestly, such practice does exist to some degree; were this not the case, no investigative dossier would ever reach a courtroom. The problem at the present time is that professional, centralised collection management arrangements have not been put into place – or, where an OTP convinces itself that such arrangements do exist, they are patently ineffective. The fact of the matter is that, as a general rule, collection management has been approached as an afterthought by international OTPs, that is, as something to be taken seriously only where suspects have been taken into custody and the awareness dawns upon senior prosecutors that they are about to proceed to trial armed with a great many allegations for which they possess insufficient evidence. What is more, international OTPs frequently confuse collection management with data (or evidence) management; the latter has been fetishised within OTPs for roughly twenty years, which explains their tendency to purchase ever-more-expensive software systems whilst improperly using relatively simple platforms such as CaseMap – where CaseMap is used at all. To take but one example, collection management at the ICTY-OTP was so deleterious during the first decade or more of the life of the ICTY that, when a chief of Prosecutions sought to redress this shortcoming by decreeing that all open files should be put into CaseMap, this task was assigned by investigative and trial teams to the most junior personnel available, including a great many interns. What was and remains required is a disciplined approach to collection management which is rooted in a systematic and professional consideration of this key function.

8.3.2. The Role of Collection Managers and Their Subordinates

Whilst the position of a dedicated collection manager remains unknown in the field of ICHL, professionalised collection management is a well-recognised and respected endeavour in many other professions. For instance, civilian as well as military security-intelligence organisations in Western States have, for a generation, routinely employed specialised collection managers during the course of large-scale collection operations.[13] This practice is instructive insofar as a good many security-intelligence operations seek to address questions of a nature very similar to those which confront international-criminal investigative teams, not least, those concerned with collecting large and diverse amounts of information on the command and control of political, military, security-intelligence, paramilitary and police structures. To this end, security-intelligence services seek, in a manner not dissimilar to complex criminal-investigative teams, to collect, collate, analyse and disseminate high-quality information. Within security-intelligence services, raw information is collected and, in turn, transformed by analytical processes into intelligence product. An investigative team, where it is working effectively, follows similar processes designed to transform information into admissible evidence. Indeed, analytical training within international OTPs has, for a decade and more, been based upon the intelligence cycle, the latter

---

[13] See, for instance, Major Carl Grebe, "Intelligence Collection Management Process", in *ARRC Journal*, 2003, vol. 7, no. 1, pp. 16–17; Clyde R. Heffter, "A Fresh Look at Collection Requirements", in *Studies in Intelligence*, 1960, vol. 4, no. 4, pp. 43–61; US Department of the Army, *Human Intelligence Collector Operations*, Washington, 2006.

expression characterising the process by which information is rendered as intelligence product.

Since the 1980s, Western military and security-intelligence organs have developed, refined and professionalised the function of collection management in accordance with their specific needs. This evolution has seen the training and deployment of specialised personnel, known as collection managers. The focus of the latter falls upon the three distinct components of collection management: (i) requirements management, (ii) mission management and (iii) asset management. During larger collection operations, each of these three areas will have its own manager.

Requirements management is the most important of the three subfields of collection management and, arguably, that which is most relevant to international-criminal investigations. In particular, the requirements manager determines which information needs to be acquired by what temporal juncture. To cite one example, in a military context specific information and intelligence needs are generated by a military commander in accordance with the operational orders which he has received from higher echelons. In turn, the said requirements are assessed within an intelligence cell in the context of what is known as the commander's intent. Priority information and intelligence requirements (in the form of questions which require answering) are identified during this process and these requirements are updated and amended during the ongoing collection and analysis operations. At the outset of an intelligence operation, requirements managers disseminate internally the information-*cum*-intelligence requirements to analytical staff and database managers in order to determine what information is already in their custody. This step reduces the likelihood that sources will be tasked with the collection of information which is already to hand. Additionally – and indeed, critically – requirements managers draft, maintain and amend collection plans. That noted, it is military or intelligence commanders who approve collection plans before they are implemented in the first instance; commanders initiate collection processes and assume something akin to ownership over same. In so doing, commanders take responsibility, just as would an investigative team leader, for any failure of an operation. Once a collection plan has been formulated, it falls to a given requirements manager to task the mission manager (see below), receiving in due course confirmation that a particular source has been activated and, in turn, product produced. However, it does not fall to the requirements manager to analyse or action the information which comes back. These functions are performed elsewhere, although evaluation reports concerning source product make their way to the requirements manager in order that he might update and amend the collection plan.

For their part, mission managers set out plans for the direct tasking of sources and asset managers, the latter being responsible for the execution of specific collection and exploitation tasks. In a nutshell, collection management as it is implemented by Western security-intelligence organs fosters a comprehensive identification of requirements; the matching of these requirements to clearly identified sources; the tasking as well as exploitation of these sources; the ongoing amendment of the collection plan; the tracking of what has been collected (that is, the questions answered that no longer need additional collection); and the identification of remaining or newly-identified gaps during the collection process.

One is left to wonder why the approach to collection management which has long been employed by Western military and security-intelligence organs has never been adopted by OTPs in order to lend structure and coherency to the collection of *prima facie* evidence during complex criminal investigations. The absence of any such initiative in the field of ICHL is presumably a function of the fact that lawyers and to a lesser degree police officers – rather than erstwhile intelligence officers – have without exception controlled the investigative arms of all the OTPs established since 1993. Whilst the engagement of counsel in investigative processes is to be welcomed, given the debacles that were witnessed at the ICTY and ICTR OTPs during their formative years when counsel were kept at arm's length from case files until the eve of trial by former police officers, it must be recalled that very few international lawyers are possessed of experience in the realm of field collection. Put another way, (good) lawyers understand evidence; it does not follow from this truism that they are particularly skilled in its collection. As such, the leader of any investigative team, and counsel most especially, would benefit from having situated at their right hand a collection specialist whose sole mission is to manage (as opposed to lead) the collection effort. Where there is no specialist to design a collection plan and monitor the execution of the same in a holistic manner, it follows that gaps in the evidentiary record, over-collection and the inefficient tasking of collection resources are sure to follow.

8.4. Evidence Review

The authors of this chapter commenced their careers in the field of ICHL in 1997 (Wiley) and 1999 (Brown); one, the other or both have served with the Canadian war-crimes programme, the ICTY, the ICTR, the ICC, the Iraqi High Tribunal and the CIJA. Of these institutions, only the CIJA has ever implemented – in accordance with standing policy – a robust process of evidence review commencing at an early phase of every investigation. Where there was any evidence review of which to speak at the other bodies named here, this invariably took place after it was deemed – by whom, it was never quite clear – that the investigation was concluded and indictments (or a like instrument) were warranted. Such reviews were left to the team which had assembled the file, perhaps encompassing the briefing of more senior managers and leaders; in other cases (for instance, at the ICTY-OTP), a general invitation was sent around the OTP inviting personnel from other teams to wade through voluminous case files and, were individuals so inclined, to comment thereupon at something akin to a public meeting. Unsurprisingly, few took up these offers, engaged as they were with their own investigations and prosecutions. The sort of imperfect (or non-existent) evidence review procedures cited here have had two principle effects upon most of the OTPs established from 1993: (i) the initiation of a great deal of investigative work during trial, that is, once trial counsel have become aware of the paucity of linkage evidence relevant to the accused; and (ii) the dismissal of cases, or findings of criminal non-culpability, by pre-trial, trial and appellate chambers. The first of these problems bedevilled the ICTY and the ICTR; the second phenomenon has proved to be distressingly commonplace at the ICC.

It is essential that evidence review procedures should be put into place OTP wide and applied from the commencement of any given investigation. By way of a start, it would be immensely helpful if individual investigative teams encouraged devil's advocacy, that is, a culture where ostensible *prima facie* evidence was subjected to ongoing challenge by all team personnel, without regard to professional rank. What is more, the sort of robust collection planning and management which has formed the core of the foregoing discussion would, if implemented as a matter of course during complex criminal investigations, lay the groundwork for effective review within investigative teams as well as by external experts. The latter could be assigned from within OTPs themselves, albeit from ranks external to the investigative team whose evidence is being reviewed.

Conversely, outside parties subjected to standard non-disclosure agreements and possessed of the requisite experience of complex ICHL investigations and prosecutions, could be retained for this purpose. On the question of outside expertise, it will be recalled that there are a great many highly-skilled, erstwhile investigators, analysts, prosecutors, trial clerks and judges languishing in semi-retirement, having been determined by the international system to be, in their early sixties, no longer fit for full-time work. This pool of immense talent is drawn upon by the CIJA as part of its evidence review arrangements; international OTPs would do well to proceed in a like manner.

8.5. Concluding Remarks

International OTP investigative practices remain insufficient, despite several important methodological advances made since the establishment of the ICTY in 1993. The strong prosecutorial records of the ICTY and the ICTR have served to hide from the casual ICHL observer a great many of the investigative shortcomings witnessed at those institutions, not least, shoddy investigative management leading to the over-collection of crime-base materials at the expense of linkage evidence gathering. In the event, the OTPs of both *ad hoc* Tribunals proved sufficiently resilient – if only just – to address evidentiary imbalances when these were identified by senior trial counsel on the eve of trial owing to the Chapter VII mandates which these institutions enjoyed along with the fact that what might be termed emergency investigative activities could be undertaken in physically-secure, post-conflict environments.

The prosecutorial records of the courts and tribunals established from 2002 relative to financial expenditure and prosecutorial output, with the arguable exception of the Special Court for Sierra Leone ('SCSL'), have proven to be altogether less admirable. By way of example, the investigative cadres of the ICC, ECCC, STL and KSC have had to contend with not-insignificant levels of political-diplomatic resistance to their work, this obstacle being compounded in certain instances by the presence of physical risk in the respective operational areas far and away higher than that faced by the ICTY and the ICTR. Necessarily, challenges beyond the control of international OTPs have served to retard the quality and quantity of investigative output. The post-2002 institutions – again, with the arguable exception of the SCSL – have compounded the difficulties faced by their investigative teams through a collective failure to implement consistently several sorely-lacking yet fundamental improvements to their *modus operandi*. Put another way, various investigative divisions have replicated many of the most serious deficiencies witnessed at the OTPs of the *ad hoc* Tribunals. One refers here, most especially, to persistent failings in the areas of collection planning, collection management and evidence review. Until these long-term shortcomings are resolved, the practice of ICHL shall continue to fall into disrepute in the eyes of conflict-affected societies, the victims of armed conflict, the States which fund the relevant international bodies and a great many of those employed by these institutions.

PART III:
SYSTEMIC CHALLENGES
IN CASE-PREPARATORY WORK-PROCESSES

9

Prioritisation of Suspected Conduct and Cases: From Idea to Practice

Devasheesh Bais[*]

9.1. Introduction

Quality of criminal investigation in fact-rich core international crimes cases can be enhanced by selecting and prioritising cases that are best suited for the allocation of the limited resources of the prosecution. Some of the systemic bottle-necks[1] hindering criminal investigations, as identified by the 'Quality Control in Criminal Investigation' project, can be pre-empted by case selection and prioritisation strategies.

In this chapter, the evolution of the case prioritisation strategies for core international crimes will be discussed and its future prospects and challenges highlighted. The chapter starts with an explanatory background to the case prioritisation strategies (Section 9.2.), and then proceeds to discuss the early beginnings of the concept (Section 9.3.), its gradual embrace by national and international prosecution services (Section 9.4.), challenges in the implementation of case prioritisation strategies in national jurisdiction (Section 9.5.), and concludes with reflections on its future (Section 9.6.). At the end of the chapter, there is a table chronologically listing the development of case prioritisation strategies for core international crimes.

---

* **Devasheesh Bais** is Advocate at the High Court of Madhya Pradesh, India, and Fellow at the Centre for International Law Research and Policy ('CILRAP'). The author wishes to thank Morten Bergsmo for his comment on the draft of this chapter.

[1] a) the long duration and high cost of many investigations of core international crimes; b) loss of overview of information and potential evidence; c) lack of clear focus in the building of the case; d) vague formulation of criminal responsibility even after the organisation has in its possession enough potential evidence [...].

See the web page of the CILRAP research project 'Quality Control in Criminal Investigation', with links to multiple resources (https://www.cilrap.org/events/190222-23-delhi/).

While the chapter is about *prioritisation*, it is often used in conjunction with *selection*, as prioritisation usually follows once cases to be investigated have been selected. Thus, the chapter refers to case selection at various points. However, this is not to say that a prioritisation exercise cannot exist without a selection process.

9.2. Background

An armed conflict, civil war, or other events where mass crimes are committed involve a large number of instances of crimes and a complex factual narrative. Consider the Syrian situation, which is now in its ninth year, having started in 2011; it involves multiple States, multiple non-State actors, with serious crimes committed, including intentionally directing attacks against a civilian population, also by means of chemical weapons, sexual slavery, persecution and torture.[2] Imagine the difficult task of any accountability mechanism that may be set up to address the criminal conduct involved in the Syrian situation.

Prosecuting and adjudicating all those numerous crimes in a fair manner and without undue delay would be an overwhelming task. This will be true even for a jurisdiction with a well-functioning criminal justice system. However, the reality is that the judicial capacity of the State where these crimes were committed may have been destroyed, or severely impaired by conflict.

Given this context, with instances of alleged crimes exceeding judicial capacity, a significant backlog of opened or potential case-files may emerge. Years would have passed before most of these cases reach the trial stage, if ever. This challenge raises two important questions:

1) How to select the cases that will actually be investigated and tried?

2) How to rank the selected cases in an order of priority according to which they will be investigated and tried?

That is, how does a prosecution service select the cases or conduct that are to be investigated, and then amongst the selected cases and conduct identify those that should be prioritised?

---

[2]   See, for instance, Report of the Independent International Commission of Inquiry on the Syrian Arab Republic, UN Doc. A/HRC/37/72, 1 February 2018 (https://legal-tools.org/doc/b01552).

The reality is that a decision on prioritisation of cases is inevitable for any prosecution service, be it national or international, as it is likely that there will always be more cases to prosecute than what the concerned prosecution service can handle simultaneously while deploying its finite resources. Thus, it is likely that any prosecutor would have to take a decision on the order in which the cases are rolled out.

In the absence of formal criteria for prioritising cases, a decision on prioritisation would be done on an informal basis, which could not only lack transparency but also consistency.[3] A prosecution service is also more susceptible to being influenced by governments, powerful organisations and individuals, and media coverage if it is not bound by formal prioritisation criteria.[4] A formalised set of criteria, designed according to the circumstances of the jurisdiction it serves, not only protect the prosecution service from political pressure or accusation of bias, but could also, with a right set of criteria, increase its effectiveness and efficiency.

9.3. The Idea

The idea started in a nascent manner with the International Criminal Tribunal for the former Yugoslavia ('ICTY'), progressed with the preparatory work on the International Criminal Court's ('ICC') Office of the Prosecutor ('OTP'), however, the real progress happened in the domestic context aided by international justice professionals and non-governmental organisations.

9.3.1. International Criminal Tribunal for the Former Yugoslavia

The Statute of the ICTY gave a general mandate "to prosecute persons responsible for serious violations of international humanitarian law committed in the territory of the former Yugoslavia since 1991".[5] Case selection and prioritisation criteria were not addressed. However, the ICTY's

---

[3] CMN, *Guidelines: Case Mapping, Selection and Prioritisation of Conflict and Atrocity-Related Crimes*, Brussels, June 2018, p. 1 (https://legal-tools.org/doc/fd5f42).

[4] *Ibid.*, p. 9.

[5] See Statute of the International Criminal Tribunal for the Former Yugoslavia, adopted 25 May 1993, amended 17 May 2002, Article 1 ('ICTY Statute') (https://legal-tools.org/doc/b4f63b).

OTP formally adopted case selection and prioritisation criteria in October 1995.[6]

These criteria were organised in five different thematic groups:

(a) the person to be targeted for prosecution:[7]

- position in the hierarchy under investigation;
- political, military, paramilitary or civilian leader;
- leadership at a municipal, regional or national level;
- nationality;
- role or participation in policy or strategy decisions;
- personal culpability for specific atrocities;
- notoriousness or responsibility for particularly heinous acts;
- the extent of direct participation in the alleged incidents;
- authority and control exercised by the suspects;
- the suspect's alleged notice and knowledge of acts by subordinates;
- arrest potential;
- evidence or witness availability;
- media or government or non-governmental target; and
- potential role-over witness or likelihood of linkage evidence.

(b) the serious nature of the crime:[8]

- number of victims;
- nature of acts;
- area of destruction;
- duration and repetition of the offence;
- location of the crime;
- linkage to other cases;

---

[6] See Morten Bergsmo, Kjetil Helvig, Ilia Utmelidze and Gorana Žagovec (eds.), *The Backlog of Core International Crimes Case Files in Bosnia and Herzegovina*, Torkel Opsahl Academic EPublisher ('TOAEP'), Oslo, 2nd edition, 2010, p. 99 (https://legal-tools.org/doc/688146).

[7] *Ibid.*, p. 99.

[8] *Ibid.*, p. 100.

- nationality of perpetrators or victims;
- arrest potential;
- evidence or witness availability;
- showcase or pattern crime; and
- media or government or non-governmental target.

(c) policy considerations:[9]

- advancement of international jurisprudence (reinforcement of existing norms, building precedent, clarifying and advancing the scope of existing protections);
- willingness and ability of national courts to prosecute the alleged perpetrator;
- potential symbolic or deterrent value of prosecution;
- public perception concerning the effective functioning of Tribunal;
- public perception concerning immediate response to ongoing atrocities; and
- public perception concerning impartiality or balance.

(d) practical considerations:[10]

- available investigative resources;
- impact that the new investigation will have on an ongoing investigation and on making existing indictments trial-ready;
- the estimated time to complete the investigation;
- timing of the investigation (for example, the impact initiating a particular investigation will have on the ability to conduct future investigations in the country);
- possibility or likelihood of arrest of the alleged perpetrator;
- consideration of other work carried out in relation to the case (including a check against Rules of Road cases);
- completeness of evidence;
- availability of exculpatory information and evidence; and

---

9   *Ibid.*, pp. 101–02.
10   *Ibid.*, pp. 102–04.

- consideration of other prosecution's investigations in the same geographical area, particularly those of opposite ethnicity perpetrators and victims.

(e) other relevant considerations:[11]

- The particular statutory offence or parts thereof, that can be charged;

- the charging theories available;

- potential legal impediments to prosecution;

- potential defences;

- theory of liability and legal framework of each potential suspect;

- the extent to which the crime base fits in with current investigations and overall strategic direction;

- the extent to which a successful investigation or prosecution of the case would further the strategic aims;

- the extent to which the case can take the investigation to higher political, military, police and civil chains of command; and

- to what extent the case fits into a larger pattern-type of ongoing or future investigations and prosecutions.

The thematic groups and their constitutive lists of factors, arranged at random, seemingly without any hierarchy, were to be considered as a set of relevant considerations informing the decision to start investigations and prosecutions.[12] However, implementing a focused case selection and prioritisation policy on the basis of this diffused list is a difficult proposition.[13] It is not surprising that these criteria were not adhered to in practice by the ICTY, as apparent in indictments against many low-level perpetrators despite a stated policy to focus on the higher-level perpetrators.[14]

---

[11] *Ibid.*, pp. 104–05.

[12] *Ibid.*, p. 99.

[13] Claudia Angermaier, "Case Selection and Prioritization Criteria in the Work of the International Criminal Tribunal for the Former Yugoslavia", in Morten Bergsmo (ed.), *Criteria for Prioritizing and Selecting Core International Crimes Case*, TOAEP, Oslo, 2nd edition, 2010, pp. 33–34 (https://legal-tools.org/doc/f5abed).

[14] Bergsmo *et al.*, 2010, p. 109, see above note 6.

The failure of this prosecution-led case selection and prioritisation effort has led Bergsmo *et al.* to observe that the development and implementation of case selection prioritisation criteria is difficult to achieve by a prosecution service.[15]

It would have been difficult to implement a focused policy based on this catalogue of criteria.[16]

9.3.2. Early Efforts at the International Criminal Court

The preparatory team[17] for the establishment of ICC-OTP, led by Morten Bergsmo as its co-ordinator, was the first to suggest the use of a case selection and prioritisation approach within the context of the ICC. This approach was born out of the concern that exercise of discretion by the OTP could be seen as "biased or lacking in independence".[18] It was thought that formal criteria for selection and prioritisation could shelter OTP's decision-making from such risks.[19]

An expert group convened by the preparatory team to present some reflections "on measures available to the Court to reduce the length of trials as well as pre-trial and trial preparation stage" found it "highly desirable" to have such criteria in place from the start of the Court's operations.[20]

---

[15] *Ibid.*, p. 111.

[16] Angermaier, 2010, pp. 33–34, see above note 13.

[17] The preparatory team for the ICC Office of the Prosecutor was instituted by the Advance Team for the establishment of the International Criminal Court. The preparatory team's work spanned from August 2002 to November 2003. The preparatory team identified several topics on which it formed expert groups to prepare non-binding reports "for the benefit of the ICC Office of the Prosecutor, ICC judges, and for those building relevant investigation and prosecution capacity in national jurisdictions". See Morten Bergsmo, "Institutional History, Behaviour and Development", in Morten Bergsmo, Klaus Rackwitz and SONG Tianying (eds.), *Historical Origins of International Criminal Law: Volume 5*, TOAEP, Brussels, 2017, pp. 1–3 (https://legal-tools.org/doc/09c8b8).

[18] *Ibid.*, p. 12.

[19] *Ibid.*

[20] Morten Bergsmo and Vladimir Tochilovsky, "Measures Available to the International Criminal Court to Reduce the Length of Proceedings", in Morten Bergsmo, Klaus Rackwitz and SONG Tianying (eds.), *Historical Origins of International Criminal Law: Volume 5*, TOAEP, Brussels, 2017, pp. 651, 653 (the report, which was submitted to ICC judges, Registry and Prosecutor, is annexed to the chapter) (https://legal-tools.org/doc/09c8b8).

In its report, the expert group, in the section on investigation strategy, began its rationale for case selection and prioritisation with the need to effectively allocate the limited resources of the OTP:

> Given the limited investigative and prosecutorial resources of the Office of the Prosecutor (OTP) and the broad scope of investigations under Article 54(1)(a), the Prosecutor may not be able to investigate each and every incident arising from a single situation or to prosecute every perpetrator. It is essential to review each potential new investigation by a set of rational standards that will allow the effective marshalling of OTP resources.[21]

In addition, it considered that "[a] clear pronunciation of the prosecution policy, given in the abstract, could prevent the public from harbouring unrealistic expectations and also avoid any appearance of political bias in particular cases".[22] Importantly, the expert group suggested that such a prosecution policy could prevent a "backlog of non-priority suspects".[23]

The report goes on to suggest that in order to limit the number of cases before the Court, the policy should set out priorities, such as focusing on suspects in leadership positions or those accused of crimes of a particular gravity.[24] Underscoring the fact that lower threshold crimes and low-level suspects should not be of concern to the Court, but instead to the domestic jurisdictions, it said, material from ICC investigations on these other suspects can be made available for domestic accountability mechanisms.[25]

Similarly, in terms of charging, the expert group considered that an excessive charging policy will lead to lengthy trials and extensive evidence and thus questioned whether the OTP should avoid charging offences of relatively minor importance.[26] However, it considered reasons

---

[21] *Ibid.*, pp. 668–69.
[22] *Ibid.*, p. 653.
[23] *Ibid.*
[24] *Ibid.*, p. 669.
[25] *Ibid.*
[26] *Ibid.*, pp. 674–75.

which may support an excessive charging policy, such as the wish to address "the totality of crimes committed and the degree of victimisation".[27]

The report of the expert group on the length of proceedings was circulated to the judges of the Court, its Registrar and Prosecutor in 2003, however, it does not seem to have had an immediate impact on the Court in terms of its case selection and prioritisation suggestions.[28]

The draft Regulations for the ICC-OTP, prepared by an expert group appointed by the preparatory team, enumerated case selection and prioritisation criteria in its section on a draft investigation plan.[29] A draft investigation plan, as per the draft Regulations, was to be prepared at the end of the preliminary examination phase to aid the OTP's decision to start an investigation pursuant to Article 53(1) or request authorisation for commencing investigations under Article 15(3).[30] In case of a positive decision, an investigation plan is developed from the draft investigation plan.[31]

The draft investigation plan was to include, *inter alia*, "an explanation why the alleged offences warrant a full investigation against the backdrop of other alleged offences where such a step might not be recommendable".[32] This element of the draft investigation plan brings forth the basic step necessary in a prioritisation exercise: drawing comparisons with other conduct and cases and prioritising some over others. The other elements of the draft plan are also of relevance in guiding a prioritisation exercise, such as the position of the suspect in the relevant chain of authority, likelihood of arrest, and time or resources needed to complete the investigation.[33]

While an abridged version of the draft Regulations was adopted as Regulations *ad interim* of the ICC-OTP, draft investigation plans were not

---

[27] *Ibid.*, p. 675.

[28] *Ibid.*, p. 652.

[29] Carlos Vasconcelos, "Draft Regulations of the Office of the Prosecutor", in Morten Bergsmo, Klaus Rackwitz and SONG Tianying (eds.), *Historical Origins of International Criminal Law: Volume 5*, TOAEP, Brussels, 2017, Annex 1 (https://legal-tools.org/doc/09c8b8).

[30] *Ibid.*, p. 865.

[31] *Ibid.*, p. 869.

[32] *Ibid.*, p. 861.

[33] *Ibid.*

part of it.[34] There was no immediate outcome of the early meticulous efforts made at the ICC for case selection and prioritisation criteria. However, as will be discussed later in this chapter, the ICC-OTP adopted a policy paper on case selection and prioritisation in 2016.

9.3.3. Bosnia and Herzegovina: The Turning Point

One of the major turning points of the concept of case selection and prioritisation happened not in an international context, but domestically. In 2004, the Bosnia and Herzegovina ('BiH') Collegium of Prosecutors adopted the "Orientation Criteria for Sensitive Rules of the Road cases" ('Orientation Criteria'), annexed to the *Book of Rules on Internal Organization and Operations of the Prosecutor's Office of BiH*.[35] The purpose of the Orientation Criteria was to select cases to be "heard before Section I for War Crimes of the Criminal and Appellate Divisions of the Court of Bosnia and Herzegovina".[36] Amongst the selected cases, the Orientation Criteria served as a means of prioritising the order in which they are investigated.[37]

The factors in the Orientation Criteria related to the general criterion of gravity, with its focus on the nature of the crimes alleged and the circumstances of the perpetrator.[38] Cases where the mode of liability was command responsibility, or which involved crimes committed by law enforcement or incumbent public officials, were to take priority.[39] Other factors included practical considerations such as general readiness to proceed and issues of witness security.[40]

The co-ordinator of the preparatory team for the establishment of ICC-OTP, Morten Bergsmo, working in 2007 as a consultant for Organisation for Security and Cooperation in Europe ('OSCE') in Bosnia-

---

[34] Bergsmo, 2017, p. 19, see above note 17.

[35] Bergsmo *et al.*, 2010, p. 81, see above note 6.

[36] OTP of BiH, Book of Rules on the Review of War Crimes Cases, 28 December 2004, Article 10(1).

[37] Bergsmo *et al.*, 2010, p. 84, see above note 6.

[38] *Ibid.*, pp. 85–87.

[39] *Ibid.*, p. 84.

[40] *Ibid.*, p. 87.

Hercegovina, wrote a report on the back-log of open case files in BiH.[41] The report included commentary on the case selection and prioritisation criteria at the Prosecutor's Office of BiH, ICTY and the ICC. The OSCE report and its follow-up had a lasting impact in BiH and the overall development of case prioritisation strategies.

The OSCE report was followed by an expert conference 'Criteria for Prioritizing and Selecting Core International Crimes Cases' in Oslo on 26 September 2008. This was the first time the issue of case selection and prioritisation was put on the agenda in a conference anywhere. An anthology of conference papers from Oslo was published on 26 March 2009, forming one of the most valuable resources on the topic.[42]

The OSCE report was widely circulated in BiH and the Oslo conference also invited wide West Balkan representation.[43] By the end of that year, on 28 December 2008, the BiH Council of Ministers adopted the National War Crimes Strategy. Its Annex A, titled "Criteria for the review of war crimes cases", listed criteria for case selection and prioritisation for the Prosecutor's Office of BiH. The National War Crimes Strategy was motivated and influenced by the OSCE report.[44]

One of the objectives of the Strategy document was to assist the prosecution of most responsible perpetrators of war crimes before the Court of BiH through a case selection and prioritisation criteria.[45] The case selection and prioritisation criteria, though in an annex, were a 'constituent part' of the National War Crimes Prosecution Strategy.[46]

The "Criteria for the review of war crimes cases" were formulated using the Orientation Criteria and the practice of ICTY and ICC as reference.[47] It classified the criteria in three categories of (a) Gravity of crimi-

---

[41] Jared O. Bell, "The Bosnian War Crimes Justice Strategy a Decade Later", FICHL Policy Brief Series No. 92 (2018), TOAEP, Brussels, 2018, p. 1 (http://www.toaep.org/pbs-pdf/92-bell/).

[42] Morten Bergsmo (ed.), *Criteria for Prioritizing and Selecting Core International Crimes Cases*, International Peace Research Institute, Oslo, 2009. A second edition was published on 23 July 2010 (http://www.toaep.org/ps-pdf/4-bergsmo-second).

[43] Bergsmo *et al.*, 2010, p. 116, see above note 6.

[44] Bell, 2018, p. 1, see above note 41.

[45] BiH Council of Ministers, National Strategy for Processing of War Crimes Cases, 28 December 2008, Section 1.2 d., reproduced in Bergsmo *et al.*, 2010, p. 168, see above note 6.

[46] *Ibid.*, "Annex A: Criteria for the review of war crimes cases".

[47] *Ibid.*

nal offenses; (b) Capacity and role of the perpetrator; and (c) Other circumstances.

The gravity criteria considered, logically foremost, whether the qualifications of one of the core international crimes (that is, genocide, crimes against humanity and war crimes) have been fulfilled.[48] The factors guiding the gravity assessment considered whether the offence involved: widespread and systematic killings; persecution; forced disappearance; serious forms of rape, torture, unlawful detention, or inflictions of sufferings on a civilian population; large number of victims or severe consequences for the victims; and particularly insidious means and methods of perpetrating the offence.[49]

The capacity and role of the perpetrator criteria included factors such as the position of the perpetrator in the hierarchy of military, police or paramilitary establishment; whether the perpetrator holds a political office or a judicial office, such as that of a judge, prosecutor, public attorney, or attorney at law; whether the perpetrator was in charge of a camp or detention centre; and modalities of participation in the perpetration of the offence, like involvement in planning and ordering the crime, manner of perpetration and the degree of intent.[50]

The third residual criteria included factors such as: relation to other cases and potential perpetrators; interests of victims and witnesses such as whether the witnesses are protected or need protection, or are insider witnesses; and a third factor considering the impact of the offence or its prosecution on the local community, such as demographic changes, societal trauma and disturbance in public order.[51]

9.4. The Idea in the Mainstream

The OSCE report, the Oslo conference, and the efforts in Bosnia-Hercegovina heralded the dawn of case prioritisation criteria. The Oslo conference and its anthology constitute the knowledge-base pursuant to which further progress has been made on several fronts, both internationally and domestically. It brought together cross-cutting research on priori-

---

[48] *Ibid.*
[49] *Ibid.*
[50] *Ibid.*
[51] *Ibid.*

tisation from domestic and international courts and established case prioritisation as a topic in international criminal justice.

Among its most significant impact is the ICC-OTP's policy paper on case selection and prioritisation. But it has also formed the intellectual basis of efforts made in domestic jurisdictions by CILRAP's Case Matrix Network ('CMN') department.

9.4.1. ICC-OTP's Policy Paper on Case Selection and Prioritisation

On 15 September 2016, the ICC-OTP released its *Policy Paper on Case Selection and Prioritisation*.[52] While it is an internal policy document of the OTP, it was subjected to wide public consultation and published to increase transparency regarding the criteria guiding OTP's decisions on case selection and prioritisation.[53]

The OTP Policy Paper lists considerations that guide the OTP in selecting cases to be investigated and prosecuted within a situation and prioritising the selected cases both within and across the situations.[54]

As the concept of prioritisation is not in the Rome Statute, the OTP used Article 54(1)(b) that allows it to take appropriate measures to ensure the effective investigation and prosecution of crimes to articulate prioritisation criteria.[55]

In order to aid the prioritisation exercise, the OTP Policy Paper establishes a master document, titled the Case Selection Document, which lists potential cases across all situations that meet the case selection criteria of the OTP Policy Paper.[56] The prioritisation criteria are used to determine the order in which cases listed in the Case Selection Document are "rolled-out over time".[57] Cases that are not prioritised still remain part of

---

[52] ICC-OTP, *Policy Paper on Case Selection and Prioritisation*, 15 September 2016 ('OTP Policy Paper') (https://legal-tools.org/doc/182205).

[53] ICC-OTP, *Report on the Implementation of the OTP Strategic Plan (2016 – 2018): Final Analysis and Evaluation of the Results*, 23 August 2019, p. 14 (https://legal-tools.org/doc/5siv5j).

[54] OTP Policy Paper, para. 1, see above note 52.

[55] *Ibid.*, para. 49.

[56] *Ibid.*, paras. 10–11.

[57] *Ibid.*, para. 48.

the Case Selection Document and could still be investigated and prosecuted when the circumstances permit such action.[58]

The OTP Policy Paper divides prioritisation criteria into two categories: strategic and operational criteria. There is no hierarchy between the two categories and the weight to be given to each constituent criterion will depend on the circumstances of each case.[59] This gives broad discretion to the OTP to prioritise cases.

The strategic criteria include:

a) The gravity of crimes alleged, involving both quantitative and qualitative aspects. The factors that guide the assessment of gravity include the scale, nature, manner of commission, and impact of the crimes;[60]

b) Degree of responsibility of alleged perpetrators, highlighting the need to prosecute those most responsible. The extent of responsibility of an accused will be determined by the nature of the unlawful behaviour; the degree of their participation and intent; the existence of discriminatory motive; and any abuse of power or official capacity.[61]

c) Representativity: The office will prioritise cases where charges represent the true extent of the criminality which has occurred within a given situation, to constitute, whenever possible, a representative sample of the main types of victimisation and involving the main types of victim communities.[62]

Beyond representative crimes, it will also prioritise investigation of crimes against or affecting children, sexual and gender-based crimes, and attacks against cultural, religious, historical and other protected objects as well as against humanitarian and peace-keeping personnel.[63]

---

[58]   *Ibid.*

[59]   *Ibid.*, para. 52.

[60]   *Ibid.*, para. 37.

[61]   *Ibid.*, para. 43.

[62]   *Ibid.*, para. 45.

[63]   *Ibid.*, para. 46.

d) "whether a person, or members of the same group, have already been subject to investigation or prosecution either by the Office or by a State for another serious crime" ;[64]

e) "the impact of investigations and prosecutions on the victims of the crimes and affected communities" ;[65]

f) "the impact of investigations and prosecutions on ongoing criminality and/or their contribution to the prevention of crimes";[66] and

g) "the impact and the ability of the Office to pursue cases involving opposing parties to a conflict in parallel or on a sequential basis".[67]

The operational criteria explore whether there are reasonable prospects of securing conviction by reviewing the quantity and quality of the available evidence, international co-operation and judicial assistance to the OTP, ability to conduct required investigations in a timely manner, security situation in the place of investigation, protection of persons co-operating with the court, ability to secure the presence of the accused.[68]

In the OTP's annual reports on preliminary examination activities, one can get a glimpse of the implementation of the case prioritisation criteria. For instance, in Ukraine, the OTP seeks to "prioritise certain types of alleged conduct believed to be most representative of the patterns of alleged crimes".[69] While in Gaza, it seeks to prioritise "incidents for which there is a range of sources and sufficient information available to enable an objective and thorough analysis".[70]

In the Strategic Plan for 2019–2021, the OTP has set a strategic goal of increasing "the speed, efficiency and effectiveness of preliminary examinations, investigations and prosecutions" which it aims to achieve by implementing, *inter alia*, a strategy of "further prioritising amongst inves-

---

[64] *Ibid.*, para. 50.

[65] *Ibid.*

[66] *Ibid.*

[67] *Ibid.*

[68] *Ibid.*, para. 41.

[69] ICC-OTP, *Report on Preliminary Examination Activities 2018*, 5 December 2018, p. 27 (https://legal-tools.org/doc/39c2c1).

[70] ICC-OTP, *Report on Preliminary Examination Activities 2019*, 5 December 2019, p. 58 (https://legal-tools.org/doc/lq7j94).

tigations and prosecutions".[71] Recognising the expectations of stakeholders to deliver more and better results while using the existing resources, the OTP plans to stringently apply case prioritisation criteria to cases identified across all situations under investigation which it warns could delay non-prioritised cases.[72] The OTP considers it necessary to undertake these 'difficult decisions' on prioritisation, in order to build viable cases while working with limited resources.[73]

The ICC-OTP should perhaps, as a means to ascertaining the effectiveness of case prioritisation, conduct a qualitative and quantitative analysis of the results delivered by implementing its case prioritisation criteria. Such a study could help ascertain the best manner and degree of implementation of case prioritising strategies at the ICC.

9.4.2. Colombia

Colombia's Office of the Attorney General adopted a directive on case selection and prioritisation criteria in 2012, and is one of the early adopters of this strategy.[74] The directive categorises prioritisation criteria in three groups: 1) Objective: The objective criterion of prioritisation examines the criminal conduct in terms of severity and its representativeness. Thus, combining considerations of gravity and representativity in the same cluster;[75] 2) Subjective: this criterion considers the qualities of the victim such as their gender, age, membership of an ethnic group or profession such as human rights defender, journalist or judicial officer. It also considers the degree of responsibility of the accused;[76] 3) Other complementary considerations: such as practical feasibility of prosecution, whether the conduct in question is being investigated by an international court, and the region or location of the crime.[77]

---

[71] ICC-OTP, *Strategic Plan 2019–2021*, 17 July 2019, paras. 18–19 ('Strategic Plan 2019–2021') (https://legal-tools.org/doc/raba4c).

[72] *Ibid.*, para. 22.

[73] *Ibid.*

[74] Colombia Office of the Attorney General, Por medio de la cual se adoptan unos criterios de priorización de situaciones y casos, y se crea un nuevo sistema de investigación penal y de gestión de aquéllos en la Fiscalía General de la Nación, 4 October 2012, Directiva No. 0001 (https://legal-tools.org/doc/e93910).

[75] *Ibid.*, pp. 30–31.

[76] *Ibid.*, pp. 28–30.

[77] *Ibid.*, pp. 31–32.

9.4.3. The Democratic Republic of the Congo

In 2018, the Democratic Republic of the Congo ('DRC') adopted Practice Direction for the Selection and Prioritisation of Crimes Against Peace and Security of Mankind, in Particular Sexual Violence at the Investigation Stage ('Practice Direction').[78] CILRAP's CMN department assisted the DRC with methodology and technical support for the development of the Practice Direction.[79] The case selection and prioritising criteria in the Practice Direction were themselves heavily influenced by a CMN report published in 2015.[80]

As a prerequisite of the case selection and prioritisation exercise, it calls for a centralised statistical database on the number of open cases, number of suspects in those cases, nature of the offence and the number of victims.[81]

The case selection and prioritisation criteria are divided into two broad sections: formal criteria, and policy and practical considerations. Formal criteria include consideration of the factual context of the commission of the crime on the basis of indicators that assess gravity, such as the number of victims, area of destruction, duration and repetition of the offence, *modus operandi* of the criminal conduct, discriminatory motive, defencelessness of victims and impact of crimes.[82] The factual context is also enriched by the location of the crime and ethnicity, tribe or nationality of the alleged perpetrators or victims, factors that are relevant in a domestic context.[83]

---

[78] DRC Conseil Supérieur de la Magistrature, Circulaire n°02/PCC-PCSM/2018 relative a la sélection et à la priorisation des affaires de crimes contre la paix et la sécurité de l'humanité, en particulier celles liées aux violences sexuelles, au stade de l'instruction pré-juridictionnelle (Memo No. 02/PCC-PCSM/2018 on the Case Selection and Prioritisation of Crimes Against Peace and Security of Mankind, in Particular Those Relating to Sexual Violence at the Preliminary Stage), 19 March 2018 ('DRC Practice Direction') (https://legal-tools.org/doc/bf85a3).

[79] CMN, "Examples of Country-Work Undertaken by the CMN" (available on its web site).

[80] CMN, *Prioritising International Sex Crimes Cases in the Democratic Republic of the Congo: Supporting the national justice system in the investigation and prosecution of core international crimes with a sexual element*, Brussels, November 2015 (https://legal-tools.org/doc/2ee277).

[81] DRC Practice Direction, Chapter III – Mapping: prerequisite of prioritisation, see above note 78.

[82] *Ibid.*, Chapter IV, Section 1, Criterion 1.

[83] *Ibid.*

The formal criteria in the Practice Direction also include assessment of the degree of responsibility of the accused and a victim-centric representativity approach that focuses on the scale and nature of the victimisation rather than the political, ethnic or religious affiliation of the accused or victims.[84]

Practical considerations for prioritising cases include strategic and practical indicators to make an "early assessment of the effectiveness and efficiency" of prosecuting a given case.[85]

9.4.4. The Central African Republic

In December 2018, the Special Criminal Court ('CPS') of the Central African Republic ('CAR'), that exercises jurisdiction over core international crimes, launched an investigation and prosecution strategy that provides selection and prioritisation criteria.[86] Its prioritisation criteria have been localised extensively and they include:

1) Feasibility of investigation in terms of security: recognising the safety and security issues persisting in the CAR, this criterion requires the prosecutor to consider the security issues, including witness and victim protection, the safety of investigators, judicial actors and all other persons who may be at security risk due to the prosecutor's activities.[87]

2) Representativity: the CPS uses a broad criterion of representativity. The cases to be prioritised should be representative of the a) victims including from different religious, ethnic and geographic groups; b) alleged perpetrators from various armed groups or State apparatus taking into account their ethnic and religious affiliations; c) geography – the incidents selected must, wherever possible, represent the different regions affected by the crisis in the CAR; d) different time periods of conflict in the CAR lasting from 2003 until the time of writing.[88] As is clear here, the CPS's use of the term representativity hints towards diversity in prosecution.

---

[84] *Ibid.*, Chapter IV, Section 1, Criteria 2 and 3.
[85] *Ibid.*, Chapter IV, Section 2.
[86] CAR Cour Pénale Spéciale, Stratégie d'enquêtes, de poursuites et d'instructions, 4 December 2018 (https://legal-tools.org/doc/61skr0).
[87] *Ibid.*, para. 64.
[88] *Ibid.*, para. 65.

3) Possibility of identification, location and arrest of the suspect.[89]

4) Availability, credibility and reliability of evidence.[90]

5) Strategic considerations such as availability of resources, the time required to complete investigation, and the potential of developing future case files.[91]

6) Public interests, such as developing trust in the CPS, emblematic value of certain incidents and crimes, and impact of prosecution in creating a deterrence to criminality.[92]

9.4.5. Representativity as a Case Prioritisation Criteria: A Missed Opportunity

The OSCE report, referenced earlier, was also published as the monograph *The Backlog of Core International Crimes Case Files in Bosnia and Herzegovina* by Morten Bergsmo *et al.*[93] This book enunciated a unique concept of representativity that has not yet been fully captured by the discourse on prioritisation.

In the words of Bergsmo *et al.*, the idea of representativity is:

> [T]hat at the end of a process of war crimes prosecutions, the accumulated case portfolio should reflect – or be representative of – the overall victimisation caused by the crimes in the conflict or situation at hand. The most serious crimes and the crimes that the most senior leaders are suspected of being most responsible for should have been prosecuted at the end of the day. The areas and communities most affected by the crimes should have seen more of these crimes or crime base prosecuted than in less affected communities. The most affected victim groups should have more of the crimes that caused the victimisation prosecuted than other groups. Organizations or structures causing the most serious crimes should have more of its responsible members – or more of the crimes caused by them – prosecuted than other such organizations or structures.[94]

---

[89] *Ibid.*, para. 66.

[90] *Ibid.*, para. 67.

[91] *Ibid.*, para. 68.

[92] *Ibid.*, para. 69.

[93] Bergsmo *et al.*, 2010, see above note 6.

[94] *Ibid.*, p. 125.

As per that text, this approach towards representativity is born out of the concerns for the interests of the victims and the ability of criminal justice to contribute to reconciliation and deterrence, while commanding trust of all its stakeholders.[95]

However, the use of the superlative 'most' (most affected areas, communities and victim groups, most serious crimes, and so on) in the formulation of Bergsmo *et al.* exudes a utilitarian approach. From this perspective, representativity does not have victims at its core – if that were the case it would not differentiate between the most affected victims and lesser affected victims. This idea is all about efficiency – bringing out the maximum benefits from the criminal justice institution. This idea of representativity embodies the rationale of prioritisation like no other criteria, that is, to have an efficient criminal justice machinery. In a way, representativity is what law intends to do: to maintain order and to do so in a way where benefits far outweigh the costs. To do it in a way that has the maximum impact is really about hammering the nail that sticks out the most.

The idea is not to seek shelter behind the poster incident or accused, which could be guided by popular media, but to tackle head-on what represents quantitatively the most serious form of victimisation.

Donors, the international community, victims, and the general populace would surely recognise the effectiveness of a criminal justice system when those who faced the greatest suffering, the incidents which caused the greatest suffering, and those who caused the greatest suffering are processed by it.

The ICC-OTP has missed the opportunity to embrace the concept of representativity fully in its Policy Paper published in 2016. When making reference to representativity, the Policy Paper talks about representing the true extent of criminality in a situation and selecting charges that constitute a representative sample of main types of victimisation and affected communities. The ICC-OTP's approach appears to be ensuring diversity and not effectiveness. As the institution that sits at the pinnacle of efforts to end impunity for mass crimes, a case prioritisation strategy that ensures effective delivery of justice through representativity could bring larger benefits to the international community.

---

[95] *Ibid.*

9.5. Challenges

In the implementation of prioritisation criteria in domestic jurisdictions, one important factor to consider is the operation of the principle of complementarity *vis-à-vis* the prioritisation criteria in the domestic jurisdiction. Should the implementation of prioritisation criteria in a domestic jurisdiction fall foul of the ICC standard of unable and unwilling, there is a possibility of those cases reaching the ICC. While prioritising a case does not entail non-prosecution of the non-prioritised cases, realistically there are bound to be delays in managing the non-prioritised caseload. Under the ICC Statute, unjustified or undue delays could be considered as the unwillingness or inability of the domestic judicial system to carry out investigation and prosecution, and could invite the attention of the ICC-OTP.[96] Similarly, a broadly-worded, practical-considerations criterion could give wide discretion to the prosecutor, and if that discretion is used to deprioritise certain cases with the intent of shielding the accused from prosecution, it is likely to be treated as unwillingness to genuinely investigate or prosecute.[97]

The key to designing the domestic prioritisation criteria is that they not be inconsistent with the ICC prioritisation criteria: the gravity of offences and degree of responsibility of the accused should remain relevant, but the main types of victimisation and affected communities should also be considered for prioritisation.

While the ICC-OTP's Policy Paper is treated as an internal document not giving rise to any rights and obligations, it remains to be seen how the ICC-OTP will treat non-compliance by a domestic prosecution service of the relevant domestic criteria of prioritisation.[98] Could the ICC-OTP consider such non-compliance as proof that the case has not been prioritised with a view to shielding the accused from criminal responsibility? It certainly can, as the ICC is likely to take into account all information available to it in order to assess the State's unwillingness and inability to prosecute core international crimes.

Thus, an ideal prioritisation criterion in a domestic jurisdiction will not only address the local needs, but also be mindful of the ICC Statute,

---

[96] Rome Statute of the International Criminal Court, 17 July 1998, Article 17(2)(b) and 17(3) (https://legal-tools.org/doc/7b9af9).

[97] *Ibid.*, Article 17(2)(a).

[98] OTP Policy Paper, para. 2, see above note 52.

its prioritisation criteria, and the operation of the principle of complementarity.

As a corollary to the ICC-aware or -sensitive domestic prioritisation criteria, the ICC itself needs to design its prioritisation criteria so that there is no impunity gap. That is, its prioritisation criteria need to be specifically designed to cover cases, in line with the Rome Statute, that are not adequately covered by the domestic prioritisation criteria, so that the operation of prioritisation criteria at the domestic level and by the ICC-OTP complement each other and there is no impunity gap for the perpetrators of the most serious crimes.

9.6. The Future

As is evident in the adoption of case prioritisation strategies in domestic jurisdictions, the idea of case prioritisation is gaining wider acceptance due to its ability to meaningfully navigate bloated mass crimes case portfolios of States with stretched criminal justice systems.

Case prioritising could also be a useful strategy for countries that suffer from judicial pendency. For instance, the Indian judicial system suffers from a massive backlog of civil and criminal cases.[99] In a recent Delhi High Court judgment on mass violence directed against the Sikh community in the aftermath of the assassination of former Prime Minister Indira Gandhi, the Court lamented the fact that it had taken 34 years to bring the perpetrators to justice:

> In India, the riots in early November 1984 in which in Delhi alone 2,733 Sikhs and nearly 3,350 all over the country were brutally murdered (these are official figures) was neither the first instance of a mass crime nor, tragically, the last. The mass killings in Punjab, Delhi and elsewhere during the country's partition remains a collective painful memory as is the killings of innocent Sikhs in November 1984. There has

---

[99] Law Commission of India, *Arrears and Backlog: Creating Additional Judicial (Wo)manpower*, July 2014, Report No. 245, p. 1 (https://legal-tools.org/doc/jwxv5v):

[T]he judicial system is unable to deliver timely justice because of <u>huge</u> backlog of cases for which the current judge strength is <u>completely</u> inadequate. Further, in addition to the already backlogged cases, the system is not being able to keep pace with the new cases being instituted, and is not being able to dispose of a comparable number of cases. The already severe problem of backlogs is, therefore, getting exacerbated by the day, leading to a dilution of the Constitutional guarantee of access to timely justice and erosion of the rule of law.

been a familiar pattern of mass killings in Mumbai in 1993, in Gujarat in 2002, in Kandhamal, Odisha in 2008, in Muzaffarnagar in U.P. in 2013 to name a few. Common to these mass crimes were the targeting of minorities and the attacks spearheaded by the dominant political actors being facilitated by the law enforcement agencies. The criminals responsible for the mass crimes have enjoyed political patronage and managed to evade prosecution and punishment. Bringing such criminals to justice poses a serious challenge to our legal system. As these appeals themselves demonstrate, decades pass by before they can be made answerable. This calls for strengthening the legal system.[100]

Countries like India that suffer from inexplicable judicial delays due to massive backlogs of cases can benefit from prioritising mass crimes cases. The criteria for prioritising mass crimes need to be suited to the particular needs of the domestic jurisdiction. There can hardly be boilerplate prioritisation criteria for domestic jurisdictions. As the case selection and prioritising strategy from the CAR shows, States should design case prioritising strategies that are best suited to their needs and realities.

As per the ICC-OTP's Strategic Plan for 2019–2021, the resources available to it are "unlikely to significantly increase", while it expects an increase in the number of situations under investigation.[101] In order to manage a larger caseload with existing resources, the ICC-OTP has aimed to increase "the speed, efficiency and effectiveness of preliminary examinations, investigations and prosecutions" through a stringent application of case prioritisation criteria. Thus, we are likely to witness a more proactive approach on case prioritisation at the ICC, the method and results of which could be quite instructive for national jurisdictions that suffer from large backlogs of cases and limited resources.

---

[100] Delhi High Court, *State through CBI v. Sajjan Kumar and others*, Judgment, 17 December 2018, Criminal Appeal No. 1099/2013 and Connected Matters, para. 367.6 (https://legal-tools.org/doc/b08482).

[101] Strategic Plan 2019–2021, para. 9, see above note 71.

Annex 1

Date	Development
October 1995	ICTY's Office of the Prosecutor formally adopts case selection and prioritisation criteria.
August 2002 to November 2003	Expert groups appointed by the preparatory team for the ICC Office of the Prosecutor prepares report "on measures available to the Court to reduce the length of trials as well as pre-trial and trial preparation stage" and draft Regulations for the OTP.
28 December 2004	BiH Collegium of Prosecutors adopted the "Orientation Criteria for Sensitive Rules of the Road cases".
2007	OSCE report on the backlog of open case files in BiH.
26 September 2008	CILRAP expert conference on 'Criteria for Prioritizing and Selecting Core International Crimes Cases' held in Oslo.
28 December 2008	The BiH Council of Ministers adopted the National War Crimes Strategy with Annex A, titled "Criteria for the review of war crimes cases".
26 March 2009	Anthology of conference papers from Oslo expert conference 'Criteria for Prioritizing and Selecting Core International Crimes Cases' published by TOAEP.
17 September 2009	The OSCE report published as the monograph *The Backlog of Core International Crimes Case Files in Bosnia and Herzegovina* by TOAEP.
4 October 2012	Colombia's Office of the Attorney General adopts the directive on case selection and prioritisation criteria.
November 2015	CILRAP's CMN releases *Prioritising International Sex Crimes Cases in the Democratic Republic of the Congo: Supporting the national justice system in the investigation and prosecution of core international crimes with a sexual element.*
15 September 2016	The ICC-OTP releases the *Policy Paper on Case Selection and Prioritisation.*
19 March 2018	The DRC adopts "Practice Direction for the Selection and Prioritisation of Crimes Against Peace and Security of Mankind, in Particular Sexual Violence at the Investigation Stage".
4 December 2018	The Special Criminal Court of Central African Republic launches the investigation and prosecution strategy with case selection and prioritisation criteria.

**A timeline on the development of the case prioritisation criteria
for core international crimes.**

10

Enhancing the Quality of Investigations: What Role Can the In-Depth Analysis Charts Play?

Olympia Bekou[*]

A number of cases before the International Criminal Court ('ICC' or 'the Court') have collapsed in recent years, owing to inadequate evidence. This brought to the fore the quality of investigations.[1] The decision to drop the charges against Laurent Gbagbo,[2] albeit not unique, led to the issue surrounding the quality of investigations receiving closer attention and the Office of the Prosecutor being brought under the spotlight for their working practices. Improving the quality of investigations is key for the success of an institution such as the ICC insofar as building successful cases begins already at the investigation stage.

Starting with the premise that putting emphasis on the investigations should not be taken as advocating for convictions, the focus of this chapter will be on how to improve the quality of the cases that are ultimately brought before the Court. What this chapter seeks to explore is one of the many areas where a (modest) change in practice might improve the quality of investigations so as to reduce the risk of cases failing – cases that would have otherwise succeeded. It goes without saying that an institution such as the ICC ought to always strive to improve the way it operates, starting already with investigations.

---

[*]   **Olympia Bekou** is Professor of Public International Law and Head, International Criminal Justice Unit, Human Rights Law Centre, School of Law, University of Nottingham.

[1]   See Morten Bergsmo, "Towards a Culture of Quality Control in Criminal Investigations", FICHL Policy Brief Series No. 94 (2019), Torkel Opsahl Academic EPublisher, Brussels, 2019 (https://www.toaep.org/pbs-pdf/94-bergsmo/).

[2]   ICC, Situation in the Republic of Côte d'Ivoire, *The Prosecutor v. Laurent Gbagbo and Charles Blé Goudé*, Trial Chamber, Reasons for oral decision of 15 January 2019 on the Requête de la Défense de Laurent Gbagbo afin qu'un jugement d'acquittement portant sur toutes les charges soit prononcé en faveur de Laurent Gbagbo et que sa mise en liberté immédiate soit ordonnée, and on the Blé Goudé Defence no case to answer motion, 16 July 2019, ICC-02/11-01/15-1263 (https://legal-tools.org/doc/440017).

Given that core international crimes are not only factually rich but also very complex, an examination of the key challenges linked to the investigation of such crimes is necessary. Comprehending the specific legal requirements and maintaining an overview of facts and evidence already at the start of investigations is required, as insufficient understanding of such complexity can affect the quality of justice delivered further down the line. As will be seen in the sections that follow, a precise and structured approach will have a positive effect on the efficiency and precision of the criminal justice process, ensuring that fair trial guarantees are upheld throughout.

Discussion in this chapter will then turn on how existing practices, namely, the use of in-depth analysis charts which had been utilised in some of the ICC's cases, can contribute towards tackling some of the challenges in preserving an overview of facts and evidence. The main argument put forward in this chapter is that adopting a similar methodology would help improve the quality of investigations. Irrespective of the typology used, means or technology employed, it will be argued that maintaining such an overview of facts and evidence is the crux of the issue at hand and constitutes a concrete way of improving the quality of investigations.

10.1. Difficulties in Linking Law to Facts in Core International Crimes Cases

One of the difficulties in relating law to facts in core international crimes cases, is the increased volume of facts. It is not uncommon to lose the overview of the facts and evidence in such cases. Applying the law to the facts, so-called 'subsumption', is more difficult. Preserving both factual and evidentiary oversight throughout the different stages of the criminal justice process constitutes a further challenge. Although the facts of a case should be seen as a single coherent knowledge-base, this frequently ends up being broken up, not least because different teams of people work on the case from one stage to another. Although inevitable, the reality of this practice is that a lot of effort ends up being duplicated with increasing costs as a result.

10.1.1. Understanding the Legal Requirements for the Prosecution of Core International Crimes

The crimes under the jurisdiction of the ICC,[3] namely, genocide, crimes against humanity, war crimes and aggression, encompass numerous constituting elements and legal requirements. These are elaborated upon in both the ICC Statute as well as the Elements of Crimes document which aids in their interpretation. Furthermore, depending on the crime in question, certain contextual elements may also need to be established.[4] It is also necessary to satisfy one of the necessary modes of liability – perpetration, ordering, command responsibility, planning, and so on.[5]

To secure a conviction, evidence must be presented to support each of the individual elements above. In addition to the legal requirements, appreciating whether adequate evidence exists, and the type of evidence needed to prove that each legal requirement has been satisfied to the requisite standard, is necessary.

Investigating and bringing charges against high level individuals – be they rebel leaders, military leaders, or Heads of State, requires establishing the evidential chain necessary to link such an individual to the criminal acts carried out by others, which can potentially be a complex endeavour.[6]

The complexity of the legal requirements of the core international crimes, together with the modes of liability and the nature of the factual situations to which these must be applied, and in order to understanding the evidence available, it is important to adopt a clear and precise structure to cases. Lack of such understanding and overview may cause delays in the justice process, negatively impacting on the precision and quality of cases, and may also lead to the erosion of the Court's credibility.

---

[3] Rome Statute of the International Criminal Court, 17 July 1998, Article 5 ('ICC Statute') (https://legal-tools.org/doc/7b9af9).

[4] For instance, genocide must be committed "in the context of a manifest pattern of similar conduct", whereas the attack in crimes against humanity must be "widespread or systematic". ICC, Elements of Crimes, 11 June 2010, Articles 6, 7 (https://legal-tools.org/doc/3c0e2d).

[5] ICC Statute, Articles 25 and 38, see above note 3.

[6] Frederik Harhoff, "It is all in the Process: Reflections on the Relation between International Criminal Trials and International Humanitarian Law", in *Nordic Journal of International Law*, 2009, vol. 78, no. 4, p. 478.

10.1.2. Applying the Legal Requirements to Large Quantities of Evidence

Investigators, prosecutors and judges must be able to process vast quantities of data efficiently and accurately. This includes also matching it to the specific legal requirements of a case. For, it is not just the legal aspects of a case that pose challenges. Facts and evidence commonly challenge both the legal analysis and established work practices in complex cases. Such cases rely on a wide range of documents and witness statements. They are inherently fact-rich. Analysing and organising materials and determining their relevancy and weight in terms of the legal aspects of the case are, therefore, necessary. Organising evidence effectively is critical to the success of the case, affecting different stages of the process, from case selection and prioritisation, to the quality of the case, to fairness and judicial economy.

To select strong cases, prosecutors must both comprehend the legal requirements and the strength of the available evidence to prove them. Maintaining a well-organised overview of the case is also important for the development of a clear prosecutorial or defence strategy by counsel, particularly where larger teams are involved who may be working on different areas of the same case.

The problem of handling large quantities of facts and evidence is by no means unique to core international crimes.[7] It is also an issue in serious fraud and organised crime cases, including human trafficking. The difficulties faced in the prosecution of core international crimes closely resemble those encountered in serious fraud cases in respect of linking lots of facts to specific legal requirements.[8] International criminal justice institutions may benefit from the experience of serious fraud agencies in that respect.

---

[7] See Bergsmo, 2019, see above note 1.

[8] Jack A. Blum, "Enterprise Crime: Financial Fraud in International Interspace", in *Trends in Organized Crime*, 1998, vol. 3, no. 3, p. 39. See also report of the Fraud Advisory Panel, *Bringing to Book: Tackling the Crisis in the Investigation and Prosecution of Serious Fraud*, 2006.

10.2. Applying the Law to the Facts in an Informed, Efficient and Precise Manner

10.2.1. Pursuing Justice and the Quality of the Process

The quality of the justice process also depends on the efficiency of the overall process and the adherence to protecting the rights of the accused. These are challenges that arise in respect of core crimes cases as well and will, therefore, be examined next.

10.2.2. The Efficiency of the Criminal Justice Process and the Fight Against Impunity

The practical challenges associated with the application of the law to the facts in core international crimes cases and the manner in which they are dealt with, influences the ability of criminal justice institutions to pursue justice efficiently and effectively, and to contribute to the fight against impunity.

One such challenge is the sheer number of potential perpetrators. In the aftermath of mass atrocity, there may be a large number of individuals suspected of having been involved in the commission of core international crimes, which may even amount to a significant part of the population.[9] Moreover, international trials are both costly and resource intensive. This in turn means that only a small number of individuals can be brought before an international court or tribunal and the process is likely to be expensive. Such low number of perpetrators being brought to justice internationally and the associated costs, is also a common source of criticism of international criminal justice institutions. If this is coupled with inefficient practices and the lack of precision, it becomes harder to meet the demand for justice, particularly where many perpetrators exist. The result of this is that cases which are being pursued may later fail owing to a lack of evidence or weaknesses that were not foreseen at an earlier stage of the process. It may also lead to handling unnecessary evidence, making the process more cumbersome for all involved, including counsel and judges.

---

[9] Scott Straus, "How Many Perpetrators Were There in the Rwandan Genocide? An Estimate", in *Journal of Genocide Research*, 2004, vol. 6, no. 1, p. 85. Morten Bergsmo, Kjetil Helvig, Ilia Utmelidze and Gorana Žagovec, *The Backlog of Core International Crimes Case Files in Bosnia and Herzegovina*, Torkel Opsahl Academic EPublisher, Oslo, 2010 (http://www.toaep.org/ps-pdf/3-bergsmo-helvig-utmelidze-zagovec-second).

Organising evidence in such a manner so as to have an up-to-date overview of the case at all times, is an important way of ensuring efficiency. For example, where evidence is weak or missing, it is counterproductive to pursue a case which is not supported by sufficient evidence. Maintaining a clear overview also aids in developing a clear prosecutorial strategy and avoids having counsel prepare for cases to progress in a number of different directions or presenting evidence with little or no relevance to the charges. Developing a precise and structured approach to the handling of evidence also avoids the duplication of work, both within teams of investigators, prosecutors, defence lawyers and judges, and between different teams or stages of the process, enhancing the efficiency as a whole and reducing the overall length of the process as well as the associated costs.

10.2.3. Promotion of the Rights of the Accused

The inability of the prosecution to outline a clear strategy for the prosecution of cases may also affect the fair trial rights of the accused. The right of the accused to be informed promptly and in detail of the nature, cause and content of the charge, and the right to have adequate time and facilities for the preparation of his or her defence are two aspects of the right to fair trial.[10] The ICC Statute guarantees these rights to accused persons appearing before the ICC.[11] However, in practice,[12] how evidence is organised and presented by the prosecution will affect how the criminal justice process is carried out. Handling evidence in precise manner and being clear as to the way in which such evidence will be linked to the legal requirements of the crime can contribute to the observation of the fundamental rights of the accused. This in turn will also ease the burden of the defence who, becoming aware of the prosecutorial strategy, would be able to channel their (modest) resources to the specific charges, in-

---

[10] International Covenant on Civil and Political Rights, 16 December 1966, Articles 14(3)(a), 14(3)(b) ('ICCPR') (https://legal-tools.org/doc/2838f3); European Convention on Human Rights, 4 November 1950, Article 6(3)(a), 6(3)(b) (https://legal-tools.org/doc/8267cb); American Convention on Human Rights, 22 November 1969, Articles 8(2)(b), 8(2)(c) (https://legal-tools.org/doc/1152cf).

[11] ICC Statute, Articles 67(1)(a), 67(1)(b), see above note 3.

[12] Jacob Katz Cogan, "International Criminal Courts and Fair Trials: Difficulties and Prospects", in *Yale Journal of International Law*, 2002, vol. 27, no. 1, p. 111.

forming the accused from the outset of the detailed nature of the charges against them.

Ensuring that accused persons are tried without undue delay is also aided by an increase in precision and efficiency.[13] This right afforded to the accused is yet another important aspect of the right to fair trial. Having an efficient, precise and informed methodology can help the ICC to overcome these difficulties and ensure the application of the rights of the accused in practice.

10.3. The 'In-depth Analysis Charts': An Overview of the Relevant Case-Law

Having outlined some of the challenges associated with core international crimes cases, the chapter will now provide an overview of the in-depth analysis charts which had been introduced by the ICC's Chambers as part of a broader engagement with questions of pre-trial disclosure. This was done whilst discussing *how* evidence should be disclosed, *what* should be disclosed, to *whom*, and *when*.[14] By exploring the merits and perceived drawbacks of the in-depth analysis charts, the chapter will argue that expanding their use also to cover investigations, will both improve the quality of investigations and will be of benefit to the judicial process as a whole.

Pre-Trial Chamber ('PTC') III explained the rationale for the development of the in-depth analysis charts. In reflecting on the Chamber's functions, it held that they help ensure "the efficient organisation of the confirmation hearing, in determining whether or not to send the case to trial and in facilitating the conduct of the trial if the charges are confirmed".[15]

---

[13] ICCPR, Article 14(3)(c), see above note 10.

[14] On 'who, what, when, why' characterisation of the disclosure theme, see Helen Brady, "Disclosure of Evidence", in Roy S. Lee (ed.), *The International Criminal Court: Elements of Crimes and Rules of Procedure and Evidence*, Transnational Publishers, Ardsley, 2001, p. 404. For background information on the introduction of in-depth analysis charts, see Olympia Bekou and Morten Bergsmo, "The In-depth Evidence Analysis Charts at the International Criminal Court", in Morten Bergsmo (ed.), *Active Complementarity: Legal Information Transfer*, Torkel Opsahl Academic EPublisher, Oslo, 2011, pp. 313–47 (http://www.toaep.org/ps-pdf/8-bergsmo); and Morten Bergsmo, Olympia Bekou and Annika Jones, "Preserving the Overview of Law and Facts: The Case Matrix", in *ibid.*, pp. 43–66.

[15] ICC, Situation in the Central African Republic, *The Prosecutor v. Jean-Pierre Bemba Gombo*, Pre-Trial Chamber, Decision on the Evidence Disclosure System and Setting a

In order to improve the efficiency of the proceedings, PTC III prescribed in *Bemba* a specific method of presenting the evidence disclosed prior to the confirmation hearing, and communication to the Chambers. The so-called 'analytical disclosure', required that all evidence disclosed by either party at the pre-confirmation stage be presented in the form of an 'in-depth analysis chart'. Therefore, "each piece of evidence [is presented] according to its relevance in relation to the constituent elements of the crimes presented by the Prosecutor". Moreover, the Chamber required that each "piece of evidence must be analysed – page by page or, where required, paragraph by paragraph [...] with one or more of the constituent elements of one or more of the crime with which the person is charged".[16] In the two Kenyan disclosure Decisions, the Single Judge specifically directed the parties to follow the disclosure regime established in the Decision in *Bemba*.[17]

Similarly, Trial Chamber II in *Katanga* required that evidence be disclosed using a 'Table of Incriminating Evidence' that follows a similar logic, and which:

> breaks down each confirmed charge into its constituent elements – contextual circumstances as well as material and mental elements – as prescribed by the *Elements of crimes*. For each element, the Prosecution shall set out the precise factual allegations which it intends to prove at trial in order to establish the constituent element in question. For each factual allegation, the Prosecution shall specify which item(s) of evidence it intends to rely on at trial in order to prove the allegation. Within each item of evidence, the Prosecution shall

---

Timetable for Disclosure between the Parties, 31 July 2008, ICC-01/05-01/08-55, para. 6 ('Bemba Pre-Trial Decision on the Evidence Disclosure System and Setting a Timetable for Disclosure between the Parties') (https://legal-tools.org/doc/15c802).

[16] *Ibid.*, para. 69.

[17] ICC, Situation in the Republic of Kenya, *The Prosecutor v. William Samoei Ruto, Henry Kiprono Kosgey and Joshua Arap Sang*, Pre-Trial Chamber, Decision Setting the Regime for Evidence Disclosure and Other Related Matters, 6 April 2011, ICC-01/09-01/11-44, paras. 21–23 (https://legal-tools.org/doc/351827); ICC, Situation in the Republic of Kenya, *The Prosecutor v. Francis Kirimi Muthaura, Uhuru Muigai Kenyatta and Mohammed Hussein Ali*, Pre-Trial Chamber, Decision Setting the Regime for Evidence Disclosure and Other Related Matters, 6 April 2011, ICC-01/09-02/11-48, paras. 22–24 (https://legal-tools.org/doc/12b91f).

identify the pertinent passage(s), which are directly relevant to the specific factual allegation.[18]

In subsequent case-law, Trial Chamber II substantively adopted the same methodology of the 'in-depth analysis charts' as outlined in *Bemba*, even if this Chamber did not use the term itself.

Whilst the Pre-Trial Chamber in *Bemba*, and the Trial Chamber in *Katanga*, have prescribed the precise format in which evidence must be disclosed to the other party, and communicated to the Chamber, the Pre-Trial Chamber *Abu Garda*[19] and also *Banda and Jerbo*,[20] adopted a less rigorous regime of analytical disclosure. The Chamber confirmed that the appropriate system of disclosure to be adopted was that developed at the confirmation of charges stages in the *Lubanga* Case[21] and the *Katanga and Ngudjolo* Case,[22] models that predate the comprehensive regime outlined in *Bemba*.[23]

Having said that, the Chamber in *Abu Garda* required that the Prosecutor provide the "Charging Document and the List of Evidence [...] in a language which the person fully understands and speaks. In doing so, the Prosecution shall further ensure that this is organised in such a manner that: i) each item of evidence is linked to the factual statement it intends to

---

[18] ICC, Situation in the Democratic Republic of the Congo, *The Prosecutor v. Germain Katanga and Mathieu Ngudjolo Chui*, Trial Chamber, Order Concerning the Presentation of Incriminating Evidence and the E-Court Protocol, 13 March 2009, ICC-01/04-01/07-956, para. 13 ('Katanga Trial Order Concerning the Presentation of Incriminating Evidence and the E-Court Protocol') (https://legal-tools.org/doc/ad5c46).

[19] ICC, Situation in Darfur, Sudan, *The Prosecutor v. Bahar Idriss Abu Garda*, Pre-Trial Chamber, Second Decision on Issues Relating to Disclosure, 15 July 2009, ICC-02/05-02/09-35 ('Abu Garda Pre-Trial Second Decision on Issues Relating to Disclosure') (https://legal-tools.org/doc/b57860).

[20] ICC, Situation in Darfur, Sudan, *The Prosecutor v. Abdallah Banda Abakaer Nourainand and Saleh Moahmmed Jerbo Jamus*, Pre-Trial Chamber, Decision on Issues Relating to Disclosure, 29 June 2010, ICC-02/05-03/09-49 (https://legal-tools.org/doc/2a3bac).

[21] ICC, Situation in the Democratic Republic of the Congo, *The Prosecutor v. Thomas Lubanga Dyilo*, Pre-Trial Chamber, Decision on the Final System of Disclosure and the Establishment of a Timetable, 15 May 2006, ICC-01/04-01/06-102 ('Lubanga Pre-Trial Decision on the Final System of Disclosure and the Establishment of a Timetable') (https://legal-tools.org/doc/052848).

[22] ICC, Situation in the Democratic Republic of the Congo, *The Prosecutor v. Germain Katanga and Mathieu Ngudjolo Chui*, Pre-Trial Chamber, Transcript, 14 December 2007, ICC-01/04-01/07-T-12-ENG (https://legal-tools.org/doc/03aafc).

[23] Abu Garda Pre-Trial Second Decision on Issues Relating to Disclosure, para. 12, see above note 19.

prove; and ii) each factual statement is linked to a specific element of crime, a mode of liability, or both",[24] reflecting the same direction as in the *Lubanga* disclosure decision.[25] A similar direction was also given, in the *Mbarushimana* case.[26] Despite the Chamber not prescribing a particular format in which that information ought to be conveyed, the underlying rationale of analytical disclosure is clearly present.

The obligation of analytical disclosure using in-depth analysis does not extend to the disclosure of Article 67(2) or Rule 77 evidence, that is, exculpatory evidence. This was confirmed by Pre-Trial Chamber I[27] and II.[28] Pre-Trial Chamber II highlighted that it only demanded in-depth analytical disclosure for incriminating evidence, whilst Pre-Trial Chamber I in *Mbarushimana* considered that contrary to the Prosecutor's interpretation of the "Decision on Issues Relating to Disclosure", that Decision only required "a concise summary of the content of each item", not a 'detailed summary'.[29]

However, a shift in the ICC's approach occurred in the *Ongwen* case where the Appeals Chamber in its judgment on the disclosure regime

---

[24] *Ibid.*, pp. 17–18.

[25] Lubanga Pre-Trial Decision on the Final System of Disclosure and the Establishment of a Timetable, Annex 1, para. 59, see above note 21.

[26] ICC, Situation in the Democratic Republic of the Congo, *The Prosecutor v. Callixte Mbarushimana*, Pre-Trial Chamber, Decision on Issues Relating to Disclosure, 30 March 2011, ICC-01/04-01/10-87, p. 18 ('Mbarushimana Pre-Trial Decision on Issues Relating to Disclosure') (https://legal-tools.org/doc/aee80d).

[27] ICC, Situation in the Democratic Republic of the Congo, *The Prosecutor v. Callixte Mbarushimana*, Pre-Trial Chamber, Decision on the "Prosecution's Application for Leave to Appeal the 'Decision on Issues relating to Disclosure' (ICC-01/04-01/10-87)", 21 April 2011, ICC-01/04-01/10-116 (https://legal-tools.org/doc/c803fc).

[28] ICC, Situation in the Republic of Kenya, *The Prosecutor v. William Samoei Ruto, Henry Kiprono Kosgey and Joshua Arap Sang*, Pre-Trial Chamber, Decision on the "Prosecution's Application for Leave to Appeal the 'Decision Setting the Regime for Evidence Disclosure and Other Related Matters' (ICC-01/09-01/11-44)", 2 May 2011, ICC-01/09-01/11-74 ('Ruto and Sang Pre-Trial Decision on the Prosecution's Application for Leave to Appeal Pre-Trial Chamber's 6 April 2011 Decision') (https://legal-tools.org/doc/7ea8aa); ICC, Situation in the Republic of Kenya, *The Prosecutor v. Francis Kirimi Muthaura, Uhuru Muigai Kenyatta and Mohammed Hussein Ali*, Pre-Trial Chamber, Decision on the "Prosecution's Application for Leave to Appeal the 'Decision Setting the Regime for Evidence Disclosure and Other Related Matters' (ICC-01/09-02/11-48)", 2 May 2011, ICC-01/09-02/11-77 (https://legal-tools.org/doc/c25cf8).

[29] Mbarushimana Pre-Trial Decision on Issues Relating to Disclosure, para. 11, see above note 26.

---

found that the Single judge was "unfair and unreasonable" in exercising her discretion when she "ordered the production and submission of in-depth analysis charts".[30] However, the Chamber did not pronounce on the value of the charts in terms of enhancing the overall efficiency and fairness of the proceedings, as this would exceed the scope of the review.[31]

Between 2015 and 2018, no in-depth analysis charts were requested by the Pre-Trial Chambers. However, the issue was 'revived' by the Single Judge in the *Al Hassan* case who asked in one of his earlier decisions whether the use of such charts was a good idea.[32] The Office of the Prosecutor again protested vociferously[33] and analytical disclosure was again halted.[34] Following that decision, in-depth analysis charts have not been utilised in subsequent cases.

The 2019 version of the Chambers Practice Manual, states that submission of any in-depth analysis charts or *similia* of the evidenced disclosed, cannot be imposed on either party[35] and that "there is no basis for the Chamber to impose on the parties a particular modality or format to argue their case and present their evidence" such as the 'in-depth analy-

---

[30] ICC, Situation in Uganda, *The Prosecutor v. Dominic Ongwen*, Appeals Chamber, Judgment on the appeal of the Prosecutor against the decision of Pre-Trial Chamber II entitled "Decision Setting the Regime for Evidence Disclosure and Other Related Matters", 17 June 2015, ICC-02/04-01/15-251, para. 46 (https://legal-tools.org/doc/0052a2).

[31] *Ibid.*, para. 45.

[32] ICC, Situation in the Republic of Mali, *The Prosecutor v. Al Hassan Ag Abdoul Aziz Ag Mohamed Ag Mahmoud*, Pre-Trial Chamber, Decision on the Evidence Disclosure Protocol and Other Related Matters, 16 May 2018, ICC-01/12-01/18-31-tENG-Corr (https://legal-tools.org/doc/89d69e). In paras. 44–47, the Single Judge summarises the advantages of using in-depth analysis charts, and in para. 51 it requests the prosecution to file its observations on this issue.

[33] ICC, Situation in the Republic of Mali, *The Prosecutor v. Al Hassan Ag Abduoul Aziz Ag Mohamed Ag Mahmoud*, OTP, Public redacted version of the "Prosecution's observations regarding the «Décision relative au système de divulgation et à d'autres questions connexes» (ICC-01/12-01/18-31)", 24 May 2018, ICC-01/12-01/18-38-Conf-Exp, 25 May 2018, ICC-01/12-01/18-38-Red2 ('Al Hassan Prosecution's observations regarding Pre-Trial Chamber's 16 May 2018 Decision') (https://legal-tools.org/doc/f53b45).

[34] ICC, Situation in the Republic of Mali, *The Prosecutor v. Al Hassan Ag Abdoul Aziz Ag Mohamed Ag Mahmoud*, Pre-Trial Chamber, Decision on the In-Depth Analysis Chart of Disclosed Evidence, 29 June 2018, ICC-01/12-01/18-61-tENG, para. 23 (https://legal-tools.org/doc/d35cef).

[35] ICC, *Chambers Practice Manual*, 2019, para. 24 (https://legal-tools.org/doc/dh0zyq).

---

sis chart', or *similia*, "of the evidence relied upon for the purposes of the confirmation hearing can be imposed on either of the parties".[36]

Regardless of the form analytical disclosure takes, for example, whether in-depth analysis charts are used, utilising the underlying methodology and not its form is what matters. It is concerning that the practice appears to have been put on the backburner for now, for the advantages it offers outweigh the perceived disadvantages, both of which will be examined in turn.

10.4. Advantages of Adopting In-depth Analysis Charts

The advantages of adopting in-depth analysis charts in the investigations and prosecutions of core international crimes cases fit in two broad categories: They offer distinct clarity and enhance fair trial.

10.4.1. Enhancing Clarity in Complex Cases

As seen already, core international crimes cases are, by definition, fact-rich and complex. Therefore, applying the law to the facts requires a structured approach which can be greatly facilitated by the use of the in-depth analysis charts. Such charts provide both a clear structure as well as precision in every step of the process.

Structuring and presenting the Prosecution case using the in-depth analysis charts is beneficial to all parties to the proceedings, including also the Prosecution. The emphasis of the ICC case-law has been on the benefits of the in-depth analysis charts for the Defence and the Chambers. However, the Office of the Prosecutor would also benefit from using them. Structuring the prosecution case according to a clear format, increases the understanding of the parties who have not been privy to the detailed investigations, for example, by other teams within the Office of the Prosecutor or within other members of the same team. The use of such charts helps maintain an overview of the case, and assists, when presenting the case, in developing the argument in a clear and logical fashion, to improve its strength.

10.4.2. Ensuring Fair Trials

Moreover, given that the "disclosure of evidence goes to the heart of the accused's right to a fair trial",[37] ensuring that the Defence has a sound

---

[36] *Ibid.*, para. 43.

grasp of the case against it, lies at the heart of this right and the principle of equality of arms. In-depth analysis charts make the case clearer and easier to understand, facilitating the development of a more viable defence strategy, and thus enhancing fair trial.

Expecting the Prosecutor to search for and disclose all evidence, incriminating and (potentially) exculpatory,[38] in contrast to the obligation to merely disclose "any material which in the actual knowledge of the Prosecutor" may be exculpatory or mitigatory,[39] goes a long way towards rebalancing the interaction between the parties.

However, an enhanced duty to disclose may lead to a substantial increase in the volume of evidence that needs to be processed, analysed, and disclosed. Where efficient modalities of evidence handling and transfer are absent, the increased workload on the prosecutorial side may cause delays which in turn may reduce the benefits of the defence whose burden is eased through gains in expediency.

10.5. Concerns Surrounding the Use of In-Depth Analysis Charts

It is true that in-depth analysis charts challenge established work processes. Despite their many merits, the Office of the Prosecutor has been reluctant to use them and raised a number of concerns which will be discussed next.

10.5.1. Lack of Legal Basis

One of the key objections to the model put forward in *Bemba* regarding evidence disclosure was that the system advanced by the Decision was not requested by any party nor was it envisaged in the ICC Statute.[40] Moreo-

---

[37] Brady, 2001, p. 404, see above note 14.

[38] ICC Statute, Articles 67(2) and 54(1)(a), see above note 3.

[39] ICTY, Rules of Procedure and Evidence, 8 July 2015, Rule 68(i) (https://legal-tools.org/doc/30df50).

[40] ICC, Situation in the Central African Republic, *The Prosecutor v. Jean-Pierre Bemba Gombo*, OTP, Prosecution's Application for Leave to Appeal Pre-Trial Chamber III's 31 July 2008 "Decision on the Evidence Disclosure System and Setting a Timetable for Disclosure between the Parties", 6 August 2008, ICC-01/05-01/08-63, paras. 3, 4 ('Bemba Prosecution's Application for Leave to Appeal Pre-Trial Chamber's 31 July 2008 Decision') (https://legal-tools.org/doc/992213). See also, ICC, Situation in the Democratic Republic of the Congo, *The Prosecutor v. Germain Katanga and Mathieu Ngudjolo Chui*, OTP, Prosecution's Application for Leave to Appeal the "Order Concerning the Presentation of Incriminating Evidence and the E-Court Protocol", 23 March 2009, ICC-01/04-01/07-982,

ver, it also moves away from the procedure adopted in *Lubanga* and *Katanga*. Furthermore, the implementation without previously consulting any of the parties was presented as being problematic. The Office of the Prosecutor argued that given that an in-depth analysis chart was not a requirement in the *Lubanga* disclosure regime, it was not necessary for a fair trial, since the duty to make full and sufficiently timely disclosure does not include the preparation of an explanatory analytical chart.[41]

The alleged lack of legal basis for prescribing in-depth analysis charts as a modality for disclosure under Article 61(3) of the ICC Statute as well as Rule 121(2) of the ICC Rules of Procedure and Evidence ('ICC RPE'), it should be noted that the Pre-Trial Chamber has the power to issue orders in order to ensure the proper conduct of disclosure. In the case of disclosure, once the case has proceeded to the Trial Chamber, the legal basis for the prescription of disclosure procedure lies firmly in Article 64(3)(a) of the ICC Statute.[42]

---

paras. 24–35 ('Katanga Prosecution's Application for Leave to Appeal Trial Chamber's 13 March 2009 Order') (https://legal-tools.org/doc/a7ba71); ICC, Situation in the Republic of Kenya, *The Prosecutor v. Francis Kirimi Muthaura, Uhuru Muigai Kenyatta and Mohammed Hussein Ali*, OTP, Prosecutor's Application for Leave to Appeal "Decision Setting the Regime for Evidence Disclosure and Other Related Matters" (ICC-01/09-02/11-48), 13 April 2011, ICC-01/09-02/11-55, para. 4 ('Kenyatta Prosecutor's Application for Leave to Appeal Pre-Trial Chamber's 6 April 2011 Decision') (https://legal-tools.org/doc/94db9c); ICC, Situation in the Republic of Kenya, *The Prosecutor v. William Samoei Ruto, Henry Kiprono Kosgey and Joshua Arap Sang*, OTP, Prosecution's Application for Leave to Appeal the "Decision Setting the Regime for Evidence Disclosure and Other Related Matters" (ICC-01/09-01/11-44), 13 April 2011, ICC-01/09-01/11-50, para. 4 ('Ruto and Sang Prosecution's Application for Leave to Appeal Pre-Trial Chamber's 6 April 2011 Decision') (https://legal-tools.org/doc/a34575); ICC, Situation in the Democratic Republic of the Congo, *The Prosecutor v. Callixte Mbarushimana*, OTP, Prosecutor's Application for Leave to Appeal the "Decision on Issues Relating to Disclosure" (ICC-01/04-01/10-87), 5 April 2011, ICC-01/04-01/10-93, para. 4 ('Mbarushimana Prosecutor's Application for Leave to Appeal Pre-Trial Chamber's 30 March 2011 Decision') (https://legal-tools.org/doc/b97718).

[41] ICC, Situation in the Central African Republic, *The Prosecutor v. Jean-Pierre Bemba Gombo*, OTP, Prosecution's Submissions on the Trial Chamber's 8 December 2009 Oral Order Requesting Updating of the In-Depth-Analysis Chart, 15 December 2009, ICC-01/05-01/08-656, paras. 7, 8 ('Bemba Prosecution's Submissions on the Trial Chamber's 8 December 2009 Oral Order') (https://legal-tools.org/doc/5218ca).

[42] Article 64(3)(a) provides: "Upon assignment of a case for trial in accordance with this Statute, the Trial Chamber assigned to deal with the case shall: Confer with the parties and adopt such procedures as are necessary to facilitate the fair and expeditious conduct of the proceedings", see above note 3. See for discussion of the Trial Chamber's discretion,

---

The concern that the analytical disclosure obligations conflict with the work product rule under Rule 81(1) of the ICC RPE, has been countered by Trial Chambers II and III which clarified that the order does not compel the Prosecutor to provide a subjective analysis of the evidence; they only require that the relevant areas be identified. The Prosecution is therefore, under no obligation to provide the Chamber or defence with any internal work product relating to the internal analysis by the Prosecutor of the evidence.[43] Given that the obligation is based on the material that has been filed as part of the Prosecution's disclosure obligations alone, and taking into account that the burden of proof lies with the Prosecutor, the only purpose of the table is to guarantee the transparency of the Prosecutor's case, enabling the Defendant to know the precise case against him or her sufficiently in advance.[44]

10.5.2. Specific Grounds for Appeal

For the purposes of establishing the grounds for appeal pursuant to Article 82(1)(d) of the ICC Statute, it has been argued that the contested provisions pertaining to the system of disclosure affect both the *fairness* and *expeditiousness* of proceedings. The Prosecutor cited decisions of the Appeals Chamber to claim that "fairness requires that the procedural and substantive rights and obligations of all parties be respected, which has been held to include fairness to the Prosecution".[45] The Prosecutor has

---

Reinhold Gallmetzer, "The Trial Chamber's Discretionary Power to Devise the Proceedings Before It and Its Exercise in the Trial of Thomas Lubanga Dyilo", in Carsten Stahn and Göran Sluiter (eds.), *The Emerging Practice of the International Criminal Court*, Martinus Nijhoff, Leiden, 2009, pp. 501–24.

[43] ICC, Situation in the Democratic Republic of the Congo, *The Prosecutor v. Germain Katanga and Mathieu Ngudjolo Chui*, Trial Chamber, Decision on the "Prosecution's Application for Leave to Appeal the 'Order concerning the Presentation of Incriminating Evidence and the E-Court Protocol'" and the "Prosecution's Second Application for Extension of Time Limit Pursuant to Regulation 35 to Submit a Table of Incriminating Evidence and related material in compliance with Trial Chamber II 'Order concerning the Presentation of Incriminating Evidence and the E-Court Protocol'", 1 May 2009, ICC-01/04-01/07-1088, para. 33 ('Katanga Trial Decision on 1 May 2009') (https://legal-tools.org/doc/1a6508), and reiterated in Bemba Prosecution's Submissions on the Trial Chamber's 8 December 2009 Oral Order, para. 24, see above note 41.

[44] Katanga Trial Decision on 1 May 2009, para. 34, see above note 43.

[45] Bemba Prosecution's Application for Leave to Appeal Pre-Trial Chamber's 1 July 2008 Decision, para. 14, see above note 40, referring to ICC, Situation in the Democratic Republic of the Congo, Pre-Trial Chamber, Decision on the Prosecution's Application for Leave to Appeal the Chamber's Decision of 17 January 2006 on the Applications for Par-

---

further submitted that "the guarantee of a fair and expeditious trial *cannot* require the Prosecution to undertake an onerous task" not otherwise provided for in the ICC Statute.[46]

The concerns relating to the increased workload imposed upon the Office of the Prosecutor as a result of the prescribed analytical modality of disclosure are valid. However, if the analytical methodology were to be adopted as standard Prosecutorial practice from the start of the process, the additional burden upon the Prosecution at the disclosure stage should be minimal. In essence, if a case would have been built upon following this analytical logic it would lead to the fewer activities being duplicated. Arguably, whilst the work of the Prosecutor might be increased and thus has the potential for slowing down the progression of proceedings, the benefits and expediency gains enjoyed by the Chambers and the Defence would outweigh any delays. Consequently, the net benefits of the adoption of the analytical system to the judicial process as a whole would mitigate any drawbacks.

10.5.3. Fairness

Owing to the burden associated with analytical disclosure upon the Office of the Prosecutor at the time of fulfilling those requirements, it has been argued that the fairness of proceedings *vis-à-vis* the Prosecution is impacted.[47] It has been submitted that not only is the burden not envisaged by the Court's instruments, but it is an "exorbitant duty" which "cannot reasonably be complied with". Moreover, the requirement fails to appreci-

---

ticipation in the Proceedings of VPRS 1, VPRS 2, VPRS 3, VPRS 4, VPRS 5 and VPRS 6, 31 March 2006, ICC-01/04-135-tEN, paras. 38–39 (https://legal-tools.org/doc/902494); ICC, Situation in Uganda, *The Prosecutor v. Dominic Ongwen*, Pre-Trial Chamber, Decision on Prosecutor's Applications for Leave to Appeal dated the 15th Day of March 2006 and to Suspend or Stay Consideration of Leave to Appeal dated the 11th day of May 2006, 10 July 2006, ICC-02/04-01/15-64, para. 24 (https://legal-tools.org/doc/601704). Also raised in Kenyatta Prosecutor's Application for Leave to Appeal Pre-Trial Chamber's 6 April 2011 Decision, paras. 19–20, see above note 40; Ruto and Sang Prosecution's Application for Leave to Appeal Pre-Trial Chamber's 6 April 2011 Decision, see above note 40.

[46] Katanga Prosecution's Application for Leave to Appeal Trial Chamber's 13 March 2009 Order, para. 26, see above note 40 (emphasis in original).

[47] *Ibid.*, para. 30; Mbarushimana Prosecutor's Application for Leave to Appeal Pre-Trial Chamber's 30 March 2011 Decision, paras. 12–15, see above note 40; Al Hassan Prosecution's observations regarding Pre-Trial Chamber's 16 May 2018 Decision, paras. 51–53, see above note 33.

---

ate the scale of the material involved, and the implications for the Prosecution's workload and functioning.[48]

Having applied this concept of fairness to the issue of analytical disclosure obligations, the Chamber swiftly determined that this was not a valid ground for appeal. Moreover, the Chamber questioned the extent to which the impugned Decision imposed novel burdens upon the Prosecutor, asserting that:

> the Prosecutor, having investigated in the situation of CAR since May 2007, has an in-depth knowledge of his own file. It is assumed that the Prosecutor conducts the analysis of the material collected on a continuous basis in order to prepare and present properly his case.[49]

Pre-Trial Chamber II further held that the required document is a "necessary and proportionate procedural tool that assists in revealing the prosecution's case against the accused, notwithstanding the resources that will be necessary for its completion".[50]

10.5.4. Expeditiousness

Another objection to the use of in-depth analysis charts relates to the expeditiousness of the proceedings. The Prosecutor argued that, given the already limited resources of the Office of the Prosecutor, the scale of the exercise involved in the in-depth analysis charts would move resources

---

[48] Bemba Prosecution's Application for Leave to Appeal Pre-Trial Chamber's 31 July 2008 Decision, paras. 26–28, see above note 40; Kenyatta Prosecutor's Application for Leave to Appeal Pre-Trial Chamber's 6 April 2011 Decision, para. 19, see above note 40; Ruto and Sang Prosecution's Application for Leave to Appeal Pre-Trial Chamber's 6 April 2011 Decision, para. 19, see above note 40.

[49] ICC, Situation in the Central African Republic, *The Prosecutor v. Jean-Pierre Bemba Gombo*, Pre-Trial Chamber, Decision on the Prosecutor's application for leave to appeal Pre-Trial Chamber III's decision on disclosure, 25 August 2008, ICC-01/05-01/08-75, para. 66 ('Bemba Pre-Trial Decision on the Prosecutor's application for leave to appeal Pre-Trial Chamber III's decision on disclosure') (https://legal-tools.org/doc/76ef50). See also Katanga Trial Order Concerning the Presentation of Incriminating Evidence and the E-Court Protocol, para. 15, see above note 18.

[50] ICC, Situation in the Central African Republic, *The Prosecutor v. Jean-Pierre Bemba Gombo*, Trial Chamber, Decision on the "Prosecution's Submissions on the Trial Chamber's 8 December 2009 Oral Order Requesting Updating of the In-Depth-Analysis Chart", 29 January 2010, ICC-01/05-01/08-682, para. 26 ('Bemba Trial Decision on the Prosecution's Submissions on Trial Chamber's 8 December 2009 Oral Order') (https://legal-tools.org/doc/fb0bb9).

away from securing timely disclosure and inspection of material thus delaying the performance of these core statutory obligations.[51]

Deciding the appropriateness of such a time and labour-intensive analysis at the pre-confirmation hearing stage of proceedings when there is no guarantee that the charges will be confirmed by the Pre-Trial Chamber and the case sent to trial is a valid concern.

'Expeditiousness' has been interpreted by the Pre-Trial Chamber to be akin to the concept of judicial proceedings "within a reasonable time".[52] Employing efficient working practices is also important for the rights of the accused.[53] Articles 67(1)(c) and 60(4) of the ICC Statute, as well as all the international and regional human rights instruments, provide that the accused is entitled to an expeditious trial with undue delay.[54]

The length, cost and bureaucracy of international judicial proceedings are commonly criticised.[55] Therefore, the Pre-Trial Chambers have

---

[51] Ruto and Sang Prosecution's Application for Leave to Appeal Pre-Trial Chamber's 6 April 2011 Decision, para. 25, see above note 40; Kenyatta Prosecutor's Application for Leave to Appeal Pre-Trial Chamber's 6 April 2011 Decision, para. 25, see above note 40; Al Hassan Prosecution's observations regarding Pre-Trial Chamber's 16 May 2018 Decision, para. 42, see above note 33.

[52] Bemba Pre-Trial Decision on the Prosecutor's application for leave to appeal Pre-Trial Chamber III's decision on disclosure, para. 17, see above note 49.

[53] ICC Statute, Article 67, see above note 3. The text of which is drawn from ICCPR, Article 14(3), see above note 10.

[54] At the European Court of Human Rights (ECtHR), see on the length of pre-trial detention, *Wemhoff v. Germany*, Judgment, 27 June 1968, ECLI:CE:ECHR:1968:0627JUD000212 264 (https://legal-tools.org/doc/e8ac3d), and the two pronged-test: 1) was it reasonable to refuse bails; 2) was the time period given the complexities of the case reasonable? This has also been applied in *Kalashnikov v. Russia*, Judgment, 15 July 2002, ECLI:CE:ECHR: 2002:0715JUD004709599 (https://legal-tools.org/doc/d5919c).

[55] On the length of proceedings generally in international criminal justice see William A. Schabas, *An Introduction to the International Criminal Court*, Cambridge University Press, Cambridge, 2007, pp. 209–10; Jean Galbraith, "The Pace of International Criminal Justice", in *Michigan Journal of International Law*, 2009, vol. 31, no. 1, p. 79; O-Gon Kwon, "The Challenge of an International Criminal Trial as Seen From the Bench", in *Journal of International Criminal Justice*, 2007, vol. 5, no. 2, pp. 362–63; Patrick L. Robinson, "Ensuring Fair and Expeditious Trials at the International Criminal Tribunal for the Former Yugoslavia", in *European Journal of International Law*, 2000, vol. 11, no. 3, p. 569; Morten Bergsmo and Vladimir Tochilovsky, "Measures Available to the International Criminal Court to Reduce the Length of Proceedings", in Morten Bergsmo, Klaus Rackwitz and SONG Tianying (eds.), *Historical Origins of International Criminal Law: Volume 5*, Torkel Opsahl Academic EPublisher, Brussels, 2017, pp. 651–93 (http://www.toaep.org/ps-pdf/24-bergsmo-rackwitz-song). For an innovative approach that should be considered

---

been keen to stress the need to focus upon the evidence that is necessary to substantiate the criminal charges, to avoid "the disclosure of a bulk of evidence by excluding those pieces extraneous to any of the counts and useless for the purposes of the confirmation hearing and of the trial".[56]

The need to address issues of both the expeditiousness of proceedings and the vindication of the rights of the accused is real.[57] Whilst expeditious proceedings are inextricably linked to the rights of the accused, caution must be taken when judicial efforts are made to improve the efficiency of proceedings, as there is a risk that when trying to speed up proceedings the rights of the accused may be undermined.[58] The adoption of the analytical method of disclosure, under which the primary obligation to expedite proceedings is placed on the Prosecutor, strikes the right balance on both.

10.5.5. Impact on Prosecutorial Discretion

A further concern raised by the Prosecutor in providing the requisite degree of analysis and linking evidence to the precise elements of crimes and modes of liability was that, since disclosure is an ongoing process and should occur as soon as possible, it would deprive the Prosecutor of the flexibility to build and adapt the case if new circumstances arise before the trial commences and would require the Prosecution to present its case in a particular mode, "even if the Prosecution determines that that mode is

---

more closely in the coming years, see Morten Bergsmo (ed.), *Abbreviated Criminal Procedures for Core International Crimes*, Torkel Opsahl Academic EPublisher, Brussels, 2017 (http://www.toaep.org/ps-pdf/9-bergsmo).

[56] Ekaterina Trendafilova, "Fairness and Expeditiousness in the International Criminal Court's Pre-Trial Proceedings", in Carsten Stahn and Göran Sluiter (eds.), *The Emerging Practice of the International Criminal Court*, Martinus Nijhoff, Leiden, 2009, p. 444. See also ICC, Situation in the Democratic Republic of the Congo, *The Prosecutor v. Germain Katanga and Mathieu Ngudjolo Chui*, Defence, Defence Observations Concerning Prosecution Table of Disclosure, 23 January 2009, ICC-01/04-01/07-845, para. 6(iii) (https://legal-tools.org/doc/9c6086).

[57] Salvatore Zappalà, *Human Rights in International Criminal Proceedings*, Oxford University Press, Oxford, 2003, p. 117.

[58] See also Robert Heinsch, "How to Achieve Fair and Expeditious Trial Proceedings before the ICC: Is It Time for A More Judge-Dominated Approach?", in Carsten Stahn and Göran Sluiter (eds.), *The Emerging Practice of the International Criminal Court*, Martinus Nijhoff, Leiden, 2009, pp. 479–80.

not the most effective means of assembling and presenting its case".[59] The appropriateness of including witness statements in the in-depth analysis charts, was questioned, since such statements are not typically classed as evidence, and given that witnesses may produce different evidence when testifying at the trial.[60]

The Chambers responded to the Prosecutorial submission that the tabular format of disclosure unduly restricts the Prosecutor's discretion to adapt the case in response to changing circumstances or the unearthing of further evidence by emphasising that they are fully appreciative of the organic nature of trials, and to that end, there is nothing to prevent the Prosecutor from submitting further evidence or asserting that the probative value of a piece of evidence has changed, providing that any developments are charted in an updated in-depth analysis chart.[61] Similarly, the concern raised in respect of the inclusion of witness statements was found to be ill founded, since "it is self-evident that a witness's evidence at trial may not coincide with his or her pre-trial statements or interviews".[62]

The concerns presented above, albeit legitimate, can be countered with equally valid arguments which do not detract from the fact that adopting in-depth analysis charts for the investigation and prosecution of core international crimes cases more broadly continues to be desirable.

10.6. In-Depth Analysis Charts and Investigations

The above analysis has demonstrated the advantages and perceived drawbacks of the adoption of the in-depth analysis charts. The logic underpinning the analytical framework, if adopted from the beginning of an investigation, could provide a valuable tool in structuring the investigation and building a solid case. Were such a framework to be adopted from the out-

---

[59] Katanga Prosecution's Application for Leave to Appeal Trial Chamber's 13 March 2009 Order, para. 32, see above note 40. Also, Bemba Prosecution's Submissions on the Trial Chamber's 8 December 2009 Oral Order, para. 13, see above note 41.

[60] Katanga Prosecution's Application for Leave to Appeal Trial Chamber's 13 March 2009 Order, para. 27, see above note 40.

[61] Bemba Trial Decision on the Prosecution's Submissions on Trial Chamber's 8 December 2009 Oral Order, para. 27, see above note 50.

[62] *Ibid.*, para. 28.

set, it would signal a step-change in the way the Court operates and would render the ICC more efficient as a result.[63]

The proposition put forward in this chapter is that the benefits of adopting the in-depth analysis charts can be seen irrespective of the stage of proceedings, be it at investigation or at pre-trial stage. The scale, complexity of the factual situation and the high number of perpetrators, the main challenges associated with core international crimes make their investigation complex. The adoption of an analytical framework from the beginning, enables the prosecution team to easily identify those areas that require further investigation or require more evidence to support the legal assertion. This in turn, strengthens the case that goes to trial which, together with properly equipped defence, improves the overall quality of justice delivered, which can then aid the Chamber to base its decision on higher quality submissions.

Should the logic be applied a stage earlier, that is, when mapping serious human rights violations which may give rise to core international crimes, any criminal investigations that may ensue would also benefit, not least because of the importance of fact-finding missions to subsequent investigations and prosecutions.[64]

---

[63] This seems to be the implicit intention of the Chamber, given that which seems to be implicitly intended given its declared presumption that the Office of the Prosecutor will have scrutinised all evidence in its possession in order to determine its worth both in terms of establishing the prosecution case, and in terms of assisting the Prosecutor it its duty to "establish the truth" under Article 54(1)(a) of the ICC Statute, see above note 3. See Bemba Pre-Trial Decision on the Evidence Disclosure System and Setting a Timetable for Disclosure between the Parties, see above note 15, reinforced by Bemba Trial Decision on the Prosecution's Submissions on Trial Chamber's 8 December 2009 Oral Order, see above note 50; and Katanga Trial Order Concerning the Presentation of Incriminating Evidence and the E-Court Protocol, see above note 18.

[64] Lyal S. Sunga, "How can UN Special Procedures Sharpen ICC Fact Finding?", in *International Journal of Human Rights*, 2011, vol. 15, no. 2, pp. 189–90: 1) taking 'facts' out of their proper context is highly misleading therefore great care must be taken; 2) Human Rights fact-finding tends to focus on State responsibility for internationally wrongful acts in order to pressure governments to comply fully with their human rights and international humanitarian law obligations, whereas criminal investigations focus on individual criminal responsibility – therefore type of evidence collected is different; 3) respective burdens of proof; special procedural requirements in criminal investigations – preservation of presumption of innocence and confidentiality of evidence and preserving the chain of custody. In particular, distinguishing the fact-finding experiences of the ICTY and the ICTR from the technological context that now exists, Sunga discusses the possibility of drawing upon information technology and applications that utilise the same logic as that underpinning

10.7. Conclusion

The chapter has sought to demonstrate challenges faced in the application of the law on core international crimes and modes of liability to fact-rich cases. The additional problems raised by the large quantities of facts and evidence that must be organised and related to the specific legal requirements have also been explored.

The introduction and use of in-depth analysis charts by the ICC as a modality of disclosure and communication of evidence within the Court was explored in order to advance the expediency and efficiency of judicial activities, but also to ensure that the rights of the accused are being properly respected. Getting the balance right by streamlining the process may help ensure a better future for investigations by providing an efficient and logical methodology upon which to structure a case.

The introduction of in-depth analysis charts constitutes one of those mechanisms which, if consistently adopted, will improve the efficiency of judicial proceedings before the Court. Of course, on their own, they cannot be a panacea for all the challenges presented by the complexities of prosecuting the serious incidents of international criminality. However, the adoption of the in-depth analysis charts as a modality for the presentation and disclosure of evidence represents a step in the right direction.

By breaking down the crimes and modes of liability into their constituent parts, and linking each piece of factual evidence to those specific parts, the analytical logic not only helps the prosecution to present and communicate the prosecution case in the clearest and most logical manner for establishing international criminal responsibility, but it also helps the other parties to the proceedings, as well as the Chambers, to process the vast amount of information that a core crimes case involves. It is this improvement in the quality of communication between the parties that will enhance the proper respect for the rights of the accused, and which in turn will strengthen the integrity and legitimacy of the judicial process before the Court. As the ICC's courtrooms are seen as 'judicial laboratories' where the Court's procedural system is tested,[65] the impact the adoption of the in-depth analysis charts has on other fora, be it international or nation-

---

the analytical disclosure regime, specifically referring to the manner in which those applications offer a "highly logical and systematic and pertinent means by which to hone raw empirical data on mass violations into a sharp case against the accused". *Ibid.*, p. 200.

[65] Harhoff, 2009, p. 472, see above note 6.

---

al, should not be underestimated. The innovative stance taken by the ICC in that respect constitutes an important breakthrough and it is hoped that their use will be expanded to investigations in order to enhance their quality.

11

Controlling the Quality of Reasoning About the Link Between Evidence and Factual Findings

Simon De Smet[*]

11.1. Introduction

Establishing facts is one of the core functions of the judicial process. This is especially true in criminal trials. No criminal trial can be considered fair and just if the fact-finding is of bad quality. Perhaps counter-intuitively, the key criterion to determine the quality of fact-finding is not whether or not the findings the fact-finder has made are true. Rather, the central criterion is whether or not the fact-finding process was *rational*. For the purposes of this discussion, a factual finding will be considered rational if it is based on conscious reflection about the available evidence.[1] This implies that findings that are formed on the basis of, for example, intuition are not appropriate in the judicial context. Another implication is that what the fact-finder may or may not believe is not the appropriate criterion for judicial findings of fact.[2] What counts is what the fact-finder can rationally accept.[3]

The reason for putting such a premium on rationality over truth is not epistemic scepticism. Finding the truth remains the ultimate aim.[4]

---

[*]   **Simon De Smet** is Affiliate Lecturer at the University of Cambridge, from where he holds a doctorate, and has worked for many years in international criminal justice. The views expressed herein are those of the author alone and do not reflect the views of the International Criminal Court. The author is grateful to Xabier Agirre for helpful comments and suggestions.

[1]   Douglas Walton, *Methods of Argumentation*, Cambridge University Press, 2013.

[2]   Simon De Smet, "The International Criminal Standard of Proof at the ICC—Beyond Reasonable Doubt or Beyond Reason?", in Carsten Stahn (ed.), *The Law and Practice of the International Criminal Court*, Oxford University Press, 2015.

[3]   L. Jonathan Cohen, *An Essay on Belief and Acceptance*, Clarendon Press, 1992.

[4]   It has been argued that 'judicial truth' is not necessarily the same as 'historical truth'. Giorgio Resta and Vincenzo Zeno Zencovich, "Judicial 'Truth' and Historical 'Truth': The Case of the Ardeatine Caves Massacre", in *Law and History Review*, 2013, vol. 31, no. 4, p.

However, it is not sufficient for judicial findings of fact to be true. The parties and the public must *see* and have *confidence* that they are true. In this sense, judicial fact-finding is as much (if not more) concerned with certainty as it is concerned with truth. Certainty, in this context, is not a measure of the strength of the subjective feeling of a given fact-finder. Rather, certainty is a rational determination about the absence of doubt. Viewed in this regard, the central focus of judicial fact-finding is the *identification of all potential sources of doubt* concerning the relevant factual propositions.[5]

In order to identify potential sources of uncertainty, it is necessary to understand the different cognitive processes of fact-finding. In essence, fact-finding involves three steps. In the initial phase, the fact-finder tries to generate plausible explanations about what might have happened. This can be referred to as the abductive phase, which is the most creative part of the fact-finding process.[6] The purpose of the abductive process is to

---

843. It is certainly true that procedural rules can have a significant influence on the epistemic activities of judicial fact-finders. However, for the purposes of this chapter, the focus is on best practices for finding the 'historical truth'.

[5] It is stressed that this chapter is concerned with the judicial fact-finding process as a whole. It makes no claims about whose responsibility it is to do what in criminal proceedings. In other words, it is not necessarily the job of the judges to identify all sources of doubt. Indeed, in many systems of criminal adjudication, it is the role of the parties to raise doubts and the judges' task is mainly to evaluate them. However, the overall proposition, that the central activity of judicial fact-finding is (or ought to be) the identification and evaluation of uncertainty, stands. Furthermore, it should also be stressed that no suggestion is made that judicial findings are only possible if there is no doubt. How much uncertainty is allowed is determined by the applicable standard of proof, which is not the subject of the current chapter. However, regardless of which standard of proof is applied, it will always be necessary to identify all major sources of doubt in order to allow the adjudicator to evaluate the strength of the evidence and measure this against the relevant threshold as defined in the standard of proof.

[6] The concept of 'abduction' was coined by Charles Peirce at the turn of the twentieth century: Charles Peirce, in Charles Hartshorne and Paul Weis (eds.), *Collected Papers of Charles Sanders Peirce: Volume 5: Pragmatism and Pragmaticism*, Harvard University Press, 1978. Although Peirce wrote about abduction more than a century ago, until recently there have been relatively few attempts to expand on his theory of abduction. One notable exception is Norwood Russell Hanson, *Patterns of Discovery: An Inquiry into the Conceptual Foundations of Science*, Cambridge University Press, 1958; Stathis Psillos, "An Explorer Upon Untrodden Ground: Peirce on Abduction", in Dov M. Gabbay, Stephan Hartmann and John Woods (eds.), *Handbook of the History of Logic: Volume 10: Inductive Logic*, North Holland, 2011, pp. 117–51. Tomas Kapitan, "Peirce and the Autonomy of Abductive Reasoning", in *Erkenntnis*, 1992, vol. 37, no. 1, pp. 1–26; more recently, Douglas Walton, *Abductive Reasoning*, University of Alabama Press, 2005; Iddo Tavory and

---

identify all reasonable hypotheses that can explain the fact(s) of interest. Abducing hypotheses requires the fact-finder to use his or her imagination and draws heavily on his or her understanding of how the world 'normally' operates. For example, if a dead body is found and the cause of death is not obvious, the fact-finder will try to formulate a number of possible scenarios that explain why the person is dead and that are compatible with the known facts. In the judicial context, such hypotheses normally take the form of explanation-narratives.[7] Simply stated, explanation-narratives are stories that are structured in a causal or chronological manner and which include the relevant fact(s). In the example, one explanation-narrative might be that the person was murdered by a jealous partner. Another explanation-narrative could be that the person committed suicide. Each explanation-narrative will 'predict' a certain number of facts. For example, the murder-explanation 'predicts' that the killer must have been near the victim at the time of death. The fact-finder can use these predictions to look for evidence that could confirm or deny them.

In the second phase, the fact-finder tests and compares the different explanation-narratives. Comparison of different explanation-narratives essentially involves looking at the internal coherence and general plausibility of the different explanation-narratives. It also involves comparing to which extent different explanation-narratives are supported or contradict-

---

Stefan Timmermans, *Abductive Analysis: Theorizing Qualitative Research*, University of Chicago Press, 2014; Atocha Aliseda, *Abductive Reasoning: Logical Investigations into Discovery and Explanations*, Springer, 2006; John R. Josephson and Susan G. Josephson, *Abductive Inference: Computation, Philosophy, Technology*, Cambridge University Press, 1994; Igor Douven, "Abduction", in Edward N. Zalta (ed.), *Stanford Encyclopedia of Philosophy*, Summer 2017 edition, 2017 (available on its web site).

[7] Paul Roth, "Narrative Explanations: The Case of History", in *History and Theory*, 1988, vol. 27, no. 1, pp. 1–13; Nancy Pennington and Reid Hastie, "Explanation-Based Decision Making: Effects on Memory Structure on Judgement", in *Journal of Experimental Psychology, Learning and Memory and Cognition*, 1988, vol. 14, no. 3, pp. 521–33; Nancy Pennington and Reid Hastie, "Evidence Evaluation in Complex Decision Making", in *Journal of Personality and Social Psychology*, 1986, vol. 51, no. 2, pp. 242–58; Michael Pardo and Ronald Allen, "Juridical Proof and the Best Explanation", in *Law and Philosophy*, 2008, vol. 27, no. 3, pp. 223–68; Doron Menashe and Mutal E. Shamash, "The Narrative Fallacy", in *International Commentary on Evidence*, 2005, vol. 3, no. 1 ; Ronald J. Allen and Michael S. Pardo, "Relative Plausibility and its Critics", in *International Journal of Evidence and Proof*, 2019, vol. 23, nos. 1–2, pp. 5–59; Reid Hastie, "The Case for Relative Plausibility Theory: Promising, but Insufficient", in *International Journal of Evidence and Proof*, 2019, vol. 23, nos. 1–2, pp. 134–40.

ed by the available evidence. This involves verifying how many (if any) predicted facts can be confirmed by evidence.

In the third and final phase, the fact-finder decides which of the explanation-narratives is the best and infers this one to be true. There is no standardised list of criteria to determine what makes one explanation-narrative better than another.[8] However, one key consideration in this regard is undoubtedly the extent to which the explanation-narrative coheres with the available evidence.

Based on this process, it is possible to identify four different types of doubt a fact-finder may identify in relation to a particular factual finding. The first is that the correct explanation-narrative may not have been identified. The second is that the evidential data-set is incomplete.[9] Third, the fact-finder may assess the trustworthiness of the available evidence incorrectly. Finally, a lot of uncertainty may arise at the level of drawing inferences from the available evidential data. The remainder of this chapter will focus on the last two sources of uncertainty.

11.2. Logical Argumentation and Evidence-Mapping

11.2.1. The Two Basic Resources of the Fact-Finder

The two basic sources of information that fact-finders have available to them to assess factual claims are evidence[10] and generalisations. Evidence is information that comes in many shapes and forms. It constitutes the link between the fact-finder and the fact or event about which he or she has no first-hand knowledge, but is expected to make findings. Generalisations are essential for every step in the reasoning of the fact-finding process because they provide the warrant that allows the fact-finder to draw inferences from the evidence. Roughly speaking, generalisations are generalised statements about how 'we' believe or know or suppose the world always or mostly or sometimes works.[11] Sometimes generalisations have a

---

[8]   Peter Lipton, *Inference to the Best Explanation*, Routledge, 2004.

[9]   See, on this crucial and often overlooked aspect of fact-finding, Dale A. Nance, *The Burdens of Proof: Discriminatory Power, Weight of Evidence and Tenacity of Belief*, Cambridge University Press, 2016.

[10] The term 'evidence' is used here in its non-technical sense and refers to any source of information tending to establish facts in the context of a legal investigation, regardless of whether it has been formally introduced by the parties and/or admitted by the court.

[11] Terence Anderson, David Schum and William Twining, *Analysis of Evidence*, Cambridge University Press, 2005; William Twining, *Rethinking Evidence: Exploratory Essays*, 2nd

firm scientific or empirical basis. In those cases, it will often be known fairly precisely when the generalisation applies and with what frequency the stated rule is true. For example, recent research has shown that drinking two alcoholic drinks every day increases the risk of having a stroke by 10–15 per cent.[12] More often, generalisations do not have such a firm empirical basis and lack precision.

Many generalisations that people routinely apply – often without being conscious of it – are based on what can be generously described as 'common sense' or 'practical knowledge'. For example, it is often assumed that a weaker party will not act aggressively towards a much stronger one. In some cases, people may apply generalisations that find their origin in prejudice. For example, some may believe that all Swiss persons are extremely punctual. Apart from having widely varying degrees of objectivity, generalisations also differ in terms of universality, applicability, and acceptance. Universal generalisations are always true. For example, it is always the case that elephants are heavier than mice, for even the fattest mouse will be considerably lighter than a new-born elephant-calf. However, universal generalisations are relatively uncommon and rarely play a significant role in most real-life cases. A different question is whether a generalisation is applicable to the case at hand. For example, the generalisation 'all Belgians drink a lot of beer' is clearly not applicable to Belgian infants.[13] Finally, while some generalisations may

---

edition, Cambridge University Press, 2006; Terence Anderson, "Generalisations and Evidential Reasoning", in Philip Dawid, William Twining and Mimi Vasilaki, (eds.), *Evidence, Inference and Enquiry*, Oxford University Press, 2011.

[12] *BBC News*, "Even one drink a day increases stroke risk, study finds", 5 April 2019 (available on its web site).

[13] This is the so-called 'reference-class problem'. Most individual entities, such as human beings, belong to many different reference classes, for which generalisations are available that could serve as a warrant for inferential reasoning. The difficulty is knowing which the relevant reference class is for the inference of interest. The problem is studied mostly in the context of statistical evidence, but it applies to every sort of generalisation. See, for example, Paul Roberts, "From Theory into Practice: Introducing the Reference Class Problem", in *International Journal of Evidence and Proof*, 2007, vol. 11, no. 4, p. 243; Dale A. Nance, "The Reference Class Problem and Mathematical Models of Inference", in *International Journal of Evidence and Proof*, 2007, vol. 11, no. 4, p. 259; Michael S. Pardo, "Reference Classes and Legal Evidence", in *International Journal of Evidence and Proof*, 2007, vol. 11, no. 4, p. 255; Robert Rhee, "Probability, Policy and the Problem of Reference Class", in *International Journal of Evidence and Proof*, 2007, vol. 11, no. 4, p. 286; Edward Cheng, "A Practical Solution to the Reference Class Problem", in *Columbia Law Review*, 2009, vol. 109, no. 8, pp. 2081–105.

be universally accepted, others may be limited to certain cultures or social groups. For example, a 2010 Gallup showed that more than half of the population in 18 Sub-Saharan countries believed in witchcraft.[14] Such culture-specific generalisations often relate to social mores and human behaviour and may be highly significant in the context of criminal proceedings.[15]

Generalisations thus come in many different forms of varying quality and validity. To a very large extent, the quality of reasoning depends on the quality of the generalisations that are used. One of the most important steps a fact-finder can take to improve the quality of his or her work is to critically evaluate the applicability and quality of the generalisations he or she is relying on. Evaluating the quality of the generalisations one is applying presupposes that one is aware that one is applying them. However, in general, people rarely reflect upon which generalisations they are applying as part of their thinking process. Part of the reason for this is probably that the significance of generalisations is not fully comprehended. But there are also practical reasons: it turns out that making express the generalisations one relies upon is a lot more difficult than one might initially think. Moreover, it really slows down the thinking process and adds a level of complexity that is generally unwanted. Yet, allowing generalisations to remain unarticulated entails the risk that serious errors may be made and invalid conclusions reached. This risk is unacceptable in the judicial context. There is therefore a need to develop a method that assists fact-finders in understanding the role of generalisations in their thinking.

One such method is argumentation theory.[16] In essence, logical argumentation is a method for articulating and analysing defeasible argu-

---

[14] Bob Tortora, "Witchcraft Believers in Sub-Saharan Africa Rate Lives Worse: Belief Widespread in Many Countries", *Gallup*, 25 August 2010 (available on its web site).

[15] In the context of international criminal proceedings, it may be difficult for international fact-finders to be aware and fully understand culture-specific generalisations. They may need the assistance of anthropologists or sociologists to develop their understanding of the local context. See Tim Kelsall, *Culture under Cross-Examination: International Justice and the Special Court for Sierra Leone*, Cambridge University Press, 2009.

[16] Argumentation theory has been developed mainly by logicians and computer scientists. Bart Verheij, "Dialectical Argumentation with Argumentation Schemes: An Approach to Legal Logic", in *Artificial Intelligence and Law*, 2003, vol. 11, nos. 2–3, pp. 167–95; Douglas Walton, *Methods of Argumentation*, Cambridge University Press, 2013. However, the method described here has a precursor in the legal field in Wigmore's charting method. See, John Henry Wigmore's *The Principles of Judicial Proof, or, the Process of Proof: As*

ments. The basic premise is that for every uncertain proposition, there are arguments in favour and arguments against. The fundamental idea behind argumentation theory is that all these arguments are mapped out in a sequential manner. This is achieved by conceiving of an argument as a dialogue between a proponent and an opponent of the proposition of interest. In practice, this will often be one and the same analyst. The proponent of the proposition starts by articulating an argument in support of it. Then the opponent has an opportunity to point out any perceived problems or weaknesses of the proponent's argument. After that, the proponent gets another opportunity to defend his or her argument by pointing out problems and weaknesses of the counter-arguments of the opponent. And so forth, until all arguments are exhausted and the dialogue ends. At this point, the totality of the arguments are evaluated to determine whether or not the proposition can be accepted. This depends on how much uncertainty is acceptable, which can be expressed as a standard of proof.

Given by Logic, Psychology and General Experience, and Illustrated in Judicial Trials, 2nd edition, Little Brown, 1931. For a contemporary take from a lawyer's perspective, see Yvonne McDermott, "Inferential Reasoning and Proof in International Criminal Trials: The Potentials of Wigmorean Analysis", in *Journal of International Criminal Justice*, 2015, vol. 13, no. 3, pp. 507–33; Yvonne McDermott, "Strengthening the Evaluation of Evidence in International Criminal Trials", in *International Criminal Law Review*, 2017, vol. 17, no. 4, pp. 682–702. John Fox, "Arguing about the Evidence: A Logical Approach", in Philip Dawid, William Twining and Mimi Vasilaki (eds.), *Evidence, Inference and Enquiry*, Oxford University Press, 2011; Paul Krause, Simon Ambler, Morten Elvang-Gøransson and John Fox, "A Logic of Argumentation for Reasoning Under Uncertainty", in *Computational Intelligence*, 1995, vol. 11, no. 1, pp. 113–31.

Argumentation theory can help fact-finders pierce the natural language barrier by making explicit the premises that are implicit in most arguments that are expressed in ordinary language. This is done by 're-constructing' the argument in a structured and graphic format. The main tool is a so-called 'argumentation map'. This is a graphical representation of all arguments that are relevant when conducting an evidentiary analysis in which each individual evidential data-point, factual proposition and generalisation is reflected as a separate node. In the model suggested here, there are three types of nodes: (1) nodes representing factual propositions, (2) nodes representing evidence, and (3) nodes representing generalisations.

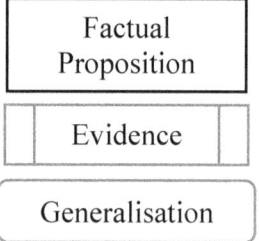

Figure 1. Argumentation map.

Nodes can be connected in two ways: supporting and attacking. Such connections are denoted by different arrows (edges), which represent logical relations between the different nodes.

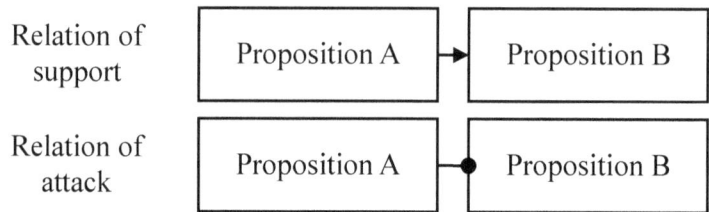

Figure 2. Logical relations between the different nodes.

In the context of evidentiary arguments, the edges usually represent the application of a particular generalisation. Most models of argumentation mapping leave the generalisation implicit. However, the main argument in this chapter is that it is important to make generalisations explicit. This can be achieved by introducing a generalisation node in the middle of the edge.

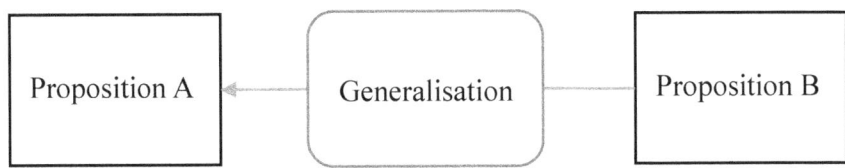

Figure 3. Generalisation node.

These are the only 'building blocks' that are required to map out any evidentiary argument.

11.2.2. Two Types of Arguments

In the context of fact-finding, there are two types of arguments. The first is at the level of the explanation-narrative, that is, the story of which the proposition of interest forms a part.[17] Arguments of this type are essentially linear, in the sense that they represent a chronological chain of events that are causally linked. To illustrate, let us consider the following hypothetical case.

In the context of an armed conflict, 20 civilians have been killed by gunfire at a checkpoint manned by a platoon belonging to one of the parties to the conflict. There is forensic evidence establishing the cause of death to be bullet wounds from a calibre that corresponds to a common type of assault rifle. The existence of these twenty civilian deaths is the *explanandum* that must be explained.

According to the prosecutor, the platoon fired on the civilians without provocation because the soldiers were executing a policy to attack the civilians. The captain of the platoon, on the other hand, testifies that his troops were manning the checkpoint until a group of ± 1,000 demonstrators arrived, chanting aggressive slogans and demanding to cross the checkpoint. When the platoon refused to allow the demonstrators to pass, the latter started throwing heavy stones and Molotov cocktails. When one of his soldiers caught fire, the captain ordered his troops to open fire on

---

[17] Floris J. Bex, *Arguments, Stories and Criminal Evidence: A Formal Hybrid Theory*, Springer, 2011; Floris J. Bex and Douglas N. Walton, "Taking the Dialectical Stance in Reasoning with Evidence and Proof", in *International Journal of Evidence and Proof*, 2019, vol. 23, nos. 1–2, pp. 90–99.

the assailants. According to the captain, the killing of the 20 civilians was thus the result of an act of legitimate self-defence.

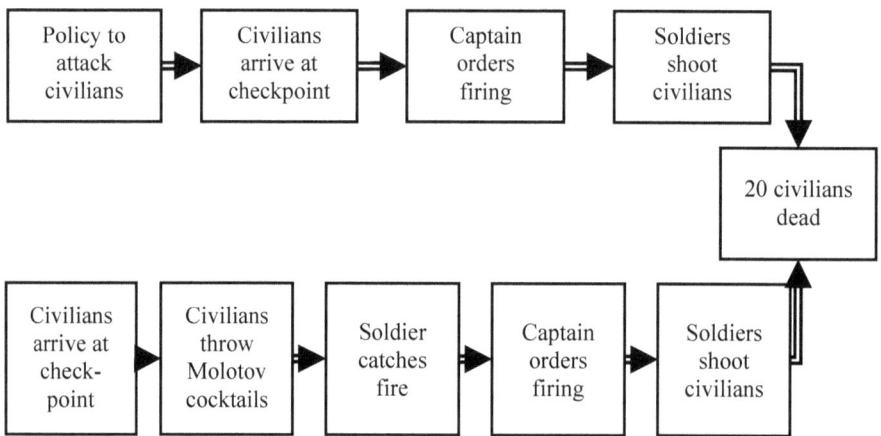

Figure 4. Hypothetical case.

In order to decide between the two explanation-narratives, the fact-finder can compare them on the basis of three criteria. The first is the inherent plausibility of each narrative, based on the fact-finder's understanding of the situation, relevant context, and the world in general. The second is to analyse the internal coherence of each narrative. A key aspect that must be considered, in this regard, is whether the causal links between the different episodes of the explanation-narratives can be verified. In a simple narrative, as in the example, this is rather straightforward, but as narratives become more intricate and extensive, a detailed coherence analysis may be quite revealing. Finally, narratives must be compared in terms of evidential coverage. Evidential coverage is a reflection of how many of the nodes in the explanation-narrative are supported by evidence, how many are unsupported (that is, gaps in the evidential coverage) and whether any of the nodes are contradicted by the available evidence.

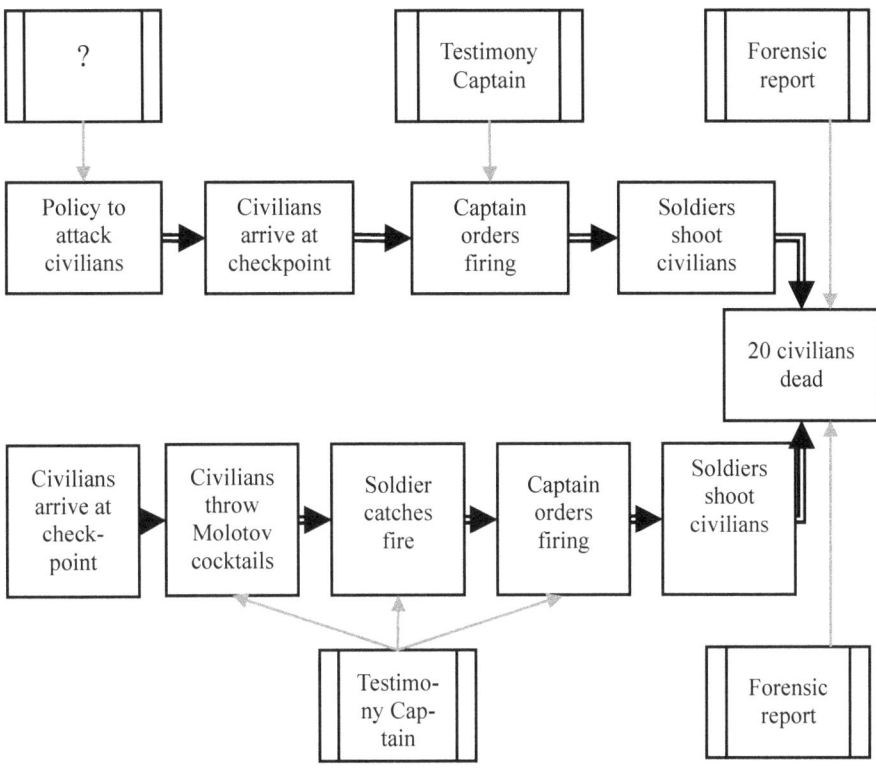

Figure 5. Evidential coverage of the hypothetical case.

As is shown in this argumentation map, the nodes representing the prosecution's explanation-narrative are less well covered by the available evidence than the ones representing the Captain's version of events. However, the only evidence supporting the relevant nodes comes from the defendant himself. This raises the question whether the better evidentiary coverage is really decisive in this case. The mere fact of there being evidence in support of a particular factual proposition does not mean that this proposition is therefore proved. The remainder of this chapter will deal with how to determine whether or not – and, if so, to what extent – a particular node is supported by evidence.

11.3. Direct Evidence Does Not Exist

It is common to make a distinction between direct and circumstantial evidence. Whereas direct evidence is said to prove the proposition immediately, circumstantial evidence requires the fact-finder to make an inference to arrive at the proposition of interest. For example, a witness who has seen the suspect shoot the victim is considered direct evidence of killing, whereas a witness who saw the suspect leaving the scene of the crime with a gun in his hand only provides circumstantial evidence of the killing. Yet, it is a mistake to think that in the first case the testimony proves the *probandum* directly, without needing inferences to be made. When a witness asserts a particular fact, be it during the investigation or in the witness box, the only certainty the fact-finder has is that the witness made this assertion. In order to conclude from the fact that a witness made a factual assertion that the asserted fact is also true requires at least one inferential step. In the case of testimony, the inference would be based on the generalisation that 'If a trustworthy witness says *that P*, then *P* is true'. Schematically, the simplest possible relation between evidence and a factual proposition looks as follows:

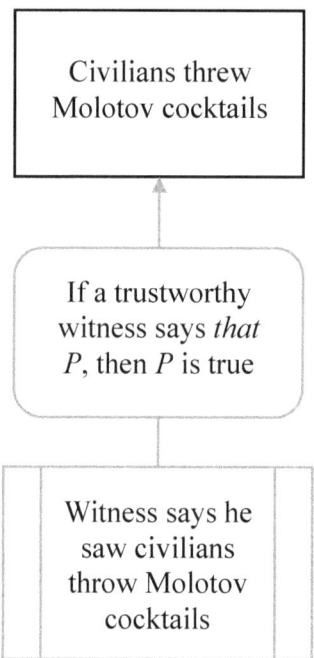

Figure 6. Relation between evidence and a factual proposition.

In reality, most factual arguments will be more complex and often involve catenate inferences. In the example, the Captain's claim of self-defence is premised on the proposition that the civilians who were shot were trying to harm the soldiers. This argument could be formulated like this:

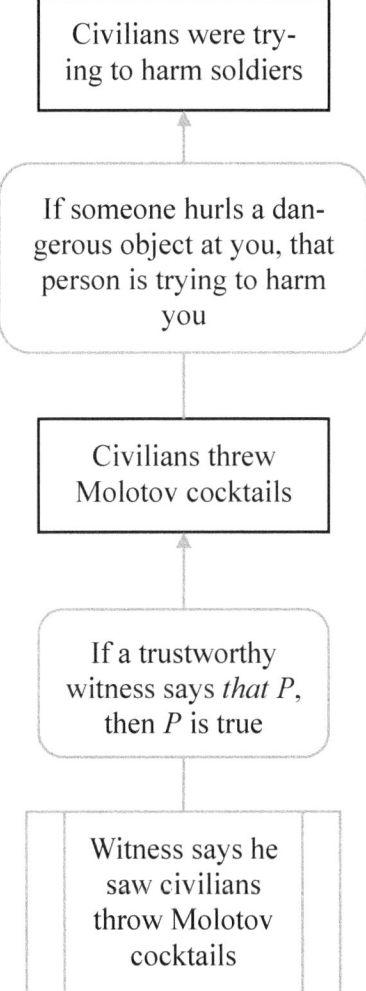

Figure 7. Captain's claim.

Each inferential step is liable to three different forms of 'attack'.[18] First, the premise may be attacked. In the example, a possible attack could be that it is claimed that the witness did not say that he actually *saw* the civilians throwing Molotov cocktails, but that he simply assumed the Molotov cocktails must have been thrown by the civilians from the fact that one of his soldiers caught fire. Such an attack can be called an *undermining attack*. Second, the generalisation that supports the inference may be attacked. This is called an *undercutting attack*. In the case of witness testimony, a possible counter-argument could be that the Captain had a reason to lie because he was being accused of a crime. Finally, the conclusion itself may be attacked as well in what is called a *rebutting attack*. In the example, a possible counter-argument could be that there never was any fire.

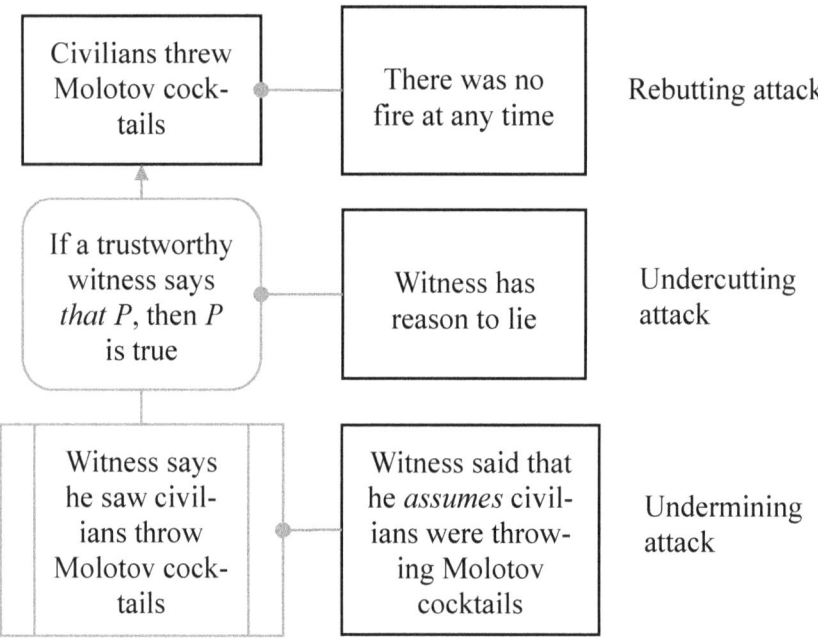

Figure 8. Three forms of attack.

---

18   Henry Prakken, "An Abstract Framework for Argumentation with Structured Arguments", in *Argument and Computation*, 2010, vol. 1, no. 2, pp. 7–22.

The fact that one of the elements of an argument is subject to attack is not necessarily the end of the story. An attack is just another argument, which must be evaluated for plausibility and validity. Moreover, an attack can itself be counter-attacked. However, if no counter-argument is formulated, then the initial attack 'succeeds' and the proponent's argument fails. In case a counter-attack can be formulated, then the fact-finder will need to make a determination as to whether or not it succeeds in 'neutralising' the initial attack. If it does, then the initial attack no longer has any effect on the original argument. However, then the opponent still has the opportunity to formulate a further argument in an attempt to neutralise the counter-attack. In the example, the opponent has made an undercutting attack, arguing that the Captain is not a trustworthy witness because he has an interest in not incriminating himself in the killing of civilians. This is a cogent argument, which, if left unaddressed, would prevent the fact-finder from concluding that the testimony of the Captain proves that civilians actually threw Molotov cocktails. However, the proponent of the argument might counter-attack by arguing that the Captain actually does not have an interest in concealing the truth because he was given immunity from prosecution. This is again a cogent and plausible argument, which, if left unanswered, succeeds in neutralising the initial attack.

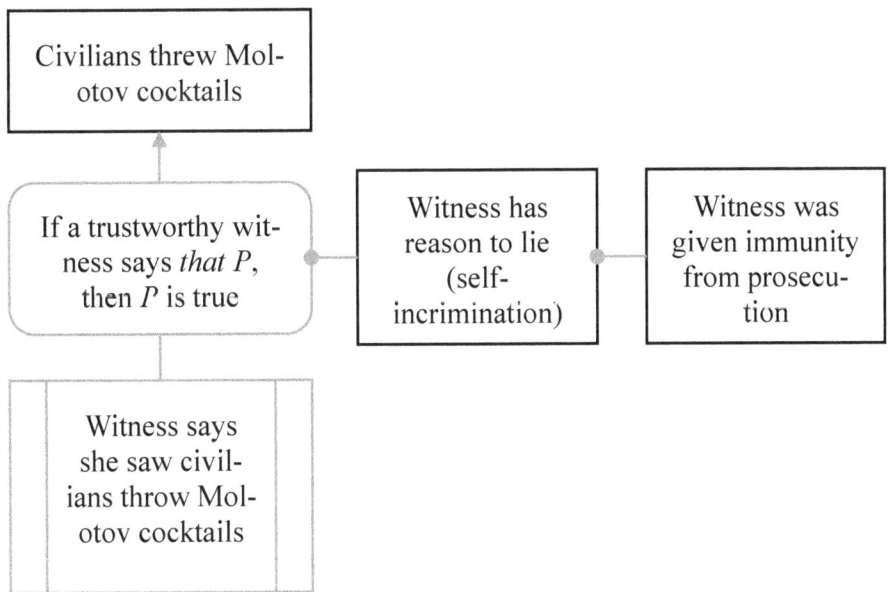

Figure 9. Attack and counter-attack.

11.4. Argumentation Schemes

While it is possible and useful to manually formulate all relevant arguments, this may be time-consuming and if the fact-finder has to process a lot of material, she may not give every step in the reasoning sufficient attention. To assist fact-finders, scholars have formulated a number of 'standardised' argumentation schemes, which apply to typical arguments that are frequently relied upon in judicial fact-finding.[19] Argumentation schemes are conceived as a list of critical questions that must be answered in relation to a particular generalisation. These questions help the fact-finder with determining whether or not the generalisation is applicable in the case at hand. They also point the fact-finder to potential sources of doubt and forces him or her to actively look for evidence in order to determine whether the generalisation can be safely applied or not.

Argumentation schemes are customisable and fact-finders may individualise them in order to match their understanding of the relevant generalisation. As an illustration, the example of the warrant for testimonial evidence will be discussed in some detail.

As a generalisation, 'If a trustworthy witness says *that P*, then *P* is true' is unassailable, but not very informative. In particular, it does not provide any indicators for when a specific testimony qualifies as trustworthy.[20] There is no universally accepted standard for when testimony is trustworthy; but it is fairly uncontroversial that a witness must be at least competent, not be unduly influenced by biases, and honest in order to be worthy of any trust. Any application of the warrant for testimonial evidence therefore presupposes that the fact-finder can confirm that the witness meets these three basic criteria.[21] Schematically, this looks as follows:

---

[19] Douglas Walton, Chris Reed and Fabrizio Macagno, *Argumentation Schemes*, Cambridge University Press, 2008; Floris Bex and Bart Verheij, "Solving a Murder Case by Asking Critical Questions: An Approach to Fact-Finding in Terms of Argumentation and Story Schemes", in *Argumentation*, 2012, vol. 26, no. 3, pp. 325–53.

[20] The term 'trustworthiness' refers to all factors that determine whether testimony can be relied upon, including credibility and reliability.

[21] The proposed model is inspired by David Schum and Jon Morris, "Assessing the Competence and Credibility of Human Sources of Intelligence Evidence: Contributions from Law and Probability", in *Law, Probability and Risk*, 2007, vol. 6, nos. 1–4, pp. 247–74. For a more empirical discussion of the evaluation of testimonial evidence by international courts, see Gabriele Chlevikaite and Barbora Hola, "Empirical Study of Insider Witnesses' Assessments at the International Criminal Court", in *International Criminal Law Review*, 2016, vol. 16, no. 4, pp. 673–702; Nancy Combs, *Fact-Finding Without Facts*, Cambridge

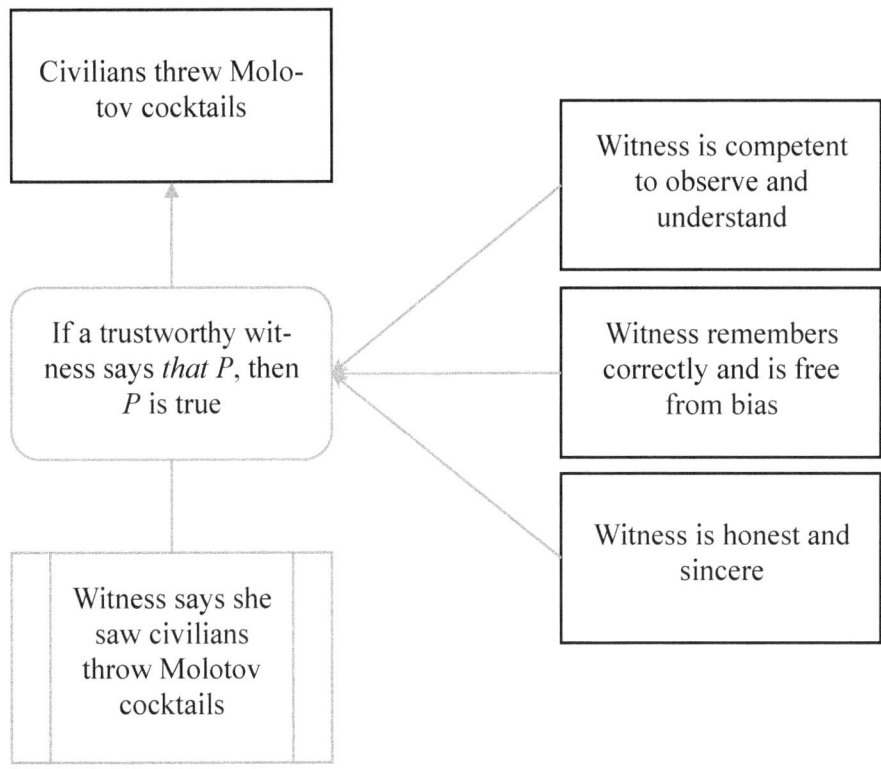

Figure 10. Three basic components of trustworthiness.

The three basic components of trustworthiness can each be un-packed further. For example, the requirement that a witness must have been competent to observe the event being testified about and capable of understanding what she observed. There are three aspects to compe-tence.[22] First, there is the question whether the witness was physically in a position to observe the event. This requires information about where the

University Press, 2010. For a more scientific approach, see, for example, Bella M. DePau-lo, James J. Lindsay, Brian E. Malone, Laura Muhlebruck, Kelly Charlton and Harris Cooper, "Cues to Deception", in *Psychological Bulletin*, 2003, vol. 129, no. 1, pp. 74–118; Aldert Vrij, *Detecting Lies and Deceit: The Psychology of Lying and the Implications for Professional Practice*, Wiley, 2000; Aldert Vrij, *Detecting Lies and Deceit: Pitfalls and Opportunities*, Wiley, 2008.

22 Competence can be defined as asking whether the witness was "in a position to know" the relevant information. See, Douglas Walton, *Witness Testimony Evidence: Argumentation, Artificial Intelligence, and Law*, Cambridge University Press, 2008.

witness was located relative to the event and whether she was able to have a 'good look'. This aspect can be called *external material competence*. Second, the fact-finder must assess the witness's *internal material competence*. This aspect raises questions about the witness's sensory and cognitive abilities. The questions range from general information about the witness, such as whether she has adequate or impaired vision, to what his or her state of consciousness was at the time she purportedly witnessed the event. Finally, witnesses must also have *substantive competence*. This relates to the witness's intellectual ability to understand what is being witnessed. This may not always be an issue when the facts testified to are very basic, such as where someone was at a given time. But in some cases, the events witnessed may not be fully understandable to an average witness. For example, recognising a particular type of vehicle or weapon may require some prior familiarity with this sort of objects. Similarly, if a witness does not understand the language in which a conversation she hears is being conducted, she is unlikely to be able to reliable testify about the content thereof.

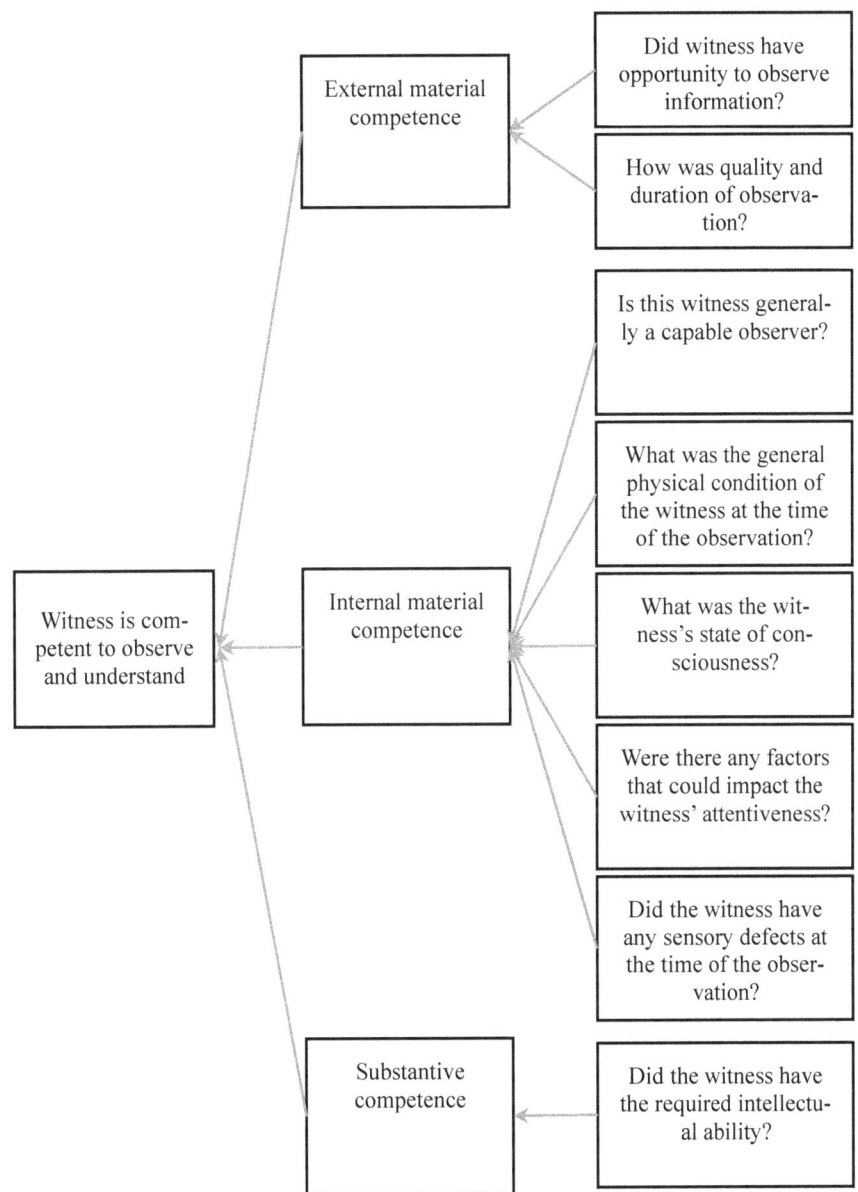

Figure 11. Three basic components of trustworthiness expanded.

A similar exercise can be done for the other two trustworthiness factors. Depending on how granular the fact-finder wishes to be, the number of critical questions can be more or less extensive. Fact-finders may also wish to apply different argumentation schemes depending on the type of witness. For example, the most relevant critical questions for a crime-base witness may be different from those for expert witness.

Once all critical questions have been defined, the fact-finder can start looking for answers. For each of the critical questions, the fact-finder needs to determine whether the available information favours the relevant trustworthiness factor or not. When there is no information available for a particular critical question or the available information is inconclusive, this constitutes a source of uncertainty. The fact that a critical question yields a negative result or no result at all does not necessarily mean that the relevant generalisation cannot be applied. Whether or not this is the case depends on two factors. The first and most important factor is how much uncertainty the fact-finder is able to accept. This depends, to a large extent, on the applicable standard of proof. However, even if the highest standard of proof in criminal proceedings – beyond reasonable doubt – is applicable, this still does not automatically mean that the warrant does not obtain if some of the critical questions are not answered favourably. Whether or not this is the case depends on the second factor, which is how much weight the fact-finder attributes to the individual critical questions and how negative the available information is. If the witness was unconscious at the time of the events she testifies about, this will obviously have a greater negative impact than if the evidence concerning his or her vision is ambiguous.

In cases when there is no evidence in relation to a particular critical question, or when the evidence is ambivalent or uncertain, the fact-finder may decide to assume that if better evidence were available, this would be favourable. In such a case the fact-finder accepts a certain risk, but this may be entirely reasonable, depending on the context. For example, if there is no specific information about the critical question whether or not the witness was conscious at the time of the event, it may be reasonable to assume that she was, based on the fact that she was able to provide information in the first place. Such arguments are obviously not free from risk, but it may be a risk that the fact-finder does not find disproportional in light of the significance of the factual proposition to which the warrant applies and the relevant context.

In any event, even if the available information is favourable in relation to a particular critical question, it is still incumbent upon the fact-finder to assess its value. Ideally, the information should come from sources other than the witness him- or herself. However, in many cases the witness will be the only source of information. This gives rise to the interesting situation where a witness is testifying about his or her own trustworthiness, which creates a 'short-circuit' in the argumentation scheme, because the information provided by the witness can only constitute a useful answer if he or she is trustworthy about this information as well. Schematically, this looks as follows.

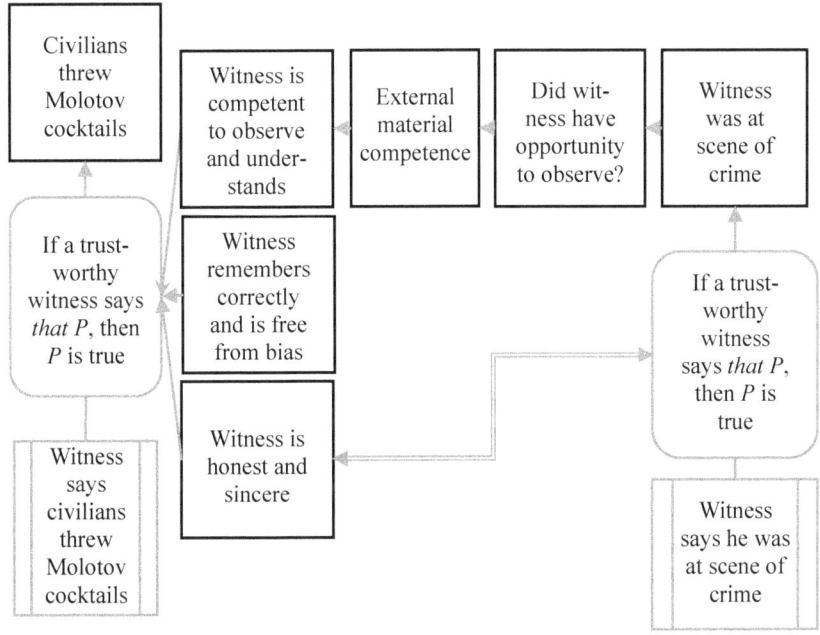

Figure 12. Witness testifying about his or her own trustworthiness.

Such 'circularity' does not denote an error in the argumentation. It simply means that in cases where there is only a single witness for a particular proposition, everything stands or falls with the fact-finder's assessment of the witness's honesty and sincerity. This is often the most difficult part of the assessment of witness testimony, where fact-finders have very little solid ground to base their conclusions on. This explains why having only one single witness is often not a strong basis for proving important factual propositions.[23]

11.5. Application of Logical Argumentation in Practice

Although this chapter has so far been limited to giving a short outline of how argument mapping and argumentation schemes can be applied for analysing witness testimony, the method can be used for most other aspects of evidentiary analysis as well. In principle, every argument that involves inferential reasoning, including analysis of causal links, can benefit from being mapped.

It will be noted that argumentation theory, even when using argumentation schemes, is extremely flexible and can fully adapt to each individual fact-finder's thinking. Indeed, it must be stressed that argumentation theory does not impose anything on the fact-finder in terms of what to think. In a very real sense, argumentation theory is just an alternative notation method for natural language, which allows the fact-finder to set out his or her reasoning with greater precision. By providing a structured and methodical approach, argument mapping can help the fact-finder to notice potential flaws or weak points in his or her reasoning, but it cannot safeguard against errors.

One great advantage of argumentation theory is that it is possible to automate part of the analytical process. In particular, it is possible to keep track of all the logical connections that are symbolised by the edges connecting the nodes.[24] This may not be of great value in relatively simple arguments like the ones discussed here. However, in cases with large quantities of evidence and especially cases with a lot of circumstantial evidence and complex catenate inferences, mapping an evidentiary argument out in its entirety may be the only way for the fact-finder to ensure that he or she does not overlook anything that is important. It also assists

---

[23] For the avoidance of doubt, this is a purely epistemic observation. It is well accepted that, from a legal point of view, a single witness can suffice and that there is no requirement of corroboration. See, for example, ICC, Rules of Procedure and Evidence, 9 September 2002, Rule 63(4): "Without prejudice to article 66, paragraph 3, a Chamber shall not impose a legal requirement that corroboration is required in order to prove any crime within the jurisdiction of the Court, in particular, crimes of sexual violence" (https://legal-tools.org/doc/8bcf6f).

[24] Phan Min Dung, "On the Acceptability of Arguments and its Fundamental Role in Non-monotonic Reasoning, Logic Programming and *n*-Person Games", in *Artificial Intelligence*, 1995, vol. 77, no. 2, pp. 321–57.

fact-finders to better understand the importance and logical implications of details in the overall argument. By helping the fact-finder to keep an overview of the available evidence and how it all fits together in a possible argument, it is easier for fact-finders to identify possible gaps in the available evidential data-set as well as potential counter-arguments. Argumentation mapping is thus not only a tool that can help in analysing an existing argument, it can also assist fact-finders with building better arguments. Crucially, mapping evidentiary arguments can support fact-finders in assessing the relative strength and (potential) weaknesses of their available evidence and guide the search for additional evidence.

11.6. Need for a Practical Tool

Although there are many significant benefits associated with using argumentation theory, it may currently be difficult to implement this method systematically in practice. The reason for this is that, whilst the theoretical framework and technology are all available, there is currently no tool that is suitable for practical use in real cases. The main challenge in developing such a tool is to design a user-friendly interface that fits on a regular computer screen and that allows the fact-finder to map very complex arguments with minimal time and effort. This requires that it must be possible for the fact-finder to zoom in and out of the argumentation map and to break down complex arguments into smaller constituent elements without losing any of the logical connections with the entirety of the argument map.

While a useful tool must include the most common argumentation schemes, it must be possible for fact-finders to customise them easily. The 'standard' argumentation schemes should be based on contemporary insights from research in the relevant field. This presupposes that those who design such a tool must be familiar with cognitive psychology, legal epistemology, and certain scientific disciplines that are recurrently relevant in criminal proceedings. For example, it may be useful to develop argumentation schemes for specialised evidence concerning DNA, ballistics, witness identification, and so on. The research relied upon in designing the argumentation schemes must be made available to the fact-finder so that he or she can fully understand the reasons behind each of the critical questions. Existing argumentation schemes should be regularly updated in light of developments in the relevant fields. In this manner, the fact-finder can be confident that he or she is always applying the most up-to-date generalisations.

To facilitate the work of the fact-finder, a user-friendly argumentation tool should be compatible with the relevant databases containing evidence or transcripts, filing, and so on. In particular, it should be simple for the fact-finder to link the propositions contained in the evidence nodes to the content contained in the databases holding the actual evidence and/or transcripts.

Finally, in order to allow teams of fact-finders to work together, it is important that argument maps can be opened and edited by multiple users at the same time. To facilitate communication between team members over time, the tool should also indicate changes made by other users.

11.7. Conclusion

Using argumentation maps does not require fact-finders to change the way they think, but it does require a certain change in mind-set. The most important change relates to shifting from natural language to a more schematic way of notating one's thoughts. Changing how to do something one is used to doing in a particular manner is not always easy. Especially lawyers, whose reliance on expressing their arguments in carefully crafted prose is deeply ingrained, may find the transition challenging at first. However, the benefits of using a more structured method for articulating evidentiary arguments are numerous. Perhaps the most significant advantage over natural language is that using argumentation maps obliges fact-finders to reflect upon the assumptions that underpin their reasoning. This may be challenging at first, but it is a price worth paying for lifting the fact-finding process out of the realm of subjective impressions and intuitions. In the end, whether one is comfortable with applying logical argumentation depends on how prepared one is to discipline oneself to restrict evidentiary analysis to arguments that can be clearly and cogently articulated. This should go some way in tackling the second bottleneck – *Factual analysis* – detailed in the concept note for the research project of which this anthology is a result.[25]

---

[25] See Morten Bergsmo, "Towards a Culture of Quality Control in Criminal Investigations", FICHL Policy Brief Series No. 94 (2019), Torkel Opsahl Academic EPublisher, Brussels, 2019, pp. 2-3 (http://www.toaep.org/pbs-pdf/94-bergsmo/).

Another key advantage of using argumentation mapping in evidentiary analysis is that it makes it a lot easier for fact-finders to keep an overview of all the relevant evidence that is available to them. As such it directly addresses the first bottleneck – *Overview of information*.[26] One of the biggest challenges fact-finders in complex criminal investigations face is keeping track of what evidence has already been collected and, most importantly, what can be proved with it. By disciplining oneself to put each piece of information into a structured argument, the fact-finder will have a better chance of identifying potential gaps in the evidential data-set early on. This will help in guiding the investigation and to focus limited resources to finding evidence that can really make a difference.

Mapping evidentiary arguments also greatly facilitates accurate communication between fact-finders. One of the greatest causes of miscommunication lies in the unarticulated assumptions that are implicit in natural language. By trying to eliminate such hidden assumptions as much as possible, it will be easier for every member of a fact-finding team to share the same level of knowledge and understanding. This facilitates debating the strengths and weaknesses of particular arguments and allows team members to contribute much more effectively. Expressing arguments in a structured manner also makes it easier to follow how an argument evolves over time. Every change in the argument, no matter how small or nuanced, can be clearly visualised and its exact implications on the rest of the argument are immediately apparent to every user of the argumentation map. Ensuring better communication is essential to making the most effective use of the available resources, both human and evidentiary. It may help to avoid duplication of efforts and should alert co-ordinators much sooner when a certain investigatory avenue is proving unfruitful. As such, argumentation mapping can contribute to addressing the third bottleneck – *Evidence review*.[27]

Crucially, argumentation mapping can be an invaluable tool for the identification of possible sources of doubt. This may help fact-finders to limit the effects of confirmation bias and coherence shifting. Human beings are inherently uncomfortable with uncertainty and instinctively aspire to clear and unambiguous conclusions. Whereas this tendency is natural and, to some extent, corresponds with the desired outcome of judicial

---

[26] *Ibid.*, p. 2.
[27] *Ibid.*, p. 3.

proceedings,[28] it is not always rational. Mapping an argument cannot prevent the fact-finder from being influenced by biases, but it should make it more difficult for such tendencies to prevail as it will force the fact-finder to confront the weaknesses of his or her arguments.

This leads to an important point that cannot be stressed enough, namely that the process of argumentation mapping, also when it is assisted by software tools, is a hundred percent controlled by the individual fact-finder(s). As a methodology, it provides a framework for articulating and evaluating evidentiary arguments. However, it is incapable of replacing the human fact-finder, because it is incapable of generating arguments by itself. Even when argumentation schemes are used, the input of the system is limited to posing a list of critical questions. It is incumbent upon the individual fact-finder to decide whether or not to pursue finding answers to all of the questions and, crucially, how to weigh the impact of those answers or the lack thereof. It therefore cannot be argued that reliance on argumentation theory impinges upon the autonomy of the fact-finder.

Still, it would be naïve to expect that a novel approach such as the one proposed in this chapter will be universally welcomed by all practitioners. As with any innovation, the method will have to go through a period of testing during which it will have to prove its added value. This is both natural and desirable. Yet, it is important to anticipate some resistance, probably mostly from lawyers, who may fear that adopting argumentation methods may infringe their 'monopoly' of framing evidentiary arguments in the context of legal proceedings. Moreover, it is probably not realistic to expect that legal proceedings will abandon the use of natural language as the main form of communication between parties and adjudicators. However, it is suggested that the quality of written and oral evidentiary submissions can greatly benefit from being based upon a duly developed and detailed argumentation map. Not only will this facilitate clarity in the exposition of the main arguments, it will also inform the drafter which details he or she must emphasise in his or her submissions. Structuring written or oral submissions on the basis of argumentation maps also has the advantage of avoiding repetition and may make it easier to divide the drafting process. While it may seem rather inefficient to

---

[28] Charles Nesson, "The Evidence or the Event? On Judicial Proof and the Acceptability of Verdicts", in *Harvard Law Review*, vol. 98, no. 7, 1985, pp. 1357–92.

'translate' arguments from natural language into argumentation maps only to have to translate them back to natural language again in the end, it should be considered that using an argumentation map as a working tool can obviate the need for drafting many intermediate documents, which are much harder to keep track of, and which involves a much greater risk of information being lost in the process. Moreover, given the inherent limitations of natural language, it is not an ideal tool for evidentiary analysis anyway. This is implicitly recognised by practitioners, who frequently make use of more or less advanced spreadsheet technology to organise the available evidence. Argumentation mapping can perform a similar role, but at a much higher level of sophistication and with many analytical benefits that are simply not attainable with ordinary techniques.

Although the last word has undoubtedly not been said in the debate about how to improve the quality of fact-finding in complex criminal investigations, it is probably safe to conclude that the time is ripe for introducing new ways of thinking about evidence and what it means to be a rational fact-finder. If this chapter has been able to contribute to this debate, it will have achieved its main objective. However, the real hope is, of course, that the ideas and methods introduced here will find application in practice sooner rather than later. To that end, practitioners and academics from a number of fields must join forces to develop a tool that makes logical argumentation techniques available and usable in real complex cases.[29] This will not happen overnight. Developing a tool that can handle the amount of information that is usually associated with core international criminal cases will require time and perseverance. But just like Rome was not built in a day or by one person; fulfilling the promise and hope of the Rome Statute relies on the sustained efforts and energy of countless individuals. It is time to get the ball rolling.

---

[29] It is noted that there are commercially available tools to help lawyers and analysts organise and analyse evidence (for example, Casemap, Relativity, Atlas.ti, and so on). However, to this author's knowledge, there is currently no programme that is powerful enough to map out and analyse evidentiary arguments with informal logic on the scale required by cases involving large-scale international crimes. The Case Matrix application – an outstanding tool to correlate evidence and elements of core international crimes – does not in its current form seek to support evidentiary argumentation as such.

12

Investigations of Criminal Responsibility by the ICC Office of the Prosecutor

Matthias Neuner[*]

12.1. Introduction

With the International Criminal Court ('ICC') operating in its seventeenth year, it is time to pause, look back and analyse its Office of the Prosecutor's ('OTP') record of investigating criminal responsibility of suspects, formulating it in the Documents containing the Charges ('DCC') and defending it in subsequent court proceedings.

The following analysis is independent, stems from a non-staff member outside the ICC's OTP and therefore centres on inferences drawn from publicly accessible legal filings, such as the OTP's arrest warrant applications, DCC's, Defence counsel submissions, and ICC judges' decisions. The reviewed filings discussed how formulations of criminal liability should be undertaken, confirmed, amended and/or why allegations of criminal responsibility advanced by the OTP had to be dismissed.

The picture emerges that at the end of its investigations, the OTP usually alleges several modes of criminal liability which, if confirmed by the Pre-Trial Chamber, sometimes were upheld by judges of the Trial and Appeals Chambers in the same variant as initially proposed. However, often the judiciary on the level of the Pre-Trial Chamber[1] or Trial Chamber,[2] and rarely the Appeals Chamber,[3] at least significantly reduced the

---

[*] **Matthias Neuner** is Trial Counsel, Office of the Prosecutor ('OTP'), Special Tribunal for Lebanon ('STL'). The views expressed herein are those of the author and do not necessarily reflect the views of the STL.

[1] The Pre-Trial Chamber has the power to dismiss a mode of liability and to ask the Prosecution to consider filing an amended DCC. Rome Statute of the International Criminal Court, 17 July 1998, Article 61(7)(b) and 61(7)(c)(ii) ('ICC Statute') (https://legal-tools.org/doc/7b9af9).

[2] The Trial Chamber has the authority to modify the legal characterisation of facts by issuing a notice to the trial's participants. ICC, Regulations of the Court, 26 May 2004, ICC-

number of the OTP's proposed modes of liability or modified the legal characterisation of facts initially alleged, or dismissed all liability of the accused. The latter occurred in *Prosecutor v. Jean-Pierre Bemba Gombo* by the Appeals Chamber and twice when the Pre-Trial Chamber was unable to confirm any of the formulations of criminal responsibility proposed by the OTP.[4] Both latter cases ended at the confirmation stage with significant investigation resources spent until then.

Non-confirmations and frequent changes of the modes of liability initially proposed by the Prosecution indicate that the OTP had submitted to the judiciary a case with allegations of criminal liability which it either was unable to defend once scrutiny by the Defence and judiciary began, or which needed changes in the formulations of criminal responsibility to correctly reflect the facts established during an investigation.

In 12 cases analysed, the OTP had initially proposed one or more mode(s) of liability which it could *not* defend during the various stages of criminal proceedings: the Pre-Trial Chambers refused to confirm the OTP's allegation of criminal liability of four suspects and refrained to elevate their status to accused persons, thereby dismissing either the entire proposed DCC or relevant sections thereof.[5] Further, though the Pre-Trial Chamber had confirmed the OTP's allegations of criminal liability against two accused, the cases ended after the Prosecution withdrew the charges before the trial could begin.[6] Against four other persons, the Trial Chamber vacated all charges after the Prosecution's case had ended with decisions on the 'no case to answer' ('NCTA') motions.[7] Based on reasons relating to criminal liability, two cases resulted in an acquittal: the case

---

BD/01-01-04, Regulation 55 ('Regulations of the Court') (https://legal-tools.org/doc/05fd20).

[3] The Appeals Chamber can overturn a Trial Chamber's finding regarding a mode of liability by dismissing it. ICC, Situation in the Central African Republic, *The Prosecutor v. Jean-Pierre Bemba Gombo*, Appeals Chamber, Judgment on the appeal of Mr Jean-Pierre Bemba Gombo against Trial Chamber III's "Judgment pursuant to Article 74 of the Statute", 8 June 2018, ICC-01/05-01/08-3636-Red, paras. 194, 196–98 ('Bemba Appeals Judgment') (https://legal-tools.org/doc/40d35b).

[4] *Prosecutor v. Bahar Idriss Abu Garda* and *Prosecutor v. Callixte Mbarushimana*.

[5] *Prosecutor v. Abu Garda, Prosecutor v. Mohammed Hussein Ali, Prosecutor v. Henry Kiprono Kosgey* and *Prosecutor v. Mbarushimana*.

[6] *Prosecutor v. Francis Kirimi Muthaura* and *Prosecutor v. Uhuru Muigau Kenyatta*.

[7] *Prosecutor v. William Samoei Ruto, Prosecutor v. Joshua Arap Sang, Prosecutor v. Laurent Koudou Gbagbo* and *Prosecutor v. Charles Blé Goudé*.

---

against Mathieu Ngudjolo Chui ended with a trial judgment and the case against Bemba with an Appeal judgment, both containing acquittals.

By contrast, the Prosecution managed to consistently maintain its initial allegation of criminal responsibility by securing convictions for the mode of liability initially alleged in three cases.[8] In the additional case of *Prosecutor v. Germain Katanga*, months after the deliberation process had begun, the Trial Chamber provided notice pursuant to Regulation 55 of a possible re-characterisation of criminal liability (other than the mode of responsibility initial alleged by the OTP) and then convicted the accused based on this new form of participation.[9] A fifth case, *Prosecutor v. Ongwen*, is in the deliberation phase at the time of writing of this analysis and therefore is not considered for this statistical evaluation.

The ratio of 4 cases in which the OTP secured convictions[10] compared to 12 cases *not* leading to any conviction of the suspects or accused persons based on the initial allegation of criminal responsibility indicate that the OTP's investigations into modes of responsibilities often resulted in identification of facts and advancement of assertions which, upon scrutiny by the Defence and the judiciary, the Prosecution could *not* defend to obtain a conviction.

This begs questions: where did it go wrong? Already during the investigative phase? And/or during the phase when the results of an investigation were turned into a draft DCC? If the OTP is more often than not unable to defend its allegations on criminal responsibility has this a mere factual background, as the discovered facts were insufficient? Or is it the result of erroneous interpretation of these facts? Or a combination of both?

---

[8] *Prosecutor v. Ahmad Al Faqi Al Mahdi*, *Prosecutor v. Thomas Lubanga Dyilo* and *Prosecutor v. Bosco Ntaganda*.

[9] ICC, Situation in the Democratic Republic of the Congo, *The Prosecutor v. Germain Katanga and Mathieu Ngudjolo Chui*, Trial Chamber, Decision on the implementation of regulation 55 of the Regulations of the Court and severing the charges against the accused persons, 21 November 2012, ICC-01/04-01/07-3319-tENG/FRA, p. 29 ('Katanga and Ngudjolo Chui Trial Decision on the Implementation of Regulation 55 and Severing the Charges') (https://legal-tools.org/doc/f5cbd0).

[10] Three cases (see above note 8) in which the OTP secured convictions based on the *same* mode of liability initially alleged. In the fourth case (*Prosecutor v. Katanga*), the OTP had pleaded facts which secured a conviction, but only after the Trial Chamber invoked Regulation 55 and re-characterised the mode of liability. The fifth case, the case against Dominic Ongwen, is not considered in this comparison, as the judges' deliberation in this case is still ongoing.

12.2. Individualisation of Guilt

Centre piece of any investigation, prosecution, trial and verdict is to identify and analyse criminal wrongdoing, meaning to attribute guilt to an individual or, if this cannot be done beyond reasonable doubt, to acquit. Thus, in the course of investigation and prosecution, the objective is to identify and define the offence(s) committed, suspects for these and to determine their individual criminal responsibility. Regarding the latter, the main question to answer is: what is the correct mode of responsibility which describes the wrongdoing most accurately? The ICC Statute distinguishes between positive or negative acts in Article 25(3): a principal 'commits' these acts by directly perpetrating, acting as direct or indirect co-perpetrator.[11] By contrast, an accomplice orders, solicits or induces,[12] aids or abets[13] in any other way contributes.[14] Further, the ICC Statute provides liability for omission: if a superior or commander omits to follow certain duties, he can be held responsible due to Article 28.

12.3. Legal Environment in Which the OTP Conducts Its Investigations

As a treaty-based organisation, the ICC has weaker powers compared to its precursors. The International Military Tribunals in Nuremberg and Tokyo had vertical powers exercised in the environment of an occupation of the German Reich and Empire of Japan. The International Criminal Tribunals for Yugoslavia and Rwanda were created by the Security Council which exercised its vertical powers under Chapter VII of the UN Charter.[15]

12.3.1. Powers Vested into the ICC

Part 9 of the ICC Statute provides powers to the Court and the OTP as its organ,[16] but only those which the States Parties have before *voluntarily* transferred to the ICC. In addition, the ICC treaty allows States Parties to

---

[11] ICC Statute, Article 25(3)(a), see above note 1.

[12] *Ibid.*, Article 25(3)(b).

[13] *Ibid.*, Articles 25(3)(c) and 25(3)(d).

[14] *Ibid.*, Article 25(3)(d).

[15] Security Council Resolution 827 (1993), UN Doc. S/RES/827 (1993), 25 May 1993 (https://legal-tools.org/doc/dc079b); Security Council Resolution 955 (1994), UN Doc. S/RES/955 (1994), 8 November 1994 (https://legal-tools.org/doc/f5ef47).

[16] ICC Statute, Articles 54(2)(a), 55(2), 57(3)(d), 58(5), 86, see above note 1.

withdraw.[17] That the Security Council refers a situation to the ICC under Chapter VII of the UN Charter and Article 13(b) of the ICC Statute does not mean that the OTP and the Court automatically get full co-operation in investigations. For example, even though the Pre-Trial Chamber issued two warrants of arrest against Omar Al Bashir,[18] the former President of the Sudan, he was not arrested by three States Parties[19] and non-States Parties of the ICC while staying on their territory.[20] Volatile security situations in (post-)conflict areas further complicate the investigations[21] as not only experiences in relation to Darfur and Libya show. Warring factions have competing interests and agendas if it comes to the OTP conducting an investigation. The result is that the OTP's access to relevant areas in

---

[17] *Ibid.*, Articles 121(6), 127.

[18] ICC, Situation in Darfur, Sudan, *The Prosecutor v. Omar Hassan Ahmad Al Bashir*, Pre-Trial Chamber, Warrant of Arrest for Omar Hassan Ahmad Al Bashir, 4 March 2009, ICC-02/05-01/09-1 (https://legal-tools.org/doc/814cca); ICC, Situation in Darfur, Sudan, *The Prosecutor v. Omar Hassan Ahmad Al Bashir*, Pre-Trial Chamber, Second Warrant of Arrest for Omar Hassan Ahmad Al Bashir, 12 July 2010, ICC-02/05-01/09-95 (https://legal-tools.org/doc/307664).

[19] For example, Al-Bashir travelled to the Federal Republic of Nigeria, the Republic of South Africa and the Kingdom of Jordan, and the ICC though finding that the last two States had failed to comply with their obligations under the ICC Statute, refrained to refer both occurrences to the Assembly of States Parties or the Security Council, because both States had commenced consultation procedures with the ICC before these visits occurred. ICC, Situation in Darfur, Sudan, *The Prosecutor v. Omar Hassan Ahmad Al Bashir*, Appeals Chamber, Judgment in the Jordan Referral re Al-Bashir Appeal, 6 May 2019, ICC-02/05-01/09-397-Corr, paras. 208–12, 215 (https://legal-tools.org/doc/0c5307); ICC, Situation in Darfur, Sudan, *The Prosecutor v. Omar Hassan Ahmad Al Bashir*, Pre-Trial Chamber, Decision under article 87(7) of the Rome Statute on the non-compliance by South Africa with the request by the Court for the arrest and surrender of Omar Al-Bashir, 6 July 2017, ICC-02/05-01/09-302, paras. 123, 139–40 (https://legal-tools.org/doc/68ffc1). For Nigeria, ICC, Situation in Darfur, Sudan, *The Prosecutor v. Omar Hassan Ahmad Al Bashir*, Trial Chamber, Decision Regarding Omar Al-Bashir's Visit to the Federal Republic of Nigeria, 15 July 2013, ICC-02/05-01/09-157 (https://legal-tools.org/doc/f97665). This visit occurred between 14 and 16 July 2013.

[20] An overview of all States visited by Al-Bashir following his arrest is provided in the web site "BashirWatch".

[21] ICC, Situation in the Democratic Republic of the Congo, *The Prosecutor v. Thomas Lubanga Dyilo*, Trial Chamber, Judgment pursuant to Article 74 of the Statute, 14 March 2012, ICC-01/04-01/06-2842, paras. 154–64 ('Lubanga Trial Judgment') (https://legal-tools.org/doc/677866); ICC, Situation in the Democratic Republic of the Congo, *The Prosecutor v. Mathieu Ngudjolo Chui*, Trial Chamber, Judgment pursuant to Article 74 of the Statute, 18 December 2012, ICC-01/04-02/12-3-tENG, paras. 115, 121 ('Ngudjolo Chui Trial Judgment') (https://legal-tools.org/doc/2c2cde).

certain countries, its field presence[22] there, and its powers of investigation are far from being vertical, but fluid, subject to political will, sometimes depend on access to and willingness to co-operate with intermediaries[23] and thus occasionally have to contain horizontal elements.

Further, the OTP's investigations may suffer from a shortcoming of direct evidence. The Trial Chamber in *Prosecutor v. Ngudjolo Chui* observed an absence of forensic findings crucial to the identification of victims, failure of the Prosecution to visit the localities where the accused lived and where preparations for the attack on Bogoro allegedly took place, failure to interview the accused and certain commanders who played a key role before the attack and to obtain civil status documents of the OTP's witnesses to more precisely determine the age of alleged child soldiers.[24] Trial Chamber II observed a "more thorough investigation [...] would have resulted in a more nuanced interpretation of certain facts [...]".[25]

The legal environment in which the OTP investigates applicable modes of criminal responsibility needs to be further considered. Article 61(4) of the ICC Statute in connection with Rule 121(4) of the Rules of Procedure and Evidence ('RPE') allow the OTP to unilaterally withdraw formulations of responsibility until 15 days before the confirmation of charges hearing. After the confirmation decision, two additional criteria have to be met before the Prosecution can amend or withdraw an alleged

---

[22]   Christian M. De Vos, "Investigating from Afar: the ICC's Evidence Problem", in *Leiden Journal of International Law*, 2013, vol. 26, no. 4, pp. 1016–19.

[23]   The OTP argued in the Lubanga case that "due to the difficulties in the DRC and the OTP's lack of a police force, it was necessary to rely on intermediaries". Lubanga Trial Judgment, para. 181, text accompanying fn. 457, see above note 21. ICC, *Guidelines Governing the Relations between the Court and Intermediaries for the Organs and Units of the Court and Counsel working with intermediaries*, March 2014, p. 2 (https://legal-tools.org/doc/e0f990):

> To facilitate activities in the field, the Court uses different forms of field presence. The effectiveness of the Court's activities also depends to a large extent on the cooperation it receives from the community, regional national (governmental) organizations and individuals operating in the country where the Court functions.

See ICC, *Code of Conduct for Intermediaries*, March 2014, sect. 5 (https://legal-tools.org/doc/eac2f0); Elena Baylis, "Outsourcing investigations", in *University of California Los Angeles Journal of International Law and Foreign Affairs*, 2009, vol. 14, no. 1, pp. 121 ff.

[24]   Ngudjolo Chui Trial Judgment, paras. 118–21, see above note 21.

[25]   *Ibid.*, para. 123.

---

mode of liability: the Defence has to be notified and the Pre-Trial Chamber needs to grant leave.[26]

12.3.2. Regulation 55

In practice, the formal amendment procedure provided by Article 61(9) to alter initial pleadings of modes of liability is rarely used. Often Regulation 55 is used. This provision allows, if the facts remain the same, a Trial Chamber to modify the legal characterisation of a pleaded mode of liability. The usage of this provision effectively reduces the Prosecution's need to pursue formal amendments of liability to those situations where it wishes to introduce other modes of liability based on *new* facts.

12.3.2.1. Diplomatic Negotiations for the ICC Could Not Identify Sufficient Common Ground

The approach adopted by Regulation 55 is based on the Latin notion *iura novit curia*, meaning the court knows the law while it is left to the parties to bring the facts. Thus, it is the judges' authority to re-characterise the pleaded modes of liability after having provided legal notice to the accused person in order to enable him to prepare and adjust his defence.[27] Common law countries disagree with this interpretation of the law. Emphasising the right of the accused to get timely informed, they argue that the Prosecutor either has to formally amend the DCC otherwise the court is bound by the legal qualifications advanced by the Prosecutor. Failing such a formal amendment, it is only possible that the accused gets convicted for a lesser mode of liability than the one he or she was charged with, but not to a higher one.[28]

Sixteen months after the ICC Statue had been adopted, ICTY Trial Chamber II ruled in *Prosecutor v. Kupreškić* that:

> [I]nternational criminal rules are still in a rudimentary state.
> […] In this state of flux the rights of the accused would not

---

[26]   ICC Statute, Article 61(9), see above note 1.

[27]   Regulation 55(3)(b) expressly refers to the accused right to effectively prepare his defence as enshrined by *ibid.*, Article 67(1)(b).

[28]   Gilbert Bitti, "Two Bones of Contention Between Civil and Common Law: The Record of the Proceedings and the Treatment of a Concursus Delictorum", in Horst Fischer, Claus Kreß and Sascha Rolf Lüder (eds.), *International and National Prosecution of Crimes under International Law: Current Developments*, Berlin Verlag Arno Spitz, Berlin, 2001, p. 282 (https://legal-tools.org/doc/b7b81a).

be satisfactorily safeguarded were one to adopt an approach akin to that of civil law countries. The task of the Defence would become exceedingly onerous [...]. On the other hand, the other requirement relating to the efficient discharge of the Tribunal's function in the interest of justice warrants the conclusion that any possible errors of the Prosecution should not stultify criminal proceedings whenever a case nevertheless appears to have been made by the Prosecution and its possible flaws in the formulation of the charge are not such as to impair or curtail the rights of the Defense.[29]

Four years before this judgment, in 1996, the French delegation had submitted a proposal relating to the ICC Statute according to which the Pre-Trial Chamber may "confirm only part of the indictment and amend it [...] by giving some facts another characterization".[30] This proposal was neither included into the Preparatory Committee's draft statute for an ICC,[31] nor by the ICC Statute adopted in Rome. On the level of the ICC RPE, the issue introducing the *iura novit curia* principle was touched upon several times in informal discussions during the fourth session of the Preparatory Commission. One informal proposal originating from ICTY's OTP was based on the ruling in *Prosecutor v. Kupreškić* and its relevant part stated:

> (1) Provided that the parties are duly notified by the Trial Chamber and given appropriate opportunity to make submissions before the conclusion of the trial, the Chamber may
>
> [...]
>
> (b) classify the particular form of participation in an offence in a different manner under Article 25(3) than that contained in the indictment.[32]

Portugal and Spain added to the excerpt of the OTP's proposal the words highlighted in italics:

---

[29] International Criminal Tribunal for the former Yugoslavia ('ICTY'), *The Prosecutor v. Kupreškić et al.*, Trial Chamber, Judgement, 14 January 2000, IT-95-16-T, paras. 740–41 (Kupreškić et al. Trial Judgment) (https://legal-tools.org/doc/5c6a53).

[30] Draft Statute of the International Criminal Court: Working paper submitted by France, UN. Doc. A/AC.249/L.3, 6 August 1996, Article 48(5)(b) (https://legal-tools.org/doc/4d28ee).

[31] Carsten Stahn, "Modification of the Legal Characterization of Facts in the ICC System: A Portrayal of Regulation", in *Criminal Law Forum*, 2005, vol. 16, no. 1, p. 10.

[32] This informal proposal is reprinted in Bitti, 2001, p. 284, see above note 28.

(2) Provided the parties are duly notified by the Trial Chamber and given appropriate opportunity to make submissions before the conclusion of the trial, the Chamber, *bearing in mind the facts included in the indictment*, may:

[...]

(b) classify the particular form of participation in an offence in a different manner under Article 25(3) than that contained in the indictment.[33]

Displaying disagreement, the common law countries informally tabled Rule 6-22*bis* which stated in its relevant part:

Relationship between the charges and the decision of the Trial Chamber, in particular with regard to concurrences of offences

(a) The Trial Chamber [...] decision shall, in accordance with Article 74(2), not exceed the facts and circumstances described in the charges and any amendment to the charges.

(b) In accordance with Article 61(9) the Prosecutor may not amend the charges after the commencement of the Trial. This shall not prevent the Prosecutor from:

[...]

(ii) with the permission of the Trial Chamber and after notice to the accused, *substituting less serious charges under Article 25(3)*.[34]

The French delegation tabled another proposal:

Provided all those who participate in the proceedings are duly notified by the Trial Chamber and given opportunity to make submissions before the conclusion of the trial, the Trial Chamber may, without adding to the facts described in the charges confirmed by the Pre-Trial Chamber, change the qualification of the facts: [...] b. regarding the particular form of participation in the crime, according to Article 25(3) of the Statute.[35]

---

[33] *Ibid.*

[34] *Ibid.*, p. 285 (emphasis added).

[35] *Ibid.*, p. 286.

As insufficient common ground could be identified, it was impossible to reconcile disagreement between the approaches favoured by the ICTY representative, Spain, Portugal and France on the one hand and the common law countries on the other.[36] Failing consensus, it was decided to not regulate this issue, but to leave it to the ICC to decide, if necessary, according to its inherent powers.[37]

12.3.2.2. Approach Adopted by the ICC Judges: Regulation 55 of the Court

The judges were aware that legal uncertainty about the power of judges to correct erroneous modes of liability charged in the DCC could affect the Prosecutorial strategy, resulting in the Prosecutor listing multiple modes of liability in order to avoid the risk of acquittal. Thus, investigations likely resulted in DCC's loaded with multiple modes of liability which could ultimately affect judicial economy as the judges would need to rule on each variant of criminal responsibility presented.

Cognisant of the lack of common ground preventing the drafters of the ICC Statute and RPE to address the situation in which a trial chamber realises during the presentation of the evidence at trial that an accused is liable according to a different mode of liability than the one charged in the DCC, the judges deliberated on what would be a fair solution taking into consideration the rights of the accused to be promptly and in detail informed as well as to an effective defence. The judges had three options: (1) to accept that the criminal liability is 'frozen' with the confirmation of the DCC, except for a formal amendment according to Article 61(9);[38] (2) to furnish the trial chamber with broader powers to have the Prosecutor *at trial* amend the facts and legal components within the DCC, including the liabilities charged within it; or (3) to furnish the trial chamber with limited powers, staying within the facts as pleaded by the Prosecutor and confirmed by the Pre-Trial Chamber in the DCC, but to grant the Trial Cham-

---

[36] Håkan Friman, "The Rules of Procedure and Evidence in the Investigative Stage", in Horst Fischer, Claus Kreß and Sascha Rolf Lüder (eds.), *International and National Prosecution of Crimes under International Law: Current Developments*, Berlin Verlag Arno Spitz, Berlin, 2001, p. 209; Bitti, 2001, p. 286, see above note 28.

[37] *Ibid.*

[38] However, the last sentence of this paragraph prohibits any adding of charges by the Prosecutor after the commencement of the trial, but allows for withdrawals only.

ber the right to re-characterise the charges. Favouring the third option, the ICC judges adopted in May 2004 Regulation 55 of the Court which stated:

Authority of the Chamber to modify the legal characterisation of facts

1. In its decision under article 74, the Chamber may change the *legal characterisation* of facts to accord with […] the form of participation of the accused under articles 25 and 28, without exceeding the facts and circumstances described in the charges and any amendments to the charges.

This approach excludes the power of a Trial Chamber to deviate from the facts pleaded in the DCC[39] and its auxiliary documents produced by the OTP,[40] but provides for the possibility to change the *legal characterisation* of these facts.[41] Regulation 55 refers expressly to the distinction introduced in Regulation 52(b) and 52(c) by allowing the Trial Chamber to only change the legal characterisation of the facts, including the form of participation under Articles 25 and 28.

With this judge-made law, the ICC's judiciary attempted to overcome the legal divide existing between common law and civil law countries about the best approach. With Regulation 55, the ICC's judges accept that the final authority to describe the scope of the statement of facts lies with the Prosecutor. However, the Trial Chamber is authorised to give the facts which the Prosecutor submitted at the conclusion of his or her investigation and which the Pre-Trial Chamber accepted in its confirmation decision, a different legal interpretation which may ultimately amount to a re-characterisation of a mode of liability. By providing notice of a possible new legal characterisation to the parties, the Trial Chamber warns the accused and thereby provides him or her with the possibility to adjust the defence accordingly. Issuing such notice indicates to the Prosecution that

---

[39] See Regulations of the Court, Regulation 52(b), see above note 2.

[40] The Appeals Chamber found that "[a]ll documents that were designed to provide information about the charges, including auxiliary documents, must be considered to determine whether an accused was informed in sufficient detail of the charges". ICC, Situation in the Democratic Republic of the Congo, *The Prosecutor v. Thomas Lubanga Dyilo*, Appeals Chamber, Judgment on the appeal of Mr Thomas Lubanga Dyilo against his conviction, 1 December 2014, ICC-01/04-01/06-3121-Red, para. 128 ('Lubanga Appeals Judgment') (https://legal-tools.org/doc/585c75); see *ibid.*, para. 134.

[41] See Regulations of the Court, Regulation 52(c), see above note 2.

the Trial Chamber is not fully convinced on the theory of liability advanced following its investigation and/or confirmation decision issued by the Pre-Trial Chamber.

12.4. Indicia of Shortcomings During the Investigation into Criminal Responsibility

Indicia of shortcomings during the investigation are that (1) a negative judicial decision regarding the mode of liability pleaded by OTP is rendered; (2) the liability language proposed by the Prosecution is vague; (3) the DCC contains too many variants of criminal responsibility, including liabilities of principal *and* accessory; (4) the Pre-Trial Chamber invoked Article 61(7)(c) to adjourn the confirmation hearing; and (5) the invocation of Regulation 55 at trial by either the Trial Chamber or the Prosecution. Each of the above indicia is discussed in the following sections.

12.4.1. Negative Judicial Decision About Mode of Liability

The rendering of a negative decision on the mode of liability by the judges is an indicator that the OTP had problems during its investigation, or at least in pleading the results thereof in its DCC. In two cases, Pre-Trial Chamber I refused to grant suspects the status of an accused by not confirming the DCC based on the OTP's inability to prove the alleged criminal responsibility to an evidentiary standard required for confirmation.[42] In *Prosecutor v. Abu Garda*, Pre-Trial Chamber I was "not satisfied that there are substantial grounds to believe that Mr. Abu Garda can be held criminally responsible as either direct or indirect co-perpetrator", and declined to confirm the charges.[43]

In *Prosecutor v. Mbarushimana* the majority of Pre-Trial Chamber I found that:

> [T]he evidence submitted by the Prosecution is not sufficient to establish substantial grounds to believe that the suspect encouraged the troops' morale through his press releases and radio messages, and, therefore, he could have not provided through his radio communications and press releases a sig-

---

[42] *Prosecutor v. Abu Garda* and *Prosecutor v. Mbarushimana*.

[43] ICC, Situation in Darfur, Sudan, *The Prosecutor v. Bahar Idriss Abu Garda*, Pre-Trial Chamber, Decision on the Confirmation of Charges, 8 February 2010, ICC-02/05-02/09-243-Red, para. 232 ('Abu Garda Pre-Trial Decision on the Confirmation of Charges') (https://legal-tools.org/doc/cb3614); see *ibid.*, paras. 233, 236.

nificant contribution to the commission of crimes by the FDLR within the meaning of article 25(3)(d) of the Statute. [...] For these reasons, the Chamber, by majority [...] declines to confirm the charges against Mr. Callixte Mbarushimana.[44]

After the OTP had closed its case in *Prosecutor v. Gbagbo and Blé Goudé*, Trial Chamber I granted the Defence's NCTA-motions.[45] Similarly, in *Prosecutor v. Ruto and Sang*, the majority of Trial Chamber V vacated the charges, as the Prosecution had at the end of its own case not proven any of the alleged modes of liability.[46]

In *Prosecutor v. Ngudjolo*, the accused was acquitted because the Trial Chamber

> could not determine beyond reasonable doubt that Mathieu Ngudjolo was, as alleged by the Prosecution, the leader of the Lendu combatants who participated in the attack on Bogoro. Therefore in the Chambers view, the Prosecution has not proven beyond reasonable doubt that Mathieu Ngudjolo committed the alleged crimes under article 25(3)(a) of the Statute, insofar as his role within Bedu-Ezekere *groupement*, as it emerges from the evidence examined, *in no way allows the Chamber to accept or even contemplate* the notion of indirect perpetration adopted by the Pre-Trial Chamber, regardless of how article 25(3)(a) of the Statute is construed.[47]

---

[44] ICC, Situation in the Democratic Republic of the Congo, *The Prosecutor v. Callixte Mbarushimana*, Pre-Trial Chamber, Decision on the Confirmation of Charges, 16 December 2011, ICC-01/04-01/10-465-Red, para. 339, p. 149 ('Mbarushimana Pre-Trial Decision on the Confirmation of Charges') (https://legal-tools.org/doc/63028f).

[45] See ICC, Situation in the Republic of Côte d'Ivoire, *The Prosecutor v. Laurent Gbagbo and Charles Blé Goudé*, Trial Chamber, Reasons for oral decision of 15 January 2019 on the "Requête de la Défense de Laurent Gbagbo afin qu'un jugement d'acquittement portant sur toutes les charges soit prononcé en faveur de Laurent Gbagbo et que sa mise en liberté immédiate soit ordonnée", and on the Blé Goudé Defence no case to answer motion, 16 July 2019, ICC-02/11-01/15-1263 ('Gbagbo and Blé Goudé Trial Reasons for Oral Decision') (https://legal-tools.org/doc/440017).

[46] ICC, Situation on the Republic of Kenya, *The Prosecutor v. William Samoei Ruto and Joshua Arap Sang*, Trial Chamber, Decision on Defence Applications for Judgments of Acquittal, 5 April 2016, ICC-01/09-01/11-2027-Red-Corr, paras. 133–34, 136–38, 143 ('Ruto and Sang Trial Decision on Defence Applications for Judgments of Acquittal') (https://legal-tools.org/doc/6baecd).

[47] Ngudjolo Chui Trial Judgment, para. 110, see above note 21 (emphasis added).

In *Prosecutor v. Bemba*, the majority of the Appeals Chamber held that

> one element of command responsibility under article 28(a) of the Statute was not properly established and Mr. Bemba cannot be held criminally liable under that provision for the crimes committed by MLC troops during the 2002-2003 CAR Operation.[48]

12.4.2. Vague Formulation of Criminal Responsibility

Imprecision in use of language regarding one aspect of criminal responsibility may be a deliberate choice of the OTP, as sometimes it is impossible to fully clarify one specific, but minor point, if otherwise the overall evidence overwhelmingly points to the accused being criminally liable. However, when such imprecision on one factual element is additionally combined with usage of multiple modes of liability in arrest warrant applications and DCCs, it is more problematic; because it indicates that, despite all efforts, the investigation could not clarify substantial aspects of the criminal responsibility. Certain omissions and misconceptions may have occurred, making it difficult for the OTP to identify the exact mode of liability of the prohibited conduct. Imprecision may also indicate that during its investigation, the OTP faced challenges in identifying and interpreting material facts. Ultimately, imprecision and inconsistency contained in arrest warrant applications and DCCs are indicative that the OTP's alleged mode of liability may suffer from misunderstandings.

In *Prosecutor v. Bemba*, the Prosecution used in its initial and amended DCCs the formulation of the Prosecutor does not exclude "any other applicable mode of liability" beside Article 25.[49] Noting such vagueness and evidence indicating a different liability, namely superior responsibility, Pre-Trial Chamber III adjourned the confirmation of charg-

---

[48] Bemba Appeals Judgment, para. 194, see above note 3.

[49] ICC, Situation in the Central African Republic, *The Prosecutor v. Jean-Pierre Bemba Gombo*, OTP, Document containing the charges, 1 October 2008, ICC-01/05-01/08-136-AnxA, para. 56 ('Bemba OTP DCC') (https://legal-tools.org/doc/94e5fb); ICC, Situation in the Central African Republic, *The Prosecutor v. Jean-Pierre Bemba Gombo*, OTP, Amended Document containing the charges, 17 October 2008, ICC-01/05-01/08-169-Anx3A, para. 57 ('Bemba OTP Amended DCC') (https://legal-tools.org/doc/bb881b).

es hearing and requested the Prosecutor to consider amending the charges.[50]

In *Prosecutor v. Abu Garda*, Pre-Trial Chamber I observed the following imprecisions in usage of language and multiple modes of liability in the DCC:

> While charging Mr Abu Garda with criminal responsibility as a co-perpetrator or as an indirect co-perpetrator, the Prosecution in the DCC *does not exclude any other applicable mode of liability*. The Chamber recalls however that in accordance with article 67(1)(a) of the Statute and rule 121(1) of the Rules, Mr Abu Garda must be informed in detail of the nature, cause and content of the charges brought against him. In addition, Regulation 52(c) of the Regulations of the Court requires the Prosecution to indicate in its DCC the precise form of participation.[51]

Regulation 52(c) expects the DCC shall include a "precise form of participation under articles 25 and 28".

In the situation in Kenya, the OTP's application for a summons to appear alleged against Ruto, Kosgey and Sang the following formulations of criminal responsibility: "the requirements of *direct/indirect* co-perpetration [...] pursuant to Article 25(3)(a) [...] have been met".[52] However, the counts listed in the same application omitted to clarify whether the Prosecution intended to see the three perpetrators as indirect co-perpetrator or direct co-perpetrators, or both. Instead, Ruto, Kosgey and Sang were simply qualified "as co-perpetrators".[53] Having charged the three men in an imprecise manner with principal liability as co-

---

[50] ICC, Situation in the Central African Republic, *The Prosecutor v. Jean-Pierre Bemba Gombo*, Pre-Trial Chamber, Decision Adjourning the Hearing pursuant to Article 61(7)(c)(ii) of the Rome Statute, 3 March 2009, ICC-01/05-01/08-388, paras. 41, 46, 49, p. 19 (letters a)–b)) ('Bemba Pre-Trial Decision Adjourning the Hearing') (https://legal-tools.org/doc/81d7a9).

[51] Abu Garda Pre-Trial Decision on the Confirmation of Charges, para. 158, see above note 43 (emphasis added).

[52] ICC, Situation in the Republic of Kenya, *The Prosecutor v. William Samoei Ruto, Henry Kiprono Kosgey and Joshua Arap Sang*, OTP, Prosecutor's Application Pursuant to Article 58 as to William Samoei Ruto, Henry Kiprono Kosgey and Joshua Arap Sang, 15 December 2010, ICC-01/09-01/11-26-Red2, para. 27 ('Ruto, Kosgey and Sang OTP Article 58 Application') (https://legal-tools.org/doc/c6cf4c).

[53] *Ibid.*, sect. F (counts 1–4).

perpetrators, meaning with liability as a principal, the Prosecution also charged the same men in the alternative with accessory liability pursuant to Article 25(3)(d).[54] Pre-Trial Chamber II noted that:

> In his application, the Prosecutor inconsistently presented different modes of liability. [...] Although the Prosecutor may generally charge in the alternative, he should be consistent throughout his Application about the actual mode(s) of liability [...]. [T]he Chamber is not persuaded it is best practice to make simultaneous findings on modes of liability presented in the alternative. A person cannot be deemed concurrently as a principal and an accessory to the same crime.[55]

12.4.3. DCC Contains Too Many Variants of Criminal Responsibility Including of Principal and Accessory

International Tribunals concur that alternative charging is permissible.[56] Alternative charging means that the Prosecutor is permitted to charge an accused person with more than one mode of responsibility.[57]

---

[54] *Ibid.*, para. 27, sect. F (counts 1–4).

[55] ICC, Situation in the Republic of Kenya, *The Prosecutor v. William Samoei Ruto, Henry Kiprono Kosgey and Joshua Arap Sang*, Pre-Trial Chamber, Decision on the Prosecutor's Application for Summons to Appear for William Samoei Ruto, Henry Kiprono Kosgey and Joshua Arap Sang, 8 March 2011, ICC-01/09-01/11-1, paras. 35–36 ('Ruto, Kosgey and Sang Pre-Trial Decision on the Prosecutor's Application for Summons to Appear') (https://legal-tools.org/doc/6c9fb0).

[56] See ICTY, *Prosecutor v. Duško Tadić*, Trial Chamber, Decision on the Defence Motion on the Form of the Indictment, 14 November 1995, IT-94-1-T, para. 17 (https://legal-tools.org/doc/8d598a); ICTY, *Prosecutor v. Mucić et al.*, Appeals Chamber, Decision on Application for Leave to Appeal by Hazim Delić (Defects in the Form of the Indictment), 6 December 1996, IT-96-21-A, para. 35 (https://legal-tools.org/doc/96e661); International Criminal Tribunal for Rwanda ('ICTR'), *The Prosecutor v. Jean-Paul Akayesu*, Trial Chamber, Judgement, 2 September 1998, ICTR-96-4-T, para. 468 (https://legal-tools.org/doc/b8d7bd); STL, *The Prosecutor v. Ayyash et al.*, Appeals Chamber, Interlocutory Decision on the Applicable Law: Terrorism, Conspiracy, Homicide, Perpetration, Cumulative Charging, 16 February 2011, STL-11-01/I, para. 298 (https://legal-tools.org/doc/ceebc3); ICC, Situation in the Democratic Republic of the Congo, *The Prosecutor v. Bosco Ntaganda*, Pre-Trial Chamber, Decision Pursuant to Article 61(7)(a) and (b) of the Rome Statute on the Charges of the Prosecutor Against Bosco Ntaganda, 9 June 2014, ICC-01/04-02/06-309, para. 100, fn. 421 ('Ntaganda Pre-Trial Decision on the Charges') (https://legal-tools.org/doc/5686c6); ICC, Situation in the Republic of Mali, *The Prosecutor v. Ahmad Al Faqi Al Mahdi*, Pre-Trial Chamber, Decision on the Confirmation of Charges Against Ahmad Al Faqi Al Mahdi, 24 March 2016, ICC-01/12-01/15-84-Red, para. 22 ('Al Mahdi Pre-Trial Decision on the Confirmation of Charges') (https://legal-tools.org/doc/bc8144); ICC, Situ-

12.4.3.1. Charging in the Alternative

In favour of charging in the alternative speaks the scope of criminality occurring in the field of international humanitarian law: to prosecute systematic wrongdoing on a large scale, some DCC's need to list more than one form of criminal liability to capture the *entire* systemic wrong. Cases may span over time periods of more than one, sometimes several years. Hence, Prosecutors appreciate the possibility to charge alternative modes of liability as a safeguard to capture the entire criminal conduct identified during an investigation and thereby to avoid impunity gaps,[58] future delays at trial,[59] and to provide early notice to the Defence.[60] Pre-Trial Chamber I declared it

> appropriate that the charges be confirmed with the various available alternatives, in order for the Trial Chamber to determine whether any of those legal characterisations is established to the applicable standard of proof at trial. [...] confirming all applicable alternative legal characterisations on the basis of the same facts is a desirable approach as it may

---

ation in the Republic of Côte d'Ivoire, *The Prosecutor v. Laurent Gbagbo*, Pre-Trial Chamber, Decision on the Confirmation of Charges Against Laurent Gbagbo, 12 June 2014, ICC-02/11-01/11-656-Red, para. 227 ('Gbagbo Pre-Trial Decision on the Confirmation of Charges') (https://legal-tools.org/doc/5b41bc).

[57] *Ibid.*

[58] ICC, Situation in the Democratic Republic of the Congo, *The Prosecutor v. Thomas Lubanga Dyilo*, Appeals Chamber, Judgment on the appeals of Mr. Lubanga Dyilo and the Prosecutor against the Decision of Trial Chamber I of 14 July 2009 entitled "Decision giving notice to the parties and participants that the legal characterisation of the facts may be subject to change in accordance with Regulation 55(2) of the Regulations of the Court", 8 December 2009, ICC-01/04-01/06-2205, para. 17 (https://legal-tools.org/doc/40d015); ICC, Situation in the Democratic Republic of the Congo, *The Prosecutor v. Germain Katanga*, Appeals Chamber, Judgment on the appeal of Mr. Germain Katanga against the decision of Trial Chamber II of 21 November 2012 entitled "Decision on the implementation of regulation 55 of the Regulations of the Court and severing the charges against the accused persons", 27 March 2013, ICC-01/04-01/07-3363, para. 22 ('Katanga Appeals Judgment on the Implementation of Regulation 55 and Severing the Charges') (https://legal-tools.org/doc/9d87d9).

[59] ICC, Situation in Uganda, *The Prosecutor v. Dominic Ongwen*, Pre-Trial Chamber, Decision on the confirmation of charges against Dominic Ongwen, 23 March 2016, ICC-02/04-01/15-422-Red, para. 35 ('Ongwen Pre-Trial Decision on the Confirmation of Charges') (https://legal-tools.org/doc/74fc6e); Gbagbo Pre-Trial Decision on the Confirmation of Charges, para. 228, see above note 56; Al Mahdi Pre-Trial Decision on the Confirmation of Charges, para. 22, see above note 56.

[60] *Ibid.*

---

reduce future delays at trial, and provides early notice to the defence of the different legal characterisations that may be considered by the trial judges. This more flexible approach is, of course, without prejudice to the possibility that trial judges, following the applicable procedure, consider other alternatives as well.[61]

On the other hand, charging too many modes of liability alternatively in a DCC blurs distinctions and opens the door for a prosecutor to remain vague regarding the ultimate issue of the accused's liability. By charging multiple modes of liability in the alternative, a prosecutor avoids settling early on a specific case theory and remains flexible until all evidence has been presented in court. This appears not fair to the accused person and the defence. Judges when faced with multiple alternative modes of liability, are not obliged to evaluate and enter findings on each and every mode of liability charged in the alternative. Rather, in their judgment, they have discretion to examine only the mode of liability that most accurately describes that conduct of the accused.[62]

12.4.3.2. Principal Versus Accomplice Liability

Article 25(3) distinguishes whether a person *commits* a crime[63] or *contributes* to it.[64] One who commits a crime is liable as a perpetrator and in all other variants as an accessory only.[65] This distinction is not merely terminological. Rather, the Appeals Chamber has explained that

> a person who is found to commit a crime him- or herself bears more blameworthiness than a person who contributes to the crime of another person or persons.[66] […] in circumstances where a plurality of individuals are involved in the

---

[61] Gbagbo Pre-Trial Decision on the Confirmation of Charges, paras. 227–28, see above note 56.

[62] ICTY, *The Prosecutor v. Šainović et al.*, Trial Chamber, Judgement: Volume 1 of 4, 26 February 2009, IT-05-87-T, para. 76 (https://legal-tools.org/doc/9eb7c3); ICC, Situation in the Republic of Côte d'Ivoire, *The Prosecutor v. Laurent Gbagbo and Charles Blé Goudé*, Trial Chamber, Dissenting Opinion Judge Herrera Carbuccia, 16 July 2019, ICC-02/11-01/15-1263-AnxC-Red, para. 485 ('Gbagbo and Blé Goudé Trial Dissenting Opinion Judge Herrera Carbuccia') (https://legal-tools.org/doc/6ak9rf).

[63] ICC Statute, Article 25(3)(a), see above note 1.

[64] *Ibid.*, Articles 25(3)(b)–25(3)(d).

[65] Lubanga Appeals Judgment, para. 462, see above note 40.

[66] *Ibid.*

---

commission of a crime, it becomes necessary to determine on what basis an individual's role is assessed to amount to that of a perpetrator or that of an accessory.[67]

Pre-Trial Chamber III held that

[t]he crimes and the mode of liability correlate to each other. Depending on the mode of participation as set out in articles 25 and 28 of the Statute, the material (objective) elements of the crime are shaped differently. It does have a bearing on the structure of *the crime* whether the person held liable for committing the crime acted as a principal, as an accomplice or as a superior.[68]

This suggests that charging a suspect with principal *and* accomplice liability, and liability as a military or civilian superior has a bearing on the structure of the crime(s) charged. Further, it would allow prosecutors to interpret the same evidence in multiple ways.

That however triggers the question whether this may be incompatible with the right of the accused to get informed, promptly and in detail,[69] of the nature of the criminal responsibility alleged.

In *Prosecutor v. Ruto, Kosgey and Sang*, Pre-Trial Chamber II held that it is

not persuaded that it is best practice to make simultaneous findings on modes of liability presented in the alternative. A person cannot be deemed concurrently as a principal and an accessory to the same crime. Thus, it is the Chamber's view that an initial decision has to be made on the basis of the material provided, as to whether there are reasonable grounds to believe that Ruto, Kosgey and Sang bear criminal responsibility for the crimes against humanity that occurred in the specific locations in the Republic of Kenya [...] either as co-perpetrators, indirect co-perpetrators, or any other form of liability presented or that the Chamber finds appropriate.[70]

---

[67] *Ibid.*, para. 463.

[68] Bemba Pre-Trial Decision Adjourning the Hearing, para. 26, see above note 50.

[69] ICC statute, Article 67(1)(a), see above note 1; Kupreškić *et al.* Trial Judgment, para. 725, see above note 29; International Covenant on Civil and Political Rights, 16 December 1966, Article 14(3) (https://legal-tools.org/doc/2838f3); European Convention on Human Rights, Article 6(3)(a), 4 November 1950 (https://legal-tools.org/doc/8267cb).

[70] Ruto, Kosgey and Sang Pre-Trial Decision on the Prosecutor's Application for Summons to Appear, para. 36, see above note 55.

Thus, if the Prosecutor omits to decide whether to consider a suspect as a principal or an accessory or (military) superior in his DCC, but charges the suspect with multiple alternative modes of liability, Pre-Trial Chamber II sees its role in deciding whether the defendant is deemed to be a principal or an accomplice. This reduces the number of modes of liability the accused has to defend himself against at trial. However, this approach is neither followed by Pre-Trial Chamber I nor adopted consistently by Pre-Trial Chamber II.

In *Prosecutor v. Ntaganda*, the DCC contained seven concurrent modes of liability: three as a principal (direct perpetration, direct co-perpetration and indirect co-perpetration, each pursuant to Article 25(3)(a)), three modes of accessorial liability (ordering and inducing, each pursuant to Article 25(3)(b) and contributing in any other way pursuant to Article 25(3)(d)), and the liability of superior responsibility (acting as military commander pursuant to Article 28(a)).[71] Pre-Trial Chamber II reduced the principal liabilities from five to four (direct participation, indirect co-perpetration, ordering and inducing), but *also* confirmed the accessory liability contributing and, parallel thereto, liability as military commander.[72]

In *Prosecutor v. Al Mahdi*, the Prosecutor charged four modes of liability concurrently in the DCC and qualified the accused as a principal (direct co-perpetration pursuant to Article 25(3)(a)) *and* accessory (further soliciting and inducing pursuant to Article 25(3)(b), aiding and abetting, or otherwise assisting the commission of a crime under Article 25(3)(c), and contributing in any other way to the commission of a crime by a group with a common purpose under Article 25(3)(d)).[73] Pre-Trial Chamber I confirmed all modes of liability advanced by the Prosecution.[74]

---

[71] Ntaganda Pre-Trial Decision on the Charges, paras. 98–99, 101, 136, 145, 153, 158, 164, see above note 56; ICC, Situation in the Democratic Republic of the Congo, *The Prosecutor v. Bosco Ntaganda*, Pre-Trial Chamber, Annex to the Decision Pursuant to Article 61(7)(a) and (b) of the Rome Statute on the Charges of the Prosecutor Against Bosco Ntaganda, 9 June 2014, ICC-01/04-02/06-309-Anx (https://legal-tools.org/doc/f8ba64).

[72] Ntaganda Pre-Trial Decision on the Charges, para. 97, p. 63 (letter b)), see above note 56.

[73] Al Mahdi Pre-Trial Decision on the Confirmation of Charges, paras. 2, 23, see above note 56.

[74] *Ibid.*, para. 23.

12.4.4. Pre-Trial Chamber Invokes Article 61(7)(c) to Adjourn the Confirmation Hearing

Article 61(7)(c) demonstrates the power of the Pre-Trial Chamber. It can order the Prosecution to consider providing further evidence and conducting further investigation and/or amending a charge contained in the DCC. The Pre-Trial Chamber can then confirm the amended charge, if it so chooses. Usage of this provision usually demonstrates that the Pre-Trial Chamber spotted during the confirmation hearing a deficiency in the OTP's investigation and/or in the draft DCC. The invocation of this provision further demonstrates that the Pre-Trial Chamber assesses the deficiency as not incurable and, by adjourning, the judges provide the Prosecution time and opportunity to correct its omission(s) resulting from the investigation and/or initial pleading.

For example, in *Prosecutor v. Gbagbo*, the majority of Pre-Trial Chamber I identified six issues and asked the Prosecution "to consider providing, to the extent possible, further evidence or conduct further investigation".[75] The first three issues identified by Pre-Trial Camber I related to modes of liability.

In *Prosecutor v. Bemba*, the initial and amended DCC contained indirect liability under Article 25(3)(a), adding that other modes of liability would not be excluded.[76] Pre-Trial Chamber III adjourned the ongoing confirmation hearing, requesting the OTP to submit and amended DCC which also included a possible liability under Article 28.[77]

12.4.5. Use of Regulation 55

Reliance on Regulation 55 to re-characterise the initially proposed mode of liability indicates that the OTP may have – during its investigation and in its DCC (as confirmed by the Pre-Trial Chamber after a cursory confirmation of charges hearing) – interpreted the facts relevant to criminal responsibility differently than the Trial Chamber, which hears at trial the

---

[75] ICC, Situation in the Republic of Côte d'Ivoire, *The Prosecutor v. Laurent Gbagbo*, Pre-Trial Chamber, Decision adjourning the hearing on the confirmation of charges pursuant to Article 61(7)(c)(i) of the Rome Statute, 3 June 2013, ICC-02/11-01/11-432, para. 44 ('Gbagbo Pre-Trial Decision Adjourning the Hearing') (https://legal-tools.org/doc/2682d8).

[76] Bemba OTP DCC, para. 56, see above note 49; Bemba OTP Amended DCC, para. 57, see above note 49.

[77] Bemba Pre-Trial Decision Adjourning the Hearing, paras. 46, 48–49, see above note 50.

entire volume of evidence. In six cases, parties to the proceedings requested usage of or the Trial Chamber invoked Regulation 55 to notify the parties of a possible modification of criminal responsibility of seven accused persons.[78]

For example, in *Prosecutor v. Muthaura and Kenyatta*, the Prosecutor alleged criminal liability as principal based on Article 25(3)(a) which the Pre-Trial Chamber confirmed.[79] Before trial, the OTP attempted to move the Trial Chamber V to re-characterise the principal liability to now also include accessory liabilities under Article 25(3)(b), 25(3)(c) and 25(3)(d).[80] Similarly, in *Prosecutor v. Ruto and Sang*, the OTP's DCC contained mainly principal liability, meaning allegations of indirect co-perpetration pursuant to Article 25(3)(a).[81] Invoking Regulation 55, the Trial Chamber V(A) expanded this notion to also include accessory liability under Article 25(3)(b), 25(3)(c) and 25(3)(d) for Ruto.[82]

In *Prosecutor v. Gbabgo*, the Prosecutor had charged the former President of Ivory Coast with five modes of liability: principal liability (indirect co-perpetration under Article 25(3)(a)), two accessory liability

---

[78] *Prosecutor v. Bemba, Prosecutor v. Gbagbo, Prosecutor v. Katanga, Prosecutor v. Kenyatta, Prosecutor v. Muthaura, Prosecutor v. Ntaganda* and *Prosecutor v. Ruto*.

[79] ICC, Situation in the Republic of Kenya, *The Prosecutor v. Francis Kirimi Muthaura, Uhuru Muigai Kenyatta and Mohammed Hussein Ali*, Pre-Trial Chamber, Decision on the Confirmation of Charges Pursuant to Article 61(7)(a) and (b) of the Rome Statute, 23 January 2012, ICC-01/09-02/11-382-Red, paras. 398–419 ('Muthaura, Kenyatta and Ali Pre-Trial Decision on the Confirmation of Charges') (https://legal-tools.org/doc/4972c0).

[80] ICC, Situation in the Republic of Kenya, *The Prosecutor v. Francis Kirimi Muthaura and Uhuru Muigai Kenyatta*, OTP, Prosecution's Submissions on the law of indirect co-perpetration under Article 25(3)(a) of the Statute and application for notice to be given under Regulation 55(2) with respect to the accused's individual criminal responsibility, 3 July 2012, ICC-01/09-02/11-444, para. 49 ('Muthaura and Kenyatta Prosecution's Submissions on the Law of Indirect Co-perpetration and Application for Notice') (https://legal-tools.org/doc/19dd29).

[81] ICC, Situation in the Republic of Kenya, *The Prosecutor v. William Samoei Ruto, Henry Kiprono Kosgey and Joshua Arap Sang*, Pre-Trial Chamber, Decision on the Confirmation of Charges Pursuant to Article 61(7)(a) and (b) of the Rome Statute, 23 January 2012, ICC-01/09-01/11-373, paras. 283, 285 ('Ruto, Kosgey and Sang Pre-Trial Decision on the Confirmation of Charges') (https://legal-tools.org/doc/96c3c2).

[82] ICC, Situation in the Republic of Kenya, *The Prosecutor v. William Samoei Ruto and Joshua Arap Sang*, Trial Chamber, Decision on Applications for Notice of Possibility of Variation of Legal Characterisation, 12 December 2013, ICC-01/09-01/11-1122, p. 20 ('Ruto and Sang Trial Decision on Applications for Notice') (https://legal-tools.org/doc/49ec33).

modes under Article 25(3)(b) and 25(3)(d), and two modes of superior and command responsibility under Article 28(a) and 28(b).[83] Pre-Trial Chamber I only confirmed liabilities based on Article 25(3) and otherwise dismissed any liability of superior and command responsibility (pursuant to Article 28(a) and 28(b)).[84] Based on the OTP's suggestion, Trial Chamber I re-characterised the alleged criminal responsibility to also include superior and command responsibility pursuant to Article 28(a) and 28(b) of the ICC Statute.[85]

12.5. Review of All Investigations Which Resulted in Decisions After a Confirmation Hearing

This section reviews the performance and consistency of the OTP in pleading and defending the modes of liability following an investigation which resulted in suspects appearing in front of a Pre-Trial Chamber at confirmation of charges hearings pursuant to Article 61. The presentation of 17 cases follows for each case a chronological approach, listing the mode(s) of liability the OTP advanced at the end of its investigation when it filed its application for an arrest warrant or summons to appear, comparing these with the DCC and, if applicable, amended DCC. Further, the rulings of the Pre-Trial Chambers on the DCC and any Trial Chamber litigation regarding Regulation 55 is observed. If a Chamber issued a NCTA-decision and/or judgment, the mode(s) of liability confirmed or dismissed in these decisions are compared with the OTP's initial positions on modes of liability.

The presentation commences with cases resulting at least in Trial Chamber judgments. Then cases are presented which ended after a trial formally opened, meaning at least after the Prosecution had presented its

---

[83] ICC, Situation in the Republic of Côte d'Ivoire, *The Prosecutor v. Laurent Gbagbo*, OTP, Version publique expurgée du Document amendé de notification des charges du 13 janvier 2014, ICC-02/11-01/11-Conf-Anx2-Corr2, notifié le 20 janvier 2014, 3 February 2014, ICC-02/11-01/11-592-Anx2-Corr2-Red, paras. 211, 232–35 ('Gbagbo OTP Amended DCC') (https://legal-tools.org/doc/5c5f60).

[84] Gbagbo Pre-Trial Decision on the Confirmation of Charges, paras. 230, 241, 244, 251, 259, 265, see above note 56.

[85] ICC, Situation in the Republic of Côte d'Ivoire, *The Prosecutor v. Laurent Gbagbo and Charles Blé Goudé*, Trial Chamber, Decision giving notice pursuant to Regulation 55(2) of the Regulations of the Court, 19 August 2015, ICC-02/11-01/15-185, para. 15.i), p. 11 ('Gbagbo and Blé Goudé Trial Decision Giving Notice Pursuant to Regulation 55(2)') (https://legal-tools.org/doc/984739).

case. Then cases are presented which ended after confirmation had occurred and before the trial opened due to the OTP withdrawing its case. Finally, cases are presented which ended at the Pre-Trial stage because the Pre-Trial Chamber could not confirm any charges.

The focus of the presentation lies on detecting whether the Prosecution managed to defend the mode(s) of liability it had identified during and immediately after its investigation.

12.5.1. Cases Ending with a Judgment

12.5.1.1. Convictions

In three cases, the Prosecutor succeeded in having the initially advanced modes of liability confirmed by the Trial Chamber by way of judgment convicting the accused.

12.5.1.1.1. Lubanga, Co-Perpetrator

Based on the OTP's request, Pre-Trial Chamber I issued an arrest warrant against Lubanga for (indirect) co-perpetration (Article 25(3)(a)).[86] Consistently the Prosecution's DCC charged Lubanga with indirect co-perpetration.[87] Pre-Trial Chamber I confirmed co-perpetration liability under Article 25(3)(a).[88] Finally, Trial Chamber I convicted Lubanga as co-perpetrator.[89] The Appeals Chamber upheld this conviction, rejecting Lubanga's appeal against co-perpetration.[90]

12.5.1.1.2. Al Mahdi

Following its investigation, the Prosecution requested an arrest warrant against Al Mahdi relying on three different modes of liability, namely co-perpetration (Article 25(3)(a)), aiding and abetting or otherwise assisting

---

[86] ICC, Situation in the Democratic Republic of the Congo, *The Prosecutor v. Thomas Lubanga Dyilo*, Pre-Trial Chamber, Decision on the Prosecutor's Application for a warrant of arrest, Article 58, 10 February 2006, ICC-01/04-01/06-1-Corr-Red, para. 96 (https://legal-tools.org/doc/af6679).

[87] ICC, Situation in the Democratic Republic of the Congo, *The Prosecutor v. Thomas Lubanga Dyilo*, OTP, Document Containing the Charges, Article 61(3)(a), 28 August 2006, ICC-01/04-01/06-356-Anx2, para. 20, 22, p. 24 (https://legal-tools.org/doc/e2fa01).

[88] ICC, Situation in the Democratic Republic of the Congo, *The Prosecutor v. Thomas Lubanga Dyilo*, Pre-Trial Chamber, Decision on the confirmation of charges, 29 January 2007, ICC-01/04-01/06-803-tEN, para. 410, p. 156 (https://legal-tools.org/doc/b7ac4f).

[89] Lubanga Trial Judgment, paras. 1351–52, 1354, 1358, see above note 21.

[90] Lubanga Appeals Judgment, paras. 473, 499, see above note 40.

(Article 25(3)(c)), and contributing in any other way (Article 25(3)(d)).[91] The Pre-Trial Chamber confirmed these three modes.[92]

The Prosecution then charged Al Mahdi with four modes of liability, including the new mode 'soliciting or inducing' (Article 25(3)(b)),[93] and the judges confirmed the DCC accordingly.[94] Particularly, the Prosecution charged him with being perpetrator and co-perpetrator, both pursuant to Article 25(3)(a).[95] Following the accused's admission of guilt, the Trial Chamber convicted him as direct co-perpetrator pursuant to Article 25(3)(a).[96] Regarding the other modes of liability, Trial Chamber VIII referring to the Appeals Chamber, noted that

> the Statute differentiates between principal (Article 25(3)(a)) and accessorial (Article 25(3)(b) to (d)) liability, with principals bearing more blameworthiness 'generally speaking and all other things being equal'. In accordance with this general rule, given that the Chamber has decided that all the elements of co-perpetration are met, there is no need to make any further findings on the accessorial liability alternatives.[97]

12.5.1.1.3. Katanga and Ngudjolo Chui

The cases against Katanga and Ngudjolo Chui resulted in a twofold outcome. Trial Chamber II acquitted Ngudjolo Chui. Also, the OTP failed to

---

[91] ICC, Situation in the Republic of Mali, *The Prosecutor v. Ahmad Al Faqi Al Mahdi*, OTP, Requête urgente du Bureau du Procureur en vue de la délivrance d'un mandat d'arrêt à l'encontre d'Ahmad Al Faqi Al Mahdi, 7 September 2015, ICC-01/12-31-US-Exp; ICC, Situation in the Republic of Mali, *The Prosecutor v. Ahmad Al Faqi Al Mahdi*, Pre-Trial Chamber, Mandat d'arrêt à l'encontre d'Ahmad AL FAQI AL MAHDI (Warrant of Arrest for Ahmad Al Faqi Al Mahdi), 18 September 2015, ICC-01/12-01/15-1-Red, pp. 3, 6 (para. 9), 8 (https://legal-tools.org/doc/c5ea5e).

[92] *Ibid.*

[93] ICC, Situation in the Republic of Mali, *The Prosecutor v. Ahmad Al Faqi Al Mahdi*, OTP, Chef d'accusation retenu par l'Accusation contre Ahmad AL FAQI AL MAHDI (Charge brought by the Prosecution against Ahmad Al Faqi Al Mahdi), 17 December 2015, ICC-01/12-01/15-62, paras. 23–24 (https://legal-tools.org/doc/a83616).

[94] Al Mahdi Pre-Trial Decision on the Confirmation of Charges, paras. 2, 23–24, pp. 22 (paras. 2–3), 26 (para. 23), 27 (para. 24), see above note 56.

[95] *Ibid.*, para. 23.

[96] ICC, Situation in the Republic of Mali, *The Prosecutor v. Ahmad Al Faqi Al Mahdi*, Trial Chamber, Judgment and Sentence, 27 September 2016, ICC-01/12-01/15-171, paras. 55–56, 59, 63 (https://legal-tools.org/doc/042397).

[97] *Ibid.*, para. 58.

secure a conviction of Katanga as co-perpetrator which the OTP had initially advanced. Instead, the judges re-characterised his liability as principal down towards accessory liability and convicted Katanga on this basis.

The OTP had initially applied for arrest warrants against Katanga and Ngudjolo Chui qualifying both as principals (co-perpetration, Article 25(3)(a)) and, in the alternative, as accessories (ordering, Article 25(3)(b)), and the Pre-Trial Chamber I issued the warrants based on both alternative modes.[98]

The OTP then submitted a DCC for both modes of liability and the Pre-Trial Chamber partially unanimously and partially by majority confirmed the principal liability as co-perpetrator through other persons.[99] Judge Ušacka dissented from the confirmation of counts six to nine, arguing that the evidence presented by the Prosecution was insufficient to link the suspects to the commission of the crimes and further contesting Katanga's knowledge of rape in one instance.[100] The dissenting judge would have adjourned the confirmation hearing on these charges pursuant to Article 61(7)(c)(i).[101]

Following the confirmation of the DCC and the Prosecution's Pre-Trial Brief, both advancing co-perpetration liability,[102] the trial against

---

[98]   ICC, Situation in the Democratic Republic of the Congo, *The Prosecutor v. Germain Katanga and Mathieu Ngudjolo Chui*, OTP, Request for arrest warrant, 25 June 2007, ICC-01/04-350-US-Exp; ICC, Situation in the Democratic Republic of the Congo, *The Prosecutor v. Germain Katanga*, Pre-Trial Chamber, Warrant of Arrest for Germain Katanga, 2 July 2007, ICC-01/04-01/07-1-tENG, pp. 5–6 (https://legal-tools.org/doc/4a8301); ICC, Situation in the Democratic Republic of the Congo, *The Prosecutor v. Mathieu Ngudjolo Chui*, Pre-Trial Chamber, Warrant of Arrest for Mathieu Ngudjolo Chui, 6 July 2007, ICC-01/04-01/07-260-tENG, p. 6 (https://legal-tools.org/doc/d03d7a).

[99]   ICC, Situation in the Democratic Republic of the Congo, *The Prosecutor v. Germain Katanga and Mathieu Ngudjolo Chui*, Pre-Trial Chamber, Decision on the confirmation of charges, 30 September 2008, ICC-01/04-01/07-717, paras. 574–76, pp. 210–12 (https://legal-tools.org/doc/67a9ec).

[100]   Partly Dissenting Opinion of Judge Anita Ušacka, in *ibid.*, paras. 23, 27.

[101]   *Ibid.*, paras. 29, 36.

[102]   ICC, Situation in the Democratic Republic of the Congo, *The Prosecutor v. Germain Katanga and Mathieu Ngudjolo Chui*, OTP, Prosecution's Pre-Trial Brief on the Interpretation of Article 25(3)(a), 19 October 2009, ICC-01/04-01/07-1541 (https://legal-tools.org/doc/76ec0a); ICC, Situation in the Democratic Republic of the Congo, *The Prosecutor v. Germain Katanga and Mathieu Ngudjolo Chui*, OTP, Document Containing the Charges as Confirmed by the Pre-Trial Chamber in accordance with the "Décision relative au dépôt d'un résumé des charges par le Procureur", 28 October 2009, ICC-01/04-01/07-1568, para. 60 (https://legal-tools.org/doc/47197f).

Katanga and Ngudjolo Chui opened in late November 2009. Both Katanga and Ngudjolo Chui testified and after the presentation of evidence as well as closing statements, Trial Chamber II retreated into deliberations in May 2012. About half a year into the deliberations, the Trial Chamber II unanimously issued a decision severing the case of Ngudjolo Chui.[103] Trial Chamber II acquitted Ngudjolo Chui because the judges could not determine that he was the leader of the Lendu combatants participating in the attack on Bogoro and his role "in no way allows the Chamber to accept or even contemplate the notion of indirect co-perpetration [...] regardless of how article 25(3)(a) of the Statute is construed".[104]

By contrast, in relation to Katanga, the majority of Trial Chamber II contemplated accessory liability, thereby re-characterising according to Regulation 55 the mode of responsibility to 'contributing in another way to the commission of crimes' pursuant to Article 25(3)(d)(ii).[105] Relying on case law of the European Court of Human Rights, the majority of Trial Chamber II argued that re-characterisation would be mostly decided at the deliberation stage, and further noted that "deliberations on the Accused's initial mode of liability under Article 25(3)(a) is already well under way".[106] Judge Van den Wyngaert dissented, arguing that the majority's approach would go beyond the facts and circumstances described in the DCC, and would be otherwise unequal.[107]

The Appeals Chamber observed that at the time of invocation of Regulation 55, the trial was still ongoing, meaning at the deliberations stage with no judgment having been rendered under Article 74.[108] Regard-

---

[103] Katanga and Ngudjolo Chui Trial Decision on the Implementation of Regulation 55 and Severing the Charges, paras. 59, 62, p. 30, see above note 9.

[104] Ngudjolo Chui Trial Judgment, para. 110, see above note 21.

[105] Katanga and Ngudjolo Chui Trial Decision on the Implementation of Regulation 55 and Severing the Charges, para. 24–34, p. 29, see above note 9. Subsequently, the OTP submitted the ICC, Situation in the Democratic Republic of the Congo, *The Prosecutor v. Germain Katanga*, OTP, Prosecution's observations on Article 25(3)(d), 8 April 2013, ICC-01/04-01/07-3367 (https://legal-tools.org/doc/e903e4).

[106] Katanga and Ngudjolo Chui Trial Decision on the Implementation of Regulation 55 and Severing the Charges, paras. 16, 18–19, see above note 9.

[107] Dissenting Opinion of Judge Christine Van den Wyngaert, in *ibid*., pp. 11, 21 (https://legal-tools.org/doc/b0367a).

[108] Katanga Appeals Judgment on the Implementation of Regulation 55 and Severing the Charges, paras. 17, 23, see above note 58; Dissenting Opinion of Judge Cuno Tarfusser, in

ing the Defence's ground of appeal that the contemplated change in legal characterisation of the facts would exceed the facts and circumstances described in the charges, the majority of the Appeals Chamber observed that

> [a]ny change from, for example, being alleged to be a principal to being alleged to have in fact been an accessory will always necessarily involve a change in the characterisation of the role. Were such a change not be permissible, it would defeat the purpose of regulation 55 [...]. The Trial Chamber would be constrained exclusively to using the precise characterisations established by the Pre-Trial Chamber at a much earlier stage of the proceedings and with a necessarily more restricted view of the case as a whole.[109]

Judge Tarfusser argued in his dissent that Regulation 55 should only apply to a shift from liability in Article 25 to Article 28, and *vice versa*.[110] He further argued that any "possible legal re-characterisation must be as specific and precise as feasible as to both legal and factual boundaries" and failing that in the present case "it is not clear what meaningful submissions could now be made by Mr. Katanga".[111]

Following the Appeals Chamber's majority upholding the invocation of Regulation 55, the Trial Chamber found that the Prosecution has not established that Katanga committed the crimes as a co-perpetrator, and modified the legal characterisation from indirect co-perpetration to Katanga contributing in any other way to the commission of a crime by a group of persons acting with a common purpose pursuant to Article 23(3)(d), and convicted the accused accordingly.[112]

---

ibid., para. 2 ('Tarfusser Dissenting Opinion in Katanga Appeals Judgment on the Implementation of Regulation 55 and Severing the Charges').

[109] Katanga Appeals Judgment on the Implementation of Regulation 55 and Severing the Charges, para. 57, see above note 58.

[110] Tarfusser Dissenting Opinion in Katanga Appeals Judgment on the Implementation of Regulation 55 and Severing the Charges, sect. II.B., see above note 58.

[111] *Ibid.*, para. 25.

[112] ICC, Situation in the Democratic Republic of the Congo, *The Prosecutor v. Germain Katanga*, Trial Chamber, Judgment pursuant to Article 74, 7 March 2014, ICC-01/04-01/07-3436-tENG, paras. 1383–421, 1596–619, pp. 658–59, annexes (https://legal-tools.org/doc/f74b4f).

12.5.1.1.4. Ntaganda

While two arrest warrant applications only contained one mode of liability, the Prosecution charged Ntaganda in the DCC with at least four different modes of liability, including under Article 25(3)(a). Based on this provision, the Trial Chamber convicted Ntaganda for several modes of liability (direct perpetration, direct and indirect co-perpetration) and did not engage in further findings based on the other modes of liability charged.

In January 2006, the Prosecution requested issuance of an arrest warrant against Ntaganda which Pre-Trial Chamber I issued based on Article 25(3)(a) liability.[113] In May 2012, the Prosecution using the phrase "without excluding any other applicable mode of liability" again, qualified Ntaganda as co-perpetrator, requesting an arrest warrant which Pre-Trial Chamber II issued, considering him as indirect co-perpetrator.[114] The DCC and its updated version both contained this same mode of liability in the variants direct perpetrator, direct and indirect co-perpetrator.[115] Further, the Prosecution added three alternative liabilities, namely ordering and inducting (Article 25(3)(b)), contributing to commission of crimes by a group of persons acting with a common purpose (Article 25(3)(d)) and command responsibility (Article 28(a)).[116] Pre-Trial Chamber II found substantial grounds that Ntaganda pursuant to Article 25(3)(a) acted as

---

[113] ICC, Situation in the Democratic Republic of the Congo, *The Prosecutor v. Bosco Ntaganda*, Pre-Trial Chamber, Warrant of Arrest, 22 August 2006, ICC-01/04-02/06-2-tENG, pp. 2, 4 (https://legal-tools.org/doc/e73e38); ICC, Situation in the Democratic Republic of the Congo, *The Prosecutor v. Bosco Ntaganda*, Pre-Trial Chamber, Warrant of Arrest, 7 March 2007, ICC-01/04-02/06-2-Corr-tENG-Red, p. 4 (https://legal-tools.org/doc/2547da).

[114] ICC, Situation in the Democratic Republic of the Congo, *The Prosecutor v. Bosco Ntaganda*, Pre-Trial Chamber, Decision on the Prosecutor's Application under Article 58, 13 July 2012, ICC-01/04-02/06-36-Red, paras. 5, 62, 66, 68, 70, 72–73, 75, 78, 82, 83, pp. 9, 20 (para. 44), 21, 36 (https://legal-tools.org/doc/18c310).

[115] ICC, Situation in the Democratic Republic of the Congo, *The Prosecutor v. Bosco Ntaganda*, OTP, Prosecution request for notice to be given of a possible re-characterisation pursuant to regulation 55(2), 9 March 2015, ICC-01/04-02/06-501, para. 3 ('Ntaganda OTP Request for Notice') (https://legal-tools.org/doc/9032ca).

[116] ICC, Situation in the Democratic Republic of the Congo, *The Prosecutor v. Bosco Ntaganda*, OTP, Document Containing the Charges, 10 January 2014, ICC-01/04-02/06-203-AnxA, paras. 111, 133, 147, pp. 36–49, 56–60 (https://legal-tools.org/doc/9aa3d9); ICC, Situation in the Democratic Republic of the Congo, *The Prosecutor v. Bosco Ntaganda*, OTP, Updated Document Containing the Charges, 14 November 2014, ICC-01/04-02/06-402-AnxA, paras. 111, 133, 147 and pp. 60–65 (https://legal-tools.org/doc/c1913a).

direct perpetrator [117] and indirect co-perpetrator, pursuant to Article 25(3)(b) ordered and induced, pursuant to Article 25(3)(d) contributed to the commission of crimes by a group acting with common purpose and pursuant to Article 28(a) acted as a military commander and thus confirmed the updated DCC.[118]

Trial Chamber VI ordered the Prosecution to produce an updated version which reflected the confirmation decision.[119] Before the trial began, the Prosecution suggested the Trial Chamber may reclassify the charges to add *direct* co-perpetration under Article 25(3)(a) "for all counts".[120] The Trial Chamber did not react.

The Trial Chamber convicted Ntaganda under Article 25(3)(a) as direct perpetrator,[121] as indirect perpetrator and as indirect co-perpetrator (Article 25(3)(a)).[122] The Chamber observed:

> a person's conduct may be capable of satisfying elements of one or more modes of liability [and] does not find it appropriate or necessary, having found Mr Ntaganda's principal liability to have been established for each of the counts charge[d], to reach any further finding on the remaining liability alternatives.[123]

Ntaganda issued a notice of appeal, challenging the Trial Chamber findings on indirect co-perpetration as flawed and further elaborated his

---

[117] The judges confirmed the proposed mode direct perpetration for counts 1–3, 10–11 and 15–17, but *not* in relation to count 12. Ntaganda OTP Request for Notice, text accompanying fn. 7, see above note 115.

[118] Ntaganda Pre-Trial Decision on the Charges, para. 97, see above note 56.

[119] ICC, Situation in the Democratic Republic of the Congo, *The Prosecutor v. Bosco Ntaganda*, Trial Chamber, Order instructing the Prosecution to prepare an updated document containing the charges, 30 October 2014, ICC-01/04-02/06-390, para. 7 (https://legal-tools.org/doc/550454).

[120] Ntaganda OTP Request for Notice, para. 1, see above note 115.

[121] For counts 1, 2 and 10, see ICC, Situation in the Democratic Republic of the Congo, *The Prosecutor v. Bosco Ntaganda*, Trial Chamber, Judgment, 8 July 2019, ICC-01/04-02/06-2359, pp. 535, 537 (https://legal-tools.org/doc/80578a).

[122] *Ibid.*, para. 11, pp. 535–38.

[123] *Ibid.*, para. 1200.

---

argument in grounds 13 to 15 of his Appeal.[124] At the time of writing, the Appeals Chamber had not issued its judgment yet.

12.5.1.2. Acquittals

The acquittal of Ngudjolo Chui was covered in the previous section already. Further, the Bemba case demonstrates flaws in the Prosecution case: the evidence generated during the investigation had led the OTP to charge the suspect with principal liability, as co-perpetrator pursuant to Article 25(3)(a). This was the liability with which the Prosecution categorised Bemba in its application for an arrest warrant and the DCC.[125] The Pre-Trial Chamber then adjourned the confirmation proceedings, ordering the Prosecution to consider superior responsibility under Article 28. The Prosecution complied and the Trial Chamber convicted under this mode in the trial judgment. This conviction did not stand on appeal where the majority of the Appeals Chamber reversed it and acquitted Bemba.

Following the Prosecution's request, Pre-Trial Chamber III confirmed the arrest warrant alleging indirect co-perpetration of Bemba "jointly with another person or through other persons under article 25(3)".[126] The Prosecution inserted this same liability in its initial and amended DCC,[127] adding that the Prosecutor does not exclude "any other

---

[124] ICC, Situation in the Democratic Republic of the Congo, *The Prosecutor v. Bosco Ntaganda*, Defence, Mr. Ntaganda's Notice of Appeal against the Judgment pursuant to Article 74 of the Statute, ICC-01/04-02/06-2359, 9 September 2019, ICC-01/04-02/06-2396, ground 13 (https://legal-tools.org/doc/a7d68d). In essence, it is alleged that Ntaganda was held liable on the basis of a common plan for which he was not charged and for which no direct evidence would exist (*ibid.*, p. 14). Otherwise, the Defence contests certain elements of the *mens rea* of Ntaganda (*ibid.*, grounds 14–15).

[125] ICC, Situation in the Central African Republic, *The Prosecutor v. Jean-Pierre Bemba Gombo*, Pre-Trial Chamber, Warrant of Arrest for Jean-Pierre Bemba Gombo, 23 May 2008, ICC-01/05-01/08-1-tENG-Corr, para. 21 ('Warrant of Arrest for Bemba') (https://legal-tools.org/doc/fb0728); ICC, Situation in the Central African Republic, *The Prosecutor v. Jean-Pierre Bemba Gombo*, OTP, Application for Warrant of Arrest under Article 58, 9 May 2008, ICC-01/05-01/08-26-Red (https://legal-tools.org/doc/a57940).

[126] Warrant of Arrest for Bemba, paras. 4, 21, see above note 125.

[127] Bemba OTP DCC, para. 56, see above note 49; Bemba OTP Amended DCC, para. 57, see above note 49; ICC, Situation in the Central African Republic, *The Prosecutor v. Jean-Pierre Bemba Gombo*, OTP, Prosecution's Written Submission Regarding the Confirmation Hearing Held on 12–15 January 2009, 26 January 2009, ICC-01/05-01/08-377, para. 5 (https://legal-tools.org/doc/7f299d).

applicable mode of liability" beside Article 25(3)(a).[128] During the confirmation hearing, Pre-Trial Chamber III observed the parties and participants had referred implicitly or explicitly to Article 28 and gained the impression "that the legal characterisation of the facts of the case may amount to a different mode of liability under article 28 of the Statute".[129] Adjourning the confirmation hearing, the judges requested the OTP to submit an amended DCC "containing the charges addressing article 28 of the Statute as a possible mode of criminal liability".[130]

After the resumption of the confirmation hearing, Pre-Trial Chamber III dismissed the liability as co-perpetrator pursuant to Article 25(3)(a), Article 28(b) and partially confirmed his liability for superior responsibility pursuant to Article 28(a).[131] Specifically, the Pre-Trial Chamber concluded that substantial grounds existed that Bemba acted with *dolus directus 2*, meaning the evidence clearly indicated that Bemba was 'aware' of the occurrence of certain crimes.[132] The dismissal of principal liability as co-perpetrator combined with confirmation of charges of command responsibility meant that the Prosecution now had to argue its case at trial with a new and rather complex mode of liability. The Pre-Trial judges' decision set aside Article 25(3)(a) and the Prosecution's initial assessment following its own investigation.

Five weeks after the Defence had opened its case, Trial Chamber III gave notice pursuant to Regulation 55: though command responsibility under Article 28(a)(i) was still the only mode of liability envisaged, the judges hinted they may re-characterise the *mens rea* of 'awareness' to the alternate form of "owing to the circumstances at the time should have known".[133] In its trial judgment, the Chamber found that Bemba 'knew'

---

[128] Bemba OTP DCC, para. 56, see above note 49; Bemba OTP Amended DCC, para. 57, see above note 49; Bemba Pre-Trial Decision Adjourning the Hearing, para. 4, see above note 50.

[129] *Ibid.*, paras. 46, 48.

[130] *Ibid.*, para. 49.

[131] ICC, Situation in the Central African Republic, *The Prosecutor v. Jean-Pierre Bemba Gombo*, Pre-Trial Chamber, Decision Pursuant to Article 61(7)(a) and (b) of the Rome Statute and the Charges of the Prosecutor Against Jean-Pierre Bemba Gombo, 15 June 2009, ICC-01/05-01/08-424, para. 344, pp. 184 (letters b)–d)), 185 (letter d)) (https://legal-tools.org/doc/07965c).

[132] *Ibid.*, paras. 478, 485–89.

[133] ICC, Situation in the Central African Republic, *The Prosecutor v. Jean-Pierre Bemba Gombo*, Trial Chamber, Decision giving notice to the parties and participants that the legal

forces under his command were committing or about to commit crimes[134] and argued it was therefore unnecessary to consider that re-characterisation of the charges pursuant to Regulation 55 to include the 'should have known' mental element is warranted.[135] Accordingly, Trial Chamber III convicted Bemba under Article 28(a) in the awareness variant.[136] However, the majority of the Appeals Chamber held that the third element of command responsibility, namely that Bemba failed to take reasonable measures, was not properly established and reversed Bemba's conviction.[137] Addressing the Prosecution, the Appeals Chamber emphasised it being axiomatic that an accused person be informed promptly and in detail of the nature, cause and content of a charge, meaning prior to the start of trial. The judges emphasised that Bemba had suffered prejudice as the OTP's second DCC did not specifically identify the redeployment of troops as a necessary and reasonable measure which Bemba should have taken.[138] The Presiding Judge pointed out that Pre-Trial Chambers face challenges because the "Prosecution was not fully prepared when it initiated confirmation proceedings".[139]

12.5.1.3. Cases Awaiting Judgment

Responding to the OTP's application, the Pre-Trial Chamber issued in 2005 an arrest warrant against Ongwen for ordering (Article 25(3)(b)) certain crimes.[140] About 10 years later, the OTP submitted its DCC, charging Ongwen with 70 counts, again referring to the liability of ordering;

---

characterisation of the facts may be subject to change in accordance with Regulation 55(2) of the Regulations of the Court, 21 September 2012, ICC-01/05-01/08-2324, para. 5 (https://legal-tools.org/doc/248406).

[134] ICC, Situation in the Central African Republic, *The Prosecutor v. Jean-Pierre Bemba Gombo*, Trial Chamber, Judgment pursuant to Article 74 of the Statute, 21 March 2016, ICC-01/05-01/08-3343, para. 717 (https://legal-tools.org/doc/edb0cf).

[135] *Ibid.*, paras. 196, 718.

[136] *Ibid.*, para. 752.

[137] Bemba Appeals Judgment, para. 194, see above note 3.

[138] *Ibid.*, paras. 187–88.

[139] ICC, Situation in the Central African Republic, *The Prosecutor v. Jean-Pierre Bemba Gombo*, Appeals Chamber, Separate Opinion Judge Christine Van den Wyngaert and Judge Howard Morrison, 8 June 2018, ICC-01/05-01/08-3636-Anx2, para. 28 (https://legal-tools.org/doc/c13ef4).

[140] ICC, Situation in Uganda, *The Prosecutor v. Dominic Ongwen*, Pre-Trial Chamber, Warrant of Arrest for Dominic Ongwen, 8 July 2005, ICC-02/04-01/15-6, para. 30, pp. 9–10 (https://legal-tools.org/doc/8bf236).

alternatively, the OTP charged Ongwen as indirect perpetrator and indirect co-perpetrator (Article 25(3)(a)), as in any other way contributing to the commission of a crime by a group of persons acting with a common purpose (Article 25(3)(d)) and for command responsibility (Article 28(a)).[141] In its pre-confirmation brief, the Prosecution stated:

> When multiple legal characterisations of the same facts are established by the evidence, it is appropriate that the charges be confirmed with all of the various modes of liability available, in order for the Trial Chamber to determine whether any of those legal characterisations is established to the applicable standard of proof at trial.[142]

Pre-Trial Chamber II found substantial grounds to believe that Dominic Ongwen committed certain crimes jointly with others and through others (Article 25(3)(a)); alternatively, it qualified Ongwen's contribution to certain crimes may be legally qualified under Articles 25(3)(b), 25(3)(d)(i) and 25(3)(d)(ii).[143] Alternatively, the judges confirmed Ongwen's liability under command responsibility (Article 28(a)).[144]

However, Judge Perrin de Brichambaut criticised that, apart from counts 50 to 61, in its reasoning, Pre-Trial Chamber II only referred to a small amount of evidence in support of Ongwen's five to six modes of liability regarding attacks on certain camps and to no evidence regarding the attack on Pajule camp.[145] The judge wrote that as

> regards the other modes of liability, the decision fails to demonstrate how each constituent element of the mode of liability charged can be proved on the available evidence. For the mode of liability under article 28(a) of the Statute, the Chamber […] restricts itself to a very general reference to

---

[141] ICC, Situation in Uganda, *The Prosecutor v. Dominic Ongwen*, OTP, Document Containing the Charges, 22 December 2015, ICC-02/04-01/15-375-AnxA-Red, paras. 9–13, pp. 12–14, 18–21, 25–28, 32–34, 43–48 (https://legal-tools.org/doc/1fd4ed).

[142] ICC, Situation in Uganda, *The Prosecutor v. Dominic Ongwen*, OTP, Pre-confirmation brief, 21st December 2015, ICC-02/04-01/15-375-Conf-AnxC, 15 February 2016, ICC-02/04-01/15-375-AnxC-Red, para. 5 (https://legal-tools.org/doc/5b9cce).

[143] Ongwen Pre-Trial Decision on the Confirmation of Charges, para. 145, pp. 76–77, 80–81, 84–85, 88–89, 97–99, 101–03, see above note 59.

[144] *Ibid.*, para. 149, pp. 76–77, 80–81, 84–85, 88–89, 97–99, 101–03.

[145] ICC, Situation in Uganda, *The Prosecutor v. Dominic Ongwen*, Pre-Trial Chamber, Separate opinion of Judge Marc Perrin de Brichambaut, 23 March 2016, ICC-02/04-01/15-422-Anx-tENG, paras. 23–24 (https://legal-tools.org/doc/a84fed).

the available evidence, without specifying any testimony or any other evidence that would enable the constituent elements of command responsibility to be established. It would have been desirable for the Chamber's decision to have specified, for each mode of liability, the evidence relied on in support of each constitutive element of a given mode of liability. That would have involved a great deal of work, given the Prosecution's aim to have 70 charges taken into consideration according to six modes of liability. By circumventing that systematic analysis, the Chamber has undermined its decision and failed to hold the Prosecution to account for its highly ambitious goal.[146]

The trial against Ongwen commenced in December 2016 and the Prosecution closed its case in April 2018. Before the Defence opened its case in September 2018, it requested leave to file a NCTA-motion, advancing reasons similar to the ones expressed in Judge Perrin de Brichambaut's separate opinion, namely the Pre-Trial Chamber's duty to set out, clearly and precisely, definitions and supplement each definition with succinct description of the main evidence it considers relevant to make out each of the modes of liability ascribed to the accused.[147] The Defence complained about the "voluminous number of modes of liability", emphasising the need to "streamline the proceedings by weeding out unnecessary charges and modes of liability that Mr Ongwen need not defend against" because "with such a multitude of crimes and modes of liability charged, a NCTA-motion will guard against violations of Mr Ongwen's right not to be compelled to testify and to remain silent".[148]

The Trial Chamber stated: "when the same acts and conduct of an accused are charged under alternative modes of liability, the additional burden on the defence would typically stem from longer legal submissions at the end of trial rather than from having a larger 'case to answer'. Noting that the confirmed charges in this case rely extensively on alternative modes of liability and characterise discrete incidents under a variety of crimes, the Chamber does not consider that the number of charges and

---

[146] *Ibid.*, paras. 25–26.

[147] ICC, Situation in Uganda, *The Prosecutor v. Dominic Ongwen*, Defence, Defence Request for Leave to File a No Case to Answer Motion and Application for Judgment of Acquittal, 5 July 2018, ICC-02/04-01/15-1300, para. 23 (https://legal-tools.org/doc/36e8de).

[148] *Ibid.*, paras. 21, 26.

modes of liability lend any greater impetus to pursue a NCTA procedure". It denied the request.[149]

During its own case, the Defence then filed a motion alleging defects in the pleading of the modes of liability, but this claim was dismissed by Trial and the Appeals Chamber as untimely without any sufficient justification, including no exceptional circumstances for its late timing.[150]

12.5.2. Cases Ending at the NCTA Stage

Two cases, against Gbagbo and Blé Goudé and Ruto, Kosgey and Sang, ended at the NCTA stage, resulting in acquittals of four accused persons.

12.5.2.1. Gbagbo and Blé Goudé

In its arrest warrant applications, the OTP considered Gbagboand Blé Goudé as indirect co-perpetrators pursuant to Article 25(3)(a) and the Pre-Trial Chamber III issued two warrant of arrest based on this liability.[151]

In its DCC's, the Prosecutor expanded the modes of liabilities against both men: it charged Blé Goudé in the alternative with four modes of liabilities under Article 25(3), namely with indirect co-perpetration (Article 25(3)(a)), ordering, soliciting and inducing (Article 25(3)(b)),

---

[149] ICC, Situation in Uganda, *The Prosecutor v. Dominic Ongwen*, Trial Chamber, Decision on Defence Request for Leave to File a No Case to Answer Motion, 18 July 2018, ICC-02/04-01/15-1309, para. 14, p. 8 (https://legal-tools.org/doc/90bb4d).

[150] ICC, Situation in Uganda, *The Prosecutor v. Dominic Ongwen*, Defence, Defence Motion on Defects in the Confirmation of Charges Decision: Defects in the Modes of Liability (Part II of the Defects Series), 1 February 2019, ICC-02/04-01/15-1431, paras. 8–12, 19–31 (https://legal-tools.org/doc/c69922); ICC, Situation in Uganda, *The Prosecutor v. Dominic Ongwen*, Trial Chamber, Decision on Defence Motions Alleging Defects in the Confirmation Decision, 7 March 2019, ICC-02/04-01/15-1476, paras. 14, 24–30, 36 (https://legal-tools.org/doc/30688a); ICC, Situation in Uganda, *The Prosecutor v. Dominic Ongwen*, Appeals Chamber, Judgment on the appeal of Mr Dominic Ongwen against Trial Chamber IX's 'Decision on Defence Motions Alleging Defects in the Confirmation Decision', 17 July 2019, ICC-02/04-01/15-1562, paras. 142, 146–53, 163.ii), 163.iv), 163.vi)–163.vii) (https://legal-tools.org/doc/56a5cc); at *ibid.*, para. 146: "Mr Ongwen did not advance any reasonable justification for raising challenges to the Confirmation Decision before the Trial Chamber more than three years after that decision was issued and after the Prosecutor presented her case at trial".

[151] ICC, Situation in the Republic of Côte d'Ivoire, Pre-Trial Chamber, Warrant of Arrest for Laurent Koudou Gbagbo, 23 November 2011, ICC-02/11-26, para. 10, p. 7 (https://legal-tools.org/doc/12e4cc); ICC, Situation in the Republic of Côte d'Ivoire, *The Prosecutor v. Charles Blé Goudé*, Pre-Trial Chamber, Warrant of Arrest for Charles Blé Goudé, 21 December 2011, ICC-02/11-02/11-1, paras. 2, 9, p. 8 (https://legal-tools.org/doc/de90c7).

aiding, abetting or otherwise assisting (Article 25(3)(c)), and contributing in any other way (Article 25(3)(d)).[152] The Pre-Trial Chamber confirmed all these modes of liability.[153] The Prosecutor charged Gbagbo with five modes of liability in the alternative: principal liability of indirect co-perpetration under Article 25(3)(a), two accessory liability modes under Article 25(3)(b) and 25(3)(d) and two modes of superior and command responsibility under Article 28(a) and 28(b).[154]

In the course of Gbagbo's confirmation hearing, the majority of Pre-Trial Chamber I emphasised the Appeals Chambers jurisprudence that an investigation should be "largely completed" at the confirmation hearing stage.[155] Addressed to the OTP, the judges considered the Prosecutor's evidence, viewed as a whole, as apparently insufficient, but emphasised that "when the evidence is insufficient", it does not need to reject the charges, but may adjourn the hearing to request the Prosecutor to provide further evidence.[156] The majority of Pre-Trial Chamber I then requested the Prosecution to consider providing further evidence or *conducting fur-*

---

[152] ICC, Situation in the Republic of Côte d'Ivoire, *The Prosecutor v. Charles Blé Goudé*, OTP, Version corrigée du Document de notification des charges, 22 août 2014, ICC-02/11-02/11-124-Anx1, 27 August 2014, ICC-02/11-02/11-124-Anx1-Corr, pp. 125–27 (https://legal-tools.org/doc/006258); ICC, Situation in the Republic of Côte d'Ivoire, *The Prosecutor v. Charles Blé Goudé*, OTP, Version publique expurgée de la Version corrigée du Document de notification des charges, 27 août 2014, ICC-02/11-02/11-124-Conf-Anx2-Corr, 10 December 2014, ICC-02/11-02/11-124-Anx2-Corr-Red, pp. 226–28 (https://legal-tools.org/doc/a4d02e).

[153] ICC, Situation in the Republic of Côte d'Ivoire, *The Prosecutor v. Charles Blé Goudé*, Pre-Trial Chamber, Decision on the confirmation of charges against Charles Blé Goudé, 11 December 2014, ICC-02/11-02/11-186, paras. 158, 166, 171, 181 (https://legal-tools.org/doc/0536d5).

[154] Gbagbo OTP Amended DCC, paras. 211, 232–35, see above note 83.

[155] Gbagbo Pre-Trial Decision Adjourning the Hearing, para. 25, see above note 75, referring to ICC, Situation in the Democratic Republic of the Congo, *The Prosecutor v. Callixte Mbarushimana*, Appeals Chamber, Judgment on the appeal of the Prosecutor against the decision of Pre-Trial Chamber I of 16 December 2011 entitled "Decision on the confirmation of charges", 30 May 2012, ICC-01/04-01/10-514, para. 44 ('Mbarushimana Appeals Judgment on the Appeal of the Prosecutor Against the Decision of Pre-Trial Chamber of 16 December 2011') (https://legal-tools.org/doc/6ead30). Critical regarding the interpretation of the Appeals Chamber's ruling in Mbarushimana is Judge Eboe-Osuji. ICC, Situation in the Republic of Kenya, *The Prosecutor v. Uhuru Muigai Kenyatta*, Trial Chamber, Corrigendum of Concurring Separate Opinion of Judge Eboe-Osuji, 2 May 2013, ICC-01/09-02/11-728-Anx3-Corr2-Red, paras. 89–90 ('Kenyatta Trial Concurring Separate Opinion of Judge Eboe-Osuji') (https://legal-tools.org/doc/d1cf87).

[156] Gbagbo Pre-Trial Decision Adjourning the Hearing, paras. 15, 37, see above note 75.

ther investigation with respect to six issues, three of them relating to the mode of liability presented by the OTP in its DCC.[157] The majority further ordered the OTP to provide within about five months' time a new amended DCC.[158] Judge Fernández de Gurmendi dissented, arguing that the request to the Prosecutor relating to issues or questions to answer would be, as well as the request for an amended DCC, *ultra vires*.[159] She also criticised to "allocate more time to the Prosecutor to adapt […] comes rather late in the process".[160]

Finally, the majority of Pre-Trial Chamber I confirmed three alternative modes of liability for Gbago, each based on Article 25(3), but dismissed his liability based on superior responsibility.[161] Judge van den Wyngaert dissented, arguing that the evidence presented by the OTP on the three modes of liability confirmed by the majority would in her view be "still insufficient" and would thus fall "below the threshold of article 61(7)".[162]

After the majority of Pre-Trial Chamber I had confirmed three alternative modes of liability and when Trial Chamber I was seized with case, the OTP suggested that the new judges give notice to the defence before the start of trial that the legal characterisation of the three confirmed modes of liability could change in order to also include liability under Article 28 against Gbagbo.[163] Five months before the trial began,

---

[157] *Ibid.*, para. 44.1.–44.3. (emphasis added).

[158] *Ibid.*, p. 23 (letter (ix)).

[159] ICC, Situation in the Republic of Côte d'Ivoire, *The Prosecutor v. Laurent Gbagbo*, Pre-Trial Chamber, Dissenting opinion of Judge Silvia Fernández de Gurmendi, 3 June 2013, ICC-02/11-01/11-432-Anx-Corr, para. 5 (https://legal-tools.org/doc/9a3b94). The judge argues:

> [a]n expansive interpretation of the Pre-Trial Chambers role is not only unsupported by law. It affects the entire architecture of the procedural system of the Court […] encroach upon functions of the trial Judges, generate duplications, and end up frustrating the judicial efficiency that Pre-Trial Chambers are called to ensure.

Ibid., para. 26.

[160] *Ibid.*, para. 8.

[161] Gbagbo Pre-Trial Decision on the Confirmation of Charges, paras. 230, 241, 244, 251, 259, 265, see above note 56.

[162] ICC, Situation in the Republic of Côte d'Ivoire, *The Prosecutor v. Laurent Gbagbo*, Pre-Trial Chamber, Dissenting Opinion of Judge Christine Van den Wyngaert, 12 June 2014, ICC-02/11-01/11-656-Anx, paras. 1, 4–8 (https://legal-tools.org/doc/f715a5).

[163] ICC, Situation in the Republic of Côte d'Ivoire, *The Prosecutor v. Laurent Gbagbo and Charles Blé Goudé*, OTP, Prosecution request for notice to be given of a possible re-

---

the judges gave pursuant to Regulation 55 notice about a possible reclassification of the liability to Article 28(a) and 28(b) and ordered the OTP to file an amended Pre-Trial Brief, identifying the facts and circumstances relating to this added liability.[164] An Appeal of the Gbagbo defence against this reclassification decision was dismissed by the Appeals Chamber five weeks before trial commenced.[165]

Following a two years long Prosecution case, Trial Chamber I ordered the parties to file mid-term briefs. The Prosecutor argued that all initially charged modes of liability, namely four of Blé Goudé and five including superior and command responsibility of Gbagbo, were proven.[166]

However, the majority of Trial Chamber I confirmed that there was no case to answer for Gbagbo and Blé Goudé and thereby acquitted both men. The majority found that

> there is no need for the defence to submit further evidence as the Prosecutor has not satisfied the burden of proof in relation to several core constitutive elements of the crimes as charged. In particular, the majority finds that the Prosecutor
>
> (i) [h]as failed to demonstrate that there was a "common plan" to keep Mr Gbagbo in power, which included the commission of crimes against civilians;
>
> [...]
>
> (iv) [h]as failed to demonstrate that public speeches by Mr Gbagbo or Mr Blé Goudé constituted ordering, soliciting or inducing that alleged crimes or that either of the

---

characterisation pursuant to regulation 55(2), 24 April 2015, ICC-02/11-01/15-43, para. 38 (https://legal-tools.org/doc/07167e).

[164] Gbagbo and Blé Goudé Trial Decision Giving Notice Pursuant to Regulation 55(2), para. 15(i), p. 11, see above note 85.

[165] ICC, Situation in the Republic of Côte d'Ivoire, *The Prosecutor v. Laurent Gbagbo and Charles Blé Goudé*, Appeals Chamber, Judgment on the appeal of Mr Laurent Gbagbo against the decision of Trial Chamber I entitled "Decision giving notice pursuant to Regulation 55(2) of the Regulations of the Court", 18 December 2015, ICC-02/11-01/15-369, paras. 57, 73 (https://legal-tools.org/doc/f08152).

[166] ICC, Situation in the Republic of Côte d'Ivoire, *The Prosecutor v. Laurent Gbagbo and Charles Blé Goudé*, OTP, Public Redacted Version of "Corrected version to Annex 1 of Prosecution's Mid-Trial Brief", 19 March 2018, ICC-02/11-01/15-1136-Conf-Anx1-Corr, 29 March 2018, ICC-02/11-01/15-1136-Anx1-Corr-Red, pp. 178–255 (https://legal-tools.org/doc/b25eea).

accused otherwise knowingly or intentionally contributed to the commission of such crimes.[167]

Judge Tarfusser observed "shortcomings affecting the performance
of the OTP, both at the investigative and at the prosecutorial stage".[168]
Judge Herrera Carbuccia dissented, finding sufficient evidence upon
which a chamber could convict so that the defence should have presented
its case.[169] She held a reasonable Trial Chamber could conclude that
Gbagbo was liable pursuant to Article 28(a) and Blé Goudé for inducing
and soliciting (Article 25(3)(b)) for certain crimes.[170]

12.5.2.2. Ruto, Kosgey and Sang

The case against Kosgey was not confirmed. Against Ruto and Sang the
DCC was confirmed and trial opened, but it ended without conviction
after the Defence's NCTA-motion was upheld by the Trial Chamber.

In mid-December 2010, the OTP requested Pre-Trial Chamber II to
issue a summons to appear against Ruto, Kosgey and Sang as principals,
referring inconsistently to direct or indirect co-perpetration under Articles
25(3)(a) or just to co-perpetration.[171] Further, in the alternative, the Prosecution alleged against all men accessory liability, namely contributing 'in
any other way' to a common purpose under Article 25(3)(d).[172] Pre-Trial
Chamber II found reasonable grounds to qualify Ruto and Kosgey as *indirect* co-perpetrators, but explicitly dismissed this form of liability for Sang

---

[167] Gbagbo and Blé Goudé Trial Reasons for Oral Decision, para. 28, see above note 45.

[168] ICC, Situation in the Republic of Côte d'Ivoire, *The Prosecutor v. Laurent Gbagbo and Charles Blé Goudé*, Trial Chamber, Opinion of Judge Cuno Tarfusser, 16 July 2019, ICC-02/11-01/15-1263-AnxA, para. 90 ('Gbagbo and Blé Goudé Trial Opinion of Judge Cuno Tarfusser') (https://legal-tools.org/doc/f6c6f3).

[169] ICC, Situation in the Republic of Côte d'Ivoire, *The Prosecutor v. Laurent Gbagbo and Charles Blé Goudé*, Trial Chamber, Dissenting Opinion to the Chamber's Oral Decision of 15 January 2019, 15 January 2019, ICC-02/11-01/15-1234, para. 48 (https://legal-tools.org/doc/bd0ffc); Gbagbo and Blé Goudé Trial Dissenting Opinion Judge Herrera Carbuccia, para. 648, see above note 62.

[170] *Ibid.*, paras. 557, 646.

[171] Ruto, Kosgey and Sang OTP Article 58 Application, para. 27, sect. F, counts 1–4, see above note 52. Ruto, Kosgey and Sang Pre-Trial Decision on the Prosecutor's Application for Summons to Appear, paras. 35–36, see above note 55.

[172] Ruto, Kosgey and Sang OTP Article 58 Application, para. 27, sect. F, counts 1–4, see above note 52.

---

against whom the judges found reasonable grounds to qualify him as an accessory pursuant to Article 25(3)(d).[173]

In August 2011, the Prosecution filed its DCC and, later, an amended version.[174] Regarding the way the OTP had pleaded the mode of liability, the majority of Pre-Trial Chamber II observed:

> In paragraph 98 of the amended DCC, the Prosecutor alleges that Mr. Ruto and Mr. Kosgey are criminally responsible as 'co-perpetrators' pursuant to Article 25(3)(a) [...]. Later, in presenting its charges in paragraphs 133 and in particular in counts 1, 3 and 5, the Prosecutor avers that Mr. Ruto and Mr. Kosgey "committed or contributed [...] in violation of Article [...] 25(3)(a)". The same holds true in relation to counts 2, 4 and 6 concerning Mr. Sang where the Prosecutor charges him under Article 25(3)(d) [...], but still claims in these counts that Mr. Sang, "as part of a group of persons, including [Mr. Ruto and Mr. Kosgey], acting with a common purpose, *committed* or contributed to the crimes".[175]

Recalling its earlier decision on summonses to appear in this case, the Pre-Trial Chamber continued that:

> although such inconsistency or lack of precision may raise an issue of deficiency of the amended DCC, the Prosecutor's clarification that the two suspects are charged under article 25(3)(a) [...] by way of presenting the elements of underlying indirect co-perpetration cures the apparent inconsistency. The same reasoning applies to the situation of Mr. Sang since the Prosecutor actually developed the legal elements of article 25(3)(d).[176]

---

[173] Ruto, Kosgey and Sang Pre-Trial Decision on the Prosecutor's Application for Summons to Appear, paras. 37–38, 57, see above note 55.

[174] ICC, Situation in the Republic of Kenya, *The Prosecutor v. William Samoei Ruto, Henry Kiprono Kosgey and Joshua Arap Sang*, OTP, Prosecution's Document Containing the Charges and List of Evidence submitted pursuant to Article 61(3) and Rule 121(3), 1 August 2011, ICC-01/09-01/11-242 (https://legal-tools.org/doc/209a4b); ICC, Situation in the Republic of Kenya, *The Prosecutor v. William Samoei Ruto, Henry Kiprono Kosgey and Joshua Arap Sang*, OTP, Document Containing the Charges, 15 August 2011, ICC-01/09-01/11-261-AnxA (https://legal-tools.org/doc/0e74d7).

[175] Ruto, Kosgey and Sang Pre-Trial Decision on the Confirmation of Charges, para. 283, see above note 81.

[176] *Ibid.*, para. 285.

Regarding the modes of liability proposed by the Prosecution in its amended DCC, the majority of Pre-Trial Chamber II confirmed the principal liability of Ruto as indirect co-perpetrator pursuant to Article 25(3)(a)[177] and accessory liability of Sang as intentionally contributing to a crime of others led by Ruto, acting with common purpose pursuant to Article 25(3)(d)(i).[178]

However, the judges declined to confirm any charges and any mode of criminal liability against Mr. Kosgey.[179] The judges based their refusal to confirm the charges on the fact that the OTP had only presented one uncorroborated and anonymous witness to detail the liability of Kosgey and otherwise alleged the suspects' presence at four meetings planning the post-election violence, but had then out of security reasons chosen to redact the dates of these meetings and revealed two of the withheld dates to the defence late, meaning only in its final written observations.[180] The judges ruled:

> in view of the prejudice experienced by the Defence, the Chamber finds that the Prosecutor has not met the evidentiary standard required at this stage of the proceedings. It follows that the Chamber needs neither to engage with the Defence challenges related to Mr. Kosgey's involvement, nor to proceed with an examination of the elements concerning his alleged criminal responsibility as provided in the Amended DCC.[181]

As a result, from the three suspects whom the OTP had in its application for a summons to appear qualified as principals, meaning as 'co-perpetrators', the Pre-Trial Chamber only confirmed Ruto as *indirect* co-perpetrator and downgraded Sang to accessory liability according to Article 25(3)(d)(i) and otherwise refused to confirm any (liability) charges against Kosgey.

About six months later, the OTP even suggested the Trial Chamber to make use of Regulation 55, thereby effectively also downgrading Ruto,

---

[177] *Ibid.*, paras. 299, 301–49.
[178] *Ibid.*, paras. 353, 355–364, 366–67.
[179] *Ibid.*, para. 293, p. 138 (letters g), j)).
[180] *Ibid.*, paras. 293–95.
[181] *Ibid.*, para. 297.

the only accused charged with responsibility as a principal, to liability of an accessory.[182] The Prosecution argued for the first time that:

> Ruto's criminal acts lend themselves to multiple legal characterizations. This is a function of the nature of the accused's conduct during the P[ost] E[lection] V[iolence] which because of its various aspects may be characterized any of the modes of liability encompassed by Article 25(3).[183]

Though the Prosecution had already submitted its DCC and amended DCC, it then argued:

> even if providing *notice* under Regulation 55(2) could somehow be equated to alternative *charging* – and it cannot – nothing in the Court's legal framework prevents the consideration of alternative modes of liability. On the contrary, [...] Pre-Trial Chamber II confirmed that "the Prosecutor may generally charge in the alternative"; the inclusion of Regulation 55 in the Court's legal framework demonstrates that alternative legal characterizations may be considered where appropriate on the facts of the case.[184]

Before the trial began, the Prosecution asked the Trial Chamber to provide notice under Regulation 55(2) that Ruto's form of individual criminal responsibility charged may be subject to legal re-characterisation under Articles 25(3)(b), 25(3)(c) or 25(3)(d) before or on the first day of trial.

So instead of using the formal procedure of amending the amended DCC under Article 61(9), the OTP asked the Trial Chamber to provide a legal notice based on Regulation 55. The requested downgrading of Ruto's liability as a principal to mere accessory liability occurred *without* any evidence having been led. In other words, after having completed its investigation, having issued two amended DCC's and after leading some evidence in the confirmation hearing, only then the OTP must have real-

---

[182] ICC, Situation in the Republic of Kenya, *The Prosecutor v. William Samoei Ruto and Joshua Arap Sang*, OTP, Prosecution's Submissions on the law of indirect co-perpetration under Article 25(3)(a) of the Statute and application for notice to be given under Regulation 55 with respect to William Samoei Ruto's individual criminal responsibility, 3 July 2012, ICC-01/09-01/11-433, paras. 24, 49 (https://legal-tools.org/doc/d90763).

[183] *Ibid.*, para. 38.

[184] *Ibid.*, para. 44.

ised during its trial preparations that it *should have* charged Ruto's liability in the alternative, referring to almost all liabilities Article 25(3) offers.

Three months into the Prosecution's case, Trial Chamber V issued notice to Ruto that the possibility existed to re-characterise his liability to Articles 25(3)(b), 25(3)(c) or 25(3)(d).[185]

16 months later and responding to a Defence request for NCTA, the majority of Trial Chamber V declared a mistrial, vacated the charges and discharged Ruto and Sang after the Prosecution had led its case.[186] Deciding on the defence's no-case to answer motion, Judge Fremr wrote:

> [i]n relation to Mr Ruto, I have found insufficient evidence to support a possible conviction for ordering any of the crimes [...] [or] on the basis of soliciting or inducing the commission of any of the crimes charged under Article 25(3)(b).[187]

Fremr continued that regarding Article 25(3)(c) liability,

> none of the alleged contributions, such as the obtaining of weapons, organisation of transport, distribution of food, etc., for which there is evidence in the record, can be sufficiently clearly linked to the alleged Network. The same is true with regard to Mr Ruto's alleged personal contributions. Equally importantly, even if certain alleged contributions could be linked to Mr Ruto, there is insufficient evidence to show that any such contributions were made 'for the purpose of facilitating the commission' of one of the charged crimes.[188]

Equally, "the available evidence would not allow a reasonable Trial Chamber to find that there was a common plan to commit the charged crimes, it is not possible to re-characterise under Article 25(3)(d)".[189] Judge Fremr also denied responsibility for Mr. Sang under Articles 25(3)(b) or 25(3)(c).[190] Judge Fremr concluded that "the available evi-

---

[185] Ruto and Sang Trial Decision on Applications for Notice, p. 20, see above note 82.

[186] Ruto and Sang Trial Decision on Defence Applications for Judgments of Acquittal, paras. 464.i.–464.ii., see above note 46.

[187] Reasons of Judge Fremr, in *ibid.*, paras. 133–34.

[188] *Ibid.*, para. 136.

[189] *Ibid.*, para. 137.

[190] *Ibid.*, para. 138.

dence does not sufficiently support any of the alternative forms of criminal responsibility to warrant the continuation of the trial on this basis".[191]

Judge Herrera Carbuccia dissented. Concerning Ruto, she concurred that for indirect co-perpetration, *prima facie* the Prosecution has not provided enough evidence.[192] However, in view of judge Herrera Carbuccia,

> there is evidence upon which a reasonable Chamber could convict Mr Ruto under Article 25(3)(b) of the Statute – ordering, soliciting or inducing –, or under Article 25(3)(c) – aiding, abetting or otherwise assisting –, or under Article 25(3)(d) – in any other way contributing to the commission of the crime.[193]

Regarding Mr. Sang, Judge Herrera Carbuccia found "the Prosecution has presented enough evidence upon which a reasonable Chamber could conclude" that he "contributed to the commission of the crimes charged" pursuant to Article 25(3)(d).[194]

The majority of Trial Chamber V vacated the charges against Ruto and Sang and discharged them without prejudice to their prosecution afresh in future.[195]

12.5.3. Cases Ending Before the Commencement of Trial

Three cases ended before trial could commence. Of these three persons did not need to face more than the Pre-Trial Chamber, while proceedings against Kenyatta and Muthaura's moved in front of the Trial Chamber but the case ended before the trial opened.

12.5.3.1. Kenyatta, Ali and Muthaura

This case never went to trial because the Pre-Trial Chamber declined to confirm any charges against one suspect, Ali , and because the Prosecution withdrew all charges against Kenyatta and Muthaura, the remaining two accused persons, before the beginning of trial.

---

[191] *Ibid.*, para. 143.

[192] ICC, Situation in the Republic of Kenya, *The Prosecutor v. William Samoei Ruto and Joshua Arap Sang*, Trial Chamber, Dissenting Opinion of Judge Herrera Carbuccia, 5 April 2016, ICC-01/09-01/11-2027-AnxI, para. 71 (https://legal-tools.org/doc/2bc8b5).

[193] *Ibid.*, para. 75.

[194] *Ibid.*, para. 76.

[195] Ruto and Sang Trial Decision on Defence Applications for Judgments of Acquittal, p. 1 (no. 1), see above note 46.

Nearing the end of its investigation, the Prosecution encountered already the first problems in convincing the Pre-Trial Chamber to issue a summons to appear against Kenyatta, Ali and Muthaura. Against Ali, the Prosecutor had applied for summons to appear based on principal liability (co-perpetration, Article 25(3)(a)) *and* accessory liability (contributing in any other way, Article 25(3)(d)).[196] However, the majority of Pre-Trial Chamber II found that the material submitted by the OTP was not sufficient to qualify Ali as a co-perpetrator and only issued the summons based on the lesser variant, meaning liability of an accessory ('contributing in any other way').[197] Further regarding two crime scenes in Kisumu and Kibera, the majority of judges failed to see reasonable grounds that these events could be attributed to Ali, Muthaura and Kenyatta.[198] However, regarding other events and allegations, the Pre-Trial Chamber's majority issued the summonses against Muthaura and Kenyatta[199] based on indirect co-perpetration,[200] though the Prosecution had against both men also alleged accessory liability under Article 25(3)(d).[201]

However, already at the confirmation stage, all judges from Pre-Trial Chamber II declined to confirm any liability of Ali under Article 25(3)(d)(i). Thus, without ever acquiring the status of an accused, Ali had not to stand trial. Pre-Trial Chamber II explained that in order to hold Ali

---

[196] ICC, Situation in the Democratic Republic of Kenya, *The Prosecutor v. Francis Kirimi Muthaura, Uhuru Muigai Kenyatta and Mohammed Hussein Ali*, Pre-Trial Chamber, Decision on the Prosecutor's Application for Summonses to Appear for Francis Kirimi Muthaura, Uhururu Muigai Kenyatta and Mohammed Hussein Ali, 8 March 2011, ICC-01/09-02/11-1, para. 13 (counts 1–5) ('Muthaura, Kenyatta and Ali Pre-Trial Decision on the Prosecutor's Application for Summonses to Appear') (https://legal-tools.org/doc/df8391).

[197] *Ibid.*, paras. 38, 46, 51.

[198] *Ibid.*, para. 32.

[199] Judge Kaul dissented, arguing the ICC lacked jurisdiction *ratione materiae* and therefore declined to issue any summons to appear against any of the three suspects. ICC, Situation in the Democratic Republic of Kenya, *The Prosecutor v. Francis Kirimi Muthaura, Uhuru Muigai Kenyatta and Mohammed Hussein Ali*, Pre-Trial Chamber, Dissenting Opinion by Judge Hans-Peter Kaul to Pre-Trial Chamber II's "Decision on the Prosecutor's Application for Summonses to Appear for Francis Kirimi Muthaura, Uhuru Muigai Kenyatta and Mohammed Hussein Ali", 15 March 2011, ICC-01/09-02/11-3, paras. 2, 36 (https://legal-tools.org/doc/521d6d).

[200] Muthaura, Kenyatta and Ali Pre-Trial Decision on the Prosecutor's Application for Summonses to Appear, paras. 39–45, see above note 196.

[201] Muthaura and Kenyatta Prosecution's Submissions on the Law of Indirect Co-perpetration and Application for Notice, para. 4, see above note 80.

---

responsible for crimes allegedly committed through the Kenya police, it is essential that it first be determined that this force indeed carried out the crimes as alleged. The judges argued no substantial grounds were provided to believe that the Kenya police participated in an attack around Nakuru and Naivasha and without being satisfied about the occurrence of this historical event as alleged by the OTP, it was "not possible to entertain further attribution of any conduct of the Kenya police to Mr. Ali and, *a fortiori*, his individual criminal responsibility".[202] Accordingly, Mr. Ali was never committed for trial, despite the OTP having alleged his criminal liability in five counts of crimes against humanity at the conclusion of its investigation.[203] Regarding Kenyatta and Muthaura, the Pre-Trial Chamber confirmed their liability as indirect co-perpetrators pursuant to Article 25(3)(a).[204]

About five months after this confirmation of liability as indirect co-perpetrators, the OTP filed own observations on Article 25(3)(a) and suggested that the judges provide, before the trial had begun, notice under Regulation 55 to both remaining accused that also other liabilities, namely under Article 25(3)(b) or 25(3)(c) could be applicable.[205]

This OTP motion based on Regulation 55 meant a change of course. First, the OTP had filed a DCC in which it had alleged *principal* liability (indirect co-perpetration) against Kenyatta and Muthaura. Then the OTP asked the Trial Chamber to reclassify and thereby *downgrade* its initial allegation (of liability as principals) to also include accessory liabilities. Procedurally, after confirmation and before the commencement of the trial, the Prosecution chose not to formally amend its DCC pursuant to Article 61(9), but to suggest instead to the Trial Chamber to consider invoking Regulation 55.

First, the wording of Regulation 55 does not provide any party or participant to a trial the right to *suggest* that a Trial Chamber invokes Regulation 55. Yet this is exactly what the Prosecution did. Secondly,

---

[202] Muthaura, Kenyatta and Ali Pre-Trial Decision on the Confirmation of Charges, paras. 420–27, see above note 79.

[203] *Ibid.*, p. 154, letter d); on the counts, para. 21, counts 2 (murder), 4 (deportation or forcible transfer), 6 (rape and other forms of sexual violence), 8 (other inhumane acts), 10 (persecution).

[204] *Ibid.*, paras. 398–419.

[205] Muthaura and Kenyatta Prosecution's Submissions on the Law of Indirect Co-perpetration and Application for Notice, paras. 24, 29–35, 49, see above note 80.

when at the conclusion of its investigation, it was possible for the prosecution to freely formulate the applicable mode(s) of liability, including to propose several of them in the alternative, then the Prosecution had chosen *not* do that, but to plead one mode of liability only, namely indirect co-perpetration.

Bearing this in mind, it is instrumental to read the application which stated "the Prosecution charged a form of individual criminal responsibility that, *in its view, appropriately captures the accused's contributions* to the crimes".[206] The Prosecution emphasising that the Pre-Trial Chamber confirmed its pleaded theory of indirect co-perpetration under Article 25(3)(a), then acknowledged:

> However, the specific facts of this case reflect that indirect co-perpetration is *not the sole manner* in which the accused's criminal responsibility can be characterized. The Prosecution acknowledges [*sic*] that the accused's criminal responsibility could equally be characterized as:
>
> - Ordering, soliciting or inducing under Article 25(3)(b);
>
> - Aiding, abetting or otherwise assisting under Article 25(3)(c); or
>
> - Contributing "[i]n any other way" [...] under Article 25(3)(d).[207]

Implicitly, the OTP thereby acknowledged that at the end of its own investigation, it had too narrowly charged the then suspects in its own DCC. Trial Chamber V did not entertain the suggestion to issue a notice pursuant to Regulation 55, but scheduled a date for trial.

Then the Prosecution referred to serious investigative challenges, including that several witnesses died or were killed and to limited co-operation of the government of Kenya, and asked the Trial Chamber to withdraw all charges against Muthaura as the available evidence would not support the charges to the beyond reasonable doubt standard required for a conviction and therefore at this present time there would be no rea-

---

[206] *Ibid.*, para. 45 (emphasis added).

[207] *Ibid.*, para. 29 (emphasis added). In the following paragraphs, the OTP listed the mode of liability indirect co-perpetration which the Pre-Trial Chamber had confirmed arguing that it is "not the only way in which [the underlying acts] can be categorized".

sonable prospect of conviction; the Trial Chamber granted the request regarding Muthaura.[208]

In April 2013, Trial Chamber V ordered the Prosecution to submit an updated DCC regarding Kenyatta. The reasoning of this decision reflects the dissatisfaction of the judges regarding the OTP's investigation. All judges concurred that the "Prosecutor should not seek to have the charges against a suspect confirmed before having conducted a full investigation in order to have sufficient overview of the evidence and the theory of the case".[209] Judge van den Wyngaert went as far as observing:

> there are serious questions as to whether the Prosecution conducted a full and thorough investigation of the case against the accused prior to confirmation. […] the facts show that the Prosecution had not complied with its obligations under article 54(1)(a) at the time when it sought confirmation and that it was still not even remotely ready when the proceedings before this Chamber started.[210]

By contrast, Judge Eboe-Osuji assessed it would be unjustifiable, if a limitation would crystallise that would forbid post-confirmation investigations generally and only allow these in exceptional circumstances.[211] Indeed, the Appeals Chamber ruled in *Prosecutor v. Lubanga*:

> The duty to establish the truth is not limited to the time before the confirmation hearing. Therefore, the Prosecutor

---

[208] ICC, Situation in the Republic of Kenya, *The Prosecutor v. Francis Kirimi Muthaura and Uhuru Muigai Kenyatta*, Trial Chamber, OTP, Prosecution notification of withdrawal of the charges against Francis Kirimi Muthaura, 11 March 2013, ICC-01/09-02/11-687, paras. 1, 9–11 (https://legal-tools.org/doc/4786c1). The Trial Chamber V granted the request in its ICC, Situation in the Republic of Kenya, *The Prosecutor v. Francis Kirimi Muthaura and Uhuru Muigai Kenyatta*, Trial Chamber, Decision on the withdrawal of charges against Mr Muthaura, 18 March 2013, ICC-01/09-02/11-696, para. 11, p. 8 (https://legal-tools.org/doc/44ecc9).

[209] ICC, Situation in the Republic of Kenya, *The Prosecutor v. Uhuru Muigai Kenyatta*, Trial Chamber, Decision on defence application pursuant to Article 64(4) and related requests, 26 April 2013, ICC-01/09-02/11-728, para. 119 ('Kenyatta Trial Decision on Defence Application Pursuant to Article 64(4) and Related Requests') (https://legal-tools.org/doc/da5089).

[210] ICC, Situation in the Republic of Kenya, *The Prosecutor v. Uhuru Muigai Kenyatta*, Trial Chamber, Concurring Opinion of Judge Christine Van den Wyngaert, 26 April 2013, ICC-01/09-02/11-728-Anx2, para. 1 (https://legal-tools.org/doc/917ec7).

[211] Kenyatta Trial Concurring Separate Opinion of Judge Eboe-Osuji, para. 87, see above note 155.

must be allowed to continue his investigation beyond the confirmation hearing, if this is necessary in order to establish the truth. This is confirmed by article 61(9) of the Statute, which stipulates inter alia that the charges may be amended before the trial has begun. As the Prosecutor rightly pointed out, this indicates that the investigation does not have to stop before the confirmation hearing.[212]

All judges of Trial Chamber V concurred that the specific investigation regarding the post-election violence in Kenya "the circumstances under which the Prosecution was operating were difficult and may have affected its ability to conduct a fuller investigation prior to confirmation".[213]

Indeed, the OTP had twice requested adjournments of the provisional trial date to undertake additional investigative steps.[214] Trial Chamber V observing that investigations into the Kenya situation has been ongoing for almost five years, acknowledged that certain unique circumstances beyond the Prosecutions control, including unexplained delay on the part of the Kenyan government facilitated loss of evidence, but identified also concerns regarding the OTP's timeliness, vigorousness and thoroughness of its investigations and ruled this alone does not provide a basis for open-ended investigations.[215] The judges noticed the OTP's admission regarding the insufficiency of its current evidence and rejected any further

---

[212] ICC, Situation in the Democratic Republic of the Congo, *The Prosecutor v. Thomas Lubanga Dyilo*, Appeals Chamber, Judgement on the Prosecutor's appeal against the decision of Pre-Trial Chamber I entitled "Decision Establishing General Principles Governing Applications to Restrict Disclosure pursuant to Rule 81 (2) and (4) of the Rules of Procedure and Evidence", 13 October 2006, ICC-01/04-01/06-568, para. 52 (https://legal-tools.org/doc/7813d4).

[213] Kenyatta Trial Decision on Defence Application Pursuant to Article 64(4) and Related Requests, para. 124, see above note 209.

[214] ICC, Situation in the Republic of Kenya, *The Prosecutor v. Uhuru Muigai Kenyatta*, OTP, Notification of the removal of a witness from the Prosecution's witness list and application for an adjournment of the provisional trial date, 19 December 2013, ICC-01/09-02/11-875, paras. 17–22, 24 (https://legal-tools.org/doc/f017e7); ICC, Situation in the Republic of Kenya, *The Prosecutor v. Uhuru Muigai Kenyatta*, OTP, Prosecution notice regarding the provisional trial date, 5 September 2014, ICC-01/09-02/11-944, paras. 4, 6 (https://legal-tools.org/doc/5d9c72).

[215] ICC, Situation in the Republic of Kenya, *The Prosecutor v. Uhuru Muigai Kenyatta*, Trial Chamber, Decision on Prosecution's application for a further adjournment, 3 December 2014, ICC-01/09-02/11-981, paras. 44–45, 49–51, 54 (https://legal-tools.org/doc/731d89).

---

adjournment.[216] Two days after this decision, the OTP provided notice that it had withdrawn all charges against Kenyatta, pointing out that this step is without prejudice to bring new charges based on the same or similar factual circumstances.[217]

12.5.3.2. Abu Garda

In its arrest warrant application, the Prosecution qualified Abu Garda as co-perpetrator pursuant to Article 25(3)(a), but added it would do so "[w]ithout excluding any other applicable mode of responsibility".[218] Pre-Trial Chamber I interpreted this vague phrase to mean that the Prosecution alleged principal liability as co-perpetrator or as indirect co-perpetrator.[219] Pre-Trial Chamber issued a summons to appear based on co-perpetration (Article 25(3)(a)).[220]

The Prosecution's DCC then charged Abu Garda with principal liability as co-perpetrator or indirect co-perpetrator and otherwise contained again the formulation "[w]ithout excluding any other applicable mode of liability".[221]

Pre-Trial Chamber I criticised the Prosecution had not excluded any other applicable mode of liability and, referring to applicable laws including Regulation 52(c) which requires the pleading of a precise form of participation, restricted itself to analyse only the mode specifically

---

[216] *Ibid.*, para. 61, p. 26.

[217] ICC, Situation in the Republic of Kenya, *The Prosecutor v. Uhuru Muigai Kenyatta*, OTP, Notice of withdrawal of the charges against Uhuru Muigai Kenyatta, 5 December 2015, ICC-01/09-02/11-983, paras. 1, 3 (https://legal-tools.org/doc/b57a97).

[218] ICC, Situation in Darfur, Sudan, *The Prosecutor v. Abdallah Banda Abakaer Nourain*, OTP, Public Redacted Version of Prosecutor's Application under Article 58 filed on 20 November, 20 November 2008, ICC-02/05-03/09-20-Red, pp. 10–11, para. 140 (https://legal-tools.org/doc/95138b).

[219] ICC, Situation in Darfur, Sudan, *The Prosecutor v. Bahar Idriss Abu Garda*, Pre-Trial Chamber, Decision on the Prosecutor's Application under Article 58, 7 May 2009, ICC-02/05-02/09-1, para. 24 (https://legal-tools.org/doc/126792).

[220] ICC, Situation in Darfur, Sudan, *The Prosecutor v. Bahar Idriss Abu Garda*, Pre-Trial Chamber, Summons to Appear for Bahr Idriss Abu Garda, 7 May 2009, ICC-02/05-02/09-2, paras. 6, 18–19 (https://legal-tools.org/doc/9a4a9e).

[221] ICC, Situation in Darfur, Sudan, *The Prosecutor v. Bahar Idriss Abu Garda*, OTP, Public Redacted Version of Prosecution's "Document Containing the Charges Submitted Pursuant to Article 61(3) of the Statute" filed on 10 September 2009, 24 September 2009, ICC-02/05-02/09-91-Red, para. 117, pp. 32–33 (counts 1–3) (https://legal-tools.org/doc/4ac1f8).

charged by the OTP.[222] Regarding the OTP's precision in the DCC, the judges noted:

> because of the inconsistencies in the allegations contained in the DCC, it is unclear whether or not the Prosecution is claiming that Mr Abu Garda directly participated in the attack [...]. At the confirmation hearing, the Prosecution continued to claim both that Mr Abu Garda directly participated in the attack and that he did not.[223]

Further, the judges found insufficient grounds to establish the existence of a common plan and lack of sufficient evidence substantiating the allegations of Abu Garda responsibility as either direct or indirect co-perpetrator or under any other liability contemplated in Article 25(3).[224]

Judge Tarfusser observed a "flimsy, inconsistent or otherwise inadequate" body of evidence which would not allow establishing a proper link between the attack as a historic event and the alleged perpetrator in terms of either direct or indirect involvement.[225] The Prosecution requested leave to appeal the decision which did not confirm the DCC, including the judges analysis of criminal liability of Abu Garda. Due to the absence of substantial grounds to believe that a common plan to the attack existed, the Pre-Trial Chamber found the OTP's challenge not essential for the determination of matters arising from judicial cause and rejected the request.[226]

12.5.3.3. Mbarushimana

In its arrest warrant application, the Prosecution qualified Mbarushimana as principal, co-perpetrator pursuant to Article 25(3)(a) and, in the alterna-

---

[222] Abu Garda Pre-Trial Decision on the Confirmation of Charges, para. 158, see above note 43.

[223] *Ibid.*, paras. 218, 220.

[224] *Ibid.*, paras. 231–32.

[225] Separate Opinion of Judge Cuno Tarfusser, in *ibid.*, paras. 4, 6.

[226] ICC, Situation in Darfur, Sudan, *The Prosecutor v. Bahar Idriss Abu Garda*, Pre-Trial Chamber, Decision on the "Prosecution's Application for Leave to Appeal the 'Decision on Confirmation of Charges'", 23 April 2010, ICC-02/05-02/09-267, para. 18, p. 15 (https://legal-tools.org/doc/840d58).

tive, as accessory for having contributed in any other way to crimes by a group with a common purpose under Article 25(3)(d).[227]

Pre-Trial Chamber I dismissed Mbarushimana's liability as a principal, meaning as co-perpetrator under Article 25(3)(a) because of no reasonable grounds existed establishing that his contribution was essential.[228] However, the judges found reasonable grounds for his liability as accessory under Article 25(3)(d) .[229]

In its DCC and oral arguments, the Prosecution emphasised Mbarushimana's position of Executive Secretary of the Forces Démocratiques de Libération du Rwanda ('FDLR'), arguing he would be the 'linchpin' of his rebel group, accentuating "his ability to transform the FDLR's crimes on the ground into political capital" and thus he knowingly and intentionally contributed in any other way under Article 25(3)(d).[230]

Following the confirmation of charges hearing, the majority of Pre-Trial Chamber I declined[231] to confirm the charges, holding that:

> the evidence submitted by the Prosecution is insufficient to substantiate the finding [...] that the Suspect's role as a leader of the FDLR qualifies a significant contribution to the commission of crimes by the FDLR in accordance with article 25(3)(d).[232]

The majority disagreed with the dissenting judge on the requirement that the FDLR leadership constituted a group of persons acting with a common purpose within the meaning of Article 25(3)(d).

In his dissent Judge Monageng endorsed the Prosecution's position that the FDLR had a specific leadership consisting out of President, two vice presidents and Mbarushimana as executive secretary and a leader of

---

[227] ICC, Situation in the Democratic Republic of the Congo, OTP, Prosecution's Application under Article 58, 20 August 2010, ICC-01/04-573-Red, paras. 21, 115, 129 (https://legal-tools.org/doc/f9b78d).

[228] ICC, Situation in the Democratic Republic of the Congo, *The Prosecutor v. Callixte Mbarushimana*, Pre-Trial Chamber, Decision on the Prosecutor's Application for a Warrant of Arrest against Callixte Mbarushimana, 28 September 2010, ICC-01/04-01/10-1, paras. 30–36 (https://legal-tools.org/doc/04d4fa).

[229] *Ibid.*, paras. 38–44.

[230] Mbarushimana Pre-Trial Decision on the Confirmation of Charges, para. 8, see above note 44.

[231] *Ibid.*, p. 149.

[232] *Ibid.*, para. 303.

the military wing.[233] He further argued with the occurrence of certain meetings from the FDLR's steering committee and High Command, adding that Mbarushimana closely co-operated with certain persons, all of which was evidence of structure and activities of a group of persons with a common purpose.[234] Thus, he would have accepted Mbarushimana's liability as contributing to a group with a common purpose pursuant to Article 25(3)(d).[235] By contrast, the majority noted that the common purpose pursued by the group "must have at least an element of criminality" and substantial grounds lacked to be satisfied that the FDLR pursued the policy of attacking the civilian population.[236] The majority further held that not just any contribution would have sufficed, but that a contribution pursuant to Article 25(3)(d) would need to be significant.[237] The majority held that there was no link between the Mbarushimana's conduct and the alleged crimes of the FDLR.[238]

The majority emphasised that the evidence presented was insufficient to establish substantial grounds to believe that the suspect denied crimes committed by the FDLR and therefore, through radio communications, radio and press releases, which among others encouraged the troops morale, he could not make a significant contribution to the commission of crimes by the FDLR pursuant to Article 25(3)(d).[239] The chamber unanimously agreed that the suspect functioning as a point of contact for external actors and his involvement in peace negotiations was no contribution to the commission of crimes pursuant to Article 25(3)(d).[240]

On 23 December 2011, the ICC released Mbarushimana who left for France.[241]

---

[233] Dissenting opinion of Judge Sanji Mmasenono Monageng, in *ibid.*, para. 51.

[234] *Ibid.*, paras. 52–54.

[235] *Ibid.*, paras. 64, 134–35.

[236] Mbarushimana Pre-Trial Decision on the Confirmation of Charges, para. 291, see above note 44.

[237] *Ibid.*, paras. 283–84.

[238] *Ibid.*, paras. 293–339.

[239] *Ibid.*, paras. 315, 339.

[240] *Ibid.*, para. 320.

[241] "Rwandan rebel leader in France after ICC release", *France24*, 23 February 2011 (available on its web site).

The Prosecution appealed the Pre-Trial Chambers decision not to confirm any charges, but the Appeals Chamber upheld the decision of the majority of the Pre-Trial Chamber.[242] Regarding the Prosecution's third ground of appeal that an error of law had occurred as any (and not only a substantial) contribution to a crime by a group of persons acting with a common purpose pursuant to Article 25(3)(d) was sufficient, the Appeals Chamber decided that such an alleged error would not have materially affected the impugned decision as the majority of the Pre-Trial Chamber had found one fundamental element of this liability, namely the existence of a group acting with a common purpose, had not been established.[243]

In a separate opinion, Judge Fernandéz de Gurmendi emphasised that the phrase "in any other way" in Article 25(3)(d) would indicate there should not be a minimum threshold or level of contribution as required by the majority of Pre-Trial Chamber I.[244]

12.6. Emerging Picture

Regarding 17 cases at the ICC, this contribution has whether the OTP could maintain consistency in advancing one or several mode(s) of criminal liability which it had determined towards the end of its investigation. This analysis is *not* about the performance of the ICC's OTP in confirmation and trial proceedings. Rather, it is about *inferences* drawn from public filings produced at these procedural stages about the quality of the OTP's earlier investigation into modes of liability.

12.6.1. Stage at Which Judicial Proceedings Coming Out of an Investigation End

Inferences on the thoroughness of each investigation can be drawn from the procedural stage which each ensuing judicial proceeding reached and how a pleaded criminal liability ended procedurally. That cases end in front of the Pre-Trial Chamber already, or Trial Chamber or Appeals Chamber is indicative of an investigation's strength (or lack thereof). That cases end after confirmation hearings, or before trial, or at the no-case to answer stage, or upon judgments being rendered provide insights about

---

[242] Mbarushimana Appeals Judgment on the Appeal of the Prosecutor Against the Decision of Pre-Trial Chamber of 16 December 2011, paras. 69, 70, see above note 155.

[243] *Ibid.*, para. 66.

[244] Separate Opinion of Judge Silvia Fernández de Gurmendi, in *ibid.*, paras. 9, 15.

the quality of investigations which occurred earlier: convictions to prison sentences indicate that the OTP's investigation was thorough. However, at the ICC, only few cases resulted in convictions while the majority of cases ended in earlier stages (with the suspects or accused being released):

Case ends at procedural stage:				
Confirmation decision	**Before trial**	**No-case to answer**	**Trial judgment**	**Appeal judgment**
Abu Garda	Muthaura	Ruto	Ngudjolo Chui	Bemba
Mbarushimana	Kenyatta	Sang	Katanga	Lubanga
Ali		Gbagbo	Ntaganda	
Kosgey		Blé Goudé	Al Mahdi	

Table 1: Procedural stages where cases ended.

A white background in the table marks the 12 cases in which a release of the suspect or accused occurred. The 4 cases against a grey background mark cases which ended in convictions. The case arising out of the investigation against Ongwen is not listed in this graphic as the trial was at the time of writing in the deliberation phase, meaning after the closure of the defence case and when this contribution was submitted for publication the parties still awaited the Trial Chamber to issue its judgment.

12.6.2. Interpreting and Pleading Modes of Liability Consistently After an Investigation

Certain public filings[245] allow drawing of inferences on the thoroughness of the OTP's investigation which preceded applications under Article 58, the confirmation hearing and trial proceedings. They also demonstrate whether the results of an investigation into the modes of liability was consistently interpreted by the OTP in its pleadings:

---

[245] For example, request for arrest warrant/summons to appear, the DCC, decision on confirmation of charges, notice for re-characterisation of facts, no-case to answer decisions, trial and appeal judgments.

Liability advanced by

In filing: Case:	OTP Arrest warrant application	PTC Decision on arrest warrant	OTP (Amended) DCC	PTC Confirmation decision	OTP suggests use of Regulation 55	TC Notice pursuant to Regulation 55	TC Decision on NCTA	TC Judgment	AC Judgment
Abu Garda	25(3)(a)	25(3)(a)	25(3)(a)	Declined					
Mba-rushimana	25(3)(a)	25(3)(d)	25(3)(d)	Declined					
Ali	25(3)(a) 25(3)(d)	25(3)(d)	25(3)(d)	Declined					
Kosgey	25(3)(a) 25(3)(d)	25(3)(a)	25(3)(a)	Declined					
Muthaura	25(3)(a) 25(3)(d)	25(3)(a)	25(3)(a)	25(3)(a)	25(3)(b) 25(3)(c) 25(3)(d)				
Kenyatta	25(3)(a) 25(3)(d)	25(3)(a)	25(3)(a)	25(3)(a)	25(3)(b) 25(3)(c) 25(3)(d)				

Ruto	25(3)(a) 25(3)(d)	25(3)(a)	25(3)(a)	25(3)(a)	**25(3)(b)** **25(3)(c)** 25(3)(d)	**25(3)(b)** **25(3)(c)** 25(3)(d) — Charges vacated
Sang	25(3)(d)	25(3)(a)	25(3)(a) 25(3)(b) 25(3)(d) 28(a) 28(b)	25(3)(a) 25(3)(b) 25(3)(d) 25(3)(d)(i)		Charges vacated
Gbagbo	25(3)(a)	25(3)(a)	25(3)(a) 25(3)(b) 25(3)(c) 25(3)(d) 28(a) 28(b)	25(3)(a) 25(3)(b) 25(3)(d) 28	28(a) 28(b)	Acquittal
Blé Goudé	25(3)(a)	25(3)(a)	25(3)(a) 25(3)(b) 25(3)(c) 25(3)(d) 28(a)	25(3)(a) 25(3)(b) 25(3)(c) 25(3)(d)		Acquittal
Ongwen	25(3)(b)	25(3)(b)	25(3)(a) 25(3)(b) 25(3)(d) 28(a)	25(3)(a) 25(3)(b) 25(3)(d) 28(a)		

| Liability advanced by | | | | | | | | | |
In filing: Case:	OTP Arrest warrant application	PTC Decision on arrest warrant	OTP (Amended) DCC	PTC Confirmation decision	OTP suggests use of Regulation 55	TC Notice pursuant to Regulation 55	TC Decision on NCTA	TC Judgment	AC Judgment
Ngudjolo Chui	25(3)(a) 25(3)(b)	25(3)(a) 25(3)(b)	25(3)(a) 25(3)(b)	25(3)(a)				Acquittal	
Al Mahdi	25(3)(a) 25(3)(c) 25(3)(d)	25(3)(a) **25(3)(b)** 25(3)(c) 25(3)(d)	25(3)(a) 25(3)(b) 25(3)(c) 25(3)(d)	25(3)(a) 25(3)(b) 25(3)(c) 25(3)(d)				25(3)(a) conviction	
Ntaganda	25(3)(a)	25(3)(a)	25(3)(a) 25(3)(b) 25(3)(d) 28(a)	25(3)(a) 25(3)(b) 25(3)(d) 28(a)	25(3)(a) 'direct co-perpetration' for all counts			25(3)(a) conviction	

Katanga	25(3)(a) 25(3)(b)	25(3)(a) 25(3)(b)	25(3)(a) 25(3)(b)	25(3)(a)		**25(3)(d)**	
Lubanga	25(3)(a)	25(3)(a)	25(3)(a)	25(3)(a)			25(3)(a) conviction
Bemba	25(3)(a)	25(3)	25(3)(a)	**28(a)** 'knew'	**28(a)** 'should have known'		**28(a)** 'knew' conviction	Acquittal

Table 2: Criminal liability of cases at different stages.

The bolded entries indicate that a liability change occurred in the judicial proceedings or was suggested by the OTP. Indicative of the struggle of the Prosecution to realistically assess the results of its investigation are the cases against Muthaura, Kenyatta and Ruto. Shortly before these cases resulted in withdrawal of or vacating of all charges, the Prosecution tried to suggest to the Trial Chamber to re-characterise the liability it had initially determined during its ongoing investigations. This suggested use of Regulation 55 would have resulted in a downgrading of liability from principal to accessory. Similarly, in the Katanga case, the judges realised at the deliberation stage that the alleged principal liability was not proven and, based on the same facts, re-characterised the allegation to accessory liability (Article 25(3)(d)). In the Bemba case, the Prosecution had misinterpreted the facts determined during its own investigation by charging principal liability under Article 25(3)(a) so the Pre-Trial Chamber had to adjourn the confirmation hearing to 'guide' the Prosecution to the correct liability: command responsibility (Article 28(a)). However, an investigation into command responsibility is complex and has a rather different dimension than an investigation into Article 25(3)(a) charges. The Prosecution finally lost its case due to failure to prove one element of command responsibility, as Bemba had taken certain measures.

12.6.3. Alternative Charging

The above table shows that nearing the conclusion of its investigation in 10 out of 17 cases, the Prosecution advanced *multiple* modes of liability in its applications for an arrest warrant or summons to appear.[246] The Pre-Trial Chambers reduced this approach by only issuing three warrants for arrests with multiple modes of liability,[247] and otherwise authorising arrest warrants and summons to appear with one mode of liability only. The Prosecution, appearing in front of the same Pre-Trial Chamber, attempted to (re-)introduce its *wider* approach on modes of liability by producing 7 out of 17 DCC's with multiple modes of liability.[248] In 4 of these 7 cases,

---

[246] *Prosecutor v. Mbarushimana, Prosecutor v. Ali, Prosecutor v. Kosgey, Prosecutor v. Muthaura, Prosecutor v. Kenyatta, Prosecutor v. Ruto, Prosecutor v. Sang, Prosecutor v. Ngudjolo Chui, Prosecutor v. Al Mahdi* and *Prosecutor v. Katanga.*

[247] *Prosecutor v. Ngudjolo Chui, Prosecutor v. Al Mahdi* and *Prosecutor v. Katanga.*

[248] *Prosecutor v. Gbagbo, Prosecutor v. Blé Goudé, Prosecutor v. Ongwen, Prosecutor v. Ngudjolo Chui, Prosecutor v. Al Mahdi, Prosecutor v. Ntaganda* and *Prosecutor v. Katanga.*

the Prosecution had initially applied only for an arrest warrant based on one mode of liability and then expanded the DCC to contain multiple modes.[249] In the Ongwen case, multiple liabilities may have been the result of further investigations, but such an expansion of modes of liability may have otherwise more reflected the OTP's charging practice and the aim to put the defendant on early notice which modes of liability he will face. However, in the Blé Goudé and Gbagbo cases, there was no reason for the Prosecution to re-assess its investigation by switching from one liability mode, as pleaded in the motion for an arrest warrant, to four modes of liability against each suspect in the DCC, because the majority of Trial Chamber held in its decision on the NCTA-motion that *none* of these liabilities had been proven to the required evidentiary standard.[250]

12.6.4. The Elephant in the Room

This analysis has referred to several judges expressing concern, sometimes even frustration about the way the ICC OTP conducted its investigation into the modes of liability. Unlike the ICTY, ICTR and SCSL, the ICC employs the notion of *iura novit curia*. However, even Regulation 55 (meaning a re-characterisation of the mode of liability) did not always enable the judges to cure earlier deficiencies in the way the OTP has conducted its investigation.

Simply put, the cases analysed in this chapter support the conclusion that in several cases, the OTP moved to have charges confirmed at a point in time when its investigation into the modes of liability was not yet ready to face judicial scrutiny. This resulted not infrequently in cases not passing the confirmation of charges hearing, or simply ending before a judgment could be issued, because the determinations of liability and the cases overall were too weak. Thus, it is time to consider a paradigm change. Judge Tarfusser was right in pronouncing that investigations constitute

> the bedrock of any criminal case; as a consequence, flaws and shortcomings at the investigative stage are not suitable

---

[249] *Prosecutor v. Gbagbo, Prosecutor v. Blé Goudé, Prosecutor v. Ongwen* and *Prosecutor v. Ntaganda*.

[250] Gbagbo and Blé Goudé Trial Reasons for Oral Decision, para. 28, see above note 45.

to be remedied in the courtroom and will inevitably com-
promise the chances of success of any resulting case.[251]

12.7. Solutions

Within each investigation, a preference should be put on establishing one
mode of liability in a solid way. An intermediate step in an investigation is
therefore the fundamental decision whether the target is liable as a principal or accessory. While it is always possible to charge a suspect in the
alternative, this option should not be used excessively, but rather sparing-
ly.[252] In other words: if the investigation division can only conclude that a
suspect is liable for three or more possible modes of liability, then it is
proposed that a request for an arrest warrant or a document containing the
charges should generally *not* yet be entertained. Rather, investigations
focused on determining the applicable mode of liability should continue
as long as sufficient evidence creates more certainty and a maximum of
two alternative modes of liability remain. It is proposed to entertain the
charging with more than two modes of liability in exceptional cases and,
if so, with hesitation and caution. One may argue that charging multiple
modes of liability is sometimes the only way to reflect the totality of
wrongdoing.[253] But experience at the ICC shows that the OTP had often
not fully concluded its analysis or investigations, and has thus exposed
itself to the risk of losing its cases in court. Requesting an arrest warrant
and confirmation of charges without having settled on the most applicable
modes of liability means that the approach was, simply put, to 'keep all
options open'. Such an approach leaves the risk of not fully understanding
one's own case. By contrast, identifying the right mode of liability is going to the core of any case – that is, to individualise guilt, to attribute
wrong to one specific person.

---

[251] Gbagbo and Blé Goudé Trial Opinion of Judge Cuno Tarfusser, para. 95, see above note
168.

[252] In 2016, the OTP had advanced that it strives to "explore and present the most appropriate
range of modes of liability to legally qualify the criminal conduct" (emphasis added). ICC-
OTP, *Policy Paper on Case Selection and Prioritisation*, 15 September 2016, para. 44
('OTP Policy Paper on Case Selection and Prioritisation') (https://legal-tools.org/doc/
182205). By contrast, the OTP's recent strategic plan introduced the new objective of developing a "more *narrow* case in terms of crimes and criminal *liability*" (emphasis added).
ICC-OTP, *Strategic Plan 2019–2021*, 17 July 2019, para. 24 (https://legal-tools.org/doc/
7ncqt3).

[253] *Ibid.*, referring in para. 24 to a "broad case representing the totality of the crimes".

Consideration should be given to quality-control mechanisms in order to adopt a different approach: to have independent teams review the results of an investigation and test the case on criminal liability for sufficiency. The 'review team' could consist of persons from within or outside the OTP, but these persons should, apart from the review itself, not have had exposure to the previous investigation in order to be able to form an independent and unbiased assessment of the status and sufficiency of the investigation.[254]

Another option is for the OTP to 'over deliver': that is, already *before* entering a new procedural stage, the OTP should strive to meet the evidentiary threshold required for the next, higher stage. For example, before the OTP issues a draft document containing the charges for a confirmation hearing which requires "substantial grounds",[255] it should have prepared its case to meet the threshold required for the NCTA stage, meaning to have identified enough "evidence on which a reasonable Trial Chamber could convict".[256]

---

[254] See OTP Policy Paper on Case Selection and Prioritisation, para. 23, see above note 252.

[255] ICC Statute, Article 61(5), see above note 1.

[256] ICC, Situation in the Republic of Kenya, *The Prosecutor v. William Samoei Ruto and Joshua Arap Sang*, Trial Chamber, Decision No. 5 on the Conduct of Trial Proceedings (Principles and Procedure on 'No Case to Answer' Motions), 3 June 2014, ICC-01/09-01/11-1334, para. 32 (https://legal-tools.org/doc/128ce5).

13

Challenges in Charge Selection: Considerations Informing the Number of Charges and Cumulative Charging Practices

Cale Davis[*]

13.1. Introduction

There is no other discretion singularly more important to whether an international criminal tribunal fulfils its mandate than a prosecutor's decision of who to charge, and what to charge them with. Prosecutors are the 'gatekeepers' to international courts,[1] tasked with determining what conduct does and does not merit prosecution. It is no exaggeration to say that in setting a court's agenda, they have the life of international criminal law in their hands.

Yet the charging discretion is also one of the most complex decisions prosecutors are called upon to make. It is marked by a plethora of pragmatic, legal, evidential, and policy considerations that need to be assessed and weighed. Prosecutors must carefully exercise their professional judgement to determine the most appropriate course of action in each case. Rarely will they be confronted with a scenario that sufficiently mirrors a previous case from which they can draw a direct historical comparison.

---

[*] **Cale Davis** (I.L.M. (Adv), LL.B. (Hons), BIR, GDLP) is a Ph.D. candidate at Leiden University. He was previously a Prosecutor at the Northern Territory DPP and a Judge's Associate at the Supreme Court of the Northern Territory in Australia. He has held teaching positions at Bond University and Charles Darwin University. This chapter is derived from research the author has conducted for his Ph.D. research. A very early version of this chapter was presented at the Quality Control in Criminal Investigations Conference in Delhi on 22 February 2019 (https://www.cilrap.org/cilrap-film/190222-davis/). The author wishes to thank Dr. Vanessa Newby for pointing him in the direction of Thomas Risse.

[1] Lovisa Bådagård and Mark Klamberg, "The Gatekeeper of the ICC: Prosecutorial Strategies for Selecting Situations and Cases at the International Criminal Court", in *Georgetown Journal of International Law*, 2017, vol. 48, no. 5, p. 639; Héctor Olásolo, "The Prosecutor of the ICC Before the Initiation of Investigations: A Quasi-Judicial or a Political Body?", in *International Criminal Law Review*, 2003, vol. 3, no. 2, p. 89.

Moreover, they must make these decisions in the knowledge that the path they choose will have consequences not only for the potential defendant, but also an innumerable number of actors with an interest in the court's work.

Perhaps for this reason, deontological, rule-based approaches to analysing and guiding the charging discretion have their attractions. Yet attempts to provide normative guidance to prosecutors on how to navigate the discretion have inevitably failed to placate critics. For example, despite the ICC-OTP's efforts to produce policy papers and strategic plans (a practice largely ignored by the ICTY, ICTR, and SCSL), Darryl Robinson has observed that "[f]or any position the Court can possibly take, perfectly plausible and powerful criticisms can inevitably be made".[2] Martti Koskenniemi's famous apology – utopia duopoly remains relevant.[3] William Schabas has argued that the policy papers fail to explain why some cases were selected while others were cast aside.[4] Deontological approaches to analysing the charging discretion have so far failed to provide sufficient nuance to be useful in any concrete sense. A different focus is required to better understand how the quality of the exercises of the charging discretion can be ensured.

It should be noted at the outset that it is misleading to speak of the 'charging discretion' as a single choice. It is not. The charging discretion is a collective of smaller discretionary choices, such as *who* to charge, *when* to charge them, and *what* to charge them with. The question of what to charge can again be broken down into the issues of the *types* of charges someone should face and the *number* of charges they should face. This may lead to the practice of cumulative charging, one of the seven bottlenecks identified by the *Quality Control in Criminal Investigations* team as being pertinent to improving the speed and cost of international criminal processes.[5] For reasons of brevity, it is this last issue concerning the number of charges that a defendant should face that this chapter shall focus on.

---

[2] Darryl Robinson, "Inescapable Dyads: Why the International Criminal Court Cannot Win", in *Leiden Journal of International Law*, 2015, vol. 28, no. 2, p. 324.

[3] Martti Koskenniemi, *From Apology to Utopia*, Cambridge University Press, 2005, p. 16.

[4] William A. Schabas, "Feeding Time at the Office of the Prosecutor", *International Criminal Justice Today*, 23 November 2016 (available on its web site).

[5] Morten Bergsmo, "Towards a Culture of Quality Control in Criminal Investigations", FICHL Policy Brief Series No. 94, Torkel Opsahl Academic EPublisher, Brussels, 2019 (https://www.toaep.org/pbs-pdf/94-bergsmo/).

This chapter has three broad purposes. First, it attempts to highlight the weaknesses of deontological approaches in analysing or guiding the charging discretion by demonstrating that the factors that affect how the discretion is exercised do not lend themselves to normative constraint. Second, it represents an attempt to turn the discussion regarding charge selection towards the views of the people exercising the discretion by drawing heavily upon the author's own interviews with international prosecutors. Third, it hopes to encourage the quality of choices to be assessed by reference to the willingness of the actor who made the decision to engage in debate and discussion regarding why the choice was made.

This chapter is divided into five core sections. Section 13.2. presents descriptive statistics to place the exercise of the charging discretion in its historical context. It reveals that the issue of how many charges to allege against individual accused is marked by both consonance and dissonance. From a purely numerical perspective, historical practice is widely varied. Section 13.3. goes on to explore the factors international prosecutors have relied upon in describing how many charges to allege. It demonstrates that these factors are numerous and context-specific. Section 13.4. posits that attempts to ensure the quality of the exercise of the charging discretion need to accept that prosecutors are trying to achieve numerous goals through their charging practices and that the charging discretion is steeped in subjectivity. Section 13.5. argues that Thomas Risse's logic of arguing provides a conceptual framework through which we can assess the quality of exercises of the charging discretion. It aims to demonstrate the importance of sharing practitioners' experiences in exercising the charging discretion and the reasons they have relied upon to justify the decisions that they have made. The voices of practitioners who work at the proverbial coalface are not given sufficient prominence in the literature. It is important their experiences be shared. By drawing these voices into the conversation, we can hope to develop a more complete picture of the challenges they face in charge selection, as well as accelerate the development of collective knowledge about desirable and undesirable conduct.

13.1.1. Interview Methodology

This chapter is based in part on a subset of thirty personal, anonymous interviews the author conducted between March and September 2018. With only two exceptions, the interview subjects held or hold the rank of

Senior Trial Attorney (or its equivalent) and above at the ICC, ICTY, ICTR, and SCSL.[6] These individuals were selected because of their senior positions within trial teams and the organisational structure of the various OTPs, allowing them to speak with authority regarding discretionary choices.

Interviews were conducted in person, via video-conference, or on the phone. To encourage the interviewees to speak openly, they were informed at the start of the interview that they would not be quoted directly by name or in a manner that identifies them personally. The open interviews were structured around two broad questions: what discretionary choices did the interviewee consider to be important in their work, and what did they consider relevant when exercising them. At the conclusion of the interviews, the recordings were transcribed by the author. The transcripts of the recordings are stored on file with the author.

Importantly, the views presented in this chapter are not offered as being universally held. Nor are they claimed to be widely held, or even held by more than one person. The point of discussing these views is simply to demonstrate that the views *are* held, and this is important in order to develop a picture regarding the factors that have influenced the decision of how many charges a defendant should be faced with.

13.2. Charging in Numbers

Before proceeding to analyse the rationales that have informed the question of how many charges to allege against an accused, it is useful to reflect on historical charging practice. This section presents descriptive statistics that contextualise this issue, while contrasting the variations in charging practices across, and within, the ICC, ICTY, ICTR, and SCSL's prosecution offices.

The descriptive statistics presented in this section are based on the charges alleged against individual accused contained in the *final charging documents* filed against each individual defendant at the ICC, ICTY, ICTR, and SCSL up to December 2018. The final charging documents are

---

[6] Of the 30 interviewees, 26 came from a common law background and 4 came from a civil law background. The predominance of common law practitioners reflects the reality that most individuals who fall into this class come from common law systems. The author is thankful for the co-operation and assistance of all the interviewees who spoke on a voluntary basis, as well as the OTPs of the MICT and the ICC for making current staff available.

the most recent official filings regarding the charges a defendant is accused of. They may be indictments, 'documents containing the charges', warrants of arrest, or summonses to appear. While some accused were never prosecuted (they may have died, or the charges may have been later withdrawn), the final charging documents are nevertheless useful because they are the ones in which the prosecutor 'nails their colours to the mast'. They represent the final assessment of what the prosecutor considers to be the charges on which there *are* grounds for a conviction.

Between 1995 (the year the first final charging document was issued) to December 2018, international criminal prosecutors at the four courts within the framework of this study have seen 195 final charging documents issued, accusing 298 defendants of 2,774 core international crimes. On average, defendants charged by the prosecutors of these courts will face 9.3 charges. The average number of charges alleged against defendants at the ICTY is 10; at the ICTR is 6; at the SCSL is 13; and at the ICC is 12.

Figure 1 presents the average number of charges alleged against individual accused for each year across the four courts. As depicted by the dotted regression line, the average number of charges alleged against defendants each year has remained largely flat. There is only a minor upward trend.

On a year-to-year basis, the averages have also remained largely consistent at the ICTY, the ICTR, and the SCSL. There is only minimal variation. The averages never exceed 20 charges. ICC-OTP practice, however, has been far less consistent. Periods of relative stability – such as between 2008 and 2014 – contrast sharply against the periods 2004-2007 and 2015-2018. Significantly higher averages are reported in 2004, 2007, and 2015. These were the years in which final charging documents containing a large number of charges were issued for Otti, Harun, Kushayb, and Ongwen. In these years, the averages spiked respectively to 30, 32, and 46 charges – roughly five times the average across all courts.

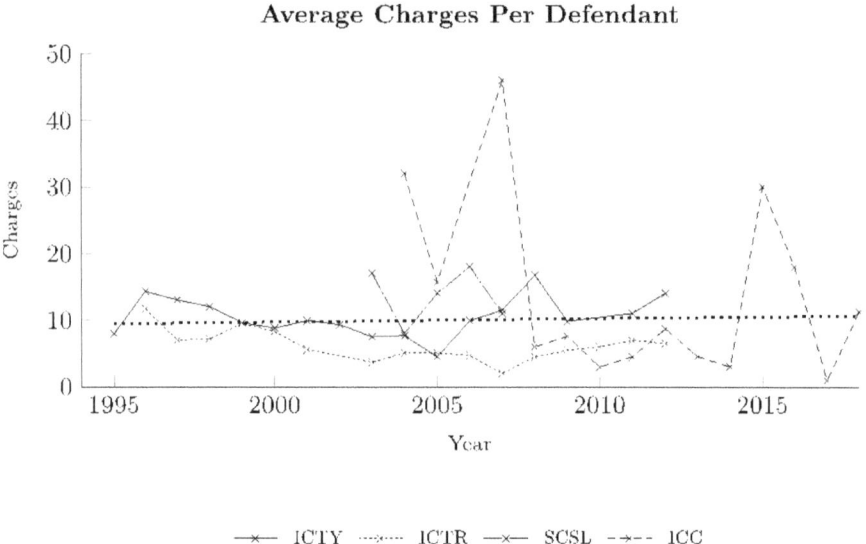

Figure 1.

One might be tempted to explain away the spikes in the ICC-OTP's averages by claiming that each case is unique and that past practice cannot, therefore, be used as a reliable benchmark against which to assess charging practices. This is undoubtedly correct. However, the explanation is not entirely satisfying, for two reasons. First, each case is *always* unique. Therefore, over a quarter of a century of charging practice, it would be reasonable to expect that in at least some of those years, at some other court, similar fluctuations would have been seen. They have not. Second, for this explanation to be convincing, we would expect to see similar spikes in *other* courts. Yet the ICC-OTP is the only prosecution office to demonstrate such significant fluctuations on a year-to-year basis.

The data in Figure 1 can be presented differently to provide additional insights into charging practices. Figure 2 is a box plot. Box plots are constructed by listing the number of charges per each individual defendant in order from lowest to highest. The 'whiskers' – the lines extending from either end of the central boxes – represent the top 25 per cent and bottom 25 per cent of observations. The boxes are the middle 50 per cent of observations. The vertical line dissecting each box represents the median observation. Box plots therefore demonstrate how observations are distributed over the range between the lowest score and the highest

score. They allow charging practices to be easily compared between
courts.

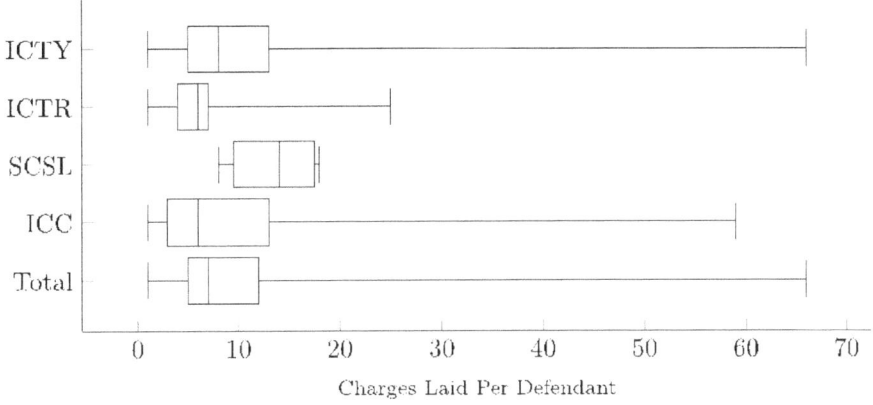

Figure 2.

The Total plot is derived from all 298 observations. It represents the
'state of the art' of charging across the four courts. Twenty-five per cent of
all defendants that have ever been prosecuted by the OTPs of ICTY, ICTR,
SCSL, and ICC faced between 1 and 4 charges each. Fifty per cent faced
between 5 and 12 charges. Twenty-five per cent faced between 13 and 66
charges. These figures show that the number of charges faced by all defendants are *not* normally distributed. They do not depict a neat, symmet-
rical 'bell curve' in which the middle 50 per cent of observations lie equi-
distant from the highest and lowest scores, and the top 25 per cent and
bottom 25 per cent of observations cover the same range of data. Instead,
the data is skewed, with the top 25 per cent of observations covering a
much higher range than the bottom 75 per cent of observations. A similar
skewness is evident at the ICC and the ICTY. The SCSL and the ICTR
display more normal distributions.[7]

What Figure 2 demonstrates is that there have been divergent practices regarding the number of charges prosecutors have alleged against
individual accused. While 75 per cent of defendants have faced between 1
and 12 charges, history has revealed that 25 per cent of the time an OTP

---

[7] The SCSL-OTP only charged 11 defendants, so the number of observations was significantly lower than the ICTY (165); ICTR (85); and ICC (37).

charges someone, they will allege a far greater number of charges against them than the 75 per cent of other cases would suggest.

The figures presented in Figures 1 and 2 require reflection. They raise important questions concerning what goals international criminal prosecutors hope to achieve through the prosecutions they commence. More charges mean prosecutors need to invest more money and more resources to prove them. It also means that defence needs to invest similar resources in casting reasonable doubt over them. With this in mind, it could be suggested that the further the proposed number of charges against an individual strays upwards from the mean figure of 9.3, the greater consideration should be given to what is hoped to be achieved by the prosecution.

13.3. Charging Rationales

The figures presented in Section 13.2. invite an inquiry into why there has been such varied practice with respect to the number of charges alleged against individual defendants. The purpose of this section is to begin this inquiry. Section 13.3.1. discusses four factors that appear to have operated to *increase* the number of charges faced by individual defendants. Yet one should not view these in isolation. As discussed in Section 13.3.2., there are other factors that appear to have operated to *reduce* the number of charges faced by individual defendants.

13.3.1. Factors Justifying More Charges

There appear to be at least four factors that have operated in favour of defendants facing more, rather than fewer, charges: the desire to obtain convictions; the aspiration of advancing the law; recording history; and finally a hope that the prosecution of the defendant will be representative of other uncharged – allegedly criminal – acts.

13.3.1.1. A Desire for Convictions

The fact that a desire to obtain convictions has militated in favour of defendants facing more charges should not come as a surprise. While Richard J. Goldstone once argued that "[w]hether there are convictions or whether there are acquittals will not be the yardstick" against which the

success of international criminal justice will be assessed,[8] there is cause
for scepticism as to whether this is universally accepted. Schabas has recognised that international criminal law 'thrives on conviction' – a hunger
that has driven international criminal law and procedure "into a more re-
pressive mode".[9] Mirjan Damaška went further, arguing that international
criminal courts possessed a *'libido puniendi'* unlike those of their domestic counterparts, driven by the famous desire to 'end impunity' – on his
account, "[h]igh acquittal rates could easily augur failure of their mission".[10]

While this sort of narrowly-focussed consequentialist reasoning
might appear unrefined in light of recent turns towards expressivist accounts of international prosecutions that draw legitimacy from the broader
effects criminal justice mechanisms have on society, it is difficult to deny
them some visceral attraction. A conviction is a vindication of the time,
effort, and resources expended on the prosecution. It validates the suffering of the victims. And given the relentless barrage of commentary about
just how few convictions the ICC-OTP has obtained, it could be used to
justify a court's very existence.

There is an additional reason why prosecutors have seen convictions as important: some defendants are seen to fall into a unique category
of extraordinary maliciousness. Completely aside from any lofty desire to
fulfil the aims of international criminal justice, this itself has, in some
instances, warranted charging a defendant with numerous crimes in order
to increase the likelihood that a conviction will be entered against them.
One prosecutor recalled that in the Prosecution's Final Trial Brief in *Galić*,
Mark Ierace SC submitted that Galić's crimes were not "committed in the
heat of battle, or with little time to reflect on their consequences. Rather,
they were continuing crimes, in which his *mens rea* was refreshed on a

---

[8]   Richard J. Goldstone, "Address Before the Supreme Court of the United States", speech
      delivered at the 1996 CEELI Leadership Award Dinner, Washington, D.C., 2 October 1996,
      quoted in Mark Ellis, "Achieving Justice Before the International War Crimes Tribunal:
      Challenges for the Defence Counsel", in *Duke Journal of Comparative and International
      Law*, 1997, vol. 7, no. 2, p. 526 (fn. 37).

[9]   William A. Schabas, "Balancing the Rights of the Accused with the Imperatives of Ac-
      countability", in Ramesh Thakur and Peter Malcontent (eds.), *From Sovereign Impunity to
      International Accountability: The Search for Justice in a World of States*, United Nations
      University Press, 2004, p. 165.

[10] Mirjan Damaška, "Reflections on Fairness in International Criminal Justice", in *Journal of
      International Criminal Justice*, 2012, vol. 10, no. 3, p. 613.

daily basis".[11] In this light, the prosecutor recalled that Galić's conduct "almost [fell] in a special category", and on their assessment, the Prosecution was justifiably "out to get him".[12] While they reflected that it would not be appropriate to "double up on war crimes and crimes against humanity" in every prosecution, the alleged maliciousness of Galić "warranted using everything in our armoury to get him" and that "on that basis alone, it was appropriate to use all relevant crimes in the *Statute* that applied to what he'd done".[13]

There is another reason why a desire to obtain convictions has led to defendants facing an inflated number of charges: ambiguity. This takes two forms: ambiguity as to what the law requires to be proved for a conviction to be entered; and ambiguity as to what evidence will emerge at trial. One prosecutor recalled questioning a "very prominent member of the OTP" regarding why comparatively low-level offenders were being faced with a large number of charges. The response, they recollected, was "because we don't know what we are going to be able to prove".[14] The prosecutor recalled saying (perhaps words to the effect of) "that's good, that's really good. So if you get four counts conviction and the other fifty-six [are] acquittals, that's a win?", and worried that the practice of overcharging would raise unrealistic expectations in the community.[15]

13.3.1.2. Advancing the Law

A desire to advance the law has also arguably influenced considerations of how many charges a defendant should face. International criminal law is in a constant state of development and transformation. Since 1993, practitioners have been 'discovering' new crimes that were not necessarily envisaged a quarter of a century ago. While judges are given most of the credit for this – Joe Powderly has correctly noted that judicial creativity involves "the sculpting of the relatively featureless granite of existing law

---

[11] ICTY, *Prosecutor v. Stanislav Galić*, Trial Chamber, Prosecution's Final Trial Brief, 28 April 2003, IT-98-29-T, para. 644 (https://www.legal-tools.org/doc/8263bd).
[12] Interview with P19.
[13] Interview with P19.
[14] Interview with P29.
[15] Interview with P29.

in order to give it form, effect, and reason"[16] – the role of prosecutors cannot be understated. After all, prosecutors provide courts with the defendants who serve as vehicles for important jurisprudential developments. It is similarly important not to understate the willingness of prosecutors to engage in the process of law development.

The historical context in which prosecutorial discretion has been exercised sheds some light on why this is the case. "Apart from Nuremberg […] and Tokyo for that matter", remarked one prosecutor, "there had been no real attempt to develop the international criminal law".[17] Prior to the creation of the ICTY, they observed, international criminal law "had been more academic than an enforceable body of law".[18] Prosecutors had before them a blank canvas, and could hand the judiciary the brushes through which modern international criminal law could be painted.

In part, a desire to advance the law can be attributed to pressure from the broader international community that enforced upon prosecutors a sense of duty to ensure the ICTY was a success. This sense of duty was felt at the highest levels of the ICTY-OTP. One prosecutor reflected that prior to Graham T. Blewitt travelling to The Hague to take up the role of Deputy Prosecutor, he travelled to the United Nations in New York and met with high-profile NGOs, members of the US State Department, international media, and others. The prosecutor recalled that Blewitt felt that all those with whom he met were "trying to impress on [him] the importance of the ICTY and what it meant for international humanitarian law", and that they were impressing on him the belief that the ICTY should not be allowed to fail.[19]

The sense of duty felt by prosecutors was accompanied by a desire to ensure that the jurisprudence that was developed by the Chambers was of a quality that would withstand legal scrutiny. An ICTY prosecutor described that they "had the *responsibility* of making sure that the judgments that came out of the trial chambers, but more particularly out of the Ap-

---

[16]   Joseph Powderly, "Judicial Interpretation at the *Ad Hoc* Tribunals: Method from Chaos?", in Shane Darcy and Joseph Powderly (eds.), *Judicial Creativity at the International Criminal Tribunals*, Oxford University Press, 2010, p. 18.

[17]   Interview with P4.

[18]   Interview with P4.

[19]   Interview with P4.

peals Chamber, would withstand international scrutiny".[20] They wanted the jurisprudence to be consistent, and saw it as a "major responsibility to put up good, sound legal arguments".[21] The prosecutor noted that the production of good jurisprudence would aid the survival of the ICTY, and that "if the Tribunal succeeded, then the creation of a permanent court had more chance of [...] being achieved than if we failed", conceding that their eye was trained on the future of international humanitarian law.[22]

Prosecutors seized the opportunity to advance the law with an enthusiastic sense of duty. One SCSL prosecutor, noting that international law contains many rules that have never been enforced, noted "you really want to build the law and you want to use the opportunity to do it".[23] Another reflected that the undeveloped state of international humanitarian law meant that its development "*needed* to be pursued" and saw the development of the law as part of their mandate (although, when questioned further about the sense of being mandated to advance the law, they explained that this was "putting it too high" and that they misspoke).[24]

The desire to advance the law had practical consequences for how the charging discretion was exercised. One ICTY prosecutor reflected that Blewitt introduced a "policy" for all investigators, and "in particular, the Senior Trial Attorneys", under which "they should not be afraid to advance legal arguments and legal theories in prosecuting the cases".[25] There are several examples of where charges appear to have been affected by this policy. In the prosecution of Stanislav Galić, the ICTY-OTP was of the view that "there was an international crime of terror and that it came within the jurisdiction of ICTY", despite there being no on-point jurisprudence to clearly justify this position.[26] The charge of inflicting terror was a "discretionary additional charge" in the indictment.[27] One prosecutor recalled that "we thought it was important to nail [the infliction of terror

---

20   Interview with P4. Emphasis added.
21   Interview with P4.
22   Interview with P4.
23   Interview with P9.
24   Interview with P4. Emphasis added.
25   Interview with P4.
26   Interview with P19.
27   Interview with P19.

upon civilians as] an express crime", explaining that they saw this as a "a responsible exercise of our power".[28]

The ICTY and ICTR-OTP was also prolific in the development of the law surrounding sexual violence in armed conflict. Several members of the Office wanted to prove the criminality of certain sexual conduct.[29] The 'dearth' of jurisprudence regarding this category of crime allowed the Office to be creative in the formulation of charges.[30] "I think it was probably always recognised that plundering and raping and pillaging was part of the process of conquering the enemy", remarked one prosecutor, adding that "it was nothing that was previously prosecuted, and the Tribunal had been urged to examine this aspect of the conflict, and of course we did that".[31] The OTPs charged sexual violence as "cruel treatment, torture, persecution, enslavement, and genocide", which led to the "rapid development of sexual violence jurisprudence".[32]

Despite the clear path the OTPs had before them to push forward novel charges and arguments, constraint needed to be exercised. Even though Blewitt had introduced the policy that Senior Trial Attorneys should not be afraid to advance "novel" legal arguments, this was on the proviso that "they had a fall-back position of a more traditional position".[33] The arguments justifying the novel position should also be reasonable. "[W]e were going to be asking the judges to make rulings that were unique", one senior ICTY prosecutor noted, "I certainly felt the obligation to ensure that what we were putting up to the judges was sound and would enable them to bring rulings that would [...] withstand international scrutiny and withstand the test of time".[34]

Another prosecutor described that they were constrained by the "spirit" that animated the provisions in the *Rome Statute*, describing the need to adhere to processes "that will look to be fair in the light of day".[35]

---

[28] Interview with P19.

[29] Interview with P29.

[30] Michelle Jarvis and Kate Vigneswaran, "Challenges to Successful Outcomes in Sexual Violence Cases", in Serge Brammertz and Michelle Jarvis (eds.), *Prosecuting Conflict-Related Sexual Violence at the ICTY*, Oxford University Press, 2016, p. 58.

[31] Interview with P4.

[32] Jarvis and Vigneswaran, 2016, p. 58, see above note 30.

[33] Interview with P4.

[34] Interview with P4.

[35] Interview with P24.

While they recognised that the nature of the ICC's cases required prosecutors to be "aggressive and forward-leaning" and "creative", they explained that the Court was "not a place to be cute or clever with the rights of the accused" and it was "not a place where you're clever with the law".[36]

Similarly, another prosecutor described that the law should be developed carefully. They explained their view that "it was fine for us to stretch the envelope, but there's no ruddy way in which we should be ripping the edges off".[37] They described that this philosophy affected the charges laid against Duško Tadić, explaining that there were some members within the Office who wanted to argue that grave breaches of the *Geneva Conventions* applied to non-international armed conflicts. The prosecutor described that, in their view, this was "just not so" and that the only way those arguments would be advanced was going to be "over [their] dead body".[38]

At the ICC-OTP, the policy decisions to focus on sexual and gender-based crimes and crimes against children has been further explained by a desire to, in the words of one prosecutor, "do what we can to protect the most vulnerable populations".[39] The prosecutor explained that this approach affected the charges laid against Bosco Ntaganda. Ntaganda was the first defendant charged by the ICC-OTP for alleged sexual offences committed against 'child soldiers' within the *Forces Patriotiques pour la Libération du Congo*, by members of that same armed group. "[P]eople think of the law of armed conflict as essentially focussed on the so-called enemy population or the opponents in the conflict", the prosecutor explained, "[b]ut we said no [...] children don't lose those protections simply because they'd been conscripted into armed forces".[40]

13.3.1.3. Recording History

A desire to record history may also have militated in favour of defendants being charged with more, rather than fewer, charges. Remarkably, while all international criminal tribunals record history through the taking and

---

[36] Interview with P24.
[37] Interview with P13.
[38] Interview with P13.
[39] Interview with P14.
[40] Interview with P14.

recording of evidence, only the ECCC has this stated as one of its express goals.[41]

One prosecutor advanced the argument that the benefits of setting an historical record warranted charging a potential defendant with all possible crimes that it was believed they committed. "I think starting at the beginning there was an unspoken policy that you should charge them with pretty much everything you could prove against them", they observed.[42] They added, "I don't think you can say that that approach was wrong. And, on the contrary, I think it is probably right".[43] The rationale for this belief, they explained, is that war crimes trials, certainly in cases where the leadership is being prosecuted, "do have a role in telling a full story even though [prosecutors are] not there to write history".[44]

The prosecutor was also in favour of laying charges that are at least arguable. They argued this by positing that if a prosecutor did *not* "try" to prove an arguable charge, revisionist historians could reflect on the conduct and deny the unalleged arguable charge ever occurred.[45] The prosecutor observed that "history will look back and say there was no genocide in Kosovo" due to the OTP not including that charge in the Kosovo indictment against Milošević, suggesting that such a charge – in their view – should have been included for this reason.[46]

13.3.1.4. Representation

Perhaps the most significant factor that has informed the number of charges a defendant will be faced with is the desire for prosecutors to lay representational charges. Representative charging is a necessary ancillary

---

[41] In their request for assistance to the United Nations, the two Cambodian Prime Ministers hoped that the United Nations would "assist the Cambodian people in establishing the truth": Identical letters dated 23 June 1997 from the Secretary-General addressed to the President of the General Assembly and to the President of the Security Council, UN Doc. S/1997/488, 24 June 1997 (https://www.legal-tools.org/doc/kcnjj4). The United Nations General Assembly hoped that the UN would assist Cambodia in investigating its 'tragic history': Situation of Human Rights in Cambodia: Resolution Adopted by the General Assembly, UN Doc. A/RES/52/135, 27 February 1998 (https://www.legal-tools.org/doc/6e9a5f).

[42] Interview with P11.

[43] Interview with P11.

[44] Interview with P11.

[45] Interview with P11.

[46] Interview with P11.

to the fact that international prosecutors must be selective in their charging decisions. Prosecutors "can't charge every crime that was committed, every murder, every act of sexual violence or mutilation".[47] There are not the resources to do so, nor the motivations. The charging discretion has therefore been used to curate a selection of charges that best represent "the overall picture" of what occurred in a situation,[48] being in "broad terms reflective of what had happened".[49] Prosecutors have identified five ways that charges can be representative.

The first is to represent *criminality*. There are two ways prosecutors have attempted to ensure that they exercise their charging discretion in way that is representative of criminality. The first is to represent the criminality of any given *situation*. Representing the criminality of a situation means that prosecutors endeavour to capture the "essence of what happened on the ground"[50] through a curated set of charges that can be said to be representative of other uncharged acts.[51] "I ensured", remarked one prosecutor, "that we had forcible transfer, deportation, crimes of sexual violence, murders [...] [I] wanted to make sure that every crime was represented somehow in that indictment".[52] Another noted that if investigations revealed incidences of "severe torture", then "the right thing to do would be to add it [to the indictment] because those victims suffered it".[53] A more self-reflective approach was offered by a different prosecutor which highlights the importance of *personal satisfaction* with how they are doing their job. The prosecutor conceded that it was impossible to satisfy even an objective observer "that you got [the charges] absolutely correct", but they personally needed to "have at least some sense of confidence that you were depicting at least a *bona fide* approximation of what had happened".[54]

At the ICC, the principle of representing criminality been enshrined in regulatory and policy documents. Regulation 34(2) of the *Regulations*

---

47 Interview with P12.
48 Interview with P12.
49 Interview with P7.
50 Interview with P14.
51 Interview with P5; Interview with P8.
52 Interview with P8.
53 Interview with P20.
54 Interview with P7.

of the Office of the Prosecutor obliges the 'joint team' to select incidents in its provisional case hypothesis that are "reflective of the most serious crimes and the main types of victimisation".[55] The *Policy Paper on Case Selection and Prioritisation* purports to commit the Prosecutor to "[representing] as much as possible the true extent of the criminality which has occurred within a given situation, in an effort to ensure, jointly with the relevant national jurisdictions, that the most serious crimes committed in each situation do not go unpunished".[56]

One of the ways through which prosecutors have attempted to satisfy themselves that they are representing a situation's criminality is through a focus on those they believe to be the 'most responsible'. The rationale for this is that persons who are purportedly the 'most responsible' are likely "responsible for a wider range of crimes over a wider area", allowing charges against them to "reflect crimes against thousands, tens of thousands of people"[57] without spending resources on multiple prosecutions of lower-ranked individuals to achieve the same *intended* representative effect.

Of course, successfully prosecuting those apparently 'most responsible' requires evidence that is probably difficult to come by. The longstanding practice of pyramidal prosecutions targets lower-ranked perpetrators with the intention of using their evidence (or the investigation into them) to develop evidence that might lead to the successful prosecution of individuals higher up a chain of command (which may or may not exist). This approach was notably adopted (although not without controversy) at the ICTY.[58] At the ICTR, it was not so relevant as "the perpetrator[s] [were] actually on the ground".[59] The ICC-OTP has expressly stated the importance of a 'build upwards strategy' in the 2012-2015 *Strategic Plan*,[60] which was a change from the original (and criticised) policy articulated in 2009 of 'focused investigations and prosecutions' under which

---

[55] ICC, *Regulations of the Office of the Prosecutor*, 23 April 2009, Regulation 34(2) (https://www.legal-tools.org/doc/a97226).

[56] ICC-OTP, *Policy Paper on Case Selection and Prioritisation*, September 2016, para. 45 (https://www.legal-tools.org/doc/182205).

[57] Interview with P12.

[58] Interview with P12; Interview with P10.

[59] Interview with P16.

[60] ICC-OTP, *Strategic Plan: June 2012-2015*, 11 October 2013, para. 43 (https://www.legal-tools.org/doc/954beb).

prosecutors would "select for prosecution those situated at the highest echelons of responsibility".[61] The policy of engaging in pyramidal prosecutions has also been established in the *Policy Paper on Preliminary Examinations* and the *Policy Paper on Case Selection and Prioritisation*.[62]

The principle of representing criminality through the exercise of the charging discretion is also arguably relevant to the prosecution of individual *accused*. In this respect, one prosecutor noted that they tried to craft their indictments so that they were representative "in terms of being reflective of the totality of the criminal conduct of the accused".[63] An experienced ICC prosecutor reflected that "it would be wrong to use your discretion to only charge somebody [...] [with] [...] forcible transfer if they've killed and tortured people, even if it might be easier",[64] reflecting the belief that a proper exercise of the charging discretion should not artificially represent the criminality of the conduct that the prosecution reasonably believes to have been committed. Under this approach, greater emphasis is placed on the individual accused's conduct in the laying of charges, as prosecutors seek to ensure that they represent the crimes they were allegedly responsible for. In practice, and in particular with respect to those individuals allegedly 'most responsible' for crimes, the distinction between representing the criminality of a situation and the criminality of an accused may not be significant.

Consistent with a desire to represent the criminality of a situation or an accused, a comparatively limited amount of evidence regarding alleged crimes of sexual violence or crimes against children – or evidence suggesting such crimes occurred comparatively rarely – does not necessarily mean they will receive less attention in the exercise of a prosecutor's charging discretion. One prosecutor, reflecting on their experiences at the ICTY, recalled that "if I put all of the [...] evidence that I had on the table that was developed during the course of the investigation, and categorised it into [...] piles according to crime, probably the smallest stack of evidence, statements and the like, would have been crimes of sexual vio-

---

[61]   ICC-OTP, *Prosecutorial Strategy: 2009-2012*, 1 February 2010, p. 6 (https://www.legal-tools.org/doc/6ed914).

[62]   ICC-OTP, *Policy Paper on Preliminary Examinations*, November 2013, fn. 72 (https://www.legal-tools.org/doc/acb906); ICC-OTP, *Policy Paper on Case Selection and Prioritisation*, September 2016, p. 14 (https://www.legal-tools.org/doc/182205).

[63]   Interview with P12.

[64]   Interview with P20.

lence".[65] Similarly, another prosecutor recalled that a decision was "certainly" made in the early days of the ICTY and ICTR to "in a sense privilege the investigation of sexual offences", "[b]ecause left to just a normal unfolding of events, the massive numbers of homicides, of murders, would have dwarfed the appearance of severity of sexual crimes".[66] Had that decision not been taken, the same prosecutor remarked, sexual violence "might not have featured as prominently as I believed it should [have], considering the impact that it had on the level of criminality in these countries".[67] The ICC adopted a similar approach in its *Policy Paper on Sexual and Gender-Based Crimes*, where it committed itself to laying charges for sexual and gender-based crimes "wherever there is sufficient evidence to support such charges",[68] irrespective of the number of alleged offences. The same applies to crimes directed against children or disproportionately affecting them.[69]

But, of course, the assessment of what is 'representative' of criminality is subjective and underpinned by a raft of personal factors. To take the charging of sexual and gender-based violence as an example, one need only point to the Women's Initiatives for Gender Justice challenging the ICC-OTP's 'failure' to prosecute a raft of crimes (including crimes of sexual violence and gender-based crimes);[70] the general criticism levelled against the ICTY-OTP to do the same; and Cecily Rose's criticism that the SCSL-OTP failed to properly plead forced marriage and crimes of sexual violence.[71] With this in mind, the ICTY prosecutor's comment that prose-

---

[65] Interview with P8.

[66] Interview with P7.

[67] Interview with P7.

[68] ICC-OTP, *Policy Paper on Sexual and Gender-Based Crimes*, June 2014, p. 6 (https://www.legal-tools.org/doc/7ede6c).

[69] ICC-OTP, *Policy on Children*, November 2016, p. 2 (https://www.legal-tools.org/doc/c2652b).

[70] ICC, Situation in the Democratic Republic of the Congo, Pre-Trial Chamber, Request submitted pursuant to rule 103(1) of the Rules of Procedure and Evidence for leave to participate as amicus curiae with confidential annex 2, 10 November 2006, ICC-01/04-316 (https://www.legal-tools.org/doc/ceb093). 'Failure' is put in inverted commas for the purposes of indicating that something can only be assessed as a 'success' or a 'failure' if there is some binding standard to assess it by, which there is not.

[71] Cecily Rose, "Troubled Indictments at the Special Court for Sierra Leone: The Pleading of Joint Criminal Enterprise and Sex-based Crimes", in *Journal of International Criminal Justice*, 2009, vol. 7, no. 2, p. 368.

cutors should "have at least some *sense* of confidence" that their charges represent the criminality of the situation is particularly poignant[72] as that is the most that can ever be achieved in what is ultimately a subjective exercise.

The second category is representing the *geographical spread* of alleged crimes. Prosecutors have attempted to represent this through the exercise of the charging discretion.[73] In this respect, prosecutors have tried to exercise the charging discretion in such a way that the locations in which alleged crimes have been committed are, they believe, reflected in the charges laid or incidents scheduled. There are three reasons for this.

The first reason is that representing the geographic spread of alleged criminal offences may show the existence of a plan or policy, which may in turn prove that the conduct was part of a 'widespread or systematic' attack constituting a crime against humanity.[74] A 'plan or policy' or 'large-scale' requirement is also included in the *Rome Statute* with respect to war crimes under Article 7. In that respect, representing the geographic spread of alleged offences is not so much a discretionary choice, but rather a tool used to prove beyond reasonable doubt a defendant's guilt.

The second reason is that a failure to represent the geographic spread of alleged offences has been considered (in what is again a subjective assessment) *unfair*. One prosecutor recounted that the ICTY-OTP deployed the historian András Reidlmayer and the demographer Ewa Tabeau to Bosnia, in part, so as not "to leave out the municipalities" the prosecutors were not going to lead detailed evidence on, because it was considered "important to show that they too were impacted by the crimes".[75] The same prosecutor considered that "it would have been unfair just to pick" a limited number of areas on which to focus.[76] In this light, 'fairly' representing the geographical spread of alleged offences was considered to outweigh the time gained to spend on other matters should less areas be pursued at trial.[77] At the ICTR, Hassan Jallow recognised the

---

[72]   Interview with P7. Emphasis added.

[73]   Interview with P5; Interview with P12; Interview with P9.

[74]   ICTY, *Prosecutor v. Dragoljub Kunarać et al.*, Appeals Chamber, Judgment, 12 June 2002, IT-96-23 and IT-96-23/1-A, para. 65 (https://www.legal-tools.org/doc/029a09).

[75]   Interview with P8.

[76]   Interview with P8.

[77]   Interview with P8.

need for indictments to cover all of Rwanda's administrative regions on the basis that a failure to do so could be seen as discriminatory, biased, or flush with favouritism.[78]

The third reason is a desire on the part of a prosecution office to properly respond to the public's perception about where offences have taken place. With respect to the work of the ICTR, one prosecutor noted that the Office wanted to cover "each of the [...] regions of Rwanda" as well as "the major killing sites that everyone thinks of if you know Rwandan topography".[79]

The third category of representation concerns *structural commission*. Some prosecutors have attempted to represent the structural means through which alleged offences were committed in the exercise of their charging discretion. The need for such an approach was expressly adopted at the ICTR, where Jallow thought it important to prosecute members of different social organisations to demonstrate the breadth of societal participation on the Rwandan atrocities. "The Prosecutor [Jallow] consciously decided", Alex Obote-Odora notes, "to include all of the various groups represented in the atrocities to ensure that different types of involvement were covered".[80] As such, the ICTR-OTP pursued cases concerning the government, military, clergy, and the media; as well as lower-level territory administration officials such as the *bourgmestres* and mayors.[81]

ICTY prosecutors also attempted to represent the structural means through which alleged offences were committed through their charging decisions. The *Milošević* indictments, for example, were drafted in such a way that they "fairly and appropriately reflected each of those avenues of perpetration that he engaged in", including his alleged use of the Ministry of the Interior, paramilitaries, and political leaders.[82]

---

[78] Hassan Jallow, "Prosecutorial Discretion and International Criminal Justice", in *Journal of International Criminal Justice*, 2005, vol. 3, no. 1, p. 153.

[79] Interview with P9.

[80] Alex Obote-Odora, "Case Selection and Prioritization Criteria at the International Criminal Tribunal for Rwanda", in Morten Bergsmo (ed.), *Criteria for Prioritizing and Selecting Core International Crimes Cases*, 2nd edition, Torkel Opsahl Academic EPublisher, Oslo, 2010, p. 56 (https://www.legal-tools.org/doc/f5abed).

[81] Interview with P9.

[82] Interview with P8.

The fourth category of representation is *temporal spread*. There is some minor evidence to support the proposition that prosecutors may also attempt to represent the time over which alleged offences were committed in the exercise of the charging discretion. An SCSL prosecutor noted that they tried to ensure their indictments represented the alleged crimes "*in tempore*" (in addition to representing their criminality and geographic spread).[83] This approach suggests prosecutors may wish to ensure that the alleged offences that are the subject of the charging discretion cover their respective court's temporal jurisdictional mandate.

The fifth category of representation is *alleged victims*. Prosecutors have also attempted to represent the types of alleged victims in the exercise of the charging discretion.[84] As one prosecutor pondered, "[a]re we responding to what the affected community suffered?"[85]

A desire to represent the alleged victims has prompted prosecutors to creatively employ the charging discretion where it was unclear whether the law covered the harms the alleged victims were alleged to have suffered. In the *Galić* indictment,[86] the Prosecutor charged the offence of 'unlawfully inflicting terror upon civilians'. Cryer termed the Prosecution's characterisation of this crime 'novel', as it had not been established before by an international criminal tribunal that such a crime existed.[87] As one prosecutor recalled, "what was important from our perspective in making that allegation was that the *victims are different* [...] [b]y killing and wounding some civilians, you terrorise not just those who were wounded, but the rest of the civilian population".[88] In this light, the Prosecution recognised that harm had been suffered by a class of persons where it was ambiguous whether such harm gave rise to criminal liability. The prosecutor additionally observed that this expansion of the law – albeit in

---

[83]   Interview with P5.

[84]   Interview with P12; Interview with P14; Interview with P19.

[85]   Interview with P14.

[86]   ICTY, *Prosecutor v. Stanislav Galić*, OTP, Indictment, 26 March 1999, IT-98-29-I (https://www.legal-tools.org/doc/527ac8).

[87]   Robert Cryer, "*Prosecutor v. Galić* and the War Crime of Terror Bombing", in *Israeli Defence Forces Law Review*, 2006, vol. 2, p. 80.

[88]   Interview with P19. Emphasis added.

---

a slightly different way to what the Prosecution intended[89] – served the
objective of general deterrence.[90]

13.3.2. Or Fewer Charges?

While the above factors can generally be classed as encouraging an increase in the number of charges faced by individual accused, some of
them – and many others – also militate in favour of defendants facing a
fewer number of criminal allegations.

13.3.2.1. The Likely Sentence

Prosecutors have, for example, considered excluding charges if they believe the alleged offender is likely to receive a *fair* sentence, with fewer
counts, taking into account the uncharged conduct. One prosecutor questioned whether it was necessary to spend time proving additional charges
and additional elements if they believed that the alleged offender would
nevertheless receive a "fair sentence".[91] The prosecutor also noted that
they did "not at all favour the kitchen sink approach of charging every
single possible charge you can" in circumstances where more serious
conduct also involved "relatively mild mistreatment", wondering aloud
whether "is it really necessary if you're charging the person with murder,
and that's […] your prime case, to charge every little possible act you
could? I don't think so".[92] Similarly, prosecutors have considered excluding charges if they believe the alleged offender is likely to receive a
lengthy sentence, with fewer counts, taking into account the uncharged
conduct. This approach has a greater punitive element than the first identified approach, however it is entirely plausible that a *fair* sentence would
be a *lengthy* sentence. One prosecutor demonstrated the relevance of this
consideration by reflecting on the *Milošević* indictments. "Why did you
bother with these huge indictments?", they recalled people wondering,

---

[89] The Chamber rejected the argument that "that actual infliction of terror is an element of the
crime of terror", observing instead that "the Prosecution is required to prove not only that
the Accused accepted the likelihood that terror would result from the illegal acts – or, in
other words, that he was aware of the possibility that terror would result – but that that was
the result which he specifically intended": ICTY, *Prosecutor v. Stanislav Galić*, Trial
Chamber, Judgment, 5 December 2003, IT-98-29-T, paras. 70, 134 (https://www.legal-
tools.org/doc/eb6006).

[90] Interview with P19.

[91] Interview with P20.

[92] Interview with P20.

"[w]hy decide to cover three wars in ten years? Wouldn't it have been enough simply to decide to prosecute Milošević for some single event, and have him sent away to prison for life for that, and then use the time, the resources, the money, to do more cases?".[93] This, they believed, would have been an "entirely plausible, entirely satisfactory argument" and a "perfectly proper approach", yet added that this was not to say it would have been the *correct* approach.[94]

13.3.2.2. Macro Managerial Considerations

One can also not disregard *macro managerial considerations*. External demands to complete the work of tribunals expediently fall into this category, as do budgetary and resource limitations. The discretion prosecutors have is how to work within them. At the ICTY, these restrictions and pressures became a significant influencing factor post the mid-2000 recognition by Carla Del Ponte that the OTP's prosecutorial policy needed to be revised, and the accompanying pressure from President Pillay and the Security Council to expedite the work of the Tribunal. In addition, the amendments to Rule 73*bis*(d) of the ICTY's *Rules of Procedure and Evidence* in July 2003 allowed the Trial Chamber to "fix a number of crime sites or incidents comprised in one or more of the charges in respect of which evidence may be presented by the Prosecutor"[95] and, in May 2006, "invite the Prosecutor to reduce the number of counts charged in the indictment".[96]

These developments "placed further pressure on the OTP in terms of determining which charges to proceed with"[97] and made one prosecutor wonder "how I was going to [...] get justice for the most victims with the limited time that I would have".[98] Reflecting on the prosecutions of Ivan Čermak and Ante Gotovina, a prosecutor remarked that the Trial Chamber's clear policy of trimming prosecutions "so as to wrap up the operation of ICTY as quickly as possible" meant the Office "had to be fairly

---

93 Interview with P11.
94 Interview with P11.
95 ICTY, *Rules of Procedure and Evidence*, 17 July 2003 (https://www.legal-tools.org/doc/9zo9md).
96 ICTY, *Rules of Procedure and Evidence*, 30 May 2006 (https://www.legal-tools.org/doc/n510a9).
97 Interview with P19.
98 Interview with P8.

prudent in terms of the number of charges that we alleged against an indictee".[99] This meant that they were not charged with "every possible crime and in relation to every possible incident", and the prosecution team was "quite selective in the drafting of the indictment as to what [they] would set out to prove".[100]

Similarly, after the arrest of Radovan Karadžić, the OTP's decision to trim the indictment against him was made in part because "the OTP had been criticised by the judges in the past" and they "had, in a number of other cases, asked the OTP to reduce by a certain percentage the indictments".[101] In the *Karadžić* and *Mladić* prosecutions, the OTP decided to "reduce the number of municipalities" in the indictment, "because if you can prove the criminal intent in 10 municipalities about a widespread and systematic attack against a civilian population, you don't need to prove it in all areas".[102] The decision about which municipalities to exclude from the indictment was based on the strength of the evidence and "gravity in terms of numbers of victims", noting that incidents with direct evidence linking the crime to the alleged perpetrator would be prioritised, even when they involved less victims (the prosecutor also observed that "you would, of course, never take a massive crime out with hundreds of victims").[103]

With the ICTR under comparable pressure to wind up its operations, Hassan Jallow started filing what he termed 'lean and mean indictments'.[104] These indictments, he claimed, contained fewer charges than their predecessors and would presumably take less time to prove.

At the SCSL, a looming completion date was one of the factors militating against the prosecution of Benjamin Yeaten. As described by one prosecutor, "we were expected to get everything done at that point by the end of 2009", and that, in culmination with other factors, meant that it was not possible to join a trial of Yeaten to the trial of Charles Taylor.[105] The

---

[99] Interview with P19.

[100] Interview with P19.

[101] Interview with P5.

[102] Interview with P5.

[103] Interview with P5.

[104] Hassan Jallow, *The ICTR and the Challenge of Completion*, paper delivered at the T.M.C. Asser Institute, The Hague, 4 October 2006, p. 2.

[105] Interview with P9.

same prosecutor later observed that "if you're a temporary court, which is now well-beyond its shelf life according to the sponsors, and you still don't have your major suspects, that's difficult".[106]

13.3.2.3. Trial Management

Trial management also falls into this category of considerations. One prosecutor recalled that, in the preparation of the Bosnia and Herzegovina indictment against Slobodan Milošević, Senior Trial Attorney Dermot Groome "set an arbitrary line that any criminal event where there were less than ten people killed, unless there was something uniquely important about that", would not be included in the indictment.[107] This "shocked" the staff, however the prosecutor could not recall how rigorously the policy was applied.[108] In any event, the prosecutor recalled that roughly the same number of witnesses would be required to prove one person was killed or ten people were killed, and that by focusing on the latter charges they "could get justice for more victims" in the time that was allocated for the trial.[109]

Another ICTY prosecutor, reflecting on the *Karadžić* indictment, bore in mind the collapse of the *Milošević* trial when determining how to abbreviate the indictment. They noted that the decision to abbreviate the indictment was driven in part by a desire "to have a manageable trial", recalling that "we thought that […] we don't want an eight-year trial and we want this to be under control".[110]

13.3.2.4. Judicial Reaction

The *prosecution's relationship with the bench* has also militated in favour of there being a limited number of charges. One prosecutor described how they could "almost feel the judge wince" when they filed "eighty-eight counts" for "about a three-day course of conduct that's basically murder".[111] This, the prosecutor suggested, indicated that laying comparatively minor charges when the course of conduct alleged involved more seri-

---

[106] Interview with P9.
[107] Interview with P8.
[108] Interview with P8.
[109] Interview with P8.
[110] Interview with P5.
[111] Interview with P20.

ous offences would be an inappropriate use of judicial resources. There is a clear interest in prosecutors having a good, professional, working relationship with the bench. Laying an unreasonable number of charges risks reflecting poorly on a prosecutor's professional judgement and creating an uncomfortable working environment.

13.4. The Challenges of Charge Selection

Section 13.3. has demonstrated that the decision of how many charges to allege against a defendant is deeply context-specific and open to subjective interpretation. There appear to be two factors that need to be considered when deciding, in light of the above, on how to best ensure the quality of these decisions.

The first factor that appears to be relevant in understanding the challenges of charge selection is that international criminal prosecutors are hoping to achieve numerous goals through their charging practices. In 2008, Damaška criticised international criminal courts for self-imposing a gargantuan number of objectives. Unlike Atlas, he argued, these courts are not "bodies of titanic strength, capable of carrying on their shoulders the burden of so many tasks".[112]

One can see this multiplicity of goals reflected in the ways that prosecutors have navigated the issue of how many charges to allege against potential defendants. Should prosecutors be trying to obtain convictions? Should they be attempting to advance the law or record history? Should they be considering the representative effect of their charging decisions, and attempt to reflect the criminality, geographical spread, means of structural commission, temporal spread, or classes of alleged victims? Or all of the above? It is incorrect to proceed on the assumption that these questions have answers.

This leads into the second, and more pragmatic issue. The charging discretion is one that is steeped in subjectivity. To again quote and appropriate Schabas, there is no 'iPhone app' that tells prosecutors what is relevant and the weight to be given to any one particular factor.[113] People are, quite simply, going to have different ideas about what are or are not relevant considerations in any given situation.

---

[112] Mirjan Damaška, "What's the point of international criminal justice?", in *Chicago-Kent Law Review*, 2008, vol. 83, no. 1, p. 331.

[113] Schabas, 2016, see above note 4.

In light of the two challenges identified above, it is evident that quality control cannot be simply a question of identifying and applying normative benchmarks. As Jan Klabbers has argued, "[i]t is tempting to give in to the kneejerk deontological reflex and devise ethical codes for experts, a set of rules that would apply to experts, whether they render advice, participate as decision makers or act as gate-keepers between expert knowledge and political decision making".[114] Yet any rules will always be simultaneously over-inclusive or under-inclusive, need to be applied by humans, and be incapable of assigning weights to different considerations while maintaining a necessary level of flexibility. "Important as rules are (legal or otherwise)", argues Klabbers, "they are, eventually, better seen as signposts than as absolutes. They offer guidance and ought to be followed, but not blindly or at all costs".[115]

13.5. Quality Control and the Value of Argument

So then what can be said for ensuring the quality of exercises of the charging discretion? As an alternative to a normative approach, it may be that quality control over the charging discretion can be understood through Thomas Risse's 'logic of arguing' – itself an advancement of Jürgen Habermas's theory of communicative action. Historically, two mainstream theories have attempted to explain why actors engage in the conduct they do. The 'logic of consequentialism', which focusses on rational choice, posits that actors will engage in conduct that complies with norms until such point that it is no longer in their best interests to do so. On the other hand, the 'logic of appropriateness' essentially claims that actors engage in conduct that complies with norms because the norm forms part of their social identity, even though it may not be in their best interests to do so.[116]

Yet Risse was dissatisfied that neither theory appropriately accounted for those situations in which there was ambiguity surrounding the

---

[114] Jan Klabbers, "The Virtues of Expertise", in Monika Ambrus *et al.* (eds.), *The Role of 'Experts' in International and European Decision-Making Processes: Advisors, Decision Makers, or Irrelevant Actors?*, Cambridge University Press, 2014, p. 90.

[115] Jan Klabbers, "Too Much, Too Little, Too Late? Reflections on Law and Ethics in the EU's Foreign Policy", in Steven Blockmans and Panos Koutrakos (eds.), *Research Handbook on the EU's Common Foreign and Security Policy*, Edward Elgar, 2018, p. 446.

[116] The terms 'logic of consequentialism' and 'logic of appropriateness' are borrowed from Risse's article.

norms that applied to a given problem (if any), or indeed how actors identified the methods through which this ambiguity would be resolved. As
such, he claimed, it was necessary to emphasise the argumentative process
in which actors engage for the purpose of "truth seeking with the aim of
reaching a mutual understanding based on reasoned consensus".[117] The
process of communication through argument "is motivated by the desire
to find out the "truth" with regard to the facts in the world or to figure out
"the right thing to do" in a commonly-defined situation".[118] It is this latter
motivation that is relevant to prosecutorial discretion.

Risse identified four preconditions that should be conducive to
achieving the desires he described. First is the "existence of a common
lifeworld provided by a high degree of international institutionalisation in
the respective issue-area". The 'common lifeworld' that Risse referred to
"consists of a shared culture, a common system of norms and rules perceived as legitimate, and the social identity of actors being capable of
communicating and acting".[119] It is the environment in which actors have
been socialised and determines the limits of their understandings. The
lifeworld establishes "the forms of the intersubjectivity of possible understanding", something in which actors move within but can never leave.[120]
Second, there should be "conscious efforts by actors to construct such a
common lifeworld through narratives that enable them to communicate in
a meaningful way"; third, "[u]ncertainty of interests and/or lack of
knowledge about the situation among the actors"; and fourth, the presence
of "[i]nternational institutions based on nonhierarchical relations enabling
dense interactions in informal network-like settings".[121] Risse's conclusion was that arguments are more likely to occur in a sphere of interaction
the greater the degree of uncertainty actors hold about their own interests
and identities; the less common knowledge they possess "about the situation in which they find themselves"; and the "more apparently irreconcil-

---

[117] Thomas Risse, ""Let's Argue!": Communicative Action in World Politics", in *International Organization*, 2000, vol. 54, no. 1, pp. 1–2.

[118] *Ibid.*, p. 12.

[119] *Ibid.*, p. 11.

[120] Jürgen Habermas, *The Theory of Communicative Action: Volume Two: Lifeworld and
Systems: A Critique of Functionalist Reason*, Thomas McCarthy trans., Polity Press, 1991,
p. 111.

[121] Risse, 2000, p. 19, see above note 117.

able differences prevent them from reaching an optimal rather than a merely satisfactory solution for a widely perceived problem".[122]

It is apparent that Risse's four preconditions are met in the context of international prosecutors exercising the charging discretion. The common lifeworld that international prosecutors occupy is evident through their engagement in the post-1993 efforts to develop systems through which international and hybrid organisations can legitimately usurp the State's monopoly over the use of coercive measures against the subjects of their jurisdiction with respect to the prosecution of genocide, aggression, war crimes, and crimes against humanity. They work in the same cities, crossing paths at conferences, professional gatherings, and social events. Their concerns lie not just with the tribunal in which they work, but the success of international criminal justice more broadly. They are guided by integrity and a desire to do what is best in the circumstances they are confronted with. International prosecutors seek to strengthen the corpus of international criminal law and procedure for the purposes of ending impunity and doing 'justice for the victims'. Yet at the same time, the discretionary power they wield is exercised in, at best, a vague normative framework that provides little to no clear practical guidance. There is ambiguity about the relevant considerations and the weight to be afforded to any of them. Finally, all international prosecutors act within international criminal courts, giving rise to a horizontal structure in which they can communicate and argue with each other on equal footing.

When seen in this light, discretionary choices are not seen as 'right' or 'wrong' in a normative sense. Instead, they can be seen as an attempt by prosecutors to determine the most appropriate conduct in the circumstances in a never-ending cycle of interpretation in which social identities are expressed and constructed, and opinions about what is 'appropriate' come and go.[123] The practice of exercising discretion is better seen as an argument between prosecutors themselves and the broader epistemic community, rather than one in which rules are applied or interests are advanced.

---

[122] *Ibid.*, p. 33.

[123] Yet, in contrast to Risse, it is unlikely that 'norms' develop through this process. For a powerful attack on the idea that something can be right or wrong (from a moral perspective), see Elizabeth Anscombe, "Modern Moral Philosophy", in *Philosophy*, 1958, vol. 33, no. 124, p. 1.

Importantly, for this collective attempt to identify the right course of action in a circumstance to succeed, the arguments must be "open to other participants and *be public in nature*".[124] This is critical for the purposes of quality control. If prosecutors do not engage with the broader epistemic community, or even each other, regarding the reasons why they took particular decisions, the quality of future decisions cannot be bettered. As such, when prosecutors do make discretionary choices, it is essential from a quality control perspective that they are willing to openly discuss the reasons why they took these decisions. Only then is it possible to fully embrace and learn from the collective knowledge and experience present among the broad international prosecutorial college. Under this approach, quality is not assessed by reference to normative standards, but rather by the willingness of prosecutors to openly discuss the motivations underpinning their decisions and persuade others as to their appropriateness while remaining open to reassessing their position based on what they see as better arguments.

13.6. Conclusion

The charging discretion is complex. This chapter has focussed on merely one aspect of it: the assessment of how many charges to allege against an individual accused. Through the empirical statistical and qualitative surveys in Sections 13.2. and 13.3., this chapter has attempted to reveal the fragmented practices and subjective rationales that have historically informed how the charging discretion has been exercised. Specifically, Section 13.4. argued that attempts to develop normative frameworks through which the quality of these decisions can be assessed are likely to be thwarted by a need for flexibility and context-specificity. In this light, Section 13.5. argued in favour of a new approach to assessing the quality of the charging discretion. When the exercise of discretion is seen as part of a process of argumentation, it becomes possible to see the quality of decisions by the extent to which prosecutors are willing to debate the motivations behind their choices with the broader epistemic community, engage with criticisms, and accept them if they are persuaded by their appropriateness.

Finally, it should be remembered that international prosecutions take place in a lifeworld with a relatively short history. International pros-

---

[124] Risse, 2000, p. 11, see above note 117.

ecutors do not have hundreds of years of domestic experience, collective knowledge, and a well-refined lifeworld to draw upon when exercising the charging discretion. The lifeworld that does exist needs to be developed. Silence is not conducive to the collective development of knowledge.

14

Rethinking Disclosure:
Embrace the Electronic Disclosure Suite

David Re[*]

14.1. Introduction and General Proposition

A fair trial requires the disclosure to an accused person of incriminating evidence to be used against them at trial, plus exculpatory material, and anything that is 'material' to defence preparation for trial. These, in a nutshell, are the long-established legal principles governing disclosure.

The consequences of violating these principles – intentionally or otherwise – are also well settled; after a declaration of a violation, witness testimony or the trial could be adjourned, or in extreme cases temporarily or permanently stayed. Potentially, the evidence could be excluded from use at trial. Personal sanctions could even be ordered against an 'offending' prosecution official. On appeal, a conviction could be overturned, or a mistrial declared.

Despite specific rules of procedure and evidence ('RPE'), and numerous decisions and judgments of international criminal courts and tribunals compelling the prosecution to disclose this material to the defence, the system is far from perfect. Enormous unnecessary prosecution, defence and judicial resources are expended in resolving disclosure issues

---

[*] **David Re** is the Presiding Judge of the Trial Chamber of the Special Tribunal for Lebanon (since 2013). Previously, he was an international judge of the Court of Bosnia and Herzegovina in Sarajevo and a senior prosecuting trial attorney at the International Criminal Tribunal for the Former Yugoslavia ('ICTY') in The Hague. In Australia he worked as a barrister, a prosecutor and a solicitor in private practice, and also as a research officer for the New South Wales Attorney General's Department. He was an NGO observer at the negotiations for the Rome Statute of the International Criminal Court in 1998. This chapter is based on a presentation at the Indian Law Institute, see David Re, "Rethinking Disclosure in Core International Cases", CILRAP Film, New Delhi, 22 February 2019 (https://www.cilrap.org/cilrap-film/190222-re/). The author thanks those who provided comments on the draft, and in particular, Judge Ekaterina Trendafilova, President, Kosovo Specialist Chambers.

and disputes. The contention here is that solutions lie in *rethinking how disclosure is handled* rather than in revising the fundamental principles.

Writing critically about the consequences of late or non-disclosure, and particularly from the defence perspective, is not particularly difficult; finding workable solutions is more challenging. This chapter therefore tries to propose a practical resolution that builds on existing precedents and also conforms with the courts' and tribunals' statutory instruments and international human rights law.

To understand why requires an appreciation of the systemic 'blockages' in the existing disclosure structures and practices.

The starting point is that international prosecutors are both the primary investigator and a party to proceedings. In investigating crimes or situations, they collect an enormous quantity of material – in documentary and digital form. But very little of it will be used as evidence at trial.

Due to the conditions often confronting investigators on the ground in conflict or post-conflict situations, the collection or seizure of material may be more sweeping than targeted. The ICTY is a case in point as in some cases it took many years for its Office of the Prosecutor to gain access, in the former Yugoslavia, to military and governmental records necessary for case presentation in court.[1] As a consequence, its officials often gathered – or seized – large 'collections' of documents, when they could, some of which took some years to catalogue.[2]

A legitimate fear may exist that the material must be collected if possible, then and there, using the principle of take now and sift later. Another more mundane reality of international criminal investigations is that inevitably more material than can ever be used in a trial is gathered, including that used for investigative leads and indeed the statements of *potential* witnesses. This is especially acute in the preliminary investigatory stages in which its ultimate direction is understandably unknown, including who if anyone may eventually be indicted.

---

[1] Based on the author's personal knowledge – from working in the ICTY's Office of the Prosecutor between 2002 and 2008 – that some States subject to the ICTY's jurisdiction had motives not to co-operate with the Tribunal and to provide access to specified documents, or classes of documents or witnesses.

[2] This too comes from the author's first-hand experience of the ICTY prosecution's evidence collection and vault.

Equally immense collections of digital material now supplement, or substitute for, these vast quantities of physical documents. Prosecutors acting as investigators now amass enormous digital evidence collections. The predictable consequence is the accumulation of far too much information, in multiple formats; greatly exceeding what could ever be of use either to an investigation or a prosecution.[3] This is accentuated by the time taken to get cases before courts, especially where accused persons may not be apprehended for years after arrest warrants are issued, which may in turn have occurred some years after the prosecution first collected the material. And additionally, perhaps without it having made a connection between the eventual accused and the material viewed in the investigation's initial stages.

One of the main challenges facing investigators in obtaining documents 'in the field' – and indeed in receiving digital evidence – is linguistic. Investigators and lawyers might not speak, read or understand the language of a situation under investigation.[4] Obtaining qualified and trusted language assistants who can review documents in the field – or even in the office – is very challenging if the language of the information found or sought is not widely spoken. Ideally, potential evidence should be reviewed before it is collected or catalogued.[5] But this may prove to be impossible.

---

[3] The author's experience is that, unfortunately, this does not necessarily restrain parties – and in particular, prosecutors – from 'dumping' extraneous 'just in case' material on exhibit and even witness lists, causing them to balloon beyond realistic judicial case management control. See, for example, STL, *Prosecutor v. Ayyash et al.*, Judgment, 18 August 2020, STL-11-01/T/TC/F3839/20200818/R331945-R334626/EN/dm, Annex A, Procedural History, paras. 61–80; see also, Separate Opinion of Judge David Re, paras. 170–220 (https://www.legal-tools.org/doc/gcoqu8).

[4] At the International Criminal Court ('ICC'), information provided to the prosecution at the preliminary examination stage may later become disclosable to the defence if an investigation and charges against an accused person eventuate.

[5] The author had personal experience of this in leading ICTY prosecution missions to examine military and government document archives in Serbia and Bosnia and Herzegovina in the 2000s, using analysts, investigators and lawyers – some utilising language assistants – and copying relevant documents *in situ* in the archives and then electronically entering them into the relevant evidence collection while there 'in the field'. This is more expensive and time-consuming as it requires an on the spot screening assessment of material for relevance, and hence more personnel are needed, but in the author's view, it is far preferable – where it is feasible – to simply 'grabbing' as many documents as possible and taking them all back to the office. Wholesale seizures may represent a false economy when the time and resources spent later examining them and searching them for disclosable material is

Having collected the information, in whatever form, the prosecution is obliged to store and catalogue it, and additionally, to search it for material disclosable to the defence. This is a labour intensive, time-consuming and potentially fruitless exercise, which is frequently delegated to junior staff.[6]

The material collected can be divided into several categories: open source material, or that which is publicly available to anyone (namely, who is motivated enough to find it); witness generated material such as 'statements' taken by prosecution officials and material provided by these witnesses; information from fact-finding bodies which can include that from the two previous categories; 'public' records, for example, government and military records; and material provided with conditions attached, such as that its existence cannot be disclosed, that is usually used to generate leads and other evidence. The conditionally provided information typically comes from governments, their specialised agencies, such as intelligence or diplomatic, and inter-governmental and non-governmental organisations ('NGOs'). Another category is of artefacts and forensic material, like blood samples, and ballistic fragments and human remains recovered from graves.

The prosecution must store and manage this material. Some will be received in an electronic form – making it easier to catalogue – while other material will be in hard copy, meaning that it must be converted into an electronic form before storing. Artefacts and biological material also have to be securely stored and electronically catalogued, usually by photographing.

The main issue here is how to ensure that the defence of an accused person has access to the things that are necessary for their trial preparation – either inculpatory, exculpatory, or 'material' to defence preparations.

---

calculated and compared to a more targeted and contemporaneous extraction of information.

[6] It can also be described as a soul-destroying task, and consequently in the author's experience it has been delegated to the most junior employees, including interns. But as tedious as this can be, such a delegation decision could be misguided; sometimes only the most experienced lawyers have the skills needed to make judgment calls about what should be disclosed. The corollary of this would be experienced prosecution staff expending valuable time on this task rather than on trial preparation. Both are necessary, but arguably their time is far better spent on the latter; hence the plea to rethink how mass disclosure is done.

The most sensitive categories are those relating to witness statements and witness generated material and information conditionally provided to a prosecutor's office with non-disclosure stipulations. The disclosure of open source material – with some caveats – should not trouble a prosecutor's office; it should be available in an easily accessible and searchable format.

'Public' documents – such as those from military and government archives – should fall into the same category. Artefacts are available for inspection, and where necessary, independent testing by experts engaged by the defence.

Disclosing fact-finding material, for example, from non-governmental organisations such as Human Rights Watch, or inter-governmental organisations like United Nations bodies with fact-finding or humanitarian assistance mandates, may present some complexities. It often contains sensitive witness-related material, the unconditional disclosure of which might potentially endanger witnesses or providers. These documents may fall into either category.

As prosecutors' offices have either collected or been given this material, they become its custodian. This imposes a colossal burden on them to search the collections to find material that is legally disclosable. A failure to search, or having searched, either not disclosing it or disclosing it late, can result in sanctions, or worse.

The prosecution – in the broadest sense of 'the office', which is of course composed of humans[7] – may not always know what is 'material' to the defence of an accused person. Appreciating what is potentially exculpatory, or may discredit a prosecution witness or evidence, is usually easier. But expecting prosecution personnel to try and find *all* of this 'material' information is both impractical and unreasonable in circumstances where the information is voluminous, and in particular where the extent of a defence is unknown.

Moreover, in what could be seen as a 'disclosure paradox', the defence may react to prosecution disclosure by modifying an existing intended defence. The prosecution disclosure could of itself therefore trigger a defence alteration in strategy (but one that was already unknown to the prosecution). So, by virtue of one disclosure that causes the defence to

---

[7] With all our non-algorithmic searching imperfections and frailties of judgment.

change its defence strategy, the prosecution could extend its own disclosure obligations further by making more things in its possession potentially material to the defence. But how is the prosecution to know this?

This burden should therefore be shifted from the prosecution to the defence to search the large bulk of information currently held in prosecution evidence collections for information material to defence preparations. Of course, anything that the prosecution intends to use as evidence at trial or has been submitted to a judge or chamber to confirm an indictment must be disclosed. But ascertaining what is material to the preparation of the defence for trial should not be solely the prosecution's role. The defence should inform the prosecution, and if necessary, the chambers, of what is *potentially* material. Equally important is ensuring that accused persons have the necessary resources, in other words funding and staffing of their defence teams, to search this material.

This role should also not be transferred to the judiciary; the chambers are not parties to adversarial proceedings and should only be brought into inter-parties disclosure disputes as a last resort in unresolvable situations.

Since 2003 the ICTY, and thereafter the International Residual Mechanism for Criminal Tribunals ('IRMCT'), has used an 'electronic disclosure suite' ('EDS'), managed by the tribunal's registry, for disclosure. All defence counsel have access to the EDS, which is where most prosecution material has been placed. The prosecution retains responsibility for searching its own restricted witness and otherwise sensitive material. This model should be followed in other international criminal law institutions. Open source, government archival and most fact-finding mission material should be replicated and placed in a separate evidence collection maintained by the court or tribunal's registry, thus creating a 'neutral' custodian. This allows a form of objective third-party oversight of part of the process.

Under this model, the prosecution would retain responsibility for maintaining its own database of witness-generated and other sensitive material, and for searching this and disclosing any relevant material. The prosecution would also retain its statutory obligation to search and to disclose anything that it *found* in its entire collection that was disclosable. Consequently, the prosecution would have no positive obligation to search the registry's (replicated) electronic disclosure suite collection for disclosable material. This is the essence of the proposal. However, the prosecution, naturally, should comprehensively review whatever it has in-house.

Chambers, in ensuring a fair trial, obviously retain an overall responsibility for supervising this process, including, if needed, examining disputed material for themselves (*ex parte* the other party) to determine whether it should be disclosed in whole, in part, or in some redacted form. But the primary responsibility should rest with the parties. Judges should not attempt to micro-manage disclosure between the parties.

For context, it is necessary to understand the legal principles governing disclosure. Placing it in its historical framework also assists. The basic principles, it must be emphasised, are not that complicated; the sting in the tail is in their application. The quantity of international decisions on disclosure since 1994 is vast; and a smattering is referenced below. Additionally, in writing this chapter, some experienced senior prosecution and defence lawyers were informally interviewed in an attempt to obtain the litigant's perspective; some of their views are referenced in the text and footnotes.

14.2. Disclosure Principles

Like most of the modern international criminal procedural rules, those regulating the disclosure of material to the defence derive from the International Military Tribunal ('IMT') at Nuremberg[8] and the International Military Tribunal for the Far East at Tokyo,[9] and their rules and practices. One fair trial right for accused persons before these tribunals was timely access to prosecution material[10] in what at each was admittedly a very expeditious trial.

---

[8] Agreement for the Prosecution and Punishment of the Major War Criminals of the European Axis, 8 August 1945 ('London Agreement'), reprinted in IMT, *Trial of the Major War Criminals Before the International Military Tribunal: Nuremberg: 14 November 1945–1 October 1946: Volume 1: Official Documents*, Nuremberg, 1947, pp. 8–9 ('Trial of the Major War Criminals Before the International Military Tribunal: Volume 1') (https://www.legal-tools.org/doc/844f64); Charter of the International Military Tribunal, Part of the London Agreement of 8 August 1945 (https://www.legal-tools.org/doc/64ffdd).

[9] Special Proclamation: Establishment of an International Military Tribunal for the Far East, 19 January 1946 (https://www.legal-tools.org/doc/242328); Charter of the International Military Tribunal for the Far East, 19 January 1946 ('Tokyo Charter') (https://www.legal-tools.org/doc/a3c41c).

[10] See, for example, Fergal Gaynor, Dov Jacobs, Mark Klamberg and Vladimir Tochilovsky, "Law of Evidence", in Göran Sluiter, Håkan Friman, Suzannah Linton, Sergey Vasiliev

To these now are added the expanded principles of international human rights law, originating in the 1948 Universal Declaration on Human Rights and thereafter developed in the 1966 International Covenant on Civil and Political Rights ('ICCPR')[11] and numerous other statutory instruments, the case law and opinions of relevant courts and advisory bodies.

The Nuremberg and Tokyo Charters[12] specified that the prosecutors had to provide relevant translated material to the defence in advance of the opening of the trial, including the indictment. The Nuremberg Rules mandated the pre-trial disclosure within 30 days of the start of the trial of the documents accompanying the indictment, but translated.[13] When the prosecution case closed, the IMT directed the defence counsel to submit the evidence they intended to rely upon, including witness names, and to what they would testify. The prosecution had no statutory right of access to the defence material and the Tribunal did not direct the defence to provide it.[14]

Under long standing international human rights law principles, accused persons have a right to be informed of the charges against them.[15]

---

and Salvatore Zappalà (eds.), *International Criminal Procedure: Principles and Rules*, Oxford University Press, Oxford, 2013, p. 1085.

[11] International Covenant on Civil and Political Rights, 16 December 1966, Article 14 provides that "everyone shall be entitled to a fair and public hearing by a competent, independent and impartial tribunal established by law" (https://www.legal-tools.org/doc/2838f3). The ICCPR entered into force in 1976. See also Universal Declaration of Human Rights, 10 December 1948, Article 10: "Everyone is entitled in full equality to a fair and public hearing by an independent and impartial tribunal, in the determination of his rights and obligations and of any criminal charge against him" (https://www.legal-tools.org/doc/de5d83).

[12] London Agreement, Article 16, see above note 8; while in Article 9(b) of the Tokyo Charter, the indictment was to be provided to the accused "in adequate time for defense", see above note 9.

[13] IMT Rules of Procedure, 29 October 1945, Rules 2(a) and 3, reprinted in Trial of the Major War Criminals Before the International Military Tribunal: Volume 1, pp. 19–23.

[14] See Gaynor, Jacobs, Klamberg and Tochilovsky, 2013, p. 1099, see above note 10.

[15] See, for example, Article 6(3)(a) of the European Convention on Human Rights, 4 November 1950 (https://www.legal-tools.org/doc/8267cb) and Article 14(3)(a) of the ICCPR, see above note 11, which provide the right "to be informed promptly, and in detail in a language which he understands of the nature and cause of the accusation against him"; see also Article 8(2)(b) of the American Convention on Human Rights, 22 November 1969 (https://www.legal-tools.org/doc/1152cf), which provides the right to "prior notification in detail to the accused of the charges against him". The case-law of the European Court of

International human rights law instruments and case law also mandate an accused person having adequate time and facilities to prepare their defence.

Article 14(3)(b) of the ICCPR provides:

> In the determination of any criminal charge against him, everyone shall be entitled to the following minimum guarantees, in full equality:
>
> [...]
>
> (b) To have adequate time and facilities for the preparation of his defence and to communicate with counsel of his own choosing.[16]

The UN Human Rights Committee in its General Comment 32 has interpreted this, finding that:

> "Adequate facilities" must include access to documents and other evidence; this access must include all materials that the prosecution plans to offer in court against the accused or that are exculpatory. Exculpatory material should be understood as including not only material establishing innocence but also other evidence that could assist the defence (e.g. indications that a confession was not voluntary). In cases of a claim that evidence was obtained in violation of article 7 of the Covenant, information about the circumstances in which such evidence was obtained must be made available to allow an assessment of such a claim. If the accused does not speak the language in which the proceedings are held, but is represented by counsel who is familiar with the language, it may be sufficient that the relevant documents in the case file are made available to counsel.[17]

Human Rights ('ECHR') holds that a fair trial requires that indictments include the charges and form of liability alleged; see, for example, ECHR, *Penev v. Bulgaria*, Judgment, 7 January 2012, ECLI:CE:ECHR:2010:0107JUD002049404, para. 44 (https://www.legal-tools.org/doc/989a14); ECHR, *Varela Geis v. Spain*, Judgment, 5 March 2013, ECLI:CE:ECHR:2013:0305JUD006100509, para. 42.

16   See above note 11.

17   General Comment No. 32: Article 14: Right to equality before courts and tribunals and to a fair trial, UN Doc. CCPR/C/GC/32, 23 August 2007, para. 33 (https://www.legal-tools.org/doc/17c458); citing Views: Communication No. 451/1991, *Harward v. Norway*, UN Doc. CCPR/C/51/D/451/1991, 18 August 1994, para. 9.5 (https://www.legal-tools.org/doc/syb36n).

Security Council Resolution 808 in 1993 established the ICTY, and the International Criminal Tribunal for Rwanda ('ICTR') was established by Resolution 955 in 1994. The Statutes of both essentially replicate the right to a fair trial set out in the ICCPR's Article 14.[18]

The Secretary-General's report on Resolution 808, stated that it was

> axiomatic that the International Tribunal must fully respect internationally recognized standards regarding the rights of the accused at all stages of its proceedings. In the view of the Secretary-General, such [...] standards are, in particular,

---

[18] ICTY Statute, 25 May 1993, Article 21 (https://www.legal-tools.org/doc/b4f63b):
1. All persons shall be equal before the International Tribunal.
2. In the determination of charges against him, the accused shall be entitled to a fair and public hearing, subject to article 22 of the Statute.
3. The accused shall be presumed innocent until proved guilty according to the provisions of the present Statute.
4. In the determination of any charge against the accused pursuant to the present Statute, the accused shall be entitled to the following minimum guarantees, in full equality:
   (a) to be informed promptly and in detail in a language which he understands of the nature and cause of the charge against him;
   (b) to have adequate time and facilities for the preparation of his defence and to communicate with counsel of his own choosing;
   (c) to be tried without undue delay;
   (d) to be tried in his presence, and to defend himself in person or through legal assistance of his own choosing; to be informed, if he does not have legal assistance, of this right; and to have legal assistance assigned to him, in any case where the interests of justice so require, and without payment by him in any such case if he does not have sufficient means to pay for it;
   (e) to examine, or have examined, the witnesses against him and to obtain the attendance and examination of witnesses on his behalf under the same conditions as witnesses against him;
   (f) to have the free assistance of an interpreter if he cannot understand or speak the language used in the International Tribunal;
   (g) not to be compelled to testify against himself or to confess guilt.

See also ICTR Statute, 8 November 1994, Article 20 (https://www.legal-tools.org/doc/8732d6); IRMCT Statute, 22 December 2010, Article 19 (https://www.legal-tools.org/doc/30782d); Statute of the Special Court for Sierra Leone ('SCSL'), 16 January 2002, Article 17 (https://www.legal-tools.org/doc/aa0e20); and Statute of the Residual Special Court for Sierra Leone ('RSCSL'), 16 January 2002, Article 17 (https://www.legal-tools.org/doc/4768bc).

---

contained in article 14 of the International Covenant on Civil and Political Rights.[19]

This implicitly included its interpretation and application. And the statutes of all international courts and tribunals contain these fair trial guarantees.[20] The International Law Commission's 1994 Draft Statute for an international criminal court also replicated Article 14 of the ICCPR.[21] The ICC Statute also mirrors these and specifies the presumption of innocence.[22]

Prosecutor's offices and defence counsel have distinct statutory roles. This cannot be emphasised enough in the context of adversarial proceedings. The Prosecutor's is to investigate *and* prosecute. The others', by contrast, is far more limited – confined to defending an accused person against charges of having committed specific crimes. This could of course also involve defence investigations.[23]

---

[19] Report of the Secretary-General Pursuant to Paragraph 2 of Security Council Resolution 808 (1993), UN Doc. S/25704, 3 May 1993, para. 106 (https://www.legal-tools.org/doc/c12981).

[20] ICTY Statute, Article 20(1) "Commencement and conduct of trial proceedings": "The Trial Chambers shall ensure that a trial is fair and expeditious and that proceedings are conducted in accordance with the rules of procedure and evidence, with full respect for the rights of the accused and due regard for the protection of victims and witnesses", see above note 18; ICTR Statute, Article 19(1), see above note 18; IRMCT Statute, Article 18(1), see above note 18; STL Statute, 30 May 2007, Articles 16(2), 16(4)(c) (https://www.legal-tools.org/doc/da0bbb); Rome Statute of the International Criminal Court, 17 July 1998, Article 64(2): "The Trial Chamber shall ensure that a trial is fair and expeditious and is conducted with full respect for the rights of the accused and due regard for the protection of victims and witnesses" ('ICC Statute') (https://www.legal-tools.org/doc/7b9af9). The SCSL Statute has no equivalent except in Article 17(4)(c) "to be tried without undue delay" under "Rights of the Accused", which mirrors the same provisions in Article 21 of the ICTY Statute and Article 20 of the ICTR Statute.

[21] Additionally, Article 41(2) "Rights of the accused", provided that "Exculpatory evidence that becomes available to the Procuracy prior to the conclusion of the trial shall be made available to the defence. In case of doubt as to the application of this paragraph or as to the admissibility of the evidence, the Trial Chamber shall decide" (https://www.legal-tools.org/doc/17ad09).

[22] ICC Statute, Articles 66 and 67, see above note 20.

[23] See, for example, STL, *Prosecutor v. Ayyash et al.*, Trial Chamber, Decision Denying Merhi Defence Motion Seeking Disclosure of Material Relating to Potential Users of Purple Phone 231, 13 September 2017, STL-11-01/T/TC/F3320/20170913/R299893-R299913/EN/dm, para. 33 ('*Ayyash et al.* Trial Decision Denying Merhi Defence Motion') (https://www.legal-tools.org/doc/e16ae3).

The right to prosecution disclosure is not unlimited. The ICC's Appeals Chamber has held that material "while not directly linked to exonerating or incriminating evidence, may otherwise be material to the preparation of the defence".[24] However, this should not be read too broadly as "the right to disclosure is not unlimited" as what it material to defence preparations "will depend upon the specific circumstances of the case".[25] The Special Tribunal for Lebanon ('STL'), for example, has held that the rules regulating disclosure therefore cannot be interpreted as allowing the defence an absolute right of access to all information just because it is in the prosecution's possession.[26]

Another core principle is that prosecutors are presumed to be acting in good faith in making their disclosure decisions.[27] The mere fact that a chamber, after itself inspecting undisclosed prosecution material, may disagree with a prosecutorial decision not to disclose and orders disclosure, does not of itself equate to bad faith.

---

[24] ICC, Situation in the Democratic Republic of the Congo, *Prosecutor v. Thomas Lubanga Dylo*, Appeals Chamber, Judgment on the appeal of Mr. Lubanga Dyilo against the Oral Decision of Trial Chamber I of 18 January 2008, 11 July 2008, ICC-01/04-01/06-1433, para. 77 ('*Lubanga* Appeals Judgment on the Appeal of Mr. Lubanga Dyilo Against the Oral Decision of Trial Chamber I') (https://www.legal-tools.org/doc/f5bc1e); ICC, Situation in Uganda, *Prosecutor v. Dominic Ongwen*, Trial Chamber, Decision on Defence Request for Disclosure and Remedy for Late Disclosure, 28 September 2018, ICC-02/04-01/15-1351, para. 18 ('*Ongwen* Trial Decision') (https://www.legal-tools.org/doc/555655).

[25] ICC, Situation in Darfur, Sudan, *Prosecutor v. Abdallah Banda Abakaer Nourain and Saleh Mohammed Jerbo Jamus*, Appeals Chamber, Judgment on the appeal of Mr Abdallah Banda Abakaer Nourain and Mr Saleh Mohammed Jerbo Jamus against the decision of Trial Chamber IV of 23 January 2013 entitled "Decision on the Defence's Request for Disclosure of Documents in the Possession of the Office of the Prosecutor", 28 August 2013, ICC-02/05-03/09-501, para. 39 ('*Banda and Jerbo* Appeals Judgment') (https://www.legal-tools.org/doc/26d917).

[26] *Ayyash et al*. Trial Decision Denying Merhi Defence Motion, paras. 32–33, see above note 23; STL, *Prosecutor v. Ayyash et al.*, Trial Chamber, Decision on Disclosure of List of Student Information, 9 April 2014 STL-11-01/T/TC/F1490/20140409/R258118-R258126/EN/dm, para. 13 (https://www.legal-tools.org/doc/0173b1).

[27] See, for example, ICTR, *Kamuhanda v. Prosecutor*, Appeals Chamber, Decision on Motion for Disclosure, 4 March 2010, ICTR-99-54A-R68, para. 14 ('*Kamuhanda* Appeals Decision on Motion for Disclosure') (https://www.legal-tools.org/doc/e61411). ICTR, *Prosecutor v. Bizimungu et al.*, Trial Chamber, Decision on Bicamumpaka's Motion for Disclosure of Exculpatory Evidence (MDR Files), 17 November 2004, ICTR-99-50-T, para. 14 (https://www.legal-tools.org/doc/3f54ee); ICTY, *Prosecutor v. Kordić and Čerkez*, Appeals Chamber, Judgement, 17 December 2004, IT-95-14/2-A, para. 183 ('*Kordić and Čerkez* Appeals Judgment') (https://www.legal-tools.org/doc/738211).

The defence may be prejudiced by the prosecution either failing to disclose something that was subject to disclosure, or by its late disclosure. Generally, before a chamber will provide a remedy for this, a party must demonstrate material prejudice.[28] If the remedy sought is disclosure, the defence "has to describe clearly and comprehensively what it requests from the Chamber when formulating its relief sought".[29]

14.2.1. Exculpatory Material

The statutory instruments of the ICTY, ICTR, IRMCT and the STL require the prosecution, as soon as practicable, to disclose to the defence any exculpatory or mitigating information in its "possession or actual knowledge". At the SCSL and its residuary mechanism the RSCSL this is expressed as "evidence known to the Prosecutor".[30] Article 67(2) of the ICC Statute, by contrast, confines this to "evidence in the Prosecutor's possession or control". These principles derive from the need to ensure a fair trial under international human rights law.

Accordingly, at the ICTY the "significance of the fulfilment of the duty placed upon the Prosecution by virtue of Rule 68 [to disclose exculpatory material] has been stressed by the Appeals Chamber, and the obli-

---

[28] ICTY, *Prosecutor v. Krstić*, Appeals Chamber, Judgement, 19 April 2004, IT-98-33-A, para. 153 (https://www.legal-tools.org/doc/86a108); ICTR, *Prosecutor v. Kajelijeli*, Appeals Chamber, Judgement, 23 May 2005, ICTR-98-44A-A, para. 262 ('*Kajelijeli* Appeals Judgment') (https://www.legal-tools.org/doc/2b7d1c); STL, *Prosecutor v. Ayyash et al.*, Trial Chamber, Decision on Motion Seeking Interim Relief for Late Disclosure, 25 November 2014, STL-11-01/T/TC/F1766/20141125/R270154-R270159/EN/dm, para. 11 (https://www.legal-tools.org/doc/0c549c).

[29] See, for example, *Ongwen* Trial Decision, para. 7, see above note 24.

[30] ICTY RPE, 11 February 1994, Rule 68(i) (https://www.legal-tools.org/doc/30df50); ICTR RPE, 29 June 1995, Rule 68(A) (https://www.legal-tools.org/doc/c6a7c6); and IRMCT RPE, 8 June 2012, Rule 73(A) (https://www.legal-tools.org/doc/n7lau1): "the Prosecutor shall, as soon as practicable, disclose to the Defence any material which in the actual knowledge of the Prosecutor may suggest the innocence or mitigate the guilt of the accused or affect the credibility of Prosecution evidence"; Rule 113(A) of the STL RPE refers to "any information in his possession or actual knowledge", 20 March 2009 (https://www.legal-tools.org/doc/lc66t7). Under Rule 68(B) of the SCSL RPE and Rule 68(B) of the RSCSL RPE, the Prosecutor must make a statement "disclosing to the Defence the existence of evidence known to the Prosecutor which in any way tends to suggest the innocence or mitigate the guilt of the accused or may affect the credibility of prosecution evidence. The Prosecutor shall be under a continuing obligation to disclose any such exculpatory material", 16 January 2002 (https://www.legal-tools.org/doc/4c2a6b, https://www.legal-tools.org/doc/lt008t).

gation to disclose under Rule 68 has been considered as important as the obligation to prosecute".[31] However, the ICTY Appeals Chamber has held that:

> The Prosecution is under no legal obligation to consult with an accused to reach a decision on what material suggests the innocence or mitigates the guilt of an accused or affects the credibility of the Prosecution's evidence. The issue of what evidence might be exculpatory evidence is primarily a facts-based judgement made by and under the responsibility of the Prosecution.[32]

While true, it must be emphasised that when making such an internal and hence *ex parte* decision, the prosecution must exercise particular care to ensure due process.

In relation to the ICTR equivalent of the EDS, the ICTR Appeals Chamber in 2008 found that the prosecution's obligation to disclose for Rule 68 material "extends simply beyond making available its entire evidence collection in a searchable format. A search engine cannot serve as a surrogate for the Prosecution's individualized consideration of the material in its possession".[33]

Regarding 'internal work product', the STL Appeals Chamber determined that what may be considered as the prosecution's internal work product may be exculpatory. It held that there "has been general acceptance that, although characterized as internal, a document may nonetheless be subject to disclosure to an accused if it suggests the innocence or mitigates the guilt of the accused or if it affects the credibility of the Prosecutor's evidence".[34]

---

[31] *Kordić and Čerkez* Appeals Judgment, para. 183, see above note 27; citing ICTY, *Prosecutor v. Blaškić*, Appeals Chamber, Judgement, 29 July 2004, IT-95-14-A, para. 264 (*'Blaškić* Appeals Judgment') (https://www.legal-tools.org/doc/88d8e6).

[32] *Kordić and Čerkez* Appeals Judgment, para. 183, see above note 27; citing *Blaškić* Appeals Judgment, para. 264, see above note 31.

[33] ICTR, *Prosecutor v. Karemera et al.*, Appeals Chamber, Decision on the Prosecution's Interlocutory Appeal Concerning Disclosure Obligations, 23 January 2008, ICTR-98-44-AR73.11, para. 10 (*'Karemera et al.* Appeals Decision on the Prosecution's Interlocutory Appeal') (https://www.legal-tools.org/doc/f13f94).

[34] STL, *In the Matter of El Sayed*, Appeals Chamber, Decision on Partial Appeal by Mr. El Sayed of Pre-Trial Judge's Decision of 12 May 2011, 19 July 2011, CH/AC/2011/01, para. 97 (*'El Sayed* Appeals Decision') (https://www.legal-tools.org/doc/d3da38); STL, *Prosecutor v. Ayyash et al.*, Trial Chamber, Decision Denying the Sabra Defence Application for

Before a Chamber can order the disclosure of exculpatory material under the applicable Rule, the Party seeking disclosure must: (i) specifically identify the material sought, (ii) present a *prima facie* showing of the probable exculpatory nature of the material, and (iii) prove that the material is in the custody or control of the Prosecution.[35]

On its face, as noted above, this may present a problem to defence counsel who may only suspect that the prosecution is holding material that may be exculpatory. No matter how well motivated prosecution officials are, the possibility always exists of undisclosed exculpatory information remaining in the prosecution's possession.[36] This possibility is amplified by assigning the searching of holdings for disclosable information to junior staff. And it is further magnified by the challenges of finding this information in collections of evidence in languages not spoken or read by the reviewing officials, including in videos, evidence on CDs or other electronic forms. It may also be delegated – with instructions of what to look for – to language assistants. Inevitably things may be overlooked. This is another reason for an electronic disclosure suite.

The obligation to disclose may be lifted if the evidence is both known to and is accessible to the Defence.[37] An example is open session

---

Disclosure of a UNIIIC Internal Memorandum on Mr. Wissam Al-Hassan (Witness PRH680) Under Rules 110(B) and 113, 7 February 2018, STL-11-01/T/TC/F3562/20180207/R306883-R306898/EN/dm, para. 12 ('*Ayyash et al.* Trial Decision re Wissam Al-Hassan') (https://www.legal-tools.org/doc/ce9a0f); STL, *Prosecutor v. Ayyash et al.*, Trial Chamber, Reasons for the Trial Chamber's Decision Dismissing the Sabra Defence Application to Order Prosecution Disclosure of Documents Related to Mr. Michael Taylor, 13 July 2018, STL-11-01/T/TC/F3710/20180713/R311213-R311231/EN/dm, para. 32 ('*Ayyash et al.* Trial Decision re Michael Taylor') (https://www.legal-tools.org/doc/e8b492).

[35] See, for example, ICTR, *Prosecutor v. Karemera et al.*, Appeals Chamber, Decision on "Joseph Nzirorera's Appeal from Decision on Tenth Rule 68 Motion", 14 May 2008, ICTR-98-44-AR73.13, para. 9 (https://www.legal-tools.org/doc/a849fd); *Kamuhanda* Appeals Decision on Motion for Disclosure, para. 14, see above note 27; *Kordić and Čerkez* Appeals Judgment, para. 179, see above note 27.

[36] This is shown by the disclosures of such information common to international trials that continue into appellate proceedings and sometimes beyond.

[37] See, for example, ICTY, *Prosecutor v. Blaškić*, Appeals Chamber, Decision on the Appellant's Motion for the Production of Material, Suspension or Extension of the Briefing Schedule, and Additional Filings, 26 September 2000, IT-95-14-A, para. 38 (https://www.legal-tools.org/doc/8ff583); ICTY, *Prosecutor v. Bralo*, Appeals Chamber, Decision on Motions for Access to *Ex Parte* Portions of the Record on Appeal and for Disclosure of Mitigating Material, 30 August 2006, IT-95-17-A, para. 30 (https://www.legal-tools.org/

testimony of a witness in another case, but if that testimony may become exculpatory in combination with undisclosed closed session testimony, the prosecution must disclose the open session testimony.[38]

14.2.2. Information that Is 'Material' to Defence Preparations for Trial

The general principle, as noted in the introduction above, is that the Prosecution must disclose evidence it intends to use at trial, or information that is material to defence preparations for trial.[39] What is 'material', however, may not always be obvious. The key is of materiality to defence preparations as opposed to relevance to the prosecution's case.[40] The international case law has interpreted this as requiring the defence to demonstrate *prima facie* that the material sought is "material to the preparation of the defence".[41]

---

doc/e97b7c); ICTR, *Niyitegeka v. Prosecutor*, Appeals Chamber, Decision on Request for Review, 30 June 2006, ICTR-96-14-R, para. 51 (https://www.legal-tools.org/doc/f70249).

[38] ICTY, *Prosecutor v. Dario Kordić*, Appeals Chamber, Decision on Appellant's Notice and Supplemental Notice of Prosecution's Non-Compliance with its Disclosure Obligation under Rule 68 of the Rules, 11 February 2004, IT-95-14/2-A, para. 20 (https://www.legal-tools.org/doc/5da353).

[39] The accused shall have access to books, documents, photographs and tangible objects in the Prosecutor's custody or control, which are material to the preparation of the defence, or are intended for use by the Prosecution as evidence at trial; ICTY RPE, Rule 66(B), see above note 30; ICTR RPE, Rule 66(B), see above note 30; SCSL RPE, Rule 66(B), see above note 30; IRMCT RPE, Rule 71(B), see above note 30; ICC RPE, 9 September 2002, Rule 77 (https://www.legal-tools.org/doc/e1b3f5); STL RPE, Rule 110(B), see above note 30.

[40] See, for example, *Prosecutor v. Ayyash et al.*, Trial Chamber, Decision on Call Data Records and Disclosure to Defence (On Remand from Appeals Chamber), 4 December 2013, STL-11-01/PT/TC/F1252/20131204/R250347-R250361/EN/djo, para. 13 ('*Ayyash et al.* Trial Decision on Call Data Records') (https://www.legal-tools.org/doc/8d7200); STL, *Prosecutor v. Ayyash et al.*, Appeals Chamber, Public Redacted Version of 19 September 2013 Decision on Appeal by Counsel for Mr. Oneissi against Pre-Trial Judge's "Decision on Issues Related to the Inspection Room and Call Data Records", 2 October 2013, STL-11-01/PT/AC/AR126.4/F0004-AR126.4/PRV/20131002/R000068-R000086/EN/af, para. 19 (https://www.legal-tools.org/doc/a64cd6).

[41] See, for example, *Karemera et al.* Appeals Decision on the Prosecution's Interlocutory Appeal, paras. 12, 14, see above note 33; ICTR, *Karemera et al. v. Prosecutor*, Appeals Chamber, Decision on Joseph Nzirorera's Appeal from Decision on Alleged Rule 66 Violation, 17 May 2010, ICTR-98-44-AR73.18, paras. 12–13 (https://www.legal-tools.org/doc/00a88f); *Banda and Jerbo* Appeals Judgment, para. 42, see above note 25; ICTR, *Prosecutor v. Bagosora et al.*, Appeals Chamber, Decision on Interlocutory Appeal Relating to Disclosure under Rule 66(B) of the Tribunal's Rules of Procedure and Evidence, 25 Sep-

---

Before disclosing evidence, the Prosecution is responsible for determining whether it is material to the Defence.[42] In doing so, the Prosecution should consider, among other things, "whether the material could reasonably lead to further investigation by the Defence and the discovery of additional evidence".[43] But the courts have also held that "[p]reparation is a broad concept" and what is material to the defence does not need to be limited to being 'directly linked exonerating or incriminating evidence' or "related to the Prosecution's case-in-chief".[44] It refers to "all objects that are relevant for the preparation of the defence" and must be interpreted broadly.[45]

---

tember 2006, ICTR-98-41-AR73, para. 9 ('*Bagosora et al*. Appeals Decision on Interlocutory Appeal') (https://www.legal-tools.org/doc/3d937e); *Lubanga* Appeals Judgment on the Appeal of Mr. Lubanga Dyilo Against the Oral Decision of Trial Chamber I, para. 77, see above note 24; ICTY, *Prosecutor v. Karadžić*, Trial Chamber, Decision on Motion to Compel Inspection of Items Material to the Sarajevo Defence Case, 8 February 2012, IT-95-5/18-T, paras. 6–9 ('*Karadžić* Trial Decision') (https://www.legal-tools.org/doc/6ab104).

[42] See, for example, SCSL, *Prosecutor v. Sesay et al.*, Trial Chamber, Decision on Defence Motion for Disclosure Pursuant to Rules 66 and 68 of the Rules, 9 July 2004, SCSL-2004-15-T, para. 28 ('*Sesay* Trial Decision on Defence Motion for Disclosure') (https://www.legal-tools.org/doc/d154fc); ICTY, *Prosecutor v. Mucić et al.*, Trial Chamber, Decision on the Motion by the Accused Zejnil Delalić for the Disclosure of Evidence, 26 September 1996, IT-96-21-T, , para. 11 ('*Mucić et al*. Trial Decision on the Motion by the Accused Zejnil Delalić for the Disclosure of Evidence') (https://www.legal-tools.org/doc/100f7a); ICTR, ICTR, *Prosecutor v. Ndayambaje*, Trial Chamber, Decision on the Defence Motion for Disclosure, 25 September 2001, ICTR-96-8-T, para. 11 (https://www.legal-tools.org/doc/049d4e).

[43] See, for example, ICTR, *Nahimana et al. v. Prosecutor*, Appeals Chamber, Decision on Motions Relating to the Appellant Hassan Ngeze's and the Prosecution's Request for Leave to Present Additional Evidence of Witnesses ABC1 and EB, 27 November 2006, ICTR-99-52-A, para. 16 ('*Nahimana et al*. Appeals Decision') (https://www.legal-tools.org/doc/f076c8), citing to ICTY, *Prosecutor v. Krstić*, Appeals Chamber, Confidential Decision on the Prosecution's Motion to be Relieved of Obligation to Disclose Sensitive Information Pursuant to Rule 66(C), 27 March 2003, IT-98-33-A, p. 4, which held that the prosecution on the request of the defence "has to permit the inspection of any material which is capable of being admitted on appeal or which may lead to the discovery of material which is capable of being admitted on appeal" (This ICTY Appeals Chamber decision appears not to be publicly available).

[44] See, for example, *Karadžić* Trial Decision, para. 9, see above note 41; *Karemera et al*. Appeals Decision on the Prosecution's Interlocutory Appeal, para. 14, see above note 33; *Bagosora et al*. Appeals Decision on Interlocutory Appeal, para. 9, see above note 41.

[45] *Lubanga* Appeals Judgment on the Appeal of Mr. Lubanga Dyilo Against the Oral Decision of Trial Chamber I, paras. 77–78, see above note 24.

The defence, the ICC Appeals Chamber held in *Lubanga*, does not need to provide

> advance revelation of his or her defences in order to receive full prosecution disclosure. The lack of any correlation between the right to receive prosecution disclosure and any disclosure obligations of the Defence is evident in that the Prosecutor is duty-bound to provide full disclosure even if an accused elects to remain silent or does not raise a defence.[46]

If the defence believes that the prosecution has failed to disclose or has withheld material information, it may seek judicial intervention, but it cannot rely on unspecific or unsubstantiated allegations or general descriptions in so doing.[47] International case law has consistently held against defence disclosure 'fishing expeditions'.[48] In lay terms, a so-called 'fishing expedition' could equate to a general Internet search for, say, a nice new washing machine.

The practical and logical difficulty with the application of this international case law, however, is that defence counsel may often only *suspect* that the prosecution has information in a class that they seek. And without providing a basis for asserting that the prosecution has this information they will be denied an order for disclosure. This conundrum has been revealed by judicial, *ex parte* to the defence, inspection of materials in the prosecution's possession that the prosecution has not found to be material to defence preparations.

Unfortunately, the results of these inspections, have gone both ways, as judicial review has sometimes resulted in orders to the prosecution to disclose withheld information. Other judicial reviews have produced the opposite result. The word 'unfortunately' is used here, because preferably, (a) the chambers should not have to do this and (b) should not – even accepting that reasonable minds could differ as to the meaning of 'material to the defence' – come to a different view as to whether something hitherto undisclosed should be handed over. A number of these decisions, with

---

[46] *Ibid.*, para. 50.

[47] See, for example, *Sesay et al.* Trial Decision on Defence Motion for Disclosure, paras. 26–27, see above note 42; *Mucić et al.* Trial Decision on the Motion by the Accused Zejnil Delalić for the Disclosure of Evidence, para. 9, see above note 42.

[48] See, for example, *Karadžić* Trial Decision, para. 8, see above note 41; *Nahimana et al.* Appeals Decision, para. 11, see above note 43.

divergent results, are footnoted below – illustrating the burden placed on a chamber in having to review such material itself.[49]

---

[49] For example, just at the STL, in *Prosecutor v. Ayyash et al.*, Trial Chamber, Decision on Sabra Motion to Lift Redactions and Disclosure of United Nations Fact-Finding Mission Documents, 9 December 2013, STL-11-01/PT/TC/F1256/20131209/R250391-R250401/EN/af ('*Ayyash et al.* Trial Decision on Sabra Motion to Lift Redactions and Disclosure of United Nations Fact-Finding Mission Documents') (https://www.legal-tools.org/doc/d42cdf), the Trial Chamber – on a defence application – ordered the Prosecution to provide it with two unredacted witness statements and an undisclosed UN fact-finding document to ascertain whether the redactions were properly made. Upon review of the documents, the Trial Chamber decided that they had been; see, STL, *Prosecutor v. Ayyash et al.*, Trial Chamber, Second Decision on Sabra Motion to Lift Redactions and Disclose United Nations Fact-Finding Mission Documents, 28 February 2014, STL-11-01/T/TC/F1436/20140228/R255770-R255773/EN/af (https://www.legal-tools.org/doc/42fe47). Conversely, see also STL, *Prosecutor v. Ayyash et al.*, Trial Chamber, Decision on the Oneissi Defence Motion for Disclosure of Requests for Assistance, 7 November 2014, STL-11-01/T/TC/F1739/20141107/R269752-R269757/EN/dm ('*Ayyash et al.* Trial Decision on the Oneissi Defence Motion for Disclosure of Requests for Assistance') (https://www.legal-tools.org/doc/8f1dbd), where the Trial Chamber on a defence application examined 38 Prosecution undisclosed requests for assistance to Lebanon, and decided that they contained nothing material to defence preparations for trial. Upon a further defence application – but based upon different reasons for requiring the material, namely that the defence needed the documents to challenge the legality of the transfer of Lebanese telecommunications data to the United Nations International Independent Investigation Commission ('UNIIIC') – the Trial Chamber reconsidered this decision and ordered the Prosecution to disclose these documents, STL, *Prosecutor v. Ayyash et al.*, Trial Chamber, Decision Reconsidering 'Decision on the Oneissi Defence Motion for Disclosure of Requests for Assistance', 7 November 2014, 6 March 2015, STL-11-01/T/TC/F1875/20150306/R272340-R272349/EN/dm (https://www.legal-tools.org/doc/b524a3). On a defence application, the Trial Chamber ordered the Prosecution to provide it with draft statements and reports of a prosecution analyst witness, STL, *Prosecutor v. Ayyash et al.*, Trial Chamber, Order on Merhi Defence Request for Disclosure of Documents Concerning Witness PRH230 (Andrew Donaldson), 20 April 2017, STL-11-01/T/TC/F3094/20170420/R294760-R294761/EN/dm (https://www.legal-tools.org/doc/1a24a6), and after examining them ordered their immediate disclosure to the Defence, STL, *Prosecutor v. Ayyash et al.*, Trial Chamber, Decision on Merhi Defence Request for Disclosure of Documents Concerning Witness PRH230, 2 June 2017, STL-11-01/T/TC/F3171/20170602/R296549-R296581/EN/dm ('*Ayyash et al.* Trial Decision on Merhi Defence Request for Disclosure of Documents Concerning Witness PRH230') (https://www.legal-tools.org/doc/5ac961); STL, *Prosecutor v. Ayyash et al.*, Trial Chamber, Corrected Version of the 'Decision on Oneissi Defence Urgent Motion for an Order to Compel Disclosure of Requests for Assistance Relevant to the Attribution of Mobile Number 3598095' of 13 October 2017, 24 October 2017, STL-11-01/T/TC/F3359/COR/20171024/R302308-R302326/EN/dm (https://www.legal-tools.org/doc/dc9bbb), in which the Trial Chamber after reviewing, *ex-parte* the defence, Prosecution requests for assistance to Lebanon, ordered the Prosecution to disclose 12 of the 13 that it reviewed. Other examples include *Ayyash et al.* Trial Decision re Wissam Al-Hassan, see above note

The chambers as the ultimate guardian of ensuring a fair trial are placed in the same position as defence counsel in not knowing whether anything else in the prosecution's holdings requires disclosure. Some judicial decisions ordering additional disclosure are based on a view different to the prosecution's of what is 'material'. As chambers must ensure a fair trial to an accused, they should generally take the most generous and liberal view of what is material to defence preparations for trial, even where the decision may be delicately balanced and may impose burdens on a prosecutor's office, over its protestations.

Also problematic is that the defence bears the onus both of showing the existence of the material sought and its materiality. The difficulty with this principle is illustrated by the very fact that judges in examining prosecution material, *ex parte* the defence, may discover additional material which in their view should be – or should have been – disclosed. This raises the issue of whether a court should act as a *general* disclosure filter, by examining prosecution disclosure, either intended or actual. The simple answer to this is 'no'.

The court, on a practical basis, cannot do this, and as one of public policy should not have to. To perform this task, it would have to have access to the prosecution's databases and search them for itself seeking material that is 'material' to defence preparations. This would blur the lines between judicial impartiality and the role of the prosecutor as both investigator and party to proceedings before a chamber. This is another reason why non-restricted prosecution material should be placed in a registry-controlled electronic disclosure suite.

As a matter of practicality, it would also be infeasible. At the ICC and STL, for example, the judges have access to material disclosed between the parties in what are termed 'disclosure batches'; at the STL the disclosure is made through the Tribunal's electronic case management system 'Legal Workflow'. This is party controlled disclosure that a chamber *may* examine for itself. Some of the material in these innocently termed 'batches' relates to evidence to be used at trial (witness and documentary) while other disclosed material concerns documents the prosecution considers material to defence preparations, including exculpatory information. Another category, sometimes voluminous, is of material that

---

34, and *Ayyash et al*. Trial Decision re Michael Taylor, see above note 34. This list is extracted to give an illustrative overview.

---

might be used in cross-examining opposing witnesses. But much of it will not be. This surely cannot be the most efficient way to conduct litigation on this important issue.

Hence, the scale of the exercise and its often-abstract nature – as the disclosures may be large and lacking in context – would make it impractical and an inefficient use of chamber resources, both judicial and staff.

The challenge, it appears, is less one of involving the judges in the day-to-day work of disclosure but rather their better understanding how the information is stored, managed, searched and retrieved. Moreover, making blanket orders to the prosecution, for example, to provide better details in disclosing material will not necessarily solve the problem of trying to make sense of some of the disclosures, given the work that would be needed to provide this level of detail. This may be beyond the resources of the prosecutor's office, and chambers must carefully balance overall institutional resources in making orders that are unnecessarily onerous to a party.

Implicit in saying this of course is that fundamental to the right to a fair trial is the defence receiving all exculpatory material and information that is material to trial preparation. This principle trumps resource considerations. But in any event, the documents should contain comprehensible metadata, preferably entered when the material is logged, which would facilitate its understanding.

14.2.3. Witness Statements and Related Information

The prosecution must disclose witness statements of the witnesses who will provide evidence at trial.[50] However, no one set definition for a 'witness statement' exists.[51] Witness statements evolve and may comprise formally recorded question and answer style interviews, whether audio or video recorded or written, statements written in a prescribed or habitual form, notes of the utterances of witnesses recorded in note or other form, drafts of formal statements, or any combination of these.

---

[50]   ICTY RPE, Rule 66(A)(ii), see above note 30; ICTR RPE, Rule 66(A)(ii), see above note 30; SCSL RPE, Rule 66(A)(ii), see above note 30; ICC RPE, Rule 76, see above note 39; STL RPE, Rule 110(A)(ii), see above note 30.

[51]   *Ayyash et al.* Trial Decision on Merhi Defence Request for Disclosure of Documents Concerning Witness PRH230, paras. 45–47, see above note 49.

Courts have grappled with the boundaries of what can be described as a witness statement and hence what must be disclosed. The ICC's Appeals Chamber, for instance, has held that witness statements within the meaning of Rule 76 are made only when witnesses "are questioned about their knowledge of [a] case".[52]

The ICTR's and ICTY's Appeals Chambers have found that "[r]ecords of questions put to the witness and answers given constitute witness statements", and "it is necessary to disclose the questions put to witnesses in order to make the statements intelligible".[53] One ICTY Trial Chamber broadened the definition to "[a]nything that a witness says or writes which is relevant to an indictment".[54]

The STL Appeals Chamber has said that its usual meaning "is an account of a person's knowledge of a crime, which is recorded through due procedure in the course of an investigation into the crime". Further, as witness statements may go through a number of drafts, all stages of the preparation of a 'witness statement' can be important, as they enable the Chamber and the opposing party to know how a witness statement has evolved.[55] Thus, the courts and tribunals have decided, it is not only the final signed witness statement that is subject to disclosure; question and answers, investigator's notes and emails can also constitute witness statements.[56]

---

[52]   ICC, Situation in the Democratic Republic of the Congo, *Prosecutor v. Ntaganda*, Appeals Chamber, Judgment on the Appeal of Mr Bosco Ntaganda Against the "Decision on Defence Request Seeking Disclosure Orders and a Declaration of Prosecution Obligations to Record Contacts with Witnesses", 20 May 2016, ICC-01/04-02/06-1330, para. 16 (https://www.legal-tools.org/doc/7790c5).

[53]   ICTR, *Niyitegeka v. Prosecutor*, Appeals Chamber, Judgement, 9 July 2004, ICTR-96-14-A, para. 33 ('*Niyitegeka* Appeals Judgment') (https://www.legal-tools.org/doc/35cd4f).

[54]   ICTY, *Prosecutor v. Haradinaj et al.*, Trial Chamber, Decision on Haradinaj Motion for Disclosure of Exculpatory Materials in Respect of Witness 81, 18 November 2011, IT-04-84*bis*-T, paras. 27, 32 (https://www.legal-tools.org/doc/680c8f).

[55]   *El Sayed* Appeals Decision, paras. 83–89, see above note 34.

[56]   SCSL, *Prosecutor v. Norman et al.*, Trial Chamber, Decision on Disclosure of Witness Statements and Cross-Examination, 16 July 2004, SCSL-04-14-PT, paras. 8–10 (https://www.legal-tools.org/doc/85781e); *Niyitegeka* Appeals Judgment, paras. 33–35, see above note 53; *El Sayed* Appeals Decision, paras. 83–87, see above note 34; *Ayyash et al.* Trial Decision on Merhi Defence Request for Disclosure of Documents Concerning Witness PRH230, para. 12, see above note 49; STL, *Prosecutor v. Ayyash et al.*, Trial Chamber, Decision Denying Merhi Defence Request Relating to Prosecution Disclosure Obligations,

---

Moreover, witness statements are the witness' product and therefore must be disclosed and do not fall under the protections of work product,[57] even if contained in a larger document which is work product. Similarly, drafts of expert reports should be disclosed.[58]

As a miscellaneous example, the payment of normal witness expenses to prosecution witnesses, such as travel and accommodation, is not necessarily disclosable as material to defence preparations for trial.[59] Additional benefits or payments are;[60] the test is whether they could go to the motivation of a witness to provide evidence and hence their credibility or reliability.

---

23 March 2018, STL-11-01/T/TC/F3607/20180323/R308136-R308149/EN/dm, para. 18 (https://www.legal-tools.org/doc/5d3790).

[57] *El Sayed* Appeals Decision, para. 78, see above note 34.

[58] See, for example, *Ayyash et al.* Trial Decision on Merhi Defence Request for Disclosure of Documents Concerning Witness PRH230, paras. 80–81, see above note 49, declining to follow a decision of the STL's Pre-Trial Judge which held that these were only disclosable if the expert referred to the draft, STL, Ayyash *et al.*, Pre-Trial Judge, Decision on Sabra's Seventh Motion for Disclosure – Experts, 24 May 2013, STL-11-01/PT/PTJ/F0913/20130524/R143164-R143183/EN/af, paras. 30–33 (https://www.legal-tools.org/doc/f91c2a).

[59] ICTR, *Prosecutor v. Bizimungu*, Trial Chamber, Decision on Prosper Mugiraneza's Motion for Records of All Payments Made Directly or Indirectly to Witness D, 28 September 2006, ICTR-99-50-T, para. 13 (https://www.legal-tools.org/doc/d8043c); STL, *Prosecutor v. Ayyash et al.*, Trial Chamber, Decision on Prosecution Witness Expenses, 9 May 2014, STL-11-01/T/TC/F1519/20140509/R258860-R258867/EN/dm (https://www.legal-tools.org/doc/6188bb).

[60] ICTR, *Prosecutor v. Karemera*, Trial Chamber, Decision on Defence Motion for Full Disclosure of Payments to Witnesses and to Exclude Testimony from Paid Witnesses, 23 August 2005, ICTR-98-44-PT, para. 7 (https://www.legal-tools.org/doc/482aea); ICC, Situation in the Central African Republic, *Prosecutor v. Bemba*, Trial Chamber, Public redacted version of "Decision on 'Defence Request for Disclosure and Investigative Assistance concerning Witnesses 169 and 178'", 11 December 2014, ICC-01/05-01/08-3077-Red, para. 2 (https://www.legal-tools.org/doc/c86b31/), referring to its Decision on the prosecution's 'Information on contacts of Witnesses 169 and 178 with other witnesses located [...]' (ICC-01/05-01/08-2827-Conf-Exp)", 25 October 2013, ICC-01/05-01/08-2845-Conf-Exp.

14.2.4. Witnesses Called by Chamber

Some international criminal courts and tribunals, such as the IRMCT and the STL, may call their own witnesses.[61] While the Rome Statute is silent on this, its trial chambers have done so.

Given the adversarial nature of international proceedings – after all, they are entitled *Prosecutor v. Defendant/Accused*, as opposed to *Trial Chamber v. Defendant/Accused/Prosecutor* – the discretion to 'step into the ring' and call witnesses must be exercised with extreme caution. This may raise tangential disclosure issues.

Trial and appellate chambers are mandated only with determining whether an accused person is guilty of the crimes charged – in a fair trial conducted according to law – rather than with attempting to determine some 'objective truth' that is possibly ascertainable by conducting an inquiry extending beyond this framework. This is of course the fundamental difference between a fact-finding mission or a truth and reconciliation commission and a criminal trial.[62]

The danger is that the chamber may decide to call a witness that the parties for good reasons have decided not to. The chamber cannot know the full 'back-story' to a witness's involvement with a party, including communications between the two. If a chamber decides to call its own witnesses its actions in doing so are disclosable to the parties and any participating victims. This includes its methodology in 'preparing' witnesses for their testimony.

---

[61] IRMCT RPE, Rule 120, see above note 30; STL RPE, Rule 165, but only after first 'hearing the Parties', see above note 30.

[62] Article 69(3) ICC Statute provides: "The parties may submit evidence relevant to the case, in accordance with article 64. The Court shall have the authority to request the submission of all evidence that it considers necessary for the determination of the truth". In an adversarial criminal trial this can only extend to examining the available evidence, and determining the 'truth' on that available evidence in the sense of whether the Prosecutor has established the guilt beyond reasonable doubt of the accused on the charges pursuant to Article 66(2). The question of 'who really did it?' if the court acquits and hence, 'the truth' is beyond the chamber's statutory function. This does not conflict with the Prosecutor's statutory duty under Article 54(1)(a): "In order to establish the truth, extend the investigation to cover all facts and evidence relevant to an assessment of whether there is criminal responsibility under this Statute, and, in doing so, investigate incriminating and exonerating circumstances equally", as the chambers and prosecution have different roles in an adversarial trial. Nor would it impede the Trial Chamber's ability to request the parties to call additional evidence.

Thus, the STL Trial Chamber, in deciding to call one witness – on a defence application to do so – held that it had the same disclosure obligations as the prosecution, and that the prosecution's obligation to disclose exculpatory or mitigating information also applies, as it is a requirement independent of whoever calls the witness.[63] Further, when required by the interests of justice, a chamber may order the prosecution to inform it of the existence of witness statements by the chamber's witnesses – where legally permitted – or to provide them to the chamber or the parties.[64]

Again, it is emphasised that chambers do not have access to internal prosecution (or defence) work product or evidence holdings to search them. Judges and their staff must therefore rely on the parties to provide information to them that is relevant to any witnesses called by chambers. The ICTY's *Krajišnik* Trial Chamber, for example, decided to call six witnesses itself after the close of the defence case, but according to a complicated formula involving its legal officers contacting the witnesses, conducting recorded preliminary interviews, compiling witness statements based on these, and providing the parties with the witness statements, while also requiring the parties to provide relevant material to the chamber.[65]

The *Blaškić* Trial Chamber made the process even more complex in calling eight witnesses itself. It required the witnesses to make 'spontaneous' in-court statements – but they could consult notes – on specified subjects, including their "perception of the accused's personality both professionally and personally".[66] It allowed the parties equal time to question

---

[63]   *Ayyash et al.* Trial Decision re Michael Taylor, para. 15, see above note 34.

[64]   *Ibid.*, para. 21; ICTY, *Prosecutor v. Krajišnik*, Trial Chamber, Procedure on Calling and Examining Chamber Witnesses, 7 April 2006, IT-00-39-T, Annex, paras. 3, 7, 10 (https://www.legal-tools.org/doc/wl8kca); ICTY, *Prosecutor v. Krajišnik*, Trial Chamber, Finalized Procedure on Chamber Witnesses; Decisions and Orders on Several Evidentiary and Procedural Matters, 24 April 2006, IT-00-39-T, para. 14 (https://www.legal-tools.org/doc/ik1mey). A chamber could use Article 69(3) of the ICC Statute to do this, see above note 20.

[65]   ICTY, *Prosecutor v. Krajišnik*, Trial Chamber, Judgement, 27 September 2006, IT-00-39-T, para. 1255 ('*Krajišnik* Trial Judgment') (https://www.legal-tools.org/doc/62a710). One of the (reluctant) witnesses was Krajišnik's former (and sentenced) co-accused, Biljana Plavšić (IT-00-39 & 40/1), who had pleaded guilty to persecutions as a crime against humanity charged on the same indictment.

[66]   See, for example, ICTY, *Prosecutor v. Blaškić*, Trial Chamber, Decision of Trial Chamber I Summoning Mr. Robert Stewart as a Witness of the Trial Chamber, 19 May 1999, IT-95-14-T, no. 3 on the list (https://www.legal-tools.org/doc/dbc860).

the witnesses – two of whom were subsequently indicted – but only on the basis of their spontaneous statements, and before the chamber itself questioned the witnesses.[67] The parties were also ordered to confidentially provide the chamber with their own statements from these witnesses and related material.[68]

What occurred in that case starkly illustrates the policy reasons for the restraint that a chamber must exercise in deciding whether to call its own witnesses. In attempting to – as the Trial Chamber explained – "ascertain the truth in respect of the crimes with which the accused has been charged",[69] it could not have been expected to know that at that time Colonel Amir Kubura and General Enver Hadžihasanović – officers serving in the military on the opposing side to the conflict – were themselves the subjects of a prosecution investigation, and two years later would be indicted by the ICTY.[70] The ICTY Trial Chamber's statutory function was to conduct a criminal trial on whether the charged accused person was guilty of the charges on the indictment before it, rather than to conduct an inquiry to ascertain the 'truth' of whatever transpired, in the manner of a truth and reconciliation commission. But this occurred in the late 1990s and, undoubtedly, lessons will have been drawn from it.

14.2.5. Witnesses Called by Participating Victims

The ICC and STL allow victims to participate in the proceedings. At the STL they may receive "all documents filed by the parties and the case file submitted by the Pre-Trial Judge to the Trial Chamber before commencement of the trial, except for confidential and *ex parte* material or for other restrictions imposed in the interest of justice". The STL Rules provide for the Trial Chamber to determine the disclosure obligations of the Legal Representatives of Victims if they have been authorised to call evidence.[71]

---

[67] ICTY, *Prosecutor v. Blaškić*, Trial Chamber, Judgement, 3 March 2000, IT-95-14-T, para. 57 (https://www.legal-tools.org/doc/e1ae55). It also "made a Defence witness appear".

[68] See, for example, ICTY, *Prosecutor v. Blaškić*, Trial Chamber, Decision of Trial Chamber I in Respect of the Appearance of General Enver Hadžihasanović, 25 March 1999, IT-95-14-T, p. 3 (https://www.legal-tools.org/doc/635aa7).

[69] *Ibid.*, p. 2.

[70] ICTY, *Prosecutor v. Hadžihasanović, Alagić and Kubura*, Prosecutor, Indictment, 5 July 2001, IT-01-47 (https://www.legal-tools.org/doc/db0960).

[71] STL RPE, Rules 87(A), 87(B) and 112*bis*, see above note 30. See also, STL, *Prosecutor v. Ayyash et al.*, Trial Chamber, Decision on the Legal Representatives of Victims' Applica-

Obvious practical difficulties would exist in allowing disclosure to all participating victims, as opposed to their legal representatives. The potential victims may be numerous, numbering in the thousands in some ICC proceedings, thus presenting real logistical and security issues. However, the participating victims have no standing giving them a procedural right to disclosure.

At the STL, participating victims may request the Trial Chamber to call witnesses and to authorise them to tender evidence,[72] while the chamber must decide on their disclosure obligations.[73] In allowing the participating victims to call witnesses and present evidence the STL Trial Chamber in *Ayyash* decided that they had to disclose to the parties the statements of all intended witnesses.[74] The ICC has also permitted participating victims to present evidence and has held that this may extend to evidence bearing on the guilt of the accused.[75]

---

tion to Call Evidence, Schedule the Presentation of Evidence and Directions on Disclosure Obligations, 31 July 2017, STL-11-01/T/TC/F3260/20170731/R297955-R297984/EN/dm, para. 98 ('*Ayyash et al.* Trial Decision on LRV Application and Directions on Disclosure Obligations') (https://www.legal-tools.org/doc/23a9e6).

[72] STL RPE, Rule 87(B), see above note 30. The ICC Appeals Chamber has ruled that, in order to allow victims to participate meaningfully in the trial, the Trial Chamber may, where appropriate, authorise them to tender evidence, ICC, Situation in the Democratic Republic of the Congo, *The Prosecutor v. Thomas Lubanga Dyilo*, Appeals Chamber, Judgment on the appeals of The Prosecutor and The Defence against Trial Chamber I's Decision on Victims' Participation of 18 January 2008, 11 July 2008, ICC-01/04-01/06-1432, paras. 97–99 ('*Lubanga* Appeals Judgment on the Appeals of the Prosecutor and the Defence Against Trial Chamber I's Decision on Victims' Participation') (https://www. legal-tools.org/doc/75cf1a).

[73] STL RPE, Rule 112*bis* "Disclosure by Victims Participating in the Proceedings" provides that "where the Trial Chamber grants a victim participating in the proceedings the right to call evidence, the Chamber shall decide on the corresponding disclosure obligations that shall be imposed", see above note 30.

[74] *Ayyash et al.* Trial Decision on LRV Application and Directions on Disclosure Obligations, para. 98, see above note 71.

[75] *Lubanga* Appeals Judgment on the Appeals of the Prosecutor and the Defence Against Trial Chamber I's Decision on Victims' Participation, paras. 93–97, see above note 72. Judges Pikis and Kirsch dissented, stating that victims cannot adduce evidence on the guilt of the accused and that their participation is confined to the expression of their views and concerns, Partly Dissenting Opinion of Judge G.M. Pikis, in *Lubanga* Appeals Judgment on the Appeals of the Prosecutor and the Defence Against Trial Chamber I's Decision on Victims' Participation, paras. 4–6, 15, see above note 72; ICC, Situation in the Democratic Republic of the Congo, *The Prosecutor v. Thomas Lubanga Dyilo*, Appeals Chamber, Partly Dissenting Opinion of Judge Philippe Kirsch, 23 July 2008, ICC-01/04-01/06-1432-Anx,

14.2.6. Material Conditionally Provided to Prosecutor's Offices

Another problematic issue is of material provided confidentially to prosecutor's offices that cannot be disclosed to the defence without the provider's consent. Often it is provided for lead investigative purposes. It could also come from fact-finding operations – NGO or governmental or intergovernmental – and contain information that is highly relevant to bringing charges. The information may be very sensitive and present security concerns to potential witnesses and providers. There could be issues of State security. Such material potentially may also contain information that is either exculpatory, impacts upon the credibility of the prosecution's evidence or is material to defence preparations for trial. If it cannot be disclosed – for example, the provider will not permit it – the Prosecutor must decide whether the case can continue.

Article 54(3)(e) of the ICC Statute allows the prosecution to obtain material and agree not to disclose at any stage of the proceedings, "documents or information that the Prosecutor obtains on the condition of confidentiality and solely for the purpose of generating new evidence, unless the provider of the information consents". In its early investigations the ICC prosecution, to its eventual regret, relied heavily on such agreements. Its inability to disclose to the defence information obtained in this manner in the *Lubanga* trial almost led to its collapse when the Trial Chamber twice stayed the proceedings.[76]

---

paras. 4–5, 23–24, 39, referring to the ICC Statute envisaging that the accused is faced by one Prosecutor, "rather than, potentially, multiple accusers" (https://www.legal-tools.org/doc/6fe269). In *Katanga*, the Appeals Chamber revisited this issue, ICC, Situation in the Democratic Republic of the Congo, *The Prosecutor v. Germain Katanga*, Appeals Chamber, Judgment on the Appeal of Mr Katanga Against the Decision of Trial Chamber II of 22 January 2010 Entitled "Decision on the Modalities of Victim Participation at Trial", 16 July 2010, ICC-01/04-01/07-2288, para. 116, reaching the same decision as in *Lubanga* (https://www.legal-tools.org/doc/e58575). It held that the Trial Chamber could permit the victims to testify on matters "including the role of the accused in the crimes charged against them, grounded on the Trial Chamber's authority to request evidence necessary for the determination of the truth, is not *per se* inconsistent with the rights of the accused and the concept of a fair trial". *Ibid.*, para. 114.

76 The second was, ICC, Situation in the Democratic Republic of the Congo, *The Prosecutor v. Thomas Lubanga Dyilo*, Trial Chamber, Redacted Decision on the Prosecution's Urgent Request for Variation of the Time-Limit to Disclose the Identity of Intermediary 143 or Alternatively to Stay Proceedings Pending Further Consultations with the VWU, 8 July 2010, ICC-01/04-01/06-2517-Red (https://www.legal-tools.org/doc/cd4f10). The Appeals Chamber reversed the stay in ICC, Situation in the Democratic Republic of the Congo, *The*

In *Lubanga* the Appeals Chamber held that a chamber must first determine – in *ex parte* proceedings open only to the Prosecutor – whether the material would have to be disclosed to the defence if it had not been obtained under that Article. If so, the Prosecutor should seek the provider's consent to disclose the material. If that is not forthcoming, the chamber must then determine whether and if any counter-balancing measures can be taken to ensure the rights of the accused to a fair trial, in spite of the non-disclosure.[77] In some instances a provider may permit the disclosure of some information or documents with appropriate redactions, maybe for reasons of State security or to protect the identity of sources.[78]

At the STL, for example, if the material to be disclosed is redacted, the following principles apply: first, the prosecution must decide whether the information it wishes to redact would ordinarily be subject to disclosure.[79] Then, if the material is to be disclosed, the application for redaction must satisfy one of the three criteria under its Rule 116(A), namely if

---

Prosecutor v. Thomas Lubanga Dyilo, Appeals Chamber, Judgment on the appeal of the Prosecutor against the decision of Trial Chamber I of 8 July 2010 entitled "Decision on the Prosecution's Urgent Request for Variation of the Time-Limit to Disclose the Identity of Intermediary 143 or Alternatively to Stay Proceedings Pending Further Consultations with the VWU", 8 October 2010, ICC-01/04-01/06-2582 (https://www.legal-tools.org/doc/8f3b61). The Appeals Chamber held the Trial Chamber had erred in not determining, at para. 61, "that a fair trial had become irreparably impossible" and consequently there was "no obstacle to imposing sanctions and allowing them [the prosecution] a reasonable opportunity to induce compliance, and, therefore, too change the very circumstances which made a fair trial prospectively impossible".

[77] ICC, Situation in the Democratic Republic of the Congo, *Prosecutor v. Lubanga*, Appeals Chamber, Judgment on the appeal of the Prosecutor against the decision of Trial Chamber I entitled "Decision on the consequences of non-disclosure of exculpatory materials covered by Article 54(3)(e) agreements and the application to stay the prosecution of the accused, together with certain other issues raised at the Status Conference on 10 June 2008", 21 October 2008, ICC-01/04-01/06-1486, para. 48 (https://www.legal-tools.org/doc/485c2d). Trial Chambers have followed this approach, for example, in ICC, Situation in the Democratic Republic of the Congo, *Prosecutor v. Ntaganda*, Trial Chamber, Decision on Prosecution request for authorisation of non-disclosure of five documents, 11 June 2015, ICC-01/04-02/06-637, para. 12 (https://www.legal-tools.org/doc/25cec7).

[78] There is also an abundance of case law at the ICTY and ICTR on disclosure related to information obtained under Rule 70 of the ICTY RPE and Rule 70 of the ICTR RPE which applies to both prosecution and defence, see above note 30.

[79] STL, *Prosecutor v. Ayyash et al.*, Trial Chamber, Decision on Prosecution's Application to Authorise Necessary Redactions Pursuant to Rule 116 Dated 18 October 2013, 8 November 2013, STL-11-01/PT/TC/F1212/20131108/R248503-R248506/EN/af (https://www.legal-tools.org/doc/38de81).

disclosure: may prejudice ongoing of future investigations, cause a grave risk to the security of a witness or their family, or for any other reason may be contrary to the public interest or the rights of third parties. The Prosecution must also support its application with a statement relating to the proposed redactions.[80]

Article 72 of the ICC Statute, "Protection of national security information" provides at first blush an absolute bar to disclosing information where a State is of the view that disclosure of such information would "prejudice its national security interests".[81] There follows a complicated statutory regime of requests, co-operation, consultations and so on, which may, by implication, eventually lead to an acquittal if the information is not disclosed to the defence.[82]

The ensuing result may be the disclosure to the defence of redacted material. This can again raise further issues of the extent of the redactions, and some ICC Pre-Trial Chambers have required the prosecution to seek its approval for each redaction. This could conflict with the principle that prosecutor's offices are deemed to be acting in good faith, but furthermore, it is difficult to see how this is an efficient use of judicial resources.

14.2.7. Extended Disclosure – In-Depth Analysis Charts

For some years, the ICC entertained what has become termed 'In-Depth Analysis Charts' or 'IDACs' prepared by the prosecution. The principle, it

---

[80] *Ibid.*, paras. 6–7; see also ICTY RPE, Rule 69, see above note 30; ICTR RPE, Rule 69, see above note 30; SCSL RPE, Rule 69, see above note 30; and ICC RPE, Rule 81(4), see above note 39.

[81] Article 72(1) starts, with "This article applies in any case where the disclosure of the information or documents of a State would, in the opinion of that State, prejudice its national security interests", see above note 20. Article 72(6) provides:

> Once all reasonable steps have been taken to resolve the matter through cooperative means, and if the State considers that there are no means or conditions under which the information or documents could be provided or disclosed without prejudice to its national security interests, it shall so notify the Prosecutor or the Court of the specific reasons for its decision, unless a specific description of the reasons would itself necessarily result in such prejudice to the State's national security interests.

See above note 20.

[82] The STL has a similar provision, although less complicated, in STL RPE, Rule 118 "Information never Subject to Disclosure without Consent of Provider", see above note 30. See also ICTY RPE, Rule 70 and IRMCT RPE, Rule 76(B) "Matters not Subject to Disclosure", see above note 30. There is no need to examine in any detail the litigation on these Rules here.

appears, was that the defence – and by extension the chambers – needed to be properly informed of the particulars of the prosecution's case, including the evidence supporting each count on an indictment. However, they took the form of gargantuan charts containing many boxes and sub-headings and links. This could be viewed as an extended form of court-ordered prosecution disclosure, perhaps of information material to the defence of an accused.

The *Bemba* Pre-Trial Chamber ordered the prosecution *and* defence to file their evidence through the registry accompanied by a chart linking each piece of evidence to the elements of the crimes charged.[83] The decision also set out a regime for managing disclosure between the parties, and the chamber's access to this material. In *Katanga*, the Trial Chamber held that by providing the defence with a clear and comprehensive overview of the evidence and how it related to the crimes, the analysis charts would ensure the accused adequate time and facilities to prepare their defence.[84] It could also conceivably assist the chamber in trial preparation and judgment drafting.

However, this practice is far from uncontroversial,[85] as other ICC chambers have ruled that they were either not necessary,[86] not useful,[87] or

---

[83] ICC, Situation in the Central African Republic, *Prosecutor v. Bemba*, Pre-Trial Chamber, Decision on the Evidence Disclosure System and Setting a Timetable for Disclosure between the Parties, 31 July 2008, ICC-01/05-01/08-55, para. 69 (https://www.legal-tools.org/doc/15c802); ICC, Situation in the Central African Republic, *Prosecutor v. Bemba*, Pre-Trial Chamber, Decision on the Submission of an Updated, Consolidated Version of the In-depth Analysis Chart of Incriminatory Evidence, 10 November 2008, ICC-01/05-01/08-232 (https://www.legal-tools.org/doc/842374).

[84] ICC, Situation in the Democratic Republic of the Congo, *Prosecutor v. Katanga and Ngudjolo*, Trial Chamber, Order concerning the Presentation of Incriminating Evidence and the E-Court Protocol, 13 March 2009, ICC-01/04-01/07-956, para. 6 (https://www.legal-tools.org/doc/ad5c46).

[85] See, for example, ICC, Situation in the Central African Republic, *Prosecutor v. Jean-Pierre Bemba Gombo, Aime Kilolo Musamba, Jean-Jacques Mangenda Kabongo, Fidele Babala Wandu and Narcisse Arido*, Pre-Trial Chamber, Decision on the "Defence request for an in-depth analysis chart" submitted by the Defence for Mr. Jean-Pierre Bemba Gombo, 28 January 2014, ICC-01/05-01/13-134, para. 5 ('*Bemba et al.* Pre-Trial Contempt Decision') (https://www.legal-tools.org/doc/596c75).

[86] ICC, Situation in the Republic of Kenya, *Prosecutor v. Muthaura and Kenyatta*, Trial Chamber, Decision on the schedule leading up to trial, 9 July 2012, ICC-01/09-02/11-451, paras. 11, 16 (https://www.legal-tools.org/doc/3b7bdc).

that the Pre-Trial Judge had no authority to order the creation of such a document.[88] Chambers that ordered IDACs did so well in advance of the hearing on the confirmation of charges or the commencement of trial. In 2015, the Appeals Chamber in *Ongwen* overturned the pre-trial decision of a Single Judge to order the prosecution to submit an IDAC but without first having sought submissions on the matter, given that this could "place a disproportionate burden on the parties and may ultimately lead to delays in the proceedings".[89] By 2017, the ICC Chambers Practice Manual emphatically stated that "[n]o submission of any "in-depth analysis chart", or *similia*, of the evidence disclosed can be imposed on either party".[90] In 2018, after initially considering whether to order the prosecution to file an IDAC with its disclosure, the Single Judge in *Al-Hassan*, declined to order one.[91]

The STL's Trial Chamber declined a defence application to order the prosecution to file a 'table of incriminating evidence' in respect of a fifth accused joined to an existing indictment after the trial of the initial

---

[87] ICC, Situation in the Republic of Kenya, *Prosecutor v. Ruto and Sang*, Trial Chamber, Transcript, 11 June 2012, ICC-01/09-01/11-T-15-ENG, p. 32 (https://www.legal-tools.org/doc/623461).

[88] *Bemba et al.* Pre-Trial Contempt Decision, paras. 5, 7, see above note 85.

[89] ICC, Situation in Uganda, *Prosecutor v. Dominic Ongwen*, Appeals Chamber, Judgment on the appeal of the Prosecutor against the decision of Pre-Trial Chamber II entitled "Decision Setting the Regime for Evidence Disclosure and Other Related Matters", 17 June 2015, ICC-02/04-01/15-251, para. 42 (https://www.legal-tools.org/doc/0052a2).

[90] ICC, *Chambers Practice Manual*, 2017, p. 10 ('ICC Chambers Practice Manual 2017') (https://www.legal-tools.org/doc/f0ee26). *Ibid.*, p. 14:

> It is up to the parties to determine the best way to persuade the Chamber: there is no basis for the Chamber to impose on the parties a particular modality/format to argue their case and present their evidence. For example, no submission of any "in-depth analysis chart", or *similia*, of the evidence relied upon for the purposes of the confirmation hearing can be imposed on either of the parties.

> This is repeated in the *Chambers Practice Manual*, 2019, para. 24 ('ICC Chambers Practice Manual 2019') (https://www.legal-tools.org/doc/dh0zyq/). As an aside, it is unclear why a document whose stated intention is to inform would use an obscure Latin term like '*similia*' – defined in English dictionaries as the plural of 'simile'. Presumably, it is intended to mean 'similar documents'.

[91] ICC, Situation in the Republic of Mali, *Prosecutor v. Al Hassan Ag Abdoul Aziz Ag Mohamed Ag Mahmoud*, Pre-Trial Chamber, Decision on the In-Depth Analysis Chart of Disclosed Evidence, 29 June 2018, ICC-01/12-01/18-61-tENG, paras. 21–23, accepting the prosecution's submissions and deciding that it would impose a disproportionate burden on the prosecution to prepare such a chart and possibly delay the proceedings by a year (https://www.legal-tools.org/doc/d35cef).

---

four accused had already commenced. It found that it had the discretionary power to order such a table but that at that stage of the proceedings the time needed to prepare the report was outweighed by its minimal practical utility, given that it would take months to prepare and divert substantial resources from the prosecution's pre-trial preparation.[92]

The prosecution's witness lists must also "list the points in the indictment as to which each witness will testify, including specific reference to counts and relevant paragraphs in the indictment".[93] As a result some chambers have required the prosecution to prepare charts linking witnesses and exhibits to evidence in addition to the information in prosecution pre-trial briefs.[94] In *Gbagbo* the Trial Chamber, at the close of the Prosecution's case, "invited" the Prosecutor to submit within thirty days, "a trial brief illustrating her case and detailing the evidence in support of the charges".[95] The Prosecution submitted a 256-page brief plus annexes, yet strangely qualified this by stating that "[i]n a case of this magnitude, and consistent with the present stage of the trial, it is not possible to recite in this Mid-Trial Brief all the relevant evidence before the Chamber".[96] To the contrary, one would have thought that this was precisely the place to

---

[92] STL, *Prosecutor v. Ayyash et al.*, Trial Chamber, Decision on Merhi Defence Request for a 'Table of Incriminating Evidence', 9 May 2014, STL-11-01/T/TC/F1524/20140509/ R259005-R259016/EN/dm, para. 27 (https://www.legal-tools.org/doc/37e63b). The Trial Chamber noted that the IDACs ordered at the ICC were of 1,000 pages in *Katanga*, 6,600 pages in *Kenyatta*, and exceeded 12,000 pages in *Ruto and Sang*.

[93] For example, ICTY RPE, Rule 65*ter*(E), see above note 30. Rules 70(M) of the IRMCT RPE, Rule 73*bis*(B) of the ICTR RPE and RSCSL RPE have no requirement to list points "including specific reference to counts and relevant paragraphs in the indictment", see above note 30. The ICC's RPE have no similar requirement, see above note 39.

[94] Linked to ICTY RPE, Rule 65*ter*(E), see above note 30. See, for example, ICTY, *Prosecutor v. Prlić et al.*, Trial Chamber, Revised Version of the Decision Adopting Guidelines on Conduct of Trial Proceedings, 28 April 2006, IT-04-74-PT, para. 9 (https://www.legal-tools. org/doc/47ef0e); SCSL, *Prosecutor v. Brima et al.*, Trial Chamber, Transcript, 30 April 2004, SCSL-04-16-T, pp. 24–25: a "proofing-chart [...] to focus on the count system indicating specifically for every count, paragraph, the testimonial or primary documentary evidence that supports those counts".

[95] ICC, Situation in the Republic of Côte d'Ivoire, *Prosecutor v. Laurent Gbagbo and Charles Blé Goudé*, Order on the further conduct of the proceedings, 9 February 2018, ICC-02/11-01/15-1124, p. 9 (https://www.legal-tools.org/doc/66a934/).

[96] ICC, *Prosecutor v. Laurent Gbagbo and Charles Blé Goudé*, OTP, Prosecution's Mid-Trial Brief submitted pursuant to Chamber's Order on the further conduct of the proceedings (ICC-02/11-01/15-1124), 19 March 2018, ICC-02/11-01/15-1136, para. 7 (https://www. legal-tools.org/doc/155267/).

"recite" all the relevant evidence. Where else, if not in what could turn out to be in effect the Prosecution's closing brief?

Evidence charts may be advantageous, but on the other hand, they could also be utterly useless, confusing and unmanageably large and obtuse. Thematic summaries of evidence, linked to the relevant source material such as the witness statements and the exhibit, could be more useful. This works for both the prosecution and defence presentation of their cases. But it is essential that they are prepared only under the supervision of senior lawyers who will appear in the case in court. It is imperative that the prosecution thoroughly knows its own case well before it gets to court – pre-trial or trial – and can present it in a manner that is easily understood. This is fundamental to a fair trial. Thus, how forcing a party to prepare – or alternatively a party itself submitting – a complicated IDAC of thousands of pages can be in the interest of justice is highly questionable.

14.3. Material Exempt from Disclosure – A Party's Internal Work Product

A party's internal work product is exempt from disclosure to an opposing party. This is something that the chambers obviously cannot access without a specific order. As it is not disclosed no one but the party itself would normally know that it exists – short of a leak, a tip-off, an accidental disclosure or a reference to it somewhere else.

An internal document is "an in-house product of a party created for its own internal use".[97] But what falls within this category may be very much in the 'eye of the beholder'. As an example, in the same way as the ICTY, in 1994, received hefty UN Commission of Experts witness material,[98] the STL's Office of the Prosecutor inherited numerous records from

---

[97] See, for example, *El Sayed* Appeals Decision, para. 78, see above note 34; *Ayyash et al.* Trial Decision on Sabra Motion to Lift Redactions and Disclosure of United Nations Fact-Finding Mission Documents, para. 14, see above note 49.

[98] Final Report of the Commission of Experts Established Pursuant to Security Council Resolution 780 (1992), in Letter Dated 24 May 1994 from the Secretary-General to the President of the Security Council, UN Doc. S/1994/674, 27 May 1994 (https://www.legal-tools.org/doc/3a3ae2). It transferred its data-base to the ICTY Prosecutor in April 1994, see Report of the International Tribunal for the Prosecution of Persons Responsible for Serious Violations of International Humanitarian Law Committed in the Territory of the Former Yugoslavia since 1991, UN Doc. A/49/342 and S/1994/1007, paras. 157–58 (https://www.legal-tools.org/doc/cacdb7). The Commission's last of three Chairs, Professor M. Cherif

the UNIIIC, many of which would either be used in court proceedings or otherwise disclosable to the defence.

An issue under judicial adjudication was the width of the definition of 'internal work product' in the STL's Rule 111 that specifically provides an exemption from prosecution disclosure of "internal documents prepared by the UNIIIC or its assistants or representatives in connection with its investigative work". In *El-Sayed*, the STL's Appeals Chamber found that "internal memoranda of the UNIIIC containing legal analysis, research, or investigatory strategies" fell outside of the prosecution's disclosure obligations. But 'investigator notes', by contrast, contain the thoughts and original work of investigators, most often in an incomplete form.[99]

Further, it held that although the prosecution is responsible for categorising documents, ensuring compliance with the Rules – including classifying and disclosing documents – is ultimately a judicial function, and judges may have to engage in a sampling exercise if there are numerous documents, rather than rubber-stamping the prosecution's contentions.[100] In exercising this function, a chamber may need to establish criteria to facilitate evaluation such as the document's contents, its function and purpose and its author.[101] However, it need not inspect every document potentially falling under the Rule.[102] And this Rule does not oblige a party to inform the other parties that it is not disclosing a document, information in a document, or the existence of a document that is a report, memoranda, or other internal document.[103] It is the contents, function, purpose and source of the document, and not the title, that is important in determining whether it is considered work product.[104]

Another consideration is that once a question is put to a witness or disclosed outside the prosecutor's office, the information can no longer be

---

Bassiouni, described a data-base of close to 80,000 documents and 300 hours of video tape. M. Cherif Bassiouni, "Appraising UN Justice-Related Fact-Finding Missions", in *Washington University Journal of Law and Policy*, 2001, vol. 5, no. 1, p. 46.

[99] *El Sayed* Appeals Decision, paras. 95–96, see above note 34.

[100] *Ibid.*, paras. 74, 117.

[101] *Ibid.*, para. 78; *Ayyash et al.* Decision on Sabra Motion to Lift Redactions and Disclosure of United Nations Fact-Finding Mission Documents, para. 14, see above note 49.

[102] *Ibid.*, para. 13.

[103] *Ibid.*, para. 10.

[104] *El Sayed* Appeals Decision, paras. 74, 117, see above note 34.

considered as internal work product.[105] A party also may implicitly waive its claim for non-disclosure of material that would otherwise be considered as internal work product, for example, by a witness revealing its content in court. However, this does not automatically extend to waiving the privilege attached to not disclosing the document itself. This will depend upon the circumstances.[106]

International criminal courts and tribunals, lacking their own internal enforcement mechanisms, rely upon State co-operation, mainly through official requests for assistance. Prosecutor's offices generate most of these, although the defence, registry and victim participants can also send international requests for assistance. The prosecution need disclose requests for assistance only if the defence can demonstrate that they are material to its preparation for trial.[107] But the difficulty with this is that the defence has to know that the request was made. This includes the request and any response. Sometimes it will be obvious, but at other times, not.

14.4. Defence Disclosure Obligations

Defence disclosure obligations are far less onerous. An alibi notice must be notified, as must a ground for excluding criminal responsibility, such as a special defence. At the ICC, the defence shall permit the Prosecutor to inspect material intended for use as evidence in confirmation proceedings or at trial.[108] Privileged material, such as communications between a client and a lawyer, is also generally immune from disclosure.[109]

---

[105] *Niyitegeka* Appeals Judgment, para. 34, see above note 53.

[106] *Ayyash et al.* Trial Decision re Michael Taylor, paras. 53–57, see above note 34.

[107] ICC, *Prosecutor v. Ayyash et al.*, Trial Chamber, Decision on the Oneissi Defence Motion for Disclosure of Documents Referred to in the Report Related to the Hard Drive of Mr. Ahmed Abu Adass, 14 October 2014, STL-11-01/T/TC/F1697/20141014/R269080-R269084/EN/dm, para. 7 (https://www.legal-tools.org/doc/22843d); *Ayyash et al.* Trial Decision on the Oneissi Defence Motion for Disclosure of Requests for Assistance, para. 36, see above note 49.

[108] ICC RPE, Rules 78 and 79, see above note 39. Rules 67(A) and 67(B) of the ICTY RPE had similar requirements, see above note 30. Rules 67(A) and 67(B) of the ICTR RPE only required "reciprocal disclosure" by the defence if it had sought the same inspection rights to prosecution material, see above note 30. Rule 72 of the IRMCT RPE requires the defence to allow prosecution inspection and copying of defence material to be used at trial and to provide copies to the prosecution of the statements of all proposed trial witnesses, see above note 30. Rule 112 of the STL RPE has similar requirements for alibi and special

14.5. Relief for Disclosure Violations

The relief that a court may grant for late or non-disclosure varies.[110] The overriding principle is that the defence must show some prejudice. The consequences could be existential for the prosecution of an accused. The result could be an adjournment, a recall of a witness, a stay of proceedings – temporary or permanent – and on appeal, admitting new evidence, an acquittal, an order for a retrial or a declaration of a mistrial. A reduction in sentence could also result.[111] A court could also order sanctions against a prosecution office or an individual prosecution lawyer for disclosure violations. Another possibility could be the exclusion of the evidence, in not permitting a party to tender it into evidence.[112] The latter could apply equally to breaches of defence disclosure obligations.[113]

14.6. The Current Practices

The disclosure practices vary between the international institutions but each follows the basic model outlined above of a prosecutorial custodian of all that it has gathered, but with strong disclosure obligations as outlined above – from which it is obvious that there are some grey areas, such as the definition of witness statements, internal work product and what may be material to defence trial preparations. The most fair, efficient and sensible is that employed by the IRMCT which comes from the ICTY's long-established practice.

---

defence notifications, prosecution inspection of material for use at trial and disclosure of defence witness statements, see above note 30.

[109] Some exceptions are in Rule 73 of the ICC RPE, see above note 39.

[110] Rule 68*bis* of the ICTY RPE and Rule 74 of the IRMCT RPE "Failure to Comply with Disclosure Obligations" allows a chamber to impose sanctions on a party that fails to comply, see above note 30. The ICC Statute and ICC RPE contain nothing to this effect.

[111] *Kajelijeli* Appeals Judgment, para. 255, see above note 28 – if found on an interlocutory appeal that "an accused's rights have been violated, but not egregiously so, it will order the Trial Chamber to reduce the accused's sentence if the accused is found guilty".

[112] There is an enormous body of case law on this topic, as each motion alleging a disclosure violation generally seeks specific relief in the form of an order rectifying the situation; there is therefore no need to refer to specific cases.

[113] A comprehensive overview of the subject is in Kelly Pitcher, *Judicial Responses to Pre-Trial Procedural Violations in International Criminal Proceedings*, Asser Press, Springer, The Hague, 2018, pp. 397–435.

14.6.1. IRMCT – Including the ICTY and ICTR

The prosecution at the IRMCT generally follows the practice of the former ICTY whose evidence collection and that of the ICTR it inherited.

The IRMCT, for ICTY related proceedings, has an electronic disclosure system or 'suite' (EDS) that contains a general collection of evidence that is made available to the relevant defence. It is a large volume of evidence, including documents, redacted witness statements and so on. In addition, case or accused specific disclosure can be made via the system.

The EDS was a prosecution initiative from around 2003 that was accepted by the ICTY President, the Registrar, and its Association of Defence Counsel. Until then the prosecution electronically searched its collection but disclosed its documents to the defence either in hard copy or on compact disc.

From December 2003, the ICTY moved to compulsory electronic disclosure. In that month the ICTY judges amended Rule 68, "Disclosure of exculpatory and other relevant material", to mandate that "the Prosecutor shall make available to the defence, in electronic form, collections of relevant material held by the Prosecutor, together with appropriate computer software with which the defence can search such collections electronically". This was without prejudice to the prosecution's obligation to disclose exculpatory material, or to take reasonable steps to obtain the consent of a provider if obtained under the obligation not to disclose it without its consent.[114]

This did not relieve the prosecution from searching its evidence collection. The ICTY's Appeals Chamber held that

> while Rule 68(ii) of the Rules allows the Prosecutor to make disclosure materials available on the EDS, it is well-established that the EDS cannot be used a substitute for positive disclosure. In this regard, *the Prosecution may satisfy its disclosure obligations by creating a case-specific file, providing an index of disclosed materials, or providing some notice to the Defence when materials are added to the file.*[115]

---

[114] Under the ICTY's RPE Rule 70, now the IRMCT's RPE Rule 76 "Matters Not Subject to Disclosure", see above note 30.

[115] ICTY, *Prosecutor v. Mladić*, Appeals Chamber, Decision on Defence Interlocutory Appeal against the Trial Chamber's Decision on EDS Disclosure Methods, 28 November 2013, IT-

And further:

> Similarly, the jurisprudence does not designate the EDS or any other form of electronic disclosure as the official method, nor does it support a conclusion that one method of electronic disclosure is to be used to the exclusion of other methods. On the contrary, the Appeals Chambers of the Tribunal and the International Criminal Tribunal for Rwanda as well as various trial chambers have found that the provision of non-EDS resources, such as descriptive indices and written notices of disclosed material, are precisely the types of assistance that make EDS materials reasonably available and accessible to the Defence, thereby helping to meet the Prosecution's disclosure obligations.[116]

The EDS contains prosecution evidence, so in that sense its content is prosecution controlled, but it is managed by the Registry. The prosecution has no access to the system to change anything, this goes through the Registry. The Registry also manages access to the system.

It was a pioneering international disclosure suite that was in use when the ICC's Office of the Prosecutor started its own document collection in 2004. In its 2009 developed practices manual, the ICTY said of disclosure:

> Given the complex nature of war crimes cases, disclosure is a major undertaking that is extremely resource-intensive. Because the ICTY's OTP seized many original documents from government archives in the former Yugoslavia, the Defence is especially reliant on the disclosure process. Disclosure in these massive cases is quite unlike disclosure in a domestic criminal trial where all the relevant evidence can be readily assembled and inspected.[117]

09-92-AR73.2, para. 25 (internal footnotes omitted; emphasis added) (https://www.legal-tools.org/doc/c42827).

[116] *Ibid.*, para. 27 (internal footnotes omitted).

[117] ICTY and United Nations Interregional Crime and Justice Research Institute ('UNICRI'), *ICTY Manual on Developed Practices*, UNICRI Publisher, Turin, 2009, p. 61 (https://www.legal-tools.org/doc/0cc55d). It also noted, at p. 62, that, "[w]hile the Prosecutor remains subject to the underlying obligation to disclose exculpatory information within the Prosecutor's actual knowledge, the new EDS represents a move towards "open book" disclosure".

The ICTY's criminal defence manual, which followed in 2011, said of the EDS:

> an Electronic Disclosure System (EDS) was instituted at the ICTY which provides the Defence access via the internet to evidentiary materials in electronic format collected by the Prosecution. This is an important means for the Defence to conduct its own independent research into matters for preparation of the case.[118]

The ICTY's prosecution document collection eventually contained over 9.3 million pages.[119] The IRMCT inherited it.

Prosecution officials would collect (or seize) documents, sometimes pursuant to search warrants issued by chambers that could be enforced in Bosnia and Herzegovina or Kosovo and either copy the documents on site or take them back to The Hague to enter them into the evidence collection. Each collection was given its own unique name, generally identifying its source, as examples, the Drina Corps or 1st Krajina Corps, referring to two distinct seized and copied Bosnian Serb Army archives. Another was entitled "Exhumations". There was an index for a collection of miscellaneous material titled "Evidence day forward".

Each document was scanned and entered into the system. In doing this it was given metadata, known as a 'MIFF', which listed the source, the type of document – such as whether it was an order, video, photograph, an exhumation report – the name of the person entering it. It also received a unique 'ERN' (or electronic registration number). Any associated ERNs were also noted. The language of the original and any translations were also recorded. Searching was through optical character recognition, or OCR, of scanned documents, however, this technology was imperfect

---

[118] UNICRI, Association of Defence Counsel Practising Before the ICTY (ADC-ICTY) and Organization for Security and Co-operation in Europe, Office for Democratic Institutions and Human Rights (ODIHR OSCE), *Manual on International Criminal Defence: ADC-ICTY Developed Practices Within the framework of the War Crimes Justice Project*, UNICRI Publisher, 2011, p. 47.

[119] The information in the following paragraphs comes from a combination of the author's own experience and an interview on 30 October 2019 with Robert Reid, the former ICTY and IRMCT Chief of Operations in the Office of the Prosecutor, who worked in that office between 1994 and 2018. His view is that generally the defence should get everything, and electronically, except restricted material which should be carefully searched by the prosecution for disclosable information.

especially with handwritten, coloured or Cyrillic documents. With improved technology these problems diminished greatly.

Separate indexes were maintained for witness related material, restricted witness material, restricted material, and confidentially provided Rule 70 documents – namely, those provided with confidentiality restrictions meaning that its existence could not be disclosed without the provider's consent.

In searching the collections for disclosable material, the prosecution could search across combinations of indexes, with the exception of the restricted indexes in combination with the non-restricted, to guard against accidental disclosure. According to the prosecution official responsible for implementing and overseeing the system, it reached a level of accuracy of 94.6 per cent in hits in searches.[120]

A dedicated prosecution information support unit, using experienced language staff, would perform searches on the indexes on specified search terms, provided by either prosecution staff or the defence. Prosecution legal teams had case management staff who would prepare documents for disclosure, namely, those containing hits on the search terms. The prosecution would, at the request of defence counsel, do searches on specified terms in the non-EDS collections described above. Lawyers would review the material before disclosing it. It would be disclosed electronically in batches, as Rule 68(B), referred to above, required.

All defence counsel had access to the EDS. It contained a general collection of all indexes, with the exception of the four prosecution restricted indexes, and for each case a new case-specific index was created to which assigned defence teams had access. The defence thus had unfettered access to the prosecution's document collection with the exception of the restricted indexes. The ICTY's information technology section, under the Registrar, maintained the EDS and had two dedicated staff. The philosophy was to provide as far as possible a level playing field pursuant to the principle of equality of arms.

The former ICTY prosecution's Chief of Operations[121] described hard-copy disclosure as labour and time intensive and generally unhelpful to the defence, as it was unsearchable. Defence counsel had to scan the

---

[120] Robert Reid, interview on 30 October 2019.
[121] *Ibid.*

documents before searching. He also described the effort involved in searching and compiling the disclosure of around 80 hard-copy boxes of documents to Slobodan Milošević who was self-represented during pre-trial and the trial.[122] When Milošević died in March 2006 the official was seconded to a judicial investigation into his death and went to the UN Detention Unit in The Hague. Milošević had been allocated a second cell for his legal work. The 80 disclosure boxes were sitting unopened in the second cell; the exercise had been futile.

A senior defence lawyer who assisted the self-represented accused Radovan Karadžić in the ICTY and IRMCT proceedings had a less sanguine view of the EDS's efficacy from a defence searching perspective. He described receiving maybe 1,500 separate disclosure batches – resulting from the prosecution's searches of its defence restricted indexes, of possibly two million pages. He was unable to search across the material and had to do it by individual CD. For material placed on the EDS, the prosecution segregated it into several folders, requiring a search across several folders. In his view, it became unmanageable. He described attempting to find material as 'a nightmare'. During the proceedings he also filed 108 motions alleging disclosure violations by the prosecution, succeeding in 84. They mostly concerned the late disclosure of witness statements.[123]

The ICTR had its own version of the ICTY's EDS but it was maintained by the prosecution. It was much smaller, containing 'only' over 200,000 documents.[124] It was an archive of general information relating to the genocide and its background, for example, of Rwandan Government and military documents, UNIMIR and diplomatic documents, and numerous media material such as speeches, radio publications. It also had specific case related folders. Both contained witness statements. Rwandan Gacaca trial documents were later added to it, thus providing material that at times contradicted witness statements already in these archives.

---

[122] ICTY, *Prosecutor v. Slobodan Milošević*, IT-02-54.

[123] Peter Robinson, interview on 29 October 2019. He helpfully numbered each motion – from one all the way to 108. The final one, filed on 14 March 2016, was titled "108th motion for finding of disclosure violation and for remedial measures". ICTY, *Prosecutor v. Radovan Karadžić*, IT-95-5/18-T.

[124] Peter Robinson, interview on 29 October 2019. The figure is imprecise.

Of it, the same experienced defence counsel said it was "rudimentary but it worked".[125] The main problem in his experience had been of information systems management, namely, how the prosecution had stored the information, giving examples of investigators storing relevant witness related material on their personal drives and folders rather than logging it into the central system. There was also a lack of metadata.

Another senior lawyer who had worked at the ICTR as defence counsel[126] was of the view the system did not work that well considering that the information essentially related to one event which was far more limited in time than the conflicts under investigation at the ICTY or ICC.

14.6.2. Special Tribunal for Lebanon

At the STL the prosecution searches its archives and discloses material in batches through the STL's own in-house developed litigation software, Legal Workflow. The STL judges, like the ICC's, also have access to some disclosure batches. An email notification is sent with each fresh disclosure to everyone who has access to it. Prosecution disclosure is specified according to the relevant Rules together with a brief description of the batches' contents.[127]

14.6.3. International Criminal Court

The ICC, before the referral of the first situation, that of Uganda, to the Court in 2004 – and hence the collection of evidence – was a *tabula rasa* in respect of prosecution document management, and hence disclosure.

---

[125] *Ibid.*, who was lead counsel for Joseph Nzirorera in ICTR, *Prosecutor v. Karemera et al.*, ICTR-98-44-T.

[126] And at another international court as a senior prosecutor.

[127] As of the date of judgment, 18 August 2020, 879 electronic disclosure batches were in Legal Workflow in relation to the *Ayyash et al.* case. This included prosecution disclosure of evidence to be used at trial and of exculpatory material and that which is material to defence preparation, and defence disclosure of documents intended to be used in questioning prosecution witnesses (so it contains some overlap of information that was disclosed more than once). The Prosecution filed pre-trial disclosure reports in late 2012 which revealed that *at that stage* it had disclosed 101,117 pages of witness statements and related material, and 211,632 pages of exhibits on its exhibit list, contained in 19,530 files released in 62 disclosure batches. Any suggestion that a Trial Chamber of three judges plus an alternative judge, with four staff, could have familiarised itself with this material in the two and half months between becoming seized of the case in October 2013 and the trial starting in mid-January 2014, is unrealistic. The Trial Chamber had access to around 444 (random) disclosure batches. The disclosure batches were by August 2020 numbered up to 3,590.

The ICTY prosecutor's office by that stage had an enormous evidence collection of millions of pages of documents in different languages and was already using its EDS for defence disclosure. It was generally seen to be efficient and was a massive improvement on hard copy disclosure and a prosecutor's office keeping for itself its entire evidence collection. It was the obvious international example to study and from which lessons could be gleaned and learned.

The ICC as an institution collectively, however, appears not to have adequately learned from this and has neither attempted to replicate nor improve on it. In saying this, the fundamental differences between the two institutions are of course recognised. The ICC has many more 'unique' situations under investigation, as well as preliminary investigations, as opposed to the different but related conflicts confined to the former Yugoslavia from 1991 to 1995, 1998 to 1999 and in 2001. In this respect there was some obvious evidentiary overlap.[128] However, it is never too late.

The ICC Prosecution stores its document collection in litigation software called Ringtail where evidence is stored according to the relevant situation. Metadata concerning documents is entered when the material is registered, including its source and date of collection. Whether it can be disclosed is also indicated in the metadata. Ringtail can be configured to run searches by actors, field, location or name. It also has a field that can be filtered as 'disclose' or 'do not disclose'.

A part of the material collected and categorised is open source. The prosecution must search this database for material that is disclosable; only then does the defence get access to it. It is disclosed to the defence through e-court. The judges also have access to this material. This disclosure occurs in Ringtail.

The informal views of several ICC prosecution senior trial lawyers were sought in relation to the efficacy of the current disclosure system;

---

[128] The predominant languages at the ICTY were its two working languages, English and French, and the languages of the former Yugoslavia, namely, Bosnian/Croatian/Serbian, Albanian and Macedonian. The ICC has collections in many more languages. The sole case from what was then called the former Yugoslav Republic of Macedonia, ICTY, *Prosecutor v. Boškoski and Tarčulovski*, IT-04-82, related to an internal armed conflict in that country in August 2001, which was unrelated to the other earlier armed conflicts in the former Yugoslavia.

some had had experience at other international tribunals, all had extensive domestic litigation experience.[129]

One described the current system as imposing a 'tremendous burden' upon limited prosecution resources especially in the lead-up to confirmation proceedings and trial. This lawyer unfavourably compared the ICC's practices in lacking an EDS, meaning that the sometimes-voluminous open source material had to be thoroughly scrutinised for potential disclosure.

To demonstrate the dimension of the disclosure issue, in one recent case four months of legal work was required to review around 80,000 documents, amounting to an estimated 80 per cent of the time of the prosecution lawyers' work during the pre-trial period.

In another, a case specific document collection contained about 100,000 documents of which only around one hundred were witness statements. There were about 500 screening interviews with witnesses. Most of the material – an estimated 80 per cent or so – was open-source; radio, television, video, news reports and so on. A lawyer described the legal team becoming bogged down in redacting material according to a pre-trial chamber order requiring a motion for each proposed redaction to witness related material.

A lawyer also referred to an unfortunate atmosphere of distrust developing between prosecution and defence legal teams on disclosure and redactions.

An ICC defence counsel, who has also worked as defence counsel at the ICTY and for its prosecution, also unfavourably compared the ICC's disclosure regime to the ICTY's.[130] In his experience, the ICTY's was better developed – although he conceded that many of the ICTY cases were sub-sets of a larger whole – and consequently defence counsel had greater confidence that they had access to the information that could be material to defence preparation. The ICTY disclosure case-law was also more consistent but by contrast "at the ICC we don't know what we

---

[129] Their views are described here with their permission but without specific attribution.

[130] Interview with Christopher Gosnell, 24 October 2019, who has been co-counsel in the *Ntaganda* case (ICC-01/04-02/06), and the Article 70 *Bemba et al.* case (ICC-01/05-01/13) at the ICC; in the *Hadžić* case (IT-04-75) at the ICTY, and also worked in the ICTY's Office of the Prosecutor (including with the author on the case of *Prosecutor v. Haradinaj et al.*).

haven't got". Also, the ICTY prosecution seemed to have had a better appreciation of its Rule 70 obligations (similar to the ICC's Article 54(3)), and hence what needed to be disclosed. This is most probably because of its years of doing it. His overall view, however, was that the ICC's disclosure metadata, although basic, and generally lacking commentary, was of a sufficient basic quality.

A particular issue, in this defence lawyer's view, was the ICC's prosecution's practice of disclosing summaries of investigator's notes of early encounters or interviews with witnesses,[131] rather than the original document itself, which could, if necessary, be disclosed in a suitably redacted form. He believed that this was time-consuming for the prosecution. (The prosecution's response to this was that this was actually the most efficient way to do it because the security interviews were not supposed to contain evidentiary material.) Moreover, investigators, rather than prosecution lawyers prepared the summaries. The defence lawyer believed that wherever possible, the prosecution should disclose that it has information in its possession from a named source, as the source itself could be exculpatory information.

A senior prosecution lawyer, by contrast, could not see how knowledge of the source *of itself* could generally be exculpatory. Further, the prosecution's general Rule 77 disclosure could contain information falling within other categories such as exculpatory information under Article 68(2).[132]

That lawyer felt that the current disclosure methodology is extremely time-consuming; it absorbs lawyer resources that could be better used for trial preparation. The most efficient approach is to identify redactions as early as possible in the process, while recognising that these early decisions may need reconsideration closer to the time of pre-trial disclosure. Over 60,000 documents, for example, had to be reviewed in one trial, which imposed an enormous burden on the prosecution lawyers in the

---

[131] Interview with Christopher Gosnell, 24 October 2019, by this he was probably referring to the ICC's basic security questionnaire used to screen all witnesses.

[132] Referring to disclosure of information in the prosecution's possession which is material to defence preparation, intended for use in confirmation proceedings or at trial, or that contain information that is either potentially exonerating, mitigating, or that affects the credibility of Prosecution evidence. It states that the Prosecutor "shall permit the defence to inspect any books, documents, photographs and other tangible objects in the possession or control of the Prosecutor".

pre-trial period. A possible solution could be to use highly trained paralegals for this task, as occurs in large domestic civil cases.

Another senior prosecution lawyer took the view that searching the prosecution's potential evidentiary holdings should not be viewed as for the purposes of defence disclosure, but rather to find out what is in it, to understand the prosecution case. It is while doing this that disclosable material is found.

The time that can elapse between investigation and arrest can also create enormous internal challenges, especially given that staff are moved from inactive to active cases. As an illustration, in one case the investigation ceased and lay dormant until the arrest of the accused eight years later, by which time only two prosecution staff remained who had worked on the original investigation. This necessitated *all* prosecution lawyers reviewing the entirety of the evidence collection for themselves, both for inculpatory and exculpatory information. In this lawyer's view this work should be done by the most senior, rather than the most junior, lawyers. The quality of the metadata, which could have been described before as 'patchy', had improved over the years.

An issue going directly to the efficiency of the current disclosure practices is the role of the judiciary in managing disclosure. This includes whether a chamber should actively oversee prosecution disclosure by, for example, positively approving proposed redactions of material for disclosure, or should trust the prosecution to do it. And how far, if at all, a chamber should involve itself in reviewing the massive quantity of material passing between the parties, while knowing that much, if not almost all of it will never be used in confirmation proceedings or at trial. ICC judges have access to all such material.

A review of the practices of the ICC chambers shows that the chambers, and particularly the pre-trial chambers, have struggled in attempting to manage the massive quantity of disclosed material passing between the parties – generally from the prosecution to the defence. The pre-trial chambers have issued numerous orders establishing disclosure regimes that have included timetables, IDACs, redaction protocols and a degree of realistic judicial supervision.

A central issue here is the meaning of the term 'evidence' in the context of inter-parties disclosure. Neither the Rome Statute nor the ICC's Rules of Procedure and Evidence define what 'evidence' is. The use of the term in both documents is therefore contextual. 'Evidence' is normally understood to mean the material (namely, the proof) that is used to support a case in proceedings, and depending upon the context, may include that collected in an investigation.[133]

In the context of court proceedings, Article 69(3) provides that the "parties may submit evidence relevant to the case", while Article 69(4) contains the standard provision that the court

> may rule on the relevance or admissibility of any evidence, taking into account, *inter alia*, the probative value of the evidence and any prejudice that such evidence may cause to a fair trial or to a fair evaluation of the testimony of a witness in accordance with the Rules of Procedure and Evidence.

For confirmation hearings, Article 61(3)(b) requires that the accused is "informed of the *evidence* on which the Prosecutor *intends to rely* at the hearing" (emphasis added). This can only be referring to the material – namely to the proof, being the documents and, if necessary, witness testimony – that will be adduced at a confirmation hearing. The words "intends to rely" could have no other meaning in that context. In the hearing, the Prosecutor presents a positive case supporting the charges, and does not produce evidence that is neither relevant nor probative of this case. Likewise, the defence may also produce such evidence in support of a case.

Significantly, Article 61(3)(b) regulates disclosure of evidence to the defence, not to the chambers. It does not regulate what the chambers should have access to. And it neither states nor implies that "evidence" includes every document passing between the parties before the confirmation hearing, in the broader disclosure sense of Article 67(2) or Rule 77. These two provisions have different purposes and operate separately to Article 61(3)(b). Under Rule 121(2)(c) all "evidence" disclosed between the parties "for the purpose of the confirmation hearing" is communicated to the Pre-Trial Chamber. The rule, however, defines neither what is

---

[133] *Black's Law Dictionary*, 19th edition, defines it as "1. Something (including testimony, documents, and tangible objects) that tends to prove or disprove the existence of an alleged fact; anything presented to the senses and offered to prove the existence or nonexistence of a fact"; "3. The collective mass of things, esp. testimony and exhibits, presented before a tribunal in a given dispute"; and "4. The body of law regulating the admissibility of what is offered as proof into the record of a legal proceeding".

meant here by "evidence" nor the words "for the purpose of the confirmation hearing".

The most rational interpretation would confine that communication to material that the parties *intend to use* in presenting their cases in the hearing before the Pre-Trial Chamber. Namely, of "evidence" as it is normally understood, that is, the exhibits and testimony (including witness statements) received by a court in determining the issues before it. Logically, this is done by submitting witness and exhibit lists, even if no hearing eventuates, as this precisely identifies the material the parties intend to use "for the purpose of the confirmation hearing". This is consistent with Rule 121(3) which requires the Prosecutor to present "the list of the evidence which he or she intends to present at the hearing". Documents falling outside of those categories cannot, reasonably, be relevant "for the purpose of the confirmation hearing", so far as a pre-trial chamber is concerned.

An expansive interpretation of the words "for the purpose of" could conceivably extend to documents that the defence uses as part of its general strategy, as opposed to those *actually* put before a pre-trial chamber in confirmation proceedings. However, the narrower and more coherent interpretation is far more consistent with Article 67(2) which requires the Prosecutor to disclose to the defence

> evidence in the Prosecutor's possession or control which he or she believes shows or tends to show the innocence of the accused, or to mitigate the guilt of the accused, or which may affect the credibility of prosecution evidence.

It is important to emphasise Article 67(2)'s purpose, namely, of codifying the Prosecutor's disclosure obligations under international human rights law, rather than defining what material a pre-trial chamber or a trial chamber should view. The term "evidence" is used, albeit somewhat loosely, but only in this context of inter-parties disclosure. This narrower interpretation is also far more consistent with Rule 77's requirement that the Prosecution discloses information that may be material to the defence preparation for trial.

The ICC's 2017 and 2019 Chambers Practice Manuals, however, attempted to interpret Rule 121(2)(c) – but without defining the concept of "evidence" – by stating:

> This should be understood as encompassing all evidence disclosed between the parties during the pre-trial proceedings,

i.e. between the person's initial appearance (or, in particular circumstances, even before) and the issuance of the confirmation decision.[134]

The manuals do not explain how this "understanding" is consistent with Article 61(3)(b). According to the manuals, this material – or "evidence" – forms part of the record of the case irrespective of whether it eventually appears on a party's evidence list.[135] Or, by extension, is ever received into evidence in a court hearing.

An example of a pre-trial chamber's view of its role in relation to the vast quantity of documents passing between the parties is of the Single Judge in *Abd-Al-Rahman* embracing the manual's over-expansive definition of "evidence" and ordering the Registry to register any "evidence disclosed between the parties and make it available to the Chamber". He held that it was of the "utmost importance" that the "parties provide all required metadata".[136]

The order, however, did not attempt to explain why the Pre-Trial Chamber needed access to every document exchanged between the parties – and in particular those that could be material to defence preparations for trial – and how having such access could expedite the proceedings. Nor did it define "evidence".[137]

These types of orders, however and unfortunately, misconceive the pre-trial chambers' role as a filtering body that decides whether a case moves forward to trial. The Court's statutory instruments do not give the pre-trial chambers an investigatory function, yet providing them with access to this material implicitly bestows this role on them. Even if the pre-trial chambers have some form of supervisory role in ensuring that the

---

[134] ICC Chambers Practice Manual 2017, p. 10, see above note 90; ICC Chambers Practice Manual 2019, para. 26, see above note 90.

[135] ICC Chambers Practice Manual 2017, p. 10, see above note 90; ICC Chambers Practice Manual 2019, para. 27, see above note 90.

[136] ICC, Situation in Darfur, Sudan, *The Prosecutor v. Ali Muhammad Ali-Abd-Al-Rahman ('Ali Kushayb')*, Pre-Trial Chamber, Order on disclosure and related matters, 17 August 2020, ICC-02/05-01/20-116, para. 11 (Judge Aitala) (https://www.legal-tools.org/doc/l59vj1/).

[137] The order then went into micro-management mode on inter-parties disclosure by ordering the Prosecution to provide "detailed" fortnightly reports "to keep the Chamber abreast of any progress made with regard to the evidence review, translation and disclosure process", *ibid.*, para. 17.

Prosecution is adhering to its disclosure obligations, they do not have an investigatory function.

The role of the trial chamber, however, is very different. Even if it is accepted – and only for arguments sake – that the pre-trial chambers should have access to vast swathes of material that the parties will not put before the chamber in the confirmation proceedings (perhaps as part of an expanded filtering function), a trial chamber cannot, as part of its statutory function require access to this irrelevant material. It is therefore essential to distinguish their different functions in assessing whether they should view the "evidence" disclosed between the parties – especially that which will not be used in hearings. Experience shows that most of the material falls into this category.

The Chambers Practice Manuals, however, state that the transmission of the record to the Trial Chamber, after confirmation of a case, "includes all evidence which has become part of the record by way of its communication to the Pre-Trial Chamber following *inter partes* disclosure".[138]

But this too is flawed. Providing the Trial Chamber with this material goes well beyond the function of the fact-finding body charged with determining whether an accused person is guilty beyond reasonable doubt. A trial chamber should not view material that will not become part of the trial record, except to decide whether it will upon the application of a party, or in the limited circumstances when it may require "the submission of all evidence that it considers necessary for the determination of the truth" pursuant to Article 69(3). Having access to all of material passing between the parties is tantamount to an impermissible fishing expedition into the Prosecutor's evidentiary holdings to ascertain whether anything is missing from the trial record. Trial chambers are conducting criminal trials not inquiries.

In taking this position the Chambers Practice Manuals are taking an overly broad interpretation of the concept of "evidence". A stricter and more realistic reading would confine it to that which a chamber receives and examines and uses in its deliberations concerning whether an accused person is guilty or not guilty of the charges. In other words, the *evidentiary* record of what is proposed for receipt into evidence, rather than eve-

---

[138] ICC Chambers Practice Manual 2017, p. 19, see above note 90; ICC Chambers Practice Manual 2019, para. 69, see above note 90.

ry document (in the broadest sense of the term) passing between the parties, regardless of its pertinence or eventual use in court. This interpretation would also better coincide with the international human rights law requirement of a fair trial which guarantees that accused persons have the right to challenge the evidence used against them. The manual, however, goes on further to assert that:

> Considering that the evidence would then be individually considered for formal admission during trial, its inclusion in the record of proceedings before professional judges is not problematic. The transmission of the complete record with all its contents is also the preferred solution because of its simplicity.[139]

It is not easy to comprehend the policy rationale for this. International criminal proceedings, in accordance with international human rights law, are adversarial. The ICC has neither an investigating judge nor chamber nor a dossier. The Prosecutor prepares an indictment in the form of a 'document containing the charges', and a case to present before a pre-trial chamber and then a trial chamber. The parties are responsible for their own investigation and case strategies. And crucially, many thousands of documents will normally have passed from the prosecution to the defence during the pre-trial phase, during which time the opposing legal teams will have familiarised themselves with this material. This is something a chamber, with a small support staff, often composed (at least in part) of junior lawyers having little if any prior domestic, criminal, litigation or even court experience, could never do.[140] It is implicitly inviting a trial chamber to rummage through thousands of irrelevant documents – most of which, sitting in their disclosure batches, will lack context – but without stating why it should do this.

Moreover, it is hard to see how transferring tens of thousands of documents *en masse* to a Trial Chamber – most of which will doubtless be irrelevant to determining the charges – has more 'simplicity' than confining the Trial Chamber's role to examining those that the parties actually

---

[139] ICC Chambers Practice Manual 2017, p. 19, see above note 90; ICC Chambers Practice Manual 2019, para. 69, see above note 90.

[140] These same legal assistants could also be tasked with obtaining statements from witnesses called by the chambers. This actually occurred in the *Krajišnik* trial. Krajišnik Trial Judgment, see above note 65.

rely upon as part of their cases, after investigating their respective cases. This can only complicate rather than simplify a trial chamber's task.

It also neglects to distinguish between two essential but different concepts. One is 'the record of the proceedings' – which is undefined in the Court's statutory instruments – but in reality is the *case record*. This could be considered to include all *potential* evidentiary material *uploaded* into Ringtail, either for disclosure or for use in court, and additionally motions, responses, decisions and orders and so on, and the judgment itself. The other is the *trial evidentiary record*. This is the material that a chamber either receives into evidence – normally when a party tenders it – or examines in deciding whether to receive it into evidence. It does this in exercising its statutory function of determining whether an accused is guilty or not guilty.

The manual does not explain how a Trial Chamber examining inter-party disclosure documents – most of which will not be used at trial and hence will not form part of the *trial evidentiary record* – is either an effi-cient use of judicial and chambers staff resources, or is in the interests of justice. It also fails to consider that the prosecution will have spent many years investigating and preparing the case, the defence less time, and their resources collectively dwarf those of a chamber of three judges and a small team of legal assistants. A Trial Chamber logistically cannot do the work of the prosecution or defence; its role is to adjudicate rather than investigate, search prosecution disclosure batches or to second-guess what the parties are doing. But the manual is appearing to invite the Trial Chamber to examine all of this material itself.

Writing in 2001, nineteen years before the Single Judge's order in *Abd-Al-Rahman* referred to above, a member of the French delegation involved in negotiating the ICC's Rules of Procedure and Evidence fur-nished a possible relatively contemporaneous policy explanation for Rule 121, which derives from a French proposal. In fairness to its author, the publication was of course written well before the ICC had any cases, and had actually started collecting *potential* evidence, and hence was yet to be confronted with the reality rather than the mere theory of disclosure and conducting expeditious proceedings.

In essence, according to the French delegate, its aim was to reduce the length of trials by giving the chambers access to all possible material, thus allowing the judges to decide for themselves what was relevant to the case. At the time particular concern was expressed at the average of 16 months then apparently being taken for ICTY trials. ICTR and ICTY trials, it was suggested, were being delayed by lengthy pre-trial disclosure motions, and this could be eliminated by providing the confirmation chamber with all the material, so that it could examine it for itself.[141]

Putting to one side the magical thinking inherent in supposing that inserting an extra judicial layer in the form of pre-trial confirmation proceedings into the proceedings would accelerate rather than slow cases,[142] the case statistics of the first ICC trial, *Lubanga*, reveal (quite predictably) that this 'initiative' did nothing to cure the 'problem' of these apparently excessively lengthy sixteen-month 'common-law' trials. The *Lubanga* trial took three years between its opening and the verdict, which was preceded by a 24-month delay between the confirmation decision and the trial's opening. It was also plagued by disclosure problems – mainly stemming from the prosecution's overuse of Article 54(3)(e) agreements – with the Trial Chamber twice staying the proceedings.[143] Moreover, the

---

[141] Gilbert Bitti, "Two Bones of Contention Between Civil and Common Law: The Record of the Proceedings and the Treatment of a Concursus Delictorum", in Horst Fischer, Claus Kreß, Sascha Rolf Lüder (eds.), *International and National Prosecution of Crimes under International Law: Current Developments*, Berlin Verlag Arno Spitz, Berlin, 2001, p. 276 (https://www.legal-tools.org/doc/b7b81a). A member of the Australian delegation to the negotiations countered these arguments in the same book: Helen J. Brady, "Setting the Record Straight: A Short Note on Disclosure and "the Record of the Proceedings"", in *ibid.*, pp. 262–72, pointing out that a number of delegations viewed the confirmation proceedings as a very short procedure – as a 'filter' that was "designed to ensure that only cases reaching a certain standard or significance go to trial – namely, those where the Prosecution puts forward sufficient evidence to establish substantial grounds to believe that the person committed the crime or crimes charged" (*ibid.*, p. 264). The difference in principle between the two views is that in the latter the confirmation proceedings are not concerned with the pre-trial chamber examining all inter-parties disclosure, instead concentrating on the evidence that the parties say is relevant to determining whether the case should proceed to trial and on what charges.

[142] This is of course premised on the Prosecutor filing a document containing the charge only in cases that have solid evidence against the accused persons that should survive confirmation proceedings.

[143] The first ICC situation was referred to the Court by the Ugandan government in January 2004 and investigations commenced in July 2004. The ICC case sheet reveals of its first case, *The Prosecutor v. Thomas Lubanga Dylio*, ICC-01/04-01/06, the following case statistics: Warrant of arrest issued: 10 February 2006; Transfer to The Hague: 16 March 2006; Confirmation of charges hearing: 9–28 November 2006; Decision on the confirmation of charges: 29 January 2007; Opening of the trial: 26 January 2009; Verdict: 14 March 2012; Sentence: 10 July 2012; Appeal judgment: 1 December 2014; Final Appeals Chamber reparations judgment: 18 July 2019.

Lubanga case could objectively be viewed as less factually and legally complex than many of its ICTY equivalents.[144]

The next trial, *Katanga*, was no better with six years and seven months passing between Germain Katanga's transfer to The Hague in October 2007, and his sentencing in May 2014; there was no appeal. The reparations litigation was completed only in March 2017. There was also a fourteen-month gap between the confirmation decision in September 2008 and the trial's opening in November 2009. The verdict was issued four years and four months later in March 2014.[145]

The third trial, *Bemba*, was worse as 10 years passed between Jean-Pierre Bemba Gombo's arrest, in June 2008, and his acquittal on appeal (by a three-two majority) in June 2018. Seventeen months had also passed between the confirmation decision in June 2009 and the trial's opening in November 2010. The Trial Chamber's verdict was issued five years and four months later, in March 2016, with the sentence following in June 2016.

Of the role of the Trial Chamber in relation to this 'record of proceedings', the French official wrote:

> But here we see that the problem is in fact the role of the judges during the trial. If the presiding judge is going to be the one to question the witnesses and to conduct the trial, it is a sheer necessity for him or her to consult the Record of proceedings, otherwise it will simply be impossible to conduct the trial. But if the Judge is only here to watch the fight between the Prosecutor and the Defence, there is no necessity for him or her to consult the Record, even if it could be useful to understand more what's going on.[146]

This approach, however, seems to be grounded in supposing the use of the procedures of domestic systems that feature an investigating judge

---

[144] Sixty-seven witnesses were called and the Trial Chamber received 1373 exhibits over 204 trial days between January 2009 and May 2011. ICC, Situation in the Democratic Republic of the Congo, *The Prosecutor v. Thomas Lubanga Dylio*, Trial Chamber, Judgment pursuant to Article 74 of the Statute, 14 March 2012, ICC-01/04-01/06-2842, para. 11 (https://www.legal-tools.org/doc/677866). Compared to 'normal' domestic trials, it is of course enormous, but comparatively not so in international proceedings.

[145] See ICC, Situation in the Democratic Republic of the Congo, *The Prosecutor v. Germain Katanga*, Case Information Sheet, 20 March 2018, ICC-PIDS-CIS-DRC-03-014/18_Eng (https://www.legal-tools.org/doc/7649d0).

[146] Bitti, 2001, p. 278, see above note 141.

and a dossier. But the experience of international trials since the first ICTY proceedings in 1994 has revealed few similarities between international and domestic criminal proceedings,[147] which moreover use hybrid procedures.

Article 64(8) of the ICC Statute permits the presiding judge to give directions on the conduct of a trial. If the presiding judge does not, the prosecution and defence shall agree on the order and manner in which the evidence shall be submitted to the Trial Chamber. Whichever is chosen, Rule 140(2) ensures that the party putting forward a witness has the right to question that witness and those of the opposing party. The Trial Chamber may question witnesses before or after the parties, and the defence has the right to question a witness last.

Each Trial Chamber to date, in the eight completed trials, and the one plea of guilty sentence hearing has conducted its proceedings by permitting the parties to call their own evidence and to question their own witnesses first.[148] That is what could be described as a 'party-driven' order of proceedings. In fact, it is difficult to see how it could be otherwise at trial, even with the chambers having access to the enormous 'case record' of actual evidence to which is added copious additional prosecution disclosure. In doing this the chambers have also at least implicitly recognised that the parties – having investigated and prepared their own cases – have distinct 'cases'.[149]

However, despite this, the Chambers Practice Manual, which presumably is intended to reflect perceived best judicial case management practice, suggests a form of micro-management of prosecution disclosure,

---

[147] ICTY and UNICRI, 2009, see above note 117.

[148] This includes all benches of civil law or mixed civil law or common law origin, including a bench of three judges in the Article 70 contempt case of *Bemba et al.*, ICC-01/05-01/13, in which one of the trial judges was Judge Marc Perrin de Brichambaut who led the French delegation in the negotiations for the ICC Statute and thereafter for its Rules of Procedure and Evidence. In that case the Accused were arrested in November 2013, the confirmation decision followed a year later in November 2014, the trial opened in September 2015 with a verdict in October 2016, followed by sentencing in March 2017 (and some resentencing in September 2018 after appellate proceedings for some accused), meaning that 22 months passed between arrests and the start of the trial, including the confirmation proceedings. In *Lubanga* the Trial Chamber called four expert witnesses and started the questioning itself; in *Katanga* it called two witnesses, and in *Bemba* one.

[149] The procedures employed in confirmation proceedings have varied; some have been live witness-free, with the parties submitting written evidence and making submissions.

even at the trial stage. In writing this, it is of course recognised that it is a manual rather than a statutory instrument and chambers are free to modify it or to disregard it entirely.

Moreover, one can only envisage with horror the adverse effects on the statistics in the *Lubanga, Katanga* and *Bemba* trials had the presiding judges (and the other Trial Chamber judges) elected to do as the French delegate suggested, namely, to trawl through thousands of pages of documents – mostly irrelevant – while forging ahead with questioning the witnesses.

Another important issue which goes to blockages in the system of disclosure and hence the trial schedule is of redacting material for defence disclosure, or in lay terms, blacking out information. The prosecution may redact information under Rules 81(2) and (4) – which relates to not prejudicing further or ongoing investigations or the protection and safety of witnesses, victims or members of their families or other third parties. The ICC Chambers Practice Manual states, sensibly, that this can be done without a chamber's authorisation unless the defence challenges it. In the event of a defence challenge, however, the prosecution must justify the redactions and specify how they fall into 1 of 13 enumerated categories.[150]

The ICTY/ICTR/IRMCT/STL judges did not and do not do any of the things described above. The parties were permitted to do their job and the chambers intervened when required. In these tribunals the judges do not (generally) examine or micro-manage inter-party disclosure.

From the above it can be safely concluded that the current ICC disclosure systems compare unfavourably to those used at the ICTY and IRMCT, even taking into account the fundamental differences between these institutions.

The ICC judicial approach in some cases has tended towards oversupervising prosecution disclosure, while the prosecution, on the other hand, has yet to embrace the relatively successful ICTY/IRMCT EDS experience of putting its open source and non-restricted witness materials into a 'neutral' Registry database. These two methodologies employed at the ICC appear to combine some of the least efficient approaches to man-

---

[150] This seems excessively bureaucratic. ICC Chambers Practice Manual 2017, pp. 29–30, see above note 90; ICC Chambers Practice Manual 2019, para. 101, see above note 90.

aging the inter-parties disclosure of information in complex international criminal proceedings.

A reform suggested by some prosecutors was to ensure that the defence is required to state, and as early as possible, its contentions with the prosecution case, or to put it more simply, to state its case. This, it was felt, would facilitate informed disclosure of material to the defence from the prosecution's restricted evidence collections. A defence lawyer was relaxed with the suggestion, but only if the defence were required to set out its case *after* prosecution disclosure was complete, explaining (quite reasonably) the difficulty of advising a client in the absence of complete disclosure of all potentially exculpatory material or that material to defence preparations.[151] This has some merit and could be part of trial judicial case management.

It would also require the court to make a declaration of an 'end of essential disclosure date' for this purpose. In so doing, the chamber would have to acknowledge, tacitly or expressly, that in international criminal law proceedings disclosure never seems to end, and can even continue past an appellate judgment.

14.6.4. Judicial Familiarity with Prosecution Evidence Collections, Searching and Disclosure

Another issue for consideration is that of judicial familiarity in the international system with how international prosecutors' offices collect, store, catalogue and search their evidence collections.[152] And, further, how defence counsel do it. At the ICTY judicial 'buy-in' was required before the prosecution could move to mandatory electronic disclosure, as in its Rule 68(B), now replicated in the IRMCT Rule 73(B).

Historically, few international judges have had first-hand experience of large and complicated domestic criminal investigations, much less international ones, before assuming international judicial office. Those who have attained international judicial office through an academic or diplomatic route, or who have no criminal law background, could not be

---

[151] Peter Robinson, interview on 29 October 2019.

[152] For example, the STL's Trial Chamber, before the commencement of the trial of *Prosecution v. Ayyash et al.*, convened a meeting of the parties to receive a judicial demonstration of searching the Prosecution's databases of telephonic call data records and how it is stored; see *Ayyash et al.* Trial Decision on Call Data Records, para. 8, see above note 40.

expected to be familiar with the more complex and technical details of the workings of criminal justice systems. This of course includes evidence gathering and storage, and as a corollary, disclosure.

But obtaining this knowledge or experience is essential to understanding the challenges of ensuring that disclosable material gets to the defence and hence to guarantee a fair trial to accused persons. International judges must familiarise themselves with how international prosecutors go about their business of collecting and storing information. It is suggested that they must delve into prosecution evidence and information systems – meaning in demonstrations – and, further in these demonstrations, attempt themselves to perform sample targeted or general searches in the systems. Without having gained some familiarity with the prosecution's evidence and information systems, it is difficult to understand how a chamber can make informed decisions on alleged disclosure breaches and hence remedies – except of course in the most obvious cases.

Overcoming this obstacle to judicial understanding, whatever its basis, is central to rethinking disclosure. Put another way, an informed judiciary that understands from the inside the challenges of disclosure is more likely to sponsor or support reform.

Relevant to this is the compilation and publication of the ICC Chambers Practice Manuals that set out guidelines for best practice on numerous matters that affect the parties, including disclosure. Best practice would suggest a period of significant consultation with all interested and affected parties – prosecution, defence, registry, victims' representatives – before finalising such a document.[153] Ironically, the opposite seems to have occurred, meaning that no consultation occurred.[154]

---

[153] "Introduction to the third edition of the Manual, May 2017", in ICC Chambers Practice Manual 2017, see above note 90:

> This update of the Chambers Practice Manual adds a new section governing issues related to the preparation phase of trial proceedings before the commencement of trial (Section B). The new section is the result of discussions held at the second Judges' retreat that took place in Limburg, the Netherlands, from 28 to 29 October 2016. Similarly to the rest of the Manual, this section is not intended as a binding instrument on ICC trial judges. Rather, it contains general recommendations and guidelines reflecting best practices. These best practices are based on the experience and expertise of judges across trials at the Court.

> Two years later nothing had changed in this respect. The 'Introduction to the fourth edition of the Manual, November 2019', states:

14.6.5. Prosecution Record Keeping

Also historically, a large part of the problem concerns Prosecution record keeping.[155] In the *ad hoc* and hybrid tribunals their temporary nature, which itself causes a turnover of personnel and a loss of corporate memory, exacerbates this.[156] And this problem is aggravated if the documents do not contain proper searchable metadata.

Prosecution offices must maintain their internal databases in a manner conducive to searching for disclosable material. This includes draft reports of any proposed in-house witnesses, whether expert or not. Correspondence with witnesses could also be disclosable. Problematically, prosecution officials may do this by emails that remain only in that person's own inbox or sent folder. There is no reason why these emails,

---

> This update of the Chambers Practice Manual is the result of discussions held at the Judges' retreat that took place in Arnhem, the Netherlands, from 3 to 4 October 2019. New content has been added in relation to deadlines for key judicial decisions and internal guidelines on trial judgment drafting and structure have been incorporated'.

Again, this occurred without consultation with or notification to anyone who would be affected by decisions taken at the judicial retreat.

[154] The *ICTY Manual on Developed Practices*, by contrast, was the result of collaboration between the ICTY and UNICRI. Its introduction stated at p. 1, that

> this Manual is aimed at preserving the legacy of the ICTY in the form of a blueprint of its practices for use by other international and domestic courts. This Manual was prepared with assistance and contributions from a number of ICTY staff members from each of the Tribunal's organs.

See above note 117. The author had some involvement in this project in its initial stages.

[155] Again, this statement comes from the author's own experience, which the interviewees for this chapter have confirmed.

[156] For example, the STL Trial Chamber in *Ayyash et al.* Trial Decision on Merhi Defence Request for Disclosure of Documents Concerning Witness PRH230, held, at para. 102,

> On the other side, this litigation has revealed that the Prosecution's record-keeping is inadequate in significant aspects with regard to its disclosure obligations. The Prosecution has admitted that, for the thousands of documents it classifies as internal work product, it has not gathered them into a central database. Instead, these documents are scattered across various computer drives, including the personal drives of Prosecution employees. As a result, searching for and identifying documents responsive to the category of records of questions and answers would have required the Prosecution to manually review around 70,000 computer files and around 60,000 emails, a process that would have taken weeks or months to complete and would have delayed Mr Donaldson's testimony in the meantime.

Internal footnotes omitted. See above note 49.

---

which may after all contain disclosable material, should not be centrally stored.

Thought must be given, and hence discipline exercised, in internally filing documents. This could include keeping electronic correspondence logs. Whichever, it should be centralised, organised and contain proper metadata.[157]

The enormous quantity of open source digital material gathered during international investigations presents challenges for prosecution offices not just in storing and searching but also in disclosing it. In cases in their early stages, especially where arrests are either a long way off or unlikely, the material should certainly be collected but it should be kept in a manner in which it can be disclosed as a whole once defence counsel become involved.

In general, the defence should be given access to it.

One lawyer interviewed raised possible privacy and security concerns for personal data found on social media platforms and other areas of the internet.[158] She considered that even if such information is 'open' in the normal sense of it being publicly accessible, its collection and processing by an international organisation may nevertheless raise some data protection issues. This is so even while recognising that the ICC and other international institutions have immunity in the execution of their functions, preventing the enforcement of privacy data protection regulations such as the European Union's General Data Protection Regulation (GDPR).[159] And, additionally, that prosecution activities could fall under an exception for certain law enforcement activities. Nonetheless, in her view, disclosure processes should comply with measures intended to protect the fundamen-

---

[157] The ICC's Office of the Prosecutor has a system of internal document management for contact with witnesses. The author had experience of a system developed for that purpose at the ICTY, namely, in which all contacts with witnesses were supposed to be recorded. Unfortunately, however, only some officials actually used it.

[158] Interview with Lindsay Freeman, Senior Legal Researcher at the UC Berkeley Human Rights Center, and former prosecution lawyer in San Francisco, 25 October 2019.

[159] Regulation (EU) 2016/679 (General Data Protection Regulation). Article 23(1)(d) permits member states to exempt (that is, restrict its application) "when such a restriction respects the essence of the fundamental rights and freedoms and is a necessary and proportionate measure in a democratic society to safeguard" for "the prevention, investigation, detection or prosecution of criminal offences or the execution of criminal penalties, including the safeguarding against and the prevention of threats to public security".

tal right to privacy. The lawyer suggests that this issue could be addressed by clear and transparent policies around digital data access, retention and deletion.

14.7. Conclusion

To conclude, disclosure is a swamp, like a mire of quicksand that can rapidly swallow the unsuspecting. The methodology, rather than the underlying legal principles, must be rethought. This requires joint and collaborative action between prosecution, defence and chambers.

The first and most obvious point is to identify the flaws and blockages in the current systems and to ascertain where they are not working well or even failing. The collection of digital evidence presents new challenges but in practice and in theory it should be easier to resolve these than it is with vast paper collections that need digitalisation before they can be searched. An EDS, it is stressed, is no panacea and will not miraculously solve the disclosure issue; but it is a model that can work if properly employed.

To summarise, the following reforms are proposed:

- As a starting point the prosecution retains, as it must, sole 'ownership' of its own witness-generated materials and in particular, evidence and information of a sensitive nature. 'Sensitive' here includes information provided with conditions, including of non-disclosure without the provider's permission; such as that it could be provided solely for generating investigating leads.

- Open-source and public documents, namely, government and other public records, provided to prosecutors' offices should be copied and provided to the court registry and maintained in an electronic disclosure suite similar in form and function to that of the ICTY and then IRMCT.

- Prosecutors' offices must ensure that their staff properly record metadata sufficient to allow any interested party to search their collections with relative ease.

- If possible, information collected by prosecution officials in the field should be scrutinised then and there for potential relevance, and when feasible, immediately entered into the system.

- Prosecutors' offices should ensure that all potentially disclosable information such as draft reports and statements of in-house witnesses and experts, and relevant communications with witnesses, are centrally stored and managed and have proper metadata.

- Prosecution internal work product should be strictly isolated from non-internal work product that is potentially disclosable.

- The primary responsibility for searching the EDS collections for information that is material to defence preparations for trial should *prima facie* shift to the defence.

- The defence should notify the prosecution of the search terms that could produce this material in searching the prosecution's non-EDS collections.

- Chambers must properly familiarise themselves with prosecution evidence and information-keeping practices and the parties' search methodology.

- Chambers should not micro-manage inter-party disclosure.

- Chambers should exercise great care before deciding to examine the inter-parties disclosure to which they have access but which is not part of the evidentiary record on which guilt or otherwise is determined. Best practice would be to avoid examining this material unless cogent reasons exist to do so.

- Chambers should consult extensively with the prosecution, defence, registry and victims' representatives before setting policies such as those in the ICC's Chambers Practice Manuals.

- The defence should be required to provide better details of contentions with the prosecution case after the chambers are satisfied that the essential disclosure is complete. This should be done as early as possible in a case.

- Each accused person must have adequate resources – staffing and facilities – to properly prepare their case for trial, which includes searching disclosed prosecution material.

But problem-fixing normally only occurs in stages, and only after acceptance that one exists. After acknowledgment comes the real challenge of taking the problem-solving leap. The suggestions above could work, but this would require all 'actors' collaboratively putting their heads together and examining them as neutrally as possible. The consultative process employed by the ICTY in 2008 in preparing its *ICTY Manual on Developed Practices* in this respect is worth emulating.

PART IV:
INVESTIGATION PLANS
AS INSTRUMENTS OF QUALITY CONTROL

15

Investigation Plans
in International Criminal Investigations:
The Example of the ICC Office of the Prosecutor

Markus Eikel[*]

15.1. Introduction

Investigation plans are a recognised best practice for international criminal investigations.[1] At the same time, they are not yet a universal practice, as many national jurisdictions investigating core international crimes do not use investigation plans.[2] This chapter supports the argumentation that investigation plans should be used as one instrument of quality control in international criminal investigations, as they support mitigating some of the bottlenecks that are identified in the concept paper of the CILRAP Quality Control Project.[3] They make sure that a criminal investigation,

---

[*]   **Markus Eikel** is Senior Investigator, International Criminal Court ('ICC'), Office of the Prosecutor ('OTP'); previously working at the International Criminal Tribunal for the Former Yugoslavia ('ICTY') (2002–04) and at the Crimes Against Humanity and War Crimes Section, Department of Justice, Canada (1997–2002); Ph.D. (University of Hamburg), M.A. (University of Hamburg), LL.M. (Leiden University). The views expressed in this chapter are those of the author and do not necessarily reflect those of the OTP. At the same time, the chapter has greatly benefited from ideas developed within the OTP Investigation Division, in particular by Michel De Smedt (Director Investigation Division) and Cristina Ribeiro (Inves-tigation Coordinator).

[1]   Robert Petit, David Akerson and Maria Warren (eds.), *Prosecuting Mass Atrocities: Lessons from the International Tribunals: A Compendium of Lessons Learned and Suggested Practices from the Offices of the Prosecutors*, 2012, p. 51, Practice 58: "For each case or situation under investigation, the prosecution office should draw an investigation plan that seeks to achieve the strategic aims of the office".

[2]   See Morten Bergsmo, "Rethinking Instruments of Quality Control in the Investigation and Preparation of Core International Crimes Cases", CILRAP Film, New Delhi, 22 February 2019 (www.cilrap.org/cilrap-film/190222-bergsmo/).

[3]   The CILRAP concept paper has identified draft indictments, indictments, and pre-trial briefs as other instruments of quality control. See Morten Bergsmo, "Towards a Culture of Quality Control in Criminal Investigations", FICHL Policy Brief Series No. 94 (2019),

like any other professional inquiry, benefits from an organised and systematic approach, addressing the relevant legal issues in a prioritised manner.[4]

The chapter is divided into four parts. Firstly, it will define the different functions that an investigation plan should fulfil within the framework of an international criminal investigation. The chapter will argue that, the more the investigation plan is in line with those functions, the better this tool achieves its quality-control role (Section 15.2.). Subsequently, the chapter will describe what role an investigation plan fulfils within the investigation cycle and how the plan helps to define the investigation strategy (Section 15.3.). Thirdly, the chapter will cover the past and current practice of drafting and reviewing investigation plans at the International Criminal Court's Office of the Prosecutor ('ICC-OTP') (Section 15.4.). At the end, the chapter provides some conclusions on how investigation plans can be best utilised in international criminal investigations to assure quality control and to mitigate some of the bottlenecks that are described in the CILRAP concept paper (Section 15.5.).

15.2. Functions of an Investigation Plan

While other contributions in this volume will cover national practices in relation to investigation plans,[5] this chapter focuses on the use of investigation plans in international investigations and prosecutions. On this level, the ICC-OTP is just one of the prosecution offices that make use of these plans. Looking at international investigating offices more generally, one can find publicly available reference points, amongst others, at the International Criminal Tribunal for the Former Yugoslavia's ('ICTY') Best

---

Torkel Opsahl Academic EPublisher, Brussels, 2019, p. 4 (http://www.toaep.org/pbs-pdf/94-bergsmo/). From the current ICC practice, one may add the Arrest Warrant ('AW'), the Arrest Warrant Application ('AWA'), and the Document Containing the Charges ('DCC') prior to the Confirmation Hearing as further instruments or variations.

[4]   Dermot Groome, "Evidence in Cases of Mass Criminality", in Ilias Bantekas and Emmanouela Mylonaki (eds.), *Criminological Approaches to International Criminal Law*, Cambridge University Press, Cambridge, 2014, p. 120; Petit, Akerson and Warren, 2012, p. 52, see above note 1.

[5]   See for India, Usha Tandon and Shreeywah Uday Lalit, "Use of Investigation Plans in Indian Criminal Justice: The Crime of Human Trafficking", CILRAP Film, New Delhi, 23 February 2019 (www.cilrap.org/cilrap-film/190223-tandon-lalit/); for Norway, Alf Butenschøn Skre, "Investigation Plans as Management Tools in Norway", CILRAP Film, New Delhi, 23 February 2019 (www.cilrap.org/cilrap-film/190223-skre/).

Practice Manual (2009),[6] the Best Practice Project jointly conducted by all *Ad Hoc* Tribunals (2012),[7] the International Criminal Tribunal for Rwanda's ('ICTR') Best Practice Guidelines on Investigating sexual and gender-based crimes ('SGBC') (2014),[8] and the Organization for Security and Cooperation in Europe's ('OSCE') Investigation Manual for Bosnia and Herzegovina.[9] All of these reference documents have sections on investigation plans, including templates. Some of these documents dedicate significant attention to different types of evidence: witnesses (both crime-base and linkage); documents; open source; and forensics. But beyond just listing possible options for evidence collection, grouped according to different categories of evidence, all documents agree that an investigation plan has four major components.

15.2.1. Case Assessment

As a key starting point, investigation plans all have an introductory section covering a legal case assessment for the case under investigation. The ICTY Manual calls this section "fundamental questions that the investigation will hopefully be able to answer through the collection of credible and reliable evidence".[10] In the words of the Manual, without such guidance, there is a strong likelihood "that efforts will lack the focus necessary to effectively and efficiently identify and collect the evidence necessary".[11] The template provided in the ICTY Manual also foresees a section on the relevant legal framework, which includes theories of legal responsibility and possible crimes that were committed and their legal elements.

The Best Practices Manual explains that the main focus of any investigation plan "should be to identify what elements of the crime or

---

[6] See ICTY and United Nations Interregional Crime and Justice Research Institute ('UNICRI'), *ICTY Manual on Developed Practices*, UNICRI Publisher, Turin, 2009 (' ICTY Manual') (https://www.legal-tools.org/doc/0cc55d/).

[7] See Petit, Akerson and Warren, 2012, see above note 1.

[8] ICTR, *Prosecution of Sexual Violence: Best Practices Manual for the Investigations and Prosecutions of Sexual-Violence Crimes in Post-Conflict Regions: Lessons Learned from the Office of the Prosecutor from the International Criminal Tribunal for Rwanda*, January 2014 ('ICTR Manual') (https://www.legal-tools.org/doc/ea03f8/).

[9] OSCE, *Investigation Manual for War Crimes, Crimes Against Humanity and Genocide in Bosnia and Herzegovina*, October 2013 ('OSCE Investigation Manual') (https://www.legal-tools.org/doc/md6eab/).

[10] ICTY Manual, p. 30, see above note 6.

[11] *Ibid.*

criminal responsibility are not sufficiently proven", based on the identification of "specific gaps or weaknesses in the evidence required proving the elements of the crimes or modes of liability".[12] The ICTR Manual identifies any 'potential charges' as an initial reference point for the investigation plan;[13] while the OSCE document refers at the outset of an investigation plan to the allegations; the person to be investigated; potential offences; and elements that need to be proven.[14]

At the ICC-OTP, the legal case assessment is ordinarily drafted by prosecution lawyers and describes what the case hypothesis or the case theory is at the time of writing the respective investigation plan. This case assessment should indicate what the assessed legal strengths and weaknesses of a case are in order to allow for a more targeted and properly prioritised collection effort, mitigating the CILRAP concept paper bottleneck 'too much evidence'. It is important that the case assessment also includes references to potential exculpatory points or lines of defence.[15]

15.2.2. Planning

The first of three important functions of the investigation plan is the planning ahead of the investigation. The Best Practices Manual specifies that, after the more specific objectives of a case are set out, "the next step is to create a plan detailing how these objectives are to be achieved".[16] The ICTY Manual dedicates a specific section to planning, noting that it is important to give thought to the implementation of the plan, so that all major tasks are completed according to a schedule.[17] The OSCE document identifies different phases for investigative planning and includes an Evidence/Information Collection Plan as well as the planning of specific tasks.[18]

In planning its way forward, the case team will address all areas of the case where additional evidence is still required. That process leads to the identification of investigative objectives, which are generally defined

---

[12] Petit, Akerson and Warren, 2012, p. 60, see above note 1.
[13] ICTR Manual, p. 2, see above note 8.
[14] OSCE Investigation Manual, pp. 194–95, see above note 9.
[15] ICTR Manual, p. 4, see above note 8.
[16] Petit, Akerson and Warren, 2012, p. 52, see above note 1.
[17] ICTY Manual, p. 32, see above note 6.
[18] OSCE Investigation Manual, pp. 195–96, see above note 9.

around certain areas of the case or legal elements requiring further evidence (for example, the overall structure of an organisation, the chain of command, specific incidents, or specific crimes).

The focus of the investigation is determined by an assessment of the case, the investigative options available, and potential arrest opportunities. A combination of these parameters leads to an investigative strategy, correlating investigative objectives with existing critical internal and external factors, including co-operation with external partners, security, protection, available resources, available investigative tools, and others.

Strategic decisions captured in the investigation plan might include giving priority to linkage evidence *vis-à-vis* crime base; collecting or not collecting certain types of evidence; suspending the investigation in certain geographical areas; or accelerating the investigation in relation to certain suspects for which arrest opportunities may arise. In the investigation plan, the case team will justify its decisions with regards to these issues and the underlying reasoning for management approval.

As a result of the investigation strategy, the investigation plan will identify concrete investigative and analytical priorities. The case team needs to prioritise those for which concrete results within the period relevant to the specific investigation plan are feasible. For each of the identified priorities, the plan will provide specific information on the concrete investigative activities the team intends to undertake, including the types of evidence to collect (such as interviews of certain witnesses or the collection of certain documents).

In order to illustrate the correlation between investigative objectives and critical factors affecting the planning, the following example is provided. A common feature from most investigations of core international crimes is the requirement to obtain additional linkage evidence, effectively connecting the suspect with the crimes that took place on the ground. Some of the investigations at the ICC-OTP are conducted without the co-operation of the situation country, that is, the country where the crimes occurred. Investigators therefore have no (or only very limited) access to the country under investigation and thereby to a pool of potential insiders often residing in country who may be able to provide the required linkage evidence. In addition, there may be only limited capacity to protect any potential insider witness who is located within the structures under investigation.[19] One way of mitigation in this case is to focus as much as possible on non-testimonial evidence, including open sources, imagery and documents.

While mitigation strategies need to be in place at the outset, the case team has to constantly re-adjust the planning, based on external factors that may change the framework of the investigation and are outside of the control of the investigation. Examples for such external factors may include: a sudden and unexpected political regime change in one of the countries that the investigation is operating in; a declining security situation in certain areas of operation; or an unexpected surrender, like the one of Dominic Ongwen in 2015 to the ICC. It is therefore important to update the planning in regular intervals and, when required, even earlier than that.[20]

15.2.3. Reporting

Reporting is a second important function of the investigation plan. The reporting takes place on two levels: 1) Has the case team done what it intended to do; and 2) in doing so, what knowledge has the case team acquired in relation to the case hypothesis or case theory? In answering these questions, the case team reports to its supervisors on the actual progress made. Robust compliance mechanisms evaluating the performance of the team from the outside will support such an assessment. The progress reporting within the plan can be undertaken in the form of a narrative. Alternatively, it could also be provided in form of a log-frame (logical framework) matrix. This format, designed in project management practice, defines objectives, results and activities based on a summary narrative combined with previously defined indicators.[21]

---

[19] For the limitations of the witness protection capacity at the ICC, see Markus Eikel, "External Support and Internal Coordination – The ICC and the Protection of Witnesses", in Carsten Stahn (ed.), *The Law and Practice of the International Criminal Court*, Oxford University Press, Oxford, 2015, pp. 1105–32.

[20] For the relevance of uncertainty in business planning, see Hugh Courtney, Jane Kirkland and Patrick Viguerie, "Strategy Under Uncertainty", *Harvard Business Review*, 1997, November–December issue, pp. 1–32.

[21] For example, see OSCE, *Project Management in the OSCE: A Manual for Programme and Project Managers*, Vienna, 2010, pp. 39–47 (https://www.legal-tools.org/doc/6jbcgx/).

The relevance of regular reporting is emphasised in the various reference manuals mentioned above.[22] For instance, the ICTY Manual recommends that the investigation "should be reviewed on a quarterly basis to assess progress towards its objectives and to evaluate how the collective knowledge of a particular event has evolved".[23] The reporting assists senior management to assess the pace of the investigation. Such an assessment puts the speed of the investigation into context, which implies also looking at the framework in which the investigation is conducted. Therefore, an investigation plan may include a table indicating the timeline of the investigation to date and the impact of main factors, such as co-operation, security and resources over time. Justifiable reasons for a delay in reaching investigative objectives may include: unforeseeable security developments; unforeseen resource shortcomings, caused by developments in other cases; or a lack of co-operation of witnesses.

The reporting function also includes an explanation as to why certain investigative activities or lines of inquiry were not pursued. For example, the case team may decide not to conduct exhumations and autopsies as it considers these investigative activities desirable, but not strictly necessary for proving the case at hand. In this scenario, the case team logs its decision and its reasoning in the investigation plan. By doing so, the case team mitigates the CILRAP policy paper bottleneck 'overview of information', here in relation to capture certain investigative decisions taken. More generally, the investigation plan serves the purpose of creating a historical record of the investigation.

15.2.4. Management

Investigation plans also fulfil a management function. One important aspect in this regard is to define the resource requirements for the team. What are the projected needs in terms of investigators and their required competencies, for example to conduct online or financial investigations, as well as other staff, including a certain language profile. Resources at international courts and tribunals are generally scarce; and it is therefore necessary to justify towards senior management the assignment of current

---

[22] Petit, Akerson and Warren, 2012, p. 52, see above note 1; ICTY Manual, p. 32, see above note 6; ICTR Manual, p. 4, see above note 8; OSCE Investigation Manual, p. 195, see above note 9.

[23] ICTY Manual, p. 32, see above note 6.

and additional staff for the specific course of the investigation. All reference documents include specific sections on resource requirements.[24] The ICTY Manual explains how necessary resources should be identified once a task-list has been generated.[25]

A second relevant management aspect is to identify the support that is required from other entities within the prosecution's office where co-ordinating aspects become relevant. The example of language support can illustrate the latter aspect. Most international criminal investigations require interpretation and translation from local languages into the official languages of an international court or tribunal, most commonly English and French. The case team needs to make sure that it defines, at the earliest possible junction, the language support required to conduct its investigative activities in order to make sure that sufficient interpretation staff can support the field missions; and that the language staff has received proper security clearance and training prior to field deployment. Planning these aspects of the case ahead may be crucial to ensure an effective implementation of investigative priorities and activities.

As a third important management function, the process of drafting an investigation plan offers an opportunity for the whole case team to take stock and develop a common understanding of where the investigation stands and what the required next steps are. Once a common understanding within the team has been reached, it becomes easier for team members to identify relevant investigative activities and inform team management of initiatives they may want to take.

15.2.5. Template Investigation Plan

Based on the reference documents mentioned in Section 15.2. above and ICC-OTP practice at the time of writing, the general template of an investigation plan could look like the one illustrated in Figure 1.

---

[24] *Ibid.*; Petit, Akerson and Warren, 2012, p. 52, see above note 1; ICTR Manual, p. 3, see above note 8; OSCE Investigation Manual, p. 195, see above note 9.

[25] ICTY Manual, p. 32, see above note 6.

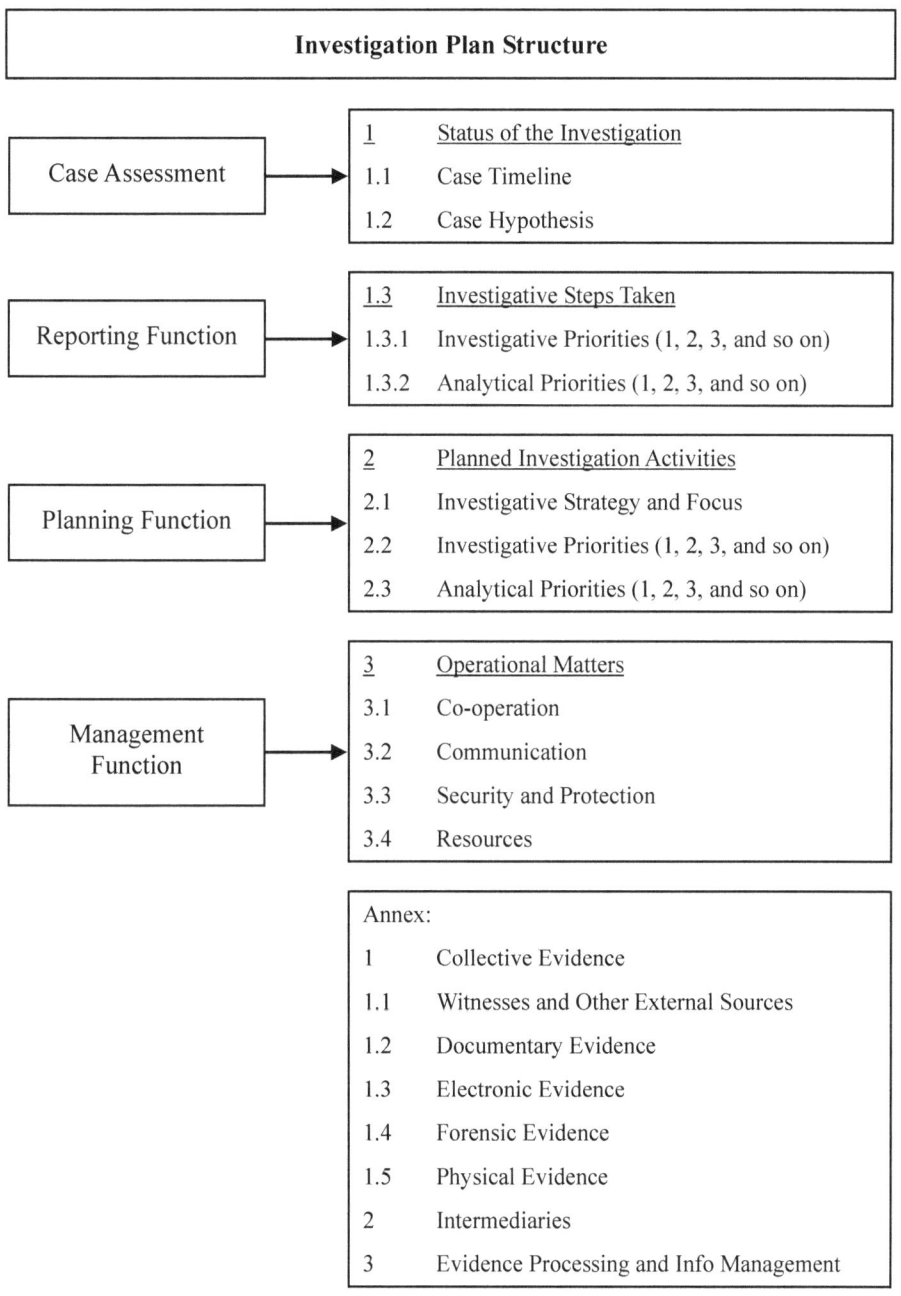

Figure 1. General template of an investigation plan.

15.3. Investigation Cycle

Building a case in international criminal investigations is a multi-staged process, from an initially very broad to a gradually narrower focus.[26] In an initial phase, the investigation looks at the totality of a situation, which includes all sides of a conflict, including all potential crimes and all potential criminal incidents. Gradually, and depending on the results of collection and analysis, the investigation will narrow its focus and develop one or more case hypotheses. Eventually, when facts are believed to be sufficiently established to avoid other hypotheses, the case team will develop a case theory, defining the criminal responsibility of specific individuals for specific crimes under a defined mode of liability.

An investigation plan needs to be placed within the circular approach of a criminal investigation. An identified case is broken down into different sub-components; for some of those, prosecution lawyers will assess the available evidence as strong; for others, the evidentiary basis may be weaker. Based on this legal assessment, the investigation plan outlines investigative strategy, investigative objectives and activities, as described in Section 15.2.2. above. Strategy and activities are implemented and then evaluated in a subsequent plan. This evaluation may come to the conclusion that certain objectives were achieved; and thereby certain weaknesses of the case as previously identified in the case assessment are now mitigated. The evaluation may also come to the conclusion that the weaknesses are not mitigated, which in turn leads to the question a) if there are other investigative methods and approaches that need to be applied in order to find the required evidence; or b) if the case theory or at least certain parts of it may need to be adjusted, as the evidence collected does not support the legal theory. The course of the investigation is best described in the form of the cycle seen in Figure 2.

---

[26] Groome, 2012, pp. 119–22, see above note 4.

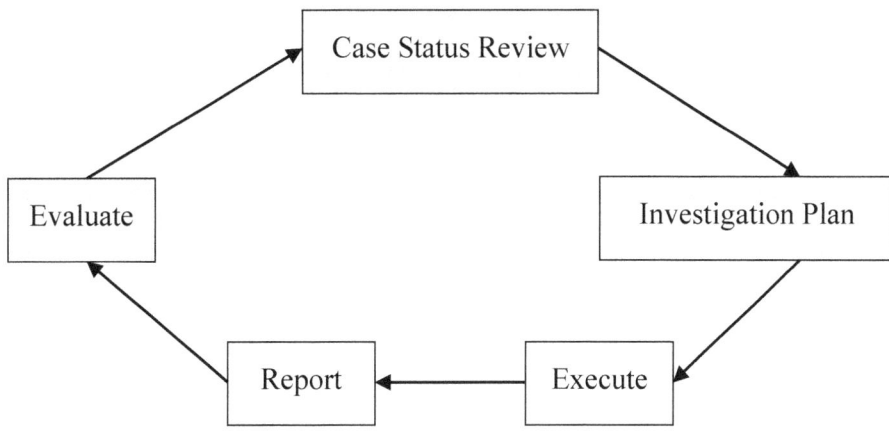

Figure 2. The course of an investigation.

Applying the investigation cycle in itself is a quality-control mechanism as it provides for an opportunity to correct or adjust the focus of the investigation.

15.4. Past and Current ICC-OTP Practice

15.4.1. Draft Regulations and Regulations *Ad Interim* 2003

Investigation plans were considered as an investigation management tool for the OTP since the early days of the ICC. The Draft Regulations of the OTP, formulated in the first half of 2003,[27] determined that the two foreseen Deputy Prosecutors (for Investigation and Prosecution) were to designate a senior prosecutor to supervise the drafting of a 'draft investigation plan' towards the end of the Preliminary Examination ('PE') of a case.

Draft Regulation 6.5. set out the various parameters relevant for the draft investigation plan.[28] The parameters covered an assessment of the anticipated focus of the investigation; an early formulation of criminal responsibility; an assessment of the available evidence and its amount; and a tentative indication of possible charges, modes of liability and po-

---

[27] Morten Bergsmo, "Institutional History, Behaviour and Development", in Morten Bergsmo, Klaus Rackwitz and SONG Tianying (eds.), *Historical Origins of International Criminal Law: Volume 5*, Torkel Opsahl Academic EPublisher, Brussels, 2017, pp. 5–6 (https://www.legal-tools.org/doc/09c8b8/); Carlos Vasconcelos, "Draft Regulations of the Office of the Prosecutor", in *ibid.*, pp. 802–04.

[28] Carlos Vasconcelos, "Draft Regulations of the Office of the Prosecutor", in *ibid.*, pp. 859–62.

tential defences. Antonio Angotti has provided an analysis of these criteria and how they relate to the bottlenecks identified in the CILRAP concept paper,[29] in Chapter 16 below. The final investigation plan, as defined in Draft Regulation 20, was one of the three essential investigation management tools (next to a Draft Charges Document and a Proof Chart); it "describes the different steps of the investigation which are necessary to achieve the aim of the investigation, the anticipated outcome of each investigative step and alternative strategies".[30] The draft investigation plan was to converge into an investigation plan, which in turn provided the grounds for the draft charges document.[31]

The Regulations *ad interim*, signed by the first ICC Prosecutor in early September 2003, were an abridged version of the Draft Regulations and contained no reference to a draft investigation plan or an investigation plan.[32] As a consequence, there was no binding regulatory framework for investigation plans at the ICC-OTP until the adoption of the Regulations in 2009. In the years prior, different investigative models were tested. As the OTP explained in the OTP Strategic Plan 2012-2015, the first such document issued under the term in office of Prosecutor Fatou Bensouda, the option of adopting investigative standards from the beginning was rejected because the OTP did not consider it mandatory to adopt specific standards before some practical experience had been gained; and because the OTP wanted to test the approaches coming from different systems.[33]

---

[29] See also Antonio Angotti, "Investigation Plans in the Draft Regulations of the Office of the Prosecutor of the International Criminal Court: An Italian Perspective", CILRAP Film, New Delhi, 23 February 2019 (www.cilrap.org/cilrap-film/190223-angotti/).

[30] Vasconcelos, 2017, p. 869 (Draft Regulation 20.2), see above note 28.

[31] See Angotti, 2019, see above note 29.

[32] ICC-OTP, *Paper on some policy issues before the Office of the Prosecutor*, September 2003, p. 7 (https://www.legal-tools.org/doc/f53870/); Bergsmo, 2017, p. 22, see above note 27; Vasconcelos, 2017, pp. 894–911, see above note 28. The OTP issued the Regulations *ad interim* as it

> considers that in the elaboration of the final Regulations, it will be indispensable to also take into account the views of the staff members that will be recruited and the experience gained by the Office in its first months of operations. The Office envisages adopting these Regulations during the first semester of 2004.

[33] ICC-OTP, *Strategic Plan June 2012-2015*, 11 October 2013, para. 42 ('OTP Strategic Plan June 2012-2015') (https://www.legal-tools.org/doc/954beb/).

15.4.2. OTP Regulations 2009

In the 2009 OTP Regulations, there is no specific reference to what the Draft Regulations referred to as 'draft investigation plan'. Once an investigation was initiated, a 'joint team', consisting of representatives of the three ICC-OTP divisions (Investigation Division (ID), Prosecution Division (PD), Jurisdiction Cooperation and Complementarity Division (JCCD)), reviewed the information and evidence collected and drafted a provisional 'case hypothesis' or different 'case hypotheses'.[34] The provisional case hypothesis identified incidents to be investigated as well as the person or persons who appeared to be the most responsible. It also included a tentative indication of possible charges, forms of individual criminal responsibility, and potentially exonerating circumstances. In each provisional case hypothesis, the team was supposed to select incidents reflective of the most serious crimes and the main types of victimisation.[35] As to the 'planning of investigative activities', the case team was supposed to "develop an evidence collection plan and a cooperation plan".[36] No further parameters were provided to define the evidence collection plan; in particular there was no reference to the main categories or the anticipated amount of evidence.

15.4.3. OTP Operations Manual 2010 and After

In 2010, the OTP released the first version of its Operations Manual ('OM').[37] This document and subsequent OM versions are internal OTP products and can therefore only be referred to in generic terms. The OM maintains a distinction between a Case Hypothesis document and an Investigation Plan in separate documents.

As for the planning of investigative activities, the OM institutionalised the practice of drafting an investigation plan. The investigation plan as viewed in the OM proposed a strategy for investigative operations and

---

[34] ICC, Regulations of the Office of the Prosecutor, 23 April 2009, ICC-BD/05-01-09, Regulation 34(1) ('Regulations of the Office of the Prosecutor') (https://www.legal-tools.org/doc/a97226/).

[35] *Ibid.*, Regulation 34(2).

[36] *Ibid.*, Regulation 35.

[37] Jens Meierhenrich, "The Evolution of the Office of the Prosecutor at the International Criminal Court: Insights from Institutional Theory", in Martha Minow, C. Cora True-Frost and Alex Whiting (eds.), *The First Global Prosecutor: Promise and Constraints*, University of Michigan Press, Ann Arbor, 2015, pp. 117–24.

took into consideration timelines and the allocation of resources within the team. The investigation plan described the investigative focus as determined in the Case Hypothesis, addressed evidentiary gaps, and included sections on the selection of different types of evidence. The case team was supposed to regularly review the investigation plan in light of the possible elements of the crimes investigated; the quality and quantity of the evidence collected; and exonerating information and likely defence theories.

Since the OM was issued, the OTP has further updated its practices on the management of investigations and the investigation plan. These practices are in the process of being integrated into the OTP's regulatory framework.

The OTP Strategic Plan 2012-2015 changed the overall directions of OTP investigations to the principle of in-depth, open-ended investigations.[38] This new approach to investigations also included a change in investigative strategy and planning; and the development of a new investigation plan template.

15.4.4. Current Practice

The ICC-OTP initially does not focus its activities on a certain structure or even a certain individual, but rather on a specific situation. During the PE phase, the ICC-OTP determines if the Court indeed has jurisdiction over certain crimes; assesses if these crimes are of sufficient gravity; makes sure that no national proceedings are undertaken covering the same crimes; and determines if the investigation would not serve the 'interests of justice'.[39] At the end of this process, as outlined in the Regulations, a preliminary case hypothesis or multiple preliminary case hypotheses are formulated, providing a potential starting point for any subsequent investigation.[40] Morten Bergsmo has argued that a draft investigation plan should be formulated towards the end of the PE; and that the formulation of this investigation plan should actually be one of the major outcomes of the PE. He suggests that the investigation plan should be a dynamic tool, preferably in the form of a digitised knowledge-base, rather than a static,

---

[38] OTP Strategic Plan June 2012-2015, para. 4, see above note 33.

[39] ICC-OTP, *Policy Paper on Preliminary Examinations*, November 2013, pp. 34–70 ('OTP Policy Paper on Preliminary Examinations') (https://www.legal-tools.org/doc/acb906/).

[40] Regulations of the Office of the Prosecutor, Regulation 34, see above note 34.

frozen document.[41] During the PE, the investigative powers of the OTP are rather limited. As the 2013 Policy Paper on PE points out,

> the Office does not enjoy investigative powers, other than for the purpose of receiving testimony at the seat of the Court, and cannot invoke the forms of cooperation specified in Part 9 of the Statute from States. As article 15 sets out, the Office may receive information on alleged crimes and may seek additional information from States, organs of the United Nations, intergovernmental and non-governmental organisations and other reliable sources that are deemed appropriate. Accordingly, the Office can send requests for information to such sources for the purpose of analysing the seriousness of the information received. For this purpose, the Office may also undertake field missions to the territory concerned in order to consult with the competent national authorities, the affected communities and other relevant stakeholders, such as civil society organisations.[42]

Once officially opened, an investigation at the ICC-OTP will develop from investigating a potential case or potential cases within a situation to investigating a defined case or cases.[43] The so-called Basic Size document, drafted by the OTP in 2015 to provide estimates for its required resource capacities, projected for the time from the opening of the investigation until the presentation of a defined case at Confirmation Hearing a period of around three years.[44] This time-estimate presupposes that the investigation progresses in an overall favourable framework, which implies a positive impact of all relevant external factors, in particular cooperation, security and resources.

It is important for investigation plans to refer to the case hypothesis or, at the later stages of the investigation, to the case theory, in particular to identify the areas of the case where the evidence is assessed as weak, and the areas where potentially exonerating material exists. Such gap analysis can be conducted in form of a written narrative, but is also possi-

---

[41] See Bergsmo, 22 February 2019, see above note 2.

[42] OTP Policy Paper on Preliminary Examinations, para. 85, see above note 39.

[43] Carsten Stahn, *A Critical Introduction to International Criminal Law*, Cambridge University Press, Cambridge, 2019, p. 347.

[44] ICC Assembly of States Parties, *Report of the Court on the Basic Size of the Office of the Prosecutor*, 17 September 2015, ICC-ASP/14/21, p. 34 (https://www.legal-tools.org/doc/b27d2a/).

ble in an evaluation matrix or evaluation table, breaking down the case into various required legal elements (that is, contextual elements for war crimes or crimes against humanity; Count 1 murder in location A; Count 2 rape in location B, and so on) and assessing the evidence collected for the different legal elements based on pre-defined criteria. This analysis should lead to a conclusion as to what legal elements would require the collection of additional evidence as a priority and therefore further deserve investigative and analytical attention.

The current practice at the OTP is to have an investigation plan written, reviewed and approved for every active investigation case. The completion of an investigation plan is one of the quality performance indicators of OTP investigations. More generally, the ICC-OTP is in the process of developing a quality assurance system at various stages of the proceedings. According to its most recent Strategic Plan, the ICC-OTP "will strengthen and refine its quality control mechanisms to ensure that all critical decisions and activities are consistently taken and properly conducted".[45] This includes a regular review of standards and practices; employing the right resources in terms of quality and quantity; and by reinforcing mechanisms to ensure that the actual collection and analysis of evidence is done thoroughly, including through the review of investigation plans.[46]

At present time, the case team drafts an investigation plan once a year; with an interim update after six months. The plan is written in a narrative form, and its structure roughly follows the template as outlined in Section 15.2.5. above. In this concept, regularly drafted investigation plans are written like different chapters of a book, providing the complete history of an investigation. An alternative way could be to conceptualise the investigation plan in a knowledge-base format, which, as one single inter-linked document, has a continuous existence and is designed as a living and growing instrument that follows the entire investigation and case preparation stage.[47]

While defining the investigation strategy, a case team at the ICC-OTP will give consideration to the following issues:

---

[45] ICC-OTP, *Strategic Plan 2019-2021*, 17 July 2019, para. 14 ('OTP Strategic Plan 2019-2021') (https://www.legal-tools.org/doc/7ncqt3/).
[46] *Ibid.*, para. 17.
[47] See Bergsmo, 22 February 2019, see above note 2.

- The requirement of an open-ended investigation;[48]

- A building-up target strategy that may consider charging mid-level perpetrators first before reaching those at the highest level of responsibility;[49]

- The OTP policy papers on SGBC and children and how the investigation strategy proactively reflects them;[50]

- Financial investigations – both for obtaining evidence on crimes and in relation to asset tracing of identified suspects;

- An investigation feasibility assessment conducted in the transition from the PE to the investigation phase and mapping out the following: general evidence collection opportunities and obstacles; co-operation issues; and a concept of operations, including the possibility of a permanent field presence of investigators.

In the office-internal process, the plan is reviewed in various steps, which ensures another quality-control layer: a) first by the case team internally; b) then peer-reviewed at Investigation Division management level in order to benefit from ideas that have worked in other cases and to ensure compliance with the investigative standards, policies and rules as developed by the Office; and c) finally discussed with and approved by senior management. This process is in line with the ICTY Manual recommendation that there should be "a careful and comprehensive review of the plan", both at the peer level and at senior management level.[51]

In the practice of the ICC-OTP, investigation plans are drafted in co-ordination with other internal plans relevant to the investigation, such as the co-operation plan and the relevant security and operational risk assessments. In a best-case scenario, the investigation plan identifies the relevant requirements; and the corresponding plans explain how these requirements can be met.

---

[48] OTP Strategic Plan June 2012-2015, para. 4, see above note 33.

[49] *Ibid.*; OTP Strategic Plan 2019-2021, para. 24, see above note 45.

[50] ICC-OTP, *Policy Paper on Sexual and Gender-Based Crimes*, 20 June 2014 (https://www. legal-tools.org/doc/7ede6c/); ICC-OTP, *Policy on Children*, 15 November 2016 (https:// www.legal-tools.org/doc/c2652b/).

[51] ICTY Manual, p. 32, see above note 6. At the ICTY, senior management approval was deemed especially important, as many investigations overlapped, which might result in conflicting priorities between different investigation teams. As cases are more separate from one another, this inherent conflict is less pronounced at the ICC-OTP.

More recently, the ICC-OTP has focused on a further integration between the PE and the investigation phase of a case. In 2015, the ICC-OTP emphasised that "it will look for ways to further integrate its preliminary examinations work into its pre-investigative planning",[52] for instance by ensuring the preservation of evidence as a 'critical challenge'.[53] The most recent OTP Strategic Plan pledged to further "explore synergies between preliminary examinations and investigations"[54] and to continue to dedicate efforts to the issue:

> Work is already underway to see how to increase the speed of the investigations through a better integration between the phase of preliminary examination and investigations with regard to (1) preservation of evidence; (2) earlier start of the planning (including, *inter alia*, identification of staff profiles requirements, specific language support, security and logistics needs), and (3) better integration of the work products and resources from the preliminary examination into the investigation.[55]

In this respect, the Prosecutor follows recommendations as provided by Pre-Trial Chamber III to broaden OTP activities prior to the official authorisation of an investigation, as the Office may take

> meaningful steps to protect victims and (potential) witnesses, [...] may receive written or oral testimony at the seat of the Court at this stage and may even, under rule 47 of the Rules, request the Pre-Trial Chamber to take measures as may be necessary to ensure the efficiency and integrity of the proceedings.[56]

While the investigation plan fulfils an important role within the investigation cycle, it does not stand in isolation, as it also serves as the overarching umbrella to reason individual investigative activities initiated

---

[52] ICC-OTP, *Strategic Plan 2016-2018*, 16 November 2015, para. 55 (https://www.legal-tools.org/doc/2dbc2d/).

[53] *Ibid.*, para. 104.

[54] OTP Strategic Plan 2019-2021, para. 2, see above note 45.

[55] *Ibid.*, para. 26.

[56] ICC, Situation in the Republic of Burundi, Pre-Trial Chamber, Public Redacted Version of "Decision Pursuant to Article 15 of the Rome Statute on the Authorization of an Investigation into the Situation in the Republic of Burundi", ICC-01/17-X-9-US-Exp, 25 October 2017, 9 November 2017, ICC-01/17-9-Red, para. 15 (https://www.legal-tools.org/doc/8f2373/).

to comply with the overall investigative strategy and objectives. These activities are captured in an Investigation Management System ('IMS'). The IMS breaks down activities in individual tasks; assigns resources and timelines to the task; documents individual investigative steps taken; and reports back on the completion of the task. The inputting into the IMS needs to follow a coherent protocol and is therefore (as data-entry into databases in general) an aspect that needs attention in terms of quality control. If the inputting is done with the requisite level of detail, accurateness and consistency, compliance rates in the system will provide a more tactical view on the progress of the investigation. The system, however, presupposes that the original tasking is done in line with the appropriate strategic directions to advance the case.

15.5. Conclusions

As a summary of this chapter, the following conclusions can be drawn, both in terms of the use of investigation plans in international criminal investigations as in relation to the regulatory framework, and the past and current practice at the ICC-OTP:

1. Based on an analysis of different manuals and templates for international criminal investigations, an investigation plan is structured into common main components and fulfils at least three main functions (planning – reporting – management). The plan best complies with its role as a quality-control tool if all functions are adequately taken care of.

2. Investigation plans are one important tool in the process of the investigation cycle. They are complemented by a legal case assessment, an investigation management system, and a Fact Analysis Database (FAD).

3. Investigation plans are most effective when aligned with the legal case assessment, in order to make sure that investigative strategy, objectives and activities directly respond to identified legal requirements and in order to allow for targeted and properly prioritised collection.

4. Investigation plans are an important contribution to maintain an overview of information – primarily in terms of capturing investigative strategies and decisions; and in creating an historical record for the investigation.

5. The investigation management system provides an overview of the progress of the investigation on a more tactical level and, with that caveat, is able to serve as a quality-control tool for assessing pace and task-compliance within the established investigative framework.

6. The regulatory framework at the ICC-OTP officially established investigation plans in 2009, with further upgrades and amendments implemented since. The ICC-OTP currently focuses on a stronger integration between the PE and the investigation/prosecution phase of a case.

7. Investigation plans at the ICC-OTP are written for every active investigation in a narrative form once a year with an update every six months. They are peer reviewed as well as reviewed by senior management.

This chapter has examined the role of investigation plans as an investigation management tool and as a quality-control tool in international criminal investigations. It has come to the conclusion that such plans, if properly applied, can contribute to overcoming some of the bottlenecks identified in the CILRAP concept paper, in particular 'overview of information', 'evidence review' and 'too much evidence'.

16

Investigation Plans in the Draft Regulations of the ICC Office of the Prosecutor: An Italian Perspective

Antonio Angotti[*]

16.1. Introduction

Investigation plans should serve as instruments of quality control, particularly when designed to enhance oversight capacity, monitoring and strategy. International criminal jurisdictions share some needs with domestic jurisdictions dealing with fact-rich criminal cases such as core international crimes cases. This chapter provides an analysis of the first example of investigation plans in the framework of the International Criminal Court ('ICC'), and compares that with related initiatives within the Italian legal system. The resulting considerations should shed new light on the needs addressed by investigation plans, when compared with alternative tools, with special attention being paid to policy concerns that shape the content of both.

16.2. The Draft Regulations

16.2.1. The Making of the Draft Regulations

The process to establish the ICC Office of the Prosecutor ('OTP' or 'Office') benefitted from contributions by more than 100 experts through several expert consultation processes. In March 2003, in the spirit of Rule 9 of the ICC Rules of Procedure and Evidence,[1] a group of legal experts joined forces with the preparatory team for the OTP to draft a set of regulations aimed at tackling several issues that the Office would likely face

---

[*] **Antonio Angotti** is an Attorney in Florence, Italy, and a Fellow at the Centre for International Law Research and Policy (CILRAP). He holds a law degree from the University of Florence and an LL.M. from Pennsylvania State University's Dickinson School of Law.

[1] International Criminal Court, Rules of Procedure and Evidence, 9 September 2002 (https://www.legal-tools.org/doc/e1b3f5/).

from its initial phase. The co-ordinator of the group was Morten Bergsmo, co-editor of this volume, who initiated the expert consultations and designed the mandate of each. The work of the group of experts on the Draft Regulations addressed several carefully selected topics,[2] including a Code of Conduct for the Office of the Prosecutor;[3] it elaborated internal procedural guidelines for the management of preliminary examinations and investigations, in particular the critical decision-making process to open an investigation; the rational management of evidence; and the training of involved personnel. While the reception of the Draft Regulations was exceptionally positive,[4] the first ICC Prosecutor only adopted parts of them *ad interim*. As described in Chapter 15 above, the practice of the OTP under the first and the second Prosecutors has evolved and come to deviate in some respects from the original Draft Regulations.[5] Regardless, this tentative chapter is written under the premise that the Draft Regulations contain procedural and substantial insights that should be fully harnessed, also for the benefit of domestic war crimes investigation and prosecution programmes.

The Draft Regulations were drawn up by a group of five legal experts: Tor-Aksel Busch (Norway), Michael Grotz (Germany), Nobuo Hayashi (Japan), Peter Lewis (United Kingdom), and Carlos Vasconcelos (Brazil). Tor-Aksel Busch was Norway's Director-General of Public Prosecutions and the country's most highly-respected prosecutor. He had professional experience as a prosecutor and judge, and extensive expertise on prosecutions.[6] Michael Grotz was one of Germany's most experienced

---

[2] The text of the ICC-OTP Draft Regulations is annexed to Carlos Vasconcelos, "Draft Regulations of the Office of the Prosecutor", in Morten Bergsmo, Klaus Rackwitz and SONG Tianying (eds.), *Historical Origins of International Criminal Law: Volume 5*, Torkel Opsahl Academic EPublisher, Brussels, 2017, pp. 834–93 ('Draft Regulations') (https://www.legal-tools.org/doc/09c8b8/). The references in this chapter pertain to Book 3 of the Draft Regulations, the Operations Manual. Vasconcelos' chapter is the leading publication on the Draft Regulations.

[3] Salim A. Nakhjavani, "The Origins and Development of the Code of Conduct", in *ibid.*, pp. 964–77.

[4] Vasconcelos, 2017, p. 804, see above note 2.

[5] Benjamin N. Schiff, *Building the International Criminal Court*, Cambridge University Press, 2012, pp. 110–15. Chapter 15 by Markus Eikel provides an overview of ICC-OTP practices, with specific regards to investigation plans as management tools.

[6] Government of Norway, "Tor-Aksel Busch ny Riksadvokat", 22 August 1997 (available on the Government of Norway's web site).

prosecutors, who had served in the Federal Ministry of Justice in various sections, and had experience in negotiations and international organisations.[7] At the time of the Draft Regulations, he was the Chairperson of the European Committee on Crime Problems of the Council of Europe.[8] Nobuo Hayashi was a Legal Officer of the Office of the Prosecutor of the International Criminal Tribunal for the former Yugoslavia ('ICTY'), where he was a leading expert on international humanitarian law and war crimes.[9] Peter Lewis was one of the leaders of the Crown Prosecution Service of England and Wales, who had been a prominent United Kingdom delegate to the Preparatory Commission for the Rules of Procedure and Evidence of the ICC.[10] He currently serves as the ICC Registrar. Carlos Vasconcelos had served as General Prosecutor in Brazil and Senior Judicial Affairs Officer at the United Nations ('UN') Transitional Administration in East Timor where he had experience with core international crimes cases. He went on to become Associate Federal Prosecutor-General in Brazil.[11]

Appropriately, prosecutorial professionalism and practical experience appear to have been prioritised in the composition of the group. As a result, the Draft Regulations adopted a strategic approach to facilitate oversight and quality control in complex prosecutorial bodies.

16.2.2. Investigative Guidelines in the Draft Regulations

The guidelines for investigations designed by the Draft Regulations revolve around three main "essential management tools to ensure focused and professional investigations",[12] namely a draft charges document, a proof chart, and an investigation plan.[13] Due to the open-ended nature of

---

[7] Curricula Vitae of Candidates Nominated by States Members of the United Nations and by Non-member States Maintaining Permanent Observer Missions at United Nations Headquarters, UN Doc. A/55/919, 27 April 2001, pp. 54–55.

[8] Council of Europe, *European Committee on Crime Problems: Abridged Report of the 48th Meeting (Strasbourg, 7-11 June 1999)*, 2 August 1999, CM(99)118, para. 2.

[9] See Nobuo Hayashi's *Curriculum Vitae* (available on the International Law and Policy Institute's web site).

[10] See Peter Lewis' *Curriculum Vitae* (available on the ICC's web site).

[11] See Carlos Vasconcelos' *Curriculum Vitae* (available at the time of writing on LinkedIn's web site).

[12] Draft Regulations, Book 3, Regulation 19, p. 869, see above note 2.

[13] *Ibid.*, Regulations 20–22, pp. 869–71.

criminal inquiries, each tool is updated to reflect the progress of the investigation and to plan ahead, anticipating a number of assessments (Draft Regulation ('DR') 19). None of the tools were seen as static or frozen in time.

In the Draft Regulations model, the draft investigation plan is situated at the crossroads between the preliminary examination phase and the investigation:[14] in fact, the decision on whether to open an investigation cannot be taken without due consideration having been given to the draft investigation plan.[15] Moving to open an ICC investigation has such significant economic and other consequences that such a decision should only be made after careful reflection involving the entire OTP senior management. If an investigation is initiated, the draft plan converges into a dynamic investigation plan, and later provides the grounds for the draft charges document (DR 20.1.).

The draft charges document draws on the results of the preliminary examination, the investigation plan, and the on-going investigation. The proof chart gives an overview of the evidence collected that proves the elements of the suspected crimes and their modes of liability, informing the draft charges document (DR 22.2.). The proof chart organises the available evidence; however, its structure should also receive guidance from the dynamic investigation plan. It is important to emphasise that the investigation plan, as the other two documents, was not designed to be static; the Draft Regulations provide for its continuous update as the investigation progresses. Rather than steering the investigation, the plan is meant to adapt to the results of the steps that have already been completed.

The Draft Regulations modelled two separate paths for *proprio motu* investigations and referrals from the United Nations Security Council ('UNSC') or States Parties. The Deputy Prosecutor in charge of investigations is ultimately responsible for preliminary examinations (DR 4.1.). In *proprio motu* proceedings, once the preliminary examinations team in charge of a specific situation has completed the assessments required by Draft Regulation 4.5.,[16] it will forward a final report to the Deputy Prosecutors in charge of investigations and prosecutions along with a reasoned recommendation on further action (DR 6.1.). Following these steps, the

---

[14]   *Ibid.*, Regulation 12.1., p. 865.

[15]   *Ibid.*, Regulations 6.3., 12.1, pp. 859, 865.

[16]   *Ibid.*, Regulation 4.5., p. 859.

two Deputy Prosecutors must consider whether the situation merits an investigation (DR 6.4.). In case of disagreement, the decision to move forward is left to the chief Prosecutor. If the Deputy Prosecutors agree that a situation does merit an investigation, then a draft investigation plan is set up under the supervision of the Deputy Prosecutor in charge of prosecutions (DR 6.3.).

The Draft Regulations provided a separate path for determining whether the OTP should open an investigation in case of referrals by States Parties or the UNSC (DR 7.-11.). The draft investigation plan, however, is always balancing between preliminary examinations and the investigation phase. After receiving a referral, the Prosecutor mandates an evaluation team whose composition represents investigations, prosecutions, analysis, and legal advisory and policy.[17] The report of the evaluation team partially mirrors the work of the preliminary examinations team described above: accordingly, the report will assess whether the situation merits an investigation (DR 11.1.-11.4.). In such case, a senior prosecutor will likewise oversee the draft investigation plan. Initially, the draft investigation plan is grounded in the information gathered during the evaluation of the situation.

In both *proprio motu* and referred situations, the draft investigation plan and the report by the preliminary examination/evaluation team are submitted to the Prosecutor along with a reasoned recommendation.[18] If an investigation is initiated, the draft evolves into the investigation plan proper, a strategic management tool to plan and prepare for the foreseeable steps of the investigation.

It should be noted that the team in charge of preparing the investigation plan is composed by the team that oversaw the draft, including members of the Investigation and Prosecution Divisions and one Legal Advisor; a senior prosecutor supervises the drafting.[19] The same team will recommend whether the Prosecutor should start an investigation, and is mandated by Draft Regulation 6.7. to pay "specific attention to the interests of justice as specified by Article 53(1) and Rule 48".[20] This seeks to promote broad involvement of the Office in the evaluation, providing the

---

[17] *Ibid.*, Regulation 9.1., p. 863.
[18] *Ibid.*, Regulation 6.7., p. 862.
[19] *Ibid.*, Regulation 6.3., p. 859.
[20] *Ibid.*, Regulation 6.7., p. 862.

Prosecutor with requisite insights and counsel on a delicate policy question.

The current practice of the ICC-OTP includes many of the assessments underlying the Draft Regulations, as explained by Markus Eikel in Chapter 15 above, and is gradually being developed in light of the Office's growing experience. Still, the model designed by the Draft Regulations stands out for the inclusive involvement of high-level OTP staff from different areas in the preparation of the draft investigation plan, the centrality of such tool, and its early adoption: "no decision [to start or not to start an investigation] is to be taken without prior establishment of a draft investigation plan" (DR 12.1.).

16.2.3. The Content of the Investigation Plan

The substance of the investigation plan as foreseen by the Draft Regulations is a list of assessments that, if duly anticipated and considered, aims to avoid several bottlenecks that affect past and present investigations of core international crimes.[21] The content of the draft investigation plan is listed in Draft Regulation 6.5. of Book 3.[22] The same provision is referred to for the content of the investigation plan proper, given that it will be a continuation of the draft (DR 20.1.).

Firstly, the Draft Regulations require an early evaluation of "whether there is a reasonable basis to believe that a crime within the jurisdiction of the Court has been or is being committed",[23] together with the background and the context of the situation.[24] The investigation plan further requires the Office to identify "the crime base incidents to be investigated and a description of likely suspects, together with the overall aim of the

---

[21] The terminology used in this chapter explicitly refers to Morten Bergsmo, "Towards a Culture of Quality Control in Criminal Investigations", FICHL Policy Brief Series No. 94 (2019), Torkel Opsahl Academic EPublisher, Brussels, 2019 (http://www.toaep.org/pbs-pdf/94-bergsmo). The Quality Control in Criminal Investigations Project defined seven particularly problematic bottlenecks: overview of information, factual analysis, evidence review, formulation of responsibility, cumulative charging, too much evidence, and disclosure. See also Morten Bergsmo, "Rethinking Instruments of Quality Control in the Investigation and Preparation of Core International Crimes Cases", CILRAP Film, New Delhi, 23 February 2019 (http://www.cilrap.org/cilrap-film/190222-bergsmo/).

[22] Draft Regulations, Book 3, Regulation 6.5., p. 861, see above note 2.

[23] *Ibid.*, Regulation 6.5.(a).

[24] *Ibid.*, Regulation 6.5.(b).

---

investigation".[25] Such provisions are aimed to outline the scope of the investigation and facilitate the overview of information, providing an established framework for factual analysis that is shared by the Office. Interestingly, the OTP is required to assess "the overall aim of the investigation" before its inception, fostering co-ordination among all the teams that will work on the case (DR 6.5.(d)).

Likewise, "the role and place of [the] likely suspects in the relevant chains of authority" must be explained from the outset.[26] Investigators and prosecutors draw, from the beginning of the investigation, a tentative and continuously updated structure for criminal responsibility. Requiring such evaluation this early expresses the relevance of such structure, aimed to prevent oversights in the formulation of responsibility, as the main connections of responsibility that need to be proven are clarified. The makers of the Draft Regulations realised that proving chains of responsibility is difficult, and therefore decided to facilitate leadership analysis. An incisive, evidence-based understanding of the power structure in a situation is indispensable in order to outline the chain of command that allegedly led to the crimes, and it depends on the proper direction of analysis expertise.[27]

A crucial provision of the Draft Regulations investigation plan requires the "preliminary indication of the main categories of and the amount of evidence that is likely to be required to prove the possible charges".[28] Given that the possible charges are grounded in alleged facts, requiring an early assessment of how such charges can be proven may instil the investigation with a sense of realism to steer clear of unsubstantiated charges. Insufficient evidence review can lead to evidence that is duly submitted but left disconnected from the charges.[29] Arguably, linking

---

[25] *Ibid.*, Regulation 6.5.(d).

[26] *Ibid.*, Regulation 6.5.(f).

[27] A tentative structure of the relevant chains of authority would likely constitute proper direction for the work of leadership analysts. See Christian A. Nielsen, "Leadership Analysis in International Criminal Justice", in Adejoké Babington-Ashaye, Aimée Comrie and Akingbolahan Adeniran (eds.), *International Criminal Investigations Law and Practice*, Eleven International Publishing, The Hague, 2018, p. 211. See also Christian Axboe Nielsen, "Analysis of Organisational Structures and Quality Control of Case Development", CILRAP Film, New Delhi, 22 February 2019 (www.cilrap.org/cilrap-film/190222-nielsen/).

[28] Draft Regulations, Book 3, Regulation 6.5.(j), p. 861, see above note 2.

[29] See ICC, Situation in the Central African Republic, *Prosecutor v. Jean-Pierre Bemba Gombo*, Pre-Trial Chamber, Decision Pursuant to Article 61(7)(a) and (b) of the Rome

investigative activities to the on-going assessment of evidence contributes to a more effective factual analysis and enables a constant evidence review, preventing possible issues in the trial phase, including the abundance of evidence which results in lengthier and costlier proceedings.[30] The case history of the ICC provides some insight on how relevant rigorous evidence review is. Inadequate review of available evidence has troubled the work of the OTP since the Kenyatta case, as Judge van den Wyngaert noted in her concurring opinion,[31] while conceding that it was far from being the only influencing factor.[32] The Trial Chamber itself noted "the failure on the part of the Prosecution to take appropriate steps to verify the credibility and reliability of evidence on which it intended to rely at trial"[33] as one of the many reasons for the outcome of the case. The lack of clear correspondence between factual findings and actual evidence was arguably among the issues[34] in the Bemba Conviction Decision that was overturned by the Appeals Chamber.[35] With regards to the Gbagbo case, reviewing the investigative results for each charge could have contributed to avoiding the overuse of hearsay or NGO reports among the evidence relied upon by the Prosecutor,[36] deemed "exceptionally weak"

Statute on the Charges of the Prosecutor, Decision, 15 June 2009, ICC-01/05-01/08-424 (https://www.legal-tools.org/doc/07965c/).

[30] Rupert Skillbeck, "Funding Justice: The Price of War Crimes Trials", in *Human Rights Brief*, 2008, vol. 15, no. 3, p. 1.

[31] ICC, Situation in the Republic of Kenya, *Prosecutor v. Uhuru Muigai Kenyatta*, Trial Chamber, Concurring Opinion of Judge Christine van den Wyngaert, 26 April 2013, ICC-01/09-02/11-728-Anx2, para. 4 (https://www.legal-tools.org/doc/917ec7/).

[32] *Ibid.*, para. 6.

[33] ICC, Situation in the Republic of Kenya, *Prosecutor v. Uhuru Muigai Kenyatta*, Trial Chamber, Decision on Prosecution's Application for a Further Adjournment, 3 December 2014, ICC-01/09-02/11-981, para. 52 (https://www.legal-tools.org/doc/731d89/).

[34] ICC, Situation in the Central African Republic, *Prosecutor v. Jean-Pierre Bemba Gombo*, Appeals Chamber, Separate Opinion of Judge Christine van den Wyngaert and Judge Howard Morrison, 8 June 2018, ICC-01/05-01/08-3636-Anx2, paras. 10, 12, 50, 64 (https://www.legal-tools.org/doc/c13ef4/).

[35] ICC, Situation in the Central African Republic, *Prosecutor v. Jean-Pierre Bemba Gombo*, Appeals Chamber, Judgment on the Appeal of Mr Jean-Pierre Bemba Gombo against Trial Chamber III's "Judgment pursuant to Article 74 of the Statute", 8 June 2018, ICC-01/05-01/08-3636-Red (https://www.legal-tools.org/doc/40d35b/).

[36] ICC, Situation in the Republic of Côte d'Ivoire, *Prosecutor v. Laurent Gbagbo and Charles Blé Goudé*, Pre-Trial Chamber, Decision adjourning the hearing on the confirmation of charges pursuant to Article 61(7)(c)(i) of the Rome Statute, 3 June 2013, ICC-02/11-01/11-432, para. 35 (https://www.legal-tools.org/doc/2682d8/).

by the Trial Chamber.[37] It may certainly be said, as it has,[38] that some of the acquittals express more complex issues; however, it is also clear that inadequate evidence review has been a crucial factor in more than one instance. Furthermore, knowing in advance which kind of evidence is needed can greatly facilitate meeting evidentiary thresholds, and fosters co-ordination among investigators and prosecutors – a recurring theme in the model foreseen by the Draft Regulations.

Policy concerns find their place in the investigation plan, as the drafters required the prosecution to provide "an explanation of how the investigation and prosecution of the alleged crimes or perpetrators is expected to fit in with the broader context of cases pursued by the Office",[39] and the reasons "why the alleged offences warrant a full investigation against the backdrop of other alleged offences where such a step might not be recommendable".[40] The view of the makers of the Draft Regulations was that a clear prosecutorial policy would be beneficial for the work of the Office. Accordingly, they required the investigation plan to provide the rationale for case selection and prioritisation. The latest OTP policy paper on the issue was published in 2016:[41] interestingly, it mandated the adoption of a Case Selection Document based on the conclusions of the preliminary examination phase,[42] similarly to what the draft investigation plan foreseen by the expert group in 2003 required. The benefits of formulating an advance assessment on case selection and prioritisation are beyond discussion, and are partially covered elsewhere in this anthology.[43]

---

[37] ICC, Situation in the Republic of Côte d'Ivoire, *Prosecutor v. Laurent Gbagbo and Charles Blé Goudé*, Trial Chamber, Transcript, 16 January 2019, ICC-02/11-01/15-T-234-ENG, p. 4 (https://www.legal-tools.org/doc/496176/).

[38] William H. Wiley, "Incisive Hypotheses on Criminal Responsibility in Team Environments", CILRAP Film, New Delhi, 22 February 2019 (www.cilrap.org/cilrap-film/190222-wiley/).

[39] Draft Regulations, Book 3, Regulation 6.5.(l), p. 861, see above note 2.

[40] *Ibid.*, Regulation 6.5.(c).

[41] ICC-OTP, *Policy Paper on Case Selection and Prioritisation*, 15 September 2016 (https://www.legal-tools.org/doc/182205/).

[42] *Ibid.*, p. 5.

[43] See Devasheesh Bais, "Prioritisation of Suspected Conduct and Cases: From Idea to Practice", CILRAP Film, New Delhi, 22 February 2019 (www.cilrap.org/cilrap-film/190222-bais/), and his Chapter 9 above.

Draft Regulation 6.5. requires the OTP to formulate "a tentative indication of possible charges, modes of liability and potential defences".[44] The assessment will be updated as the investigation progresses, and ensures that investigative activities remain directed towards the trial phase. Both aspects are crucial to avoid target-driven investigations: investigative results and accusatory hypotheses should be allowed to inform each other, if the aim of the system is to do justice rather than meeting a target.[45] Such indication requires investigators to ensure that the results of their work speak to the charges that will later be discussed in Court, and to perform evidence review for each allegation from an initial stage. Finally, the provision implies an early thinking-process about possible charges which, as it matures, may guide – and simultaneously be shaped by – the sharpness of the focus of the investigation. The process of articulating and discussing possible charges guides fact-finders and -reviewers towards constantly asking questions that are relevant to formulating tentative charging hypotheses, by that aiding clarity about the emerging theory of responsibility, thus reducing the reliance on broad indictments as a veil concealing lack of clarity of analysis.[46] This is also in the interest of the defence. Thinking about possible charges while the investigation is ongoing and upholding the requirement of an updated formulation within the investigation plan may limit the use of cumulative charging, avoiding undue burdening of the defence and the trial process.[47]

The Draft Regulations mandated several assessments that are more focused on the practical aspects of investigations and prosecutions. For instance, the likelihood of arresting the suspects is tentatively evaluated

---

[44] Draft Regulations, Book 3, Regulation 6.5.(e), p. 861, see above note 2.

[45] On the issues related to target-driven investigations, see Morten Bergsmo and William H. Wiley, "Human Rights Professionals and the Criminal Investigation and Prosecution of Core International Crimes", in Siri Skåre, Ingvild Burkey and Hege Mørk (eds.), *Manual on Human Rights Monitoring: An Introduction for Human Rights Field Officers*, Norwegian Centre for Human Rights, Oslo, 2008, p. 8 (https://www.legal-tools.org/doc/8362d5/).

[46] See ICC, Situation in the Republic of Kenya, *Prosecutor v. Ruto et al.*, Pre-Trial Chamber, Decision on the Confirmation of Charges Pursuant to Article 61(7)(a) and (b) of the Rome Statute, 23 January 2012, ICC-01/09-01/11-373, para. 99 (https://www.legal-tools.org/doc/96c3c2/).

[47] See ICC, Situation in the Central African Republic, *Prosecutor v. Jean-Pierre Bemba Gombo*, Pre-Trial Chamber, Decision on the Prosecutor's Application for a Warrant of Arrest, 10 June 2008, ICC-01/05-01/08-14-tENG, para. 25 (https://www.legal-tools.org/doc/fb80c6/).

before the decision on whether to open an investigation is taken.[48] Given the relevancy of this issue, among the most visible in the context of international justice and the ICC specifically,[49] it deserves consideration from the early stages of the process.

Other required evaluations include issues of "State co-operation and security",[50] and the "assessment of the admissibility of a possible case under Article 17 of the Statute":[51] complementarity, including the evaluation of the genuineness of the will and ability to prosecute through national proceedings, *ne bis in idem*, and the 'sufficient gravity' threshold. The three provisions project the investigation to the next phase, and potentially reduce resource-intensive efforts with little value. If issues of State co-operation or suspect apprehension are foreseeable, the Office should consider this in the planning. Article 17 assessments, if timely, may likewise prevent unfruitful action.

Importantly, the fourth provision on practical matters requires the Office to estimate the foreseeable costs in term of resources and staff.[52] The budget of the Court is finite, and does not allow for limitless investigations; a mismanaged resource-intensive investigation might prejudice the results of another. In order to prevent this scenario, the drafters of the Draft Regulations required the Office to plan its involvement ahead, with a view to reducing overall expenditure and promoting efficiency. In this regard, and notwithstanding any controversy, is it appropriate to mention the Decision of Pre-Trial Chamber II of the ICC on the Afghanistan situation, according to which the foreseeable scarcity of resources plays a relevant role in the evaluation of the interests of justice.[53] Accordingly, the

---

[48] Draft Regulations, Book 3, Regulation 6.5.(g): "The whereabouts, if known, of the possible suspects and the likelihood to arrest them", p. 861, see above note 2.

[49] David Scheffer, "Proposal for an International Criminal Court Arrest Procedures Protocol", in *Northwestern Journal of International Human Rights*, 2014, vol. 12, no. 3, p. 229.

[50] Draft Regulations, Book 3, Regulation 6.5.(k), p. 861, see above note 2.

[51] *Ibid.*, Regulation 6.5.(h): "An assessment of the admissibility of a possible case under Article 17 of the Statute".

[52] *Ibid.*, Regulation 6.5.(i): "A preliminary indication of resources, time and staff likely to be required to complete the investigation".

[53] ICC, Situation in the Islamic Republic of Afghanistan, Pre-Trial Chamber, Decision Pursuant to Article 15 of the Rome Statute on the Authorisation of an Investigation, 12 April 2019, ICC-02/17-33, para. 95 ('Afghanistan Pre-Trial Decision') (https://www.legal-tools.org/doc/2fb1f4/).

current practice at the OTP outlined in Chapter 15 pays specific regards to resource management.

The investigation plan model of the Draft Regulations further includes a specific evaluation of "potential dangers to the integrity of the investigation or the life or well-being of victims and witnesses that could arise once the victims are informed of the intention of the Chief Prosecutor to seek authorisation"[54] to initiate an investigation pursuant to Article 15(3) of the Rome Statute. Witness interference is unfortunately common within ICC cases,[55] and has been crucial to the outcome of some proceedings.[56] A dedicated assessment might facilitate upholding Article 68(1) of the Rome Statute on the protection of witness and victims.

Finally, the draft investigation plan allows the inclusion of relevant information that does not fit in the categories discussed above, namely "any other matter that may be of relevance for a decision to start an investigation in the light of the specific situation".[57] The provision is meant for the draft investigation plan only, since the document is relevant for the decision to open an investigation. It is noteworthy that the Draft Regulations encourage the investigation and prosecution teams to express their concerns or policy-related advice with the inclusion of a dedicated entry in the investigation plan. By doing so, one could argue, the decision to start an investigation would involve key actors of the Office of the Prosecutor to a significant degree.

16.2.4. An Overall Assessment of the Draft Regulations' Approach to Investigation Plans

It is beyond argument that investigation plans are significantly beneficial for investigations of core international crimes and fact-rich criminal cases. As mentioned in Chapter 15 above, the ICC institutionalised the use of such plans in 2010. The Draft Regulations chose to anticipate many inves-

---

[54] Draft Regulations, Book 3, Regulation 6.5.(m): "Potential dangers to the integrity of the investigation or the life or well-being of victims and witnesses that could arise once the victims are informed of the intention of the Chief Prosecutor to seek authorisation, in accordance with Rule 50(1) of the Rules of Procedure and Evidence", p. 861, see above note 2.

[55] Open Society Justice Initiative, "Witness Interference in Cases before the International Criminal Court" (available on the Open Society's web site).

[56] See Afghanistan Pre-Trial Decision, para. 95, see above note 53.

[57] Draft Regulations, Book 3, Regulation 6.5.(n), p. 862, see above note 2.

---

tigative assessments, requiring them to be formulated before a decision to open an investigation is finally taken. They gather from past experiences of international criminal justice. In doing so, the Draft Regulations chose to involve some of the highest ranked professionals in the OTP.

By way of example, the six-year younger ICTY Manual on Developed Practices ('ICTY Manual') from 2009 includes a model investigation plan which should likewise be adopted "prior to commencing any significant investigative activity",[58] and has several points in common with Draft Regulation 6.5. The ICTY Manual investigation plan is explicitly aimed to link the lines of enquiry with the foreseeable evidentiary results, promoting constant evidence review; the plan requires an estimate of the resources and time that will likely be employed, and specifically includes assessments of the background of the crimes and the alleged offenders; the "charging theory and the characterization of the crimes", the position and the authority of the alleged perpetrators.[59] The ICTY Manual provides the requirement of an on-going review of the results of the investigations and a series of evidence-specific assessments with regards to the required categorisation of the foreseeable "avenues of investigation".[60]

The investigation plan provided by the ICC-OTP Draft Regulations follows a different approach and considers a number of aspects which add to the wisdom distilled in light of the practice at the ICTY. For instance, the ICTY Manual investigation plan does not require policy assessments and statements – which is likely due to the inherent differences among the mandates of the ICTY and the ICC – but both investigation plans include the explanation of the aim of an investigation. The Draft Regulations investigation plan, however, brings the formulation of a 'charging theory' a step forward, requiring a tentative draft indictment. Likewise, assessing the position and the authority of the individual alleged perpetrators, as was the ICTY practice, is conceptually different from the Draft Regulations' requirement of formulating "the role and place of these likely suspects in the relevant chains of authority"[61] and, as such, the latter arguably

---

[58]   ICTY and United Nations Interregional Crime and Justice Research Institute ('UNICRI'), *ICTY Manual on Developed Practices*, UNICRI Publisher, Turin, 2009, p. 30 (https://www.legal-tools.org/doc/0cc55d).

[59]   *Ibid.*, p. 14.

[60]   *Ibid.*, p. 30.

[61]   Draft Regulations, Book 3, Regulation 6.5.(f), p. 861, see above note 2.

enables leadership-analysis to a greater extent. Regarding evidence, the ICTY Manual is remarkably hands-on and practically useful, since it requires assessments of the foreseeable categories of evidence (in terms of potential witnesses, physical evidence, and documentary evidence) for each investigative avenue.[62] The Draft Regulations further add the required assessment of the likely amount of evidence that is directly linked to proving the possible charges. Finally, it can be argued that the inclusion of mandatory evaluations of the potential dangers to victims, witnesses, and to the integrity of the investigation would benefit the ICTY Manual investigation plan; the same could be said for the pre-emptive assessment of foreseeable issues of State co-operation as well. Chapter 15 outlines how the ICC is learning from the practice of the past tribunals, as similar assessments are conducted albeit with other tools that are distinct from investigation plans.

The Draft Regulations were composed in 2003. Subsequent developments in the field of international justice may suggest the inclusion of additional assessments or strategic choices. For instance, a planning tool for tackling the issue of disclosure could certainly find its place within the provisions of Draft Regulation 6.5. (see Chapter 14 above by David Re). Nevertheless, the content foreseen by the expert group in 2003 still has high relevancy in light of the lessons learned during the first 17 years of the ICC. Arguably, the guidelines on the timing of the formulation of the draft investigation plan, the involvement of operational lawyers and investigators as well as senior management in that exercise, and the early thinking about possible legal classifications are directly relevant to the serious problems the ICC-OTP has encountered in several of its cases to date.

16.3. An Italian Perspective

16.3.1. An Introduction to Criminal Investigations in the Italian Legal System

With regards to criminal procedure, one of the most visible differences between the ICC and the Italian national legal system is the absence of the preliminary examination stage in the latter. This difference is, of course, due to the principle of mandatory prosecutions, applied by Article 112 of

---

[62]   ICTY and UNICRI, 2009, p. 30, see above note 58.

the Italian Constitution.[63] Consequently, the decision to open an investigation is taken automatically, as soon as the notice of a prosecutable crime is brought to the attention of the authorities.[64] Generally, the duty to investigate rests with the offices of the prosecutor of the district court with territorial jurisdiction on the alleged crimes.[65] It must be noted, however, that Italian legal scholarship has consistently interpreted the principle of mandatory prosecutions to implicitly exclude criminal pursuits without a reasonable prospect of securing a conviction.[66]

Italian prosecutors ("pubblici ministeri") have the same selection procedure, requirements and appointment as judges; in fact, they are magistrates. The prosecutor in charge of a case leads the investigation, and coordinates the work of tasked officers and other staff. Police authorities are directed by the prosecutors appointed to their offices,[67] similar to the Norwegian model described in Chapter 18 below by Alf Butenschøn Skre. Italy has adopted a hybrid procedural model, which is predominantly accusatory.[68] Hence, prosecutors qualify as parties to the proceedings, but they have an obligation to seek the truth and must search for evidence that is favourable to the accused person.[69] Nonetheless, it is their responsibility to strategically pursue successful prosecutions.[70] In the words of the renowned jurist Piero Calamandrei, Italian prosecutors are "lawyers without passion, judges without impartiality".[71]

---

[63] Italy, Costituzione della Repubblica Italiana [The Constitution of the Italian Republic], 1 January 1948 ('Constitution of Italy') (https://www.legal-tools.org/doc/8e3867/).

[64] Italy, Codice di Procedura Penale (Code of Criminal Procedure), 22 September 1988, Article 335 ('CPP') (https://www.legal-tools.org/doc/aee4e8/).

[65] *Ibid.*, Article 51.1(a).

[66] Francesca Ruggieri, "Nota Introduttiva", in Claudio Botti, Domenico Manzione and Enrico Marzaduri (eds.), "Il principio di Obbligatorietà dell'Azione Penale Oggi: Confini e Prospettive", in *Criminalia 2010: Annuario di scienze penalistiche*, Edizioni ETS, Pise, 2011, p. 301.

[67] CPP, Article 58, see above note 64.

[68] Court of Cassation of Italy, Judgment, 14 December 1996, no. 6599.

[69] CPP, Article 358, see above note 64; Court of Cassation of Italy, Judgment, 23 February 1998, no. 1125.

[70] Court of Cassation of Italy, Judgment, 20 December 2005, no. 6743.

[71] Piero Calamandrei, *Elogio dei Giudici Scritto da un Avvocato*, Ponte alle Grazie, Milan, 1989, p. 56.

Starting from the opening of an investigation, the proceedings are subject to judicial oversight,[72] more so when the rights of the accused are significantly impacted. Such is the case, for instance, of wiretaps,[73] arrests "in flagrante delicto",[74] or the compulsory extraction of biological material.[75] The Code of Criminal Procedure provides that the judge overseeing the investigation phase must either authorise said measures or evaluate the prosecutor's decisions *ex post* in case of urgency which did not allow the prosecutor to seek an authorisation beforehand. Investigations are directed by prosecutors while being subjected to selective scrutiny by a pre-trial judge. Investigative choices are the domain of the offices of the prosecutor, fulfilling their functions in an organic procedure which involves the judiciary from the outset.

With a notable exception – the possibility of a pre-trial judge ordering additional investigation of select matters in a small number of instances specified by law – prosecutors are exclusively charged with choosing and implementing strategic approaches. In order for a prosecutor to properly discharge this function, the Italian legal system offers a series of guarantees of independence from external influence, albeit not as marked as the ones provided for the judges. Prosecutors are particularly independent during hearings, as the law grants them "full autonomy".[76] However, the hierarchical structure of the offices of the prosecutors implies a limitation of the independence of individual prosecutors from legitimate internal influence,[77] which is important to understand before dealing with the issue of strategic co-ordination of investigative activities.

The consequences of the Italian prosecutorial hierarchy have wider effects during pre-trial phases, including investigations,[78] due to the priority granted to the promotion of uniform approaches. The chief prosecutors at the district-court level determine their offices' organisational and

---

[72] CPP, Article 328, see above note 64.

[73] *Ibid.*, Article 267.

[74] *Ibid.*, Article 391.

[75] *Ibid.*, Article 359*bis*.

[76] *Ibid.*, Article 53.

[77] Marco Bignami, "L'Indipendenza Interna del Pubblico Ministero", in *Questione Giustizia*, 2018, no. 1, p. 80.

[78] Jessica De Vivo, *L'indipendenza del Pubblico Ministero: Profili Costituzionali e Ordinamentali*, doctoral thesis, Università degli Studi di Milano-Bicocca, 2018, p. 47.

strategic aspects,[79] and thus have the necessary autonomy to co-ordinate with other offices at the same level. Accordingly, the instruments of strategic planning examined in this chapter are either co-ordinating agreements among offices of the prosecutors of different courts, or guidelines adopted within a specific office. Both encompass best practices in light of jurisprudential and normative developments.

16.3.2. Strategic Tools to Direct Criminal Investigations

The first Italian strategic tool for investigations examined in this chapter is an organisational agreement at the court of appeals' level, encompassing several court districts and entered into by the prosecutors themselves. It is a protocol to co-ordinate the offices of the prosecutor of different Sicilian district courts, in order to identify a working method to address "the vagueness of certain legal provisions and the obvious lack of consolidated jurisprudence" with regards to a 2006 legislative reform on environmental crimes.[80]

The protocol is explicitly aimed to "provide operational directions, uniform for the whole District"[81] within the normative gaps left by primary and secondary sources of law, similar to the Draft Regulations or the current Regulations of the ICC Office of the Prosecutor.[82] In light of the identified issues, the protocol provides several tools to enhance the effectiveness of the investigations of specific environmental crimes. The document identifies a range of minor offences, dubbed 'spy-crimes', which strongly suggest the commission of more serious environmental crimes. As such, the protocol provides for investigative direction, and establishes a shared IT monitoring tool. One of the main issues was the need to shorten the duration of investigations to counter the effects of the statute of limitations. Hence, the protocol sets out an obligation for each office to forward any notice of certain alleged crimes to a number of prosecutorial

---

[79] Bignami, 2018, p. 83, see above note 77.
[80] Italy, Office of the Prosecutor of the Court of Appeals of Caltanissetta, Protocollo Organizzativo in Materia di Reati Ambientali ex Legge n. 68/2015 [Organisational Protocol on Environmental Crimes Pursuant to Law No. 68/2015], 22 March 2016, no. 955/2016 ('Organisational Protocol on Environmental Crimes').
[81] *Ibid.*, p. 2.
[82] ICC, Regulations of the Office of the Prosecutor, 23 April 2009, ICC-BD/05-01-09, Regulation 1.2 (https://www.legal-tools.org/doc/a97226/).

offices.[83] A significant portion of the document covers the interpretation of key legal provisions, indicating an appropriate course of action for issues ranging from jurisdiction to elements of the crimes: in other words, investigative and prosecutorial direction within the framework of a common statement of policy. While much different from an investigation plan, the document represents an effort to further a strategic approach to investigations, largely consisting in tools and directions for advance planning. To some extent, it provides for investigative planning, as the protocol mandates assessment and procedures for each investigation of relevant crimes. However, the lack of an individual planning approach renders the document more related to a very detailed policy paper on a select crime area.

Other offices of the prosecutor have pursued similar goals, albeit in different guises: circulars ("circolari"), internal dispatches containing guidelines with administrative binding effects on hierarchically subordinated offices. Such is the case of the Office of the Prosecutor of the district court of Bari in Puglia, another region of southern Italy.[84] As a relevant contextual factor it is fair to state that southern Italy has suffered the direct consequences of constant organised criminal activities which notoriously allow and profit from illegal practices within their controlled territories.[85] Therefore, environmental crimes are a matter of particular concern to certain Italian regions. Against this background, the Chief Prosecutor of Bari issued a series of relevant circulars,[86] of which the latest is

---

[83] The targeted crimes are environmental pollution, environmental disaster, trafficking and abandoning highly radioactive material, organised activities aimed at the trafficking of waste. See Organisational Protocol on Environmental Crimes, p. 2, see above note 80.

[84] Italy, Office of the Prosecutor of the District Court of Bari, Nuova Circolare Relativa ai Reati Contravvenzionali in Materia Ambientale di cui al Testo Unico Ambiente – D. Lgs. N. 152/2006, come Modificato dalla L. n. 68/2015 [New Circular on Environmental Criminal Misdemeanours Pursuant to the Consolidated Law on the Environment – Legislative Decree No. 152/2006, as Amended by Law No. 68/2018], 21 December 2017 ('New Circular on Environmental Criminal Misdemeanours').

[85] Antonio Pergolizzi, "L'Economia Avvelenata del Crimine Ambientale", in *Moneta e Credito*, 2018, vol. 71, no. 284, p. 341. It is important to note that – regardless of visible action on the ground – such activities burden Italy as a whole, along with other, if not all, States, more so in case of environmental crimes.

[86] Italy, Office of the Prosecutor of the District Court of Bari, Circolare prot. 936/2016 [Circular Protocol No. 936/2016], 8 February 2016; Italy, Office of the Prosecutor of the District Court of Bari, Circolare prot. 5648/2018 [Circular Protocol No. 5648/2018], 19 July 2016.

---

mainly aimed to discipline the application of the statute of limitations to minor offences.[87] The document expresses the office's policy on the concerned norms in terms of scope and procedural aspects, indicating mandatory steps and a statement of best practices. The circular reads as the detailed account of the tasks that must be performed by the office. Compared to investigation plans, and to the ICC-OTP Draft Regulations in particular, the circular lacks the element of advance planning for individual circumstances, and disproportionally covers practical matters and procedural guidelines.

A third example from Italian prosecution offices focuses on ensuring a uniform procedure or method to deal with specific crimes, which has been a priority for the Office of the Prosecutor of the district court of Macerata particularly for the crimes of stalking[88] and abuse or mistreatment within the family.[89] The office has drafted two crime-specific directives[90] which are very similar in content: both documents discuss the elements of the crimes in light of consolidated jurisprudence, and outline a step-by-step procedure starting from the acquisition of the notice that an alleged crime has been committed. The directives focus on obtaining evidence, with special regards to the weight of foreseeable means of proof, such as the interview of the victim *vis-à-vis* potential witnesses. Furthermore, the document provides a variety of guidelines on the steps to be followed during the investigation, including recommended courses of action and criteria for the prioritisation of investigative activities. The latter portion of the directives is particularly detailed, and provides an overview of the whole investigation phase which may contribute towards advanced planning. Such in-depth indication of tasks to be undertaken functions as a check-list of sorts, enabling better oversight. Interestingly,

---

[87] New Circular on Environmental Criminal Misdemeanours, p. 2, see above note 84.

[88] Italy, Codice Penale (Penal Code), 19 October 1930, Article 612*bis* ('CP') (https://www.legal-tools.org/doc/46945d/).

[89] *Ibid.*, Article 572.

[90] Italy, Office of the Prosecutor of the District Court of Macerata, Direttive per le Indagini in Materia di Reato ex art. 572 c.p. [Directives for Investigations of the Crime Pursuant to Article 572 of the Penal Code], 15 January 2014; Italy, Office of the Prosecutor of the District Court of Macerata, Direttive per le Indagini in Materia di Reato ex art. 612 *bis* c.p. [Directives for Investigations of the Crime as Provided by Article 612*bis* of the Penal Code], 15 January 2014.

attached to both documents are forms that outline how the interview of the victims should be conducted in light of the guidelines.

The main characteristic that these tools have in common with the content and the purpose of the investigation plan as provided by the ICC-OTP Draft Regulations is that they are adopted in advance, to direct the steps and the progress of an investigation prospectively. Italian prosecution authorities do recognise that organised planning leads to more effective investigations. However, the equivalent of an investigation plan is not currently provided for by the Italian legal system, and neither protocols nor circulars or directives can replace the functions that investigation plans tend to perform. For instance, the body of each of the documents is largely composed of interpretation of norms. While certainly useful, if translated into the ICC framework, they resemble thematic policy papers, which do not adequately cater to the strategic needs of individual investigations. This function is performed by the two directives of the Macerata district court's Office of the Prosecutor, albeit only partially. The instructions contained in the documents, if applied to an individual case, can answer many of the questions raised by an investigation plan. However, the Italian directives are static, since they pertain to every case of a particular crime, and do not translate into or require the actual planning of individual casework. Nevertheless, not unlike the ICC-OTP Draft Regulations investigation plan, the above-mentioned tools can foster an organised approach and greatly facilitate the sharing of knowledge and best practices among and within offices. Co-ordinating investigative practices likely results, ultimately, in the consolidation of a common method and better oversight.

16.3.2.1. An Assessment of Current Developments in the Uniformity of Criminal Pursuits

Recent developments have shown the increasing priority afforded to the planning of criminal investigations by the Italian judiciary. In September 2017, the Superior Council of Magistrates[91] included the drafting and

---

[91] The Superior Council of Magistrates is the overseeing body for career judges and prosecutors, mandated by the Italian Constitution and performing a quasi-normative function on its area of influence, namely judicial activities left out from existing primary and secondary sources of law. Albeit debated in Italian academia with regards to issues of legitimacy, there is unanimous consensus that the Council exercises a *de facto* normative power. See the Constitution of Italy, Articles 104–07, see above note 63; Giuseppe Volpe, "Le Origini

adoption of investigative planning tools within the suggested, non-mandatory content of the organisational plan that all offices of the prosecutor are bound to implement periodically.[92] The term that is employed is "investigative protocols" aimed to discipline "homogeneous categories of proceedings".[93] The aim of such protocols is, according to the Office of the Prosecutor of Tivoli in the central Lazio region, to render more effective the use of existing resources while enabling the prosecutor to make more uniform and hastier assessments. Adopting directives containing investigative protocols enhances "the overall saving of resources and operational results, for the sake of the victims as well".[94]

A paradigmatic example is, in fact, a directive pertaining to gender-based crimes, implemented by the same Office of the Prosecutor in Tivoli.[95] The reasons for employing a more strategic approach are similar to the advantages of investigation plans: the directive mentions the effectiveness of criminal pursuits, resource-effective management, and the explicit aim to enhance monitoring.[96] Such provisions enable swifter investigations and limit superfluous activities, with the effect of "offering an actual perception of protection and care to the victims".[97] The directive provides guidelines on substantial matters and procedural steps, and is not designed to constitute a proper plan for investigations. Hence, it cannot be adapted to the developments of individual proceedings. Nevertheless,

---

dell'Organizzazione Corporativa della Magistratura", in Alessandro Pace, Sergio Bartole, and Roberto Romboli (eds.), *Problemi Attuali della Giustizia in Italia*, Jovene, Naples, 2009, p. 82; Alessandro Pace, "I Poteri Normativi del CSM", in *Rassegna Parlamentare*, 2010, no. 2, pp. 3–6.

[92] Italy, Consiglio Superiore della Magistratura, Circolare sulla Organizzazione degli Uffici di Procura [Circular on the Organisation of the Offices of the Prosecutor], 16 November 2017.

[93] *Ibid.*, Article 7.5(o).

[94] Italy, Office of the Prosecutor of the District Court of Tivoli, Direttiva alla Polizia Giudiziaria n. 1/2019, in materia di truffe commesse a mezzo internet [Directive to the Police No. 1/2019 Regarding Frauds Committed Through the Internet], 8 April 2019, n. prot. 562/2019, p. 3.

[95] Italy, Office of the Prosecutor of the District Court of Tivoli, Direttiva n. 2/2019: Protocolli Investigativi e Buone Prassi per la Polizia Giudiziaria in Materia di Reati di Violenze di Genere [Directive No. 2/2019: Investigative Protocols and Best Practices for the Police with Regards to Gender-Based Violent Crimes], 3 May 2019, n. prot. 686/2019 ['Directive No. 2/2019'].

[96] *Ibid.*, p. 3.

[97] *Ibid.*, p. 4.

updating and amending the directive according to future developments is an important priority of the document, which provides several means to that end: firstly, it encourages follow-up meetings and consultations aimed to facilitate the work of police personnel; secondly, the directive is expressly subject to on-going monitoring; and thirdly, it enables police bureaus to directly request clarifications and amendments (specific issues are dealt with in thematic circulars).[98] While neither the directive nor the circulars are updated to reflect the developments within individual cases, possible modifications are foreseen and facilitated in their implementation. The consultation process leading to the adoption of similar documents is an expression of a co-operative approach. As such, the directives are adopted with the participation of all the prosecutors of the office, and its administrative staff when relevant. If appropriate, the adoption of investigative directives follows a series of meetings and contacts with the police bureaus involved in the work affected by the document, "in order to pre-emptively deal with the issues affecting the police bureaus" involved in the consultations.[99] Furthermore, the directive on gender-based crimes followed a meeting among the directors of several police authorities, and the gathering of the opinions of a relevant NGO in the field and the unit of the prosecutor's office specialised in victims' care. The reasons for the inclusive policy are stated in the document:

> judicial experience has proven that an effective and prompt response to such crimes is only possible through the involvement and the accountability of every individual who, in any way, takes part in the prevention and the repression of the offences [...] such synergy is required in order to fully protect and care for the victims.[100]

This comprehensive framework is complemented by the provision of continuous co-ordination and training initiatives for involved police personnel. The aims of such directives resonate with the strategic nature of investigation plans. Their formulation shares and gathers information and best practices widely within the office and other relevant authorities. The directives are updated to reflect possible developments via either newer directives with abrogative effect or specifically-themed circulars.[101]

---

[98] *Ibid.*, pp. 3–4.
[99] *Ibid.*, p. 3
[100] *Ibid.*, p. 8.
[101] *Ibid.*, pp. 3–4.

Finally, the directive itself is a statement of a policy that is, to some extent, shared with all the members of the office thanks to the consultation process that ultimately led to its adoption. This is similar to the ICC-OTP Draft Regulation investigation plan, although the most significant differences with the Italian directives rest in the content which, for the latter, must necessarily be tailored to address a set of crimes rather than individual investigations.

Addressing a category of crimes, the directive contains statements on case prioritisation for the set of crimes defined by its scope. A number of offences have high priority, indicating that proceedings for the crimes of stalking, mistreatment and sexual violence should reach the trial phase as soon as possible.[102] The directive mandates very detailed procedures for the foreseeable police and prosecutorial activities, considering different practical scenarios and suggesting adequate responses. Much space is given to the description of desirable investigative activities and on the overall treatment of victims throughout the proceedings. The statement of the tasks to be undertaken on a case-by-case basis provides implicit criteria for the prioritisation of evidence. For instance, in the wake of sexual violence allegations, police officers are required to gather biological evidence and call in specialised personnel among the first mandatory steps.[103] Investigations of alleged domestic violence cases should prioritise the search for evidence aimed to assess the immediate dangers for the victims.[104] The directive contains more detailed guidelines on how to gather evidence, the kind of evidence required in connection with the alleged offences, while also focusing on the assessments and measures deemed necessary to preserve the well-being of victims and the integrity of the investigation.

Unless otherwise specified, the indications contained in the directive must be regarded as mandatory for the individuals under the Office of the Prosecutor's authority. The directive of the Office of the Prosecutor of the Tivoli district court, in fact, states that such documents "must be regarded as strictly mandatory in order for their goals to be accomplished, with the consequence that any significant instance of incorrect

---

[102] *Ibid.*, p. 6.

[103] *Ibid.*, p. 13.

[104] *Ibid.*, p. 14.

compliance [with the directive's provisions] must be reported to the police bureaus".[105]

The initiatives undertaken by the Italian offices of the prosecutor to ensure a uniform, strategic and effective approach to criminal pursuits may be adopted in the form of directives, circulars or protocols. As such, they can be considered, at best, close to the bottom of the hierarchy of the sources of law. The force of law is reserved to few sources in the Italian legal system, while regulations, with one exception,[106] are the recognised source of binding secondary norms. This leaves directives, circulars and similar documents with a limited administrative force through which a body invested with adequate power can self-regulate.[107] Hence, they are binding only in an administrative, and perhaps disciplinary, manner. Far from being provided by the law, the uniformity of criminal pursuits is currently being developed at the local level, under the administrative authority of individual offices of the prosecutor.

While steps are certainly being taken,[108] the diffusion of the power to make strategic and managerial investigative choices likely results in a fragmentation of practice, inherently contradicting the aims such initiatives are directed towards. In practical terms, unless considerable effort is employed in co-ordination, the locally-sourced and -developed practices result in a myriad of best practices which differ on the basis of where the offence has been allegedly committed. While this is an issue that disproportionately concerns domestic jurisdictions, it is fair to argue that the adoption of detailed directives by the higher-ups within the prosecutorial hierarchy might share and balance the benefits already provided by such efforts.

---

[105] *Ibid.*, p. 3.

[106] The exception consists in the statutes of local governments, such as townships.

[107] Floriana Lisena, *Manuale di Diritto Costituzionale*, Nel Diritto, Rome, 2016, p. 110.

[108] Offices of the Prosecutor can enter into the protocols explained above. Furthermore, the directives adopted by one office likely influence others, see Directive No. 2/2019, see above note 95. Albeit belonging to the same normative rank as directives, the resolutions of the Superior Council of Magistrates have by definition nationwide impact, and relevant guidelines and best practices have been adopted, see Italy, Consiglio Superiore della Magistratura, Risoluzione sulle linee guida in tema di organizzazione e buone prassi per la trattazione dei procedimenti relativi a reati di violenza di genere e domestica [Resolution on the Guidelines on the Organisation and Best Practices in Dealing with Proceedings Regarding Gender-Based and Domestic Violent Crimes], 9 May 2018.

16.3.3. Reasons for the Absence of Investigation Plans in Italy

The Italian offices of the prosecutors have been tackling issues similar to the ones that the expert group tasked with the ICC-OTP Draft Regulations aimed to address with the provision of a mandatory investigation plan from the earliest stages of the process. However functional directives, circulars and protocols may be to strategy, planning, and policy, they are not suited or intended to monitor, manage and oversee individual investigations. The Italian initiatives do result in a somewhat increased oversight capacity, as the uniformity of expected practices inherently facilitates scrutiny and the predictability of management. At the same time, they are markedly different from the "management tools to ensure focused and professional investigations" envisioned by the ICC-OTP Draft Regulations.[109] Hence, there is no widely adopted instrument to strategically manage and monitor individual investigations in Italy, that resembles an investigation plan. My argument is that this absence is far from being solely determined by the lack of will or capacity by part of the competent authorities. Indeed, there are other, perhaps more practical reasons.

First and foremost, Italian prosecutors are largely educated in their legal system from the beginning of their studies. The public selection procedure is strict, and every applicant has studied the same norms. The majority of police investigators, likewise, grew up, studied and worked in the same legal and cultural framework. The fact that the working language is the mother tongue of most involved personnel is an additional consideration. The uniformity of the backgrounds of the individuals involved in an investigation likely increases the predictability of their work, perhaps reducing the need for planning a common approach.

Secondly, the scope and timing of criminal investigations must be taken into consideration, as most national investigations in fact-rich cases operate in an on-going, ever-evolving and functioning criminal reality. Often, these investigations are, or become related to, crimes that are still being committed: such is arguably the case for organised crime, serious fraud, transnational human trafficking, and smuggling. By way of example, an investigation might begin with an alleged tax fraud through coin-operated gambling devices in bars. A wiretap could expose the fraud as a part of a money-laundering scheme of a local organised crime syndicate.

---

[109] Draft Regulations, Book 3, Regulation 19, p. 869, see above note 2.

Organised crime investigations may start as a branch but evolve into a tree. In such cases, the suspected individuals are operating in functioning criminal frameworks until their apprehension. Normally, such investigations are gradually built on the results of on-going surveillance. Defining the objectives and the intended direction of an investigation beforehand is arguably more difficult.

Another relevant factor is the level of detail of the working normative framework, as procedural norms provide guidance and requirements for prosecutorial activities: every additional legal requirement and definition shapes the work of the prosecution. The Italian Code of Criminal Procedure sets out how evidence should be collected and used in great detail. Furthermore, the said provisions are constantly discussed and interpreted by the Italian Court of Cassation, whose Criminal Section has issued 32,496 fully reasoned judgments in 2018,[110] with only 8,535 with simplified reasons for the judgment, and an overall total of 57,177 judgments.[111] This wealth of jurisprudential interpretations arguably results in more detailed guidance for the prosecution. It has been said that there is an inherent uncertainty in international law,[112] which warrants better planning.

Together with extensive legal interpretation, an Italian office of the prosecutor can count on the best practices developed over decades of investigative activities in the same territory, and sometimes regarding the same actors. For example, the Italian authorities have been investigating and prosecuting Sicilian mafia-type organisations at least since 1885, if not earlier.[113] The need for planning ahead is arguably reduced if there are

---

[110] Court of Cassation of Italy, *La Cassazione Penale – Annuario Statistico 2018*, 9 January 2019, p. 12 (available on the Court of Cassation of Italy's web site).

[111] Court of Cassation of Italy, *Relazione sull'Amministrazione della Giustizia nell'Anno 2018*, 25 January 2019, p. 123 (available on the Court of Cassation of Italy's web site).

[112] Jörg Kammerhofer, "Uncertainty in the Formal Sources of International Law: Customary International Law and Some of Its Problems", in *European Journal of International Law*, 2004, vol. 15, no. 3, p. 551.

[113] The prosecutions first emerged in the second half of 1800, with the 'Stuppagghieri' trial of 1878 in Palermo. The more widely known 'Fratellanza di Favara' trials took place in Agrigento in 1885. The first official document that mentions the "mafia" as a criminal organisation was a report authored by the Prefect of Palermo, a representative of the Ministry of the Interior, on the 25 April 1865, see John Dickie, *Cosa Nostra: Storia della Mafia Siciliana*, Laterza, Rome, 2015.

established practices to follow, especially if the geographical, social, and political backgrounds do not vary much between cases.

Finally, as mentioned above, the Italian Constitution applies the principle of mandatory prosecutions. Accordingly, there are no budgetary limits to criminal investigations. A prosecutor must be able to employ every tool provided by the law in order to fulfil his mandate to prosecute every reported crime. On the contrary, the ICC-OTP is constrained by its annually-adopted budget, and must necessarily plan its work more extensively.

16.3.4. Lessons to be Learned

Different solutions cater to different needs. My view is that the reasons for the absence of investigation plans in Italy mitigate for their adoption in international jurisdictions and hybrid tribunals. The Italian authorities in charge of investigations are largely composed of individuals with uniform backgrounds and common cultural roots. Their work is perhaps more predictable than in a multicultural team working in a recently created jurisdiction, on cases that usually involve a new country to study and understand. The offices of the Italian prosecutors operate without budget constraints, and do not ordinarily plan the costs of investigative activities. Investigations evolve according to the movements of a criminal reality which is still operational, and rely on a wealth of established practices, norms, and jurisprudence that provide detailed guidance.

In my view, Italy would benefit from the adoption of investigation plans for fact-rich criminal cases, especially if mandated by a primary source of law and disciplined by nationwide regulations which would equally bind all relevant prosecution offices. However, the need to strategically plan and manage investigations from the outset is arguably more urgent in jurisdictions bound by yearly budgets, composed by heterogeneous teams of individuals representing a rich variety of legal systems,[114] and which usually operate in unfamiliar settings.

---

[114] As of July, 2017, the professional staff of the ICC represented 90 nationalities, see ICC Assembly of States Parties, *Report of the Bureau on Equitable Geographical Representation and Gender Balance in the Recruitment of Staff of the International Criminal Court*, 22 November 2017, ICC-ASP/16/35, p. 3 (https://www.legal-tools.org/doc/2f9b58/).

16.4. The Relevancy to Current International Criminal Law Discourse

We often remember the "gift of hope to future generations"[115] that the International Criminal Court represented in the words of former UN Secretary-General Kofi Annan. And we learned – more so during the last trying years – that, as the Minister of Foreign Affairs of Italy concluded in his address at the end of the UN Diplomatic Conference in Rome:

> the project to institute an International Criminal Court is one of those that belong to the highest reaches of international political achievements. We can expect no indulgence if we fail in our endeavour.[116]

Accordingly, every perceived failure and shortcoming of the ICC is met by varying degree of dismay. Our scrutiny, I argue, should be aimed towards finding out which aspects of the international criminal justice process can and need to be improved. Less energy should be dedicated to disillusionment and disappointment.

The Quality Control Project reminds us of how the process is segmented and subject to the same challenges affecting other jurisdictions, including Italy, in addition to a set of difficulties that are inherent to international criminal justice. There are a number of overarching issues that seem to affect the whole process, such as individual integrity, undue State encroachment, and appointments of and performance by high officials. Nevertheless, the existence of seemingly less tangible problems does not exempt us from addressing what should and could be fixed.

This book focuses on challenges faced during criminal investigations, and on bottlenecks that they cause. This chapter concentrates on investigative strategy and management, paying special attention to the investigation plan, an instrument used by both national and international jurisdictions, for similar reasons. Criminal investigations led pursuant to a measure of advance planning, such as the model foreseen by the ICC-OTP Draft Regulations, lend themselves to systematic oversight. The results of

---

[115] Statement by the United Nations Secretary-General Kofi Annan at the Ceremony Held at Campidoglio Celebrating the Adoption of the Statute of the International Criminal Court, 18 July 1998 (https://www.legal-tools.org/doc/8b0ab6/).

[116] Address of H.E. Mr. Lamberto Dini, Minister of Foreign Affairs of Italy to the UN Diplomatic Conference on the Establishment of an International Criminal Court, 17 June 1998 (https://www.legal-tools.org/doc/680833/).

questioning the implementation of a formulated plan are necessarily more precise than scrutiny of whether opportunity has been duly employed. In this regard, we can also draw from the Italian experience of not having a properly defined investigation plan. The needs of criminal investigations are currently been addressed with crime-specific guidelines, rather than strategic management of individual proceedings. Nevertheless, as one of the directives clearly states, any significant lack of compliance with the directive's provisions must be reported to the competent police bureaus, presumably to ensure uniformity of approach. Similar to investigation plans, Italian directives, protocols, and circulars tend to promote oversight, and thus quality control. Yet, investigation plans are essential tools for the complex investigations of core international crimes, as the current ICC model, described in Chapter 15 above, shows. Notwithstanding the on-going evolution of ICC-OTP practice, the Draft Regulations still have lessons to teach. The centrality of investigations plans, their early adoption, and the high-level composition of the drafting team all suggest that we should make an even better use of such management and planning tools.

I wish to conclude this chapter with an invitation, which in my view is inherent to the entire Quality Control Project. We should take notice of the overarching, less tangible issues, and think of solutions. But, in the meantime, we should roll up our figurative sleeves and work on the 'plumbing'[117] of international criminal law. If better results – results of higher quality, in other words – are being demanded, then it is appropriate that the discourse turns to quality control mechanisms.

---

[117] This expression draws from the eloquent closing speech by Gregory S. Gordon, on the occasion of the 'Quality Control in Criminal Investigation' conference in New Delhi. In his words, referencing Roger Clark, legal scholars can be divided in two categories: philosophers and plumbers, with the latter being more dedicated to the underlying mechanisms of the law, see Gregory S. Gordon, "Synthesis of Conference Papers and Deliberations", CILRAP Film, New Delhi, 23 February 2019 (https://www.cilrap.org/cilrap-film/190223-gordon/).

17

Use of Investigation Plans
in Indian Criminal Justice:
The Crime of Human Trafficking

Usha Tandon and Shreeyash Uday Lalit[*]

17.1. Introduction

The prosecutorial systems in India and international jurisdictions have a sea of difference on account of factors such as the judges, investigative agencies, nature and source of funding, subject matter of the substantive law, as well as the authorisation under which the prosecutorial system has power to conduct an investigation. These factors influence how the prosecutorial system will function and who will exercise the checks and balances. Notwithstanding the fact that the investigation by the International Criminal Court's ('ICC') Office of the Prosecutor ('OTP') is conducted only for genocide, crimes against humanity, war crimes and crimes of aggression, there is much in common between the two jurisdictions as regards the need for investigation plans. The ICC-OTP conducts investigations in fact-rich and complex crimes, necessitating a high degree of assessment, planning, co-operation, reporting and management. This is similar to the hurdles faced by the Indian investigative agencies in fact-rich and complex cases such as human trafficking.

It can hardly be contradicted that real-time case assessment, planning, reporting and management is rarely undertaken by the Indian investigating officers in investigations that are not fact-intensive. However, in so far as the crime of human trafficking is concerned, there has been a

---

[*] **Usha Tandon** is a Professor of Law and Professor-in-Charge, Campus Law Centre, University of Delhi. She has 29 years of teaching experience, and is a recognised scholar in human development, focusing on women empowerment and environmental protection. **Shreeyash Uday Lalit** is an Advocate at the Supreme Court of India and holds an LL.M. degree from the University of Cambridge. The authors acknowledge the excellent research assistance provided by Mr. Kartikay Aggarwal, Law Clerk, Supreme Court of India, and meticulous editing of the final draft by Mr. Subham Kumar Jain.

growing need to use investigation plans on account of the complicated web of transactions, the co-ordination required between different branches of police in order to freeze the proceeds of crime, the sensitivity required in order to address and de-brief the victims of human trafficking, as well as a fast-paced response team that may be able to deal with the exigencies of an emergent situation.

This chapter first offers some thoughts on the ICC-OTP (Section 17.2.), before delving into Indian criminal justice in order to assess the difficulties faced by Indian investigative agencies (Section 17.3.). Thereafter, we proceed to consider points of divergence between the Indian investigative system and the ICC-OTP investigations (Section 17.4.). Next, we discuss the provisions of Indian law dealing with the offence of human trafficking (Section 17.5.). The Chapter then undertakes an analysis of the checklists and soft-law compliance through which the Indian procedural law regulates an investigation (Section 17.6.). Lastly, it considers whether the Indian model is the most appropriate for our domestic jurisdiction and whether any suggestions could be taken from investigations conducted by the ICC-OTP (Section 17.7.).

17.2. Draft Regulations of the ICC-OTP

On 5 September 2013, the Code of Conduct for the Office of the Prosecutor ('OTP Code') adopted by the ICC-OTP entered into force,[1] a little over a year after the commencement of the term of the second ICC Prosecutor, Mrs. Fatou Bensouda.[2] Though the Code fills an important void in the regulation of OTP ethical conduct, its provenance and content mean that much depend on the manner in which it is applied in the future. Prior to the OTP Code's entry into force in 2013, no document specifically regulated the conduct of members of the ICC-OTP in contrast with the judges and non-OTP counsel practicing before the Court.[3] Some viewed this difference as unjustified and undesirable.[4] The preparatory team of the ICC-

---

[1]   International Criminal Court, Code of Conduct for the Office of the Prosecutor, 2013 ('OTP Code') (https://www.legal-tools.org/doc/3e11eb/).

[2]   International Criminal Court, "Ms Fatou Bensouda" (available on its web site).

[3]   International Criminal Court, Code of Professional Conduct for counsel, 2 December 2005 ('ICC Code') (https://www.legal-tools.org/doc/f9ed33/); International Criminal Court, Code of Judicial Ethics, 9 March 2005 (https://www.legal-tools.org/doc/383f8f/).

[4]   Arman Sarvarian, *Professional Ethics at the International Bar*, Oxford University Press, Oxford, 2013, p. 203.

OTP carefully prepared a draft Code of Conduct in 2003, in consultation with various experts, including from the International Association of Prosecutors and the Coalition for the International Criminal Court, but the controversial first Prosecutor Mr. Luis Moreno-Ocampo simply refused to accept such a Code, however well-drafted it was.[5] This contrasted with other international criminal courts and tribunals. For example, the International Criminal Tribunal for the former Yugoslavia ('ICTY') and the International Criminal Tribunal for Rwanda ('ICTR') adopted ethical codes for members of the prosecution in the Tribunals' early days,[6] whereas a code applicable to all counsel appearing before the Special Court for Sierra Leone ('SCSL') was adopted in 2005,[7] and a code applicable to all counsel appearing before the Special Tribunal for Lebanon ('STL') was adopted in 2011.[8]

The 2003 draft Code of Conduct was prepared through a broadly-based expert-consultation process designed by the leader of the preparatory team of the ICC-OTP. Among the outcomes of this work were the Draft Regulations of the OTP presented to the first Prosecutor in September 2003, and then adopted in an abridged version *ad interim*. They are discussed in further detail by Antonio Angotti in Chapter 16 above. The Draft Regulations are significant. In particular, in Book 3: Operations Manual of the Draft Regulations, there is an extremely pertinent Part 2 relating to the management of preliminary examinations, Article 53(1) evaluation, and the start of investigation. Regulation 6 provides for a 'Pre-

---

[5] See Salim A. Nakhjavani, "The Origins and Development of the Code of Conduct", in Morten Bergsmo, Klaus Rackwitz and SONG Tianying (eds.), *Historical Origins of International Criminal Law: Volume 5*, Torkel Opsahl Academic EPublisher, Brussels, 2017, pp. 951-1006 (http://www.toaep.org/ps-pdf/24-bergsmo-rackwitz-song). The preparatory team was led by Morten Bergsmo, co-editor of this volume.

[6] International Criminal Tribunal for the former Yugoslavia, Standards of Professional Conduct for Prosecution Counsel, 14 September 1999 (https://www.legal-tools.org/doc/nz7gv4/); International Criminal Tribunal for Rwanda, Prosecutor's Regulation No. 2, 14 September 1999 (https://www.legal-tools.org/doc/cf3184/).

[7] Special Court for Sierra Leone, Code of Professional Conduct for Counsel with the Right of Audience before the SCSL, 14 May 2005 ('SCSL Code') (https://www.legal-tools.org/doc/a3420b/).

[8] Special Tribunal for Lebanon, Code of Professional Conduct for Counsel Appearing Before the Tribunal, 28 February 2011 ('STL Code') (https://www.legal-tools.org/doc/240aa0/).

liminary Examination Report' and a 'Draft Investigation Plan' to be pre-pared by the OTP.[9]

The Draft Investigation Plan as envisaged in Regulation 6 offers a significant check in terms of quality control in investigations, by providing for a plan or a roadmap to be used by investigators from the start of the investigation. This is an extremely useful construct in the Indian context. Cases of mass riot, lynching, corruption, and rackets in trafficking

---

[9] Regulation 6.5. provides that the OTP shall prepare a draft investigation plan along the following lines:

(a)   an assessment of whether there is a reasonable basis to believe that a crime within the jurisdiction of the Court has been or is being committed (article 53(1)(a) of the Statute);

(b)   the relevant background of the situation, placing the alleged offences in a broader geographical, social and cultural context;

(c)   an explanation why the alleged offences warrant a full investigation against the backdrop of other alleged offences where such a step might not be recommendable;

(d)   an identification of the crime base incidents to be investigated and a description of likely suspects, together with the overall aim of the investigation;

(e)   a tentative indication of possible charges, modes of liability and potential defences, if any, as provided for in article 31 of the Statute;

(f)   an explanation of the role and place of these likely suspects in the relevant chains of authority;

(g)   the whereabouts, if known, of the possible suspects and the likelihood to arrest them;

(h)   an assessment of the admissibility of a possible case under article 17 of the Statute;

(i)   a preliminary indication of resources, time and staff likely to be required to complete the investigation;

(j)   a preliminary indication of the main categories of evidence and the amount of evidence that is likely to be required to prove the possible charges;

(k)   matters of State co-operation and security;

(l)   an explanation of how the investigation and prosecution of the alleged crimes or perpetrators is expected to fit in with the broader context of cases pursued by the Office;

(m)   potential dangers to the integrity of the investigation or the life or well-being of victims and witnesses that could arise once the victims are informed of the intention of the Chief Prosecutor to seek authorization, in accordance with rule 50(1) of the Rules of Procedure and Evidence;

(n)   any other matter that may be of relevance for a decision to start an investigation in the light of the specific situation.

For more information on the Draft Regulations, see Chapter 16 above and Carlos Vasconcelos, "Draft Regulations of the Office of the Prosecutor", in Morten Bergsmo, Klaus Rackwitz and SONG Tianying (eds.), *Historical Origins of International Criminal Law: Volume 5, op. cit.*, pp. 861–62.

---

pose extremely onerous problems on account of the sheer volume of data that requires to be processed, the complexity of the case, and the time element that is lost in the whole process due to inefficiency – which leads to a reduced quality of criminal investigation on account of degraded witness testimony and insufficient evidential backing.

As described by Markus Eikel in Chapter 15 above, the ICC-OTP has nevertheless developed a practice that draws on key elements of the Draft Regulations, including the use of investigation plans. Eikel clearly explains the complex normative environment in which the ICC-OTP undertakes investigations holistically. Four key components of investigation plans used by international criminal tribunals may be identified as i) link to legal case-assessment, ii) planning, iii) reporting and iv) management.[10]

At the outset, it would be pertinent to note that ICC investigations benefit from robust preliminary examination which assists the formulation of an investigation plan with greater depth of analysis. In contrast to the same, it would be relevant to visit the Indian criminal justice system to determine how the investigation proceeds, and assess how the investigatory guidelines in India help elevate the standard of investigative quality in criminal prosecutions.

17.3. An Overview of the Indian Criminal Justice System

The Indian Criminal Justice system is largely premised on three statutes, the premise of which were largely enacted in the Victorian era. These statutes are the Indian Penal Code (1860), Indian Evidence Act (1872), and the Criminal Procedure Code (1973) ('CrPC'). The CrPC contains the procedural law for the investigation, prosecution and trial of offences.

17.3.1. Investigation v. Inquiry

Under the Indian CrPC, investigation, defined under Section 2(h), "includes all the proceedings under this code for the collection of evidence

---

[10] See Chapter 14 as well as various documents such as ICTY and United Nations Interregional Crime and Justice Research Institute ('UNICRI'), *ICTY Manual on Developed Practices*, UNICRI Publisher, Turin, 2009 (https://www.legal-tools.org/doc/0cc55d/); ICTR, *Prosecution of Sexual Violence: Best Practices Manual for the Investigation and Prosecution of Sexual Violence Crimes in Post-Conflict Regions: Lessons Learned from the Office of the Prosecutor for the International Criminal Tribunal for Rwanda*, January 2014 (https://www.legal-tools.org/doc/ea03f8/); ICC, Regulations of the Office of the Prosecutor, 23 April 2009 (https://www.legal-tools.org/doc/a97226/).

conducted by a police officer or by any person (other than a magistrate) who is authorised by a Magistrate in this behalf".[11] Thus, investigation under the CrPC has been defined in contradistinction to inquiry under Section 2(g) of the CrPC, where the latter amounts to a judicial proceeding under Section 2(i) of the CrPC but the former does not.

Inquiry under Section 2(g) of the CrPC is defined so as to mean every inquiry other than a trial conducted under the Code by a Magistrate or Court.[12] The term inquiry has been used in a wider sense. It includes all such proceedings which do not require an adjudication upon a guilt or determination of an offence. It would also include proceedings which precede the stage of trial.[13]

The meaning of the word 'inquiry' in the CrPC was interpreted by the Supreme Court in *V.C. Shukla v. State Through C.B.I.*[14] The judgment sets out the history of the definitions in the successive Codes of Criminal Procedure since 1872 of the words 'inquiry' and 'trial'. Thus, 'inquiry' is "a judicial act and not [akin] to the steps taken by the Police which are either investigation after the stage of Section 154 CrPC or termed as 'Preliminary Inquiry'", which is "prior to the registration of the FIR, even though, no entry in the General Diary or the Station Diary or the Daily Diary has been made".[15]

17.3.2. Initiation of a Criminal Process

In India, the criminal investigation process and prosecution can be initiated in several ways, which are elaborated as under:

---

[11] India, High Court of Karnatakan, *State of Mysore v. Laxmi Trading Co. and Others*, Judgment, 6 July 1962, (1963) 1 Cr LJ 269; Supreme Court of India, *Union of India v. Prakash P. Hinduja and Another*, Judgment, 7 July 2003, (2003) 6 SCC 195.

[12] India, High Court of Gujarat, *Kanbi Bechar Lala and Others v. State and Another*, Judgment, 12 March 1962, 1963 LLR 57; India, High Court of Kerala, *State of Kerala v. Ramanatha Iyer*, Judgment, 26 February 1965, 1965 Ker LT 978; India, High Court of Patna, *Tuneshwar Prasad Singh and Another v. State of Bihar*, Judgment, 20 January 1978, 1978 Cr LJ 1080.

[13] India, High Court of Madhya Pradesh, *Arun Debe v. State of M.P.*, Judgment, 18 August 1990, 1991 Cr LJ 840.

[14] Supreme Court of India, *V.C. Shukla v. State Through C.B.I.*, Judgment, 7 December 1979, AIR 1980 SC 962.

[15] Supreme Court of India, *Lalita Kumari v. Government of U.P. and Others*, Judgment, 12 November 2013, 2014 Cr LJ 470: AIR 2014 SC 187: (2014) 2 SCC 1.

---

i) An informant can report the commission of a cognisable offence[16] to the police officer, or the police officer can himself take cognisance of the commission of a cognisable offence having been committed in his presence. In such a situation, any police officer, even without the orders of a Magistrate, whether on the basis of a complaint or report or knowledge of the commission of a cognisable offence, can investigate the cognisable case under Section 156(1) of the CrPC.

ii) If the complainant feels that a police officer has failed to investigate a cognisable offence, the complainant can approach the Magistrate with a criminal complaint under Section 190 of the CrPC, to take cognisance of such offence. Upon the filing of such complaint, the Magistrate can take cognisance of the case and either conduct the inquiry, or in the alternative, order the Police to register a First Information Report ('FIR') and investigate the offence under Section 156(3) of the CrPC.

iii) In the case of a non-cognisable offence,[17] the police is not bound to investigate, and the judicial process can be set in motion only by using the mechanism provided under Section 190 of the CrPC, by filing a criminal complaint before the competent court.

Since we are considering only warrants cases in this chapter, the same are usually initiated only upon the filing of an FIR by an informant under Section 154 of the CrPC, or upon information received by the police station under Section 157(1) of the CrPC, in pursuance of which the police ought to investigate the cognisable offence as under Section 156(1) of the CrPC. If there is a failure to investigate the same, upon the presentation of a complaint to the Magistrate under Section 190 of the CrPC, the Magistrate may either take cognisance and conduct an inquiry, or order

---

[16] In the Indian Criminal Justice System, offences under the CrPC are classified as cognisable and non-cognisable. Generally, serious offences such as rape, murder, and so on are considered cognisable; whereas less serious offences such as nuisance, mischief, and so on are classified as non-cognisable offences. In cognisable offences, the police can arrest a person without warrant and may start investigation without the order from the court.

[17] In non-cognisable offences, the police cannot arrest a person without warrant and investigation cannot be initiated without the order from the court.

the registration of a FIR under Section 156(3) of the CrPC and order the commencement of the investigation.[18]

---

[18] The various stages involved in the process of investigation in the Indian criminal justice system are as follows:

    i)   Stage of Evidence: Once a FIR has been registered by the police, the evidence is mainly divided into three parts: Recording of Statements under Section 161 of the CrPC; Collecting of Evidence in form of documents and others; Recording of confessions or statements under Section 164 of the CrPC before the Magistrate.

    ii)   Recording of 164 Statement: It is not compulsory for the Magistrate to record statement under Section 164 of the CrPC. However, in cases where the offence has been committed under Section 354, 354A, 354B, 354C, 354D, 376(1), 376(2), 376A, 376B, 376C, 376D, 376E, or 509 of IPC, the Magistrate has to record the statement of the victim of such offence.

    iii)   Stage of Section 173 (Final Report): Once the three stages of evidence are completed, the police has to submit a final report to the magistrate empowered to take cognisance of such report which includes all the evidence collected by the Investigating Agency and on which prosecution proposes to rely upon. When upon investigation, there is insufficient evidence to send the accused to the magistrate, the police authority must file a report under Section 169 of the CrPC and release the accused on furnishing a bond and to appear before the Magistrate empowered to take cognisance, if and when so required. Thus, the final report can only be of two kinds: Closure Report, or Charge Sheet or Final Report.

    iv)   Commitment of the Case under Section 209: Once the Charge Sheet is filed by the investigation agency before the Magistrate, irrespective of whether it is sessions triable case or not, the Magistrate will take cognisance of the case under Section 190(1)(b) of the CrPC and issue warrant under Section 204 of the CrPC to the accused to secure his presence before him, and further can direct the investigation agency to hand over the Charge Sheet to the accused under Section 207 of the CrPC. If the offences are sessions triable, then the Magistrate will commit the case and send all the papers and proceedings of the case to the District and Session court for the trial to begin.

    v)   Opening of the case: The Prosecutor appointed will have to open the case by explaining to the Court about the charges slapped on the accused in the Charge Sheet. The provision of discharge of the accused is provided in Section 227 of the CrPC whereas framing of charges is provided in Section 228 of the CrPC. Before framing of charges, the accused may file an application before the court, and, if on perusing the record of the case along with the documents presented and hearing the prosecution and the accused, the Court finds that there is not sufficient cause to continue the proceedings, the Court shall discharge the accused under Section 227 of the CrPC. In any event if the Court rejects the application filed under Section 227 of the CrPC, it may proceed to frame charges under Section 228 of the CrPC. The Court at this stage can even add or delete any charge if the material available on record does not support the said charge. The Court shall read out the charges to the accused and ask if he agrees with the said charges and pleads guilty for the same.

17.3.3. Preliminary Enquiry under the Criminal Procedure Code

The courts have held in a line of cases that registration of FIR is compulsory on receipt of any information or complaint that discloses a cognisable offence under Section 154 of the CrPC and no preliminary enquiry is permissible therein. However, there are cases where such an offence is not *prima facie* made out and the police may need to carry out investigation in order to ascertain the correct position.

In *Lalita Kumari v. Government of U.P.*,[19] the Supreme Court of India observed that although a preliminary enquiry may be conducted before registration of FIR, the purpose of the same shall be limited to determining if a cognisable offence is disclosed or not. Hence the scope of preliminary enquiry, before the registration of FIR, is to ascertain whether the information received reveals commission of any cognisable offence, and does not extend to verification of the veracity of such information.[20] Such verification is to be done only after the registration of FIR.[21]

The Madras High Court similarly held in *CHANGEIndia v. Commissioner of Police and Others*[22] – where the court was dealing with a petition filed under Section 482 of the CrPC to direct the Inspector of Police, Crime Branch, Crime Investigation Department, Anti Human Trafficking Cell (Anti Vice Squad) – to register FIR on the complaint sent by the petitioner against owners or management of the unregistered, illegal Balagurukulam Orphanage for Children, and to conduct an effective investigation into the allegation of child trafficking. The court reiterated the ratio laid down in the *Lalita Kumari* judgment and ordered the respondent to comply with the same.

Under Chapter XV of the CrPC, which covers the position before actual commencement in a court or before a Magistrate, and particularly under Sections 200 and 202 of the CrPC, the scope of preliminary enquiry in case of complaints to the Magistrate is very limited. Section 200 states,

---

See generally K.N. Chandrasekharan Pillai, *R.V. Kelkar's Criminal Procedure*, Eastern Book Company, Lucknow, 2017.

[19] See above note 15.

[20] *Ibid.*

[21] India, High Court of Karnataka, *Mareppa v. The State of Karnataka and Others*, Judgment, 5 June 2017, (2017) 4 AIR Kant R 465.

[22] India, High Court of Judicature at Madras, *CHANGEIndia v. Commissioner of Police and Others*, 20 September 2017, 2017 SCC OnLine Mad 26925.

"the Magistrate taking cognizance of an offence on complaint shall examine upon oath the complainant and the witnesses, if any". The mandate of Section 202 does not require the Magistrate to issue process in all situations. It empowers him to ascertain, either by himself or police officer or any other person, whether adequate grounds are present to proceed further.[23] The aim is to ascertain, from the perusal of complaint and statements recorded, if there is *prima facie* evidence to support the allegations and proceed against the accused,[24] who according to the complainant has committed an offence. Therefore, at this stage, the Magistrate is not required to meticulously appreciate the evidence as if he were the trial court.[25] Under Section 203, the Magistrate can dismiss the complaint if there is insufficient ground to proceed based on the statement of the complainant, the witnesses and the inquiry or investigation carried out under Section 202. However, Section 204 provides for issue of process subject to the satisfaction of the Magistrate that sufficient ground exists for doing so. The expression "sufficient ground" used in Sections 203 and 204 is only to indicate that *prima facie* case is made out against the accused and not that sufficient grounds exist to convict him.[26]

17.4. Points of Divergence From ICC-OTP Investigation

In moving forward, it would be pertinent to consider the points of difference or divergence in investigation conducted by the Indian investigative agencies from the investigation conducted by the ICC-OTP. Notwithstanding the obvious issue that the OTP has to extensively rely upon third party sources at the preliminary examination stage, there are various other theoretical and statutory differences.

17.4.1. Robust Preliminary Examination v. Mandatory Investigation

The OTP Policy Paper on Preliminary Examinations reveals that "in accordance with the Rome Statute, the OTP is responsible for determining

---

[23] Supreme Court of India, *S.K. Sinha, Chief Enforcement Officer v. Videocon International Ltd. and Others*, Judgment, 25 January 2008, (2008) 2 SCC 492.

[24] India, High Court of Judicature at Allahabad, *Durga Prasad and Others v. State of U.P. and Another*, Judgment, 6 December 2012, 2012 SCC OnLine All 4067.

[25] Supreme Court of India, *Kewal Krishan v. Suraj Bhan*, Judgment, 1 August 1980, 1980 Supp SCC 499.

[26] Supreme Court of India, *Shivjee Singh v. Nagendra Tiwary and Others*, Judgment, 6 July 2010, AIR 2010 SC 2261.

---

whether there is a reasonable basis to proceed with an investigation into a situation pursuant to the criteria established by the Rome Statute, subject to judicial authorisation as appropriate".[27] This in effect entails an examination on three different counts: (i) jurisdiction (temporal, material, territorial and personal); (ii) admissibility (complementarity and gravity); and (iii) interests of justice.

The aforementioned three factors are visible through a reading of Article 53(1) and Article 15(3) of the ICC Statute, where the standard of proof has been set as a "reasonable basis to proceed". Given the fact that the ICC jurisdiction is complementary to the domestic jurisdiction insofar as criminal offences are concerned, the standard of proof becomes higher than usual, since the OTP not only has to assess complementarity through an examination of the existence of relevant national proceedings in relation to potential cases being considered for investigation, but it also has to assess the scale, nature and manner of commission of the crimes, and their impact, bearing in mind the potential cases that would be likely to arise from an investigation of the situation.[28]

As a result, the ICC-OTP prefers to consider as much additional information as possible under Article 15(2), from other sources such as States, organs of the United Nations ('UN'), inter-governmental or non-governmental organisations, or other reliable sources that the OTP deems appropriate, and may also consider and receive written or oral testimony at the seat of the Court.[29] This, in effect, necessitates a highly reliable and expansive preliminary examination in order to assess the aforesaid factors.

In light of the Indian regime, the same can be easily contrasted, on account of the mandatory investigations that need to be conducted by the police upon the commission of cognisable offences. As stated above, the Supreme Court of India in *Lalita Kumari v. Government of U.P.*[30] has held that if the information discloses the commission of a cognisable offence, then no preliminary inquiry is permissible and the registration of a FIR under Section 154 of the CrPC is mandatory. However, "if the information

---

[27] ICC-OTP, *Policy Paper on Preliminary Examinations*, November 2013 (https://www.legal-tools.org/doc/acb906/).

[28] *Ibid.*

[29] Hanna Kuczyńska, *The Accusation Model Before the International Criminal Court: Study of Convergence of Criminal Justice Systems*, Springer, 2015.

[30] See above note 15.

received does not disclose a cognizable offence but indicates the necessity for an inquiry, a preliminary inquiry may be conducted only to ascertain whether cognizable offence is disclosed or not".[31] Furthermore, upon such preliminary inquiry, if it is clear that the case discloses the commission of a cognisable offence, the FIR under Section 154 of the CrPC must be registered. "In cases where preliminary inquiry ends up in closing the complaint, a copy of the entry of such closure must be supplied to the first informant forthwith and not later than one week. It must disclose reasons in brief for closing the complaint and not proceeding further."[32]

Thus, the Supreme Court of India held that "the scope of preliminary inquiry is not to verify the veracity or otherwise of the information received but only to ascertain whether the information reveals any cognizable offence".[33] It gave examples of cases in which preliminary inquiry may be made, such as matrimonial disputes, family disputes, commercial offences, medical negligence cases, corruption cases, "cases where there is abnormal delay or laches in initiating criminal prosecution, for example, over 3 months delay in reporting the matter without satisfactorily explaining the reasons for delay".[34]

Furthermore, the requirement of a preliminary inquiry, especially in cases of cognisable offences, has been made time bound wherein the preliminary inquiry is required to be completed within seven days. The fact of such delay and the cause of it also has to be reflected in the General Diary entry.

17.4.2. Admissibility of Statements Before Investigative Agency

Under the Rules of Procedure and Evidence of the ICC, the procedure with regards to the collection of evidence during investigation has been delineated in Section III of Chapter V. Rule 111 allows a record of questioning to be taken, wherein the formal statements made by any person who is questioned in connection with an investigation or proceedings, shall be recorded and signed by the interviewee or his or her counsel. The record would also note the time, date and place of and all persons present during the questioning. It is important to note that when someone does not

---

[31] *Ibid.*, para. 111(ii).
[32] *Ibid.*, para. 111(iii).
[33] *Ibid.*, para. 111(v).
[34] *Ibid.*, para. 111(vi)(e).

sign the record, then the reasons for the same also have to be noted in accordance with Rule 111.

This is in complete opposition to the requirement under the Indian CrPC wherein statements made before the police are inadmissible as evidence, let alone recorded. Under Section 161(1) of the CrPC, a police officer making an investigation can orally examine any person acquainted with the facts and circumstances of the case, including the accused himself. Under Section 161(2) of the CrPC, the person being examined would be bound to answer the questions, other than those which would expose him to criminal liability. Moreover, the statement would be reduced into writing by the police under Section 161(3) of the CrPC.

It is important to note the bar imposed on Section 161 by Section 162 of the CrPC, wherein the latter mandates that no statement made by any person to a police officer in the course of investigation shall be signed by the said person (if it is reduced into writing). The only purpose of statements under Section 161 of the CrPC is to seek contradiction when these statements are compared to the admissible statements. Thus, under the Indian Evidence Act, former statements made by a witness can be used to contradict him,[35] to impeach his credit,[36] to corroborate him,[37] or to refresh his memory.[38] But "Section 162 CrPC imposes an absolute bar to the use of statements covered by it for any purpose save for the purposes provided, however garbed the use may be".[39]

17.4.3. Separation of Investigation from Prosecution

Though the Prosecutors in India are considered as an important part in the state machinery and are charged with a statutory duty to be fair and im-

---

[35] Indian Evidence Act, 15 March 1872, Section 145 ('Indian Evidence Act') (https://www.legal-tools.org/doc/675509/). See Supreme Court of India, *Hazari Lal v. Delhi Administration*, Judgment, 15 February 1980, AIR 1980 SC 873: (1980) 2 SCC 390.

[36] Indian Evidence Act, Section 155, see above note 35.

[37] *Ibid.*, Section 157. See India, High Court of Kerala, *Peethambaran Prasad v. State of Kerala*, Judgment, 27 February 1998, 1998 Cr LJ 2122.

[38] Indian Evidence Act, Section 159, see above note 35.

[39] India, High Court of Judicature at Allahabad, *Munshi v. State*, Judgment, 11 October 1966, 1967 All LJ 695.

partial, they are not part of the investigating agency or the forwarding agency.[40]

The issue was studied by the Law Commission of India as early as in 1958.[41] It was of the considered view that looking to the nature of duties that police forces "have to discharge in bringing a case in court, it is not possible for them to exhibit that degree of detachment which is necessary in a prosecutor".[42] Therefore the Law Commission suggested that public prosecutors should be completely separated from the Police Department. It recommended the following:

> In every district a separate Prosecution Department may be constituted and placed in charge of an official who may be called a "Director of Public Prosecutions". The entire prosecution machinery in the District should be under his control. The departments of the machinery of criminal justice, namely, the Investigation Department and the Prosecuting Department should thus be completely separated from each other.[43]

In 1995, in *S.B. Shahane v. State of Maharashtra*[44] the Supreme Court of India held:

> When Assistant Public Prosecutors are appointed under [...] the Code for conducting prosecutions in courts of Magistrates in a district fairly and impartially, separating them from the police officers of the Police Department and freeing them from the administrative or disciplinary control of officers of the Police Department, are the inevitable consequential actions required to be taken by the State Government which appoints such Public Prosecutors, inasmuch as, taking of such actions are statutory obligations impliedly imposed upon it under sub-section (3) of section 25 CrPC.

---

[40] India, High Court of Judicature at Allahabad, *Jai Pal Singh Naresh and Others v. State of U.P. and Others*, Judgment, 6 August 1975, 1976 Cri LJ 32 (All); Supreme Court of India, *Hitendra Vishnu Thakur v. State of Maharashtra*, Judgment, 12 July 1994, (1994) 4 SCC 602.

[41] Law Commission of India, "Prosecuting Agency – Director of Public Prosecutions", in *14th Report: Reform on Judicial Administration: Vol. II*, 1958, p. 770.

[42] *Ibid.*, para. 12.

[43] *Ibid.*, para. 15.

[44] Supreme Court of India, *S.B. Shahane and Others v. State of Maharashtra and Another*, Judgment, 21 April 1995, 1995 Supp (3) SCC 37.

Thus, there is a clear and perceptible difference in the functioning of prosecutors under the Indian CrPC and at the ICC-OTP: the latter functionaries routinely conduct investigations and also prosecute the accused persons concerned. Even if there is a separation brought about in the OTP by ensuring that the persons investigating are not the same who are prosecuting, yet the very fact that the officers performing the two functions are working under the aegis of the OTP is enough to demonstrate a clearly distinct way of functioning *vis-à-vis* prosecutors under the Indian CrPC.

17.4.4. Collection of Evidence at the Request of the Defence

Under the Indian CrPC, investigation extends until the stage of charge – that is, until formal charges are framed in the case. As we have noted previously, the accused, at any time before framing of charges against him, can file an application under Section 227 of the CrPC to discharge him from the charges in the charge sheet.

However, the material that is supplied to the Court at the stage of framing of charges is only the prosecution material.[45] Therefore, at the stage of framing of charges, the only material that is available to the Court is the Final Police Report under Section 173 of the CrPC which contains all documents and witness statements which the Prosecution proposes to rely upon and examine. There is no requirement on the part of Investigating Officer to submit the material favourable to defence as part of the Final Report. For that purpose, the accused can, at any stage, request summons for production of all documents under Section 91 of the CrPC, which the police is believed to be in possession or power of, requiring them to "attend and produce it, or to produce it, at the time and place stated in the summons or order". When interpreted harmoniously with the provisions relevant to framing of charges, it becomes clear that:

> while ordinarily the Court has to proceed on the basis of material produced with the charge-sheet for dealing with the is-

---

[45] Please see CrPC, Section 173:

> (5) When such report is in respect of a case to which section 170 applies, the police officer shall forward to the Magistrate along with the report –
>
> (a) all documents or relevant extracts thereof on which the prosecution proposes to rely other than those already sent to the Magistrate during investigation;
>
> (b) the statements-recorded under section 161 of all the persons whom the prosecution proposes to examine as its witnesses.

sue of charge but if the court is satisfied that there is material of sterling quality which has been withheld by the investigator/prosecutor, the court is not debarred from summoning or relying upon the same even if such document is not a part of the charge-sheet.[46]

This position of the Indian CrPC is in contradistinction to the position in the ICC Rules of Procedure and Evidence which permits the Pre-Trial Chamber, under Rule 116, Section III, Chapter V to issue an order or seek co-operation under Article 57(3)(b) of the ICC Statute for collection of evidence at the request of the defence, if "such order would facilitate the collection of evidence that may be material to the proper determination of the issues being adjudicated, or to the proper preparation of the person's defence".

17.5. Human Trafficking in India: A Fact-Rich Crime

Trafficking of persons is a complex crime with incalculable elements. The multi-dimensional nature of the problem, involvement of international organised mafia, deficient legislation, laxity in law enforcement, official complicity and the trauma of the victims make it a challenging crime for investigation and prosecution. Millions of women and girls are victims of sex trafficking in India, trapped in false promises of employment or sham marriages. Many trafficked persons are subjected to forced labour.

In January 2019, the UN's fourth Global Report on Trafficking in Persons (2018) released by United Nations Office on Drugs and Crime ('UNODC') again recorded high numbers of cases of human trafficking, mainly targeting women and girls.[47] Though Article 23(1) of the Constitution of India prohibits trafficking in human beings and forced labour, unfortunately, India is a source, transit and destination country for human trafficking. While noting that "[t]rafficking in women and children is the gravest form of abuse and exploitation of human beings", the High Court of Delhi in *Bachpan Bachao Andolan v. Union of India* observed:

> Thousands of Indians are trafficked every day to some destination or the other and are forced to lead lives of slavery.

---

[46] Supreme Court of India, *Nitya Dharmananda v. Gopal Sheelum Reddy*, Judgment, 7 December 2017, (2018) 2 SCC 93.

[47] UNODC, *Global Report on Trafficking in Persons 2018*, p. 10. This report is based on information collected from 142 countries, encompassing more than 94 per cent of the world's population.

> They are forced to survive in brothels, factories, guesthouses, dance bars, farms and even in the homes of well-off Indians, with no control over their bodies and lives.[48]

"Trafficking in women and children has become an increasingly lucrative business especially since the risk of being prosecuted is very low".[49] As noted by the Supreme Court of India in one of the cases:[50]

> It is highly deplorable and heart-rending to note that many poverty-stricken children and girls in the prime of youth are taken to 'flesh market' and forcibly pushed into the 'flesh trade' which is being carried on in utter violation of all cannons of morality, decency and dignity of humankind. There cannot be two opinions – indeed there is none – that this obnoxious and abominable crime committed with all kinds of unthinkable vulgarity should be eradicated at all levels by drastic steps.

Since 2011, the US State Department, in its annual report on trafficking in persons, has been placing India in 'Tier Two', as "the Government of India does not fully meet the minimum standards for the elimination of trafficking; however, it is making significant efforts to do so".[51] The crime of human trafficking involves, *inter alia*, the issues of prosecution of traffickers and rehabilitation of rescued victims.

This chapter is mainly concerned with the investigation of the crime of human trafficking in India, so the discussion that follows focuses on the provisions of law involving prosecution.

17.5.1. Indian Penal Code (1860)

Section 370 of the Indian Penal Code provides for the definition as well as the punishment for the offence of trafficking. Following the recommenda-

---

[48] India, High Court of Delhi, *Bachpan Bachao Andolan and Others v. Union of India and Others*, Judgment, December 24 2010, Writ Petition (Crl.) No. 82/2009.

[49] Supreme Court of India, *Bachpan Bachao Andolan v. Union of India*, Judgment, 18 April 2011, (2011) 5 SCC 1.

[50] Supreme Court of India, *Vishal Jeet v. Union of India*, Judgment, 2 May 1990, (1990) 3 SCC 318.

[51] US Department of State, "India", in *Trafficking in Persons Report*, June 2018 (available on its web site).

tions of Justice J.S. Verma Committee Report,[52] the Criminal Law (Amendment) Act (2013) has amended the entire section "so as to enlarge the scope of the offence,[53] and include within its purview not just slavery, but trafficking in general – of minors as well as adults, and also forced or bonded labour, prostitution, organ transplantation etc".[54] While sub-section (1)[55] of Section 370 provides for the ingredients of the offence, sub-section (2) to (7)[56] provide for the punishment in varying situations.

---

[52] J.S. Verma, Leila Seth and Gopal Subramaniam, *Report of the Committee on Amendments to Criminal Law*, 23 January 2013 (https://www.legal-tools.org/doc/8712ed/, for the 2013 Act, see https://www.legal-tools.org/doc/8f62ce/).

[53] *Ibid.* Chapter 6 of Justice J.S. Verma Committee's Report is on Trafficking of Woman and Children, wherein the entire issue of trafficking has been discussed at length.

[54] India, High Court of Gujarat at Ahmedabad, *Vinod v. State of Gujarat and Another*, Judgment, 5 May 2017, (2017) 4 GLR 2804.

[55] Indian Penal Code, 1860, Section 370(1):
> Whoever, for the purpose of exploitation, (a) recruits, (b) transports, (c) harbours, (d) transfers, or (e) receives, a person or persons, by –
> *First.* – using threats, or
> *Secondly.* – using force, or any other form of coercion, or
> *Thirdly.* – by abduction, or
> *Fourthly.* – by practising fraud, or deception, or
> *Fifthly.* – by abuse of power, or
> *Sixthly.* – by inducement, including the giving or receiving of payments or benefits, in order to achieve the consent of any person having control over the person recruited, transported, harboured, transferred or received, commits the offence of trafficking.
> *Explanation 1.* – The expression "exploitation" shall include any act of physical exploitation or any form of sexual exploitation, slavery or practices similar to slavery, servitude, or the forced removal of organs.
> *Explanation 2.* – The consent of the victim is immaterial in determination of the offence of trafficking.

[56] Indian Penal Code, 1860, Section 370:
> (2) Whoever commits the offence of trafficking shall be punished with rigorous imprisonment for a term which shall not be less than seven years, but which may extend to ten years, and shall also be liable to fine.
> (3) Where the offence involves the trafficking of more than one person, it shall be punishable with rigorous imprisonment for a term which shall not be less than ten years but which may extend to imprisonment for life, and shall also be liable to fine.
> (4) Where the offence involves the trafficking of a minor, it shall be punishable with rigorous imprisonment for a term which shall not be less than ten years, but which may extend to imprisonment for life, and shall also be liable to fine.
> (5) Where the offence involves the trafficking of more than one minor, it shall be punishable with rigorous imprisonment for a term which shall not be less than

The penalty under normal circumstance of trafficking range from seven years to ten years rigorous imprisonment and fine.

The consent of the victim is immaterial in determining the offence of human trafficking. Trafficking of a minor attracts the rigorous imprisonment from ten years to life imprisonment and fine. If more than one child is trafficked, then the offender gets more stringent punishment that may not be less than 14 years, but may extend to life imprisonment and fine. Repeat offenders are awarded imprisonment for life (which means imprisonment for the remainder of that person's natural life), as well as fine. Another important provision relates to the complicit official who gets the same punishment as prescribed for repeat offenders.

17.5.2. Immoral Traffic Prevention Act (1956)

Enacted in pursuance to the 1949 UN International Convention for the Suppression of Traffic in Persons and of the Exploitation of Prostitution of Others, the Immoral Traffic Prevention Act (1956) ('ITPA')[57] is projected as the main legislative tool for preventing and combating trafficking in human beings in India.[58] The ITPA provides for the offence of trafficking where commercial sexual exploitation is being undertaken. Trafficking and prostitution are not synonymous under the ITPA. However, if the displacement of a person has been undertaken with a view to undertake commercial sexual exploitation and commodification of the said person through prostitution, then, the same can be punishable under the ITPA.

---

fourteen years, but which may extend to imprisonment for life, and shall also be liable to fine.

(6) If a person is convicted of the offence of trafficking of minor on more than one occasion, then such person shall be punished with imprisonment for life, which shall mean imprisonment for the remainder of that person's natural life, and shall also be liable to fine.

(7) When a public servant or a police officer is involved in the trafficking of any person then, such public servant or police officer shall be punished with imprisonment for life, which shall mean imprisonment for the remainder of that person's natural life, and shall also be liable to fine.

[57] Initially known as the Suppression of Immoral Traffic in Women and Girls Act (1956) (SITA).

[58] National Human Rights Commission ('NHRC'), *Integrated Plan of Action to Prevent and Combat Human Trafficking with Special Focus on Children and Women*; Sankar Sen and P.M. Nair, *A Report on Trafficking of Women and Children in India 2002-2003* (available on NHRC's web site).

The biggest criticism of ITPA is that it failed to define 'trafficking' and as a matter of fact deals mainly with prostitution.[59]

ITPA criminalises keeping a brothel,[60] living on the earnings of prostitution,[61] inducing a person for the sake of prostitution,[62] detaining a person for prostitution.[63] Complicit officials are dealt with stringent punishment for seven years to life imprisonment and fine, in cases involving seduction for prostitution of a person in custody.[64] Punishment in ITPA ranges from one year to life imprisonment depending on the severity of offence.

17.5.2.1. Procedural Law under ITPA

Any offence punishable under ITPA is a cognisable offence under Section 14, in which the police can arrest the alleged accused without warrant. There are, however, several procedural compliances required under the ITPA. The investigating agency has to appoint a Special Police Officer under Section 13 who is obligated to conduct a raid or search. He is also required to conduct a search only in the presence of two or more respectable inhabitants of the area. Thus, an ITPA prosecution would necessarily run afoul of due procedure if these mandatory compliances are not met. A checklist would then become necessary in order to ensure compliance.

Some of the procedural requirements provided in the ITPA have been dealt with by the Madras High Court. Section 15 ITPA provides for search without warrant, however the same is subject to certain caveats as given in sub-section (1). Whether the non-compliance with the same would render the search void was considered by the Madras High Court in the case of *Masti Health and Beauty Private Limited v. Commissioner of Police*,[65] wherein it held the following:

> 28. A careful look at the provisions of Section 15 would show that a Special Police Officer or a Trafficking Police Of-

---

[59] Verma, Seth and Subramaniam, 2013, see above note 52.

[60] India, Immoral Traffic (Prevention) Act, 30 December 1956, Section 3.

[61] *Ibid.*, Section 4.

[62] *Ibid.*, Section 5.

[63] *Ibid.*, Section 6.

[64] *Ibid.*, Section 9.

[65] India, High Court of Judicature at Madras, *Masti Health and Beauty Private Limited v. Commissioner of Police*, Judgment, 9 December 2014, 2014 SCC OnLine Mad 11927 ('Masti Health Case').

ficer can enter upon any premises and cause a search without warrant, only after satisfying the following:

(i) he should have reasonable grounds for believing that an offence punishable under this Act has been or is being committed;

(ii) he must believe that such an offence is committed in respect of a person living in the premises;

(iii) he should believe that the search of the premises with warrant cannot be made without undue delay; and

(iv) he must record the grounds of his belief before entering the premises.

Thus, the Madras High Court in *Masti Health* observed that the Special Police Officer must record the grounds of his belief before searching without warrant, wherein such belief must record that an offence was committed under ITPA for a person living in the premises where the search is conducted, and that the search cannot be delayed until such warrant is procured. These steps have to be scrupulously followed, as observed by the Madras High Court in paragraph 67 of *Masti Health*, failing which the search without warrant would be vitiated.

Another judgment on the procedural law to be complied with under ITPA was given by the Delhi High Court in *Kumari Sangeeta v. State*.[66] It made an observation with regards to the statutory requirement of conducting a search without warrant under Section 15(6A) only in the presence of two women police officers. It stated that the requirement under Section 15(6A), although worded as "shall" has to be read in conjunction with Section 13(3) ITPA, which provides that the presence of two women police officers shall be mandatory only when such officers are available. If they are not available, then it has to be left to the discretion of the Special Police Officer conducting the search without warrant, and the same cannot be a ground to vitiate the search *in toto*. Paragraph 35 of the *Kumari Sangeeta* throws light on that aspect:

> 35. A careful perusal of Sub-section (6A) of Section 15 of the Act reveals that the Special Police Officer would be accompanied by at least two women Police Officers. However, again it has been left to the discretion of the Special Police

---

66 India, High Court of Delhi, *Kumari Sangeeta and Another v. State and Others*, Judgment, 1 May 1995, 1995 SCC OnLine Del 337.

Officer to include two [women] Police Officers at the time of the search and at the time of the interrogation. This intention of the legislature is crystal from the subsequent last lines of Sub-section (6A) inasmuch as it provides that if no woman Police Officer is available in that eventuality interrogation shall be done only in the presence of a lady member of a recognised welfare institution or organisation.

With regards to the "shall" requirement under Section 15(2) ITPA, the Karnataka High Court has given a resounding judgment in *Shivaraj v. State of Karnataka*.[67] Section 15(2) ITPA provides that in a search without warrant under ITPA, the Special Police Officer shall call upon two respectable inhabitants of the place, one of whom shall be a woman. However, in a situation where the Special Police Officer was only able to call upon only two male inhabitants (none of them were women), the Karnataka High Court was called in to opine on the validity of such a search. The High Court held the following in paragraph 8 of *Shivaraj*:

8. From a plain reading of sub-section 2 of the above Section 15 it is evident that the raid could be conducted only in the presence of two or more witnesses of the locality. The interpretation by the learned Government Pleader that the proviso does not require a woman to be present at the raid as a witness is incorrect. It is mandatory. What the proviso indicates is that two persons who should be present to witness the raid should be respectable people from the locality, and one should be a woman, and if no woman could be found in the locality, a woman could be brought from some other locality to witness the raid. Therefore, in the present case on hand there is no dispute that the witnesses who accompanied the police at the raid were two men and there was no woman present. In which event, the search would be illegal and cannot be cited in support of the prosecution case. Therefore, the entire exercise of a trial and further prosecution is futile. The petition is therefore allowed. The proceedings before the court below are quashed.

As can be seen from the aforementioned judgments, the procedural requirements shift as depending upon the interpretation of the High Courts in different cases. A certain provision which reads as 'may' can be

---

[67] India, High Court of Karnataka, *Shivaraj v. State of Karnataka*, Judgment, 12 July 2016, 2016 SCC OnLine Kar 5077.

read as 'shall', thereby making it mandatory. For example, the Supreme Court in *Shri A.C. Aggarwal, Sub Divisional Magistrate, Delhi v. Mst. Ram Kali, etc.*[68] observed that although Section 190(1)(b) of the CrPC states that the Magistrate "may take cognizance", however the Magistrate is bound to take cognisance of any cognisable offence brought to his notice and he has no discretion in the matter.[69] On the other hand, there are also judgments given by several high courts where 'shall' has been read as 'may', that is, a provision has been read to be discretionary although a literal interpretation of the same would suggest that it is mandatory, *viz. Kumari Sangeeta* as pronounced by the Delhi High Court. Each provision is thus subject to judicial rules of statutory interpretation, which may not necessarily be comprehensible to a police officer lacking formal legal education. This necessitates the need for an investigation plan that is updated with new pronouncement of judgments that have interpreted a provision differently as compared to its literal interpretation.

17.5.3. The Trafficking of Persons (Prevention, Protection and Rehabilitation) Bill (2018)

The Trafficking of Persons (Prevention, Protection and Rehabilitation) Bill (2018) introduced in the Rajya Sabha (Upper House) in December 2018, seeks to create a law for investigation of all types of trafficking of persons, and protection and rehabilitation of rescued victims. The Bill categorises and criminalises 11 purposes of trafficking as aggravated forms of trafficking, such as forced labour, begging, administering narcotic drugs, pretext of marriage, bearing children, and inducing early sexual maturity by administering chemical substances or hormones.[70] The punishment for aggravated trafficking is higher than for simple trafficking ranging from ten years to life imprisonment and fine.[71] The intent behind the Bill is to set up various authorities at the district, state and national levels for rescue of trafficked persons and investigation of offences, such

---

[68] Supreme Court of India, *Shri A.C. Aggarwal, Sub Divisional Magistrate, Delhi and Another v. Mst. Ram Kali, etc.*, Judgment, 16 August 1967, AIR 1968 SC 1.

[69] India, High Court of Delhi, *Nagarwala v. State*, Judgment, 24 November 1971, 1972 RLR 73.

[70] India, The Trafficking of Persons (Prevention, Protection and Rehabilitation) Bill (2018), 26 July 2018, Section 31 ('The Trafficking of Persons (Prevention, Protection and Rehabilitation) Bill').

[71] *Ibid.*, Section 32

as anti-trafficking police officers, Anti Trafficking Units and National Anti-Trafficking Bureau.[72] It provides for Special Public Prosecutors and the setting up of designated courts in each district, to complete trials of trafficking cases within a year.[73] All offences under the Bill are cognisable and non-bailable.[74] The Bill provides for the attachment of property used for the apprehension of commission of trafficking.[75] And in case of conviction, such properties shall be forfeited to the government, which may sell the properties and remit the sale proceeds to the Rehabilitation Fund.[76]

17.5.4. Other Laws

Indian law criminalises trafficking for the purpose of sex, various forms of forced labour, and begging under various legislations. For instance, trafficking of children for sexual purposes is liable to punishment under the Protection of Children from Sexual Offences Act (2012) providing stringent punishment up to life imprisonment. Whereas, the Scheduled Castes and Scheduled Tribes (Prevention of Atrocities) Act (1989) punishes the accused of bonded labour up to five years imprisonment, the Bonded Labour System (Abolition) Act (1976) punishes him up to three years imprisonment. The Juvenile Justice (Care and Protection of Children) Act (2015) criminalises employment of children for begging,[77] sale

---

[72] *Ibid.*, Sections 15–19. Ministry of Home Affairs of India has sanctioned a Comprehensive Scheme "Strengthening law enforcement response in India against Trafficking in Persons through Training and Capacity Building", wherein it is proposed to establish 330 Anti Human Trafficking Units (AHTUs) throughout the country and impart training to 10,000 police officers through Training of Trainers. Ministry of Home Affairs of India, "Anti Trafficking Cell" (available on its web site). AHTUs continued to serve as the primary investigative force for human trafficking crimes. US Department of State, 2018, see above note 51.

[73] The Trafficking of Persons (Prevention, Protection and Rehabilitation) Bill, Sections 46–48, see above note 70.

[74] *Ibid.*, Section 52.

[75] *Ibid.*, Section 29.

[76] *Ibid.*, Section 30.

[77] India, Juvenile Justice (Care and Protection of Children) Act (2015), 31 December 2015, Section 76 (https://www.legal-tools.org/doc/7d2f03/).

---

and procurement of children for any purpose,[78] and use of children by militant groups.[79]

17.6. Locating Investigation Plans to Combat Human Trafficking

Having perused the Indian procedural law, substantive law and the points of divergence of the Indian criminal investigation from that of the ICC-OTP, let us consider the investigation plans, or lack thereof, employed by the Indian criminal justice agencies. It would not be wrong to suggest that the ICC-OTP investigation plans embark upon a significantly robust analysis, having secured material through preceding preliminary examination which may serve as an edifice.

Over the past few years, the Indian Government has realised the need for a checklist that guides investigators in understanding whether the prosecution is covering all bases or not. This checklist works in the form of an investigation plan, as it helps the investigator navigate the difficult terrain of case assessment, planning and management. These checklists are referred to as Standard Operating Procedures ('SOP') that encapsulate mandatory and discretionary requirements with which investigators need to comply.

17.6.1. Standard Operating Procedure of UNODC and the Government of India

The SOP prepared by the UNODC in conjunction with the Government of India[80] offers a detailed breakdown of these compliances. It lists the different kinds of material objects that can be collected, and who and where to collect them. Material objects include the following:

- *Diaries, notebooks, account books, registers, and so on in the brothel:*

  The purpose of this is to prove the existence of brothel, name of victims (already trafficked, likely to be trafficked), number of victims, details of payments, earnings, names of 'customers', accomplices, conspirators, abettors, traffickers and others.

---

[78] *Ibid.*, Section 81.

[79] *Ibid.*, Section 83.

[80] UNODC and the Government of India, *Standard Operating Procedures (SOP) on Investigating Crimes of Trafficking for Commercial Sexual Exploitation*, New Delhi, 2007 (https://www.legal-tools.org/doc/376b95/).

- *Travel documents like bus or train tickets of the accused persons:*

  This can be used to prove the movement of persons during trafficking to link source-transit-destination areas and to link the offenders in the process of the crime.

- *Rent agreements, rent receipts, house tax receipts:*

  Ownership or lease or rent agreements can help pin the location of the accused persons. This helps prove the existence and address of the brothel, the people who are managing it and their income and their earnings.

- *Receipts and registers reflecting expenditure on medicines, contraceptives, and so on:*

  Medical history can help prove the sexual exploitation of the victims.

- *Photographs, albums, video cassettes, DVDs:*

  This can prove the sexual exploitation of victims and the existence of an organised network of criminals.

- *Vehicles used for transporting victims:*

  The transportation of victims from one place to another, linking up places of exploitation and thereby the exploiter's networks, is crucial for these investigations.

- *Documents, including personal belongings, relating to the income, expenditures or assets of inmates of the place:*

  To establish aspects of illegal detention, level of exploitation of the victims, the debt bondage of the victims and also to assess the illegal assets acquired by the exploiters.

After the collection of material objects, the SOP then lists the step-wise compliance required of the investigator, including the following:

a. *Interrogation of the suspects or accused:*

  This includes uncovering the entire organised network of human trafficking, including the source, transit and destination of the victims; the demand and supply patterns; the push and pull factors. Interrogation ought to also help the investigator in unearthing the contacts, sources and witnesses in this source-transit-destination conundrum.

b. *Interrogation strategies for the suspects or accused:*

This includes associating other agencies for investigation, including the income tax department, financial institutions where huge assets may likely get disclosed, immigration department if the accused persons are foreigners, different police agencies if the crimes are committed over different jurisdictions.

c. *Arrest of accused persons:*

If the brothel is run by a woman, the investigator has to bear in mind that the compliance with Section 46(4) CrPC is a must, providing that no woman can be arrested after sunset and before sunrise, except in exceptional circumstances with prior permission from a Magistrate.

d. *Eviction of offenders and closure of brothels:*

Under Section 18(1) ITPA, the Magistrate has the power to order eviction from places of commercial sexual exploitation. On receipt of information from the police, the process can be initiated by the Magistrate. The most crucial aspect is that eviction can be ordered under ITPA even before conviction and even without a FIR.

e. *Organised crime approach:*

Since human trafficking is a 'basket of crimes',[81] the investigator has to take care to note the linkage of source-transit-destination during investigation, to explore the angle of conspiracy since there are always multiple offenders involved in human trafficking, to share criminal intelligence with police agencies, to confiscate assets under Section 105A CrPC, to collect intelligence on income, expenditure and assets and link those assets with proceeds of crime so that the same may be frozen through action initiated under the Prevention of Money Laundering Act (2002) through a Provisional Attachment Order.

f. *Recording of statements under Section 161 CrPC:*

When a rescued girl or woman is to be interviewed, the same is "to be done only by a woman police official. If the woman police official is not available, then the same is to be done only in the presence

---

[81] P.M. Nair, *Trafficking Women and Children for Sexual Exploitation: Handbook for Law Enforcement Agencies in India: Revised Edition 2007*, United Nations Development Fund for Women (UNIFEM) and UNODC, New Delhi, 2007 (https://www.legal-tools.org/doc/de8afd/).

of a female member of an NGO. This is a mandatory compliance required under Section 15(6A) ITPA". Furthermore, a statement can only be taken in a place where the girl or woman is comfortable, as required under Section 160 CrPC.

g. *Recording of statements under Section 164 CrPC:*

This is usually a preferred option undertaken by investigators. The reason for the same is that victims are likely to be repatriated or sent back to their place of residence, which would make them unavailable for questioning. Another reason is that they may be reluctant to record evidence in order not to relive the trauma of the offence, or that they may be suffering from some medical ailment, on account of which travelling to meet the investigator may be unfeasible.

h. *Production of rescued person before the Magistrate or Child Welfare Committee:*

An adult person rescued under Section 15 or 16 ITPA has to be produced before a Magistrate as required under Section 15(5) or Section 16(2) ITPA respectively. A child on the other hand has to be produced before the Child Welfare Committee in accordance with the requirements of the Juvenile Justice Act.

i. *Age assessment of the victims:*

This is extremely important to be undertaken as the investigator needs to exercise caution against deceptions. Some victims may get pressurised or coerced into declaring themselves as adults so that the offenders may not retaliate against them or their family. Thus, it is crucial for the investigator to conduct a preliminary age assessment on the spot, in order to preclude all such deceptions.

17.6.2. NHRC Standard Operating Procedure

Another checklist for a general investigation plan is provided in the NHRC SOP for Combating Trafficking of Persons in India.[82] This is the latest SOP from the governmental institutions. It delineates a step-wise questionnaire for the investigator involved, in order to assess whether all steps are completed as provided in the checklist. Some of these advisories are as follows:

---

[82] National Human Rights Commission India, *Standard Operating Procedure (SOP) for Combating Trafficking of Persons in India*, New Delhi, 2017.

- Whether a bone ossification test is required, and if yes, then whether it has been conducted?
- Whether the statement of the victim has been recorded by the magistrate under Section 164 CrPC?
- Whether there is a chain of evidence linking previous cases, train tickets, phone records, internet search or communication prints, money trail?
- Whether the investigating officer has checked for missing persons or child cases or other related cases registered?
- What is the best evidence available and whether it has been checked?
- Whether the assistance of various forms of media, such as radio, TV, newspapers as well as alternate sources such as NGOs and Legal Services Authorities have been utilized?
- Whether a financial investigation has been carried out and the feasibility of provision attachment of proceeds of crime has been evaluated?

These requirements are crisper and more cogent as compared to the SOP of UNODC. They demonstrate the requirements that are more proximate and necessary in order to achieve a higher quality investigation. None of the requirements as mentioned in the checklist are mandatory guidelines. However, non-compliance with each such guideline can generate enough doubt in the mind of a judge to distrust the prosecution story. That is an evaluation that has to be made on a case-to-case basis. However, what is important is that the SOP assists the investigator in achieving an investigation that cannot be called into question at the time of trial. This significantly guides the investigator in determining the weak links of his case, which can be used by him as a feedback loop to plan and manage the investigation in a manner that makes the case more robust.

17.6.3. General Investigation Plans

As can be seen from the above, there are various compliances in the form of a checklist that are necessary; while some are advisable but not necessary. For example, taking a statement under Section 164 of the CrPC before a Magistrate is advisable but not necessary;[83] therefore, its non-

---

[83] See Supreme Court of India, *Jogendra Nahak and Others v. State of Orissa and Others*, Judgment, 4 August 1999, AIR 1999 SC 2565. The Supreme Court notes at paragraph 24:

compliance will not render a prosecution null and void. On the other hand, non-compliance of Section 15(6A) ITPA which requires a woman police officer to be present at the time of arrest, would bring the arrest mechanism into suspicion and may vitiate the whole prosecution story. If there are suspicious circumstances that make the prosecution story dubious, then the same will get negated and the burden of proof will not be discharged. If the compliances are met, then a Prosecutor is also satisfied that there is enough evidence in the case to secure a conviction. However, if there are several non-compliances with the checklist, the burden on the prosecutor increases as there are gaping holes in the prosecution story which cannot be filled *post facto*. Thus, investigators get to perceive a direct consequence of their non-compliances with the checklist.

A prime example is that of stand-alone evidence of a prosecutrix. The test of a sterling witness[84] is that the evidence should be of a very high quality and calibre whose version should not be assailable. The relevant test of such a witness testimony is that that the statement should be truthful and free from contradictions. "It should be natural and consistent with the case of the prosecution qua the accused."[85] In a situation where the investigator discovers a prosecutrix, he may be inclined to only take the statement of the prosecutrix under Section 161 of the CrPC and not corroborate the same with any independent witnesses. This strategy may be a folly as it is possible that at the stage of trial, the court may not find the witness testimony to be wholly reliable. In such a situation, the court may need corroboration from independent and impartial witnesses. As stated in *Lallu Manjhi v. State of Jharkhand*,[86] the Supreme Court faced

---

On the other hand, if door is opened to such persons to get in and if the Magistrates are put under the obligation to record their statements, then too many persons sponsored by culprits might throng before the portals of the Magistrate courts for the purpose of creating record in advance for the purpose of helping the culprits. In the present case, one of the arguments advanced by accused for grant of bail to them was based on the statements of the four Appellants recorded by the Magistrate under Section 164 of the Code. It is not part of the investigation to open up such a vista nor can such step be deemed necessary for the administration of justice.

[84] See Supreme Court of India, *Rai Sandeep v. State (NCT of Delhi)*, Judgment, 7 August 2012, (2012) 8 SCC 21 ('Sandeep Case Judgment'); Supreme Court of India, *Tameezuddin v. State (NCT of Delhi)*, Judgment, 26 August 2009, (2009) 15 SCC 566; Supreme Court of India, *Lallu Manjhi and Another v. State of Jharkhand*, Judgment, 7 January 2003, (2003) 2 SCC 401 ('Manjhi Case Judgment').

[85] Sandeep Case Judgment, see above note 84.

[86] Manjhi Case Judgment, see above note 84.

---

with a testimony may classify the same into one of three categories: (i) wholly reliable; (ii) wholly unreliable; or (iii) neither wholly reliable or wholly unreliable. Thus, the strategy of the investigator to only obtain the statement of the prosecutrix may end up being fallacious, as it is possible that the prosecutrix may display material contradictions at the stage of cross-examination *vis-à-vis* her Section 164 statement or her Section 161 statements. In such a situation, if the court finds the testimony to be not wholly reliable thereby requiring corroboration, the same may put the investigator in a fix as he may not have taken any statement from an independent witness under Section 161 of the CrPC. Any new statement taken under Section 161 of the CrPC would also make the case hypothesis dubious, since it would be assailable on account of there being a doubt that the same is an after-thought, embellishment or a product of tutoring by the investigator. This example confirms why general investigation plans are necessary, as they may guide the investigator to cover all the possible lacuna that exist in the case.

Another example is that of best evidence. The Supreme Court of India notes in *Tomaso Bruno v. State of U.P.*[87] at paragraph 42:

> The courts below have ignored the importance of best evidence i.e. CCTV camera in the instant case and also have not noticed the absence of symptoms of strangulation in the medical reports. Upon consideration of the facts and circumstances of the case, we are of the view that the circumstances and the evidence adduced by the prosecution do not form a complete chain pointing to the guilt of the accused and the benefit of doubt is to be given to the accused and the conviction of the appellants is liable to be set aside.

Thus, at any point in time, the investigator needs to be cognisant of the best evidence available in order to increase the quality control of investigation. The SOPs thus guide the investigator in assessing the availability and feasibility of extracting the best evidence in a case theory; as non-production of such evidence can create an adverse inference against the prosecution under Section 114(g) Indian Evidence Act (1872).

In contradistinction to general investigation plans, the ICC-OTP undertakes a fact-specific investigation plan wherein it links the facts of

---

[87] Supreme Court of India, *Tomaso Bruno and Another v. State of U.P.*, Judgment, 20 January 2015, Criminal Appeal No. 142/2015.

the matter to a case hypothesis or theory, in order to decipher the underlying elements of the prosecution story, which includes the witnesses, evidence, persons involved, and ways and means to secure new evidence. Thereafter, the ICC-OTP enters into the planning phase, where a plan of action is chalked out, which includes the broad investigative objectives, how these objectives can be achieved in light of existing critical factors and identified risks, what the mitigation strategies and alternative planning scenarios are, and how they can be executed. This leads into the reporting phase where the ICC-OTP reports back with regard to the ongoing investigation and provides a feedback loop so that the case hypothesis or theory can be constantly improved in order to update itself with any new events. This includes an assessment of what the investigation was able to achieve in terms of the objectives that it had set out, and what were the reasons for failure or delay. Thus, an historic record is created through the use of the reporting phase. Finally, the last element is that of management where the ICC-OTP undertakes to manage the investigation, wherein it conducts a value assessment of what is required in the foreseeable future, and what support can be sought from other units or agencies, whether domestic or international.

Thus, a crucial difference needs to be observed. As can be seen from the SOP, these are various soft compliances that are required of the investigator in the Indian criminal justice system. These soft compliances, or checklists, provide a detailed plan for the investigating officer to undertake. These plans are not fact-specific investigation plans, but general investigation plans, for they provide for general guidelines on what the investigating officer ought to undertake and pursue, irrespective of what the facts of the case are. Some of these compliances are not in the form of hard law, as they do not entail hard consequences on account of non-compliance. Such compliances only exist in the form of advisories, that is, it is advisable for the investigating officer to undertake the compliance in order to create a complete case theory; however, non-compliance will not necessarily vitiate the prosecution hypothesis.

The SOP guides the investigating officer how to best collect the material objects, which can be crucial for proving the existence and address of a brothel, the movement of persons during trafficking, the sexual exploitation of a victim, the existence of an organised crime network, and the aspects of illegal detention. As stated earlier, an investigating officer has the discretion to deviate from the checklists as provided in the SOP, as the same would not render the case hypothesis nugatory. However, he is advised to complete the checklists as the same would strengthen the prosecution story and remove the loopholes in the case.

17.7. Conclusion: What Can We Learn and Unlearn From the ICC-OTP?

It is most alarming that far from being isolated incidents, the trafficking in persons has become a booming industry: a well-engineered and organised racket.[88] Though, India has "demonstrated increasing efforts by nearly tripling the number of victims identified". But the "investigation, prosecution and conviction are disproportionately low relative to the scale of human trafficking".[89]

Quality control in investigation and prosecution of the cases of human trafficking requires the use of sound investigation plans. The investigation plans devised by the ICC-OTP are made in real time, since the case theory is being assessed, planned, reported, and then managed depending on the facts of the prosecution case and how the investigation is panning out. One of the important reasons why the same is done is due to the fact-intensive nature of inquiry, thereby necessitating a holistic appreciation and revision of the case assessment, coupled with a good planning, reporting and management routine in real time.

In that light, the Indian investigative agencies would greatly benefit from similar case assessment, planning, reporting and management phases where the focus of the investigation can be realigned towards the prosecution objectives. The fluid and interpretative style of functioning of the Indian judicial system makes it even more necessary for the investigative and prosecutorial systems to work in tandem with the strategy to be deployed at the trial stage. As we have seen previously through the evolving law on ITPA as pronounced by the high courts in *Masti Health, Kumari Sangeeta* and *Shivaraj*,[90] the interpretation of procedural requirements ought to be clear to the investigative agencies, so that they can comply

---

[88] Mohan Parasaran, "Foreword", in Usha Tandon and Sidharth Luthra, *Human Rights: Trafficking of Women and Children: Legal and Policy Framework*, Central Law Publications, New Delhi, 2016.

[89] US Department of State, 2018, see above note 51. The conviction rate of cases of sex trafficking across the country was only 22 per cent in 2012. Pranav Garimella, "Human Trafficking Cases Jump in India; Convictions Decline!", *IndiaSpend*, 27 September 2013.

[90] Masti Health Case, see above note 65.

well in advance and not at a belated stage. When a criminal case reaches the high courts under Section 482 of the CrPC for quashing of the charge sheet or FIR, there is not enough flexibility for the investigating officer to realign the investigation and comply with the interpretation of procedural requirements by the high courts. This completely defeats the purpose of an error-free investigation as the same is constantly subject to judicial review of procedural legislation.

Another reason for importing the fact-specific investigation plans to India is that the investigating officers are often divorced from an evidential and juristic appreciation of oral and documentary evidence, thereby leading to a lesser quality of investigation, as they may not necessarily be aware as to how the prosecution may pan out at the trial stage. Thus, a higher degree of planning and reporting may help the investigating officer refocus the investigation objectives, plan the investigative strategy, keeping in mind the risks involved and the mitigation strategies, and then attempt to assess the reasons for the failure or delay, so that the investigator may re-plan his investigation to focus on what may help strengthen the prosecution. One example of this is the case of *Tomaso Bruno*[91] as discussed earlier, which went on to invalidate the prosecution story on the reason that the best evidence, that is, the CCTV footage, was not presented, resulting in an adverse inference to be drawn against the prosecution because the investigator did not procure the CCTV footage. This example indicates that a stronger appreciation of evidence and higher quality control at the investigation stage would significantly improve the outcome of prosecutions. Although the Indian investigators do not benefit from a similarly robust preliminary examination as conducted by the ICC-OTP, that does not preclude them from conducting an exhaustive investigation that may subsume a similar amount of evidence and interaction with witnesses.

However, the pros cannot be seen without analysing the cons. Implementing a real-time fact-specific investigation plan may burden the Indian investigative agencies with procedural necessities, in an already overburdened workforce. The Indian investigative and prosecutorial divisions suffer from various external and internal issues, some of them being deficiency of formal education, lack of adequate budgeting and manpower, lack of technological assistance in the investigative processes which again squares back to the reason of lack of funding, constant fluctuations and

---

[91]   See above note 87.

changes in the law either though judicial pronouncements or legislative amendments, and a dearth of investigators qualified with formal legal education in order to holistically appreciate the outcome of compliance or non-compliance of procedural requirements. Thus, importing a fact-specific investigation plan similar to that used by the ICC-OTP may be too onerous for the Indian investigative agencies to implement.

The question then crops up, as to how the pros and cons can be harmonised in order to produce the best possible result, to tackle the crime of human trafficking, in light of the constrains faced by the Indian investigative agencies. The solution is in the nature of general investigation plans, as devised through the Standard Operating Procedures devised by the UNODC and Government of India, as well as the National Human Rights Commission of India. These general investigation plans, as discussed earlier, guide the investigators in ensuring that they do not miss out on complying with a requirement, failure of which may be fatal at the stage of trial. Secondly, with a significantly less-qualified workforce operating as investigators, such general investigation plans can function as constant updates for the officers, so that they may be abreast with the evolving set of changes in the procedural and substantive law. Thirdly, a general investigation plan acts as a feed-back loop for an investigator, so that he or she is constantly aware of what the non-compliance with a procedural requirement may entail.

18

_____

Investigation Plans as a Tool for Managing Investigations in Norway

Alf Butenschøn Skre[*]

18.1. Introduction

There appears to be a need for more empirical research on which policies and practices of criminal investigations may help maximise efficiency and reliability. The reason for lack of scientific empirical knowledge in this domain could be that the possibilities for scientific research are limited due to rules of confidentiality and non-disclosure in law enforcement authorities,[1] as well as a possible lack of interest amongst some communities of practitioners in criminal investigations to engage with the scientific community[2] and _vice versa_. In addition, differences between areas of criminal law, and differences of criminal procedure and legal traditions, pose challenges for anyone with an ambition to make universal recommendations for policies and procedures in criminal investigations.

The policy and practice of investigation plans in Norway is one domestic experience that may warrant attention from decision-makers responsible for criminal investigations in fact-rich cases. One example of a fact-rich case processed in the criminal justice system of Norway is the trial of the perpetrator of the 22 July 2011 terrorist attacks, which included

---

[*] **Alf Butenschøn Skre** is a Public Prosecutor at the office of the Director of Public Prosecutions in Norway. He has previously practiced in a law firm in Oslo and served as a Senior Adviser at the Norwegian National Human Rights Institution. He holds a master's degree in law and a bachelor's degree in political science from the University of Oslo. The views expressed in this chapter are those of the author. They do not purport to reflect the views of the office of the Director of Public Prosecutions.

[1] As suggested in Ivar A. Fahsing, _The Making of an Expert Detective: Thinking and Deciding in Criminal Investigations_, doctoral thesis, University of Gothenburg, 2016, p. 6.

[2] As suggested in Richard Reyes, "Tactical Criminal Investigations: Understanding the Dynamics to Obtain the Best Results without Compromising the Investigation", in _Journal of Forensic Science and Criminal Investigation_, 2017, vol. 2, no. 2.

charges of intentionally killing 77 individual persons and seriously injuring 22 persons.[3] The final judgement in that case was issued only 13 months after the attack took place.

A cornerstone of managing fact-rich investigations in Norway is the use of investigation plans. The term 'investigation plan' is understood to denote a written outline of factual hypotheses and legal bases of criminal responsibility or innocence, and a schedule that assigns responsibility within the investigation team for investigative steps that must be taken in order to bring the investigation to a conclusion.[4]

This chapter provides a brief overview of the domestic context (Section 18.2.), outlines the use of investigation plans in Norway (Section 18.3.), and offers brief concluding remarks on the possible relevance of the Norwegian experience with investigation plans for other jurisdictions (Section 18.4.).

18.2. A Brief Overview of the Norwegian Context

Criminal justice policies that have been put in place in Norway should not necessarily be assumed to be appropriate in other national or international jurisdictions. Norway is a relatively small country in Northern Europe, with a population of some 5.3 million[5] and one of the highest gross domestic products per capita in the world.[6]

Moreover, there are important differences in criminal procedure between national and international jurisdictions. Two basic features of the Norwegian criminal justice system should be pointed out in this regard.

First, the legal framework for criminal procedure in Norway does not include a formal stage of preliminary investigations or pre-investigation in the same way as the International Criminal Court ('ICC'). Criminal investigations are opened if there are 'reasonable grounds' to investigate whether any criminal act that requires prosecution has taken

---

[3]   Oslo District Court, Judgement, 24 August 2012, TOSLO-2011-188627-24 (https://www. legal-tools.org/doc/8ej2w6/).

[4]   See National Police Directorate of Norway, Guidelines for investigation plans version 1.0, 2017.

[5]   As per the fourth quarter of 2019. See Statistics Norway, "Population", 27 February 2020 (available on its web site).

[6]   In 2018, Norway had the sixth highest GDP per capita according to the International Monetary Fund. See International Monetary Fund, "World Economic Outlook Database", April 2019 (available on its web site)

place.[7] Although some specialised law enforcement agencies have developed routines for the examination of whether there are 'reasonable grounds' to open an investigation (or, alternatively decline to open an investigation or refer the matter to another law enforcement agency), the vast majority of criminal matters in Norway are investigated without any preceding preliminary investigation stage.[8] This stands in contrast to jurisdictions with a legal framework for the conduct of preliminary examinations, as is the case, for example, in the Statute and Rules of Procedure and Evidence of the ICC.[9]

Second, the evidentiary threshold under Norwegian law for issuing an indictment is 'proof of guilt beyond a reasonable doubt',[10] and the prosecutor in charge of the matter must be certain that the necessary evidence will be available for presentation at trial. In other words, there is a higher evidentiary threshold for submitting charges from the prosecution service to the courts for trial than, for example, to confirm charges and commit the person to a Trial Chamber for trial at the ICC, cf. Article 61(7) of the ICC Statute.

Third, the lowest tier of the public prosecution service in Norway is integrated in the police organisation.[11] This stands in contrast to many

---

[7] Norway, Lov om rettergangsmåten i straffesaker (Straffeprosessloven) [Criminal Procedure Act], 22 May 1981, Section 224 ('CPA') (https://www.legal-tools.org/doc/76cf36/). See also Norway, Forskrift om ordningen av påtalemyndigheten (Påtaleinstruksen) [Regulation on Prosecutions], 28 June 1985, Sections 7-5 to 7-6 (https://www.legal-tools.org/doc/ya13nv/).

[8] See Runar Torgersen, "The Concern for Quality Control and Norwegian Preliminary Examination Practice", in Morten Bergsmo and Carsten Stahn (eds.), *Quality Control in Preliminary Examination: Volume 1*, Torkel Opsahl Academic EPublisher, Brussels, 2018 (https://www.legal-tools.org/doc/4762c4/).

[9] See, for example, Rome Statute of the International Criminal Court, 17 July 1998, Article 15(2) ('ICC Statute') (https://www.legal-tools.org/doc/7b9af9/) and ICC, Rules of Procedure and Evidence, 9 September 2002, Rule 104 (https://www.legal-tools.org/doc/8bcf6f/). See also Morten Bergsmo and Carsten Stahn (eds.), *Quality Control in Preliminary Examination: Volumes 1 and 2*, Torkel Opsahl Academic EPublisher, Brussels, 2018 (http://www.toaep.org/ps-pdf/32-bergsmo-stahn and http://www.toaep.org/ps-pdf/33-bergsmo-stahn).

[10] Director of Public Prosecutions, "Kvalitetskrav til straffesaksbehandlingen i politiet og ved statsadvokatembetene mv. (Kvalitetsrundskrivet)" [Requirements for the quality of handling criminal matters by police and public prosecutors], 8 November 2018, Circular no. 3/2018, p. 15 ('Circular no. 3/2018') (https://www.legal-tools.org/doc/9jp1eq/).

[11] The prosecution service in Norway is organised in three hierarchical tiers: 1) The Director of Public Prosecutions (Riksadvokaten), 2) Public Prosecutors (Statsadvokatene) with lim-

jurisdictions where there is organisational separation between the police and the prosecution service. Although there is a clear distinction in the line of command between police officers and prosecutors, the integration of part of the prosecution service into the police districts is meant to facilitate close collaboration with investigators and the prosecutors' oversight throughout the investigation.

The development and use of investigation plans should be seen in light of the following indicators of quality in criminal investigations, formulated by the Director of Public Prosecutions in Norway, the country's chief prosecutor:[12]

- *Fulfilling the duty to investigate and prosecute*. As mentioned above, the threshold for opening investigations is met if there are reasonable grounds to do so (Section 224 of the CPA). However, even if this threshold is met, the prosecution service in Norway has discretion to decide whether to open an investigation. The most important factors that guide such discretionary decisions are a) the likelihood that a crime has been committed, b) the gravity of the crime, and c) the extent of resources deemed necessary to conduct an investigation of the matter.[13] Once a year, the chief prosecutor issues a yearly circular in which goals and rules of prioritisation are set for the prosecution service. In recent years circulars have mostly pointed out the following categories of crimes for prioritisation: murder, other serious violent crime that endangers life or health (including arson), violence against children, domestic abuse, and hate crime. Serious forms of the following crimes should also be given priority: sexual crimes, international and organised crime, economic crimes, environmental crimes, computer related crimes, and serious traffic offences.[14]

- *Appropriate scope of investigation and appropriate use of resources*. The purpose of investigations under Norwegian law is to gather the information necessary to a) decide whether to issue an indictment, b) adjudicate the question of guilt in a court of law, and c) execute an

---

ited regional or thematic jurisdiction who report to the Director of Public Prosecutions, and 3) Prosecutors integrated in the police organisation.

[12] Circular no. 3/2018, Section 4, see above note 10.

[13] *Ibid.*, p. 7.

[14] *Ibid.*, p. 6.

adjudicated punishment (Section 226 of the CPA). The Director of Public Prosecutions has stated that the scope of an investigation must be guided by its purpose, and so that the information gathered is of relevance to those purposes. In this regard, the Director of prosecutions has stressed that the prosecutor in charge of the matter has an overarching responsibility to ensure that the investigation is purpose-driven and conducted with the necessary expeditiousness and efficiency.[15] As described in more detail below, investigation plans – which are considered conducive to a higher level of efficiency and quality – are mandatory in some category of cases, and *recommended* in all serious cases.[16] It is also stressed by the Director of Public Prosecutions that all investigations, and any trying of a case before the courts, must be proportional to the seriousness and complexity of the case. Prosecutors in charge of complex matters are encouraged to make active use of a provision in the CPA that enables the prosecutor to waive prosecution for charges that – if the person is found guilty – will not result in any material punishment for the charged person, given the other charges that are brought.[17]

- *High rate of solved cases.* While procedural safeguards and the rights of the accused are to be respected at all times, and the evidentiary threshold must be met in all cases, a high rate of solved cases is a self-evident ambition of the prosecution service.[18]

- *Adequate penal reaction.* In the Norwegian criminal system, sentencing is based largely on analysis of relevant precedents in case law, rather than detailed quantitative sentencing guidelines. Prosecutors have a particular responsibility to ensure that the development of penal reactions are in line with the priorities set by the Director of Public Prosecutions. Unnecessary delays in the handling of a criminal matter by the police or prosecution service can lead to a discretionary reduction of the sentence when the matter is adjudi-

---

[15] *Ibid.*, p. 10.

[16] *Ibid.*, p. 11.

[17] See CPA, Section 70: "Prosecution may be waived when, as a result of the rules on sentencing in cases of more than one committed offence, no or only an immaterial punishment would be applicable to the offender" (author's translation), see above note 7.

[18] Circular no. 3/2018, p. 15, see above note 10.

cated. A lack of efficiency thereby harms the goal of achieving adequate penal reactions.[19]

- *Compliance with applicable rules of procedure and code of criminal procedure.*[20]

- *Swift handling of cases.* Under Section 226 of the CPA, investigations are to be carried out as swiftly as possible.[21] Norwegian prosecutors are also under an obligation to ensure that cases are brought within a reasonable time under Article 6 of the European Convention on Human Rights. The need for expeditiousness relates to the obvious need of the accused and of victims to obtain a decision within reasonable time. However, the Director of Public Prosecutions has also stressed that swift handling of cases is conducive of a higher rate of solved cases. This is in part because many types of evidence are 'perishable' and may deteriorate over time. Swift handling of cases is also conducive to more efficient resource management – recommencing an investigation after an hiatus can cause personnel to spend more time recalling and revisiting details of the case that would otherwise be at the forefront of their attention.

- *Objectivity.* Evaluations of cases where a miscarriage of justice has taken place often point to a lack of objectivity on the part of the police and the prosecution service. The criterion of objectivity is described as a non-derogable safeguard in all criminal matters. In addition to protecting the accused against a miscarriage of justice, the criterion of objectivity helps ensure a higher quality of evidence. Prosecutors must assess whether a particular case at hand require the use of measures that reduce the risk of errors as a result of a lack of objectivity. Such measures include increasing the number of key personnel, requesting assistance from the National Criminal Investigation Service or another police district, or a meeting with the district attorney.[22]

---

[19] *Ibid.*, p. 16.

[20] *Ibid.*, p. 18.

[21] Council of Europe, Convention for the Protection of Human Rights and Fundamental Freedoms, 4 November 1950 (https://legal-tools.org/doc/8267cb).

[22] Circular no. 3/2018, p. 22–23, see above note 10.

- *Appropriate care for victims and next of kin.* The Director of Public Prosecutions has stressed the role of victims of crime and their next of kin in modern criminal proceedings. Police and the prosecution service are required to treat such persons with care and respect, and to respond expeditiously to enquiries *et cetera*. Victims and next of kin will have a right to a designated contact person within the police, and in many cases also an attorney that will safeguards their rights.[23]

- *Promoting the general public's trust in criminal prosecutions.* The Director of Public Prosecutions has pointed out that the level of trust enjoyed in the general public depends not only on whether cases are solved, but also how handling of cases is communicated to the public, and how investigations are portrayed by the media. In this regard, the Director has encouraged an open and accommodating attitude to media enquiries, while maintaining the duty of professional secrecy and the presumption of innocence.[24]

- *Appropriate co-operation with the courts and relevant parties and others involved in the case.* The Director of prosecutions has highlighted the need for professional and appropriate co-operation during investigations and during trial. There is an expectation that prosecutors – in order to enable other involved parties and the court to manage the case effectively – provide comprehensive documents describing evidence for trial, as well as informative documents containing the charges and clear introductory statements.[25]

- *Appropriate editing and storage of case files and handling of evidence.*[26]

- *Contribute to development of case law.* The prosecution service has an ambition to contribute to unity and clarity of the law, as well as appropriate legal developments, by requesting leave to appeal to the Supreme Court in appropriate cases that raise legal questions with implications for other cases.[27]

---

23 *Ibid.*, p. 23–24.
24 *Ibid.*, p. 24.
25 *Ibid.*, p. 26.
26 *Ibid.*, p. 28–29.
27 *Ibid.*, p. 29.

Investigation plans are just one of several management tools used to pursue the concept of quality described above. Other tools include:

- document containing the reasons to initiate an investigation, in certain cases of *proprio motu* investigations;

- document containing draft charges that are refined continuously in the course of the investigation;

- evidence memoranda that are used to develop and analyse the evidence base; and

- review conferences and peer review mechanisms that allow for quality control by colleagues in the prosecution service who are not otherwise assigned to the case.

18.3. Investigation Plans in Norway

18.3.1. Function and Areas of Application

In a circular of 2018, the Director of Public Prosecutions stated that investigation plans promote "more structured investigative work, progress and quality, as well as providing notoriety and an overview of the case to support decisions during the investigation".[28] A working group appointed by the Director of Public Prosecutions in 2018 to give recommendations on how the prosecution service can conduct trial hearings in large criminal matters more efficiently pointed to the importance of undertaking collection of evidence aimed at confirming or falsifying hypotheses defined in the investigation plan and draft indictment, in order to avoid overload of evidence.[29] This entails that the investigation should as far as possible be a closed-ended project. In fact-rich cases, a well-written investigation plan is paramount to achieving correct investigative processes and outcomes, as well as an appropriate allocation of resources.

The investigation plan should be prepared immediately after the report of an alleged crime, and be developed as a 'living document' throughout the investigation, in response to results of the investigative steps taken. Responsibility for the investigation plan rests with the prose-

---

[28] *Ibid.*, p. 11. Author's translation from Norwegian.

[29] The author was the legal secretary of the working group. The working group's report is published as Director of Public Prosecutions, *Effektivisering av domstolsbehandlingen av større straffesaker* [Increasing efficiency in the court-processing of larger criminal cases], 2018, Paper Series no. 1/2018 (https://www.legal-tools.org/doc/911e3e/).

cutor in charge of the matter, although the plan is frequently drafted by the main investigator in consultation with the prosecutor.

The investigation plan is often created by use of a digital project-management platform available on the Norwegian police computer network. In other words, it is not necessarily a physical, printed document or a digital document *file* as such. The plan could be the sum of input that has been entered into a specific module in a project management system, and as such could be described as a knowledge-base. The system used by the Norwegian police for this purpose is located on the servers of the police force and can be accessed by authorised personnel if they are able to establish a secure internet connection, thus facilitating the flow of information within the team. The availability of the investigation plan in 'real-time' allows team members to plan and conduct investigation steps on the basis of the latest available data and analysis. This can allow for more open and continuous flow of information within the team than would be achieved by using an investigation plan in the form of a static or frozen document. Using the investigation plan as a living document does, however, create the need for a reliable mechanism to log changes made to the investigation plan. This is particularly important with a view to being able to reconstruct decisions made during an investigation, for example as part of an evaluation that goes back to the start of the process.

The Director of Public Prosecutions has recommended the use of investigation plans in investigations of serious crime.[30] Moreover, the Director has instructed the use of investigation plans in four categories of investigations where there has arguably been a perceived need to enhance the quality and efficiency of investigations. The first of these categories were cases concerning *rape*, where the use of investigation plans was made mandatory in 2013. The decision had a backdrop of publicly voiced concerns regarding the speed and quality of rape investigations. These issues could make the criminal case more burdensome than necessary for the victim and the accused, and public perceptions of problems in rape investigations could potentially cause victims not to report instances of rape.[31] Investigation plans had already been used to a certain extent in

---

[30] Letter from the Director of Public Prosecutions to the Prosecution Service, 30 March 2015.

[31] See, for example, Letter from the Director of Public Prosecutions to the Prosecution Service, 8 November 2013. The Parliament of Norway had also expressed that the quality and speed of processing rape cases needed to be improved, see Prop. 1 S (2012–2013).

such cases. For example, the National Crime Investigation Service, which is a national investigation agency for organised and serious crime, did use investigation plans in all cases handled by them, and many police districts used investigation plans in cases that were seen as complex or particularly serious. There was a clear experience from the operational level of the prosecution service that structured investigation planning, when used, enhanced both quality and efficiency of investigations.

In 2015, instructions were given to use investigation plans in cases concerning *sexual assault on children* and cases concerning *abuse in close relationships*.[32] Another two years later, such instructions were given also for cases where there was a suspicion of *murder*.[33]

Investigation plans may be omitted in these four types of investigations if the case is so simple (both on the facts and the legal aspects) that an investigation plan is clearly unnecessary.

18.3.2. Eight Mandatory Elements of Investigation Plans in Norway

There is no authoritative template for investigation plans in Norway, but the contents of investigation plans have been gradually more standardised through guidelines on the minimum requirements of investigation plans.[34] Investigation plans must contain eight elements, which are described below.

I. **Factual hypotheses**

    The investigation plan must contain factual hypotheses that are coherent with the available facts collected thus far, and that appear relevant to the investigation. The identified hypotheses create a vantage point for developing an offence-driven and closed-ended investigation. Identifying all reasonable hypotheses is inducive to exploring avenues for finding potentially exculpatory evidence.

    Example 1:

---

[32] Letter from the Director of Public Prosecutions to the Prosecution Service, 30 March 2015.

[33] Director of Public Prosecutions, "Mål og prioriteringer for straffesaksbehandlingen i 2017 – politiet og statsadvokatene" [Goals and priorities for the processing of criminal cases in 2017 – the police and the prosecutors], 28 February 2017, Circular no. 1/2017.

[34] See Letter from the Director of Public Prosecutions to the Prosecution Service, 8 November 2013 and National Police Directorate of Norway, Guidelines for investigation plans version 1.0, 2017.

Alleged purchase of sexual services from a young girl who was in psychiatric treatment. Hypotheses that were entered in the investigation plan were as follows:

H1: The accused had sexual intercourse with the victim.

    H1.1: The accused had sexual intercourse with the victim.

    H1.2: The accused paid to have sexual intercourse with the victim.

    H1.3: The accused obtained sexual intercourse by exploiting the victim's vulnerability and then paid the victim.

H2: The accused did not have sexual intercourse with the victim.

    H2.1: The victim has given an untrue statement caused by her mental illness.

    H2.2: The victim has given an untrue statement as a result of influence in the form of leading questions posed by family members and/or her therapist.

H3: The victim was forced to have sexual intercourse with the accused for payment.

H4: The accused has had sexual intercourse with several minors. He contacts them through [web site] and then meets them at [location].

Example 2:

The suspect was observed by several eyewitnesses as he exerted brutal violence over some time until the victim died. The suspect admitted the *actus reus* elements, but gave a confused statement regarding the circumstances.

H1 (Murder – premeditated):

There is a known pre-existing connection between the suspect and victim, and the suspect killed the victim after premeditation over time.

H2 (Murder – wilful):

Regardless of whether there is a pre-existing connection between the victim and suspect, the murder was committed because of circumstances occurring at the time, resulting in the death of the victim.

H3 (Murder – insanity):

There was no pre-existing connection between the suspect and victim and no particular events that led to the violence. The crime was committed without pre-meditation or explicable causes.

H4 (Self-defence):

Regardless of any pre-existing connection between the suspect and victim, a situation occurred in which the suspect felt he had to defend himself against the victim. The situation resulted in death for the victim.

Because the use of investigation plans is not regulated in detail, there is room for variation in how hypotheses are formulated in practice, and there is room for debate as to what constitutes best practice. In a publication from the Norwegian Police Academy, Professor Eivind Kolflaath[35] proposes the following principles to guide the creation of hypotheses in investigation plans, which the present author endorses as a vantage point for further discussion:[36]

Principles of content

Contents in *each individual hypothesis*:

(1) The hypothesis must be a possible expla-nation to information in the case. *Id est*, the hypothesis must relate to the facts of the case, not the legal requirements.

(2) The hypothesis must be testable, that is, there must exist investigative steps that could strengthen or weaken the hypothesis (either directly or indirectly through test-ing of another hypothesis).

Contents in *the set of hypotheses*:

---

[35] Faculty of Law of the University of Bergen. Professor Kolflaath has published extensively on theories of evidence and probability in law.

[36] The present author's translation from Norwegian to English, from Eivind Kolflaath, "Hy-poteser i etterforskningsplaner" [Hypotheses in Investigation Plans], in Egil H. Olsvik and Patrick Risan (eds.), *Etterforskning under lupen* [Investigations Examined], Politihøg-skolen, Oslo, 2019, pp. 97–98.

(3) Every hypothesis in the set must be different from the others.

(4) The set of hypotheses must cover all remaining realistic possibilities.

Principles of formulation

(1) Formulations of hypotheses must be complete sentences (although cross-references to such formulations may be done by way of abridged phrases for sake of convenience).

(2) Formulations of hypotheses must be unambiguous, unless ambiguity may be eliminated using principles of interpretation (see below).

Principles of interpretation

(1) Formulations of hypotheses shall be interpreted literally. No assumptions should be made about factual or legal aspects that are not explicitly stated in the hypothesis.

(2) Formulations of hypotheses shall be interpreted as hypotheses on the facts of the case, that is, not as a hypothesis about any particular legal classification.

II. Legal classifications

The plan must contain reference to sections of the Criminal Code – or any other statute containing relevant penal sanctions – that would appear relevant to one or more of the factual hypotheses in the case. In practice, the sections of the penal code are often noted in conjunction with the relevant alternative factual hypotheses. The choice of legal classifications is a way of selecting parts of the totality of possible crime committed for investigation and prosecution, that is, determining the focus and scope of the investigation. In selecting which legal classifications to include in the investigation plan, it is of course very important to make a critical assessment as to what should be included. Several contributions in this volume[37] – and a policy brief by Morten Bergsmo in 2019 that broached the issue of

---

[37] Devasheesh Bais, "Prioritisation of Suspected Conduct and Cases: From Idea to Practice", Chapter 9 above; Cale Davis, "Challenges in Charge Selection: Considerations Informing the Number of Charges and Cumulative Charging Practices", Chapter 13 above.

quality control in criminal investigations of core international crimes[38] – have pointed to the importance of exercising prosecutorial discretion in order to 'frame' the case in an appropriate way.

A working group appointed by the Director of Public Prosecutions to make recommendations on how the prosecution service could handle complex and large cases more efficiently at the trial stage emphasised the need to take a clear position on the purpose and objectives of the case.[39] In other words, it should be clearly stated what it is that justifies the use of resources to investigate and prosecute *this* alleged instance of crime, when there are *other* cases waiting in a backlog. When that justification is clearly stated from the outset, it will become clear that some acts possibly committed by the suspect constitute the very essence of the case, while other acts (although possibly criminal acts) and other possible modes of liability, hold less demand of our attention – in fact they may inadvertently distract and unnecessarily complicate the investigation. It was a clear recommendation from the working group to weed out acts falling in the second category, in other words removing instances *within the case* that do not justify prioritisation.

Without such a guiding principle, and without a strong will to eliminate less serious instances from the investigation, the working group found that there is a clear risk that the investigator will find himself in an open-ended, evidence-driven investigation with a significant potential to swell far out of proportion. At the same time, the working group acknowledged the need to balance this perspective against the perspective of victims of the crimes that could be ejected from the case and their need for reparations.

III.   Based on the facts and on the legal elements of the statutes identified in item II, the prosecutor in charge of the matter **formulates factual questions** that the investigation should aim to answer. This can be done in many ways, and there is no detailed manual on best practice for how to formulate this in an investigation plan. The pinpointing of the factual topics of inquiry and investigative steps will

---

[38]   Morten Bergsmo, "Towards a Culture of Quality Control in Criminal Investigations", FICHL Policy Brief Series No. 94 (2019), Torkel Opsahl Academic EPublisher, Brussels, 2019 (http://www.toaep.org/pbs-pdf/94-bergsmo/). See in particular Sections 3.4 and 3.5.

[39]   Director of Public Prosecutions, 2018, see above note 29.

of course be useful to ensure that involved team members fully understand how to carry out their work in a way that is most useful to the investigation, that is, that they give appropriate attention to what is seen by the prosecutor as the most salient issues. An example of such formulation is given in *Example 3* below, which concerns the investigation of a murder case. Due to evidence gathered at the crime scene, the police had a strong suspicion against the suspect, but it was unclear whether the motive was purely profit-based, or if other mental factors had influenced the suspect.

Example 3:

> The main aim of gathering of information in [location] is to establish the suspect's movements in [location] before and after the time of the murder. It is most important to document his movements between […] and […], but also movements before this period will be of significant interest to the case. […] In questioning friends and acquaintances, it will be important to clarify whether the suspect has a history of drug use, mental health and other circumstances that could be of importance to the question of criminal liability/defence of insanity.

In addition to items I to III described above, investigation plans should include the following five elements:

IV. Based on the factual questions formulated pursuant to item III above, relevant investigative steps should be identified. The investigative steps should be ranked according to priority and tactical considerations.

V. The plan must assign responsibility within the investigation team for outstanding actions, and a deadline for completion of each step. The plan should show when deadlines have not been met, and any consequences expected as a consequence of the fact that the deadline was missed.

VI. The need for documentation from external sources (such as reports from technical analysts, expert opinions, and medical journals) and actions required to obtain such documents.

VII. A deadline for completing the investigation, and assignment of responsibility for the necessary final steps in closing the investigation.

VIII. The plan should include contingency planning in case the lead prosecutor, lead investigator or main investigator should become unavailable to continue working on the case.

In addition to these eight elements, investigation plans will in practice often include a description of resources required in order to complete the investigation.

18.4. Relevance for Other Jurisdictions?

On the whole, public prosecutors in Norway view investigation plans as a useful tool in clarifying the scope of the investigation, organising tasks in an efficient manner and to provide a record of decision points in the course of the investigation.[40] A key function of investigation plans in large investigations is to provide a common platform for the investigation team and the prosecutor in charge to facilitate thought-processes as described above in this chapter. In this way investigation plans help by providing guidance to investigators, thus avoiding unnecessarily lengthy investigations resulting in voluminous and unfocused gathering of evidence.

The Quality Control in Criminal Investigation Project of the Centre for International Law Research and Policy (CILRAP) has identified seven bottlenecks for the prosecution's investigation and case-preparation in matters of core international crimes.[41] For reasons described above, the proper use of investigation plans as a tool to ensure that the investigation meets strict evidentiary requirements before an indictment is issued, may help address in part the following of the bottlenecks identified in the project:

- overview of information;
- evidence-review;
- formulation of responsibility;
- cumulative charging; and
- too much evidence.

---

[40] Responses provided by all public prosecutors to the Director of Public Prosecutions regarding the utility of investigation plans were described in a letter from the Director of Public Prosecutions to the Prosecution Service on 30 March 2015.

[41] Bergsmo, 2019, see above note 38.

PART V:
JUDICIAL AND PROSECUTORIAL PARTICIPATION IN INVESTIGATION AND CASE PREPARATION

19

Quality Control in Case Preparation
and the Role of the Judiciary of the
International Criminal Court

Gilbert Bitti[*]

When starting a discussion on quality control in 'case preparation', it is necessary to first agree on what is a good quality case and what is a well-prepared case.

With regard to the quality of the case, there is a need to first determine what the scope of a 'good' case is. More specifically, does a good quality case need to be representative of the victimisation in a situation? In other words, could a case be qualified as good even if the harm suffered by the victims is not fully represented by that case due to its very limited scope? Second, it is also necessary to agree on the goal of building a case. Is a 'good' case, a case that is construed in a way that maximises the chances for the Prosecutor to win it, even if the price to pay is to avoid some aspects difficult to prove but important for the victims, or is a 'good' case a case that centres on establishing the truth?

With regard to case preparation, several aspects should be considered: (i) the need to respect the rights of the defence, which requires, *inter alia*,[1] avoiding an over-collection of evidence (especially with regard to crime base evidence) and to properly define the case (especially with regard to its factual scope and the modes of liability), thereby preventing the defence from being flooded with tons of evidentiary material to analyse and from facing a case which is too vague and contains 'many possible

---

[*] **Gilbert Bitti** is Senior Legal Adviser, Pre-Trial Division, International Criminal Court ('ICC'). The views expressed in this chapter are solely those of the author and do not reflect the views of the ICC.

[1] Other aspects are important with regard to the rights of the defence, such as the duty for the Prosecutor to investigate equally exonerating and incriminating circumstances, and the need to prepare as soon as possible to comply with the requirements concerning disclosure and translation of evidence collected.

options'; (ii) the need to protect the rights of victims (for example, the need to conduct as early as possible financial investigations for the purposes of reparations); and (iii) the need to protect witnesses and to plan such a protection sufficiently in advance to avoid delays in the proceedings. The role of the judiciary is to ensure respect and protection of the rights of all those participating in the procedure.

With regard to the role of the judiciary at the ICC in the quality control of case preparation, two issues are of great importance: the timing of case preparation (Section 19.1.) and the framing of the charges when preparing a case (Section 19.2.).

19.1. The Timing of Case Preparation

With regard to the timing of case preparation, the role of the judiciary has been up until now to insist on the need for the case to be prepared as soon as possible. The need for early case preparation will first be analysed with regard to the conduct of the preliminary examination (Section 19.1.1.) and thereafter with regard to the conduct of the investigation (Section 19.1.2.).

19.1.1. Case Preparation and Conduct of the Preliminary Examination

The problems related to the conduct of preliminary examinations by the Office of the Prosecutor ('OTP'), will first be analysed (Section 19.1.1.1.), and then the necessity to adequately prepare for the investigation already at the stage of the preliminary examination (Section 19.1.1.2.).

19.1.1.1. The Problems Related to the Conduct of Preliminary Examinations

It is important for case preparation to start already before the formal investigation is initiated.

In Part 2 of the OTP Draft Regulations,[2] which dealt with the management of preliminary examinations, Regulation 3.1. provided that the Deputy Prosecutor (Investigations) was to be responsible for the preliminary examination of all information received under Article 15 of the

---

[2]   ICC-OTP, Draft Regulations of the Office of the Prosecutor, 3 June 2003 ('Draft Regulations') (https://www.legal-tools.org/doc/siibwo/).

Rome Statute of the International Criminal Court,[3] and would report to the Prosecutor on the state of the preliminary examinations (Regulation 3.5.). The Deputy Prosecutor was to establish standing Article 15 preliminary examination teams, composed of persons from the investigation and analysis sections within the Investigation Division, a lawyer from the Prosecution Division, and a legal adviser from the Legal Advisory Section (Regulation 4.1.). The preliminary examination teams were envisaged to first make an assessment of the credibility and reliability of the sources of information and, to the extent possible, preliminarily characterise the nature of alleged crimes, identify those involved, recommend targets of a possible investigation, and assess the likelihood of a successful completion of such an investigation (Regulation 4.5.). Obviously, the logic of those teams was to prepare an investigation and future cases, while taking into consideration issues related to complementarity (see the same Regulation 4.5.). Those Draft Regulations were not approved by the first ICC Prosecutor.

In this regard, the creation of a Jurisdiction, Complementarity and Cooperation Division ('JCCD') in the first years of the Court, which integrates a section on preliminary examinations, was motivated by the willingness to push for a positive approach to complementarity,[4] although this was, according to some,[5] too often in vein. In this regard, waiting for a State reaction to crimes within the jurisdiction of the Court, may have been at the detriment of the preservation of crucial evidence. It is important to envisage the preservation of evidence in a strategic and systematic way, including the necessary protection of witnesses, and to plan very early on for an investigation. The JCCD rather focuses on the analysis of the criteria provided for in Article 53(1) of the Statute, and diplomatic exchanges with States especially with regard to the application of the principle of complementarity. While the Statute requires such an analysis and stresses the importance of the principle of complementarity between the Court and States, this cannot be at the expense of the fight against

---

[3]   Rome Statute of the International Criminal Court, 17 July 1998 ('Statute') (https://www.legal-tools.org/doc/7b9af9/).

[4]   See ICC-OTP, Report on Prosecutorial Strategy, 14 September 2006, pp. 4–5 (https://www.legal-tools.org/doc/6e3bf4/).

[5]   See Human Rights Watch, *Pressure Point: The ICC's Impact on National Justice: Lessons from Colombia, Georgia, Guinea and the United Kingdom*, 3 May 2018 (https://www.legal-tools.org/doc/442f1c/).

impunity which requires a prompt response from the OTP with regard to the collection of evidence. In the current structure adopted by the OTP, the JCCD is given priority with regard to the initiation of OTP activities in a situation, allowing the JCCD to retain control according to a recent report presented by an independent panel of experts[6] and therefore delaying the preparation for the investigation, with the unfortunate consequence that evidence could be lost.

It is important to understand that, as soon as the OTP becomes aware of crimes committed which could be under the jurisdiction of the Court, the immediate reaction of national jurisdictions towards those crimes needs to be monitored. As is well-known, there is a duty for national jurisdictions to react quickly and thoroughly in order to preserve evidence, especially regarding the crimes under the jurisdiction of the ICC.

The jurisprudence of both the Inter-American Court of Human Rights ('IACtHR') and the European Court of Human Rights ('ECtHR') is clear on this topic. The ECtHR insists especially on the requirement of promptness with regard to the start of the investigation,[7] as a prompt response by the national authorities in charge of the investigation is "regarded as essential in maintaining public confidence in their adherence to the rule of law and in preventing any appearance of collusion in or tolerance of unlawful acts".[8] Promptness goes hand in hand with effectiveness and national authorities in charge of the investigation must take all reasonable steps they can to secure the evidence concerning the incident, including, *inter alia*, eyewitness testimony and forensic evidence.[9] Furthermore, the investigation must be independent from the executive and the victims must be able to participate effectively in the investigation.[10]

---

[6] See ICC-OTP, "Annex 1: ICC OTP Kenya Cases: Review and Recommendations: Executive Summary of the Report of the External Independent Experts", in "Full Statement of the Prosecutor, Fatou Bensouda, on external expert review and lessons drawn from the Kenya situation", 26 November 2019, paras. E.10 and E.14 ('Kenya Cases: Review and Recommendations: Executive Summary of the Report of the External Independent Experts') (https://www.legal-tools.org/doc/32p2hy/).

[7] See ECtHR, *El-Masri v. The Former Yugoslav Republic of Macedonia*, Grand Chamber, Judgment, 13 December 2012, ECLI:CE:ECHR:2012:1213JUD003963009, para. 183 ('El-Masri Judgment') (https://www.legal-tools.org/doc/3f5063/).

[8] See ECtHR, *McKerr v. The United Kingdom*, Judgment, 4 May 2001, ECLI:CE:ECHR:2001:0504JUD002888395, para. 114 (https://www.legal-tools.org/doc/fa3ca4/).

[9] *Ibid.*, para. 113.

[10] See El-Masri Judgment, paras. 184–85, see above note 7.

The IACtHR has found that the obligation to employ due diligence is "particularly stringent and important" in the face of serious human rights violations – including forced disappearances, extra judicial executions, torture and other cruel, inhuman or degrading treatment – and requires the investigating body to "use all available means to carry out such steps and inquiries as are necessary to achieve the goal pursued within a reasonable time".[11] Efforts to investigate promptly should be increased in these cases

> because the passage of time has a directly proportionate relationship to the limitations to – and, in some cases, the impossibility of – obtaining evidence and/or testimony, making it difficult and even rendering ineffective or invalid, the probative measures taken in order to elucidate the facts investigated, identify the possible authors and participants, and determine possible criminal responsibilities.[12]

Moreover, the IACtHR has established that "it is necessary to act with special promptness when, owing to the design of the domestic laws, the possibility of filing a civil action for damages depends on the criminal proceeding".[13] This is precisely the case at the ICC where the right of victims to claim compensation is entirely dependent on the existence of an investigation and prosecutions; as stated by Pre-Trial Chamber I:

> any delay in the start of the investigation is a delay for the victims to be in a position to claim reparations for the harm suffered as a result of the commission of the crimes within the jurisdiction of this Court.[14]

---

[11]   IACtHR, *Rochela Massacre v. Colombia*, Judgment, 11 May 2007, para. 156 (https://www. legal-tools.org/doc/0c7f35/). See also IACtHR, *Serrano-Cruz Sisters v. El Salvador*, Judgment, 1 March 2005, para. 166 (https://www.legal tools.org/doc/5ae34f/); IACtHR, *Pueblo Bello Massacre v. Colombia*, Judgment, 31 January 2006, paras. 151–52, 184–88 (https://www.legal-tools.org/doc/cb12ef/); IACtHR, *Ticona Estrada et al. v. Bolivia*, Judgment, 27 November 2008, paras. 79–82 (https://www.legal-tools.org/doc/2cikyj/).

[12]   IACtHR, *Contreras et al. v. El Salvador*, Judgment, 31 August 2011, para. 145 (https:// www.legal-tools.org/doc/owwoho/). See also IACtHR, *Heliodoro Portugal v. Panama*, Judgment, 12 August 2008, para. 150 (https://www.legal-tools.org/doc/4c42c7/).

[13]   IACtHR, *Gonzales Lluy et al. v. Ecuador*, Judgment, 1 September 2015, para. 312 (https:// www.legal-tools.org/doc/08ca92/). See also IACtHR, *Suárez Peralta v. Ecuador*, Judgment, 21 May 2013, para. 102 (https://www.legal-tools.org/doc/ikrdxc/).

[14]   ICC, Request under Regulation 46(3) of the Regulations of the Court, Pre-Trial Chamber, Decision on the "Prosecution's Request for a Ruling on Jurisdiction under Article 19(3) of the Statute", 6 September 2018, ICC-RoC46(3)-01/18-37, para. 88 ('Pre-Trial Decision on

It is against those standards that the OTP should assess the reaction of prosecutorial and judicial national authorities, especially with regard to the promptness of their response. Impunity for grave violations of human rights is "caused or facilitated notably by the lack of diligent reaction of institutions or state agents".[15] What matters here for the OTP is to analyse the concrete and prompt investigative steps taken by the national authorities, not any kind of political response or general commitment to act.

In case those national jurisdictions do not react, either because they do not have the capacity or because of mostly political unwillingness to do so, the OTP should react and start preserving evidence, even if the means at the disposal of the OTP are limited at that stage.[16] This presupposes that investigators and analysts are involved very quickly and have the capacity to react when they receive information from victims, non-governmental organisations ('NGOs'), the United Nations ('UN') or foreign Governments. Otherwise, crucial evidence may be lost and this affects the entirety of the proceedings before the Court.

In its decision on the authorisation of an investigation in the situation in Burundi, Pre-Trial Chamber III[17] stressed two important issues in relation to what the Court can do at the preliminary examination stage: (1) there is a possibility to involve the judiciary in the preservation of evidence already at the stage of the preliminary examination in accordance with Rule 47 of the Rules, as the Pre-Trial Chamber may either appoint a counsel or a judge to be present during the taking of the testimony at the seat of the Court; and (2) there is also a possibility for the OTP, in coordination with the Victims and Witnesses Unit, to already start taking

---

the Prosecution's Request for a Ruling on Jurisdiction') (https://www.legal-tools.org/doc/73aeb4/).

[15] See Directorate General of Human Rights and Rule of Law, Council of Europe, "Guidelines adopted by the Committee of Ministers on 30 March 2011 at the 1110th meeting of the Ministers' Deputies", in *Eradicating impunity for serious human rights violations: Guidelines and reference texts*, Strasbourg, 2011, p. 7; see also Guiding principles for the search for disappeared persons, UN Doc. CED/C/7, 8 May 2019, Principle 6, requiring that investigative activities start immediately and that evidence be preserved.

[16] See Article 15(2) of the Statute, see above note 3 and Rule 47 of the Rules of Procedure and Evidence, 9 September 2002 ('Rules') (https://www.legal-tools.org/doc/8bcf6f/).

[17] ICC, Situation in the Republic of Burundi, Pre-Trial Chamber, Public Redacted Version of "Decision Pursuant to Article 15 of the Rome Statute on the Authorization of an Investigation into the Situation in the Republic of Burundi", 9 November 2017, ICC-01/17-9-Red, para. 15 ('Burundi Article 15 Decision') (https://www.legal-tools.org/doc/8f2373/).

---

measures for the protection of witnesses at the stage of the preliminary examination. Indeed, although States are not obliged to co-operate at that stage, nothing prevents the OTP from asking their voluntary co-operation for the protection of victims and witnesses. The same is true for the voluntary co-operation which could be offered by NGOs or by inter-governmental organisations, including the UN. Therefore, the preliminary examination could be a much more operational stage than it is now, geared towards investigation and case preparation.

Furthermore, the ICC judiciary has been underlining for years that preliminary examinations are too long and should be concluded within a reasonable time.[18] This has been recently reiterated, taking into consideration the rights of the victims to have access to justice.[19] Again, the quality of the investigation and the preparation of the case have implications for all those involved in the situation under preliminary examination or under investigation, especially the victims, whose rights to truth, justice and reparations are at stake.

For example, complementarity considerations are cited by the Prosecutor for explaining an 11-year long preliminary examination in the situation in Afghanistan (from 2006 until 2017), although the Prosecutor notes in her request under Article 15 of the Statute that, due to an amnesty law passed in 2007, near "total impunity has been the rule not the exception".[20] This is also true for other situations. In her request to be authorised to start an investigation in the situation in Georgia from 2015, the Prosecutor noted that "the timing of this Application has been determined largely by issues of admissibility as they relate to the progress of national

---

[18] ICC, Situation in the Central African Republic, Pre-Trial Chamber, Decision Requesting Information on the Status of the Preliminary Examination of the Situation in the Central African Republic, 30 November 2006, ICC-01/05-6 (https://www.legal-tools.org/doc/76e607/).

[19] ICC, Situation on the Registered Vessels of the Union of the Comoros, the Hellenic Republic and the Kingdom of Cambodia, Pre-Trial Chamber, Decision on the "Application for Judicial Review by the Government of the Union of the Comoros", 15 November 2018, ICC-01/13-68, paras. 119–20 (https://www.legal-tools.org/doc/a268c5/); see also Pre-Trial Decision on the Prosecution's Request for a Ruling on Jurisdiction, paras. 84–88, see above note 14.

[20] ICC, Situation in the Islamic Republic of Afghanistan, OTP, Public redacted version of "Request for authorisation of an investigation pursuant to article 15", 20 November 2017, ICC-02/17-7-Red, para. 5 ('Situation in Afghanistan OTP Request for Authorisation of an Investigation') (https://www.legal-tools.org/doc/db23eb/).

proceedings".[21] This statement should be compared with the following conclusion by Judge Peter Kovacs, in his separate opinion to the decision authorising the investigation in the situation in Georgia:

> The report presented suggests that at least during the period between December 2011 and 30 October 2014, the Georgian authorities were not investigating the serious incidents which are of concern to the ICC Prosecutor. Nor does this report reveal whether those low-level perpetrators referred to belong to those most responsible for the commission of the crimes in the course of the 2008 conflict. As such, said investigations do not fulfil the required admissibility test before the Court. Moreover, notably at this stage of the Georgian investigation, no charge had been presented against any perpetrator, be it a low or high ranking one. In this regard, a six-year investigation without any charge being presented against a single perpetrator raises serious doubts as to the seriousness of such an investigation. To meet the admissibility test, a national investigation should not be confined to simply "collect evidence" but should aim at prosecutions. Therefore, the Prosecutor could have reached the conclusion that the admissibility test was not met way before October 2015.[22]

If one compares the first report on preliminary examinations issued by the OTP in 2011[23] and the last one issued in 2019[24], it is striking to note that the situations in Colombia and Guinea were at what is referred to by the OTP as 'Phase 3' of the preliminary examination stage (that is, the stage concerning analysis of complementarity) in 2011 and were still at that stage in 2019.

The length of preliminary examinations seems also to be the result of a sequential approach on the part of the OTP, namely by first assessing

---

[21] ICC, Situation in Georgia, OTP, Corrected Version of "Request for authorisation of an investigation pursuant to article 15", 16 October 2015, ICC-01/15-4-Corr, para. 13 (https://www.legal-tools.org/doc/75ab1e/).

[22] ICC, Situation in Georgia, Pre-Trial Chamber, Separate Opinion of Judge Péter Kovács, 27 January 2016, ICC-01/15-12-Anx-Corr, para. 47 (https://www.legal-tools.org/doc/28b159/).

[23] ICC-OTP, *Report on Preliminary Examination activities*, 13 December 2011, pp. 14 (Colombia) and 21 (Guinea) (https://www.legal-tools.org/doc/4aad1d/).

[24] ICC-OTP, *Report on Preliminary Examination activities*, 5 December 2019, pp. 24 (Colombia) and 37 (Guinea) (https://www.legal-tools.org/doc/lq7j94/).

jurisdiction and then assessing complementarity which delays even further the preliminary examination of a situation.[25] Such a sequential approach is not required by the Statute.

Respect for complementarity when national prosecutorial and judicial authorities do not react promptly could simply end up in impunity both at the national and international levels. In this regard, it must be underlined that the respect for complementarity and the fight against impunity must go hand in hand; this is the logic of the Statute which provides, even when there is an actual litigation on complementarity, for preservation of evidence, with the involvement of the ICC Pre-Trial Chamber.[26]

The principle of complementarity should not be a reason to delay early investigative steps or to unduly prolong preliminary examinations in the hope that, *one day*, national authorities will start an investigation, which in fact they are under the obligation to start immediately. Complementarity may be respected also *after* those investigative steps are taken or after the investigation is initiated by the ICC-OTP in case it appears that national authorities are willing and able to genuinely investigate and prosecute.

The Appeals Chamber has determined that the factual situation on the basis of which the admissibility of a case is to be established is "ambulatory".[27] Therefore, the Prosecutor can revisit the issue of admissibility, with regard to its complementarity component, after the investigation has been initiated, by keeping under review the progress, if any, made by national authorities. In this regard, the Prosecutor may at any time decide not to prosecute in accordance with Article 53(2)(b) of the Statute, in case

---

[25] Situation in Afghanistan OTP Request for Authorisation of an Investigation, para. 25, where it is stated that by

> the end of 2013, [the OTP] had obtained sufficiently credible and detailed information on approximately 200 incidents prioritised for analysis to enable a determination that there was a reasonable basis to believe that crimes against humanity and war crimes had been committed. [...] *Since then*, the Prosecution has focused on analysing the admissibility of potential cases [...].

Emphasis added, see above note 20.

[26] See Articles 18(6) and 19(8) of the Statute, see above note 3.

[27] ICC, Situation in the Democratic Republic of the Congo, *The Prosecutor v. Germain Katanga and Mathieu Ngudjolo Chui*, Appeals Chamber, Judgment on the Appeal of Mr. Germain Katanga against the Oral Decision of Trial Chamber II of 12 June 2009 on the Admissibility of the Case, 25 September 2009, ICC-01/04-01/07-1497, para. 56 (https://www.legal-tools.org/doc/ba82b5/).

national authorities become active, willing and able to genuinely investigate the cases identified by the Prosecutor. In such a case, the result of the early investigate steps taken by the OTP could be provided to national authorities in accordance with Article 93(10) of the Statute, provided that the conditions of its application are respected, especially the protection of witnesses. Such steps could therefore be useful in assisting genuine national investigations and prosecutions, thus reinforcing the global fight against impunity.

Furthermore, the Statute provides ample opportunities for States to make the Court respect the primacy of their national jurisdictions *after* the initiation of an investigation. Article 18(2) of the Statute allows a State, whether Party or not to the Statute, to request the Prosecutor to defer the investigation with regard to its nationals or others within its jurisdiction. The Prosecutor shall defer to the State's investigation, unless she applies to the Pre-Trial Chamber for a decision to authorise the investigation. In such a case, the State in question has procedural standing before the Pre-Trial Chamber and may appeal the Pre-Trial Chamber's ruling on admissibility in accordance with Article 18(4) of the Statute. Furthermore, any State may also challenge the admissibility of a particular case in accordance with Article 19 of the Statute.

In case the Prosecutor decides to defer to the State's investigation in accordance with Article 18(2) of the Statute, she will be in a much better position to properly assess the national investigations and prosecutions than at the stage of the preliminary examination. Indeed, after the initiation of an investigation, States Parties are under an obligation to respond without undue delay to any request of the Prosecutor concerning the progress of their national investigations and prosecutions, in accordance with Article 18(5) of the Statute, an obligation which they do not have at the preliminary examination stage.[28] As a matter of fact, in the situation in Afghanistan, as noted by the Prosecutor with regard to crimes allegedly committed by members of the Afghan authorities, the Government of Afghanistan did not provide "any information on national proceedings to the Office, despite multiple requests for such information from the Office since 2008".[29] Moreover, the Prosecutor's deferral to the State's investiga-

---

[28] Burundi Article 15 Decision, para. 15, see above note 17.

[29] See ICC-OTP, *Report on Preliminary Examination Activities*, 14 November 2016, para. 217 (https://www.legal-tools.org/doc/f30a53/); see also Situation in Afghanistan OTP Re-

tion is open for review after six months or at any time when there has been a significant change of circumstances, in accordance with Article 18(3) of the Statute. This could prove to be a more powerful incentive for national investigations and prosecutions than the Prosecutor waiting for an indefinite period of time at the preliminary examination stage for hypothetical national proceedings.

19.1.1.2. The Necessity to Adequately Prepare for the Investigation

Recently, Pre-Trial Chamber III has emphasised the need for the Prosecutor to have very early on a clear strategy with regard to the preservation of evidence, including by involving in this regard the Pre-Trial Chamber in accordance with Article 56 of the Statute:

> As a final remark, the Chamber considers that, considering the complexity of the situation, the specific circumstances of the victims, and the difficulties for the Trial Chambers to evaluate testimonial evidence when witnesses testify a long time after the events, it is advisable for the Prosecutor to use the dispositions of article 56 of the Statute to preserve evidence which may not be available for the purposes of a potential future trial or whose reliability may be undermined by lapse of time.[30]

In this regard, it would be better for the OTP to have an *investigation plan* at the time it is presenting its request under Article 15(3) of the Statute for an authorisation to start an investigation. That investigation plan should involve investigators and analysts and envisage all the necessary measures which should be taken with regard to the preservation of evidence, including the protection of potential witnesses, taking into consideration the possible challenges with regard to the upcoming investigation, especially with regard to the access to evidence, both exculpatory

---

quest for Authorisation of an Investigation, paras. 23 and 27, where it appears that after more than 11 years of preliminary examination at the time of the Prosecutor requested authorisation to investigate in Afghanistan, almost half – 14 out of 29 formal requests for information – of the OTP requests for additional information remained unanswered, see above note 20.

[30] ICC, Situation in the People's Republic of Bangladesh/Republic of the Union of Myanmar, Pre-Trial Chamber, Decision Pursuant to Article 15 of the Rome Statute on the Authorisation of an Investigation into the Situation in the People's Republic of Bangladesh/Republic of the Union of Myanmar, 14 November 2019, ICC-01/19-27, para. 134 (https://www.legal-tools.org/doc/kbo3hy/).

and inculpatory, and the co-operation States are likely to offer. This was foreseen in Regulation 6 of the Draft Regulations in 2003, but it is not provided for in the Regulations of the OTP finally adopted in 2009.[31] It is suggested, as a step further, that such an investigation plan should be submitted to the Pre-Trial Chamber together with the request under Article 15(3) of the Statute, in order to ensure that the judiciary is informed of how the investigation should unfold if authorised and that there is a follow-up by a judicial body on this issue.

For the moment, what the OTP is presenting to the Pre-Trial Chamber together with its request under Article 15 of the Statute and the material supporting it, is described in Regulation 49 of the Regulations of the Court (the 'Regulations'). This information solely relates to: (1) the place and time of the alleged commission of the crimes; (2) the persons involved, if identified, or a description of the persons or groups of persons involved; and (3) an appendix with the chronology of the relevant events, maps showing relevant information, including the location of the alleged crimes and an explanatory glossary of relevant names of persons, locations and institutions.

The jurisprudence of Pre-Trial Chambers since the very first request presented by the OTP for an authorisation to start an investigation in the situation in Kenya, requires the OTP to present – and this is done usually in a confidential way[32] – the following information: (1) the incidents that

---

[31] ICC, Regulations of the Office of the Prosecutor, 23 April 2009, ICC-BD/05-01-09 (https://www.legal-tools.org/doc/a97226/). See especially Regulation 29 which only refers to an internal report, Regulation 35 only refers to an "evidence collection plan" and a "co-operation plan". Those OTP Regulations do not provide any detail and leave total liberty to the Prosecutor.

[32] See for the Situation in the Republic of Afghanistan, OTP, Annex 1: Public Redacted Version: List of Annexes, 20 November 2017, ICC-02/17-7-Anx1-Red (https://www.legal-tools.org/doc/11af23/), referring to confidential annexes:

- ANNEX 2A - CONF *EXP*: Indicative list of most serious incidents attributed to members of the Taliban and other anti-government armed groups;
- ANNEX 2B - CONF-*EXP*: Indicative list of alleged most serious incidents attributed to the Afghan National Security Forces;
- ANNEX 2C - CONF *EXP*: Indicative list of most serious incidents attributed to members of United States Armed Forces and the Central Intelligence Agency;
- ANNEX 3A - CONF *EXP*: Preliminary list of persons or groups that appear to be the most responsible for the most serious crimes: Taliban and affiliated armed groups;

are likely to be the focus of an investigation; and (2) the groups of persons involved that are likely to be the target of an investigation for the purpose of identifying the potential cases under consideration.[33] To a certain extent, it obliges the OTP to identify, but mostly for admissibility purposes under Articles 53(1)(b) and 17 of the Statute, who and what it plans to investigate.

This, however, falls short of a proper investigation plan[34] which, according to the Draft Regulations should also include, *inter alia*: (1) a tentative indication of possible charges, modes of liability and potential defences, if any, as provided for in Article 31 of the Statute; (2) an explanation of the role and place of the likely suspects in the relevant chains of authority; (3) the whereabouts, if known, of the possible suspects and the likelihood to arrest them; (4) a preliminary indication of resources, time and staff likely to be required to complete the investigation – in order to prepare a request to the Assembly of States Parties to get appropriate funding; (5) a preliminary indication of the main categories of evidence and the amount of evidence that is likely to be required to prove the possible charges, and of the evidence which is likely to be available to the OTP, both exculpatory and incriminatory; (6) matters relevant to State cooperation and security; and (7) issues relevant to the protection of victims and witnesses. To this list, it would be useful to add, taking into consideration the ICC mandate with regard to victims, issues relevant to the freezing of assets and property of the potential suspects and of the instru-

---

- ANNEX 3B - CONF *EXP*: Preliminary list of persons or groups that appear to be the most responsible for the most serious crimes: Afghan National Security Forces; and
- ANNEX 3C - CONF *EXP*: Preliminary list of persons or groups that appear to be the most responsible for the most serious crimes: United States Armed Forces and the Central Intelligence Agency;

See also:

- ANNEX 4A - CONF *EXP*: Map of alleged incidents referred to in confidential *ex parte* Annex 2A;
- ANNEX 4B - CONF EXP: Map of locations of Afghan detention facilities referred to in confidential *ex parte* Annex 2B; and
- ANNEX 4C - CONF EXP: Map of alleged United States detention sites in Afghanistan referred to in confidential *ex parte* Annex 2C.

[33] ICC, Situation in the Republic of Kenya, Pre-Trial Chamber, Decision Requesting Clarification and Additional Information, 18 February 2010, ICC-01/09-15, para. 14 (https://www.legal-tools.org/doc/df9549/).

[34] See Draft Regulations, Book 3, Part II, Regulation 6.5., see above note 2.

mentalities and proceeds of crimes for the ultimate benefit of victims. While some of the requirements mentioned in the Draft Regulations may be difficult to provide as such an early stage – that is, the indication of modes of liability and potential defences – an investigation plan would certainly be a useful tool provided that, first, its development does not delay the request for authorisation to investigate under Article 15 of the Statute and, second, there is sufficient flexibility in order to adapt to the results of the collection of evidence. Such an investigation plan should be established irrespective of the trigger mechanism used to activate the Court's jurisdiction.

A Pre-Trial chamber could require the OTP to present such an investigation plan together with the request for the authorisation of an investigation submitted in accordance with Article 15(3) of the Statute. This should be possible without changing the applicable law before the ICC. In this regard, Rule 50(4) of the Rules already provides that the Pre-Trial Chamber, in deciding on the procedure to be followed, may request additional information from the Prosecutor. Other provisions in the Statute and the Rules could justify the Pre-Trial Chamber asking for such an investigation plan, such as Article 68 of the Statute on the protection of victims and witnesses, Article 57(3)(e) of the Statute and Rule 99 of the Rules giving power to the Pre-Trial Chamber to request, *proprio motu*, the freezing of assets and property belonging to the suspect or instrumentalities and proceeds of crimes, and Articles 56 and 57(3)(c) of the Statute giving *proprio motu* power to the Pre-Trial Chamber to preserve evidence, to provide for the protection and privacy of victims and witnesses and the protection of national security information. Given the multiple powers the Pre-Trial Chamber enjoys during the investigation, both to ensure the rights of those involved in the proceedings and to ensure judicial supervision of the Prosecutor in the course of the investigation, it would be justified for the Pre-Trial Chamber to be informed in advance of the Prosecutor's investigation plan in order to ensure a proper judicial supervision during the entire investigation, especially with regard to the preservation of evidence in accordance with Article 56 of the Statute, as recently underlined by Pre-Trial Chamber III. It is to be underlined, however, that judicial supervision does not mean that the Pre-Trial Chamber would replace the OTP in its investigation.

19.1.2. Case Preparation and Conduct of the Investigation

The need to have an external review on the conduct of the investigation by the OTP will first be analysed (Section 19.1.2.1.) and thereafter the need to complete the investigation already at the pre-trial stage of the case (Section 19.1.2.2.).

19.1.2.1. The Need for an External Review on the Conduct of the Investigation

After the *formal start of an investigation*, there would certainly be an advantage to have an external review of the proper implementation of the investigation plan. This could be entrusted to the judiciary, through reports from the OTP to the Pre-Trial Chamber, at regular intervals, throughout the investigation, containing explanations of the eventual deviations from the investigation plan. To a certain extent, such a periodical review of the investigation – but not the plan which was never given to a Pre-Trial Chamber – was started by Pre-Trial Chamber I during the first years of the ICC, in the situation in the Democratic Republic of the Congo[35] and in the situation in Darfur, Sudan.[36] Those attempts were fiercely opposed by the OTP[37] and were not continued.

At the ICC, it would certainly be useful to have a periodical review of the investigation plan by a judge in the Pre-Trial Chamber assigned with the situation, but also more generally a review of the cases the Prosecutor plans to bring to Chambers in order for that judge to identify eventually flaws in those cases for prosecution purposes and issue recommendations to the OTP on what evidence is missing or what should be envisaged in a different way with regard to the theory of the case. Furthermore, that judge would be in charge of ensuring the OTP conducts its investigation in accordance with Article 54(1)(a) of the Statute, that is, investigat-

---

[35] ICC, Situation in the Democratic Republic of the Congo, Pre-Trial Chamber, Decision to Convene a Status Conference, 17 February 2005, ICC-01/04-9 (https://www.legal-tools.org/doc/236413/).

[36] ICC, Situation in Darfur, Sudan, Pre-Trial Chamber, Decision Inviting Observations in Application of Rule 103 of the Rules of Procedure and Evidence, 24 July 2006, ICC-02/05-10 (https://www.legal-tools.org/doc/657682/).

[37] ICC, Situation in the Democratic Republic of the Congo, OTP, Submission of the Redacted Version of the Prosecutor's Position on Pre-Trial Chamber I's 17 February 2005 Decision to Convene a Status Conference, 11 March 2005, ICC-01/04-12 and ICC-01/04-12-Anx (https://www.legal-tools.org/doc/5475b7/ and https://www.legal-tools.org/doc/764580/).

ing equally exonerating and incriminating circumstances. It could also be interesting to involve the Office of Public Counsel for the Defence[38] or an *ad hoc* counsel representing the interests of the defence, in order to ensure that early preservation of exonerating evidence is thoroughly pursued. Such recommendations would not be binding on the Prosecutor but would allow the opening of new lines of investigation or a change in the theory of the case taking into consideration the evidence collected so far. They would also contribute to avoiding more litigation. However, those recommendations would be filed in the record and would be accessible to the judges at the pre-trial, trial and appeals stages.

It is worth noting that the Statute already provides for the judges to issue recommendations with regard to the preservation of evidence and to appoint a counsel to represent the interests of the defence during the investigation (see Article 56(2) of the Statute). This would be another way for the judges to get involved very early on in the process and to have an early judicial review in order to avoid problems later on in the proceedings. It would be easier for the Prosecutor to take those recommendations into consideration at a very early stage of the process, where the cases are still in the making and nobody is arrested. To try to correct those mistakes at the confirmation of charges stage is often too late or far more difficult. Furthermore, this would allow an early intervention in a very confidential way.

19.1.2.2. The Need to Complete the Investigation at the Pre-Trial Stage of the Case

With regard to *the conduct of the investigation* as a whole, Pre-Trial Chambers have very early underlined in their jurisprudence that it was crucial for the investigation to be completed before the confirmation of charges hearing.[39] Unfortunately, this attempt was not supported by the Appeals Chamber,[40] in order to give maximum flexibility to the OTP. This

---

[38] See Regulation 77 of the Regulations of the Court, 26 May 2004 (https://www.legal-tools.org/doc/2988d1/).

[39] ICC, Situation in the Democratic Republic of the Congo, *The Prosecutor v. Thomas Lubanga Dyilo*, Pre-Trial Chamber, Decision Establishing General Principles Governing Applications to Restrict Disclosure pursuant to Rule 81 (2) and (4) of the Rules of Procedure and Evidence, 19 May 2006, ICC-01/04-01/06-108-Corr, para. 39 (https://www.legal-tools.org/doc/6ddc24/).

[40] ICC, Situation in the Democratic Republic of the Congo, *The Prosecutor v. Thomas Lubanga Dyilo*, Appeals Chamber, Judgment on the Prosecutor's appeal against the deci-

was probably a mistake unfortunately committed by the Appeals Chamber in its early years, a mistake which the Appeals Chamber finally realised (too late maybe?) and tried to correct in 2012 by stating that the investigation should largely be completed at the stage of the confirmation of charges hearing.[41] It is worth mentioning that the OTP itself realised the necessity to be trial-ready at the stage of the confirmation of the charges. This change in policy unfortunately only intervened in the 2012-2015 Strategic Plan where the OTP declared:

> Thirdly, the Office will aim at presenting cases at confirmation hearing that are as trial ready as possible. If meeting such a threshold would not be possible at the moment of applying for an arrest warrant or summons to appear (e.g. arrest opportunity, witnesses only willing to cooperate after an arrest), the Office intends to only proceed with the application if there are sufficient prospects to further collect evidence to be trial-ready within a reasonable timeframe.[42]

Therefore, the practice followed during the early years of the ICC produced unfortunate results especially in the situation in the Republic of Kenya. It is interesting here to quote the dissenting opinion of the dearly-missed Judge Hans-Peter Kaul on the decisions concerning the confirmation of the two cases first emanating from that situation:

> Another example of such unsatisfactory investigation would be an approach which de facto is aiming, in a first phase, (only) at gathering enough evidence to reach the "sufficiency standard" within the meaning of article 61(7) of the Statute, maybe in the expectation or hope that in a further phase after

---

    sion of Pre-Trial Chamber I entitled "Decision Establishing General Principles Governing Applications to Restrict Disclosure pursuant to Rule 81 (2) and (4) of the Rules of Procedure and Evidence", 13 October 2006, ICC-01/04-01/06-568, paras. 52–54 (https://www.legal-tools.org/doc/7813d4/).

[41] ICC, Situation in the Democratic Republic of the Congo, *The Prosecutor v. Callixte Mbarushimana*, Appeals Chamber, Judgment on the appeal of the Prosecutor against the decision of Pre-Trial Chamber I of 16 December 2011 entitled "Decision on the confirmation of charges", 30 May 2012, ICC-01/04-01/10-514, para. 44 ('Mbarushimana Appeals Judgment on the Appeal of the Prosecutor Against the Decision on the Confirmation of Charges') (https://www.legal-tools.org/doc/6ead30/).

[42] ICC-OTP, *Strategic Plan June 2012-2015*, 11 October 2013, p. 14 (https://www.legal-tools.org/doc/954beb/). It is interesting to note that in the same strategic plan the OTP announced that there would be an increase in the number of investigators and analysts (para. 45, p. 22).

the confirmation proceedings, additional and more convincing evidence may be assembled to attain the 'beyond reasonable doubt' threshold, as required by article 66(3) of the Statute. I believe that such an approach, as tempting as it might be for the Prosecutor, would be risky, if not irresponsible: if after the confirmation of the charges it turns out as impossible to gather further evidence to attain the decisive threshold of 'beyond reasonable doubt', the case in question may become very difficult or may eventually collapse at trial, then with many serious consequences, including for the entire Court and the victims who have placed great hopes in this institution.[43]

Both cases in the situation in Kenya then collapsed at the trial stage.[44] It is to be recalled in this respect that, during the pre-trial stage, two cases, each against three persons, were presented by the OTP.[45] The OTP requested and obtained three summonses to appear against Francis Kirimi Muthaura, Uhuru Muigai Kenyatta, Mohammed Hussein Ali, William Samoei Ruto, Henry Kiprono Kosgey and Joshua Arap Sang.[46]

---

[43] ICC, Situation in the Republic of Kenya, *The Prosecutor v. Francis Kirimi Muthaura, Uhuru Muigai Kenyatta and Mohammed Hussein Ali*, Pre-Trial Chamber, Dissenting Opinion by Judge Hans-Peter Kaul, in Decision on the Confirmation of Charges Pursuant to Article 61(7)(a) and (b) of the Rome Statute, 23 January 2012, ICC-01/09-02/11-382-Red, para. 52 (https://www.legal-tools.org/doc/4972c0/); see also ICC, Situation in the Republic of Kenya, *The Prosecutor v. William Samoei Ruto, Henry Kiprono Kosgey and Joshua Arap Sang*, Pre-Trial Chamber, Dissenting Opinion by Judge Hans-Peter Kaul, in Decision on the Confirmation of Charges Pursuant to Article 61(7)(a) and (b) of the Rome Statute, 23 January 2012, ICC-01/09-01/11-373, para. 47 ('Ruto, Kosgey and Sang Pre-Trial Dissenting Opinion by Judge Hans-Peter Kaul') (https://www.legal-tools.org/doc/96c3c2/).

[44] See also in this regard, Kenya Cases: Review and Recommendations: Executive Summary of the Report of the External Independent Experts, E.17, see above note 6.

[45] ICC, Situation in the Republic of Kenya, *The Prosecutor v. Francis Kirimi Muthaura, Uhuru Muigai Kenyatta and Mohammed Hussein Ali*, OTP, Prosecutor's Application Pursuant to Article 58 as to Francis Kirimi Muthaura, Uhuru Muigai Kenyatta and Mohammed Hussein Ali, 15 December 2010, ICC-01/09-02/11-35-Red2 (https://www.legal-tools.org/doc/fd1a68/); see also ICC, Situation in the Republic of Kenya, *The Prosecutor v. William Samoei Ruto, Henry Kiprono Kosgey and Joshua Arap Sang*, OTP, Prosecutor's Application Pursuant to Article 58 as to William Samoei Ruto, Henry Kiprono Kosgey and Joshua Arap Sang, 15 December 2010, ICC-01/09-01/11-26-Red2 (https://www.legal-tools.org/doc/c6cf4c/).

[46] ICC, Situation in the Republic of Kenya, *The Prosecutor v. Francis Kirimi Muthaura, Uhuru Muigai Kenyatta and Mohammed Hussein Ali*, Pre-Trial Chamber, Decision on the Prosecutor's Application for Summonses to Appear for Francis Kirimi Muthaura, Uhuru Muigai Kenyatta and Mohamed Hussein Ali, 8 March 2011, ICC-01/09-02/11-1 (https://

At the confirmation of charges stage, the charges against two of them (Mohammed Hussein Ali and Henry Kiprono Kosgey) were dismissed in their entirety. For the four others, charges were confirmed partially. It is often forgotten that between 2006 and 2012, 29% of the cases at the ICC did not even go to trial. In this regard, the above-mentioned change in policy adopted by the OTP in its 2012-2015 Strategic Plan was certainly a positive development which must be kept for the future as good practice. All cases where the confirmation of charges procedure started thereafter were confirmed, albeit sometimes only partially.

Out of the four persons sent to trial in the two cases in the situation in Kenya, none were convicted. With regard to Francis Kirimi Muthaura and Uhuru Muigai Kenyatta, the trial did not even start. The Prosecutor decided, in March 2013, to withdraw all charges against Francis Kirimi Muthaura as she considered that she had no reasonable prospect of conviction.[47] With regard to Uhuru Muigai Kenyatta, the Prosecutor decided to withdraw the charges in December 2014.[48]

With regard to the case against William Samoei Ruto and Joshua Arap Sang, the proceedings were stopped in 2016, after the Prosecutor's case ended, as the Trial Chamber concluded that "the evidence does not support the Network or existence of an organisational policy in the sense of Article 7(2)(a) of the Statute".[49] Back in 2012, this was already the conclusion of Judge Hans-Peter Kaul at the stage of the confirmation of charges:

---

www.legal-tools.org/doc/df8391/); see also ICC, Situation in the Republic of Kenya, *The Prosecutor v. William Samoei Ruto, Henry Kiprono Kosgey and Joshua Arap Sang*, Pre-Trial Chamber, Decision on the Prosecutor's Application for Summons to Appear for William Samoei Ruto, Henry Kiprono Kosgey and Joshua Arap Sang, 8 March 2011, ICC-01/09-01/11-1 (https://www.legal-tools.org/doc/6c9fb0/).

[47] ICC, Situation in the Republic of Kenya, *The Prosecutor v. Francis Kirimi Muthaura and Uhuru Muigai Kenyatta*, OTP, Prosecution notification of withdrawal of the charges against Francis Kirimi Muthaura, 11 March 2013, ICC-01/09-02/11-687 (https://www.legal-tools.org/doc/9d2c58/).

[48] ICC, Situation in the Republic of Kenya, *The Prosecutor v. Uhuru Muigai Kenyatta*, OTP, Notice of withdrawal of the charges against Uhuru Muigai Kenyatta, 5 December 2014, ICC-01/09-02/11-983 (https://www.legal-tools.org/doc/b57a97/).

[49] ICC, Situation in the Republic of Kenya, *The Prosecutor v. William Samoei Ruto and Joshua Arap Sang*, Trial Chamber, Reasons of Judge Fremr, in Public redacted version of Decision on Defence Applications for Judgments of Acquittal, 5 April 2016, ICC-01/09-01/11-2027-Red-Corr, para. 131 (https://www.legal-tools.org/doc/6baecd/).

as to the alleged existence of the various components of the 'Network' [...], according to my reading of the evidence, [they] did either not exist in that form or are reflective of the tribal component of the 'Network'. My conclusion therefore was that the violence during the 2007/2008 violence was in essence ethnically driven.[50]

It is interesting to compare this sequence of events with the sequence of events in the Laurent Gbagbo case. In 2013, Pre-Trial Chamber I adjourned the confirmation of charges hearing, by majority, underlining that it was "difficult for the Chamber to determine whether the perpetrators acted pursuant to or in furtherance of a policy to attack a civilian population as required by article 7(2)(a) of the Statute".[51] It therefore requested the Prosecutor to conduct a further investigation especially with regard to "the incidents allegedly constituting the attack against the 'pro-Ouattara civilian population' and whether the alleged physical perpetrators were acting pursuant to or in furtherance of the alleged policy".[52]

Six years later, Trial Chamber I reached the following conclusion: the Prosecutor has failed to demonstrate (1) the existence of the alleged policy to attack the civilian population on the basis of the alleged pattern of violence and other circumstantial evidence cited in support; and (2) that the crimes as alleged in the charges were committed pursuant to or in furtherance of a State or organisational policy to attack the civilian population.[53]

One could draw several conclusions from those cases: (1) a warning at the pre-trial stage means a problem at trial and a serious risk that the trial may collapse; (2) the problems in a particular case do not change

---

[50] Ruto, Kosgey and Sang Pre-Trial Dissenting Opinion by Judge Hans-Peter Kaul, para. 12, see above note 43.

[51] ICC, Situation in the Republic of Côte d'Ivoire, *The Prosecutor v. Laurent Gbagbo*, Pre-Trial Chamber, Decision adjourning the hearing on the confirmation of charges pursuant to article 61(7)(c)(i) of the Rome Statute, 3 June 2013, ICC-02/11-01/11-432, para. 36 (https://www.legal-tools.org/doc/2682d8/).

[52] *Ibid.*, para. 44.

[53] ICC, Situation in the Republic of Côte d'Ivoire, *The Prosecutor v. Laurent Gbagbo and Charles Blé Goudé*, Trial Chamber, Reasons for oral decision of 15 January 2019 on the Requête de la Défense de Laurent Gbagbo afin qu'un jugement d'acquittement portant sur toutes les charges soit prononcé en faveur de Laurent Gbagbo et que sa mise en liberté immédiate soit ordonnée, and on the Blé Goudé Defence no case to answer motion, 16 July 2019, ICC-02/11-01/15-1263, para. 28 (https://www.legal-tools.org/doc/440017/).

between pre-trial and trial: the warning in both cases was on the contextual elements of crimes against humanity and the cases collapsed at trial on those same contextual elements; (3) the fact that, as common law lawyers at the ICC tend to repeat too often, witnesses do not appear at the pre-trial stage and therefore it is not possible to foresee what they will say at trial, does not mean that weaknesses and contradictions in their written statements will disappear at the trial stage. What is absolutely clear is that a bad witness statement at pre-trial does not become good evidence at trial. There is no magic for the Prosecutor at trial so that suddenly all problems would be solved and the witnesses would start to say exactly what the Prosecutor needs to demonstrate.

The involvement of the judiciary early on in the proceedings certainly provides a useful check on the Prosecutor's case and the quality of its evidence and preparation, although the OTP has not seen it in that way, unfortunately. The pre-trial stage should be an opportunity for the Prosecutor to revise her cases, to strengthen the evidence, and reformulate the theory of the case when the evidence does not correspond to it.

Other aspects of the investigation should also be dealt with as soon as possible by the OTP during the investigation, in particular the protection of witnesses and the freezing of assets, proceeds and instrumentalities of crimes. Very often the protection of witnesses only starts after the arrest of the suspect, which could be a cause of delay in pre-confirmation proceedings as witnesses have to be relocated before disclosure or, alternatively, numerous requests for anonymous summaries have to be made by the OTP at the pre-trial stage, which is a source of delay in the proceedings. Furthermore, those anonymous summaries cannot be used at trial which is again a source of delay between the end of the pre-trial proceedings and the beginning of the trial.

With regard to the freezing of assets and properties belonging to the suspect and proceeds and instrumentalities of crimes, this should be done as a priority during the investigation and not after the arrest, as it simply means that nothing will be frozen because the suspect will seek to hide his assets and the proceeds of crimes. All relevant information shall be presented to the Pre-Trial Chamber, or the competent judge at the national level, at the time the Prosecutor requests the issuance of a warrant of arrest so that the orders for freezing are issued at the same time the warrant of arrest is issued. Very often those judicial orders are essential to allow co-operation from other States with regard to the freezing of assets.

There are other important ways in which the judiciary may assist in the preparation of the case to ensure its quality. Especially for core international crimes, it is necessary to collect evidence very early on in order to eventually be in a position to use it much later. It is extremely difficult to proceed successfully with a case when people are still in power and this is true both at the national and the international levels. The actual prosecution may therefore take place years or decades after the facts. There is a need to organise accordingly the preservation of the evidence in order to be in a position to use it in court many years later. The involvement of the judiciary in the early preservation of that evidence in order to successfully use it later should also be envisaged. Such an involvement may increase the probative value of the evidence collected with the intervention of a judge or of a counsel, representing the interests of 'future' accused, appointed by a judge. This is true at the ICC through Article 56 of the Statute, but this should also be explored at the national level.

The involvement of the judiciary is also crucial in the framing of the charges, as will be discussed next.

19.2. The Framing of the Charges

When framing the charges, the degree of specificity which must be reached with regard to the facts has been the subject of intense debate at the ICC. This debate is intrinsically linked to the ICC's specific procedural framework which departs from the one applicable at the *ad hoc* Tribunals,[54] where there was no Pre-Trial Chamber and the Prosecutor could amend the indictment at will, including during the course of the trial. The procedural compromises made in Rome are still difficult for the Judges to digest in order to finally reach an agreement on how to apply the unique ICC procedural framework. More than 17 years after the entry into force of the Statute, there are still sharp disagreements among the ICC Judges on fundamental issues regarding key aspects of the proceedings before the ICC.

Terminology is, as usual, of the essence in this debate, and the initial question is simply: what is a charge? With regard to the definition of

---

[54] Reference is made here to the International Criminal Tribunal for the former Yugoslavia and the International Criminal Tribunal for Rwanda which are no longer operational.

the charges, a combined reading of Article 74[55] of the Statute and Regulation 52 of the Regulations indicates that a 'charge' is comprised of the factual allegations together with their legal characterisation. This can be deduced from the wording of Regulation 52 of the Regulations, which makes reference to "a statement of facts, including the time and place of the alleged crimes" (Regulation 52(b) of the Regulations) and "a legal characterisation of the facts" (Regulation 52(c) of the Regulations). This understanding has been reflected in the jurisprudence:

> [A] 'charge' must be understood further to a combined reading of article 74(2) of the Statute and regulation 52 of the Regulations of the Court as: a statement of the facts and circumstances *including* the time and place of the alleged crimes; and a legal characterisation of the fact to accord both with the crimes under articles 6, 7, or 8 of the Statute and the precise form of participation under articles 25 and 28 of the Statute.[56]

In that same decision, Trial Chamber II stated that "under no circumstances can a charge be a mere statement of the legal characterisation".[57] Although the question seems to revolve around the degree of specificity of the facts mentioned in the charges, it is linked also to the moment when that specificity must be reached and to the respective roles of the Prosecutor and the Pre-Trial and Trial Chambers in this respect. This issue arose quite dramatically in the Appeals Chamber Judgement in the case against Jean-Pierre Bemba.[58]

---

[55] Article 74(2), second sentence, of the Statute provides that the "decision shall not exceed the facts and circumstances described in the charges and any amendments to the charges", see above note 3.

[56] ICC, Situation in the Democratic Republic of the Congo, *The Prosecutor v. Germain Katanga and Mathieu Ngudjolo Chui*, Trial Chamber, Decision on the Filing of a Summary of the Charges by the Prosecutor, 21 October 2009, ICC-01/04-01/07-1547-tENG, para. 10 ('Katanga and Ngudjolo Chui Trial Decision on the Filing of a Summary of the Charges by the Prosecutor') (https://www.legal-tools.org/doc/7e906f/).

[57] *Ibid.*

[58] ICC, Situation in the Central African Republic, *The Prosecutor v. Jean-Pierre Bemba Gombo*, Appeals Chamber, Judgment on the appeal of Mr Jean-Pierre Bemba Gombo against Trial Chamber III's "Judgment pursuant to Article 74 of the Statute", 8 June 2018, ICC-01/05-01/08-3636-Red ('Bemba Appeals Judgement') (https://www.legal-tools.org/doc/40d35b/); see also Bemba Appeals Judgement, Dissenting Opinion of Judge Sanji Mmasenomo Monageng and Judge Piotr Hofmański, 8 June 2018, ICC-01/05-01/08-3636-Anx1-Red ('Bemba Dissenting Opinion') (https://www.legal-tools.org/doc/dc2518/);

To try to understand the different approaches in this debate, the ICC practice before the Bemba Appeals Judgement will be analysed first (Section 19.2.1.), then the different views expressed by the (very divided) Appeals Chamber in the Bemba Appeals Judgement (Section 19.2.2.), and, finally, the (emerging) jurisprudence after the Bemba Appeals Judgement (Section 19.2.3.).

19.2.1. The ICC Practice Before the Bemba Appeals Judgement

Back in 2009, the Prosecutor tried to make a distinction between the 'facts of the case' and the 'facts constituting the charges' in the Katanga and Ngudjolo Chui case, which would have allowed the Prosecutor to introduce more and/or different criminal acts at trial, provided that those criminal acts generally fell within the crimes confirmed by the Pre-Trial Chamber (that is, 'rape' or 'murder' for example). The Prosecutor's attempt to modify the factual basis of the charges at trial was rejected by Trial Chamber II:

> Irrespective even of this requirement for precision, the Chamber is unable to accept the distinction made by the Prosecutor between the facts constituting the charges and the facts of the case. The core legal texts make no distinction of this sort, but only between the "facts and circumstances" and the "legal characterisations" on the one hand - both of which constitute the charges - and the evidence on the other. Even if the Prosecutor intends to define in the instant case, the "facts of the case" as mere "[TRANSLATION] concise summaries of the evidence", in practice, the distinction he advocates and the resulting use of the term "fact" may constitute a source of ambiguity, confusion and contention at trial. It is appropriate to prevent the Chamber from having to consider new facts, which have not expressly been accepted by the Pre-Trial Chamber as this would run contrary to the provisions of the Statute. To grant the Trial Chamber the power to not only modify the legal characterisation of the facts, as permitted by regulation 55 of the Regulations of the Court, but also to modify the facts of which it is seized or to

Bemba Appeals Judgement, Separate opinion Judge Christine van den Wyngaert and Judge Howard Morrison, 8 June 2018, ICC-01/05-01/08-3636-Anx2 ('Bemba Separate Opinion') (https://www.legal-tools.org/doc/c13ef4/); and Bemba Appeals Judgement, Concurring Separate Opinion of Judge Eboe-Osuji, 8 June 2018, ICC-01/05-01/08-3636-Anx3 ('Bemba Concurring Opinion') (https://www.legal-tools.org/doc/b31f6b/).

deal with new facts, would confer upon it power not be-
stowed by the core legal texts.[59]

However, with regard to what has to be understood by 'facts', the
discussion within the ICC did not stop there. A (new) distinction was introduced in the jurisprudence of the Court in 2011, between 'material'
facts and 'subsidiary' facts:

> It is important to bear in mind the distinction between, on the
> one hand, the facts and circumstances underlying the charges
> (that is, "the facts and circumstances described in the charg-
> es" within the meaning of article 74(2) of the Statute and
> regulation 55(1) of the Regulations) and, on the other hand,
> other facts which are not mentioned in the charge but which
> are subsidiary or otherwise related to them, in particular
> since proof of the material facts may be inferred from them.
> Furthermore, these subsidiary facts are also relevant to the
> extent that they provide background information.[60]

The purpose of such a distinction, as with the distinction between
the 'facts of the case' and the 'facts constituting the charges', was to allow
the Pre-Trial Chamber to confirm charges not defined in an exhaustive
manner: some examples of rapes or murders would justify the confirmation of the charge of rape or murder in a certain place and at a certain
moment (both being eventually broadly defined), without further precision and therefore not precluding the addition of other criminal acts at
trial. Subsequent jurisprudence was nevertheless inconsistent with regard
to the distinction between material and subsidiary facts. While that distinction was made in the decision on the confirmation of the charges in
the case against Callixte Mbarushimana,[61] no such distinction was made

---

[59] Katanga and Ngudjolo Chui Trial Decision on the Filing of a Summary of the Charges by
the Prosecutor, para. 19, see above note 56.

[60] ICC, Situation in Darfur, Sudan, *The Prosecutor v. Abdallah Banda Abakaer Nourain and
Saleh Mohammed Jerbo Jamus*, Pre-Trial Chamber, Corrigendum of the "Decision on the
Confirmation of Charges", 7 March 2011, ICC-02/05-03/09-121-Corr-Red, para. 36
(https://www.legal-tools.org/doc/5ac9eb/).

[61] ICC, Situation in the Democratic Republic of the Congo, *The Prosecutor v. Callixte Mbarushimana*, Pre-Trial Chamber, Decision on the confirmation of charges, 16 December
2011, ICC-01/04-01/10-465-Red, paras. 81–82 (https://www.legal-tools.org/doc/63028f/).

in the decisions on the confirmation of the charges in the cases arising from the situation in Kenya.[62]

This distinction was endorsed by Pre-Trial Chamber I in the Laurent Gbagbo case,[63] but rejected by the Appeals Chamber in the very same case, stating that the applicable law before the Court did not make a distinction between 'material' and 'subsidiary' facts, but simply referred to 'facts'.[64]

However, the distinction appeared again in the Pre-Trial Practice Manual (the 'Practice Manual') which was signed in September 2015, by the then President of the Pre-Trial Division. On this issue, the Practice Manual states the following:

> The charges on which the Prosecutor intends to bring the person to trial to be presented prior to the confirmation hearing (cf. article 61(3)(a) of the Statute) shall be spelt out in a clear, exhaustive and self-contained way and shall include all, and not more than, the "material facts and circumstances" (*i.e.* the facts and circumstances that must be described in the charges (cf. article 74(2) of the Statute) and which are the only facts subject to judicial determination to the applicable standard of proof at confirmation and trial stages, respectively) and their legal characterisation. There shall be no confusion between the material facts described in the charges and the "subsidiary facts" (*i.e.* those facts that are relied upon by the Prosecutor as part of his/her argumentation in support of

---

[62] ICC, Situation in the Republic of Kenya, *The Prosecutor v. Francis Kirimi Muthaura, Uhuru Muigai Kenyatta and Mohammed Hussein Ali*, Pre-Trial Chamber, Decision on the Confirmation of Charges Pursuant to Article 61(7)(a) and (b) of the Rome Statute, 23 January 2012, ICC-01/09-02/11-382-Red, see above note 43; and ICC, Situation in the Republic of Kenya, *The Prosecutor v. William Samoei Ruto, Henry Kiprono Kosgey and Joshua Arap Sang*, Pre-Trial Chamber, Decision on the Confirmation of Charges Pursuant to Article 61(7)(a) and (b) of the Rome Statute, 23 January 2012, ICC-01/09-01/11-373, see above note 43.

[63] ICC, Situation in the Republic of Côte d'Ivoire, *The Prosecutor v. Laurent Gbagbo*, Pre-Trial Chamber, Decision on the date of the confirmation of charges hearing and proceedings leading thereto, 14 December 2012, ICC-02/11-01/11-325, para. 27 (https://www.legal-tools.org/doc/c5cddf/).

[64] ICC, Situation in the Republic of Côte d'Ivoire, *The Prosecutor v. Laurent Gbagbo*, Appeals Chamber, Judgment on the appeal of the Prosecutor against the decision of Pre-Trial Chamber I of 3 June 2013 entitled "Decision adjourning the hearing on the confirmation of charges pursuant to article 61(7)(c)(i) of the Rome Statute", 16 December 2013, ICC-02/11-01/11-572, para. 37 (https://www.legal-tools.org/doc/1bffda/).

---

the charges and, as such, are functionally "evidence"). Indeed, the Prosecutor may present submissions by which
he/she proposes a narrative of the relevant events and an
analysis of facts and evidence in order to persuade the Pre-
Trial Chamber to confirm the charges. However, these submissions in support of the charges should not be confused
with the charges. These submissions/argumentation can be
included either in the same document containing the charges
or in a separate filing (a sort of a "[pre-]confirmation brief").
If the Prosecutor chooses to include submissions in the document containing the charges rather than in a separate filing,
the two sections – "charges" and "submissions" – must be
kept clearly separate, and no footnotes containing cross-
references or reference to evidence must be included in the
charges.[65]

With regard to the role of the Pre-Trial Chamber in the process of
the confirmation of the charges, the Practice Manual added:

Findings on the substantial grounds to believe standard are
made exclusively with respect to the material facts described
in the charges, and there is no requirement that each item of
evidence or each subsidiary fact relied upon by either party
be addressed or referred to in the confirmation decision – nor
would this be realistic or otherwise providing any benefit.[66]

Thereafter, the distinction between material and subsidiary facts
was made in the decision on the confirmation of charges in the Dominic
Ongwen case.[67]

With regard to the respective roles of the Pre-Trial Chamber, the
Prosecutor and the Trial Chamber with regard to the framing of the charges, Trial Chamber II in the Germain Katanga and Mathieu Ngudjolo Chui
case underlined that the Pre-Trial Chamber's decision on the confirmation

---

[65] Practice Manual, 4 September 2015, pp. 11–12 (https://www.legal-tools.org/doc/dd93f1/).
[66] *Ibid.*, p. 16.
[67] ICC, Situation in Uganda, *The Prosecutor v. Dominic Ongwen*, Pre-Trial Chamber, Decision on the confirmation of charges against Dominic Ongwen, 23 March 2016, ICC-02/04-
01/15-422-Red, see the part of the decision on the "charges confirmed" (https://www.legal-
tools.org/doc/74fc6e/).

of the charges *crystallised* the charges.[68] Trial Chamber VII, by majority, came to the following conclusion:

> It follows from the above that the Statute foresees a shift of authority to define the factual scope of the case: while at the stage of submitting the DCC [Document containing the Charges] this authority rests squarely with the prosecution, at the confirmation stage, such authority passes over to the Pre-Trial Chamber. In other words, at the confirmation stage the Pre-Trial Chamber has the sole authority to define the parameters of the case for the purpose of ensuing trial proceedings; the confirmation of charges decision rendered under Article 61(7)(a) of the Statute sets out the charges, which, as such, also binds the Trial Chamber.[69]

19.2.2. The Bemba Appeals Judgement: A Divided Chamber with Multiple Views

The issue of the framing of the charges arose again in the Bemba Appeals Judgement, more precisely with regard to Jean-Pierre Bemba Gombo's second ground of appeal which was upheld by the majority of the Appeals Chamber. In that case, the defence challenged the overly broad definition of the charges which were defined, with regard to the facts, according to geographic and temporal parameters, that is, the territory of the Central African Republic ('CAR') and from October 2002 until March 2003. Moreover, the defence criticised the fact that Mr. Bemba was convicted for individual acts of murder, rape and pillaging committed against particular victims at specific times and places that had not been confirmed by the Pre-Trial Chamber.[70]

During the confirmation process, in the Amended Document Containing the Charges, the Prosecutor listed a number of alleged criminal acts of murder, rape and pillaging, but, through the use of expressions such as 'include' or 'include but are not limited to', indicated that this list

---

[68] Katanga and Ngudjolo Chui Trial Decision on the Filing of a Summary of the Charges by the Prosecutor, para. 31, see above note 56.

[69] ICC, Situation in the Central African Republic, *The Prosecutor v. Jean-Pierre Bemba Gombo, Aimé Kilolo Musamba, Jean-Jacques Mangenda Kabongo, Fidèle Babala Wandu and Narcisse Arido*, Trial Chamber, Decision on the Submission of Auxiliary Documents, 10 June 2015, ICC-01/05-01/13-992, para. 12 ('Bemba Trial Decision on the Submission of Auxiliary Documents') (https://www.legal-tools.org/doc/6a4ba2/).

[70] Bemba Appeals Judgement, para. 99, see above note 58.

was not complete or exhaustive.[71] The Pre-Trial Chamber confirmed in broad terms charges of murder as a war crime and as a crime against humanity, rape as a war crime and as a crime against humanity, and pillaging as a war crime, finding substantial grounds to believe that these crimes had been perpetrated against civilians by the *Mouvement de Libération du Congo* ('MLC') soldiers in the CAR from 26 October 2002 until 15 March 2003, without limiting its findings to a specific number of acts of murder, rape or pillaging.[72]

Analysing the scope of the conviction decision, the Appeals Chamber rejected, once more, the distinction between 'material' and 'subsidiary' facts:

> The Appeals Chamber therefore rejects, by majority, Judge Monageng and Judge Hofmański dissenting, the Prosecutor's submission, at the appeal hearing, that Mr Bemba was charged with, and convicted of, generally crimes of murder, rape and pillaging committed by MLC soldiers on the territory of the CAR from 26 October 2002 to 15 March 2003, which constituted the [*sic*] "the facts and circumstances" in the present case, and that the criminal acts were merely "subsidiary facts" or "evidence", "used in this case to establish the material fact".[73]

Turning thereafter to the question of the necessary precision in the description of the factual basis of the charges, the Appeals Chamber criticised both the Trial Chamber and the Pre-Trial Chamber stating:

> The Appeals Chamber recalls that the Confirmation Decision in its operative part was equally broad as the disposition of the Conviction Decision: the charges against Mr Bemba were "confirmed" in relation to categories of crimes, without any further qualification. Clearly this broad formulation would have been an insufficient basis to bring Mr Bemba to trial and cannot be said to amount to a description of "facts and circumstances" in terms of article 74 (2) of the Statute.[74]

The Appeals Chamber added:

---

[71] *Ibid.*, para. 75.

[72] *Ibid.*, para. 76.

[73] *Ibid.*, para. 104.

[74] *Ibid.*, para. 107.

> Simply listing the categories of crimes with which a person is to be charged or stating, in broad general terms, the temporal and geographical parameters of the charge is not sufficient to comply with the requirements of regulation 52 (b) of the Regulations of the Court and does not allow for a meaningful application of article 74 (2) of the Statute.[75]

The Appeals Chamber then considered that the criminal acts that the Prosecutor added after the decision on the confirmation of the charges was issued could not be said to have been part of the "facts and circumstances described in the charges" in terms of Article 74(2) of the Statute. In order to add those additional criminal acts of murder, rape and pillage, an amendment to the charges would have been required.[76]

The Appeals Chamber does not develop on which Chamber, Pre-Trial or Trial, should have been in charge of deciding on the amendment of the charges, for the simple reason that the majority itself was divided on this issue. Whereas the Bemba Separate Opinion[77] insists on the role of the Pre-Trial Chamber to confirm the charges including all alleged criminal acts, the Bemba Concurring Opinion underlines that the Trial Chamber should not be precluded from giving leave to the amendment of the charges after the trial has begun.[78]

It is interesting to analyse the strong disagreement expressed in the Bemba Dissenting Opinion with regard to this issue of the framing of the charges. The arguments put forward mainly relate to the dissenting Judges' understanding of the respective roles of the Prosecutor and the Pre-Trial Chamber and are informed by what they call the 'Prosecutor's discretion' to formulate the charges:

> We consider that it is for the Prosecutor to define the factual scope of a case and that the identification of the broad parameters of a case may suffice to serve article 74 (2)'s purpose of delineating the jurisdiction of the trial chamber.[79]
>
> [...] In our view, the pre-trial chamber is tasked with determining whether there is a case to be tried – "whether

---

[75] *Ibid.*, para. 110.

[76] *Ibid.*, para. 115.

[77] Bemba Separate Opinion, para. 25, see above note 58.

[78] Bemba Concurring Opinion, paras. 122 and 140, see above note 58.

[79] Bemba Dissenting Opinion, para. 20, see above note 58.

there is sufficient evidence to establish substantial grounds to believe that the person committed each of the crimes charged" – and not with confirming or crystallising the totality of the factual allegations underpinning these charges for the purposes of the trial. Again for this purpose, we consider that the pre-trial chamber may confirm the crimes charged in a broad manner depending on the nature of the charges brought by the Prosecutor.[80]

[…]

In this regard, we note that articles 58 and 61 of the Statute vest the Prosecutor with exclusive authority to frame the charges, with the role of the pre-trial chamber being restricted, under article 61 (7) of the Statute, to confirming the charges, declining to confirm the charges or adjourning the hearing and requesting the Prosecutor to consider amending a charge or providing further evidence or conducting further investigation with respect to a particular charge. Read together, we consider these provisions to reflect adherence to the accusatorial principle. They are aimed at ensuring that responsibility for framing the charges and determining the scope of the criminal trial remains with the Prosecutor throughout the proceedings, subject to the confirmation or non-confirmation of the charges by the pre-trial chamber.[81]

We further consider that the Prosecutor has discretion to formulate the charges in a manner appropriate to the type of case she wishes to bring. From the perspective of article 74 (2) of the Statute, it is important that the charges are described in a way that enables the chamber, as well as the parties and participants, to determine with certainty which sets of historical events, in the course of which crimes within the jurisdiction of the Court are alleged to have been committed, form part of the charges, and which do not. This delineation can be made based on specific criminal acts; however, depending on the case, the delineation may also be made based on broader parameters, for instance, by specifying a period of time and a geographical area over which criminal acts

---

[80] *Ibid.*, para. 21; compare with Katanga and Ngudjolo Chui Trial Decision on the Filing of a Summary of the Charges by the Prosecutor, para. 31, see above note 56.

[81] Bemba Dissenting Opinion, para. 26, see above note 58; compare with Bemba Trial Decision on the Submission of Auxiliary Documents, para. 12, see above note 69.

were allegedly committed by an identifiable group of perpetrators against an identifiable group of victims.[82]

It is this understanding of the ICC procedural framework which led
the dissenting Judges to conclude that the Prosecutor could rely at trial on
criminal acts not relied upon during the confirmation process, subject to
appropriate notification to the accused.[83] Such an understanding begs the
question, as raised in the Bemba Separate Opinion,[84] of what is the purpose of the confirmation process: if the Pre-Trial Chamber is only here to
confirm an 'historical set of events' and whether there is a case to be tried,
leaving the Prosecutor freedom to modify the case at trial, there seems to
be no real difference with the (very light) process of the indictment confirmation which existed before the *ad hoc* tribunals and the (much more
substantial) process of the charges confirmation at the ICC. No reference
is made in the Bemba Dissenting Opinion to the fact that the Pre-Trial
Chamber is supposed to commit the person to a Trial Chamber for a *trial
on the charges as confirmed* (Article 61(7)(a) of the Statute). The difference between the confirmation process before the *ad hoc* tribunals and
before the ICC has already been underlined by the Appeals Chamber.[85]

More than 20 years after the adoption of the Statute, nostalgia for
the system followed by the *ad hoc* Tribunals seems to have developed,
which was obviously rejected during the negotiations on the Statute. Otherwise, it would have been extremely easy to simply copy and paste into
the Statute the system followed by the *ad hoc* Tribunals, which was already in place at the time of the negotiations on the Statute. More specifically, the disappearance of the indictment in the Statute and the fact that
the basis for the trial is a judicial decision taken by the Pre-Trial Chamber
seem to have been for some a trauma.

There is a temptation to reduce the scope of intervention and even
the role of the Pre-Trial Chamber, probably with a view to proving that
this ICC novelty is largely useless – as those who oppose it anyway will
try to make it useless – hoping that one day maybe the Statute will be
changed to go back to the (beloved) *ad hoc* Tribunals procedural scheme.

---

[82] Bemba Dissenting Opinion, para. 27, see above note 58.

[83] *Ibid.*, para. 36.

[84] Bemba Separate Opinion, para. 28.

[85] Mbarushimana Appeals Judgment on the Appeal of the Prosecutor Against the Decision on
the Confirmation of Charges, para. 43, see above note 41.

The OTP has certainly contributed to that debate with a view to keeping a maximum of freedom, meaning a minimal intervention by the judiciary at the pre-trial stage.

The intervention of the Pre-Trial Chamber was precisely meant to avoid having a Prosecutor who is not ready before trial,[86] changing the case at will during trial, thereby making the case a moving target at the expense of the defence and delaying the proceedings. There is an absolute need to understand that the solution is not to give more freedom during the proceedings to the Prosecutor, but to make sure that (s)he is ready as soon as possible and to have judicial checks on the investigation and on the preparation of the case as early as possible. In this regard, those judicial checks must be reinforced and not abolished. It is crucial to have early judicial checks, provided of course that those checks are made by judges having the appropriate knowledge and experience. Judicial intervention is meant to reinforce the investigation and the case preparation for the benefit of the fight against impunity.

19.2.3. The ICC Jurisprudence After the Bemba Appeals Judgement

After the Bemba Appeals Judgement, Pre-Trial Chamber I, which was at the time of the issuance of the Bemba Appeals Judgement the only pre-trial chamber seized with a case, was put in the awkward position of being confronted with a jurisprudence by the Appeals Chamber which, first, rejected the crucial distinction made by the Practice Manual in the confirmation of charges process between 'subsidiary' and 'material' facts and, second, requested more precision in the factual description of the charges.

In the Al Hassan case, Pre-Trial Chamber I therefore tried to build on the Bemba Appeals Judgement by requiring the Prosecutor to be sufficiently precise and exhaustive in its presentation and description of the criminal acts contained in the charges, by means of a distinction with regard to this requirement depending on the nature of the crime:

> As a result the Chamber emphasizes the need for the Prosecution to be as precise and exhaustive as possible in respect of those facts in its DCC [Document Containing the Charges]. Nonetheless, the Chamber is of the view that the degree of precision to be expected from the Prosecutor in its description of the facts depends on the nature of the crimes in

---

[86] See Bemba Separate Opinion, para. 28, see above note 58.

question and the circumstances of the Prosecutor's case before it. Where crimes such as torture or rape are concerned, the Prosecutor must describe the criminal acts in issue, stating the date and place of the acts, along with the number of victims, or at the very least a precise estimate of that number, and their identities as far as possible. However, where the nature of the crimes is such that they are directed against a group or collectivity of people, as in the case of the crime of persecution, a like degree of precision cannot be expected of the Prosecutor in its description of the facts; nonetheless, the Prosecutor must endeavour to give the most precise possible statements of place, time and approximate number of victims, along with the necessary particulars to make out the elements of the crimes.[87]

This rather new approach pushed the Prosecutor to be more precise in its presentation of facts in the DCC, which is the longest in the ICC history (457 pages long).[88] The DCC, despite the existence of at least two Appeals Chamber decisions – including the Bemba Appeals Judgement – rejecting such a concept, still refers to 'material' facts,[89] and when giving a list of alleged victims, still uses expressions such as 'for example' or 'at least',[90] indicating that the list may not be exhaustive.

The decision on the confirmation of the charges issued by Pre-Trial Chamber I, which is 467 pages long, is equally by far the longest confir-

---

[87] ICC, Situation in the Republic of Mali, *The Prosecutor v. Al Hassan Ag Abdoul Aziz Ag Mohamed Ag Mahmoud*, Pre-Trial Chamber, Decision on the Defence Request concerning the Time Limit for the Prosecutor to File the Document Containing a Detailed Description of the Charges, 5 October 2018, ICC-01/12-01/18-143-tENG, para. 30 (https://www.legal-tools.org/doc/dd8f47/); see also ICC, Situation in the Republic of Mali, *The Prosecutor v. Al Hassan Ag Abdoul Aziz Ag Mohamed Ag Mahmoud*, Pre-Trial Chamber, Decision on the Admissibility Challenge raised by the Defence for Insufficient Gravity of the Case, 27 September 2019, ICC-01/12-01/18-459-tENG, paras. 55–56 (https://www.legal-tools.org/doc/z1jsl3/).

[88] ICC, Situation in the Republic of Mali, *The Prosecutor v. Al Hassan Ag Abdoul Aziz Ag Mohamed Ag Mahmoud*, OTP, Version publique expurgée de la «Version amendée et corrigée du Document contenant les charges contre M. Al HASSAN Ag ABDOUL AZIZ Ag Mohamed Ag Mahmoud», ICC-01/12-01/18-335-Conf-Corr, 11 mai 2019, 2 July 2019, ICC-01/12-01/18-335-Corr-Red (https://www.legal-tools.org/doc/1e4aac/).

[89] *Ibid.*, see Part 9 of the DCC, pp. 428, 439, 444, 446 and 453.

[90] *Ibid.*, see paras. 1046, 1056, 1058, 1085 and 1087.

mation of charges decision in the history of the ICC.[91] For most of the crimes, the decision identifies precisely the alleged victims – and does not use expressions such as 'for example' or 'included but not limited to' therefore indicating that the list is exhaustive – with the exception of the alleged victims of the crime of persecution.[92] Further, there is no reference to a distinction between 'subsidiary' and 'material' facts.

This is a first attempt by a pre-trial chamber to try to adapt to the requirements established in the Bemba Appeals Judgement with regard to the precision of the charges. The Trial Chamber VI Judgement in the Bosco Ntaganda[93] case seems to go in the same direction by trying to distinguish between different categories of crimes: whereas certain charges can be properly framed only at the level of individual criminal acts, others, such as deportation, may only be properly framed more broadly. However, the Chamber also indicates:

> Further, the Chamber may consider whether a specific type of criminal act (e.g. murder as a crime against humanity) is committed in narrowly confined temporal and geographical space and/or other parameters. These charges can be framed by these parameters and need not be framed at the level of individual criminal acts, as long as they fall within the specific parameters of the charge as confirmed by the pre-trial chamber.[94]

This is a clear indication that the Trial Chamber wanted to avoid setting a too rigid rule with regard to the required level of precision in the charges. It is precisely this aspect that the defence is now challenging

---

[91] ICC, Situation in the Republic of Mali, *The Prosecutor v. Al Hassan Ag Abdoul Aziz Ag Mohamed Ag Mahmoud*, Pre-Trial Chamber, Rectificatif à la Décision relative à la confirmation des charges portées contre Al Hassan Ag Abdoul Aziz Ag Mohamed Ag Mahmoud, 13 November 2019, ICC-01/12-01/18-461-Corr-Red (https://www.legal-tools.org/doc/9lml5x/).

[92] *Ibid.*, see especially pp. 452–65.

[93] ICC, Situation in the Democratic Republic of the Congo, *The Prosecutor v. Bosco Ntaganda*, Trial Chamber, Judgement, 8 July 2019, ICC-01/04-02/06-2359, paras. 39–40 (https://www.legal-tools.org/doc/80578a/).

[94] *Ibid.*, para. 41.

before the Appeals Chamber, arguing that such a ruling is in contradiction with the Bemba Appeals Judgement.[95]

The Bemba Appeals Judgement is therefore not the end but just the beginning of a long judicial discussion to come on this subject with a view to finding a balance between the necessity to spell out the facts in the charges in a clear and exhaustive a way as possible, avoiding to have a confirmation of charges or a conviction on the basis of 'samples',[96] while at the same time taking into consideration the diversity of forms of mass criminality that the Court may face.

19.3. Conclusion

The involvement of the judiciary in case preparation at the ICC has certainly been useful in assisting to correct early mistakes. OTP policies have changed or are changing in several ways and it is worth highlighting some positive developments.

With regard to the need to be trial-ready at the pre-trial stage of a case, the OTP has recently underlined that it "considers this approach to be more important than ever and will build upon and further strengthen this strategy in 2019-2021".[97]

The OTP is also indicating a willingness to reduce the length of preliminary examinations and to increase the preparation for an effective investigation during those preliminary examinations. The OTP is indicating in this regard that "it will continue its efforts to expedite the conduct of preliminary examinations"[98] and that JCCD "has developed methods to ensure the work done at the preliminary examination stage can be fully exploited by investigative teams and evidence is preserved during preliminary examinations".[99] Furthermore, the OTP is working "to effect an even closer integration of the work of SAS [the Situation Analysis Section

---

[95]   ICC, Situation in the Democratic Republic of the Congo, *The Prosecutor v. Bosco Ntaganda*, Defence Team of Mr. Bosco Ntaganda, Defence Appeal Brief – Part I, 11 November 2019, ICC-01/04-02/06-2443, para. 21 (https://www.legal-tools.org/doc/dstrmv/).

[96]   See Bemba Separate Opinion, para. 23, see above note 58.

[97]   ICC-OTP, Strategic Plan 2019-2021, 17 July 2019, para. 14 (https://www.legal-tools.org/doc/7ncqt3/).

[98]   *Ibid.*, para. 21.

[99]   *Ibid.*, para. 18.

within JCCD] with that of ID [Investigation Division] and PD [Prosecution Division]".[100] To that effect, the OTP is

> now beginning to assign ID and PD staff to situations under preliminary examination, to collaborate with SAS staff in preparing for any eventual investigation, and to assist in taking any necessary steps to preserve evidence.[101]

There is also a notable evolution with regard to the balance the OTP tries to achieve between the respect for the complementarity principle and the fight against impunity. One may compare in this regard the OTP's response to the reports concerning the serious acts of violence in the Democratic Republic in the Congo ('DRC'), particularly in the Kasaï provinces, with its response to the upsurge of violence in the Republic of Mali, more precisely in the Mopti region.

On 31 March 2017, in reaction to the events in the Kasaï provinces, the Prosecutor urged the competent authorities in the DRC, in accordance with the principle of complementarity, to "take all necessary measures to conduct genuine investigations so as to shed light on the alleged abuses and bring to justice all perpetrators involved".[102] The focus was on the primary responsibility of States Parties to act and no mention was made of any direct action to be taken by the OTP. The OTP visit to the DRC took place more than a year later, in May 2018.

By contrast, on 25 March 2019, in reaction to the events in the Mopti region, the Prosecutor stated that in

> complementarity with the national criminal justice system in Mali, my Office will take all necessary steps to ensure the investigation and prosecution of those who participated in or otherwise contributed to what appears to be egregious crimes which may fall under the jurisdiction of the [ICC]. As an *immediate* step, a delegation from my Office will, no later

---

[100] See in the regard, "Full Statement of the Prosecutor, Fatou Bensouda, on external expert review and lessons drawn from the Kenya situation", 26 November 2019, p. 11, see above note 6.

[101] *Ibid.*, p. 13.

[102] See ICC-OTP, "Statement of the Prosecutor of the International Criminal Court, Mrs Fatou Bensouda, regarding the situation in the Kasaï provinces, Democratic Republic of the Congo", 31 March 2017; see also ICC-OTP, "Statement by the ICC Prosecutor, Fatou Bensouda, at the conclusion of her visit to the DRC: "The fight against impunity and the critical prevention of crimes under the Rome Statute are essential to social stability"", 4 May 2018.

than this week, meet with the relevant authorities on these matters.[103]

The OTP willingness to get involved just after the commission of crimes is to be welcomed and contrasts with the more passive approach taken in the DRC with respect to the alleged crimes committed in the Kasaï provinces. In such instances, the OTP should have recourse to Article 56 of the Statute and involve the judiciary for the immediate preservation of evidence, in case it appears that the national authorities do not take urgently such measures.

It is finally worth mentioning that not everything depends on the evolution of OTP's policies. The type and extent of judiciary involvement in the quality control of case preparation is still a bone of contention among the judges and leads to conflicting jurisprudence. In this regard the judiciary will have to find a way to reach an agreement on the way the compromises made in Rome shall work in practice, for the benefit of the entire institution and more generally for the fight against impunity.

---

[103] See ICC-OTP, "Statement of the ICC Prosecutor, Fatou Bensouda, on reported upsurge of violence and mass killings in Mopti region, central Mali", 25 March 2019. Emphasis added.

20

___

The Judiciary and Enhancement of the Classification of Alleged Conduct

Eleni Chaitidou[*]

When contemplating possible improvements to the quality of investigations, attention is usually on the work-processes of investigators, as partially reflected by Part II of this anthology. An aspect less obvious is whether and to what extent judicial intervention at the investigation and pre-trial phase can impact and improve the quality of investigations.

Unless equipped with investigative powers, judges do not engage in fact-finding work, do not select the targets of the investigation, do not decide who and what should be prosecuted, and do not advise on the sufficiency and quality of evidence collected. That remains the responsibility of investigators and prosecutors. Judges are on the receiving end. They verify that the evidence presented supports the factual allegations attributed to the accused, and that the legal characterisation of the factual allegations (or, in other words, the classification of alleged conduct), as proposed by the prosecuting authorities, is accurate.

Why would judges address the classification of alleged conduct or seek to enhance such classification at all? To begin with, judges are not passive observers in criminal proceedings who are bound by the submissions advanced by the Prosecutor or the Defence, but they are a neutral authority and the ultimate decision-makers as regards the determination of the facts, their attribution to the accused, and the interpretation and appli-

___

[*] **Eleni Chaitidou** is Senior Legal Officer at the Kosovo Specialist Chambers, on leave from the International Criminal Court ('ICC') at the time of writing this chapter. The views expressed in the chapter are those of the author alone and do not necessarily reflect the views of the ICC or the Kosovo Specialist Chambers. The chapter is based on a speech the author gave on 23 February 2019 at the conference 'Quality Control in Criminal Investigation', co-organised by the Centre for International Law Research and Policy (CILRAP) and the Indian Law Institute in New Delhi. All decisions discussed in this paper can be accessed in the ICC Legal Tools Database (https://www.legal-tools.org).

cation of the law in question. The truth-finding mandate compels the judges to search for the 'judicial truth', as it transpires from the evidence, and to attribute responsibility to the accused that reflects what has actually happened. The mandate includes the accurate legal classification of the accused's conduct that best reflects his or her culpability. The accurate legal classification provides the accused with clarity about the accusations levied against him or her. It also allows the victims to accept and embrace the judicial process and its outcome. Lastly, the classification assists in articulating in abstract the behaviour considered to be unacceptable, thus fostering social cohesion.

At the International Criminal Court ('ICC' or 'Court'), the interference of the Judiciary in first instance regarding the classification of alleged conduct can occur at different stages of the proceedings. It can occur, for example, at the stage when the Prosecutor[1] requests the Pre-Trial Chamber to authorise the commencement of the investigation (Article 15 of the Rome Statute),[2] when the Pre-Trial Chamber reviews the Prosecutor's decision not to initiate an investigation into a situation (Article 53(3)), when the Pre-Trial Chamber issues a warrant of arrest or summons to appear (Article 58), when the Pre-Trial Chamber decides whether to confirm or decline to confirm the charges or to adjourn the hearing (Article 61(7)), when the Trial Chamber decides to re-characterise the facts of the case (Regulation 55 of the Regulations of the Court) or, ultimately, decides on the innocence or guilt of the accused at trial (Article 74).

Mindful of the subject-matter of the research project of which this anthology forms part, the chapter examines judicial intervention of ICC judges in proceedings at the situation level, during which the investigation takes place, and the pre-trial stage of a case, and describes how Pre-Trial Chambers addressed the Prosecutor's classification of conduct. The topic invites the reader to reflect on past practice of ICC Chambers and to assess whether certain ideas and approaches may be borrowed from the ICC and applied by investigating and prosecuting authorities in other jurisdictions.

---

[1]   The ICC Prosecutor at the time of writing was Fatou Bensouda, from Gambia (2012–2021).

[2]   Rome Statute of the International Criminal Court, 17 July 1998 ('ICC Statute') (https://www.legal-tools.org/doc/7b9af9/). All articles mentioned in this chapter without reference to the legal instrument, are those of the ICC Statute.

20.1. Judicial Intervention at the ICC

In contrast to the *ad hoc* tribunals (that is, the international criminal tribunals for the former Yugoslavia and Rwanda) or other internationalised criminal tribunals (for example, the Special Court for Sierra Leone or the Extraordinary Chambers in the Courts of Cambodia), the ICC is not established to enquire into the criminal responsibility of potential perpetrators in one pre-defined situation. Rather, the ICC Prosecutor decides, independently of the political will of States and the Security Council, to intervene in situations where there are grounds to believe that crimes under the jurisdiction of the Court have been committed. This reality sets the ICC apart from any other international(ised) criminal tribunal and mirrors its permanent nature and universal orientation.

20.1.1. Preliminary Examinations

The Court does not intervene automatically when there is suspicion that crimes within its jurisdiction have been committed. For the ICC to become active, the powers of the Court must be triggered. This occurs in three ways: a situation[3] has been referred to the Court by a State Party (Articles 13(a), 14) or the Security Council, acting under Chapter VII of the United Nations ('UN') Charter (Article 13(b)), or the Prosecutor, having analysed the seriousness of information gathered and received,[4] has decided to open an investigation *proprio motu* (Articles 13(c), 15).[5] The

---

[3] As indicated by the word 'situation', the State Party or Security Council may not refer a particular case, that is, an accusation against a particular individual for a specific conduct, but only a situation. Referrals containing information about certain potential perpetrators may be indicative for the Prosecutor, but do not instruct her to prosecute those individuals. Rather, the Prosecutor is free to enquire into the criminal responsibility of any person involved in the commission of crimes within the given situation, subject to the jurisdictional parameters set forth in Article 12, see above note 2.

[4] The Prosecutor may receive information (referred to as 'communications') from a variety of sources, such as governments, international organisations, non-governmental organisations or individuals, see Article 15(1) and 15(2), see above note 2 and Rule 104 of the Rules of Procedure and Evidence, 9 September 2002 (https://www.legal-tools.org/doc/e1b3f5/). All Rules mentioned in this chapter without reference to the legal instrument are those of the ICC's Rules of Procedure and Evidence.

[5] The Court may also receive a declaration under Article 12(3) by a non-State Party which accepts the Court's jurisdiction with respect to the crimes in question. Nevertheless, the exercise of jurisdiction must be triggered according to three mechanisms set forth in Article 13, see above note 2.

term 'situation' is understood to denote a conflict scenario that is delineated by temporal, geographical or personal parameters.[6]

The receipt of a referral or the receipt of information about crimes within the jurisdiction of the Court does not mark the opening of an ICC investigation. Rather, it compels the Prosecutor to start a preliminary examination.[7] During the preliminary examination, the Prosecutor is duty-bound to analyse – within a reasonable time[8] – the seriousness of the information received or made available against the cumulative criteria under Article 53(1)[9] with a view to deciding whether to open an investigation at the ICC or not. The assessment of the information under Article 53(1) is conducted against the lowest evidentiary threshold in the Statute ("reasonable basis to proceed"), requiring that there exists merely a sensible or reasonable justification for a belief that a crime falling within the jurisdic-

---

[6] ICC, Situation in the Democratic Republic of the Congo, Pre-Trial Chamber, Decision on the Applications for Participation in the Proceedings of VPRS 1, VPRS 2, VPRS 3, VPRS 4, VPRS 5 and VPRS 6, 17 January 2006, ICC-01/04-101-tEN-Corr, para. 65 (https://www.legal-tools.org/doc/2fe2fc/); ICC, Situation in Uganda, Pre-Trial Chamber, Decision on victims' applications for participation a/0010/06, a/0064/06 to a/0070/06, a/0081/06 to a/0104/06, and a/0111/06 to a/0127/06, 10 August 2007, ICC-02/04-101, paras. 88–103 (https://www.legal-tools.org/doc/8f9181/). For a comprehensive analysis of the jurisdictional confines of a situation, see Rod Rastan, "Situation and Case: Defining the Parameters", in Carsten Stahn and Mohamed M. El Zeidy (eds.), *The International Criminal Court and Complementarity: From Theory to Practice*, vol. I, Cambridge University Press, 2011, p. 421.

[7] See the use of the mandatory 'shall' in Article 15(2), first sentence, see above note 2, and Rule 104(1), see above note 4.

[8] ICC, Situation in the Central African Republic, Pre-Trial Chamber, Decision Requesting Information on the Status of the Preliminary Examination of the Situation in the Central African Republic, 30 November 2006, ICC-01/05-6, p. 4 (https://www.legal-tools.org/doc/76e607/); ICC, Situation in Bangladesh/Myanmar, Pre-Trial Chamber, Decision on the "Prosecution's Request for a Ruling on Jurisdiction under Article 19(3) of the Statute", 6 September 2018, ICC-RoC46(3)-01/18-37, para. 84 ('Rohingya Preliminary Ruling') (https://www.legal-tools.org/doc/73aeb4/); ICC, Situation on the Registered Vessels of the Union of the Comoros, the Hellenic Republic and the Kingdom of Cambodia, Pre-Trial Chamber, Decision on the "Application for Judicial Review by the Government of the Union of the Comoros", 15 November 2018, ICC-01/13-68, para. 119 ('Comoros Second Review Decision') (https://www.legal-tools.org/doc/a268c5/).

[9] Rules 48 and 104, see above note 4. ICC, Situation in Egypt, Pre-Trial Chamber, Decision on the "Request for review of the Prosecutor's decision of 23 April 2014 not to open a Preliminary Examination concerning alleged crimes committed in the Arab Republic of Egypt, and the Registrar's Decision of 25 April 2014", 12 September 2014, ICC-RoC46(3)-01/14-3, para. 6 (https://www.legal-tools.org/doc/bfbb8f/); Rohingya Preliminary Ruling, para. 82, see above note 8.

tion of the Court has been committed.[10] The Article 53(1) criteria, which are applicable irrespective of the trigger mechanism,[11] involve an assessment as to whether

(i) the crime(s), as alleged, fall(s) within the jurisdiction of the Court (Article 53(1)(a));[12] this assessment involves the classification of alleged conduct, including contextual circumstances, that underlies the referral or constitutes the focus of the Article 15(1) information;

(ii) the potential case(s) within the context of the situation would be admissible before the Court (Article 53(1)(b));[13] and

---

[10] ICC, Situation in the Republic of Kenya, Pre-Trial Chamber, Decision Pursuant to Article 15 of the Rome Statute on the Authorization of an Investigation into the Situation in the Republic of Kenya, 31 March 2010, ICC-01/09-19-Corr, paras. 27–35 ('Kenya Authorisation Decision') (https://www.legal-tools.org/doc/f0caaf/); ICC, Situation in Georgia, Pre-Trial Chamber, Decision on the Prosecutor's request for authorization of an investigation, 27 January 2016, ICC-01/15-12, para. 25 ('Georgia Authorisation Decision') (https://www.legal-tools.org/doc/a3d07e/); ICC, Situation in the Republic of Burundi, Pre-Trial Chamber, Public Redacted Version of "Decision Pursuant to Article 15 of the Rome Statute on the Authorization of an Investigation into the Situation in the Republic of Burundi", ICC-01/17-X-9-US-Exp, 25 October 2017, 9 November 2017, ICC-01/17-9-Red, para. 30 ('Burundi Authorisation Decision') (https://www.legal-tools.org/doc/8f2373/).

[11] Kenya Authorisation Decision, paras. 23–24, see above note 10. See also ICC Office of the Prosecutor ('OTP'), *Policy Paper on Preliminary Examinations*, 1 November 2013, paras. 34–35 ('2013 Policy Paper on Preliminary Examinations') (https://www.legal-tools.org/doc/acb906/).

[12] The jurisdiction of the Court is ascertained on the basis of four different parameters, of which the last two are in the alternative: material (jurisdiction *ratione materiae* – Article 5), temporal (jurisdiction *ratione temporis* – Article 11), territorial (jurisdiction *ratione loci* – Article 12(2)(a) or 12(3)) or personal (jurisdiction *ratione personae* – Article 12(2)(b), 12(3), 26), see above note 2; ICC, Situation in the Democratic Republic of the Congo, *Prosecutor v. Thomas Lubanga Dyilo*, Appeals Chamber, Judgment on the Appeal of Mr. Thomas Lubanga Dyilo against the Decision on the Defence Challenge to the Jurisdiction of the Court pursuant to article 19(2)(a) of the Statute of 3 October 2006, 14 December 2006, ICC-01/04-01/06-772, paras. 21–22 (https://www.legal-tools.org/doc/1505f7/); Kenya Authorisation Decision, paras. 38–39, see above note 10.

[13] Admissibility concerns the question of whether the Court should exercise its recognised jurisdiction over a particular situation or case. The admissibility of the potential cases (consisting of the group of persons likely to be the focus of an investigation and crimes committed during incidents that are likely to be the focus of the investigation) is analysed on the basis of the two criteria set forth in Article 17 (complementarity and gravity). Complementarity (Article 17(1)(a)–(c)) in the present context involves the enquiry whether domestic proceedings are, or have been, conducted in relation to groups of persons and the crimes allegedly committed during those incidents which together would likely form the object of the ICC investigation. Gravity (Article 17(1)(d)) in the present context enquires whether the likely set of potential cases is serious enough to justify further action by the

(iii) "taking into account the gravity of the crime and the interests of victims, there are nonetheless substantial reasons to believe that an investigation would not serve the interests of justice" (Article 53(1)(c)).

The nature of preliminary examinations informs the manner in which the aforementioned criteria are analysed. Article 53(1)(a) and (b) entail the application of exacting legal requirements, while Article 53(1)(c) contains an element of discretion.[14] Considering the lack of investigative powers of the Prosecutor at this phase, the information available must not be "comprehensive", "conclusive", "clear, univocal or not contradictory".[15] Rather, "if the information available to the Prosecutor at the pre-investigative stage allows for reasonable inferences that at least one crime within the jurisdiction of the Court has been committed and that the case would be admissible, the Prosecutor shall open an investigation".[16] If the information basis is not adequate, the Prosecutor may revert to States or other reliable sources, such as the UN or non-governmental organisations, in order to receive further additional information, or receive written or oral testimonies at the seat of the Court.[17] The Prosecutor regularly confirms that the analysis, even though provisional, is thorough at this stage.[18]

Court. The assessment covers: (i) the group of persons that are likely to form the object of the investigation and which bear the greatest responsibility; and (ii) the crimes committed within the incidents that are likely to be focus of the investigation; in making the assessment, gravity is examined following a quantitative and qualitative approach, see above note 2. See for a comprehensive discussion Kenya Authorisation Decision, paras. 40–62, see above note 10.

[14] ICC, Situation on Registered Vessels of the Union of Comoros, the Hellenic Republic and the Kingdom of Cambodia, Pre-Trial Chamber, Decision on the request of the Union of the Comoros to review the Prosecutor's decision not to initiate an investigation, 16 July 2015, ICC-01/13-34, para. 14 ('Comoros First Review Decision') (https://www.legal-tools.org/doc/2f876c/).

[15] Kenya Authorisation Decision, para. 27, see above note 10; Comoros First Review Decision, para. 13, see above note 14; Georgia Authorisation Decision, para. 25, see above note 10.

[16] Comoros First Review Decision, para. 13, see above note 14.

[17] Article 15(2), see above note 2 and Rule 47, see above note 4.

[18] See, for example, 2013 Policy Paper on Preliminary Examinations, para. 81:

Phase 2 analysis entails a thorough factual and legal assessment of the crimes allegedly committed in the situation at hand with a view to identifying the potential cases falling within the jurisdiction of the Court. The Office will pay particular consideration to

---

Preliminary examinations are the exclusive domain of the ICC Prosecutor. Judges do not intervene in this phase. It is incumbent upon the Prosecutor to give consideration to the Article 53(1) criteria, including the classification of alleged conduct at issue and thus establish the Court's subject-matter jurisdiction. Recently, however, the Prosecutor approached the Pre-Trial Chambers under Regulation 46(3) of the Regulations of the Court[19] or Article 19(3)[20] requesting a ruling on discrete legal questions. For example, in April 2018 the Prosecutor requested that a Pre-Trial Chamber rule on whether the Court may exercise jurisdiction over the alleged deportation of Rohingya people from the Republic of Myanmar to the People's Republic of Bangladesh.[21] On 22 January 2020, the Prosecutor requested Pre-Trial Chamber I[22] to rule on the scope of the Court's

---

crimes committed on a large scale, as part of a plan or pursuant to a policy. The Office may further gather information on relevant national proceedings if such information is available at this stage. Phase 2 leads to the submission of an 'Article 5 report' to the Prosecutor, in reference to the material jurisdiction of the Court as defined in article 5 of the Statute

See above note 11; ICC-OTP, *Report on Preliminary Examination Activities 2019*, 5 December 2019, para. 10: "All information gathered is subjected to a fully independent, impartial and thorough analysis"; and para. 13: "The Office takes no longer than is necessary to complete a thorough assessment of the statutory criteria to arrive at an informed decision" (https://www.legal-tools.org/doc/lq7j94/).

[19] Regulation 46(3) of the Regulations of the Court, 26 May 2004 (https://www.legal-tools.org/doc/2988d1/) reads:

Any matter, request or information not arising out of a situation assigned to a Pre-Trial Chamber in accordance with sub-regulation 2, shall be directed by the President of the Pre-Trial Division to a Pre-Trial Chamber according to a roster established by the President of that Division.

[20] Article 19(3) reads:

The Prosecutor may seek a ruling from the Court regarding a question of jurisdiction or admissibility. In proceedings with respect to jurisdiction or admissibility, those who have referred the situation under article 13, as well as victims, may also submit observations to the Court.

See above note 2.

[21] ICC-OTP, Prosecution's Request for a Ruling on Jurisdiction under Article 19, 9 April 2018, ICC-RoC46(3)-01/18-1, para. 1 ('Rohingya Request') (https://www.legal-tools.org/doc/4af756/). Pre-Trial Chamber I confirmed that the Court would have territorial jurisdiction over the crime of deportation but also over the crimes of other inhumane acts (Article 7(1)(k)) and persecution (Article 7(1)(h)), see Rohingya Preliminary Ruling, paras. 50–78, see above note 8.

[22] Following Palestine's referral, the situation in Palestine was assigned to Pre-Trial Chamber I, pursuant to Regulation 45(1) ("The Prosecutor shall inform the Presidency in writing as soon as a situation has been referred to the Prosecutor by a State Party under article 14 or

territorial jurisdiction in the situation of Palestine and to 'confirm' the boundaries of the territory over which the ICC may exercise jurisdiction.[23] Thus, notwithstanding the Prosecutor's exclusive authority, she twice engaged the judges at this early stage arguing, *inter alia*, that a judicial resolution of the matters "would assist in her further deliberations",[24] ensure that a possible investigation is placed on the "soundest legal foundation" before she embarks on a course of action and would "facilitate the practical conduct of [the] investigation".[25] It is not excluded that, for the same reasons, preliminary rulings may be requested in the future in relation to the classification of alleged conduct underpinning a referral or the Article 15(1) information. In particular, pronouncements on the interpretation of the crimes under the ICC jurisdiction could be useful for the Prosecutor's further course of action. That said, whereas such preliminary judicial rulings assist the Prosecutor in taking the next steps, they are without prejudice to subsequent determinations on the same matter in light of the facts and the evidence presented at a later stage.

Upon conclusion of the preliminary examination, the Prosecutor decides either that there is a reasonable basis to proceed with an investigation or that the information provided does not constitute a reasonable basis to commence an investigation.[26] Her decision is summarised in a report, which includes her preliminary findings regarding the legal characterisation of the alleged conduct.

---

by the Security Council under article 13, sub-paragraph (b); [...]") and Regulation 46 (2) ("The Presidency shall assign a situation to a Pre-Trial Chamber as soon as the Prosecutor has informed the Presidency in accordance with regulation 45, paragraph 1. [...]") of the Regulations of the Court, see above note 19.

23   ICC-OTP, Situation in the State of Palestine, Prosecution request pursuant to article 19(3) for a ruling on the Court's territorial jurisdiction in Palestine, 22 January 2020, ICC-01/18-12 ('Palestine Request') (https://www.legal-tools.org/doc/clur6w/). At the time of writing, the request is still pending before Pre-Trial Chamber I.

24   Rohingya Request, para. 3, see above note 21.

25   Palestine Request, paras. 5–6, see above note 23.

26   In the past, the Prosecutor's conclusions not to proceed with an investigation were summarised in a report and made public, see, for example, on 23 June 2014 regarding the situation in the Republic of Korea: ICC-OTP, *Situation in the Republic of Korea: Article 5 Report*, 23 June 2014 (https://www.legal-tools.org/doc/ef1f7f/); on 21 September 2018 regarding the situation in the Gabonese Republic: ICC-OTP, *Situation in the Gabonese Republic: Article 5 Report*, 21 September 2018 (https://www.legal-tools.org/doc/9aad5c/).

20.1.2. Authorisation to Commence the Investigation

If the Prosecutor decides in the affirmative, that there is a reasonable basis to proceed with an investigation, the trigger mechanisms determine the subsequent course of action: in case of a referral, the Prosecutor is free to commence the investigation into the situation, within the boundaries of the referral.[27] In this case, the judges do not intervene and will have the first opportunity to espouse their views on the classification of alleged conduct when the Prosecutor requests the issuance of a warrant of arrest or a summons to appear for a suspect. In case of the Prosecutor's *proprio motu* initiative, she must first submit a request to a Pre-Trial Chamber seeking its authorisation to commence the investigation.[28] Upon such judicial authorisation,[29] the Prosecutor may commence the investigation, within the boundaries of the authorisation.

In the context of Article 15 authorisation proceedings the legal characterisation of the alleged conduct is reviewed by the Pre-Trial Chamber as a consequence of its statutory responsibility to analyse whether indeed, as proposed by the Prosecutor, there is a reasonable basis to believe that one or more crimes within the jurisdiction of the Court have been or are being committed.[30] To this end, the judges review the

---

[27] If the referral involves the crime of aggression, the special procedure under Articles 15*bis* and 15*ter* applies, see above note 2.

[28] Article 15(3), see above note 2.

[29] Article 15(4), see above note 2.

[30] Article 15(4) in conjunction with Article 53(1), see above note 2 and Rule 48, see above note 4. When reviewing the Prosecutor's request for authorisation to commence an investigation under Article 15(3), all Pre-Trial Chambers have consistently held that the Article 53(1) criteria must be examined by the Pre-Trial Chamber under Article 15(4), see the first and seminal Kenya Authorisation Decision, paras. 17–25, see above note 10. The Appeals Chamber recently narrowed down significantly the review powers of the Pre-Trial Chambers and opined that the Pre-Trial Chambers are only mandated to determine under Article 15(4) whether there is "a reasonable factual basis for the Prosecutor to proceed with an investigation, in the sense of whether crimes have been committed, and that potential case(s) arising from such investigation appear to fall within the Court's jurisdiction", see ICC, Situation in the Islamic Republic of Afghanistan, Appeals Chamber, Judgment on the appeal against the decision on the authorisation of an investigation into the situation in the Islamic Republic of Afghanistan, 5 March 2020, ICC-02/17-138, para. 1 ('Afghanistan Appeals Judgment') (https://www.legal-tools.org/doc/x7kl12/). In a separate opinion, Judge Ibañez Carranza pointed out that these findings were rendered in passing and are *ultra petita*, constituting at best *obiter dicta*, see ICC, Situation in the Islamic Republic of Afghanistan, Appeals Chamber, Separate Opinion of Judge Luz del Carmen Ibañez Carranza to the Judgment on the appeal against the decision of Pre-Trial Chamber II on the authorization

---

Prosecutor's request together with the supporting material.[31] In addition, the judges of the Pre-Trial Chamber receive representations of victims, who present their views as to whether an investigation should be opened.[32] In so doing, the victims also describe the conduct of known perpetrators or groups of perpetrators and the harm suffered. Such description may overlap with the Prosecutor's submissions, but may also be an addition to the Prosecutor's factual narrative of the situation. At the end of the review exercise, the Chamber sets the scope of the authorised investigation in terms of its geographical and temporal reach as well as its subject-matter.

Authorisation proceedings under Article 15 have taken place in several situations, namely in relation to the situations in Kenya, Côte d'Ivoire, Georgia, Burundi, Myanmar/Bangladesh and Afghanistan. The practice hitherto shows that the judges follow largely the classification of conduct as identified by the Prosecutor.[33] Only occasionally did the judges go beyond the Prosecutor's classification when they added a legal characterisa-

---

of an investigation into the situation in the Islamic Republic of Afghanistan, 6 March 2020, ICC-02/17-138-Anx-Corr (https://www.legal-tools.org/doc/bfdi78/). Irrespective of how the test under Article 15(4) will be shaped in the future by the Pre-Trial Chambers, the issue of legal classification of the conduct remains an integral part of the Pre-Trial Chamber's analysis under Article 15(4). See also Kenya Authorisation Decision, paras. 37–39, see above note 10.

[31] Article 15(4) stipulates that the Pre-Trial Chamber render its decision "upon examination of the request and the supporting material", see above note 2.

[32] Article 15(3), second sentence, see above note 2, and Rule 50, see above note 4.

[33] For example, in the authorisation request regarding the commencement of an investigation into the situation in Kenya, the Prosecutor at the time had determined that murder, rape and other forms of sexual violence, deportation or forcible transfer of population and other inhumane acts as crimes against humanity had allegedly been committed, see ICC, Situation in the Republic of Kenya, OTP, Request for authorization of an investigation pursuant to Article 15, 26 November 2009, ICC-01/09-3, para. 48 (https://www.legal-tools.org/doc/c63dcc/). The Pre-Trial Chamber confirmed the Prosecutor's classification in its entirety, see Kenya Authorisation Decision, paras. 139–71, see above note 10. In relation to the situation in Burundi, the Prosecutor had determined that murder, imprisonment or severe deprivation of liberty, torture, rape and other forms of sexual violence, enforced disappearance and persecution as crimes against humanity had occurred, see ICC, Situation in Burundi, OTP, Public version of "Request for authorization of an investigation pursuant to article 15", 6 September 2017, ICC-01/17-5-US-Exp, 15 November 2017, ICC-01/17-5-Red, paras. 80–139 ('Burundi Authorisation Request') (https://www.legal-tools.org/doc/e47402/). Pre-Trial Chamber III largely confirmed the Prosecutor's classification and added attempted murders, but did not mention other forms of sexual violence in its analysis, see Burundi Authorisation Decision, see above note 10.

---

tion of alleged conduct as described in the request and/or the supporting material and/or the victims' representations. Importantly, these additions remained within the geographical and temporal parameters of the situation as delineated by the Prosecutor.

Two examples, in which the Pre-Trial Chambers amended the Prosecutor's classification regarding selected examples of conduct, illustrate the Pre-Trial Chambers' approach.

- **Burundi Situation**: The Prosecutor requested authorisation to commence an investigation into allegations of crimes against humanity committed by members of the Burundian Government, military, intelligence service, police and a youth movement associated with the ruling party, against the civilian population believed to be actual or perceived opponents to the President and the ruling party. The Prosecutor submitted that, on evidence at the time, there was no reasonable basis to believe that the situation could be characterised as a non-international armed conflict as (i) the violence had not reached the degree of intensity, and (ii) the level of organisation of the anti-government entities was insufficient in order to characterise the situation as such. Nevertheless, the Prosecutor confirmed that she would keep these allegations under review, if authorisation was given.[34]

  The Pre-Trial Chamber, upon analysis of the supporting material, determined that the Prosecutor had acted "too restrictively" and had imposed requirements on the supporting material that cannot reasonably be met in the absence of an investigation. It encouraged the Prosecutor to draw reasonable conclusions at this stage, "provided those conclusions do not appear manifestly unreasonable".[35] As a result, it authorised the Prosecutor to extend her investigation into all crimes under the Statute, including war crimes, as long as they remained within the parameters of the authorised investigation.[36]

- **Côte d'Ivoire Situation**: The Prosecutor requested authorisation to commence an investigation into allegations of crimes against hu-

---

[34] Burundi Authorisation Request, paras. 6, 35, see above note 33.
[35] Burundi Authorisation Decision, paras. 138, 141, see above note 10.
[36] *Ibid.*, para. 193.

manity and war crimes committed in the context of post-election violence in 2010–11 between security forces loyal to outgoing President Laurent Gbagbo, associated groups and militias ('pro-Gbagbo forces'), on the one hand, and supporters and armed groups loyal to incoming President Ouattara ('pro-Ouattara forces'), on the other hand.[37] The Prosecutor argued that both sides had committed crimes to varying degrees. However, in relation to the pro-Ouattara forces in particular the Prosecutor submitted that, on evidence at the time, there was no reasonable basis to believe that they had committed crimes against humanity.[38] Nevertheless, the Prosecutor confirmed that the determinations were made without prejudice to other possible crimes within the Court's jurisdiction, including whether pro-Ouattara forces had committed crimes against humanity.[39]

The Pre-Trial Chamber, upon analysis of the supporting material, determined that there was a reasonable basis to believe that pro-Ouattara forces had committed alleged crimes against humanity against the civilian population, as well as other crimes not presented by the Prosecutor, such as pillaging, cruel treatment and torture.[40] It also added further crimes purportedly committed by the pro-Gbagbo forces not presented by the Prosecutor, such as torture and other inhumane acts.[41]

Why do judges review and, as the case may be, amend the Prosecutor's classification of alleged conduct at the stage of the authorisation of the investigation? In the first place, the drafters of the Statute purposefully subjected the Prosecutor's conclusions to the independent review of the Pre-Trial Chamber, before the commencement of an investigation.[42] In-

---

[37] ICC, Situation in Côte d'Ivoire, OTP, Request for authorization of an investigation pursuant to article 15, 23 June 2011, ICC-02/11-3, para. 39 (https://www.legal-tools.org/doc/1b1939/).

[38] *Ibid.*, para. 75.

[39] *Ibid.*, paras. 39, 75.

[40] ICC, Situation in Côte d'Ivoire, Pre-Trial Chamber, Corrigendum to "Decision Pursuant to Article 15 of the Rome Statute on the Authorisation of an Investigation into the Situation in the Republic of Côte d'Ivoire", 15 November 2011, ICC-02/11-14-Corr, paras. 92–105, 162–69 (https://www.legal-tools.org/doc/e0c0eb/).

[41] *Ibid.*, paras. 83–86.

[42] Pre-Trial Chamber II in the Kenya situation clarified that the purpose of the Article 15(4) supervision is "to prevent the Court from proceeding with unwarranted, frivolous, or politically motivated investigations that could have a negative effect on its credibility", see

deed, the Article 15 procedure compensates the absence of a referral and constitutes an impartial check on the powers of the independent Prosecutor.[43] Thus, the supervisory role of the Pre-Trial Chamber entails that it is not bound by the Prosecutor's conclusions, including the classification of alleged conduct, but is at liberty to view them differently. This approach ensures objectivity, meaning that the review exercise is free of any appearance of bias. In the second place, divergence in the classification of conduct is a natural consequence of the fact that the information basis of the Pre-Trial Chamber is broader than that of the Prosecutor. As mentioned earlier, during the authorisation proceedings, victims are entitled to make representations to the Pre-Trial Chamber. They may provide new information on facts that may move the Chamber, in turn, to classify the conduct differently.

If the Pre-Trial Chamber does not agree with the classification of the reported factual allegations and declines to authorise the commencement of the investigation, for example for lack of subject-matter jurisdiction, the Prosecutor has no authority to proceed. Unless subjected to appellate review, the matter is closed. If, however, the investigation is authorised, it is upon the Prosecutor to investigate within the parameters of the authorised investigation and to frame the charges against individuals.[44] Hence, what matters is that the Prosecutor describes in the authorisation request the factual allegations with sufficient specificity so that the material parameters of the future investigation are clear to the judges. Pre-Trial Chambers reassured the Prosecutor on several occasions that the Prosecutor's Office is not bound by the incidents described in the application or the authorisation decision.[45] As a corollary, any of the legal classifications

---

Kenya Authorisation Decision, para. 32, see above note 10. The same reasoning has been echoed by other Pre-Trial Chambers.

[43] Comoros First Review Decision, para. 9, see above note 14.

[44] ICC, Situation in the Democratic Republic of the Congo, Appeals Chamber, Judgment on victim participation in the investigation stage of the proceedings in the appeal of the OPCD against the decision of Pre-Trial Chamber I of 7 December 2007 and in the appeals of the OPCD and the Prosecutor against the decision of Pre-Trial Chamber I of 24 December 2007, 19 December 2008, ICC-01/04-556, para. 52 ('Appeals Judgment on Victims Participation During Investigation') (https://www.legal-tools.org/doc/dca981/); ICC, Situation in Uganda, *Prosecutor v. Dominic Ongwen*, Pre-Trial Chamber, Decision on the confirmation of charges against Dominic Ongwen, 23 March 2016, ICC-02/04-01/15-422-Red, para. 106 ('Ongwen Confirmation Decision') (https://www.legal-tools.org/doc/74fc6e/).

[45] Kenya Authorisation Decision, para. 75, see above note 10; Georgia Authorisation Decision, para. 63, see above note 10; Burundi Authorisation Decision, para. 193:

of alleged conduct undertaken by the Pre-Trial Chamber is preliminary in nature and not restricting the Prosecutor's investigation. Indeed, it would be illogical to bind the Prosecutor to a classification that is based on a limited information basis formed during the pre-investigative phase.[46] What the judges achieve by amending the classification is to invite the Prosecutor to explore the classification of the reported conduct not envisaged before with a view to gaining clarity and overcoming any doubts. Further, as the example Burundi shows, the Prosecutor is encouraged to look into all possible crimes committed, in line with her duty to "establish the truth [and] extend the investigation to cover all facts and evidence".[47] Moreover, as the example Côte d'Ivoire shows, the Prosecutor is encouraged to look equally into crimes committed by all actors involved, in line with her (and the Court's) duty of independence and impartiality. In this respect, the Pre-Trial Chamber can enhance the investigation of the Prosecutor.

20.1.3. Review of the Prosecutor's Decision Not to Commence an Investigation

If after the preliminary examination the Prosecutor decides not to open an investigation, the Prosecutor must notify the referring entity[48] and/or those

---

[T]he Prosecutor is not restricted to the incidents and crimes set out in the present decision but may, on the basis of the evidence, extend her investigation to other crimes against humanity or other article 5 crimes, *i.e.* war crimes and genocide, as long as they remain within the parameters of the authorized investigation.

See above note 10; ICC, Situation in Côte d'Ivoire, Pre-Trial Chamber, Decision on the "Prosecution's provision of further information regarding potentially relevant crimes committed between 2002 and 2010", 22 February 2012, ICC-02/11-36, paras. 14–15 (https://www.legal-tools.org/doc/de6177/); ICC, Situation in the People's Republic of Bangladesh/Republic of the Union of Myanmar, Pre-Trial Chamber, Decision Pursuant to Article 15 of the Rome Statute on the Authorisation of an Investigation into the Situation in the People's Republic of Bangladesh/Republic of the Union of Myanmar, 14 November 2019, ICC-01/19-27, paras. 126–30 (https://www.legal-tools.org/doc/kbo3hy/); see also Afghanistan Appeals Judgment, paras. 2, 61, see above note 30.

[46] Pre-Trial Chamber II in the Kenya situation had authorised the investigation only in respect to crimes against humanity. It held that allowing the Prosecutor to investigate acts constituting other crimes would not be consistent with the purpose of the Article 15 authorisation proceedings, see Kenya Authorisation Decision, paras. 208–09, see above note 10. This approach was not followed by Pre-Trial Chambers in any of the subsequent authorisation decisions.

[47] Article 54(1)(a), see above note 2.

[48] Rule 105(1), see above note 4.

---

who provided the information,[49] including the reasons for the conclusion reached.[50] The Prosecutor's decision not to proceed is reviewable by the Pre-Trial Chamber, either upon request of the referring entity (Article 53(3)(a))[51] or, if the Prosecutor's decision is based solely on the criterion of Article 53(1)(c), *proprio motu* by the Pre-Trial Chamber (Article 53(3)(b)).[52] In the context of the Article 53(3)(a) review, the Pre-Trial Chamber does not undertake the assessment of the Article 53(1) criteria *ex novo*, but reviews only those issues that are raised by the challenging entity.[53] In so doing, the Pre-Trial Chamber examines whether the "validity of the decision is materially affected by an error, whether it is an error of procedure, an error of law, or an error of fact".[54] The classification of alleged conduct may be part of the Pre-Trial Chamber's review exercise in relation to any of the Article 53(1) criteria, but in particular the ascertainment of the Court's jurisdiction.[55] If errors are found that have a bearing on the Prosecutor's conclusion not to investigate, the Pre-Trial Chamber may request the Prosecutor to reconsider, in whole or in part, her previous decision not to proceed.[56] Upon such reconsideration, the Prosecutor takes a "final decision" on the matter.[57] In case the Pre-Trial Chamber does not

---

[49] Article 15(6), first sentence, see above note 2, and Rules 49, 105(2), see above note 4.

[50] Rules 49(1) and 105(3), see above note 4. In case the Prosecutor decides not to proceed based on the criterion of Article 53(1)(c), that is, that an investigation would not serve the interests of justice, the Prosecutor must inform, in addition, the Pre-Trial Chamber promptly after making that decision, see Rule 105(4).

[51] Rule 107, see above note 4.

[52] Rule 109, see above note 4.

[53] Comoros First Review Decision, para. 10, see above note 14.

[54] *Ibid.*, para. 12. As will be explained below, the Appeals Chamber provided further clarifications as to the review of factual errors.

[55] Article 53(1)(a), see above note 2.

[56] Article 53(3)(a), see above note 2, Rule 108(2), see above note 4.

[57] Rule 108(3), see above note 4. See also ICC, Situation on Registered Vessels of the Union of the Comoros, the Hellenic Republic and the Kingdom of Cambodia, Appeals Chamber, Decision on the admissibility of the Prosecutor's appeal against the "Decision on the request of the Union of the Comoros to review the Prosecutor's decision not to initiate an investigation", ICC-01/13-51, 6 November 2015, para. 56 ('Comoros Appeals Decision') (https://www.legal-tools.org/doc/a43856/). Once the Prosecutor has taken a final decision, he or she shall notify the Pre-Trial Chamber and others who participated in the review, see Rule 108(3).

confirm the Prosecutor's decision taken solely under Article 53(1)(c), then the Prosecutor shall proceed with the investigation.[58]

Review proceedings under Article 53(3)(a) have taken place in the situation regarding the vessels registered in the Union of the Comoros ('Mavi Marmara'), the Hellenic Republic ('Eleftheri Mesogios/Sofia'), and the Kingdom of Cambodia ('Rachel Corrie'). The Union of the Comoros, for which the Statute entered into force on 1 November 2006, referred the situation to the ICC Prosecutor with a letter dated 14 May 2013.[59] The acts to be investigated in the referral can be summarised briefly as follows.

Sixty-four miles from the coast of the Gaza Strip, the Israeli Defence Forces purportedly intercepted between 31 May 2010 and at least 5 June 2010 three vessels registered in the Union of the Comoros, the Hellenic Republic and the Kingdom of Cambodia. On board of those vessels were about 700 persons who purportedly attempted to break the Israeli blockade claiming to deliver humanitarian goods to the Gaza population. The interception operation allegedly resulted in the death of 10 passengers, the bodily harm of 50–55 passengers as well as other harm suffered by a significant number of passengers.

Upon receipt of the referral, the Prosecutor conducted the preliminary examination of the information received against the Article 53(1) criteria, at the end of which she decided not to initiate an investigation.

Whereas the Prosecutor accepted the existence of an international armed conflict, or alternatively, a non-international armed conflict, and the commission of certain war crimes, she declined to qualify the conduct as crimes against humanity arguing that there was no widespread or systematic attack directed against the civilian population. In addition, the Prosecutor concluded that the potential cases emanating from the situation would not satisfy the gravity threshold as stipulated in Article 17(1)(d) considering, *inter alia*, the limited scope of the situation, the small num-

---

[58] Rule 110(2), see above note 4.

[59] ICC-OTP, Letter attached to the notification of the Prosecutor to the President of the Court, 14 May 2013, ICC-01/13-1-Anx1, p. 2 (https://www.legal-tools.org/doc/d5e455/), which is appended to ICC, Situation on Registered Vessels of the Union of Comoros, the Hellenic Republic and the Kingdom of Cambodia, Presidency, Decision assigning the Situation on Registered Vessels of the Union of the Comoros, the Hellenic Republic and the Kingdom of Cambodia to Pre-Trial Chamber I, 5 July 2013, ICC-01/13-1 (https://www.legal-tools.org/doc/8e4e80/).

ber of victims, the nature of the crimes, the manner of the commission of the crimes and the impact of the crimes. Hence, since potential cases would be inadmissible, pursuant to Articles 53(1)(b) and 17(1)(d), further action by the Court was, in her view, unjustified.[60]

Subsequently, the Union of the Comoros requested Pre-Trial Chamber I to review the Prosecutor's negative decision.[61] The referring State based its review request essentially on two grounds: the Prosecutor's purported (i) failure to take into account alleged crimes that fall outside the jurisdiction of the Court (that is, beyond the vessels) when assessing gravity, and (ii) errors in assessing the gravity factors.

On 16 July 2015, Pre-Trial Chamber I determined, by majority, that the Prosecutor had made a series of errors when assessing, *inter alia*, the gravity of the potential cases.[62] In this context, the Prosecutor's classification of alleged conduct became highly relevant, in particular when assessing the gravity of the crimes committed within the incidents that would likely form the object of the Court's investigation.

The Majority Judges took issue, for example, with the Prosecutor's conclusion regarding the nature of the crimes, challenging the Prosecutor's determination that the documented mistreatment and harassment of the passengers did not amount to the war crimes of torture and inhuman treatment under Article 8(2)(a)(ii). Thus, in the view of the Majority, the Prosecutor failed to take into account those crimes in addition to other crimes as part of the gravity test.[63] Further, the Majority found several errors in the Prosecutor's factual assessment regarding the manner of the commission of the crimes. In the opinion of the Majority, these errors rendered unsustainable the Prosecutor's conclusion with respect to the

---

[60] ICC, Situation on Registered Vessels of the Union of Comoros, the Hellenic Republic and the Kingdom of Cambodia, OTP, Article 53(1) Report, 6 November 2014, ICC-01/13-6-AnxA (https://www.legal-tools.org/doc/6b833a/).

[61] ICC, Situation on Registered Vessels of the Union of Comoros, the Hellenic Republic and the Kingdom of Cambodia, Union of the Comoros, Application for Review pursuant to Article 53(3) (a) of the Prosecutor's Decision of 6 November 2014 not to initiate an investigation in the Situation, 29 January 2015, ICC-01/13-3-Red (https://www.legal-tools.org/doc/b60981/).

[62] Comoros First Review Decision, see above note 14. The dissenting opinion of Judge Péter Kovács is appended to the decision, 16 July 2015, ICC-01/13-34-Anx-Corr (https://www.legal-tools.org/doc/0fceb2/).

[63] Comoros First Review Decision, paras. 27–30, see above note 14.

question whether the crimes "were systematic or resulted from a deliberate plan or policy to attack, kill or injure civilians".[64] The latter determination is aimed at the Prosecutor's assessment that the conduct described in the information available did not amount to crimes against humanity.

The Prosecutor was requested to reconsider her decision not to initiate an investigation into the situation referred to by the Union of the Comoros and to notify the Pre-Trial Chamber of her final decision.[65]

What are the consequences of the Chamber's classification of alleged conduct and how does this impact the investigation, if initiated after review? The purpose of the Article 53(3)(a) review proceedings is "to give referring entities the opportunity to challenge, and have the Chamber

---

[64] *Ibid.*, paras. 31–45.

[65] The Prosecutor sought to appeal this decision without leave from the Pre-Trial Chamber under Article 82(1)(a). Following the dismissal of the Prosecutor's direct appeal against the Pre-Trial Chamber's decision (Comoros Appeals Decision, see above note 57), the Prosecutor notified the Pre-Trial Chamber of her reconsideration decision (ICC, Situation on Registered Vessels of the Union of the Comoros, the Hellenic Republic and the Kingdom of Cambodia, OTP, Final Decision of the Prosecution concerning the "Article 53(1) Report" (ICC-01/13-6-AnxA), dated 6 November 2014, 29 November 2017, ICC-01/13-57-Anx1 (https://www.legal-tools.org/doc/298503/)). This reconsideration decision was challenged for a second time by the Union of the Comoros and the Pre-Trial Chamber, in a second review decision, concluded that the Prosecutor had not, in fact, complied with its earlier pronouncements. Hence, the reconsideration decision was not 'final' within the meaning of Rule 108(3). The Prosecutor's appeal of the second review decision was unsuccessful and she was instructed to reconsider her decision not to initiate an investigation by taking into account the findings of the Pre-Trial Chamber by 2 December 2019 (ICC, Situation on Registered Vessels of the Union of the Comoros, the Hellenic Republic and the Kingdom of Cambodia, Appeals Chamber, Judgment on the appeal of the Prosecutor against Pre-Trial Chamber I's 'Decision on the "Application for Judicial Review by the Government of the Union of the Comoros"', 2 September 2019, ICC-01/13-98 ('Comoros Appeals Judgment') (https://www.legal-tools.org/doc/802549/)). The Prosecutor filed her 'final' decision within the deadline proscribed (ICC, Situation on Registered Vessels of the Union of the Comoros, the Hellenic Republic and the Kingdom of Cambodia, OTP, Final decision of the Prosecutor concerning the "Article 53(1) Report" (ICC-01/13-6-AnxA), dated 6 November 2014, as revised and refiled in accordance with the Pre-Trial Chamber's request of 15 November 2018 and the Appeals Chamber's judgment of 2 September 2019, 2 December 2019, ICC-01/13-99-Anx1 (https://www.legal-tools.org/doc/jrysaj/)). The Union of the Comoros challenged the Prosecutor's reconsideration decision for a third time (ICC, Situation on Registered Vessels of the Union of the Comoros, the Hellenic Republic and the Kingdom of Cambodia, Union of the Comoros, Application for Judicial Review by the Government of the Comoros, 2 March 2020, ICC-01/13-100 (https://www.legal-tools.org/doc/bj2tbv/)). At the time of writing, a decision of Pre-Trial Chamber I is pending.

test, the validity of the Prosecutor's decision not to investigate".[66] In contrast to the authorisation proceedings developed above, the Pre-Trial Chamber's duty under Article 53(3)(a) is fundamentally different. It is triggered only upon request and is restricted to the points of disagreement between the Prosecutor and the referring entity.[67] If the Pre-Trial Chamber finds that the Prosecutor's conclusion suffered from errors, then it may request the Prosecutor to reconsider her previous decision not to initiate an investigation. Such request for reconsideration, despite the discretionary wording in Article 53(3)(a) ('request'), obliges the Prosecutor (i) to reconsider her previous decision, and (ii) to do so in light of the Pre-Trial Chamber's review decision.[68] As to the binding effect of the Pre-Trial Chamber's pronouncements in its request for reconsideration, the Appeals Chamber differentiated between errors of law and fact: given the Chamber's authority to interpret the Court's applicable law, the Pre-Trial Chamber may give directions to the Prosecutor on questions of substantive or procedural law;[69] however, it cannot give directions as to how the Prosecutor is to assess the facts and which results she should reach.[70] Lastly, the final decision on whether to open an investigation is for the Prosecutor to take.[71]

Any classification of alleged conduct that the Pre-Trial Chamber undertakes at this stage is for the purpose of exercising judicial oversight over the Prosecutor's conclusion not to initiate an investigation. If the Prosecutor committed an error, she is duty-bound to comply with the Pre-Trial Chamber's findings of law, in particular the interpretation of crimes, when reconsidering the facts anew.[72] However, the final result is for the Prosecutor to take: once she has corrected the legal error, she may change

---

[66] Comoros First Review Decision, para. 9, see above note 14.

[67] *Ibid.*; Comoros Appeals Judgment, para. 76, see above note 65.

[68] Comoros Second Review Decision, paras. 95–100, 110, 113, see above note 8; Comoros Appeals Judgment, para. 77, see above note 65.

[69] *Ibid.*, para. 78.

[70] *Ibid.*, paras. 76, 80, 82. That said, the Appeals Chamber conceded that the Pre-Trial Chamber may direct the Prosecutor to take into account available information, *ibid.*, para. 80.

[71] Comoros Second Review Decision, para. 109, see above note 8; Comoros Appeals Decision, paras. 56, 59, see above note 57; Comoros Appeals Judgment, para. 76, see above note 65.

[72] *Ibid.*, para. 78: "[…] where questions of law arise, the only authoritative interpretation of the relevant law is that espoused by the Chambers of this Court and not the Prosecutor".

her view and initiate an investigation. Relevant legal findings of the Pre-Trial Chamber regarding the classification of alleged conduct may prove useful during the investigation. The Prosecutor's adherence thereto ensures consistency in the application of the law and equal treatment across situations. However, it is also conceivable that, even though the Prosecutor corrected the legal error in accordance with the directions of the Pre-Trial Chamber, she may reach the same conclusion as before and still not initiate an investigation, depending on the particular circumstances of the situation.

Matters are different when it comes to the Article 53(3)(b) review of the Prosecutor's conclusion not to open an investigation solely on considerations regarding the interests of justice. The Prosecutor's decision not to initiate an investigation will be "effective only if confirmed by the Pre-Trial Chamber". If the Prosecutor's decision is not confirmed, the Prosecutor "shall proceed with the investigation".[73] The Prosecutor has hitherto not invoked considerations of interests of justice in order to take a decision not to initiate an investigation. In any event, classification of alleged conduct may play only a tangential role (at best, in the context of the considerations regarding the 'gravity of the crime') which is only one of many factors to be considered, as suggested in Article 53(1)(c).

20.1.4. Investigation

Investigating international crimes is complex and time-consuming. The ICC is seated in The Hague[74] while the crime scenes are located thousands of kilometres away. At the early phase of an investigation, the Prosecutor must develop quickly an overall understanding of the situation. Understandably, the limited analysis during the preliminary examination may not be sufficient to proceed to the next phase and enable her to request, for example, a warrant of arrest. In-house investigators travel regularly into the field, oftentimes to dangerous and/or challenging regions and at personal risk to their health and safety. They interview witnesses and collect evidence on incidents and resulting victimisation as well as groups and potential perpetrators and their involvement in the incidents. Once back in The Hague, investigators and analysts process the information collected, label, register and store it.

---

[73] Rule 110(2), see above note 4.
[74] Article 3(1), see above note 2.

During the investigation, it is upon the Prosecutor to identify, amidst a plurality of individuals and incidents, specific perpetrators and specific conduct with a view to bringing those deemed responsible to justice.[75] Notably, the Statute instructs the Prosecutor, "in order to establish the truth, [to] extend the investigation to cover all facts and evidence relevant to an assessment of whether there is criminal responsibility under [the] Statute and, in doing so, to investigate incriminating and exonerating circumstances equally".[76] Judges are not part of this process and remain inactive throughout the investigation phase, unless the Prosecutor requests certain measures, such as the preservation of evidence in the context of a unique investigative opportunity[77] or the protection of victims.[78] Their involvement is certainly triggered if and when, any time after the initiation of the investigation, the Prosecutor approaches the Pre-Trial Chamber with a request for the issuance of a warrant of arrest or summons to appear.

20.1.5. Warrant of Arrest or Summons to Appear

A concrete 'case' emerges when the Prosecutor identifies a particular suspect and the conduct for which that person is allegedly responsible.[79] Hence, 'case' proceedings start with the Prosecutor's request seeking the issuance of a warrant of arrest or a summons to appear pursuant to Article 58.

The Pre-Trial Chamber, or a Single Judge acting on its behalf, issues a warrant of arrest, on the application of the Prosecutor, if, having examined the Prosecutor's application and the evidence or other infor-

---

[75] Appeals Judgment on Victims Participation During Investigation, para. 45, see above note 44.

[76] Article 54(1)(a), see above note 2.

[77] Article 56, see above note 2.

[78] Articles 57(3)(c) and 68(1), see above note 2.

[79] See, for example, Kenya Authorisation Decision, para. 44, see above note 10; ICC, Situation in Libya, *Prosecutor v. Saif Al-Islam Gaddafi and Abdullah Al-Senussi*, Pre-Trial Chamber, Decision on the admissibility of the case against Abdullah Al-Senussi, 11 October 2013, ICC-01/11-01/11-466-Red, para. 66(i) (https://www.legal-tools.org/doc/af6104/); ICC, Situation in the Republic of Kenya, *Prosecutor v. Francis Muthaura et al.*, Appeals Chamber, Judgment on the appeal of the Republic of Kenya against the decision of Pre-Trial Chamber II of 30 May 2011 entitled "Decision on the Application by the Government of Kenya Challenging the Admissibility of the Case Pursuant to Article 19(2)(b) of the Statute", 30 August 2011, ICC-01/09-02/11-274, para. 39 (https://www.legal-tools.org/doc/c21f06/).

mation, (a) there are "reasonable grounds to believe" that the suspect has committed a crime within the jurisdiction of the Court; and (b) the arrest of the suspect appears necessary.[80] Alternatively, the Pre-Trial Chamber may issue upon request a summons to appear, with or without conditions, if it is satisfied that the summons is sufficient to ensure the person's appearance.[81] If the conditions under Article 58 are fulfilled, the Pre-Trial Chamber is under an obligation to issue the warrant of arrest.[82] If the Pre-Trial Chamber considers that further information or evidence is necessary, it may request the Prosecutor to present more evidence.[83] Accordingly, the Chamber has no discretion to decline the request for reasons other than evidentiary or legal.[84]

The evidentiary threshold applicable at this stage is commonly understood to involve the existence of information that satisfies an objective observer that the suspect may have committed the crime(s).[85] The Pre-

---

[80] Article 58(1), see above note 2. The arrest of the suspect appears necessary (i) to ensure his or her appearance at trial; (ii) to ensure that the suspect does not obstruct or endanger the investigation or the court proceedings; or (iii) where applicable, to prevent the suspect from continuing with the commission of the crime or a related crime which is within the jurisdiction of the Court and which arises out of the same circumstances.

[81] Article 58(7), see above note 2.

[82] ICC, Situation in the Democratic Republic of the Congo, Appeals Chamber, Judgment on the Prosecutor's appeal against the decision of Pre-Trial Chamber I entitled "Decision on the Prosecutor's Application for Warrants of Arrest, Article 58", 13 July 2006, ICC-01/04-169, para. 44 (https://www.legal-tools.org/doc/8c20eb/).

[83] ICC, Situation in the Democratic Republic of the Congo, *Prosecutor v. Thomas Lubanga Dyilo*, Pre-Trial Chamber, Redacted Version of the Decision concerning Supporting Materials in Connection with the Prosecution's Application REDACTED pursuant to article 58, 9 March 2006, ICC-01/04-01/06-27, p. 3 (https://www.legal-tools.org/doc/021949/); ICC, Situation in the Democratic Republic of the Congo, *Prosecutor v. Bosco Ntaganda*, Pre-Trial Chamber, Decision concerning Supporting Materials in Connection with the Prosecution's Application for Warrants of Arrest pursuant to article 58, 20 January 2006, ICC-01/04-02/06-323-Red (https://www.legal-tools.org/doc/e9a4da/).

[84] Christopher K. Hall and Cedric Ryngaert, "Article 58", in Otto Triffterer and Kai Ambos (eds.), *The Rome Statute of the International Criminal Court: A Commentary*, 3rd edition, C.H. Beck/Hart/Nomos, 2016, mn. 10; William A. Schabas, "Article 58", in William A. Schabas (ed.), *The International Criminal Court: A Commentary on the Rome Statute*, Oxford University Press, Oxford, 2010, p. 705.

[85] See, for example, ICC, Situation in the Democratic Republic of the Congo, *Prosecutor v. Bosco Ntaganda*, Pre-Trial Chamber, Decision on the Prosecutor's Application under Article 58, 13 July 2012, ICC-01/04-02/06-36-Red, para. 16 (https://www.legal-tools.org/doc/18c310/); ICC, Situation in the Central African Republic, *Prosecutor v. Jean-Pierre Bemba Gombo*, Pre-Trial Chamber, Decision on the Prosecutor's Application for a Warrant of Ar-

---

Trial Chamber does not have to be certain that the person concerned committed the crimes. Rather, the evidence must only establish *a* reasonable conclusion, possibly amongst several other reasonable conclusions available, and not the *only* reasonable conclusion.[86]

A review of the decisions pertaining to the issuance of warrants of arrest (or summonses to appear) reveals that in the vast majority of cases, the Pre-Trial Chambers confirmed the Prosecutor's proposed classification of alleged conduct. Only in a few instances, did the Pre-Trial Chambers reject or suggest amendment of the proposed classification of alleged conduct. Without claiming to be complete, three scenarios emerge from the case-law of the ICC.

The first scenario concerns the situation where the alleged conduct as described in the Article 58 application is proven, but its classification does not, in the view of the Judges, fully and accurately reflect the conduct, as it transpires from the evidence. Since the legal characterisation of the conduct is 'incomplete', the Pre-Trial Chamber indicates an additional classification.

- **Kenyatta *et al.* case**: In the Article 58 application seeking the issuance of summonses to appear for Messrs Muthaura, Kenyatta and Ali, the Prosecutor alleged, *inter alia*, that the Mungiki – an organisation controlling core societal activities in poor residential areas in Nairobi – attacked the civilian population in, amongst other, Nakuru and Naivasha during the 2007–08 post-election violence pursuant to a policy established to that effect during the 2007–08 post-election

---

rest against Jean-Pierre Bemba Gombo, 10 June 2008, ICC-01/05-01/08-14-tENG, para. 24 ('Bemba Warrant of Arrest Decision') (https://www.legal-tools.org/doc/fb80c6/); ICC, Situation in the Democratic Republic of the Congo, *Prosecutor v. Germain Katanga and Mathieu Ngudjolo Chui*, Appeals Chamber, Judgment in the Appeal of Mathieu Ngudjolo Chui of 27 March 2008 against the Decision of Pre-Trial Chamber I on the Application of the Appellant for Interim Release, 9 June 2008, ICC-01/04-01/07-572, para. 18 (https://www.legal-tools.org/doc/69bee9/).

[86] ICC, Situation in the Democratic Republic of the Congo, *Prosecutor v. Sylvestre Mudacumura*, Pre-Trial Chamber, Decision on the Prosecutor's Application under Article 58, 13 July 2012, ICC-01/04-01/12-1-Red, para. 19 ('Mudacumura Article 58 Decision') (https://www.legal-tools.org/doc/ecfae0/); ICC, Situation in Darfur, Sudan, *Prosecutor v. Omar Hassan Ahmad Al Bashir*, Appeals Chamber, Judgment on the appeal of the Prosecutor against the "Decision on the Prosecution's Application for a Warrant of Arrest against Omar Hassan Ahmad Al Bashir", 3 February 2010, ICC-02/05-01/09-73, para. 33 (https://www.legal-tools.org/doc/9ada8e/).

violence. The Prosecutor also mentioned that this was made possible due to the inactivity of the Kenyan police forces and presented evidence in this regard.[87]

The Chamber accepted that the attack had been carried out in furtherance of an organisational policy within the meaning of Article 7(2)(a), but raised the question whether evidence pointed to the existence of a 'State policy' by abstention. Eventually, it left it to the Prosecutor to clarify it at a later stage.[88]

The second scenario concerns the situation where the alleged conduct as described in the Article 58 application is proven, but it does not, in the view of the judges, fulfil the legal requirements of the proposed crimes or forms of criminal responsibility. One of the reasons for this is that the Pre-Trial Chamber adopts a different interpretation of the applicable law than the Prosecutor. In this instance, the judges do not confirm the classification of alleged conduct for legal reasons.

- **Bemba case**: In the request for the issuance of a warrant of arrest for Mr. Bemba, the Prosecutor alleged that, in the context of a conflict in the Central African Republic between October 2002 and March 2003, Mr. Bemba was responsible for, *inter alia*, other forms of sexual violence involving the undressing of civilians in public, thereby humiliating them.[89]

    The Pre-Trial Chamber disagreed with the Prosecutor's classification of the undressing of persons in public as other forms of sexual violence. It found that the facts submitted did not fulfil the legal requirements of the crime of sexual violence since the conduct was not of comparable gravity to the other crimes listed in Article

---

[87] ICC, Situation in the Republic of Kenya, *Prosecutor v. Francis Kirimi Muthaura et al.*, Pre-Trial Chamber, Decision on the Prosecutor's Application for Summonses to Appear for Francis Kirimi Muthaura, Uhuru Muigai Kenyatta and Mohammed Hussein Ali, 8 March 2011, ICC-01/09-02/11-1, paras. 22–24 ('Kenyatta et al. Summons Decision') (https://www.legal-tools.org/doc/df8391/).

[88] *Ibid.*, para. 24.

[89] ICC, Situation in the Central African Republic, *Prosecutor v. Jean-Pierre Bemba Gombo*, OTP, Prosecutor's Application for Warrant of Arrest under Article 58, 9 May 2008, ICC-01/05-01/08-26-Red, p. 9 (https://www.legal-tools.org/doc/a57940/); ICC, Situation in the Central African Republic, *Prosecutor v. Jean-Pierre Bemba Gombo*, OTP, Prosecutor's Submission on Further Information and Materials, 27 May 2008, ICC-01/05-01/08-29-Red, p. 8 (https://www.legal-tools.org/doc/6eaf15/).

7(1)(g).[90] The Pre-Trial Chamber did not classify these factual allegations under a different crime and did not include them in the warrant of arrest.

- **Kenyatta *et al.* case**: In the Article 58 application seeking the issuance of summonses to appear for Messrs Muthaura, Kenyatta and Ali, the Prosecutor alleged that in the context of the 2007–08 post-election violence in Kenya they were responsible for other forms of sexual violence as crimes against humanity (Article 7(1)(g)) in the form of forced circumcisions of men.[91] The crime of 'other inhumane acts' (Article 7(1)(k)) had been pleaded by the Prosecutor as well.[92]

    The Pre-Trial Chamber did not follow the legal characterisation of the alleged acts of circumcision, as proposed by the Prosecutor, and opined that this conduct was better characterised as 'other inhumane acts' within the meaning of Article 7(1)(k), paying special heed to the serious injury to the body of the victims.[93]

The third scenario concerns the situation where the classification is rejected since the evidence does not support the alleged conduct, as presented by the Prosecutor. This may concern crimes or forms of criminal responsibility. In this instance, the judges do not confirm the classification of the alleged conduct for evidentiary reasons.

- **Kenyatta *et al.* case**: In the Article 58 application seeking the issuance of summonses to appear for Messrs Muthaura, Kenyatta and Ali, the Prosecutor alleged that in the context of the 2007–08 post-election violence in Kenya they were responsible for rapes committed in, amongst other, Naivasha and Nakuru.

    In the summonses to appear, the Pre-Trial Chamber did not include the crime of rape as a crime against humanity allegedly committed in Naivasha since the Prosecutor had failed to present evidence substantiating his allegation that rapes had been committed as part of the attack.[94]

---

90   Bemba Warrant of Arrest Decision, paras. 39–40, see above note 85.
91   Kenyatta et al. Summons Decision, para. 27, see above note 87.
92   *Ibid.*, p. 7.
93   *Ibid.*, para. 27.
94   *Ibid.*, para. 26.

- **Ruto *et al.* case**: in the Article 58 application seeking the issuance of summonses to appear for Messrs Ruto, Kosgey and Sang, the Prosecutor alleged that Mr. Sang, a radio broadcaster in Kenya, was criminally responsible for the commission of crimes against humanity, jointly with others, as an indirect co-perpetrator.[95] In the alternative, the Prosecutor alleged that Mr. Sang was an accessory, having contributed to a crime committed by a group of persons within the meaning of Article 25(3)(d).[96]

  The Chamber declined to follow the Prosecutor's assessment that Sang was a principal perpetrator. It held that his role as a radio broadcaster and his involvement in (only) two preparatory meetings did not allow for the conclusion that his actions were essential contributions to the common plan to commit crimes against humanity, in that he had the power to frustrate the commission of the crimes by not fulfilling his task.[97] Accordingly, the Chamber determined that there were reasonable grounds to believe that Mr. Sang was (only) an accessory to the alleged crimes.[98]

- **Mudacumura case**: In the request for the issuance of a warrant of arrest for Mr. Mudacumura, the Prosecutor alleged that he was responsible, *inter alia*, for the commission of crimes against humanity committed between January 2009 and September 2010 in the North and South Kivu Provinces in the Democratic Republic of the Congo.[99]

  The Chamber declined to classify the conduct as crimes against humanity arguing that the evidence did not support the existence of an organisational policy to attack a civilian population within the meaning of Article 7(2)(a) and did not demonstrate that the civilian population had been the primary target of such attack.[100]

---

[95] ICC, Situation in the Republic of Kenya, *Prosecutor v. William Samoei Ruto et al.*, Pre-Trial Chamber, Decision on the Prosecutor's Application for Summons to Appear for William Samoei Ruto, Henry Kiprono Kosgey and Joshua Arap Sang, 8 March 2011, ICC-01/09-01/11-1, paras. 13, 35–36 ('Ruto et al. Summons Decision') (https://www.legal-tools.org/doc/6c9fb0/).

[96] *Ibid.*, para. 50.

[97] *Ibid.*, para. 44.

[98] *Ibid.*, para. 57.

[99] Mudacumura Article 58 Decision, paras. 7, 25, see above note 86.

[100] *Ibid.*, paras. 26–29.

As a result, the Pre-Trial Chamber rejected to qualify the conduct as crimes against humanity and included in the warrant of arrest only war crimes.

Can the Pre-Trial Chamber's classification of alleged conduct and amendments thereto in the warrant of arrest or summons to appear enhance the quality of the Prosecutor's ongoing investigation? What can be discerned from the past practice is that the judges' review of the Prosecutor's allegations appears to be comprehensive, meticulous and always guided by the supporting material furnished by the Prosecutor.[101] In adopting this approach, the judges demonstrate that they act sensibly and with circumspection: based on the ICC warrant of arrest, domestic authorities are obligated to arrest the suspect and deprive him or her of his or her liberty.[102] A person sought with an ICC warrant of arrest quickly bears the stigma of a 'war criminal' in the public eye and will find it difficult to dispel the allegations once they are made. As a result, any warrant of arrest or summons to appear must be adequately reasoned and be based on solid legal and evidentiary foundations.

As regards the factual allegations made, it is noteworthy that the Pre-Trial Chambers do not add new facts which they may discover in the supporting material during the review into the warrant of arrest or summons to appear. Under the Statute, they are not mandated to establish the case and, therefore, lack investigative powers. Their main responsibility lies in verifying that the evidence presented by the Prosecutor supports the factual allegations. As regards the classification of alleged conduct, on the other hand, the Pre-Trial Chamber is not bound by the Prosecutor's *legal* characterisation of the facts and may advance its own classification in the warrant of arrest or summons to appear.[103] Despite their prerogative, prac-

---

[101] In the *Lubanga* case, the Prosecutor had argued at the time that the Chamber should "trust the Prosecution's summary", to which the Chamber responded that it is instructed by the Statute to review not only the Article 58 application but also the supporting material, see ICC, Situation in the Democratic Republic of the Congo, *Prosecutor v. Thomas Lubanga Dyilo*, Pre-Trial Chamber, Decision on the Prosecutor's Application for a warrant of arrest, Article 58, 10 February 2006, ICC-01/04-01/06-1-Corr-Red, para. 10 ('Lubanga Warrant of Arrest Decision') (https://www.legal-tools.org/doc/af6679/).

[102] *Ibid.*, para. 11.

[103] For example, Bemba Warrant of Arrest Decision, para. 25: "It is for the Chamber to characterize the facts put forward by the Prosecutor", see above note 85; Lubanga Warrant of Arrest Decision, para. 16: "However, the Chamber considers that it is not bound by the

tice shows that Pre-Trial Chambers follow largely the classification of conduct proposed by the Prosecutor. If they do not follow the Prosecutor's legal characterisation of facts, it is in the first place for evidentiary reasons and only in the second place for legal reasons.

The Pre-Trial Chamber's detailed and thorough review of the evidence regarding the alleged conduct and the determination of the corresponding classification can also be beneficial for the Prosecutor in her preparation of the next procedural steps. She can consider the Chamber's analysis as a 'test' of her case theory, albeit admittedly against a low(er) evidentiary threshold. It is, as it were, a first external review of the strength of the evidence and classification of alleged conduct. Especially when the Pre-Trial Chamber does not confirm the classification proposed, either for legal or evidentiary reasons, the Prosecutor may take it as a stimulus, a suggestion, to reconsider certain aspects of the case or intensify the investigation on the 'problematic' aspects of the case. Weaknesses in the evidence (which may translate in re-classification of alleged conduct, should they have been identified by the Pre-Trial Chamber) should be addressed as a matter of priority during the ongoing investigation.

At the same time, the Prosecutor is in a rather comfortable position: at the stage of the warrant of arrest, the person is not charged yet. The Prosecutor presents the charges in the document containing the charges ('DCC'), which is notified to the suspect at a later stage. In the DCC the Prosecutor is at liberty to add or withdraw factual allegations, without judicial permission, to the factual allegations set forth in the warrant of arrest or summons to appear, and is only limited by the rule of speciality under Article 101.[104] If facts are added or withdrawn in the DCC, this may affect the classification of conduct. Importantly, the Prosecutor is also not required to follow the Pre-Trial Chamber's legal characterisation con-

---

Prosecution's legal characterisation of the conduct referred to in the Prosecution's Application", see above note 101.

[104] ICC, Situation in Uganda, *Prosecutor v. Dominic Ongwen*, Pre-Trial Chamber, Decision Postponing the Date of the Confirmation of Charges Hearing, 6 March 2015, ICC-02/04-01/15-206, para. 32 ('Ongwen Postponement Decision') (https://www.legal-tools.org/doc/5a0ab1/); ICC, Situation in the Democratic Republic of the Congo, *Prosecutor v. Callixte Mbarushimana*, Pre-Trial Chamber, Decision on the confirmation of charges, 16 December 2011, ICC-01/04-01/10-465-Red, para. 88 ('Mbarushimana Confirmation Decision') (https://www.legal-tools.org/doc/63028f/).

tained in the warrant of arrest or summons to appear.[105] In the DCC she may include other crimes or forms of criminal responsibility without judicial permission. However, if she insists on a classification previously rejected by the Pre-Trial Chamber at the Article 58 stage without furnishing further evidence or explanations, she risks that the Pre-Trial Chamber will take the same decision at the next procedural stage, which will be addressed in the following section.

20.1.6. Confirmation of Charges

After the suspect is arrested and surrendered to the Court, he or she appears before the Pre-Trial Chamber which sets the date of the confirmation of charges hearing.[106] In that hearing, the Pre-Trial Chamber hears the arguments of both parties and of participating victims with a view to assessing whether the case should proceed to trial.

Thirty days prior to the hearing, the Prosecutor submits the DCC together with the list of evidence on which she intends to rely at the hearing.[107] The DCC is the Prosecutor's assertion to bring the person to trial for the factual allegations the person is believed to be responsible, including the time and place of the alleged crimes. In addition, the Prosecutor attaches a legal characterisation to such factual allegations that corresponds to the crimes and the precise forms of criminal responsibility set out in the Statute.[108] Together, the facts and the legal characterisation make the 'charge'[109] which must be specified with clarity and in detail in

---

[105] ICC, Situation in the Democratic Republic of the Congo, *Prosecutor v. Thomas Lubanga Dyilo*, Appeals Chamber, Judgment on the Prosecutor's appeal against the decision of Pre-Trial Chamber I entitled "Decision Establishing General Principles Governing Applications to Restrict Disclosure pursuant to Rule 81(2) and (4) of the Rules of Procedure and Evidence", 13 October 2006, ICC-01/04-01/06-568, para. 53 ('Lubanga Redactions Appeals Judgment') (https://www.legal-tools.org/doc/7813d4/).

[106] Article 60(1), see above note 2 and Rule 121(1), third sentence, see above note 4.

[107] Article 61(3), see above note 2 and Rule 121(3), see above note 4.

[108] Regulation 52 of the Regulations of the Court, see above note 19.

[109] Article 74(2), see above note 2 and Regulations 52(b) and (c) of the Regulations of the Court, see above note 19. See also, for example, ICC, Situation in the Republic of Mali, *Prosecutor v. Al Hassan Ag Abdoul Aziz Ag Mohamed Ag Mahmoud*, Pre-Trial Chamber, Decision on the Defence Request concerning the Time Limit for the Prosecutor to File the Document Containing a Detailed Description of the Charges, 5 October 2018, ICC-01/12-01/18-143-tENG, para. 30 ('Al Hassan DCC Decision') (https://www.legal-tools.org/doc/dd8f47/); ICC, Situation in the Democratic Republic of the Congo, *Prosecutor v. Germain Katanga and Mathieu Ngudjolo Chui*, Trial Chamber, Decision on the Filing of a Sum-

the DCC.[110] Only a specific DCC will put the suspect formally on notice about the nature and cause of the charges and allow him or her to prepare an adequate defence.[111]

At the confirmation hearing, the Pre-Trial Chamber is tasked to decide whether there is sufficient evidence to establish substantial grounds to believe that the suspect committed each of the crimes charged by the Prosecutor.[112] It is a higher threshold than that applied in other tribunals when confirming indictments.[113] The threshold of 'substantial grounds to

---

mary of the Charges by the Prosecutor, 21 October 2009, ICC-01/04-01/07-1547-tENG, para. 10 ('Katanga and Ngudjolo Decision on Summary of Charges') (https://www.legal-tools.org/doc/7e906f/).

[110] Al Hassan DCC Decision, para. 30, see above note 109; ICC, Situation in the Central African Republic II, *Prosecutor v. Alfred Yekatom and Patrice-Edouard Ngaïssona*, Pre-Trial Chamber, Decision on the "Prosecution's Request to Postpone the Confirmation Hearing and All Related Disclosure Deadlines", 15 May 2019, ICC-01/14-01/18-199, paras. 41–42 ('Yekatom/Ngaïssona Postponement Decision') (https://www.legal-tools.org/doc/a751e6/); ICC, Situation in the Republic of Côte d'Ivoire, *Prosecutor v. Laurent Gbagbo*, Pre-Trial Chamber, Decision on the Date of the Confirmation of Charges Hearing and Proceedings Leading Thereto, 14 December 2012, ICC-02/11-01/11-325, para. 25 (https://www.legal-tools.org/doc/c5cddf/); Katanga and Ngudjolo Decision on Summary of Charges, para. 19, see above note 109. See also European Court of Human Rights ('ECtHR'), *Pélissier and Sassi v. France*, Grand Chamber, Judgment, 25 March 1999, ECLI:CE:ECHR:1999:0325JUD002544494, para. 51 ('Pélissier and Sassi v. France Judgment') (https://www.legal-tools.org/doc/e092c3/); ECtHR, *Mattoccia v. Italy*, Judgment, 25 July 2000, ECLI:CE:ECHR:2000:0725JUD002396994, para. 59 ('Mattoccia v. Italy Judgment') (https://www.legal-tools.org/doc/5e07d3/); ECtHR, *Penev v. Bulgaria*, Judgment, 7 January 2010, ECLI:CE:ECHR:2010:0107JUD002049404, paras. 33, 42 (https://www.legal-tools.org/doc/989a14/).

[111] See also ICTY, *Prosecutor v. Kupreškić et al.*, Appeals Chamber, Judgment, 23 October 2001, IT-95-16-A, para. 88 (https://www.legal-tools.org/doc/c6a5d1/); ICTR, *Prosecutor v. Ntagerura et al.*, Appeals Chamber, Judgment, 7 July 2006, ICTR-99-46-A, para. 22 (https://www.legal-tools.org/doc/816b44/); ICTR, *Prosecutor v. Nsengiyumva*, Trial Chamber, Decision on the Defence Motion Raising Objections on Defects in the Form of the Indictment and to Personal Jurisdiction on the Amended Indictment, 12 May 2000, ICTR-96-12-I, p. 2, para. 1 (https://www.legal-tools.org/doc/0f23f1/). Similarly, Pélissier and Sassi v. France Judgment, para. 54, see above note 110; Mattoccia v. Italy Judgment, para. 60, see above note 110.

[112] Article 61(7), first sentence, see above note 2.

[113] At other international(ised) tribunals, the Pre-Trial Judge, being satisfied that a *prima facie* case has been established by the Prosecutor, confirms the indictment, see ICTR Statute, 8 November 1994, Article 18 (https://www.legal-tools.org/doc/8732d6/); ICTY Statute, 25 May 1993, Article 19 (https://www.legal-tools.org/doc/b4f63b/); SCSL, Rules of Procedure and Evidence, 16 January 2002, Rule 47(E) (https://www.legal-tools.org/doc/4c2a6b/); STL, Rules of Procedure and Evidence, 20 March 2009, Rule 68(F) (https://www.legal-

---

believe' is fulfilled if, after an exacting scrutiny of the evidence, the charges are "sufficiently compelling going beyond mere theory or suspicion".[114] On the basis of the confirmation hearing, the Pre-Trial Chamber may either confirm the charges in relation to which there is sufficient evidence or decline to confirm the charges because of insufficiency of the evidence.[115] If the charges are confirmed, the person is committed to a Trial Chamber for the charges as confirmed. Declining to confirm the charges does not mean the person is acquitted. Rather, it means that there was not sufficient evidence to proceed to trial. The Prosecutor is, however, free to revert to the Pre-Trial Chamber and to request confirmation of the charges based on additional evidence.[116] If the Pre-Trial Chamber cannot take a final decision, it may adjourn the hearing[117] and request the Prose-

---

tools.org/doc/lc66t7/). The *prima facie* case has been understood to be a "credible case which would (if not contradicted by the Defence) be a sufficient basis to convict the accused on the charge", see ICTY, *Prosecutor v. Kordić et al.*, Trial Chamber, Decision on the Review of the Indictment, 10 November 1995, IT-95-14-I, p. 3 (https://www.legal-tools.org/doc/0c369d/); STL, *Prosecutor v. Ayyash et al.*, Appeals Chamber, Interlocutory Decision on the Applicable Law: Criminal Association and Review of the Indictment, 18 October 2017, STL-17-07/I/AC/R176bis/F0021/20171018/R000800-R000844/EN/dm, para. 110 (https://www.legal-tools.org/doc/829cbe/); ICTR, *Prosecutor v. Bikindi*, Trial Chamber, Confirmation of the Indictment, 5 July 2001, ICTR-2001-72-1, para. 5 (https://www.legal-tools.org/doc/a5e4c7/). At the Kosovo Specialist Chambers, the evidentiary threshold applicable at the stage of the confirmation of the indictment is "well-grounded suspicion", Article 39(2) of the Law on the Specialist Chambers and Specialist Prosecutor's Office, 3 August 2015, Law No. 05/L-053 (https://www.legal-tools.org/doc/8b71c3/). According to Article 19.1.12. of the 2012 Kosovo Criminal Procedure Code, 28 December 2012, "well-grounded suspicion" means that the evidence "would satisfy an objective observer that a criminal offence has occurred and the defendant has committed the offence".

[114] See, for example, ICC, Situation in the Central African Republic II, *Prosecutor v. Alfred Yekatom and Patrice-Edouard Ngaïssona*, Pre-Trial Chamber, Decision on the confirmation of charges against Alfred Yekatom and Patrice-Edouard Ngaïssona, 11 December 2019, ICC-01/14-01/18-403-Red, para. 14 ('Yekatom/Ngaïssona Confirmation Decision') (https://www.legal-tools.org/doc/f0s9c6/); Ongwen Confirmation Decision, para. 14, see above note 44; Mbarushimana Confirmation Decision, para. 41, see above note 104; ICC, Situation in Darfur, Sudan, *Prosecutor v. Bahar Idriss Abu Garda*, Pre-Trial Chamber, Decision on the Confirmation of Charges, 8 February 2010, ICC-02/05-02/09-243-Red, para. 41 (https://www.legal-tools.org/doc/cb3614/).

[115] Article 61(7)(a) and (b), see above note 2.

[116] Article 61(8), see above note 2.

[117] Article 61(7)(c), see above note 2. See also ICC, Situation in the Central African Republic, *Prosecutor v. Jean-Pierre Bemba Gombo*, Pre-Trial Chamber, Decision Adjourning the Hearing pursuant to Article 61(7)(c)(ii) of the Rome Statute, 3 March 2009, ICC-01/05-

cutor to consider (i) providing further evidence or conducting further investigation with respect to a particular charge;[118] or (ii) amending a charge because the evidence submitted appears to establish a different crime within the jurisdiction of the Court.[119] Before addressing the question of classification of alleged conduct by the judges at the confirmation stage, a few preliminary remarks on three important aspects are necessary: (i) the completion of the investigation, (ii) the communication of evidence to the Pre-Trial Chamber, and (iii) the analysis of the evidence.

20.1.6.1. Preliminary Remarks

First, before undertaking the classification of the factual allegations, it is crucial to investigate comprehensively and to determine with specificity, at the latest when charging the person, what is the conduct for which the person is brought to trial. If there is uncertainty as to the exact contours of the alleged conduct, it is difficult to give it the proper classification. Admittedly, the nature of international crimes is different from ordinary crimes as they often concern a plurality of incidents occurring over a prolonged period of time, across large swathes of the territory, and involve high numbers of perpetrators and victims. Nevertheless, despite the complexity of the relevant conduct, it is necessary to frame the charges in such a manner that will inform the suspect in a meaningful way. Recently, Pre-Trial Chamber I summarised its expectations as to the factual specificity of the DCC as follows:

> the Chamber is of the view that the degree of specificity expected from the Prosecutor in her description of the facts depends on the nature of the crimes in question and the circumstances of the case brought by the Prosecutor before the Chamber. Where crimes such as torture or rape are concerned, the Prosecutor must describe the criminal acts in issue, stating the date and place of the acts, along with the number of victims, or at the very least a clear estimate of that

---

01/08-388, para. 14 ('Bemba Adjournment Decision') (https://www.legal-tools.org/doc/81d7a9/).

[118] Pre-Trial Chamber I adjourned the hearing in the *Laurent Gbagbo* case and requested the Prosecutor to consider conducting further investigation in relation to the contextual elements and certain incidents.

[119] Pre-Trial Chamber III adjourned the hearing in the *Bemba* case and requested the Prosecutor to consider adding his criminal responsibility as a commander to the responsibility as a principal perpetrator.

---

number, and their identities as far as at all possible. However, where by their nature the crimes are directed against a group or collectivity of people, as in the case of the crime of persecution, a like degree of specificity cannot be expected of the Prosecutor's description of the facts; nonetheless, the Prosecutor must endeavour to pinpoint as much as possible places, times and approximate numbers of victims and to provide the necessary particulars to make out the elements of the crimes.[120]

Setting the contours of the case will also facilitate the gathering of evidence during the investigation. Chambers have been acutely aware of the challenges and complexities of the Prosecutor's investigations. However, they also must ensure that proceedings unfold expeditiously with due regard for the rights of the Defence. On a number of occasions the ICC judges insisted that the Prosecutor (who controls the timing when proceedings are triggered before the Court) *largely* complete the investigation at the stage of the confirmation of charges so that the case is trial-ready and further delays in the proceedings are avoided.[121] The ambition

---

[120] Al Hassan DCC Decision, para. 30, see above note 109; this approach was followed thereafter in the Yekatom/Ngaïssona Postponement Decision, paras. 41–42, see above note 110.

[121] Lubanga Redactions Appeals Judgment, para. 54, see above note 105; ICC, Situation in the Democratic Republic of the Congo, *Prosecutor v. Callixte Mbarushimana*, Appeals Chamber, Judgment on the appeal of the Prosecutor against the decision of Pre-Trial Chamber I of 16 December 2011 entitled "Decision on the confirmation of charges", 30 May 2012, ICC-01/04-01/10-514, para. 44 ('Mbarushimana Appeals Judgment') (https://www.legal-tools.org/doc/6ead30/); ICC, Situation in the Republic of Kenya, *Prosecutor v. William Samoei Ruto et al.*, Pre-Trial Chamber, Dissenting Opinion by Judge Hans-Peter Kaul, in Decision on the Confirmation of Charges Pursuant to Article 61(7)(a) and (b) of the Rome Statute, 23 January 2012, ICC-01/09-01/11-373, paras. 42–52 (https://www.legal-tools.org/doc/96c3c2/); ICC, Situation in the Republic of Kenya, *Prosecutor v. Francis Kirimi Muthaura et al.*, Pre-Trial Chamber, Dissenting Opinion by Judge Hans-Peter Kaul, in Decision on the Confirmation of Charges Pursuant to Article 61(7)(a) and (b) of the Rome Statute, 23 January 2012, ICC-01/09-02/11-382-Red, paras. 47–57 (https://www.legal-tools.org/doc/4972c0/); ICC, Situation in the Republic of Kenya, *Prosecutor v. Uhuru Muigai Kenyatta*, Pre-Trial Chamber, Corrigendum to "Decision on the 'Prosecution's Request to Amend the Final Updated Document Containing the Charges Pursuant to Article 61(9) of the Statute'", 21 March 2013, ICC-01/09-02/11-700-Corr, paras. 35–36 ('Kenyatta Amendment Decision') (https://www.legal-tools.org/doc/d70f13/); ICC, Situation in the Democratic Republic of the Congo, *Prosecutor v. Bosco Ntaganda*, Pre-Trial Chamber, Decision on the "Prosecution's Urgent Request to Postpone the Date of the Confirmation Hearing" and Setting a New Calendar for the Disclosure of Evidence Between the Parties, 17 June 2013, ICC-01/04-02/06-73, para. 31 ('Ntaganda Postponement Decision') (https://www.legal-tools.org/doc/f65c8a/); ICC, Situation in the Republic of Côte d'Ivoire, *Prose-

of the Prosecutor and the Chambers must be that soon after the confirmation of the charges, the trial commences on the charges as confirmed.

Second, an evidentiary record largely completed in time enables the Prosecutor to analyse whether the factual allegations are supported by the evidence collected as a whole. The analysis should not only concentrate on how many pieces of evidence support a particular factual allegation but, more importantly, whether the proven factual allegation fulfils the legal requirements of the crime or form of criminal responsibility that the Prosecutor advances in the DCC. This point will be further elaborated below when addressing the analysis of evidence.

For the judges to take an informed decision and to agree or disagree with the classification of alleged conduct proposed by the Prosecutor, it is necessary that they have full access to the evidence. At the ICC, two approaches were followed in the pre-trial phase of the cases. In some cases it was argued that the Pre-Trial Chamber should only receive the evidence on which the parties rely.[122] Evidence which the Prosecutor discloses to

---

cutor v. Laurent Gbagbo, Pre-Trial Chamber, Decision adjourning the hearing on the confirmation of charges pursuant to article 61(7)(c)(i) of the Rome Statute, 3 June 2013, ICC-02/11-01/11-432, para. 25 ('Gbagbo Adjournment Decision') (https://www.legal-tools.org/doc/2682d8/); Ongwen Postponement Decision, para. 32, see above note 104; ICC, Situation in the Central African Republic II, *Prosecutor v. Alfred Yekatom and Patrice-Edouard Ngaïssona*, Pre-Trial Chamber, Second Decision on Disclosure and Related Matters, 4 April 2019, ICC-01/14-01/18-163, para. 28 ('Yekatom and Ngaïssona Second Disclosure Decision') (https://www.legal-tools.org/doc/35f5b8/).

122 ICC, Situation in the Democratic Republic of the Congo, *Prosecutor v. Thomas Lubanga Dyilo*, Pre-Trial Chamber, Decision on the Final System of Disclosure and the Establishment of a Timetable, 15 May 2006, ICC-01/04-01/06-102, paras. 41–43 ('Lubanga Disclosure Decision') (https://www.legal-tools.org/doc/052848/); ICC, Situation in the Democratic Republic of the Congo, *Prosecutor v. Germain Katanga*, Pre-Trial Chamber, Transcript of Hearing, 14 December 2007, ICC-01/04-01/07-T-12-ENG, p. 4, lines 14–22 (https://www.legal-tools.org/doc/03aafc/); ICC, Situation in Darfur, Sudan, *Prosecutor v. Bahar Idriss Abu Garda*, Pre-Trial Chamber, Second Decision on issues relating to Disclosure, 15 July 2009, ICC-02/05-02/09-35, paras. 6–12 ('Abu Garda Second Disclosure Decision') (https://www.legal-tools.org/doc/b57860/); ICC, Situation in Darfur, Sudan, *Prosecutor v. Abdallah Banda Abakaer Nourain and Saleh Mohamed Jerbo Jamus*, Pre-Trial Chamber, Decision on issues relating to disclosure, 29 June 2010, ICC-02/05-03/09-49, paras. 5–6 ('Banda and Jerbo Disclosure Decision') (https://www.legal-tools.org/doc/2a3bac/); ICC, Situation in the Democratic Republic of the Congo, *Prosecutor v. Callixte Mbarushimana*, Pre-Trial Chamber, Decision on issues relating to disclosure, 30 May 2011, ICC-01/04-01/10-87, paras. 9–10 ('Mbarushimana Disclosure Decision') (https://www.legal-tools.org/doc/aee80d/); ICC, Situation in the Republic of Côte d'Ivoire, *Prosecutor v. Laurent Gbagbo*, Pre-Trial Chamber, Decision establishing a disclosure system and a cal-

---

the Defence but on which it does not rely, such as potentially exculpatory evidence or evidence that is material to the preparation of the defence, so-called Rule 77 material, need not be communicated to the Pre-Trial Chamber as such communication would alter the nature of the confirmation hearing and infringe the right of the Defence to decide whether to rely on disclosed evidentiary material.[123] In other cases it was required that all evidence disclosed between the parties, be it incriminating or exculpatory, be communicated in their entirety to the Chamber.[124] This ap-

---

endar for disclosure, 24 January 2012, ICC-02/11-01/11-30, paras. 15, 19–20 ('Gbagbo Disclosure Decision') (https://www.legal-tools.org/doc/3637f7/); ICC, Situation in the Republic of Côte d'Ivoire, *Prosecutor v. Charles Blé Goudé*, Pre-Trial Chamber, Decision establishing a system of disclosure of evidence, 14 April 2014, ICC-02/11-02/11-57, para. 6 (https://www.legal-tools.org/doc/226a9a/).

[123] For example, Lubanga Disclosure Decision, paras. 50–58, see above note 122.

[124] ICC, Situation in the Central African Republic, *Prosecutor v. Jean-Pierre Bemba Gombo*, Pre-Trial Chamber, Decision on the Evidence Disclosure System and Setting a Timetable for Disclosure between the Parties, 31 July 2008, ICC-01/05-01/08-55, para. 19 ('Bemba Disclosure Decision') (https://www.legal-tools.org/doc/15c802/); ICC, Situation in the Republic of Kenya, *Prosecutor v. William Samoei Ruto et al.*, Pre-Trial Chamber, Decision Setting the Regime for Evidence Disclosure and Other Related Matters, 6 April 2011, ICC-01/09-01/11-44, paras. 4–6 ('Ruto *et al.* Disclosure Decision') (https://www.legal-tools.org/doc/351827/); ICC, Situation in the Republic of Kenya, *Prosecutor v. Francis Kirimi Muthaura et al.*, Pre-Trial Chamber, Decision Setting the Regime for Evidence Disclosure and Other Related Matters, 6 April 2011, ICC-01/09-02/11-48, paras. 5–7 ('Muthaura *et al.* Disclosure Decision') (https://www.legal-tools.org/doc/12b91f/); ICC, Situation in the Democratic Republic of the Congo, *Prosecutor v. Bosco Ntaganda*, Pre-Trial Chamber, Decision Setting the Regime for Evidence Disclosure and Other Related Matters, 12 April 2013, ICC-01/04-02/06-47, paras. 8–12 ('Ntaganda Disclosure Decision') (https://www.legal-tools.org/doc/4b9b48/); ICC, Situation in the Central African Republic, *Prosecutor v. Jean-Pierre Bemba Gombo et al.*, Pre-Trial Chamber, Transcript of Hearing, 4 December 2013, ICC-01/05-01/13-T-2-Red-ENG, p. 31, line 25 to p. 32, line 3 (https://www.legal-tools.org/doc/d06553/); ICC, Situation in the Central African Republic, *Prosecutor v. Jean-Pierre Bemba Gombo et al.*, Pre-Trial Chamber, Transcript of Hearing, 5 December 2013, ICC-01/05-01/13-T-3-Red2-ENG, p. 12, lines 22–25 (https://www.legal-tools.org/doc/93e80f/); ICC, Situation in Uganda, *Prosecutor v. Dominic Ongwen*, Pre-Trial Chamber, Decision Setting the Regime for Evidence Disclosure and Other Related Matters, 27 February 2015, ICC-02/04-01/15-203, paras. 9–13 (https://www.legal-tools.org/doc/43ce00/); ICC, Situation in the Republic of Mali, *Prosecutor v. Ahmad Al Faqi Al Mahdi*, Pre-Trial Chamber, Decision on issues related to disclosure and exceptions thereto, 30 September 2015, ICC-01/12-01/15-9, para. 2 (https://www.legal-tools.org/doc/eff9b5/); ICC, Situation in the Republic of Mali, *Prosecutor v. Al Hassan Ag Abdoul Aziz Ag Mahmoud*, Pre-Trial Chamber, Decision on the Evidence Disclosure Protocol and Other Related Matters, 16 May 2018, ICC-01/12-01/18-31-tENG-Corr, paras. 12–16 (https://www.legal-tools.org/doc/89d69e/); ICC, Situation in the Central African Republic II, *Prosecutor v. Alfred Yekatom*, Pre-Trial Chamber, Public Redacted Version of Decision Disclosure and Related Mat-

proach was justified with the wording of Rule 121(2)(c),[125] the Pre-Trial Chamber's duty to contribute to the search for the truth, its filtering function to allow only those cases to go to trial for which there is sufficient evidence, and its duty to delineate the scope of the trial which is binding on the Trial Chamber.[126] Today, the system of disclosure of evidence at the pre-trial phase is harmonised as it is commonly accepted that the Pre-Trial Chambers have access to the entire evidentiary material disclosed between the parties regardless of whether they rely on it.[127] This approach allows the Pre-Trial Chambers to independently assess the evidence available, request, if need be, the submission of all evidence necessary for the determination of the truth,[128] and arrive at its own conclusion.[129]

Third, a related topic is the manner in which the evidence is presented. Evidently, an organised presentation of the pre-trial evidence is conducive to the smooth conduct of the proceedings and the better understanding of the charges. Pre-trial proceedings are characterised by a fast pace and processing of a large amount of information within a very short period of time. The Prosecutor presents the DCC together with the list of incriminating evidence, on which she relies, only 30 days in advance of the confirmation hearing. The Defence has thereafter 15 days to present evidence in favour of the suspect, if it chooses to do so.[130] This tight time schedule does not give the Defence much time to analyse evidence, especially if disclosed only shortly before the confirmation hearing. Unlike at trial, the Pre-Trial Chamber only exceptionally hears witnesses and does not discuss the evidence with the parties in a series of hearings. Several Pre-Trial Chambers explored ways to make the processing of voluminous

---

ters, 23 January 2019, ICC-01/14-01/18-64-Red, paras. 11–12 (https://www.legal-tools. org/doc/30e9b1/); Yekatom and Ngaïssona Second Disclosure Decision, p. 16, para. (a), see above note 121.

[125] Rule 121(2)(c) reads: "All evidence disclosed between the Prosecutor and the person for the purposes of the confirmation bearing shall be communicated to the Pre-Trial Chamber", see above note 4.

[126] See Bemba Disclosure Decision, paras. 8–25, see above note 124.

[127] Recent pre-trial proceedings in the cases concerning Al Hassan Ag Abdoul Aziz Ag Mahmoud, Alfred Yekatom and Patrice-Edouard Ngaïssona followed this approach. See also ICC, *Chambers Practice Manual*, 4th edition, 2019, paras. 26–27 ('Chambers Practice Manual') (https://www.legal-tools.org/doc/dh0zyq/).

[128] Article 69(3), see above note 2.

[129] Bemba Disclosure Decision, para. 16, see above note 124.

[130] Article 61(6)(c), see above note 2, Rule 121(6), see above note 4.

evidence take place under satisfactory conditions, in particular for the Defence. One Pre-Trial Chamber requested that the Prosecutor explain only the exculpatory evidence and Rule 77 material by summarising it and explaining its relevance.[131] Another Pre-Trial Chamber requested that the Prosecutor analyse incriminating evidence and organise it in an in-depth-analysis chart ('IDAC') according to the constitutive legal requirements of the crimes, including contextual elements, and the forms of criminal responsibility.[132] A third Pre-Trial Chamber ordered that incriminating evidence be set out in a document termed 'element-based chart' according to the legal requirements of the crimes and forms of criminal responsibility. It also ordered the Prosecutor to organise the list of incriminating evidence in such a manner that each factual statement is linked with the specific element of crime and/or form of criminal responsibility.[133] The Appeals Chamber clarified that the Pre-Trial Chambers may not compel the parties to produce such analytical documents without seeking prior submissions from them on the utility and practical implications.[134] In recent cases Pre-Trial Chambers have refrained from ordering analytical documents highlighting, *inter alia*, the additional burden placed on the Prose-

---

[131] Abu Garda Second Disclosure Decision, paras. 13–16, see above note 122; Banda and Jerbo Disclosure Decision, para. 5, see above note 122; Mbarushimana Disclosure Decision, para. 11, see above note 122.

[132] Bemba Disclosure Decision, paras. 64–73, see above note 124; ICC, Situation in the Central African Republic, *Prosecutor v. Jean-Pierre Bemba Gombo*, Pre-Trial Chamber, Decision on the Submission of an Updated, Consolidated Version of the In-depth Analysis Chart of Incriminatory Evidence, 10 November 2008, ICC-01/05-01/08-232 ('Bemba Updated IDAC Decision') (https://www.legal-tools.org/doc/842374/); Ruto *et al.* Disclosure Decision, paras. 21–23, see above note 124; Muthaura *et al.* Disclosure Decision, paras. 22–24, see above note 124; Ntaganda Disclosure Decision, paras. 29–32, see above note 124.

[133] Gbagbo Disclosure Decision, para. 40, p. 31, see above note 122; ICC, Situation in the Republic of Côte d'Ivoire, *Prosecutor v. Charles Blé Goudé*, Pre-Trial Chamber, Second decision on issues related to disclosure of evidence, 5 May 2014, ICC-02/11-02/11-67, paras. 14–15 (https://www.legal-tools.org/doc/62fa3c/). In the Blé Goudé case, the same Pre-Trial Chamber refrained from ordering a particular structure of the list of evidence and left it to the Prosecutor to organise the evidence "consecutively in any clear order", see *ibid.*, para. 14.

[134] ICC, Situation in Uganda, *Prosecutor v. Dominic Ongwen*, Appeals Chamber, Judgment on the appeal of the Prosecutor against the decision of Pre-Trial Chamber II entitled "Decision Setting the Regime for Evidence Disclosure and Other Related Matters", 17 June 2015, ICC-02/04-01/15-251 (https://www.legal-tools.org/doc/0052a2/).

cutor or the risk for delays in the proceedings, in particular the postponement of the confirmation hearing.[135]

The analytical documents, such as the IDAC or the 'element-based
chart', organise the evidence presentation in a law-driven way, linking the
relevant evidence to the factual allegation with which the Prosecutor intends to prove the existence of a particular legal requirement of the applicable law.[136] It provides an immediate overview of whether the evidence
is sufficient in support of a particular legal requirement, as alleged by the
Prosecutor. The list of evidence, or a footnoted DCC do not provide the
same level of analysis as they are not organised according to the legal
requirements of the applicable law. The level of analysis also cannot be
achieved by summarising witness statements or other pieces of evidence,
as has been proposed by another presenter at the New Delhi expert conference.[137] Summaries of evidence do not filter the relevant pieces of information in relation to specific legal requirements of the applicable law,
but merely reproduce the gist of information contained in the evidence.

---

[135] ICC, Situation in the Republic of Mali, *Prosecutor v. Al Hassan Ag Abdoul Aziz Ag
Mahmoud*, Pre-Trial Chamber, Decision on the In-Depth Analysis Chart of Disclosed Evidence, 29 June 2018, ICC-01/12-01/18-61-tENG, paras. 22–23 (https://www.legal-tools.
org/doc/d35cef/); Yekatom and Ngaïssona Second Disclosure Decision, para. 24, see above
note 121. Contrary, ICC, Situation in the Republic of Kenya, *Prosecutor v. William Samoei
Ruto et al.*, Pre-Trial Chamber, Decision on the "Prosecution's Application for leave to
Appeal the 'Decision Setting the Regime for Evidence Disclosure and Other Related Matters' (ICC-01/09-01/11-44)", 2 May 2011, ICC-01/09-01/11-74, para. 27 (https://www.
legal-tools.org/doc/7ea8aa/); ICC, Situation in the Republic of Kenya, *Prosecutor v. Francis Kirimi Muthaura et al.*, Pre-Trial Chamber, Decision on the "Prosecution's Application
for leave to Appeal the 'Decision Setting the Regime for Evidence Disclosure and Other
Related Matters' (ICC-01/09-02/11-48)", 2 May 2011, ICC-01/09-02/11-77, para. 25
(https://www.legal-tools.org/doc/c25cf8/).

[136] Pre-Trial Chamber III, the first Chamber to order an IDAC, established and proposed a
model which was adopted in all other cases before it, see ICC, Situation in the Central African Republic, *Prosecutor v. Jean-Pierre Bemba Gombo*, Pre-Trial Chamber, Annex, 10
November 2008, ICC-01/05-01/08-232-Anx (https://www.legal-tools.org/doc/b6b329/),
appended to Bemba Updated IDAC Decision, see above note 132. The model of the element-based chart is to be found, for example, in ICC, Situation in the Republic of Côte
d'Ivoire, *Prosecutor v. Laurent Gbagbo*, Pre-Trial Chamber, Annex III, 24 January 2012,
ICC-02/11-01/11-30-AnxIII (https://www.legal-tools.org/doc/3d7817/), appended to
Gbagbo Disclosure Decision, see above note 122.

[137] See David Re, "David Re, Rethinking Disclosure in Core International Crimes Cases",
CILRAP Film, New Delhi, 22 February 2019 (www.cilrap.org/cilrap-film/190222-re/).

Auxiliary documents, presented in addition to the documents required by law, are not foreign to large and complex proceedings as those before the ICC.[138] It is worth highlighting that at trial the Office of the Prosecutor readily prepares and submits other voluminous auxiliary documents, such as pre-trial briefs, which provide further explanations on the evidence with a view to assisting the Defence and the Trial Chamber. Outsiders observe that analytical documents organise the evidence according to the legal elements, assist in navigating through large amounts of evidence, expedite the proceedings, and provide the Defence "maximum notice and a clear understanding" of the case.[139] A 2014 expert report on the effectiveness of the ICC recommended that the IDAC be submitted "as early as practical before the commencement of the confirmation of charges hearing".[140]

Various Pre-Trial Chambers have stressed in the context of setting disclosure deadlines prior to the confirmation hearing:

> the Prosecutor is the triggering force of the proceedings, in the sense that the determination as to whether, and when, an application for a warrant of arrest or a summons to appear is to be filed before the Chamber falls squarely within his prerogatives. The Single Judge thus expects that, before approaching the Chamber with his application for summonses to appear [...] the Prosecutor has carefully reviewed the evidence in his possession at that time, both incriminating and exculpatory. Furthermore, this material has been in his domain for sufficient time for him to be able to disclose to the

---

[138] Michael G. Karnavas, "The Kosovo Specialist Chambers' Rules of Procedure and Evidence: More of the Same Hybridity with Added Prosecutorial Transparency", in *International Criminal Law Review*, 2020, vol. 20, no. 1, p. 94.

[139] *Ibid.*, p. 94; Morten Bergsmo and Olympia Bekou, "The In-depth Evidence Analysis Charts at the International Criminal Court", in Morten Bergsmo (ed.), *Active Complementarity: Legal Information Transfer*, Torkel Opsahl Academic EPublisher, Oslo, 2011, pp. 313–47 (http://www.toaep.org/ps-pdf/8-bergsmo); Roger S. Clark, "Elements of Crimes in Early Confirmation Decisions of Pre-Trial Chambers of the International Criminal Court", in *New Zealand Yearbook of International Law*, 2008, vol. 6, pp. 209-238; Johan D. van der Vyver, "Time is of the essence: The In-depth Analysis Chart in Proceedings before the International Criminal Court", in *Criminal Law Bulletin*, vol. 48, no. 4, pp. 601–16.

[140] Guénaël Mettraux et al., "The Confirmation Process", in *Expert Initiative on Promoting Effectiveness at the International Criminal Court*, December 2014, para. 31 (https://www.legal-tools.org/doc/3dae90/).

Defence or to request for redactions, if need be, within a short period of time.[141]

The above reasons which the Pre-Trial Chambers have brought forward in the context of disclosure must apply *a fortiori* for the analysis of the evidence. During the investigation, the Prosecutor continuously takes possession of incriminating evidence and, undoubtedly and demonstrably, analyses it with a view to formulating the charges in the DCC. The IDAC or element-based chart is nothing else but the outcome of such analysis that underlies the DCC.

The judges of the Kosovo Specialist Chambers, who adopted the Rules of Procedure and Evidence in March 2017, acknowledged the necessity of such analysis at the pre-trial stage and included in said instrument that the Specialist Prosecutor, when presenting the indictment, submit not only the evidentiary material but also a "detailed outline demonstrating the relevance of each item of evidentiary material to each allegation, with particular reference to the conduct of the suspect with respect to the alleged crime(s)".[142]

20.1.6.2. Classification of Alleged Conduct at the Confirmation of Charges Stage

By the time of writing, the Pre-Trial Chambers have confirmed charges relating to Article 5 crimes and offences against the administration of justice against 22 suspects,[143] and declined to confirm charges against four

---

[141] For example, ICC, Situation in the Republic of Kenya, *Prosecutor v. Francis Kirimi Muthaura et al.*, Pre-Trial Chamber, Decision on the "Prosecution's application requesting disclosure after a final resolution of the Government of Kenya's admissibility challenge" and Establishing a Calendar for Disclosure Between the Parties, 20 April 2011, ICC-01/09-02/11-64, para. 17 (https://www.legal-tools.org/doc/1f9ef0/). This finding was rehearsed with approval in Gbagbo Disclosure Decision, para. 38, see above note 122; recently also remarked in Yekatom/Ngaïssona Postponement Decision, para. 32, see above note 110.

[142] Rule 86(3)(b) of the Rules of Procedure and Evidence before the Kosovo Specialist Chambers, 17 March 2017 (https://www.legal-tools.org/doc/opmwoy/).

[143] These persons are: Thomas Lubanga Dyilo, Germain Katanga, Mathieu Ngudjolo Chui, Bosco Ntaganda, Dominic Ongwen, Jean-Pierre Bemba Gombo, Aimé Kilolo Musamba, Jean-Jacques Mangenda Kabongo, Fidèle Babala Wandu, Narcisse Arido, Abdallah Banda Abakaer Nourain, Saleh Mohammed Jerbo Jamus, William Samoei Ruto, Joshua Arap Sang, Francis Kirimi Muthaura, Uhuru Muigai Kenyatta, Laurent Gbagbo, Charles Blé Goudé, Ahmad Al Faqi Al Mahdi, Al Hassan Ag Abdoul Aziz Ag Mahmoud, Alfred Yekatom and Patrice-Edouard Ngaïssona.

---

suspects for insufficiency of the evidence.[144] When the Pre-Trial Chamber confirms the charges, it considers the evidence to be sufficient to establish 'substantial grounds to believe' that the suspect indeed committed the crimes, as charged, and adopts the classification of alleged conduct as proposed by the Prosecutor. The Prosecutor thus can assume that there is a strong likelihood the Trial Chamber will enter a conviction on the basis of the confirmed classification of alleged conduct, provided the evidence satisfies the evidentiary threshold applicable at trial ('beyond reasonable doubt'). If the Pre-Trial Chamber concludes that the evidence presented does not support the factual allegations, it declines to confirm the charge(s) concerned or those parts of the charge(s) affected by evidentiary deficiencies. As is the case with warrants of arrest, the classification of alleged conduct is not confirmed for evidentiary reasons. If, however, the judges are of the view that, on the basis of the evidence presented, a different classification of the alleged conduct should be adopted, they can remedy the deficiency detected through the avenue the Statute offers: adjourning the hearing and requesting the Prosecutor to reconsider the classification of alleged conduct pursuant to Article 61(7)(c)(ii). In other words, judges cannot change the legal classification themselves. In case the judges are of the view that the evidence is insufficient (and they do not wish to decline to confirm the charges outright), they may revert to the Prosecutor and request that she consider providing further evidence or conducting further investigation with respect to a particular charge pursuant to Article 61(7)(c)(i).

Pre-Trial Chambers have adjourned the confirmation hearings in two cases, namely in the *Bemba* case and in the *Laurent Gbagbo* case.

- **Bemba case**: The Chamber requested the Prosecutor to consider amending the charges because the evidence submitted appeared to establish a different form of criminal responsibility, namely Mr. Bemba's responsibility as a military commander or superior under Article 28 instead of his responsibility of an indirect co-perpetrator under Article 25(3)(a).[145] After the Prosecutor re-submitted an amended DCC (and corresponding IDAC), the Pre-Trial Chamber declined to confirm Mr. Bemba's criminal responsibility as a prin-

---

[144] These persons are: Callixte Mbarushimana, Bahar Idriss Abu Garda, Henry Kiprono Kosgey, and Mohammed Hussein Ali.

[145] Bemba Adjournment Decision, paras. 46 and 49, see above note 117.

cipal perpetrator and confirmed his responsibility as a military commander.[146] The fact that the Trial Chamber discussed the evidence on the basis of Article 28 and ultimately convicted Mr. Bemba for his responsibility as a military commander, demonstrates that the intervention of the Pre-Trial Chamber as regards the classification was, as such, correct.

- **Gbagbo case**: The Chamber requested the Prosecutor to consider providing further evidence or conducting further investigation with respect to the existence of the contextual elements of crimes against humanity with which Mr. Gbagbo was charged.[147] The Prosecutor conducted further investigative activities, re-submitted an amended DCC, and the Chamber, by majority, confirmed the charges as presented by the Prosecutor.[148] The fact that the majority of Trial Chamber I acquitted Messrs Gbagbo and Blé Goudé, *inter alia*, because of lack of evidence concerning the existence of a State or organisational policy to commit an attack against the civilian population within the meaning of Article 7(2)(a),[149] is a further indication that the evidentiary problem was correctly identified by the Pre-Trial Chamber but could not be overcome at trial.

---

[146] ICC, Situation in the Central African Republic, *Prosecutor v. Jean-Pierre Bemba Gombo*, Pre-Trial Chamber, Decision Pursuant to Article 61(7)(a) and (b) of the Rome Statute on the Charges of the Prosecutor Against Jean-Pierre Bemba Gombo, 15 June 2009, ICC-01/05-01/08-424, paras. 344, 501 ('Bemba Confirmation Decision') (https://www.legal-tools.org/doc/07965c/).

[147] Gbagbo Adjournment Decision, paras. 44–45, see above note 121.

[148] ICC, Situation in the Republic of Côte d'Ivoire, *Prosecutor v. Laurent Gbagbo*, Pre-Trial Chamber, Decision on the confirmation of charges against Laurent Gbagbo, 12 June 2014, ICC-02/11-01/11-656-Red ('Gbagbo Confirmation Decision') (https://www.legal-tools.org/doc/5b41bc/). The dissenting Judge, while agreeing that "several incidents supporting the crimes against humanity allegation are now better supported by evidence", could not agree with her colleagues on the confirmation since, in her view, the evidence in the record did not suffice to commit Gbagbo to trial for the charges under the forms of criminal responsibility as pleaded by the Prosecutor, see ICC, Situation in the Republic of Côte d'Ivoire, *Prosecutor v. Laurent Gbagbo*, Pre-Trial Chamber, Dissenting Opinion of Judge Christine van den Wyngaert, 12 June 2014, ICC-02/11-01/11-656-Anx ('Dissenting Opinion of Judge Christine van den Wyngaert') (https://www.legal-tools.org/doc/f715a5/).

[149] ICC, Situation in the Republic of Côte d'Ivoire, *Prosecutor v. Laurent Gbagbo and Charles Blé Goudé*, Trial Chamber, Transcript of Hearing, 15 January 2019, ICC-02/11-01/15-T-232-ENG, p. 3 (https://www.legal-tools.org/doc/4fe93a/).

Which conclusions for the Prosecutor's investigation can be drawn from the Pre-Trial Chamber's review of the charges at the confirmation stage? To find a response to this question, the purpose of the confirmation stage must first be called to mind. All Pre-Trial Chambers are unanimous in stipulating that its purpose, *inter alia*, lies in filtering those cases that merit to be discussed at trial.[150] What exactly this means has been described by Judge Christine van den Wyngaert as follows: the Pre-Trial Chamber verifies whether there is sufficient evidence to "sustain a possible conviction on the assumption that [evidentiary] questions are resolved in favour of the Prosecutor at trial".[151] It follows that the confirmation of charges is not an end in itself, but serves to 'weed out' the weak cases and to 'test' the sufficiency of evidence for trial. As a consequence, and mindful of the serious consequences of confirmation for the accused, the victims and the Court as a whole, the scrutiny of the Prosecutor's evidence is thorough and rigorous, undertaken against a relatively high intermediate evidentiary threshold. *All* factual allegations included in the DCC are assessed in light of the evidence presented. The fact that the evidentiary threshold at the confirmation stage is not the same as at trial does not mean that the Pre-Trial Chamber does not assess *all* factual allegations in detail.[152] The requisite evidentiary threshold and the scope of the factual

---

[150] See, for example, ICC, Situation in the Democratic Republic of the Congo, *Prosecutor v. Thomas Lubanga Dyilo*, Pre-Trial Chamber, Decision on the confirmation of charges, 29 January 2007, ICC-01/04-01/06-803-tEN, para. 37 ('Lubanga Confirmation Decision') (https://www.legal-tools.org/doc/b7ac4f/); Gbagbo Adjournment Decision, para. 18, see above note 121; ICC, Situation in the Republic of Mali, *Prosecutor v. Ahmad Al Faqi Al Mahdi*, Pre-Trial Chamber, Decision on the confirmation of charges against Ahmad Al Faqi Al Mahdi, 24 March 2016, ICC-01/12-01/15-84-Red, para. 15 ('Al Mahdi Confirmation Decision') (https://www.legal-tools.org/doc/bc8144/); ICC, Situation in the Republic of Mali, *Prosecutor v. Al Hassan Ag Abdoul Aziz Ag Mohamed Ag Mahmoud*, Pre-Trial Chamber, Rectificatif à la Décision relative à la confirmation des charges portées contre Al Hassan Ag Abdoul Aziz Ag Mohamed Ag Mahmoud, 30 September 2019, ICC-01/12-01/18-461-Corr-Red, para. 42 ('Al Hassan Confirmation Decision') (https://www.legal-tools.org/doc/9lml5x/); Mbarushimana Appeals Judgment, para. 39, see above note 121; Bemba Confirmation Decision, para. 28, see above note 146; Ongwen Confirmation Decision, para. 14, see above note 44; Yekatom/Ngaïssona Confirmation Decision, para. 14, see above note 114.

[151] Dissenting Opinion of Judge Christine van den Wyngaert, para. 4, see above note 148.

[152] Contrary, ICC, Situation in the Democratic Republic of the Congo, *Prosecutor v. Bosco Ntaganda*, Trial Chamber, Decision on Updated DCC, 6 February 2015, ICC-01/04-02/06-450, para. 28: "The Pre-Trial Chamber is not required to consider each factual allegation in detail but rather only to determine whether there is sufficient evidence to establish substantial grounds to believe that the crimes charged were committed" (https://www.legal-tools.

---

enquiry are distinct notions and should not be conflated. Upon confirmation of the charges, the accused will defend him- or herself only against those factual allegations that are contained in the confirmation decision.[153] The Trial Chamber will enter a conviction only on the factual allegations as described in the confirmation decision.[154] As a result, the factual scope of the case is 'fixed' at the confirmation stage and the Prosecutor is not authorised to introduce new facts into trial that have not been contemplated by the Pre-Trial Chamber. On the other hand, factual allegations that are not proven against the evidentiary threshold of 'substantial grounds to believe' are not confirmed and, therefore, not retained in the charges. This may concern discrete factual allegations underlying a crime or form of criminal responsibility, or crimes and forms of criminal responsibility as a whole.

The classification, which is part and parcel of the 'charge', is of course also reviewed by the Pre-Trial Chamber. If the alleged conduct is proven and fulfils the legal requirements of the crime(s) and form(s) of criminal responsibility, then the Pre-Trial Chamber confirms the classification proposed by the Prosecutor. The confirmed classification of alleged conduct informs authoritatively the accused of the legal subject-matter of the ensuing trial. The confirmation decision also restricts the Prosecutor's authority as she is no longer at liberty to amend the classification of alleged conduct on her own. Notably, while the legal classification given by

---

org/doc/7cec26/). See also ICC, *Situation in the Central African Republic, Prosecutor v. Jean-Pierre Bemba Gombo*, Appeals Chamber, Dissenting Opinion of Judge Sanji Mmasenono Monageng and Judge Piotr Hofmański, 8 June 2018, ICC-01/05-01/08-3636-Anx1-Red, para. 34 (https://www.legal-tools.org/doc/dc2518/):

> In such a case, allegations of such criminal acts are primarily vehicles to prove a broader allegation and it may therefore not be necessary for the pre-trial chamber to assess all criminal acts put forward by the Prosecutor. The pre-trial chamber may then [...] rely on all or some of those acts to confirm the crimes charged.

This particular understanding of the scope of the Pre-Trial Chamber's factual enquiry offered by Trial Chamber VI and two dissenting appellate judges cannot explain why Pre-Trial Chambers have significantly reduced the factual scope of specific charges, such as in the Situation in the Republic of Kenya cases.

[153] ICC, *Situation in the Central African Republic, Prosecutor v. Jean-Pierre Bemba Gombo et al.*, Trial Chamber, Decision on the Submission of Auxiliary Documents, 10 June 2015, ICC-01/05-01/13-992, paras. 12–13 (https://www.legal-tools.org/doc/6a4ba2/); Katanga and Ngudjolo Decision on Summary of Charges, paras. 17, 19, see above note 109.

[154] Cf. Articles 61(7)(a), 64(8)(a), 74(2), see above note 2 and Regulation 55 of the Regulations of the Court, see above note 19.

---

the Pre-Trial Chamber when issuing a warrant of arrest is not binding on the Prosecutor at the confirmation stage, the Prosecutor must proceed at the trial stage with the prosecution of the accused in relation to the crimes and forms of criminal responsibility as confirmed in the Article 61 decision. Should the Prosecutor be in disagreement with or change her mind regarding the classification of alleged conduct after the charges are confirmed, she can either (i) request to amend the charges with permission of the Pre-Trial Chamber,[155] or (ii) request that the Trial Chamber trigger the application of Regulation 55 of the Regulations of the Court and inform the parties that it may give the factual allegations a different classification. However, in both instances the ultimate decision whether the classification is subject to change lies with the respective Chamber and not the Prosecutor.[156] It is clear from the foregoing that under the Statute the classification of alleged conduct, in contrast to the facts, may not remain static in the course of the proceedings and be subject to change. As a result, it appears that the confirmation of the facts of the case is more important than the confirmation of the classification of alleged conduct.

Should, however, the Pre-Trial Chamber wish to amend the classification of alleged conduct at the confirmation stage, it must do so through the avenue of Article 61(7)(c)(ii) and provide the Prosecutor with the opportunity to amend the charge. It cannot change the classification of alleged conduct on its own. This conforms with the division of responsibilities set out in the Statute which vests the responsibility to frame the charges in the DCC in the Prosecutor, including the classification of alleged conduct. Regulation 55 of the Regulations of the Court is not applicable at the confirmation stage.[157] In this regard, Pre-Trial Chamber I's

---

[155] Article 61(9), see above note 2.

[156] Kenyatta Amendment Decision, para. 19, see above note 121; ICC, Situation in the Central African Republic, *Prosecutor v. Jean-Pierre Bemba Gombo et al.*, Trial Chamber, Decision on Prosecution Application to Provide Notice pursuant to Regulation 55, 15 September 2015, ICC-01/05-01/13-1250, para. 8 (https://www.legal-tools.org/doc/ea422e/); ICC, Situation in the Central African Republic, *Prosecutor v. Jean-Pierre Bemba Gombo et al.*, Trial Chamber, Decision on Prosecution's Re-application for Regulation 55(2) Notice, 15 January 2016, ICC-01/05-01/13-1553 (https://www.legal-tools.org/doc/8ddec3/); ICC, Situation in the Republic of Côte d'Ivoire, *Prosecutor v. Laurent Gbagbo and Charles Blé Goudé*, Trial Chamber, Decision giving notice pursuant to Regulation 55(2) of the Regulations of the Court, 19 August 2015, ICC-02/11-01/15-185, para. 10 (https://www.legal-tools.org/doc/984739/).

[157] In the Regulations of the Court, Regulation 55 is placed under Chapter 3 "Proceedings before the Court" Section 3 entitled "Trial", see above note 19. Its wording clearly ad-

approach in the *Lubanga* case to reclassify *proprio motu* the contextual elements of war crimes in the confirmation decision[158] was criticised for not being in conformity with the statutory framework.[159]

Lastly a few brief observations on the issue of confirming charges for the same facts in the alternative. This issue has provoked much controversy, in particular from the Defence, and concerns mainly the confirmation of several forms of criminal responsibility in the alternative (forms of principal perpetratorship and accessoryship). While in the first cases, the Office of the Prosecutor charged Messrs Lubanga, Katanga, Ngudjolo, and Bemba, with only one or two forms of criminal responsibility,[160] it changed its approach in later cases and adopted a broad charging policy.[161] The same development is mirrored in the jurisprudence of the Pre-

---

dresses the Trial Chamber. Furthermore, there is no provision in the statutory framework that renders this Regulation applicable at the pre-trial stage. Lastly, mindful of the norm hierarchy, the Pre-Trial Chamber is duty-bound to apply Article 61(7)(c)(ii) and not a Regulation that is subject to the Statute (Article 52).

[158] Lubanga Confirmation Decision, paras. 202–04, see above note 150.

[159] Olympia Bekou, *"Prosecutor v Thomas Lubanga Dyilo* – Decision on the Confirmation of Charges", in *Human Rights Law Review*, 2008, vol. 8, no. 2, p. 354.

[160] In the *Lubanga* case, the Prosecutor charged Mr. Lubanga as co-perpetrator, see ICC, Situation in the Democratic Republic of the Congo, *Prosecutor v. Thomas Lubanga Dyilo*, OTP, Document Containing the Charges, Article 61(3)(a), 28 August 2006, ICC-01/04-01/06-356-Anx2, paras. 20–24 (https://www.legal-tools.org/doc/e2fa01/), Lubanga Confirmation Decision, para. 319, see above note 150. In the *Katanga* and *Ngudjolo* case, the Prosecutor charged both suspects as co-perpetrators and, in the alternative, as accessories for having ordered the commission of the crimes, see ICC, Situation in the Democratic Republic of the Congo, *Prosecutor v. Germain Katanga and Mathieu Ngudjolo Chui*, OTP, Amended Document Containing the Charges Pursuant to Article 61(3)(a) of the Statute, 26 June 2008, ICC-01/04-01/07-649-Anx1A, paras. 90–94 (https://www.legal-tools.org/doc/9cc58b/). In the *Bemba* case, the Prosecutor charged Mr. Bemba as indirect co-perpetrator. After the Pre-Trial Chamber adjourned the hearing and requested the Prosecutor to consider amending the charges by considering Mr. Bemba's criminal responsibility as a military commander or superior, the Prosecutor charged Mr. Bemba alternatively for his responsibility under Article 28, see ICC, Situation in the Central African Republic, *Prosecutor v. Jean-Pierre Bemba Gombo*, OTP, Public Redacted Version of the Amended Document containing the charges filed on 30 March 2009, 30 March 2009, ICC-01/05-01/08-395-Anx3, paras. 57–59, 86 (https://www.legal-tools.org/doc/d7f72e/).

[161] For example, in the *Al Hassan* case, the Prosecutor charged Mr. Al Hassan as direct perpetrator, co-perpetrator and indirect co-perpetrator. In addition, Mr. Al Hassan was charged as accessory for having solicited or induced the commission of the crimes, for having aided and abetted the commission of the crimes, and for having contributed in any other way to the crimes committed by a group of persons acting with a common purpose. The forms of criminal responsibility were further specified for each crime charged. See ICC, Situation

---

Trial Chambers. While the Pre-Trial Judges adopted a strict approach in the first cases[162] they changed their approach in later cases, "taking stock of the experience of the Court", and accepted different forms of criminal responsibility for the accused's conduct in the alternative when the evidence was deemed sufficient to sustain each alternative.[163] The judges

---

in the Republic of Mali, *Prosecutor v. Al Hassan Ag Abdoul Aziz Ag Mohamed Ag Mahmoud*, OTP, Version publique expurgée de la "Version amendée et corrigée du Document contenant les charges contre M. Al Hassan Ag Abdoul Aziz Ag Mohamed Ag Mahmoud", ICC-01/12-01/18-335-Conf-Corr, 11 mai 2019, 2 July 2019, ICC-01/12-01/18-335-Corr-Red, para. 208 (https://www.legal-tools.org/doc/1e4aac/). In the *Yekatom and Ngaïssona* case, the Prosecutor charged Mr. Yekatom as direct perpetrator and co-perpetrator and as an accessory for having ordered, solicited and/or induced the commission of the crimes, for having assisted in the commission of the crimes, and for having contributed in any other way to the crimes committed by a group of persons acting with a common purpose. In addition, Mr. Yekatom was charged for his responsibility as military commander. Mr. Ngaïssona was charged as co-perpetrator and as an accessory for having assisted in the commission of the crimes and for having contributed in any other way to the crimes committed by a group of persons acting with a common purpose. The forms of criminal responsibility were further set out for each suspect individually and specified for each crime charged. See ICC, Situation in the Central African Republic II, *Prosecutor v. Alfred Yekatom and Patrice-Edouard Ngaïssona*, OTP, Public redacted version of "Document Containing the Charges", ICC-01/14-01/18-282-Conf-AnxB1, 19 August 2019, 18 September 2019, ICC-01/14-01/18-282-AnxB1-Red, paras. 120–26, 185–99 (https://www.legal-tools.org/doc/9e589d/).

162 Pre-Trial Chamber I held that if there was sufficient evidence to establish principal perpetratorship, the question of accessorial forms of criminal responsibility or command/superior responsibility became moot, see Lubanga Confirmation Decision, para. 321, see above note 150; ICC, Situation in the Democratic Republic of the Congo, *Prosecutor v. Germain Katanga and Mathieu Ngudjolo Chui*, Pre-Trial Chamber, Decision on the confirmation of charges, 30 September 2008, ICC-01/04-01/07-717, para. 471 (https://www.legal-tools.org/doc/67a9ec/). Pre-Trial Chamber II in the *Bemba* case adopted a similar approach and considered the assessment of Article 28 only necessary if Mr. Bemba's responsibility as a principal perpetrator could not be established, see Bemba Confirmation Decision, para. 342, see above note 146. See also Ruto et al. Summons Decision, para. 36, see above note 95.

163 See Chambers Practice Manual, para. 67, see above note 127; ICC, Situation in the Democratic Republic of the Congo, *Prosecutor v. Bosco Ntaganda*, Pre-Trial Chamber, Decision Pursuant to Article 61(7)(a) and (b) of the Rome Statute on the Charges of the Prosecutor Against Bosco Ntaganda, 9 June 2014, ICC-01/04-02/06-309, para. 100 (https://www.legal-tools.org/doc/5686c6/); Gbagbo Confirmation Decision, paras. 227–28, see above note 148; ICC, Situation in the Republic of Côte d'Ivoire, *Prosecutor v. Charles Blé Goudé*, Pre-Trial Chamber, Decision on the confirmation of charges against Charles Blé Goudé, 11 December 2014, ICC-02/11-02/11-186, para. 133 (https://www.legal-tools.org/doc/0536d5/); Al Mahdi Confirmation Decision, para. 22, see above note 150; Ongwen Confirmation Decision, paras. 33, 35, see above note 44; Al Hassan Confirmation Decision, pp. 452–65, see above note 150; Yekatom/Ngaïssona Confirmation Decision, pp. 100–07, see

---

advanced two reasons in support of this approach: confirming alternative forms of responsibility may reduce future delays at trial and provides early notice to the accused of the different legal characterisations that may be considered by the trial judges.[164] Some presenters at the New Delhi expert conference expressed a degree of sympathy for this approach.[165] While it is possible to confirm charges in the alternative against a lower evidentiary threshold with a view to discussing them at trial, conducting a trial on the basis of numerous forms of criminal responsibility evidently places a higher burden on the Defence. The accused is presented with a catalogue of forms of criminal responsibility for either all or selected crimes – that is, as such, neither meaningful nor informative.[166] Since the Defence cannot foresee which form of criminal responsibility the Trial Chamber will ultimately choose in its final judgment, it must extend its investigation to cover all legal elements of the alternatives. This is also a matter of time and costs for the Defence teams (as it is equally for the Prosecutor). In the courtroom, evidence must be elicited from witnesses that could *potentially* be relevant for a number of forms of criminal responsibility, thus prolonging the duration of the trial. Moreover, Defence counsel are compelled to build various strands of defence strategies in relation to each and every alternative. There is no hard rule according to which the Pre-Trial Chamber ought to proceed. If the evidence clearly evinces the principal perpetratorship of the accused, it is at least debatable whether there is a need for the Pre-Trial Chamber to confirm, in addition, his or her criminal responsibility as an accessory. In any event, should the classification of the alleged conduct prove not to be sustainable at trial, there is the possibility to apply Regulation 55 of the Regulations of the Court, an in-

---

above note 114. The policy change was also informed by the developments at trial, in particular the acquittal of Mr. Ngudjolo and the conviction of Mr. Katanga after the Majority of Trial Chamber II re-characterised his conduct pursuant to Regulation 55 of the Regulations of the Court.

[164] For example, Gbagbo Confirmation Decision, para. 228, see above note 148; Ongwen Confirmation Decision, para. 35, see above note 44.

[165] See Cale J. Davis, "Cumulative Charging and Challenges in Charge Selection", CILRAP Film, New Delhi, 22 February 2019 (www.cilrap.org/cilrap-film/190222-davis/).

[166] Karnavas, 2020, p. 94, see above note 138: "Pleading all modes of liability in the alternative is hardly specific, even if it technically meets the notice requirement".

---

strument that was introduced to strengthen the efficiency of trial proceedings and to close "accountability gaps".[167]

20.2. Conclusions

Have the ICC Pre-Trial Chambers, when assessing the classification of alleged conduct, contributed to the improvement of the Prosecutor's investigation or the preparation of the cases? I leave this answer to the informed observer of the Court's proceedings. Importantly, the impact of the Pre-Trial Chambers' classification of alleged conduct must be evaluated in light of the stage of the proceedings, in which such classification is undertaken, and the role of the Pre-Trial Chamber. At the situation stage, during which the Prosecutor decides whether to open an investigation and, if in the affirmative, conducts the investigation, the pronouncements of Pre-Trial Chambers on the legal characterisation of alleged conduct are mainly indicative.[168] Pronouncements on the interpretation of the law, on the other hand, contribute to the establishment of settled jurisprudence. These findings should be taken into account already at the early stages of the investigation. This approach ensures a neat and thorough analysis of the evidence collected in light of the applicable law, as established by the Court. With the appearance of a suspect, the Statute foresees a shift of authority and the Prosecutor's authority is subjected to increasing judicial control. Yet, it appears that of paramount importance throughout the pre-trial phase is not so much the classification of alleged conduct, but the delineation of the factual scope of the case. This is so because under the statutory regime, and throughout the criminal process, the Chambers retain flexibility to react to changes in the factual basis of the case and to choose the most appropriate classification. Conversely, this flexibility

---

[167] ICC, Situation in the Democratic Republic of the Congo, *Prosecutor v. Thomas Lubanga Dyilo*, Appeals Chamber, Judgment on the appeals of Mr Lubanga Dyilo and the Prosecutor against the Decision of Trial Chamber I of 14 July 2009 entitled "Decision giving notice to the parties and participants that the legal characterisation of the facts may be subject to change in accordance with Regulation 55(2) of the Regulations of the Court", 8 December 2009, ICC-01/04-01/06-2205, para. 77 (https://www.legal-tools.org/doc/40d015/). See also Hans-Peter Kaul, "Developments at the International Criminal Court/Construction Site for More Justice: The International Criminal Court after Two Years", in *American Journal of International Law*, 2005, vol. 99, no. 2, pp. 370–84.

[168] This does not apply, of course, if the Pre-Trial Chamber were to reject a request for authorisation to commence an investigation because the alleged conduct does not appear to fulfil the legal requirements of any of the crimes under the Court's jurisdiction.

does not exist in relation to the 'facts and circumstances' of the case once the charges have been confirmed. That said, the classification of alleged conduct undertaken by the Pre-Trial Chambers is far from futile. In particular when confirming the classification proposed by the Prosecutor, the Pre-Trial Chamber gives notice to the accused on which basis the trial will unfold and signals that the classification is likely to pass the test at trial, provided the requisite evidentiary threshold at trial is satisfied.

What can investigators and prosecutors learn from the ICC experience? Four points seem to be important:

- **Investigation**. Conduct a comprehensive investigation from the outset and identify the exact factual contours of the case. Collect relevant evidence of sufficient probative value during the investigation with a view to providing a solid basis for a future judicial assessment against the highest evidentiary threshold. A potentially longer investigation phase should be accepted in the interest of proper case preparation.

- **Law-driven analysis of evidence**. Already at the investigation stage, commence to build up the analysis of the evidence on a continuous basis applying exacting standards. Prefer the use of law-driven analysis tools over fact-driven analysis tools. Of essence is not whether a particular factual allegation has been proven by a high number of pieces of evidence but whether the particular factual allegation, as proven by the evidence, fulfils the legal elements of the crime or form of criminal responsibility. Findings of the Chambers on the law should be taken into account when conducting such analysis.

- **Labelling**. Critically review the classification of alleged conduct and pursue the classification of crimes or forms of criminal responsibility that are squarely supported by the evidence.

- **Quality beats quantity**. Criminal proceedings involving the prosecution of international crimes generate voluminous evidence which is difficult to handle. Ways to reduce the amount of evidence should be explored. Sometimes, less is more.

21

The Role of the Judiciary in the Enhancement of Quality in the National Investigation and Preparation of Core International Crimes

Leïla Bourguiba[*]

21.1. Introductory Remarks

When frustration is rising over inefficiency of international criminal tribunals, voices praising national criminal proceedings' idyllic efficiency can often be heard. These voices are sometimes those of persons with long-standing experience from domestic practice. It is natural that investigators, prosecutors, judges and lawyers draw on their strong past experience and their habitual practice in their national jurisdiction. This experience is obviously precious as seasoned professionals have usually learned from their past mistakes and are therefore more likely to anticipate practical, factual and legal difficulties and offer solutions to solving them.

Nonetheless, having both worked at the International Criminal Court ('ICC') as well as within a national specialised unit in charge of investigating and prosecuting core international crimes, I believe it is relevant to compare the work of international tribunals to such a national unit, especially when it is exercising universal jurisdiction. There are synergies between them and challenges that are common, such as reasonable time, costs, challenging fact-finding in fact-rich criminal cases, complexity of the cases, and diversity of contexts, including cultural differences and geographical distance.

---

[*] **Leïla Bourguiba** is Associated-judge, representing the United Nations High Commissioner, before the French National Appeals Court for Asylum, and Board member of the Research Institute on Mediterranean and Middle East countries (ReMMO). She has served as an Associate Legal Officer at the Pre-trial Chamber of the International Criminal Court (2006–12) and as a Legal Advisor at the French War crimes and Crimes against Humanity Unit within the *Tribunal de grande instance* of Paris (2012–18). The chapter is submitted in her personal capacity and does not necessarily reflect the views of any of the institutions she has or is working for.

The project conference in New Delhi in February 2019 and this anthology brought about stimulating exchanges. Sharing experiences is a key tool for improvement. The Specialised French Unit for the investigation and prosecution of genocide, crimes against humanity and war crimes ('Specialised Unit') remains a relatively young unit created in 2012, yet it is part of an old judicial institution with long traditions and deep-rooted practices. Unlike the situation where some professionals bring their longstanding national experience to the work of international tribunals, within the Unit the situation was inverse. Its creation and blended composition brought national investigators, prosecutors and judges together with professionals whose experience was primarily gained in international tribunals. This sometimes increased the sensitivity to protect national law and practises. This was particularly the case – and understandably so – when the practises and procedures followed in international tribunals were questioned and perceived as the main reason for their lack of efficiency.

The quality of the national prosecutors and investigative judges at the time of creation of the Specialised Unit, and their genuine dedication in making the Specialised Unit efficient, helped to overcome these tensions. Quickly indeed, the particularities of the cases before the Unit led the professionals to constantly challenge their routine ways of operating, and to be open to new tools and approaches while respecting the coherence of French national criminal law and procedure.

The expectations of CLIRAP's Quality Control in Criminal Investigation Project are high. But they need to be demanding to foster reflection and blend in some new ideas to enhance the quality of the investigation and prosecution of core international crimes. This chapter-contribution to the reflection process attempts to shed light on how the judiciary can help to enhance the quality of the investigation and preparation of core international crimes cases.

Without delving into the specifics of the French criminal justice system, it is, however, necessary to understand the practical experience of the investigative judges of the Specialised Unit in order to gain a clear comprehension of its fundamental characteristics (Section 21.2.) and its jurisdictional nature (Section 21.3.). To overcome the challenges arising from such complex cases in a newly established Unit, investigative judges have developed tools and practices to reduce the geographical and cultural gaps (Section 21.4.), track the fragilities and procedural difficulties (Section 21.5.), and efficiently frame the legal and factual scope of the cases ahead of the trial (Section 21.6.).

21.2. Introduction to the French Specialised Unit

The French Specialised Unit was essentially created to speed up the investigation and prosecution of a number of pending cases related to the genocide of Tutsis in Rwanda in 1994 (Section 21.2.1.), expanding from that starting point to include other cases. It is a dedicated Unit, yet with limited staffing and other resources compared to the challenges induced by the exponential increase in cases (Section 21.2.2.).

21.2.1. Efficiency of the Proceedings as an Essential *Raison d'être*

The creation of the Unit is in itself a step towards efficiency. On 8 May 2003, the Council of the European Union ('EU') adopted the Council Decision on the investigation and prosecution of genocide, crimes against humanity and war crimes. Already in 2003, thus only a year after the entering into force of the Rome Statute of the ICC, the EU Council underlined the "need to set up or designate specialist units within the competent law enforcement authorities with particular responsibility for investigating and, as appropriate, prosecuting" genocide, crimes against humanity and war crimes.[1] At that time, different French judges were already seized with complaints related to the genocide of Tutsis in Rwanda in 1994[2] and the proceedings were not advancing satisfactorily.

In 2004, a year after the EU Decision, the European Court of Human Rights ('ECtHR') in the case *Mutimura v. France*, found that France had violated Article 6(1) of the European Convention on Human Rights. The case related to a civil party criminal complaint lodged in France against a Rwandan clergyman for his alleged participation in acts of genocide against Tutsis in his parish in Rwanda in 1994, which resulted in a judicial investigation for genocide and torture. At the time of the complaint in 1995, the clergyman was residing in France and serving as a curate.[3]

---

[1] Council of the European Union, Council Decision 2003/335/JHA of 8 May 2003 on the investigation and prosecution of genocide, crimes against humanity and war crimes, Article 4 (https://www.legal-tools.org/doc/e41495).

[2] See Section 21.3. below on the triggering jurisdiction mechanism.

[3] On 2 October 2015, the investigative judges of the Specialist Unit issued an order dismissing the proceedings for lack of sufficient evidence.

Before the ECtHR, the plaintiff submitted that the case was pending for almost four years before the investigative judge, hence the criminal complaint as well as the civil party application ("constitution de partie civile") had not been examined within a reasonable time. The French government, on the other hand, submitted that the case was legally and factually complex. In particular, it underlined that the facts were grave and of extreme scale as the person was suspected of acts of genocide committed in a foreign country. It added that the investigation of crimes committed abroad by a foreigner against foreigners, in a country such as Rwanda with which France had no agreement of mutual legal assistance, was by nature complex, in particular as regards gathering evidence, all the more since the suspect denied the imputed conduct. Furthermore, this was the first case linked to the Tutsi genocide in Rwanda in 1994 that the French courts had to deal with. Altogether, the French government submitted that this explained and justified the length of the proceedings. On 8 June 2004, having examined the circumstances of each imputed cause of delay, the ECtHR found that indeed the length of the proceedings did not satisfy the reasonable time requirement of Article 6(1) of the Convention and thus held unanimously that there was a violation.

Despite the EU Decision and the ECtHR's ruling, it took nonetheless some time for France to decide to set up the Specialised Unit. In fact, its creation was essentially prompted by the increasing number of cases related to the Tutsi genocide in Rwanda in 1994 brought before French courts.

It was only in 2011 that Law No. 2011-1862 of 13 December 2011 (which entered into force on 1 January 2012) offered a window opportunity to include a provision leading to the creation of the Specialised Unit. According to the parliamentary debates, it became necessary to better concentrate the investigative resources, as (i) such investigations require deep knowledge of the specific historical and cultural contexts in which the crimes were committed, and (ii) the crimes were mostly committed abroad so they require complex and lengthy investigation steps.

As a result, the Parliament found 'indispensable' that a team of magistrates in this new Specialised Unit be exclusively dedicated to such cases, as well as that investigators exclusively assigned to war crimes, crimes against humanity and genocide investigations be at the disposal of these magistrates.[4] So the Specialised Unit was intended to provide a better balance between efficiency and compliance with important procedural principles.

21.2.2. Composition and Activities of the Specialised Unit

The Specialised Unit is part of the *Tribunal de grande instance de Paris* (first instance). Article 628-1 of the Criminal Code of Procedure states that, for the prosecution, investigation and judgement of genocide, crimes against humanity and war crimes, the Specialised Unit does not exercise exclusive jurisdiction but concurrent jurisdiction with other tribunals in France.

Unlike the ICC, as soon as the Specialised Unit was created, and even before its staff and all judges were recruited, it already inherited dozens of cases,[5] mainly related to the genocide of Tutsis in Rwanda. In fact, case files were already opened, in some cases since a decade, and were spread all over the country at different prosecutors and judges' offices. Thus, it turned vital to define work-processes and priorities as quickly as possible, and to draw on each other's background.

As of October 2018, the Specialised Unit (prosecutors and investigative judges) was dealing with situations involving 15 different geographical areas, including crimes allegedly committed in Syria, Iraq, Libya, Chad, the Democratic Republic of Congo, Uganda, Afghanistan, Rwanda or Chechenia.[6] This represents in total more than 105 files including 43 preliminary investigations. Most cases related to Syria, Central African Republic and Rwanda. In fact, in less than three years, the Spe-

---

[4] M. Yves Détraigne, *Rapport fait au nom de la commission des lois constitutionnelles, de législation, du suffrage universel, du Règlement et d'administration générale sur le projet de loi relatif à la répartition des contentieux et à l'allègement de certaines procédures juridictionnelles*, March 2011, Senate report no. 394, p. 27. See also, M. Marcel Bonnot, *Rapport fait au nom de la commission des lois constitutionnelles, de la législation et de l'administration générale de la république sur le projet de loi (n° 3373), adopté par le Sénat après engagement de la procédure accélérée, relatif à la répartition des contentieux et à l'allègement de certaines procédures juridictionnelles*, June 2011, National Assembly report no. 3604, pp. 30, 108–14.

[5] Already, before the creation of the Unit, the Directorate for Criminal Matters and Pardons invited the local public prosecutors to ask the *Cour de cassation* (Supreme Court), for the proper administration of justice, to transfer their cases related to the genocide in Rwanda to the *Tribunal de Grande instance* of Paris (First Instance Tribunal).

[6] See Interview with Prosecutor Aurélia Devos, Ministère de la Justice, "Crimes contre l'humanité : bilan du pôle du TGI de Paris", 17 October 2018 (available on its web site).

cialised Unit experienced a 400 per cent growth in the number of ongoing investigations (including preliminary investigations as well as "informations judiciaires")[7].

In light of these figures, it was vital to keep a regular rhythm in the advancement of the investigations and not to overlook any case. The first investigative judges created a 'dashboard', regularly updated, allowing easy checks of workflow status. They held regular meetings with the investigators during which challenges and issues could be raised and priorities set or revised if need be. Moreover, to avoid anticipated further delays, the investigative judges identified as early as possible the main interlocutors to address requests for co-operation as their execution is not guaranteed in a timely manner.

Undoubtedly, the creation of the Specialised Unit and its visibility among NGOs led to a further increase in the number of complaints filed and investigations opened. An additional explanation to the rapid exponential growth is a 2015 asylum law reform.[8] According to the new law, the Director of the Office for the Protection of Refugees and Stateless Persons shall transmit to the Public Prosecutor all relevant information linked to a decision motivated by an exclusion clause,[9] as defined in Article 1F of the 1951 Refugee Convention.[10]

The figures mentioned above and the variety of situations under scrutiny by the Specialised Unit are, again, a clear indication of the need to create specialised units within the judiciary in order to centralise the information and specialise the investigative efforts.

---

[7] French criminal law provides for two phases of a criminal investigation: preliminary investigations ("enquêtes préliminaires") led by prosecutors and judicial investigations ("informations judiciaires") handled by investigative judges.

[8] France, LOI n° 2015-925 du 29 juillet 2015 relative à la réforme du droit d'asile [Law No. 2015-925 of 29 July 2015 on the asylum law reform], 29 July 2015.

[9] *Ibid.*, Article 10.

[10] Convention Relating to the Status of Refugees, 28 July 1951 (https://www.legal-tools.org/doc/9b8e7a). The exclusion clause allows for the rejection of an asylum or stateless protection request when there are 'serious reasons' for considering that the applicant: (a) has committed a crime against peace, a war crime, or a crime against humanity, as defined in the international instruments drawn up to make provision in respect of such crimes; (b) has committed a serious non-political crime outside the country of refuge prior to his admission to that country as a refugee; or (c) has been found guilty of acts contrary to the purposes and principles of the United Nations.

The Specialised Unit is not the only unit of its kind in France. Indeed, to address complex cases like health scandals, organised crime or financial crime, France has opted to create special task forces of magistrates and specialised assistants. As a result, in these units, prosecutors and investigative judges are assisted by doctors, veterinarians, accountants or customs-officers. The War Crimes Unit responds to the same scheme and includes specialised assistants as well. According to Article 628-9 of the French Criminal Code of Procedure, the specialised assistants participate in the proceedings under the supervision of the Unit's magistrates and may submit to the judges analytical and summary documents which can be filed into the record of the case.

According to Decree No. 2012-682 of 7 May 2012, the assistants must be specialised in criminal law and criminal procedure, public international law, international humanitarian law, history or ethnology.

To complete this scheme, at the time of the creation of the Specialised Unit, a team of a dozen *gendarmes*-investigators carried out the investigations under the supervision of prosecutors and the investigative judges. As the number of cases grew and the *gendarmes* were sometimes involved in contributing to the investigation of domestic criminal cases, it was necessary to also create a dedicated investigation team. On 5 November 2013, by decree, the government established a new centralised investigative unit, the Central office for combatting Crimes against humanity, genocides and war crimes.[11] It became operational in early 2014 and includes both *gendarmes* and police officers. Depending of the needs, it may also rely on external consultants.

---

[11] The Central Office's mandate includes core international crimes as well as hate crimes. It thus also implies investigating into domestic cases which do not have an international dimension.

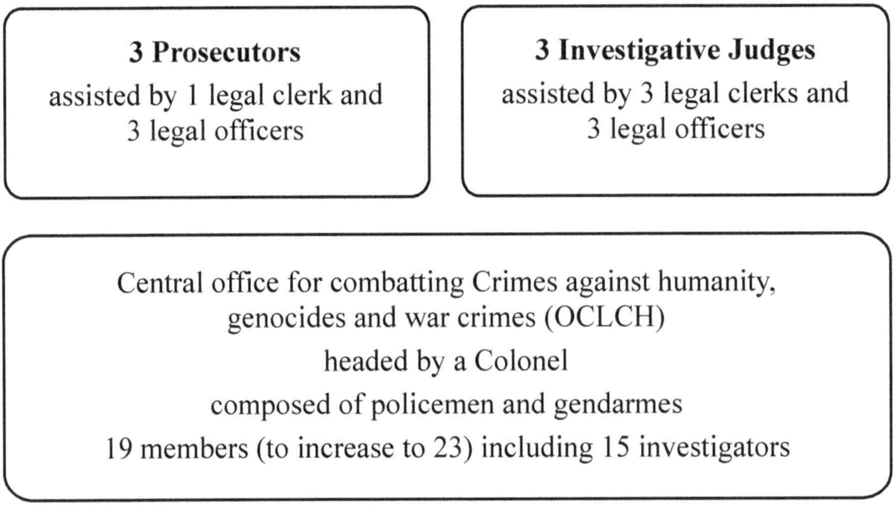

3 Prosecutors	3 Investigative Judges
assisted by 1 legal clerk and 3 legal officers	assisted by 3 legal clerks and 3 legal officers

Central office for combatting Crimes against humanity, genocides and war crimes (OCLCH)

headed by a Colonel

composed of policemen and gendarmes

19 members (to increase to 23) including 15 investigators

Figure 1: Actual scheme.

21.3. The Triggering of Jurisdiction: A Self-Imposed Filter for Selection of Cases

Bearing in mind the figures, it is obviously important to rightly calibrate the scope of the case. However, unlike the ICC where a case is selected out of a situation under investigation, the jurisdiction triggering mechanism in France serves as a filter in the selection of cases (Section 21.3.1.), which has an impact on investigation techniques (Section 21.3.2.).

21.3.1. *À la Carte* Triggering Mechanism of Universal Jurisdiction

France has recognised crimes against humanity and genocide as crimes in the Criminal Code in 1994 and war crimes in 2010. French tribunals can thus exercise territorial jurisdiction over these crimes, and extraterritorial jurisdiction in cases of:

- active personality jurisdiction (French nationality of the suspect);
- passive personality jurisdiction (French nationality of the victim);
- France's national interests, harm to the forum State's own national interests; and
- universal jurisdiction, for acts that are not linked to the French nationality of the suspect or of the victim or to harm to France's national interests.

The material scope of universal jurisdiction is restrictively enumerated in Articles 689-1 to 689-13 of the Criminal Code of Procedure, which limits it to offenses included in treaties ratified by France. More specifically, in relation to the prosecution and investigation of core international crimes, France has deliberately widened its jurisdiction.

Chronologically, it first provided for universal jurisdiction for torture under the meaning of Article 1 of the Convention against Torture and other Cruel, Inhuman or Degrading Treatment of 10 December 1984.[12] A presence-link is required to trigger the exercise of universal jurisdiction, which must be demonstrated[13] at the initiation of the proceedings (complaint or the prosecutor's initial indictment, the so-called "réquisitoire introductive")[14].

Next, following the conflicts in Rwanda and in the former Yugoslavia, France adapted its legislation to fulfil its obligations of full co-operation, as set forth in Resolutions 827 and 955 by the United Nations Security Council establishing respectively the International Criminal Tribunal for the former Yugoslavia and the International Criminal Tribunal for Rwanda.[15] While in these resolutions, as in many international treaties,

---

[12] Convention against Torture and Other Cruel, Inhuman or Degrading Treatment or Punishment, 10 December 1984 (https://www.legal-tools.org/doc/713f11). The same mechanism is provided for in relation to the International Convention for the Protection of All Persons from Enforced Disappearance, 20 December 2006 (https://www.legal-tools.org/doc/0d0674) (Article 689-13 of the French Code de procédure pénale ('Criminal Code of Procedure'), 23 December 1958 (https://www.legal-tools.org/doc/388101)).

[13] Besides hypothesis of clear effective presence of the suspect on French territory (residence, arrest in France), indicia suggesting the presence of the suspect on French territory can also be sufficient to initiate criminal proceedings (presumed presence), such as driving licence issued in France, paying regular visits to a relative healing at the hospital (France, Cour de cassation, Criminal Chamber, 10 January 2007, 04-87.245).

[14] It does not matter if the suspect has thereafter left French territory. See France, Cour de cassation, Criminal Chamber, 23 October 2002, 02-85.379.

[15] See, France, Loi n° 95-1 du 2 janvier 1995 portant adaptation de la législation française aux dispositions de la résolution 827 du Conseil de sécurité des Nations Unies instituant un tribunal international en vue de juger les personnes présumées responsables de violations graves du droit international humanitaire commises sur le territoire de l'ex-Yougoslavie depuis 1991 [Law No. 95-1 of 2 January 1995 adapting French legislation to Resolution 827 of the United Nations Security Council establishing the International Criminal Tribunal for the former Yugoslavia], 2 January 1995, and France, Loi n° 96-432 du 22 mai 1996 portant adaptation de la législation française aux dispositions de la résolution 955 du Conseil de sécurité des Nations unies instituant un tribunal international en vue de juger les personnes présumées responsables d'actes de génocide ou d'autres violations graves du

---

universal jurisdiction is not required as such, what is imposed is the obligation to prosecute or extradite (*aut dedere, aut judicare*). France decided that it may also exercise criminal jurisdiction when the suspect of crimes provided for in these resolutions and treaties is found ("se trouve") on French territory at the initiation of the proceedings.

On 9 August 2010, Law No. 2010-930 adapted the French Criminal Code to the Statute of the ICC.[16] It inserted Article 689-11 in the Code of Criminal Procedure allowing for the exercise of universal jurisdiction for crimes falling within the jurisdiction of the ICC. It should be noted that the legislator was, however, ever-careful and subjected the exercise of this universal jurisdiction to four locks:[17]

i)   *Residency*: the legislator opted for a more restrictive nexus than mere presence of the suspect on the territory;

ii) *Subsidiarity*: the public prosecutor can only proceed with a prosecution if no international or national tribunal has requested the surrender or extradition of the suspect;[18]

iii) *Double criminality*: with the exception of genocide, in relation to crimes against humanity and war crimes and offenses, the acts must also be punishable under the legislation of the State where they have been committed or that State or the State of nationality of the suspect is a State Party to the Rome Statute of the ICC;

iv) *Prosecutor's discretion*: proceedings can only be initiated at the request of the public prosecutor.

---

droit international humanitaire commis en 1994 sur le territoire du Rwanda et, s'agissant des citoyens rwandais, sur le territoire d'Etats voisins [Law No. 96-432 of 22 May 1996 adapting French legislation to Resolution 955 of the United Nations Security Council establishing the International Criminal Tribunal for Rwanda], 22 May 1996.

[16] France, LOI n° 2010-930 du 9 août 2010 portant adaptation du droit pénal à l'institution de la Cour pénale internationale, 9 August 2010. This law notably criminalises direct and public incitement to commit genocide; amends the definition of crimes against humanity to conform to the definition of Article 7 of the Rome Statute; inserts Title IV*bis* in the Criminal Code wherein, for the first time in the Criminal Code, acts that may constitute war crimes or offenses are listed.

[17] As modified by LOI n° 2019-222 du 23 mars 2019 de programmation 2018-2022 et de réforme pour la justice, 23 March 2019.

[18] Article 689-11 of the Criminal Code of Procedure specifies that the public prosecutor has to ensure that there are no proceedings initiated by the ICC; that no other international tribunal, competent to prosecute the person, has asked for his/her surrender; and that no State has requested his or her extradition, see above note 12.

By introducing this last requirement, the French legislator explicitly restricted the civil party complaint mechanism to trigger the prosecution of core international crimes pursuant to universal jurisdiction. This however, has a practical drawback, because victims are thus encouraged to file a civil party complaint for an alleged crime of torture within the meaning of the Convention against Torture, whilst the act might amount as well to a crime against humanity, in order to avoid the cumulative demanding four locks discussed above.

It follows that the presence or residence of the person suspected of having committed core international crimes is the key element in triggering the exercise of universal jurisdiction. This has important consequences for the manner investigations and prosecutions are led, and for the role of the judiciary in the pre-trial process.

21.3.2. *In Personam* Investigations: A Self-Imposed Calibration

It should be recalled that the ICC's case law distinguishes between 'situations', which are generally defined by temporal, territorial and personal parameters, and 'cases' comprising specific incidents arising from a given situation.[19] A case starts when the Prosecutor identifies one or more crimes within the jurisdiction of the Court that might have been committed, and one or more suspects allegedly responsible for their commission. This triggers challenges in the defining criterion for the selection of cases and in delineating their scope. In this regard, the situation experienced by the French Specialised Unit is different.

Triggered by the presence or residence of the suspect on French territory, the jurisdiction of the Specialised Unit is determined by the person (*in personam*) rather than the facts denounced (*in rem*), as it is the case for the prosecution of most crimes.

This extraordinary *in personam* triggering of jurisdiction acts as a first filter. The public prosecutor is thus not called upon to make choices on the selection of areas, regions, incidents, groups of persons, militia or individuals to be the subject of his or her investigation and prosecution. The investigation does not start from a crime scene to undercover the per-

---

[19] See, for instance, ICC, Situation in the Democratic Republic of the Congo, Pre-Trial Chamber, Decision on the applications for participation in the proceedings of VPRS 1, VPRS 2, VPRS 3, VPRS 5 and VPRS 6, 17 January 2006, ICC-01/04-101-tEN-Corr, para. 65 (https://www.legal-tools.org/doc/2fe2fc).

sons or chain of command allegedly responsible for its commission, the case is in fact *ab initio* delineated by the identity of the alleged suspect, because of his presence or residence on French territory. This has several procedural consequences. First, the prosecutor's initial indictment must be filed against a named suspect. As a result, only an additional indictment ("réquisitoire supplétif") can authorise the extension of the case to other potential suspects. Requesting it to extend to other individuals may impact on the length of the investigations.

It further creates an uncomfortable situation where investigative steps are undertaken to establish whether the alleged perpetrator is present or residing on French territory before addressing the facts; then the facts are being characterised before establishing the jurisdiction of the Unit. Under this scheme, one can wonder how confirmation bias can be mitigated during the investigations? Accordingly, it is the role of investigative judges to ensure that investigations not only gather incriminating evidence but also exculpatory material or elements that can mitigate the suspect's guilt, contributing to the quality of investigations. In addition, the fact that pre-trial investigations are increasingly incorporating adversarial mechanisms, allowing an early involvement of the Defence, contributes to mitigating the risks of potential confirmation bias. To that end as well, the judges have developed new working methods.

21.4. Reducing the Gap from Geographical Distance to Factual Proximity

The cases inherited by the Unit had already been under investigation for several years, if not a decade. By shortage of available time, the previous investigative judges[20] sometimes lacked focus in the case-delineation. This resulted in wasteful over-collection of potential evidence, including a number of books and reports. Facing such fact-rich cases, the Specialised Unit's investigative judges were aware of the importance of first understanding the context (Section 21.4.2.) as well as their own limits in this respect (21.4.1.).

---

[20] Before the creation of the Specialised Unit, the cases related to core international crimes were dealt by prosecutors and investigative judges who simultaneously had to deal with tens of ordinary crimes cases, often involving detained persons.

21.4.1. Acceptance of the Limitations of Lawyers

Prior to the creation of the Specialised Unit, France was not ignorant of
mass crimes. It had already experienced within its own judicial system the
investigation and prosecution of crimes against humanity and war crimes,
having held important and highly publicised trials related to World War II
and issuing landmark decisions.[21] This experience is still very vivid in
French memory and often used as historic and legal reference.

However, previous experiences may be reassuring but misleading as
well. As a matter of fact, a perfect analogy between the experience of the
World War II trials and the Specialised Unit's current activities is not possible. Following World War II, France tried French citizens whose acts
had been committed on French soil and constituted acts of complicity in
crimes against humanity. In this scenario, judges knew the context in
which the crimes had been committed, shared historical and sociological
background with the victims, witnesses and suspects, and were often contemporary to the facts under judicial scrutiny. Today, on the other hand,
the Specialised Unit is mostly investigating and prosecuting crimes under
universal jurisdiction for acts committed abroad, by and against non-
French nationals.

While international criminal law has developed legal concepts
aimed at capturing the particularities of mass crimes, one should accept
that these legal concepts may not be adequate to efficiently fulfil the mission to punish the most serious conduct and efficiently prevent recurrence.
Significantly, in some cases it may even be that exclusively relying on
such concepts could lead to miscarriage of justice.

From experience, judges and international lawyers assisting them in
adjudicating the facts, are aware of and the first to be frustrated by shortage of access to background and contextual information, which are essential to better understand and capture the facts and acts committed in a
country, culture and social setting that is foreign and unknown to them.

Judgements issued by different international(ised) tribunals, such as
the International Criminal Tribunal for Rwanda, the Special Court for
Sierra Leone ('SCSL') as well as the ICC, have been criticised for focus-

---

[21] For the prosecution of a French national for involvement in the deportation of Jews, see,
for example, France, Cour de cassation, Klaus Barbie, Cass crim, 3 June 1998; and France,
Cour de cassation, Maurice Papon, Cass crim, 23 January 1997.

ing too much on legal discussions, but missing to understand and deal with the facts in accordance with the cultural settings of the affected communities, on behalf of which they have assumed the responsibility of doing justice.[22]

For instance, the social scientist Tim Kelsall, presenting his experience as an expert at the SCSL, deplored the lack of contextual familiarity of the SCSL, which prevented an accurate understanding of the chain of command. He criticised the SCSL for relying on its own understanding of a hierarchical organisation, including the concept of command responsibility, instead of understanding the specific context of the creation of these groups in that situation, which developed as a militarisation of a social network.[23]

At the same time, difficulties at the ICC – where the judges have deplored the lack of evidence or issues of witness credibility – may well be seen as a consequence of a factual misrepresentation, which has weakened cases presented by the Prosecutor. It is submitted, without entertaining or entering into the long-discussed controversy between 'judicial' and 'historic' truth, that the dedication of most legal staff both at the ICC and the Specialised Unit is towards the accomplishment of the purpose of these institutions, which is not to develop legal theory or focus on the impact that their work may have on the historical account of the events. Rather, most of the staff work towards fulfilling their mandate as set out in the preamble of the ICC Statute: contribute to putting an end to impunity for the perpetrators of these crimes and thus to their prevention.

Julien Seroussi, a social scientist who both worked at the ICC and at the Specialised Unit, calls for an acknowledgment of the "inevitable limitations to knowledge" and highlights the importance of "folk sociological

---

[22] See, for instance, Tim Kelsall, *Culture under Cross-Examination: International Justice and the Special Court for Sierra Leone*, Cambridge University Press, 2009, and Nancy Combs, *Fact-Finding Without Facts: The Uncertain Evidentiary Foundations of International Criminal Convictions*, Cambridge University Press, 2010. See also Christian De Vos, Sara Kendall and Carsten Stahn (eds.), *Contested Justice: The Politics and Practice of the International Criminal Court Interventions*, Cambridge University Press, 2015.

[23] Kelsall, 2009, see above note 22.

theories" ('FSTs'), also called the "sociological consciousness" of international lawyers in the establishment of facts.[24]

He submits that FSTs "developed within the space that separates the legal from the historical truth", and are aimed at ensuring "the advancement of the law while respecting the facts to the maximum extent possible".[25] Building on his own experience at the ICC, Julien Seroussi emphasises that FSTs help "international lawyers [...] to overcome their ignorance". While his analysis focused on the work of international criminal tribunals, it seems also applicable to cases when judges adjudicate facts based on universal jurisdiction, as the challenges largely echo those of international criminal tribunals.

Stating that FST's "may give plausible, cheap and useful explanations to international judges who face empirical limitations to fact-finding", the author nonetheless calls for extreme caution as

> the discrepancy between what may appear plausible to international judges before the beginning of a trial and what they discover after an examination of complex factual elements in war-torn societies can have debilitating effects on their initial theories – as well as immediate effects on the legal procedure and validity of their original reasoning.[26]

As a result, better and stronger FSTs should be used when adjudicating facts before international criminal tribunals as well as national tribunals, as weak FSTs may indeed have devastating consequences in the long-term. In this regard, the judges of the Specialised Unit have developed factual toolkits.

21.4.2. Developing Tools for the Work on Facts

Geographical distance is common to the work of the ICC and that of the Specialised Unit. This geographical distance notably leads to evidence gathering difficulties, but one should not be misled or hide behind it, blindly accepting one of its insidious consequences: 'factual distance'.

---

[24] Julien Seroussi, "How Do International Lawyers Handle Facts? The Role of Folk Sociological Theories at the International Criminal Court", in *The British Journal of Sociology*, 2018, vol. 69, no. 4, pp. 962–83.

[25] *Ibid.*, p. 966.

[26] *Ibid.*, p. 967.

This challenge is being addressed at the ICC by the Prosecutor's Office. It comprises an Investigative Analysis Section ('IAS') within the Investigations Division ('ID') wherein analysts are expected to produce:

> accurate and source analytical products in response to the requirements of the Integrated Teams, including reports of different kinds (on incidents, crime pattern, profiles, groups and networks etc.), relational charts, timelines and GIS (Geographic Information Systems), in compliance with IAS standards, and taking into account the social context of the crimes and background of the alleged perpetrators.[27]

The link between the quality of the products of the IAS and successful investigations and prosecutions is obvious. Unfortunately, though, their analysis is not shared with the ICC Pre-trial Chambers and remains undisclosed, as investigation notes and internal memoranda fall within the scope of Rule 81(1) of the Rules of Procedure and Evidence, not subject to disclosure. Instead of deep analytical information, in several cases Chambers received only a few pages, usually at the beginning of the Prosecutor's Document Containing the Charges ('DCC'), providing succinct contextual background (geographical features, main historical events, and so on). In the recent DCC in the Uganda situation, such sections seem to have disappeared.[28]

Arguably, judges are not to be blamed for their lack of knowledge and misconceptions about the situation and the underlying facts if they are not given the tools to address them. This is of particular importance as, *in fine*, it is they who decide whether to commit a person to trial or on his or her guilt. Therefore, the development of tools to better capture the essence of the context where the alleged crimes have been committed has to be encouraged at the earliest stages, and as soon as the judiciary gets involved. Such tools should be accessible to everyone, allowing the parties to contribute to the judiciary's role in establishing the truth within the contradictory setting of judicial proceedings.

This idea was implemented at the Specialised Unit as soon as it entered into motion. In that setting, prosecutors, and pre-trial and trial judges

---

[27] Excerpt of a job description published on the ICC web site.

[28] ICC, Situation in Uganda, *The Prosecutor v. Dominic Ongwen*, Document Containing the Charges, 22 December 2015, ICC-02/04-01/15-375-AnxA-Red (https://www.legal-tools.org/doc/1fd4ed).

decided to be pro-active and not wait for the story-telling, if any, to be submitted by any of the parties. They were of the view that, to adjudicate the facts independently and impartially, they also needed to have an independent understanding of the context in which such facts occurred at the earliest stage possible. Of course, such knowledge was not only of benefit to judges and prosecutors, as it was shared with the parties and participants to the proceedings.

To that end, the investigative judges in charge of maintaining the case record quickly decided to create the so-called "Cote Context". It consists in a separate folder within the electronic case file, which is available to the parties, and wherein information related to the 'context' is filed. For the purposes of this tool, the context is understood in its plain and ordinary meaning, that is, the "situation within which something exists or happens, and that can help explain it".[29] Accordingly, it includes relevant books, international reports or decisions, as well as NGOs reports. The tool serves two objectives: (1) to physically isolate information not directly related to the crimes and the individual criminal liability of a person, in order not to overload, blur or distract the analysis of the heart of the case; and (2) to give key elements of understanding of the facts under examination.

Furthermore, the first investigative judges also decided to include in their team a social scientist as one of their specialist assistants, who became an essential member of the team. As a member of the Unit, he was subjected to professional secrecy and the duty to keep the investigations confidential. His access to the files puts him in a better position to identify, in co-ordination with the judges, the relevant elements that need to be contextualised. As a result, the social scientist helped identifying other relevant social and political scientists, ethnologists and anthropologists who were heard by the investigative judges, helping to build bridges between legal and social issues. Their testimonies were thereafter filed in the record of the case, as part of the "Cote Context". For instance, considering that the Specialised Unit has several cases related to the genocide of Tutsis in Rwanda, the investigations collected a series of documents, indictments, testimonies and decisions emanating from the Gacaca courts. In order to grasp fully the functioning of these popular tribunals, an historian who thoroughly worked on that subject was heard during the pre-trial

---

[29] Cambridge Dictionary.

stage of the investigations and later called to testify before the trial chamber.

These types of interviews have proven precious. They have helped to ensure that the judge assesses the evidence and the involvement of a person in the commission of alleged crimes with a better understanding of the context in which the facts occurred, be it political, sociological or anthropological. This mitigates the risk of misrepresentations of the facts that can turn critical at trial, as experienced during the Katanga and Ngudjolo trial at the ICC. It also proved important in efficiently approaching and hearing witnesses and victims.

Of course, as much as the ICC has been criticised for focusing on legal issues more than on the facts, the Specialised Unit should be careful not to overwhelm itself by focusing too much on the facts to the detriment of the law. This is a constant concern that the investigative judges of the Unit have to keep in mind, regularly tracking factual and legal fragilities of the cases and addressing procedural and substantive issues as they arise.

21.5. Fragility Trackers and Solvers of Procedural Issues

During the pre-trial investigation, the judges proceed with a regular interim assessment of the public prosecutor's charging choices (Section 21.5.1.) and shall ensure that any procedural issue be addressed as soon as possible (Section 21.5.2.).

21.5.1. Regular Interim Assessments

As mentioned above, following the 2010 Law, the French Public Prosecutor enjoys autonomy in presenting charges throughout the pre-trial stage of the proceedings. Nonetheless, the investigative judges of the Specialised Unit shall exercise scrutiny over the Public Prosecutor's choices. Such judicial oversight is exercised at different stages of the pre-trial investigations, with positive effects on the quality of the prosecution and the efficient preparation of a focused trial.

When the initial indictment ("réquisitoire introductive") as well as any additional indictments ("réquisitoire supplétif") are filed, the pre-trial judge can assess the legal characterisation of the facts as decided by the public prosecutor. Such intermediate assessment proceeds first when hearing the suspect at the first appearance ("interrogatoire de première comparution"), at the end of which the pre-trial judge may place him under judicial examination ("mis en examen"). As provided by Article 80-1 of the

Code of Criminal Procedure, under penalty of nullity, the investigating judge may place under judicial examination only those persons against whom there are strong and concordant indicia making it probable that they may have participated in the commission of the offences investigated as a perpetrator or an accomplice. This assessment is made after an adversarial debate, where the pre-trial judge shall hear or give the opportunity to be heard to the person concerned, before placing him or her under judicial examination.[30] Throughout the pre-trial investigations, the person concerned may request, every six months, the end of his judicial examination. The pre-trial judge can only decide upon such request after hearing the observations of the public prosecutor. If the pre-trial judge decides to maintain the judicial examination of the person concerned, he or she shall issue a reasoned decision detailing the strong and concordant indicia against the person.[31] Accordingly, at each of these stages, the investigative judges exercise judicial control over the evidence so far gathered and the legal characterisation presented by the public prosecutor.[32]

In order to facilitate this regular interim assessment and to keep an overview of the content of these factually rich cases, the investigative judges' team has intuitively organised its evolving cases in a chart. Yet, it has not adopted the In-depth-Analysis Chart as used in some cases at the ICC whereby pieces of evidence are linked to constitutive elements of the crimes.[33]

---

[30] Article 80-1 of the Criminal Code of Procedure, see above note 12.

[31] *Ibid.*, Article 80-1-1.

[32] For the sake of clarity, it is underlined that according to French criminal procedure, the person suspected can, at this stage of the procedure, appeal the investigative judge order. His appeal is examined by the Investigative Chamber of the Court of Appeal which will decide whether or not the person shall be placed under the status of person under judicial examination or, if there exist indicia making plausible that he participated in the crime, under the status of assisted witness (Article 113-2 of the Criminal Code of Procedure, see above note 12). The difference between the two statuses is thus the evidentiary threshold.

[33] ICC, Situation in the Republic of Kenya, *The Prosecutor v. Francis Kirimi Muthaura, Uhuru Muigai Kenyatta and Mohammed Hussein Ali*, Pre-Trial Chamber, Decision Setting the Regime for Evidence Disclosure and Other related matters, 6 April 2011, ICC-01/09-02/11-48, para. 22 (https://www.legal-tools.org/doc/12b91f):

> this analysis should be presented in the form of a summary table which shows the relevance of the evidence presented in relation to the constituent elements of the crimes with which the person is charged. It should enable the Chamber to verify that for each constituent element of any crime with which the person is charged, including their contextual elements, as well as for each constituent element of the mode of participation in

The investigative judges' team of the Specialised Unit customised the chart to the Unit's specific needs, organising it per items of facts, linking them with the available evidence, and identifying issues of credibility and possible contradictions. The chart also indicates whether the evidence collected in relation to a fact is considered incriminating or potentially exculpatory and, for each item of fact, a short analysis is made, assessing the evidence so far gathered, including the alleged involvement of the suspect.

The chart and intermediate analysis are live and constantly updated throughout the investigation. This dynamic document helps the coherence of the investigations and acts as a guide to keep the investigations focused.

The chart is an internal working document, which is only accessible to the investigative judges and their team on a shared platform.[34] This enables immediate and constant dissemination of the information and its update. The chart is not shared with the Trial Chamber either.

21.5.2. Procedural Issues

Over the years, it has become apparent that once the indictments are filed by the public prosecutor, the investigative judges must promptly identify any potential issues or hesitations in relation to their jurisdiction. This is essential because pre-trial investigations can last for several years. In fact, even investigations that are conducted with a regular rhythm, taking advantage of the different field missions in the year and the smooth cooperation of the authorities, may last up to five years. It thus engages limited staff and financial resources for a long period of time. Accordingly, any doubt as to the jurisdiction of the Specialised Unit must be raised as early as possible, even *proprio motu* by the investigative judges as allowed by law, for such investment not to go to waste. They need to shoul-

---

the offence with which he or she is charged, there are one or more corresponding pieces of evidence, either incriminating or exculpatory, which the Chamber must assess in light of the criteria set under Article 61(7) of the Statute.

See also, ICC, Situation in the Central African Republic, *The Prosecutor v. Jean-Pierre Bemba*, Pre-Trial Chamber, Decision on the Evidence Disclosure System and Setting a Timetable for Disclosure between the Parties, 31 July 2008, ICC-01/05-01/08-55, paras. 66–70 (https://www.legal-tools.org/doc/15c802). For more information, see Chapter 20 above by Eleni Chaitidou.

[34] As mentioned earlier, according to Article 628-9 of the French Criminal Code of Procedure the specialist assistant (legal officer or analyst) may submit to the judges analytical and summary documents which may remain internal working documents, see above note 12.

der their duty to solve key legal issues, such as possible *ne bis in idem,* lack of jurisdiction or statute of limitation challenges, in order to ensure that investigations and prosecutions are on the right track. They should not wait for the issue to be raised by the parties as this may occur once the proceedings are well advanced, sometimes at the closure of the investigations. It should be noted that under Article 181 of the French Code of Criminal Procedure, when the indictment becomes final, all procedural errors, if any, are solved. In other words, when the file is communicated to the trial chamber, prosecutors and lawyers are not allowed to raise the nullity of any investigation steps. They are thus encouraged to raise them before the investigative judge, but it is sometimes if not often raised late during the pre-trial investigations.[35]

This is a typical situation where, overwhelmed by the facts of a specific case as well as the number of other pending cases, critical legal issues may remain unidentified for a moment.

21.6. Interface between Pre-Trial Investigations and the Trial: The Judiciary's Role in Defining the Parameters of the Trial

To enhance case preparation for trial, a thorough pre-trial brief is prepared by the investigative judges (Section 21.6.1.) and serve as a tool for the presiding judge of the trial together with the complete case record of the investigation (Section 21.6.2.).

21.6.1. Pre-Trial Brief in the Form of a Judicial Indictment Order

As developed above, in the exercise of its extraordinary universal jurisdiction, the scope of the investigative judge's jurisdiction has been largely vested on the public prosecutor's shoulders. This is a departure from the French Civil Law tradition, explained by the peculiarity of this extraterritorial exercise of jurisdiction.

However, despite this shift, the judiciary remains vested with the power and duty to write the pre-trial brief known in France as the "ordon-

---

[35] Only the investigative chambers can rescind an act of investigation during the pre-trial phase, such as phone surveillance, requisition, seizure, geolocation, hearing of person suspected or of witnesses, expert assessment, civil party application, DNA or print test, and so on. Once the investigation phase concludes, it is assumed that all the investigation acts are valid, in the interest of the expeditiousness of the proceedings.

nance de mise en accusation" ('indictment order').[36] This indictment order is of critical importance, as it will form the basis of the trial.[37] Its drafting process provides checks and balances as in the Specialised Unit at least two judges, sometimes three, are co-seized of each case.

In this judicial process committing a suspect to trial, two documents are essential: (1) the public prosecutor's final request ("réquisitoire définitif"), and (2) the judge's indictment order. The first is a document filed by the public prosecutor before the pre-trial judge. It has to be motivated, and the parties may submit observations. As to the second document, Article 176 of the Code of Criminal Procedure vests in the per-trial judge the task of judicially scrutinising the charges. The judiciary thus examines whether there exists sufficient evidence of a crime committed by the person under judicial examination. In the affirmative, the pre-trial judge orders the suspect's indictment before the *Cour d'assises* (Criminal Trial Chamber).

The indictment order shall contain, under penalty of nullity, (i) the accused's identity and (ii) a statement of the facts and their legal characterisation. It shall also (iii) state precisely the grounds for whether or not there is sufficient evidence against the person; (iv) be rendered in light of the public prosecutor's request and the parties' observations; and (v) specify the incriminating and exculpatory pieces of evidence.[38] It is therefore, like at the ICC, the judicial indictment order that constitutes the reference document before the Criminal Trial Chamber containing the charges against the suspect and delimitating the factual scope of the trial.

Moving now from the text to actual practise, when dealing with factually rich cases there is the important challenge of presenting the confirmed charges in a clear and exhaustive manner. To that end, the confirmed facts and their legal characterisation shall be clearly identifiable in the order to prepare the trial properly.

---

[36] At the end of the pre-trial investigation of the case, the investigative judge may, *inter alia*, issue (i) a discharge order pursuant to Article 177 of the Criminal Code of Procedure ("ordonnance de non lieu") or (ii) an indictment order pursuant to Article 181 ("ordonnance de mise en accusation"). It can also order, in the course of the investigation, a partial discharge pursuant to Article 182 ("ordonnance de non lieu partiel").

[37] Article 231 of the Criminal Code of Procedure, see above note 12.

[38] See *ibid.*, Articles 176 and 184.

In addition, the indictment order shall cast light on the strong and weak aspects of the criminal case, pointing out the incriminating and exculpatory material contained in the case record and forming the basis of the investigative judges' reasoning to dismiss the case or commit the suspect to trial. The indictment order is subjected to checks and balance before the commencement of the trial, as it may be appealed by the parties before the Investigative Chamber.

A clearly-reasoned decision by the investigative judges allows to better manage the trial, avoiding the waste of time litigating uncontested, non-controversial or secondary matters. It helps the parties to focus their respective presentation of evidence on issues of actual dispute, increasing the prospects of a trial focused on the real issues at stake, identifying and narrowing down the number of issues to be discussed at trial and, as a result, reducing the length of the trial. For instance, before the Specialised Unit in the joint case against *M. Ngenzi and M. Barahiera*, about 200 witnesses were heard during the pre-trial investigations. In light of the impartial judicial assessment of the witnesses as developed in the indictment order, 92 witnesses out of 200 were finally called to testify during the first instance trial.[39]

Judicial involvement during pre-trial investigations does not, however, prevent the debate on the merits of the case. If the indictment order clearly delineates the factual scope of the case, the presiding judge of the trial is not prevented from asking the jury to analyse questions that have appeared necessary as a result of the trial hearings, even if they do not directly result from the indictment order. In such a scenario, the presiding judge will read these additional questions before the closing statements of the victims' representative, the public prosecutor, and the defence counsel.[40] At the same time, the first genocide trials held in France in relation to the genocide of Tutsis in Rwanda have demonstrated that the orality of the trial proceedings might cast further light on elements, facts or witnesses than the pre-trial stage allowed. Re-characterisation of facts may therefore still happen at trial.

---

[39] These figures include 33 witnesses called to testify by the Defence, 50 by the Prosecution, and 1 by a victim.

[40] France, Cour de cassation, Criminal Chamber, 8 February 2017, 16-81.962.

21.6.2. The Preparation and Transmission of a Case Record as a Tool for a Prepared and Focused Trials

In the French system, as well within the context of the Specialised Unit's work, the indictment order that establishes the parameters of the trial is transferred together with the full case record.

The record of the case contains the document initiating the proceedings (the prosecutor's initial request or the civil party complaint) and all documents and incriminating and exonerating evidence gathered during the pre-trial investigations, including witness statements, documentary evidence, requests by parties, and orders by the investigative judges.

The dynamic constitution of the case record offers the advantage of ensuring that incriminating as well as exculpatory material are made available to the parties, especially to the Defence of a person under judicial examination, as soon as such material becomes available, well in advance of the start of the trial. The defence counsel can thus consult the case record and request a copy thereof,[41] subject to confidentiality.[42] Aware of the consequences of potential breaches to confidentiality, and in order to maintain the principle of access to the file,[43] the witness and victim protection scheme has been enhanced to adapt the legislation to the specificity of such cases.[44]

The defence's access to the case record increases its capacity of preparation before the commencement of the trial. This can only be welcomed in light of the complexity of the cases and the length of the proceedings. Actually, compared to ordinary crimes, defence teams in core international crimes cases in France often find themselves in a difficult situation to prepare efficiently. France has incorporated adversarial elements into its criminal procedure, notably during the pre-trial investigations. In light of the different challenges presented by the investigation of

---

[41] Articles 113-3, 114 and 114-1 of the Criminal Code of Procedure, see above note 12.

[42] Pre-trial investigations are confidential.

[43] Access to the case record is given to the Defence Counsel of the person under judicial examination as well as to the Defence Counsel of the 'assisted witness' ("témoin assisté"). The assisted witness includes any person mentioned by name in an initial or subsequent prosecutor's submission and who is not under judicial examination. See Articles 113 and following of the Criminal Code of Procedure.

[44] France, LOI n° 2016-731 du 3 juin 2016 renforçant la lutte contre le crime organisé, le terrorisme et leur financement, et améliorant l'efficacité et les garanties de la procédure pénale, 3 June 2016.

---

core crimes pursuant to universal jurisdiction, the early defence involvement can be instrumental in identifying and gathering exculpatory evidence as well as in challenging requests by victims or the prosecutor and judicial orders.[45] This runs up against the cost and time available to do so. Indeed, investigations can last for several years, a trial a few months, and the case-record may be voluminous. Without financial means, a dynamic involvement of the defence throughout the proceedings can be very challenging, as only a few lawyers will have the means and resources to focus their efforts on one case only, to the detriment of the proper functioning of their practice.

The legal aid scheme does not provide for any additional means for core international crimes cases, such as expenses for travel costs for site visits. Yet, in most cases, the suspects benefit from the legal aid scheme. It is important to reflect on the need to improve this situation. The Bar Association's involvement may also be one of the venues to further explore, for instance by setting up a contingency fund to assist counsel taking core international crimes cases under the legal aid scheme. This might help to level the playing field.

Finally, the case record is chronologically organised and therefore a useful tool in understanding the lines of investigation followed. If the pre-trial stage was conducted efficiently, the case record will provide the trial chamber with a complete account, clearly distinguishing between contextual aspects and the heart of the criminal case brought against the accused. This will allow even outsiders to understand the line of reasoning in the investigation and the subsequent decision committing the person to trial. The indictment order will thus serve as an efficient tool for the presiding judge of the trial chamber[46] to organise the court sessions, the calling of evidence, and the questioning of witnesses. Held before a jury, only the presiding judge will have access to the case record. Parts of the indictment

---

[45] French Law does not expressly foresee the possibility for the defence to undertake independent investigations. While no provision prevents the defence from doing so, it is nonetheless not generally accepted in practise as it is assumed that the defence should rely on the prosecutors and investigative judges' investigations, duty bound to look for incriminating and exculpatory evidence.

[46] The trial is held before a trial chamber composed of the presiding judge, two assessor-judges, and a trial jury composed of six jurors when the court of assizes rules at first instance and nine jurors when it rules on appeal (Article 296 of the Criminal Code of Procedure, see above note 12).

order will be read at the beginning of the trial and this is how members of the jury will get knowledge of its content.[47] When presenting, concisely, the imputed facts as contained in the indictment order, the presiding judge will also indicate the incriminating and exculpatory elements therein mentioned, as well as the legal characterisation of the imputed facts.[48]

Finally, following feedback from the trial judges who sat on the first trial on the Tutsi genocide in Rwanda, it will become regular practise to call to testify at trial the Director of Investigation of the case. He or she will explain how the investigation proceeded, any challenges encountered, and how they overcame them. This testimony will be given after the hearings dedicated to context, and will help navigate from the broad context to the heart of the case.

21.7. Conclusion

With the creation of the Specialised Unit, the French Parliament wanted to concentrate better the investigation's means and to encourage a deeper knowledge of the specific historical and cultural contexts of the commission of alleged crimes. After seven years of existence, it is fair to submit that the Specialised Unit is on the right track. The investigative judges' efforts were instrumental in raising and addressing issues such as jurisdiction or *ne bis in idem* challenges as early as possible during the pre-trial investigations. The efforts deployed in ensuring a good knowledge of the context in which the crimes were committed enhanced the quality of the investigations and turned useful for a good preparation of the trial. At the same time, by ensuring the existence of an organised and complete case-record, accessible to the parties, investigative judges ensured that they were trial-ready and that the lines of investigation will be understood, yet without preventing the debate at trial.

However, there is still some room for improvement. In light of the increased number of cases under investigation, it appears essential to give the staffing and material means to the Specialised Unit so that it can take additional cases while not affecting the expeditiousness of the proceedings. In addition, it is equally important to find further support for the Defence.

---

[47] In addition to the presiding judge, during the trial, the two assessor-judges as well as members of the jury may question the accused or witnesses (*ibid.*, Article 311).

[48] *Ibid.*, Article 327.

At the same time, it is fundamental that the Specialised Unit is not
seen as a unit specialised only on physically storing folders of core international crimes cases. It should rather develop an expertise over the years,
which will turn beneficial for the efficiency and expeditiousness of the
proceedings. Judges should be encouraged to stay within the Specialised
Unit long enough to complete the investigations without adverse effect on
their career advancement. Mobility of judges and their teams should be as
limited as possible in order to preserve institutional memory and expertise.
This is even more important because the trial judges to date are not specialised in international criminal law, and trials are held before popular
juries.

Finally, one should recall the words of Judge Jorda, former President of the ICTY and presiding judge of Pre-trial Chamber I of the ICC:
"a trial should never last more than 18 months total".[49] I agree with the
importance of keeping the trial within a reasonable time-frame. Too
lengthy trials cease to be understandable or followed by the victims and,
more broadly, the affected communities. On the other hand, while acknowledging the difficulties in gathering a jury for several months, I believe that, for certain cases, a trial held in less than two months is neither
efficient nor effective. In fact, leaving little time to the jury to rest and
reflect does not afford the jurors the necessary time to grasp the peculiari-
ties of the context in which the crimes were committed and the cultural
and sociological dimensions of victims and perpetrators. They also need
to have sufficient time to properly hear the evidence and understand the
tremendous amount of information contained in the case file. Perhaps, to
address the challenges of keeping a jury for months, such trials should be
held before professional judges, without a jury, as is currently done in
terrorism-related cases.

---

[49]   See interview with Judge Claude Jorda: Franck Petit, "A trial should never last more than
18 months total", in *International Justice Tribune*, 19 December 2005 (available on its web
site).

22

The Importance of Successful Co-operation Between Police Investigators and the Prosecution Service to Secure Efficient and Fair Court Proceedings and Verdicts

Tor-Geir Myhrer[*]

22.1. Introduction

The level of co-operation between investigators and the prosecutor during investigations varies considerably in different countries and legal systems. Even in Norway, where the first level of the prosecution service is an integrated part of the police, often located in the same building as the investigators, the co-operation is frequently limited to questions where it is mandatory. This chapter presents some reflections on how co-operation between investigator and prosecutor during a criminal investigation can contribute to improved quality of cases, and thus also more efficient and fair court proceedings. The chapter is written from a Norwegian perspective: a civil law country, with mainly statute legislation. But as the experiences from England and Wales mentioned below indicate, the problems discussed here are probably of a universal character, independent of the legal system.

'Quality' is defined as "an activity, which is conducted according to certain agreed standards".[1] Criminal investigation is in Norway regulated

---

[*] **Tor-Geir Myhrer** is a Professor at the Norwegian Police University College (Oslo). He holds Dr. Juris and Cand. Jur. degrees, and has been one of Norway's most prominent prosecutors and served as an expert adviser on criminal law reform since 1988. He has published extensively on criminal procedure, police law (in particular use of police force), data protection, immigration law and legal ethics.

[1] Tor-Geir Myhrer, *Kvalitet i etterforskningen: Særlig om påtaleansvarliges rolle og betydning* (*Quality in the Investigation: The Role and Responsibilities of the Police Prosecutor*), Politihøgskolen (Norwegian Police University College), Oslo, 2015, p. 9.

by the Criminal Procedure Act. The Act in force today is from 1981.[2] It continued the main features from the previous act which dates back to 1890. Even though criminal investigation has been carried out under more or less the same organisational and procedural regulations for nearly 130 years, it is only the last ten years that the following question has been asked: which are the standards (essential elements) that define the quality of an investigation?[3]

The number of sub-standards or essential elements may differ, but there is no need to discuss all aspects in this chapter. We shall instead concentrate on the elements where the co-operation between the investigator and the prosecutor is essential for the efficiency and successful outcome of the proceedings. But first we should address one pivotal question.

22.2. What Is the Purpose of an Investigation?

Why does good co-operation with the prosecutor influence the quality of the investigation? Why cannot the investigation simply be the first leg in a relay-run independently of the next, and the result of the investigation be the baton one delivers to the prosecutor who is running the next leg? The reason is that an investigation is not simply a fact-finding mission, but a mission with a clearly defined purpose: to obtain the necessary information for deciding whether an indictment should be sought; and, if so, to serve as a preparation for the trial, both on deciding the question of guilt and the sentencing.[4]

Accordingly, the questions concerning the facts come first, then deciding whether the facts amount to a criminal offence. In many investigations the answers to these questions are clear from the start, but this is not always the case. When the starting point of the investigation is an accident, a fire or simply a dead body found in the woods, these questions are the first that need answers. Sometimes it is clear from the start that a crime has taken place, but not what kind: is it a homicide, manslaughter or has someone with an obligation to care left a sick or injured person to die? More often the main question in an investigation is to establish whether

---

[2] See Lov 1981-05-22 nr 25: Lov om rettergangsmåten i straffesaker (https://legal-tools.org/doc/76cf36). You find an English translation (The Criminal Procedure Act) in the ICC Legal Tools Database under persistent URL https://legal-tools.org/doc/612318.

[3] *Ibid.*

[4] Norway, The Criminal Procedure Act, 22 May 1981, Section 226, see note 2 above.

somebody is responsible for what has happened and who they are. On this the prosecutor normally has little to offer. When the suspects have been identified, the most difficult part of an investigation may be to find proof that they have acted with the requisite guilt. As discussed below, co-operation between investigator and prosecutor can be useful at this point.

In fiction and popular literature, this is where the investigation stops. In real life, it has to continue, collecting information for purpose of the sentencing. Even in cases where the accused do not confess, the evidence on the issue of guilt is often so overwhelming that the only, or at least the most interesting question, is the extent of the punishment. The evidence regarding the facts of the matter, for the suspect's degree of participation in the crime and his or her guilt, will always give important information relevant to the sentencing. But it is normally not sufficient. If it is a crime with a victim, information about the victim and possible connection with the offender is important, as well as how the crime has affected and possibly will affect the victim or persons close to her or him. The prosecutor (and the court) also need information about issues such as the accused's personal situation at the time of the crime and at present, and how a sentence will affect family and plans for the future. Information about previous investigations and convictions might also be important if they show a pattern relevant to the present case.

It follows from this that it is essential for the quality and efficiency of the investigation to have good knowledge about what information the prosecutor needs for deciding on the indictment, and what is important for the presentation and argumentation in court. The best way an investigator can obtain this, is to co-operate with the prosecutor during the investigation.

I find the views in Chapter 10 of Lord Justice Auld's *Review of the Criminal Courts of England and Wales* (2002) illustrating. The Crown Prosecution Service ('CPS') in England and Wales was established 1986. Until then, the police had carried out both the investigation and decided on the indictment. It is easy to understand that the CPS from the start deemed it important to demonstrate that they were an independent authority, separate from the police. But as a consequence, the police could run the investigation as an independent and isolated first leg in the law enforcement relay, and subsequently hand it over to the CPS. In the book *Effective Prosecution*, the authors summarised the findings of Lord Justice Auld in this way:

> He identified that one of the biggest problems was the large number of cases incorrectly often overcharged by the police. This were subsequently altered and discontinued at court after CPS review of the charge at a very late stage. He pointed out that this led to late guilty pleas and ineffective trials, with consequential disappointment for victims and costs to the CJS [Criminal Justice System].[5]

As a remedy for this Auld prescribed:

> The prosecutor should take control of cases at the charge or, where appropriate, pre-charge, stage, fix on the right charges from the start and keep to them, assume a more direct role than at present on disclosure and develop a more proactive role in shaping the case for trial, communicating appropriately and promptly with all concerned.[6]

The quotation above use the phrase "prosecutor should take control of cases". I think it is more appropriate to talk of a 'co-operation'. The investigators have their skills and competence, and the prosecutors have theirs. What is needed is that they co-operate and work together in partnership. It is important, however, to emphasise that such co-operation is not a universal remedy that will fix all shortcomings in an investigation. Moreover, it may not even be needed in all circumstances. Other important factors are the skills, competence and experience of the investigators and prosecutors, the complexity of the facts of the case, and the challenges linked to the criminal law or the criminal procedure law that have to be employed.

Sometimes investigators tend to see co-operation with prosecutors as a mark of distrust in their competence, or even as a defeat. From my experience as a public prosecutor for more than 20 years, this is hard to understand. How can it be a defeat to seek or receive information important for safeguarding that the investigation fulfils its purpose?

In the following, I discuss some situations or areas where co-operation between investigators and prosecutors is particularly important in order to secure proper quality of the investigation.

---

[5] Yvonne Moreno OBE and Paul Hughes, *Effective Prosecution: Working in Partnership with the CPS*, Oxford University Press, Oxford, 2008, p. 28.

[6] Robin Auld, *Review of the criminal courts of England and Wales*, Stationery Office, London, 2001, p. 399.

22.3. What Should be Investigated?

This question comprises two different situations: the *first* is a question concerning the amount of investigative resources. The number of crimes will in most countries and cultures probably always exceed the capacity. This brings up the question: on what kind of crimes should the investigative resources be employed and how 'minor' can they be? This is usually regulated in general instructions, although not always successfully, and will not be discussed her.

The topic of this chapter is the *second* situation, namely how comprehensive and all-embracing should an investigation be in cases that comprise a) many different types of crimes of varied degrees of seriousness, or b) a large number of the same crime? I will discuss situation a), which is often seen in different forms of economic crimes, but can also occur in more organised forms of traditional crimes. This situation may be relatively common in war crimes justice.

The investigation of such cases will normally benefit from some tailoring from the start, and this should be done in co-operation with the prosecutor. The main reasons for tailoring the case are that pursuing and investigating every possible crime is both very time consuming, and may also complicate the presentation in court. An essential quality standard is that investigations are carried out within reasonable time. And bringing all possible crimes to court will often not influence sentencing.[7] The extra time and resources will accordingly not be proportionate. The main consideration when tailoring the case must be that the resources are used on the most serious crimes. The maximum sentence for the crime is an indication of its seriousness, but how the court will in fact rule is also important. Normally, court experience will place the prosecutor in a better position to decide which crime(s) can be left out without having a negative impact on the final sentencing in the case as a whole.

The relative seriousness of the crime is, however, not the only consideration. Offences that are rather minor compared with other conduct in the case, could be important because they show a certain motivation or a general attitude. Even if they do not influence the sentencing, they might

---

[7] If the legal system in question measures a penalty for each crime and then accumulates all in one final sentence, this may not be correct. However, whether the defendant's total is reduced from, for example, 80 to 75 years of imprisonment is normally of limited importance.

be important for the prosecutor to have them investigated and included in the indictment. They can be used to argue for guilt for the main crimes. If the accused in a trial for economic crimes in his or her defence puts that the missing report, application or approval is an oversight or omission caused by work pressure, it might be difficult to be believed if the same form of behaviour is shown under other circumstances (such as not filling out a missing tax declaration when returning from holiday where valuable goods have been purchased abroad).

22.4. What Are the Crucial Elements of the Crime?

Basically, the prosecutor must prove that a certain event or a certain state of affairs, which is forbidden by the criminal law, has been caused by the accused person's conduct, and that this conduct was accompanied by a prescribed state of mind or mental state.[8]

How straightforward or complicated this is, depends on how complex the facts of the case are, and the character and number of the elements that have to be proven under the relevant criminal law. It follows from this that the need for co-operation between investigator and prosecutor will vary considerably with the competence and experience of the investigators, and with how complicated the facts and the law related to the case are. In this chapter I will limit myself to pointing out some areas where the quality of the investigation and the ambition to have efficient and fair court proceedings will benefit from an early co-operation between investigator and prosecutor.

Clearly, the more complex the legal and factual variables are, the greater is the need and benefits of a co-operation between investigators and prosecutor. Although both are crimes against property, there is a big difference between investigating a simple theft and a complicated suspicion of money laundering. Under Norwegian criminal law the latter is defined as:

> by converting or transferring assets or by other means conceals or obscures where the proceeds of a criminal act he/she has personally committed are located or originate from, who

---

[8]   David Ormerod and Karl Laird, *Smith and Hogan's Criminal Law*, Oxford University Press, Oxford, chap. 4.

controls them, their movements or rights associated with
them.[9]

It is frequently not the elements in the definition of the crime in
themselves that create the problem. Rather, do all – or, if not, which – of
the elements need to be covered by the accused's guilty mind (*mens rea*)?
When this has been clarified, the question of how to prove the guilty mind
arises. Unless the accused gives a full confession covering the mental
element, the guilty *mind* needs to be proven by elements from the *physical*
world. This is an area where a close co-operation between prosecutor and
investigator is especially important. In a fruitful co-operation the prosecutor will clearly indicate what information is required, and the investigator
present what is possible to retrieve with the resources and investigative
methods available.

Another area where proving criminal liability can be challenging,
and where co-operation may be beneficial for the quality of the investigation, is when other forms of participation than commission need to be
considered. Attempt and participation as an accomplice are the most
common examples. It can be particularly complicated when the two are
combined. Such complications can occur even if the investigation against
the person who is responsible for the commission of the crime, is fairly
straightforward. Let me use an example based on a real incident.

In a city there are two competing gangs. In an enclosed gateway to
the building where gang A has their residence, a member of gang B is
caught on CCTV as he leaves a stolen car loaded with explosives. He immediately runs from the gateway, and the car explodes within seconds and
destroys the building, causing a fire, and two members of gang A are
killed.

Since it can be proven that the chauffeur of the car knew that the
two members of gang A slept in the building, he is charged with murder.
But what about the peripheral member of gang B who stole the car the
previous night? What line of inquiry must be carried out and evidence
gathered to decide and eventually prove her guilt for murder, manslaughter, criminal damage or simply just car theft? When it is clear what kind of
evidence is needed, the investigator must indicate what is possible to obtain with the resources and investigative methods available. Depending on

---

[9]   Norway, Lov 2005-05-20 nr. 28: Lov om straff (Straffeloven) (The Penal Code), 20 May
2005, Section 337 (https://legal-tools.org/doc/aa2cee).

the answer to these questions, the investigator and the prosecutor might have to return to the question discussed above: how broad should the investigation be? How important is it for evidential or tactical reasons to clarify whether the car thief can also be charged with murder? Co-operation at this point will prevent that time and manpower are spent on a line of investigation with slim chances of success, or that the investigation is prolonged in a disproportionate way.

If the driver is stopped and apprehended by the police in the immediate vicinity because of failure to stop at a red light, and subsequently is discovered to be carrying explosives, the situation gets even more complex. Can he be charged with attempted murder? And what about the car thief? If her intent to murder cannot be proven, 'attempted manslaughter' is no alternative.

This example demonstrates another area where co-operation between investigator and prosecutor is beneficial for efficient court proceedings. Most prosecutors have experienced that even indictments based on the most thorough investigation fall apart during court hearings. The reason is often that witnesses change their statements, do not any more remember, do not show up, or use their right. For example, a close relative selects not to give a statement in court in front of the defendant.

If consulted during an investigation an experienced prosecutor will often ask: what if 'this or that' happens in court? By this question the prosecutor may bring the investigators to consider whether the same offence can *also* be viewed as a different crime, with other or fewer elements to satisfy. When the offence is also investigated from this point of view, the prosecutor may be in a position to change the indictment (if allowed)[10] to this alternative crime during the court hearing, if the evidence for the principal crimes does not hold up.

Co-operation with the prosecutor could also make the criminal activity be investigated as another offence. When a person is found in possession of large quantities of stolen goods, it is sometimes difficult to prove that he or she has stolen the goods and thus guilty of aggravated theft. To avoid this fragile point in the chain of evidence, it is often useful

---

[10] As long as it is the same offence, the prosecutor will in many countries be allowed to make such amendments in the indictment, see, for example, the Norwegian Criminal Procedure Act, Section 38, in note 2 above.

with a subsidiary line of investigation, and subsequently a subsidiary charge for receiving proceeds from crime.

22.5. Argumentation for the Sentencing

The degree of co-operation needed between investigator and prosecutor related to sentencing depends on the roles of the police investigator and the prosecutor in the criminal system in question. It is obviously more challenging to argue for a penalty if the system – like in Norway or at the International Criminal Court – requires that the police investigators and the prosecutor conduct their function objectively.[11] The investigation shall clarify both the evidence against the suspect and that in his or her favour. If, on the other hand, the identification and presentation of mitigating circumstances is primarily a task for the defence, then the prosecutor's argumentation for the sentencing is easier. However, it is often wise to investigate possible mitigating facts.

The most decisive circumstances and facts will normally be presented to the court as part of the evidence for the accused's guilt. This will be the situation for aggravating circumstances such as:

- the crime was committed by means or methods which were particularly dangerous, in a particularly reckless manner, or with a considerable potential for harm;
- a more serious outcome could easily have been the consequence;
- committed by multiple persons acting together, or as a planned or organised enterprise; or
- was committed in the course of public service or was perpetrated by violating a special trust.

Other aggravating circumstances are not linked to the elements of the crime. Such facts will often need special attention during the investigation if the prosecutor shall be able to present sufficient evidence as a basis for the sentencing argumentation. This will normally be necessary for an argument that the offence was perpetrated by exploiting or misguiding young persons, persons in a very difficult life situation, who are mentally disabled or in a dependent relationship with the offender. This will also be the case for evidence showing that the offence has affected persons who are defenceless or particularly vulnerable. The same applies if

---

[11] *Ibid.*, Sections 55 and 226.

the crime was motivated by the victims' religion or life stance, skin colour, national or ethnic origin, sexual orientation, disability or other circumstances relating to groups with a particular need for protection.

Co-operation between investigator and prosecutor on these topics should normally provide quality control on two points: first, and most importantly, the relevant topic is actually investigated; secondly, clarification of the level of proof needed. Elements decisive for ascertaining guilt need to be proven beyond reasonable doubt. For aggravating circumstances, the requirements are less, but it can often be unclear what the demands are.

If it is required that the investigation and prosecution are carried out objectively, an insufficient investigation of mitigating circumstances will create an impression of a biased inquiry. That could damage the convincing effect of the evidence of guilt. Many mitigating circumstances are, as the aggravating, closely linked to the elements of the crime or evidence of a guilty mind. However, such circumstances may in relation to the argumentation on sentencing still need special attention during the investigation. This applies to circumstances such as:

- the offender has prevented, reversed or limited the harm or loss of welfare caused by the offence, or sought to do so;

- the offence was to a significant degree occasioned by the circumstances of the aggrieved party; or

- the offender had, at the time of the act, reduced capacity to realistically assess his or her relationship to the outside world due to mental illness, mental disability, impairment of consciousness[12] or a state of severe mental agitation.

Other mitigating circumstances need a more dedicated line of inquiry during the investigation. Let me mention two. First, the ultimate purpose of criminal law is to prevent new crimes. It is therefore important for the sentencing if there is valid proof that the defendant has changed her or his lifestyle in a manner that improves the prospect of rehabilitation. A sentence, which do not ruin this prospect, is often preferable.

The second circumstance is when the offender himself/herself has been severely affected by the offence, or the criminal sanction will impose

---

[12] Not caused by self-induced intoxication.

a heavy burden due to advanced age, illness or other circumstances. I will illustrate this with an example based on a real incident.

A man in his early twenties appeared in court charged with reckless driving. He had probably fallen asleep at the wheel causing an accident that killed his girlfriend who was a passenger in his car. There was no question about the defendant's guilt, nor was it exceptional that he was still on crutches some ten months after the accident. What entirely influenced the atmosphere during the trial was the evidence given that whenever someone visited the grave of the young woman, they could see marks from his crutches in the soft soil or in the snow. This information was not in the case file and unknown to the prosecutor, but was known to some of the investigators.

Such mitigating circumstances will often influence the line of argumentation and possibly also the request for a sentence. For the prosecutor to adjust this during trial could be challenging and also influence the efficiency of court proceedings. If the information on how the offence has affected the defendant is simply ignored by the prosecutor, it might create an impression of a not entirely fair (and objective) criminal prosecution. A good co-operation with the investigators, who are normally closer to both the defendant and the victims than the prosecutor, could prevent or reduce the potential for such occurrence as well as unexpected information during trial.

22.6. Procedural Requirements and Safeguards

In the previous sections of this chapter, the dominant idea has been that co-operation between investigators and prosecutor will improve the quality of the investigation in its function as preparation for the trial. When it comes to procedural requirements and safeguards, the involvement from the prosecutor gets a stronger element of control. The reason is that evidence obtained in a way that contradict with procedural requirements, may not be allowed as evidence in court. It is equally important that this is frequently not just a question of efficiency, in the sense that the trial has to be postponed; very often the error cannot be remedied, causing the chain of evidence to fall apart.

There are numerous procedural questions for which guidance from and involvement by the prosecutor might be beneficial for the quality of the investigation. The discussion in this chapter will be limited to four rather broad questions.

First, in the countries where there is a legal obligation that the investigation shall be conducted objectively, this requirement must have the prosecutor's constant attention when co-operating with the investigator. Very often this is primarily a question of ensuring that all probable hypotheses or explanations of what has happened have been followed up as a line of investigation. Even where the principle of objectivity is not a legal requirement, such control over the investigation might be advantageous for tactical reasons. If the defence launches an alternative explanation during the trial, it is always better to be able to respond that this hypothesis has already been checked and rejected, than simply to argue that the hypothesis is not probable. Experienced investigators will often have formed and followed up all probable lines of inquiry. If that is not the case, the role of the prosecutor will be to use her or his role to make the investigation as robust as possible.

The second area for the prosecutor's guidance or quality control is evidence obtained by use of coercive measures like search and seizure, covert CCTV, or surveillance of telephones or other (electronic) forms of communication. Use of such coercive measures is normally restricted to special types of crimes or offences with a high maximum sentencing frame. A certain level of suspicion is often required. It differs from country to country whether such coercive measures can be decided by the investigators themselves, superior officers, the prosecutor, or by the court. Nevertheless, it is important that the prosecutor makes sure that this part of the investigation is, or has been, conducted in conformity with the legal requirements. But what if it is not? If the flawed evidence cannot be allowed in court, it must be considered whether it may be remedied, or if it will in fact taint other evidence and ultimately lead to the case being dropped. Illegally obtained CCTV images might be used to identify witnesses who could be interviewed about their observations at the same time and place, but illegal search and seizure is more difficult to deal with. Ultimately, the result might be that the case has to be dropped.

A third area for quality control is the privilege against self-incrimination – the right to silence. Case law from treaty-based human rights courts or committees has raised the importance of this in the last decades. In many countries the formal interviewing is taped or videoed. The challenge is therefore often the questioning of the suspect that takes place in the stressful and shocking situation shortly after or during an arrest. A statement given at this early stage might influence which options the suspect feels that he or her will have during the following interrogation secured on tape and video and with a lawyer present. The prosecutor has to ascertain personally that the suspect initially was given proper notice of the consequences of being questioned; that this may form a basis for criminal prosecution. It is important that this can be proven if contested by the defence.

'Proper notice of the consequences' is of course impossible if the suspect is not even aware that he is dealing with the police. This directs me to the fourth area of quality control: provocative and/or undercover police investigative work. Books can be (and have been) written about the procedural challenges connected with such investigative methods. Here I restrict myself to underline what may be the most important checkpoint for the prosecutor: where the nature of the offence so warrants, there is nothing that precludes that the investigation be based on evidence obtained through an undercover police operation. However, the use of undercover agents must be restricted: the police may act undercover but not incite. This is often a question of who has taken the first initiative *vis-à-vis* the crime; the undercover agent or the suspect? And, importantly, can this be proven?

22.7. Final Remarks

When reading this chapter, as well as when I give lectures on the subject, I find the observations rather obvious and commonplace, perhaps even banal. So why is not such co-operation between prosecutor and investigators standard routine? Even in Norway – where, as mentioned above, the first level of the prosecution service is an integrated part of the police – the co-operation during the investigation is often limited to questions where it is mandatory, primarily decisions on use of some coercive measures. From the prosecutor's perspective, there are typically three conditions for a more extensive co-operation to happen: a) time and opportunity, b) competence and will-power, and c) acceptance and demand.

In Norway, time and opportunity seem to be the most important factor. The prosecutors are either in court or occupied with preparing a case for imminent trial. There is limited time to involve themselves in ongoing investigations. Even though the case files are digital and accessible from both the investigators' and prosecutor's computer, the 'opportunity' is still very much linked to geographical proximity. To pop into the office or have a brief discussion when meeting in the corridor or in the canteen seems easier and more likely to happen than accessing the file on the computer, asking a question, or writing a comment.

Competence and will-power are probably closely inter-linked. If the prosecutor perceives that her or his competence is inferior to that of the investigators, the will may also be lacking to become involved in the investigation. More complicated types of crimes are, however, normally handled by experienced prosecutors, and the willingness might in these circumstances be influenced by the third factor: acceptance and demand.

Whether investigators accept and value involvement of the prosecutor in the investigation varies over time and from country to country. When I started as a prosecutor some 40 years ago, co-operation with the prosecutor was not accepted as organisational routine, but was more based on the personal relation between investigator and prosecutor. Today it is different.[13] I have no wide or profound knowledge about the climate of such co-operation in other countries, but if the attitude presented in fiction is of any value, the prosecutor will frequently be seen as an opponent rather than a partner. One important way to change this is for the prosecutor to accentuate the value of the investigators' competence and experience, but at the same time, to demonstrate how their own competence create an added value to the quality of the investigation.

---

[13] Myhrer, 2015, pp. 120–23, see above note 1.

23

Some Reflections on the Role of Military Justice Mechanisms in the International Criminal Justice System

Gilad Noam[*]

23.1. Introduction

In February 2019, I had the honour of participating in the 'Quality Control in Criminal Investigation' conference in New Delhi. The conference offered various observations and insights, from practitioners and academics alike, from both domestic and international perspectives. Conference participants highlighted the importance of the investigation phase, which, when conducted with appropriate scrutiny, while adhering to rigorous professional standards, facilitates and improves the overall quality of criminal proceedings, in both the international and domestic spheres.

This chapter focuses on the domestic sphere. The importance of exploring national investigation systems stems from the fact that the primary obligation to investigate violations of international law rests upon States, as reflected, *inter alia*, in the principle of complementarity.

States may adopt various models to fulfil their obligations to investigate alleged criminal conduct during armed conflicts, in particular allegations of violations of the law of armed conflict ('LOAC'), which may amount to war crimes. States can generally rely either on a military justice system, or on a civilian one, though this is not a strict dichotomy. States that rely mainly on a military justice system may nonetheless incorporate certain civilian elements into their system of examinations and investigations, and *vice versa*: States, the investigative system of which is rooted in

---

[*] Dr. **Gilad Noam**, Senior Director, International Justice Division, Ministry of Justice of the State of Israel, adjunct lecturer, Hebrew University Faculty of Law and College of Management School of Law. The chapter was written in my personal academic capacity, and does not necessarily reflect the positions of the State of Israel.

the civilian sector, may rely to some extent on investigative steps carried out by the military system.

Each approach has its pros and cons. Understanding the structure and the work of national investigation mechanisms can shed some light on, and offer a better understanding of, the unique challenges that arise in this context and the ways in which such challenges could be addressed, hence drawing some lessons for the benefit of the international criminal justice system as a whole.

In this regard, two main observations emerge from an examination of the relevant national practice. Firstly, the International Criminal Court's ('ICC') complementarity assessment should give due regard to the manner in which national investigation systems are commonly structured. In particular, the standards applied by the Court in determining the competence of national systems and the capability of national proceedings to deal with alleged LOAC violations, must take into account the common practice in that State, as well as States' practice more generally as evidence of the contents of the obligation to investigate LOAC violations.[1] Secondly, international investigations can draw on the experience of national investigation systems, and refine their capabilities for addressing the challenges associated with investigations of alleged violations of LOAC accordingly.

This chapter will resort to the work of the Public Commission to Examine the Maritime Incident of 31 May 2010 (Turkel Commission), which was established by the Government of Israel.[2] In addition to examining the maritime incident itself, the Commission was further requested to examine "whether the mechanism for examining and investigating

---

[1]   See, Article 21(1) of the Rome Statute with regard to applicable law in the ICC, which provides, *inter alia*, that the Court shall apply, where appropriate "the principles and rules of international law, including the established principles of the international law of armed conflict". Rome Statute of the International Criminal Court, 17 July 1998, Article 21(1) ('ICC Statute') (https://www.legal-tools.org/doc/7b9af9/).

[2]   Resolution No. 1796 of the 32nd Government of Israel, *Appointment of an Independent Public Commission, Chaired by Supreme Court Justice (ret.) Jacob Turkel, to Examine the Maritime Incident of 31 May 2010* (14 June 2010). The Commission was headed by retired Supreme Court Justice Jacob Turkel, and was composed of Israeli experts in the fields of law, diplomacy and security, as well as esteemed foreign observers such as Professor Tim McCormack, Brig. Gen, (Ret.) Kenneth Watkin, and Lord David Trimble. The Commission was also assisted in its work by a number of renowned international legal experts: Professor Claus Kreß, Professor Gabriella Blum and Professor Michael Schmitt.

complaints and claims raised in relation to violations of the laws of armed conflict, as conducted in Israel generally, [...] conforms with the obligations of the State of Israel under the rules of international law".[3] In February 2013 the Commission issued a comprehensive report which examined not only the international legal standards on this matter, but also conducted a comparative analysis of investigation mechanisms in six States, with a view to establishing what are considered "best practices" in this field.[4] The comparative analysis demonstrates the diverse practice in terms of the manner in which states have designed their investigations systems. The Commission's comparative survey, a unique and ground-breaking effort, will serve as the basis for this chapter's modest presentation of this issue. Naturally, this chapter will also base itself on Israeli practice, which was the focus of the Commission's work. The Israeli investigation system has also undergone progressive developments in recent years, based, *inter alia*, on the Commission's recommendations.

This chapter will proceed as follows. Section 23.2. reviews key characteristics of State investigation systems of alleged violations of LOAC. Section 23.3. presents the work of the Turkel Commission, and some of the changes that took place in Israeli investigation mechanisms in recent years. Lastly, Section 23.4. offers some thoughts on the possible implications of this survey on international investigations.

23.2. National Investigation Mechanisms: Structure and Standards

Law-abiding States employ a wide range of investigative mechanisms in order to fulfil their obligation to investigate violations of LOAC. In some

---

[3] *Ibid.*; Second Report, The Turkel Commission, Public Commission to Examine the Maritime Incident of 31 May 2010, Israel's Mechanisms for Examining and Investigating Complaints and Claims of Violations of the Laws of Armed Conflict According to International Law, February 2013, p. 33 ('Turkel Commission Report') (https://www.legal-tools.org/doc/e8437b/).

[4] *Ibid.*, p. 43:

Admittedly, each country has its own considerations when it chooses the appropriate tools and mechanisms for the purpose of fulfilling its obligations under international law. Such considerations relate to the circumstances of that country and its inhabitants, its government institutions, and its constitutional and legal system. Despite the differences in national approaches, the survey provides a wide range of mechanisms that countries may adopt in order to examine and investigate violations of international humanitarian law. It also assists in critically assessing the pros and cons of the different systems when considering the legal and operational needs and realities in Israel.

States, distinct military justice systems are those that regularly examine complaints regarding violations of LOAC. Although these systems differ – for example, with regard to the role commanders play in the process, or with regard to the division between legal advisors and those responsible for criminal enforcement – the main characteristic they all share is that all phases of the criminal process (including the preliminary phases of examinations and investigations) are conducted within the military. The United States, Canada, Australia, the United Kingdom, and Israel, are all examples of States that have such distinct military justice systems.[5] In contrast, other States, such as Germany and the Netherlands, chose to entrust civilian bodies with the task of investigating violations of LOAC by the military.[6] However, such States may nevertheless choose to employ an internal disciplinary system as part of their armed forces, or rely on the work of military police in prosecutions held before civilian courts.[7] States that have chosen to use distinct military justice systems, usually also incorporate into their work, to a varying degree, elements of their civilian system.[8]

The comparative analysis conducted by the Turkel Commission demonstrates the diverse practice in terms of the manner in which States have designed their investigation mechanisms. As noted, each possible model has its pros and cons. Civilian justice systems, for instance, due to their remoteness from the military, may be perceived as more objective. In contrast, distinct military justice systems may benefit from better legal expertise with regard to LOAC, and from greater operational knowledge in matters related to application of such laws. Given that the Israeli system is based on the military model, I will focus on some characteristics of military justice systems.

23.2.1. Military Investigations: The Applicable Standards

The Turkel Commission concluded that the existence and utilization of military justice systems is not only commonly accepted and in line with

---

[5] *Ibid.*, pp. 177–203.
[6] *Ibid.*, p. 155.
[7] *Ibid.*, p. 178.
[8] See, for example, in Australia, *ibid.*, p. 189.

international standards, but also that their use was "expressly envisaged" by international law.[9]

The Commission identified the standards for conducting effective investigations in situations in which LOAC (international humanitarian law, as referred to by the Commission), applies. The four general principles that the Commission identified as applying to such investigations are independence, impartiality, effectiveness and thoroughness, and promptness.[10] The Commission found that the principle of transparency, derived from international human rights law, is not explicitly recognized in LOAC, and that investigators and prosecutors are not obliged to comply with the rules of transparency that relate to specific victims' rights in such situations. The Commission found, however, that to the extent that the circumstances allow, it is desirable to promote aspects of transparency that relate to public scrutiny, through means such as the publication of guidelines, establishing reporting mechanisms, and making statistics and relevant information publicly available.[11]

The Commission acknowledged that adjustments must be made when applying the aforementioned principles to investigations of operational activities that take place in the context of an armed conflict. Such adjustments are required in view of "the surrounding circumstances as well as the underlying principles governing international humanitarian

---

[9] *Ibid.*, pp. 123–24. For example, Article 84 of the Third Geneva Convention refers to the military justice system of States Parties as the default system in which both the State's own military personnel as well as prisoners of war should be brought to trial. Convention (III) relative to the Treatment of Prisoners of War (IV), 12 August 1949, Article 84 (https://www.legal-tools.org/doc/365095/).

[10] Turkel Commission Report, see above note 3, p. 114. The Commission distinguished between two uses of the term 'effective'. The four principles are meant to ensure an 'effective investigation' in the broad sense, namely, that an investigation will be carried out when needed, with the aim of identifying those responsible and committing them to justice. In the narrow sense, the principle of "effectiveness and thoroughness" is concerned with the means of the investigation in order to discover the truth (*ibid.*, fn. 193); see also Noam Lubell, Jelena Pejić and Claire Simmons, *Guidelines on Investigating Violations of International Humanitarian Law: Law, Policy and Good Practice*, 2019, pp. 24–30.

[11] Turkel Commission Report, pp. 145–46, see above note 3; See also Lubell, Pejić and Simmons, p. 31, see above note 10.

law", and "the extent to which they apply is determined by the overall purpose of achieving an 'effective investigation'".[12]

As explained by the Turkel Commission, numerous challenges arise with respect to the practical ability to conduct an investigation effectively and thoroughly while hostilities are still taking place.[13] Nevertheless, the Commission found that even if during an armed conflict the thoroughness and effectiveness of an investigation, "may not translate to the same evidentiary standards as during peacetime, the standards must still be high enough to reach conclusive and reliable findings".[14] The evidence that is available "must be *thoroughly* secured and all feasible reporting must be completed".[15] Similarly, with respect to the standard of promptness, the Commission found that when applied to an armed conflict, "determining the reasonableness of a delay must be assessed according to the surrounding circumstances and according to the scope and scale of the violence".[16]

To be sure, investigations of operational activities in situations of armed conflict may encounter numerous practical challenges, even after the end of active hostilities. The conflict might have led to the destruction of evidence, witnesses may be difficult to locate, and opposing authorities may still be reluctant to co-operate and assist in such investigations. An effective inquiry is one which upholds the aforementioned principles, subject to the inevitable need for adjustments, which will depend on the particular set of circumstances.

23.2.2. Advantages of Military Justice Systems

Military justice systems benefit from unique specialization. Military lawyers are not only best familiar with LOAC on the theoretical level, but they also have a good understanding of military conduct and operational considerations, and thus of the implementation of LOAC norms in the operational theatre. Such understanding is essential for conducting effective and professional investigations. Military investigations teams are composed also of non-lawyers with operational background, whose essen-

---

[12] Turkel Commission Report, p. 139, see above note 3; See also Lubell, Pejić and Simmons, p. 9, see above note 10.
[13] Turkel Commission Report, p. 141, see above note 3.
[14] *Ibid.*, p. 142.
[15] *Ibid.*, p. 143 (emphasis supplied).
[16] *Ibid.*

tial expertise contributes much to the work of the teams. In many cases, understanding individual battlefield incidents requires knowledge of the broader operational picture, without which the investigations are at risk of reaching inaccurate conclusions. For instance, the understanding of what would constitute a military advantage that arises from a particular attack as part of the assessment of proportionality,[17] might require a broader understanding of operational considerations that pertain to the hostilities at hand, and an isolated examination of a particular attack may not provide the full picture.[18] Military justice systems usually enjoy a profound and constantly cultivated understanding of operational procedures and directives and other relevant information that is crucial for deciphering the factual picture and for formulating the evidentiary basis for criminal charges in appropriate cases.

The unique expertise of military justice systems lies also in the accumulated experience in dealing with investigations of violations of LOAC, which are fundamentally different from investigations of criminal offenses in the civilian context. When investigating allegations of war crimes, the surrounding circumstances are inherently violent and involve the use of armed force. The challenge is to differentiate between legitimate and lawful use of military power, and violations of LOAC that implicate individual criminal responsibility.[19] Military justice systems have experience and knowledge that helps to better identify those instances in which members of the armed forces deviate from conduct that is expected from law-abiding troops in combat situations, giving due regard to the operational circumstances and to challenges which stem from the 'fog of the battle' in which military forces operate.

---

[17] Protocol I Additional to the Geneva Conventions of 12 August, 1949, and Relating to the Protection of Victims of International Armed Conflicts, 8 June 1977, Article 51(1)(b) (https://www.legal-tools.org/doc/d9328a/); ICC Statute, Article 8(2)(b)(iv), see above note 1.

[18] See, John J. Merriam and Michael N. Schmitt, "Israeli Targeting: A Legal Appraisal", in *Naval War College Review*, 2015, vol. 64, no. 4, pp. 15, 18, 28–29, arguing that "[t]o understand why Israel adopts particular interpretations of the LOAC and how the nation applies them in practice, one must comprehend the operational and strategic dilemmas it faces".

[19] There is also need to differentiate between violations of the LOAC in general, and violations that amount to war crimes, see Turkel Commission Report, pp. 94–99, see above note 3.

All of the above does not detract from the need to review the way in which a particular military justice system operates in light of the investigative standards noted above, and to consider improvements through the adoption of best practices. The next part illustrates some of the processes that the Israeli system has undertaken in recent years, following the Turkel Commission's Report.

23.3. Israel's Mechanism for Examining and Investigating Complaints and Claims Raised in Relation to Violations of the LOAC: The Turkel Commission's Report and Subsequent Developments

Several States, including States that were included in the Turkel Commission's comparative analysis, have in recent decades carried out reforms of their mechanisms dedicated to investigating violations of the LOAC. The changes have taken place in pursuit of best practice, sometimes influenced by the respective States' membership in international legal institutions, particularly the European Court of Human Rights and the ICC, and sometimes as a result of internal review procedures that took place in response to concrete instances.[20]

The Government of Israel established the Turkel Commission to examine various aspects of the maritime incident of 31 May 2010.[21] Extending the Commission's mandate to also include an examination of whether Israel's mechanism generally conforms with the obligations of the State of Israel under international law (that is, not only with regard to the maritime incident),[22] stemmed from, *inter alia*, criticisms with regard to the manner in which Israel investigates complaints and claims of violations of LOAC.[23]

---

[20] *Ibid.*, pp. 157–58.

[21] On the maritime incident and the background for the establishment of the Commission, see The Public Commission to Examine the Maritime Incident of 31 May 2010: The Turkel Commission Report Part One, January 2011 (https://www.legal-tools.org/doc/f2aae4/).

[22] Resolution No. 1796 of the 32nd Government of Israel, see above note 2.

[23] Turkel Commission Report, pp. 33–35, see above note 3. In particular, reports of committees appointed by the UN Human Rights Council in the aftermath of the military operations in the Gaza Strip in 2008-2009 ('Operation Cast Lead') and in 2014 ('Operation Protective Edge') criticized the Israeli system, albeit noticing the progress along the years and speaking favourably of the establishment of the Turkel Commission and its work. See Human Rights Council, Human Rights in Palestine and Other Occupied Arab Territories, Report of the United Nations Fact-Finding Mission on the Gaza Conflict, UN Doc.

Following a comprehensive review, the Turkel Commission concluded that the mechanisms in Israel and the methods they employ generally comply with Israel's obligations under the rules of international law.[24] The Commission nevertheless made a number of recommendations for the adoption of practices and operating methods which would improve the system.[25] Since the Turkel Commission published its Report in 2013, many of the recommendations have been implemented, and improvements and lessons-learned processes to that effect are ongoing.[26] Below, I will introduce some of the main changes made to Israel's system in recent years.

The Turkel Commission recommended the establishment of a mechanism for carrying out a fact-finding assessment, to assist the Mili-

---

A/HRC/12/48, 25 September 2009 (https://www.legal-tools.org/doc/ca9992/); Human Rights Council, Report of the Committee of independent experts in international humanitarian and human rights laws to monitor and assess any domestic, legal or other proceedings undertaken by both the Government of Israel and the Palestinian side, in the light of General Assembly resolution 64/254, including the independence, effectiveness, genuineness of these investigations and their conformity with international standards, UN Doc. A/HRC/15/50, 23 September 2010 (https://www.legal-tools.org/doc/h22u4b/); Human Rights Council, Report of the Committee of independent experts in international humanitarian and human rights law established pursuant to Council resolution 13/9, UN Doc. A/HRC/16/24, 18 March 2011(https://www.legal-tools.org/doc/3bd812/); Human Rights Council, Report of the detailed findings of the independent commission of inquiry established pursuant to Human Rights Council resolution S-21/1, UN Doc. A/HRC/29/CRP.4, 24 June 2015, paras. 601–67 (https://www.legal-tools.org/doc/a67ee2/).

24   Turkel Commission Report, p. 49, see above note 3.

25   *Ibid.*, emphasizing that "where the Commission saw a need for amendments or changes to the mechanisms and operating methods, it does not necessarily indicate essential flaws, but rather it is a blueprint for optimal improvement".

26   Following the publication of the Turkel Commission's Report, the Israeli Government appointed a team to review and implement the Turkel Commission's recommendations. In August 2015, the team published a detailed report on the status of implementation of the recommendations as of that time. See Team for the Review and Implementation of the Second Report of the Public Commission for the Examination of the Maritime Incident of May 31st 2010 Regarding Israel's Mechanisms for Examining and Investigating Complaints and Claims of Violations of the Law of Armed Conflict According to International Law, August 2015 ('Implementation Report'). The team submitted its report to the Prime Minister, and recommended the establishment of a small monitoring team that will continue to observe the process of implementation. The Ministerial Committee on National Security approved the recommendations of the implementation team. See The Ministerial Committee on National Security approves the implementation of the Turkel Commission's Second Report.

tary Advocate General ('MAG') in making a determination as to whether a criminal investigation is warranted in particular instances.[27] This mechanism does not detract from the MAG's discretion to decide on the initiation of a criminal investigation based on the facts known to him or her,[28] but it provides an additional tool that may assist the MAG in making such a decision by gathering additional information when required.[29] The Turkel Commission's recommendation to establish a professional fact-finding assessment mechanism resulted mainly from difficulties that it found with the practice of using operational debriefings for such purpose.[30] It recommended that the mechanism be composed of experts on the theatres of military operations, international law and investigations.

Accordingly, the General Staff Mechanism for Fact Finding Assessments ('FFA') was founded and became functional during operation 'Protective Edge' in Gaza in 2014.[31] The FFA is headed by a Major General who, like the other members of the mechanism, was outside the chain of command when the incidents that they examine took place. The FFA is comprised of investigative teams of officers, who hold operational expertise, legal qualifications, and professional investigative experience. It is vested with broad-ranging powers in order to ensure that it can obtain all the information required, and members of the Israeli Defense Forces are obligated to co-operate with it. The FFA's role is to conduct prompt and thorough examinations of every incident referred to it by the MAG, in order to gather sufficient information to determine whether the conduct in question is of a criminal nature. The FFA has dealt with numerous inci-

---

[27] Turkel Commission Report, p. 382, see above note 3.

[28] See for example, the MAG's decision to open a criminal investigation as reported in Decisions of the IDF Military Advocate General Regarding Exceptional Incidents that occurred during Operation 'Protective Edge' – Update No. 1 (Part 2) (10 September 2014): "The MAG Corps received an operational incident report indicating a suspicion that an IDF soldier stole money while in the Gaza Strip. Subsequently, the MAG ordered an immediate criminal investigation into the incident".

[29] The implementing team noted in its report (Implementation Report, para. 53, see above note 26) that the MAG has additional tools available to him to complete the factual assessment, including obtaining relevant factual information from the command operational debrief.

[30] In the Commission's view, operational debriefings should primarily serve the operational needs of the army, rather than focus on questions of criminality as a basis for a decision to initiate an investigation.

[31] Implementation Report, para. 49, see above note 26.

dents of various types, most notably with exceptional incidents (such as attacks resulting in significant civilian casualties), particularly incidents related to operation Protective Edge and violent events across the fence between Israel and the Gaza Strip.[32] In addition to supporting the MAG's decision-making process, the FFA findings also inform the IDF's 'lessons-learned' process so that steps may be considered to minimize the risk of such incidents in the future.

Examples of other changes in Israel's military justice system following the Turkel Commission's recommendations include: the establishment of a department for operational matters within the Military Police (Military Police Criminal Investigative Unit for Operational Affairs ('CIUO')), alongside the MAG Corps for Operational Matters within the military prosecution (which was established back in 2007);[33] and incorporating the reporting procedure into the IDF Directives.[34]

Several recommendations of the Turkel Commission aimed at strengthening the independence of the military justice system, by focusing on the MAG, who heads the system.[35] According to military orders, while the MAG is subordinate to the IDF Chief of Staff in rank, and is part of the military's General Staff, the MAG, and the entire MAG Corps, are only subject to the authority of the law, and not to the chain of command, in making legal and investigative determinations. In order to support the independence of the MAG, the Commission recommended, *inter alia*, that the MAG's tenure be fixed, and that the MAG shall be given a fixed rank,

---

[32] See The Supreme Court sitting as the High Court of Justice, *Yesh Din et al. v. IDF Chief of Staff et al.*, 24 May 2018, HCJ 3003/18, para. 63 (President E. Hayut's Verdict). With regard to Operation Protective Edge, as of August 2018, approximately 220 incidents have been referred by the MAG for examination by the FFA Mechanism. On the status of the examinations and investigations, see Decisions of the IDF Military Advocate General Regarding Exceptional Incidents that Allegedly Occurred during Operation 'Protective Edge' – Update 6 (15 August 2018).

[33] Turkel Commission Report, p. 397, see above note 3. See also, "The IDF Military Justice System", Israel Defense Force (available on its web site).

[34] Turkel Commission Report, p. 374, see above note 3; Israel's State Comptroller Public Report on Operation 'Protective Edge', IDF Activity from the Perspective of International Law, Particularly with Regard to Mechanisms of Examination and Oversight of Civilian and Military Echelons, 14 March 2018, pp. 94–96, and recommendations for further improvements in that regard in *ibid.*, pp. 96–98.

[35] Turkel Commission Report, pp. 389–96, see above note 3.

such that the promotion of the MAG from Brigadier-General to Major-General is not subject to the discretion of the Chief of the General Staff.[36] These recommendations were implemented. In April 2015, a new Directive was published by the Attorney General, clarifying the relationship between the military justice system and the general legal system headed by the Attorney General. The Directive also clarifies the independent legal status of the MAG and the framework for professional guidance provided to the MAG by the Attorney General. The Directive further refers to the established guidelines regarding the Attorney General's involvement in the MAG's decisions.[37]

Finally, it should be noted that the Turkel Commission's work also contributed to improvements in the civilian system, primarily by strengthening the oversight capabilities of the civilian system *vis-à-vis* the military justice system. The authority of the Attorney General to review appeals on the MAG's decisions regarding investigations and prosecutions of serious violations of international law has been regularized and formalized in the form of an official Attorney General guideline.[38] In addition, following the Commission's recommendation,[39] a unit within the office of the Deputy Attorney General (International Law) which deals with matters pertaining to LOAC, has been established. This unit adds a civilian echelon dealing with these matters, in addition to the work of the MAG's Corps. These changes further strengthen the ability of Israel's legal system to deal effectively with claims regarding violations of LOAC.

23.4. Implications for International Investigations

What implications does national practice have for investigations by international institutions, including the ICC? The starting point in answering this question is that international proceedings are complementary to domestic proceedings. As a rule, international proceedings can hardly be justified in situations in which domestic systems function according to the

---

[36] *Ibid.*, pp. 391–92.
[37] Implementation Report, paras. 74–76, see above note 26.
[38] Turkel Commission Report, pp. 407–408, see above note 3; Attorney General Guideline 4.5003 (5775): "The review of decisions of the Military Advocate General regarding incidents involving the death of an individual in the course of Israel Defense Forces operational activity, when serious violations of customary international law are alleged"; *ibid.*, paras. 114–16.
[39] Turkel Commission Report, p. 403, see above note 3.

aforementioned international principles.[40] The complementary nature of international criminal proceedings goes beyond the perception of complementarity as an issue of admissibility before the ICC.[41] The awareness of those spearheading international proceedings of the challenges that arise at the domestic level in relation to examinations and investigations of alleged violations of LOAC, as well as the way in which States deal with these challenges, is in other words of critical importance. Realizing that such challenges may be inherent to the complex investigative effort in the context of an armed conflict can prevent wrong conclusions as to whether domestic systems function properly. The standard, including that demanded by the principle of complementarity, is essentially one of process rather than of result.

International investigations are complementary to national investigations in another, less noticed, aspect, which relates to the substance of the process. Investigations of violations of the LOAC must consider in-

---

[40] See, for example, William Schabas, "Complementarity in Practice: Some Uncomplimentary Thoughts", in *Criminal Law Forum*, 2008, vol. 19, no. 1; Charles Chernor Jalloh, "Kenya vs. The ICC Prosecutor", in *Harvard International Law Journal*, 2012, vol. 53; Anna Bishop, "Failure of Complementarity: The Future of the International Criminal Court Following the Libyan Admissibility Challenge", in *Minnesota Journal of International Law*, 2013, vol. 22; Sarah M.H. Nouwen, *Complementarity in the Line of Fire: The Catalysing Effect of the International Criminal Court in Uganda and Sudan*, Cambridge University Press, 2013.

[41] The complementary nature of the ICC as an institution is reflected, *inter alia*, in the preamble and Article 1 of the Rome Statute of the International Criminal Court, see above note 1 ("shall be complementary to national criminal jurisdictions"). This notion of complementarity goes beyond its function as an admissibility device (reflected in Articles 17, 18 and 19 of the ICC Statue). See, generally, Carsten Stahn, "Revitalizing Complementarity a Decade after the Stocktaking Exercise", Policy Brief Series No. 115 (2020), Torkel Opsahl Academic EPublisher, Brussels, 2020, p. 1: "Complementarity has several dimensions. In its most narrow form it is an admissibility device [...] it is also a means to organize the interaction between international and domestic jurisdictions in a more holistic sense. This may be called the 'systemic function of complementarity'" (https://www.toaep.org/pbs-pdf/115-stahn/); Justin Tillier, "The ICC Prosecutor and Positive Complementarity: Strengthening the Rule of Law", in *International Criminal Law Review*, 2013, vol. 13, no. 3, pp. 507–08: "The Preamble of the Rome Statue [...] sets an ambitious goal – ending impunity, but the Preamble also provides a strict limitation on the implementation of this goal – the ICC shall be complementary to national criminal jurisdictions. This means that national judiciaries have the primary responsibility for preventing and punishing atrocities in their own territories, and the ICC remains a Court of last resort"; see also David Hughes, "Investigation as Legitimisation: The Development, Use and Misuse of Informal Complementarity", in *Melbourne Journal of International Law*, 2018, vol. 19, no. 1.

formation and evidence at the disposal of the military. For example, in order to establish criminal intent for a specific conduct or analyse targeting decisions, it is vital to build on information that the *attacker* had *at the time* of the relevant conduct. Information relating to the processes used in order to determine the lawfulness of potential targets is also crucial. Many investigations, both in the national and international spheres, commence following allegations brought by victims of hostilities, based on their effects and outcomes. The perspective offered by victims is very important for conducting a thorough factual assessment. Sometimes victims possess crucial information that is not known to the military.

International investigators should be cognizant of the relative advantages of domestic systems, in particular in cases involving alleged violation of LOAC in which capable domestic military justice systems are available. As described above, this relative advantage stems from the legal and operational expertise of such domestic systems, as well as their proximity to the scene and the exclusive information they may possess. In many cases, international investigations rely heavily on materials and evidence from victims or those who represent them, while State investigations have critical access to exclusive information, which is normally sensitive and classified in situations with ongoing or recurring conflict. International prosecutors should seek to "expend greater effort in ensuring that cases brought to trial are fully investigated and supported by sufficient evidence".[42] While there is no doubt that international judicial bodies are accountable to victims and communities affected by international crimes, who have understandable interests in the initiation of international proceedings, such expectations from international bodies cannot come at the expense of quality control or professionalism when conducting criminal processes.

Considering the unique expertise gained in state investigative bodies in the context of international investigations, international bodies should consider not merely deference to law-abiding states, but also referring victims and the information that they provided to the relevant national mechanisms. Some commentators have defined such a policy as "posi-

---

[42] Richard J. Goldstone, "Acquittals by the International Criminal Court", *EJIL: Talk!*, 18 January 2019 (available on its web site).

tive complementarity".[43] The inherent potential of national justice systems of States that are committed to the rule of law, reinforces the conclusion that this policy is a worthy one.

That is not to say that national military justice systems are flawless. Examinations and investigations in situations that inherently involve violence and national sentiments, are never easy, and States do not always prioritize such endeavours. The role of jurists committed to international law is to support such systems and strive to improve them.[44]

Professional international review of domestic investigation systems is sometimes necessary. However, considering also the challenges faced by international judicial institutions, and the difficulty of investigating "from a distance", it is fundamentally important to invest resources in

---

[43] ICC-OTP, Prosecutorial Strategy 2009-2012, 1 February 2010, paras. 16–17 (https://www.legal-tools.org/doc/6ed914/): "The positive approach to complementarity means that the Office will encourage genuine national proceedings where possible […]"; Tillier, see above note 42; Luis Moreno-Ocampo, "A Positive Approach to Complementarity: The Impact of the Office of the Prosecutor", in Mohamed M. El Zeidy and Carsten Stahn (eds.), *The International Criminal Court and Complementarity: From Theory to Practice*, Cambridge University Press, 2011, pp. 21–32; William W. Burke-White, "Reframing Positive Complementarity: Reflections on the First Decade and Insights from the US Federal Criminal Justice System", in El Zeidy and Stahn (eds.), *The International Criminal Court and Complementarity*, Cambridge University Press, 2014, pp. 341-60; Katharine A. Marshall, "Prevention and Complementarity in the International Criminal Court: A Positive Approach", in *Human Rights Brief*, 2010, vol. 17, no. 2; Rod Rastan, "Complementarity: Contest or Collaboration", in Morten Bergsmo (ed.), *Complementarity and the Exercise of Universal Jurisdiction for Core International Crimes*, Torkel Opsahl Academic EPublisher, 2010, pp. 112–13:

> Drawing on these lessons learned, the ICC Prosecutor's Office stated early on that it would adopt a policy to encourage and assist national investigations and prosecutions. The stated objective was not to compete for case allocation with national courts, but to ensure that the most serious crimes did not go unpunished through adoption of a policy of coordinated action between the ICC and national authorities. This approach, labelled "positive complementarity", has been described by the Prosecutor's Office as meaning that it "encourages genuine national proceedings where possible; relies on national and international networks; and participates in a system of international cooperation".

[44] See SONG Tianying, "Positive Complementarity and the Receiving End of Justice: The Case of Myanmar", Policy Brief Series No. 104 (2020), Torkel Opsahl Academic EPublisher, Brussels, 2020 (https://www.toaep.org/pbs-pdf/104-song/).

strengthening the role of the domestic component within the international criminal justice system.[45] International proceedings are a last resort.

---

[45] Phil Clark, *Distant Justice: The Impact of the International Criminal Court on African Politics*, Cambridge University Press, 2018, chap. 5.

INDEX

A

Adichie, Chimamanda Ngozi, 247
adversarial techniques (investigations). *See* devil's advocate, red team
Afghanistan, 345
age (estimation). *See* estimation (age)
Agirre, Xabier Aranburu, 289, 290
AKUTAGAWA Ryūnosuke, 130
American Bar Association, 270
analysis, 11, 14, 42, 118, 243, 273, 543, *See* also investigation plans
  analysts, role of, 15, 123, 277, 284, 291, 537, 545, 551
  crime pattern, 496
  data, collation of, 127, 554
  dedicated analysis section, 123
  dissemination, 128
  evidence-based, 285
  external experts, 288
  forensic, 34
  intelligence cycle, 125
  intelligence-led model, 26
  investigation plans, 810
  judiciary, 293
  law-driven (evidence analysis), 992
  organisational structures, 274, 284, 541
  peer-review, 296
  regional expertise, 287
  situation analysis, 279
  strategic, 279
  target-driven, 287
Analysis of Competing Hypotheses, 235, 248, 505, 521, 527
anchoring effect. *See* bias
Andreotti, Giulio, 163
Annan, Kofi, 848
Anti-Torture Initiative, 305
Arendt, Hannah, 72
argumentation (theory), 617, 632
  mapping, 636
  maps, 634

  rebutting attack, 624
  schemes, 633
  undercutting attack, 624
  undermining attack, 624
Aristotle, 243
Arlacchi, Pino, 161
Arthashastra, 131, 148, 193, 199, 200
Association for the Prevention of Torture, 305
asymmetrical skepticism, 482
Auld, Robin Ernest, 1023
Australia
  Police v. Kennedy case (Supreme Court, South Australia), 388

B

Barrett-Lennard, Godfrey, 311
Beccaria, Cesare, 167, 193, 201
Bekou, Olympia, 53
Bentham, Jeremy, 172
Bergsmo, Morten, 26, 53, 69, 119, 130, 263, 285, 464, 569, 581, 814, 822, 899
Between Expert Reliability. *See* reliability (between expert), *See* reliability
beyond reasonable doubt, 87, 251, 269, 333, 383, 390, 433, *489*, 630, 889, 922
bias
  anchoring effect, 400, 480
  cascade effect, 495
  cognitive, 16, 43, 73, 286
  cognitive load, 502, 523
  Common-Civil Law, 10
  confirmation, 7, 73, 293, 462, 465
  cultural, 147, 194
  debiasing techniques, 524
  definition (source evaluation), 136
  descriptive (confirmation), 501
  emotional, 16, 509, 526
  estimation (age), 331, 378, 384, 399, 421, 426
  ethno-centric, 151
  forensic, 378, 491, 506
  framing effect, 480

L

Lakoff, Robin, 154
law of armed conflict. *See jus in bello*
Lebanon
    Mehlis Report, 465
legal information services (IT), ii, 34, *See
    also* information technology (tools)
legal positivism, 72
Lewis, Peter, 823
Lord's Resistance Army, 93

M

Manusmriti, 128, 131
McHenry, Teresa, 6
Mégret, Frédéric, 37
Mehlis, Detlev, 466
Menchú Tum, Rigoberta, 138, 145
mens rea, 1027
military justice
    cf. civilian justice, 1036, 1038
    distinct system (model), 1038
    expertise (investigations), 1041
    independence, 1045
Moore, Charles C., 175
Moreno-Ocampo, Luis, xviii, 75, 83, 95,
    853
motivated cognition, 513
multiculturalism, 153

N

Nazi reports on war crimes, 138
Netherlands, the, 113, 468
Neuner, Matthias, 6
Nicholson, Peter, 292
Nickerson, Raymond, 462
non-governmental   organisations
    (investigations), 68, 83, 85, 92, 105,
    422, 739
Norway, 32, 888
    22 July 2011 terrorist attacks, 887
    co-operation   (investigators   and
        prosecutors), 1033
    co-operation (requirements), 1033
    criminal procedure, 888
    Criminal Procedure Act, 1021

Director of Public Prosecutions, 890,
    895
duty to investigate, 890
dynamic investigation plan, 32
evidence, collection of, 1023
evidentiary threshold, 889
investigation plans (definition), 888
investigation plans (legal framework),
    891
investigation plans (structure), 896
investigative strategy, 890, 900
length of investigations, 892
Ministry of Foreign Affairs, i
money laundering (elements), 1026
National Crime Investigation Service,
    896
objectivity (investigations), 892
preliminary investigations, lack of, 889
resource management, 900
victims' care (investigations), 893
violence (sexual), 896
Norwegian Centre for Human Rights, 305
Nuremberg trials, 118, 142, 329, 642
    Charter (IMT), 742
    Einsatzgruppen trial, xxi
    International Military Tribunal, 741
Nyāya Sūtra, 131

O

objectivity (investigations)
    co-operation   (investigators   and
        prosecutors),   1032,   *See*   also
        investigators (co-operation)
Obote-Odora, Alex, 723
offence-driven investigations, 469
old evidence, 76, 135, 374
open sources, reliance on, 68, 78, 93, 99,
    217, 861, 948
Organisation   for   Security   and   Co-
    operation in Europe, 14, 572
    Investigation Manual for Bosnia and
        Herzegovina, 802
Osiel, Mark, 148
Otto, M.C., 128
Oxburgh, Gavin, 311

TOAEP TEAM

Editors

Antonio Angotti, Editor
Olympia Bekou, Editor
Mats Benestad, Editor
Morten Bergsmo, Editor-in-Chief
Alf Butenschøn Skre, Senior Executive Editor
Eleni Chaitidou, Editor
CHAN Icarus, Editor
CHEAH Wui Ling, Editor
FAN Yuwen, Editor
Manek Minhas, Editor
Gareth Richards, Senior Editor
Nikolaus Scheffel, Editor
SIN Ngok Shek, Editor
SONG Tianying, Editor
Moritz Thörner, Editor
ZHANG Yueyao, Editor

Editorial Assistants

Pauline Brosch
Marquise Lee Houle
Genevieve Zingg

Law of the Future Series Co-Editors

Dr. Alexander (Sam) Muller
Professor Larry Cata Backer
Professor Stavros Zouridis

Nuremberg Academy Series Editor

Dr. Viviane Dittrich, Deputy Director, International Nuremberg Principles Academy

Scientific Advisers

Professor Danesh Sarooshi, Principal Scientific Adviser for International Law
Professor Andreas Zimmermann, Principal Scientific Adviser for Public International Law
Professor Kai Ambos, Principal Scientific Adviser for International Criminal Law
Dr.h.c. Asbjørn Eide, Principal Scientific Adviser for International Human Rights Law

Editorial Board

Dr. Xabier Agirre, International Criminal Court
Dr. Claudia Angermaier, Austrian judiciary
Ms. Neela Badami, Narasappa, Doraswamy and Raja
Dr. Markus Benzing, Freshfields Bruckhaus Deringer, Frankfurt

OTHER VOLUMES IN THE PUBLICATION SERIES

Morten Bergsmo, Mads Harlem and Nobuo Hayashi (editors):
Importing Core International Crimes into National Law
Torkel Opsahl Academic EPublisher
Oslo, 2010
FICHL Publication Series No. 1 (Second Edition, 2010)
ISBN: 978-82-93081-00-5

Nobuo Hayashi (editor):
National Military Manuals on the Law of Armed Conflict
Torkel Opsahl Academic EPublisher
Oslo, 2010
FICHL Publication Series No. 2 (Second Edition, 2010)
ISBN: 978-82-93081-02-9

Morten Bergsmo, Kjetil Helvig, Ilia Utmelidze and Gorana Žagovec:
The Backlog of Core International Crimes Case Files in Bosnia and Herzegovina
Torkel Opsahl Academic EPublisher
Oslo, 2010
FICHL Publication Series No. 3 (Second Edition, 2010)
ISBN: 978-82-93081-04-3

Morten Bergsmo (editor):
Criteria for Prioritizing and Selecting Core International Crimes Cases
Torkel Opsahl Academic EPublisher
Oslo, 2010
FICHL Publication Series No. 4 (Second Edition, 2010)
ISBN: 978-82-93081-06-7

Morten Bergsmo and Pablo Kalmanovitz (editors):
Law in Peace Negotiations
Torkel Opsahl Academic EPublisher
Oslo, 2010
FICHL Publication Series No. 5 (Second Edition, 2010)
ISBN: 978-82-93081-08-1

Morten Bergsmo, César Rodríguez Garavito, Pablo Kalmanovitz and Maria Paula Saffon (editors):
Distributive Justice in Transitions
Torkel Opsahl Academic EPublisher
Oslo, 2010
FICHL Publication Series No. 6 (2010)
ISBN: 978-82-93081-12-8

Morten Bergsmo, César Rodriguez-Garavito, Pablo Kalmanovitz and Maria Paula Saffon (editors):
Justicia Distributiva en Sociedades en Transición
Torkel Opsahl Academic EPublisher
Oslo, 2012
FICHL Publication Series No. 6 (2012)
ISBN: 978-82-93081-10-4

Morten Bergsmo (editor):
Complementarity and the Exercise of Universal Jurisdiction for Core International Crimes
Torkel Opsahl Academic EPublisher
Oslo, 2010
FICHL Publication Series No. 7 (2010)
ISBN: 978-82-93081-14-2

Morten Bergsmo (editor):
Active Complementarity: Legal Information Transfer
Torkel Opsahl Academic EPublisher
Oslo, 2011
FICHL Publication Series No. 8 (2011)
ISBN print: 978-82-93081-56-2
ISBN e-book: 978-82-93081-55-5

Morten Bergsmo (editor):
Abbreviated Criminal Procedures for Core International Crimes
Torkel Opsahl Academic EPublisher
Brussels, 2017
FICHL Publication Series No. 9 (2018)
ISBN print: 978-82-93081-20-3
ISBN e-book: 978-82-8348-104-4

Sam Muller, Stavros Zouridis, Morly Frishman and Laura Kistemaker (editors):
The Law of the Future and the Future of Law
Torkel Opsahl Academic EPublisher
Oslo, 2010
FICHL Publication Series No. 11 (2011)
ISBN: 978-82-93081-27-2

Morten Bergsmo, Alf Butenschøn Skre and Elisabeth J. Wood (editors):
Understanding and Proving International Sex Crimes
Torkel Opsahl Academic EPublisher
Beijing, 2012
FICHL Publication Series No. 12 (2012)
ISBN: 978-82-93081-29-6

Morten Bergsmo (editor):
Thematic Prosecution of International Sex Crimes
Torkel Opsahl Academic EPublisher
Beijing, 2012
FICHL Publication Series No. 13 (2012)
ISBN: 978-82-93081-31-9

Terje Einarsen:
The Concept of Universal Crimes in International Law
Torkel Opsahl Academic EPublisher
Oslo, 2012
FICHL Publication Series No. 14 (2012)
ISBN: 978-82-93081-33-3

莫滕·伯格斯默 凌岩(主编):
国家主权与国际刑法
Torkel Opsahl Academic EPublisher
Beijing, 2012
FICHL Publication Series No. 15 (2012)
ISBN: 978-82-93081-58-6

Morten Bergsmo and LING Yan (editors):
State Sovereignty and International Criminal Law
Torkel Opsahl Academic EPublisher
Beijing, 2012
FICHL Publication Series No. 15 (2012)
ISBN: 978-82-93081-35-7

Morten Bergsmo and CHEAH Wui Ling (editors):
Old Evidence and Core International Crimes
Torkel Opsahl Academic EPublisher
Beijing, 2012
FICHL Publication Series No. 16 (2012)
ISBN: 978-82-93081-60-9

YI Ping:
戦争と平和の間——発足期日本国際法学における「正しい戦争」の観念とその帰結
Torkel Opsahl Academic EPublisher
Beijing, 2013
FICHL Publication Series No. 17 (2013)
ISBN: 978-82-93081-66-1

Morten Bergsmo and SONG Tianying (editors):
On the Proposed Crimes Against Humanity Convention
Torkel Opsahl Academic EPublisher
Brussels, 2014
FICHL Publication Series No. 18 (2014)
ISBN: 978-82-93081-96-8

Morten Bergsmo, CHEAH Wui Ling and YI Ping (editors):
Historical Origins of International Criminal Law: Volume 1
Torkel Opsahl Academic EPublisher
Brussels, 2014
FICHL Publication Series No. 20 (2014)
ISBN: 978-82-93081-11-1

Morten Bergsmo, CHEAH Wui Ling and YI Ping (editors):
Historical Origins of International Criminal Law: Volume 2
Torkel Opsahl Academic EPublisher
Brussels, 2014
FICHL Publication Series No. 21 (2014)
ISBN: 978-82-93081-13-5

Morten Bergsmo, CHEAH Wui Ling, SONG Tianying and YI Ping (editors):
Historical Origins of International Criminal Law: Volume 3
Torkel Opsahl Academic EPublisher
Brussels, 2015
FICHL Publication Series No. 22 (2015)
ISBN print: 978-82-8348-015-3
ISBN e-book: 978-82-8348-014-6

Morten Bergsmo, CHEAH Wui Ling, SONG Tianying and YI Ping (editors):
Historical Origins of International Criminal Law: Volume 4
Torkel Opsahl Academic EPublisher
Brussels, 2015
FICHL Publication Series No. 23 (2015)
ISBN print: 978-82-8348-017-7
ISBN e-book: 978-82-8348-016-0

Morten Bergsmo, Klaus Rackwitz and SONG Tianying (editors):
Historical Origins of International Criminal Law: Volume 5
Torkel Opsahl Academic EPublisher
Brussels, 2017
FICHL Publication Series No. 24 (2017)
ISBN print: 978-82-8348-106-8
ISBN e-book: 978-82-8348-107-5

Morten Bergsmo and SONG Tianying (editors):
Military Self-Interest in Accountability for Core International Crimes
Torkel Opsahl Academic EPublisher
Brussels, 2015
FICHL Publication Series No. 25 (2015)
ISBN print: 978-82-93081-61-6
ISBN e-book: 978-82-93081-81-4

Wolfgang Kaleck:
Double Standards: International Criminal Law and the West
Torkel Opsahl Academic EPublisher
Brussels, 2015
FICHL Publication Series No. 26 (2015)
ISBN print: 978-82-93081-67-8
ISBN e-book: 978-82-93081-83-8

LIU Daqun and ZHANG Binxin (editors):
Historical War Crimes Trials in Asia
Torkel Opsahl Academic EPublisher
Brussels, 2016
FICHL Publication Series No. 27 (2015)
ISBN print: 978-82-8348-055-9
ISBN e-book: 978-82-8348-056-6

Mark Klamberg (editor):
Commentary on the Law of the International Criminal Court
Torkel Opsahl Academic EPublisher
Brussels, 2017
FICHL Publication Series No. 29 (2017)
ISBN print: 978-82-8348-100-6
ISBN e-book: 978-82-8348-101-3

Stian Nordengen Christensen:
Counterfactual History and Bosnia-Herzegovina
Torkel Opsahl Academic EPublisher
Brussels, 2018
Publication Series No. 30 (2018)
ISBN print: 978-82-8348-102-0
ISBN e-book: 978-82-8348-103-7

Stian Nordengen Christensen:
Possibilities and Impossibilities in a Contradictory Global Order
Torkel Opsahl Academic EPublisher
Brussels, 2018
Publication Series No. 31 (2018)
ISBN print: 978-82-8348-104-4
ISBN e-book: 978-82-8348-105-1

Morten Bergsmo and Carsten Stahn (editors):
Quality Control in Preliminary Examination: Volume 1
Torkel Opsahl Academic EPublisher
Brussels, 2018
Publication Series No. 32 (2018)
ISBN print: 978-82-8348-123-5
ISBN e-book: 978-82-8348-124-2

Morten Bergsmo and Carsten Stahn (editors):
Quality Control in Preliminary Examination: Volume 2
Torkel Opsahl Academic EPublisher
Brussels, 2018
Publication Series No. 33 (2018)
ISBN print: 978-82-8348-111-2
ISBN e-book: 978-82-8348-112-9

Morten Bergsmo and Emiliano J. Buis (editors):
Philosophical Foundations of International Criminal Law: Correlating Thinkers
Torkel Opsahl Academic EPublisher
Brussels, 2018
Publication Series No. 34 (2018)
ISBN print: 978-82-8348-117-4
ISBN e-book: 978-82-8348-118-1

Morten Bergsmo and Emiliano J. Buis (editors):
Philosophical Foundations of International Criminal Law: Foundational Concepts
Torkel Opsahl Academic EPublisher
Brussels, 2019
Publication Series No. 35 (2019)
ISBN print: 978-82-8348-119-8
ISBN e-book: 978-82-8348-120-4

Terje Einarsen and Joseph Rikhof:
A Theory of Punishable Participation in Universal Crimes
Torkel Opsahl Academic EPublisher
Brussels, 2018
Publication Series No. 37 (2018)
ISBN print: 978-82-8348-127-3
ISBN e-book: 978-82-8348-128-0

All volumes are freely available online at http://www.toaep.org/ps/. For printed copies, see http://www.toaep.org/about/distribution/. For reviews of earlier books in this Series in academic journals and yearbooks, see http://www.toaep.org/reviews/.

Lightning Source UK Ltd.
Milton Keynes UK
UKHW052126270121
377669UK00011BB/956/J